PEARSON CUSTOM
MATHEMATICS

Precalculus: Functions and Graphs
Custom Edition for Cal Poly San Luis Obispo
MATH 116/117

PEARSON

This special edition published in cooperation with Pearson Learning Solutions.

Printed in the United States of America.

18 17

Please visit our website at *www.pearsonlearningsolutions.com.*

Attention bookstores: For permission to return any unsold stock, contact us at *pe-uscustomreturns@pearson.com.*

Pearson Learning Solutions, 501 Boylston Street, Suite 900, Boston, MA 02116
A Pearson Education Company
www.pearsoned.com

ISBN 10: 1-256-57465-1
ISBN 13: 978-1-256-57465-1

Table of Contents

Function Gallery

Constant Function

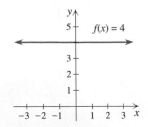

Domain $(-\infty, \infty)$
Range $\{4\}$
Constant on $(-\infty, \infty)$
Symmetric about y-axis

Identity Function

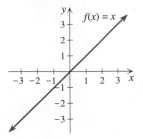

Domain $(-\infty, \infty)$
Range $(-\infty, \infty)$
Increasing on $(-\infty, \infty)$
Symmetric about origin

Linear Function

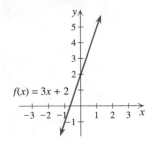

Domain $(-\infty, \infty)$
Range $(-\infty, \infty)$
Increasing on $(-\infty, \infty)$

Absolute Value Function

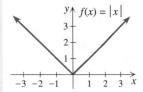

Domain $(-\infty, \infty)$
Range $[0, \infty)$
Increasing on $[0, \infty)$
Decreasing on $(-\infty, 0]$
Symmetric about y-axis

Square Function

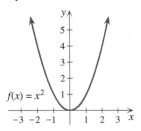

Domain $(-\infty, \infty)$
Range $[-0, \infty)$
Increasing on $[0, \infty)$
Decreasing on $(-\infty, 0]$
Symmetric about y-axis

Square-Root Function

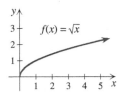

Domain $[0, \infty)$
Range $[0, \infty)$
Increasing on $[0, \infty)$

Cube Function

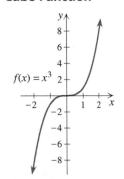

Domain $(-\infty, \infty)$
Range $(-\infty, \infty)$
Increasing on $(-\infty, \infty)$
Symmetric about origin

Cube-Root Function

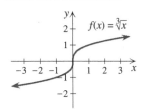

Domain $(-\infty, \infty)$
Range $(-\infty, \infty)$
Increasing on $(-\infty, \infty)$
Symmetric about origin

Greatest Integer Function

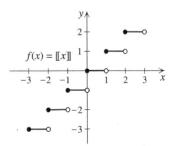

Domain $(-\infty, \infty)$
Range $\{n \,|\, n \text{ is an integer}\}$
Constant on $[n, n + 1)$
  for every integer n

FUNCTION
gallery... Some Inverse Functions

Linear

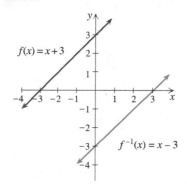

$f(x) = x + 3$

$f^{-1}(x) = x - 3$

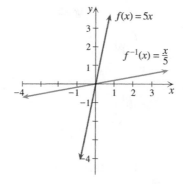

$f(x) = 5x$

$f^{-1}(x) = \frac{x}{5}$

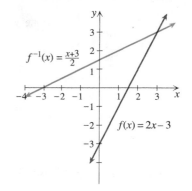

$f^{-1}(x) = \frac{x+3}{2}$

$f(x) = 2x - 3$

Powers and Roots

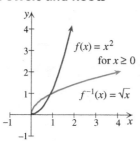

$f(x) = x^2$
for $x \geq 0$

$f^{-1}(x) = \sqrt{x}$

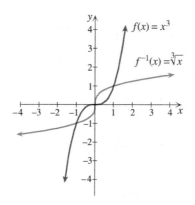

$f(x) = x^3$

$f^{-1}(x) = \sqrt[3]{x}$

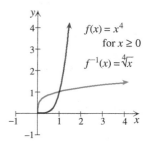

$f(x) = x^4$
for $x \geq 0$

$f^{-1}(x) = \sqrt[4]{x}$

FUNCTION
gallery... Polynomial Functions

Linear: $f(x) = mx + b$

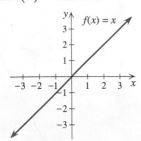
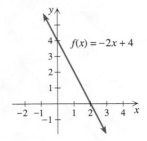

Slope 1, *y*-intercept $(0, 0)$ Slope 3, *y*-intercept $(0, -2)$ Slope -2, *y*-intercept $(0, 4)$

Quadratic: $f(x) = ax^2 + bx + c$ **or** $f(x) = a(x - h)^2 + k$

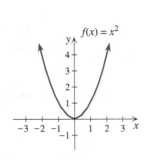
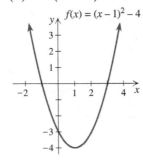
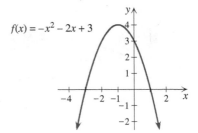

Vertex $(0, 0)$ Vertex $(1, -4)$ Vertex $(-1, 4)$
Range $[0, \infty)$ Range $[-4, \infty)$ Range $(-\infty, 4]$

Cubic: $f(x) = ax^3 + bx^2 + cx + d$

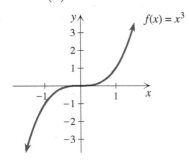
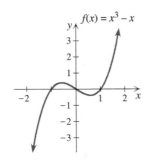
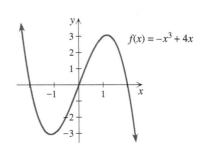

Quartic or Fourth-Degree: $f(x) = ax^4 + bx^3 + cx^2 + dx + e$

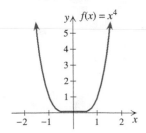
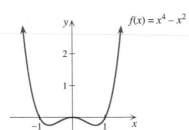
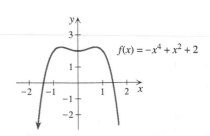

gallery... Some Basic Rational Functions

Horizontal Asymptote *x*-axis and Vertical Asymptote *y*-axis

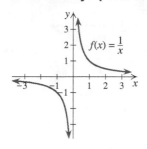

$f(x) = \dfrac{1}{x}$

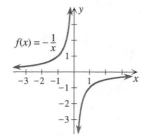

$f(x) = -\dfrac{1}{x}$

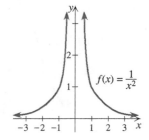

$f(x) = \dfrac{1}{x^2}$

Various Asymptotes

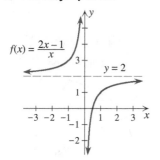

$f(x) = \dfrac{2x - 1}{x}$

$y = 2$

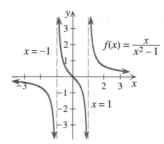

$x = -1$

$f(x) = \dfrac{x}{x^2 - 1}$

$x = 1$

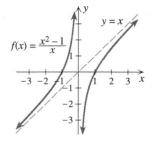

$f(x) = \dfrac{x^2 - 1}{x}$

$y = x$

5

→ **FUNCTION**

gallery... Exponential and Logarithmic Functions

Exponential: $f(x) = a^x$**, domain** $(-\infty, \infty)$**, range** $(0, \infty)$

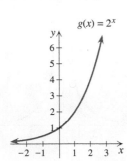

$g(x) = 2^x$

Increasing on $(-\infty, \infty)$
y-intercept $(0, 1)$

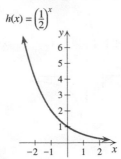

$h(x) = \left(\frac{1}{2}\right)^x$

Decreasing on $(-\infty, \infty)$
y-intercept $(0, 1)$

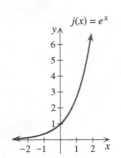

$j(x) = e^x$

Increasing on $(-\infty, \infty)$
y-intercept $(0, 1)$

Logarithmic: $f^{-1}(x) = \log_a(x)$**, domain** $(0, \infty)$**, range** $(-\infty, \infty)$

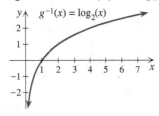

$g^{-1}(x) = \log_2(x)$

Increasing on $(0, \infty)$
x-intercept $(1, 0)$

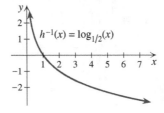

$h^{-1}(x) = \log_{1/2}(x)$

Decreasing on $(0, \infty)$
x-intercept $(1, 0)$

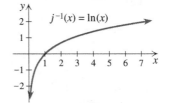

$j^{-1}(x) = \ln(x)$

Increasing on $(0, \infty)$
x-intercept $(1, 0)$

FUNCTION gallery... Some Basic Functions of Algebra with Transformations

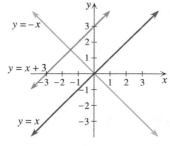

Linear

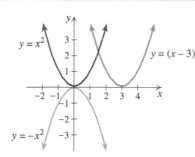

Quadratic

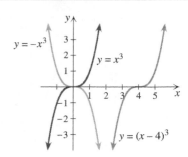

Cubic

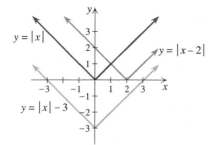

Absolute value

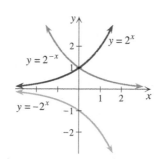

Exponential

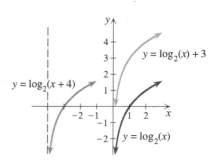

Logarithmic

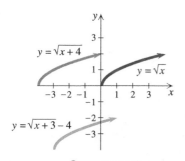

Square root

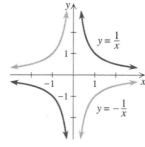

Reciprocal

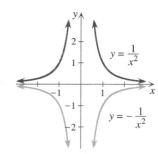

Rational

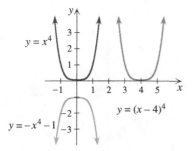

Fourth degree

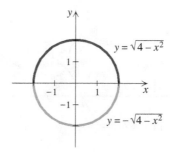

Semicircle

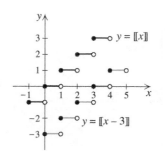

Greatest integer

7

FUNCTION gallery... The Sine and Cosine Functions

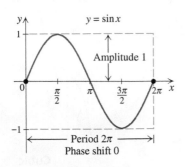

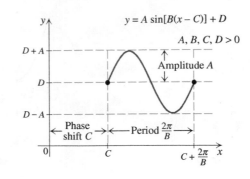

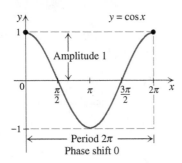

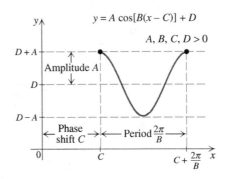

FUNCTION gallery... Periods of Sine, Cosine, and Tangent ($B > 1$)

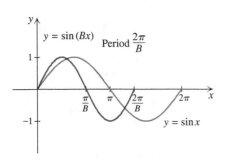

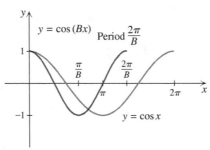

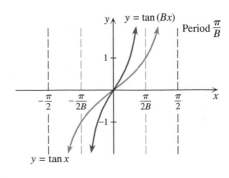

Fundamental cycles

FUNCTION gallery... Trigonometric Functions

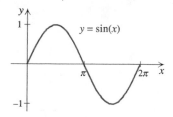

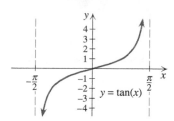

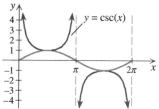

Domain (k any integer)	$(-\infty, \infty)$	$(-\infty, \infty)$	$x \neq \dfrac{\pi}{2} + k\pi$
Range	$[-1, 1]$	$[-1, 1]$	$(-\infty, \infty)$
Period	2π	2π	π
Fundamental cycle	$[0, 2\pi]$	$[0, 2\pi]$	$\left[-\dfrac{\pi}{2}, \dfrac{\pi}{2}\right]$

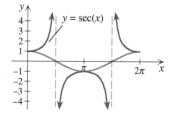

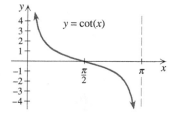

Domain (k any integer)	$x \neq k\pi$	$x \neq \dfrac{\pi}{2} + k\pi$	$x \neq k\pi$
Range	$(-\infty, -1] \cup [1, \infty)$	$(-\infty, -1] \cup [1, \infty)$	$(-\infty, \infty)$
Period	2π	2π	π
Fundamental cycle	$[0, 2\pi]$	$[0, 2\pi]$	$[0, \pi]$

FUNCTION
gallery... Inverse Trigonometric Functions

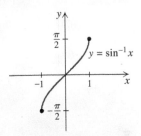

Domain [−1, 1]
Range $\left[-\frac{\pi}{2}, \frac{\pi}{2}\right]$

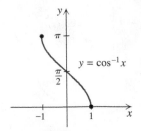

Domain [−1, 1]
Range $[0, \pi]$

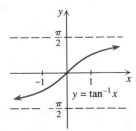

Domain $(-\infty, \infty)$
Range $\left(-\frac{\pi}{2}, \frac{\pi}{2}\right)$

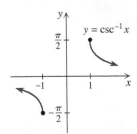

Domain $(-\infty, -1] \cup [1, \infty)$
Range $\left[-\frac{\pi}{2}, 0\right) \cup \left(0, \frac{\pi}{2}\right]$

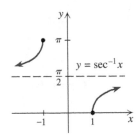

Domain $(-\infty, -1] \cup [1, \infty)$
Range $\left[0, \frac{\pi}{2}\right) \cup \left(\frac{\pi}{2}, \pi\right]$

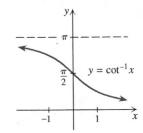

Domain $(-\infty, \infty)$
Range $(0, \pi)$

FUNCTION
gallery... **Functions in Polar Coordinates**

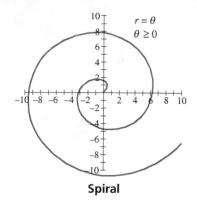

Spiral

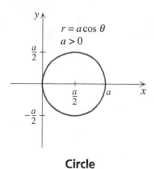

Circle

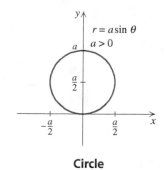

Circle

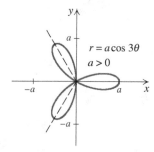

Three-Leaf Rose

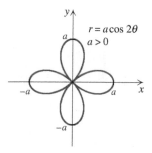

Four-Leaf Rose

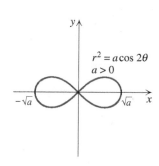

Lemniscate

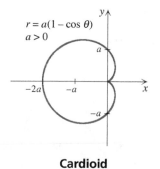

Cardioid

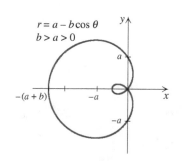

Limaçon

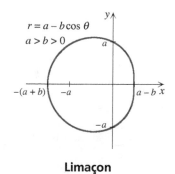

Limaçon

Equations, Inequalities, and Modeling

Even infamous Heartbreak Hill couldn't break the winning spirit of Ethiopian runner Dire Tune as she focused on first place. It was the 112th running of the Boston Marathon, a 26.2-mile ordeal that one runner called "14 miles of fun, 8 miles of sweat, and 4 miles of hell!"

Sporting events like the 2008 Marathon have come a long way since the first Olympic Games were held over 2500 years ago. Today, sports and science go hand in hand. Modern athletes often use mathematics to analyze the variables that help them increase aerobic capacity, reduce air resistance, or strengthen muscles.

▶WHAT YOU WILL learn... In this chapter you will see examples of sports applications while you learn to solve equations and inequalities. By the time you reach the finish line, you will be using algebra to model and solve problems.

1 **Equations in One Variable**

2 **Constructing Models to Solve Problems**

3 **Equations and Graphs in Two Variables**

4 **Linear Equations in Two Variables**

5 **Scatter Diagrams and Curve Fitting**

6 **Complex Numbers**

7 **Quadratic Equations**

8 **Linear and Absolute Value Inequalities**

Winslow Townson/AP Images

From Chapter 1 of *Precalculus: Functions and Graphs*. Fourth Edition. Mark Dugopolski. Copyright © 2013 by Pearson Education, Inc. All rights reserved.

1 Equations in One Variable

One of our main goals in algebra is to develop techniques for solving a wide variety of equations. In this section we will solve linear equations and other similar equations.

Definitions

An **equation** is a statement (or sentence) indicating that two algebraic expressions are equal. The verb in an equation is the equality symbol. For example, $2x + 8 = 0$ is an equation. If we replace x by -4, we get $2 \cdot (-4) + 8 = 0$, a true statement. So we say that -4 is a **solution** or **root** to the equation or -4 **satisfies** the equation. If we replace x by 3, we get $2 \cdot 3 + 8 = 0$, a false statement. So 3 is not a solution.

Whether the equation $2x + 8 = 0$ is true or false depends on the value of x, and so it is called an **open sentence.** The equation is neither true nor false until we choose a value for x. The set of all solutions to an equation is called the **solution set** to the equation. To **solve** an equation means to find the solution set. The solution set for $2x + 8 = 0$ is $\{-4\}$. The equation $2x + 8 = 0$ is an example of a linear equation.

Definition: Linear Equation in One Variable

> A **linear equation in one variable** is an equation of the form $ax + b = 0$, where a and b are real numbers, with $a \neq 0$.

Note that other letters can be used in place of x. For example, $3t + 5 = 0$, $2w - 6 = 0$, and $-2u + 7 = 0$ are linear equations.

Solving Linear Equations

The equations $2x + 8 = 0$ and $2x = -8$ both have the solution set $\{-4\}$. Two equations with the same solution set are called **equivalent** equations. Adding the same real number to or subtracting the same real number from each side of an equation results in an equivalent equation. Multiplying or dividing each side of an equation by the same nonzero real number also results in an equivalent equation. These **properties of equality** are stated in symbols in the following box.

Properties of Equality

> If A and B are algebraic expressions and C is a real number, then the following equations are equivalent to $A = B$:
>
> | | |
> |---|---|
> | $A + C = B + C$ | **Addition property of equality** |
> | $A - C = B - C$ | **Subtraction property of equality** |
> | $CA = CB \, (C \neq 0)$ | **Multiplication property of equality** |
> | $\dfrac{A}{C} = \dfrac{B}{C} \, (C \neq 0)$ | **Division property of equality** |

We can use an algebraic expression for C in the properties of equality, because the value of an algebraic expression is a real number. However, this can produce nonequivalent equations. For example,

$$x = 0 \qquad \text{and} \qquad x + \frac{1}{x} = 0 + \frac{1}{x}$$

appear to be equivalent by the addition property of equality. But the first is satisfied by 0 and the second is not. When an equation contains expressions that are undefined for some real number(s) then we must check all solutions carefully.

Any linear equation, $ax + b = 0$, can be solved in two steps. Subtract b from each side and then divide each side by a ($a \neq 0$), to get $x = -b/a$. Although the equations in our first example are not exactly in the form $ax + b = 0$, they are often called linear equations because they are equivalent to linear equations.

EXAMPLE 1 Using the properties of equality

Solve each equation.

a. $3x - 4 = 8$ **b.** $\dfrac{1}{2}x - 6 = \dfrac{3}{4}x - 9$ **c.** $3(4x - 1) = 4 - 6(x - 3)$

Solution

a.

$$3x - 4 = 8$$

$$3x - 4 + 4 = 8 + 4 \qquad \text{Add 4 to each side.}$$

$$3x = 12 \qquad \text{Simplify.}$$

$$\frac{3x}{3} = \frac{12}{3} \qquad \text{Divide each side by 3.}$$

$$x = 4 \qquad \text{Simplify.}$$

Since the last equation is equivalent to the original, the solution set to the original equation is $\{4\}$. We can check by replacing x by 4 in $3x - 4 = 8$. Since $3 \cdot 4 - 4 = 8$ is correct, we are confident that the solution set is $\{4\}$.

b. Multiplying each side of the equation by the least common denominator, LCD, will eliminate all of the fractions:

$$\frac{1}{2}x - 6 = \frac{3}{4}x - 9$$

$$4\left(\frac{1}{2}x - 6\right) = 4\left(\frac{3}{4}x - 9\right) \qquad \text{Multiply each side by 4, the LCD.}$$

$$2x - 24 = 3x - 36 \qquad \text{Distributive property}$$

$$2x - 24 - 3x = 3x - 36 - 3x \qquad \text{Subtract } 3x \text{ from each side.}$$

$$-x - 24 = -36 \qquad \text{Simplify.}$$

$$-x = -12 \qquad \text{Add 24 to each side.}$$

$$(-1)(-x) = (-1)(-12) \qquad \text{Multiply each side by } -1.$$

$$x = 12 \qquad \text{Simplify.}$$

Check 12 in the original equation. The solution set is $\{12\}$.

c. $3(4x - 1) = 4 - 6(x - 3)$

$$12x - 3 = 4 - 6x + 18 \qquad \text{Distributive property}$$

$$12x - 3 = 22 - 6x \qquad \text{Simplify.}$$

$$18x - 3 = 22 \qquad \text{Add } 6x \text{ to each side.}$$

$$18x = 25 \qquad \text{Add 3 to each side.}$$

$$x = \frac{25}{18} \qquad \text{Divide each side by 18.}$$

Check 25/18 in the original equation. The solution set is $\left\{\frac{25}{18}\right\}$.

You can use a graphing calculator to calculate the value of each side of the equation when x is 25/18 as shown in Fig. 1.

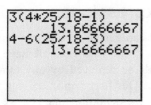

Figure 1

▶**TRY THIS.** Solve $5(3x - 2) = 5 - 7(x - 1)$. ∎

15

Note that checking the equation in Example 1(c) with a calculator did not prove that 25/18 is the correct solution. The properties of equality that were applied correctly in each step guarantee that we have the correct solution. The values of the two sides of the equation could agree for the 10 digits shown on the calculator and disagree for the digits not shown. Since that possibility is extremely unlikely, the calculator check does support our belief that we have the correct solution.

Identities, Conditional Equations, and Inconsistent Equations

An equation that is satisfied by every real number for which both sides are defined is an **identity.** Some examples of identities are

$$3x - 1 = 3x - 1, \qquad 2x + 5x = 7x, \qquad \text{and} \qquad \frac{x}{x} = 1.$$

The solution set to the first two identities is the set of all real numbers, R. Since $0/0$ is undefined, the solution set to $x/x = 1$ is the set of nonzero real numbers, $\{x \mid x \neq 0\}$.

A **conditional equation** is an equation that is satisfied by at least one real number but is not an identity. The equation $3x - 4 = 8$ is true only on condition that $x = 4$, and it is a conditional equation. The equations of Example 1 are conditional equations.

An **inconsistent equation** is an equation that has no solution. Some inconsistent equations are

$$0 \cdot x + 1 = 2, \qquad x + 3 = x + 5, \qquad \text{and} \qquad 9x - 9x = 8.$$

Note that each of these inconsistent equations is equivalent to a false statement: $1 = 2$, $3 = 5$, and $0 = 8$, respectively.

EXAMPLE 2 Classifying an equation

Determine whether the equation $3(x - 1) - 2x(4 - x) = (2x + 1)(x - 3)$ is an identity, an inconsistent equation, or a conditional equation.

Solution

$$3(x - 1) - 2x(4 - x) = (2x + 1)(x - 3)$$
$$3x - 3 - 8x + 2x^2 = 2x^2 - 5x - 3 \qquad \text{Simplify each side.}$$
$$2x^2 - 5x - 3 = 2x^2 - 5x - 3$$

Since the last equation is equivalent to the original and the last equation is an identity, the original equation is an identity.

▶**TRY THIS.** Determine whether $x(x - 1) - 6 = (x - 3)(x + 2)$ is an identity, an inconsistent equation, or a conditional equation. ■

Equations Involving Rational Expressions

Recall that division by zero is undefined and we can't have zero in the denominator of a fraction. Since the rational expressions in the next example have variables in their denominators, these variables can't be replaced by any numbers that would cause zero to appear in a denominator. Our first step in solving these equations is to multiply by the LCD and eliminate the denominators. But we must check our solutions in the original equations and discard any that cause undefined expressions.

EXAMPLE 3 | Equations involving rational expressions

Solve each equation and identify each as an identity, an inconsistent equation, or a conditional equation.

a. $\dfrac{y}{y-3} + 3 = \dfrac{3}{y-3}$ **b.** $\dfrac{1}{x-1} - \dfrac{1}{x+1} = \dfrac{2}{x^2-1}$ **c.** $\dfrac{1}{2} + \dfrac{1}{x-1} = 1$

Solution

a. Since $y - 3$ is the denominator in each rational expression, $y - 3$ is the LCD. Note that using 3 in place of y in the equation would cause 0 to appear in the denominators. So we know up front that 3 *is not a solution to this equation.*

$$(y-3)\left(\dfrac{y}{y-3} + 3\right) = (y-3)\dfrac{3}{y-3} \qquad \text{Multiply each side by the LCD.}$$

$$(y-3)\dfrac{y}{y-3} + (y-3)3 = 3 \qquad \text{Distributive property}$$

$$y + 3y - 9 = 3$$

$$4y - 9 = 3$$

$$4y = 12 \qquad \text{Add 9 to each side.}$$

$$y = 3 \qquad \text{Divide each side by 4.}$$

If we replace y by 3 in the original equation, then we get two undefined expressions. So 3 is not a solution to the original equation. The original equation has no solution. The equation is inconsistent.

b. Since $x^2 - 1 = (x-1)(x+1)$, the LCD is $(x-1)(x+1)$. Note that using 1 or -1 for x in the equation would cause 0 to appear in a denominator.

$$\dfrac{1}{x-1} - \dfrac{1}{x+1} = \dfrac{2}{x^2-1}$$

$$(x-1)(x+1)\left(\dfrac{1}{x-1} - \dfrac{1}{x+1}\right) = (x-1)(x+1)\dfrac{2}{x^2-1} \qquad \text{Multiply by the LCD.}$$

$$(x-1)(x+1)\dfrac{1}{x-1} - (x-1)(x+1)\dfrac{1}{x+1} = 2 \qquad \text{Distributive property}$$

$$x + 1 - (x-1) = 2$$

$$2 = 2$$

Since the last equation is an identity, the original equation is also an identity. The solution set is $\{x \mid x \neq 1 \text{ and } x \neq -1\}$, because 1 and -1 cannot be used for x in the original equation.

c. Note that we cannot use 1 for x in the original equation. To solve the equation multiply each side by the LCD:

$$\dfrac{1}{2} + \dfrac{1}{x-1} = 1$$

$$2(x-1)\left(\dfrac{1}{2} + \dfrac{1}{x-1}\right) = 2(x-1)1 \qquad \text{Multiply by the LCD.}$$

$$x - 1 + 2 = 2x - 2$$

$$x + 1 = 2x - 2$$

$$3 = x$$

Check 3 in the original equation. The solution set is $\{3\}$, and the equation is a conditional equation.

▶**TRY THIS.** Solve $\dfrac{2}{x-3} - \dfrac{3}{x+3} = \dfrac{4}{x^2-9}$. ∎

In Example 3(a) the final equation had a root that did not satisfy the original equation, because the domain of the rational expression excluded the root. Such a root is called an **extraneous root.** If an equation has no solution, then its solution set is the **empty set** (the set with no members). The symbol $\varnothing$ is used to represent the empty set.

EXAMPLE 4 Using a calculator in solving an equation

Solve

$$\frac{7}{2.4x} + \frac{3}{5.9} = \frac{1}{8.2}$$

with the aid of a calculator. Round the answer to three decimal places.

Solution

We could multiply each side by the LCD, but since we are using a calculator, we can subtract 3/5.9 from each side to isolate x.

$$\frac{7}{2.4x} + \frac{3}{5.9} = \frac{1}{8.2}$$

$$\frac{7}{2.4x} = \frac{1}{8.2} - \frac{3}{5.9}$$

$$\frac{7}{2.4x} \approx -0.38652336 \qquad \text{Use a calculator to simplify.}$$

$$\frac{7}{2.4} \approx -0.38652336x \qquad \text{Multiply each side by } x.$$

$$\frac{7}{2.4(-0.38652336)} \approx x \qquad \text{Divide each side by } -0.38652336.$$

$$x \approx -7.546 \qquad \text{Round to three decimal places.}$$

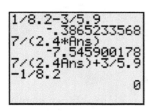

Figure 2

The solution set is $\{-7.546\}$. Since -0.38652336 is an approximate value, the sign $\approx$ (for "approximately equal to") is used instead of the equal sign. To get three-decimal-place accuracy in the final answer, use as many digits as your calculator allows until you get to the final computation.

Figure 2 shows the computations and the check. Note how the ANS key is used.

▶**TRY THIS.** Solve $\dfrac{2}{3.4x} - \dfrac{1}{8.9} = \dfrac{4}{4.7}$ with the aid of a calculator. ∎

Equations Involving Absolute Value

To solve equations involving absolute value, remember that $|x| = x$ if $x \geq 0$, and $|x| = -x$ if $x < 0$. The absolute value of x is greater than or equal to 0 for any real number x. So an equation such as $|x| = -6$ has no solution. Since a number and its opposite have the same absolute value, $|x| = 4$ is equivalent to $x = 4$ or $x = -4$. The only number that has 0 absolute value is 0. These ideas are summarized as follows.

Basic Absolute Value Equations

Absolute value equation	Equivalent statement	Solution set
$\lvert x \rvert = k \ (k > 0)$	$x = -k$ or $x = k$	$\{-k, k\}$
$\lvert x \rvert = 0$	$x = 0$	$\{0\}$
$\lvert x \rvert = k \ (k < 0)$		$\varnothing$

EXAMPLE 5 Equations involving absolute value

Solve each equation.

a. $\lvert x - 5 \rvert = 4$ **b.** $2\lvert x + 8 \rvert - 6 = 0$

Solution

a. First write an equivalent statement without using absolute value symbols.

$$\lvert x - 5 \rvert = 4$$

$$x - 5 = -4 \qquad \text{or} \qquad x - 5 = 4$$

$$x = 1 \qquad \text{or} \qquad x = 9$$

The solution set is $\{1, 9\}$. Check that $\lvert 1 - 5 \rvert = 4$ and $\lvert 9 - 5 \rvert = 4$.

b. First isolate $\lvert x + 8 \rvert$.

$$2\lvert x + 8 \rvert - 6 = 0$$

$$2\lvert x + 8 \rvert = 6$$

$$\lvert x + 8 \rvert = 3$$

Now write an equivalent statement without absolute value symbols.

$$x + 8 = -3 \qquad \text{or} \qquad x + 8 = 3$$

$$x = -11 \qquad \text{or} \qquad x = -5$$

The solution set is $\{-11, -5\}$. Check that $2\lvert -11 + 8 \rvert - 6 = 0$ and $2\lvert -5 + 8 \rvert - 6 = 0$.

▶**TRY THIS.** Solve $\lvert 2x - 3 \rvert = 5$. ∎

Equation-Solving Overview

In solving equations, there are usually many different sequences of correct steps that lead to the correct solution. If the approach that you try first does not work, *try another approach*, but learn from your failures as well as your successes. Solving equations successfully takes patience and practice.

Equations Used as Models

Equations are often used to describe or **model** real situations. In the coming sections we will learn how to write equations that model real situations. In the next example you are simply given an equation and asked to solve it.

Equations, Inequalities, and Modeling

EXAMPLE 6 | An equation used as a model

If x is the number of years after 1990 and y is the median income in dollars for working women in the United States, then the equation $y = 355.9x + 11,075.3$ models the real data (www.infoplease.com). In what year (to the nearest year) is the median income $20,000?

Solution

Since y is 20,000, we solve the following equation to find x:

$$20,000 = 355.9x + 11,075.3$$

$$8924.7 = 355.9x \qquad \text{Subtract 11,075.3 from each side.}$$

$$25.08 \approx x \qquad \text{Divide each side by 355.9.}$$

So to the nearest year the median income reaches $20,000 in 25 years after 1990, or 2015.

▶TRY THIS. In what year (to the nearest year) will the median income be $25,000? ∎

➤ FOR thought... True or False? Explain.

1. The number 3 is in the solution set to $5(4 - x) = 2x - 1$.

2. The equation $3x - 1 = 8$ is equivalent to $3x - 2 = 7$.

3. The equation $x + \sqrt{x} = -2 + \sqrt{x}$ is equivalent to $x = -2$.

4. The solution set to $x - x = 7$ is the empty set.

5. The equation $12x = 0$ is an inconsistent equation.

6. The equation $x - 0.02x = 0.98x$ is an identity.

7. The equation $|x| = -8$ is equivalent to $x = 8$ or $x = -8$.

8. The equations $\frac{x}{x-5} = \frac{5}{x-5}$ and $x = 5$ are equivalent.

9. To solve $-\frac{2}{3}x = \frac{3}{4}$, we should multiply each side by $-\frac{2}{3}$.

10. If a and b are real numbers, then $ax + b = 0$ has a solution.

➤ EXERCISES 1

Fill in the blank.

1. A statement that two algebraic expressions are equal is an _____.

2. An equation of the form $ax + b = 0$ with $a \neq 0$ is a _____ equation.

3. Equations with the same solution set are _____ equations.

4. The set of all solutions to an equation is the _____.

5. An _____ is an equation that is satisfied by all real numbers for which both sides are defined.

6. An _____ is an equation that has no solution.

7. A _____ is an equation that has at least one solution but is not an identity.

8. A number that satisfies the final equation but not the original equation is an _____.

Determine whether each given number is a solution to the equation following it.

9. $3, 2x - 4 = 9$

10. $-2, \frac{1}{x} - \frac{1}{2} = -1$

11. $-3, (x - 1)^2 = 16$

12. $4, \sqrt{3x + 4} = -4$

Solve each equation and check your answer.

13. $3x - 5 = 0$

14. $-2x + 3 = 0$

15. $-3x + 6 = 12$

16. $5x - 3 = -13$

17. $8x - 6 = 1 - 6x$

18. $4x - 3 = 6x - 1$

19. $7 + 3x = 4(x - 1)$

20. $-3(x - 5) = 4 - 2x$

21. $-\dfrac{3}{4}x = 18$

22. $\dfrac{2}{3}x = -9$

23. $\dfrac{x}{2} - 5 = -12 - \dfrac{2x}{3}$

24. $\dfrac{x}{4} - 3 = \dfrac{x}{2} + 3$

25. $\dfrac{3}{2}x + \dfrac{1}{3} = \dfrac{1}{4}x - \dfrac{1}{6}$

26. $\dfrac{x}{2} + \dfrac{x}{5} = \dfrac{x}{6} - \dfrac{1}{3}$

Solve each equation. Identify each equation as an identity, an inconsistent equation, or a conditional equation.

27. $3(x - 6) = 3x - 18$

28. $2a + 3a = 6a$

29. $2x + 3x = 4x$

30. $4(y - 1) = 4y - 4$

31. $2(x + 3) = 3(x - 1)$

32. $2(x + 1) = 3x + 2$

33. $3(x - 6) = 3x + 18$

34. $2x + 3x = 5x + 1$

35. $\dfrac{3x}{x} = 3$

36. $\dfrac{x(x + 2)}{x + 2} = x$

Solve each equation involving rational expressions. Identify each equation as an identity, an inconsistent equation, or a conditional equation.

37. $\dfrac{1}{w - 1} - \dfrac{1}{2w - 2} = \dfrac{1}{2w - 2}$

38. $\dfrac{1}{x} + \dfrac{1}{x - 3} = \dfrac{9}{x^2 - 3x}$

39. $\dfrac{1}{x} - \dfrac{1}{3x} = \dfrac{1}{2x} + \dfrac{1}{6x}$

40. $\dfrac{1}{5x} - \dfrac{1}{4x} + \dfrac{1}{3x} = -\dfrac{17}{60}$

41. $\dfrac{z + 2}{z - 3} = \dfrac{5}{-3}$

42. $\dfrac{2x - 3}{x - 4} = \dfrac{5}{x - 4}$

43. $\dfrac{1}{x - 3} - \dfrac{1}{x + 3} = \dfrac{6}{x^2 - 9}$

44. $\dfrac{4}{x - 1} - \dfrac{9}{x + 1} = \dfrac{3}{x^2 - 1}$

45. $4 + \dfrac{6}{y - 3} = \dfrac{2y}{y - 3}$

46. $\dfrac{x}{x + 6} - 3 = 1 - \dfrac{6}{x + 6}$

47. $\dfrac{t}{t + 3} + 4 = \dfrac{2}{t + 3}$

48. $\dfrac{3x}{x + 1} - 5 = \dfrac{x - 11}{x + 1}$

Use a calculator to help you solve each equation. Round each approximate answer to three decimal places.

49. $0.27x - 3.9 = 0.48x + 0.29$

50. $x - 2.4 = 0.08x + 3.5$

51. $0.06(x - 3.78) = 1.95$

52. $0.86(3.7 - 2.3x) = 4.9$

53. $2a + 1 = -\sqrt{17}$

54. $3c + 4 = \sqrt{38}$

55. $\dfrac{0.001}{y - 0.333} = 3$

56. $1 + \dfrac{0.001}{t - 1} = 0$

57. $\dfrac{x}{0.376} + \dfrac{x}{0.135} = 2$

58. $\dfrac{1}{x} + \dfrac{5}{6.72} = 10.379$

59. $(x + 3.25)^2 = (x - 4.1)^2$

60. $0.25(2x - 1.6)^2 = (x - 0.9)^2$

61. $(2.3 \times 10^6)x + 8.9 \times 10^5 = 1.63 \times 10^4$

62. $(-3.4 \times 10^{-9})x + 3.45 \times 10^{-8} = 1.63 \times 10^4$

Solve each absolute value equation.

63. $|x| = 8$

64. $|x| = 2.6$

65. $|x - 4| = 8$

66. $|x - 5| = 3.6$

67. $|x - 6| = 0$

68. $|x - 7| = 0$

69. $|x + 8| = -3$

70. $|x + 9| = -6$

71. $|2x - 3| = 7$

72. $|3x + 4| = 12$

73. $\dfrac{1}{2}|x - 9| = 16$

74. $\dfrac{2}{3}|x + 4| = 8$

75. $2|x + 5| - 10 = 0$

76. $6 - 4|x + 3| = -2$

77. $8|3x - 2| = 0$

78. $5|6 - 3x| = 0$

79. $2|x| + 7 = 6$

80. $5 + 3|x - 4| = 0$

Solve each equation.

81. $x - 0.05x = 190$

82. $x + 0.1x = 121$

83. $0.1x - 0.05(x - 20) = 1.2$

84. $0.03x - 0.2 = 0.2(x + 0.03)$

85. $(x + 2)^2 = x^2 + 4$

86. $(x - 3)^2 = x^2 - 9$

87. $(2x - 3)^2 = (2x + 5)^2$

88. $(3x - 4)^2 + (4x + 1)^2 = (5x + 2)^2$

89. $\dfrac{x}{2} + 1 = \dfrac{1}{4}(x - 6)$

90. $-\dfrac{1}{6}(x + 3) = \dfrac{1}{4}(3 - x)$

91. $\dfrac{y - 3}{2} + \dfrac{y}{5} = 3 - \dfrac{y + 1}{6}$

92. $\dfrac{y - 3}{5} - \dfrac{y - 4}{2} = 5$

93. $5 + 7|x + 6| = 19$

94. $9 - |2x - 3| = 6$

95. $9 - 4|2x - 3| = 9$

96. $-7 - |3x + 1| = |3x + 1| - 7$

97. $8 - 5|5x + 1| = 12$

98. $5|7 - 3x| + 2 = 4|7 - 3x| - 1$

99. $\dfrac{3}{x - 2} + \dfrac{4}{x + 2} = \dfrac{7x - 2}{x^2 - 4}$

100. $\dfrac{2}{x - 1} - \dfrac{3}{x + 2} = \dfrac{8 - x}{x^2 + x - 2}$

101. $\dfrac{4}{x + 3} - \dfrac{3}{2 - x} = \dfrac{7x + 1}{x^2 + x - 6}$

102. $\dfrac{3}{x} - \dfrac{4}{1 - x} = \dfrac{7x - 3}{x^2 - x}$

103. $\dfrac{x - 2}{x - 3} = \dfrac{x - 3}{x - 4}$

104. $\dfrac{y - 1}{y + 4} = \dfrac{y + 1}{y - 2}$

Solve each problem.

105. *Working Mothers* The percentage of working mothers y can be modeled by the equation

$$y = 0.0102x + 0.644$$

where x is the number of years since 1990 (U.S. Census Bureau, www.census.gov).

a. Use the accompanying graph to estimate the year in which 70% of mothers were in the work force.

b. Is the percentage of mothers in the labor force increasing or decreasing?

c. Use the equation to find the year in which 90% of mothers will be in the labor force.

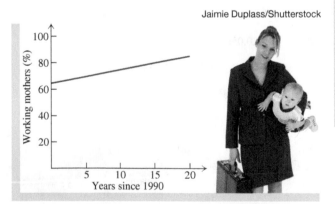
Jaimie Duplass/Shutterstock

Figure for Exercises 105 and 106

106. *Working Mothers* Use the equation in the previous exercise to find the year in which 64.4% of mothers were in the labor force.

107. *Cost Accounting* An accountant has been told to distribute a bonus to the employees that is 15% of the company's net income. Since the bonus is an expense to the accountant, it must be subtracted from the income to determine the net income. If the company has an income of \$140,000 before the bonus, then the accountant must solve

$$B = 0.15(140,000 - B)$$

to find the bonus B. Find B.

108. *Corporate Taxes* For a class C corporation in Louisiana, the amount of state income tax S is deductible on the federal return and the amount of federal income tax F is deductible on the state return. With \$200,000 taxable income and a 30% federal tax rate, the federal tax is $0.30(200,000 - S)$. If the state tax rate is 6% then the state tax satisfies

$$S = 0.06(200,000 - 0.30(200,000 - S)).$$

Find the state tax S and the federal tax F

109. *Production Cost* An automobile manufacturer, who spent \$500 million to develop a new line of cars, wants the cost of development and production to be \$12,000 per vehicle. If the production costs are \$10,000 per vehicle, then the cost per vehicle for development and production of x vehicles is $(10,000x + 500,000,000)/x$ dollars. Solve the equation

$$\frac{10,000x + 500,000,000}{x} = 12,000$$

to find the number of vehicles that must be sold so that the cost of development and production is \$12,000 per vehicle.

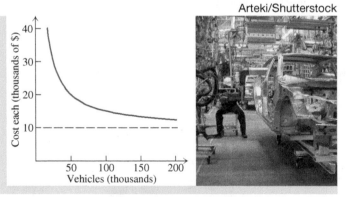
Arteki/Shutterstock

Figure for Exercise 109

110. *Harmonic Mean* The *harmonic mean* of the numbers $x_1, x_2, \ldots, x_n$ is defined as

$$HM = \frac{n}{\dfrac{1}{x_1} + \dfrac{1}{x_2} + \cdots + \dfrac{1}{x_n}}.$$

The accompanying table shows the gross domestic product (GDP) for the top five countries in trillions of U.S. dollars (www.worldbank.org).

a. What is the harmonic mean for the GDP for these five countries?

b. If France is included, the harmonic mean for the six countries is $2.93 trillion. What is the GDP for France?

Table for Exercise 110

Country	GDP ($ trillions)	
U.S.	12.5	
Japan	4.5	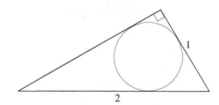
Germany	2.8	
China	2.2	
U.K.	2.2	

Krom/Shutterstock

111. *Inscribed Circle* A right triangle has sides of length 1 and 2 as shown in the accompanying figure. Find the exact radius of the inscribed circle.

Figure for Exercise 111

112. *Inscribed Circle* A right triangle has sides of length 1 and 1 as shown in the accompanying figure. Find the exact radius of the inscribed circle.

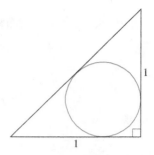

Figure for Exercise 112

FOR WRITING/DISCUSSION

113. *Definitions* Without looking back in the text, write the definitions of linear equation, identity, and inconsistent equation. Use complete sentences.

114. *Cooperative Learning* Each student in a small group should write a linear equation, an identity, an inconsistent equation, and an equation that has an extraneous root. The group should solve each equation and determine whether each equation is of the required type.

THINKING OUTSIDE THE BOX I

Nines Nine people applying for credit at the Highway 99 Loan Company listed nine different incomes each containing a different number of digits. Each of the nine incomes was a whole number of dollars and the maximum income was a nine-digit number. The loan officer found that the arithmetic mean of the nine incomes was $123,456,789. What are the nine incomes?

POP QUIZ 1

Solve each equation and identify each as an identity, inconsistent equation, or a conditional equation.

1. $7x - 6 = 0$

2. $\frac{1}{4}x - \frac{1}{6} = \frac{1}{3}$

3. $3(x - 9) = 3x - 27$

4. $|w - 1| = 6$

5. $2(x + 6) = 2x + 6$

6. $(x + 1)^2 = x^2 + 1$

→ LINKING

concepts... For Individual or Group Explorations

Modeling Oxygen Uptake in Runners

Scott Thomas/Digital Vision/Getty Images

In a study of oxygen uptake rate for marathon runners (Costill and Fox, Medicine and Science in Sports, Vol. 1) it was found that the power expended in kilocalories per minute is given by the formula $P = M(av - b)$ where M is the mass of the runner in kilograms and v is the speed in meters per minute. The constants a and b have values

$$a = 1.02 \times 10^{-3} \text{ kcal/kg m} \quad and \quad b = 2.62 \times 10^{-2} \text{ kcal/kg min.}$$

a) Runners with masses of 60 kg, 65 kg, and 70 kg are running together at 400 m/min. Find the power expenditure for each runner.

b) With a constant velocity, does the power expended increase or decrease as the mass of the runner increases?

c) Runners of 80 kg, 84 kg, and 90 kg are all expending power at the rate of 38.7 kcal/min. Find the velocity at which each is running.

d) With a constant power expenditure, does the velocity increase or decrease as the mass of the runner increases?

e) A 50-kg runner in training has a velocity of 480 m/min while carrying a weight of 2 kg. Assume that her power expenditure remains constant when the weight is removed, and find her velocity without the weight.

f) Why do runners in training carry weights?

g) Use a computer to create graphs showing power expenditure versus mass with a velocity fixed at 400 m/min and velocity versus mass with a fixed power expenditure of 40 kcal/min.

2 Constructing Models to Solve Problems

In Section 1 we solved equations. In this section we will use those skills in problem solving. To solve a problem we construct a mathematical model of the problem. Sometimes we use well-known formulas to model real situations, but we must often construct our own models.

Formulas and Functions

A **formula** is an equation involving two or more variables. Consider the uniform-motion formula $D = RT$. If you know the value of R (rate) and the value of T (time), you can determine the value of D (distance). This formula is a rule by which we can determine D: *Multiply the rate and time to get the distance.* We may also call this formula a *function.*

Definition: Function

> A **function** is a rule for determining the value of one variable from the values of one or more other variables. We say that the first variable **is a function of** the other variable(s).

So D is a function of R and T. We also say that $D = RT$ expresses D as a function of R and T.

Formulas and functions are used to **model** real-life situations. The function $D = RT$ models the relationship between distance, rate, and time in uniform motion. The formula $P = 2L + 2W$ models the relationship between the perimeter, length, and width of a rectangle. Since P is determined by the values of L and W, we say that P is a function of L and W. A list of common formulas that are commonly used as mathematical models is given inside the back cover of this text.

The formula $C = \frac{5}{9}(F - 32)$ is used to determine the Celsius temperature from the Fahrenheit temperature. So C is a function of F. This formula is **solved for** C. When a formula is solved for a specified variable, that variable is isolated on one side of the equal sign and must not occur on the other side. The formula $F = \frac{9}{5}C + 32$ expresses F as a function of C. It is solved for F.

EXAMPLE 1 Solving a formula for a specified variable

Solve the formula $S = P + Prt$ for P.

Solution

$$P + Prt = S \qquad \text{Write the formula with } P \text{ on the left.}$$

$$P(1 + rt) = S \qquad \text{Factor out } P.$$

$$P = \frac{S}{1 + rt} \qquad \text{Divide each side by } 1 + rt.$$

The formula $S = P + Prt$ expresses S as a function of P, r, and t. The formula $P = \frac{S}{1 + rt}$ expresses P as a function of S, r, and t.

▶**TRY THIS.** Solve $A = \frac{1}{2}hb_1 + \frac{1}{2}hb_2$ for h. ∎

In some situations we know the values of all variables except one. After we substitute values for those variables, the formula is an equation in one variable. We can then solve the equation to find the value of the remaining variable.

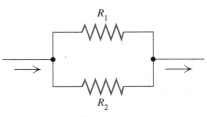

R_1

R_2

Figure 3

EXAMPLE 2 Finding the value of a variable in a formula

The total resistance R (in ohms) in the parallel circuit shown in Fig. 3 is modeled by the formula

$$\frac{1}{R} = \frac{1}{R_1} + \frac{1}{R_2}.$$

The subscripts 1 and 2 indicate that R_1 and R_2 represent the resistance for two different receivers. If $R = 7$ ohms and $R_1 = 10$ ohms, then what is the value of R_2?

Solution

Substitute the values for R and R_1 and solve for R_2.

$$\frac{1}{7} = \frac{1}{10} + \frac{1}{R_2} \qquad \text{The LCD of 7, 10, and } R_2 \text{ is } 70R_2.$$

$$70R_2 \cdot \frac{1}{7} = 70R_2 \left(\frac{1}{10} + \frac{1}{R_2} \right) \qquad \text{Multiply each side by } 70R_2.$$

$$10R_2 = 7R_2 + 70$$

$$3R_2 = 70$$

$$R_2 = \frac{70}{3}$$

Check the solution in the original formula. The resistance R_2 is 70/3 ohms, or about 23.3 ohms.

▸**TRY THIS.** Find b_1 if $A = 20$, $h = 2$, $b_2 = 3$, and $A = \frac{1}{2}h(b_1 + b_2)$. ■

Constructing Your Own Models

Applied problems in mathematics often involve solving an equation. The equations for some problems come from known formulas, as in Example 2, while in other problems we must write an equation that models a particular problem situation.

The best way to learn to solve problems is to study a few examples and then solve lots of problems. We will first look at an example of problem solving, then give a problem-solving strategy.

EXAMPLE 3 Solving a problem involving sales tax

Jeannie Fung bought a Ford Mustang GT for a total cost of $18,966, including sales tax. If the sales tax rate is 9%, then what amount of tax did she pay?

Solution

There are two unknown quantities here, the price of the car and the amount of the tax. Represent the unknown quantities as follows:

$$x = \text{the price of the car}$$

$$0.09x = \text{the amount of sales tax}$$

The price of the car plus the amount of sales tax is the total cost of the car. We can model this relationship with an equation and solve it for x:

$$x + 0.09x = 18{,}966$$

$$1.09x = 18{,}966$$

$$x = \frac{18{,}966}{1.09} = 17{,}400$$

$$0.09x = 1566$$

You can check this answer by adding $17,400 and $1566 to get $18,966, the total cost. The amount of tax that Jeannie Fung paid was $1566.

▸**TRY THIS.** Joe bought a new computer for $1506.75, including sales tax at 5%. What amount of tax did he pay? ■

No two problems are exactly alike, but there are similarities. The following strategy will assist you in solving problems on your own.

STRATEGY

Problem Solving

1. Read the problem as many times as necessary to get an understanding of the problem.
2. If possible, draw a diagram to illustrate the problem.
3. Choose a variable, write down what it represents, and if possible, represent any other unknown quantities in terms of that variable.

4. Write an equation that models the situation. You may be able to use a known formula, or you may have to write an equation that models only that particular problem.

5. Solve the equation.

6. Check your answer by using it to solve the original problem (not just the equation).

7. Answer the question posed in the original problem.

In the next example we have a geometric situation. Notice how we are following the strategy for problem solving.

EXAMPLE 4 | Solving a geometric problem

In 1974, Chinese workers found three pits that contained life-size sculptures of warriors, which were created to guard the tomb of an emperor (www.chinatour.com). The largest rectangular pit has a length that is 40 yards longer than three times the width. If its perimeter is 640 yards, what are the length and width?

Solution

First draw a diagram as shown in Fig. 4. Use the fact that the length is 40 yards longer than three times the width to represent the width and length as follows:

$$x = \text{the width in yards}$$

$$3x + 40 = \text{the length in yards}$$

Figure 4

The formula for the perimeter of a rectangle is $2L + 2W = P$. Replace W by x, L by $3x + 40$, and P by 640.

$$2L + 2W = P \qquad \text{Perimeter formula}$$
$$2(3x + 40) + 2x = 640 \qquad \text{Substitution}$$
$$6x + 80 + 2x = 640$$
$$8x + 80 = 640$$
$$8x = 560$$
$$x = 70$$

If $x = 70$, then $3x + 40 = 250$. Check that the dimensions of 70 yards and 250 yards give a perimeter of 640 yards. We conclude that the length of the pit is 250 yards and its width is 70 yards.

▶**TRY THIS.** The length of a rectangle is 20 cm shorter than five times its width. If the perimeter is 800 cm, then what is the length? ■

The next problem is called a **uniform-motion** problem because it involves motion at a constant rate. Of course, people do not usually move at a constant rate, but their average speed can be assumed to be constant over some time interval. The problem also illustrates how a table can be used as an effective technique for organizing information.

EXAMPLE 5 | Solving a uniform-motion problem

A group of hikers from Tulsa hiked down into the Grand Canyon in 3 hours 30 minutes. Coming back up on a trail that was 4 miles shorter, they hiked 2 mph slower and it took them 1 hour longer. What was their rate going down?

Solution

Let x represent the rate going down into the canyon. Make a table to show the distance, rate, and time for both the trip down and the trip back up. Once we fill in any two entries in a row of the table, we can use $D = RT$ to obtain an expression for the third entry:

	Rate	Time	Distance
Down	x mi/hr	3.5 hr	$3.5x$ mi
Up	$x - 2$ mi/hr	4.5 hr	$4.5(x - 2)$ mi

Using the fact that the distance up was 4 miles shorter, we can write the following equation:

$$4.5(x - 2) = 3.5x - 4$$
$$4.5x - 9 = 3.5x - 4$$
$$x - 9 = -4$$
$$x = 5$$

After checking that 5 mph satisfies the conditions given in the problem, we conclude that the hikers traveled at 5 mph going down into the canyon.

▶**TRY THIS.** Bea hiked uphill from her car to a waterfall in 6 hours. Hiking back to her car over the same route, she averaged 2 mph more and made the return trip in half the time. How far did she hike? ■

Average speed is not necessarily the average of your speeds. For example, if you drive 70 mph for 3 hours and then 30 mph for 1 hour, you will travel 240 miles in 4 hours. Your average speed for the trip is 60 mph, which is not the average of 70 and 30.

EXAMPLE 6 | Average speed

Shelly drove 40 miles from Peoria to Bloomington at 20 mph. She then drove back to Peoria at a higher rate of speed so that she averaged 30 mph for the whole trip. What was her speed on the return trip?

Solution

Let x represent the speed on the return trip. Make a table as follows:

	Rate	Time	Distance
Going	20 mph	2 hr	40 mi
Returning	x mph	$40/x$ hr	40 mi
Round trip	30 mph	$2 + 40/x$ hr	80 mi

Use $D = RT$ to write an equation for the round trip and solve it.

$$80 = 30\left(2 + \frac{40}{x}\right)$$

$$80 = 60 + \frac{1200}{x}$$

$$20 = \frac{1200}{x}$$

$$20x = 1200$$

$$x = 60$$

So the speed on the return trip was 60 mph. It is interesting to note that the distance between the cities does not affect the solution. You should repeat this example using d as the distance between the cities.

▶TRY THIS. Dee drove 20 miles to work at 60 mph. She then drove back home at a lower rate of speed, averaging 50 mph for the round trip. What was her speed on the return trip? ■

The next example involves mixing beverages with two different concentrations of orange juice. In other **mixture problems,** we may mix chemical solutions, candy, or even people.

EXAMPLE 7 | Solving a mixture problem

A beverage producer makes two products, Orange Drink, containing 10% orange juice, and Orange Delight, containing 50% orange juice. How many gallons of Orange Delight must be mixed with 300 gallons of Orange Drink to create a new product containing 40% orange juice?

300 gallons   x gallons   x + 300 gallons

Figure 5

Solution

Let x represent the number of gallons of Orange Delight and make a sketch as in Fig. 5. Next, we make a table that shows three pertinent expressions for each product: the amount of the product, the percent of orange juice in the product, and the actual amount of orange juice in that product.

	Amount of Product	Percent Orange Juice	Amount Orange Juice
Drink	300 gal	10%	0.10(300) gal
Delight	x gal	50%	0.50x gal
Mixture	x + 300 gal	40%	0.40(x + 300) gal

We can now write an equation expressing the fact that the actual amount of orange juice in the mixture is the sum of the amounts of orange juice in the Orange Drink and in the Orange Delight:

$$0.40(x + 300) = 0.10(300) + 0.50x$$

$$0.4x + 120 = 30 + 0.5x$$

$$90 = 0.1x$$

$$900 = x$$

Mix 900 gallons of Orange Delight with the 300 gallons of Orange Drink to obtain the proper mixture.

▶TRY THIS. How many gallons of a 40% acid solution must be mixed with 30 gallons of a 20% acid solution to obtain a mixture that is 35% acid? ■

Work problems are problems in which people or machines are working together to accomplish a task. A typical situation might have two people painting a house at different rates. Suppose Joe and Frank are painting a house together for 2 hours and Joe paints at the rate of one-sixth of the house per hour while Frank paints at the rate of one-third of the house per hour. Note that

$$\left(\frac{1}{6} \text{ of house per hour}\right)(2 \text{ hr}) = \frac{1}{3} \text{ of house}$$

and

$$\left(\frac{1}{3} \text{ of house per hour}\right)(2 \text{ hr}) = \frac{2}{3} \text{ of house}.$$

The product of the rate and the time gives the fraction of the house completed by each person, and these fractions have a sum of 1 because the entire job is completed. Note how similar this situation is to a uniform-motion problem where $RT = D$.

EXAMPLE 8 | Solving a work problem

Aboard the starship *Nostromo*, the human technician, Brett, can process the crew's medical history in 36 minutes. However, the android Science Officer, Ash, can process the same records in 24 minutes. After Brett worked on the records for 1 minute, Ash joined in and both crew members worked until the job was done. How long did Ash work on the records?

Solution

Let x represent the number of minutes that Ash worked and $x + 1$ represent the number of minutes that Brett worked. Ash works at the rate of 1/24 of the job per minute, while Brett works at the rate of 1/36 of the job per minute. The following table shows all of the pertinent quantities.

	Rate	Time	Work Completed
Ash	$\frac{1}{24}$ job/min	x min	$\frac{1}{24}x$ job
Brett	$\frac{1}{36}$ job/min	$x + 1$ min	$\frac{1}{36}(x + 1)$ job

The following equation expresses the fact that the work completed together is the sum of the work completed by each worker alone.

$$\frac{1}{24}x + \frac{1}{36}(x + 1) = 1$$

$$72\left[\frac{1}{24}x + \frac{1}{36}(x + 1)\right] = 72 \cdot 1 \quad \text{Multiply by the LCD 72.}$$

$$3x + 2x + 2 = 72$$

$$5x = 70$$

$$x = 14$$

Ash worked for 14 minutes.

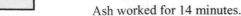 Check 14 in the original equation as shown in Fig. 6.

Figure 6

►**TRY THIS.** A tank can be filled by a small pipe in 12 hours or a large pipe in 8 hours. How long will it take to fill the tank if the small pipe is used alone for 2 hours and then both pipes are used until the tank is full? ∎

► FOR thought... True or False? Explain.

1. If we solve $P + Prt = S$ for P, we get $P = S - Prt$.

2. The perimeter of any rectangle is the product of its length and width.

3. If n is an odd integer, then $n + 1$ and $n + 3$ represent odd integers.

4. The equation $y = x + 2$ expresses y as a function of x.

5. Two numbers that have a sum of -3 can be represented by x and $-3 - x$.

6. If P is the number of professors and S is the number of students at the play, and there are twice as many professors as students, then $2P = S$.

7. If you need \$100,000 for your house, and the agent gets 9% of the selling price, then the agent gets \$9000, and the house sells for \$109,000.

8. If John can mow the lawn in x hours, then he mows the lawn at the rate of $1/x$ of the lawn per hour.

9. If George hiked $3x$ miles and Anita hiked $4(x - 2)$ miles, and George hiked 5 more miles than Anita, then $3x + 5 = 4(x - 2)$.

10. Two numbers that differ by 9 can be represented as 9 and $x + 9$.

► EXERCISES 2

Fill in the blank.

1. A _____ is an equation that involves two or more variables.

2. If the value of y can be determined from the value of x, then y is a _____ of x.

3. Motion at a constant rate is _____ motion.

4. In uniform motion, distance is a function of _____ and _____.

Solve each formula for the specified variable. The use of the formula is indicated in parentheses.

5. $I = Prt$ for r (simple interest)

6. $D = RT$ for R (uniform motion)

7. $F = \dfrac{9}{5}C + 32$ for C (temperature)

8. $C = \dfrac{5}{9}(F - 32)$ for F (temperature)

9. $A = \dfrac{1}{2}bh$ for b (area of a triangle)

10. $A = \dfrac{1}{2}bh$ for h (area of a triangle)

11. $Ax + By = C$ for y (equation of a line)

12. $Ax + By = C$ for x (equation of a line)

13. $\dfrac{1}{R} = \dfrac{1}{R_1} + \dfrac{1}{R_2} + \dfrac{1}{R_3}$ for R_1 (resistance)

14. $\dfrac{1}{R} = \dfrac{1}{R_1} + \dfrac{1}{R_2} + \dfrac{1}{R_3}$ for R_2 (resistance)

15. $a_n = a_1 + (n - 1)d$ for n (arithmetic sequence)

16. $S_n = \dfrac{n}{2}(a_1 + a_n)$ for a_1 (arithmetic series)

17. $S = \dfrac{a_1 - a_1 r^n}{1 - r}$ for a_1 (geometric series)

18. $S = 2LW + 2LH + 2HW$ for H (surface area)

19. *The 2.4-Meter Rule* A 2.4-meter sailboat is a one-person boat that is about 13 ft in length, has a displacement of about 550 lb, and a sail area of about 81 ft^2. To compete in the 2.4-meter class, a boat must satisfy the formula

$$2.4 = \frac{L + 2D - F\sqrt{S}}{2.37},$$

where L = length, F = freeboard, D = girth, and S = sail area. Solve the formula for D.

20. *Finding the Freeboard* Solve the formula in the previous exercise for F.

Find the requested formula.

21. Write a formula that expresses rate R as a function of distance D and time T in uniform motion

22. Write a formula that expresses time T as a function of distance D and rate R in uniform motion.

23. Write a formula that expresses the width W of a rectangle as a function of its area A and length L.

24. Write a formula that expresses the width W of a rectangle as a function of its perimeter P and length L.

25. Write a formula that expresses the radius r of a circle as a function of its diameter d.

26. Write a formula that expresses the diameter d of a circle as a function of its radius r.

Use the appropriate formula to solve each problem.

27. *Simple Interest* If $51.30 in interest is earned on a deposit of $950 in one year, then what is the simple interest rate?

28. *Simple Interest* If you borrow $100 and pay back $105 at the end of one month, then what is the simple annual interest rate?

29. *Uniform Motion* How long does it take an SR-71 Blackbird, one of the fastest U.S. jets, to make a surveillance run of 5570 mi if it travels at an average speed of Mach 3 (2228 mph)?

30. *Circumference of a Circle* If the circumference of a circular sign is 72π in., then what is the radius?

31. *Fahrenheit Temperature* If the temperature at 11 P.M. on New Year's Eve in Times Square was 23°F, then what was the temperature in degrees Celsius?

32. *Celsius Temperature* If the temperature at 1 P.M. on July 9 in Toronto was 30°C, then what was the temperature in degrees Fahrenheit?

Solve each problem.

33. *Cost of a Car* Jeff knows that his neighbor Sarah paid $40,230, including sales tax, for a new Buick Park Avenue. If the sales tax rate is 8%, then what is the cost of the car before the tax?

34. *Real Estate Commission* To be able to afford the house of their dreams, Dave and Leslie must clear $128,000 from the sale of their first house. If they must pay $780 in closing costs and 6% of the selling price for the sales commission, then what is the minimum selling price for which they will get $128,000?

35. *Adjusting the Saddle* The saddle height on a bicycle should be 109% of the inside leg measurement of the rider (www.harriscyclery.com). See the figure. If the saddle height is 37 in., then what is the inside leg measurement?

109% of the inside leg measurement

Figure for Exercise 35

36. *Target Heart Rate* For a cardiovascular workout, fitness experts recommend that you reach your target heart rate and stay at that rate for at least 20 minutes (www.healthstatus.com). To find your target heart rate find the sum of your age and your resting heart rate, then subtract that sum from 220. Find 60% of that result and add it to your resting heart rate. If the target heart rate for a 30-year-old person is 144, then what is that person's resting heart rate?

37. *Classic Car Auction* A buyer paid $50,600, including the buyer's premium, for a 1963 Corvette at a Mecum auction. If Mecum adds a 10% buyer's premium to the sale price of the car, then what was the sale price of the car?

38. *Art Auction* A buyer paid 2.835 million pounds, including a buyer's premium, for a Salvador Dali painting at a Sotheby's auction. If Sotheby's adds a 5% buyer's premium to the winning bid, then what was the winning bid?

39. *Investment Income* Tara paid one-half of her game-show winnings to the government for taxes. She invested one-third of her winnings in Jeff's copy shop at 14% interest and one-sixth of her winnings in Kaiser's German Bakery at 12% interest. If she earned a total of $4000 on the investments in one year, then how much did she win on the game show?

40. *Construction Penalties* Gonzales Construction contracted Kentwood High and Memorial Stadium for a total cost of $4.7 million. Because the construction was not completed on time, Gonzales paid 5% of the amount of the high school contract in penalties and 4% of the amount of the stadium contract in penalties. If the total penalty was $223,000, then what was the amount of each contract?

41. *Trimming a Garage Door* A carpenter used 30 ft of molding in three pieces to trim a garage door. If the long piece was 2 ft longer than twice the length of each shorter piece, then how long was each piece?

Figure for Exercise 41

42. *Increasing Area of a Field* Julia's soybean field is 3 m longer than it is wide. To increase her production, she plans to increase both the length and width by 2 m. If the new field is 46 m² larger than the old field, then what are the dimensions of the old field?

43. *Fencing a Feed Lot* Peter plans to fence off a square feed lot and then cross-fence to divide the feed lot into four smaller square feed lots. If he uses 480 ft of fencing, then how much area will be fenced in?

Figure for Exercise 43

44. *Fencing Dog Pens* Clint is constructing two adjacent rectangular dog pens. Each pen will be three times as long as it is wide, and the pens will share a common long side. If Clint has 65 ft of fencing, what are the dimensions of each pen?

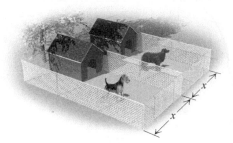

Figure for Exercise 44

45. *Racing Speed* Bobby and Rick are in a 10-lap race on a one-mile oval track. Bobby, averaging 90 mph, has completed two laps just as Rick is getting his car onto the track. What speed does Rick have to average to be even with Bobby at the end of the tenth lap?

HINT Bobby does 8 miles in the same time as Rick does 10 miles.

46. *Rowing a Boat* Boudreaux rowed his pirogue from his camp on the bayou to his crab traps. Going down the bayou, he caught a falling tide that increased his normal speed by 2 mph, but coming back it decreased his normal speed by 2 mph. Going with the tide, the trip took only 10 min; going against the tide, the trip took 30 min. How far is it from Boudreaux's camp to his crab traps?

HINT With the tide his rate is $x + 2$ mph and against the tide it is $x - 2$ mph.

47. *Average Speed* Junior drove his rig on Interstate 10 from San Antonio to El Paso. At the halfway point he noticed that he had been averaging 80 mph, while his company requires his average speed to be 60 mph. What must be his speed for the last half of the trip so that he will average 60 mph for the entire trip?

HINT The distance from San Antonio to El Paso is irrelevant. Use d or simply make up a distance.

48. *Basketball Stats* Two-thirds of the way through the basketball season, Tina Thompson of the Houston Comets has an average of 18 points per game. What must her point average be for the remaining games to average 22 points per game for the season?

49. *Start-Up Capital* Norma invested the start-up capital for her Internet business in two hedge funds. After one year one of the funds returned 5% and the other returned 6%, for a total return of $5880. If the amount on which she made 6% was $10,000 larger than the amount on which she made 5%, then what was the original amount of her start-up capital?

50. *Combining Investments* Brent lent his brother Bob some money at 8% simple interest, and he lent his sister Betty half as much money at twice the interest rate. Both loans were for one year. If Brent made a total of 24 cents in interest, then how much did he lend to each one?

51. *Percentage of Minority Workers* At the Northside assembly plant, 5% of the workers were classified as minority, while at the Southside assembly plant, 80% of the workers were classified as minority. When Northside and Southside were closed, all workers transferred to the new Eastside plant to make up its entire work force. If 50% of the 1500 employees at Eastside are minority, then how many employees did Northside and Southside have originally?

52. *Mixing Alcohol Solutions* A pharmacist needs to obtain a 70% alcohol solution. How many ounces of a 30% alcohol solution must be mixed with 40 ounces of an 80% alcohol solution to obtain a 70% alcohol solution?

HINT Add x ounces of 30% solution to 40 ounces of 80% solution to get $x + 40$ ounces of 70% solution.

53. *Harvesting Wheat* With the old combine, Nikita's entire wheat crop can be harvested in 72 hr, but a new combine can do the same job in 48 hr. How many hours would it take to harvest the crop with both combines operating?

HINT The rate for the old combine is 1/72 crop/hr and for the new one it is 1/48 crop/hr. Together the rate is $1/x$ crop/hr.

54. *Processing Forms* Rita can process a batch of insurance claims in 4 hr working alone. Eduardo can process a batch of insurance claims in 2 hr working alone. How long would it take them to process a batch of claims if they worked together?

55. *Batman and Robin* Batman can clean up all of the crime in Gotham City in 8 hr working alone. Robin can do the same job alone in 12 hr. If Robin starts crime fighting at 8 A.M. and Batman joins him at 10 A.M., then at what time will they have all of the crime cleaned up?

56. *Scraping Barnacles* Della can scrape the barnacles from a 70-ft yacht in 10 hr using an electric barnacle scraper. Don can do the same job in 15 hr using a manual barnacle scraper. If Don starts scraping at noon and Della joins him at 3 P.M., then at what time will they finish the job?

57. *Planning a Race Track* If Mario plans to develop a circular race track one mile in circumference on a square plot of land, then what is the minimum number of acres that he needs? (One acre is equal to 43,560 ft^2.)

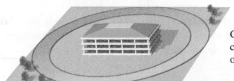

Circular track has a circumference of one mile.

Figure for Exercise 57

58. *Volume of a Can of Coke* If a can of Coke contains 12 fluid ounces and the diameter of the can is 2.375 in., then what is the height of the can? (One fluid ounce equals approximately 1.8 in.^{3}.)

59. *Area of a Lot* Julio owns a four-sided lot that lies between two parallel streets. If his 90,000-ft^2 lot has 500-ft frontage on one street and 300-ft frontage on the other, then how far apart are the streets?

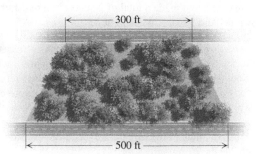

Figure for Exercise 59

60. *Width of a Football Field* If the perimeter of a football field in the NFL, including the end zones, is 1040 ft and the field is 120 yd long, then what is the width of the field in feet?

61. *Depth of a Swimming Pool* A circular swimming pool with a diameter of 30 ft and a horizontal bottom contains 22,000 gal of water. What is the depth of the water in the pool? (One cubic foot contains approximately 7.5 gal of water.)

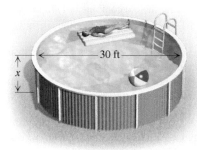

Figure for Exercise 61

62. *Depth of a Reflecting Pool* A rectangular reflecting pool with a horizontal bottom is 100 ft by 150 ft and contains 200,000 gal of water. How deep is the water in the pool?

63. *Olympic Track* To host the Summer Olympics, a city plans to build an eight-lane track. The track will consist of parallel 100-m straightaways with semicircular turns on either end as shown in the figure. The distance around the outside edge of the oval track is 514 m. If the track is built on a rectangular lot as shown in the drawing, then how many hectares (1 hectare = 10,000 m^2) of land are needed in the rectangular lot?

64. *Green Space* If the inside radius of the turns is 30 m and grass is to be planted inside and outside the track of Exercise 63, then how many square meters of the rectangular lot will be planted in grass?

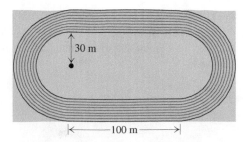

Figure for Exercises 63 and 64

65. *Taxable Income* According to the IRS (Internal Revenue Service, www.irs.gov), a single taxpayer with a taxable income between $82,400 and 171,850 in 2010 paid $16,781.25, plus 28% of the amount over $82,400. If Lorinda paid $22,280.17 in federal income tax for 2010, then what was her taxable income in 2010?

66. *Higher Bracket* According to the IRS (Internal Revenue Service, www.irs.gov), a single taxpayer with a taxable income over $373,650 in 2010 paid $108,421.25 plus 35% of the amount over $373,650. If Glen paid $284,539.85 in federal income tax for 2010, then what was his taxable income for 2010?

67. *Diluting Baneberry* How much water must Poison Ivy add to a 4-liter solution that contains 5% extract of baneberry to get a solution that contains 3% extract of baneberry?

68. *Strengthening Vinegar* A food chemist has 200 gallons of vinegar that is 4% acetic acid. How much acetic acid must be added to get the acetic acid up to 5%?

69. *Mixing Gasoline* A chemist has 500 gallons of gasoline that contain 5% ethanol. How many gallons of gasoline containing 12% ethanol should she add to get a mixture that contains 10% ethanol?

70. *Diluting Antifreeze* A mechanic is working on a car with a 20-qt radiator containing a 60% antifreeze solution. How much of the solution should he drain and replace with pure water to get a solution that is 50% antifreeze?

71. *Mixing Dried Fruit* The owner of a health-food store sells dried apples for $1.20 per quarter-pound, and dried apricots for $1.80 per quarter-pound. How many pounds of each must he mix together to get 20 lb of a mixture that sells for $1.68 per quarter-pound?

72. *Mixing Breakfast Cereal* Raisins sell for $4.50/lb, and bran flakes sell for $2.80/lb. How many pounds of raisins should be mixed with 12 lb of bran flakes to get a mixture that sells for $3.14/lb?

73. *Coins in a Vending Machine* Dana inserted eight coins, consisting of dimes and nickels, into a vending machine to purchase a Snickers bar for 55 cents. How many coins of each type did she use?

74. *Cost of a Newspaper* Ravi took eight coins from his pocket, which contained only dimes, nickels, and quarters, and bought the Sunday Edition of *The Daily Star* for 75 cents. If the number of nickels he used was one more than the number of dimes, then how many of each type of coin did he use?

75. *Active Ingredients* A pharmacist has 200 milliliters of a solution that is 40% active ingredient. How much pure water should she add to the solution to get a solution that is 25% active ingredient?

76. *Mixed Nuts* A manager bought 12 pounds of peanuts for $30. He wants to mix $5 per pound cashews with the peanuts to get a batch of mixed nuts that is worth $4 per pound. How many pounds of cashews are needed?

77. *Salt Solution I* A chemist has 5 gallons of salt solution with a concentration of 0.2 pound per gallon and another solution with a concentration of 0.5 pound per gallon. How many gallons of the stronger solution must be added to the weaker solution to get a solution that contains 0.3 pound per gallon?

78. *Salt Solution II* Suppose the 5-gallon solution in the previous problem is contained in a 5-gallon container. The chemist plans to remove some amount of the 0.2 pound per gallon solution and replace it with 0.5 pound per gallon solution so that he ends up with 5 gallons of a 0.3 pound per gallon solution. What amount should he remove?

79. *Draining a Pool I* A small pump can drain a pool in 8 hours. A large pump could drain the same pool in 5 hours. How long (to the nearest minute) will it take to drain the pool if both pumps are used simultaneously?

80. *Draining a Pool II* Suppose that the pumps in the previous exercise could not be used simultaneously and that the pool was drained in exactly 6 hours. How long was each pump used?

81. *Alcohol Solution* How many gallons of a 15% alcohol solution and how many gallons of a 10% alcohol solution should be mixed together to obtain 20 gallons that contain 12% alcohol?

82. *Alcohol Solution* How many quarts of a 20% alcohol solution and how many quarts of pure alcohol should be mixed together to obtain 100 quarts that contain 30% alcohol?

83. *Dining In* Revenue for restaurants and supermarkets can be modeled by the equations $R = 13.5n + 190$ and $S = 7.5n + 225$, where n is the number of years since 1986 (Forbes, www.forbes.com).
   a. Use the accompanying graph to estimate the year in which restaurant and supermarket revenue were equal.
   b. Use the equations to find the year in which restaurant and supermarket revenue were equal.

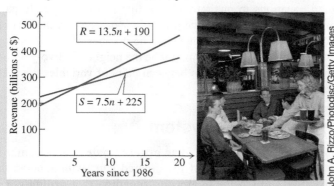

Figure for Exercises 83 and 84

84. *Dining Out* Use the equations in the previous exercise to find the year in which restaurant revenue will double supermarket revenue.

FOR WRITING/DISCUSSION

85. *Working Together* If one lost hiker can pick a gallon of wild berries in 2 hr, then how long should it take two lost hikers working together to pick one gallon of wild berries? If one mechanic at Spee-Dee Oil Change can change the oil in a Saturn in 6 min, then how long should it take two mechanics working together to change the oil in a Saturn? How long would it take 60 mechanics? Are your answers reasonable? Explain.

86. *Average Speed* Imagine that you are cruising down I-75 headed to spring break in Florida.
   a. Suppose that you cruise at 70 mph for 3 hours and then at 60 mph for 1 hour. What is your average speed for those 4 hours? When is the average speed over two time intervals actually the average of the two speeds? Explain your answer.

   b. Suppose that you cruise at 60 mph for 180 miles and then cruise at 40 mph for 160 miles. What is your average speed? When is the average speed over two distance intervals actually the average of the two speeds? Explain your answer.

▶ RETHINKING

87. Solve $2x - 3 = 8$.

88. Solve $\dfrac{x}{2} + \dfrac{1}{3} = \dfrac{x}{9} + \dfrac{1}{6}$.

89. Solve $x - 0.001x = 9990$.

90. Solve $|2x - 3| = 8$.

91. Solve $|2x - 3| = -8$.

92. Solve $|2x - 3| = 0$.

THINKING OUTSIDE THE BOX II

Roughing It Milo and Bernard are planning a three-day canoe trip on the Roaring Fork River. Their friend Vince will drop them off at the Highway 14 bridge. From there they will paddle upstream for 12 hours on the first day and 9 hours on the second day. They have been on this river before and know that their average paddling rate is twice the rate of the current in the river. At what time will they have to start heading downstream on the third day to meet Vince at the Highway 14 bridge at 5 P.M.?

POP QUIZ 2

1. Solve $dx + dy = w$ for y.

2. If the length of a rectangle is 3 feet longer than the width and the perimeter is 62 feet, then what is the width?

3. How many liters of water should be added to 3 liters of a 70% alcohol solution to obtain a 50% alcohol solution?

LINKING

For Individual or Group Explorations

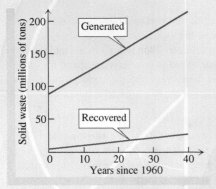

A Recycling Model

In 1960 the United States generated 87.1 million tons of municipal solid waste and recovered (or recycled) only 4.3% of it (U.S. EPA, www.epa.gov). The amount of municipal solid waste generated in the United States can be modeled by the formula $w = 3.14n + 87.1$, while the amount recovered can be modeled by the formula $w = 0.576n + 3.78$, where w is in millions of tons and n is the number of years since 1960.

a) Use the graph to estimate the first year in which the United States generated over 100 million tons of municipal solid waste.

b) Use the formulas to determine the year in which the United States generated 150 million more tons than it recovered.

c) Find the year in which 13% of the municipal solid waste generated will be recovered.

d) Find the years in which the recovery rates will be 14%, 15%, and 16%.

e) Will the recovery rate ever reach 25%?

f) According to this model, what is the maximum percentage of solid waste that will ever be recovered?

3 Equations and Graphs in Two Variables

In Section 1 we studied equations in one variable. In this section we study pairs of variables. For example, p might represent the price of gasoline and n the number of gallons that you consume in a month; x might be the number of toppings on a medium pizza and y the cost of that pizza; or h might be the height of a two-year-old child and w the weight. To study relationships between pairs of variables we use a two-dimensional coordinate system.

Table 1

Toppings x	Cost y
0	$ 5
1	7
2	9
3	11
4	13

Sergey Shandin/Shutterstock

The Cartesian Coordinate System

If x and y are real numbers then (x, y) is called an **ordered pair** of real numbers. The numbers x and y are the **coordinates** of the ordered pair, with x being the **first coordinate** or **abscissa**, and y being the **second coordinate** or **ordinate**. For example, Table 1 shows the number of toppings on a medium pizza and the

corresponding cost. The ordered pair $(3, 11)$ indicates that a three-topping pizza costs \$11. The order of the numbers matters. In this context, $(11, 3)$ would indicate that an 11-topping pizza costs \$3.

To picture ordered pairs of real numbers we use the **rectangular coordinate system** or **Cartesian coordinate system,** named after the French mathematician René Descartes (1596–1650). The Cartesian coordinate system consists of two number lines drawn perpendicular to one another, intersecting at zero on each number line as shown in Fig. 7. The point of intersection of the number lines is called the **origin.** The horizontal number line is the **x-axis** and its positive numbers are to the right of the origin. The vertical number line is the **y-axis** and its positive numbers are above the origin. The two number lines divide the plane into four regions called **quadrants,** numbered as shown in Fig. 7. The quadrants do not include any points on the axes. We call a plane with a rectangular coordinate system the **coordinate plane** or the **xy-plane.**

Just as every real number corresponds to a point on the number line, every ordered pair of real numbers (a, b) corresponds to a point P in the xy-plane. For this reason, ordered pairs of numbers are often called **points.** So a and b are the coordinates of (a, b) or the coordinates of the point P. Locating the point P that corresponds to (a, b) in the xy-plane is referred to as **plotting** or **graphing** the point, and P is called the *graph* of (a, b). In general, a **graph** is a set of points in the rectangular coordinate system.

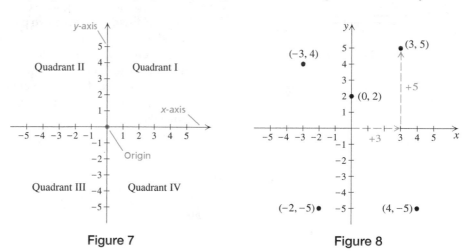

Figure 7   Figure 8

EXAMPLE 1 Plotting points

Plot the points $(3, 5)$, $(4, -5)$, $(-3, 4)$, $(-2, -5)$, and $(0, 2)$ in the xy-plane.

Solution

The point $(3, 5)$ is located three units to the right of the origin and five units above the x-axis as shown in Fig. 8. The point $(4, -5)$ is located four units to the right of the origin and five units below the x-axis. The point $(-3, 4)$ is located three units to the left of the origin and four units above the x-axis. The point $(-2, -5)$ is located two units to the left of the origin and five units below the x-axis. The point $(0, 2)$ is on the y-axis because its first coordinate is zero.

▶**TRY THIS.** Plot $(-3, -2)$, $(-1, 3)$, $(5/2, 0)$, and $(2, -3)$. ∎

Note that for points in quadrant I, both coordinates are positive. In quadrant II the first coordinate is negative and the second is positive, while in quadrant III, both coordinates are negative. In quadrant IV the first coordinate is positive and the second is negative.

The Pythagorean Theorem and the Distance Formula

You have probably studied the Pythagorean theorem in an algebra or a trigonometry course that you have taken. This theorem states that the *sum of the squares of the legs of any right triangle is equal to the square of the hypotenuse.*

The Pythagorean Theorem

The triangle shown here is a right triangle if and only if $a^2 + b^2 = c^2$.

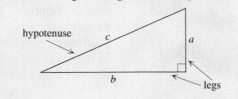

We will not prove the Pythagorean theorem here. If you want to see a proof, try an Internet search for the Pythagorean theorem. You will get many sites with numerous proofs. This author found one site with 79 proofs, including one by a former president of the United States. Here we will show how the Pythagorean theorem leads to a formula for the distance between two points in the plane and the equation for a circle.

If a and b are real numbers, then the distance between them on the number line is $|a - b|$. Now consider the points $A(x_1, y_1)$ and $B(x_2, y_2)$ shown in Fig. 9. Let AB represent the length of line segment $\overline{AB}$. Now $\overline{AB}$ is the hypotenuse of the right triangle in Fig. 9. Since A and C lie on a horizontal line, the distance between them is $|x_2 - x_1|$. Likewise $CB = |y_2 - y_1|$. Since the sum of the squares of the legs of a right triangle is equal to the square of the hypotenuse (the Pythagorean theorem) we have

$$d^2 = |x_2 - x_1|^2 + |y_2 - y_1|^2.$$

Since the distance between two points is a nonnegative real number, we have $d = \sqrt{(x_2 - x_1)^2 + (y_2 - y_1)^2}$. The absolute value symbols are replaced with parentheses, because $|a - b|^2 = (a - b)^2$ for any real numbers a and b.

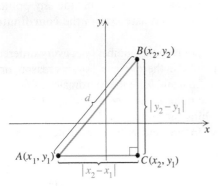

Figure 9

The Distance Formula

The distance d between the points (x_1, y_1) and (x_2, y_2) is given by the formula

$$d = \sqrt{(x_2 - x_1)^2 + (y_2 - y_1)^2}.$$

EXAMPLE 2 Finding the distance between two points

Find the exact distance between each pair of points.

a. $(5, -3), (-1, -6)$ **b.** $(\pi/2, 0), (\pi/3, 1)$

Solution

a. Let $(x_1, y_1) = (5, -3)$ and $(x_2, y_2) = (-1, -6)$. These points are shown on the graph in Fig. 10. Substitute these values into the distance formula:

$$d = \sqrt{(-1 - 5)^2 + (-6 - (-3))^2}$$
$$= \sqrt{(-6)^2 + (-3)^2}$$
$$= \sqrt{36 + 9} = \sqrt{45} = 3\sqrt{5}$$

The exact distance between the points is $3\sqrt{5}$.

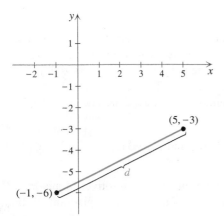

Figure 10

b. Use the distance formula as follows.

$$d = \sqrt{\left(\frac{\pi}{2} - \frac{\pi}{3}\right)^2 + (0 - 1)^2}$$

$$= \sqrt{\left(\frac{3\pi}{6} - \frac{2\pi}{6}\right)^2 + (-1)^2} \quad \text{Get common denominators.}$$

$$= \sqrt{\left(\frac{\pi}{6}\right)^2 + 1} = \sqrt{\frac{\pi^2}{36} + 1} = \sqrt{\frac{\pi^2 + 36}{36}} = \frac{\sqrt{\pi^2 + 36}}{6}$$

The exact distance between the points is $\sqrt{\pi^2 + 36}/6$.

▶**TRY THIS.** Find the distance between $(-3, -2)$ and $(-1, 4)$. ∎

Note that the distance between two points is the same regardless of which point is chosen as (x_1, y_1) or (x_2, y_2).

The Midpoint Formula

When you average two test scores (by finding their sum and dividing by 2), you are finding a number midway between the two scores. Likewise, the midpoint of the line segment with endpoints -1 and 7 in Fig. 11 is $(-1 + 7)/2$ or 3. In general, $(a + b)/2$ is the midpoint of the line segment with endpoints a and b shown in Fig. 12.

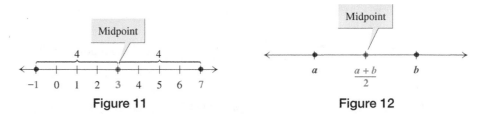

Figure 11   Figure 12

Theorem:
Midpoint on a Number Line

If a and b are real numbers, then $\frac{a + b}{2}$ is midway between them on the number line.

PROOF The distance between two numbers on the number line is the absolute value of their difference. So

$$\left| a - \frac{a + b}{2} \right| = \left| \frac{2a}{2} - \frac{a + b}{2} \right| = \left| \frac{a - b}{2} \right| = \frac{|a - b|}{2}$$

and

$$\left| b - \frac{a + b}{2} \right| = \left| \frac{2b}{2} - \frac{a + b}{2} \right| = \left| \frac{b - a}{2} \right| = \frac{|b - a|}{2}.$$

Since $|a - b| = |b - a|$, the distances from $\frac{a + b}{2}$ to a and from $\frac{a + b}{2}$ to b are equal. Since $\frac{a + b}{2}$ is equidistant from a and b, it must be between a and b. ∎

We can find the midpoint of a line segment in the xy-plane in the same manner.

Theorem:
The Midpoint Formula

The midpoint of the line segment with endpoints (x_1, y_1) and (x_2, y_2) is

$$\left(\frac{x_1 + x_2}{2}, \frac{y_1 + y_2}{2} \right).$$

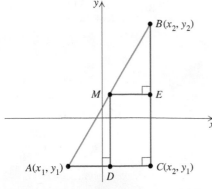

Figure 13

PROOF Start with a line segment with endpoints $A(x_1, y_1)$ and $B(x_2, y_2)$, as shown in Fig. 13. Let M be the midpoint of $\overline{AB}$. Draw horizontal and vertical line segments that form three right triangles, as shown in Fig. 13. Since M is the midpoint of $\overline{AB}$, the two small right triangles are congruent. So D is the midpoint of $\overline{AC}$ and E is the midpoint of $\overline{BC}$. Since the midpoint on a number line is found by adding and dividing by two, the x-coordinate of D is $\frac{x_1 + x_2}{2}$ and the y-coordinate of E is $\frac{y_1 + y_2}{2}$. So the midpoint M is $\left(\frac{x_1 + x_2}{2}, \frac{y_1 + y_2}{2}\right)$. ∎

EXAMPLE 3 Finding the midpoint

Find the midpoint of the line segment with the given endpoints.

a. $(5, -3), (-1, -6)$ **b.** $(\pi/2, 0), (\pi/3, 1)$

Solution

a. To get the midpoint, add the corresponding coordinates and divide by 2:

$$\left(\frac{5 + (-1)}{2}, \frac{-3 + (-6)}{2}\right) = \left(\frac{4}{2}, \frac{-9}{2}\right) = \left(2, -\frac{9}{2}\right)$$

The midpoint is $(2, -9/2)$.

b. To get the midpoint, add the corresponding coordinates and divide by 2:

$$\left(\frac{\frac{\pi}{2} + \frac{\pi}{3}}{2}, \frac{0 + 1}{2}\right) = \left(\frac{\frac{3\pi}{6} + \frac{2\pi}{6}}{2}, \frac{1}{2}\right) = \left(\frac{\frac{5\pi}{6}}{2}, \frac{1}{2}\right) = \left(\frac{5\pi}{12}, \frac{1}{2}\right)$$

The midpoint is $(5\pi/12, 1/2)$.

▶**TRY THIS.** Find the midpoint of the line segment with endpoints $(4, -1)$ and $(3, 1/2)$. ∎

EXAMPLE 4 Using the midpoint formula

Prove that the diagonals of the parallelogram with vertices $(0, 0)$, $(1, 3)$, $(5, 0)$, and $(6, 3)$ bisect each other.

Solution

The parallelogram is shown in Fig. 14. The midpoint of the diagonal from $(0, 0)$ to $(6, 3)$ is

$$\left(\frac{0 + 6}{2}, \frac{0 + 3}{2}\right),$$

or $(3, 1.5)$. The midpoint of the diagonal from $(1, 3)$ to $(5, 0)$ is

$$\left(\frac{1 + 5}{2}, \frac{3 + 0}{2}\right),$$

or $(3, 1.5)$. Since the diagonals have the same midpoint, they bisect each other.

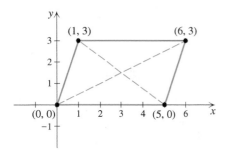

Figure 14

▶ **TRY THIS.** Prove that the diagonals of the square with vertices $(0, 0)$, $(4, 1)$, $(3, 5)$, and $(-1, 4)$ bisect each other. ∎

The Circle

An ordered pair is a **solution to** or **satisfies** an equation in two variables if the equation is correct when the variables are replaced by the coordinates of the ordered pair. For example, $(3, 11)$ satisfies $y = 2x + 5$ because $11 = 2(3) + 5$ is correct. The

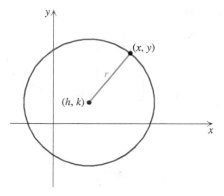

Figure 15

solution set to an equation in two variables is the set of all ordered pairs that satisfy the equation. The graph of (the solution set to) an equation is a geometric object that gives us a visual image of an algebraic object. Circles provide a nice example of this relationship between algebra and geometry.

A **circle** is the set of all points in a plane that lie a fixed distance from a given point in the plane. The fixed distance is called the **radius,** and the given point is the **center.** The distance formula can be used to write an equation for the circle shown in Fig. 15 with center (h, k) and radius r for $r > 0$. A point (x, y) is on the circle if and only if it satisfies the equation

$$\sqrt{(x - h)^2 + (y - k)^2} = r.$$

Since both sides of $\sqrt{(x - h)^2 + (y - k)^2} = r$ are positive, we can square each side to get the following **standard form** for the equation of a circle.

Theorem: Equation for a Circle in Standard Form

The equation for a circle with center (h, k) and radius r for $r > 0$ is

$$(x - h)^2 + (y - k)^2 = r^2.$$

A circle centered at the origin has equation $x^2 + y^2 = r^2$.

Note that squaring both sides of an equation produces an equivalent equation only when both sides are positive. If we square both sides of $\sqrt{x} = -3$, we get $x = 9$. But $\sqrt{9} \neq -3$ since the square root symbol always represents the nonnegative square root.

EXAMPLE 5 Graphing a circle

Sketch the graph of the equation $(x - 1)^2 + (y + 2)^2 = 9$.

Solution

To determine the center and radius of this circle, compare its equation to the standard form:

$$(x - h)^2 + (y - k)^2 = r^2$$

$$(x - 1)^2 + (y + 2)^2 = 9$$

$$(x - 1)^2 + (y - (-2))^2 = 3^2$$

It is clear that $h = 1$, but you must rewrite (or at least think of) $y + 2$ as $y - (-2)$ to determine that $k = -2$. So the center of the circle is $(1, -2)$ and the radius is 3. You can draw the circle as in Fig. 16 with a compass or computer. To draw a circle by hand, locate the points that lie 3 units above, below, right, and left of the center, as shown in Fig. 16. Then sketch a circle through these points.

To support these results with a graphing calculator you must first solve the equation for y:

$$(x - 1)^2 + (y + 2)^2 = 9$$

$$(y + 2)^2 = 9 - (x - 1)^2$$

$$y + 2 = \pm\sqrt{9 - (x - 1)^2}$$

$$y = -2 \pm \sqrt{9 - (x - 1)^2}$$

Now enter y_1 and y_2 as in Fig. 17(a) on the next page. Set the viewing window as in Fig. 17(b). The graph in Fig. 17(c) supports our previous conclusion. A circle looks round only if the same unit distance is used on both axes. Some calculators

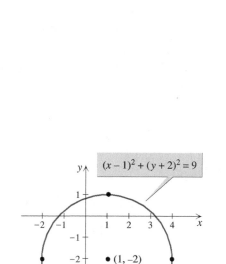

Figure 16

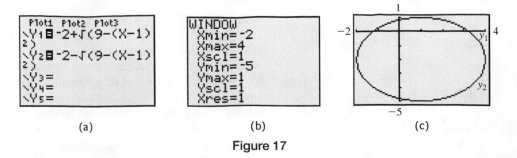

(a)   (b)   (c)

Figure 17

automatically draw the graph with the same unit distance on both axes given the correct command (Zsquare on a TI-83).

▶**TRY THIS.** Sketch the graph of $(x + 2)^2 + (y - 4)^2 = 25$. ∎

Note that an equation such as $(x - 1)^2 + (y + 2)^2 = -9$ is not satisfied by any pair of real numbers, because the left-hand side is a nonnegative real number, while the right-hand side is negative. The equation $(x - 1)^2 + (y + 2)^2 = 0$ is satisfied only by $(1, -2)$. Since only one point satisfies $(x - 1)^2 + (y + 2)^2 = 0$, its graph is sometimes called a degenerate circle with radius zero.

In the next example we start with a description of a circle and write its equation.

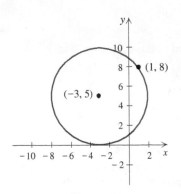

Figure 18

EXAMPLE 6 Writing an equation of a circle

Write the standard equation for the circle with the center $(-3, 5)$ and passing through $(1, 8)$ as shown in Fig. 18.

Solution

The radius of this circle is the distance between $(-3, 5)$ and $(1, 8)$:

$$r = \sqrt{(1 - (-3))^2 + (8 - 5)^2} = \sqrt{16 + 9} = 5$$

Now use $h = -3$, $k = 5$, and $r = 5$ in the standard equation of the circle $(x - h)^2 + (y - k)^2 = r^2$.

$$(x - (-3))^2 + (y - 5)^2 = 5^2$$

So the equation of the circle is $(x + 3)^2 + (y - 5)^2 = 25$.

▶**TRY THIS.** Write the standard equation for the circle with center $(2, -1)$ and passing through $(3, 6)$. ∎

A circle in standard form could be rewritten as follows:

$$(x + 3)^2 + (y - 5)^2 = 4 \qquad \text{Standard form for a circle}$$
$$x^2 + 6x + 9 + y^2 - 10y + 25 = 4 \qquad \text{Square the binomials.}$$
$$x^2 + 6x + y^2 - 10y = -30$$

To find the center and radius of the circle that is given by the last equation, we go back to standard form by *completing the square*.

Completing the square means finding the third term of a perfect square trinomial when given the first two. That is, if we start with $x^2 + bx$, then what third term will make a perfect square trinomial? Since

$$\left(x + \frac{b}{2}\right)^2 = x^2 + 2 \cdot \frac{b}{2} \cdot x + \left(\frac{b}{2}\right)^2 = x^2 + bx + \left(\frac{b}{2}\right)^2$$

adding $\left(\frac{b}{2}\right)^2$ to $x^2 + bx$ completes the square. For example, the perfect square trinomial that starts with $x^2 + 6x$ is $x^2 + 6x + 9$. Note that 9 can be found by taking one-half of 6 and squaring.

Rule for Completing the Square of $x^2 + bx + ?$

The last term of a perfect square trinomial (with $a = 1$) is the square of one-half of the coefficient of the middle term. In symbols, the perfect square trinomial whose first two terms are $x^2 + bx$ is

$$x^2 + bx + \left(\frac{b}{2}\right)^2.$$

EXAMPLE 7 Changing an equation of a circle to standard form

Graph the equation $x^2 + 6x + y^2 - 5y = -\frac{1}{4}$.

Solution

Complete the square for both x and y to get the standard form.

$$x^2 + 6x + 9 + y^2 - 5y + \frac{25}{4} = -\frac{1}{4} + 9 + \frac{25}{4} \qquad \left(\frac{1}{2} \cdot 6\right)^2 = 9, \left(\frac{1}{2} \cdot 5\right)^2 = \frac{25}{4}$$

$$(x + 3)^2 + \left(y - \frac{5}{2}\right)^2 = 15 \qquad \text{Factor the trinomials on the left side.}$$

The graph is a circle with center $\left(-3, \frac{5}{2}\right)$ and radius $\sqrt{15}$. See Fig. 19.

▶**TRY THIS.** Graph the equation $x^2 + 3x + y^2 - 2y = 0$. ∎

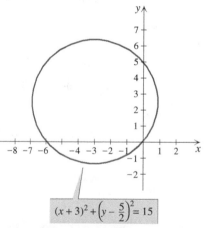

$$(x + 3)^2 + \left(y - \frac{5}{2}\right)^2 = 15$$

Figure 19

HISTORICAL NOTE

Euclid of Alexandria (325–265 B.C.) was a Greek mathematician who lived in Alexandria, Egypt, during the reign of Ptolemy I (323 B.C.–283 B.C.). He is considered to be the "father of geometry." His most popular work, *Elements*, is one of the most successful textbooks in the history of mathematics. Within it, the properties of geometrical objects are deduced from a small set of axioms, thereby founding the axiomatic method of mathematics.

Whether an equation of the form $x^2 + y^2 + Ax + By = C$ is a circle depends on the values of A, B, and C. We can always complete the squares for $x^2 + Ax$ and $y^2 + By$ as in Example 7. Since a circle must have a positive radius, this equation is the equation of a circle only if the right side of the equation turns out to be positive *after* completing the squares. If the right side turns out to be zero, then only one point satisfies the equation. If the right side turns out to be negative, then no points satisfy the equation.

The Line

For the circle, we started with the geometric definition and developed the algebraic equation. We would like to do the same thing for lines, but geometric definitions of lines are rather vague. Euclid's definition was "length without breadth." A modern geometry textbook states that a line is "a straight set of points extending infinitely in both directions." Another modern textbook defines lines algebraically as the graph

Equations, Inequalities, and Modeling

of an equation of the form $Ax + By = C$. So we will accept the following theorem without proof.

Theorem: Equation of a Line in Standard Form

If A, B, and C are real numbers, then the graph of the equation

$$Ax + By = C$$

is a straight line, provided A and B are not both zero. Every straight line in the coordinate plane has an equation in the form $Ax + By = C$, the **standard form** for the equation of a line.

An equation of the form $Ax + By = C$ is called a **linear equation in two variables.** The equations

$$2x + 3y = 5, \qquad x = 4, \qquad \text{and} \qquad y = 5$$

are linear equations in standard form. An equation such as $y = 3x - 1$ that can be rewritten in standard form is also called a linear equation.

There is only one line containing any two distinct points. So to graph a linear equation we simply find two points that satisfy the equation and draw a line through them. We often use the point where the line crosses the x-axis, the **x-intercept,** and the point where the line crosses the y-axis, the **y-intercept.** Since every point on the x-axis has y-coordinate 0, we find the x-intercept by replacing y with 0 and then solving the equation for x. Since every point on the y-axis has x-coordinate 0, we find the y-intercept by replacing x with 0 and then solving for y. If the x- and y-intercepts are both at the origin, then you must find another point that satisfies the equation.

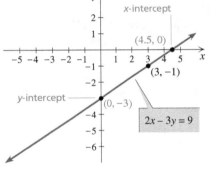

Figure 20

EXAMPLE 8 Graphing lines and showing the intercepts

Graph each equation. Be sure to find and show the intercepts.

a. $2x - 3y = 9$ **b.** $y = 40 - x$

Solution

a. Since the y-coordinate of the x-intercept is 0, we replace y by 0 in the equation:

$$2x - 3(0) = 9$$
$$2x = 9$$
$$x = 4.5$$

To find the y-intercept, we replace x by 0 in the equation:

$$2(0) - 3y = 9$$
$$-3y = 9$$
$$y = -3$$

The x-intercept is $(4.5, 0)$ and the y-intercept is $(0, -3)$. Locate the intercepts and draw the line as shown in Fig. 20. To check, locate a point such as $(3, -1)$, which also satisfies the equation, and see if the line goes through it.

b. If $x = 0$, then $y = 40 - 0 = 40$ and the y-intercept is $(0, 40)$. If $y = 0$, then $0 = 40 - x$ or $x = 40$. The x-intercept is $(40, 0)$. Draw a line through these points as shown in Fig. 21. Check that $(10, 30)$ and $(20, 20)$ also satisfy $y = 40 - x$ and the line goes through these points.

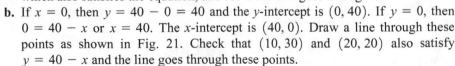 The calculator graph shown in Fig. 22 is consistent with the graph in Fig. 21. Note that the viewing window is set to show the intercepts.

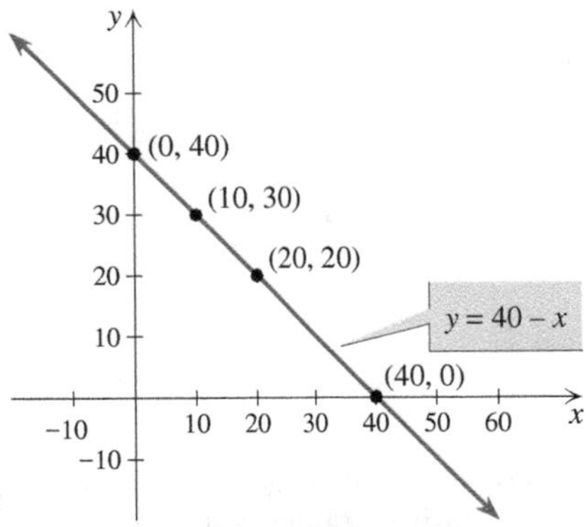

►TRY THIS. Graph $2x + 5y = 10$ and determine the intercepts. ∎

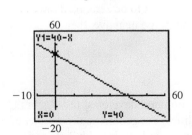

Figure 21

Figure 22

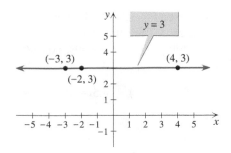

Figure 23

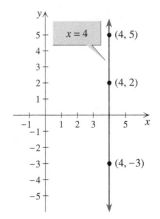

Figure 24

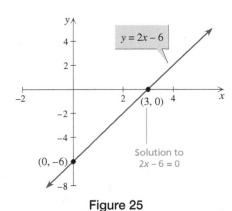

Figure 25

EXAMPLE 9 | Graphing horizontal and vertical lines

Sketch the graph of each equation in the rectangular coordinate system.

a. $y = 3$ **b.** $x = 4$

Solution

a. The equation $y = 3$ is equivalent to $0 \cdot x + y = 3$. Because x is multiplied by 0, we can choose any value for x as long as we choose 3 for y. So ordered pairs such as $(-3, 3)$, $(-2, 3)$, and $(4, 3)$ satisfy the equation $y = 3$. The graph of $y = 3$ is the horizontal line shown in Fig. 23.

b. The equation $x = 4$ is equivalent to $x + 0 \cdot y = 4$. Because y is multiplied by 0, we can choose any value for y as long as we choose 4 for x. So ordered pairs such as $(4, -3)$, $(4, 2)$, and $(4, 5)$ satisfy the equation $x = 4$. The graph of $x = 4$ is the vertical line shown in Fig. 24.

Note that you cannot graph $x = 4$ using the Y= key on your calculator. You can graph it on a calculator using polar coordinates or parametric equations.

▶**TRY THIS.** Graph $y = 5$ in the rectangular coordinate system. ∎

In the context of two variables the equation $x = 4$ has infinitely many solutions. Every ordered pair on the vertical line in Fig. 24 satisfies $x = 4$. In the context of one variable, $x = 4$ has only one solution, 4.

Using a Graph to Solve an Equation

Graphing and solving equations go hand in hand. For example, the graph of $y = 2x - 6$ in Fig. 25 has x-intercept $(3, 0)$, because if $x = 3$ then $y = 0$. Of course, 3 is also the solution to the corresponding equation $2x - 6 = 0$ (where y is replaced by 0). For this reason, the solution to an equation is also called a **zero** or **root** of the equation. Every x-intercept on a graph provides us a solution to the corresponding equation. However, an x-intercept on a graph may not be easy to identify. In the next example we see how a graphing calculator identifies an x-intercept and thus gives us the approximate solution to an equation.

EXAMPLE 10 | Using a graph to solve an equation

Use a graphing calculator to solve $0.55(x - 3.45) + 13.98 = 0$.

Solution

First graph $y = 0.55(x - 3.45) + 13.98$ using a viewing window that shows the x-intercept as in Fig. 26(a). Next press ZERO or ROOT on the CALC menu. The calculator can find a zero between a *left bound* and a *right bound*, which you must

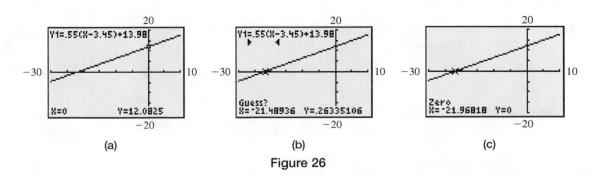

(a)   (b)   (c)

Figure 26

enter. The calculator also asks you to make a guess. See Fig. 26(b). The more accurate the guess, the faster the calculator will find the zero. The solution to the equation rounded to two decimal places is -21.97. See Fig. 26(c). As always, consult your calculator manual if you are having difficulty.

▶**TRY THIS.** Use a graphing calculator to solve $0.34(x - 2.3) + 4.5 = 0$. ∎

FOR thought... True or False? Explain.

1. The point $(2, -3)$ is in quadrant II.

2. The point $(4, 0)$ is in quadrant I.

3. The distance between (a, b) and (c, d) is
$$\sqrt{(a - b)^2 + (c - d)^2}.$$

4. The equation $3x^2 + y = 5$ is a linear equation.

5. The solution to $7x - 9 = 0$ is the x-coordinate of the x-intercept of $y = 7x - 9$.

6. $\sqrt{7^2 + 9^2} = 7 + 9$

7. The origin lies midway between $(1, 3)$ and $(-1, -3)$.

8. The distance between $(3, -7)$ and $(3, 3)$ is 10.

9. The x-intercept for the graph of $3x - 2y = 7$ is $(7/3, 0)$.

10. The graph of $(x + 2)^2 + (y - 1)^2 = 5$ is a circle centered at $(-2, 1)$ with radius 5.

EXERCISES 3

Fill in the blank.

1. If x and y are real numbers, then (x, y) is an _____ pair of real numbers.

2. The first coordinate in (x, y) is the _____ and the second coordinate is the _____.

3. Ordered pairs are graphed in the rectangular coordinate system or the _____ coordinate system.

4. The intersection of the x-axis and the y-axis is the _____.

5. The set of all points in a plane that lie a fixed distance from a given point in the plane is a _____.

6. Finding the third term of a perfect square trinomial when given the first two is _____.

7. An equation of the form $Ax + By = C$ is a _____ in two variables.

8. The point where a line crosses the y-axis is the _____.

In Exercises 9–18, for each point shown in the xy-plane, write the corresponding ordered pair and name the quadrant in which it lies or the axis on which it lies.

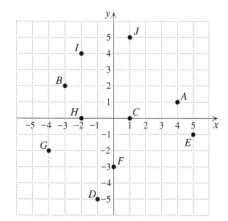

9. A **10.** B **11.** C **12.** D

13. E **14.** F **15.** G **16.** H

17. I **18.** J

For each pair of points find the distance between them and the midpoint of the line segment joining them.

19. $(1, 3), (4, 7)$ **20.** $(-3, -2), (9, 3)$

21. $(-1, -2), (1, 0)$ **22.** $(-1, 0), (1, 2)$

23. $(12, -11), (5, 13)$ **24.** $(-4, -7), (4, 8)$

25. $(-1, 1), (-1 + 3\sqrt{3}, 4)$

26. $(1 + \sqrt{2}, -2), (1 - \sqrt{2}, 2)$

27. $(1.2, 4.8), (-3.8, -2.2)$ **28.** $(-2.3, 1.5), (4.7, -7.5)$

29. $(a, 0), (b, 0)$ **30.** $(a, 0), \left(\dfrac{a+b}{2}, 0\right)$

31. $(\pi, 0), (\pi/2, 1)$ **32.** $(0, 0), (\pi/2, 1)$

Determine the center and radius of each circle and sketch the graph

33. $x^2 + y^2 = 16$ **34.** $x^2 + y^2 = 1$

35. $(x + 6)^2 + y^2 = 36$ **36.** $x^2 + (y - 2)^2 = 16$

37. $y^2 = 25 - (x + 1)^2$ **38.** $x^2 = 9 - (y - 3)^2$

39. $(x - 2)^2 = 8 - (y + 2)^2$

40. $(y + 2)^2 = 20 - (x - 4)^2$

Write the standard equation for each circle.

41. Center at $(0, 0)$ with radius 7

42. Center at $(0, 0)$ with radius 5

43. Center at $(-2, 5)$ with radius $1/2$

44. Center at $(-1, -6)$ with radius $1/3$

45. Center at $(3, 5)$ and passing through the origin

46. Center at $(-3, 9)$ and passing through the origin

47. Center at $(5, -1)$ and passing through $(1, 3)$

48. Center at $(-2, -3)$ and passing through $(2, 5)$

Determine the center and radius of each circle and sketch the graph. See the rule for completing the square in Example 6.

49. $x^2 + y^2 = 9$ **50.** $x^2 + y^2 = 100$

51. $x^2 + y^2 + 6y = 0$ **52.** $x^2 + y^2 = 4x$

53. $x^2 + 6x + y^2 + 8y = 0$

54. $x^2 - 8x + y^2 - 10y = -5$ **55.** $x^2 - 3x + y^2 + 2y = \dfrac{3}{4}$

56. $x^2 + 5x + y^2 - y = \dfrac{5}{2}$ **57.** $x^2 - 6x + y^2 - 8y = 0$

58. $x^2 + 10x + y^2 - 8y = -40$

59. $x^2 + y^2 = 4x + 3y$ **60.** $x^2 + y^2 = 5x - 6y$

61. $x^2 + y^2 = \dfrac{x}{2} - \dfrac{y}{3} - \dfrac{1}{16}$ **62.** $x^2 + y^2 = x - y + \dfrac{1}{2}$

Write the standard equation for each of the following circles.

63. a. **b.**

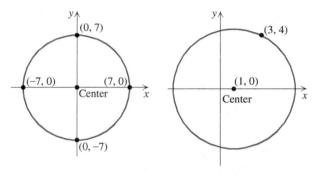

c.

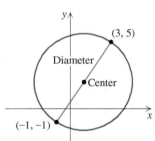

64. a. **b.**

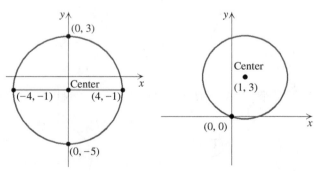

c.

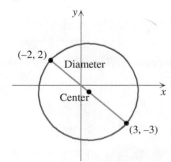

Write the equation of each circle in standard form. The coordinates of the center and the radius for each circle are integers.

65. a.

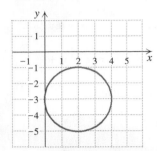

b.

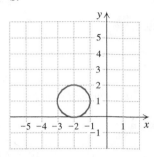

c.

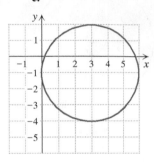

d.

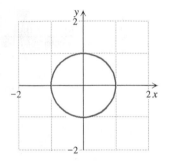

66. a.

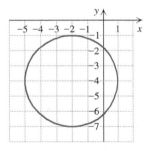

b.

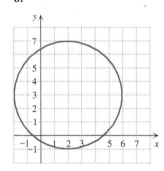

c.

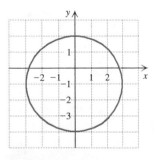

d.

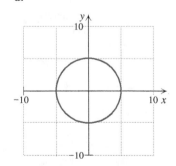

Sketch the graph of each linear equation. Be sure to find and show the x- and y-intercepts.

67. $y = 3x - 4$

68. $y = 5x - 5$

69. $3x - y = 6$

70. $5x - 2y = 10$

71. $x = 3y - 90$

72. $x = 80 - 2y$

73. $\frac{2}{3}y - \frac{1}{2}x = 400$

74. $\frac{1}{2}x - \frac{1}{3}y = 600$

75. $2x + 4y = 0.01$

76. $3x - 5y = 1.5$

77. $0.03x + 0.06y = 150$

78. $0.09x - 0.06y = 54$

Graph each equation in the rectangular coordinate system.

79. $x = 5$

80. $y = -2$

81. $y = 4$

82. $x = -3$

83. $x = -4$

84. $y = 5$

85. $y - 1 = 0$

86. $5 - x = 4$

Find the solution to each equation by reading the accompanying graph.

87. $2.4x - 8.64 = 0$

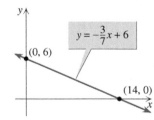

88. $8.84 - 1.3x = 0$

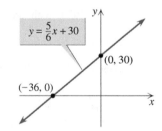

89. $-\frac{3}{7}x + 6 = 0$

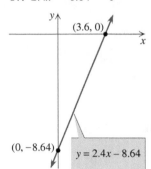

90. $\frac{5}{6}x + 30 = 0$

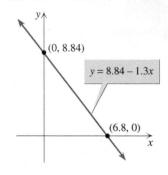

Use a graphing calculator to estimate the solution to each equation to two decimal places. Then find the solution algebraically and compare it with your estimate.

91. $1.2x + 3.4 = 0$

92. $3.2x - 4.5 = 0$

93. $1.23x - 687 = 0$

94. $-2.46x + 1500 = 0$

95. $0.03x - 3497 = 0$

96. $0.09x + 2000 = 0$

97. $4.3 - 3.1(2.3x - 9.9) = 0$

98. $9.4x - 4.37(3.5x - 9.76) = 0$

Solve each problem.

99. *First Marriage* The median age at first marriage for women went from 20.8 in 1970 to 25.1 in 2000 as shown in the accompanying figure (U.S. Census Bureau, www.census.gov).
   a. Find the midpoint of the line segment in the figure and interpret your result.

b. Find the distance between the two points shown in the figure and interpret your result.

Figure for Exercise 99

100. *Unmarried Couples* The number of unmarried-couple households h (in millions) can be modeled using the equation $h = 0.171n + 2.913$, where n is the number of years since 1990 (U.S. Census Bureau, www.census.gov).
a. Find and interpret the n-intercept for the line. Does it make sense?

b. Find and interpret the h-intercept for the line.

Figure for Exercise 100

101. *Capsize Control* The capsize screening value C is an indicator of a sailboat's suitability for extended offshore sailing. C is determined by the formula

$$C = 4D^{-1/3}B,$$

where D is the displacement of the boat in pounds and B is its beam (or width) in feet. Sketch the graph of this equation for B ranging from 0 to 20 ft, assuming that D is fixed at 22,800 lb. Find C for the Island Packet 40, which has a displacement of 22,800 pounds and a beam of 12 ft 11 in. (Island Packet Yachts, www.ipy.com).

102. *Limiting the Beam* The International Offshore Rules require that the capsize screening value C (from the previous exercise) be less than or equal to 2 for safety. What is the maximum allowable beam (to the nearest inch) for a boat with a displacement of 22,800 lb? For a fixed displacement, is a boat more or less likely to capsize as its beam gets larger?

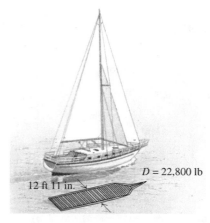

Figure for Exercises 101 and 102

103. Show that the points $A(-4, -5)$, $B(1, 1)$, and $C(6, 7)$ are colinear.

HINT Points A, B, and C lie on a straight line if $AB + BC = AC$.

104. Show that the midpoint of the hypotenuse of any right triangle is equidistant from all three vertices.

FOR WRITING/DISCUSSION

105. *Finding Points* Can you find two points such that their coordinates are integers and the distance between them is 10? $\sqrt{10}$? $\sqrt{19}$? Explain.

106. *Plotting Points* Plot at least five points in the xy-plane that satisfy the inequality $y > 2x$. Give a verbal description of the solution set to $y > 2x$.

107. *Cooperative Learning* Work in a small group to plot the points $(-1, 3)$ and $(4, 1)$ on graph paper. Assuming that these two points are adjacent vertices of a square, find the other two vertices. Now select your own pair of adjacent vertices and "complete the square." Now generalize your results. Start with the points (x_1, y_1) and (x_2, y_2) as adjacent vertices of a square and write expressions for the coordinates of the other two vertices. Repeat this exercise assuming that the first two points are opposite vertices of a square.

108. *Distance to the Origin* Let m and n be any real numbers. What is the distance between $(0, 0)$ and $(2m, m^2 - 1)$? What is the distance between $(0, 0)$ and $(2mn, m^2 - n^2)$?

▶ RETHINKING

109. Identify each equation as an identity, inconsistent equation, or conditional equation.
a. $2x + 4 = 5$

b. $2x + 4 = 2(x + 2)$

c. $2x + 4 = 2x$

110. Solve $\dfrac{4}{x - 3} + \dfrac{1}{x + 3} = \dfrac{x}{x^2 - 9}$.

111. Solve $\dfrac{x - 2}{x + 3} = \dfrac{x + 4}{x + 9}$.

112. The Wilsons got $180,780 for their house after paying a sales commission that was 8% of the selling price. What was the selling price?

113. Solve $ax + b = cx + d$ for x.

114. Solve $\dfrac{1}{a} + \dfrac{1}{b} = \dfrac{1}{x}$ for x.

THINKING OUTSIDE THE BOX III

Methodical Mower Eugene is mowing a rectangular lawn that is 300 ft by 400 ft. He starts at one corner and mows a swath of uniform width around the outside edge in a clockwise direction. He continues going clockwise, widening the swath that is mowed and shrinking the rectangular section that is yet to be mowed. When he is half done with the lawn, how wide is the swath?

POP QUIZ 3

1. Find the distance between $(-1, 3)$ and $(3, 5)$.

2. Find the center and radius for the circle
$$(x - 3)^2 + (y + 5)^2 = 81.$$

3. Find the center and radius for the circle
$$x^2 + 4x + y^2 - 10y = -28.$$

4. Find the equation of the circle that passes through the origin and has center at $(3, 4)$.

5. Find all intercepts for $2x - 3y = 12$.

6. Which point is on both of the lines $x = 5$ and $y = -1$?

LINKING concepts... For Individual or Group Explorations

Denis Pepin/Shutterstock

Modeling Energy Requirements

Clinical dietitians must design diets for patients that meet their basic energy requirements and are suitable for the condition of their health. The basic energy requirement B (in calories) for a male is given by the formula

$$B = 655.096 + 9.563W + 1.85H - 4.676A,$$

where W is the patient's weight in kilograms, H is the height in centimeters, and A is the age in years (www.eatwell.com). For a female the formula is

$$B = 66.473 + 13.752W + 5.003H - 6.755A.$$

a) Find your basic energy requirement.

b) Replace H and A with your actual height and age. Now draw a graph showing how B depends on weight for suitable values of W.

c) For a fixed height and age, does the basic energy requirement increase or decrease as weight increases?

d) Replace W and H with your actual weight and height. Now draw a graph showing how B depends on age for suitable values of A.

e) For a fixed weight and height, does the basic energy requirement increase or decrease as a person gets older?

f) Replace W and A with your actual weight and height. Now draw a graph showing how B depends on height for suitable values of H.

g) For a fixed weight and age, does the basic energy requirement increase or decrease for taller persons?

h) For the three graphs that you have drawn, explain how to determine whether the graph is increasing or decreasing from the formula for the graph.

4 Linear Equations in Two Variables

In Section 3 we graphed lines, including horizontal and vertical lines. We learned that every line has an equation in standard form $Ax + By = C$. In this section we will continue to study lines.

Slope of a Line

A road that rises 4 feet in a horizontal run of 100 feet has a grade of $\frac{4}{100}$ or 4%. A roof that rises 5 feet in a horizontal run of 12 feet has a 5-12 pitch. See Fig. 27. Grade and pitch are measurements of *steepness.*

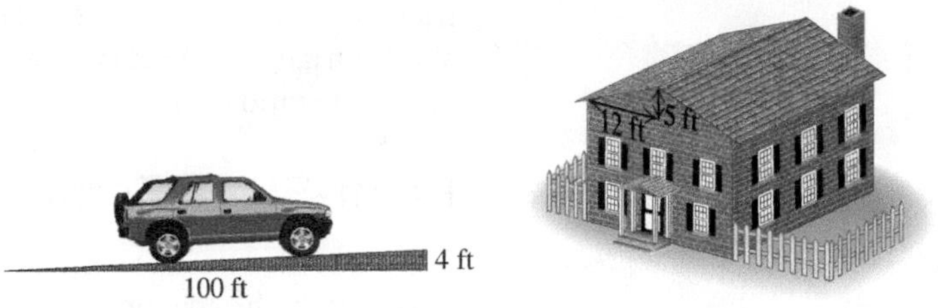

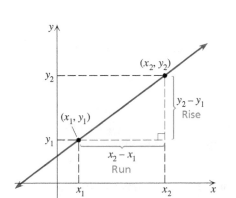

Figure 27

The steepness or *slope* of a line in the *xy*-coordinate system is the ratio of the **rise** (the change in *y*-coordinates) to the **run** (the change in *x*-coordinates) between two points on the line. The notation Δx (read "delta *x*") is often used to represent the change in the *x*-coordinates. Likewise, Δy is used to represent the change in *y*-coordinates. So

$$\text{slope} = \frac{\text{change in } y\text{-coordinates}}{\text{change in } x\text{-coordinates}} = \frac{\Delta y}{\Delta x} = \frac{\text{rise}}{\text{run}}.$$

If (x_1, y_1) and (x_2, y_2) are the coordinates of the two points in Fig. 28, then the rise is $y_2 - y_1$ and the run is $x_2 - x_1$:

Figure 28

Definition: Slope

> The **slope** of the line through (x_1, y_1) and (x_2, y_2) with $x_1 \neq x_2$ is
>
> $$\frac{y_2 - y_1}{x_2 - x_1}.$$

Note that if (x_1, y_1) and (x_2, y_2) are two points for which $x_1 = x_2$ then the line through them is a vertical line. Since this case is not included in the definition of slope, a vertical line does not have a slope. We also say that the slope of a vertical line is un-defined. If we choose two points on a horizontal line then $y_1 = y_2$ and $y_2 - y_1 = 0$. For any horizontal line the rise between two points is 0 and the slope is 0.

EXAMPLE 1 Finding the slope

In each case find the slope of the line that contains the two given points.

a. $(-3, 4), (-1, -2)$ **b.** $(-3, 7), (5, 7)$ **c.** $(-3, 5), (-3, 8)$

Solution

a. Use $(x_1, y_1) = (-3, 4)$ and $(x_2, y_2) = (-1, -2)$ in the formula:

$$\text{slope} = \frac{y_2 - y_1}{x_2 - x_1} = \frac{-2 - 4}{-1 - (-3)} = \frac{-6}{2} = -3$$

The slope of the line is -3.

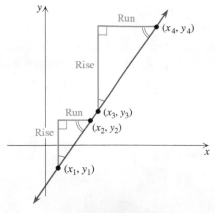

Figure 29

b. Use $(x_1, y_1) = (-3, 7)$ and $(x_2, y_2) = (5, 7)$ in the formula:

$$\text{slope} = \frac{y_2 - y_1}{x_2 - x_1} = \frac{7 - 7}{5 - (-3)} = \frac{0}{8} = 0$$

The slope of this horizontal line is 0.

c. The line through $(-3, 5)$ and $(-3, 8)$ is a vertical line and so it does not have a slope.

▶**TRY THIS.** Find the slope of the line that contains $(-2, 5)$ and $(-1, -3)$.   ■

The slope of a line is the same number regardless of which two points on the line are used in the calculation of the slope. To understand why, consider the two triangles shown in Fig. 29. These triangles have the same shape and are called similar triangles. Because the ratios of corresponding sides of similar triangles are equal, the ratio of rise to run is the same for either triangle.

Point-Slope Form

Suppose that a line through (x_1, y_1) has slope m. Every other point (x, y) on the line must satisfy the equation

$$\frac{y - y_1}{x - x_1} = m$$

because any two points can be used to find the slope. Multiply both sides by $x - x_1$ to get $y - y_1 = m(x - x_1)$, which is the **point-slope form** of the equation of a line.

Theorem: Point-Slope Form

> The equation of the line (in point-slope form) through (x_1, y_1) with slope m is
> $$y - y_1 = m(x - x_1).$$

In Section 3 we started with the equation of a line and graphed the line. Using the point-slope form, we can start with a graph of a line or a description of the line and write the equation for the line.

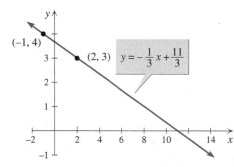

Figure 30

EXAMPLE 2 The equation of a line given two points

In each case graph the line through the given pair of points. Then find the equation of the line and solve it for y if possible.

a. $(-1, 4), (2, 3)$ **b.** $(2, 5), (-6, 5)$ **c.** $(3, -1), (3, 9)$

Solution

a. Find the slope of the line shown in Fig. 30 as follows:

$$m = \frac{y_2 - y_1}{x_2 - x_1} = \frac{3 - 4}{2 - (-1)} = \frac{-1}{3} = -\frac{1}{3}$$

Now use a point, say $(2, 3)$, and $m = -\frac{1}{3}$ in the point-slope form:

$$y - y_1 = m(x - x_1)$$

$$y - 3 = -\frac{1}{3}(x - 2) \qquad \text{The equation in point-slope form}$$

$$y - 3 = -\frac{1}{3}x + \frac{2}{3}$$

$$y = -\frac{1}{3}x + \frac{11}{3} \qquad \text{The equation solved for } y$$

b. The slope of the line through $(2, 5)$ and $(-6, 5)$ shown in Fig. 31 is 0. The equation of this horizontal line is $y = 5$.

c. The line through $(3, -1)$ and $(3, 9)$ shown in Fig. 32 is vertical and it does not have slope. Its equation is $x = 3$.

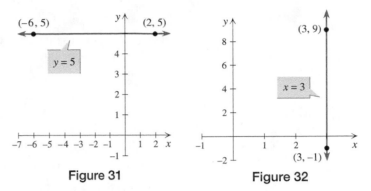

Figure 31   Figure 32

▶**TRY THIS.** Find the equation of the line that contains $(-2, 5)$ and $(-1, -3)$ and solve the equation for y. ∎

Slope-Intercept Form

The line $y = mx + b$ goes through $(0, b)$ and $(1, m + b)$. Between these two points the rise is m and the run is 1. So the slope is m. Since $(0, b)$ is the y-intercept and m is the slope, $y = mx + b$ is called slope-intercept form. Any equation in standard form $Ax + By = C$ can be rewritten in **slope-intercept form** by solving the equation for y provided $B \neq 0$. If $B = 0$, then the line is vertical and has no slope.

Theorem:
Slope-Intercept Form

> The equation of a line (in slope-intercept form) with slope m and y-intercept $(0, b)$ is
>
> $$y = mx + b.$$
>
> Every nonvertical line has an equation in slope-intercept form.

If you know the slope and y-intercept for a line then you can use slope-intercept form to write its equation. For example, the equation of the line through $(0, 9)$ with slope 4 is $y = 4x + 9$. In the next example we use the slope-intercept form to determine the slope and y-intercept for a line.

EXAMPLE 3 | Find the slope and y-intercept

Identify the slope and y-intercept for the line $2x - 3y = 6$.

Solution

First solve the equation for y to get it in slope-intercept form:

$$2x - 3y = 6$$

$$-3y = -2x + 6$$

$$y = \frac{2}{3}x - 2$$

So the slope is $\frac{2}{3}$ and the y-intercept is $(0, -2)$.

▶**TRY THIS.** Identify the slope and y-intercept for $3x + 5y = 15$. ∎

Given any point and a slope, we can find the equation of the line using the point-slope form. We can also use the slope-intercept form as shown in the next example.

53

EXAMPLE 4 Using slope-intercept form with any point and a slope

Find the equation of the line in slope-intercept form through $(-2, 3)$ with slope $1/2$.

Solution

Since $(-2, 3)$ must satisfy the equation of the line, we can use $x = -2$, $y = 3$, and $m = 1/2$ in the slope-intercept form to find b:

$$y = mx + b \qquad \text{Slope-intercept form}$$

$$3 = \frac{1}{2}(-2) + b \qquad x = -2, y = 3, \text{ and } m = \tfrac{1}{2}.$$

$$3 = -1 + b$$

$$4 = b$$

So the equation is $y = \frac{1}{2}x + 4$.

▶**TRY THIS.** Find the equation of the line in slope-intercept form through $(4, -6)$ with slope $1/4$. ■

Using Slope to Graph a Line

Slope is the ratio $\frac{\text{rise}}{\text{run}}$ that results from moving from one point to another on a line. A positive rise indicates a motion upward and a negative rise indicates a motion downward. A positive run indicates a motion to the right and a negative run indicates a motion to the left. If you start at any point on a line with slope $\frac{1}{2}$, then moving up 1 unit and 2 units to the right will bring you back to the line. On a line with slope -3 or $\frac{-3}{1}$, moving down 3 units and 1 unit to the right will bring you back to the line.

EXAMPLE 5 Graphing a line using its slope and y-intercept

Graph each line.

a. $y = 3x - 1$ **b.** $y = -\dfrac{2}{3}x + 4$

Solution

a. The line $y = 3x - 1$ has y-intercept $(0, -1)$ and slope 3 or $\frac{3}{1}$. Starting at $(0, -1)$ we obtain a second point on the line by moving up 3 units and 1 unit to the right. So the line goes through $(0, -1)$ and $(1, 2)$ as shown in Fig. 33.

b. The line $y = -\frac{2}{3}x + 4$ has y-intercept $(0, 4)$ and slope $-\frac{2}{3}$ or $\frac{-2}{3}$. Starting at $(0, 4)$ we obtain a second point on the line by moving down 2 units and then 3 units to the right. So the line goes through $(0, 4)$ and $(3, 2)$ as shown in Fig. 34.

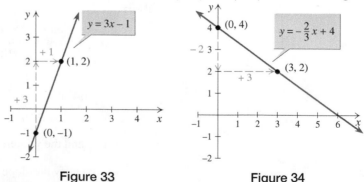

Figure 33   Figure 34

▶**TRY THIS.** Use the slope and y-intercept to graph $y = -\frac{3}{2}x + 1$. ■

As the x-coordinate increases on a line with positive slope, the y-coordinate increases also. As the x-coordinate increases on a line with negative slope, the y-coordinate decreases. Figure 35 shows some lines of the form $y = mx$ with positive slopes and negative slopes. Observe the effect that the slope has on the position of the line. Note that lines with positive slope go up as you move from left to right and lines with negative slope go down as you move from left to right as shown in Fig. 36.

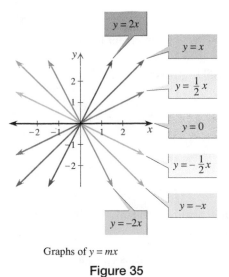

Graphs of $y = mx$

Figure 35

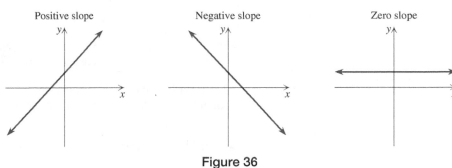

Figure 36

The Three Forms for the Equation of a Line

There are three forms for the equation of a line. The following strategy will help you decide when and how to use these forms.

STRATEGY

Finding the Equation of a Line

Standard form	$Ax + By = C$
Slope-intercept form	$y = mx + b$
Point-slope form	$y - y_1 = m(x - x_1)$

1. Since vertical lines have no slope, they can't be written in slope-intercept or point-slope form.
2. All lines can be described with an equation in standard form.
3. For any constant k, $y = k$ is a horizontal line and $x = k$ is a vertical line.
4. If you know two points on a line, then find the slope.
5. If you know the slope and a point on the line, use point-slope form. If the point is the y-intercept, then use slope-intercept form.
6. Final answers are usually written in slope-intercept or standard form. Standard form is often simplified by using only integers for the coefficients.

EXAMPLE 6 Standard form using integers

Find the equation of the line through $\left(0, \frac{1}{3}\right)$ with slope $\frac{1}{2}$. Write the equation in standard form using only integers.

Solution

Since we know the slope and y-intercept, start with slope-intercept form:

$$y = \frac{1}{2}x + \frac{1}{3} \qquad \text{Slope-intercept form}$$

$$-\frac{1}{2}x + y = \frac{1}{3}$$

$$-6\left(-\frac{1}{2}x + y\right) = -6 \cdot \frac{1}{3} \qquad \text{Multiply by } -6 \text{ to get integers.}$$

$$3x - 6y = -2 \qquad \text{Standard form with integers}$$

Any integral multiple of $3x - 6y = -2$ would also be standard form, but we usually use the smallest possible positive coefficient for x.

▶**TRY THIS.** Find the equation of the line through $\left(0, \frac{1}{2}\right)$ with slope $\frac{3}{4}$ and write the equation in standard form using only integers. ∎

Parallel Lines

Two lines in a plane are said to be **parallel** if they have no points in common. Any two vertical lines are parallel, and slope can be used to determine whether nonvertical lines are parallel. For example, the lines $y = 3x - 4$ and $y = 3x + 1$ are parallel because their slopes are equal and their y-intercepts are different.

Theorem: Parallel Lines

> Two nonvertical lines in the coordinate plane are parallel if and only if their slopes are equal.

A proof to this theorem is outlined in Exercises 113 and 114.

EXAMPLE 7 Writing equations of parallel lines

Find the equation in slope-intercept form of the line through $(1, -4)$ that is parallel to $y = 3x + 2$.

Solution

Since $y = 3x + 2$ has slope 3, any line parallel to it also has slope 3. Write the equation of the line through $(1, -4)$ with slope 3 in point-slope form:

$$y - (-4) = 3(x - 1) \qquad \text{Point-slope form}$$

$$y + 4 = 3x - 3$$

$$y = 3x - 7 \qquad \text{Slope-intercept form}$$

The line $y = 3x - 7$ goes through $(1, -4)$ and is parallel to $y = 3x + 2$.
The graphs of $y_1 = 3x - 7$ and $y_2 = 3x + 2$ in Fig. 37 support the answer.

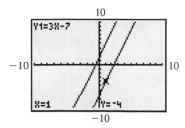

Figure 37

▶**TRY THIS.** Find the equation in slope-intercept form of the line through $(2, 4)$ that is parallel to $y = -\frac{1}{2}x + 9$. ∎

Perpendicular Lines

Two lines are **perpendicular** if they intersect at a right angle. Slope can be used to determine whether lines are perpendicular. For example, lines with slopes such as 2/3 and −3/2 are perpendicular. The slope −3/2 is the opposite of the reciprocal of

2/3. In the following theorem we use the equivalent condition that the product of the slopes of two perpendicular lines is -1, provided they both have slopes.

Theorem:
Perpendicular Lines

> Two lines with slopes m_1 and m_2 are perpendicular if and only if $m_1 m_2 = -1$.

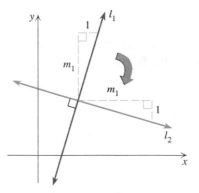

Figure 38

PROOF The phrase "if and only if" means that there are two statements to prove. First we prove that if l_1 with slope m_1 and l_2 with slope m_2 are perpendicular, then $m_1 m_2 = -1$. Assume that $m_1 > 0$. At the intersection of the lines draw a right triangle using a rise of m_1 and a run of 1, as shown in Fig. 38. Rotate l_1 (along with the right triangle) 90 degrees so that it coincides with l_2. Now use the triangle in its new position to determine that $m_2 = \frac{1}{-m_1}$ or $m_1 m_2 = -1$.

The second statement to prove is that $m_1 m_2 = -1$ or $m_2 = \frac{1}{-m_1}$ implies that the lines are perpendicular. Start with the two intersecting lines and the two congruent right triangles, as shown in Fig. 38. It takes a rotation of 90 degrees to get the vertical side marked m_1 to coincide with the horizontal side marked m_1. Since the triangles are congruent, rotating 90 degrees makes the triangles coincide and the lines coincide. So the lines are perpendicular. ∎

EXAMPLE 8 | Writing equations of perpendicular lines

Find the equation of the line perpendicular to the line $3x - 4y = 8$ and containing the point $(-2, 1)$. Write the answer in slope-intercept form.

Solution

Rewrite $3x - 4y = 8$ in slope-intercept form:

$$-4y = -3x + 8$$

$$y = \frac{3}{4}x - 2 \qquad \text{Slope of this line is 3/4.}$$

Since the product of the slopes of perpendicular lines is -1, the slope of the line that we seek is $-4/3$. Use the slope $-4/3$ and the point $(-2, 1)$ in the point-slope form:

$$y - 1 = -\frac{4}{3}(x - (-2))$$

$$y - 1 = -\frac{4}{3}x - \frac{8}{3}$$

$$y = -\frac{4}{3}x - \frac{5}{3}$$

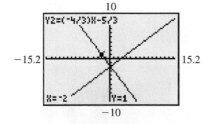

Figure 39

The last equation is the required equation in slope-intercept form. The graphs of these two equations should look perpendicular.

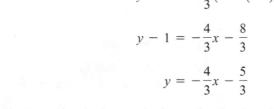 If you graph $y_1 = \frac{3}{4}x - 2$ and $y_2 = -\frac{4}{3}x - \frac{5}{3}$ with a graphing calculator, the graphs will not appear perpendicular in the standard viewing window because each axis has a different unit length. The graphs appear perpendicular in Fig. 39 because the unit lengths were made equal with the ZSquare feature of the TI-83.

▶**TRY THIS.** Find the equation in slope-intercept form of the line through $(-2, 1)$ that is perpendicular to $2x - y = 8$. ∎

Applications

In Section 3 the distance formula was used to establish some facts about geometric figures in the coordinate plane. We can also use slope to prove that lines are parallel or perpendicular in geometric figures.

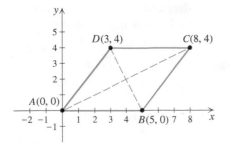

Figure 40

EXAMPLE 9 | The diagonals of a rhombus are perpendicular

Given a rhombus with vertices $(0, 0)$, $(5, 0)$, $(3, 4)$, and $(8, 4)$, prove that the diagonals of this rhombus are perpendicular. (A rhombus is a four-sided figure in which the sides have equal length.)

Solution

Plot the four points A, B, C, and D as shown in Fig. 40. You should show that each side of this figure has length 5, verifying that the figure is a rhombus. Find the slopes of the diagonals and their product:

$$m_{AC} = \frac{4 - 0}{8 - 0} = \frac{1}{2} \qquad m_{BD} = \frac{0 - 4}{5 - 3} = -2$$

$$m_{AC} \cdot m_{BD} = \frac{1}{2}(-2) = -1$$

Since the product of the slopes of the diagonals is -1, the diagonals are perpendicular.

▶**TRY THIS.** Prove that the triangle with vertices $(0, 0)$, $(5, 2)$, and $(1, 12)$ is a right triangle. ∎

If the value of one variable can be determined from the value of another variable, then we say that the first variable is a function of the second variable. This idea was discussed in Section 2. Because the area of a circle can be determined from the radius by the formula $A = \pi r^2$, we say that A is a function of r. If y is determined from x by using the slope-intercept form of the equation of a line $y = mx + b$, then **y is a linear function of x.** The formula $F = \frac{9}{5}C + 32$ expresses F as a linear function of C.

EXAMPLE 10 | A linear function

From ABC Wireless the monthly cost for a cell phone with 100 minutes per month is $35, or 200 minutes per month for $45. See Fig. 41. The cost in dollars is a linear function of the time in minutes.

a. Find the formula for C.
b. What is the cost for 400 minutes per month?

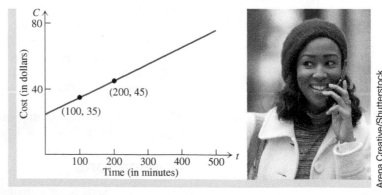

Figure 41

Solution

a. First find the slope:

$$m = \frac{C_2 - C_1}{t_2 - t_1} = \frac{45 - 35}{200 - 100} = \frac{10}{100} = 0.10$$

The slope is \$0.10 per minute. Now find b by using $C = 35$, $t = 100$, and $m = 0.10$ in the slope-intercept form $C = mt + b$:

$$35 = 0.10(100) + b$$
$$35 = 10 + b$$
$$25 = b$$

So the formula is $C = 0.10t + 25$.

b. Use $t = 400$ in the formula $C = 0.10t + 25$:

$$C = 0.10(400) + 25 = 65$$

The cost for 400 minutes per month is \$65.

▶**TRY THIS.** The cost of a truck rental is \$70 for 100 miles and \$90 for 200 miles. Write the cost as a linear function of the number of miles. ■

Note that in Example 10 we could have used the point-slope form $C - C_1 = m(t - t_1)$ to get the formula $C = 0.10t + 25$. Try it.

The situation in the next example leads naturally to an equation in standard form.

[**EXAMPLE 11**] Interpreting slope

A manager for a country market will spend a total of \$80 on apples at \$0.25 each and pears at \$0.50 each. Write the number of apples she can buy as a linear function of the number of pears. Find the slope and interpret your answer.

Solution

Let a represent the number of apples and p represent the number of pears. Write an equation in standard form about the total amount spent:

$$0.25a + 0.50p = 80$$
$$0.25a = 80 - 0.50p$$
$$a = 320 - 2p \qquad \text{Solve for } a.$$

The equation $a = 320 - 2p$ or $a = -2p + 320$ expresses the number of apples as a function of the number of pears. Since p is the first coordinate and a is the second, the slope is -2 apples per pear. So if the number of apples is decreased by 2, then the number of pears can be increased by 1 and the total is still \$80. This makes sense because the pears cost twice as much as the apples.

▶**TRY THIS.** A manager will spend \$3000 on file cabinets at \$100 each and bookshelves at \$150 each. Write the number of file cabinets as a function of the number of bookshelves and interpret the slope. ■

► FOR thought... True or False? Explain.

1. The slope of the line through $(2, 2)$ and $(3, 3)$ is $3/2$.

2. The slope of the line through $(-3, 1)$ and $(-3, 5)$ is 0.

3. Any two distinct parallel lines have equal slopes.

4. The graph of $x = 3$ in the coordinate plane is the single point $(3, 0)$.

5. Two lines with slopes m_1 and m_2 are perpendicular if $m_1 = -1/m_2$.

6. Every line in the coordinate plane has an equation in slope-intercept form.

7. The slope of the line $y = 3 - 2x$ is 3.

8. Every line in the coordinate plane has an equation in standard form.

9. The line $y = 3x$ is parallel to the line $y = -3x$.

10. The line $x - 3y = 4$ contains the point $(1, -1)$ and has slope $1/3$.

► EXERCISES 4

Fill in the blank.

1. The change in y-coordinate between two points on a line is the _____.

2. The change in x-coordinate between two points on a line is the _____.

3. The rise divided by the run is the _____ of a line.

4. The equation $y - y_1 = m(x - x_1)$ is the _____ form of the equation of a line.

5. The equation $y = mx + b$ is the _____ form of the equation of a line.

6. Two lines that have no points in common are _____.

7. Two lines with slopes m_1 and m_2 are _____ if and only if $m_1 m_2 = -1$.

8. If the value of one variable can be determined from the value of another variable, then the first variable _____ the second variable.

Find the slope of the line containing each pair of points.

9. $(-2, 3), (4, 5)$

10. $(-1, 2), (3, 6)$

11. $(1, 3), (3, -5)$

12. $(2, -1), (5, -3)$

13. $(5, 2), (-3, 2)$

14. $(0, 0), (5, 0)$

15. $\left(\dfrac{1}{8}, \dfrac{1}{4}\right), \left(\dfrac{1}{4}, \dfrac{1}{2}\right)$

16. $\left(-\dfrac{1}{3}, \dfrac{1}{2}\right), \left(\dfrac{1}{6}, \dfrac{1}{3}\right)$

17. $(5, -1), (5, 3)$

18. $(-7, 2), (-7, -6)$

Find the equation of the line through the given pair of points. Solve it for y if possible.

19. $(-1, -1), (3, 4)$

20. $(-2, 1), (3, 5)$

21. $(-2, 6), (4, -1)$

22. $(-3, 5), (2, 1)$

23. $(3, 5), (-3, 5)$

24. $(-6, 4), (2, 4)$

25. $(4, -3), (4, 12)$

26. $(-5, 6), (-5, 4)$

Write an equation in slope-intercept form for each of the lines shown.

27.

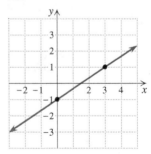

28.

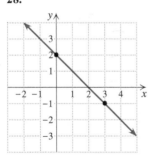

29.

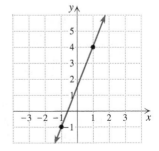

30.

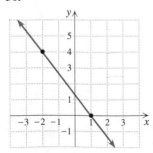

31.

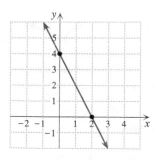

32.

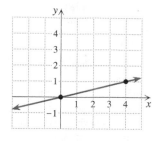

33.

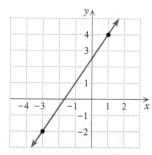

34.

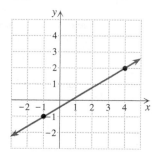

Write each equation in slope-intercept form and identify the slope and y-intercept of the line.

35. $3x - 5y = 10$

36. $2x - 2y = 1$

37. $y - 3 = 2(x - 4)$

38. $y + 5 = -3(x - (-1))$

39. $y + 1 = \frac{1}{2}(x - (-3))$

40. $y - 2 = -\frac{3}{2}(x + 5)$

41. $y - 4 = 0$

42. $-y + 5 = 0$

Find the equation of each line in slope-intercept form.

43. The line through $(-8, 5)$ with slope $1/4$

44. The line through $(6, 9)$ with slope $-1/3$

45. The line through $(-3, -2)$ with slope $-1/2$

46. The line through $(4, 3)$ with slope $2/3$

Use the y-intercept and slope to sketch the graph of each equation.

47. $y = \frac{1}{2}x - 2$

48. $y = \frac{2}{3}x + 1$

49. $y = -3x + 1$

50. $y = -x + 3$

51. $y = -\frac{3}{4}x - 1$

52. $y = -\frac{3}{2}x$

53. $x - y = 3$

54. $2x - 3y = 6$

55. $y - 5 = 0$

56. $6 - y = 0$

Find the equation of the line through the given pair of points in standard form using only integers.

57. $(3, 0)$ and $(0, -4)$

58. $(-2, 0)$ and $(0, 3)$

59. $(2, 3)$ and $(-3, -1)$

60. $(4, -1)$ and $(-2, -6)$

61. $(-4, 2)$ and $(-4, 5)$

62. $(-3, 6)$ and $(9, 6)$

63. $\left(2, \frac{2}{3}\right), \left(-\frac{1}{2}, -2\right)$

64. $\left(\frac{3}{4}, -3\right), \left(-5, \frac{1}{8}\right)$

65. $\left(\frac{1}{2}, \frac{1}{4}\right), \left(-\frac{1}{3}, \frac{1}{5}\right)$

66. $\left(-\frac{3}{8}, \frac{1}{4}\right), \left(\frac{1}{2}, -\frac{1}{6}\right)$

Find the slope of each line described.

67. A line parallel to $y = 0.5x - 9$

68. A line parallel to $3x - 9y = 4$

69. A line perpendicular to $3y - 3x = 7$

70. A line perpendicular to $2x - 3y = 8$

71. A line perpendicular to the line $x = 4$

72. A line parallel to $y = 5$

Write an equation in standard form using only integers for each of the lines described. In each case make a sketch.

73. The line with slope 2, going through $(1, -2)$

74. The line with slope -3, going through $(-3, 4)$

75. The line through $(1, 4)$, parallel to $y = -3x$

76. The line through $(-2, 3)$ parallel to $y = \frac{1}{2}x + 6$

77. The line parallel to $5x - 7y = 35$ and containing $(6, 1)$

78. The line parallel to $4x + 9y = 5$ and containing $(-4, 2)$

79. The line perpendicular to $y = \frac{2}{3}x + 5$ and containing $(2, -3)$

80. The line perpendicular to $y = 9x + 5$ and containing $(5, 4)$

81. The line perpendicular to $x - 2y = 3$ and containing $(-3, 1)$

82. The line perpendicular to $3x - y = 9$ and containing $(0, 0)$

83. The line perpendicular to $x = 4$ and containing $(2, 5)$

84. The line perpendicular to $y = 9$ and containing $(-1, 3)$

Find the value of a in each case.

85. The line through $(-2, 3)$ and $(8, 5)$ is perpendicular to $y = ax + 2$.

86. The line through $(3, 4)$ and $(7, a)$ has slope $2/3$.

87. The line through $(-2, a)$ and $(a, 3)$ has slope $-1/2$.

88. The line through $(-1, a)$ and $(3, -4)$ is parallel to $y = ax$.

Either prove or disprove each statement. Use a graph only as a guide. Your proof should rely on algebraic calculations

89. The points $(-1, 2)$, $(2, -1)$, $(3, 3)$, and $(-2, -2)$ are the vertices of a parallelogram.

90. The points $(-1, 1)$, $(-2, -5)$, $(2, -4)$, and $(3, 2)$ are the vertices of a parallelogram.

91. The points $(-5, -1)$, $(-3, -4)$, $(3, 0)$, and $(1, 3)$ are the vertices of a rectangle.

92. The points $(-5, -1)$, $(1, -4)$, $(4, 2)$, and $(-1, 5)$ are the vertices of a square.

93. The points $(-5, 1)$, $(-2, -3)$, and $(4, 2)$ are the vertices of a right triangle.

94. The points $(-4, -3)$, $(1, -2)$, $(2, 3)$, and $(-3, 2)$ are the vertices of a rhombus.

Use a graphing calculator to solve each problem.

95. Graph $y_1 = (x - 5)/3$ and $y_2 = x - 0.67(x + 4.2)$. Do the lines appear to be parallel? Are the lines parallel?

96. Graph $y_1 = 99x$ and $y_2 = -x/99$. Do the lines appear to be perpendicular? Should they appear perpendicular?

97. Graph $y = (x^3 - 8)/(x^2 + 2x + 4)$. Use TRACE to examine points on the graph. Write a linear function for the graph. Explain why this function is linear.

98. Graph $y = (x^3 + 2x^2 - 5x - 6)/(x^2 + x - 6)$. Use TRACE to examine points on the graph. Write a linear function for the graph. Factor $x^3 + 2x^2 - 5x - 6$ completely.

Solve each problem.

99. *Celsius to Fahrenheit Formula* Fahrenheit temperature F is a linear function of Celsius temperature C. The ordered pair $(0, 32)$ is an ordered pair of this function because $0°C$ is equivalent to $32°F$, the freezing point of water. The ordered pair $(100, 212)$ is also an ordered pair of this function because $100°C$ is equivalent to $212°F$, the boiling point of water. Use the two given points and the point-slope formula to write F as a function of C. Find the Fahrenheit temperature of an oven at $150°C$.

100. *Cost of Business Cards* Speedy Printing charges $23 for 200 deluxe business cards and $35 for 500 deluxe business cards. Given that the cost is a linear function of the number of cards printed, find a formula for that function and find the cost of 700 business cards.

101. *Volume Discount* Mona Kalini gives a walking tour of Honolulu to one person for $49. To increase her business, she advertised at the National Orthodontist Convention that she would lower the price by $1 per person for each additional person. Write the cost per person c as a function of the number of people n on the tour. How much does she make for a tour with 40 people?

HINT Find the equation of the line through $(1, 49)$, $(2, 48)$, $(3, 47)$, etc.

102. *Ticket Pricing* At $10 per ticket, Willie Williams and the Wranglers will fill all 8000 seats in the Assembly Center. The manager knows that for every $1 increase in the price, 500 tickets will go unsold. Write the number of tickets sold n as a function of the ticket price p. How much money will be taken in if the tickets are $20 each?

HINT Find the equation of the line through $(10, 8000)$, $(11, 7500)$, $(12, 7000)$, etc.

103. *Lindbergh's Air Speed* Charles Lindbergh estimated that at the start of his historic flight the practical economical air speed was 95 mph and at 4000 statute miles from the starting point it was 75 mph (www.charleslindbergh.com). Assume that the practical economical air speed S is a linear function of the distance D from the starting point as shown in the accompanying figure. Find a formula for that function.

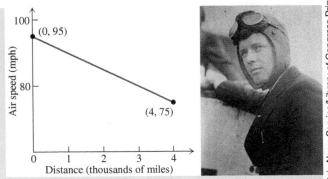

Figure for Exercise 103

104. *Speed over Newfoundland* In Lindbergh's flying log he recorded his air speed over Newfoundland as 98 mph, 1100 miles into his flight. According to the formula from Exercise 103, what should have been his air speed over Newfoundland?

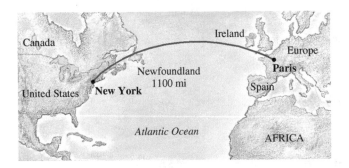

Figure for Exercise 104

105. *Computers and Printers* An office manager will spend a total of $60,000 on computers at $2000 each and printers at $1500 each. Write the number of computers purchased as a function of the number of printers purchased. Find and interpret the slope.

HINT Start with standard form.

106. *Carpenters and Helpers* Because a job was finished early, a contractor will distribute a total of $2400 in bonuses to 9 carpenters and 3 helpers. The carpenters all get the same amount and the helpers all get the same amount. Write the amount of a helper's bonus as a function of the amount of a carpenter's bonus. Find and interpret the slope.

107. *Integral Coordinates* Find all points on the line through $(-9, 14)$ and $(21, -4)$ that lie between these two points and have integral coordinates.

108. *Parallelograms* The points $(-1, 2)$, $(4, 1)$, and $(2, -3)$ are the vertices of a parallelogram in the coordinate plane. Find all possibilities for the fourth vertex.

The distance d from the point (x_1, y_1) to the line $Ax + By = C$ is given by the formula

$$d = \frac{|Ax_1 + By_1 - C|}{\sqrt{A^2 + B^2}}.$$

Find the exact distance from each given point to the given line.

109. $(3, -6), 5x - 12y = 2$

110. $(-4, 8), 3x + 4y = 9$

111. $(1, 3), y = 5x - 4$

112. $(-2, 5), y = -4x + 1$

FOR WRITING/DISCUSSION

113. *Equal Slopes* Show that if $y = mx + b_1$ and $y = mx + b_2$ are equations of lines with equal slopes, but $b_1 \neq b_2$, then they have no point in common.

HINT Assume that they have a point in common and see that this assumption leads to a contradiction.

114. *Unequal Slopes* Show that the lines $y = m_1x + b_1$ and $y = m_2x + b_2$ intersect at a point with x-coordinate $(b_2 - b_1)/(m_1 - m_2)$ provided $m_1 \neq m_2$. Explain how this exercise and the previous exercise prove the theorem that two nonvertical lines are parallel if and only if they have equal slopes.

▶ RETHINKING

115. Solve $3 - 5|x - 4| = 0$.

116. Hall can shovel the snow from a long driveway in 24 minutes. If Shanna helps, they can do the job in 18 minutes. How long would it take Shanna to do the job alone?

117. The diameter of a circle has endpoints $(1, 3)$ and $(3, 9)$. Find the equation of the circle.

118. Find the center and radius of the circle $x^2 + 3x + y^2 - 4y = 0$.

119. Solve $-5|x - 4| = 0$.

120. Find the midpoint of the line segment with endpoints $(\pi/2, 1)$ and $(\pi, 1)$.

THINKING OUTSIDE THE BOX IV AND V

Army of Ants An army of ants is marching across the kitchen floor. If they form columns with 10 ants in each column, then there are 6 ants left over. If they form columns with 7, 11, or 13 ants in each column, then there are 2 ants left over. What is the smallest number of ants that could be in this army?

Summing Angles Consider the angles shown in the accompanying figure. Show that the degree measure of angle A *plus* the degree measure of angle B is equal to the degree measure of angle C.

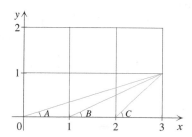

Figure for Thinking Outside the Box V

POP QUIZ 4

1. Find the slope of the line through $(-4, 9)$ and $(5, 6)$.

2. Find the equation of the line through $(3, 4)$ and $(6, 8)$.

3. What is the slope of the line $2x - 7y = 1$?

4. Find the equation of the line with y-intercept $(0, 7)$ that is parallel to $y = 3x - 1$.

5. Find the equation of the line with y-intercept $(0, 8)$ that is perpendicular to $y = \frac{1}{2}x + 4$.

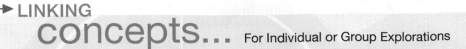

concepts...

For Individual or Group Explorations

The Negative Income Tax Model

One idea for income tax reform is that of a negative income tax. Under this plan families with an income below a certain level receive a payment from the government in addition to their income while families above a certain level pay taxes. In one proposal a family with an earned income of $6000 would receive a $4000 payment, giving the family a disposable income of $10,000. A family with an earned income of $24,000 would pay $2000 in taxes, giving the family a disposable income of $22,000. A family's disposable income D is a linear function of the family's earned income E.

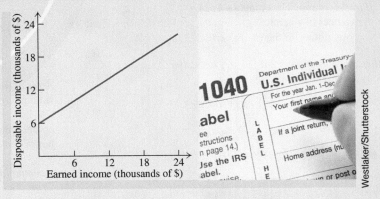

a) Use the given data to write a formula for D as a linear function of E.

b) What is the disposable income for a family with an earned income of $60,000?

c) Find the break-even point, the income at which a family pays no taxes and receives no payment.

d) What percentage of their earned income is paid in taxes for a family with an earned income of $25,000? $100,000? $2,000,000?

e) What is the maximum percentage of earned income that anyone will pay in taxes?

f) Compare your answer to part (e) with current tax laws. Does this negative income tax favor the rich, poor, or middle class?

5 Scatter Diagrams and Curve Fitting

The Cartesian coordinate system is often used to illustrate real data and relationships between variables. In this section we will graph real data and see how to fit lines to that data.

Scatter Diagrams and Types of Relationships

In statistics we often gather paired data, such as height and weight of an individual. We seek a relationship between the two variables. We can graph pairs of data as

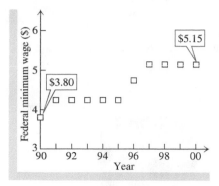

Figure 42

ordered pairs in the Cartesian coordinate system as shown in Fig. 42. The graph is called a **scatter diagram** because real data are more likely to be scattered about rather than perfectly lined up. If a pattern appears in the scatter diagram, then there is a relationship between the variables. If the points in the scatter diagram look like they are scattered about a line, then the relationship is **linear.** Otherwise the relationship is **nonlinear.**

EXAMPLE 1 Classifying scatter diagrams

For each given scatter diagram determine whether there is a relationship between the variables. If there is a relationship then determine whether it is linear or nonlinear.

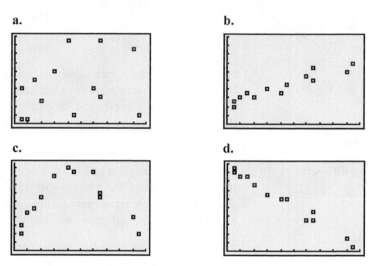

Solution

a. The points are just scattered about and it does not appear that there is a relationship between the variables.

b. It appears that there is a linear relationship between the variables.

c. It appears that there is a pattern to the data and that there is a nonlinear relationship between the variables.

d. It appears that there is a linear relationship between the variables.

▶**TRY THIS.** Determine whether the variables depicted in the following scatter diagrams have a linear or nonlinear relationship.

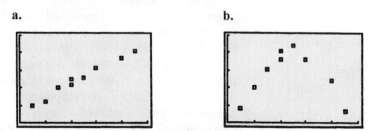

Using a scatter diagram to determine whether there is a relationship between variables is not precise. We will see a more precise method in Example 3.

Finding a Line of Best Fit

If there appears to be a linear relationship in a scatter diagram, we can draw in a line and use it to make predictions.

EXAMPLE 2 | Fitting a line to data

The following table shows the relationship between the size of a house in square feet and the selling price of the house in dollars.

Size (sq ft)	Price (thousands of dollars)
1100	259
1200	280
1350	299
1625	335
2200	419

Sascha Burkard/Shutterstock

a. Make a scatter diagram using the given data.
b. Draw a line that appears to fit the data.
c. Use your graph to estimate the cost of a house with 1500 square feet.
d. Use your graph to estimate the cost of a house with 2400 square feet.

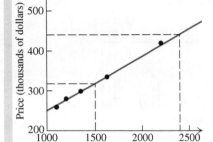

Figure 43

Solution

Make a scatter diagram and draw a line to fit the data as shown in Fig. 43. From the graph it appears that a house with 1500 square feet would cost about $320,000. A house with 2400 square feet would cost approximately $450,000. Of course, answers will vary depending on the line that is drawn.

▶**TRY THIS.** The following table shows the average cost of a gallon of regular unleaded gas in selected years. Predict the cost of a gallon of regular gas in 2011 by using a scatter diagram for the given data.

Year	1999	2001	2005	2007	2008
Price per gallon (dollars)	1.17	1.64	2.48	2.93	4.15

Making a prediction within the range of the data (as in Example 2c) is called **interpolating** and making a prediction outside the range of the data (as in Example 2d) is called **extrapolating.** Remember that a prediction made by extrapolating or interpolating the data is a guess and it may be incorrect.

We could have drawn many different lines to fit the data in Example 2. However, there is one line that is preferred over all others. It is called the **line of best fit** or the **regression line.** The line that best fits the data minimizes the total "distance" between the points in the scatter diagram and the line. More details on the line of best fit can be found in any introductory statistics text and we will not give them here. However, it is relatively easy to find an equation for the regression line because a graphing calculator performs all of the computations for you. The calculator even indicates how well the equation fits the data by giving a number r called the **correlation coefficient.** The correlation coefficient is between -1 and 1. If $r = 1$ (a **positive correlation**) the data are perfectly in line, and increasing values of one variable correspond to increasing values of the other. If $r = -1$ (a **negative correlation**) the data are also perfectly in line, but increasing values of one variable correspond to decreasing values of the other. If $r = 0$ (or r is close to 0) the data are scattered about with no linear correlation. The closer r is to 1 or -1, the more the scatter diagram will look linear. See Fig. 44.

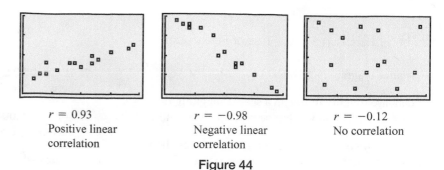

$r = 0.93$
Positive linear
correlation

$r = -0.98$
Negative linear
correlation

$r = -0.12$
No correlation

Figure 44

Temp (°F)	% Injured
46	4.7
72	12.3
59	6.5
56	5.9
54	6.6
70	10.3
68	8.4
48	4.0

Jupiterimages/Photos.com/Thinkstock

Source: Larry Tye, "Ambulatory Laboratory Marathon Is a Unique Research Arena," *Boston Globe*, 20 April 1992, p. 28.

EXAMPLE 3 Finding the line of best fit

The table shows the temperature at the start of the race and the percentage of runners injured in eight runnings of the Boston Marathon.

a. Use a graphing calculator to make a scatter diagram and find the equation of the regression line for the data.

b. Use the regression equation to estimate the percentage of runners that would be injured if the marathon was run on a day when the temperature was 82°F.

c. Use the regression equation to estimate the temperature at the start of the race for a race in which 9% of the runners were injured.

Solution

a. First enter the data into the calculator using the STAT EDIT feature as shown in Fig. 45(a). Enter the temperature in the first list or x-list and the percent injured in the second list or y-list. Consult your calculator manual if you have trouble or your calculator does not accept data in this manner. Use the STAT CALC feature and the choice LinReg, to find the equation as shown in Fig. 45(b). The calculator gives the equation in the form $y = ax + b$ where $a \approx 0.27$ and $b \approx -8.46$. So the equation is $y = 0.27x - 8.46$. Since $r \approx 0.94$, the equation is a good model for the data. The scatter diagram and the regression line are shown in Fig. 45(c).

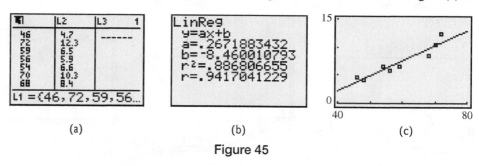

(a) (b) (c)

Figure 45

b. If $x = 82$, then $y = 0.27(82) - 8.46 = 13.68$. When the temperature is 82°F about 13.7% of the runners would be injured.

c. If 9% of the runners are injured, then $9 = 0.27x - 8.46$. Solve for x to get $x \approx 64.7$. So the temperature should be about 65°F if 9% are injured.

▶**TRY THIS.** Predict the cost in 2010 to the nearest cent by using linear regression and the given data. Use the equation given by the calculator to make the prediction.

Year	1980	1985	1990	2000	2005
Cost ($)	12	21	33	49	61

■

The percentage of runners injured in the Boston Marathon is a function of many variables, one of which is temperature. Linear regression removes all of the variables except temperature. With linear regression we get a formula that determines the approximate percentage of runners who are injured as a function of temperature alone.

FOR thought... True or False? Explain.

1. A scatter diagram is a graph.

2. If data are roughly in line in a scatter diagram, then there is a linear relationship between the variables.

3. If there is no pattern in a scatter diagram, then there is a nonlinear relationship between the variables.

4. The line of best fit is the regression line.

5. If $r = 0.999$, then there is a positive correlation between the variables.

6. If $r = -0.998$, then there is a negative correlation between the variables.

7. If $r = 0.002$, then there is a positive correlation between the variables.

8. If $r = -0.001$, then there is a negative correlation between the variables.

9. If we make a prediction outside the range of the data, then we are interpolating.

10. If we make a prediction within the range of the data, then we are extrapolating.

EXERCISES 5

Fill in the blank.

1. The graph of pairs of data in the Cartesian coordinate system is a _____.

2. The line that best fits the data is the line of best fit or the _____ line.

For each given scatter diagram determine whether there is a linear relationship, a nonlinear relationship, or no relationship between the variables.

3.

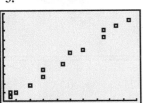

4.

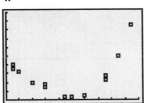

5.

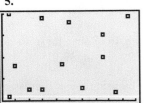

6.

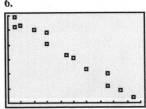

7.

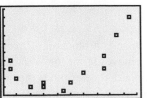

8.

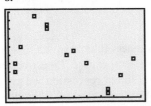

9.

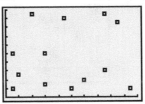

10.

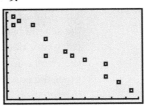

Draw a scatter diagram for each given data set. Use graph paper. From your graph determine whether there is a linear relationship between the variables.

11.

Height (in.)	Weight (lb)
24	52
30	62
32	66
18	40
22	50
36	68
40	78
28	60
22	42

12.

Age (yr)	Income (thousands of $)
33	24
30	23
32	26
30	22
38	36
35	34
32	30
40	44
39	42

13.

ACT Score	Grade Point Average
18	2.2
26	3.4
20	2.8
17	2.0
19	2.6
23	3.2
25	3.6
30	4.0

14.

Distance (mi)	Time (min)
8	34
5	20
6	26
16	70
12	50
6	32
20	90
18	70

19.

Pressure (lb / in.^{2})	Volume (in.^{3})
122	40
110	50
125	38
132	?
141	30
138	32
117	40
144	26
?	25

20.

Rate (ft / sec)	Time (sec)
10.0	6
10.1	6
10.2	5.7
10.3	?
10.4	5.6
10.5	5.4
10.6	5.5
10.7	5.4
10.8	5.2
?	5.0

15.

Height (in.)	Grade Point Average
61	4.0
59	1.9
66	3.8
72	1.6
62	2.5
74	3.8
60	1.2
68	2.6
65	2.0

16.

Price (thousands of $)	Miles per gal
16	40
18	20
22	16
24	33
29	8
32	30
35	40
38	12
40	66

Solve each problem.

21. *Fossil Fuels* The amount of coal used to generate electricity in the United States is shown in the accompanying table (Energy Information Administration, www.eia.doe.gov).

Table for Exercise 21

Year	Amount (thousand tons)
2001	964,433
2002	977,507
2003	1,005,116
2004	1,016,268
2005	1,037,485
2006	1,026,636
2007	1,046,424

A.S. Zain/Shutterstock

a. Use linear regression on your graphing calculator to find the regression equation. Let $x = 1$ correspond to 2001.

b. Use the regression equation to predict the amount of coal used for electricity in 2010.

c. Interpret the slope of the regression equation.

22. *Earthquakes* The accompanying table shows the number of earthquakes worldwide with magnitude between 5.0 and 9.9 (U.S. Geological Survey, www.usgs.gov).

Table for Exercise 22

Year	Number of Earthquakes
2000	1518
2001	1385
2002	1361
2003	1358
2004	1672
2005	1844
2006	1865
2007	2190

Thinkstock

a. Use linear regression on your graphing calculator to find the regression equation. Let $x = 0$ correspond to 2000.

Draw a scatter diagram using the given ordered pairs and a line that you think fits the data. Use graph paper. Complete the missing entries in the table by reading them from your graph. Answers may vary.

17.

Weight (thousands of lb)	Stopping Distance (ft)
2.0	96
2.4	110
2.7	130
2.8	130
2.8	142
?	160
3.7	180
3.8	180
4.0	?

18.

Prime Rate (%)	Unemployment Rate (%)
8.2	6.1
5.1	3.0
?	4.6
9.7	7.7
5.5	3.2
7.3	5.2
5.5	3.7
7.8	5.6
9.9	?

b. Use the regression equation to predict the number of earthquakes in 2015.

c. According to the regression equation, in what year were there no earthquakes?

23. *Money Supply* The M1 money supply is a measure of money in its most liquid forms, including currency and checking accounts. The accompanying table shows the M1 in billions of dollars in the United States (www.economagic.com).

Table for Exercise 23

Year	M1 Money Supply ($ billions)	
2001	1121	
2002	1096	
2003	1221	
2004	1290	
2005	1354	
2006	1375	
2007	1369	
2008	1388	

Mikeledray/Shutterstock

a. Use linear regression on your graphing calculator to find the regression equation. Let $x = 1$ correspond to 2001.

b. Use the regression equation to predict the year in which the M1 money supply will reach $2 trillion.

c. According to the regression equation, what was the M1 money supply in 1995?

24. *Price of Oil* The accompanying table shows the price of West Texas Intermediate Crude at the beginning of each year for the years 2000 through 2008 (www.economagic.com).

Table for Exercise 24

Year	Price ($/barrel)	
2000	27.18	
2001	29.58	
2002	19.67	
2003	32.94	
2004	34.27	
2005	46.84	
2006	65.51	
2007	54.57	
2008	92.95	

Vadim Ponomarenko/Shutterstock

a. Use linear regression on your graphing calculator to find the regression equation. Let $x = 0$ correspond to 2000.

b. Use the regression equation to predict the year in which the price will reach $200 per barrel.

c. According to the regression equation, what was the price in 1999?

25. *Injuries in the Boston Marathon* A study of the 4386 male runners in the Boston Marathon showed a high correlation between age and the percentage of injured runners for men aged 59 and below (*The Boston Globe,* www.boston.com/marathon). The bar graph shows the percentage of injured men age 59 and below grouped into five categories. There appears to be a relationship between the age group A and the percentage p of those injured. Use the linear regression feature of a graphing calculator to find an equation that expresses p in terms of A. Find the percentage of runners that are predicted to be injured in age group 4 according to the equation and compare the answer to the actual percentage injured.

Beth Anderson/Pearson Education, Inc.

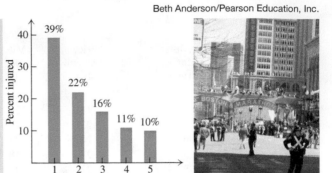

1: under 20, 2: 20–29, 3: 30–39, 4: 40–49, 5: 50–59

Figure for Exercise 25

26. *Injuries in the Boston Marathon* Use the equation of Exercise 25 to predict the percentage of runners injured in age group 6 (60-plus). Actually, 21% of the runners in the 60-plus age group were injured. Can you offer an explanation for the difference between the predicted and the actual figures?

▶ **RETHINKING**

27. Solve $(x - 5)^2 = (x + 7)^2$.

28. The length of a rectangle is 3 feet more than its width. If the perimeter is 46 feet, then what is the width?

29. Find the center and radius of the circle $x^2 + 8x + y^2 - 10y = 0$.

30. Write the equation of the line through $(-1, -2)$ and $(3, 1)$ in slope-intercept form.

31. Find the slope of the line $3x - 5y = -11$.

32. Write the equation of the line through $(5, -2)$ with slope $(-1/2)$ in standard form using only integers.

THINKING OUTSIDE THE BOX VI

Counting Coworkers Chris and Pat work at Tokyo Telemarketing. One day Chris said to Pat, "19/40 of my coworkers are female." Pat replied, "That's strange, 12/25 of my coworkers are female." If both are correct, then how many workers are there at Tokyo Telemarketing and what are the genders of Chris and Pat?

➤ POP QUIZ 5

1. Use your calculator to find the regression equation for the data given in the table:

Year	01	02	03	04	05
Cost ($)	10	12	13	16	17

2. Use the regression equation to estimate the cost in 2010.

3. Use the regression equation to estimate the cost in 1998.

6 Complex Numbers

Our system of numbers developed as the need arose. Numbers were first used for counting. As society advanced, the rational numbers were formed to express fractional parts and ratios. Negative numbers were invented to express losses or debts. When it was discovered that the exact size of some very real objects could not be expressed with rational numbers, the irrational numbers were added to the system, forming the set of real numbers. The set of real numbers was later expanded to the set of complex numbers, which includes the real and imaginary numbers. The imaginary numbers are the most abstract numbers in our system. They will be used in Section 7 to solve quadratic equations.

Definitions

There are no even roots of negative numbers in the set of real numbers. So, the real numbers are inadequate or incomplete in this regard. The imaginary numbers were invented to complete the set of real numbers. Using real and imaginary numbers, every nonzero real number has *two* square roots, *three* cube roots, *four* fourth roots, and so on. (Actually finding all of the roots of any real number is done in trigonometry.)

The imaginary numbers are based on the symbol $\sqrt{-1}$. Since there is no real number whose square is -1, a new number called i is defined such that $i^2 = -1$.

Definition:
Imaginary Number i

> The **imaginary number i** is defined by
> $$i^2 = -1.$$
> We may also write $i = \sqrt{-1}$.

A complex number is formed as a real number plus a real multiple of i.

Definition:
Complex Numbers

> The set of **complex numbers** is the set of all numbers of the form $a + bi$, where a and b are real numbers.

In $a + bi$, a is called the **real part** and b is called the **imaginary part.** Two complex numbers $a + bi$ and $c + di$ are **equal** if and only if their real parts are equal ($a = c$) and their imaginary parts are equal ($b = d$). If $b = 0$, then $a + bi$ is a **real number.** If $b \neq 0$, then $a + bi$ is an imaginary number.

The form $a + bi$ is the **standard form** of a complex number, but for convenience we use a few variations of that form. If either the real or imaginary part of a complex number is 0, then that part can be omitted. For example,

$$0 + 3i = 3i, \qquad 2 + 0i = 2, \qquad \text{and} \qquad 0 + 0i = 0.$$

If b is a radical, then i is usually written before b. For example, we write $2 + i\sqrt{3}$ rather than $2 + \sqrt{3}i$, which could be confused with $2 + \sqrt{3i}$. If b is negative, a subtraction symbol can be used as in $3 + (-2)i = 3 - 2i$. A complex number with fractions, such as $\frac{1}{3} - \frac{2}{3}i$, may be written as $\frac{1 - 2i}{3}$.

> **EXAMPLE 1** Standard form of a complex number

Determine whether each complex number is real or imaginary and write it in the standard form $a + bi$.

a. $3i$ **b.** 87 **c.** $4 - 5i$ **d.** 0 **e.** $\dfrac{1 + \pi i}{2}$

Solution

a. The complex number $3i$ is imaginary, and $3i = 0 + 3i$.
b. The complex number 87 is a real number, and $87 = 87 + 0i$.
c. The complex number $4 - 5i$ is imaginary, and $4 - 5i = 4 + (-5)i$.
d. The complex number 0 is real, and $0 = 0 + 0i$.
e. The complex number $\frac{1 + \pi i}{2}$ is imaginary, and $\frac{1 + \pi i}{2} = \frac{1}{2} + \frac{\pi}{2}i$.

▶**TRY THIS.** Determine whether $i - 5$ is real or imaginary and write it in standard form. ■

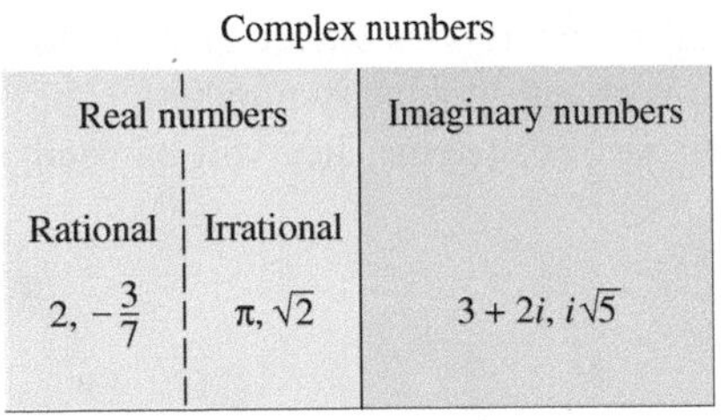

The real numbers can be classified as rational or irrational. The complex numbers can be classified as real or imaginary. The relationship between these sets of numbers is shown in Fig. 46.

Complex numbers

Real numbers		Imaginary numbers
Rational	Irrational	
$2, -\frac{3}{7}$	$\pi, \sqrt{2}$	$3 + 2i, i\sqrt{5}$

Figure 46

Addition, Subtraction, and Multiplication

Now that we have defined complex numbers, we define the operations of arithmetic with them.

Definition: Addition, Subtraction, and Multiplication

> If $a + bi$ and $c + di$ are complex numbers, we define their sum, difference, and product as follows.
>
> $$(a + bi) + (c + di) = (a + c) + (b + d)i$$
> $$(a + bi) - (c + di) = (a - c) + (b - d)i$$
> $$(a + bi)(c + di) = (ac - bd) + (bc + ad)i$$

It is not necessary to memorize these definitions, because the results can be obtained by performing the operations as if the complex numbers were binomials with i being a variable, replacing i^2 with -1 wherever it occurs.

> **EXAMPLE 2** Operations with complex numbers

Perform the indicated operations with the complex numbers.

a. $(-2 + 3i) + (-4 - 9i)$ **b.** $(-1 - 5i) - (3 - 2i)$ **c.** $2i(3 + i)$
d. $(3i)^2$ **e.** $(-3i)^2$ **f.** $(5 - 2i)(5 + 2i)$

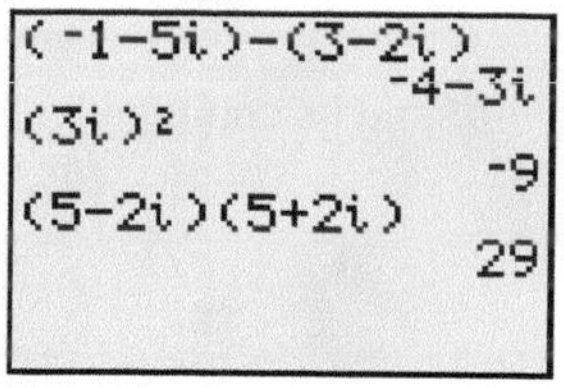

Solution

a. $(-2 + 3i) + (-4 - 9i) = -2 + (-4) + 3i + (-9i) = -6 - 6i$
b. $(-1 - 5i) - (3 - 2i) = -1 - 5i - 3 + 2i = -4 - 3i$
c. $2i(3 + i) = 6i + 2i^2 = 6i + 2(-1) = -2 + 6i$
d. $(3i)^2 = 3^2i^2 = 9(-1) = -9$
e. $(-3i)^2 = (-3)^2i^2 = 9(-1) = -9$
f. $(5 - 2i)(5 + 2i) = 25 - 4i^2 = 25 - 4(-1) = 29$

Check these results with a calculator that does computations with complex numbers, as in Fig. 47.

▶**TRY THIS.** Find the product $(4 - 3i)(1 + 2i)$. ∎

Figure 47

We can find whole-number powers of i by using the definition of multiplication. Since $i^1 = i$ and $i^2 = -1$, we have

$$i^3 = i^1 \cdot i^2 = i(-1) = -i \quad \text{and} \quad i^4 = i^1 \cdot i^3 = i(-i) = -i^2 = -(-1) = 1.$$

The first eight powers of i are listed here.

$$i^1 = i \qquad i^2 = -1 \qquad i^3 = -i \qquad i^4 = 1$$
$$i^5 = i \qquad i^6 = -1 \qquad i^7 = -i \qquad i^8 = 1$$

This list could be continued in this pattern, but any other whole-number power of i can be obtained from knowing the first four powers. We can simplify a power of i by using the fact that $i^4 = 1$ and $(i^4)^n = 1$ for any integer n.

EXAMPLE 3 Simplifying a power of i

Simplify.

a. i^{83} b. i^{-46}

Solution

a. Divide 83 by 4 and write $83 = 4 \cdot 20 + 3$. So

$$i^{83} = (i^4)^{20} \cdot i^3 = 1^{20} \cdot i^3 = 1 \cdot i^3 = -i.$$

b. Since $-46 = 4(-12) + 2$, we have

$$i^{-46} = (i^4)^{-12} \cdot i^2 = 1^{-12} \cdot i^2 = 1(-1) = -1.$$

▶**TRY THIS.** Simplify i^{35}. ∎

Division of Complex Numbers

The complex numbers $a + bi$ and $a - bi$ are called **complex conjugates** of each other.

EXAMPLE 4 Complex conjugates

Find the product of the given complex number and its conjugate.

a. $3 - i$ b. $4 + 2i$ c. $-i$

Solution

a. The conjugate of $3 - i$ is $3 + i$, and $(3 - i)(3 + i) = 9 - i^2 = 10$.
b. The conjugate of $4 + 2i$ is $4 - 2i$, and $(4 + 2i)(4 - 2i) = 16 - 4i^2 = 20$.
c. The conjugate of $-i$ is i, and $-i \cdot i = -i^2 = 1$.

▶**TRY THIS.** Find the product of $3 - 5i$ and its conjugate. ∎

In general we have the following theorem about complex conjugates.

Theorem:
Complex Conjugates

If a and b are real numbers, then the product of $a + bi$ and its conjugate $a - bi$ is the real number $a^2 + b^2$. In symbols,

$$(a + bi)(a - bi) = a^2 + b^2.$$

We use the theorem about complex conjugates to divide imaginary numbers, in a process that is similar to rationalizing a denominator.

EXAMPLE 5 | Dividing imaginary numbers

Write each quotient in the form $a + bi$.

a. $\dfrac{8 - i}{2 + i}$ **b.** $\dfrac{1}{5 - 4i}$ **c.** $\dfrac{3 - 2i}{i}$

Solution

a. Multiply the numerator and denominator by $2 - i$, the conjugate of $2 + i$:

$$\frac{8 - i}{2 + i} = \frac{(8 - i)(2 - i)}{(2 + i)(2 - i)} = \frac{16 - 10i + i^2}{4 - i^2} = \frac{15 - 10i}{5} = 3 - 2i$$

Check division using multiplication: $(3 - 2i)(2 + i) = 8 - i$.

b. $\dfrac{1}{5 - 4i} = \dfrac{1(5 + 4i)}{(5 - 4i)(5 + 4i)} = \dfrac{5 + 4i}{25 + 16} = \dfrac{5 + 4i}{41} = \dfrac{5}{41} + \dfrac{4}{41}i$

Check: $\left(\dfrac{5}{41} + \dfrac{4}{41}i\right)(5 - 4i) = \dfrac{25}{41} - \dfrac{20}{41}i + \dfrac{20}{41}i - \dfrac{16}{41}i^2$

$$= \frac{25}{41} + \frac{16}{41} = 1.$$

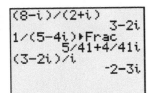

Figure 48

You can also check with a calculator that handles complex numbers, as in Fig. 48. □

c. $\dfrac{3 - 2i}{i} = \dfrac{(3 - 2i)(-i)}{i(-i)} = \dfrac{-3i + 2i^2}{-i^2} = \dfrac{-2 - 3i}{1} = -2 - 3i$

Check: $(-2 - 3i)(i) = -2i - 3i^2 = 3 - 2i$.

▶**TRY THIS.** Write $\dfrac{4}{1 + i}$ in the form $a + bi$. ■

Roots of Negative Numbers

In Examples 2(d) and 2(e), we saw that both $(3i)^2 = -9$ and $(-3i)^2 = -9$. This means that in the complex number system there are two square roots of -9, $3i$ and $-3i$. For any positive real number b, we have $(i\sqrt{b})^2 = -b$ and $(-i\sqrt{b})^2 = -b$. So there are two square roots of $-b$. They are $i\sqrt{b}$ and $-i\sqrt{b}$. We call $i\sqrt{b}$ the **principal square root** of $-b$ and make the following definition.

Definition: Square Root of a Negative Number

For any positive real number b, $\sqrt{-b} = i\sqrt{b}$.

In the real number system, $\sqrt{-2}$ and $\sqrt{-8}$ are undefined, but in the complex number system they are defined as $\sqrt{-2} = i\sqrt{2}$ and $\sqrt{-8} = i\sqrt{8}$. Even though we now have meaning for a symbol such as $\sqrt{-2}$, *all operations with complex numbers must be performed after converting to the $a + bi$ form.* If we perform operations with roots of negative numbers using properties of the real numbers, we can get contradictory results:

$$\sqrt{-2} \cdot \sqrt{-8} = \sqrt{(-2)(-8)} = \sqrt{16} = 4 \qquad \text{Incorrect}$$

$$i\sqrt{2} \cdot i\sqrt{8} = i^2 \cdot \sqrt{16} = -4 \qquad \text{Correct}$$

The product rule $\sqrt{a} \cdot \sqrt{b} = \sqrt{ab}$ is used *only* for nonnegative numbers a and b.

EXAMPLE 6 Square roots of negative numbers

Write each expression in the form $a + bi$, where a and b are real numbers.

a. $\sqrt{-8} + \sqrt{-18}$

b. $\dfrac{-4 + \sqrt{-50}}{4}$

c. $\sqrt{-27}(\sqrt{9} - \sqrt{-2})$

Solution

The first step in each case is to replace the square roots of negative numbers by expressions with i.

a. $\sqrt{-8} + \sqrt{-18} = i\sqrt{8} + i\sqrt{18} = 2i\sqrt{2} + 3i\sqrt{2}$

$$= 5i\sqrt{2}$$

b. $\dfrac{-4 + \sqrt{-50}}{4} = \dfrac{-4 + i\sqrt{50}}{4} = \dfrac{-4 + 5i\sqrt{2}}{4}$

$$= -1 + \frac{5}{4}i\sqrt{2}$$

c. $\sqrt{-27}(\sqrt{9} - \sqrt{-2}) = 3i\sqrt{3}(3 - i\sqrt{2}) = 9i\sqrt{3} - 3i^2\sqrt{6}$

$$= 3\sqrt{6} + 9i\sqrt{3}$$

▶**TRY THIS.** Write $\dfrac{2 - \sqrt{-12}}{2}$ in the form $a + bi$. ∎

▶FOR thought... True or False? Explain.

1. The multiplicative inverse of i is $-i$.

2. The conjugate of i is $-i$.

3. The set of complex numbers is a subset of the set of real numbers.

4. $(\sqrt{3} - i\sqrt{2})(\sqrt{3} + i\sqrt{2}) = 5$

5. $(2 + 5i)(2 + 5i) = 4 + 25$

6. $5 - \sqrt{-9} = 5 - 9i$

7. $(3i)^2 + 9 = 0$

8. $(-3i)^2 + 9 = 0$

9. $i^4 = 1$

10. $i^{18} = 1$

EXERCISES 6

Fill in the blank.

1. Numbers of the form $a + bi$ where a and b are real numbers are _____.

2. In $a + bi$, a is the _____ and b is the _____.

3. A number of the form $a + bi$ with $b \neq 0$ is an _____.

4. The _____ square root of $-b$ where b is a positive real number is $i\sqrt{b}$.

Determine whether each complex number is real or imaginary and write it in the standard form $a + bi$.

5. $6i$

6. $-3i + \sqrt{6}$

7. $\dfrac{1 + i}{3}$

8. -72

9. $\sqrt{7}$

10. $-i\sqrt{5}$

11. $\dfrac{\pi}{2}$

12. 0

Perform the indicated operations and write your answers in the form $a + bi$, where a and b are real numbers.

13. $(3 - 3i) + (4 + 5i)$

14. $(-3 + 2i) + (5 - 6i)$

15. $(1 - i) - (3 + 2i)$

16. $(6 - 7i) - (3 - 4i)$

17. $(1 - i\sqrt{2}) + (3 + 2i\sqrt{2})$

18. $(5 + 3i\sqrt{5}) + (-4 - 5i\sqrt{5})$

19. $\left(5 + \dfrac{1}{3}i\right) - \left(\dfrac{1}{2} - \dfrac{1}{2}i\right)$

20. $\left(\dfrac{1}{2} - \dfrac{2}{3}i\right) - \left(3 - \dfrac{1}{4}i\right)$

21. $-6i(3 - 2i)$

22. $-3i(5 + 2i)$

23. $(2 - 3i)(4 + 6i)$

24. $(3 - i)(5 - 2i)$

25. $(4 - 5i)(6 + 2i)$

26. $(3 + 7i)(2 + 5i)$

27. $(5 - 2i)(5 + 2i)$

28. $(4 + 3i)(4 - 3i)$

29. $(\sqrt{3} - i)(\sqrt{3} + i)$

30. $(\sqrt{2} + i\sqrt{3})(\sqrt{2} - i\sqrt{3})$

31. $(3 + 4i)^2$

32. $(-6 - 2i)^2$

33. $(\sqrt{5} - 2i)^2$

34. $(\sqrt{6} + i\sqrt{3})^2$

35. i^{17}

36. i^{24}

37. i^{98}

38. i^{19}

39. i^{-1}

40. i^{-2}

41. i^{-3}

42. i^{-4}

43. i^{-13}

44. i^{-27}

45. i^{-38}

46. i^{-66}

Find the product of the given complex number and its conjugate.

47. $3 - 9i$

48. $4 + 3i$

49. $\dfrac{1}{2} + 2i$

50. $\dfrac{1}{3} - i$

51. i

52. $-i\sqrt{5}$

53. $3 - i\sqrt{3}$

54. $\dfrac{5}{2} + i\dfrac{\sqrt{2}}{2}$

Write each quotient in the form $a + bi$.

55. $\dfrac{1}{2 - i}$

56. $\dfrac{1}{5 + 2i}$

57. $\dfrac{-3i}{1 - i}$

58. $\dfrac{3i}{-2 + i}$

59. $\dfrac{-3 + 3i}{i}$

60. $\dfrac{-2 - 4i}{-i}$

61. $\dfrac{1 - i}{3 + 2i}$

62. $\dfrac{4 + 2i}{2 - 3i}$

63. $\dfrac{2 - i}{3 + 5i}$

64. $\dfrac{4 + 2i}{5 - 3i}$

Write each expression in the form $a + bi$, where a and b are real numbers.

65. $\sqrt{-4} - \sqrt{-9}$

66. $\sqrt{-16} + \sqrt{-25}$

67. $\sqrt{-4} - \sqrt{16}$

68. $\sqrt{-3} \cdot \sqrt{-3}$

69. $(\sqrt{-6})^2$

70. $(\sqrt{-5})^3$

71. $\sqrt{-2} \cdot \sqrt{-50}$

72. $\dfrac{-6 + \sqrt{-3}}{3}$

73. $\dfrac{-2 + \sqrt{-20}}{2}$

74. $\dfrac{9 - \sqrt{-18}}{-6}$

75. $-3 + \sqrt{3^2 - 4(1)(5)}$

76. $1 - \sqrt{(-1)^2 - 4(1)(1)}$

77. $\sqrt{-8}(\sqrt{-2} + \sqrt{8})$

78. $\sqrt{-6}(\sqrt{2} - \sqrt{-3})$

Evaluate the expression $\dfrac{-b + \sqrt{b^2 - 4ac}}{2a}$ for each choice of a, b, and c.

79. $a = 1, b = 2, c = 5$

80. $a = 5, b = -4, c = 1$

81. $a = 2, b = 4, c = 3$

82. $a = 2, b = -4, c = 5$

Evaluate the expression $\dfrac{-b - \sqrt{b^2 - 4ac}}{2a}$ for each choice of a, b, and c.

83. $a = 1, b = 6, c = 17$

84. $a = 1, b = -12, c = 84$

85. $a = -2, b = 6, c = 6$

86. $a = 3, b = 6, c = 8$

Perform the indicated operations. Write the answers in the form $a + bi$ *where a and b are real numbers.*

87. $(3 - 5i)(3 + 5i)$

88. $(2 - 4i)(2 + 4i)$

89. $(3 - 5i) + (3 + 5i)$

90. $(2 - 4i) + (2 + 4i)$

91. $\dfrac{3 - 5i}{3 + 5i}$

92. $\dfrac{2 - 4i}{2 + 4i}$

93. $(6 - 2i) - (7 - 3i)$

94. $(5 - 6i) - (8 - 9i)$

95. $i^5(i^2 - 3i)$

96. $3i^7(i - 5i^3)$

FOR WRITING/DISCUSSION

97. Explain in detail how to find i^n for any positive integer n.

98. Find a number $a + bi$ such that $a^2 + b^2$ is irrational.

99. Let $w = a + bi$ and $\overline{w} = a - bi$, where a and b are real numbers. Show that $w + \overline{w}$ is real and that $w - \overline{w}$ is imaginary. Write sentences (containing no mathematical symbols) stating these results.

100. Is it true that the product of a complex number and its conjugate is a real number? Explain.

101. Prove that the reciprocal of $a + bi$, where a and b are not both zero, is $\dfrac{a}{a^2 + b^2} - \dfrac{b}{a^2 + b^2}i$.

102. Evaluate $i^{0!} + i^{1!} + i^{2!} + \cdots + i^{100!}$, where $n!$ (read "n factorial") is the product of the integers from 1 through n if $n \geq 1$ and $0! = 1$.

▶ RETHINKING

103. Solve $\dfrac{x}{2} + 4 = \dfrac{x}{6} - 3$.

104. Solve $\dfrac{1}{x - 1} + \dfrac{x}{x + 1} = \dfrac{x^2}{x^2 - 1}$.

105. Write a formula that expresses the width W of a rectangle as a function of its perimeter P and its length L.

106. Write a formula that expresses the diameter d of a circle as a function of its circumference C.

107. E10 consists of 10% ethanol and 90% gasoline. E20 is 20% ethanol and 80% gasoline. How many gallons of ethanol must be added to 50 gallons of E10 to obtain E20?

108. How many gallons of gasoline must be added to 50 gallons of E20 to obtain E10? See the previous exercise.

THINKING OUTSIDE THE BOX VII & VIII

Reversing the Digits Find a four-digit integer x such that $4x$ is another four-digit integer whose digits are in the reverse order of the digits of x.

Summing Reciprocals There is only one way to write 1 as a sum of the reciprocals of three different positive integers:

$$\frac{1}{2} + \frac{1}{3} + \frac{1}{6} = 1$$

Find all possible ways to write 1 as a sum of the reciprocals of four different positive integers.

► POP QUIZ 6

1. Find the sum of $3 + 2i$ and $4 - i$.

2. Find the product of $4 - 3i$ and $2 + i$.

3. Find the product of $2 - 3i$ and its conjugate.

4. Write $\dfrac{5}{2 - 3i}$ in the form $a + bi$.

5. Find i^{27}.

6. What are the two square roots of -16?

7 Quadratic Equations

One of our main goals is to solve polynomial equations. In Section 1 we learned to solve equations of the form $ax + b = 0$, the linear equations. Linear equations are first-degree polynomial equations. In this section we will solve second-degree polynomial equations, the quadratic equations.

Definition

Quadratic equations have second-degree terms that linear equations do not have.

Definition:
Quadratic Equation

> A **quadratic equation** is an equation of the form
> $$ax^2 + bx + c = 0,$$
> where a, b, and c are real numbers with $a \neq 0$.

The condition that $a \neq 0$ in the definition ensures that the equation actually does have an x^2-term. There are several methods for solving quadratic equations. Which method is most appropriate depends on the type of quadratic equation that we are solving. We first consider the factoring method.

Solving Quadratic Equations by Factoring

Many second-degree polynomials can be factored as a product of first-degree binomials. When one side of an equation is a product and the other side is 0, we can write an equivalent statement by setting each factor equal to zero. This idea is called the **zero factor property.**

The Zero Factor Property

> If A and B are algebraic expressions, then the equation $AB = 0$ is equivalent to the compound statement $A = 0$ or $B = 0$.

EXAMPLE 1 Quadratic equations solved by factoring

Solve each equation by factoring.

a. $x^2 - x - 12 = 0$
b. $(x + 3)(x - 4) = 8$

Solution

a.
$$x^2 - x - 12 = 0$$

$(x - 4)(x + 3) = 0$ Factor the left-hand side.

$x - 4 = 0$ or $x + 3 = 0$ Zero factor property

$x = 4$ or $x = -3$

Check: $(-3)^2 - (-3) - 12 = 0$ and $4^2 - 4 - 12 = 0$. The solution set is $\{-3, 4\}$.

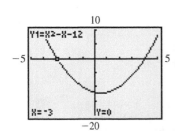

The graph of $y = x^2 - x - 12$ intersects the x-axis at $(-3, 0)$ and $(4, 0)$ as shown in Fig. 49. □

Figure 49

b. We must first rewrite the equation with 0 on one side, because the zero factor property applies only when the factors have a product of 0.

$$(x + 3)(x - 4) = 8$$

$x^2 - x - 12 = 8$ Multiply on the left-hand side.

$x^2 - x - 20 = 0$ Get 0 on the right-hand side.

$(x - 5)(x + 4) = 0$ Factor.

$x - 5 = 0$ or $x + 4 = 0$ Zero factor property

$x = 5$ or $x = -4$

Check in the original equation. The solution set is $\{-4, 5\}$.

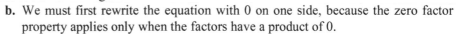

The graph of $y = x^2 - x - 20$ intersects the x-axis at $(-4, 0)$ and $(5, 0)$ as shown in Fig. 50.

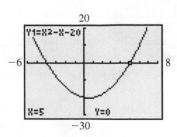

Figure 50

▶**TRY THIS.** Solve $x^2 - 7x - 18 = 0$ by factoring. ■

Equations, Inequalities, and Modeling

The Square Root Property

An equation of the type $x^2 = k$ can be solved by factoring a difference of two squares:

$$x^2 - k = 0$$

$$(x + \sqrt{k})(x - \sqrt{k}) = 0 \qquad \text{Factor.}$$

$$x + \sqrt{k} = 0 \qquad \text{or} \quad x - \sqrt{k} = 0 \qquad \text{Zero factor property}$$

$$x = -\sqrt{k} \quad \text{or} \qquad x = \sqrt{k}$$

If $k > 0$, then $x^2 = k$ has two real solutions. If $k < 0$, then $\sqrt{k}$ is an imaginary number and $x^2 = k$ has two imaginary solutions. If $k = 0$, then 0 is the only solution to $x^2 = k$. Instead of solving equations of this type by factoring, it is worth remembering this result as the square root property.

The Square Root Property

> For any real number k, the equation $x^2 = k$ is equivalent to $x = \pm\sqrt{k}$.

EXAMPLE 2 Using the square root property

Find all complex solutions to each equation.

a. $x^2 - 9 = 0$
b. $2x^2 - 1 = 0$
c. $(2x - 1)^2 = 0$
d. $(x - 3)^2 + 8 = 0$

Solution

a. Before using the square root property, isolate x^2.

$$x^2 - 9 = 0$$

$$x^2 = 9$$

$$x = \pm\sqrt{9} = \pm 3 \qquad \text{Square root property}$$

Check: $3^2 - 9 = 0$ and $(-3)^2 - 9 = 0$. The solution set is $\{-3, 3\}$.

b. $2x^2 - 1 = 0$

$$2x^2 = 1$$

$$x^2 = \frac{1}{2}$$

$$x = \pm\sqrt{\frac{1}{2}} = \pm\frac{1}{\sqrt{2}} = \pm\frac{1 \cdot \sqrt{2}}{\sqrt{2} \cdot \sqrt{2}} = \pm\frac{\sqrt{2}}{2}$$

Check: $2\left(\pm\frac{\sqrt{2}}{2}\right)^2 - 1 = 2\left(\frac{1}{2}\right) - 1 = 0$. The solution set is $\left\{\pm\frac{\sqrt{2}}{2}\right\}$.

c. $(2x - 1)^2 = 0$

$$2x - 1 = \pm\sqrt{0} \qquad \text{Square root property}$$

$$2x - 1 = 0$$

$$2x = 1$$

$$x = \frac{1}{2}$$

The solution set is $\left\{\frac{1}{2}\right\}$.

d. $(x - 3)^2 + 8 = 0$

$$(x - 3)^2 = -8$$

$$x - 3 = \pm\sqrt{-8} \qquad \text{Square root property}$$

$$x = 3 \pm 2i\sqrt{2} \qquad \sqrt{-8} = i\sqrt{8} = i\sqrt{4}\sqrt{2} = 2i\sqrt{2}$$

The solution set is $\{3 - 2i\sqrt{2}, 3 + 2i\sqrt{2}\}$. Note that there are no real solutions to this equation, because the square of every real number is nonnegative.

▶**TRY THIS.** Solve $(x - 3)^2 = 16$ by the square root property. ∎

In Section 3 we learned that the solution to an equation in one variable corresponds to an x-intercept on a graph in two variables. Note that the solutions to $x^2 - 9 = 0$ and $(2x - 1)^2 = 0$ in Example 2 correspond to the x-intercepts on the graphs of $y = x^2 - 9$ and $y = (2x - 1)^2$ in Figs. 51(a) and 51(b). Because there are no real solutions to $(x - 3)^2 + 8 = 0$ in Example 2(d), the graph of $y = (x - 3)^2 + 8$ in Fig. 51(c) has no x-intercepts.

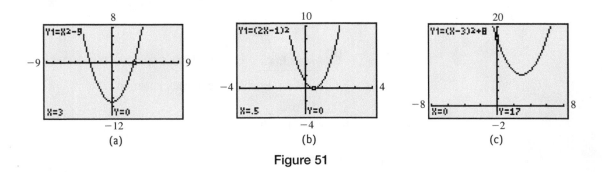

Figure 51

We will study graphs and their properties extensively in the coming chapters. In this chapter we will point out, using calculator graphs, how graphs in two variables can help us understand the solutions to equations and inequalities in one variable. So even if you are not using a graphing calculator, you should pay close attention to the calculator graphs shown in this chapter.

Completing the Square

Solving quadratic equations by factoring is limited to equations that we can factor. However, we can solve any quadratic equation by completing the square and then using the square root property. We used completing the square in Section 3 to convert an equation of a circle into standard form.

Since it is simplest to complete the square when the leading coefficient of the polynomial is 1, we divide by the leading coefficient before completing the square. This is illustrated in part (b) of the next example.

EXAMPLE 3 | Solving a quadratic equation by completing the square

Solve each equation by completing the square.

a. $x^2 + 6x + 7 = 0$
b. $2x^2 - 3x - 4 = 0$

Solution

a. Since $x^2 + 6x + 7$ is not a perfect square trinomial, we must find a perfect square trinomial that has $x^2 + 6x$ as its first two terms. Since one-half of 6 is 3 and $3^2 = 9$, our goal is to get $x^2 + 6x + 9$ on the left-hand side:

$$x^2 + 6x + 7 = 0$$

$$x^2 + 6x = -7 \qquad \text{Subtract 7 from each side.}$$

$$x^2 + 6x + 9 = -7 + 9 \qquad \text{Add 9 to each side.}$$

$$(x + 3)^2 = 2 \qquad \text{Factor the left-hand side.}$$

$$x + 3 = \pm\sqrt{2} \qquad \text{Square root property}$$

$$x = -3 \pm \sqrt{2}$$

Check in the original equation. The solution set is $\{-3 - \sqrt{2}, -3 + \sqrt{2}\}$.

b. $2x^2 - 3x - 4 = 0$

$$x^2 - \frac{3}{2}x - 2 = 0 \qquad \text{Divide each side by 2 to get } a = 1.$$

$$x^2 - \frac{3}{2}x = 2 \qquad \text{Add 2 to each side.}$$

$$x^2 - \frac{3}{2}x + \frac{9}{16} = 2 + \frac{9}{16} \qquad \frac{1}{2} \cdot \frac{3}{2} = \frac{3}{4} \text{ and } \left(\frac{3}{4}\right)^2 = \frac{9}{16}.$$

$$\left(x - \frac{3}{4}\right)^2 = \frac{41}{16} \qquad \text{Factor the left-hand side.}$$

$$x - \frac{3}{4} = \pm\frac{\sqrt{41}}{4} \qquad \text{Square root property}$$

$$x = \frac{3}{4} \pm \frac{\sqrt{41}}{4} = \frac{3 \pm \sqrt{41}}{4}$$

(a)

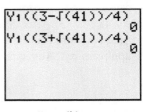

(b)

Figure 52

The solution set is $\left\{\dfrac{3 - \sqrt{41}}{4}, \dfrac{3 + \sqrt{41}}{4}\right\}$.

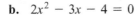 To check, enter $y_1 = 2x^2 - 3x - 4$ as in Fig. 52(a). On the home screen in Fig. 52(b), enter y_1 followed in parentheses by the x-value at which you want to calculate y_1.

▶**TRY THIS.** Solve $2x^2 - 4x - 1 = 0$ by completing the square. ∎

STRATEGY

Completing the Square

The goal is to get a perfect square trinomial on one side of the equation.

1. If the coefficient of x is not 1, divide by it.
2. To complete $x^2 + bx$, add $(b/2)^2$ to both sides of the equation.
3. Factor the perfect square trinomial.
4. Apply the square root property.
5. Simplify the results.

The Quadratic Formula

The method of completing the square can be applied to any quadratic equation

$$ax^2 + bx + c = 0, \qquad \text{where } a \neq 0.$$

Assume for now that $a > 0$, and divide each side by a.

$$x^2 + \frac{b}{a}x + \frac{c}{a} = 0$$

$$x^2 + \frac{b}{a}x = -\frac{c}{a} \qquad \text{Subtract } \tfrac{c}{a} \text{ from each side.}$$

$$x^2 + \frac{b}{a}x + \frac{b^2}{4a^2} = -\frac{c}{a} + \frac{b^2}{4a^2} \qquad \tfrac{1}{2} \cdot \tfrac{b}{a} = \tfrac{b}{2a} \text{ and } \left(\tfrac{b}{2a}\right)^2 = \tfrac{b^2}{4a^2}.$$

Now factor the perfect square trinomial on the left-hand side. On the right-hand side get a common denominator and add.

$$\left(x + \frac{b}{2a}\right)^2 = \frac{b^2 - 4ac}{4a^2} \qquad \tfrac{c}{a} \cdot \tfrac{4a}{4a} = \tfrac{4ac}{4a^2}$$

$$x + \frac{b}{2a} = \pm\sqrt{\frac{b^2 - 4ac}{4a^2}} \qquad \text{Square root property, assuming } b^2 - 4ac \geq 0$$

$$x = -\frac{b}{2a} \pm \frac{\sqrt{b^2 - 4ac}}{2a} \qquad \text{Because } a > 0, \sqrt{4a^2} = 2a.$$

$$x = \frac{-b \pm \sqrt{b^2 - 4ac}}{2a}$$

We assumed that $a > 0$ so that $\sqrt{4a^2} = 2a$ would be correct. If a is negative, then $\sqrt{4a^2} = -2a$, and we get

$$x = -\frac{b}{2a} \pm \frac{\sqrt{b^2 - 4ac}}{-2a}.$$

However, the negative sign in $-2a$ can be deleted because of the $\pm$ symbol preceding it. For example, $5 \pm (-3)$ gives the same values as 5 ± 3. After deleting the negative sign on $-2a$, we get the same formula for the solution. It is called the **quadratic formula.** Its importance lies in its wide applicability. Any quadratic equation can be solved by using this formula.

The Quadratic Formula

> The solutions to $ax^2 + bx + c = 0$, with $a \neq 0$, are given by the formula
> $$x = \frac{-b \pm \sqrt{b^2 - 4ac}}{2a}.$$

EXAMPLE 4 Using the quadratic formula

Use the quadratic formula to find all real or imaginary solutions to each equation.

a. $x^2 + 8x + 6 = 0$ **b.** $x^2 - 6x + 11 = 0$ **c.** $4x^2 + 9 = 12x$

Solution

a. For $x^2 + 8x + 6 = 0$ we use $a = 1$, $b = 8$, and $c = 6$ in the formula:

$$x = \frac{-8 \pm \sqrt{8^2 - 4(1)(6)}}{2(1)} = \frac{-8 \pm \sqrt{40}}{2} = \frac{-8 \pm 2\sqrt{10}}{2}$$

$$= \frac{2(-4 \pm \sqrt{10})}{2} = -4 \pm \sqrt{10}$$

The solution set is $\{-4 - \sqrt{10}, -4 + \sqrt{10}\}$.

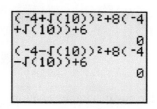

Figure 53

Check by using a calculator as in Fig. 53. □

b. Use $a = 1$, $b = -6$, and $c = 11$ in the quadratic formula:

$$x = \frac{-(-6) \pm \sqrt{(-6)^2 - 4(1)(11)}}{2(1)}$$

$$= \frac{6 \pm \sqrt{-8}}{2} = \frac{6 \pm 2i\sqrt{2}}{2} = 3 \pm i\sqrt{2}$$

Check by evaluating $x^2 - 6x + 11$ with $x = 3 + i\sqrt{2}$ as follows:

$$(3 + i\sqrt{2})^2 - 6(3 + i\sqrt{2}) + 11 = 9 + 6i\sqrt{2} + (i\sqrt{2})^2 - 18 - 6i\sqrt{2} + 11$$

$$= 9 + 6i\sqrt{2} - 2 - 18 - 6i\sqrt{2} + 11$$

$$= 0$$

The reader should check $3 - i\sqrt{2}$. The imaginary solutions are $3 - i\sqrt{2}$ and $3 + i\sqrt{2}$.

The solutions can be checked with a calculator as in Fig. 54. □

Figure 54

c. To use the quadratic formula, the equation must be in the form $ax^2 + bx + c = 0$. So rewrite the equation as $4x^2 - 12x + 9 = 0$. Now use $a = 4$, $b = -12$, and $c = 9$ in the formula:

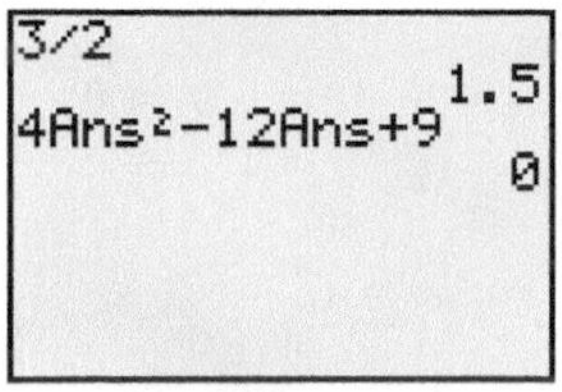

$$x = \frac{-(-12) \pm \sqrt{(-12)^2 - 4(4)(9)}}{2(4)} = \frac{12 \pm \sqrt{0}}{8} = \frac{3}{2}$$

You should check that $4\left(\frac{3}{2}\right)^2 - 12\left(\frac{3}{2}\right) + 9 = 0$. The solution set is $\left\{\frac{3}{2}\right\}$.

You can check with a calculator as in Fig. 55.

Figure 55

▶**TRY THIS.** Solve $2x^2 - 3x - 2 = 0$ by the quadratic formula. ∎

To decide which of the four methods to use for solving a given quadratic equation, use the following strategy.

STRATEGY

Solving $ax^2 + bx + c = 0$

1. If $b = 0$, solve $ax^2 + c = 0$ for x^2 and apply the square root property.

2. If $ax^2 + bx + c$ can be easily factored, then solve by factoring. If $a < 0$ multiply each side of the equation by -1 for easier factoring.

3. If the equation cannot be solved by the square root property or factoring, then use the quadratic formula.

4. Completing the square can be used on any quadratic equation, but the quadratic formula is usually easier.

5. Graph $y = ax^2 + bx + c$. The x-coordinates of the x-intercepts on the graph are the solution(s) to $ax^2 + bx + c = 0$. The graph may not give exact solutions, but you can easily check your solutions from the other methods with a graph.

The Discriminant

The expression $b^2 - 4ac$ in the quadratic formula is called the **discriminant,** because its value determines the number and type of solutions to a quadratic equation. If $b^2 - 4ac > 0$, then $\sqrt{b^2 - 4ac}$ is real and the equation has two real solutions. If $b^2 - 4ac < 0$, then $\sqrt{b^2 - 4ac}$ is not a real number and there are no real solutions.

There are two imaginary solutions. If $b^2 - 4ac = 0$, then $-b/(2a)$ is the only solution. See Table 2.

Table 2 Number of real solutions to a quadratic equation

Value of $b^2 - 4ac$	Number of Real Solutions
Positive	2
Zero	1
Negative	0

EXAMPLE 5 Using the discriminant

For each equation, state the value of the discriminant and the number of real solutions.

a. $x^2 + 8x + 6 = 0$ **b.** $5x^2 - 4x + 1 = 0$ **c.** $4x^2 + 12x + 9 = 0$

Solution

a. Find the value of $b^2 - 4ac$ using $a = 1$, $b = 8$, and $c = 6$:

$$b^2 - 4ac = 8^2 - 4(1)(6) = 40$$

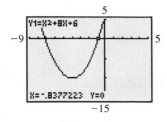

Figure 56

The value of the discriminant is 40 and the equation has two real solutions.

The graph of $y = x^2 + 8x + 6$ has two x-intercepts as shown in Fig. 56. ☐

b. Find the value of the discriminant for the equation $5x^2 - 4x + 1 = 0$:

$$b^2 - 4ac = (-4)^2 - 4(5)(1) = -4$$

Because the discriminant is negative, the equation has no real solutions.

The graph of $y = 5x^2 - 4x + 1$ has no x-intercepts as shown in Fig. 57. ☐

c. For $4x^2 + 12x + 9 = 0$, we have $b^2 - 4ac = 12^2 - 4(4)(9) = 0$. So the equation has one real solution.

The graph of $y = 4x^2 + 12x + 9$ has one x-intercept as shown in Fig. 58.

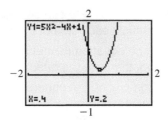

Figure 57

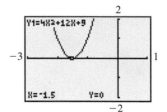

Figure 58

▶**TRY THIS.** State the value of the discriminant and the number of real solutions to $5x^2 - 7x + 9 = 0$. ∎

The number of solutions to polynomial equations is a topic of considerable interest in algebra. The number of solutions to any polynomial equation of degree n is less than or equal to n (the fundamental theorem of algebra). Notice how the number of solutions to linear and quadratic equations agrees with these results.

Using Quadratic Models in Applications

The problems that we solve in this section are very similar to those in Section 2. However, in this section the mathematical model of the situation results in a quadratic equation.

EXAMPLE 6 A problem solved with a quadratic equation

It took Susan 30 minutes longer to drive 275 miles on I-70 west of Green River, Utah, than it took her to drive 300 miles east of Green River. Because of a sand storm and a full load of cantaloupes, she averaged 10 mph less while traveling west of Green River. What was her average speed for each part of the trip?

Solution

Let x represent Susan's average speed in mph east of Green River and $x - 10$ represent her average speed in mph west of Green River. We can organize all of the given information as in the following table. Since $D = RT$, the time is determined by $T = D/R$.

	Distance	Rate	Time
East	300 mi	x mi/hr	$\dfrac{300}{x}$ hr
West	275 mi	$x - 10$ mi/hr	$\dfrac{275}{x - 10}$ hr

The following equation expresses the fact that her time west of Green River was $\frac{1}{2}$ hour greater than her time east of Green River.

$$\frac{275}{x - 10} = \frac{300}{x} + \frac{1}{2}$$

$$2x(x - 10) \cdot \frac{275}{x - 10} = 2x(x - 10)\left(\frac{300}{x} + \frac{1}{2}\right)$$

$$550x = 600(x - 10) + x(x - 10)$$

$$-x^2 - 40x + 6000 = 0$$

$$x^2 + 40x - 6000 = 0$$

$$(x + 100)(x - 60) = 0 \qquad \text{Factor.}$$

$$x = -100 \quad \text{or} \quad x = 60$$

The solution $x = -100$ is a solution to the equation, but not a solution to the problem. The other solution, $x = 60$, means that $x - 10 = 50$. Check that these two average speeds are a solution to the problem. Susan's average speed east of Green River was 60 mph, and her average speed west of Green River was 50 mph.

▶**TRY THIS.** It took Josh 30 minutes longer to drive 100 miles than it took Bree to drive 90 miles. If Josh averaged 5 mph less than Bree, then what was the average speed of each driver? ■

In the next example we use the formula for the height of a projectile under the influence of gravity. Although we can use any letters we want for variables, it is customary to use s (upper case or lower case) for height and t for time.

EXAMPLE 7 Applying the quadratic formula

In tennis a lob can be used to buy time to get into position. The approximate height S in feet for a tennis ball that is hit straight upward at v_0 ft/sec from a height of s_0 ft is modeled by

$$S = -16t^2 + v_0 t + s_0,$$

where t is time in seconds.

a. Use Fig. 59 to estimate the time that it takes a ball to return to the court when it is hit straight upward with velocity 60 ft/sec from a height of 5 ft.

b. Find the time for part (a) by using the quadratic formula.

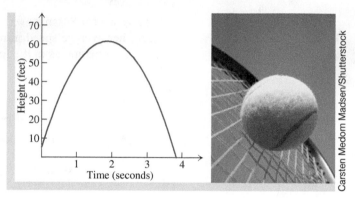

Figure 59

Solution

a. At the t-intercept in Fig. 59, $S = 0$. Since the t-intercept is approximately $(3.7, 0)$, the ball is in the air for about 3.7 sec.

b. We are looking for the value of t for which the height S is zero. Use $v_0 = 60$, $s_0 = 5$, and $S = 0$ in the given formula:

$$0 = -16t^2 + 60t + 5$$

Use the quadratic formula to solve the equation:

$$t = \frac{-60 \pm \sqrt{60^2 - 4(-16)(5)}}{2(-16)} = \frac{-60 \pm \sqrt{3920}}{-32} = \frac{-60 \pm 28\sqrt{5}}{-32}$$

$$= \frac{15 \pm 7\sqrt{5}}{8}$$

Figure 60

Now $(15 - 7\sqrt{5})/8 \approx -0.082$ and $(15 + 7\sqrt{5})/8 \approx 3.83$. Since the time at which the ball returns to the earth must be positive, it will take exactly $(15 + 7\sqrt{5})/8$ seconds or approximately 3.83 seconds for the ball to hit the earth. Check as shown in Fig. 60. Due to round-off errors the calculator answer is not zero, but really close to zero $(-1 \times 10^{-11} = -0.00000000001)$.

▶**TRY THIS.** A ball is tossed straight upward. Its height h in feet at time t in seconds is given by $h = -16t^2 + 40t + 6$. For how long is the ball in the air? ∎

Quadratic equations often arise from applications that involve the Pythagorean theorem from geometry: *A triangle is a right triangle if and only if the sum of the squares of the legs is equal to the square of the hypotenuse.*

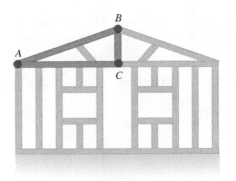

Figure 61

EXAMPLE 8 Using the Pythagorean theorem

In the house shown in Fig. 61 the ridge of the roof at point B is 6 feet above point C. If the distance from A to C is 18 feet, then what is the length of a rafter from A to B?

Solution

Let x be the distance from A to B. Use the Pythagorean theorem to write the following equation.

$$x^2 = 18^2 + 6^2$$
$$x^2 = 360$$
$$x = \pm\sqrt{360} = \pm 6\sqrt{10}$$

Since x must be positive in this problem, $x = 6\sqrt{10}$ feet or $x \approx 18.97$ feet.

▶**TRY THIS.** One leg of a right triangle is 2 feet longer than the other leg. If the hypotenuse is 6 feet, then what are the lengths of the legs? ■

Quadratic Regression

In Section 5 we used a graphing calculator to find the line of best fit. In the next example we will use the quadratic regression feature of a calculator to find an equation of the form $y = ax^2 + bx + c$ that fits a set of data points.

EXAMPLE 9 Quadratic regression

The accompanying table shows the average monthly temperature in degrees Fahrenheit for Athens, Georgia, for the year 2008.

Month	Temp.
Jan	49.2
Feb	45.0
Mar	54.5
Apr	65.6
Jun	77.4
Jul	81.4
Aug	80.7
Sep	71.5
Oct	60.4
Nov	53.1

Hunta/Shutterstock

a. Use quadratic regression on your graphing calculator to find the regression equation.
b. Draw the scatter diagram and the regression curve on the calculator.
c. According to the regression equation, what should be the average temperature for May and for December?

Solution

a. Use the number of the month starting at 1 and enter the data using the STAT EDIT menu. Note that May is missing from the table. Use 6 for June. Choose quadratic regression from the STAT CALC menu to get the equation

$$y = -1.17x^2 + 15.6x + 25.0.$$

b. The regression curve and the scatter diagram are shown in Fig. 62.

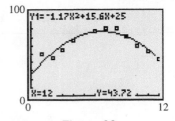

Figure 62

Equations, Inequalities, and Modeling

c. Let $x = 5$ in the equation to get the average monthly temperature for May of 73.8°. Use $x = 12$ in the equation to get the average monthly temperature for December of 43.7°.

▶**TRY THIS.** Use quadratic regression and the given data to predict the cost in 2010.

Year	1980	1985	1990	2000	2005
Cost ($)	11.9	8.15	7.04	12.3	18.40

■

► FOR thought... True or False? Explain.

1. The equation $(x - 3)^2 = 4$ is equivalent to $x - 3 = 2$.

2. Every quadratic equation can be solved by factoring.

3. The trinomial $x^2 + \frac{2}{3}x + \frac{4}{9}$ is a perfect square trinomial.

4. The equation $(x - 3)(2x + 5) = 0$ is equivalent to $x = 3$ or $x = \frac{5}{2}$.

5. All quadratic equations have two distinct solutions.

6. If $x^2 - 3x + 1 = 0$, then $x = \frac{3 \pm \sqrt{5}}{2}$.

7. If $b = 0$, then $ax^2 + bx + c = 0$ cannot be solved by the quadratic formula.

8. All quadratic equations have at least one real solution.

9. For $4x^2 + 12x + 9 = 0$ the discriminant is 0.

10. A quadratic equation with real coefficients might have only one real solution

► EXERCISES 7

Fill in the blank.

1. An equation of the form $ax^2 + bx + c = 0$ where $a, b,$ and c are real numbers with $a \neq 0$ is a _____ equation.

2. The equation $ax^2 + bx + c = 0$ can be solved by using the _____ formula.

3. The expression $b^2 - 4ac$ in the quadratic formula is the _____.

4. According to the _____ property, $x^2 = k$ is equivalent to $x = \pm\sqrt{k}$.

Solve each equation by factoring

5. $x^2 - x - 20 = 0$

6. $x^2 + 2x - 8 = 0$

7. $a^2 + 3a = -2$

8. $b^2 - 4b = 12$

9. $2x^2 - 5x - 3 = 0$

10. $2x^2 - 5x + 2 = 0$

11. $6x^2 - 7x + 2 = 0$

12. $12x^2 - 17x + 6 = 0$

13. $(y - 3)(y + 4) = 30$

14. $(w - 1)(w - 2) = 6$

Use the square root property to find all real or imaginary solutions to each equation.

15. $x^2 - 5 = 0$

16. $x^2 - 8 = 0$

17. $3x^2 + 2 = 0$

18. $2x^2 + 16 = 0$

19. $(x - 3)^2 = 9$

20. $(x + 1)^2 = \frac{9}{4}$

21. $(3x - 1)^2 = 0$

22. $(5x + 2)^2 = 0$

23. $\left(x - \frac{1}{2}\right)^2 = \frac{25}{4}$

24. $(3x - 1)^2 = \frac{1}{4}$

25. $(x + 2)^2 = -4$

26. $(x - 3)^2 = -20$

27. $\left(x - \frac{2}{3}\right)^2 = \frac{4}{9}$

28. $\left(x + \frac{3}{2}\right)^2 = \frac{1}{2}$

Find the perfect square trinomial whose first two terms are given.

29. $x^2 - 12x$

30. $y^2 + 20y$

31. $r^2 + 3r$

32. $t^2 - 7t$

33. $w^2 + \dfrac{1}{2}w$

34. $p^2 - \dfrac{2}{3}p$

Find the real or imaginary solutions by completing the square.

35. $x^2 + 6x + 1 = 0$

36. $x^2 - 10x + 5 = 0$

37. $n^2 - 2n - 1 = 0$

38. $m^2 - 12m + 33 = 0$

39. $h^2 + 3h - 1 = 0$

40. $t^2 - 5t + 2 = 0$

41. $2x^2 + 5x = 12$

42. $3x^2 + x = 2$

43. $3x^2 + 2x + 1 = 0$

44. $5x^2 + 4x + 3 = 0$

Find the real or imaginary solutions to each equation by using the quadratic formula

45. $x^2 + 3x - 4 = 0$

46. $x^2 + 8x + 12 = 0$

47. $2x^2 - 5x - 3 = 0$

48. $2x^2 + 3x - 2 = 0$

49. $9x^2 + 6x + 1 = 0$

50. $16x^2 - 24x + 9 = 0$

51. $2x^2 - 3 = 0$

52. $-2x^2 + 5 = 0$

53. $x^2 + 5 = 4x$

54. $x^2 = 6x - 13$

55. $x^2 - 2x + 4 = 0$

56. $x^2 - 4x + 9 = 0$

57. $-2x^2 + 2x = 5$

58. $12x - 5 = 9x^2$

59. $4x^2 - 8x + 7 = 0$

60. $9x^2 - 6x + 4 = 0$

Use a calculator and the quadratic formula to find all real solutions to each equation. Round answers to two decimal places.

61. $3.2x^2 + 7.6x - 9 = 0$

62. $1.5x^2 - 6.3x - 10.1 = 0$

63. $3.25x^2 - 4.6x + 20 = 42$

64. $4.76x^2 + 6.12x = 55.3$

For each equation, state the value of the discriminant and the number of real solutions.

65. $9x^2 - 30x + 25 = 0$

66. $4x^2 + 28x + 49 = 0$

67. $5x^2 - 6x + 2 = 0$

68. $3x^2 + 5x + 5 = 0$

69. $7x^2 + 12x - 1 = 0$

70. $3x^2 - 7x + 3 = 0$

Find the solutions to each equation by reading the accompanying graph.

71. $6x^2 + x - 2 = 0$

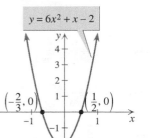

72. $-2x^2 - 2x + 12 = 0$

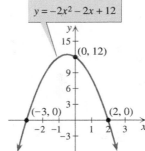

73. $-0.5x^2 + x + 7.5 = 0$

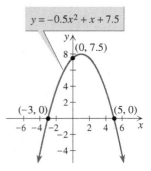

74. $0.5x^2 - 2.5x + 2 = 0$

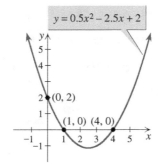

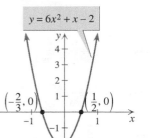 *For each equation of the form $ax^2 + bx + c = 0$, determine the number of real solutions by examining the graph of $y = ax^2 + bx + c$*

75. $1.44x^2 - 8.4x + 12.25 = 0$

76. $4.41x^2 - 5.46x + 1.69 = 0$

77. $x^2 + 3x + 15 = 0$

78. $-2x^2 + 5x - 40 = 0$

79. $x^2 + 3x - 160 = 0$

80. $-x^2 + 5x - 6.1 = 0$

Use the method of your choice to find all real solutions to each equation.

81. $x^2 = \dfrac{4}{3}x + \dfrac{5}{9}$

82. $x^2 = \dfrac{2}{7}x + \dfrac{2}{49}$

83. $x^2 - \sqrt{2} = 0$

84. $\sqrt{2}x^2 - 1 = 0$

85. $12x^2 + x\sqrt{6} - 1 = 0$

86. $-10x^2 - x\sqrt{5} + 1 = 0$

87. $x(x + 6) = 72$

88. $x = \dfrac{96}{x + 4}$

89. $x = 1 + \dfrac{1}{x}$

90. $x = \dfrac{1}{x}$

91. $\dfrac{28}{x} - \dfrac{7}{x^2} = 7$

92. $\dfrac{20}{x} - \dfrac{46}{x^2} = 2$

93. $\dfrac{x - 12}{3 - x} = \dfrac{x + 4}{x + 7}$

94. $\dfrac{x - 9}{x - 2} = -\dfrac{x + 3}{x + 1}$

95. $\dfrac{x - 8}{x + 2} = -\dfrac{1 - 2x}{x + 3}$

96. $\dfrac{x - 1}{x} = \dfrac{3x}{x + 1}$

97. $\dfrac{2x + 3}{2x + 1} = \dfrac{8}{2x + 3}$

98. $\dfrac{2x + 3}{6x + 5} = \dfrac{2}{2x + 3}$

Use the methods for solving quadratic equations to solve each formula for the indicated variable.

99. $A = \pi r^2$ for r

100. $S = 2\pi rh + 2\pi r^2$ for r

101. $x^2 + 2kx + 3 = 0$ for x

102. $hy^2 - ky = p$ for y

103. $2y^2 + 4xy = x^2$ for y

104. $\dfrac{\dfrac{1}{x + h} - \dfrac{1}{x}}{h} = 1$ for x

Find an exact solution to each problem. If the solution is irrational, then find an approximate solution also.

105. *Demand Equation* The demand equation for a certain product is $P = 40 - 0.001x$, where x is the number of units sold per week and P is the price in dollars at which each one is sold. The weekly revenue R is given by $R = xP$. What number of units sold produces a weekly revenue of \$175,000?

106. *Average Cost* The total cost in dollars of producing x items is given by $C = 0.02x^3 + 5x$. For what number of items is the average cost per item equal to \$5.50?
HINT Average cost is total cost divided by the number of items.

107. *Height of a Ball* A juggler tosses a ball into the air with an initial velocity of 40 ft/sec from an initial height of 4 ft. Find how long it takes for the ball to return to a height of 4 ft
HINT The formula $S = -16t^2 + v_0 t + s_0$ gives the height S in feet at time t in seconds where v_0 is the initial velocity and s_0 is the initial height.

108. *Height of a Sky Diver* A sky diver steps out of an airplane at 5000 ft. Use the formula $S = -16t^2 + v_0 t + s_0$ to find how long it takes the sky diver to reach 4000 ft.

109. *Diagonal of a Football Field* A football field is 100 yd long from goal line to goal line and 160 ft wide. If a player ran diagonally across the field from one goal line to the other, then how far did he run?

110. *Dimensions of a Flag* If the perimeter of a rectangular flag is 34 in. and the diagonal is 13 in., then what are the length and width?

111. *Long Shot* To avoid hitting the ball out, a tennis player in one corner of the 312 yd^2 court hits the ball to the farthest corner of the opponent's court as shown in the diagram. If the length L of the tennis court is 2 yd longer than twice the width W, then how far did the player hit the ball?

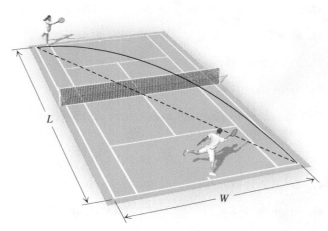

Figure for Exercise 111

112. *Open-Top Box* Imogene wants to make an open-top box for packing baked goods by cutting equal squares from each corner of an 11 in. by 14 in. piece of cardboard as shown in the diagram. She figures that for versatility the area of the bottom must be 80 in.^{2}. What size square should she cut from each corner?

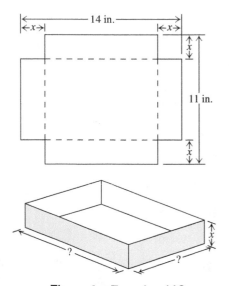

Figure for Exercise 112

113. *Finding the Displacement* The sail area-displacement ratio *S* measures the amount of power available to drive a sailboat in moderate to heavy winds (Ted Brewer Yacht Design, www.tedbrewer.com). For the Sabre 402 shown in the figure, the sail area *A* is 822 ft² and $S = 18.8$. The displacement *d* (in pounds) satisfies $2^{-12}d^2S^3 - A^3 = 0$. Find *d*.

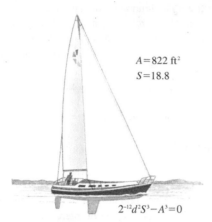

$A = 822 \text{ ft}^2$
$S = 18.8$

$2^{-12}d^2S^3 - A^3 = 0$

Figure for Exercise 113

114. *Charleston Earthquake* The Charleston, South Carolina, earthquake of 1886 registered 7.6 on the Richter scale and was felt over an area of 1.5 million square miles (U.S. Geological Survey, www.usgs.gov). If the area in which it was felt was circular and centered at Charleston, then how far away was it felt?

115. *Radius of a Pipe* A large pipe is placed next to a wall and a 1-ft-high block is placed 5 ft from the wall to keep the pipe in place as shown in the figure. What is the radius of the pipe?
HINT Draw in the radius at several locations.

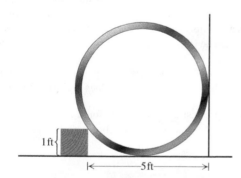

1 ft

5 ft

Figure for Exercise 115

116. *Another Pipe* A small pipe is placed against a wall as in the previous exercise, but no block is used to keep it in place. There is a point on the edge of this pipe that is both 5 in. from the ground and 10 in. from the wall. Find two possibilities for the radius of the pipe.

117. *Speed of a Tortoise* When a tortoise crosses a highway, his speed is 2 ft/hr faster than normal. If he can cross a 24-ft lane in 24 min less time than he can travel that same distance off the highway, then what is his normal speed?

118. *Speed of an Electric Car* An experimental electric-solar car completed a 1000-mi race in 35 hr. For the 600 mi traveled during daylight the car averaged 20 mph more than it did for the 400 mi traveled at night. What was the average speed of the car during the daytime?

119. *Initial Velocity of a Basketball Player* Vince Carter is famous for his high leaps and "hang time," especially while slam-dunking. If Carter leaped for a dunk and reached a peak height at the basket of 1.07 m, what was his upward velocity in meters per second at the moment his feet left the floor? The formula $v_1^2 = v_0^2 + 2gS$ gives the relationship between final velocity v_1, initial velocity v_0, acceleration of gravity g, and his height S. Use $g = -9.8$ m/sec² and the fact that his final velocity was zero at his peak height. Use $S = \frac{1}{2}gt^2 + v_0t$ to find the amount of time he was in the air.

Saim Nadir/Shutterstock

Figure for Exercise 119

120. *Hazards of Altitude* As shown in the table (www.nasa.gov), atmospheric pressure *a* (atm) decreases as height above sea level *h* (in feet) increases. The equation

$$a = 3.89 \times 10^{-10}h^2 - 3.48 \times 10^{-5}h + 1$$

can be used to model this relationship.
a. Mountain climbers begin to deteriorate at 18,000 ft. Find *a* at that height.

b. The atmospheric pressure at the highest human settlements is 0.52 atm. Find the height for $a = 0.52$.

c. Use the quadratic regression feature of your graphing calculator and the data given in the table to find an equation expressing atmospheric pressure *a* in terms of *h*.

Table for Exercise 120

Altitude (ft)	Atmospheric Pressure (atm)
28,000	0.33
20,000	0.46
18,000	
	0.52
10,000	0.69
0	1

Sam D. Cruz/Shutterstock

121. *Teen Birth Rate* The accompanying table gives the number of births per 1000 females ages 15–19 (www.infoplease.com).

   a. Use your graphing calculator to find a quadratic regression equation that expresses the birth rate in terms of the year.

   b. In what year will the birth rate reach zero according to the quadratic equation of part (a)?

Table for Exercise 121

Year	Births per 1000 Females (ages 15–19)
1980	53.0
1985	51.0
1990	59.9
1995	56.8
2000	47.7
2005	41.4

Niderlander/Shutterstock

122. *Teen Birth Rate* Use the data in the previous exercise.

   a. Find the equation of the regression line that expresses the birth rate in terms of the year.

   b. In what year will the birth rate reach zero according to the regression line?

123. *Computer Design* Using a computer design package, Tina can write and design a direct-mail package in two days less time than it takes to create the same package using traditional design methods. If Tina uses the computer and her assistant Curt uses traditional methods, and together they complete the job in 3.5 days, then how long would it have taken Curt to do the job alone using traditional methods?

   HINT Curt's rate is $1/x$ job/day and Tina's rate is $1/(x - 2)$ job/day.

124. *Making a Dress* Rafael designed a sequined dress to be worn at the Academy Awards. His top seamstress, Maria, could sew on all the sequins in 10 hr less time than his next-best seamstress, Stephanie. To save time, he gave the job to both women and got all of the sequins attached in 17 hr. How long would it have taken Stephanie working alone?

125. *Percentage of White Meat* The Kansas Fried Chicken store sells a Party Size bucket that weighs 10 lb more than the Big Family Size bucket. The Party size bucket contains 8 lb of white meat, while the Big Family Size bucket contains 3 lb of white meat. If the percentage of white meat in the Party Size is 10 percentage points greater than the percentage of white meat in the Big Family Size, then how much does the Party Size bucket weigh?

126. *Mixing Antifreeze in a Radiator* Steve's car had a large radiator that contained an unknown amount of pure water. He added two quarts of antifreeze to the radiator. After testing, he decided that the percentage of antifreeze in the radiator was not large enough. Not knowing how to solve mixture problems, Steve decided to add one quart of water and another quart of antifreeze to the radiator to see what he would get. After testing he found that the last addition increased the percentage of antifreeze by three percentage points. How much water did the radiator contain originally?

▶ **RETHINKING**

127. Find the equation (in standard form) of the line through $(-2, 6)$ that is parallel to $4x - 5y = 8$.

128. Find the product $(3 - 2i)(3 + 2i)$.

129. Chandra invested in a CD that returned 5% and a mutual fund that returned 6% after one year. The amount invested in the mutual fund was $4000 more than the amount invested in the CD, and the total amount of interest was $1230. How much did she invest in the CD?

130. Find the radius of the circle $x^2 + y^2 = 3y$.

131. Find the additive inverse of $2 + 3i$.

132. Use the linear regression feature of a graphing calculator to find the equation of the regression line for the points $(-2, 1)$, $(-1, 2)$, $(0, 5)$, $(1, 4)$, and $(2, 4)$.

THINKING OUTSIDE THE BOX IX

As the Crow Flies In Perfect City the avenues run east and west, the streets run north and south, and all of the blocks are square. A crow flies from the corner of 1st Ave and 1st Street to the corner of mth Ave and nth Street, "as the crow flies." Assume that m and n are positive integers greater than 1 and the streets and avenues are simply lines on a map. If the crow flies over an intersection, then he flies over only two of the blocks that meet at the intersection.

   a. If $m - 1$ and $n - 1$ are relatively prime (no common factors), then how many city blocks does the crow fly over?

   b. If d is the greatest common factor for m and n, then how many city blocks does the crow fly over?

POP QUIZ 7

1. Solve $x^2 = 2$.

2. Solve $x^2 - 2x = 48$ by factoring.

3. Solve $x^2 - 4x = 1$ by completing the square.

4. Solve $2x^2 - 4x = 3$ by the quadratic formula.

5. How many real solutions are there to $5x^2 - 9x + 5 = 0$?

LINKING

concepts... For Individual or Group Explorations

Baseball Statistics

Michael Karlin/Shutterstock

Baseball fans keep up with their favorite teams through charts where the teams are ranked according to the percentage of games won. The chart usually has a column indicating the games behind (GB) for each team. If the win-loss record of the number one team is (A, B), then the games behind of another team whose win-loss record is (a, b) is calculated by the formula

$$GB = \frac{(A - a) + (b - B)}{2}.$$

a) Find *GB* for Atlanta and Philadelphia in the following table.

Team	Won	Lost	Pct.	GB
New York	38	24	.613	—
Atlanta	35	29	.547	?
Philadelphia	34	31	.523	?

b) In the following table Pittsburgh has a higher percentage of wins than Chicago, and so Pittsburgh is in first place. Find *GB* for Chicago.

Team	Won	Lost	Pct.	GB
Pittsburgh	18	13	.581	—
Chicago	22	16	.579	?

c) Is Chicago actually behind Pittsburgh in terms of the statistic *GB*?

d) Another measure of how far a team is from first place, called the deficit *D*, is the number of games that the two teams would have to play against each other to get equal percentages of wins, with the higher-ranked team losing all of the games. Find the deficits for Atlanta, Philadelphia, and Chicago.

e) Is it possible for *GB* or *D* to be negative? Does it make any sense if they are?

f) Compare the values of *D* and *GB* for each of the three teams. Which is a better measure of how far a team is from first place?

8 Linear and Absolute Value Inequalities

An equation states that two algebraic expressions are equal, while an **inequality** or **simple inequality** is a statement that two algebraic expressions are not equal in a particular way. Inequalities are stated using less than ($<$), less than or equal to ($\leq$), greater than ($>$), or greater than or equal to ($\geq$). In this section we study some basic inequalities.

Interval Notation

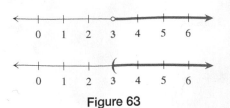

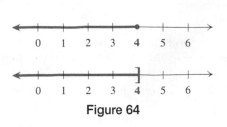

Figure 63

Figure 64

The solution set to an inequality is the set of all real numbers for which the inequality is true. The solution set to the inequality $x > 3$ is written as $\{x \mid x > 3\}$ and consists of all real numbers to the right of 3 (but not including 3) on the number line. This set is also called the **interval** of numbers greater than 3, and it is written in **interval notation** as $(3, \infty)$. To graphically show that 3 is not in the interval, you can use a parenthesis or an open circle as shown on the graphs in Fig. 63. In this text, a parenthesis is used because it matches the interval notation. The infinity symbol (∞) is not a number. It indicates that there is no bound on the numbers greater than 3.

The solution set to $x \leq 4$ is written in set notation as $\{x \mid x \leq 4\}$ and it consists of the number 4 along with all real numbers to the left of 4 on the number line. It is written in interval notation as $(-\infty, 4]$. The symbol $-\infty$ indicates that all numbers to the left of 4 on the number line are in the interval. To graphically show that 4 is in the interval, you can use a bracket or a solid circle as shown on the graphs in Fig. 64. In this text, a bracket is used because it matches the interval notation. Open circles and solid circles will be used occasionally on some two-dimensional graphs in this text.

Intervals that use the infinity symbol are **unbounded** intervals. The following summary lists the different types of unbounded intervals used in interval notation and the graphs of those intervals on a number line. An unbounded interval with an endpoint is **open** if the endpoint is not included in the interval and **closed** if the endpoint is included.

SUMMARY

Interval Notation for Unbounded Intervals

Set	Interval notation	Type	Graph
$\{x \mid x > a\}$	(a, ∞)	Open	
$\{x \mid x < a\}$	$(-\infty, a)$	Open	
$\{x \mid x \geq a\}$	$[a, \infty)$	Closed	
$\{x \mid x \leq a\}$	$(-\infty, a]$	Closed	
Real numbers	$(-\infty, \infty)$	Open	

We use a parenthesis when an endpoint of an interval is not included in the solution set and a bracket when an endpoint is included. A bracket is never used next to ∞ because infinity is not a number. On the graphs above, the number lines are shaded, showing that the solutions include all real numbers in the given interval.

EXAMPLE 1 Interval notation

Write an inequality whose solution set is the given interval.

a. $(-\infty, -9)$ **b.** $[0, \infty)$

Solution

a. The interval $(-\infty, -9)$ represents all real numbers less than -9. It is the solution set to $x < -9$.
b. The interval $[0, \infty)$ represents all real numbers greater than or equal to 0. It is the solution set to $x \geq 0$.

▶**TRY THIS.** Write an inequality whose solution set is $(-\infty, 5]$. ■

Linear Inequalities

Replacing the equal sign in the general linear equation $ax + b = 0$ by any of the symbols $<, \leq, >$, or $\geq$ gives a **linear inequality.** Two inequalities are **equivalent** if they have the same solution set. We solve linear inequalities like we solve linear equations by performing operations on each side to get equivalent inequalities. However, the rules for inequalities are slightly different from the rules for equations.

Adding any real number to both sides of an inequality results in an equivalent inequality. For example, adding 3 to both sides of $-4 < 5$ yields $-1 < 8$, which is true. Adding or subtracting the same number simply moves the original numbers to the right or left along the number line and does not change their order.

The order of two numbers will also be unchanged when they are multiplied or divided by the same positive real number. For example, $10 < 20$, and after dividing both numbers by 10 we have $1 < 2$. However, multiplying or dividing any two numbers by a negative number will change their order. For example, $-2 < -1$, but after multiplying both numbers by -1 we have $2 > 1$. See Fig. 65. Likewise, $-10 < 20$, but after dividing both numbers by -10 we have $1 > -2$. *When an inequality is multiplied or divided by a negative number, the direction of the inequality symbol is reversed.* These ideas are stated symbolically in the following box for $<$, but they also hold for $>, \leq$, and $\geq$.

Multiplying by –1 changes the order

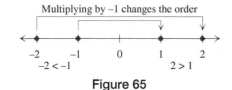

$-2 < -1$ $2 > 1$

Figure 65

Properties of Inequality

> If A and B are algebraic expressions and C is a nonzero real number, then the inequality $A < B$ is equivalent to
>
> 1. $A \pm C < B \pm C$,
> 2. $CA < CB$ (for C positive), $CA > CB$ (for C negative),
> 3. $\dfrac{A}{C} < \dfrac{B}{C}$ (for C positive), $\dfrac{A}{C} > \dfrac{B}{C}$ (for C negative).

EXAMPLE 2 Solving a linear inequality

Solve $-3x - 9 < 0$. Write the solution set in interval notation and graph it.

Solution

Isolate the variable as is done in solving equations.

$$-3x - 9 < 0$$

$$-3x - 9 + 9 < 0 + 9 \qquad \text{Add 9 to each side.}$$

$$-3x < 9$$

$$x > -3 \qquad \text{Divide each side by } -3, \text{ reversing the inequality.}$$

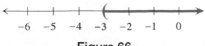

Figure 66

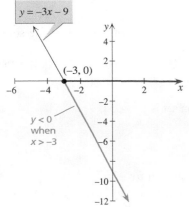

Figure 67

The solution set is the interval $(-3, \infty)$ and its graph is shown in Fig. 66. Checking the solution to an inequality is generally not as simple as checking an equation, because usually there are infinitely many solutions. We can do a "partial check" by checking one number in $(-3, \infty)$ and one number not in $(-3, \infty)$. For example, $0 > -3$ and $-3(0) - 9 < 0$ is correct, while $-6 < -3$ and $-3(-6) - 9 < 0$ is incorrect.

▶**TRY THIS.** Solve $2 - 5x \le 7$. Write the solution set in interval notation and graph it. ∎

We can read the solution to an inequality in one variable from a graph in two variables in the same manner that we read the solution to an equation in one variable. Figure 67 shows the graph of $y = -3x - 9$. From this figure we see that the y-coordinates on this line are negative when the x-coordinates are greater than -3. In other words, $-3x - 9 < 0$ when $x > -3$.

We can also perform operations on each side of an inequality using a variable expression. Addition or subtraction with variable expressions will give equivalent inequalities. However, we must always watch for undefined expressions. *Multiplication and division with a variable expression are usually avoided because we do not know whether the expression is positive or negative.*

> **EXAMPLE 3** Solving a linear inequality

Solve $\frac{1}{2}x - 3 \ge \frac{1}{4}x + 2$ and graph the solution set.

Solution

Multiply each side by the LCD to eliminate the fractions.

$$\frac{1}{2}x - 3 \ge \frac{1}{4}x + 2$$

$$4\left(\frac{1}{2}x - 3\right) \ge 4\left(\frac{1}{4}x + 2\right) \quad \text{Multiply each side by 4.}$$

$$2x - 12 \ge x + 8$$

$$x - 12 \ge 8$$

$$x \ge 20$$

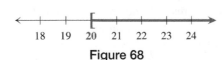

Figure 68

The solution set is the interval $[20, \infty)$. See Fig. 68 for its graph.

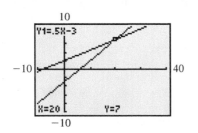

Figure 69

The algebraic solution to $\frac{1}{2}x - 3 \ge \frac{1}{4}x + 2$ proves that the graph of $y = \frac{1}{2}x - 3$ is at or above the graph of $y = \frac{1}{4}x + 2$ when $x \ge 20$, as it appears to be in Fig. 69. Conversely, the graphs in Fig. 69 support the conclusion that $x \ge 20$ causes the inequality to be true.

▶**TRY THIS.** Solve $\frac{1}{2}x + \frac{1}{3} \le \frac{1}{3}x + 1$ and graph the solution set. ∎

Compound Inequalities

A **compound inequality** is a sentence containing two simple inequalities connected with "and" or "or." The solution to a compound inequality can be an interval of real numbers that does not involve infinity, a **bounded** interval of real numbers. For example, the solution set to the compound inequality $x \ge 2$ and $x \le 5$ is the set of real numbers between 2 and 5, inclusive. This inequality is also written as $2 \le x \le 5$. Its solution set is $\{x \mid 2 \le x \le 5\}$, which is written in interval notation as $[2, 5]$. Because $[2, 5]$ contains both of its endpoints, the interval is **closed.** The following summary lists the different types of bounded intervals used in interval notation and the graphs of those intervals on a number line.

Interval Notation for Bounded Intervals

Set	Interval notation	Type	Graph
$\{x \mid a < x < b\}$	(a, b)	Open	
$\{x \mid a \leq x \leq b\}$	$[a, b]$	Closed	
$\{x \mid a \leq x < b\}$	$[a, b)$	Half open or half closed	
$\{x \mid a < x \leq b\}$	$(a, b]$	Half open or half closed	

The notation $a < x < b$ is used only when x is between a and b, and a is less than b. We do *not* write inequalities such as $5 < x < 3, 4 > x < 9$, or $2 < x > 8$.

The **intersection** of sets A and B is the set $A \cap B$ (read "A intersect B"), where $x \in A \cap B$ if and only if $x \in A$ and $x \in B$. (The symbol $\in$ means "belongs to.") The **union** of sets A and B is the set $A \cup B$ (read "A union B"), where $x \in A \cup B$ if and only if $x \in A$ or $x \in B$. In solving compound inequalities it is often necessary to find intersections and unions of intervals.

EXAMPLE 4 Intersections and unions of intervals

Let $A = (1, 5), B = [3, 7)$, and $C = (6, \infty)$. Write each of the following sets in interval notation.

a. $A \cup B$ **b.** $A \cap B$ **c.** $A \cup C$ **d.** $A \cap C$

Solution

a. Graph both intervals on the number line, as shown in Fig. 70(a). The union of two intervals is the set of points that are in one, the other, or both intervals. For a union, nothing is omitted. The union consists of all points shaded in the figure. So $A \cup B = (1, 7)$.

b. The intersection of A and B is the set of points that belong to both intervals. The intersection consists of the points that are shaded twice in Fig. 70(a). So $A \cap B = [3, 5)$.

(a)　　　　　　　　　　　　(b)

Figure 70

c. Graph both intervals on the number line, as shown in Fig. 70(b). For a union, nothing is omitted. So $A \cup C = (1, 5) \cup (6, \infty)$. Note that $A \cup C$ cannot be written as single interval.

d. Since there are no points shaded twice in Fig. 70(b), $A \cap C = \varnothing$.

▶**TRY THIS.** Find $A \cup B$ and $A \cap B$ if $A = (1, 6)$ and $B = [4, 9)$. ■

The solution set to a compound inequality using the connector "or" is the union of the two solution sets, and the solution set to a compound inequality using "and" is the intersection of the two solution sets.

EXAMPLE 5 Solving compound inequalities

Solve each compound inequality. Write the solution set using interval notation and graph it.

a. $2x - 3 > 5$ and $4 - x \leq 3$ **b.** $4 - 3x < -2$ or $3(x - 2) \leq -6$
c. $-4 \leq 3x - 1 < 5$

Solution

a. $\quad 2x - 3 > 5 \qquad$ and $\qquad 4 - x \leq 3$

$\qquad\qquad 2x > 8 \qquad$ and $\qquad\quad -x \leq -1$

$\qquad\qquad\;\, x > 4 \qquad$ and $\qquad\qquad x \geq 1$

Graph $(4, \infty)$ and $[1, \infty)$ on the number line, as shown in Fig. 71(a). The intersection of the intervals is the set of points that are shaded twice in Fig. 71(a). So the intersection is the interval $(4, \infty)$, and $(4, \infty)$ is the solution set to the compound inequality. Its graph is shown in Fig. 71(b).

(a)   (b)

Figure 71

b. $\quad 4 - 3x < -2 \quad$ or $\quad 3(x - 2) \leq -6$

$\qquad\qquad -3x < -6 \quad$ or $\qquad x - 2 \leq -2$

$\qquad\qquad\;\;\; x > 2 \quad$ or $\qquad\quad\; x \leq 0$

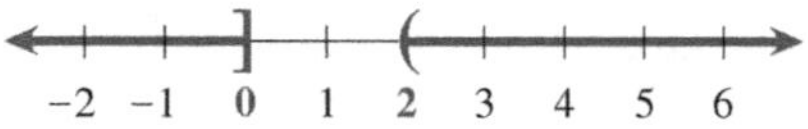

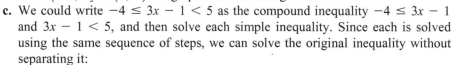

Figure 72

The union of the intervals $(2, \infty)$ and $(-\infty, 0]$ consists of all points that are shaded in Fig. 72. This set cannot be written as a single interval. So the solution set is $(-\infty, 0] \cup (2, \infty)$. Its graph is shown in Fig. 72.

c. We could write $-4 \leq 3x - 1 < 5$ as the compound inequality $-4 \leq 3x - 1$ and $3x - 1 < 5$, and then solve each simple inequality. Since each is solved using the same sequence of steps, we can solve the original inequality without separating it:

$$-4 \leq 3x - 1 < 5$$

$$-4 + 1 \leq 3x - 1 + 1 < 5 + 1 \qquad \text{Add 1 to each part of the inequality.}$$

$$-3 \leq 3x < 6$$

$$\frac{-3}{3} \leq \frac{3x}{3} < \frac{6}{3} \qquad\qquad\qquad \text{Divide each part by 3.}$$

$$-1 \leq x < 2$$

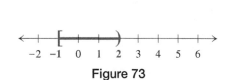

Figure 73

The solution set is the half-open interval $[-1, 2)$, graphed in Fig. 73.

▶**TRY THIS.** Solve $2x > -4$ and $4 - x \geq 0$ and graph the solution set. ∎

It is possible that all real numbers satisfy a compound inequality or no real numbers satisfy a compound inequality.

EXAMPLE 6 Solving compound inequalities

Solve each compound inequality.

a. $3x - 9 \leq 9$ or $4 - x \leq 3$

b. $-\dfrac{2}{3}x < 4$ and $\dfrac{3}{4}x < -6$

Solution

a. Solve each simple inequality and find the union of their solution sets:

$$3x - 9 \le 9 \quad \text{or} \quad 4 - x \le 3$$
$$3x \le 18 \quad \text{or} \quad -x \le -1$$
$$x \le 6 \quad \text{or} \quad x \ge 1$$

The union of $(-\infty, 6]$ and $[1, \infty)$ is the set of all real numbers, $(-\infty, \infty)$.

b. Solve each simple inequality and find the intersection of their solution sets:

$$-\frac{2}{3}x < 4 \quad \text{and} \quad \frac{3}{4}x < -6$$
$$\left(-\frac{3}{2}\right)\left(-\frac{2}{3}x\right) > \left(-\frac{3}{2}\right)4 \quad \text{and} \quad \left(\frac{4}{3}\right)\left(\frac{3}{4}x\right) < \left(\frac{4}{3}\right)(-6)$$
$$x > -6 \quad \text{and} \quad x < -8$$

Since $(-6, \infty) \cap (-\infty, -8) = \varnothing$, there is no solution to the compound inequality.

▶**TRY THIS.** Solve $3x + 2 > -1$ and $5 < -3 - 4x$. ■

Absolute Value Inequalities

We studied absolute value equations in Section 1. Absolute value inequalities are closely related to absolute value equations. Remember that the absolute value of a number is its distance from 0 on the number line. The equation $|x| = 3$ means that x is exactly three units from 0 on the number line. Since 3 and -3 are three units from 0, both 3 and -3 satisfy the equation. The inequality $|x| < 3$ means that x is less than three units from 0. See Fig. 74. Any number between -3 and 3 is less than three units from 0. So $|x| < 3$ is equivalent to $-3 < x < 3$ and the solution set is the open interval $(-3, 3)$.

The inequality $|x| > 5$ means that x is more than five units from 0 on the number line, which is equivalent to the compound inequality $x > 5$ or $x < -5$. See Fig. 75. So the solution to $|x| > 5$ is the union of two intervals, $(-\infty, -5) \cup (5, \infty)$. These ideas about absolute value inequalities are summarized as follows.

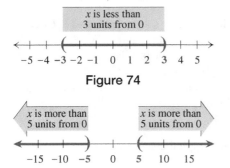

Figure 74

Figure 75

SUMMARY

Basic Absolute Value Inequalities (for $k > 0$)

Absolute value inequality	Equivalent statement	Solution set in interval notation	Graph of solution set
$\lvert x \rvert > k$	$x < -k$ or $x > k$	$(-\infty, -k) \cup (k, \infty)$	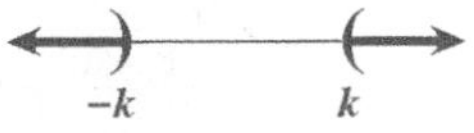
$\lvert x \rvert \ge k$	$x \le -k$ or $x \ge k$	$(-\infty, -k] \cup [k, \infty)$	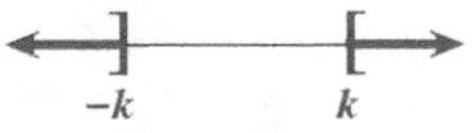
$\lvert x \rvert < k$	$-k < x < k$	$(-k, k)$	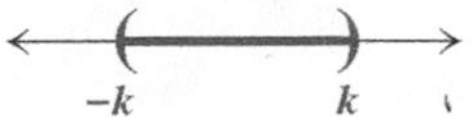
$\lvert x \rvert \le k$	$-k \le x \le k$	$[-k, k]$	

In the next example we use the rules for basic absolute value inequalities to solve more complicated absolute value inequalities.

EXAMPLE 7 | Absolute value inequalities

Solve each absolute value inequality and graph the solution set.

a. $|3x + 2| < 7$ **b.** $-2|4 - x| \leq -4$ **c.** $|7x - 9| \geq -3$

Solution

a.

$$|3x + 2| < 7$$

$$-7 < 3x + 2 < 7 \qquad \text{Write the equivalent compound inequality.}$$

$$-7 - 2 < 3x + 2 - 2 < 7 - 2 \qquad \text{Subtract 2 from each part.}$$

$$-9 < 3x < 5$$

$$-3 < x < \frac{5}{3} \qquad \text{Divide each part by 3.}$$

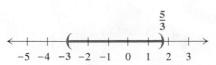

Figure 76

The solution set is the open interval $\left(-3, \frac{5}{3}\right)$. The graph is shown in Fig. 76.

b.

$$-2|4 - x| \leq -4 \qquad \text{Divide each side by } -2, \text{ reversing the inequality.}$$

$$|4 - x| \geq 2$$

$$4 - x \leq -2 \quad \text{or} \quad 4 - x \geq 2 \qquad \text{Write the equivalent compound inequality.}$$

$$-x \leq -6 \quad \text{or} \qquad -x \geq -2$$

$$x \geq 6 \quad \text{or} \qquad x \leq 2 \qquad \text{Multiply each side by } -1.$$

Figure 77

The solution set is $(-\infty, 2] \cup [6, \infty)$. Its graph is shown in Fig. 77. Check 8, 4, and 0 in the original inequality. If $x = 8$, we get $-2|4 - 8| \leq -4$, which is true. If $x = 4$, we get $-2|4 - 4| \leq -4$, which is false. If $x = 0$, we get $-2|4 - 0| \leq -4$, which is true.

c. The expression $|7x - 9|$ has a nonnegative value for every real number x. So the inequality $|7x - 9| \geq -3$ is satisfied by every real number. The solution set is $(-\infty, \infty)$, and its graph is shown in Fig. 78.

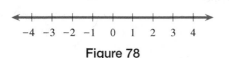

Figure 78

▶**TRY THIS.** Solve $|x - 6| - 3 \leq -2$ and graph the solution set.   ∎

Modeling with Inequalities

Inequalities occur in applications just as equations do. In fact, in real life, equality in anything is usually the exception. The solution to a problem involving an inequality is generally an interval of real numbers. In this case we often ask for the range of values that solve the problem.

EXAMPLE 8 | An application involving inequality

Remington scored 74 on his midterm exam in history. If he is to get a B, the average of his midterm and final exam must be between 80 and 89 inclusive. In what range must his final exam score lie for him to get a B in the course? Both exams have a maximum of 100 points possible.

Solution

Let x represent Remington's final exam score. The average of his midterm and final must satisfy the following inequality.

$$80 \leq \frac{74 + x}{2} \leq 89$$

$$160 \leq 74 + x \leq 178$$

$$86 \leq x \leq 104$$

His final exam score must lie in the interval [86, 104]. Since 100 is the maximum possible score, we can shorten the interval to [86, 100].

▶**TRY THIS.** Kelly's commissions for her first two sales of the Whirlwind Vacuum Cleaner were $80 and $90. In what range must her third commission lie for her average to be between $100 and $110? ∎

When discussing the error made in a measurement, we may refer to the *absolute error* or the *relative error*. For example, if L is the actual length of an object and x is the length determined by a measurement, then the absolute error is $|x - L|$ and the relative error is $|x - L|/L$.

EXAMPLE 9 | Application of absolute value inequality

A technician is testing a scale with a 50-lb block of steel. The scale passes this test if the relative error when weighing this block is less than 0.1%. If x is the reading on the scale, then for what values of x does the scale pass this test?

Solution

If the relative error must be less than 0.1%, then x must satisfy the following inequality:

$$\frac{|x - 50|}{50} < 0.001$$

Solve the inequality for x:

$$|x - 50| < 0.05$$

$$-0.05 < x - 50 < 0.05$$

$$49.95 < x < 50.05$$

So the scale passes the test if it shows a weight in the interval (49.95, 50.05).

▶**TRY THIS.** A gas pump is certified as accurate if the relative error when dispensing 10 gallons of gas is less than 1%. If x is the actual amount of gas dispensed, then for what values of x is the pump certified as accurate? ∎

►FOR thought... True or False? Explain.

1. The inequality $-3 < x + 6$ is equivalent to $x + 6 > -3$.

2. The inequality $-2x < -6$ is equivalent to $\frac{-2x}{-2} < \frac{-6}{-2}$.

3. The smallest real number that satisfies $x > 12$ is 13.

4. The number -6 satisfies $|x - 6| > -1$.

5. $(-\infty, -3) \cap (-\infty, -2) = (-\infty, -2)$

6. $(5, \infty) \cap (-\infty, -3) = (-3, 5)$

7. All negative numbers satisfy $|x - 2| < 0$.

8. The compound inequality $x < -3$ or $x > 3$ is equivalent to $|x| < -3$.

9. The inequality $|x| + 2 < 5$ is equivalent to $-5 < x + 2 < 5$.

10. The fact that the difference between your age y and my age m is at most 5 years is written $|y - m| \leq 5$.

EXERCISES 8

Fill in the blank.

1. The set $\{x \mid x > a\}$ is written in _____ notation as (a, ∞).

2. An _____ interval does not include its endpoints.

3. A _____ interval includes its endpoints.

4. An interval that involves the infinity symbol is an _____ interval.

5. Two simple inequalities connected with "and" or "or" is a _____ inequality.

6. The _____ of sets A and B is the set of all elements that are in both A and B.

For each interval write an inequality whose solution set is the interval, and for each inequality, write the solution set in interval notation.

7. $(-\infty, 12)$ 8. $(-\infty, -3]$ 9. $[-7, \infty)$

10. $(1.2, \infty)$ 11. $x \geq -8$ 12. $x < 54$

13. $x < \pi/2$ 14. $x \geq \sqrt{3}$

Solve each inequality. Write the solution set using interval notation and graph it.

15. $3x - 6 > 9$ 16. $2x + 1 < 6$

17. $7 - 5x \leq -3$ 18. $-1 - 4x \geq 7$

19. $\dfrac{1}{2}x - 4 < \dfrac{1}{3}x + 5$ 20. $\dfrac{1}{2} - x > \dfrac{x}{3} + \dfrac{1}{4}$

21. $\dfrac{7 - 3x}{2} \geq -3$ 22. $\dfrac{5 - x}{3} \leq -2$

23. $\dfrac{2x - 3}{-5} \geq 0$ 24. $\dfrac{5 - 3x}{-7} \leq 0$

25. $-2(3x - 2) \geq 4 - x$ 26. $-5x \leq 3(x - 9)$

Solve each inequality by reading the accompanying graph.

27. $1.8x + 6.3 < 0$ 28. $1.2x - 3 \geq 0$

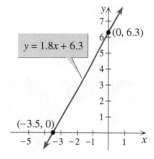

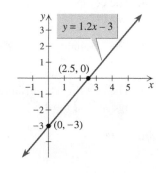

29. $6.3 - 4.5x \geq 0$ 30. $-5.1 - 1.7x < 0$

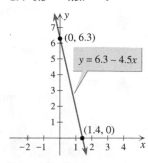

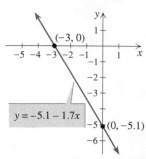

Solve the inequalities in Exercises 31–34 by reading the following graphs.

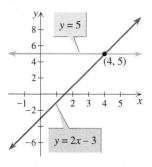

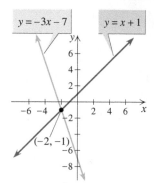

31. $2x - 3 > 5$ 32. $5 \geq 2x - 3$

33. $x + 1 \leq -3x - 7$ 34. $x + 1 > -3x - 7$

Write as a single interval.

35. $(-3, \infty) \cup (5, \infty)$ 36. $(-\infty, 0) \cup (-\infty, 6)$

37. $(3, 5) \cup (-3, \infty)$ 38. $(4, 7) \cap (3, \infty)$

39. $(-\infty, -2) \cap (-5, \infty)$ 40. $(-3, \infty) \cap (2, \infty)$

41. $(-\infty, -5) \cap (-2, \infty)$ 42. $(-\infty, -3) \cup (-7, \infty)$

43. $(-\infty, 4) \cup [4, 5]$ 44. $[3, 5] \cup [5, 7]$

Solve each compound inequality. Write the solution set using interval notation and graph it.

45. $5 > 8 - x$ and $1 + 0.5x < 4$

46. $5 - x < 4$ and $0.2x - 5 < 1$

47. $\dfrac{2x - 5}{-2} < 2$ and $\dfrac{2x + 1}{3} > 0$

48. $\dfrac{4 - x}{2} > 1$ and $\dfrac{2x - 7}{-3} < 1$

49. $1 - x < 7 + x$ or $4x + 3 > x$

50. $5 + x > 3 - x$ or $2x - 3 > x$

51. $\dfrac{1}{2}(x + 1) > 3$ or $0 < 7 - x$

52. $\dfrac{1}{2}(x + 6) > 3$ or $4(x - 1) < 3x - 4$

53. $1 - \dfrac{3}{2}x < 4$ and $\dfrac{1}{4}x - 2 \le -3$

54. $\dfrac{3}{5}x - 1 > 2$ and $5 - \dfrac{2}{5}x \ge 3$

55. $1 < 3x - 5 < 7$ **56.** $-3 \le 4x + 9 \le 17$

57. $-2 \le 4 - 6x < 22$ **58.** $-13 < 5 - 9x \le 41$

Solve each absolute value inequality. Write the solution set using interval notation and graph it.

59. $|3x - 1| < 2$ **60.** $|4x - 3| \le 5$

61. $|5 - 4x| \le 1$ **62.** $|6 - x| < 6$

63. $|x - 1| \ge 1$ **64.** $|x + 2| > 5$

65. $|5 - x| > 3$ **66.** $|3 - 2x| \ge 5$

67. $5 \ge |4 - x|$ **68.** $3 < |2x - 1|$

69. $|5 - 4x| < 0$ **70.** $|3x - 7| \ge -5$

71. $|4 - 5x| < -1$ **72.** $|2 - 9x| \ge 0$

73. $3|x - 2| + 6 > 9$ **74.** $3|x - 1| + 2 < 8$

75. $\left|\dfrac{x - 3}{2}\right| > 1$ **76.** $\left|\dfrac{9 - 4x}{2}\right| < 3$

Write an inequality of the form $|x - a| < k$ or of the form $|x - a| > k$ so that the inequality has the given solution set.
HINT $|x - a| < k$ means that x is less than k units from a and $|x - a| > k$ means that x is more than k units from a on the number line.

77. $(-5, 5)$ **78.** $(-2, 2)$

79. $(-\infty, -3) \cup (3, \infty)$ **80.** $(-\infty, -1) \cup (1, \infty)$

81. $(4, 8)$ **82.** $(-3, 9)$

83. $(-\infty, 3) \cup (5, \infty)$ **84.** $(-\infty, -1) \cup (5, \infty)$

For each graph write an absolute value inequality that has the given solution set.

85.

86.

87.

88.

89.

90.

Recall that $\sqrt{w}$ is a real number only if $w \ge 0$ and $1/w$ is a real number only if $w \ne 0$. For what values of x is each of the following expressions a real number?

91. $\sqrt{x - 2}$ **92.** $\sqrt{3x - 1}$ **93.** $\dfrac{1}{\sqrt{2 - x}}$

94. $\dfrac{5}{\sqrt{3 - 2x}}$ **95.** $\sqrt{|x| - 3}$ **96.** $\sqrt{5 - |x|}$

Solve each problem.

97. *Price Range for a Car* Yolanda is shopping for a used car in a city where the sales tax is 10% and the title and license fee is $300. If the maximum that she can spend is $8000, then she should look at cars in what price range?

98. *Price of a Burger* The price of Elaine's favorite Big Salad at the corner restaurant is 10 cents more than the price of Jerry's hamburger. After treating a group of friends to lunch, Jerry is certain that for 10 hamburgers and 5 salads he spent more than $9.14, but not more than $13.19, including tax at 8% and a 50 cent tip. In what price range is a hamburger?

99. *Final Exam Score* Lucky scored 65 points on his Psychology 101 midterm. If the average of his midterm and final must be between 79 and 90 inclusive for a B, then for what range of scores on the final exam would Lucky get a B? Both tests have a maximum of 100 points.
    HINT Write a compound inequality with his average between 79 and 90 inclusive.

100. *Bringing Up Your Average* Felix scored 52 points and 64 points on his first two tests in Sociology 212. What must he get on the third test to get an average for the three tests of at least 70? All tests have a maximum of 100 points.

101. *Weight Average with Whole Numbers* Ingrid scored 65 points on her calculus midterm. If her final exam counts twice as much as her midterm exam, then for what range of scores on her final would she get an average between 79 and 90? Both tests have a maximum of 100 points.

102. *Weighted Average with Fractions* Elizabeth scored 64, 75, and 80 on three equally weighted tests in French. If the final exam score counts for two-thirds of the grade and the other tests count for one-third, then what range of scores on the final exam would give her a final average over 70? All tests have a maximum of 100 points.
    HINT For this weighted average multiply the final exam score by 2/3 and the average of the other test scores by 1/3.

103. *Maximum Girth* United Parcel Service (UPS) defines girth of a box as the sum of the length, twice the width, and twice the height. The maximum length that can be shipped with UPS is 108 in. and the maximum girth is 130 in. If a box has a length of 40 in. and a width of 30 in. then in what range must the height fall?

104. *Raising a Batting Average* At one point during the 2008 season, a baseball player had 97 hits in 387 times at bat for an average of 0.251.

   a. How many more times would he have to bat to get his average over 0.300, assuming he got a hit every time?

   b. How many more times would he have to bat to get his average over 0.300, assuming he got a hit 50% of the time?

Figure for Exercise 104

105. *Bicycle Gear Ratio* The gear ratio r for a bicycle is defined by the following formula

$$r = \frac{Nw}{n},$$

where N is the number of teeth on the chainring (by the pedal), n is the number of teeth on the cog (by the wheel), and w is the wheel diameter in inches. The following chart gives uses for the various gear ratios.

Ratio	Use	
$r < 90$	down hill	
$70 < r \leq 90$	level	
$50 < r \leq 70$	mild hill	
$35 < r \leq 50$	long hill	

Suzanne Tucker/Shutterstock

A bicycle with a 27-in.-diameter wheel has 50 teeth on the chainring and 5 cogs with 14, 17, 20, 24, and 29 teeth. Find the gear ratio with each of the five cogs. Does this bicycle have a gear ratio for each of the four types of pedaling described in the table?

106. *Selecting the Cogs* Use the formula from the previous exercise to answer the following.

   a. If a single-speed 27-in. bicycle has 17 teeth on the cog, then for what numbers of teeth on the chainring will the gear ratio be between 60 and 80?

   b. If a 26-in. bicycle has 40 teeth on the chainring, then for what numbers of teeth on the cog will the gear ratio be between 60 and 75?

107. *Expensive Models* Two of the ten most expensive cars in the world are the BMW Z8 and the Mercedes Benz CL 600 (www.forbes.com). The prices of these two cars differ by more than $10,000. The price of the Z8 is $130,645.

   a. Assuming that you do not know which model is more expensive, write an absolute value inequality that describes this situation. Use x for the price of the CL 600.

   b. What are the possibilities for the price of the CL 600?

108. *Differences in Prices* There is less than a $5100 difference between the base price of a $21,195 Subaru Forester 2.5X and a comparable Ford (www.subaru.com).

   a. Write an absolute value inequality that describes this situation. Use x for the price of the Ford.

   b. What are the possibilities for the price of the Ford?

109. *Controlling Temperature* Michelle is trying to keep the water temperature in her chemistry experiment at 35°C. For the experiment to work, the relative error for the actual temperature must be less than 1%. Write an absolute value inequality for the actual temperature. Find the interval in which the actual temperature must lie.

110. *Laying Out a Track* Melvin is attempting to lay out a track for a 100-m race. According to the rules of competition, the relative error of the actual length must be less than 0.5%. Write an absolute value inequality for the actual length. Find the interval in which the actual length must fall.

111. *Acceptable Bearings* A spherical bearing is to have a circumference of 7.2 cm with an error of no more than 0.1 cm. Use an absolute value inequality to find the acceptable range of values for the diameter of the bearing.

112. *Acceptable Targets* A manufacturer makes circular targets that have an area of 15 ft². According to competition rules, the area can be in error by no more than 0.5 ft². Use an absolute value inequality to find the acceptable range of values for the radius.

Area: 15 ± 0.5 ft²

Figure for Exercise 112

113. *Per Capita Income* The 2007 per capita income for the United States was \$38,611 (U.S. Census Bureau, www.census.gov). The accompanying table shows the per capita income for 2007 for selected states.

Table for Exercise 113

State	Per Capita Income
Alabama	32,404
Colorado	41,042
Georgia	33,457
Iowa	35,023
Maryland	46,021
Missouri	34,389
New Jersey	49,194
Ohio	34,874
S. Carolina	31,013
Vermont	36,670

Monkey Business Images/Shutterstock

a. If a is the per capita income for a state, then for which states is $|a - 38{,}611| < 3000$?

b. For which states is $|a - 38{,}611| > 5000$?

114. *Making a Profit* A strawberry farmer paid \$4200 for planting and fertilizing her strawberry crop. She must also pay \$2.40 per flat (12 pints) for picking and packing the berries and \$300 rent for space in a farmers' market where she sells the berries for \$11 per flat. For what number of flats will her revenue exceed her costs?

▶ **RETHINKING**

115. Solve $x^2 + 2x = 0$.

116. Solve $x^2 + 2x = 9$.

117. Find the equation of the line (in standard form) through $(3, -4)$ that is perpendicular to $2x - y = 1$.

118. Find the distance between the points $(-3, 5)$ and $(2, 8)$ and the midpoint of the line segment joining the points.

119. Solve $3y - w = ay + 9$ for y.

120. Solve $5|2x - 9| = 0$.

THINKING OUTSIDE THE BOX X

One in a Million If you write the integers from 1 through 1,000,000 inclusive, then how many ones will you write?

POP QUIZ 8

Solve each inequality. Write the solution set using interval notation.

1. $x - \sqrt{2} \geq 0$

2. $6 - 2x < 0$

3. $x > 4$ or $x \geq -1$

4. $x - 1 > 5$ and $2x < 18$

5. $|x| > 6$

6. $|x - 1| \leq 2$

LINKING

concepts... For Individual or Group Explorations

Modeling the Cost of Copying

A company can rent a copy machine for five years from American Business Machines for \$105 per month plus \$0.08 per copy. The same copy machine can be purchased for \$6500 with a per copy cost of \$0.04 plus \$25 per month for a maintenance contract. After five years the copier is worn out and worthless. To help the company make its choice, ABM sent the accompanying graph (see next page).

a) Write a formula for the total cost of renting and using the copier for five years in terms of the number of copies made during five years.

(continued on next page)

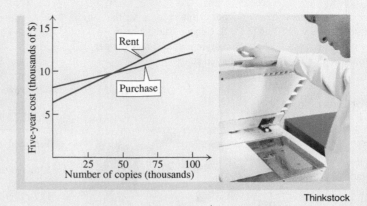

Thinkstock

b) Write a formula for the total cost of buying and using the copier for five years in terms of the number of copies made during five years.

c) For what number of copies does the total cost of renting exceed $10,000?

d) For what number of copies does the total cost of buying exceed $10,000?

e) Use an absolute value inequality and solve it to find the number of copies for which the two plans differ by less than $1000.

f) For what number of copies is the cost of renting equal to the cost of buying?

g) If the company estimates that it will make between 40,000 and 50,000 copies in five years, then which plan is better?

Highlights

1 Equations in One Variable

Linear Equation	$ax + b = 0$ where a and b are real numbers with $a \neq 0$.	$5x - 10 = 0$
Properties of Equality	An equivalent equation is obtained by adding, subtracting, multiplying, or dividing each side of an equation by the same nonzero real number.	$5x = 10$ $x = 2$
Solution Set	The set of all real numbers that satisfy an equation	Solution set to $5x - 10 = 0$ is $\{2\}$.
Identity	An equation satisfied by all real numbers for which both sides are defined	$\frac{y}{y} = 1$, solution set: $(-\infty, 0) \cup (0, \infty)$
Conditional Equation	An equation that has at least one solution but is not an identity	$2z - 1 = 0$ Solution set: $\{1/2\}$
Inconsistent Equation	An equation that has no solutions	$w = w + 1$, solution set: $\varnothing$
Absolute Value Equations	$\lvert x \rvert = k$ for $k > 0 \Leftrightarrow x = k$ or $x = -k$	$\lvert t \rvert = 1 \Leftrightarrow t = 1$ or $t = -1$
	$\lvert x \rvert = k$ for $k < 0$ is inconsistent	$\lvert m \rvert = -2$, solution set: $\varnothing$
	$\lvert x \rvert = 0 \Leftrightarrow x = 0$	$\lvert q - 4 \rvert = 0 \Leftrightarrow q = 4$

2 Constructing Models to Solve Problems

Formula	An equation in two or more variables that is usually of an applied nature	$A = \pi r^2, P = 2L + 2W$ $E = mc^2, F = \frac{9}{5}C + 32$
Function	A rule for determining the value of one variable from the values of one or more other variables. The first variable is a function of the other variable(s).	$A = \pi r^2$ Area of a circle is a function of its radius.
Solving for a Variable	The properties of equality are used to solve a formula for one variable in terms of the others.	$P = 2L + 2W$ $2L = P - 2W$ $L = (P - 2W)/2$

3 Equations and Graphs in Two Variables

Distance Formula	Distance between (x_1, y_1) and (x_2, y_2) is $\sqrt{(x_2 - x_1)^2 + (y_2 - y_1)^2}$.	For $(1, 2)$ and $(4, -2)$, $\sqrt{(4 - 1)^2 + (-2 - 2)^2} = 5$.
Midpoint Formula	The midpoint of the line segment with endpoints (x_1, y_1) and (x_2, y_2) is $\left(\frac{x_1 + x_2}{2}, \frac{y_1 + y_2}{2}\right)$.	For $(0, -4)$ and $(6, 2)$, $\left(\frac{0 + 6}{2}, \frac{-4 + 2}{2}\right) = (3, -1)$.
Equation of a Circle	The graph of $(x - h)^2 + (y - k)^2 = r^2 \, (r > 0)$ is a circle with center (h, k) and radius r.	Circle: $(x - 1)^2 + (y + 2)^2 = 9$ Center $(1, -2)$, radius 3
Linear Equation: Standard Form	$Ax + By = C$ where A and B are not both zero, $x = h$ is a vertical line, $y = k$ is a horizontal line.	$2x + 3y = 6$ is a line. $x = 5$ is a vertical line. $y = 7$ is a horizontal line.

4 Linear Equations in Two Variables

Slope Formula	The slope of a line through (x_1, y_1) and (x_2, y_2) is $(y_2 - y_1)/(x_2 - x_1)$ provided $x_1 \neq x_2$.	$(1, 2), (3, -6)$ slope $\frac{-6 - 2}{3 - 1} = -4$
Slope-Intercept Form	$y = mx + b$, slope m, y-intercept $(0, b)$, y is a linear function of x.	$y = 2x + 5$, slope 2, y-intercept $(0, 5)$
Point-Slope Form	The line through (x_1, y_1) with slope m is $y - y_1 = m(x - x_1)$.	Point $(-3, 2)$, $m = 5$ $y - 2 = 5(x - (-3))$
Parallel Lines	Two nonvertical lines are parallel if and only if their slopes are equal.	$y = 7x - 1$ and $y = 7x + 4$ are parallel.
Perpendicular Lines	Two lines with slopes m_1 and m_2 are perpendicular if and only if $m_1 m_2 = -1$.	$y = \frac{1}{2}x + 4$ and $y = -2x - 3$ are perpendicular.

5 Scatter Diagrams and Curve Fitting

Scatter Diagram	A graph of a set of ordered pairs	
Linear Relationship	If the points in a scatter diagram appear to be scattered about a line, then there is a linear relationship between the two variables.	

6 Complex Numbers

Standard Form	Numbers of the form $a + bi$ where a and b are real numbers, $i = \sqrt{-1}$, and $i^2 = -1$	$2 + 3i, -\pi + i\sqrt{2}, 6, 0, \frac{1}{2}i$
Add, Subtract, Multiply	Add, subtract, and multiply like binomials with variable i, using $i^2 = -1$ to simplify.	$(3 - 2i)(4 + 5i)$ $= 12 + 7i - 10i^2$ $= 22 + 7i$

Divide	Divide by multiplying the numerator and denominator by the complex conjugate of the denominator.	$6/(1 + i)$ $= \dfrac{6(1 - i)}{(1 + i)(1 - i)} = 3 - 3i$
Square Roots of Negative Numbers	Square roots of negative numbers must be converted to standard form using $\sqrt{-b} = i\sqrt{b}$, for $b > 0$, before doing computations.	$\sqrt{-4} \cdot \sqrt{-9} = 2i \cdot 3i = -6$

7 Quadratic Equations

Quadratic Equation	$ax^2 + bx + c = 0$ where a, b, and c are real and $a \neq 0$	$x^2 + 2x - 3 = 0$
Methods for Solving Quadratic Equations	Factoring: factor the quadratic polynomial and set the factors equal to zero.	$(w + 3)(w - 1) = 0 \Rightarrow$ $w + 3 = 0$ or $w - 1 = 0$
	Square root property: $x^2 = k$ is equivalent to $x = \pm\sqrt{k}$.	$m^2 = 5 \Rightarrow m = \pm\sqrt{5}$
	Completing the square: complete the square and then apply the square root property.	$(w + 1)^2 = 4 \Rightarrow$ $w + 1 = \pm 2$
	Quadratic formula: solutions to $ax^2 + bx + c = 0$ are $x = \dfrac{-b \pm \sqrt{b^2 - 4ac}}{2a}$.	$t^2 + 2t - 3 = 0 \Rightarrow$ $t = \dfrac{-2 \pm \sqrt{2^2 - 4(1)(-3)}}{2(1)}$

8 Linear and Absolute Value Inequalities

Linear Inequalities	The inequality symbol is reversed if the inequality is multiplied or divided by a negative number.	$4 - 2x > 10$ $-2x > 6$ $x < -3$
Absolute Value Inequalities	$\|x\| > k \,(k > 0) \Leftrightarrow x > k$ or $x < -k$ $\|x\| < k \,(k > 0) \Leftrightarrow -k < x < k$ $\|x\| \leq 0 \Leftrightarrow x = 0$ $\|x\| \geq 0 \Leftrightarrow x$ is any real number	$\|y\| > 1 \Leftrightarrow y > 1$ or $y < -1$ $\|z\| < 2 \Leftrightarrow -2 < z < 2$ $\|2b - 5\| \leq 0 \Leftrightarrow 2b - 5 = 0$ All real numbers satisfy $\|3s - 7\| \geq 0$.

Chapter Review Exercises

Find all real solutions to each equation.

1. $3x - 2 = 0$

2. $3x - 5 = 5(x + 7)$

3. $\dfrac{1}{2}y - \dfrac{1}{3} = \dfrac{1}{4}y + \dfrac{1}{5}$

4. $\dfrac{1}{2} - \dfrac{w}{5} = \dfrac{w}{4} - \dfrac{1}{8}$

5. $\dfrac{2}{x} = \dfrac{3}{x - 1}$

6. $\dfrac{5}{x + 1} = \dfrac{2}{x - 3}$

7. $\dfrac{x + 1}{x - 1} = \dfrac{x + 2}{x - 3}$

8. $\dfrac{x + 3}{x - 8} = \dfrac{x + 7}{x - 4}$

For each pair of points, find the distance between them and the midpoint of the line segment joining them.

9. $(-3, 5), (2, -6)$

10. $(-1, 1), (-2, -3)$

11. $(1/2, 1/3), (1/4, 1)$

12. $(0.5, 0.2), (-1.2, 2.1)$

Sketch the graph of each equation. For the circles, state the center and the radius. For the lines state the intercepts.

13. $x^2 + y^2 = 25$

14. $(x - 2)^2 + y^2 = 1$

15. $x^2 + 4x + y^2 = 0$

16. $x^2 - 6x = 2y - y^2 - 1$

17. $x + y = 25$

18. $2x - y = 40$

19. $y = 3x - 4$

20. $y = -\dfrac{1}{2}x + 4$

21. $x = 5$

22. $y = 6$

Solve each problem.

23. Write in standard form the equation of the circle that has center $(-3, 5)$ and radius $\sqrt{3}$.

24. Find the center and radius for the circle $x^2 + y^2 = x - 2y + 1$.

25. Find the x- and y-intercepts for the graph of $3x - 4y = 12$.

26. What is the y-intercept for the graph of $y = 5$?

27. Find the slope of the line that goes through $(3, -6)$ and $(-1, 2)$.

28. Find the slope of the line $3x - 4y = 9$.

29. Find the equation (in slope-intercept form) for the line through $(-2, 3)$ and $(5, -1)$.

30. Find the equation (in standard form using only integers) for the line through $(-1, -3)$ and $(2, -1)$.

31. Find the equation (in standard form using only integers) for the line through $(2, -4)$ that is perpendicular to $3x + y = -5$.

32. Find the equation (in slope-intercept form) for the line through $(2, -5)$ that is parallel to $2x - 3y = 5$.

Solve each equation for y.

33. $2x - 3y = 6$

34. $x(y - 2) = 1$

35. $xy = 1 + 3y$

36. $x^2y = 1 + 9y$

37. $ax + by = c$

38. $\dfrac{1}{y} = \dfrac{1}{x} + \dfrac{1}{2}$

Evaluate the discriminant for each equation, and use it to determine the number of real solutions to the equation.

39. $x^2 + 2 = 4x$

40. $y^2 + 2 = 3y$

41. $4w^2 = 20w - 25$

42. $2x^2 - 3x + 10 = 0$

Write each expression in the form $a + bi$, where a and b are real numbers.

43. $(3 - 7i) + (-4 + 6i)$

44. $(-6 - 3i) - (3 - 2i)$

45. $(4 - 5i)^2$

46. $7 - i(2 - 3i)^2$

47. $(1 - 3i)(2 + 6i)$

48. $(0.3 + 2i)(0.3 - 2i)$

49. $(2 - 3i) \div i$

50. $(-2 + 4i) \div (-i)$

51. $(1 - i) \div (2 + i)$

52. $(3 + 6i) \div (4 - i)$

53. $\dfrac{1 + i}{2 - 3i}$

54. $\dfrac{3 - i}{4 - 3i}$

55. $\dfrac{6 + \sqrt{-8}}{2}$

56. $\dfrac{-2 - \sqrt{-18}}{2}$

57. $\dfrac{-6 + \sqrt{(-2)^2 - 4(-1)(-6)}}{-8}$

58. $\dfrac{-9 - \sqrt{(-9)^2 - 4(-3)(-9)}}{-6}$

59. $i^{34} + i^{19}$

60. $\sqrt{6} + \sqrt{-3}\sqrt{-2}$

Find all real or imaginary solutions to each equation. Use the method of your choice on each problem.

61. $x^2 - 5 = 0$

62. $3x^2 - 54 = 0$

63. $x^2 + 8 = 0$

64. $x^2 + 27 = 0$

65. $2x^2 + 1 = 0$

66. $3x^2 + 2 = 0$

67. $(x - 2)^2 = 17$

68. $(2x - 1)^2 = 9$

69. $x^2 - x - 12 = 0$

70. $2x^2 - 11x + 5 = 0$

71. $b^2 + 10 = 6b$

72. $4t^2 + 17 = 16t$

73. $s^2 - 4s + 1 = 0$

74. $3z^2 - 2z - 1 = 0$

75. $4x^2 - 4x - 5 = 0$

76. $9x^2 - 30x + 23 = 0$

77. $x^2 - 2x + 2 = 0$

78. $x^2 - 4x + 5 = 0$

79. $\dfrac{1}{x} + \dfrac{1}{x - 1} = \dfrac{3}{2}$

80. $\dfrac{2}{x - 2} - \dfrac{3}{x + 2} = \dfrac{1}{2}$

Solve each equation.

81. $|3q - 4| = 2$

82. $|2v - 1| = 3$

83. $|2h - 3| = 0$

84. $4|x - 3| = 0$

85. $|5 - x| = -1$

86. $|3y - 1| = -2$

Solve each inequality. State the solution set using interval notation and graph the solution set.

87. $4x - 1 > 3x + 2$

88. $6(x - 3) < 5(x + 4)$

89. $5 - 2x > -3$

90. $7 - x > -6$

91. $\dfrac{1}{2}x - \dfrac{1}{3} > x + 2$

92. $0.06x + 1000 > x + 60$

93. $-2 < \dfrac{x - 3}{2} \le 5$

94. $-1 \le \dfrac{3 - 2x}{4} < 3$

95. $3 - 4x < 1$ and $5 + 3x < 8$

96. $-3x < 6$ and $2x + 1 > -1$

97. $-2x < 8$ or $3x > -3$

98. $1 - x < 6$ or $-5 + x < 1$

99. $|x - 3| > 2$

100. $|4 - x| \le 3$

101. $|2x - 7| \le 0$

102. $|6 - 5x| < 0$

103. $|7 - 3x| > -4$

104. $|4 - 3x| \ge 1$

Solve each equation or inequality by reading the accompanying graph.

105. $x - 0.5(30 - x) = 0$

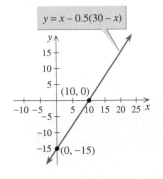

$y = x - 0.5(30 - x)$

$(10, 0)$

$(0, -15)$

106. $x^2 + 4x - 780 = 0$

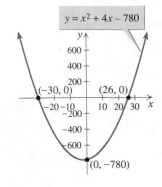

$y = x^2 + 4x - 780$

$(-30, 0)$ $(26, 0)$

$(0, -780)$

107. $0.6x - 4.8 < 0$

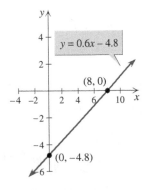

$y = 0.6x - 4.8$

$(8, 0)$

$(0, -4.8)$

108. $36 - 1.2x \geq 0$

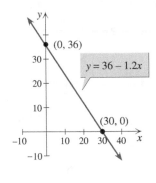

$(0, 36)$

$y = 36 - 1.2x$

$(30, 0)$

Solve each problem. Use an equation or an inequality as appropriate. For problems in which the answer involves an irrational number, find the exact answer and an approximate answer.

109. *Folding Sheet Metal* A square is to be cut from each corner of an 8-in. by 11-in. rectangular piece of copper and the sides are to be folded up to form a box as shown in the figure. If the area of the bottom is to be 50 in.², what is the length of the side of the square to be cut from the corner?

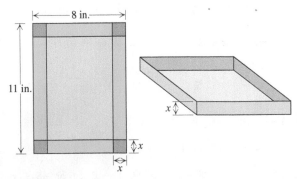

8 in.

11 in.

x

x

Figure for Exercise 109

■ **Foreshadowing Calculus**

Making an open-top box as in Exercise 109 is a classic problem in calculus. However, in calculus we usually find the value of x that maximizes the volume of the box.

110. *Peeling Apples* Bart can peel a batch of 3000 lb of apples in 12 hr with the old machine, while Mona can do the same job in 8 hr using the new machine. If Bart starts peeling at 8 A.M. and Mona joins him at 9 A.M., then at what time will they finish the batch working together?

111. *Meeting Between Two Cities* Lisa, an architect from Huntsville, has arranged a business luncheon with her client, Taro Numato from Norwood. They plan to meet at a restaurant off the 300-mi highway connecting their two cities. If they leave their offices simultaneously and arrive at the restaurant simultaneously, and Lisa averages 50 mph while Taro averages 60 mph, then how far from Huntsville is the restaurant?

112. *Driving Speed* Lisa and Taro agree to meet at the construction site located 100 mi from Norwood on the 300-mi highway connecting Huntsville and Norwood. Lisa leaves Huntsville at noon, while Taro departs from Norwood 1 hr later. If they arrive at the construction site simultaneously and Lisa's driving speed averaged 10 mph faster than Taro's, then how fast did she drive?

113. *Fish Population* A channel was dug to connect Homer and Mirror Lakes. Before the channel was dug, a biologist estimated that 20% of the fish in Homer Lake and 30% of the fish in Mirror Lake were bass. After the lakes were joined, the biologist made another estimate of the bass population in order to set fishing quotas. If she decided that 28% of the total fish population of 8000 were bass, then how many fish were in Homer Lake originally?

114. *Support for Gambling* Eighteen pro-gambling representatives in the state house of representatives bring up a gambling bill every year. After redistricting, four new representatives are added to the house, causing the percentage of pro-gambling representatives to increase by 5 percentage points. If all four of the new representatives are pro-gambling and they still do not constitute a majority of the house, then how many representatives are there in the house after redistricting?

115. *Hiking Distance* The distance between Marjorie and the dude ranch was $4\sqrt{34}$ mi straight across a rattlesnake-infested canyon. Instead of crossing the canyon, she hiked due north for a long time and then hiked due east for the shorter leg of the journey to the ranch. If she averaged 4 mph and it took her 8 hr to get to the ranch, then how far did she hike in a northerly direction?

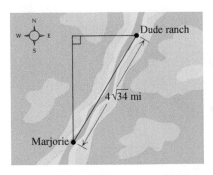

Dude ranch

$4\sqrt{34}$ mi

Marjorie

Figure for Exercise 115

116. *Golden Rectangle* The *golden rectangle* of the ancient
Greeks was thought to be the rectangle with the shape that was
most pleasing to the eye. The golden rectangle was defined as
a rectangle that would retain its original shape after removal of
a *W* by *W* square from one end, as shown in the figure. So the
length and width of the original rectangle must satisfy

$$\frac{L}{W} = \frac{W}{L - W}.$$

If the length of a golden rectangle is 20 m, then what is its
width? If the width of a golden rectangle is 8 m, then what is
its length?

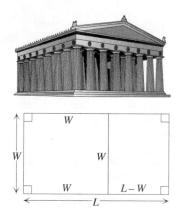

Figure for Exercise 116

117. *Price Range for a Haircut* A haircut at Joe's Barber Shop
costs $50 less than a haircut at Renee's French Salon. In fact,
you can get five haircuts at Joe's for less than the cost of one
haircut at Renee's. What is the price range for a haircut at
Joe's?

118. *Selling Price of a Home* Elena must get at least $120,000 for
her house in order to break even with the original purchase
price. If the real estate agent gets 6% of the selling price, then
what should the selling price be?

119. *Dimensions of a Picture Frame* The length of a picture frame
must be 2 in. longer than the width. If Reginald can use between 32 and 50 in. of frame molding for the frame, then what
are the possibilities for the width?

120. *Saving Gasoline* If Americans drive 10^{12} mi per year and
the average gas mileage is raised from 27.5 mpg to 29.5 mpg,
then how many gallons of gasoline are saved?

121. *Increasing Gas Mileage* If Americans continue to drive
10^{12} mi per year and the average gas mileage is raised from
29.5 to 31.5 mpg, then how many gallons of gasoline are saved?
If the average mpg is presently 29.5, then what should it be increased to in order to achieve the same savings in gallons as the
increase from 27.5 to 29.5 mpg?

122. *Thickness of Concrete* Alfred used 40 yd^3 of concrete to
pour a section of interstate highway that was 12 ft wide and
54 ft long. How many inches thick was the concrete?

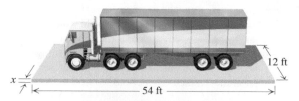

Figure for Exercise 122

123. *U.S. Cell Phone Subscribers* The number of cell phone subscribers in the United States reached 256 million in 2008, up
from 34 million in 1995, as seen in the accompanying graph.
a. Find the equation of the line that passes through the two
given points.

b. Use the equation to estimate the number of cell phone
subscribers in the United States in 2012.

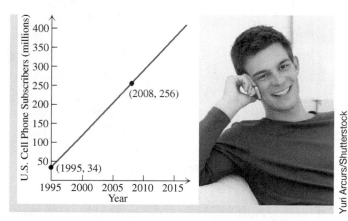

Figure for Exercise 123

124. *Worldwide Cell Phone Subscribers* The number of cell
phone subscribers worldwide reached approximately 3300
million in 2007, up from 145 million in 1996, as seen in the
accompanying graph.
a. Find the equation of the line that passes through the two
given points.

b. Use the equation to estimate the number of worldwide
cell phone subscribers in 2015.

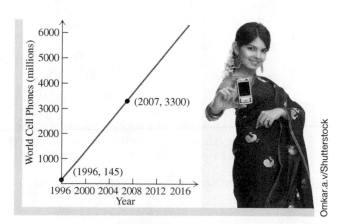

Figure for Exercise 124

125. *Percent of Body Fat* The average 20-year-old woman has 23% body fat and the average 50-year-old woman has 47% body fat (Infoplease, www.infoplease.com). Assuming that the percentage of body fat is a linear function of age, find the function. Use the function to determine the percentage of body fat in the average 65-year-old woman.

126. *Olympic Gold* In 2004 Shawn Crawford won the 200-meter race with a time of 19.79 seconds (www.infoplease.com). In 2008 Usain Bolt won the race with a time of 19.30 seconds. Assuming the winning time is decreasing linearly, as shown in the accompanying figure, express the winning time as a linear function of the year. Use the function to predict the winning time in the 2012 Olympics.

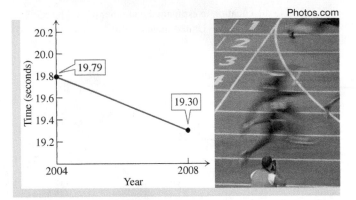

Photos.com

Figure for Exercise 126

127. *Price of Prescription Drugs* The accompanying table shows the average price of a prescription drug in the United States for the years 2000 through 2007 (U.S. Census Bureau, www.census.gov).

Table for Exercise 127

Year	Average Price ($)
2000	45.79
2001	50.06
2002	55.37
2003	59.52
2004	63.59
2005	64.86
2006	68.26
2007	72.16

GeoM/Shutterstock

a. Use linear regression with a graphing calculator to find a linear equation that expresses the price as a function of the year. Let $x = 0$ correspond to the year 2000.

b. Use the equation from part (a) to predict the average price in 2015.

128. *Number of Prescriptions* The accompanying table shows the number of prescriptions written in the United States for the years 2000 through 2007 (U.S. Census Bureau, www.census.gov).

Table for Exercise 128

Year	Number (in millions)
2000	2865
2001	3009
2002	3139
2003	3215
2004	3274
2005	3279
2006	3420
2007	3516

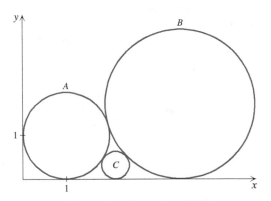

Rob Byron/Shutterstock

a. Use linear regression with a graphing calculator to find a linear equation that expresses the number of prescriptions as a function of the year. Let $x = 0$ correspond to the year 2000.

b. Use the equation from part (a) to predict the number of prescriptions of 2012.

129. *Tangent Circles* Circle A with center $(1, 1)$ and radius 1 is drawn in the first quadrant as shown in the accompanying figure. Circle B with radius 2 and circle C are placed as shown so that each circle is tangent to the other two circles and the x-axis. Find the equations of circles A, B, and C.

Figure for Exercise 129

THINKING OUTSIDE THE BOX XI & XII

Unlucky Number What is the smallest positive integer that is 13 times the sum of its digits?

Run for Your Life A hiker is one-fourth of the way through a narrow train tunnel when he looks over his shoulder to see a train approaching the tunnel at 30 mph. He quickly figures that if he runs in either direction at his top speed he can just make it out of the tunnel. What is his top running speed?

Chapter Test

Find all real or imaginary solutions to each equation.

1. $2x + 1 = x - 6$

2. $\dfrac{1}{2}x - \dfrac{1}{6} = \dfrac{1}{3}x$

3. $3x^2 - 2 = 0$

4. $x^2 + 1 = 6x$

5. $x^2 + 14 = 9x$

6. $\dfrac{x - 1}{x + 3} = \dfrac{x + 2}{x - 6}$

7. $x^2 = 2x - 5$

8. $x^2 + 1 = 0$

Sketch the graph of each equation in the xy-coordinate system.

9. $3x - 4y = 120$

10. $x^2 + y^2 = 400$

11. $x^2 + y^2 + 4y = 0$

12. $y = -\dfrac{2}{3}x + 4$

13. $y = 4$

14. $x = -2$

Perform the indicated operations, and write the answer in the form a + bi, where a and b are real.

15. $(4 - 3i)^2$

16. $\dfrac{2 - i}{3 + i}$

17. $i^6 - i^{35}$

18. $\sqrt{-8}(\sqrt{-2} + \sqrt{6})$

Solve each problem.

19. Find the slope of the line $3x - 5y = 8$.

20. Find the slope of the line through $(-3, 6)$ and $(5, -4)$.

21. Find the slope-intercept form of the equation of the line that goes through $(1, -2)$ and is perpendicular to the line $2x - 3y = 6$.

22. Find the equation of the line in slope-intercept form that goes through $(3, -4)$ and is parallel to the line through $(0, 2)$ and $(3, -1)$.

23. Find the exact distance between $(-3, 1)$ and $(2, 4)$.

24. Find the midpoint of the line segment with endpoints $(-1, 1)$ and $(1, 0)$.

25. Find the value of the discriminant for $x^2 - 5x + 9 = 0$. How many real solutions are there for this equation?

26. Solve $5 - 2y = 4 + 3xy$ for y.

Solve each inequality in one variable. State the solution set using interval notation and graph it on the number line.

27. $3 - 2x > 7$

28. $\dfrac{x}{2} > 3$ and $5 < x$

29. $|2x - 1| \le 3$

30. $2|x - 3| + 1 > 5$

Solve each problem.

31. Terry had a square patio. After expanding the length by 20 ft and the width by 10 ft, the area was 999 ft^2. What was the original area?

32. How many gallons of 20% alcohol solution must be mixed with 10 gal of a 50% alcohol solution to obtain a 30% alcohol solution?

33. *Median Price* The median price of a home in San Diego was $311,000 in 1997 and $495,000 in 2007.
   a. Assuming that the price is a linear function of the year, write a formula for that function.

   b. Use the formula to predict the median price to the nearest thousand in 2015.

34. *Number of Farms* The accompanying table gives the number of farms in the United States for the years 2001 through 2007. (U.S. Department of Agriculture, www.usda.gov).

Table for Exercise 34

Year	Farms (in thousands)
2001	2149
2002	2135
2003	2127
2004	2113
2005	2099
2006	2090
2007	2082

Jon Kroninger/Shutterstock

   a. Find the equations that express the number of farms as a function of the year by using linear regression and quadratic regression. Let $x = 1$ correspond to 2001.

   b. Predict the number of farms in the United States in 2012 using linear regression and quadratic regression.

CONCEPTS OF
calculus...

Limits

In algebra we can evaluate algebraic expressions for any acceptable value of the variable. The following tables show values of $x^2 + 5$ for certain values of x.

x	2.9	2.99	2.999
$x^2 + 5$	13.41	13.9401	13.994001

x	3.1	3.01	3.001
$x^2 + 5$	14.61	14.0601	14.006001

In calculus we look for trends. What happens to the value of $x^2 + 5$ as x gets closer and closer to 3? From the tables we see that the closer x is to 3, the closer $x^2 + 5$ is to 14. We say that the limit of $x^2 + 5$ as x approaches 3 is 14, and abbreviate this statement as $\lim_{x \to 3}(x^2 + 5) = 14$ or $\lim_{x \to 3} x^2 + 5 = 14$.

Note that we get 14 if we evaluate $3^2 + 5$, but that is not the idea of limits. We are looking for the trend as x approaches but never actually reaches a number. In fact, we often let x approach a number for which the expression cannot be evaluated.

Exercises

1. a. Fill in the second row of each table.

x	1.9	1.99	1.999
$5x - 4$			

x	2.1	2.01	2.001
$5x - 4$			

b. Can you evaluate $5x - 4$ for $x = 2$?

c. What is $\lim_{x \to 2}(5x - 4)$?

2. a. Fill in the second row of each table.

x	0.6	0.66	0.666
$\dfrac{24x^2 - 25x + 6}{3x - 2}$			

x	0.7	0.67	0.667
$\dfrac{24x^2 - 25x + 6}{3x - 2}$			

b. Can you evaluate $\dfrac{24x^2 - 25x + 6}{3x - 2}$ for $x = 2/3$?

c. What is $\lim_{x \to 2/3} \dfrac{24x^2 - 25x + 6}{3x - 2}$?

3. a. Fill in the second row of each table.

x	0.01	0.0001	0.000001
$(1 + \lvert x \rvert)^{1/\lvert x \rvert}$			

x	-0.01	-0.0001	-0.00001
$(1 + \lvert x \rvert)^{1/\lvert x \rvert}$			

b. Can you evaluate $(1 + \lvert x \rvert)^{1/\lvert x \rvert}$ for $x = 0$?

c. What is $\lim_{x \to 0}(1 + \lvert x \rvert)^{1/\lvert x \rvert}$?

4. a. Use a calculator in radian mode to fill in the second row of each table.

x	0.1	0.001	0.0001
$\dfrac{\sin(x)}{x}$			

x	-0.1	-0.001	-0.0001
$\dfrac{\sin(x)}{x}$			

b. Can you evaluate $\dfrac{\sin(x)}{x}$ for $x = 0$?

c. What is $\lim_{x \to 0} \dfrac{\sin(x)}{x}$?

Answers to Exercises

Section 1

For Thought: **1.** T **2.** T **3.** F **4.** T **5.** F **6.** T
7. F **8.** F **9.** F **10.** F

Exercises:

1. equation **3.** equivalent **5.** identity **7.** conditional equation
9. No **11.** Yes **13.** $\{5/3\}$ **15.** $\{-2\}$ **17.** $\{1/2\}$
19. $\{11\}$ **21.** $\{-24\}$ **23.** $\{-6\}$ **25.** $\{-2/5\}$
27. R, identity **29.** $\{0\}$, conditional **31.** $\{9\}$, conditional
33. $\varnothing$, inconsistent **35.** $\{x \mid x \neq 0\}$, identity
37. $\{w \mid w \neq 1\}$, identity **39.** $\{x \mid x \neq 0\}$, identity
41. $\{9/8\}$, conditional **43.** $\{x \mid x \neq 3 \text{ and } x \neq -3\}$, identity
45. $\varnothing$, inconsistent **47.** $\{-2\}$, conditional **49.** $\{-19.952\}$
51. $\{36.28\}$ **53.** $\{-2.562\}$ **55.** $\{1/3\}$ **57.** $\{0.199\}$
59. $\{0.425\}$ **61.** $\{-0.380\}$ **63.** $\{-8, 8\}$ **65.** $\{-4, 12\}$
67. $\{6\}$ **69.** $\varnothing$ **71.** $\{-2, 5\}$ **73.** $\{-23, 41\}$
75. $\{-10, 0\}$ **77.** $\{2/3\}$ **79.** $\varnothing$ **81.** $\{200\}$ **83.** $\{4\}$
85. $\{0\}$ **87.** $\{-1/2\}$ **89.** $\{-10\}$ **91.** $\{5\}$
93. $\{-8, -4\}$ **95.** $\{3/2\}$ **97.** $\varnothing$
99. $\{x \mid x \neq 2 \text{ and } x \neq -2\}$, identity
101. $\{x \mid x \neq -3 \text{ and } x \neq 2\}$, identity **103.** $\varnothing$, inconsistent
105. a. About 1995 **b.** Increasing **c.** 2015
107. $18,260.87 **109.** 250,000 **111.** $(\sqrt{3} - 1)/2$

Section 2

For Thought: **1.** F **2.** F **3.** F **4.** T **5.** T **6.** F
7. F **8.** T **9.** F **10.** F

Exercises:

1. formula **3.** uniform **5.** $r = \dfrac{I}{Pt}$ **7.** $C = \dfrac{5}{9}(F - 32)$

9. $b = \dfrac{2A}{h}$ **11.** $y = \dfrac{C - Ax}{B}$ **13.** $R_1 = \dfrac{RR_2R_3}{R_2R_3 - RR_3 - RR_2}$

15. $n = \dfrac{a_n - a_1 + d}{d}$ **17.** $a_1 = \dfrac{S(1 - r)}{1 - r^n}$

19. $D = \dfrac{5.688 - L + F\sqrt{S}}{2}$ **21.** $R = D/T$ **23.** $W = A/L$

25. $r = d/2$ **27.** 5.4% **29.** 2.5 hr **31.** $-5°C$
33. $37,250 **35.** 33.9 in. **37.** $46,000 **39.** $60,000
41. 16 ft, 7 ft, 7 ft **43.** 6400 ft^2 **45.** 112.5 mph **47.** 48 mph
49. $106,000 **51.** Northside 600, Southside 900 **53.** 28.8 hr
55. 2 P.M. **57.** 64.85 acres **59.** 225 ft **61.** 4.15 ft
63. 1.998 hectares **65.** $102,039 **67.** 8/3 liters
69. 1250 gallons **71.** 4 lb apples, 16 lb apricots
73. 3 dimes, 5 nickels **75.** 120 milliliters **77.** 2.5 gal
79. 3 hr 5 min **81.** 8 gal of 15%, 12 gal of 10%
83. a. About 1992 **b.** 1992 **85.** 1 hr, 3 min, 6 sec, no
87. $\{11/2\}$ **89.** $\{10,000\}$ **91.** $\varnothing$

Section 3

For Thought: **1.** F **2.** F **3.** F **4.** F **5.** T **6.** F
7. T **8.** T **9.** T **10.** F

Exercises:

1. ordered **3.** Cartesian **5.** circle **7.** linear equation
9. $(4, 1)$, I **11.** $(1, 0)$, x-axis **13.** $(5, -1)$, IV
15. $(-4, -2)$, III **17.** $(-2, 4)$, II **19.** 5, $(2.5, 5)$
21. $2\sqrt{2}$, $(0, -1)$ **23.** 25, $(17/2, 1)$

25. $6, \left(\dfrac{-2 + 3\sqrt{3}}{2}, \dfrac{5}{2}\right)$ **27.** $\sqrt{74}$, $(-1.3, 1.3)$

29. $|a - b|, \left(\dfrac{a + b}{2}, 0\right)$ **31.** $\dfrac{\sqrt{\pi^2 + 4}}{2}, \left(\dfrac{3\pi}{4}, \dfrac{1}{2}\right)$

33. $(0, 0)$, 4

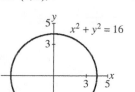

35. $(-6, 0)$, 6

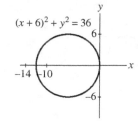

37. $(-1, 0)$, 5

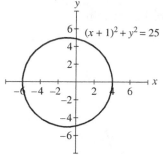

39. $(2, -2)$, $2\sqrt{2}$

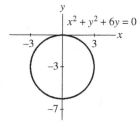

41. $x^2 + y^2 = 49$ **43.** $(x + 2)^2 + (y - 5)^2 = 1/4$
45. $(x - 3)^2 + (y - 5)^2 = 34$ **47.** $(x - 5)^2 + (y + 1)^2 = 32$
49. $(0, 0)$, 3 **51.** $(0, -3)$, 3

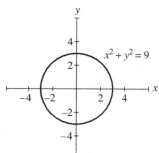

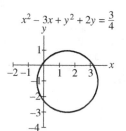

53. $(-3, -4)$, 5

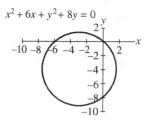

55. $(3/2, -1)$, 2

57. $(3, 4)$, 5

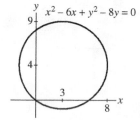

59. $(2, 3/2)$, 5/2

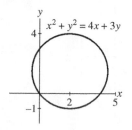

61. $(1/4, -1/6), 1/6$

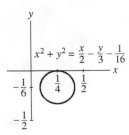

$$x^2 + y^2 = \frac{x}{2} - \frac{y}{3} - \frac{1}{16}$$

63. a. $x^2 + y^2 = 49$ **b.** $(x - 1)^2 + y^2 = 20$
c. $(x - 1)^2 + (y - 2)^2 = 13$
65. a. $(x - 2)^2 + (y + 3)^2 = 4$ **b.** $(x + 2)^2 + (y - 1)^2 = 1$
c. $(x - 3)^2 + (y + 1)^2 = 9$ **d.** $x^2 + y^2 = 1$
67. $(0, -4), (4/3, 0)$ **69.** $(0, -6), (2, 0)$

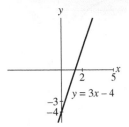

$y = 3x - 4$

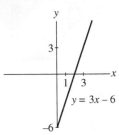

$y = 3x - 6$

71. $(0, 30), (-90, 0)$ **73.** $(0, 600), (-800, 0)$

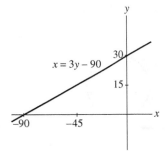

$x = 3y - 90$

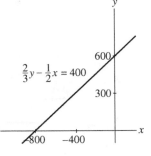

$\frac{2}{3}y - \frac{1}{2}x = 400$

75. $(0, 0.0025), (0.005, 0)$ **77.** $(0, 2500), (5000, 0)$

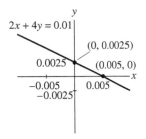

$2x + 4y = 0.01$

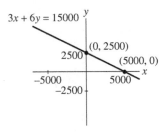

$3x + 6y = 15000$

79.   **81.**

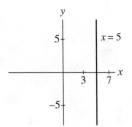

$x = 5$

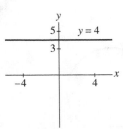

$y = 4$

83.   **85.**

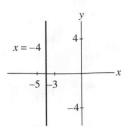

$x = -4$

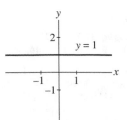

$y = 1$

87. $\{3.6\}$ **89.** $\{14\}$ **91.** $\{-2.83\}$ **93.** $\{558.54\}$
95. $\{116{,}566.67\}$ **97.** $\{4.91\}$
99. a. $(15, 22.95)$ The median age at first marriage in 1985 was 22.95.
b. 30.3; because of the units, distance is meaningless.
101. $C = 1.8$

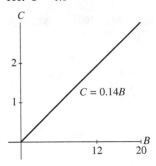

$C = 0.14B$

109. a. Conditional equation   **b.** Identity   **c.** Inconsistent equation
111. $\varnothing$ **113.** $x = \dfrac{d - b}{a - c}$

Section 4

For Thought: **1.** F   **2.** F   **3.** F   **4.** F   **5.** T   **6.** F
7. F   **8.** T   **9.** F   **10.** T

Exercises:
1. rise   **3.** slope   **5.** slope-intercept   **7.** perpendicular
9. $\dfrac{1}{3}$ **11.** -4 **13.** 0   **15.** 2   **17.** No slope
19. $y = \dfrac{5}{4}x + \dfrac{1}{4}$ **21.** $y = -\dfrac{7}{6}x + \dfrac{11}{3}$ **23.** $y = 5$
25. $x = 4$ **27.** $y = \dfrac{2}{3}x - 1$ **29.** $y = \dfrac{5}{2}x + \dfrac{3}{2}$
31. $y = -2x + 4$ **33.** $y = \dfrac{3}{2}x + \dfrac{5}{2}$ **35.** $y = \dfrac{3}{5}x - 2, \dfrac{3}{5}, (0, -2)$
37. $y = 2x - 5, 2, (0, -5)$ **39.** $y = \dfrac{1}{2}x + \dfrac{1}{2}, \dfrac{1}{2}, \left(0, \dfrac{1}{2}\right)$
41. $y = 4, 0, (0, 4)$ **43.** $y = \dfrac{1}{4}x + 7$ **45.** $y = -\dfrac{1}{2}x - \dfrac{7}{2}$
47.   **49.**

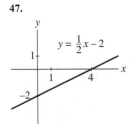

$y = \dfrac{1}{2}x - 2$

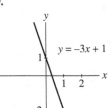

$y = -3x + 1$

51.

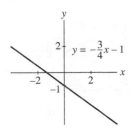

53.

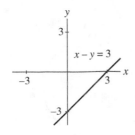

55.

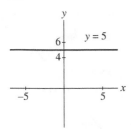

57. $4x - 3y = 12$ **59.** $4x - 5y = -7$ **61.** $x = -4$
63. $16x - 15y = 22$ **65.** $3x - 50y = -11$ **67.** 0.5   **69.** -1
71. 0   **73.** $2x - y = 4$ **75.** $3x + y = 7$ **77.** $5x - 7y = 23$
79. $3x + 2y = 0$ **81.** $2x + y = -5$ **83.** $y = 5$ **85.** -5
87. 8   **89.** T   **91.** T   **93.** F   **95.** Yes, no
97. $y = x - 2, x^3 - 8 = (x - 2)(x^2 + 2x + 4)$
99. $F = \frac{9}{5}C + 32, 302°F$ **101.** $c = 50 - n, \$400$
103. $S = -0.005D + 95$
105. $c = -\frac{3}{4}p + 30, -\frac{3}{4}$; if p increases by 4 then c decreases by 3.
107. $(-4, 11), (1, 8), (6, 5), (11, 2), (16, -1)$ **109.** 85/13
111. $\sqrt{26}/13$ **115.** $\{17/5, 23/5\}$ **117.** $(x - 2)^2 + (y - 6)^2 = 10$
119. $\{4\}$

Section 5

For Thought: **1.** T   **2.** T   **3.** F   **4.** T   **5.** T   **6.** T
7. F   **8.** F   **9.** F   **10.** F

Exercises:
1. scatter diagram   **3.** Linear   **5.** No relationship   **7.** Nonlinear
9. Linear   **11.** Linear   **13.** Linear   **15.** No relationship
17. $(3.3, 160), (4.0, 193)$ **19.** $(132, 34), (148, 25)$
21. a. $y = 13,450x + 956,753$ **b.** 1,091,253 thousand tons
c. Coal use for electricity increases by 13,450 thousand tons per year.
23. a. $y = 44.8x + 1075.3$ **b.** 2021   **c.** \$851 billion
25. $p = -0.069A + 0.403, 12.7\%$ **27.** $\{-1\}$ **29.** $(-4, 5), \sqrt{41}$
31. 3/5

Section 6

For Thought: **1.** T   **2.** T   **3.** F   **4.** T   **5.** F   **6.** F
7. T   **8.** T   **9.** T   **10.** F

Exercises:
1. complex numbers   **3.** imaginary number   **5.** Imaginary, $0 + 6i$
7. Imaginary, $\frac{1}{3} + \frac{1}{3}i$ **9.** Real, $\sqrt{7} + 0i$ **11.** Real, $\frac{\pi}{2} + 0i$
13. $7 + 2i$ **15.** $-2 - 3i$ **17.** $4 + i\sqrt{2}$ **19.** $\frac{9}{2} + \frac{5}{6}i$
21. $-12 - 18i$ **23.** 26   **25.** $34 - 22i$
27. 29   **29.** 4   **31.** $-7 + 24i$ **33.** $1 - 4i\sqrt{5}$ **35.** i
37. -1 **39.** $-i$ **41.** i **43.** $-i$ **45.** -1 **47.** 90
49. 17/4   **51.** 1   **53.** 12   **55.** $\frac{2}{5} + \frac{1}{5}i$ **57.** $\frac{3}{2} - \frac{3}{2}i$

59. $3 + 3i$ **61.** $\frac{1}{13} - \frac{5}{13}i$ **63.** $\frac{1}{34} - \frac{13}{34}i$ **65.** $-i$
67. $-4 + 2i$ **69.** -6 **71.** -10 **73.** $-1 + i\sqrt{5}$
75. $-3 + i\sqrt{11}$ **77.** $-4 + 8i$ **79.** $-1 + 2i$ **81.** $\frac{-2 + i\sqrt{2}}{2}$
83. $-3 - 2i\sqrt{2}$ **85.** $\frac{3 + \sqrt{21}}{2}$ **87.** 34   **89.** 6
91. $-\frac{8}{17} - \frac{15}{17}i$ **93.** $-1 + i$ **95.** $3 - i$
103. $\{-21\}$ **105.** $W = \frac{P - 2L}{2}$ **107.** 6.25 gal ethanol

Section 7

For Thought: **1.** F   **2.** F   **3.** F   **4.** F   **5.** F   **6.** T
7. F   **8.** F   **9.** T   **10.** T

Exercises:
1. quadratic   **3.** discriminant   **5.** $\{-4, 5\}$ **7.** $\{-2, -1\}$
9. $\left\{-\frac{1}{2}, 3\right\}$ **11.** $\left\{\frac{2}{3}, \frac{1}{2}\right\}$ **13.** $\{-7, 6\}$ **15.** $\{\pm\sqrt{5}\}$
17. $\left\{\pm i\frac{\sqrt{6}}{3}\right\}$ **19.** $\{0, 6\}$ **21.** $\{1/3\}$ **23.** $\{-2, 3\}$
25. $\{-2 \pm 2i\}$ **27.** $\left\{0, \frac{4}{3}\right\}$ **29.** $x^2 - 12x + 36$
31. $r^2 + 3r + \frac{9}{4}$ **33.** $w^2 + \frac{1}{2}w + \frac{1}{16}$ **35.** $\{-3 \pm 2\sqrt{2}\}$
37. $\{1 \pm \sqrt{2}\}$ **39.** $\left\{\frac{-3 \pm \sqrt{13}}{2}\right\}$ **41.** $\left\{-4, \frac{3}{2}\right\}$
43. $\left\{\frac{-1 \pm i\sqrt{2}}{3}\right\}$ **45.** $\{-4, 1\}$ **47.** $\left\{-\frac{1}{2}, 3\right\}$
49. $\left\{-\frac{1}{3}\right\}$ **51.** $\left\{\pm\frac{\sqrt{6}}{2}\right\}$ **53.** $\{2 \pm i\}$ **55.** $\{1 \pm i\sqrt{3}\}$
57. $\left\{\frac{1}{2} \pm \frac{3}{2}i\right\}$ **59.** $\left\{1 \pm \frac{\sqrt{3}}{2}i\right\}$ **61.** $\{-3.24, 0.87\}$
63. $\{-1.99, 3.40\}$ **65.** 0, 1   **67.** $-4, 0$ **69.** 172, 2
71. $\left\{-\frac{2}{3}, \frac{1}{2}\right\}$ **73.** $\{-3, 5\}$ **75.** 1   **77.** 0   **79.** 2
81. $\left\{-\frac{1}{3}, \frac{5}{3}\right\}$ **83.** $\{\pm\sqrt[4]{2}\}$ **85.** $\left\{-\frac{\sqrt{6}}{6}, \frac{\sqrt{6}}{12}\right\}$
87. $\{-12, 6\}$ **89.** $\left\{\frac{1 \pm \sqrt{5}}{2}\right\}$ **91.** $\{2 \pm \sqrt{3}\}$ **93.** $\{-6, 8\}$
95. $\varnothing$ **97.** $\{1/2\}$ **99.** $r = \pm\sqrt{\frac{A}{\pi}}$
101. $x = -k \pm \sqrt{k^2 - 3}$ **103.** $y = x\left(-1 \pm \frac{\sqrt{6}}{2}\right)$
105. 5000 or 35,000   **107.** 2.5 sec   **109.** 340 ft
111. $2\sqrt{205} \approx 28.6$ yd   **113.** 18,503.4 pounds   **115.** $6 - \sqrt{10}$ ft
117. 10 ft/hr   **119.** 4.58 m/sec, 0.93 sec
121. a. $y = -0.067x^2 + 1.26x + 51.14$ where x is years since 1980
b. 2019
123. $\frac{9 + \sqrt{53}}{2} \approx 8.14$ days   **125.** 40 lb or 20 lb
127. $4x - 5y = -38$ **129.** \$9000   **131.** $-2 - 3i$

Section 8

For Thought: **1.** T   **2.** F   **3.** F   **4.** T   **5.** F   **6.** F
7. F   **8.** F   **9.** F   **10.** T

Exercises:
1. interval   **3.** closed   **5.** compound   **7.** $x < 12$
9. $x \geq -7$ **11.** $[-8, \infty)$ **13.** $(-\infty, \pi/2)$
15. $(5, \infty)$ **17.** $[2, \infty)$

19. $(-\infty, 54)$

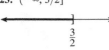

54

21. $(-\infty, 13/3]$

$\frac{13}{3}$

23. $(-\infty, 3/2]$

$\frac{3}{2}$

25. $(-\infty, 0]$

0

27. $(-\infty, -3.5)$ **29.** $(-\infty, 1.4]$ **31.** $(4, \infty)$ **33.** $(-\infty, -2]$
35. $(-3, \infty)$ **37.** $(-3, \infty)$ **39.** $(-5, -2)$ **41.** $\varnothing$
43. $(-\infty, 5]$

45. $(3, 6)$

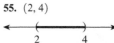

3   6

47. $(1/2, \infty)$

$\frac{1}{2}$

49. $(-3, \infty)$

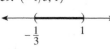

-3

51. $(-\infty, \infty)$

53. $\varnothing$
55. $(2, 4)$

2   4

57. $(-3, 1]$

-3 1

59. $(-1/3, 1)$

$-\frac{1}{3}$ 1

61. $[1, 3/2]$

1    $\frac{3}{2}$

63. $(-\infty, 0] \cup [2, \infty)$

0   2

65. $(-\infty, 2) \cup (8, \infty)$

2   8

67. $[-1, 9]$

-1 9

69. $\varnothing$ **71.** $\varnothing$

73. $(-\infty, 1) \cup (3, \infty)$

1   3

75. $(-\infty, 1) \cup (5, \infty)$

1   5

77. $|x| < 5$ **79.** $|x| > 3$ **81.** $|x - 6| < 2$ **83.** $|x - 4| > 1$
85. $|x| \geq 9$ **87.** $|x - 7| \leq 4$ **89.** $|x - 5| > 2$ **91.** $[2, \infty)$
93. $(-\infty, 2)$ **95.** $(-\infty, -3] \cup [3, \infty)$ **97.** $[\$0, \$7000]$
99. $[93, 100]$ **101.** $(86, 100]$ **103.** $(0 \text{ in.}, 15 \text{ in.}]$
105. 96, 79, 68, 56, 47, yes   **107. a.** $|x - 130{,}645| > 10{,}000$
b. $x > 140{,}645$ or $x < 120{,}645$
109. $\dfrac{|x - 35|}{35} < 0.01$, $(34.65°, 35.35°)$ **111.** $[2.26 \text{ cm}, 2.32 \text{ cm}]$

113. a. Colorado, Vermont
b. Alabama, Georgia, Maryland, New Jersey, S. Carolina

115. $\{-2, 0\}$ **117.** $x + 2y = -5$ **119.** $y = \dfrac{w + 9}{3 - a}$

Chapter Review Exercises

1. $\{2/3\}$ **3.** $\left\{\dfrac{32}{15}\right\}$ **5.** $\{-2\}$ **7.** $\left\{-\dfrac{1}{3}\right\}$

9. $\sqrt{146}$, $(-1/2, -1/2)$ **11.** $\dfrac{\sqrt{73}}{12}$, $\left(\dfrac{3}{8}, \dfrac{2}{3}\right)$

13. $(0, 0)$, 5

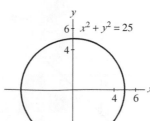

15. $(-2, 0)$, 2

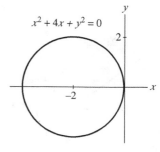

17. $(25, 0)$, $(0, 25)$

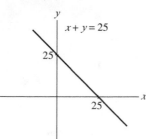

19. $(4/3, 0)$, $(0, -4)$

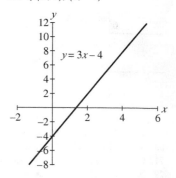

21. $(5, 0)$

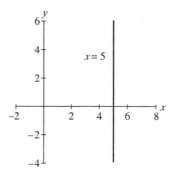

23. $(x + 3)^2 + (y - 5)^2 = 3$ **25.** $(4, 0)$, $(0, -3)$
27. -2 **29.** $y = -\dfrac{4}{7}x + \dfrac{13}{7}$ **31.** $x - 3y = 14$
33. $y = \dfrac{2}{3}x - 2$ **35.** $y = \dfrac{1}{x - 3}$ **37.** $y = -\dfrac{a}{b}x + \dfrac{c}{b}$
39. 8, two real   **41.** 0, one real   **43.** $-1 - i$ **45.** $-9 - 40i$
47. 20   **49.** $-3 - 2i$ **51.** $\dfrac{1}{5} - \dfrac{3}{5}i$ **53.** $-\dfrac{1}{13} + \dfrac{5}{13}i$
55. $3 + i\sqrt{2}$ **57.** $\dfrac{3}{4} - \dfrac{\sqrt{5}}{4}i$ **59.** $-1 - i$ **61.** $\{\pm\sqrt{5}\}$
63. $\{\pm 2i\sqrt{2}\}$ **65.** $\left\{\pm i\dfrac{\sqrt{2}}{2}\right\}$ **67.** $\{2 \pm \sqrt{17}\}$
69. $\{-3, 4\}$ **71.** $\{3 \pm i\}$ **73.** $\{2 \pm \sqrt{3}\}$
75. $\left\{\dfrac{1 \pm \sqrt{6}}{2}\right\}$ **77.** $\{1 \pm i\}$ **79.** $\left\{\dfrac{1}{3}, 2\right\}$
81. $\left\{\dfrac{2}{3}, 2\right\}$ **83.** $\{3/2\}$ **85.** No solutions
87. $(3, \infty)$

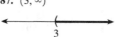

3

89. $(-\infty, 4)$

4

91. $(-\infty, -14/3)$

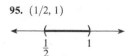
$-\dfrac{14}{3}$

93. $(-1, 13]$

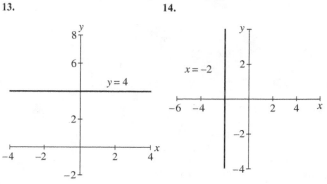

95. $(1/2, 1)$

$\dfrac{1}{2} \quad 1$

97. $(-4, \infty)$

-4

99. $(-\infty, 1) \cup (5, \infty)$

$1 \quad 5$

101. $\{7/2\}$

$\dfrac{7}{2}$

103. $(-\infty, \infty)$

105. $\{10\}$

107. $(-\infty, 8)$ **109.** $\dfrac{19 - \sqrt{209}}{4} \approx 1.14$ in.   **111.** 136.4 mi

113. 1600   **115.** 20 mi   **117.** (0, $12.50)   **119.** (7 in., 11.5 in.)

121. 2.15×10^9 gal, 31.8 mpg

123. a. $y = 17.08x - 34{,}034$ **b.** 331 million

125. $p = 0.008a + 0.07$, 59%

127. a. $y = 3.67x + 47.11$ **b.** $102.16

129. $(x - 1)^2 + (y - 1)^2 = 1$,
$(x - 1 - 2\sqrt{2})^2 + (y - 2)^2 = 4$,
$(x - 5 + 2\sqrt{2})^2 + (y - 6 + 4\sqrt{2})^2 = (6 - 4\sqrt{2})^2$

Chapter Test

1. $\{-7\}$ **2.** $\{1\}$ **3.** $\left\{\pm \dfrac{\sqrt{6}}{3}\right\}$ **4.** $\{3 \pm 2\sqrt{2}\}$

5. $\{2, 7\}$ **6.** $\{0\}$ **7.** $\{1 \pm 2i\}$ **8.** $\{\pm i\}$

9.

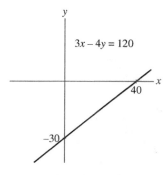
$3x - 4y = 120$

10.

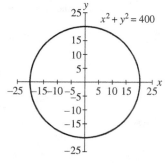
$x^2 + y^2 = 400$

11.

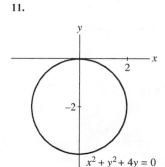
$x^2 + y^2 + 4y = 0$

12.

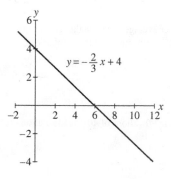
$y = -\dfrac{2}{3}x + 4$

13.

$y = 4$

14.

$x = -2$

15. $7 - 24i$ **16.** $\dfrac{1}{2} - \dfrac{1}{2}i$ **17.** $-1 + i$ **18.** $-4 + 4i\sqrt{3}$

19. $3/5$ **20.** $-5/4$ **21.** $y = -\dfrac{3}{2}x - \dfrac{1}{2}$ **22.** $y = -x - 1$

23. $\sqrt{34}$ **24.** $\left(0, \dfrac{1}{2}\right)$ **25.** -11, none   **26.** $y = \dfrac{1}{3x + 2}$

27. $(-\infty, -2)$

-2

28. $(6, \infty)$

6

29. $[-1, 2]$

$-1 \quad 2$

30. $(-\infty, 1) \cup (5, \infty)$

$1 \quad 5$

31. 289 ft^2 **32.** 20 gal

33. a. $y = 18.4x + 311$ where x is the number of years since 1997 and y is in thousands of dollars.   **b.** $642,000

34. a. $y = -11.39x + 2159.14$,
$y = 0.30x^2 - 13.77x + 2162.71$
b. 2,022,000, 2,041,000

Solutions to Try This Exercises

1.1 $5(3x - 2) = 5 - 7(x - 1)$

$$15x - 10 = 5 - 7x + 7$$
$$22x = 22$$
$$x = 1$$

Check: $5(3 \cdot 1 - 2) = 5 - 7(1 - 1)$
$$5 = 5$$

The solution set is $\{1\}$.

1.2 $x(x - 1) - 6 = (x - 3)(x + 2)$
$$x^2 - x - 6 = x^2 - x - 6$$

Since both sides are identical, it is an identity.

1.3
$$\frac{2}{x - 3} - \frac{3}{x + 3} = \frac{4}{x^2 - 9}$$

$$(x - 3)(x + 3)\left(\frac{2}{x - 3} - \frac{3}{x + 3}\right) = (x^2 - 9)\frac{4}{x^2 - 9}$$

$$2(x + 3) - 3(x - 3) = 4$$
$$-x + 15 = 4$$
$$-x = -11$$
$$x = 11$$

Check: $\dfrac{2}{11 - 3} - \dfrac{3}{11 + 3} = \dfrac{1}{28}, \dfrac{4}{11^2 - 9} = \dfrac{1}{28}$

The solution set to this conditional equation is $\{11\}$.

1.4 $\dfrac{2}{3.4x} - \dfrac{1}{8.9} = \dfrac{4}{4.7}$

$$\frac{2}{3.4x} = \frac{4}{4.7} + \frac{1}{8.9}$$

$$\frac{2}{3.4} = x\left(\frac{4}{4.7} + \frac{1}{8.9}\right)$$

$$\frac{\frac{2}{3.4}}{\frac{4}{4.7} + \frac{1}{8.9}} = x$$

$$x \approx 0.611$$

Check: $\dfrac{2}{3.4(0.611)} - \dfrac{1}{8.9} \approx 0.851, \dfrac{4}{4.7} \approx 0.851$

The solution set is $\{0.611\}$.

1.5 $|2x - 3| = 5$

$2x - 3 = 5$	or	$2x - 3 = -5$
$2x = 8$	or	$2x = -2$
$x = 4$	or	$x = -1$

Check: $|2 \cdot 4 - 3| = 5$ and $|2 \cdot (-1) - 3| = 5$
The solution set is $\{-1, 4\}$.

1.6 Solve the following equation.

$$25,000 = 355.9x + 11,075.3$$
$$13,924.7 = 355.9x$$
$$x \approx 39$$

So 39 years after 1990, or in 2029 the median income will reach $25,000.

2.1 $A = \dfrac{1}{2}hb_1 + \dfrac{1}{2}hb_2$

$$2A = hb_1 + hb_2$$
$$2A = h(b_1 + b_2)$$
$$h = \frac{2A}{b_1 + b_2}$$

2.2 $A = \dfrac{1}{2}h(b_1 + b_2)$

$$20 = \frac{1}{2} \cdot 2(b_1 + 3)$$
$$20 = b_1 + 3$$
$$17 = b_1$$

2.3 Let x represent the price of the computer and $0.05x$ the amount of tax.

$$x + 0.05x = 1506.75$$
$$1.05x = 1506.75$$
$$x = 1435$$
$$0.05x = 71.75$$

The amount of tax was $71.75.

2.4 Let x represent the width and $5x - 20$ represent the length.

$$2W + 2L = P$$
$$2x + 2(5x - 20) = 800$$
$$12x - 40 = 800$$
$$12x = 840$$
$$x = 70$$
$$5x - 20 = 330$$

So the length is 330 cm.

2.5 Let x represent her rate uphill and $x + 2$ her rate downhill. The distance is $6x$ or $3(x + 2)$.

$$6x = 3(x + 2)$$
$$6x = 3x + 6$$
$$3x = 6$$
$$x = 2$$
$$6x = 12$$

The total distance hiked is 24 miles.

2.6 Let x represent her speed on the return trip. Her time to work is 1/3 hr and her time for the return trip is $20/x$. Her average speed of 50 mph is the total distance divided by the total time:

$$\frac{20 + 20}{\frac{1}{3} + \frac{20}{x}} = 50$$

$$40 = 50\left(\frac{1}{3} + \frac{20}{x}\right)$$

$$\frac{4}{5} = \frac{1}{3} + \frac{20}{x}$$

$$15x \cdot \frac{4}{5} = 15x\left(\frac{1}{3} + \frac{20}{x}\right)$$

$$12x = 5x + 300$$
$$7x = 300$$
$$x = 42\frac{6}{7}$$

Her average speed on the return trip was $42\frac{6}{7}$ mph.

2.7 Let x represent the number of gallons of 40% acid solution.

$$0.40x + 0.20(30) = 0.35(x + 30)$$
$$0.40x + 6 = 0.35x + 10.5$$
$$0.05x = 4.5$$
$$x = 90$$

Use 90 gallons of 40% acid solution.

2.8 Let x represent the number of hours the small pipe is used and $x - 2$ represent the number of hours the large pipe is used.

$$\frac{1}{12}x + \frac{1}{8}(x - 2) = 1$$
$$\frac{1}{12}x + \frac{1}{8}x - \frac{1}{4} = 1$$
$$24\left(\frac{1}{12}x + \frac{1}{8}x - \frac{1}{4}\right) = 24 \cdot 1$$
$$2x + 3x - 6 = 24$$
$$5x = 30$$
$$x = 6$$

It will take 6 hours to fill the tank.

3.1

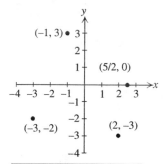

3.2 $\sqrt{(-3 - (-1))^2 + (-2 - 4)^2} = \sqrt{4 + 36} = \sqrt{40} = 2\sqrt{10}$

3.3 Add the corresponding coordinates and divide by 2:

$$\left(\frac{4 + 3}{2}, \frac{-1 + 1/2}{2}\right) = \left(\frac{7}{2}, \frac{-1/2}{2}\right) = \left(\frac{7}{2}, -\frac{1}{4}\right)$$

3.4 The midpoint of the diagonal with endpoints $(0, 0)$ and $(3, 5)$ is $(3/2, 5/2)$. The midpoint of the diagonal with endpoints $(4, 1)$ and $(-1, 4)$ is also $(3/2, 5/2)$. So the diagonals bisect each other.

3.5 The circle has center $(-2, 4)$ and radius 5.

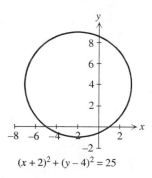

$$(x + 2)^2 + (y - 4)^2 = 25$$

3.6 The radius is the distance from the center $(2, -1)$ to $(3, 6)$:

$$\sqrt{(2 - 3)^2 + (-1 - 6)^2} = \sqrt{50}$$

The equation is $(x - 2)^2 + (y + 1)^2 = 50$.

3.7 Complete the squares:

$$x^2 + 3x + \frac{9}{4} + y^2 - 2y + 1 = 0 + \frac{9}{4} + 1$$
$$\left(x + \frac{3}{2}\right)^2 + (y - 1)^2 = \frac{13}{4}$$

The graph is a circle with center $(-3/2, 1)$ and radius $\sqrt{13}/2$ or about 1.8.

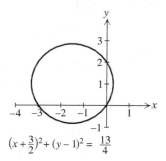

$$(x + \tfrac{3}{2})^2 + (y - 1)^2 = \frac{13}{4}$$

3.8 If $x = 0$, then $5y = 10$ or $y = 2$. If $y = 0$, then $2x = 10$ or $x = 5$. Draw a line through the intercepts $(0, 2)$ and $(5, 0)$.

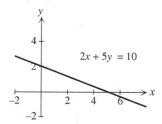

3.9 The ordered pairs $(-2, 5)$, $(0, 5)$, and $(2, 5)$ satisfy $y = 5$. So the graph is a horizontal line.

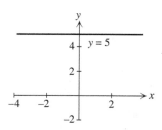

3.10 Graph $y = 0.34(x - 2.3) + 4.5$ and find the x-intercept. The x-intercept is $(-10.93529, 0)$ and the solution to the equation is approximately -10.93529.

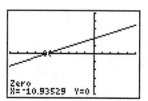

4.1 slope $= \frac{-3 - 5}{-1 - (-2)} = \frac{-8}{1} = -8$

4.2 Use the slope -8 from the preceding answer and the point $(-2, 5)$ in point-slope form.

$$y - 5 = -8(x - (-2))$$
$$y - 5 = -8x - 16$$
$$y = -8x - 11$$

4.3 Solve the equation for y:

$$3x + 5y = 15$$
$$5y = -3x + 15$$
$$y = -\frac{3}{5}x + 3$$

The slope is $-\frac{3}{5}$ and the y-intercept is $(0, 3)$.

4.4 Use $m = 1/4$ and $(x, y) = (4, -6)$ in $y = mx + b$:

$$-6 = \frac{1}{4} \cdot 4 + b$$
$$-6 = 1 + b$$
$$-7 = b$$

So the equation is $y = \frac{1}{4}x - 7$.

4.5 Start at the y-intercept $(0, 1)$ and use the slope $-3/2$ to locate a second point $(2, -2)$ which is down 3 and 2 to the right from $(0, 1)$:

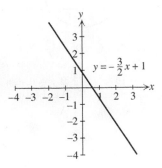

4.6 Use slope-intercept form:

$$y = \frac{3}{4}x + \frac{1}{2}$$
$$4y = 3x + 2$$
$$-3x + 4y = 2$$
$$3x - 4y = -2$$

4.7 The slope of any line parallel to $y = -\frac{1}{2}x + 9$ is $-\frac{1}{2}$. Use slope $-\frac{1}{2}$ and $(2, 4)$ in the point-slope form:

$$y - 4 = -\frac{1}{2}(x - 2)$$
$$y - 4 = -\frac{1}{2}x + 1$$
$$y = -\frac{1}{2}x + 5$$

4.8 Write $2x - y = 8$ as $y = 2x - 8$. The slope of any line perpendicular to $y = 2x - 8$ is $-\frac{1}{2}$. Use $-\frac{1}{2}$ and $(-2, 1)$ in point-slope form:

$$y - 1 = -\frac{1}{2}(x - (-2))$$
$$y - 1 = -\frac{1}{2}x - 1$$
$$y = -\frac{1}{2}x$$

4.9 The slope of the side with endpoints $(0, 0)$ and $(5, 2)$ is $\frac{2 - 0}{5 - 0}$ or $\frac{2}{5}$. The slope of the side with endpoints $(5, 2)$ and $(1, 12)$ is $\frac{12 - 2}{1 - 5}$ or $-\frac{5}{2}$. So the sides are perpendicular and the triangle is a right triangle.

4.10 Find the equation of the line through $(100, 70)$ and $(200, 90)$. The slope is $\frac{90 - 70}{200 - 100}$ or 0.20. Use the point-slope formula with C for cost in dollars and m for miles:

$$C - 70 = 0.20(m - 100)$$
$$C - 70 = 0.20m - 20$$
$$C = 0.20m + 50$$

4.11 Let F be the number of file cabinets and B be the number of bookshelves. Solve $100F + 150B = 3000$ for F:

$$100F = -150B + 3000$$
$$F = -1.5B + 30$$

The slope -1.5 means that increasing B by 1 causes F to decrease by 1.5.

5.1 a. Since the points appear to be approximately in line, the relationship is linear.

b. Since the points appear to be in an approximate parabolic shape, the relationship is nonlinear.

5.2 Graph the data and draw a line that approximately fits the data. At 2011 the second coordinate should be about 4.5. So the cost in 2011 should be about $4.50.

5.3 Enter the data into your calculator and find the regression equation $C = 1.926x + 12.093$ where x is the number of years after 1980. $C(30) \approx \$69.87$.

6.1 The complex number $i - 5$ is imaginary because the coefficient of i is nonzero. In standard form it is written as $-5 + i$.

6.2 $(4 - 3i)(1 + 2i) = 4 - 3i + 8i - 6i^2$
$= 4 + 5i - 6(-1) = 10 + 5i$

6.3 $i^{35} = (i^4)^8 i^3 = 1^8(-i) = -i$

6.4 $(3 - 5i)(3 + 5i) = 9 - 25i^2 = 34$

6.5 $\frac{4}{1 + i} = \frac{4(1 - i)}{(1 + i)(1 - i)}$

$= \frac{4 - 4i}{2} = 2 - 2i$

6.6 $\frac{2 - \sqrt{-12}}{2} = \frac{2 - 2i\sqrt{3}}{2} = 1 - i\sqrt{3}$

7.1 $x^2 - 7x - 18 = 0$
$(x - 9)(x + 2) = 0$
$x - 9 = 0$ or $x + 2 = 0$
$x = 9$ or $\quad x = -2$

The solution set is $\{-2, 9\}$.

7.2 $(x - 3)^2 = 16$
$x - 3 = \pm\sqrt{16}$
$x = 3 \pm 4$
$x = 7$ or -1

The solution set is $\{-1, 7\}$.

7.3 $2x^2 - 4x - 1 = 0$

$$x^2 - 2x - \frac{1}{2} = 0$$

$$x^2 - 2x + 1 = \frac{1}{2} + 1$$

$$(x - 1)^2 = \frac{3}{2}$$

$$x - 1 = \pm\sqrt{\frac{3}{2}}$$

$$x = 1 \pm \frac{\sqrt{6}}{2} = \frac{2 \pm \sqrt{6}}{2}$$

The solution set is $\left\{\frac{2 - \sqrt{6}}{2}, \frac{2 + \sqrt{6}}{2}\right\}$.

7.4 $2x^2 - 3x - 2 = 0$

$$x = \frac{3 \pm \sqrt{(-3)^2 - 4(2)(-2)}}{2(2)}$$

$$= \frac{3 \pm \sqrt{25}}{4} = \frac{3 \pm 5}{4}$$

The solution set is $\left\{-\frac{1}{2}, 2\right\}$.

7.5 $b^2 - 4ac = (-7)^2 - 4(5)(9) = -131$

Since the discriminant is negative, the equation has no real solutions.

7.6 Let x be Josh's average speed and $x + 5$ be Bree's average speed. Their times differ by one-half hour:

$$\frac{100}{x} - \frac{90}{x + 5} = \frac{1}{2}$$

$$2x(x + 5)\left(\frac{100}{x} - \frac{90}{x + 5}\right) = 2x(x + 5)\frac{1}{2}$$

$$200x + 1000 - 180x = x^2 + 5x$$
$$-x^2 + 15x + 1000 = 0$$
$$x^2 - 15x - 1000 = 0$$
$$(x - 40)(x + 25) = 0$$
$$x = 40 \text{ or } x = -25$$

Josh averaged 40 mph and Bree 45 mph.

7.7 The ball is back on the earth when $h = 0$:

$$-16t^2 + 40t + 6 = 0$$

$$t = \frac{-40 \pm \sqrt{(40)^2 - 4(-16)(6)}}{2(-16)}$$

$$t = \frac{-40 \pm \sqrt{1984}}{-32} = \frac{-40 \pm 8\sqrt{31}}{-32}$$

$$t = \frac{5 \pm \sqrt{31}}{4} \approx 2.64 \quad \text{or} \quad -0.14$$

The ball is in the air for $(5 + \sqrt{31})/4$ or about 2.64 seconds.

7.8 Let x and $x + 2$ represent the lengths of the legs.

$$x^2 + (x + 2)^2 = 6^2$$
$$2x^2 + 4x + 4 = 36$$
$$x^2 + 2x - 16 = 0$$

$$x = \frac{-2 \pm \sqrt{2^2 - 4(1)(-16)}}{2(1)} = \frac{-2 \pm \sqrt{68}}{2}$$

$$= \frac{-2 \pm 2\sqrt{17}}{2} = -1 \pm \sqrt{17}$$

The short leg is $-1 + \sqrt{17}$ or about 3.1 ft and the long leg is $1 + \sqrt{17}$ or about 5.1 ft.

7.9 Let x be the number of years after 1980. Quadratic regression yields
$$C = 0.0495x^2 - 0.973x + 11.850.$$
So $C(30) \approx \$27.21$.

8.1 The interval $(-\infty, 5]$ consists of all real numbers that are less than or equal to 5, and that is the solution set to $x \leq 5$.

8.2 $2 - 5x \leq 7$
$$-5x \leq 5$$
$$x \geq -1$$
The solution set is $[-1, \infty)$ and it is graphed as follows.

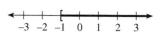

8.3 $\frac{1}{2}x + \frac{1}{3} \leq \frac{1}{3}x + 1$

$$6\left(\frac{1}{2}x + \frac{1}{3}\right) \leq 6\left(\frac{1}{3}x + 1\right)$$

$$3x + 2 \leq 2x + 6$$
$$x \leq 4$$
The solution set is $(-\infty, 4]$ and it is graphed as follows.

8.4 $A \cup B$ consists of all real numbers between 1 and 9. So $A \cup B = (1, 9)$. $A \cap B$ consists of all real numbers that belong to both A and B. So $A \cap B = [4, 6)$.

8.5 $\quad 2x > -4$ and $4 - x \geq 0$
$$x > -2 \text{ and } \quad -x \geq -4$$
$$x > -2 \text{ and } \quad x \leq 4$$
The solution set is $(-2, 4]$.

8.6 $3x + 2 > -1$ and $5 < -3 - 4x$
$$3x > -3 \text{ and } 4x < -8$$
$$x > -1 \text{ and } x < -2$$
Since $(-\infty, -2) \cap (-1, \infty) = \varnothing$, the solution set is the empty set, $\varnothing$.

8.7 $|x - 6| - 3 \leq -2$
$$|x - 6| \leq 1$$
$$-1 \leq x - 6 \leq 1$$
$$5 \leq x \leq 7$$
The solution set is $[5, 7]$.

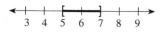

8.8 Let x be the third commission.

$$100 < \frac{80 + 90 + x}{3} < 110$$

$$300 < 170 + x < 330$$
$$130 < x < 160$$

The third commission must be in the interval $(130, 160)$ or between \$130 and \$160.

8.9 $\qquad \frac{|x - 10|}{10} < 0.01$

$$|x - 10| < 0.1$$
$$-0.1 < x - 10 < 0.1$$
$$9.9 < x < 10.1$$

If the actual amount dispensed is between 9.9 and 10.1 gallons, then the pump is certified as accurate.

Equations, Inequalities, and Modeling

For Thought

1. True, since $5(1) = 6 - 1$.

2. True, since $x = 3$ is the solution to both equations.

3. False, -2 is not a solution of the first equation since $\sqrt{-2}$ is not a real number.

4. True

5. False, $x = 0$ is the solution.   **6.**   True

7. False, since $|x| = -8$ has no solution.

8. False, $\dfrac{x}{x-5}$ is undefined at $x = 5$.

9. False, since we should multiply by $-\dfrac{3}{2}$.

10. False, $0 \cdot x + 1 = 0$ has no solution.

1 Exercises

1. equation

3. equivalent

5. identity

7. conditional equation

9. No, since $2(3) - 4 = 2 \neq 9$.

11. Yes, since $(-4)^2 = 16$.

13. Since $3x = 5$, the solution set is $\left\{\dfrac{5}{3}\right\}$.

15. Since $-3x = 6$, the solution set is $\{-2\}$.

17. Since $14x = 7$, the solution set is $\left\{\dfrac{1}{2}\right\}$.

19. Since $7 + 3x = 4x - 4$, the solution set is $\{11\}$.

21. Since $x = -\dfrac{4}{3} \cdot 18$, the solution set is $\{-24\}$.

23. Multiplying by 6 we get

$$
\begin{aligned}
3x - 30 &= -72 - 4x \\
7x &= -42.
\end{aligned}
$$

The solution set is $\{-6\}$.

25. Multiply both sides of the equation by 12.

$$
\begin{aligned}
18x + 4 &= 3x - 2 \\
15x &= -6 \\
x &= -\frac{2}{5}.
\end{aligned}
$$

The solution set is $\left\{-\dfrac{2}{5}\right\}$.

27. Note, $3(x - 6) = 3x - 18$ is true by the distributive law. It is an identity and the solution set is R.

29. Note, $5x = 4x$ is equivalent to $x = 0$. A conditional equation whose solution set is $\{0\}$.

31. Equivalently, we get $2x + 6 = 3x - 3$ or $9 = x$. A conditional equation whose solution set is $\{9\}$.

33. Using the distributive property, we find

$$
\begin{aligned}
3x - 18 &= 3x + 18 \\
-18 &= 18.
\end{aligned}
$$

The equation is inconsistent and the solution set is $\emptyset$.

35. An identity and the solution set is $\{x | x \neq 0\}$.

37. Multiplying $2(w - 1)$, we get

$$
\begin{aligned}
\frac{1}{w-1} - \frac{1}{2w-2} &= \frac{1}{2w-2} \\
2 - 1 &= 1.
\end{aligned}
$$

An identity and the solution set is $\{w | w \neq 1\}$

39. Multiply by $6x$.

$$
\begin{aligned}
6 - 2 &= 3 + 1 \\
4 &= 4
\end{aligned}
$$

An identity with solution set $\{x | x \neq 0\}$.

41. Multiply by $3(z - 3)$.

$$
\begin{aligned}
3(z + 2) &= -5(z - 3) \\
3z + 6 &= -5z + 15 \\
8z &= 9
\end{aligned}
$$

A conditional equation with solution set $\left\{\dfrac{9}{8}\right\}$.

43. Multiplying by $(x-3)(x+3)$.

$$(x+3)-(x-3) = 6$$
$$6 = 6$$

An identity with solution set $\{x|x \neq 3, x \neq -3\}$.

45. Multiply by $(y-3)$.

$$4(y-3)+6 = 2y$$
$$4y-6 = 2y$$
$$y = 3$$

Since division by zero is not allowed, $y=3$ does not satisfy the original equation. We have an inconsistent equation and so the solution set is $\emptyset$.

47. Multiply by $t+3$.

$$t+4t+12 = 2$$
$$5t = -10$$

A conditional equation with solution set $\{-2\}$.

49. Since $-4.19 = 0.21x$ and $\dfrac{-4.19}{0.21} \approx -19.952$,

the solution set is approximately $\{-19.952\}$.

51. Divide by 0.06.

$$x-3.78 = \frac{1.95}{0.06}$$
$$x = 32.5 + 3.78$$
$$x = 36.28$$

The solution set is $\{36.28\}$.

53.

$$2a = -1-\sqrt{17}$$
$$a = \frac{-1-\sqrt{17}}{2}$$
$$a \approx \frac{-1-4.1231}{2}$$
$$a \approx -2.562$$

The solution set is approximately $\{-2.562\}$.

55.

$$0.001 = 3(y-0.333)$$
$$0.001 = 3y-0.999$$
$$1 = 3y$$
$$\frac{1}{3} = y$$

The solution set is $\left\{\dfrac{1}{3}\right\}$.

57. Factoring x, we get

$$x\left(\frac{1}{0.376}+\frac{1}{0.135}\right) = 2$$
$$x(2.6596+7.4074) \approx 2$$
$$10.067x \approx 2$$
$$x \approx 0.199$$

The solution set is approximately $\{0.199\}$.

59.

$$x^2+6.5x+3.25^2 = x^2-8.2x+4.1^2$$
$$14.7x = 4.1^2-3.25^2$$
$$14.7x = 16.81-10.5625$$
$$14.7x = 6.2475$$
$$x = 0.425$$

The solution set is $\{0.425\}$.

61.

$$(2.3\times10^6)x = 1.63\times10^4-8.9\times10^5$$
$$x = \frac{1.63\times10^4-8.9\times10^5}{2.3\times10^6}$$
$$x \approx -0.380$$

The solution set is approximately $\{-0.380\}$.

63. Solution set is $\{\pm8\}$.

65. Since $x-4=\pm8$, we get $x=4\pm8$.

The solution set is $\{-4,12\}$.

67. Since $x-6=0$, we find $x=6$.

The solution set is $\{6\}$.

69. Since the absolute value of a real number is not a negative number, the equation $|x+8|=-3$ has no solution. The solution set is $\emptyset$.

71. Since $2x - 3 = 7$ or $2x - 3 = -7$, we get $2x = 10$ or $2x = -4$. The solution set is $\{-2, 5\}$.

73. Multiplying $\frac{1}{2}|x - 9| = 16$ by 2 we obtain $|x - 9| = 32$. Then $x - 9 = 32$ or $x - 9 = -32$. The solution set is $\{-23, 41\}$.

75. Since $2|x + 5| = 10$, we find $|x + 5| = 5$. Then $x + 5 = \pm 5$ or $x = \pm 5 - 5$.

The solution set is $\{-10, 0\}$.

77. Dividing $8|3x - 2| = 0$ by 8, we obtain $|3x - 2| = 0$. Then $3x - 2 = 0$ and the solution set is $\{2/3\}$.

79. Subtracting 7, we find $2|x| = -1$ and

$|x| = -\frac{1}{2}$. Since an absolute value is not equal to a negative number, the solution set is $\emptyset$.

81. Since $0.95x = 190$, the solution set is $\{200\}$.

83.

$$\begin{aligned} 0.1x - 0.05x + 1 &= 1.2 \\ 0.05x &= 0.2 \end{aligned}$$

The solution set is $\{4\}$.

85. Simplifying $x^2 + 4x + 4 = x^2 + 4$, we obtain $4x = 0$. The solution set is $\{0\}$.

87. Since $|2x - 3| = |2x + 5|$, we get $2x - 3 = 2x + 5$ or $2x - 3 = -2x - 5$. Solving for x, we find $-3 = 5$ (an inconsistent equation) or $4x = -2$. The solution set is $\{-1/2\}$.

89. Multiply by 4.

$$\begin{aligned} 2x + 4 &= x - 6 \\ x &= -10 \end{aligned}$$

The solution set is $\{-10\}$.

91. Multiply by 30.

$$\begin{aligned} 15(y - 3) + 6y &= 90 - 5(y + 1) \\ 15y - 45 + 6y &= 90 - 5y - 5 \\ 26y &= 130 \end{aligned}$$

The solution set is $\{5\}$.

93. Since $7|x + 6| = 14$, $|x + 6| = 2$. Then $x + 6 = 2$ or $x + 6 = -2$. The solution set is $\{-4, -8\}$.

95. Since $-4|2x - 3| = 0$, we get $|2x - 3| = 0$. Then $2x - 3 = 0$ and the solution set is $\{3/2\}$.

97. Since $-5|5x + 1| = 4$, we find $|5x + 1| = -4/5$. Since the absolute value is not a negative number, the solution set is $\emptyset$.

99. Multiply by $(x - 2)(x + 2)$.

$$\begin{aligned} 3(x + 2) + 4(x - 2) &= 7x - 2 \\ 3x + 6 + 4x - 8 &= 7x - 2 \\ 7x - 2 &= 7x - 2 \end{aligned}$$

An identity with solution set $\{x \mid x \neq 2, x \neq -2\}$.

101. Multiply $(x + 3)(x - 2)$ to

$$\frac{4}{x + 3} + \frac{3}{x - 2} = \frac{7x + 1}{(x + 3)(x - 2)}.$$

Then we find

$$\begin{aligned} 4(x - 2) + 3(x + 3) &= 7x + 1 \\ 4x - 8 + 3x + 9 &= 7x + 1 \\ 7x + 1 &= 7x + 1. \end{aligned}$$

An identity and the solution set is $\{x \mid x \neq 2 \text{ and } x \neq -3\}$.

103. Multiply by $(x - 3)(x - 4)$.

$$\begin{aligned} (x - 4)(x - 2) &= (x - 3)^2 \\ x^2 - 6x + 8 &= x^2 - 6x + 9 \\ 8 &= 9 \end{aligned}$$

An inconsistent equation and so the solution set is $\emptyset$.

105. a) About 1995

b) Increasing

c) Let $y = 0.90$. Solving for x, we find

$$\begin{aligned} 0.90 &= 0.0102x + 0.644 \\ \frac{0.90 - 0.644}{0.0102} &= x \\ 25 &\approx x. \end{aligned}$$

In the year 2015 $(= 1990 + 25)$, 90% of mothers will be in the labor force.

107. Since $B = 21,000 - 0.15B$, we obtain $1.15B = 21,000$ and the bonus is

$$B = \frac{21,000}{1.15} = \$18,260.87.$$

109. Rewrite the left-hand side as a sum.

$$10,000 + \frac{500,000,000}{x} = 12,000$$

$$\frac{500,000,000}{x} = 2,000$$

$$500,000,000 = 2000x$$

$$250,000 = x$$

Thus, $250,000$ vehicles must be sold.

111. The third side of the triangle is $\sqrt{3}$ by the Pythagorean Theorem. Then draw radial lines from the center of the circle to each of the three sides. Consider the square with side r that is formed with the $90°$ angle of the triangle. Then the side of length $\sqrt{3}$ is divided into two segments of length r and $\sqrt{3} - r$. Similarly, the side of length 1 is divided into segments of length r and $1 - r$.

Note, the center of the circle lies on the bisectors of the angles of the triangle. Using congruent triangles, the hypotenuse consists of line segments of length $\sqrt{3} - r$ and $1 - r$. Since the hypotenuse is 2, we have

$$(\sqrt{3} - r) + (1 - r) = 2$$

$$\sqrt{3} - 1 = 2r.$$

Thus, the radius is

$$r = \frac{\sqrt{3} - 1}{2}.$$

For Thought

1. False, $P(1 + rt) = S$ implies $P = \dfrac{S}{1 + rt}$.

2. False, since the perimeter is twice the sum of the length and width. **3.** False, since $n + 1$ and $n + 3$ are even integers if n is odd.

4. True

5. True, since $x + (-3 - x) = -3$. **6.** False

7. False, for if the house sells for x dollars then

$$x - 0.09x = 100,000$$

$$0.91x = 100,000$$

$$x = \$109,890.11.$$

8. True

9. False, a correct equation is $4(x - 2) = 3x - 5$.

10. False, since 9 and $x + 9$ differ by x.

2 Exercises

1. formula

3. uniform

5. $r = \dfrac{I}{Pt}$

7. Since $F - 32 = \dfrac{9}{5}C$, $C = \dfrac{5}{9}(F - 32)$.

9. Since $2A = bh$, we get $b = \dfrac{2A}{h}$.

11. Since $By = C - Ax$, we obtain $y = \dfrac{C - Ax}{B}$.

13. Multiplying by $RR_1R_2R_3$, we find

$$R_1R_2R_3 = RR_2R_3 + RR_1R_3 + RR_1R_2$$

$$R_1R_2R_3 - RR_1R_3 - RR_1R_2 = RR_2R_3$$

$$R_1(R_2R_3 - RR_3 - RR_2) = RR_2R_3.$$

Then $R_1 = \dfrac{RR_2R_3}{R_2R_3 - RR_3 - RR_2}$.

15. Since $a_n - a_1 = (n - 1)d$, we obtain

$$n - 1 = \frac{a_n - a_1}{d}$$

$$n = \frac{a_n - a_1}{d} + 1$$

$$n = \frac{a_n - a_1 + d}{d}.$$

17. Since $S = \dfrac{a_1(1 - r^n)}{1 - r}$, we obtain

$$a_1(1 - r^n) = S(1 - r)$$

$$a_1 = \frac{S(1 - r)}{1 - r^n}.$$

19. Multiplying by 2.37, one obtains

$$2.4(2.37) = L + 2D - F\sqrt{S}$$
$$5.688 - L + F\sqrt{S} = 2D$$

and $D = \dfrac{5.688 - L + F\sqrt{S}}{2}$.

21. $R = D/T$

23. Since $LW = A$, we have $W = A/L$.

25. $r = d/2$

27. By using the formula $I = Prt$, one gets

$$51.30 = 950r \cdot 1$$
$$0.054 = r.$$

The simple interest rate is 5.4%.

29. Since $D = RT$, we find

$$5570 = 2228 \cdot T$$
$$2.5 = T.$$

and the surveillance takes 2.5 hours.

31. Note, $C = \dfrac{5}{9}(F - 32)$. If $F = 23^{o}F$, then

$$C = \frac{5}{9}(23 - 32) = -5^{o}C.$$

33. If x is the cost of the car before taxes, then

$$1.08x = 40,230$$
$$x = \$37,250.$$

35. Let S be the saddle height and let L be the inside measurement.

$$S = 1.09L$$
$$37 = 1.09L$$
$$\frac{37}{1.09} = L$$
$$33.9 \approx L$$

The inside leg measurement is 33.9 inches.

37. If x is the sales price, then $1.1x = \$50,600$. Solving for x,

$$x = \frac{50,600}{1.1} = \$46,000.$$

39. Let x be the amount of her game-show winnings.

$$0.14\frac{x}{3} + 0.12\frac{x}{6} = 4000$$
$$6\left(0.14\frac{x}{3} + 0.12\frac{x}{6}\right) = 24000$$
$$0.28x + 0.12x = 24000$$
$$0.40x = 24000$$
$$x = \$60,000.$$

Her winnings is \$60,000.

41. If x is the length of the shorter piece in feet, then the length of the longer side is $2x + 2$. Then we obtain

$$x + x + (2x + 2) = 30$$
$$4x = 28$$
$$x = 7.$$

The length of each shorter piece is 7 ft and the longer piece is $(2 \cdot 7 + 2)$ or 16 ft.

43. If x is the length of the side of the larger square lot then $2x$ is the amount of fencing needed to divide the square lot into four smaller lots. The solution to $4x + 2x = 480$ is $x = 80$. The side of the larger square lot is 80 feet and its area is 6400 ft^2.

45. Note, Bobby will complete the remaining 8 laps in $\dfrac{8}{90}$ of an hour. If Ricky is to finish at the same time as Bobby, then Ricky's average speed s over 10 laps must satisfy $\dfrac{10}{s} = \dfrac{8}{90}$. $\left(\text{Note: } time = \dfrac{distance}{speed}\right)$. The equation is equivalent to $900 = 8s$. Thus, Ricky's average speed must be 112.5 mph.

47. Let d be the halfway distance between San Antonio and El Paso, and let s be the speed in the last half of the trip. Junior took $\dfrac{d}{80}$ hours to get to the halfway point and the last half took $\dfrac{d}{s}$ hours to drive. Since the total distance is $2d$ and $distance = rate \times time$,

$$
\begin{aligned}
2d &= 60\left(\frac{d}{80} + \frac{d}{s}\right) \\
160sd &= 60\left(sd + 80d\right) \\
160sd &= 60sd + 4800d \\
100sd &= 4800d \\
100d(s - 48) &= 0.
\end{aligned}
$$

Since $d \neq 0$, the speed for the last half of the trip was $s = 48$ mph.

49. If x is the part of the start-up capital invested at 5% and $x + 10,000$ is the part invested at 6%, then

$$
\begin{aligned}
0.05x + 0.06(x + 10,000) &= 5880 \\
0.11x + 600 &= 5880 \\
0.11x &= 5280 \\
x &= 48,000.
\end{aligned}
$$

Norma invested $\$48,000$ at 5% and $\$58,000$ at 6% for a total start-up capital of $\$106,000$.

51. Let x and $1500 - x$ be the number of employees from the Northside and Southside, respectively. Then

$$
\begin{aligned}
(0.05)x + 0.80(1500 - x) &= 750 \\
0.05x + 1200 - 0.80x &= 750 \\
450 &= 0.75x \\
600 &= x.
\end{aligned}
$$

There were 600 and 900 employees at the Northside and Southside, respectively.

53. Let x be the number of hours it takes both combines working together to harvest an entire wheat crop.

	rate
old	1/72
new	1/48
combined	1/x

Then $\dfrac{1}{72} + \dfrac{1}{48} = \dfrac{1}{x}$. Multiply both sides by

$144x$ and get $2x + 3x = 144$. The solution is $x = 28.8$ hr which is the time it takes both combines to harvest the entire wheat crop.

55. Let t be the number of hours since 8:00 a.m.

	rate	time	work completed
Batman	1/8	$t - 2$	$(t - 2)/8$
Robin	1/12	t	$t/12$

$$
\begin{aligned}
\frac{t - 2}{8} + \frac{t}{12} &= 1 \\
24\left(\frac{t - 2}{8} + \frac{t}{12}\right) &= 24 \\
3(t - 2) + 2t &= 24 \\
5t - 6 &= 24 \\
t &= 6
\end{aligned}
$$

At 2 p.m., all the crime have been cleaned up.

57. Since there are 5280 feet to a mile and the circumference of a circle is $C = 2\pi r$,

the radius r of the race track is $r = \dfrac{5280}{2\pi}$.

Since the length of a side of the square plot is twice the radius, the area of the plot is

$$
\left(2 \cdot \frac{5280}{2\pi}\right)^2 \approx 2,824,677.3 \text{ ft}^2.
$$

Dividing this number by $43,560$ results to 64.85 acres which is the acreage of the square lot.

59. The area of a trapezoid is $A = \dfrac{1}{2}h(b_1 + b_2)$.

$$
\begin{aligned}
90,000 &= \frac{1}{2}h(500 + 300) \\
90,000 &= 400h \\
225 &= h
\end{aligned}
$$

Thus, the streets are 225 ft apart.

61. Since the volume of a circular cylinder is $V = \pi r^2 h$, we have $\dfrac{22,000}{7.5} = \pi 15^2 \cdot h$.

Solving for h, we get $h = 4.15$ ft, the depth of water in the pool.

63. Let r be the radius of the semicircular turns. Since the circumference of a circle is given by $C = 2\pi r$, we have $514 = 2\pi r + 200$. Solving for r, we get

$$r = \frac{157}{\pi} \approx 49.9747 \text{ m}.$$

Note, the width of the rectangular lot is $2r$. Then the dimension of the rectangular lot is 99.9494 m by 199.9494 m; its area is $19,984.82$ m^2, which is equivalent to 1.998 hectares.

65. Let x be Lorinda's taxable income.

$$
\begin{aligned}
16,781.25 + 0.28(x - 82,400) &= 22,280.17 \\
0.28(x - 82,400) &= 5498.92 \\
x - 82,400 &= 19,639 \\
x &= 102,039.
\end{aligned}
$$

Lorinda's taxable income is $102,039.

67. Let x be the amount of water to be added. The volume of the resulting solution is $4 + x$ liters and the amount of pure baneberry in it is $0.05(4)$ liters. Since the resulting solution is a 3% extract, we have

$$
\begin{aligned}
0.03(4 + x) &= 0.05(4) \\
0.12 + 0.03x &= 0.20 \\
x &= \frac{0.08}{0.03} \\
x &= \frac{8}{3}.
\end{aligned}
$$

The amount of water to be added is $\frac{8}{3}$ liters.

69. Let x be the number of gallons of gasoline with 12% ethanol that needs to be added. The volume of the resulting solution is $500 + x$ gallons and the amount of ethanol is $(500 + x)0.1$ gallons.

$$
\begin{aligned}
500(0.05) + 0.12x &= (500 + x)0.1 \\
0.02x &= 25 \\
x &= 1250.
\end{aligned}
$$

The amount of gasoline with 5% ethanol to be added is 1250 gallons.

71. The costs of x pounds of dried apples is $(1.20)4x$ and the cost of $(20 - x)$ pounds of dried apricots is $4(1.80)(20 - x)$. Since the 20 lb-mixture costs $1.68 per quarter-pound, we obtain

$$
\begin{aligned}
4(1.68)(20) &= (1.20)4x + 4(1.80)(20 - x) \\
134.4 &= 4.80x + 144 - 7.20x \\
2.40x &= 9.6 \\
x &= 4.
\end{aligned}
$$

The mix needs 4 lb of dried apples and 16 lb of dried apricots.

73. Let x and $8 - x$ be the number of dimes and nickels, respectively. Since the candy bar costs 55 cents, we have $55 = 10x + 5(8 - x)$. Solving for x, we find $x = 3$. Thus, Dana has 3 dimes and 5 nickels.

75. Let x be the amount of water needed. The volume of the resulting solution is $200 + x$ ml and the amount of active ingredient in it is $0.4(200)$ or 80 ml. Since the resulting solution is a 25% extract, we have

$$
\begin{aligned}
0.25(200 + x) &= 80 \\
200 + x &= 320 \\
x &= 120.
\end{aligned}
$$

The amount of water needed is 120 ml.

77. Let x be the number of gallons of the stronger solution. The amount of salt in the new solution is $5(0.2) + x(0.5)$ or $(1 + 0.5x)$ lb, and the volume of new solution is $(5 + x)$ gallons. Since the new solution contains 0.3 lb of salt per gallon, we obtain

$$
\begin{aligned}
0.30(5 + x) &= 1 + 0.5x \\
1.5 + 0.3x &= 1 + 0.5x \\
0.5 &= 0.2x.
\end{aligned}
$$

Then $x = 2.5$ gallons, the required amount of the stronger solution.

Equations, Inequalities, and Modeling

79. Let x be the number of hours it takes both pumps to drain the pool simultaneously.

	The part drained in 1 hr
Together	$1/x$
Large pump	$1/5$
Small pump	$1/8$

It follows that

$$\frac{1}{5} + \frac{1}{8} = \frac{1}{x}.$$

Multiplying both sides by $40x$, we find $8x + 5x = 40$. Then $x = 40/13$ hr, or about 3 hr and 5 min.

81. Let x and $20 - x$ be the number of gallons of the needed 15% and 10% alcohol solutions, respectively. Since the resulting mixture is 12% alcohol, we find

$$\begin{aligned} 0.15x + 0.10(20 - x) &= 20(0.12) \\ 0.05x &= 0.4 \\ x &= 8. \end{aligned}$$

Then 8 gallons of the 15% alcohol solution and 12 gallons of the 10% alcohol solution are needed.

83. a) About 1992

b) Since the revenues are equal, we obtain

$$\begin{aligned} 13.5n + 190 &= 7.5n + 225 \\ 6n &= 35 \\ n &\approx 5.8. \end{aligned}$$

In the year 1992 (=1986+6), restaurant revenues and supermarket revenues were the same.

85. If h is the number of hours it will take two hikers to pick a gallon of wild berries, then

$$\begin{aligned} \frac{1}{2} + \frac{1}{2} &= \frac{1}{h} \\ 1 &= \frac{1}{h} \\ 1 &= h. \end{aligned}$$

Two hikers can pick a gallon of wild berries in 1 hr.

If m is the number of minutes it will take two mechanics to change the oil of a Saturn, then

$$\begin{aligned} \frac{1}{6} + \frac{1}{6} &= \frac{1}{m} \\ \frac{1}{3} &= \frac{1}{m} \\ m &= 3. \end{aligned}$$

Two mechanics can change the oil in 3 minutes.

If w is the number of minutes it will take 60 mechanics to change the oil, then

$$\begin{aligned} 60 \cdot \frac{1}{6} &= \frac{1}{w} \\ w &= \frac{1}{10} \text{ min} \\ w &= 6 \text{ sec.} \end{aligned}$$

So, 60 mechanics working together can change the oil in 6 sec (an unreasonable situation and answer).

87. Since $2x = 11$, the solution set is $\{11/2\}$.

89.

$$\begin{aligned} 0.999x &= 9990 \\ x &= 10,000 \end{aligned}$$

The solution set is $\{10,000\}$.

90.

$$\begin{aligned} 2x - 3 &= \pm 8 \\ 2x &= 3 \pm 8 \\ 2x &= -5, 11 \\ x &= -\frac{5}{2}, \frac{11}{2} \end{aligned}$$

The solution set is $\{-5/2, 11/2\}$.

91. The empty set $\emptyset$ since the absolute value of a number is nonnegative.

For Thought

1. False, the point $(2, -3)$ is in Quadrant IV.

2. False, the point $(4, 0)$ does not belong to any quadrant.

3. False, since the distance is $\sqrt{(a-c)^2 + (b-d)^2}$.

4. False, since $Ax + By = C$ is a linear equation.

5. True, since the x-intercept can be obtained by replacing y by 0.

6. False, since $\sqrt{7^2 + 9^2} = \sqrt{130} \approx 11.4$

7. True

8. True

9. True

10. False, it is a circle of radius $\sqrt{5}$.

3 Exercises

1. ordered

3. Cartesian

5. circle

7. linear equation

9. $(4, 1)$, Quadrant I

11. $(1, 0)$, x-axis

13. $(5, -1)$, Quadrant IV

15. $(-4, -2)$, Quadrant III

17. $(-2, 4)$, Quadrant II

19. Distance is $\sqrt{(4-1)^2 + (7-3)^2} = \sqrt{9 + 16} = \sqrt{25} = 5$, midpoint is $(2.5, 5)$

21. Distance is $\sqrt{(-1-1)^2 + (-2-0)^2} = \sqrt{4+4} = 2\sqrt{2}$, midpoint is $(0, -1)$

23. Distance is $\sqrt{(12-5)^2 + (-11-13)^2} = \sqrt{49 + 576} = \sqrt{625} = 25$, and the midpoint is $\left(\dfrac{12+5}{2}, \dfrac{-11+13}{2} \right) = \left(\dfrac{17}{2}, 1 \right)$

25. Distance is $\sqrt{(-1 + 3\sqrt{3} - (-1))^2 + (4-1)^2} = \sqrt{27 + 9} = 6$, midpoint is $\left(\dfrac{-2 + 3\sqrt{3}}{2}, \dfrac{5}{2} \right)$

27. Distance is $\sqrt{(1.2 + 3.8)^2 + (4.4 + 2.2)^2} = \sqrt{25 + 49} = \sqrt{74}$, midpoint is $(-1.3, 1.3)$

29. Distance is $\sqrt{(a-b)^2 + 0} = |a - b|$, midpoint is $\left(\dfrac{a+b}{2}, 0 \right)$

31. Distance is $\dfrac{\sqrt{\pi^2 + 4}}{2}$, midpoint is $\left(\dfrac{3\pi}{4}, \dfrac{1}{2} \right)$

33. Center $(0, 0)$, radius 4

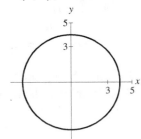

35. Center $(-6, 0)$, radius 6

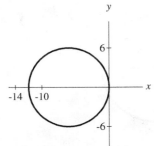

37. Center $(-1, 0)$, radius 5

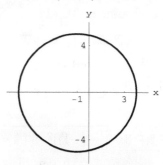

39. Center $(2, -2)$, radius $2\sqrt{2}$

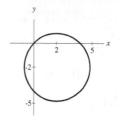

41. $x^2 + y^2 = 49$

43. $(x + 2)^2 + (y - 5)^2 = 1/4$

45. The distance between $(3, 5)$ and the origin is $\sqrt{34}$ which is the radius. The standard equation is $(x - 3)^2 + (y - 5)^2 = 34$.

47. The distance between $(5, -1)$ and $(1, 3)$ is $\sqrt{32}$ which is the radius. The standard equation is $(x - 5)^2 + (y + 1)^2 = 32$.

49. Center $(0, 0)$, radius 3

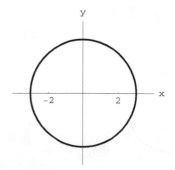

51. Completing the square, we have

$$
\begin{aligned}
x^2 + (y^2 + 6y + 9) &= 0 + 9 \\
x^2 + (y + 3)^2 &= 9.
\end{aligned}
$$

The center is $(0, -3)$ and the radius is 3.

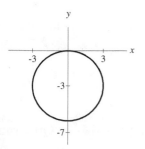

53. Completing the square, we obtain

$$
\begin{aligned}
(x^2 + 6x + 9) + (y^2 + 8y + 16) &= 9 + 16 \\
(x + 3)^2 + (y + 4)^2 &= 25.
\end{aligned}
$$

The center is $(-3, -4)$ and the radius is 5.

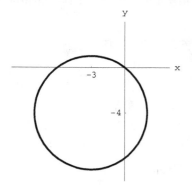

55. Completing the square, we find

$$
\begin{aligned}
\left(x^2 - 3x + \frac{9}{4}\right) + \left(y^2 + 2y + 1\right) &= \frac{3}{4} + \frac{9}{4} + 1 \\
\left(x - \frac{3}{2}\right)^2 + (y + 1)^2 &= 4.
\end{aligned}
$$

The center is $\left(\dfrac{3}{2}, -1\right)$ and the radius is 2.

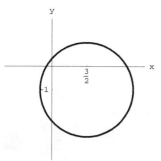

57. Completing the square, we obtain

$$
\begin{aligned}
(x^2 - 6x + 9) + (y^2 - 8y + 16) &= 9 + 16 \\
(x - 3)^2 + (y - 4)^2 &= 25.
\end{aligned}
$$

The center is $(3, 4)$ and the radius is 5.

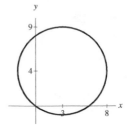

59. Completing the square, we obtain

$$(x^2 - 4x + 4) + \left(y^2 - 3y + \frac{9}{4}\right) = 4 + \frac{9}{4}$$

$$(x - 2)^2 + \left(y - \frac{3}{2}\right)^2 = \frac{25}{4}.$$

The center is $\left(2, \dfrac{3}{2}\right)$ and the radius is $\dfrac{5}{2}$.

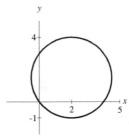

61. Completing the square, we obtain

$$\left(x^2 - \frac{1}{2}x + \frac{1}{16}\right) + \left(y^2 + \frac{1}{3}y + \frac{1}{36}\right) = \frac{1}{36}$$

$$\left(x - \frac{1}{4}\right)^2 + \left(y + \frac{1}{6}\right)^2 = \frac{1}{36}.$$

The center is $\left(\dfrac{1}{4}, -\dfrac{1}{6}\right)$ and the radius is $\dfrac{1}{6}$.

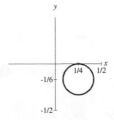

63. a. Since the center is $(0, 0)$ and the radius is 7, the standard equation is $x^2 + y^2 = 49$.

b. The radius, which is the distance between $(1, 0)$ and $(3, 4)$, is given by

$$\sqrt{(3 - 1)^2 + (4 - 0)^2} = \sqrt{20}.$$

Together with the center $(1, 0)$, it follows that the standard equation is

$$(x - 1)^2 + y^2 = 20.$$

c. Using the midpoint formula, the center is

$$\left(\frac{3 - 1}{2}, \frac{5 - 1}{2}\right) = (1, 2).$$

The diameter is

$$\sqrt{(3 - (-1))^2 + (5 - (-1))^2} = \sqrt{52}.$$

Since the square of the radius is

$$\left(\frac{1}{2}\sqrt{52}\right)^2 = 13,$$

the standard equation is

$$(x - 1)^2 + (y - 2)^2 = 13.$$

65. a. Since the center is $(2, -3)$ and the radius is 2, the standard equation is

$$(x - 2)^2 + (y + 3)^2 = 4.$$

b. The center is $(-2, 1)$, the radius is 1, and the standard equation is

$$(x + 2)^2 + (y - 1)^2 = 1.$$

c. The center is $(3, -1)$, the radius is 3, and the standard equation is

$$(x - 3)^2 + (y + 1)^2 = 9.$$

d. The center is $(0, 0)$, the radius is 1, and the standard equation is

$$x^2 + y^2 = 1.$$

67. $y = 3x - 4$ goes through $(0, -4)$, $\left(\dfrac{4}{3}, 0\right)$.

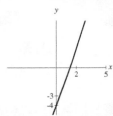

69. $3x - y = 6$ goes through $(0, -6)$, $(2, 0)$.

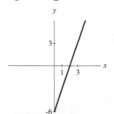

71. $x = 3y - 90$ goes through $(0, 30)$, $(-90, 0)$.

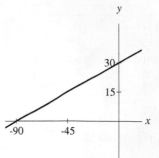

73. $\dfrac{2}{3}y - \dfrac{1}{2}x = 400$ goes through $(0, 600)$, $(-800, 0)$.

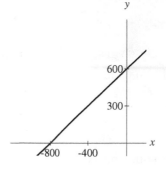

75. Intercepts are $(0, 0.0025)$, $(0.005, 0)$.

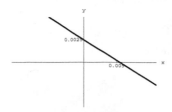

77. Intercepts are $(0, 2500)$, $(5000, 0)$.

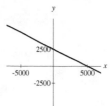

79. $x = 5$

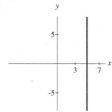

81. $y = 4$

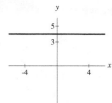

83. $x = -4$

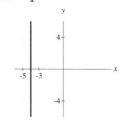

85. Solving for y, we have $y = 1$.

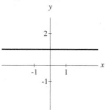

87. Since the x-intercept of $y = 2.4x - 8.64$ is $(3.6, 0)$, the solution set of $2.4x - 8.64 = 0$ is $\{3.6\}$.

89. Since the x-intercept of $y = -\dfrac{3}{7}x + 6$ is $(14, 0)$, the solution set of $-\dfrac{3}{7}x + 6 = 0$ is $\{14\}$.

91. The solution is $x = -\dfrac{3.4}{12} \approx -2.83$.

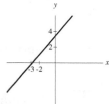

93. The solution is $\dfrac{687}{1.23} \approx 558.54$

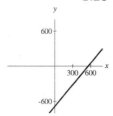

95. The solution is $\dfrac{3497}{0.03} \approx 116,566.67$

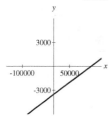

97. Note,

$$
\begin{aligned}
4.3 - 3.1(2.3x) + 3.1(9.9) &= 0 \\
4.3 - 7.13x + 30.69 &= 0 \\
34.99 - 7.13x &= 0 \\
x &= \frac{3499}{713} \\
x &\approx 4.91.
\end{aligned}
$$

The solution set is $\{4.91\}$.

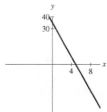

99. a) The midpoint is

$$
\left(\frac{0+30}{2}, \frac{20.8+25.1}{2} \right) = (15, 22.95).
$$

The median of age at first marriage in 1985 was 22.95 years.

b) The distance is

$$
\sqrt{(2000-1970)^2 + (25.1-20.8)^2} \approx 30.3
$$

Because of the units, the distance is meaningless.

101. Given $D = 22,800$ lbs, the graph of

$$
C = \frac{4B}{\sqrt[3]{22,800}} \text{ is given below.}
$$

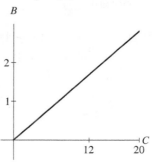

For Island Packet 40, $C = \dfrac{4\left(12 + \frac{11}{12}\right)}{\sqrt[3]{22,800}} \approx 1.8$.

103. By the distance formula, we find

$$
AB = \sqrt{(1+4)^2 + (1+5)^2} = \sqrt{25+36} = \sqrt{61}.
$$

Similarly, we obtain

$$
BC = \sqrt{61}
$$

and

$$
AC = \sqrt{244} = 2\sqrt{61}.
$$

Since

$$
AB + BC = AC
$$

we conclude that A, B, and C are collinear.

105. The distance between $(10,0)$ and $(0,0)$ is 10. The distance between $(1,3)$ and the origin is $\sqrt{10}$.

If two points have integer coordinates, then the distance between them is of the form $\sqrt{s^2 + t^2}$ where s^2, t^2 lies in the set

$$
\{0, 1, 2^2, 3^2, 4^2, ...\} = \{0, 1, 4, 9, 16, ...\}.
$$

Note, there exists no pair s^2 and t^2 in $\{0, 1, 4, 9, 16, ...\}$ satisfying $s^2 + t^2 = 19$. Thus, one cannot find two points with integer coordinates whose distance between them is $\sqrt{19}$.

109. a) Conditional equation, satisfied only by $x = 1/2$.

b) Identity, both sides are equivalent to $2x+4$.

c) Inconsistent equation, equation has no solution.

111. Cross-multiply to obtain

$$(x-2)(x+9) = (x+3)(x+4)$$
$$x^2 + 7x - 18 = x^2 + 7x + 12$$
$$-18 = 12$$

Inconsistent, the solution set is $\emptyset$.

113.

$$ax + b = cx + d$$
$$ax - cx = d - b$$
$$x(a - c) = d - b$$
$$x = \frac{d-b}{a-c}$$

For Thought

1. False, the slope is $\frac{3-2}{3-2} = 1$.

2. False, the slope is $\frac{5-1}{-3-(-3)} = \frac{4}{0}$ which is undefined.

3. False, slopes of vertical lines are undefined.

4. False, it is a vertical line. **5.** True

6. False, $x = 1$ cannot be written in the slope-intercept form.

7. False, the slope is -2.

8. True **9.** False **10.** True

4 Exercises

1. rise

3. slope

5. slope-intercept

7. perpendicular

9. $\frac{5-3}{4+2} = \frac{1}{3}$

11. $\frac{3+5}{1-3} = -4$

13. $\frac{2-2}{5+3} = 0$

15. $\frac{1/2 - 1/4}{1/4 - 1/8} = \frac{1/4}{1/8} = 2$

17. $\frac{3-(-1)}{5-5} = \frac{4}{0}$, no slope

19. The slope is $m = \frac{4-(-1)}{3-(-1)} = \frac{5}{4}$. Since $y+1 = \frac{5}{4}(x+1)$, we get $y = \frac{5}{4}x + \frac{5}{4} - 1$ or $y = \frac{5}{4}x + \frac{1}{4}$.

21. The slope is $m = \frac{-1-6}{4-(-2)} = -\frac{7}{6}$. Since $y + 1 = -\frac{7}{6}(x-4)$, we obtain $y = -\frac{7}{6}x + \frac{14}{3} - 1$ or $y = -\frac{7}{6}x + \frac{11}{3}$.

23. The slope is $m = \frac{5-5}{-3-3} = 0$. Since $y - 5 = 0(x-3)$, we get $y = 5$.

25. Since $m = \frac{12-(-3)}{4-4} = \frac{15}{0}$ is undefined, the equation of the vertical line is $x = 4$.

27. The slope of the line through $(0,-1)$ and $(3,1)$ is $m = \frac{2}{3}$. Since the y-intercept is $(0,-1)$, the line is given by $y = \frac{2}{3}x - 1$.

29. The slope of the line through $(1,4)$ and $(-1,1)$ is $m = \frac{5}{2}$. Solving for y in $y - 1 = \frac{5}{2}(x+1)$, we get $y = \frac{5}{2}x + \frac{3}{2}$.

31. The slope of the line through $(0,4)$ and $(2,0)$ is $m = -2$. Since the y-intercept is $(0,4)$, the line is given by $y = -2x + 4$.

33. The slope of the line through $(1,4)$ and $(-3,-2)$ is $m = \frac{3}{2}$. Solving for y in $y - 4 = \frac{3}{2}(x-1)$, we get $y = \frac{3}{2}x + \frac{5}{2}$.

35. $y = \frac{3}{5}x - 2$, slope is $\frac{3}{5}$, y-intercept is $(0,-2)$

37. Since $y - 3 = 2x - 8$, $y = 2x - 5$. The slope is 2 and y-intercept is $(0, -5)$.

39. Since $y + 1 = \dfrac{1}{2}x + \dfrac{3}{2}$, $y = \dfrac{1}{2}x + \dfrac{1}{2}$.

The slope is $\dfrac{1}{2}$ and y-intercept is $\left(0, \dfrac{1}{2}\right)$.

41. Since $y = 4$, the slope is $m = 0$ and the y-intercept is $(0, 4)$.

43.

$$
\begin{aligned}
y - 5 &= \frac{1}{4}(x + 8) \\
y - 5 &= \frac{1}{4}x + 2 \\
y &= \frac{1}{4}x + 7
\end{aligned}
$$

45.

$$
\begin{aligned}
y + 2 &= -\frac{1}{2}(x + 3) \\
y + 2 &= -\frac{1}{2}x - \frac{3}{2} \\
y &= -\frac{1}{2}x - \frac{7}{2}
\end{aligned}
$$

47. $y = \dfrac{1}{2}x - 2$ goes through the points $(0, -2), (2, -1),$ and $(4, 0)$.

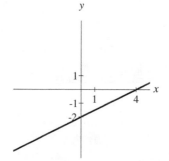

49. $y = -3x + 1$ goes through $(0, 1), (1, -2)$

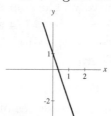

51. $y = -\dfrac{3}{4}x - 1$ goes through $(0, -1), (-4/3, 0)$

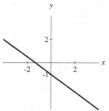

53. $x - y = 3$ goes through $(0, -3), (3, 0)$

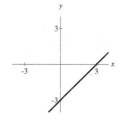

55. $y = 5$ is a horizontal line

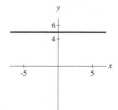

57. Since $m = \dfrac{4}{3}$ and $y - 0 = \dfrac{4}{3}(x - 3)$, we have $4x - 3y = 12$.

59. Since $m = \dfrac{4}{5}$ and $y - 3 = \dfrac{4}{5}(x - 2)$, we obtain $5y - 15 = 4x - 8$ and $4x - 5y = -7$.

61. $x = -4$ is a vertical line.

63. Note, the slope is

$$
m = \frac{\dfrac{2}{3} + 2}{2 + \dfrac{1}{2}} = \frac{8/3}{5/2} = \frac{16}{15}.
$$

Using the point-slope form, we obtain a standard equation of the line using only integers.

$$
\begin{aligned}
y - \frac{2}{3} &= \frac{16}{15}(x - 2) \\
15y - 10 &= 16(x - 2) \\
15y - 10 &= 16x - 32 \\
-16x + 15y &= -22 \\
16x - 15y &= 22
\end{aligned}
$$

65. The slope is

$$m = \dfrac{\dfrac{1}{4} - \dfrac{1}{5}}{\dfrac{1}{2} + \dfrac{1}{3}} = \dfrac{1/20}{5/6} = \dfrac{3}{50}.$$

Using the point-slope form, we get a standard equation of the line using only integers.

$$
\begin{aligned}
y - \frac{1}{4} &= \frac{3}{50}\left(x - \frac{1}{2}\right) \\
100y - 25 &= 6\left(x - \frac{1}{2}\right) \\
100y - 25 &= 6x - 3 \\
-22 &= 6x - 100y \\
3x - 50y &= -11
\end{aligned}
$$

67. 0.5   **69.** −1   **71.** 0

73. Since $y + 2 = 2(x - 1)$, $2x - y = 4$

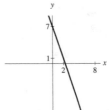

75. Since slope of $y = -3x$ is -3 and $y - 4 = -3(x - 1)$, we obtain $3x + y = 7$.

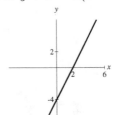

77. Since the slope of $5x - 7y = 35$ is $\dfrac{5}{7}$, we obtain

$y - 1 = \dfrac{5}{7}(x - 6)$. Multiplying by 7, we get $7y - 7 = 5x - 3$ or equivalently $5x - 7y = 23$.

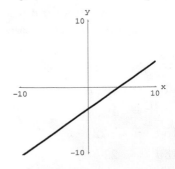

79. Since the slope of $y = \dfrac{2}{3}x + 5$ is $\dfrac{2}{3}$, we obtain

$y + 3 = -\dfrac{3}{2}(x - 2)$. Multiplying by 2, we find $2y + 6 = -3x + 6$ or equivalently $3x + 2y = 0$.

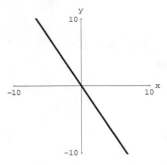

81. Since slope of $y = \dfrac{1}{2}x - \dfrac{3}{2}$ is $\dfrac{1}{2}$ and $y - 1 = -2(x + 3)$, we find $2x + y = -5$.

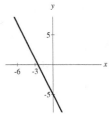

83. Since $x = 4$ is a vertical line, the horizontal line through $(2, 5)$ is $y = 5$.

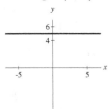

85. Since $\dfrac{5 - 3}{8 + 2} = \dfrac{1}{5} = -\dfrac{1}{a}$, we find $a = -5$.

87. Since $\dfrac{a - 3}{-2 - a} = -\dfrac{1}{2}$, we obtain $2a - 6 = 2 + a$ and $a = 8$.

89. Plot the points $A(-1, 2)$, $B(2, -1)$, $C(3, 3)$, and $D(-2, -2)$, respectively. The slopes of the opposite sides are $m_{AC} = m_{BD} = 1/4$ and $m_{AD} = m_{BC} = 4$. Since the opposite sides are parallel, it is a parallelogram.

91. Plot the points $A(-5, -1)$, $B(-3, -4)$, $C(3, 0)$, and $D(1, 3)$, respectively. The slopes of the opposite sides are $m_{AB} = m_{CD} = -3/2$ and $m_{AD} = m_{BC} = 2/3$. Since the adjacent sides are perpendicular, it is a rectangle.

93. Plot the points $A(-5, 1)$, $B(-2, -3)$, and $C(4, 2)$, respectively. The slopes of the sides are $m_{AB} = -4/3$, $m_{BC} = 5/6$ and $m_{AC} = 1/9$. It is not a right triangle since no two sides are perpendicular.

95. Yes, they appear to be parallel. However, they are not parallel since their slopes are not equal, i.e., $\dfrac{1}{3} \neq 0.33$.

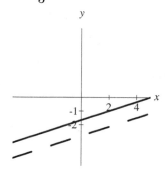

97. Since $x^3 - 8 = (x - 2)(x^2 + 2x + 4)$, we obtain $\dfrac{x^3 - 8}{x^2 + 2x + 4} = x - 2$. A linear function for the graph is $y = x - 2$.

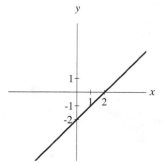

99. The slope is $\dfrac{212 - 32}{100 - 0} = \dfrac{9}{5}$.

Since $F - 32 = \dfrac{9}{5}(C - 0)$, $F = \dfrac{9}{5}C + 32$.

When $C = 150$, $F = \dfrac{9}{5}(150) + 32 = 302^{o}\text{F}$.

101. Thee linear function through $(1, 49)$ and $(2, 48)$
is $c = 50 - n$. With $n = 40$ people in a tour she would charge \$10 each and make \$400.

103. The slope is $\dfrac{75 - 95}{4000} = -0.005$. Since $S - 95 = -0.005(D - 0)$, we obtain $S = -0.005D + 95$.

105. Let c and p be the number of computers and printers, respectively. Since $60000 = 2000c + 1500p$, we have

$$2000c = -1500p + 60000$$
$$c = -\dfrac{3}{4}p + 30.$$

The slope is $-\dfrac{3}{4}$, i.e., if 4 more printers are purchased then 3 fewer computers must be bought.

107. Using the equation of the line given by $y = -\dfrac{3x}{5} + \dfrac{43}{5}$, the y-values are integers exactly for $x = -4, 1, 6, 11$ in $[-9, 21]$. The points with integral coordinates are $(-4, 11)$, $(1, 8)$, $(6, 5)$, and $(11, 2)$.

109.

$$d = \dfrac{|5(3) - 12(-6) - 2|}{\sqrt{5^2 + (-12)^2}}$$
$$d = \dfrac{85}{\sqrt{169}}$$
$$d = \dfrac{85}{13}$$

111.

$$d = \dfrac{|(-5)(1) + (1)(3) + 4|}{\sqrt{(-5)^2 + 1^2}}$$
$$d = \dfrac{2}{\sqrt{26}}$$
$$d = \dfrac{2\sqrt{26}}{26}$$
$$d = \dfrac{\sqrt{26}}{13}$$

113. Let $b_1 \neq b_2$. If $y = mx + b_1$ and $y = mx + b_2$ have a point (s, t) in common, then $ms + b_1 = ms + b_2$. After subtracting ms from both sides, we get $b_1 = b_2$; a contradiction. Thus, $y = mx + b_1$ and $y = mx + b_2$ have no points in common if $b_1 \neq b_2$.

115.

$$3 = 5|x - 4|$$
$$\frac{3}{5} = |x - 4|$$
$$\pm\frac{3}{5} = x - 4$$
$$4 \pm \frac{3}{5} = x$$

The solution set is $\{17/5, 23/5\}$.

117. The midpoint or center is $((1+3)/2, (3+9)/2)$ or $(2, 6)$. The radius is

$$\sqrt{(2-1)^2 + (6-3)^2} = \sqrt{10}.$$

The circle is given by

$$(x - 2)^2 + (x - 6)^2 = 10.$$

119. Note, $|x - 4| = \frac{0}{-5} = 0$.

Then $x = 4$, and the solution set is $\{4\}$.

For Thought

1. True, a scatter diagram is a graph consisting of ordered pairs.

2. True

3. False, it is possible for the variables to have no relationship.

4. True

5. True, in fact, if $r = 1$, the data is perfectly in line.

6. True. In addition, if $r = -1$ then the data is perfectly in line.

7. False, since $r = 0.002$ is close to zero, we say that there is no positive correlation.

8. False, since $r = -0.001$ is approximatley zero, we say that there is no negative correlation.

9. False, interpolating is making a prediction within the range of the data.

10. False, extrapolating is making a prediction outside the range of the data.

5 Exercises

1. scatter diagram

3. Linear relationship

5. No relationship

7. Nonlinear relationship

9. Linear relationship

11. Linear relationship

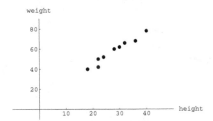

13. Linear relationship

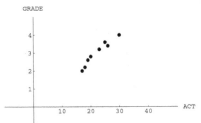

15. No relationship

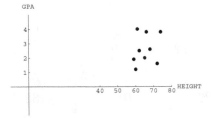

Equations, Inequalities, and Modeling

17. The missing entries are $(3.3, 160)$ and $(4.0, 193)$.

19. Missing entries are $(132, 34)$ and $(148, 25)$.

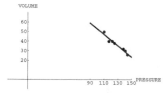

21. a) With a graphing calculator, we find

$$y = 13,450x + 956,752.7$$

or

$$y = 13,450x + 956,753$$

b) If $x = 10$, then

$$y = 13,450(10) + 956,752.7 \approx 1,091,253$$

c) The coal use increases by 13,450 thousand tons per year.

23. a) With a graphing calculator, we find

$$y = 44.8x + 1075.3$$

b) Let $y = 2000$. The solution to

$$2000 = 44.8x + 1075.3$$

is $x = \dfrac{924.7}{44.8} \approx 21$.

In 2021, money supply will be $2 trillion.

c) If $x = -5$, then

$$44.8(-5) + 1075.3 \approx 851.$$

In 1995, money supply was $851 billion.

25. With a calculator, we get $p = -0.069A + 0.403$. If $A = 4$, then

$$p = -0.069(4) + 0.403 = 0.127.$$

Thus, 12.7% of the runners in age group 4 are predicted to be injured.

27. Note, $x - 5 = x + 7$ has no solution.

$$
\begin{aligned}
x - 5 &= \pm(x + 7) \\
x - 5 &= -(x + 7) \\
2x &= -2 \\
x &= -1
\end{aligned}
$$

The solution set is $\{-1\}$.

29. Completing the square:

$$
\begin{aligned}
(x + 4)^2 + (y - 5)^2 &= 16 + 25 \\
(x + 4)^2 + (y - 5)^2 &= 41
\end{aligned}
$$

The center is $(-4, 5)$ with radius $R = \sqrt{41}$

31. Since $y = \frac{3}{5}x + \frac{11}{5}$, the slope is $\frac{3}{5}$.

For Thought

1. True, since $i \cdot (-i) = 1$.

2. True, since $\overline{0 + i} = 0 - i = -i$.

3. False, the set of real numbers is a subset of the complex numbers.

4. True, $(\sqrt{3} - i\sqrt{2})(\sqrt{3} + i\sqrt{2}) = 3 + 2 = 5$.

5. False, since $(2 + 5i)(2 + 5i) = 4 + 20i + 25i^2 = 4 + 20i - 25 = -21 + 20i$.

6. False, $5 - \sqrt{-9} = 5 - 3i$.

7. True, since $(3i)^2 + 9 = (-9) + 9 = 0$.

8. True, since $(-3i)^2 + 9 = (-9) + 9 = 0$.

9. True, since $i^4 = i^2 \cdot i^2 = (-1)(-1) = 1$.

10. False, $i^{18} = (i^4)^4 i^2 = (1)^4(-1) = -1$.

6 Exercises

1. complex numbers

3. imaginary number

5. $0 + 6i$, imaginary

7. $\frac{1}{3} + \frac{1}{3}i$, imaginary

9. $\sqrt{7} + 0i$, real

11. $\dfrac{\pi}{2} + 0i$, real

13. $7 + 2i$

15. $1 - i - 3 - 2i = -2 - 3i$

17. $1 + 3 - i\sqrt{2} + 2i\sqrt{2} = 4 + i\sqrt{2}$

19. $5 - \dfrac{1}{2} + \dfrac{1}{3}i + \dfrac{1}{2}i = \dfrac{9}{2} + \dfrac{5}{6}i$

21. $-18i + 12i^2 = -12 - 18i$

23. $8 + 12i - 12i - 18i^2 = 26 + 0i$

25. $(4 - 5i)(6 + 2i) = 24 + 8i - 30i + 10 = 34 - 22i$

27. $(5 - 2i)(5 + 2i) = 25 - 4i^2 = 25 - 4(-1) = 29$

29. $(\sqrt{3} - i)(\sqrt{3} + i) = 3 - i^2 = 3 - (-1) = 4$

31. $9 + 24i + 16i^2 = -7 + 24i$

33. $5 - 4i\sqrt{5} + 4i^2 = 1 - 4i\sqrt{5}$

35. $\left(i^4\right)^4 \cdot i = (1)^4 \cdot i = i$

37. $\left(i^4\right)^{24} i^2 = 1^{24}(-1) = -1$

39. Since $i^4 = 1$, we get $i^{-1} = i^{-1}i^4 = i^3 = -i$.

41. Since $i^4 = 1$, we get $i^{-3} = i^{-3}i^4 = i^1 = i$.

43. Since $i^{16} = 1$, we get $i^{-13} = i^{-13}i^{16} = i^3 = -i$.

45. Since $i^{-4} = 1$, we get $i^{-38} = i^2 i^{-40} = i^2(i^{-4})^{10} = i^2(1) = -1$.

47. $(3 - 9i)(3 + 9i) = 9 - 81i^2 = 90$

49. $\left(\dfrac{1}{2} + 2i\right)\left(\dfrac{1}{2} - 2i\right) = \dfrac{1}{4} - 4i^2 = \dfrac{1}{4} + 4 = \dfrac{17}{4}$

51. $i(-i) = -i^2 = 1$

53. $(3 - i\sqrt{3})(3 + i\sqrt{3}) = 9 - 3i^2 = 9 - 3(-1) = 12$

55. $\dfrac{1}{2 - i} \cdot \dfrac{2 + i}{2 + i} = \dfrac{2 + i}{5} = \dfrac{2}{5} + \dfrac{1}{5}i$

57. $\dfrac{-3i}{1 - i} \cdot \dfrac{1 + i}{1 + i} = \dfrac{-3i + 3}{2} = \dfrac{3}{2} - \dfrac{3}{2}i$

59.

$$\dfrac{-3 + 3i}{i} \cdot \dfrac{-i}{-i} = \dfrac{3i - 3i^2}{1} = 3i - 3(-1) = 3 + 3i$$

61.

$$\dfrac{1 - i}{3 + 2i} \cdot \dfrac{3 - 2i}{3 - 2i} = \dfrac{3 - 5i - 2}{13} = \dfrac{1}{13} - \dfrac{5}{13}i$$

63.

$$\dfrac{2 - i}{3 + 5i} \cdot \dfrac{3 - 5i}{3 - 5i} = \dfrac{6 - 10i - 3i - 5}{34} = \dfrac{1}{34} - \dfrac{13}{34}i$$

65. $2i - 3i = -i$

67. $-4 + 2i$

69. $\left(i\sqrt{6}\right)^2 = -6$

71. $(i\sqrt{2})(i\sqrt{50}) = i^2\sqrt{2}\cdot 5\sqrt{2} = (-1)(2)(5) = -10$

73.

$$\dfrac{-2}{2} + \dfrac{i\sqrt{20}}{2} = -1 + i\dfrac{2\sqrt{5}}{2} = -1 + \sqrt{5}i$$

75. $-3 + \sqrt{9 - 20} = -3 + i\sqrt{11}$

77. $2i\sqrt{2}\left(i\sqrt{2} + 2\sqrt{2}\right) = 4i^2 + 8i = -4 + 8i$

79. $\dfrac{-2 + \sqrt{-16}}{2} = \dfrac{-2 + 4i}{2} = -1 + 2i$

81. $\dfrac{-4 + \sqrt{16 - 24}}{4} = \dfrac{-4 + 2\sqrt{2}i}{4} = \dfrac{-2 + i\sqrt{2}}{2}$

83. $\dfrac{-6 - \sqrt{-32}}{2} = \dfrac{-6 - 4i\sqrt{2}}{2} = -3 - 2i\sqrt{2}$

85. $\dfrac{-6 - \sqrt{36 + 48}}{-4} = \dfrac{-6 - 2\sqrt{21}}{-4} = \dfrac{3 + \sqrt{21}}{2}$

87. $(3 - 5i)(3 + 5i) = 3^2 + 5^2 = 34$

89. $(3 - 5i) + (3 + 5i) = 6$

91.

$$\dfrac{3 - 5i}{3 + 5i} \cdot \dfrac{3 - 5i}{3 - 5i} = \dfrac{9 - 15i - 15i - 25}{34} =$$
$$-\dfrac{16}{34} - \dfrac{30}{34}i = -\dfrac{8}{17} - \dfrac{15}{17}i$$

93. $(6 - 2i) - (7 - 3i) = 6 - 7 - 2i + 3i = -1 + i$

95. $i^5(i^2 - 3i) = i(-1 - 3i) = -i + 3 = 3 - i$

97. If r is the remainder when n is divided by 4, then $i^n = i^r$. The possible values of r are $0, 1, 2, 3$ and for i^r they are $1, i, -1, -i$, respectively.

99. Note, $w + \overline{w} = (a + bi) + (a - bi) = 2a$ is a real number and $w - \overline{w} = (a + bi) - (a - bi) = 2bi$ is an imaginary number.

When a complex number is added to its complex conjugate the sum is twice the real part of the complex number. When the complex conjugate of a complex number is subtracted from the complex number, the difference is an imaginary number.

101. The reciprocal is $\dfrac{1}{a + bi} = \dfrac{a - bi}{(a + bi)(a - bi)} =$

$$\dfrac{a - bi}{a^2 + b^2} = \dfrac{a}{a^2 + b^2} - \dfrac{b}{a^2 + b^2}i$$

103. Multiply both sides of the equation by 6.

$$
\begin{aligned}
3x + 24 &= x - 18 \\
2x &= -42
\end{aligned}
$$

The solution set is $\{-21\}$.

105. Since $P = 2W + 2L$, we obtain

$$
\begin{aligned}
2W &= P - 2L \\
W &= \dfrac{P - 2L}{2}.
\end{aligned}
$$

107. Let x be the number of gallons of ethanol that is needed.

$$
\begin{aligned}
\dfrac{50(.1) + x}{x + 50} &= 0.2 \\
5 + x &= 0.2x + 10. \\
0.8x &= 5 \\
x &= 6.25 \text{ gallons}
\end{aligned}
$$

Thinking Outside the Box

VII. 2178

VIII. $\dfrac{1}{2} + \dfrac{1}{3} + \dfrac{1}{10} + \dfrac{1}{15}$, $\dfrac{1}{2} + \dfrac{1}{3} + \dfrac{1}{9} + \dfrac{1}{18}$

$\dfrac{1}{2} + \dfrac{1}{3} + \dfrac{1}{8} + \dfrac{1}{24}$, $\dfrac{1}{2} + \dfrac{1}{3} + \dfrac{1}{7} + \dfrac{1}{42}$

$\dfrac{1}{2} + \dfrac{1}{4} + \dfrac{1}{6} + \dfrac{1}{12}$, $\dfrac{1}{2} + \dfrac{1}{4} + \dfrac{1}{5} + \dfrac{1}{20}$

6 Pop Quiz

1. $3 + 4 + 2i - i = 7 + i$

2. $(4 - 3i)(2 + i) = 8 + 4i - 6i + 3 = 11 - 2i$

3. $(2 - 3i)(2 + 3i) = 2^2 + 3^2 = 13$

4.
$$\dfrac{5}{2 - 3i} \cdot \dfrac{2 + 3i}{2 + 3i} = \dfrac{10 + 15i}{13} = \dfrac{10}{13} + \dfrac{15}{13}i$$

5. Since $i^4 = 1$, we get $i^{27} = i^3 \cdot i^{24} =$
$(-i)(i^4)^6 = (-i)(1)^6 = -i.$

6. $\pm 4i$

For Thought

1. False, since $x = 1$ is a solution of the first equation and not of the second equation.

2. False, since $x^2 + 1 = 0$ cannot be factored with real coefficients.

3. False, $\left(x + \dfrac{2}{3}\right)^2 = x^2 + \dfrac{4}{3}x + \dfrac{9}{4}$.

4. False, the solutions to $(x - 3)(2x + 5) = 0$ are
$$x = 3 \text{ and } x = -\dfrac{5}{2}.$$

5. False, $x^2 = 0$ has only $x = 0$ as its solution.

6. True, since $a = 1, b = -3$, and $c = 1$, then by the quadratic formula we obtain
$$x = \dfrac{3 \pm \sqrt{9 - 4}}{2} = \dfrac{3 \pm \sqrt{5}}{2}.$$

7. False, the quadratic formula can be used to solve any quadratic equation.

8. False, $x^2 + 1 = 0$ has only imaginary zeros.

9. True, for $b^2 - 4ac = 12^2 - 4(4)(9) = 0$.

10. True, $x^2 - 6x + 9 = (x - 3)^2 = 0$ has only one real solution, namely, $x = 3$.

7 Exercises

1. quadratic

3. discriminant

5. Since $(x-5)(x+4) = 0$, the solution set is $\{5, -4\}$.

7. Since $a^2 + 3a + 2 = (a+2)(a+1) = 0$, the solution set is $\{-2, -1\}$.

9. Since $(2x+1)(x-3) = 0$, the solution set is $\left\{-\dfrac{1}{2}, 3\right\}$.

11. Since $(2x-1)(3x-2) = 0$, the solution set is $\left\{\dfrac{1}{2}, \dfrac{2}{3}\right\}$.

13. Note, $y^2 + y - 12 = 30$. Subtracting 30 from both sides, one obtains $y^2 + y - 42 = 0$ or $(y+7)(y-6) = 0$. The solution set is $\{-7, 6\}$.

15. Since $x^2 = 5$, the solution set is $\{\pm\sqrt{5}\}$.

17. Since $x^2 = -\dfrac{2}{3}$, we find $x = \pm i\dfrac{\sqrt{2}}{\sqrt{3}}$.

The solution set is $\left\{\pm i\dfrac{\sqrt{6}}{3}\right\}$.

19. Since $x - 3 = \pm 3$, we get $x = 3 \pm 3$.

The solution set is $\{0, 6\}$.

21. By the square root property, we get $3x - 1 = \pm 0 = 0$. Solving for x, we obtain $x = \dfrac{1}{3}$. The solution set is $\left\{\dfrac{1}{3}\right\}$.

23. Since $x - \dfrac{1}{2} = \pm\dfrac{5}{2}$, it follows that $x = \dfrac{1}{2} \pm \dfrac{5}{2}$. The solution set is $\{-2, 3\}$.

25. Since $x + 2 = \pm 2i$, the solution set is $\{-2 \pm 2i\}$.

27. Since $x - \dfrac{2}{3} = \pm\dfrac{2}{3}$, we get

$$x = \frac{2}{3} \pm \frac{2}{3} = \frac{4}{3}, 0.$$

The solution set is $\left\{\dfrac{4}{3}, 0\right\}$.

29. $x^2 - 12x + \left(\dfrac{12}{2}\right)^2 = x^2 - 12x + 6^2 = x^2 - 12x + 36$

31. $r^2 + 3r + \left(\dfrac{3}{2}\right)^2 = r^2 + 3r + \dfrac{9}{4}$

33. $w^2 + \dfrac{1}{2}w + \left(\dfrac{1}{4}\right)^2 = w^2 + \dfrac{1}{2}w + \dfrac{1}{16}$

35. By completing the square, we derive

$$\begin{aligned}
x^2 + 6x &= -1 \\
x^2 + 6x + 9 &= -1 + 9 \\
(x+3)^2 &= 8 \\
x + 3 &= \pm 2\sqrt{2}.
\end{aligned}$$

The solution set is $\{-3 \pm 2\sqrt{2}\}$.

37. By completing the square, we find

$$\begin{aligned}
n^2 - 2n &= 1 \\
n^2 - 2n + 1 &= 1 + 1 \\
(n-1)^2 &= 2 \\
n - 1 &= \pm\sqrt{2}.
\end{aligned}$$

The solution set is $\{1 \pm \sqrt{2}\}$.

39.

$$\begin{aligned}
h^2 + 3h &= 1 \\
h^2 + 3h + \frac{9}{4} &= 1 + \frac{9}{4} \\
\left(h + \frac{3}{2}\right)^2 &= \frac{13}{4} \\
h + \frac{3}{2} &= \pm\frac{\sqrt{13}}{2}
\end{aligned}$$

The solution set is $\left\{\dfrac{-3 \pm \sqrt{13}}{2}\right\}$.

41.

$$\begin{aligned}
x^2 + \frac{5}{2}x &= 6 \\
x^2 + \frac{5}{2}x + \frac{25}{16} &= 6 + \frac{25}{16} \\
\left(x + \frac{5}{4}\right)^2 &= \frac{121}{16} \\
x &= -\frac{5}{4} \pm \frac{11}{4}
\end{aligned}$$

The solution set is $\left\{-4, \dfrac{3}{2}\right\}$.

43.

$$x^2 + \frac{2}{3}x = -\frac{1}{3}$$
$$x^2 + \frac{2}{3}x + \frac{1}{9} = -\frac{3}{9} + \frac{1}{9}$$
$$\left(x + \frac{1}{3}\right)^2 = -\frac{2}{9}$$
$$x = -\frac{1}{3} \pm i\frac{\sqrt{2}}{3}$$

The solution set is $\left\{\dfrac{-1 \pm i\sqrt{2}}{3}\right\}$.

45. Since $a = 1, b = 3, c = -4$ and

$$x = \frac{-3 \pm \sqrt{3^2 - 4(1)(-4)}}{2(1)} = \frac{-3 \pm \sqrt{25}}{2} =$$

$\dfrac{-3 \pm 5}{2}$, the solution set is $\{-4, 1\}$.

47. Since $a = 2, b = -5, c = -3$ and

$$x = \frac{5 \pm \sqrt{(-5)^2 - 4(2)(-3)}}{2(2)} = \frac{5 \pm \sqrt{49}}{4} =$$

$\dfrac{5 \pm 7}{4}$, the solution set is $\left\{-\dfrac{1}{2}, 3\right\}$.

49. Since $a = 9, b = 6, c = 1$ and

$$x = \frac{-6 \pm \sqrt{6^2 - 4(9)(1)}}{2(9)} = \frac{-6 \pm 0}{18},$$

the solution set is $\left\{-\dfrac{1}{3}\right\}$.

51. Since $a = 2, b = 0, c = -3$ and

$$x = \frac{0 \pm \sqrt{0^2 - 4(2)(-3)}}{2(2)} = \frac{\pm\sqrt{24}}{4} =$$

$\dfrac{\pm 2\sqrt{6}}{4}$, the solution set is $\left\{\pm\dfrac{\sqrt{6}}{2}\right\}$.

53. In $x^2 - 4x + 5 = 0$, $a = 1, b = -4, c = 5$.

Then $x = \dfrac{4 \pm \sqrt{(-4)^2 - 4(1)(5)}}{2(1)} =$

$\dfrac{4 \pm \sqrt{-4}}{2} = \dfrac{4 \pm 2i}{2}$.

The solution set is $\{2 \pm i\}$.

55. Note, $a = 1, b = -2$, and $c = 4$.

Then $x = \dfrac{2 \pm \sqrt{4 - 16}}{2} = \dfrac{2 \pm 2i\sqrt{3}}{2}$.

The solution set is $\left\{1 \pm i\sqrt{3}\right\}$.

57. Since $2x^2 - 2x + 5 = 0$, we find $a = 2, b = -2$,

and $c = 5$. Then $x = \dfrac{2 \pm \sqrt{4 - 40}}{4} = \dfrac{2 \pm 6i}{4}$.

The solution set is $\left\{\dfrac{1}{2} \pm \dfrac{3}{2}i\right\}$.

59. Since $a = 4, b = -8, c = 7$ and

$$x = \frac{8 \pm \sqrt{64 - 112}}{8} = \frac{8 \pm \sqrt{-48}}{8} =$$

$\dfrac{8 \pm 4i\sqrt{3}}{8}$, the solution set is $\left\{1 \pm \dfrac{\sqrt{3}}{2}i\right\}$.

61. Since $a = 3.2, b = 7.6$, and $c = -9$,

$$x = \frac{-7.6 \pm \sqrt{(7.6)^2 - 4(3.2)(-9)}}{2(3.2)} \approx$$

$\dfrac{-7.6 \pm \sqrt{172.96}}{6.4} \approx \dfrac{-7.6 \pm 13.151}{6.4}$.

The solution set is $\{-3.24, 0.87\}$.

63. Note, $a = 3.25, b = -4.6$, and $c = -22$.

Then $x = \dfrac{4.6 \pm \sqrt{(-4.6)^2 - 4(3.25)(-22)}}{2(3.25)}$

$= \dfrac{4.6 \pm \sqrt{307.16}}{6.5}$. The solution set

is $\{-1.99, 3.40\}$.

65. The discriminant is $(-30)^2 - 4(9)(25) = 900 - 900 = 0$. Only one solution and it is real.

67. The discriminant is $(-6)^2 - 4(5)(2) = 36 - 40 = -4$. There are no real solutions.

69. The discriminant is

$$12^2 - 4(7)(-1) = 144 + 28 = 172.$$

There are two distinct real solutions.

71. Note, x-intercepts are $\left(-\dfrac{2}{3}, 0\right)$ and $\left(\dfrac{1}{2}, 0\right)$.

The solution set is $\left\{-\dfrac{2}{3}, \dfrac{1}{2}\right\}$.

73. Since the x-intercepts are $(-3, 0)$ and $(5, 0)$,

the solution set is $\{-3, 5\}$.

75. Note, the graph of $y = 1.44x^2 - 8.4x + 12.25$ has exactly one x-intercept.

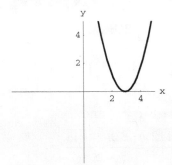

77. Note, the graph of $y = x^2 + 3x + 15$ has no x-intercept.

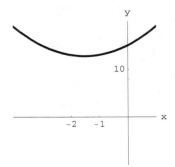

Thus, $x^2 + 3x + 15 = 0$ has no real solution.

79. The graph of $y = x^2 + 3x - 160$ has two x-intercepts.

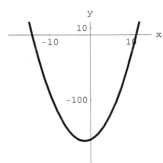

Then $x^2 + 3x - 160 = 0$ has two real solutions.

81. Set the right-hand side to 0.

$$x^2 - \frac{4}{3}x - \frac{5}{9} = 0$$
$$9x^2 - 12x - 5 = 0$$
$$(3x + 1)(3x - 5) = 0$$

The solution set is $\left\{ -\frac{1}{3}, \frac{5}{3} \right\}$.

83. Since $x^2 = \sqrt{2}$, $x = \pm\sqrt{\sqrt{2}} = \pm\sqrt[4]{2}$.

The solution set is $\left\{ \pm\sqrt[4]{2} \right\}$.

85. By the quadratic formula,

$$x = \frac{-\sqrt{6} \pm \sqrt{(-\sqrt{6})^2 - 4(12)(-1)}}{2(12)} =$$
$$\frac{-\sqrt{6} \pm \sqrt{54}}{24} = \frac{-\sqrt{6} \pm 3\sqrt{6}}{24} = \frac{2\sqrt{6}}{24}, \frac{-4\sqrt{6}}{24}.$$

The solution set is $\left\{ -\frac{\sqrt{6}}{6}, \frac{\sqrt{6}}{12} \right\}$.

87. Since $x^2 + 6x - 72 = (x + 12)(x - 6) = 0$, the solution set is $\{-12, 6\}$.

89. Multiply by x to get $x^2 = x + 1$. So $x^2 - x - 1 = 0$ and by the quadratic formula,

$$x = \frac{1 \pm \sqrt{1 - 4(1)(-1)}}{2} = \frac{1 \pm \sqrt{5}}{2}.$$

The solution set is $\left\{ \frac{1 \pm \sqrt{5}}{2} \right\}$.

91. Multiply by x^2 to get $28x - 7 = 7x^2$. Applying the quadratic formula to $7x^2 - 28x + 7 = 0$, we obtain

$$x = \frac{28 \pm \sqrt{588}}{14} = \frac{28 \pm 14\sqrt{3}}{14}.$$

The solution set is $\left\{ 2 \pm \sqrt{3} \right\}$.

93. Multiplying by $(3 - x)(x + 7)$,

$$
\begin{aligned}
(x - 12)(x + 7) &= (x + 4)(3 - x) \\
x^2 - 5x - 84 &= -x^2 - x + 12 \\
2x^2 - 4x - 96 &= 0 \\
2(x - 8)(x + 6) &= 0
\end{aligned}
$$

the solution set is $\{8, -6\}$.

95. Multiplying by $(x + 2)(x + 3)$, we find

$$
\begin{aligned}
(x - 8)(x + 3) &= (x + 2)(2x - 1) \\
x^2 - 5x - 24 &= 2x^2 + 3x - 2 \\
0 &= 2x^2 - 8x + 22 \\
0 &= x^2 - 4x + 11 \\
-11 + 4 &= x^2 - 4x + 4 \\
-7 &= (x - 2)^2.
\end{aligned}
$$

Since the left side is not a negative number, the solution set is the empty set $\emptyset$.

97. Multiplying by $(2x + 1)(2x + 3)$, we find

$$
\begin{aligned}
(2x + 3)^2 &= 8(2x + 1) \\
4x^2 + 12x + 9 &= 16x + 8 \\
4x^2 - 4x + 1 &= 0 \\
(2x - 1)^2 &= 0.
\end{aligned}
$$

Thus, the solution set is $\left\{\dfrac{1}{2}\right\}$.

99. Since $r^2 = \dfrac{A}{\pi}$, $r = \pm\sqrt{\dfrac{A}{\pi}}$.

101. We use the quadratic formula to solve

$$
x^2 + (2k)x + 3 = 0.
$$

Since $a = 1, b = 2k$, and $c = 3$, we obtain

$$
\begin{aligned}
x &= \frac{-2k \pm \sqrt{(2k)^2 - 4(1)(3)}}{2(1)} \\
x &= \frac{-2k \pm \sqrt{4k^2 - 12}}{2} \\
x &= \frac{-2k \pm \sqrt{4\left(k^2 - 3\right)}}{2} \\
x &= \frac{-2k \pm 2\sqrt{k^2 - 3}}{2} \\
x &= -k \pm \sqrt{k^2 - 3}.
\end{aligned}
$$

103. We use the quadratic formula to solve

$$
2y^2 + (4x)y - x^2 = 0.
$$

Since $a = 2, b = 4x$, and $c = -x^2$, we obtain

$$
y = \frac{-4x \pm \sqrt{(4x)^2 - 4(2)(-x^2)}}{2(2)} =
$$

$$
\frac{-4x \pm \sqrt{16x^2 + 8x^2}}{4} = \frac{-4x \pm \sqrt{24x^2}}{4}
$$

$$
\frac{-4x \pm 2|x|\sqrt{6}}{4} = x\left(-1 \pm \frac{\sqrt{6}}{2}\right)
$$

and note that we used $|x| = \sqrt{x^2}$.

105. From the revenue function,

$$
\begin{aligned}
x(40 - 0.001x) &= 175,000 \\
40x - 0.001x^2 &= 175,000
\end{aligned}
$$

By applying the quadratic formula to $0.001x^2 - 40x + 175,000 = 0$, we get

$$
\begin{aligned}
x &= \frac{40 \pm \sqrt{(40)^2 - 4(0.001)(175,000)}}{0.002} \\
x &= \frac{40 \pm \sqrt{900}}{0.002} = \frac{40 \pm 30}{0.002} \\
x &= 5000 \text{ or } 35,000
\end{aligned}
$$

Then 5000 units or 35,000 units must be produced weekly.

107. The height S (in feet) of the ball from the ground t seconds after it was tossed is given by $S = -16t^2 + 40t + 4$. When the height is 4 feet,

$$
\begin{aligned}
-16t^2 + 40t + 4 &= 4 \\
-16t^2 + 40t &= 0 \\
-8t(2t - 5) &= 0 \\
t &= 0, \frac{5}{2}.
\end{aligned}
$$

The ball returns to a height of 4 ft in 2.5 sec.

109. Let d be the diagonal distance across the field from one goal to the other. By the Pythagorean Theorem, we obtain $d = \sqrt{300^2 + 160^2} = 340$ ft.

111. Let w and $2w + 2$ be the length and width. From the given area of the court, we obtain

$$
\begin{aligned}
(2w + 2)w &= 312 \\
2w^2 + 2w - 312 &= 0 \\
w^2 + w - 156 &= 0 \\
(w - 12)(w + 13) &= 0
\end{aligned}
$$

Then $w = 12$ yd and the length is 26 yd. The distance between two opposite corners (by the Pythagorean Theorem) is $\sqrt{12^2 + 26^2} = 2\sqrt{205} \approx 28.6$ yd.

113. Substituting the values of S and A, we find that the displacement is

$$\frac{1}{2^{12}}d^2(18.8)^3 - 822^3 = 0$$

$$\frac{1}{2^{12}}d^2(18.8)^3 = 822^3$$

$$d = \sqrt{\frac{822^3(2^{12})}{18.8^3}}$$

$$d \approx 18,503.4 \text{ lbs.}$$

115. By choosing an appropriate coordinate system, we can assume the circle is given by $(x+r)^2+(y-r)^2 = r^2$ where $r > 0$ is the radius of the circle and $(-5, 1)$ is the common point between the block and the circle. Note, the radius is less than 5 feet. Substitute $x = -5$ and $y = 1$. Then we obtain

$$(-5 + r)^2 + (1 - r)^2 = r^2$$
$$r^2 - 10r + 25 + 1 - 2r + r^2 = r^2$$
$$r^2 - 12r + 26 = 0.$$

The solutions of the last quadratic equation are $r = 6 \pm \sqrt{10}$. Since $r < 5$, the radius of the circle is $r = 6 - \sqrt{10}$ ft.

117. Let x be the normal speed of the tortoise in ft/hr.

	distance	rate	time
hwy	24	$x+2$	$24/(x+2)$
off hwy	24	x	$24/x$

Since 24 minutes is $2/5$ of an hour, we get

$$\frac{2}{5} + \frac{24}{x+2} = \frac{24}{x}$$
$$2x(x+2) + 24(5)x = 24(5)(x+2)$$
$$2x^2 + 4x + 120x = 120x + 240$$
$$x^2 + 2x - 120 = 0$$
$$(x+12)(x-10) = 0$$
$$x = -12, 10.$$

The normal speed of the tortoise is 10 ft/hr.

119. Using $v_1^2 = v_0^2 + 2gS$ with $S = 1.07$ and $v_1 = 0$, we find that

$$v_0^2 + 2(-9.8)(1.07) = 0$$
$$v_0^2 - 20.972 = 0$$
$$v_0 = \pm\sqrt{20.972} \approx \pm 4.58.$$

His initial upward velocity is 4.58 m/sec.

Using $S = \frac{1}{2}gt^2 + v_0t$ with $S = 0$ and $v_o = 4.58$, we find that his time t in the air satisfies

$$\frac{1}{2}(-9.8)t^2 + 4.58t = 0$$
$$t(4.58 - 4.9t) = 0$$
$$t \approx 0, 0.93.$$

Carter is in the air for 0.93 seconds.

121. a) Let x be the number of years since 1980. With the aid of a graphing calculator, the quadratic regression curve is approximately

$$y = -0.067x^2 + 1.26x + 51.14$$

b) Using the regression curve in part a) and the quadratic formula, we find that the positive solution to

$$0 = ax^2 + bx + c$$

is

$$x = \frac{-b - \sqrt{b^2 - 4ac}}{2a} \approx 39.$$

In the year 2019, the extrapolated birth rate will be zero.

123. Let x and $x-2$ be the number of days it takes to design a direct mail package using traditional methods and a computer, respectively.

	rate
together	$2/7$
computer	$1/(x-2)$
traditional	$1/x$

$$\frac{1}{x-2} + \frac{1}{x} = \frac{2}{7}$$

$$7x + (7x - 14) = 2(x^2 - 2x)$$

$$0 = 2x^2 - 18x + 14$$

$$0 = x^2 - 9x + 7$$

$$x = \frac{9 \pm \sqrt{81 - 28}}{2}$$

$$x = \frac{9 \pm \sqrt{53}}{2}$$

$$x \approx 8.14, 0.86$$

Curt using traditional methods can do the job in 8.14 days. Note, $x \approx 0.86$ days has to be excluded since $x - 2$ is negative when $x \approx 0.86$.

125. Let x and $x - 10$ be the number of pounds of white meat in a Party Size bucket and a Big Family Size bucket, respectively. From the ratios, we obtain

$$\frac{8}{x} = \frac{3}{x-10} + 0.10$$

$$8(x - 10) = 3x + 0.10x(x - 10)$$

$$0 = 0.10x^2 - 6x + 80$$

$$0 = x^2 - 60x + 800$$

$$0 = (x - 40)(x - 20)$$

$$x = 40, 20$$

A Party Size bucket weighs 20 or 40 lbs.

127. Since the lines are parallel, we find C such that the point $(-2, 6)$ satisfies

$$4x - 5y = C$$

Then $-8 - 30 = C$ or $C = -38$. The standard form is $4x - 5y = -38$

129. Let x be the amount she invested in a CD.

$$0.05x + (x + 4000)0.06 = 1230$$

$$0.11x + 240 = 1230$$

$$0.11x = 990$$

$$x = \$9000$$

131. $2 - 3i$

For Thought

1. True

2. False, since $-2x < -6$ is equivalent to

$$\frac{-2x}{-2} > \frac{-6}{-2}.$$

3. False, since there is a number between any two distinct real numbers.

4. True, since $|-6 - 6| = |-12| = 12 > -1$.

5. False, $(-\infty, -3) \cap (-\infty, -2) = (-\infty, -3)$.

6. False, $(5, \infty) \cap (-\infty, -3) = \phi$.

7. False, no real number satisfies $|x - 2| < 0$.

8. False, it is equivalent to $|x| > 3$.

9. False, $|x| + 2 < 5$ is equivalent to $-3 < x < 3$.

10. True

7 Exercises

1. interval

3. closed

5. compound

7. $x < 12$

9. $x \geq -7$

11. $[-8, \infty)$

13. $(-\infty, \pi/2)$

15. Since $3x > 15$ implies $x > 5$, the solution set is $(5, \infty)$ and the graph is

17. Since $10 \leq 5x$ implies $2 \leq x$, the solution set is $[2, \infty)$ and the graph is

19. Multiply 6 to both sides of the inequality.

$$3x - 24 < 2x + 30$$

$$x < 54$$

The solution is the interval $(-\infty, 54)$ and the graph is

21. Multiplying the inequality by 2, we find

$$
\begin{aligned}
7 - 3x &\geq -6 \\
13 &\geq 3x \\
13/3 &\geq x.
\end{aligned}
$$

The solution is the interval $(-\infty, 13/3]$ and the graph is

23. Multiply the inequality by -5 and reverse the direction of the inequality.

$$
\begin{aligned}
2x - 3 &\leq 0 \\
2x &\leq 3 \\
x &\leq \frac{3}{2}
\end{aligned}
$$

The solution is the interval $(-\infty, 3/2]$ and the graph is

25. Multiply the left-hand side.

$$
\begin{aligned}
-6x + 4 &\geq 4 - x \\
0 &\geq 5x \\
0 &\geq x.
\end{aligned}
$$

The solution is the interval $(-\infty, 0]$ and the graph is

27. Using the portion of the graph below the x-axis, the solution set is $(-\infty, -3.5)$.

29. Using the part of the graph on or above the x-axis, the solution set is $(-\infty, 1.4]$.

31. By taking the part of the line $y = 2x - 3$ above the horizontal line $y = 5$ and by using $(4, 5)$, the solution set is $(4, \infty)$.

33. Note, the graph of $y = -3x - 7$ is above or on the graph of $y = x + 1$ for $x \leq -2$. Thus, the solution set is $(-\infty, -2]$.

35. $(-3, \infty)$

37. $(-3, \infty)$

39. $(-5, -2)$

41. ϕ

43. $(-\infty, 5]$

45. Solve each simple inequality and find the intersection of their solution sets.

$$
\begin{aligned}
x > 3 \quad &\text{and} \quad 0.5x < 3 \\
x > 3 \quad &\text{and} \quad x < 6
\end{aligned}
$$

The intersection of these values of x is the interval $(3, 6)$ and whose graph is

47. Solve each simple inequality and find the intersection of their solution sets.

$$
\begin{aligned}
2x - 5 > -4 \quad &\text{and} \quad 2x + 1 > 0 \\
x > \frac{1}{2} \quad &\text{and} \quad x > -\frac{1}{2}
\end{aligned}
$$

The intersection of these values of x is the interval $(1/2, \infty)$ and the graph is

49. Solve each simple inequality and find the union of their solution sets.

$$
\begin{aligned}
-6 < 2x \quad &\text{or} \quad 3x > -3 \\
-3 < x \quad &\text{or} \quad x > -1
\end{aligned}
$$

The union of these values of x is $(-3, \infty)$ and the graph is

51. Solve each simple inequality and find the union of their solution sets.

$$
\begin{aligned}
x + 1 > 6 \quad &\text{or} \quad x < 7 \\
x > 5 \quad &\text{or} \quad x < 7
\end{aligned}
$$

The union of these values of x is $(-\infty, \infty)$ and the graph is

53. Solve each simple inequality and find the intersection of their solution sets.

$$
\begin{aligned}
2 - 3x < 8 \quad &\text{and} \quad x - 8 \leq -12 \\
-6 < 3x \quad &\text{and} \quad x \leq -4 \\
-2 < x \quad &\text{and} \quad x \leq -4
\end{aligned}
$$

The intersection is empty and there is no solution.

55.

$$6 < 3x < 12$$
$$2 < x < 4$$

The solution set is the interval $(2, 4)$ and the graph is

57.

$$-6 \le -6x < 18$$
$$1 \ge x > -3$$

The solution set is the interval $(-3, 1]$ and the graph is

59. Solve an equivalent compound inequality.

$$-2 < 3x - 1 < 2$$
$$-1 < 3x < 3$$
$$-\frac{1}{3} < x < 1$$

The solution set is the interval $(-1/3, 1)$ and the graph is

61. Solve an equivalent compound inequality.

$$-1 \le 5 - 4x \le 1$$
$$-6 \le -4x \le -4$$
$$\frac{3}{2} \ge x \ge 1$$

The solution set is the interval $[1, 3/2]$ and the graph is

63. Solve an equivalent compound inequality.

$$x - 1 \ge 1 \quad \text{or} \quad x - 1 \le -1$$
$$x \ge 2 \quad \text{or} \quad x \le 0$$

The solution set is $(-\infty, 0] \cup [2, \infty)$ and the graph is

65. Solve an equivalent compound inequality.

$$5 - x > 3 \quad \text{or} \quad 5 - x < -3$$
$$2 > x \quad \text{or} \quad 8 < x$$

The solution set is $(-\infty, 2) \cup (8, \infty)$ and the graph is

67. Solve an equivalent compound inequality.

$$-5 \le 4 - x \le 5$$
$$-9 \le -x \le 1$$
$$9 \ge x \ge -1$$

The solution set is the interval $[-1, 9]$ and the graph is

69. No solution since an absolute value is never negative.

71. No solution since an absolute value is never negative.

73. Note, $3|x - 2| > 3$ or $|x - 2| > 1$.
We solve an equivalent compound inequality.

$$x - 2 > 1 \quad \text{or} \quad x - 2 < -1$$
$$x > 3 \quad \text{or} \quad x < 1$$

The solution set is $(-\infty, 1) \cup (3, \infty)$ and the graph is

75. Solve an equivalent compound inequality.

$$\frac{x - 3}{2} > 1 \quad \text{or} \quad \frac{x - 3}{2} < -1$$
$$x - 3 > 2 \quad \text{or} \quad x - 3 < -2$$
$$x > 5 \quad \text{or} \quad x < 1$$

The solution set is the interval $(-\infty, 1) \cup (5, \infty)$ and the graph is

77. $|x| < 5$

79. $|x| > 3$

81. Since 6 is the midpoint of 4 and 8, the inequality is $|x - 6| < 2$.

83. Since 4 is the midpoint of 3 and 5, the inequality is $|x - 4| > 1$.

85. $|x| \geq 9$

87. Since 7 is the midpoint, the inequality is $|x - 7| \leq 4$.

89. Since 5 is the midpoint, the inequality is $|x - 5| > 2$.

91. Since $x - 2 \geq 0$, the solution set is $[2, \infty)$.

93. Since $2 - x > 0$ is equivalent to $2 > x$, the solution set is $(-\infty, 2)$.

95. Since $|x| \geq 3$ is equivalent to $x \geq 3$ or $x \leq -3$, the solution set is $(-\infty, -3] \cup [3, \infty)$.

97. If x is the price of a car excluding sales tax then it must satisfy $0 \leq 1.1x + 300 \leq 8000$.

This is equivalent to $0 \leq x \leq \dfrac{7700}{1.1} = 7000$.

The price range of Yolanda's car is the interval [\$0, \$7000].

99. Let x be Lucky's score on the final exam.

$$
\begin{aligned}
79 &\leq \frac{65 + x}{2} \leq 90 \\
158 &\leq 65 + x \leq 180 \\
93 &\leq x \leq 115.
\end{aligned}
$$

Since $x \leq 100$, the final exam score must lie in $[93, 100]$.

101. Let x be Ingrid's final exam score. Since $\dfrac{2x + 65}{3}$ is her weighted average, we obtain

$$
\begin{aligned}
79 &< \frac{2x + 65}{3} < 90 \\
237 &< 2x + 65 < 270 \\
172 &< 2x < 205 \\
86 &< x < 102.5
\end{aligned}
$$

Since $x \leq 100$, Ingrid's final exam score must lie in $(86, 100]$.

103. If h is the height of the box, then

$$
\begin{aligned}
40 + 2(30) + 2h &\leq 130 \\
100 + 2h &\leq 130 \\
2h &\leq 30.
\end{aligned}
$$

The range of the height is (0 in., 15 in.].

105. By substituting $N = 50$ and $w = 27$ into $r = \dfrac{Nw}{n}$ we find $r = \dfrac{1350}{n}$. Moreover if $n = 14$, then $r = \dfrac{1350}{14} = 96.4 \approx 96$. Similarly, the other gear ratios are the following.

n	14	17	20	24	29
r	96	79	68	56	47

Yes, the bicycle has a gear ratio for each of the four types.

107. Let x be the price of a CL 600.

a) Then $|x - 130{,}645| > 10{,}000$

b) The above inequality is equivalent to

$$x - 130{,}645 > 10{,}000 \quad \text{or} \quad x - 130{,}645 < -10{,}000$$
$$x > 140{,}645 \quad \text{or} \quad x < 120{,}645.$$

Thus, the price of a CL 600 is less than \$120,645 or over \$140,645.

109. If x is the actual temperature, then

$$\left| \frac{x - 35}{35} \right| < 0.01$$

$$-0.35 < x - 35 < 0.35$$
$$34.65 < x < 35.35.$$

The actual temperature must lie in the interval $(34.65°, 35.35°)$.

111. If c is the actual circumference, then $c = \pi d$ and

$$
\begin{aligned}
|\pi d - 7.2| &\leq 0.1 \\
-0.1 \leq \pi d - 7.2 &\leq 0.1 \\
7.1 \leq \pi d &\leq 7.3 \\
2.26 \leq d &\leq 2.32.
\end{aligned}
$$

The actual diameter must lie in the interval [2.26 cm, 2.32 cm].

113. a) The inequality $|a - 38,611| < 3000$ is equivalent to

$$-3000 < \quad a - 38,611 \quad < 3000$$
$$35,611 < \qquad a \qquad < 41,611.$$

The states within this range are Colorado and Vermont.

b) The inequality $|a - 38,611| > 5000$ is equivalent to

$$a - 38,611 > 5000 \quad \text{or} \quad a - 38,611 < -5000$$
$$a > 43,611 \quad \text{or} \quad a < 33,6111$$

The states satisfying the inequality are Alabama, Georgia, Maryland, New Jersey, and South Carolina.

115.

$$x(x+2) = 0$$
$$x > 0, -2$$

The solution set is $\{-2, 0\}$.

117. Since the slope of $2x - y = 1$ is 2, the slope of a perpendicular line is $-\frac{1}{2}$. Then

$$y + 4 = -\frac{1}{2}(x - 3)$$
$$-2y - 8 > x - 3$$
$$-5 > x + 2y.$$

The standard form is $x + 2y = -5$.

119. Solving for y, we find

$$3y - ay = w + 9$$
$$y(3 - a) = w + 9$$
$$y = \frac{w + 9}{3 - a}$$

Chapter Review Exercises

1. Since $3x = 2$, the solution set is $\{2/3\}$.

3. Multiply by 60 to get $30y - 20 = 15y + 12$, or $15y = 32$. The solution set is $\{32/15\}$.

5. Multiply by $x(x - 1)$ to get $2x - 2 = 3x$. The solution set is $\{-2\}$.

7. Multiply by $(x + 1)(x - 3)$ and get $-2x - 3 = x - 2$. Then $-1 = 3x$. The solution set is $\{-1/3\}$.

9. The distance is $\sqrt{(-3 - 2)^2 + (5 - (-6))^2} = \sqrt{(-5)^2 + 11^2} = \sqrt{25 + 121} = \sqrt{146}$.

The midpoint is

$$\left(\frac{-3 + 2}{2}, \frac{5 - 6}{2}\right) = \left(-\frac{1}{2}, -\frac{1}{2}\right).$$

11. Distance is $\sqrt{\left(\frac{1}{2} - \frac{1}{4}\right)^2 + \left(\frac{1}{3} - 1\right)^2} =$

$$\sqrt{\left(\frac{1}{4}\right)^2 + \left(-\frac{2}{3}\right)^2} = \sqrt{\frac{1}{16} + \frac{4}{9}} = \sqrt{\frac{73}{144}} =$$

$\frac{\sqrt{73}}{12}$. Midpoint is $\left(\frac{1/2 + 1/4}{2}, \frac{1/3 + 1}{2}\right) =$

$\left(\frac{3/4}{2}, \frac{4/3}{2}\right) = \left(\frac{3}{8}, \frac{2}{3}\right).$

13. Circle with radius 5 and center at the origin.

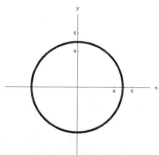

15. Equivalently, by using the method of completing the square, the circle is given by $(x + 2)^2 + y^2 = 4$. It has radius 2 and center $(-2, 0)$.

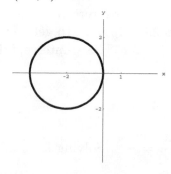

17. The line $y = -x + 25$ has intercepts $(0, 25)$, $(25, 0)$.

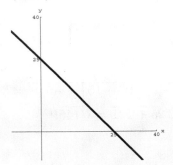

19. The line $y = 3x - 4$ has intercepts $(0, -4)$, $(4/3, 0)$.

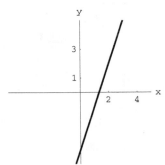

21. Vertical line $x = 5$ has intercept $(5, 0)$.

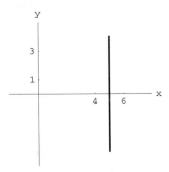

23. Simplify $(x - (-3))^2 + (y - 5)^2 = \left(\sqrt{3}\right)^2$.
The standard equation is $(x+3)^2 + (y-5)^2 = 3$.

25. Substitute $y = 0$ in $3x - 4y = 12$. Then $3x = 12$ or $x = 4$. The x-intercept is $(4, 0)$. Substitute $x = 0$ in $3x - 4y = 12$ to get $-4y = 12$ or $y = -3$. The y-intercept is $(0, -3)$.

27. $\dfrac{2 - (-6)}{-1 - 3} = \dfrac{8}{-4} = -2$

29. Note, $m = \dfrac{-1 - 3}{5 - (-2)} = -\dfrac{4}{7}$. Solving for y in

$y - 3 = -\dfrac{4}{7}(x + 2)$, we obtain $y = -\dfrac{4}{7}x + \dfrac{13}{7}$.

31. Note, the slope of $3x + y = -5$ is -3. The standard form for the line through $(2, -4)$ with slope $\dfrac{1}{3}$ is derived below.

$$
\begin{aligned}
y + 4 &= \tfrac{1}{3}(x - 2) \\
3y + 12 &= x - 2 \\
-x + 3y &= -14 \\
x - 3y &= 14
\end{aligned}
$$

33. Since $2x - 6 = 3y$, $y = \dfrac{2}{3}x - 2$.

35. Note, $y(x - 3) = 1$. Then $y = \dfrac{1}{x - 3}$.

37. Note, $by = -ax + c$. Then $y = -\dfrac{a}{b}x + \dfrac{c}{b}$ provided $b \neq 0$.

39. The discriminant of $x^2 - 4x + 2$ is $(-4)^2 - 4(2) = 8$. There are two distinct real solutions.

41. The discriminant is $(-20)^2 - 4(4)(25) = 0$. Only one real solution.

43. $3 - 4 - 7i + 6i = -1 - i$

45. $16 - 40i - 25 = -9 - 40i$

47. $2 + 6i - 6i + 18 = 20$

49. $\dfrac{2 - 3i}{i} \cdot \dfrac{-i}{-i} = \dfrac{-2i - 3}{1} = -3 - 2i$

51. $\dfrac{1 - i}{2 + i} \cdot \dfrac{2 - i}{2 - i} = \dfrac{1 - 3i}{5} = \dfrac{1}{5} - \dfrac{3}{5}i$

53. $\dfrac{1 + i}{2 - 3i} \cdot \dfrac{2 + 3i}{2 + 3i} = \dfrac{-1 + 5i}{13} = -\dfrac{1}{13} + \dfrac{5}{13}i$

55. $\dfrac{6 + 2i\sqrt{2}}{2} = 3 + i\sqrt{2}$

57. $\dfrac{-6 + \sqrt{-20}}{-8} = \dfrac{-6 + 2i\sqrt{5}}{-8} = \dfrac{3}{4} - \dfrac{\sqrt{5}}{4}i$

59. $i^{32}i^2 + i^{16}i^3 = (1)(-1) + (1)(-i) = -1 - i$

61. Since $x^2 = 5$, the solution set is $\{\pm\sqrt{5}\}$.

63. Since $x^2 = -8$, the solution set is $\{\pm 2i\sqrt{2}\}$.

65. Since $x^2 = -\dfrac{2}{4}$, the solution set is $\left\{\pm i \dfrac{\sqrt{2}}{2}\right\}$.

67. Since $x - 2 = \pm\sqrt{17}$, we get $x = 2 \pm \sqrt{17}$. The solution set is $\left\{2 \pm \sqrt{17}\right\}$.

69. Since $(x+3)(x-4) = 0$, the solution set is $\{-3, 4\}$.

71. We apply the method of completing the square.

$$
\begin{aligned}
b^2 - 6b + 10 &= 0 \\
b^2 - 6b + 9 &= -1 \\
(b - 3)^2 &= -1 \\
b - 3 &= \pm i
\end{aligned}
$$

The solution set is $\{3 \pm i\}$.

73. We apply the method of completing the square.

$$
\begin{aligned}
s^2 - 4s &= -1 \\
s^2 - 4s + 4 &= -1 + 4 \\
(s - 2)^2 &= 3 \\
s - 2 &= \pm\sqrt{3}
\end{aligned}
$$

The solution set is $\left\{2 \pm \sqrt{3}\right\}$.

75. Use the quadratic formula to solve $4x^2 - 4x - 5 = 0$.

$$
\begin{aligned}
x &= \frac{4 \pm \sqrt{(-4)^2 - 4(4)(-5)}}{2(4)} \\
&= \frac{4 \pm \sqrt{96}}{8} \\
&= \frac{4 \pm 4\sqrt{6}}{8} \\
&= \frac{1 \pm \sqrt{6}}{2}
\end{aligned}
$$

The solution set is $\left\{\dfrac{1 \pm \sqrt{6}}{2}\right\}$.

77. Subtracting 1 from both sides, we find

$$
\begin{aligned}
x^2 - 2x + 1 &= -1 \\
(x - 1)^2 &= -1 \\
x - 1 &= \pm i.
\end{aligned}
$$

The solution set is $\{1 \pm i\}$.

79. Multiplying by $2x(x - 1)$, we obtain

$$
\begin{aligned}
2(x - 1) + 2x &= 3x(x - 1) \\
0 &= 3x^2 - 7x + 2 \\
0 &= (x - 2)(3x - 1).
\end{aligned}
$$

The solution set is $\left\{\dfrac{1}{3}, 2\right\}$.

81. Solve an equivalent statement

$$
\begin{aligned}
3q - 4 = 2 \quad &\text{or} \quad 3q - 4 = -2 \\
3q = 6 \quad &\text{or} \quad 3q = 2.
\end{aligned}
$$

The solution set is $\{2/3, 2\}$.

83. We obtain

$$
\begin{aligned}
|2h - 3| &= 0 \\
2h - 3 &= 0 \\
h &= \frac{3}{2}.
\end{aligned}
$$

The solution set is $\left\{\dfrac{3}{2}\right\}$.

85. No solution since absolute values are nonnegative.

87. The solution set of $x > 3$ is the interval $(3, \infty)$ and the graph is

89. The solution set of $8 > 2x$ is the interval $(-\infty, 4)$ and the graph is

91. Since $-\dfrac{7}{3} > \dfrac{1}{2}x$, the solution set is $(-\infty, -14/3)$ and the graph is

93. After multiplying the inequality by 2 we have

$$
\begin{aligned}
-4 < x - 3 &\le 10 \\
-1 < x &\le 13.
\end{aligned}
$$

The solution set is the interval $(-1, 13]$ and the graph is

95. The solution set of $\dfrac{1}{2} < x$ and $x < 1$ is the interval $(1/2, 1)$ and the graph is

97. The solution set of $x > -4$ or $x > -1$ is the interval $(-4, \infty)$ and the graph is

99. Solving an equivalent statement, we get

$$x - 3 > 2 \quad \text{or} \quad x - 3 < -2$$
$$x > 5 \quad \text{or} \quad x < 1.$$

The solution set is $(-\infty, 1) \cup (5, \infty)$ and the graph is

101. Since an absolute value is nonnegative, $2x - 7 = 0$. The solution set is $\{7/2\}$ and the graph is

103. Since absolute values are nonnegative, the solution set is $(-\infty, \infty)$ and

the graph is

105. The solution set is $\{10\}$ since the x-intercept is $(10, 0)$.

107. Since the x-intercept is $(8, 0)$ and the y-values are negative in quadrants 3 and 4, the solution set is $(-\infty, 8)$.

109. Let x be the length of one side of the square. Since dimensions of the base are $8 - 2x$ and $11 - 2x$, we obtain

$$
\begin{aligned}
(11 - 2x)(8 - 2x) &= 50 \\
4x^2 - 38x + 38 &= 0 \\
2x^2 - 19x + 19 &= 0 \\
x = \frac{19 \pm \sqrt{209}}{4} &\approx 8.36, 1.14.
\end{aligned}
$$

But $x = 8.36$ is too big and so $x = 1.14$ inch.

111. Let x be the number of hours it takes Lisa or Taro to drive to the restaurant. Since the sum of the driving distances is 300, we obtain

$300 = 50x + 60x$. Thus, $x = \dfrac{300}{110} \approx 2.7272$ and Lisa drove $50(2.7272) \approx 136.4$ miles.

113. Let x and $8000 - x$ be the number of fish in Homer Lake and Mirror lake, respectively. Then

$$
\begin{aligned}
0.2x + 0.3(8000 - x) &= 0.28(8000) \\
-0.1x + 2400 &= 2240 \\
1600 &= x.
\end{aligned}
$$

There were originally 1600 fish in Homer Lake.

115. Let x be the distance she hiked in the northern direction. Then she hiked $32 - x$ miles in the eastern direction. By the Pythagorean Theorem, we obtain

$$
\begin{aligned}
x^2 + (32 - x)^2 &= (4\sqrt{34})^2 \\
2x^2 - 64x + 480 &= 0 \\
2 \cdot (x - 20)(x - 12) &= 0 \\
x &= 20, 12.
\end{aligned}
$$

Since the eastern direction was the shorter leg of the journey, the northern direction was 20 miles.

117. Let x and $x + 50$ be the cost of a haircut at Joe's and Renee's, respectively. Since 5 haircuts at Joe's is less than one haircut at Renee's, we have

$$5x < x + 50.$$

Thus, the price range of a haircut at Joe's is $x < \$12.50$ or $(0, \$12.50)$.

119. Let x and $x + 2$ be the length and width of a picture frame in inches, respectively. Since there are between 32 and 50 inches of molding, we get

$$
\begin{aligned}
32 &< 2x + 2(x + 2) < 50 \\
32 &< 4x + 4 < 50 \\
28 &< 4x < 46 \\
7 \text{ in.} &< x < 11.5 \text{ in.}
\end{aligned}
$$

The set of possible widths is $(7 \text{ in}, 11.5 \text{ in})$.

121. If the average gas mileage is increased from 29.5 mpg to 31.5 mpg, then the amount of gas saved is

$$\frac{10^{12}}{29.5} - \frac{10^{12}}{31.5} \approx 2.15 \times 10^9 \text{ gallons.}$$

Suppose the mileage is increased to x from 29.5 mpg. Then x must satisfy

$$\frac{10^{12}}{29.5} - \frac{10^{12}}{x} = \frac{10^{12}}{27.5} - \frac{10^{12}}{29.5}$$
$$\frac{1}{29.5} - \frac{1}{x} = \frac{1}{27.5} - \frac{1}{29.5}$$
$$-\frac{1}{x} \approx -0.031433$$
$$x \approx 31.8.$$

The mileage must be increased to 31.8 mpg.

123. a) Using a calculator, the regression line is given by

$$y \approx 17.08x - 34,034$$

where x is the year and y is the number of millions of cell users.

b) If $x = 2012$, the number of millions of cell users is

$$y \approx 17.08(2012) - 34,034 \approx 331.$$

There will be 331 million cell users in 2012.

125. Let a be the age in years and p be the percentage. The equation of the line passing through $(20, 0.23)$ and $(50, 0.47)$ is

$$p = 0.008a + 0.07.$$

If $a = 65$, then $p = 0.008(65) + 0.07 \approx 0.59$. Thus, the percentage of body fat in a 65-year old woman is 59%.

127. a) Using a calculator, the regression line is given by

$$y \approx 3.67x + 47.11$$

where $x = 0$ corresponds to 2000.

b) If $x = 15$, then the average price of a prescription in 2015 is

$$y \approx 3.67(15) + 47.11 \approx \$102.16.$$

129. a) Circle A is given by

$$(x - 1)^2 + (y - 1)^2 = 1.$$

b) Draw a right triangle with sides 1 and x, and with hypotenuse 3 such that the hypotenuse has as endpoints the centers of circles A and B. Here, x is the horizontal distance between the centers of A and B. Since

$$1 + x^2 = 9$$

we obtain $x = 2\sqrt{2}$. Then the center of B is $(1 + 2\sqrt{2}, 2)$. Thus, circle B is given by

$$\left(x - 1 - 2\sqrt{2}\right)^2 + (y - 2)^2 = 4.$$

c) Let r and (a, r) be the radius and center of circle C. Draw a right triangle with sides $a - 1$ and $1 - r$, and with hypotenuse $1 + r$ such that the hypotenuse has as endpoints the centers of circles A and C. Then

$$(1 + r)^2 = (1 - r)^2 + (a - 1)^2.$$

Next, draw a right triangle with sides $1 + 2\sqrt{2} - a$ and $2 - r$, and with hypotenuse $2 + r$ such that the hypotenuse has as endpoints the centers of circles B and C. Then

$$(2 + r)^2 = (2 - r)^2 + (1 + 2\sqrt{2} - a)^2.$$

The solution of the two equations are

$$a = 5 - 2\sqrt{2}, \quad r = 6 - 4\sqrt{2}.$$

Hence, circle C is given by

$$(x - 5 + 2\sqrt{2})^2 + (y - 6 + 4\sqrt{2})^2 = (6 - 4\sqrt{2})^2$$

Chapter Test

1. Since $2x - x = -6 - 1$, the solution set is $\{-7\}$.

2. Multiplying the original equation by 6, we get $3x - 2x = 1$. The solution set is $\{1\}$.

3. Since $x^2 = \dfrac{2}{3}$, one obtains

$$x = \pm \frac{\sqrt{2}}{\sqrt{3}} = \pm \frac{\sqrt{6}}{3}.$$

The solution set is $\left\{ \pm \dfrac{\sqrt{6}}{3} \right\}$.

4. By completing the square, we obtain

$$
\begin{aligned}
x^2 - 6x &= -1 \\
(x-3)^2 &= -1 + 9 \\
(x-3)^2 &= 8 \\
x - 3 &= \pm\sqrt{8}.
\end{aligned}
$$

The solution set is $\{3 \pm 2\sqrt{2}\}$.

5. Since $x^2 - 9x + 14 = (x-2)(x-7) = 0$, the solution set is $\{2, 7\}$.

6. After cross-multiplying, we get

$$
\begin{aligned}
(x-1)(x-6) &= (x+3)(x+2) \\
x^2 - 7x + 6 &= x^2 + 5x + 6 \\
-7x &= 5x \\
0 &= 12x
\end{aligned}
$$

The solution set is $\{0\}$.

7. We use the method of completing the square.

$$
\begin{aligned}
x^2 - 2x &= -5 \\
(x-1)^2 &= -5 + 1 \\
(x-1)^2 &= -4 \\
x - 1 &= \pm 2i
\end{aligned}
$$

The solution set is $\{1 \pm 2i\}$.

8. Since $x^2 = -1$, the solution set is $\{\pm i\}$.

9. The line $3x - 4y = 120$ passes through $(0, -30)$ and $(40, 0)$.

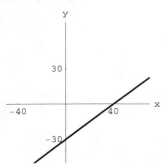

10. Circle with center $(0, 0)$ and radius 20.

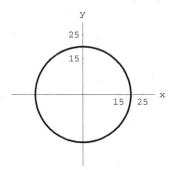

11. By using the method of completing the square, we obtain $x^2 + (y+2)^2 = 4$. A circle with center $(0, -2)$ and radius 2.

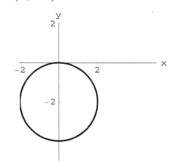

12. The line $y = -\dfrac{2}{3}x + 4$ passes through $(0, 4)$ and $(6, 0)$.

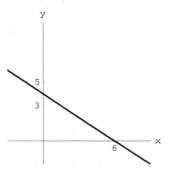

13. The horizontal line $y = 4$.

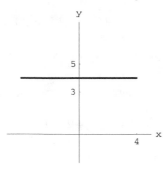

14. The vertical line $x = -2$.

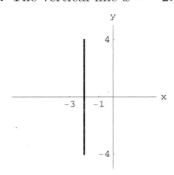

15. $16 - 24i - 9 = 7 - 24i$

16. $\dfrac{2 - i}{3 + i} \cdot \dfrac{3 - i}{3 - i} = \dfrac{5 - 5i}{10} = \dfrac{1}{2} - \dfrac{1}{2}i$

17. $i^4 i^2 - i^{32} i^3 = (1)(-1) - (1)(-i) = -1 + i$

18. $2i\sqrt{2}(i\sqrt{2} + \sqrt{6}) = -4 + 2i\sqrt{12} = -4 + 4i\sqrt{3}$

19. Since $y = \dfrac{3}{5}x - \dfrac{8}{5}$, the slope is $\dfrac{3}{5}$.

20. $\dfrac{-4 - 6}{5 - (-3)} = \dfrac{-10}{8} = -\dfrac{5}{4}$

21. We rewrite $2x - 3y = 6$ as $y = \dfrac{2}{3}x - 2$. Note, the slope of $y = \dfrac{2}{3}x - 2$ is $\dfrac{2}{3}$. Then we use $m = -\dfrac{3}{2}$ and the point $(1, -2)$.

$$
\begin{aligned}
y + 2 &= -\frac{3}{2}(x - 1) \\
y &= -\frac{3}{2}x + \frac{3}{2} - 2.
\end{aligned}
$$

The perpendicular line is $y = -\dfrac{3}{2}x - \dfrac{1}{2}$.

22. The slope is $\dfrac{-1 - 2}{3} = -1$. We use the point $(3, -4)$.

$$
\begin{aligned}
y + 4 &= -(x - 3) \\
y &= -x + 3 - 4.
\end{aligned}
$$

The parallel line is $y = -x - 1$.

23. $\sqrt{(-3 - 2)^2 + (1 - 4)^2} = \sqrt{25 + 9} = \sqrt{34}$

24. $\left(\dfrac{-1 + 1}{2}, \dfrac{1 + 0}{2} \right) = \left(0, \dfrac{1}{2} \right)$

25. Since the discriminant is negative, namely, $(-5)^2 - 4(1)(9) = -11$, then there are no real solutions.

26. We solve for y.

$$
\begin{aligned}
5 - 4 &= 3xy + 2y \\
1 &= y(3x + 2) \\
\frac{1}{3x + 2} &= y
\end{aligned}
$$

27. Since $-4 > 2x$, the solution set is $(-\infty, -2)$ and the graph is

28. The solution set to $x > 6$ and $x > 5$ is the interval $(6, \infty)$ and the graph is

29. Solving an equivalent statement, we obtain

$$
\begin{aligned}
-3 &\leq 2x - 1 \leq 3 \\
-2 &\leq 2x \leq 4 \\
-1 &\leq x \leq 2.
\end{aligned}
$$

The solution set is the interval $[-1, 2]$ and the graph is

30. We rewrite $|x - 3| > 2$ without any absolute values. Then

$$
\begin{aligned}
x - 3 > 2 \quad &\text{or} \quad x - 3 < -2 \\
x > 5 \quad &\text{or} \quad x < 1.
\end{aligned}
$$

The solution set is $(-\infty, 1) \cup (5, \infty)$ and the graph is

31. If x is the original length of one side of the square, then

$$
\begin{aligned}
(x + 20)(x + 10) &= 999 \\
x^2 + 30x + 200 &= 999 \\
x^2 + 30x - 799 &= 0 \\
\frac{-30 \pm \sqrt{900 + 4(799)}}{2} &= x \\
\frac{-30 \pm 64}{2} &= x \\
17, -47 &= x.
\end{aligned}
$$

Thus, $x = 17$ and the original area is $17^2 = 289$ ft^2.

32. Let x be the number of gallons of the 20% solution. From the concentrations,

$$
\begin{aligned}
0.3(10 + x) &= 0.5(10) + 0.2x \\
3 + 0.3x &= 5 + 0.2x \\
0.1x &= 2 \\
x &= 20.
\end{aligned}
$$

Then 20 gallons of the 20% solution are needed.

33. a) Using a calculator, the regression line is given by

$$y \approx 18.4x + 311$$

where $x = 0$ corresponds to 1997 and y is the median price of a home in thousands of dollars.

b) If $x = 18$, then

$$y \approx 18.4(18) + 311 \approx 642.$$

The predicted median price in 2015 is $642,000.

34. a) Using a calculator, the regression line is given by

$$y \approx -11.39x + 2159.14$$

where $x = 1$ corresponds to 2001 and y is the number of thousands of farms.
Similarly, the quadratic regression curve is

$$y \approx 0.30x^2 - 13.77x + 2162.71$$

b) If $x = 12$ in the regression line, then

$$y \approx -11.39(12)x + 2159.14 \approx 2022$$

In 2012, the predicted number of farms is 2,022,000.
If $x = 12$ in the regression curve, then

$$y \approx 0.30(12)^2 - 13.77(12) + 2162.71 \approx 2041$$

In 2012, the predicted number of farms is 2,041,000.

Functions and Graphs

The rainforests cover less than an eighth of a percent of the earth's surface, yet they are home to over half of our animal and plant species. Rainforests are also a source of foods such as chocolate, vanilla, pineapples, and cinnamon, and about twenty percent of all medicines.

However, the rainforests are disappearing at an alarming rate and along with them a thousand species of plants and animals per year. Destroying the rainforests will irrevocably change our planet's future.

Depletion of the rainforests is only one of many ecological issues that include the ozone layer, global warming, and hazardous waste. In assessing these problems, scientists often look for relationships between variables.

►WHAT YOU WILL learn... In this chapter you will study relationships between variables, using graphic, numeric, and algebraic points of view.

1 Functions

2 Graphs of Relations and Functions

3 Families of Functions, Transformations, and Symmetry

4 Operations with Functions

5 Inverse Functions

6 Constructing Functions with Variation

Tom Brakefield/Stockbyte/
Getty Images

From Chapter 2 of *Precalculus: Functions and Graphs*. Fourth Edition. Mark Dugopolski. Copyright © 2013 by Pearson Education, Inc.

1 Functions

The Function Concept

If you spend $10 on gasoline, then the price per gallon determines the number of gallons that you get. There is a rule: The number of gallons is $10 divided by the price per gallon. The number of hours that you sleep before a test might be related to your grade on the test, but does not determine your grade. There is no rule that will determine your grade from the number of hours of sleep. If the value of a variable y is determined by the value of another variable x, then y is a function of x. The phrase "is a function of" means "is determined by." If there is more than one value for y corresponding to a particular x-value, then y is not determined by x and y is not a function of x.

EXAMPLE 1 Using the phrase "is a function of"

Decide whether a is a function of b, b is a function of a, or neither.

a. Let a represent a positive integer smaller than 100 and b represent the number of divisors of a.
b. Let a represent the age of a U.S. citizen and b represent the number of days since his/her birth.
c. Let a represent the age of a U.S. citizen and b represent his/her annual income.

Solution

a. We can determine the number of divisors of any positive integer smaller than 100. So b is a function of a. We cannot determine the integer knowing the number of its divisors, because different integers have the same number of divisors. So a is not a function of b.
b. The number of days since a person's birth certainly determines the age of the person in the usual way. So a is a function of b. However, you cannot determine the number of days since a person's birth from their age. You need more information. For example, the number of days since birth for two 1-year-olds could be 370 and 380 days. So b is not a function of a.
c. We cannot determine the income from the age or the age from the income. We would need more information. Even though age and income are related, the relationship is not strong enough to say that either one is a function of the other.

▶TRY THIS. Let p be the price of a grocery item and t be the amount of sales tax at 5% on that item. Determine whether p is a function of t, t is a function of p, or neither. ■

A function is a rule by which the value of one variable is determined from the value of one or more other variables. In this section we will continue studying functions of a single variable. The formula $A = \pi r^2$ is a function because it provides a rule for finding the value of A from the value of the single variable r. We can also make an equivalent definition in terms of sets, as follows.

Definition: Function

> A **function** is a rule that assigns each element in one set to a unique element in a second set.

$A = \pi r^2$ is a function by this definition because it assigns each element in a set of radii to a unique element in a set of areas. Understanding this definition depends on knowing the meanings of the words *rule*, *assigns*, and *unique*. Using the language of ordered pairs we can make the following equivalent definition in which we don't use those words.

Definition: Function

> A **function** is a set of ordered pairs in which no two ordered pairs have the same first coordinate and different second coordinates.

If we start with two related variables, we can identify one as the first variable and the other as the second variable and consider the set of ordered pairs containing their corresponding values. If the set of ordered pairs satisfies the function definition, then we say that the second variable is a function of the first. The variable corresponding to the first coordinate is the **independent variable,** and the variable corresponding to the second coordinate is the **dependent variable.**

Identifying Functions

Any set of ordered pairs is called a **relation.** A relation can be indicated by a verbal description, a graph, a formula or equation, or a table, but there is always an underlying set of ordered pairs. Not every relation is a function. A function is a special relation.

When a relation is given by a graph, we can visually check whether there are two ordered pairs with the same first coordinate and different second coordinates. For example, the circle shown in Fig. 1 is not the graph of a function, because there are two points on the circle with the same first coordinate. These points lie on a vertical line. In general, if there is a vertical line that crosses a graph more than once, the graph is not the graph of a function. This criterion is known as the **vertical line test.**

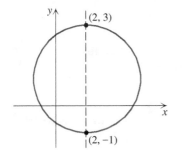

Figure 1

**Theorem:
The Vertical Line Test**

> A graph is the graph of a function if and only if there is no vertical line that crosses the graph more than once.

Every nonvertical line is the graph of a function, because every vertical line crosses a nonvertical line exactly once. Note that the vertical line test makes sense only because we always put the independent variable on the horizontal axis.

EXAMPLE 2 Identifying a function from a graph

Determine which of the graphs shown in Fig. 2 are graphs of functions.

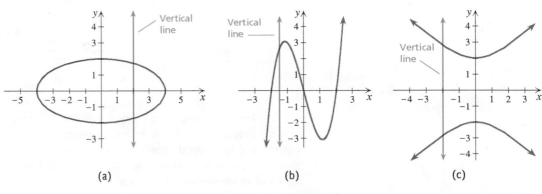

Figure 2

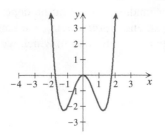

Figure 3

Solution

For each graph we want to decide whether y is a function of x. That is, can y be uniquely determined from x? In parts (a) and (c) we can draw a vertical line that crosses the graph more than once. So in each case there is an x-coordinate that corresponds to two different y-coordinates. In parts (a) and (c) we cannot always determine a unique value of y from a given x-coordinate. So y is not a function of x in parts (a) and (c). The graph in Fig. 2(b) is the graph of a function because every vertical line appears to cross the graph at most once. In this case we can determine y for a given x-coordinate and y is a function of x.

▶**TRY THIS.** Use the graph in Fig. 3 to determine whether y is a function of x. ■

A calculator is a virtual function machine. Built-in functions on a calculator are marked with symbols such as $\sqrt{x}$, x^2, $x!$, 10^x, e^x, $\ln(x)$, $\sin(x)$, $\cos(x)$, etc. When you provide an x-coordinate and use one of these symbols, the calculator finds the appropriate y-coordinate. The ordered pairs certainly satisfy the definition of function because the calculator will not produce two different second coordinates corresponding to one first coordinate.

In the next example we determine whether a relation is a function when the relation is given as a list of ordered pairs or as a table.

EXAMPLE 3 | Identifying a function from a list or table

Determine whether each relation is a function.

a. $\{(1, 3), (2, 3), (4, 9)\}$ **b.** $\{(9, -3), (9, 3), (4, 2), (0, 0)\}$

c.

Quantity	Price Each
1–5	$9.40
5–10	$8.75

Solution

a. This set of ordered pairs is a function because no two ordered pairs have the same first coordinate and different second coordinates.

b. This set of ordered pairs is not a function because both $(9, 3)$ and $(9, -3)$ are in the set and they have the same first coordinate and different second coordinates.

c. The quantity 5 corresponds to a price of $9.40 and also to a price of $8.75. Assuming that quantity is the first coordinate, the ordered pairs $(5, \$9.40)$ and $(5, \$8.75)$ both belong to this relation. If you are purchasing items whose price was determined from this table, you would certainly say that something is wrong, the table has a mistake in it, or the price you should pay is not clear. The price is not a function of the quantity purchased.

▶**TRY THIS.** Determine whether each relation is a function.

a. $\{(4, 5), (5, 5), (5, 7)\}$ **b.**

Time (minutes)	Cost ($)
0–30	40
31–60	75

■

We have seen and used many functions as formulas. For example, the formula $c = \pi d$ defines a set of ordered pairs in which the first coordinate is the diameter of a circle and the second coordinate is the circumference. Since each diameter corresponds to a unique circumference, the circumference is a function of the diameter. If the set of ordered pairs satisfying an equation is a function, then we say that the equation is a function or the equation defines a function. Other well-known formulas such as $C = \frac{5}{9}(F - 32)$, $A = \pi r^2$, and $V = \frac{4}{3}\pi r^3$ are also functions, but, as we will see in the next example, not every equation defines a function. The variables in the next example and all others in this text represent real numbers unless indicated otherwise.

EXAMPLE 4 | Identifying a function from an equation

Determine whether each equation defines y as a function of x.

a. $|y| = x$ **b.** $y = x^2 - 3x + 2$ **c.** $x^2 + y^2 = 1$ **d.** $3x - 4y = 8$

Solution

a. We must determine whether there are any values of x for which there is more than one y-value satisfying the equation. We arbitrarily select a number for x and see. If we select $x = 2$, then the equation is $|y| = 2$, which is satisfied if $y = \pm 2$. Both $(2, 2)$ and $(2, -2)$ satisfy $|y| = x$. So this equation does *not* define y as a function of x.

b. If we select any number for x, then y is calculated by the equation $y = x^2 - 3x + 2$. Since there is only one result when $x^2 - 3x + 2$ is calculated, there is only one y for any given x. So this equation *does* define y as a function of x.

c. Is it possible to pick a number for x for which there is more than one y-value? If we select $x = 0$, then the equation is $0^2 + y^2 = 1$ or $y = \pm 1$. So $(0, 1)$ and $(0, -1)$ both satisfy $x^2 + y^2 = 1$ and this equation does *not* define y as a function of x. Note that $x^2 + y^2 = 1$ is equivalent to $y = \pm\sqrt{1 - x^2}$, which indicates that there are many values for x that would produce two different y-coordinates.

d. The equation $3x - 4y = 8$ is equivalent to $y = \frac{3}{4}x - 2$. Since there is only one result when $\frac{3}{4}x - 2$ is calculated, there is only one y corresponding to any given x. So $3x - 4y = 8$ *does* define y as a function of x.

▶**TRY THIS.** Determine whether $x^3 + y^2 = 0$ defines y as a function of x. ∎

Domain and Range

A relation is a set of ordered pairs. The **domain** of a relation is the set of all first coordinates of the ordered pairs. The **range** of a relation is the set of all second coordinates of the ordered pairs. The relation

$$\{(19, 2.4), (27, 3.0), (19, 3.6), (22, 2.4), (36, 3.8)\}$$

shows the ages and grade point averages of five randomly selected students. The domain of this relation is the set of ages, $\{19, 22, 27, 36\}$. The range is the set of grade point averages, $\{2.4, 3.0, 3.6, 3.8\}$. This relation matches elements of the domain (ages) with elements of the range (grade point averages), as shown in Fig. 4. This relation is not a function because two 19-year-old students have different grade point averages.

For some relations, all of the ordered pairs are listed, but for others, only an equation is given for determining the ordered pairs. When the domain of the relation is not stated, it is understood that the domain consists of only values of the independent

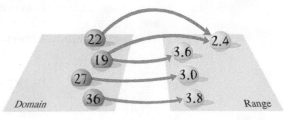

Figure 4

variable that can be used in the expression defining the relation. When we use x and y for the variables, we always assume that x is the independent variable and y is the dependent variable.

EXAMPLE 5 Determining domain and range

State the domain and range of each relation and whether the relation is a function.

a. $\{(-1, 1), (3, 9), (3, -9)\}$ **b.** $y = \sqrt{2x - 1}$ **c.** $x = |y|$

Solution

a. The domain is the set of first coordinates $\{-1, 3\}$, and the range is the set of second coordinates $\{1, 9, -9\}$. Note that an element of a set is not listed more than once. Since $(3, 9)$ and $(3, -9)$ are in the relation, the relation is not a function.

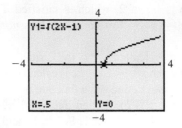

Figure 5

b. Since y is determined uniquely from x by the formula $y = \sqrt{2x - 1}$, y is a function of x. In our discussions of functions, x and y must be real numbers. Now $\sqrt{2x - 1}$ is a real number only if $2x - 1 \geq 0$, or $x \geq 1/2$. So the domain of the function is the set of all real numbers greater then or equal to $1/2$, which is written in set notation as $\{x \mid x \geq 1/2\}$ or in interval notation as $[1/2, \infty)$. Since interval notation is simpler, we will use it. If $2x - 1 \geq 0$ and $y = \sqrt{2x - 1}$, we have $y \geq 0$. So the range of the function is the interval $[0, \infty)$. The graph of $y = \sqrt{2x - 1}$ shown in Fig. 5 supports these answers because the points that are plotted appear to have $x \geq 1/2$ and $y \geq 0$. □

c. The expression $|y|$ is defined for any real number y. So the range is the interval of all real numbers, $(-\infty, \infty)$. Since $|y|$ is nonnegative, the values of x must be nonnegative. So the domain is $[0, \infty)$. Since ordered pairs such as $(2, 2)$ and $(2, -2)$ satisfy $x = |y|$, this equation does not give y as a function of x.

▶**TRY THIS.** Determine whether $y = \sqrt{x + 3}$ is a function and find its domain and range. ∎

In Example 5(b) and (c) we found the domain and range by examining an equation defining a relation. If the relation is a function as in Example 5(b), you can easily draw the graph with a graphing calculator and use it to support your answer. However, to choose an appropriate viewing window you must know the domain and range to begin with. So it is best to use a calculator graph to support your conclusions about domain and range rather than to make conclusions about domain and range. □

Function Notation

A function defined by a set of ordered pairs can be named with a letter. For example,

$$f = \{(2, 5), (3, 8)\}.$$

Since the function f pairs 2 with 5 we write $f(2) = 5$, which is read as "the value of f at 2 is 5" or simply "f of 2 is 5." We also have $f(3) = 8$.

A function defined by an equation can also be named with a letter. For example, the function $y = x^2$ could be named by a new letter, say g. We can then use $g(x)$, read "g of x" as a symbol for the second coordinate when the first coordinate is x. Since y and $g(x)$ are both symbols for the second coordinate we can write $y = g(x)$ and $g(x) = x^2$. Since $3^2 = 9$, the function g pairs 3 with 9 and we write $g(3) = 9$. This notation is called **function notation.**

EXAMPLE 6 Using function notation

Let $h = \{(1, 4), (6, 0), (7, 9)\}$ and $f(x) = \sqrt{x - 3}$. Find each of the following.

a. $h(7)$ **b.** w, if $h(w) = 0$ **c.** $f(7)$ **d.** x, if $f(x) = 5$

Solution

a. The expression $h(7)$ is the second coordinate when the first coordinate is 7 in the function named h. So $h(7) = 9$.

b. We are looking for a number w for which $h(w) = 0$. That is, the second coordinate is 0 for some unknown first coordinate w. By examining the function h we see that $w = 6$.

c. To find $f(7)$ replace x by 7 in $f(x) = \sqrt{x - 3}$:

$$f(7) = \sqrt{7 - 3} = \sqrt{4} = 2$$

d. To find x for which $f(x) = 5$ we replace $f(x)$ by 5 in $f(x) = \sqrt{x - 3}$:

$$5 = \sqrt{x - 3}$$

$$25 = x - 3$$

$$28 = x$$

▶**TRY THIS.** Let $f(x) = x - 3$.　**a.** Find $f(4)$.　**b.** Find x if $f(x) = 9$.　■

Function notation such as $f(x) = 3x + 1$ provides a rule for finding the second coordinate: Multiply the first coordinate (whatever it is) by 3 and then add 1. The x in this notation is called a **dummy variable** because the letter used is unimportant. We could write $f(t) = 3t + 1$,

$$f(\text{first coordinate}) = 3(\text{first coordinate}) + 1,$$

or even $f(\ ) = 3(\ ) + 1$ to convey the same idea. Whatever appears in the parentheses following f must be used in place of x on the other side of the equation.

EXAMPLE 7 Using function notation with variables

Given that $f(x) = x^2 - 2$ and $g(x) = 2x - 3$, find and simplify each of the following expressions.

a. $f(a)$　**b.** $f(a + 1)$　**c.** $f(x + h) - f(x)$　**d.** $g(x - 2)$　**e.** $g(x + h) - g(x)$

Solution

a. Replace x by a in $f(x) = x^2 - 2$ to get $f(a) = a^2 - 2$.

b. $f(a + 1) = (a + 1)^2 - 2$ 　　　　　Replace x by $a + 1$ in $f(x) = x^2 - 2$.

$$= a^2 + 2a + 1 - 2$$

$$= a^2 + 2a - 1$$

c. $f(x + h) - f(x) = (x + h)^2 - 2 - (x^2 - 2)$ 　Replace x with $x + h$ to get $f(x + h)$.

$$= (x + h)^2 - x^2$$

$$= x^2 + 2hx + h^2 - x^2$$

$$= 2hx + h^2$$

d. $g(x - 2) = 2(x - 2) - 3$ 　　　　　Replace x by $x - 2$ in $g(x) = 2x - 3$.

$$= 2x - 7$$

e. $g(x + h) - g(x) = 2(x + h) - 3 - (2x - 3)$

$$= 2x + 2h - 3 - 2x + 3$$

$$= 2h$$

▶**TRY THIS.** Let $f(x) = x^2 - 4$. Find and simplify $f(x + 2)$.　■

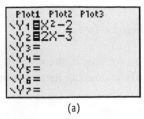

(a)

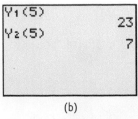

(b)

Figure 6

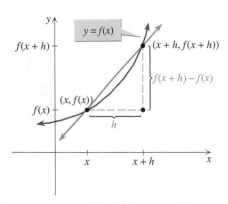

A graphing calculator uses subscripts to indicate different functions. For example, if $y_1 = x^2 - 2$ and $y_2 = 2x - 3$, then $y_1(5) = 23$ and $y_2(5) = 7$ as shown in Fig. 6(a) and (b). □

If a function describes some real application, then a letter that fits the situation is usually used. For example, if watermelons are $3 each, then the cost of x watermelons is given by the function $C(x) = 3x$. The cost of five watermelons is $C(5) = 3 \cdot 5 = \$15$. In trigonometry the abbreviations sin, cos, and tan are used rather than a single letter to name the trigonometric functions. The dependent variables are written as $\sin(x)$, $\cos(x)$, and $\tan(x)$.

The Average Rate of Change of a Function

The slope of the line through (x_1, y_1) and (x_2, y_2) is $\frac{y_2 - y_1}{x_2 - x_1}$. We now extend that idea to any function (linear or not).

Definition: Average Rate of Change from x_1 to x_2

> If (x_1, y_1) and (x_2, y_2) are two ordered pairs of a function, we defined the **average rate of change** of the function as x varies from x_1 to x_2, as the change in y-coordinates divided by the change in x-coordinates, $\Delta y / \Delta x$, or
>
> $$\frac{y_2 - y_1}{x_2 - x_1}.$$

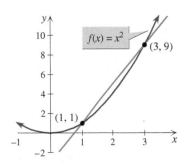

Figure 7

Note that the x-values can be specified with interval notation. For example, the average rate of change $f(x) = x^2$ on $[1, 3]$ is found as follows:

$$\frac{\Delta y}{\Delta x} = \frac{f(3) - f(1)}{3 - 1} = \frac{9 - 1}{3 - 1} = 4$$

The average rate of change is simply the slope of the line that passes through two points on the graph of the function as shown in Fig. 7.

It is not necessary to have a formula for a function to find an average rate of change, as is shown in the next example.

EXAMPLE 8 Finding the average rate of change

The population of California was 29.8 million in 1990 and 33.9 million in 2000 (U.S. Census Bureau, www.census.gov). What was the average rate of change of the population over that time interval?

Solution

The population is a function of the year. The average rate of change of the population is the change in population divided by the change in time:

$$\frac{\Delta p}{\Delta t} = \frac{33.9 - 29.8}{2000 - 1990} = \frac{4.1}{10} = 0.41$$

The average rate of change of the population was 0.41 million people/year or 410,000 people/year. Note that 410,000 people/year is an average and that the population did not actually increase by 410,000 every year.

▶**TRY THIS.** A BMW was purchased for $28,645 in 2003 and sold for $13,837 in 2009. What was the average rate of change of the car's value for that time interval? ■

The average rate of change of a function between two points that are labeled as shown in Fig. 8 is called the *difference quotient*.

Figure 8

**Definition:
Difference Quotient**

The **difference quotient** is the expression $\dfrac{f(x + h) - f(x)}{h}$.

Note that h is the change in value of the x-coordinates. So using Δx in place of h, the difference quotient is written as

$$\frac{f(x + \Delta x) - f(x)}{\Delta x}.$$

In calculus it is often necessary to find and simplify the difference quotient for a function.

EXAMPLE 9 Finding a difference quotient

Find and simplify the difference quotient for each of the following functions.

a. $j(x) = 3x + 2$ **b.** $f(x) = x^2 - 2x$ **c.** $g(x) = \sqrt{x}$ **d.** $y = \dfrac{5}{x}$

Solution

a.
$$\frac{j(x + h) - j(x)}{h} = \frac{3(x + h) + 2 - (3x + 2)}{h}$$

$$= \frac{3x + 3h + 2 - 3x - 2}{h}$$

$$= \frac{3h}{h} = 3$$

b.
$$\frac{f(x + h) - f(x)}{h} = \frac{[(x + h)^2 - 2(x + h)] - (x^2 - 2x)}{h}$$

$$= \frac{x^2 + 2xh + h^2 - 2x - 2h - x^2 + 2x}{h}$$

$$= \frac{2xh + h^2 - 2h}{h}$$

$$= 2x + h - 2$$

c.
$$\frac{g(x + h) - g(x)}{h} = \frac{\sqrt{x + h} - \sqrt{x}}{h}$$

$$= \frac{(\sqrt{x + h} - \sqrt{x})(\sqrt{x + h} + \sqrt{x})}{h(\sqrt{x + h} + \sqrt{x})} \qquad \text{Rationalize the numerator}$$

$$= \frac{x + h - x}{h(\sqrt{x + h} + \sqrt{x})}$$

$$= \frac{1}{\sqrt{x + h} + \sqrt{x}}$$

d. Use the function notation $f(x) = \dfrac{5}{x}$ for the function $y = \dfrac{5}{x}$:

$$\frac{f(x + h) - f(x)}{h} = \frac{\dfrac{5}{x + h} - \dfrac{5}{x}}{h} = \frac{\left(\dfrac{5}{x + h} - \dfrac{5}{x}\right)x(x + h)}{h \cdot x(x + h)}$$

$$= \frac{5x - 5(x + h)}{hx(x + h)} = \frac{-5h}{hx(x + h)} = \frac{-5}{x(x + h)}$$

▶**TRY THIS.** Find and simplify the difference quotient for $f(x) = x^2 - x$. ∎

Note that in Examples 9(b), 9(c), and 9(d) the average rate of change of the function depends on the values of x and h, while in Example 9(a) the average rate of change of the function is constant. In Example 9(c) the expression does not look much different after rationalizing the numerator than it did before. However, we did remove h as a factor of the denominator, and in calculus it is often necessary to perform this step.

Constructing Functions

In the next example we find a formula for, or **construct,** a function relating two variables in a geometric figure.

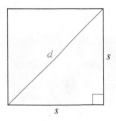

Figure 9

EXAMPLE 10 | Constructing a function

Given that a square has diagonal of length d and side of length s, write the area A as a function of the length of the diagonal.

Solution

The area of any square is given by $A = s^2$. The diagonal is the hypotenuse of a right triangle as shown in Fig. 9. By the Pythagorean theorem, $d^2 = s^2 + s^2$, $d^2 = 2s^2$, or $s^2 = d^2/2$. Since $A = s^2$ and $s^2 = d^2/2$, we get the formula

$$A = \frac{d^2}{2}$$

expressing the area of the square as a function of the length of the diagonal.

▶**TRY THIS.** A square has perimeter P and sides of length s. Write the side as a function of the perimeter. ∎

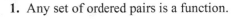

FOR thought... True or False? Explain.

1. Any set of ordered pairs is a function.

2. If $f = \{(1, 1), (2, 4), (3, 9)\}$, then $f(5) = 25$.

3. The domain of $f(x) = 1/x$ is $(-\infty, 0) \cup (0, \infty)$.

4. Each student's exam grade is a function of the student's IQ.

5. If $f(x) = x^2$, then $f(x + h) = x^2 + h$.

6. The domain of $g(x) = |x - 3|$ is $[3, \infty)$.

7. The range of $y = 8 - x^2$ is $(-\infty, 8]$.

8. The equation $x = y^2$ does not define y as a function of x.

9. If $f(t) = \dfrac{t - 2}{t + 2}$, then $f(0) = -1$.

10. The set $\left\{\left(\frac{3}{8}, 8\right), \left(\frac{4}{7}, 7\right), (0.16, 6), \left(\frac{3}{8}, 5\right)\right\}$ is a function.

EXERCISES 1

Fill in the blank.

1. Any set of ordered pairs is a _____.

2. A set of ordered pairs in which no two have the same first coordinate and different second coordinates is a _____.

3. For a set of ordered pairs, the variable corresponding to the first coordinate is the _____ variable and the variable corresponding to the second coordinate is the _____ variable.

4. For a set of ordered pairs, the set of all first coordinates is the _____ and the set of all second coordinates is the _____.

5. The expression $\dfrac{f(x + h) - f(x)}{h}$ is the _____.

6. If (x_1, y_1) and (x_2, y_2) are two ordered pairs of a function,

then $\dfrac{y_2 - y_1}{x_2 - x_1}$ is the _____ of the function on $[x_1, x_2]$.

For each pair of variables determine whether a is a function of b, b is a function of a, or neither.

7. *a* is the radius of any U.S. coin and *b* is its circumference.

8. *a* is the length of any rectangle with a width of 5 in. and *b* is its perimeter.

9. *a* is the length of any piece of U.S. paper currency and *b* is its denomination.

10. *a* is the diameter of any U.S. coin and *b* is its value.

11. *a* is the universal product code for an item at Wal-Mart and *b* is its price.

12. *a* is the final exam score for a student in your class and *b* is his/her semester grade.

13. *a* is the time spent studying for the final exam for a student in your class and *b* is the student's final exam score.

14. *a* is the age of an adult male and *b* is his shoe size.

15. *a* is the height of a car in inches and *b* is its height in centimeters.

16. *a* is the cost for mailing a first-class letter and *b* is its weight.

Use the vertical line test on each graph in Exercises 17–22 to determine whether y is a function of x.

17.

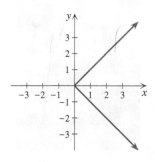

18.

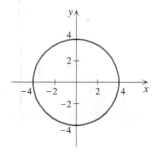

19.

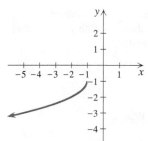

20.

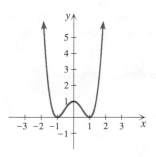

21.

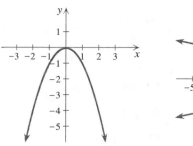

22.

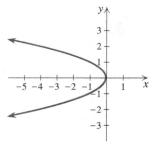

Determine whether each relation is a function.

23. $\{(-1, -1), (2, 2), (3, 3)\}$

24. $\{(0.5, 7), (0, 7), (1, 7), (9, 7)\}$

25. $\{(25, 5), (25, -5), (0, 0)\}$

26. $\{(1, \pi), (30, \pi/2), (60, \pi/4)\}$

27.

x	y
3	6
4	9
3	12

28.

x	y
1	6.98
5	5.98
9	6.98

29.

x	y
−1	1
1	1
−5	1
5	1

30.

x	y
1	1
2	4
3	9
4	16

Determine whether each equation defines y as a function of x.

31. $y = 3x - 8$

32. $y = x^2 - 3x + 7$

33. $x = 3y - 9$

34. $x = y^3$

35. $x^2 = y^2$

36. $y^2 - x^2 = 9$

37. $x = \sqrt{y}$

38. $x = \sqrt[3]{y}$

39. $y + 2 = |x|$

40. $y - 1 = x^2$

41. $x = |2y|$

42. $x = y^2 + 1$

Determine the domain and range of each relation.

43. $\{(-3, 1), (4, 2), (-3, 6), (5, 6)\}$

44. $\{(1, 2), (2, 4), (3, 8), (4, 16)\}$

45. $\{(x, y) \mid y = 4\}$

46. $\{(x, y) \mid x = 5\}$

47. $y = |x| + 5$

48. $y = x^2 + 8$

49. $x + 3 = |y|$

50. $x + 2 = \sqrt{y}$

51. $y = \sqrt{x - 4}$

52. $y = \sqrt{5 - x}$

53. $x = -y^2$

54. $x = -|y|$

Let $f = \{(2, 6), (3, 8), (4, 5)\}$ and $g(x) = 3x + 5$. Find the following.

55. $f(2)$

56. $f(4)$

57. $g(2)$

58. $g(4)$

59. x, if $f(x) = 8$

60. x, if $f(x) = 6$

61. x, if $g(x) = 26$

62. x, if $g(x) = -4$

63. $f(4) + g(4)$

64. $f(3) - g(3)$

Let $f(x) = 3x^2 - x$ and $g(x) = 4x - 2$. Find the following.

65. $f(a)$

66. $f(w)$

67. $g(a + 2)$

68. $g(a - 5)$

69. $f(x + 1)$

70. $f(x - 3)$

71. $g(x + h)$

72. $f(x + h)$

73. $f(x + 1) - f(x)$

74. $g(x + 2) - g(x)$

75. $f(x + h) - f(x)$

76. $g(x + h) - g(x)$

The following problems involve average rate of change.

77. *Depreciation of a Mustang* If a new Mustang is valued at $20,000 and five years later it is valued at $8000, then what is the average rate of change of its value during those five years?

Guy Spangenberg/PhotoLibrary New York

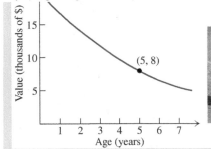

Figure for Exercise 77

78. *Cost of Gravel* Wilson's Sand and Gravel will deliver 12 yd³ of gravel for $240, 30 yd³ for $528, and 60 yd³ for $948. What is the average rate of change of the cost as the number of cubic yards varies from 12 to 30? What is the average rate of change as the number of cubic yards varies from 30 to 60?

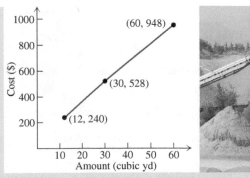

Dianne Maire/Shutterstock

Figure for Exercise 78

79. *Dropping a Watermelon* If a comedian drops a watermelon from a height of 64 ft, then its height (in feet) above the ground is given by the function $h(t) = -16t^2 + 64$ where t is time (in seconds). To get an idea of how fast the watermelon is traveling when it hits the ground find the average rate of change of the height on each of the time intervals $[0, 2]$, $[1, 2]$, $[1.9, 2]$, $[1.99, 2]$, and $[1.999, 2]$.

80. *Bungee Jumping* Billy Joe McCallister jumped off the Tallahatchie Bridge, 70 ft above the water, with a bungee cord tied to his legs. If he was 6 ft above the water 2 sec after jumping, then what was the average rate of change of his altitude as the time varied from 0 to 2 sec?

81. *Deforestation* In 1988 tropical forest covered 1970 million hectares. In 2008 tropical forest covered 1768 million hectares (1 hectare = 10,000 m²). What was the average rate of change in hectares per year of the area of tropical forest over those 20 years?

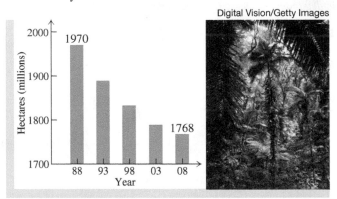
Digital Vision/Getty Images

Figure for Exercises 81 and 82

82. *Elimination* If the deforestation described in the previous exercise continues at the same rate, then in which year will the tropical moist forest be totally eliminated?

Find the difference quotient $\dfrac{f(x + h) - f(x)}{h}$ *for each function and simplify it.*

83. $f(x) = 4x$

84. $f(x) = \dfrac{1}{2}x$

85. $f(x) = 3x + 5$

86. $f(x) = -2x + 3$

87. $y = x^2 + x$

88. $y = x^2 - 2x$

89. $y = -x^2 + x - 2$

90. $y = x^2 - x + 3$

91. $g(x) = 3\sqrt{x}$

92. $g(x) = -2\sqrt{x}$

93. $f(x) = \sqrt{x + 2}$

94. $f(x) = \sqrt{\dfrac{x}{2}}$

95. $g(x) = \dfrac{1}{x}$

96. $g(x) = \dfrac{3}{x}$

97. $g(x) = \dfrac{3}{x + 2}$

98. $g(x) = 3 + \dfrac{2}{x - 1}$

Solve each problem.

99. *Constructing Functions* Consider a square with side of length s, diagonal of length d, perimeter P, and area A.
   a. Write A as a function of s.

   b. Write s as a function of A.

   c. Write s as a function of d.

   d. Write d as a function of s.

   e. Write P as a function of s.

   f. Write s as a function of P.

   g. Write A as a function of P.

   h. Write d as a function of A.

100. *Constructing Functions* Consider a circle with area A, circumference C, radius r, and diameter d.
   a. Write A as a function of r.

   b. Write r as a function of A.

   c. Write C as a function of r.

   d. Write d as a function of r.

   e. Write d as a function of C.

   f. Write A as a function of d.

   g. Write d as a function of A.

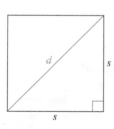

Figure for Exercise 99

Figure for Exercise 100

101. *Cost of Window Cleaning* A window cleaner charges $50 per visit plus $35 per hour. Express the total charge as a function of the number of hours worked, n.

102. *Below Sea Level* The accompanying table shows the depth below sea level d and the atmospheric pressure A (www.sportsfigures.espn.com). The equation $A(d) = 0.03d + 1$ expresses A as a function of d.
   a. Find the atmospheric pressure for a depth of 100 ft, where nitrogen narcosis begins.

   b. Find the depth at which the pressure is 4.9 atm, the maximum depth for intermediate divers.

Table for Exercise 102

Depth (ft)	Atmospheric Pressure (atm)
21	1.63
60	2.8
100	
	4.9
200	7.0
250	8.5

Dennis Sabo/Shutterstock

103. *Computer Spending* The amount spent online for computers in the year $2000 + n$ can be modeled by the function $C(n) = 0.95n + 5.8$ where n is a whole number and $C(n)$ is billions of dollars.
   a. What does $C(4)$ represent and what is it?

   b. Find the year in which online spending for computers will reach $15 billion?

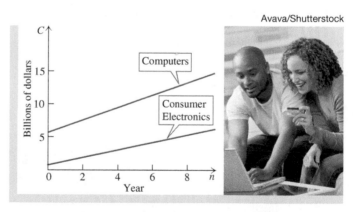

Avava/Shutterstock

Figure for Exercises 103 and 104

104. *Electronics Spending* The amount spent online for consumer electronics (excluding computers) in the year $2000 + n$ can be modeled by the function $E(n) = 0.5n + 1$ where n is a whole number and $E(n)$ is billions of dollars.
   a. What does $E(4) + C(4)$ represent and what is it?

   b. Find the year in which the total spending for computers and electronics will reach $20 billion?

   c. In which category is spending growing faster? See the accompanying figure.

175

105. *Pile of Pipes* Six pipes, each with radius a, are stacked as shown in the accompanying figure. Construct a function that gives the height h of the pile in terms of a.

HINT Connect the centers of three circles to form an equilateral triangle.

Figure for Exercise 105

106. *Angle Bisectors* The angle bisectors of any triangle meet at a single point. Let a be the length of the hypotenuse of a 30-60-90 triangle and d be the distance from the vertex of the right angle to the point where the angle bisectors meet. Write d as function of a.

HINT Draw a diagram and label as many sides and angles as you can.

107. *Concert Revenue* The revenue in dollars from the sale of concert tickets at x dollars each is given by the function

$$R(x) = 20,000x - 500x^2.$$

Find the difference quotient when $x = 18$ and $h = 0.1$ and when $x = 22$ and $h = 0.1$. Interpret your answers.

108. *Surface Area* The amount of tin A (in square inches) needed to make a tin can with radius r inches and volume 36 in.^{3} can be found by the function

$$A(r) = \frac{72}{r} + 2\pi r^2.$$

Find the difference quotient when $r = 1.4$ and $h = 0.1$ and when $r = 2$ and $h = 0.1$. Interpret your answers.

FOR WRITING/DISCUSSION

109. *Find a Function* Give an example of a function and an example of a relation that is not a function, from situations that you have encountered outside of this textbook.

110. *Cooperative Learning* Work in a small group to consider the equation $y^n = x^m$ for any integers n and m. For which integers n and m does the equation define y as a function of x?

▶ RETHINKING

111. Solve $\dfrac{3}{2}x + \dfrac{5}{6} = \dfrac{5}{9}x + \dfrac{1}{3}$.

112. There are twice as many males as females in a classroom. If the total number of people is 36, then how many males are in the classroom?

113. Find the distance between the points $(-6, 3)$ and $(-4, -3)$.

114. Find the equation of the line through the points $(-1, 2)$ and $(5, 3)$. Write the answer in slope-intercept form.

115. Solve $(x - 3)(x + 2) = 36$.

116. Solve $|2x - 9| < 13$. Write the solution set in interval notation.

THINKING OUTSIDE THE BOX XIII

Lucky Lucy Lucy's teacher asked her to evaluate $(20 + 25)^2$. As she was trying to figure out what to do she mumbled, "twenty twenty-five." Her teacher said, "Good, 2025 is correct." Find another pair of two-digit whole numbers for which the square of their sum can be found by Lucy's method.

POP QUIZ 1

1. Is the radius of a circle a function of its area?

2. Is $\{(2, 4), (1, 8), (2, -4)\}$ a function?

3. Does $x^2 + y^2 = 1$ define y as a function of x?

4. What is the domain of $y = \sqrt{x - 1}$?

5. What is the range of $y = x^2 + 2$?

6. What is $f(2)$ if $f = \{(1, 8), (2, 9)\}$?

7. What is a if $f(a) = 1$ and $f(x) = 2x$?

8. If the cost was \$20 in 1998 and \$40 in 2008, then what is the average rate of change of the cost for that time period?

9. Find and simplify the difference quotient for $f(x) = x^2 + 3$.

►LINKING
concepts... For Individual or Group Explorations

Modeling Debt and Population Growth

The following table gives the U.S. federal debt in billions of dollars as a function of the year and the population in millions of people as a function of the year (U.S. Treasury Department, www.treas.gov). Do parts (a) through (e) for each function.

Year	Debt	Pop.
1940	51	131.7
1950	257	150.7
1960	291	179.3
1970	381	203.3
1980	909	226.5
1990	3207	248.7
2000	5666	274.8

SVLuma/Shutterstock

a) Draw an accurate graph of the function.

b) Find the average rate of change of the function over each ten-year period.

c) Take the average rate of change for each ten-year period (starting with 1950–1960) and subtract from it the average rate of change for the previous ten-year period.

d) Are the average rates of change for the function positive or negative?

e) Are the answers to part (c) mostly positive or mostly negative?

f) Judging from the graphs and the average rates of change, which is growing out of control, the federal debt or the population?

g) Explain the relationship between your answer to part (f) and your answer to part (e).

2 Graphs of Relations and Functions

When we graph the set of ordered pairs that satisfy an equation, we are combining algebra with geometry. The graph of any equation of the form $(x - h)^2 + (y - k)^2 = r^2$ is a circle and that the graph of any equation of the form $Ax + By = C$ is a line. In this section we will see that graphs of equations have many different geometric shapes.

Graphing Equations

The circle and the line provide nice examples of how algebra and geometry are interrelated. When you see an equation that you recognize as the equation of a circle or a line, sketching a graph is easy to do. Other equations have graphs that are not such familiar shapes. Until we learn to recognize the kinds of graphs that other equations have, we graph other equations by calculating enough ordered pairs to determine the shape of the graph. When you graph equations, try to anticipate what the graph will look like, and after the graph is drawn, pause to reflect on the shape of the graph and the type of equation that produced it. You might wish to look ahead to the Function Gallery in Section 3, which shows the basic functions that we will be studying.

Of course, a graphing calculator can speed up this process. Remember that a graphing calculator shows only finitely many points and a graph usually consists of infinitely many points. After looking at the display of a graphing calculator, you must still decide what the entire graph looks like.

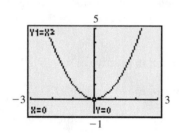

Figure 10

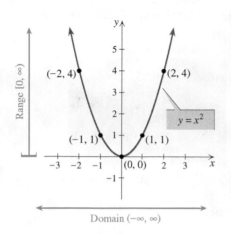

Figure 11

EXAMPLE 1 The square function

Graph the equation $y = x^2$ and state the domain and range. Determine whether the relation is a function.

Solution

Make a table of ordered pairs that satisfy $y = x^2$:

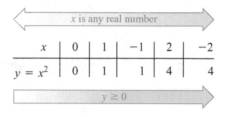

x	0	1	-1	2	-2
$y = x^2$	0	1	1	4	4

These ordered pairs indicate a graph in the shape shown in Fig. 10. The domain is $(-\infty, \infty)$ because any real number can be used for x in $y = x^2$. Since all y-coordinates are nonnegative, the range is $[0, \infty)$. Because no vertical line crosses this curve more than once, $y = x^2$ is a function.

The calculator graph shown in Fig. 11 supports these conclusions.

▶**TRY THIS.** Determine whether $y = \frac{1}{2}x^2$ is a function, graph it, and state the domain and range. ■

The graph of $y = x^2$ is called a **parabola.** The graph of the **square-root function** $y = \sqrt{x}$ is half of a parabola.

EXAMPLE 2 The square-root function

Graph $y = \sqrt{x}$ and state the domain and range of the relation. Determine whether the relation is a function.

Solution

Make a table listing ordered pairs that satisfy $y = \sqrt{x}$:

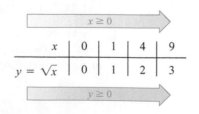

x	0	1	4	9
$y = \sqrt{x}$	0	1	2	3

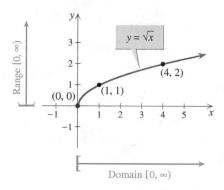

$y = \sqrt{x}$

(4, 2)

(1, 1)

(0, 0)

Range [0, ∞)

Domain [0, ∞)

Figure 12

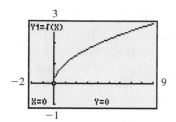

Figure 13

Plotting these ordered pairs suggests the graph shown in Fig. 12. The domain of the relation is $[0, \infty)$ and the range is $[0, \infty)$. Because no vertical line can cross this graph more than once, $y = \sqrt{x}$ is a function. The calculator graph in Fig. 13 supports these conclusions.

▶**TRY THIS.** Determine whether $y = \sqrt{1 - x}$ is a function, graph it, and state the domain and range. ∎

In the next example we graph $x = y^2$ and see that its graph is also a parabola.

EXAMPLE 3 | A parabola opening to the right

Graph $x = y^2$ and state the domain and range of the relation. Determine whether the relation is a function.

Solution

Make a table listing ordered pairs that satisfy $x = y^2$. In this case choose y and calculate x:

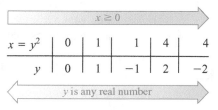

	$x \geq 0$				
$x = y^2$	0	1	1	4	4
y	0	1	−1	2	−2
	y is any real number				

Note that these ordered pairs are the same ones that satisfy $y = x^2$ except that the coordinates are reversed. For this reason the graph of $x = y^2$ in Fig. 14 has the same shape as the parabola in Fig. 10 and it is also a parabola. The domain of $x = y^2$ is $[0, \infty)$ and the range is $(-\infty, \infty)$. Because we can draw a vertical line that crosses this parabola twice, $x = y^2$ does not define y as a function of x. Because $x = y^2$ is equivalent to $y = \pm\sqrt{x}$, the top half of the graph of $x = y^2$ is $y = \sqrt{x}$ and the bottom half is $y = -\sqrt{x}$.

To support these conclusions with a graphing calculator, graph $y_1 = \sqrt{x}$ and $y_2 = -\sqrt{x}$ as shown in Fig. 15.

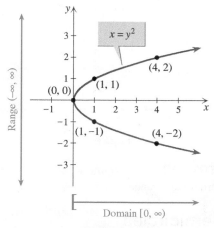

$x = y^2$

(4, 2)

(0, 0) (1, 1)

(1, −1) (4, −2)

Range (−∞, ∞)

Domain [0, ∞)

Figure 14

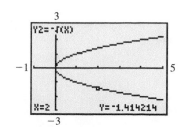

Figure 15

▶**TRY THIS.** Determine whether $x = -y^2$ is a function, graph it, and state the domain and range. ∎

In the next example we graph the **cube function** $y = x^3$ and the **cube-root function** $y = \sqrt[3]{x}$.

179

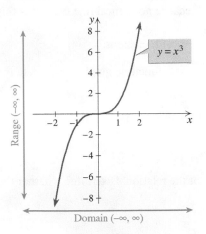

Figure 16

EXAMPLE 4 | Cube and cube-root functions

Graph each equation. State the domain and range.

a. $y = x^3$ **b.** $y = \sqrt[3]{x}$

Solution

a. Make a table listing ordered pairs that satisfy $y = x^3$:

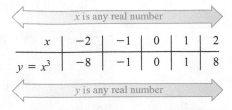

x	-2	-1	0	1	2
$y = x^3$	-8	-1	0	1	8

These ordered pairs indicate a graph in the shape shown in Fig. 16. The domain is $(-\infty, \infty)$ and the range is $(-\infty, \infty)$. By the vertical line test, this graph is the graph of a function because no vertical line crosses the curve more than once.

b. Make a table listing ordered pairs that satisfy $y = \sqrt[3]{x}$. Note that this table is simply the table for $y = x^3$ with the coordinates reversed.

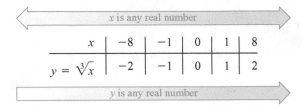

x	-8	-1	0	1	8
$y = \sqrt[3]{x}$	-2	-1	0	1	2

These ordered pairs indicate a graph in the shape shown in Fig. 17. The domain is $(-\infty, \infty)$ and the range is $(-\infty, \infty)$. Because no vertical line crosses this graph more than once, $y = \sqrt[3]{x}$ is a function.

The calculator graph in Fig. 18 supports these conclusions.

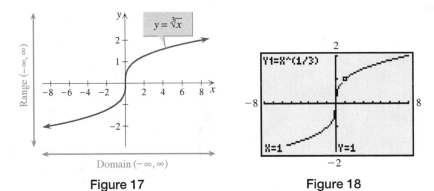

Figure 17 **Figure 18**

▶**TRY THIS.** Determine whether $y = -\sqrt[3]{x}$ is a function, graph it, and state the domain and range. ∎

Semicircles

The graph of $x^2 + y^2 = r^2 (r > 0)$ is a circle centered at the origin of radius r. A circle does not pass the vertical line test, and is not the graph of a function. We can find an equivalent equation by solving for y:

$$x^2 + y^2 = r^2$$
$$y^2 = r^2 - x^2$$
$$y = \pm\sqrt{r^2 - x^2}$$

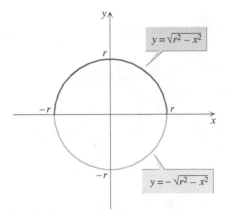

Figure 19

The equation $y = \sqrt{r^2 - x^2}$ does define y as a function of x. Because y is nonnegative in this equation, the graph is the top semicircle in Fig. 19. The top semicircle passes the vertical line test. Likewise, the equation $y = -\sqrt{r^2 - x^2}$ defines y as a function of x, and its graph is the bottom semicircle in Fig. 19.

EXAMPLE 5 Graphing a semicircle

Sketch the graph of each function and state the domain and range of the function.

a. $y = -\sqrt{4 - x^2}$ **b.** $y = \sqrt{9 - x^2}$

Solution

a. Rewrite the equation in the standard form for a circle:

$$y = -\sqrt{4 - x^2}$$
$$y^2 = 4 - x^2 \qquad \text{Square each side.}$$
$$x^2 + y^2 = 4 \qquad \text{Standard form for the equation of a circle}$$

The graph of $x^2 + y^2 = 4$ is a circle of radius 2 centered at $(0, 0)$. Since y must be negative in $y = -\sqrt{4 - x^2}$, the graph of $y = -\sqrt{4 - x^2}$ is the semicircle shown in Fig. 20. We can see from the graph that the domain is $[-2, 2]$ and the range is $[-2, 0]$.

b. Rewrite the equation in the standard form for a circle:

$$y = \sqrt{9 - x^2}$$
$$y^2 = 9 - x^2 \qquad \text{Square each side.}$$
$$x^2 + y^2 = 9 \qquad \text{Standard form for the equation of a circle}$$

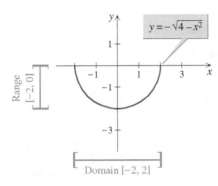

Figure 20

The graph of $x^2 + y^2 = 9$ is a circle with center $(0, 0)$ and radius 3. But this equation is not equivalent to the original. The value of y in $y = \sqrt{9 - x^2}$ is nonnegative. So the graph of the original equation is the semicircle shown in Fig. 21. We can read the domain $[-3, 3]$ and the range $[0, 3]$ from the graph.

▶**TRY THIS.** Graph $y = -\sqrt{9 - x^2}$ and state the domain and range. ■

Piecewise Functions

For some functions, different formulas are used in different regions of the domain. Since these functions are pieced together from two or more functions, they are called **piecewise functions.** The simplest example of such a function is the **absolute value function** $f(x) = |x|$, which can be written as

$$f(x) = \begin{cases} x & \text{for} \quad x \geq 0 \\ -x & \text{for} \quad x < 0. \end{cases}$$

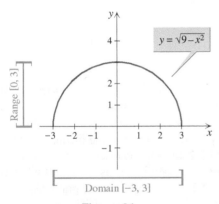

Figure 21

For $x \geq 0$ the equation $f(x) = x$ is used to obtain the second coordinate, and for $x < 0$ the equation $f(x) = -x$ is used. The graph of the absolute value function is shown in the next example. Note how the graph is pieced together from the graphs of $y = x$ and $y = -x$.

EXAMPLE 6 The absolute value function

Graph the equation $y = |x|$ and state the domain and range. Determine whether the relation is a function.

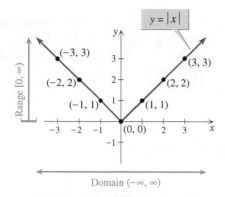

Figure 22

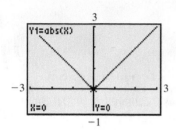

Figure 23

Solution

If $x \geq 0$ use $y = x$ to determine ordered pairs that satisfy $y = |x|$. If $x < 0$ use $y = -x$:

$x \ (x \geq 0)$	0	1	2	3
$y = x$	0	1	2	3

$x \ (x < 0)$	-1	-2	-3
$y = -x$	1	2	3

Plot these ordered pairs to get the V-shaped graph shown in Fig. 22. Because no vertical line crosses the graph more than once, $y = |x|$ is a function. Note that x can be any real number, but y is nonnegative. So the domain is $(-\infty, \infty)$ and the range is $[0, \infty)$.

To support these conclusions with a graphing calculator, graph $y_1 = \text{abs}(x)$ as shown in Fig. 23.

▶**TRY THIS.** Determine whether $y = |x| + 2$ is a function, graph it, and state the domain and range. ■

In the next example we graph two more piecewise functions.

EXAMPLE 7 Graphing a piecewise function

Sketch the graph of each function and state the domain and range.

a. $f(x) = \begin{cases} 1 & \text{for } x < 2 \\ -1 & \text{for } x \geq 2 \end{cases}$ **b.** $f(x) = \begin{cases} x^2 - 4 & \text{for } -2 \leq x \leq 2 \\ x - 2 & \text{for } x > 2 \end{cases}$

Solution

a. For $x < 2$ the graph is the horizontal line $y = 1$. For $x \geq 2$ the graph is the horizontal line $y = -1$. Note that $(2, -1)$ is on the graph shown in Fig. 24 but $(2, 1)$ is not, because when $x = 2$ we have $y = -1$. The domain is the interval $(-\infty, \infty)$ and the range consists of only two numbers, -1 and 1. The range is not an interval. It is written in set notation as $\{-1, 1\}$. Note that the graph consists of two separate sections that do not touch each other.

b. Make a table of ordered pairs using $y = x^2 - 4$ for x between -2 and 2 and $y = x - 2$ for $x > 2$.

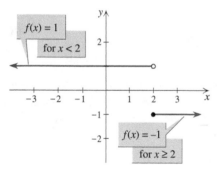

Figure 24

x	-2	-1	0	1	2
$y = x^2 - 4$	0	-3	-4	-3	0

x	2.1	3	4	5
$y = x - 2$	0.1	1	2	3

For x in the interval $[-2, 2]$ the graph is a portion of a parabola as shown in Fig. 25. For $x > 2$, the graph is a portion of a straight line through $(2.1, 0.1)$, $(3, 1)$, $(4, 2)$, and $(5, 3)$. The domain is $[-2, \infty)$, and the range is $[-4, \infty)$.

To graph a piecewise function on your calculator, use the inequality symbols from the TEST menu as shown in Fig. 26(a). On the calculator, an inequality or a compound inequality has a value of 1 when it is satisfied and 0 when it is not satisfied. So $y_1 = (x^2 - 4)/(x \geq -2 \text{ and } x \leq 2)$ will be graphed as the parabola $y = x^2 - 4$ only when both inequalities are satisfied. The word "and" is found in the TEST LOGIC menu. To graph $y = x - 2$ only for $x > 2$ enter $y_2 = (x - 2)/(x > 2)$. The calculator graph is shown in Fig. 26(b).

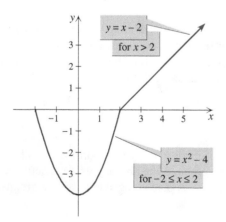

Figure 25

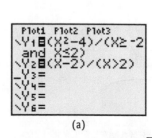
(a)

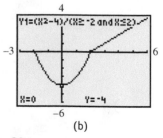
(b)

Figure 26

▶**TRY THIS.** Graph $y = \begin{cases} x & \text{for } x \geq 0 \\ -2x & \text{for } x < 0 \end{cases}$ and state the domain and range. ■

Piecewise functions are often found in shipping charges. For example, if the weight in pounds of an order is in the interval $(0, 1]$, the shipping and handling charge is \$3. If the weight is in the interval $(1, 2]$, the shipping and handling charge is \$4, and so on. The next example is a function that is similar to a shipping and handling charge. This function is referred to as the **greatest integer function** and is written $f(x) = [x]$ or $f(x) = \text{int}(x)$. The symbol $[x]$ is defined to be the largest integer that is less than or equal to x. For example, $[5.01] = 5$, because the greatest integer less than or equal to 5.01 is 5. Likewise, $[3.2] = 3$, $[-2.2] = -3$, and $[7] = 7$.

EXAMPLE 8 | Graphing the greatest integer function

Sketch the graph of $f(x) = [x]$ and state the domain and range.

Solution

For any x in the interval $[0, 1)$ the greatest integer less than or equal to x is 0. For any x in $[1, 2)$ the greatest integer less than or equal to x is 1. For any x in $[-1, 0)$ the greatest integer less than or equal to x is -1. The definition of $[x]$ causes the function to be constant between the integers and to "jump" at each integer. The graph of $f(x) = [x]$ is shown in Fig. 27. The domain is $(-\infty, \infty)$, and the range is the set of integers.

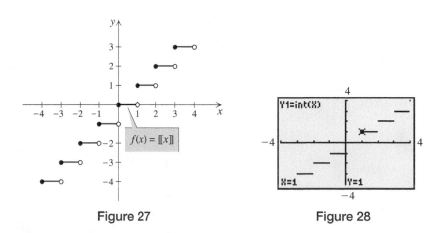

| Figure 27 | Figure 28 |

The calculator graph of $y_1 = \text{int}(x)$ looks best in dot mode as in Fig. 28, because in connected mode the calculator connects the disjoint pieces of the graph. The calculator graph in Fig. 28 supports our conclusion that the graph of this function looks like the one drawn in Fig. 27. Note that the calculator is incapable of showing whether the endpoints of the line segments are included.

▶**TRY THIS.** Graph $y = -[x]$ and state the domain and range. ■

In the next example we vary the form of the greatest integer function, but the graph is still similar to the graph in Fig. 27.

EXAMPLE 9 | A variation of the greatest integer function

Sketch the graph of $f(x) = [x - 2]$ for $0 \le x \le 5$.

Solution

If $x = 0$, $f(0) = [-2] = -2$. If $x = 0.5$, $f(0.5) = [-1.5] = -2$. In fact, $f(x) = -2$ for any x in the interval $[0, 1)$. Similarly, $f(x) = -1$ for any x in the interval $[1, 2)$.

183

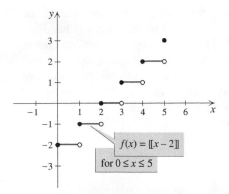

Figure 29

Definition: Increasing, Decreasing, Constant

This pattern continues with $f(x) = 2$ for any x in the interval $[4, 5)$, and $f(x) = 3$ for $x = 5$. The graph of $f(x) = [x - 2]$ is shown in Fig. 29.

▶**TRY THIS.** Graph $y = [x + 2]$ and state the domain and range. ∎

Increasing, Decreasing, and Constant

Imagine a point moving from left to right along the graph of a function. If the y-coordinate of the point is getting larger, smaller, or staying the same, then the function is said to be *increasing, decreasing,* or *constant,* respectively. More precisely we make the following definition.

> If $a < b$ implies $f(a) < f(b)$ for any a and b in the domain of f, then f is an **increasing** function.
>
> If $a < b$ implies $f(a) > f(b)$ for any a and b in the domain of f, then f is a **decreasing** function.
>
> If $a < b$ implies $f(a) = f(b)$ for any a and b in the domain of f, then f is a **constant** function.

(EXAMPLE **10**) Increasing, decreasing, or constant functions

Determine whether each function is increasing, decreasing, or constant by examining its graph.

a.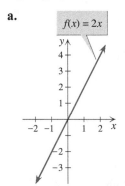

b.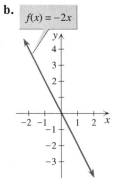

c.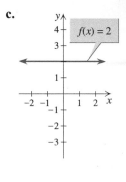

Solution

If a point is moving left to right along the graph of $f(x) = 2x$, then its y-coordinate is increasing. So $f(x) = 2x$ is an increasing function. If a point is moving left to right along the graph of $f(x) = -2x$, then its y-coordinate is decreasing. So $f(x) = -2x$ is a decreasing function. The function $f(x) = 2$ has a constant y-coordinate and it is a constant function.

▶**TRY THIS.** Determine whether $f(x) = -3x$ is increasing, decreasing, or constant by examining its graph. ∎

We can also discuss whether a function is increasing, decreasing, or constant on a subset of its domain. For example, the absolute value function $f(x) = |x|$, which we graphed in Example 6, is decreasing on the interval $(-\infty, 0]$ and increasing on the interval $[0, \infty)$.

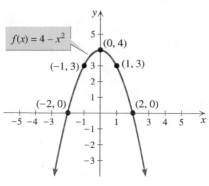

Figure 30

EXAMPLE 11 Increasing, decreasing, or constant on an interval

Sketch the graph of each function and identify any intervals on which the function is increasing, decreasing, or constant.

a. $f(x) = 4 - x^2$ **b.** $g(x) = \begin{cases} 0 & \text{for} & x \le 0 \\ \sqrt{x} & \text{for} & 0 < x < 4 \\ 2 & \text{for} & x \ge 4 \end{cases}$

Solution

a. The graph of $f(x) = 4 - x^2$ includes the points $(-2, 0)$, $(-1, 3)$, $(0, 4)$, $(1, 3)$, and $(2, 0)$. The graph is shown in Fig. 30. The function is increasing on the interval $(-\infty, 0]$ and decreasing on $[0, \infty)$.

b. The graph of g is shown in Fig. 31. The function g is constant on the intervals $(-\infty, 0]$ and $[4, \infty)$, and increasing on $[0, 4]$.

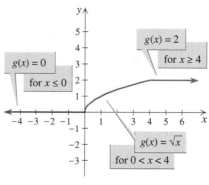

Figure 31

▶**TRY THIS.** Graph $f(x) = \begin{cases} x & \text{for} & x \ge 0 \\ -2x & \text{for} & x < 0 \end{cases}$ and identify any intervals on which the function is increasing, decreasing, or constant. ■

FOR thought... True or False? Explain

1. The range of $y = -x^2$ is $(-\infty, 0]$.

2. The function $y = -\sqrt{x}$ is increasing on $[0, \infty)$.

3. The function $f(x) = \sqrt[3]{x}$ is increasing on $(-\infty, \infty)$.

4. If $f(x) = [\![x + 3]\!]$, then $f(-4.5) = -2$.

5. The range of the function $f(x) = \frac{|x|}{x}$ is the interval $(-1, 1)$.

6. The range of $f(x) = [\![x - 1]\!]$ is the set of integers.

7. The only ordered pair that satisfies $(x - 5)^2 + (y + 6)^2 = 0$ is $(5, -6)$.

8. The domain of the function $y = \sqrt{4 - x^2}$ is the interval $[-2, 2]$.

9. The range of the function $y = \sqrt{16 - x^2}$ is the interval $[0, \infty)$.

10. The function $y = \sqrt{4 - x^2}$ is increasing on $[-2, 0]$ and decreasing on $[0, 2]$.

EXERCISES 2

Fill in the blank.

1. The graph of $y = x^2$ is a _____.

2. The absolute value function is an example of a _____ function.

Make a table listing ordered pairs that satisfy each equation. Then graph the equation. Determine the domain and range, and whether y is a function of x.

3. $y = 2x$ 4. $x = 2y$ 5. $x - y = 0$

6. $x - y = 2$ 7. $y = 5$ 8. $x = 3$

9. $y = 2x^2$ 10. $y = x^2 - 1$ 11. $y = 1 - x^2$

12. $y = -1 - x^2$ 13. $y = 1 + \sqrt{x}$ 14. $y = 2 - \sqrt{x}$

15. $x = y^2 + 1$ 16. $x = 1 - y^2$ 17. $x = \sqrt{y}$

18. $x - 1 = \sqrt{y}$ 19. $y = \sqrt[3]{x} + 1$ 20. $y = \sqrt[3]{x} - 2$

21. $x = \sqrt[3]{y}$ 22. $x = \sqrt[3]{y} - 1$ 23. $y^2 = 1 - x^2$

24. $x^2 + y^2 = 4$ 25. $y = \sqrt{1 - x^2}$ 26. $y = -\sqrt{25 - x^2}$

27. $y = x^3$ 28. $y = -x^3$ 29. $y = 2|x|$

30. $y = |x - 1|$ 31. $y = -|x|$ 32. $y = -|x + 1|$

33. $x = |y|$ 34. $x = |y| + 1$

Make a table listing ordered pairs for each function. Then sketch the graph and state the domain and range.

35. $f(x) = \begin{cases} 2 & \text{for } x < -1 \\ -2 & \text{for } x \geq -1 \end{cases}$

36. $f(x) = \begin{cases} 3 & \text{for } x < 2 \\ 1 & \text{for } x \geq 2 \end{cases}$

37. $f(x) = \begin{cases} x + 1 & \text{for } x > 1 \\ x - 3 & \text{for } x \leq 1 \end{cases}$

38. $f(x) = \begin{cases} 5 - x & \text{for } x \leq 2 \\ x + 1 & \text{for } x > 2 \end{cases}$

39. $f(x) = \begin{cases} \sqrt{x + 2} & \text{for } -2 \leq x \leq 2 \\ 4 - x & \text{for } x > 2 \end{cases}$

40. $f(x) = \begin{cases} \sqrt{x} & \text{for } x \geq 1 \\ -x & \text{for } x < 1 \end{cases}$

41. $f(x) = \begin{cases} \sqrt{-x} & \text{for } x < 0 \\ \sqrt{x} & \text{for } x \geq 0 \end{cases}$

42. $f(x) = \begin{cases} 3 & \text{for } x < 0 \\ 3 + \sqrt{x} & \text{for } x \geq 0 \end{cases}$

43. $f(x) = \begin{cases} x^2 & \text{for } x < -1 \\ -x & \text{for } x \geq -1 \end{cases}$

44. $f(x) = \begin{cases} 4 - x^2 & \text{for } -2 \leq x \leq 2 \\ x - 2 & \text{for } x > 2 \end{cases}$

45. $f(x) = [x + 1]$

46. $f(x) = 2[x]$

47. $f(x) = [x] + 2$ for $0 \leq x < 4$

48. $f(x) = [x - 3]$ for $0 < x \leq 5$

From the graph of each function in Exercises 49–56, state the domain, the range, and the intervals on which the function is increasing, decreasing, or constant.

49. a.

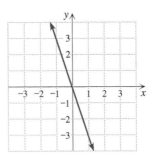

b.

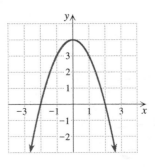

50. a.

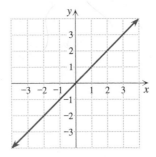

b.

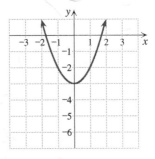

51. a.

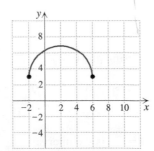

b.

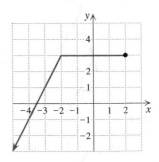

52. **a.**

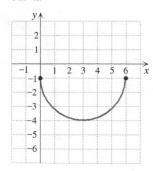

b.

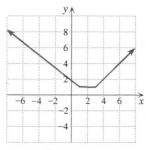

Make a table listing ordered pairs for each function. Then sketch the graph and state the domain and range. Identify any intervals on which f is increasing, decreasing, or constant.

57. $f(x) = 2x + 1$

58. $f(x) = -3x$

59. $f(x) = |x - 1|$

60. $f(x) = |x| + 1$

61. $f(x) = \dfrac{|x|}{x}$

62. $f(x) = \dfrac{2x}{|x|}$

63. $f(x) = \sqrt{9 - x^2}$

64. $f(x) = -\sqrt{1 - x^2}$

53. **a.**

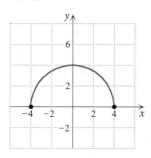

b.

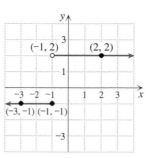

65. $f(x) = \begin{cases} x + 1 & \text{for } x \geq 3 \\ x + 2 & \text{for } x < 3 \end{cases}$

66. $f(x) = \begin{cases} \sqrt{-x} & \text{for } x < 0 \\ -\sqrt{x} & \text{for } x \geq 0 \end{cases}$

67. $f(x) = \begin{cases} x + 3 & \text{for } x \leq -2 \\ \sqrt{4 - x^2} & \text{for } -2 < x < 2 \\ -x + 3 & \text{for } x \geq 2 \end{cases}$

54. **a.**

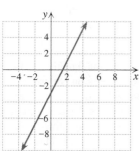

b.

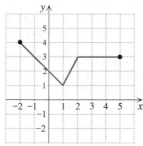

68. $f(x) = \begin{cases} 8 + 2x & \text{for } x \leq -2 \\ x^2 & \text{for } -2 < x < 2 \\ 8 - 2x & \text{for } x \geq 2 \end{cases}$

Write a piecewise function for each given graph.

69.

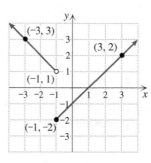

70.

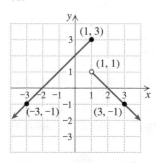

55. **a.**

b.

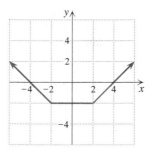

71.

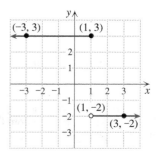

72.

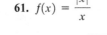

56. **a.**

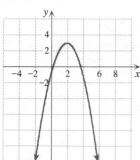

b.

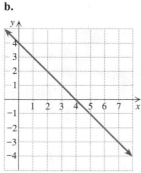

73.

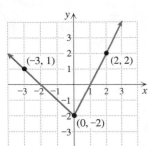

74.

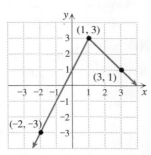

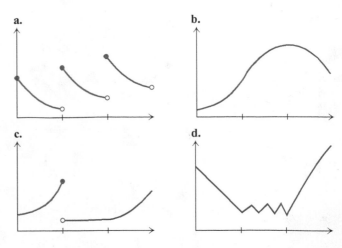

Figure for Exercises 83 to 86

Use the minimum and maximum features of a graphing calculator to find the intervals on which each function is increasing or decreasing. Round approximate answers to two decimal places.

75. $y = 3x^2 - 5x - 4$

76. $y = -6x^2 + 2x - 9$

77. $y = x^3 - 3x$

78. $y = x^4 - 11x^2 + 18$

79. $y = 2x^4 - 12x^2 + 25$

80. $y = x^5 - 13x^3 + 36x$

81. $y = |20 - |x - 50||$

82. $y = x + |x + 30| - |x + 50|$

Select the graph (a, b, c, or d) that best depicts each of the following scenarios.

83. Profits for Cajun Drilling Supplies soared during the seventies, but went flat when the bottom fell out of the oil industry in the eighties. Cajun saw a period of moderate growth in the nineties.

84. To attain a minimum therapeutic level of Flexeril in her blood, Millie takes three Flexeril tablets, one every four hours. Because the half-life of Flexeril is four hours, one-half of the Flexeril in her blood is eliminated after four hours.

85. The bears dominated the market during the first quarter with massive sell-offs. The second quarter was an erratic period in which investors could not make up their minds. The bulls returned during the third quarter, sending the market to record highs.

86. Medicare spending soared during the eighties. Congress managed to slow the rate of growth of Medicare during the nineties and actually managed to decrease Medicare spending in the first decade of the twenty-first century.

Draw a graph that pictures each situation. Explain any choices that you make. Identify the independent and dependent variables. Determine the intervals on which the dependent variable is increasing, decreasing, or constant. Answers may vary.

87. Captain Janeway left the holodeck at 7:45 to meet Tuvok, her chief of security, on the Bridge. After walking for 3 minutes, she realized she had forgotten her tricorder and returned to get it. She picked up the tricorder and resumed her walk, arriving on the Bridge at 8:00. After 15 minutes the discussion was over, and Janeway returned to the holodeck. Graph Janeway's distance from the holodeck as a function of time.

88. Starting from the pit, Helen made three laps around a circular race track at 40 seconds per lap. She then made a 30-second pit stop and two and a half laps before running off the track and getting stuck in the mud for the remainder of the five-minute race. Graph Helen's distance from the pit as a function of time.

89. Winona deposited $30 per week into her cookie jar. After 2 years she spent half of her savings on a stereo. After spending 6 months in the outback she proceeded to spend $15 per week on CDs until all of the money in the jar was gone. Graph the amount in her cookie jar as a function of time.

90. Michael started buying Navajo crafts with $8000 in his checking account. He spent $200 per day for 10 days on pottery, then $400 per day for the next 10 days on turquoise and silver jewelry. For the next 20 days, he spent $50 per day on supplies while he set up his retail shop. He rested for 5 days, then took in $800 per day for the next 20 days from the resale of his collection. Graph the amount in his checking account as a function of time.

Solve each problem.

91. *Motor Vehicle Ownership* World motor vehicle ownership in developed countries can be modeled by the function

$$M(t) = \begin{cases} 17.5t + 250 & \text{for} \quad 0 \le t \le 20 \\ 10t + 400 & \text{for} \quad 20 < t \le 40 \end{cases}$$

where t is the number of years since 1970 and $M(t)$ is the number of motor vehicles in millions in the year $1970 + t$ (World Resources Institute, www.wri.org). See the accompanying figure. How many vehicles were there in developed countries in 1988? How many will there be in 2010? What was the average rate of change of motor vehicle ownership from 1984 to 1994?

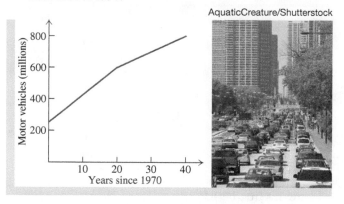

AquaticCreature/Shutterstock

Figure for Exercise 91

92. *Motor Vehicle Ownership* World motor vehicle ownership in developing countries and Eastern Europe can be modeled by the function

$$M(t) = 6.25t + 50$$

where t is the number of years since 1970 and $M(t)$ is in millions of vehicles (World Resources Institute, www.wri.org). Graph this function. What is the expected average rate of change of motor vehicle ownership from 1990 through 2010? Is motor vehicle ownership expected to grow faster in developed or developing countries in the period 1990 through 2010? (See the previous exercise.)

93. *Water Bill* The monthly water bill in Hammond is a function of the number of gallons used. The cost is $10.30 for 10,000 gal or less. Over 10,000 gal, the cost is $10.30 plus $1 for each 1000 gal over 10,000 with any fraction of 1000 gal charged at a fraction of $1. On what interval is the cost constant? On what interval is the cost increasing?

94. *Gas Mileage* The number of miles per gallon obtained with a new Toyota Prius is a function of the speed at which it is driven. Is this function increasing or decreasing on its domain? Explain.

95. *Filing a Tax Return* An accountant determines the charge for filing a tax return by using the function $C = 50 + 40\lceil t \rceil$ for $t > 0$, where C is in dollars and t is in hours. Sketch the graph of this function. For what values of t is the charge over $235?

96. *Shipping Machinery* The cost in dollars of shipping a machine is given by the function $C = 200 + 37\lceil w/100 \rceil$ for $w > 0$, where w is the weight of the machine in pounds. For which values of w is the cost less than $862?

97. *Delivering Concrete* A concrete company charges $150 for delivering less than 3 yd³ of concrete. For 3 yd³ and more, the charge is $50/yd³ with a fraction of a yard charged as a fraction of $50. Use function notation to write the charge as a function of the number x of cubic yards delivered, where $0 < x \le 10$, and graph this function.

98. *Parking Charges* A garage charges $4/hr up to 3 hr, with any fraction of an hour charged as a whole hour. Any time over 3 hr is charged at the all-day rate of $15. Use function notation to write the charge as a function of the number of hours x, where $0 < x \le 8$, and graph this function.

FOR WRITING/DISCUSSION

99. *Steps* Find an example of a function in real life whose graph has "steps" like that of the greatest integer function. Graph your function and find a formula for it if possible.

100. *Cooperative Learning* Select two numbers a and b. Then define a piecewise function using different formulas on the intervals $(-\infty, a]$, (a, b), and $[b, \infty)$ so that the graph does not "jump" at a or b. Give your function to a classmate to graph and check.

▶ RETHINKING

101. Find the domain and range of the function $f(x) = \sqrt{x - 2} + 3$.

102. Solve $|13x - 55| = -9$.

103. Solve $|13x - 55| = 0$.

104. Solve $|13x - 55| = 9$.

105. Solve $4x^2 - 20x + 25 = 0$.

106. Solve $2w^2 - 5w - 9 = 0$.

THINKING OUTSIDE THE BOX XIV

Best-Fitting Pipe A work crew is digging a pipeline through a frozen wilderness in Alaska. The cross section of the trench is in the shape of the parabola $y = x^2$. The pipe has a circular cross section. If the pipe is too large, then the pipe will not lie on the bottom of the trench.

a. What is the radius of the largest pipe that will lie on the bottom of the trench?

b. If the radius of the pipe is 3 and the trench is in the shape of $y = ax^2$, then what is the largest value of a for which the pipe will lie in the bottom of the trench?

POP QUIZ 2

1. Find the domain and range for $y = 1 - \sqrt{x}$.

2. Find the domain and range for $y = \sqrt{9 - x^2}$.

3. Find the range for $f(x) = \begin{cases} 2x & \text{for } x \geq 1 \\ 3 - x & \text{for } x < 1 \end{cases}$.

4. On what interval is $y = x^2$ increasing?

5. On what interval is $y = |x - 3|$ decreasing?

LINKING

concepts...   For Individual or Group Explorations

Bronwyn Kidd/Photodisc/Getty Images

Social Security and Life Expectancy

The average annual Social Security benefit in 2009 was about $13,800. The amount of a retiree's benefit depends on the retiree's lifetime earnings, the person's full retirement age, and the age at the time of retirement. The following function gives the annual benefit in dollars for a person retiring in 2009 at ages 62 through 70 with a full retirement benefit of $12,000 at full retirement age of 66.

$$B = \begin{cases} 600a - 28{,}200 & 62 \leq a < 64 \\ 804a - 41{,}064 & 64 \leq a < 67 \\ 960a - 51{,}360 & 67 \leq a \leq 70 \end{cases}$$

a) Graph the benefit function.

b) What is the annual benefit for a person who retires at age 64?

c) At what age does a person receive an annual benefit of $14,880?

d) What is the average rate of change of the benefit for the ages 62 through 63? Ages 64 through 66? Ages 66 through 70?

e) Do the answers to part (d) appear in the annual benefit formula?

The life expectancy L for a U.S. white male with present age a can be modeled by the formula

$$L = 67.0166(1.00308)^a.$$

f) Bob is a white male retiring in 2009 at age 62. What total amount can he be expected to draw from Social Security before he dies? Figure his Social Security benefit using the formula given above.

g) Bill is a white male retiring in 2009 at age 70. What total amount can he be expected to draw from Social Security before he dies? Figure his Social Security benefit using the formula given above.

3 Families of Functions, Transformations, and Symmetry

If a, h, and k are real numbers with $a \neq 0$, then $y = af(x - h) + k$ is a **transformation** of the function $y = f(x)$. All of the transformations of a function form a **family of functions**. For example, any function of the form $y = a\sqrt{x - h} + k$ is in the square-root family, any function of the form $y = a|x - h| + k$ is in the absolute value family, and any function of the form $y = a(x - h)^2 + k$ is in the square or quadratic family. All of the functions in a family of functions have similar graphs. The graph of any function in the square or quadratic family is called a **parabola**. We will now see what effect each of the numbers a, h, and k has on the graph of the original function $y = f(x)$.

Horizontal Translation

According to the order of operations, the first operation to perform in the formula $y = af(x - h) + k$ is to subtract h from x. Then $f(x - h)$ is multiplied by a, and finally k is added on. The order is important here and we will study the effects of these numbers in the order h, a, and k. Subtracting h from x causes the graph of $y = f(x)$ to move horizontally.

Definition: Translation to the Right or Left

> If $h > 0$, then the graph of $y = f(x - h)$ is a **translation of h units to the right** of the graph of $y = f(x)$. If $h < 0$, then the graph of $y = f(x - h)$ is a **translation of $|h|$ units to the left** of the graph of $y = f(x)$.

EXAMPLE 1 Translations to the right or left

Graph $f(x) = \sqrt{x}$, $g(x) = \sqrt{x - 3}$, and $h(x) = \sqrt{x + 5}$ on the same coordinate plane.

Solution

First sketch $f(x) = \sqrt{x}$ through $(0, 0)$, $(1, 1)$, and $(4, 2)$ as shown in Fig. 32. Since the first operation of g is to subtract 3, we get the corresponding points by adding 3 to each x-coordinate. So g goes through $(3, 0)$, $(4, 1)$, and $(7, 2)$. Since the first operation of h is to add 5, we get corresponding points by subtracting 5 from the x-coordinates. So h goes through $(-5, 0)$, $(-4, 1)$, and $(-1, 2)$.

The calculator graphs of f, g, and h are shown in Fig. 33. On many calculators the radical does not contain the radicand. Be sure to note the difference between $y = \sqrt{}(x) - 3$ and $y = \sqrt{}(x - 3)$ on a calculator.

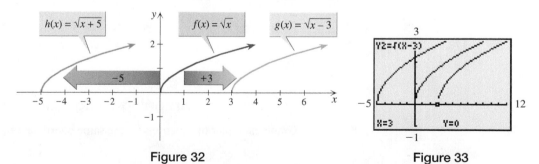

Figure 32   **Figure 33**

▶**TRY THIS.** Graph $f(x) = \sqrt{x}$, $g(x) = \sqrt{x - 2}$, and $h(x) = \sqrt{x + 1}$ on the same coordinate plane. ∎

Notice that $y = \sqrt{x - 3}$ lies 3 units to the *right* and $y = \sqrt{x + 5}$ lies 5 units to the *left* of $y = \sqrt{x}$. The next example shows two more horizontal translations.

EXAMPLE 2 | Horizontal translations

Sketch the graph of each function.

a. $f(x) = |x - 1|$ **b.** $f(x) = (x + 3)^2$

Solution

a. The function $f(x) = |x - 1|$ is in the absolute value family, and its graph is a translation one unit to the right of $g(x) = |x|$. Calculate a few ordered pairs to get an accurate graph. The points $(0, 1)$, $(1, 0)$, and $(2, 1)$ are on the graph of $f(x) = |x - 1|$ shown in Fig. 34.

b. The function $f(x) = (x + 3)^2$ is in the square family, and its graph is a translation three units to the left of the graph of $g(x) = x^2$. Calculate a few ordered pairs to get an accurate graph. The points $(-3, 0)$, $(-2, 1)$, and $(-4, 1)$ are on the graph shown in Fig. 35.

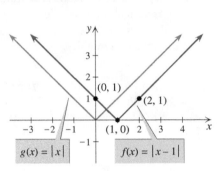

Figure 34

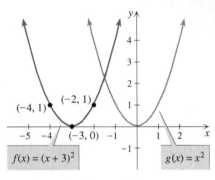

Figure 35

▶**TRY THIS.** Graph $f(x) = (x - 2)^2$. ■

Reflection

In the formula $y = af(x - h) + k$, we multiply $f(x - h)$ by a before adding k. So next we study the effect that a has on the graph. We first consider the case where $a = -1$. Multiplying by -1 is the same as taking the opposite, so we usually just write $y = -f(x)$. All points of the graph of $y = -f(x)$ can be obtained by simply changing the signs of all of the y-coordinates of the points on the graph of $y = f(x)$. This causes the graphs to be mirror images of each other with respect to the x-axis.

Definition: Reflection

> The graph of $y = -f(x)$ is a **reflection** in the x-axis of the graph of $y = f(x)$.

EXAMPLE 3 | Graphing using reflection

Graph each pair of functions on the same coordinate plane.

a. $f(x) = x^2$, $g(x) = -x^2$
b. $f(x) = x^3$, $g(x) = -x^3$
c. $f(x) = |x|$, $g(x) = -|x|$

Solution

a. The graph of $f(x) = x^2$ goes through $(0, 0)$, $(\pm 1, 1)$, and $(\pm 2, 4)$. The graph of $g(x) = -x^2$ goes through $(0, 0)$, $(\pm 1, -1)$, and $(\pm 2, -4)$ as shown in Fig. 36.

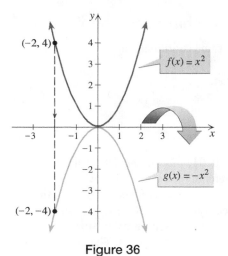

Figure 36

b. Make a table of ordered pairs for f as follows:

x	-2	-1	0	1	2
$f(x) = x^3$	-8	-1	0	1	8

Sketch the graph of f through these ordered pairs as shown in Fig. 37. Since $g(x) = -f(x)$, the graph of g can be obtained by reflecting the graph of f in the x-axis. Each point on the graph of f corresponds to a point on the graph of g with the opposite y-coordinate. For example, the point $(2, 8)$ on the graph of f corresponds to the point $(2, -8)$ on the graph of g. Both graphs are shown in Fig. 37.

c. The graph of f is the familiar V-shaped graph of the absolute value function as shown in Fig. 38. Since $g(x) = -f(x)$, the graph of g can be obtained by reflecting the graph of f in the x-axis. Each point on the graph of f corresponds to a point on the graph of g with the opposite y-coordinate. For example, $(2, 2)$ on f corresponds to $(2, -2)$ on g. Both graphs are shown in Fig. 38.

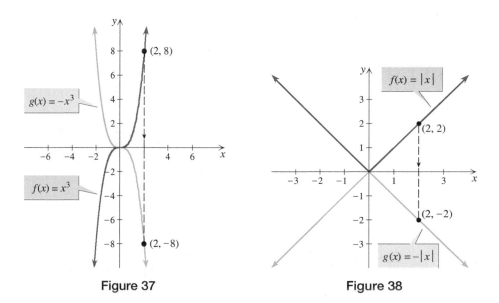

Figure 37

Figure 38

▶**TRY THIS.** Graph $f(x) = \sqrt{x}$ and $g(x) = -\sqrt{x}$ on the same coordinate plane. ■

We do not include reflections in the y-axis in our function families, but it is interesting to note that you get a reflection in the y-axis simply by replacing x with $-x$ in the formula for the function. For example, graph $y_1 = \sqrt{x}$ and $y_2 = \sqrt{-x}$ on your graphing calculator.

Stretching and Shrinking

If $a > 1$ then all of the y-coordinates on $y = af(x)$ are obtained by multiplying the y-coordinates on the graph of $y = f(x)$ by a. So the graph of $y = f(x)$ is *stretched* by a factor of a. If $0 < a < 1$ then the graph of $y = f(x)$ is *shrunk* by a factor of a. If a is negative, then reflection occurs along with the stretching or shrinking.

Definitions:
Stretching and Shrinking

The graph of $y = af(x)$ is obtained from the graph of $y = f(x)$ by

1. **stretching** the graph of $y = f(x)$ by a when $a > 1$, or
2. **shrinking** the graph of $y = f(x)$ by a when $0 < a < 1$.

EXAMPLE 4 Graphing using stretching and shrinking

In each case graph the three functions on the same coordinate plane.

a. $f(x) = \sqrt{x}$, $g(x) = 2\sqrt{x}$, $h(x) = \dfrac{1}{2}\sqrt{x}$

b. $f(x) = x^2$, $g(x) = 2x^2$, $h(x) = \dfrac{1}{2}x^2$

Solution

a. The graph of $f(x) = \sqrt{x}$ goes through $(0, 0)$, $(1, 1)$, and $(4, 2)$ as shown in Fig. 39. The graph of g is obtained by stretching the graph of f by a factor of 2. So g goes through $(0, 0)$, $(1, 2)$, and $(4, 4)$. The graph of h is obtained by shrinking the graph of f by a factor of $\frac{1}{2}$. So h goes through $(0, 0)$, $\left(1, \frac{1}{2}\right)$, and $(4, 1)$. The functions f, g, and h are shown on a graphing calculator in Fig. 40. Note how the viewing window affects the shape of the graph. The curves do not appear as separated on the calculator as they do in Fig. 39. □

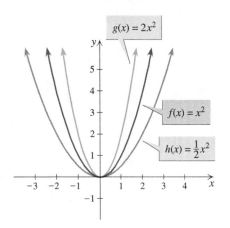

Figure 41

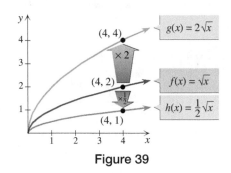

Figure 39

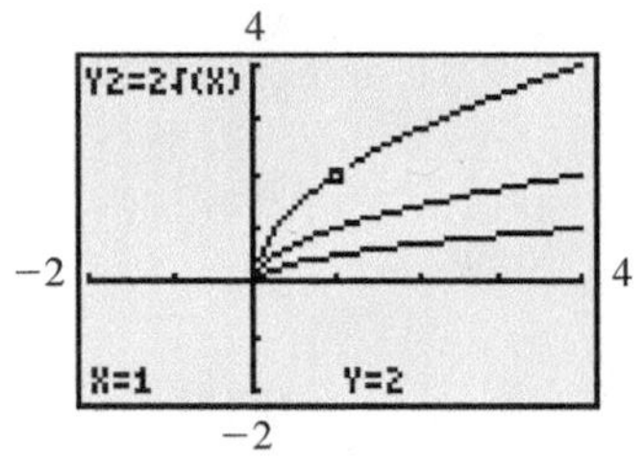

Figure 40

b. The graph of $f(x) = x^2$ is the familiar parabola shown in Fig. 41. We stretch it by a factor of 2 to get the graph of g and shrink it by a factor of $\frac{1}{2}$ to get the graph of h.

▶**TRY THIS.** Graph $f(x) = |x|$, $g(x) = 3|x|$, and $h(x) = \frac{1}{3}|x|$ on the same coordinate plane. ■

Note that the graph of $y = 2x^2$ has exactly the same shape as the graph of $y = x^2$ if we simply change the scale on the y-axis as in Fig. 42.

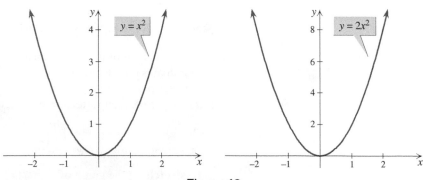

Figure 42

Vertical Translation

In the formula $y = af(x - h) + k$, the last operation is addition of k. If we add the constant k to all y-coordinates on the graph of $y = f(x)$, the graph will be translated up or down depending on whether k is positive or negative.

Definition: Translation Upward or Downward

If $k > 0$, then the graph of $y = f(x) + k$ is a **translation of k units upward** of the graph of $y = f(x)$. If $k < 0$, then the graph of $y = f(x) + k$ is a **translation of $|k|$ units downward** of the graph of $y = f(x)$.

EXAMPLE 5 Translations upward or downward

Graph the three given functions on the same coordinate plane.

a. $f(x) = \sqrt{x}, g(x) = \sqrt{x} + 3, h(x) = \sqrt{x} - 5$
b. $f(x) = x^2, g(x) = x^2 + 2, h(x) = x^2 - 3$

Solution

a. First sketch $f(x) = \sqrt{x}$ through $(0, 0)$, $(1, 1)$, and $(4, 2)$ as shown in Fig. 43. Since $g(x) = \sqrt{x} + 3$ we can add 3 to the y-coordinate of each point to get $(0, 3)$, $(1, 4)$, and $(4, 5)$. Sketch g through these points. Every point on f can be moved up 3 units to obtain a corresponding point on g. For $h(x) = \sqrt{x} - 5$, we subtract 5 from the y-coordinates on f to obtain points on h. So h goes through $(0, -5)$, $(1, -4)$, and $(4, -3)$.

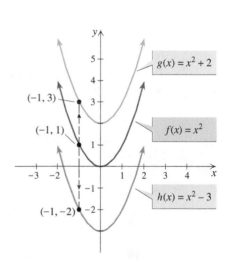

Figure 45

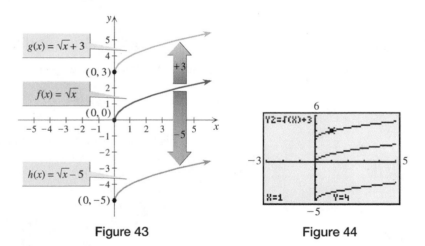

Figure 43   Figure 44

The relationship between f, g, and h can be seen with a graphing calculator in Fig. 44. You should experiment with your graphing calculator to see how a change in the formula changes the graph. □

b. First sketch the familiar graph of $f(x) = x^2$ through $(\pm 2, 4)$, $(\pm 1, 1)$, and $(0, 0)$ as shown in Fig. 45. Since $g(x) = f(x) + 2$, the graph of g can be obtained by translating the graph of f upward two units. Since $h(x) = f(x) - 3$, the graph of h can be obtained by translating the graph of f downward three units. For example, the point $(-1, 1)$ on the graph of f moves up to $(-1, 3)$ on the graph of g and down to $(-1, -2)$ on the graph of h as shown in Fig. 45.

▶**TRY THIS.** Graph $f(x) = \sqrt{x}, g(x) = \sqrt{x} + 1$, and $h(x) = \sqrt{x} - 2$ on the same coordinate plane. ■

Multiple Transformation

Any combination of stretching, shrinking, reflecting, horizontal translation, and vertical translation transforms one function into a new function. If a transformation does not change the shape of a graph, then it is a **rigid** transformation. If the shape changes, then it is **nonrigid.** Stretching and shrinking are nonrigid transformations. Translating (horizontally or vertically) and reflection are rigid transformations.

When graphing a function involving more than one transformation, $y = af(x - h) + k$, apply the transformations in the order that we discussed them: *h*-*a*-*k*. Remember that this order is simply the order of operations.

To graph $y = af(x - h) + k$ apply the transformations in the following order:

1. Horizontal translation (*h*)

2. Reflecting/stretching/shrinking (*a*)

3. Vertical translation (*k*).

Note that the order in which you reflect and stretch or reflect and shrink does not matter. It does matter that you do vertical translation last. For example, if $y = x^2$ is reflected in the *x*-axis and then translated up one unit, the equation for the graph is $y = -x^2 + 1$. If $y = x^2$ is translated up one unit and then reflected in the *x*-axis, the equation for the graph in the final position is $y = -(x^2 + 1)$ or $y = -x^2 - 1$. Changing the order has resulted in different functions.

EXAMPLE 6 Graphing using several transformations

Use transformations to graph each function.

a. $y = -2(x - 3)^2 + 4$ **b.** $y = 4 - 2\sqrt{x + 1}$

Solution

a. This function is in the square family. So the graph of $y = x^2$ is translated 3 units to the right, reflected and stretched by a factor of 2, and finally translated 4 units upward. See Fig. 46.

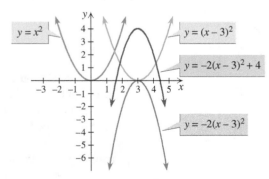

Figure 46

b. Rewrite the function as $y = -2\sqrt{x + 1} + 4$ and recognize that it is in the square root family. So we start with the graph of $y = \sqrt{x}$. The graph of $y = \sqrt{x + 1}$ is a horizontal translation one unit to the left of $y = \sqrt{x}$. Stretch by a factor of 2 to get $y = 2\sqrt{x + 1}$. Reflect in the *x*-axis to get $y = -2\sqrt{x + 1}$.

Finally, translate 4 units upward to get the graph of $y = -2\sqrt{x+1} + 4$. All of these graphs are shown in Fig. 47.

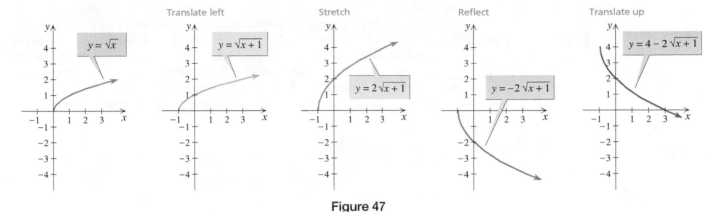

Figure 47

▶**TRY THIS.** Graph $y = 4 - 2|x + 1|$. ∎

The Linear Family of Functions

The function $f(x) = x$ is called the **identity function** because the coordinates in each ordered pair are identical. Its graph is a line through $(0, 0)$ with slope 1. A member of the **linear family,** a **linear function** is a transformation of the identity function: $f(x) = a(x - h) + k$ where $a \neq 0$. Since a, h, and k are real numbers, we can rewrite this form as a multiple of x plus a constant. So a linear function has the form $f(x) = mx + b$, with $m \neq 0$ (the slope-intercept form). If $m = 0$, then the function has the form $f(x) = b$ and it is a **constant function.**

EXAMPLE 7 Graphing linear functions using transformations

Sketch the graphs of $y = x$, $y = 2x$, $y = -2x$, and $y = -2x - 3$.

Solution

The graph of $y = x$ is a line through $(0, 0)$, $(1, 1)$, and $(2, 2)$. Stretch the graph of $y = x$ by a factor of 2 to get the graph of $y = 2x$. Reflect in the x-axis to get the graph of $y = -2x$. Translate downward three units to get the graph of $y = -2x - 3$. See Fig. 48.

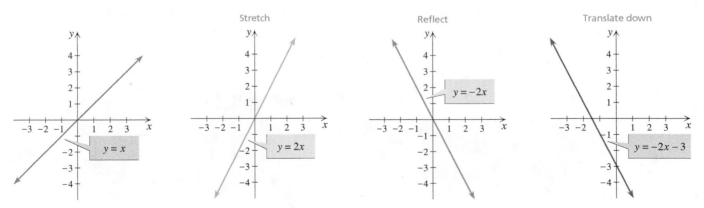

Figure 48

▶**TRY THIS.** Graph $y = -2x + 5$. ∎

Symmetry

The graph of $g(x) = -x^2$ is a reflection in the x-axis of the graph of $f(x) = x^2$. If the paper were folded along the x-axis, the graphs would coincide. See Fig. 49. The symmetry that we call reflection occurs between two functions, but the graph of $f(x) = x^2$ has a symmetry within itself. Points such as $(2, 4)$ and $(-2, 4)$ are on the graph and are equidistant from the y-axis. Folding the paper along the y-axis brings all such pairs of points together. See Fig. 50. The reason for this symmetry about the y-axis is the fact that $f(-x) = f(x)$ for any real number x. We get the same y-coordinate whether we evaluate the function at a number or at its opposite.

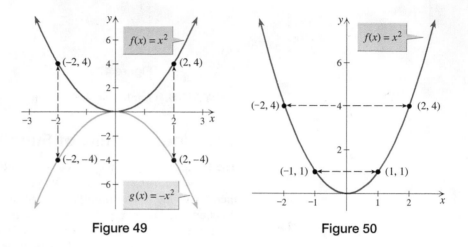

| Figure 49 | Figure 50 |

Definition: Symmetric about the y-Axis

If $f(-x) = f(x)$ for every value of x in the domain of the function f, then f is called an **even function** and its graph is **symmetric about the y-axis.**

Consider the graph of $f(x) = x^3$ shown in Fig. 51. On the graph of $f(x) = x^3$ we find pairs of points such as $(2, 8)$ and $(-2, -8)$. The odd exponent in x^3 causes the second coordinate to be negative when the sign of the first coordinate is changed from positive to negative. These points are equidistant from the origin and on opposite sides of the origin. So the symmetry of this graph is about the origin. In this case $f(x)$ and $f(-x)$ are not equal, but $f(-x) = -f(x)$.

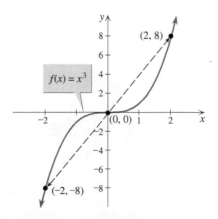

Figure 51

Definition: Symmetric about the Origin

> If $f(-x) = -f(x)$ for every value of x in the domain of the function f, then f is called an **odd function** and its graph is **symmetric about the origin.**

A graph might look like it is symmetric about the y-axis or the origin, but the only way to be sure is to use the definitions of these terms as shown in the following example. Note that an odd power of a negative number is negative and an even power of a negative number is positive. So for any real number x we have $(-x)^n = -x^n$ if n is odd and $(-x)^n = x^n$ if n is even.

EXAMPLE 8 Determining symmetry in a graph

Discuss the symmetry of the graph of each function.

a. $f(x) = 5x^3 - x$ **b.** $f(x) = |x| + 3$ **c.** $f(x) = x^2 - 3x + 6$

Solution

a. Replace x by $-x$ in the formula for $f(x)$ and simplify:

$$f(-x) = 5(-x)^3 - (-x) = -5x^3 + x$$

Is $f(-x)$ equal to $f(x)$ or the opposite of $f(x)$? Since $-f(x) = -5x^3 + x$, we have $f(-x) = -f(x)$. So f is an odd function and the graph is symmetric about the origin.

b. Since $|-x| = |x|$ for any x, we have $f(-x) = |-x| + 3 = |x| + 3$. Because $f(-x) = f(x)$, the function is even and the graph is symmetric about the y-axis.

c. In this case, $f(-x) = (-x)^2 - 3(-x) + 6 = x^2 + 3x + 6$. So $f(-x) \neq f(x)$, and $f(-x) \neq -f(x)$. This function is neither even nor odd and its graph has neither type of symmetry.

▶**TRY THIS.** Discuss the symmetry of the graph of $f(x) = -2x^2 + 5$. ∎

Do you see why functions symmetric about the y-axis are called *even* and functions symmetric about the origin are called *odd?* In general, a function defined by a polynomial with even exponents only, such as $f(x) = x^2$ or $f(x) = x^6 - 5x^4 + 2x^2 + 3$, is symmetric about the y-axis. (The constant term 3 has even degree because $3 = 3x^0$.) A function with only odd exponents such as $f(x) = x^3$ or $f(x) = x^5 - 6x^3 + 4x$ is symmetric about the origin. A function containing both even- and odd-powered terms such as $f(x) = x^2 + 3x$ has neither symmetry. For other types of functions (such as absolute value) you must examine the function more carefully to determine symmetry.

Note that functions cannot have x-axis symmetry. A graph that is symmetric about the x-axis fails the vertical line test. For example, the graph of $x = y^2$ is symmetric about the x-axis, but the graph fails the vertical line test and y is not a function of x.

Reading Graphs to Solve Inequalities

Using transformations we can graph more quickly and use those graphs to solve a wide variety of inequalities in one variable.

EXAMPLE 9 Using a graph to solve an inequality

Solve the inequality $(x - 1)^2 - 2 < 0$ by graphing.

Solution

The graph of $y = (x - 1)^2 - 2$ is obtained by translating the graph of $y = x^2$ one unit to the right and two units downward. See Fig. 52. To find the x-intercepts we solve $(x - 1)^2 - 2 = 0$:

$$(x - 1)^2 = 2$$
$$x - 1 = \pm\sqrt{2}$$
$$x = 1 \pm \sqrt{2}$$

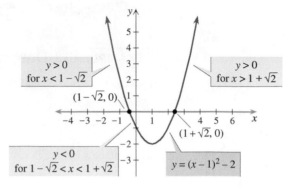

$y > 0$
for $x < 1 - \sqrt{2}$

$y > 0$
for $x > 1 + \sqrt{2}$

$(1 - \sqrt{2}, 0)$

$(1 + \sqrt{2}, 0)$

$y < 0$
for $1 - \sqrt{2} < x < 1 + \sqrt{2}$

$y = (x - 1)^2 - 2$

Figure 52

The x-intercepts are $(1 - \sqrt{2}, 0)$ and $(1 + \sqrt{2}, 0)$. If the y-coordinate of a point on the graph is negative, then the x-coordinate satisfies $(x - 1)^2 - 2 < 0$. So the solution set to $(x - 1)^2 - 2 < 0$ is the open interval $(1 - \sqrt{2}, 1 + \sqrt{2})$.

Although a graphing calculator will not find the exact solution to this inequality, you can use TRACE to support the answer and see that y is negative between the x-intercepts. See Fig. 53.

▶**TRY THIS.** Solve $2 - |x - 1| \le 0$ by graphing. ■

Note that the solution set to $(x - 1)^2 - 2 \ge 0$ can also be obtained from the graph in Fig. 52. If the y-coordinate of a point on the graph is positive or zero, then the x-coordinate satisfies $(x - 1)^2 - 2 \ge 0$. So the solution set to $(x - 1)^2 - 2 \ge 0$ is $(-\infty, 1 - \sqrt{2}] \cup [1 + \sqrt{2}, \infty)$.

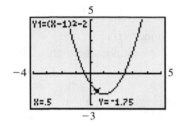

Figure 53

▶ **FUNCTION**
gallery... Some Basic Functions and Their Properties

Constant Function

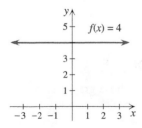

Domain $(-\infty, \infty)$
Range {4}
Constant on $(-\infty, \infty)$
Symmetric about y-axis

Identity Function

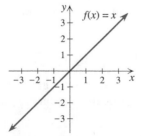

Domain $(-\infty, \infty)$
Range $(-\infty, \infty)$
Increasing on $(-\infty, \infty)$
Symmetric about origin

Linear Function

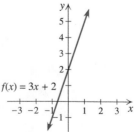

Domain $(-\infty, \infty)$
Range $(-\infty, \infty)$
Increasing on $(-\infty, \infty)$

Absolute Value Function

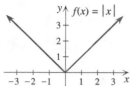

Domain $(-\infty, \infty)$
Range $[0, \infty)$
Increasing on $[0, \infty)$
Decreasing on $(-\infty, 0]$
Symmetric about y-axis

Square Function

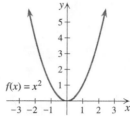

Domain $(-\infty, \infty)$
Range $[0, \infty)$
Increasing on $[0, \infty)$
Decreasing on $(-\infty, 0]$
Symmetric about y-axis

Square-Root Function

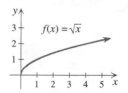

Domain $[0, \infty)$
Range $[0, \infty)$
Increasing on $[0, \infty)$

Cube Function

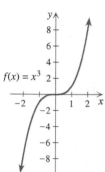

Domain $(-\infty, \infty)$
Range $(-\infty, \infty)$
Increasing on $(-\infty, \infty)$
Symmetric about origin

Cube-Root Function

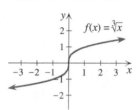

Domain $(-\infty, \infty)$
Range $(-\infty, \infty)$
Increasing on $(-\infty, \infty)$
Symmetric about origin

Greatest Integer Function

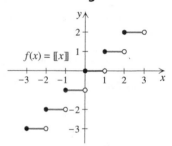

Domain $(-\infty, \infty)$
Range $\{n \mid n$ is an integer$\}$
Constant on $[n, n + 1)$
  for every integer n

FOR thought... True or False? Explain.

1. The graph of $f(x) = (-x)^4$ is a reflection in the x-axis of the graph of $g(x) = x^4$.

2. The graph of $f(x) = x - 4$ lies four units to the right of the graph of $f(x) = x$.

3. The graph of $y = |x + 2| + 3$ is a translation two units to the right and three units upward of the graph of $y = |x|$.

4. The graph of $f(x) = -3$ is a reflection in the x-axis of the graph of $g(x) = 3$.

5. The functions $y = x^2 + 4x + 1$ and $y = (x + 2)^2 - 3$ have the same graph.

6. The graph of $y = -(x - 3)^2 - 4$ can be obtained by moving $y = x^2$ three units to the right and down four units, and then reflecting in the x-axis.

7. If $f(x) = -x^3 + 2x^2 - 3x + 5$, then $f(-x) = x^3 + 2x^2 + 3x + 5$.

8. The graphs of $f(x) = -\sqrt{x}$ and $g(x) = \sqrt{-x}$ are identical.

9. If $f(x) = x^3 - x$, then $f(-x) = -f(x)$.

10. The solution set to $|x| - 1 \le 0$ is $[-1, 1]$.

201

EXERCISES 3

Fill in the blank.

1. Translating and reflecting are _____ transformations.

2. Stretching and shrinking are _____ transformations.

3. The graph of a function of the form $y = a(x - h)^2 + k$ where $a \neq 0$ is a _____.

4. The graph of $y = f(x - h)$ is a _____ of the graph of $y = f(x)$.

5. The graph of $y = -f(x)$ is a _____ of the graph of $y = f(x)$.

6. The function $f(x) = x$ is the _____ function.

7. The function $f(x) = mx + b$ with $m \neq 0$ is a _____ function.

8. The function $f(x) = b$ is a _____ function.

9. If $f(-x) = -f(x)$ for every x in the domain of f, then f is an _____ function.

10. If $f(-x) = f(x)$ for every x in the domain of f, then f is an _____ function.

Sketch the graphs of each pair of functions on the same coordinate plane.

11. $f(x) = |x|$, $g(x) = |x| - 4$

12. $f(x) = \sqrt{x}$, $g(x) = \sqrt{x} + 3$

13. $f(x) = x$, $g(x) = x + 3$ 14. $f(x) = x^2$, $g(x) = x^2 - 5$

15. $y = x^2$, $y = (x - 3)^2$ 16. $y = |x|$, $y = |x + 2|$

17. $y = \sqrt{x}$, $y = \sqrt{x + 9}$ 18. $y = x^2$, $y = (x - 1)^2$

19. $f(x) = \sqrt{x}$, $g(x) = -\sqrt{x}$ 20. $f(x) = x$, $g(x) = -x$

21. $y = \sqrt{x}$, $y = 3\sqrt{x}$

22. $y = \sqrt{1 - x^2}$, $y = 4\sqrt{1 - x^2}$

23. $y = x^2$, $y = \frac{1}{4}x^2$ 24. $y = |x|$, $y = \frac{1}{3}|x|$

25. $y = \sqrt{4 - x^2}$, $y = -\sqrt{4 - x^2}$

26. $f(x) = x^2 + 1$, $g(x) = -(x^2 + 1)$

Match each function in Exercises 27–34 with its graph (a)–(h).

27. $y = x^2$ 28. $y = (x - 4)^2 + 2$

29. $y = (x + 4)^2 - 2$ 30. $y = -2(x - 2)^2$

31. $y = -2(x + 2)^2$

32. $y = -\frac{1}{2}x^2 - 4$

33. $y = \frac{1}{2}(x + 4)^2 + 2$

34. $y = -2(x - 4)^2 - 2$

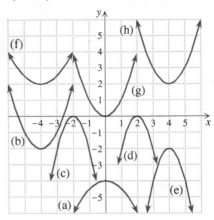

Figure for Exercises 27 to 34

Write the equation of each graph after the indicated transformation(s).

35. The graph of $y = \sqrt{x}$ is translated two units upward.

36. The graph of $y = \sqrt{x}$ is translated three units downward.

37. The graph of $y = x^2$ is translated five units to the right.

38. The graph of $y = x^2$ is translated seven units to the left.

39. The graph of $y = x^2$ is translated ten units to the right and four units upward.

40. The graph of $y = \sqrt{x}$ is translated five units to the left and twelve units downward.

41. The graph of $y = \sqrt{x}$ is stretched by a factor of 3, translated five units upward, then reflected in the x-axis.

42. The graph of $y = x^2$ is translated thirteen units to the right and six units downward, then reflected in the x-axis.

43. The graph of $y = |x|$ is reflected in the x-axis, stretched by a factor of 3, then translated seven units to the right and nine units upward.

44. The graph of $y = x$ is stretched by a factor of 2, reflected in the x-axis, then translated eight units downward and six units to the left.

Use transformations to graph each function and state the domain and range.

45. $y = (x - 1)^2 + 2$

46. $y = (x + 5)^2 - 4$

47. $y = |x - 1| + 3$

48. $y = |x + 3| - 4$

49. $y = 3x - 40$

50. $y = -4x + 200$

51. $y = \dfrac{1}{2}x - 20$

52. $y = -\dfrac{1}{2}x + 40$

53. $y = -\dfrac{1}{2}|x| + 40$

54. $y = 3|x| - 200$

55. $y = -\dfrac{1}{2}|x + 4|$

56. $y = 3|x - 2|$

57. $y = -\sqrt{x - 3} + 1$

58. $y = -\sqrt{x + 2} - 4$

59. $y = -2\sqrt{x + 3} + 2$

60. $y = -\dfrac{1}{2}\sqrt{x + 2} + 4$

Determine algebraically whether the function is even, odd, or neither. Discuss the symmetry of each function.

61. $f(x) = x^4$

62. $f(x) = x^4 - 2x^2$

63. $f(x) = x^4 - x^3$

64. $f(x) = x^3 - x$

65. $f(x) = (x + 3)^2$

66. $f(x) = (x - 1)^2$

67. $f(x) = |x - 2|$

68. $f(x) = |x| - 9$

69. $f(x) = x$

70. $f(x) = -x$

71. $f(x) = 3x + 2$

72. $f(x) = x - 3$

73. $f(x) = x^3 - 5x + 1$

74. $f(x) = x^6 - x^4 + x^2$

75. $f(x) = 1 + \dfrac{1}{x^2}$

76. $f(x) = (x^2 - 2)^3$

77. $f(x) = \sqrt{x}$

78. $f(x) = \sqrt{9 - x^2}$

79. $f(x) = |x^2 - 3|$

80. $f(x) = \sqrt{x^2 + 3}$

Match each function with its graph (a)–(h).

81. $y = 2 + \sqrt{x}$

82. $y = \sqrt{2 + x}$

83. $y = \sqrt{x^2}$

84. $y = \sqrt{\dfrac{x}{2}}$

85. $y = \dfrac{1}{2}\sqrt{x}$

86. $y = 2 - \sqrt{x - 2}$

87. $y = -2\sqrt{x}$

88. $y = -\sqrt{-x}$

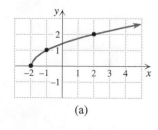

(a)

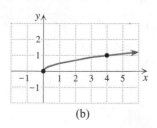

(b)

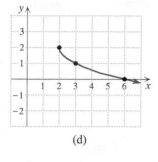

(c)

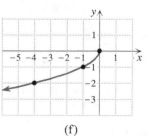

(d)

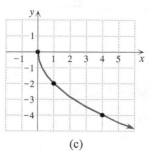

(e)

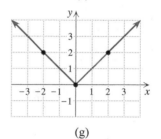

(f)

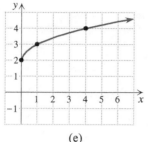

(g)

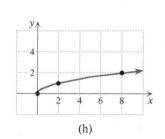

(h)

Figure for Exercises 81 to 88

Solve each inequality by reading the corresponding graph.

89. $x^2 - 1 \geq 0$

90. $2x^2 - 3 < 0$

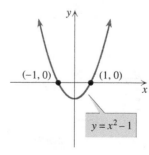

$y = x^2 - 1$

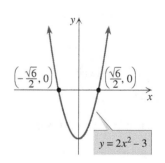

$y = 2x^2 - 3$

91. $|x - 2| - 3 > 0$

92. $2 - |x + 1| \geq 0$

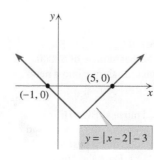

$y = |x - 2| - 3$

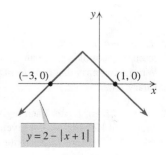

$y = 2 - |x + 1|$

Solve each inequality by graphing an appropriate function. State the solution set using interval notation.

93. $(x - 1)^2 - 9 < 0$

94. $\left(x - \dfrac{1}{2}\right)^2 - \dfrac{9}{4} \geq 0$

95. $5 - \sqrt{x} \geq 0$

96. $\sqrt{x + 3} - 2 \geq 0$

97. $(x - 2)^2 > 3$

98. $(x - 1)^2 < 4$

99. $\sqrt{25 - x^2} > 0$

100. $\sqrt{4 - x^2} \geq 0$

Use a graphing calculator to find an approximate solution to each inequality by reading the graph of an appropriate function. Round to two decimal places.

101. $\sqrt{3}x^2 + \pi x - 9 < 0$

102. $x^3 - 5x^2 + 6x - 1 > 0$

Graph each of the following functions by transforming the given graph of $y = f(x)$.

103. a. $y = 2f(x)$

  b. $y = -f(x)$

  c. $y = f(x + 1)$

  d. $y = f(x - 3)$

  e. $y = -3f(x)$

  f. $y = f(x + 2) - 1$

  g. $y = f(x - 1) + 3$

  h. $y = 3f(x - 2) + 1$

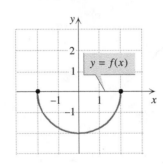

Figure for Exercise 103

104. a. $y = -f(x)$

  b. $y = 2f(x)$

  c. $y = -3f(x)$

  d. $y = f(x + 2)$

  e. $y = f(x - 1)$

  f. $y = f(x - 2) + 1$

  g. $y = -2f(x + 4)$

  h. $y = 2f(x - 3) + 1$

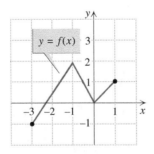

Figure for Exercise 104

Solve each problem.

105. *Across-the-Board Raise* Each teacher at C. F. Gauss Elementary School is given an across-the-board raise of $2000. Write a function that *transforms* each old salary x into a new salary $N(x)$.

106. *Cost-of-Living Raise* Each registered nurse at Blue Hills Memorial Hospital is first given a 5% cost-of-living raise and then a $3000 merit raise. Write a function that *transforms* each old salary x into a new salary $N(x)$. Does the order in which these raises are given make any difference? Explain.

107. *Unemployment Versus Inflation* The Phillips curve shows the relationship between the unemployment rate x and the inflation rate y. If the equation of the curve is $y = 1 - \sqrt{x}$ for a certain Third World country, then for what values of x is the inflation rate less than 50%?

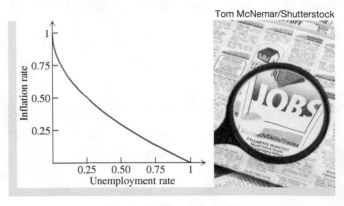

Tom McNemar/Shutterstock

Figure for Exercise 107

108. *Production Function* The production function shows the relationship between inputs and outputs. A manufacturer of custom windows produces y windows per week using x hours of labor per week, where $y = 1.75\sqrt{x}$. How many hours of labor are required to keep production at or above 28 windows per week?

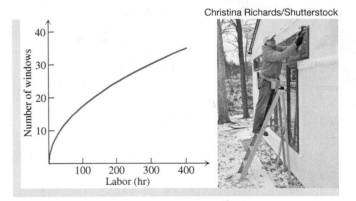

Christina Richards/Shutterstock

Figure for Exercise 108

FOR WRITING/DISCUSSION

109. Graph each pair of functions (without simplifying the second function) on the same screen of a graphing calculator and explain what each exercise illustrates.

  a. $y = x^4 - x^2$, $y = (-x)^4 - (-x)^2$

  b. $y = x^3 - x$, $y = (-x)^3 - (-x)$

  c. $y = x^4 - x^2$, $y = (x + 1)^4 - (x + 1)^2$

  d. $y = x^3 - x$, $y = (x - 2)^3 - (x - 2) + 3$

110. Graph $y = x^3 + 6x^2 + 12x + 8$ on a graphing calculator. Explain how this graph could be obtained as a transformation of a simpler function.

▶ RETHINKING

111. Find and simplify $f(a + 2) - f(a)$ given that $f(x) = x^2 + 1$.

112. Find the domain and range of the function $y = -\sqrt{36 - x^2}$.

113. Solve $2 - 3|x| \leq 0$. Write the solution set in interval notation.

114. Simplify i^{83}.

115. Solve $ay - 3 + by = cy - 5$ for y.

116. Express $\dfrac{-2 + i}{4 + 2i}$ in the form $a + bi$.

THINKING OUTSIDE THE BOX XV

Lucky Lucy Ms. Willis asked Lucy to come to the board to find the mean of a pair of one-digit positive integers. Lucy slowly wrote the numbers on the board. While trying to think of what to do next, she rested the chalk between the numbers to make a mark that looked like a decimal point to Ms. Willis. Ms. Willis said "correct" and asked her to find the mean for a pair of two-digit positive integers. Being a quick learner, Lucy again wrote the numbers on the board, rested the chalk between the numbers, and again Ms. Willis said "correct." Lucy had to demonstrate her ability to find the mean for a pair of three-digit and a pair of four-digit positive integers before Ms. Willis was satisfied that she understood the concept. What four pairs of integers did Ms. Willis give to Lucy? Explain why Lucy's method will not work for any other pairs of one-, two-, three-, or four-digit positive integers.

POP QUIZ 3

1. What is the equation of the curve $y = \sqrt{x}$ after it is translated 8 units upward?

2. What is the equation of the curve $y = x^2$ after it is translated 9 units to the right?

3. What is the equation of the curve $y = x^3$ after it is reflected in the x-axis?

4. Find the domain and range for $y = -2\sqrt{x - 1} + 5$.

5. If the curve $y = x^2$ is translated 6 units to the right, stretched by a factor of 3, reflected in the x-axis, and translated 4 units upward, then what is the equation of the curve in its final position?

6. Is $y = \sqrt{4 - x^2}$ even, odd, or neither?

▶ LINKING concepts... For Individual or Group Explorations

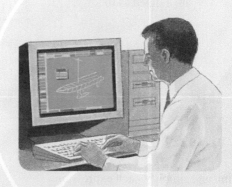

Designing a Racing Boat

According to International America's Cup Class rules, the basic dimensions of any yacht competing for the silver trophy must satisfy the inequality

$$16.96 + 9.8D^{1/3} - L - 1.25S^{1/2} \geq 0,$$

where L is the length in meters, S is the sail area in square meters, and D is the displacement in cubic meters (Americas Cup, www.americascup.org). Use a graphing utility to get approximate answers to the following questions.

a) A team of British designers wants its new boat to have a length of 20.85 m and a displacement of 17.67 m³. Write the inequality that must be satisfied by the sail area S. Use the graphing technique described in this section to find the interval in which S must lie.

b) A team of Australian designers wants its new boat to have a sail area of 312.54 m² and length of 21.45 m. Write the inequality that must be satisfied by the displacement D. Use the graphing technique to find the interval in which D must lie.

c) A team of American designers wants its new boat to have a sail area of 310.28 m² and a displacement of 17.26 m³. Write the inequality that must be satisfied by the length L. Use the graphing technique to find the interval in which L must lie.

d) When two of the three variables are fixed, the third variable either has a maximum or minimum value. Explain how you can determine whether it is a maximum or minimum by looking at the original inequality.

4 Operations with Functions

In Sections 2 and 3 we studied the graphs of functions to see the relationships between types of functions and their graphs. In this section we will study various ways in which two or more functions can be combined to make new functions. The emphasis here will be on formulas that define functions.

Basic Operations with Functions

A college student is hired to deliver new telephone books and collect the old ones for recycling. She is paid $6 per hour plus $0.30 for each old phone book she collects. Her salary for a 40-hour week is a function of the number of phone books collected. If x represents the number of phone books collected in one week, then the function $S(x) = 0.30x + 240$ gives her salary in dollars. However, she must use her own car for this job. She figures that her car expenses average $0.20 per phone book collected plus a fixed cost of $20 per week for insurance. We can write her expenses as a function of the number of phone books collected, $E(x) = 0.20x + 20$. Her profit for one week is her salary minus her expenses:

$$P(x) = S(x) - E(x)$$

$$= 0.30x + 240 - (0.20x + 20)$$

$$= 0.10x + 220$$

By subtracting, we get $P(x) = 0.10x + 220$. Her weekly profit is written as a function of the number of phone books collected. In this example we obtained a new function by subtracting two functions. In general, there are four basic arithmetic operations defined for functions.

Definition: Sum, Difference, Product, and Quotient Functions

For two functions f and g, the **sum, difference, product,** and **quotient functions,** functions $f + g$, $f - g$, $f \cdot g$, and f/g, respectively, are defined as follows:

$$(f + g)(x) = f(x) + g(x)$$

$$(f - g)(x) = f(x) - g(x)$$

$$(f \cdot g)(x) = f(x) \cdot g(x)$$

$$(f/g)(x) = f(x)/g(x) \quad \text{provided that } g(x) \neq 0.$$

Plot1 Plot2 Plot3
\Y1◼3√(X)-2
\Y2◼X²+5
\Y3=
\Y4=
\Y5=
\Y6=
\Y7=

(a)

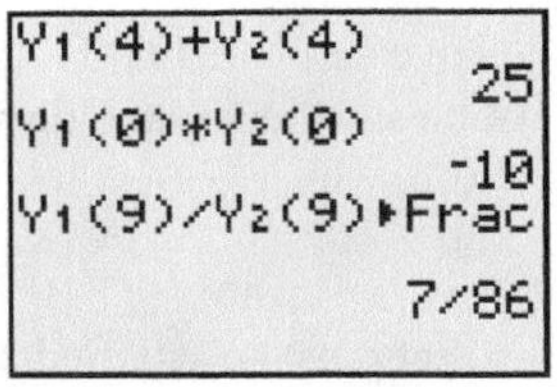

Y1(4)+Y2(4)
         25
Y1(0)*Y2(0)
        -10
Y1(9)/Y2(9)▶Frac
        7/86

(b)

Figure 54

EXAMPLE 1 Evaluating functions

Let $f(x) = 3\sqrt{x} - 2$ and $g(x) = x^2 + 5$. Find and simplify each expression.

a. $(f + g)(4)$ **b.** $(f - g)(x)$ **c.** $(f \cdot g)(0)$ **d.** $\left(\dfrac{f}{g}\right)(9)$

Solution

a. $(f + g)(4) = f(4) + g(4) = 3\sqrt{4} - 2 + 4^2 + 5 = 25$

b. $(f - g)(x) = f(x) - g(x) = 3\sqrt{x} - 2 - (x^2 + 5) = 3\sqrt{x} - x^2 - 7$

c. $(f \cdot g)(0) = f(0) \cdot g(0) = (3\sqrt{0} - 2)(0^2 + 5) = (-2)(5) = -10$

d. $\left(\dfrac{f}{g}\right)(9) = \dfrac{f(9)}{g(9)} = \dfrac{3\sqrt{9} - 2}{9^2 + 5} = \dfrac{7}{86}$

▱ Parts (a), (c), and (d) can be checked with a graphing calculator as shown in Figs. 54(a) and (b).

▶**TRY THIS.** Let $h(x) = x^2$ and $j(x) = 3x$. Find $(h + j)(5)$, $(h \cdot j)(2)$, and $(h/j)(a)$. ∎

Think of $f + g$, $f - g$, $f \cdot g$, and f/g as generic names for the sum, difference, product, and quotient of the functions f and g. If any of these functions has a particular meaning, as in the phone book example, we can use a new letter to identify it. The domain of $f + g$, $f - g$, $f \cdot g$, or f/g is the intersection of the domain of f with the domain of g. Of course, we exclude from the domain of f/g any number for which $g(x) = 0$.

EXAMPLE 2 | The sum, product, and quotient functions

Let $f = \{(1, 3), (2, 8), (3, 6), (5, 9)\}$ and $g = \{(1, 6), (2, 11), (3, 0), (4, 1)\}$. Find $f + g$, $f \cdot g$, and f/g. State the domain of each function.

Solution

The domain of $f + g$ and $f \cdot g$ is $\{1, 2, 3\}$ because that is the intersection of the domains of f and g. The ordered pair $(1, 9)$ belongs to $f + g$ because

$$(f + g)(1) = f(1) + g(1) = 3 + 6 = 9.$$

The ordered pair $(2, 19)$ belongs to $f + g$ because $(f + g)(2) = 19$. The pair $(3, 6)$ also belongs to $f + g$. So

$$f + g = \{(1, 9), (2, 19), (3, 6)\}.$$

Since $(f \cdot g)(1) = f(1) \cdot g(1) = 3 \cdot 6 = 18$, the pair $(1, 18)$ belongs to $f \cdot g$. Likewise, $(2, 88)$ and $(3, 0)$ also belong to $f \cdot g$. So

$$f \cdot g = \{(1, 18), (2, 88), (3, 0)\}.$$

The domain of f/g is $\{1, 2\}$ because $g(3) = 0$. So

$$\frac{f}{g} = \left\{ \left(1, \frac{1}{2}\right), \left(2, \frac{8}{11}\right) \right\}.$$

▶**TRY THIS.** Let $h = \{(2, 10), (4, 0), (6, 8)\}$ and $j = \{(2, 5), (6, 0)\}$. Find $h + j$ and h/j and state the domain of each function. ∎

In Example 2 the functions are given as sets of ordered pairs, and the results of performing operations with these functions are sets of ordered pairs. In the next example the sets of ordered pairs are defined by means of equations, so the result of performing operations with these functions will be new equations that determine the ordered pairs of the function.

EXAMPLE 3 | The sum, quotient, product, and difference functions

Let $f(x) = \sqrt{x}$, $g(x) = 3x + 1$, and $h(x) = x - 1$. Find each function and state its domain.

a. $f + g$ **b.** $\dfrac{g}{f}$ **c.** $g \cdot h$ **d.** $g - h$

Solution

a. Since the domain of f is $[0, \infty)$ and the domain of g is $(-\infty, \infty)$, the domain of $f + g$ is $[0, \infty)$. Since $(f + g)(x) = f(x) + g(x) = \sqrt{x} + 3x + 1$, the equation defining the function $f + g$ is

$$(f + g)(x) = \sqrt{x} + 3x + 1.$$

b. The number 0 is not in the domain of g/f because $f(0) = 0$. So the domain of g/f is $(0, \infty)$. The equation defining g/f is

$$\left(\frac{g}{f}\right)(x) = \frac{3x + 1}{\sqrt{x}}.$$

c. The domain of both g and h is $(-\infty, \infty)$. So the domain of $g \cdot h$ is $(-\infty, \infty)$. Since $(3x + 1)(x - 1) = 3x^2 - 2x - 1$, the equation defining the function $g \cdot h$ is

$$(g \cdot h)(x) = 3x^2 - 2x - 1.$$

d. The domain of both g and h is $(-\infty, \infty)$. So the domain of $g - h$ is $(-\infty, \infty)$. Since $(3x + 1) - (x - 1) = 2x + 2$, the equation defining $g - h$ is

$$(g - h)(x) = 2x + 2.$$

▶**TRY THIS.** Let $h(x) = \sqrt{x}$ and $j(x) = x$. Find $h + j$ and h/j and state the domain of each function. ■

Composition of Functions

It is often the case that the output of one function is the input for another function. For example, the number of hamburgers purchased at $1.49 each determines the subtotal. The subtotal is then used to determine the total (including sales tax). So the number of hamburgers actually determines the total, and that function is called the *composition* of the other two functions. The composition of functions is defined using function notation as follows.

Definition: Composition of Functions

If f and g are two functions, the **composition** of f and g, written $f \circ g$, is defined by the equation

$$(f \circ g)(x) = f(g(x)),$$

provided that $g(x)$ is in the domain of f. The composition of g and f, written $g \circ f$, is defined by

$$(g \circ f)(x) = g(f(x)),$$

provided that $f(x)$ is in the domain of g.

Note that $f \circ g$ is not the same as the function $f \cdot g$, the product of f and g. It might be helpful for you to read the composition symbol $\circ$ as "after." This reading makes the order clear. So $(f \circ g)(x)$ is read "f after g of x." So f is applied after g is applied to x.

For the composition $f \circ g$ to be defined at x, $g(x)$ must be in the domain of f. So the domain of $f \circ g$ is the set of all values of x in the domain of g for which $g(x)$ is in the domain of f. The diagram shown in Fig. 55 will help you to understand the composition of functions.

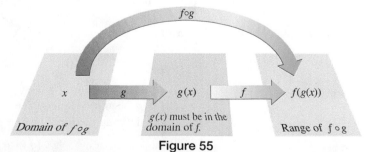

Figure 55

EXAMPLE 4 Composition of functions defined by sets

Let $g = \{(1,4), (2,5), (3,6)\}$ and $f = \{(3,8), (4,9), (5,10)\}$. Find $f \circ g$.

Solution

Since $g(1) = 4$ and $f(4) = 9$, $(f \circ g)(1) = 9$. So the ordered pair $(1, 9)$ is in $f \circ g$. Since $g(2) = 5$ and $f(5) = 10$, $(f \circ g)(2) = 10$. So $(2, 10)$ is in $f \circ g$. Now $g(3) = 6$, but 6 is not in the domain of f. So there are only two ordered pairs in $f \circ g$:

$$f \circ g = \{(1,9), (2,10)\}$$

▶**TRY THIS.** Let $h = \{(2,0), (4,0), (6,8)\}$ and $j = \{(0,7), (6,0)\}$. Find $j \circ h$ and state the domain. ∎

In the next example we find specific values of compositions that are defined by equations.

EXAMPLE 5 Evaluating compositions defined by equations

Let $f(x) = \sqrt{x}$, $g(x) = 2x - 1$, and $h(x) = x^2$. Find the value of each expression.

a. $(f \circ g)(5)$ **b.** $(g \circ f)(5)$ **c.** $(h \circ g \circ f)(9)$

Solution

a. $(f \circ g)(5) = f(g(5))$ Definition of composition

$\qquad\qquad = f(9)$ $g(5) = 2 \cdot 5 - 1 = 9$

$\qquad\qquad = \sqrt{9}$

$\qquad\qquad = 3$

b. $(g \circ f)(5) = g(f(5)) = g(\sqrt{5}) = 2\sqrt{5} - 1$

c. $(h \circ g \circ f)(9) = h(g(f(9))) = h(g(3)) = h(5) = 5^2 = 25$

You can check these answers with a graphing calculator as shown in Figs. 56(a) and (b). Enter the functions using the Y = key, then go back to the home screen to evaluate. The symbols Y_1, Y_2, and Y_3 are found in the variables menu (VARS) on a TI-83.

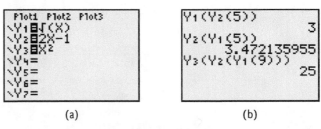

(a)   (b)

Figure 56

▶**TRY THIS.** Let $h(x) = \sqrt{x - 1}$ and $j(x) = 2x$. Find $(h \circ j)(5)$ and $(j \circ h)(5)$. ∎

In Example 4, the domain of g is $\{1, 2, 3\}$ while the domain of $f \circ g$ is $\{1, 2\}$. To find the domain of $f \circ g$, we remove from the domain of g any number x such that $g(x)$ is not in the domain of f. In the next example we construct compositions of functions defined by equations and determine their domains.

EXAMPLE 6 Composition of functions defined by equations

Let $f(x) = \sqrt{x}$, $g(x) = 2x - 1$, and $h(x) = x^2$. Find each composition function and state its domain.

a. $f \circ g$ **b.** $g \circ f$ **c.** $h \circ g$ **d.** $f \circ h$ **e.** $f \circ g \circ h$

Solution

a. In the composition $f \circ g$, $g(x)$ must be in the domain of f. The domain of f is $[0, \infty)$. If $g(x)$ is in $[0, \infty)$, then $2x - 1 \geq 0$, or $x \geq \frac{1}{2}$. So the domain of $f \circ g$ is $[\frac{1}{2}, \infty)$. Since

$$(f \circ g)(x) = f(g(x)) = f(2x - 1) = \sqrt{2x - 1},$$

the function $f \circ g$ is defined by the equation $(f \circ g)(x) = \sqrt{2x - 1}$, for $x \geq \frac{1}{2}$.

b. Since the domain of g is $(-\infty, \infty)$, $f(x)$ is certainly in the domain of g. So the domain of $g \circ f$ is the same as the domain of f, $[0, \infty)$. Since

$$(g \circ f)(x) = g(f(x)) = g(\sqrt{x}) = 2\sqrt{x} - 1,$$

the function $g \circ f$ is defined by the equation $(g \circ f)(x) = 2\sqrt{x} - 1$. Note that $g \circ f$ is generally not equal to $f \circ g$, but in Section 5 we will study special types of functions for which they are equal.

c. Since the domain of h is $(-\infty, \infty)$, $g(x)$ is certainly in the domain of h. So the domain of $h \circ g$ is the same as the domain of g, $(-\infty, \infty)$. Since

$$(h \circ g)(x) = h(g(x)) = h(2x - 1) = (2x - 1)^2 = 4x^2 - 4x + 1,$$

the function $h \circ g$ is defined by $(h \circ g)(x) = 4x^2 - 4x + 1$.

d. The domain of $f(x) = \sqrt{x}$ is the set of nonnegative real numbers. Since x^2 is nonnegative, $h(x)$ is in the domain of f. So the domain of $f \circ h$ is the same as the domain of h, the set of all real numbers or $(-\infty, \infty)$. Since

$$(f \circ h)(x) = f(h(x)) = f(x^2) = \sqrt{x^2} = |x|,$$

the function $f \circ h$ is defined by $(f \circ h)(x) = |x|$.

e. Apply the functions in the order h, g, and then f:

$$(f \circ g \circ h)(x) = (f \circ g)(x^2) = f(2x^2 - 1) = \sqrt{2x^2 - 1}$$

Since the square root of a negative number is not allowed, we must have $2x^2 - 1 \geq 0$. Solve this inequality by reading the graph of $y = 2x^2 - 1$. (See Section 3, Example 9.) The graph of $y = 2x^2 - 1$ is a parabola with x-intercepts $(\pm \sqrt{2}/2, 0)$. The y-coordinates are negative between the intercepts and non-negative otherwise. So $(f \circ g \circ h)(x) = \sqrt{2x^2 - 1}$ and its domain is $(-\infty, -\sqrt{2}/2] \cup [\sqrt{2}/2, \infty)$.

▶**TRY THIS.** Let $h(x) = \sqrt{x + 3}$ and $j(x) = 3x$. Find $h \circ j$ and state its domain. ∎

In Example 6 we composed some simple functions to get more complicated functions. Now we will reverse that process. We start with a function that involves several operations and express it as a composition of simpler functions. *The order of operations is the key to this process.* For example, consider $H(x) = (x + 3)^2$. By the order of operations, we add 3 to x first, then square the result. So H is a composition of a function that adds 3 ($f(x) = x + 3$) and a function that squares ($g(x) = x^2$).

Since we write compositions from right to left, we have $H = g \circ f$. To check, we find $(g \circ f)(x)$:

$$(g \circ f)(x) = g(f(x)) = g(x + 3) = (x + 3)^2$$

Note that $(f \circ g)(x) = x^2 + 3$ and it is not the same as $H(x)$. The order is important.

EXAMPLE 7 Writing a function as a composition

Let $f(x) = \sqrt{x}$, $g(x) = x - 3$, and $h(x) = 2x$. Write each given function as a composition of appropriate functions chosen from f, g, and h.

a. $F(x) = \sqrt{x - 3}$ **b.** $G(x) = x - 6$ **c.** $H(x) = 2\sqrt{x} - 3$

Solution

a. By the order of operations, to evaluate $F(x) = \sqrt{x - 3}$ we first subtract 3 from x ($g(x) = x - 3$) and then find the square root of the result ($f(x) = \sqrt{x}$). Writing these functions from right to left, we have $F = f \circ g$. Check as follows:

$$(f \circ g)(x) = f(g(x)) = f(x - 3) = \sqrt{x - 3} = F(x)$$

b. This one is a bit tricky, because $G(x) = x - 6$ involves only one operation and none of the functions given involve a 6. However, you can subtract 6 by subtracting 3 ($g(x) = x - 3$) and then again subtracting 3. So $G = g \circ g$. Check as follows:

$$(g \circ g)(x) = g(g(x)) = g(x - 3) = x - 3 - 3 = x - 6 = G(x)$$

c. By the order of operations, to evaluate $H(x) = 2\sqrt{x} - 3$, we first find the square root ($f(x) = \sqrt{x}$), next we multiply by 2 ($h(x) = 2x$), and finally we subtract 3 ($g(x) = x - 3$). Writing these functions from right to left, we have $H = g \circ h \circ f$. Check as follows:

$$(g \circ h \circ f)(x) = g(h(f(x))) = g(h(\sqrt{x})) = g(2\sqrt{x}) = 2\sqrt{x} - 3$$

▶**TRY THIS.** Write $K(x) = 2\sqrt{x - 3}$ as a composition of f, g, and h. ■

■ **Foreshadowing Calculus**

One of the big topics in calculus is the instantaneous rate of change of a function. To find the instantaneous rate of change, we often view a complicated function as a composition of simpler functions as is done in Example 7.

Applications

In applied situations, functions are often defined with formulas rather than function notation. In this case, composition can be simply a matter of substitution.

EXAMPLE 8 Composition with formulas

The radius of a circle is a function of the diameter ($r = d/2$) and the area is a function of the radius ($A = \pi r^2$). Construct a formula that expresses the area as a function of the diameter.

Solution

The formula for A as a function of d is obtained by substituting $d/2$ for r:

$$A = \pi r^2 = \pi \left(\frac{d}{2}\right)^2 = \pi \frac{d^2}{4}$$

The function $A = \pi d^2 / 4$ is the composition of $r = d/2$ and $A = \pi r^2$.

▶**TRY THIS.** The diameter of a circle is a function of the radius ($d = 2r$) and the radius is a function of the circumference ($r = C/(2\pi)$). Construct a formula that expresses d as a function of C. ■

In the next example we find a composition using function notation for the salary of the phone book collector mentioned at the beginning of this section.

EXAMPLE 9 | Composition with function notation

A student's salary (in dollars) for collecting x phone books is given by $S(x) = 0.30x + 240$. The amount of withholding (for taxes) is given by $W(x) = 0.20x$, where x is the salary. Express the withholding as a function of the number of phone books collected.

Solution

Note that x represents the number of phone books in $S(x) = 0.30x + 240$ and x represents salary in $W(x) = 0.20x$. So we can replace the salary x in $W(x)$ with $S(x)$ or $0.30x + 240$, which also represents salary:

$$W(S(x)) = W(0.30x + 240) = 0.20(0.30x + 240) = 0.06x + 48$$

Use a new letter to name this function, say T. Then $T(x) = 0.06x + 48$ gives the amount of withholding (for taxes) as a function of x, where x is the number of phone books.

▶**TRY THIS.** The revenue for a sale of x books at \$80 each is given by $R(x) = 80x$. The commission for a revenue of x dollars is given by $C(x) = 0.10x$. Express the commission as a function of the number of books sold. ∎

➤ FOR thought... True or False? Explain.

1. If $f = \{(2, 4)\}$ and $g = \{(1, 5)\}$, then $f + g = \{(3, 9)\}$.

2. If $f = \{(1, 6), (9, 5)\}$ and $g = \{(1, 3), (9, 0)\}$, then $f/g = \{(1, 2)\}$.

3. If $f = \{(1, 6), (9, 5)\}$ and $g = \{(1, 3), (9, 0)\}$, then $f \cdot g = \{(1, 18), (9, 0)\}$.

4. If $f(x) = x + 2$ and $g(x) = x - 3$, then $(f \cdot g)(5) = 14$.

5. If $s = P/4$ and $A = s^2$, then A is a function of P.

6. If $f(3) = 19$ and $g(19) = 99$, then $(g \circ f)(3) = 99$.

7. If $f(x) = \sqrt{x}$ and $g(x) = x - 2$, then $(f \circ g)(x) = \sqrt{x} - 2$.

8. If $f(x) = 5x$ and $g(x) = x/5$, then $(f \circ g)(x) = (g \circ f)(x) = x$.

9. If $F(x) = (x - 9)^2$, $g(x) = x^2$, and $h(x) = x - 9$, then $F = h \circ g$.

10. If $f(x) = \sqrt{x}$ and $g(x) = x - 2$, then the domain of $f \circ g$ is $[2, \infty)$.

➤ EXERCISES 4

Fill in the blank.

1. For two functions f and g, the function $f + g$ is the _____ function.

2. For two functions f and g, the function $f \circ g$ is the _____ of f and g.

Let $f(x) = x - 3$ and $g(x) = x^2 - x$. Find and simplify each expression.

3. $(f + g)(2)$ **4.** $(g + f)(3)$ **5.** $(f - g)(-2)$

6. $(g - f)(-6)$ **7.** $(f \cdot g)(-1)$ **8.** $(g \cdot f)(0)$

9. $(f/g)(4)$ 10. $(g/f)(4)$ 11. $(f + g)(a)$

12. $(f - g)(b)$ 13. $(f \cdot g)(a)$ 14. $(f/g)(b)$

Let $f = \{(-3, 1), (0, 4), (2, 0)\}$, $g = \{(-3, 2), (1, 2), (2, 6),$ $(4, 0)\}$, and $h = \{(2, 4), (1, 0)\}$. Find each function and state the domain of each function.

15. $f + g$ 16. $f + h$ 17. $f - g$ 18. $f - h$

19. $f \cdot g$ 20. $f \cdot h$ 21. g/f 22. f/g

Let $f(x) = \sqrt{x}$, $g(x) = x - 4$, and $h(x) = \frac{1}{x - 2}$. Find an equation defining each function and state the domain of the function.

23. $f + g$ 24. $f + h$ 25. $f - h$ 26. $h - g$

27. $g \cdot h$ 28. $f \cdot h$ 29. g/f 30. f/g

Let $f = \{(-3, 1), (0, 4), (2, 0)\}$, $g = \{(-3, 2), (1, 2), (2, 6),$ $(4, 0)\}$, and $h = \{(2, 4), (1, 0)\}$. Find each function.

31. $f \circ g$ 32. $g \circ f$ 33. $f \circ h$

34. $h \circ f$ 35. $h \circ g$ 36. $g \circ h$

Let $f(x) = 3x - 1$, $g(x) = x^2 + 1$, and $h(x) = \frac{x + 1}{3}$. Evaluate each expression. Round approximate answers to three decimal places.

37. $f(g(-1))$ 38. $g(f(-1))$ 39. $(f \circ h)(5)$

40. $(h \circ f)(-7)$ 41. $(f \circ g)(4.39)$ 42. $(g \circ h)(-9.87)$

43. $(g \circ h \circ f)(2)$ 44. $(h \circ f \circ g)(3)$

45. $(f \circ g \circ h)(2)$ 46. $(h \circ g \circ f)(0)$

47. $(f \circ h)(a)$ 48. $(h \circ f)(w)$

49. $(f \circ g)(t)$ 50. $(g \circ f)(m)$

Let $f(x) = x - 2$, $g(x) = \sqrt{x}$, and $h(x) = \frac{1}{x}$. Find an equation defining each function and state the domain of the function.

51. $f \circ g$ 52. $g \circ f$ 53. $f \circ h$

54. $h \circ f$ 55. $h \circ g$ 56. $g \circ h$

57. $f \circ f$ 58. $g \circ g$ 59. $h \circ g \circ f$

60. $f \circ g \circ h$ 61. $h \circ f \circ g$ 62. $g \circ h \circ f$

Let $f(x) = |x|$, $g(x) = x - 7$, and $h(x) = x^2$. Write each of the following functions as a composition of functions chosen from f, g, and h.

63. $F(x) = x^2 - 7$ 64. $G(x) = |x| - 7$

65. $H(x) = (x - 7)^2$ 66. $M(x) = |x - 7|$

67. $N(x) = (|x| - 7)^2$ 68. $R(x) = |x^2 - 7|$

69. $P(x) = |x - 7| - 7$ 70. $Q(x) = (x^2 - 7)^2$

71. $S(x) = x - 14$ 72. $T(x) = x^4$

For each given function $f(x)$, find two functions $g(x)$ and $h(x)$ such that $f = h \circ g$. Answers may vary.

73. $f(x) = x^3 - 2$ 74. $f(x) = (x - 2)^3$

75. $f(x) = \sqrt{x + 5}$ 76. $f(x) = \sqrt{x} + 5$

77. $f(x) = \sqrt{3x - 1}$ 78. $f(x) = 3\sqrt{x} - 1$

79. $f(x) = 4|x| + 5$ 80. $f(x) = |4x + 5|$

Use the two given functions to write y as a function of x.

81. $y = 2a - 3, a = 3x + 1$

82. $y = -4d - 1, d = -3x - 2$

83. $y = w^2 - 2, w = x + 3$

84. $y = 3t^2 - 3, t = x - 1$

85. $y = 3m - 1, m = \frac{x + 1}{3}$ 86. $y = 2z + 5, z = \frac{1}{2}x - \frac{5}{2}$

Find each function from the given verbal description of the function.

87. If m is n minus 4, and y is the square of m, then write y as a function of n.

88. If u is the sum of t and 9, and v is u divided by 3, then write v as a function of t.

89. If w is equal to the sum of x and 16, z is the square root of w, and y is z divided by 8, then write y as a function of x.

90. If a is the cube of b, c is the sum of a and 25, and d is the square root of c, then write d as a function of b.

Graph each function on a graphing calculator without simplifying the given expression. Examine the graph and write a function for the graph. Then simplify the original function and see whether it is the same as your function. Is the domain of the original function equal to the domain of the function after it is simplified?

91. $y = ((x - 1)/(x + 1) + 1)/((x - 1)/(x + 1) - 1)$

92. $y = ((3x + 1)/(x - 1) + 1)/((3x + 1)/(x - 1) - 3)$

Define $y_1 = \sqrt{x + 1}$ and $y_2 = 3x - 4$ on your graphing calculator. For each function y_3, defined in terms of y_1 and y_2, determine the domain and range of y_3 from its graph on your calculator and explain what each graph illustrates.

93. $y_3 = y_1 + y_2$ 94. $y_3 = 3y_1 - 4$

95. $y_3 = \sqrt{y_2 + 1}$ 96. $y_3 = \sqrt{y_1 + 1}$

Define $y_1 = \sqrt[3]{x}$, $y_2 = \sqrt{x}$, and $y_3 = x + 4$. For each function y_4, determine the domain and range of y_4 from its graph on your calculator and explain what each graph illustrates.

97. $y_4 = y_1 + y_2 + y_3$ 98. $y_4 = \sqrt{y_1 + 4}$

Solve each problem.

99. *Profitable Business* Charles buys factory-reconditioned hedge trimmers for $40 each and sells them on eBay for $68 each. He has a fixed cost of $200 per month. If x is the number of hedge trimmers he sells per month, then his revenue and cost (in dollars) are given by $R(x) = 68x$ and $C(x) = 40x + 200$. Find a formula for the function $P(x) = R(x) - C(x)$. For what values of x is his profit positive?

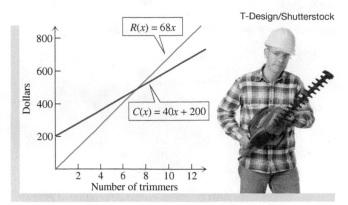

T-Design/Shutterstock

Figure for Exercise 99

100. *Profit* The revenue in dollars that a company receives for installing x alarm systems per month is given by $R(x) = 3000x - 20x^2$, while the cost in dollars is given by $C(x) = 600x + 4000$. The function $P(x) = R(x) - C(x)$ gives the profit for installing x alarm systems per month. Find $P(x)$ and simplify it.

101. Write the area A of a square with a side of length s as a function of its diagonal d.

HINT Write down the formulas involving the area, perimeter, and diagonal of square.

102. Write the perimeter of a square P as a function of the area A.

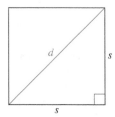

Figure for Exercises 101 and 102

103. *Deforestation in Nigeria* In Nigeria deforestation occurs at the rate of about 5.2% per year. If x is the total forest area of Nigeria at the start of 2000, then $f(x) = 0.948x$ is the amount of forest land in Nigeria at the start of 2001. Find and interpret $(f \circ f)(x)$. Find and interpret $(f \circ f \circ f)(x)$.

104. *Doubling Your Money* On the average, money invested in bonds doubles every 12 years. So $f(x) = 2x$ gives the value of x dollars invested in bonds after 12 years. Find and interpret $(f \circ f)(x)$. Find and interpret $(f \circ f \circ f)(x)$.

105. *Hamburgers* If hamburgers are $1.20 each, then $C(x) = 1.20x$ gives the pre-tax cost in dollars for x hamburgers. If sales tax is 5%, then $T(x) = 1.05x$ gives the total cost when the pre-tax cost is x dollars. Write the total cost as a function of the number of hamburgers.

106. *Laying Sod* Southern Sod will deliver and install 20 pallets of St. Augustine sod for $2200 or 30 pallets for $3200 not including tax.
  a. Write the cost (not including tax) as a linear function of x, where x is the number of pallets.

  b. Write a function that gives the total cost (including tax at 9%) as a function of x, where x is the cost (not including tax).

  c. Find the function that gives the total cost as a function of x, where x is the number of pallets.

107. *Displacement-Length Ratio* The displacement-length ratio D indicates whether a sailboat is relatively heavy or relatively light:

$$D = (d \div 2240) \div x$$

where d is the displacement in pounds and

$$x = (L \div 100)^3$$

where L is the length at the waterline in feet (*Sailing*, www.sailing.com). Assuming that the displacement is 26,000 pounds, write D as a function of L and simplify it.

108. *Sail Area-Displacement Ratio* The sail area-displacement ratio S measures the sail power available to drive a sailboat:

$$S = A \div y$$

where A is the sail area in square feet and

$$y = (d \div 64)^{2/3}$$

where d is the displacement in pounds. Assuming that the sail area is 6500 square feet, write S as a function of d and simplify it.

109. *Area of a Window* A window is in the shape of a square with a side of length s, with a semicircle of diameter s adjoining the top of the square. Write the total area of the window W as a function of s.

HINT Start with the formulas for the area of a square and the area of a circle.

Figure for Exercises 109 and 110

110. *Area of a Window* Using the window of Exercise 109, write the area of the square *A* as a function of the area of the semicircle *S*.

111. *Packing a Square Piece of Glass* A glass prism with a square cross section is to be shipped in a cylindrical cardboard tube that has an inside diameter of *d* inches. Given that *s* is the length of a side of the square and the glass fits snugly into the tube, write *s* as a function of *d*.

HINT Use the Pythagorean theorem and the formula for the area of a circle.

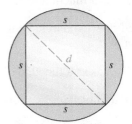

Figure for Exercise 111

112. *Packing a Triangular Piece of Glass* A glass prism is to be shipped in a cylindrical cardboard tube that has an inside diameter of *d* inches. Given that the cross section of the prism is an equilateral triangle with side of length *p* and the prism fits snugly into the tube, write *p* as a function of *d*.

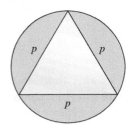

Figure for Exercise 112

FOR WRITING/DISCUSSION

113. Sears often has Super Saturday sales during which everything is 10% off, even items already on sale. If a coat is on sale at 25%, then is it 35% off on Super Saturday? What operation with functions is at work here? Explain your answers.

114. We can combine two functions to obtain a new function by addition, subtraction, multiplication, division, and composition. Are any of these operations commutative? Associative? Explain your answers and give examples.

▶ **RETHINKING**

115. Find and simplify the difference quotient for the function $f(x) = 1 + \frac{3}{x}$.

116. Let $f(x) = \begin{cases} x & \text{for} & x \geq 1 \\ -x & \text{for} & x < 1 \end{cases}$. Find the domain, the range, and the interval on which the function is increasing.

117. Find the domain and range for $f(x) = -5\sqrt{x-3} + 2$.

118. Solve $4(x-3)^2 - 6 = 0$.

119. Solve $5 - 3x < 6 + 2x$.

120. Find the slope of the line $3x - 9y = 7$.

THINKING OUTSIDE THE BOX XVI & XVII

Thirty-Percent Reduction If each of the numbers in the expression $ab^2c^3d^4$ is decreased by 30%, then the value of the expression is decreased by what percent? Give the answer to the nearest tenth of a percent.

Whole-Number Expression What is the largest whole number *N* that cannot be expressed as $N = 3x + 11y$ where *x* and *y* are whole numbers?

POP QUIZ 4

1. Write the area of a circle as a function of its diameter.

Let $f(x) = x^2$ and $g(x) = x - 2$. Find and simplify.

2. $(f + g)(3)$ **3.** $(f \cdot g)(4)$ **4.** $(f \circ g)(5)$

Let $m = \{(1, 3), (4, 8)\}$ and $n = \{(3, 5), (4, 9)\}$. Find each function.

5. $m + n$ **6.** $n \circ m$

Let $h(x) = x^2$ and $j(x) = \sqrt{x + 2}$. Find the domain of each function.

7. $h + j$ **8.** $h \circ j$ **9.** $j \circ h$

LINKING concepts... For Individual or Group Explorations

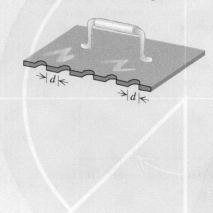

Modeling Glue Coverage

Frank is designing a notched trowel for spreading glue. The notches on the trowel are in the shape of semicircles. The diameter of each notch and the space between consecutive notches are d inches as shown in the figure. Suppose that the trowel is used to make parallel beads of glue on one square foot of floor.

a) Write the number of parallel beads made as a function of d.

b) The cross section of each parallel bead is a semicircle with diameter d. Write the area of a cross section as a function of d.

c) Write the volume of one of the parallel beads as a function of d.

d) Write the volume of glue on one square foot of floor as a function of d.

e) Write the number of square feet that one gallon of glue will cover as a function of d. (Use 1 ft^3 = 7.5 gal.)

f) Suppose that the trowel has square notches where the sides of the squares are d inches in length and the distance between consecutive notches is d inches. Write the number of square feet that one gallon of glue will cover as a function of d.

5 Inverse Functions

It is possible for one function to undo what another function does. For example, squaring undoes the operation of taking a square root. The composition of two such functions is the identity function. In this section we explore this idea in detail.

One-to-One Functions

Consider a medium pizza that costs $5 plus $2 per topping. Table 1 shows the ordered pairs of the function that determines the cost. Note that for every number of toppings there is a unique cost and for every cost there is a unique number of toppings. There is a **one-to-one correspondence** between the domain and range of this function and the function is a *one-to-one function*. For a function that is not one-to-one, consider a Wendy's menu. Every item corresponds to a unique price, but the price $0.99 corresponds to many different items.

Table 1

Toppings x	Cost y
0	$ 5
1	7
2	9
3	11
4	13

Kevin Sanchez/Cole Group/Photodisc/ Getty Images

Definition:
One-to-one Function

> If a function has no two ordered pairs with different first coordinates and the same second coordinate, then the function is called **one-to-one.**

The definition of function requires that every element of the domain corresponds to exactly one element of the range. For a one-to-one function we have the additional requirement that every element of the range corresponds to exactly one element of the domain.

EXAMPLE 1 One-to-one with ordered pairs

Determine whether each function is one-to-one.

a. $\{(1, 3), (2, 5), (3, 4), (4, 9), (5, 0)\}$
b. $\{(4, 16), (-4, 16), (2, 4), (-2, 4), (5, 25)\}$
c. $\{(3, 0.99), (5, 1.99), (7, 2.99), (8, 3.99), (9, 0.99)\}$

Solution

a. This function is one-to-one because no two ordered pairs have different first co-ordinates and the same second coordinate.
b. This function is not one-to-one because the ordered pairs $(4, 16)$ and $(-4, 16)$ have different first coordinates and the same second coordinate.
c. This function is not one-to-one because the ordered pairs $(3, 0.99)$ and $(9, 0.99)$ have different first coordinates and the same second coordinate.

▶**TRY THIS.** Determine whether the function $\{(-1, \pi), (0, 3.14), (1, 22/7)\}$ is one-to-one. ■

If a function is given as a short list of ordered pairs, then it is easy to determine whether the function is one-to-one. A graph of a function can also be used to determine whether a function is one-to-one using the **horizontal line test.**

Horizontal Line Test

> If each horizontal line crosses the graph of a function at no more than one point, then the function is one-to-one.

The graph of a one-to-one function never has the same y-coordinate for two different x-coordinates on the graph. So if it is possible to draw a horizontal line that crosses the graph of a function two or more times, then the function is not one-to-one.

EXAMPLE 2 The horizontal line test

Use the horizontal line test to determine whether the functions shown in Fig. 57 are one-to-one.

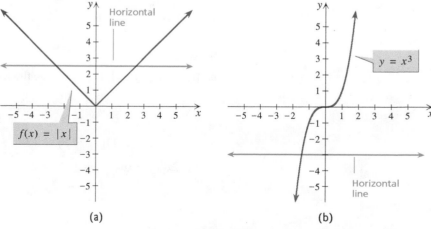

(a)   (b)

Figure 57

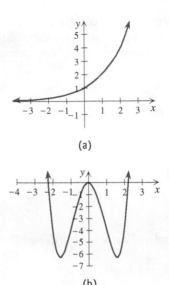

(a)

(b)

Figure 58

Solution

The function $f(x) = |x|$ is not one-to-one because it is possible to draw a horizontal line that crosses the graph twice as shown in Fig. 57(a). The function $y = x^3$ in Fig. 57(b) is one-to-one because it appears to be impossible to draw a horizontal line that crosses the graph more than once.

▶**TRY THIS.** Use the horizontal line test to determine whether the functions shown in Fig. 58 are one-to-one. ■

The horizontal line test explains the visual difference between the graph of a one-to-one function and the graph of a function that is not one-to-one. Because no graph of a function is perfectly accurate, conclusions made from a graph alone may not be correct. For example, from the graph of $y = x^3 - 0.01x$ shown in Fig. 59(a) we would conclude that the function is one-to-one. However, another view of the same function in Fig. 59(b) shows that the function is not one-to-one.

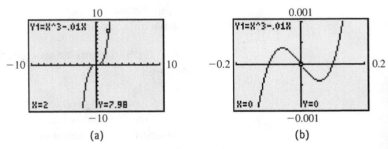

(a)   (b)

Figure 59

Using the equation for a function we can often determine conclusively whether the function is one-to-one. A function f is not one-to-one if it is possible to find two different numbers x_1 and x_2 such that $f(x_1) = f(x_2)$. For example, for the function $f(x) = x^2$, it is possible to find two different numbers, 2 and -2, such that $f(2) = f(-2)$. So $f(x) = x^2$ is not one-to-one. To prove that a function f is one-to-one, we must show that $f(x_1) = f(x_2)$ implies that $x_1 = x_2$.

EXAMPLE 3 | Using the definition of one-to-one

Determine whether each function is one-to-one.

a. $f(x) = \dfrac{2x + 1}{x - 3}$ **b.** $g(x) = |x|$

Solution

a. If $f(x_1) = f(x_2)$, then we have the following equation:

$$\frac{2x_1 + 1}{x_1 - 3} = \frac{2x_2 + 1}{x_2 - 3}$$

$$(2x_1 + 1)(x_2 - 3) = (2x_2 + 1)(x_1 - 3) \qquad \text{Multiply by the LCD.}$$

$$2x_1x_2 - 6x_1 + x_2 - 3 = 2x_2x_1 - 6x_2 + x_1 - 3$$

$$7x_2 = 7x_1$$

$$x_2 = x_1$$

Since $f(x_1) = f(x_2)$ implies that $x_1 = x_2$, $f(x)$ is a one-to-one function.

b. If $g(x_1) = g(x_2)$, then $|x_1| = |x_2|$. But this does not imply that $x_1 = x_2$, because two different numbers can have the same absolute value. For example $|3| = |-3|$ but $3 \neq -3$. So g is not one-to-one.

▶**TRY THIS.** Determine whether $h(x) = 5x^2$ is one-to-one. ∎

Inverse Functions

Consider again the function given in Table 1, which determines the cost of a pizza from the number of toppings. Because that function is one-to-one we can make a table in which the number of toppings is determined from the cost, as shown in Table 2. Of course we could just read Table 1 backward, but we make a new table to emphasize that there is a new function under discussion. Table 2 is the *inverse function* for the function in Table 1.

Table 2

Cost x	Toppings y	
$ 5	0	
7	1	
9	2	
11	3	
13	4	

Kevin Sanchez/Cole Group/Photodisc/ Getty Images

A function is a set of ordered pairs in which no two ordered pairs have the same first coordinates and different second coordinates. If we interchange the x- and y-coordinates in each ordered pair of a function, as in Tables 1 and 2, the resulting set of ordered pairs might or might not be a function. If the original function is one-to-one, then the set obtained by interchanging the coordinates in each ordered pair is a function, the inverse function. If a function is one-to-one, then it has an inverse function or it is **invertible**.

Definition:
Inverse Function

> The **inverse** of a one-to-one function f is the function f^{-1} (read "f inverse"), where the ordered pairs of f^{-1} are obtained by interchanging the coordinates in each ordered pair of f.

In this notation, the number -1 in f^{-1} does not represent a negative exponent. It is merely a symbol for denoting the inverse function.

EXAMPLE 4 | Finding an inverse function

For each function, determine whether it is invertible. If it is invertible, then find the inverse.

a. $f = \{(-2, 3), (4, 5), (2, 3)\}$ **b.** $g = \{(3, 1), (5, 2), (7, 4), (9, 8)\}$

Solution

a. This function f is *not* one-to-one because of the ordered pairs $(-2, 3)$ and $(2, 3)$. So f is not invertible.
b. The function g is one-to-one, and so g is invertible. The inverse of g is the function $g^{-1} = \{(1, 3), (2, 5), (4, 7), (8, 9)\}$.

▶**TRY THIS.** Determine whether $h = \{(2, 1), (3, 4), (4, 0)\}$ is invertible. If it is invertible, then find the inverse function. ∎

EXAMPLE 5 Using inverse function notation

Let $f = \{(1, 3), (2, 4), (5, 7)\}$. Find f^{-1}, $f^{-1}(3)$, and $(f^{-1} \circ f)(1)$.

Solution

Interchange the x- and y-coordinates of each ordered pair of f to find f^{-1}:

$$f^{-1} = \{(3, 1), (4, 2), (7, 5)\}$$

To find the value of $f^{-1}(3)$, notice that $f^{-1}(3)$ is the second coordinate when the first coordinate is 3 in the function f^{-1}. So $f^{-1}(3) = 1$. To find the composition, use the definition of composition of functions:

$$(f^{-1} \circ f)(1) = f^{-1}(f(1)) = f^{-1}(3) = 1$$

▶**TRY THIS.** Let $h = \{(2, 1), (3, 4), (4, 0)\}$. Find $h(3)$, $h^{-1}(4)$, and $(h \circ h^{-1})(1)$. ∎

Since the coordinates in the ordered pairs are interchanged, the domain of f^{-1} is the range of f, and the range of f^{-1} is the domain of f. If f^{-1} is the inverse function of f, then certainly f is the inverse of f^{-1}. The functions f and f^{-1} are inverses of each other.

Inverse Functions Using Function Notation

Suppose that the cost of a pizza is $5 plus $2 per topping. The cost C can be determined from the number of toppings T by the function $C = 2T + 5$. We can easily solve this formula for T to get $T = \frac{C - 5}{2}$. This formula can be used to determine the number of toppings from the cost. The functions $C = 2T + 5$ and $T = \frac{C - 5}{2}$ are inverse functions.

When we use the variables x and y, we always like to keep x as the independent variable and y as the dependent variable. So in the pizza situation $y = 2x + 5$ is a function that determines the cost y from the number of toppings x. The inverse function $y = \frac{x - 5}{2}$ is used to determine the number of toppings from the cost, but now x is the cost and y is the number of toppings. The roles of x and y are switched. Using function notation we write $f(x) = 2x + 5$ and $f^{-1}(x) = \frac{x - 5}{2}$. The one-to-one function f pairs members of the domain of f with members of the range of f, and the inverse function f^{-1} exactly reverses those pairings, as shown in Fig. 60.

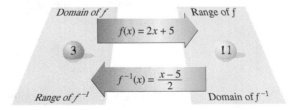

Figure 60

Table 3

Function	Inverse
$f(x) = 2x$	$f^{-1}(x) = x/2$
$f(x) = x - 5$	$f^{-1}(x) = x + 5$
$f(x) = x^3$	$f^{-1}(x) = \sqrt[3]{x}$
$f(x) = 1/x$	$f^{-1}(x) = 1/x$
$f(x) = -x$	$f^{-1}(x) = -x$

Note that the inverse of $f(x) = 2x + 5$ can be obtained by thinking of f as a composition of multiplying by 2 and adding 5 to the result. To reverse this composition you must subtract 5 and then divide the result by 2. Think of putting on your socks and then your shoes. To get back to bare feet, you must remove your shoes and then remove your socks. So $f^{-1}(x) = \frac{x - 5}{2}$. Note that $f^{-1}(x) \neq \frac{x}{2} - 5$. The *quantity* $x - 5$ must be divided by 2. The inverses of some of the common functions that we use are shown in Table 3.

EXAMPLE 6 | Finding an inverse by reversing a composition

Find the inverse of each function.

a. $f(x) = 2x + 1$ **b.** $g(x) = \dfrac{x^3 + 5}{2}$

Solution

a. The function $f(x) = 2x + 1$ is a composition of multiplying x by 2 and then adding 1. So the inverse function is a composition of subtracting 1 and then dividing by 2: $f^{-1}(x) = (x - 1)/2$. See Fig. 61.

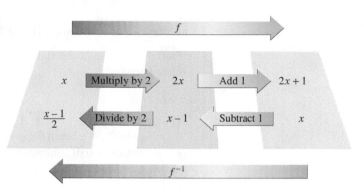

Figure 61

b. The function $g(x) = (x^3 + 5)/2$ is a composition of cubing x, adding 5, and dividing by 2. The inverse is a composition of multiplying by 2, subtracting 5, and then taking the cube root: $g^{-1}(x) = \sqrt[3]{2x - 5}$. See Fig. 62.

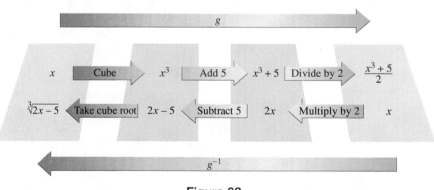

Figure 62

▶**TRY THIS.** Find the inverse of $f(x) = \frac{2}{3}x + 6$. ■

Graphs of f and f^{-1}

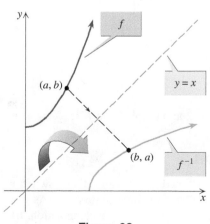

Figure 63

The inverse of a one-to-one function contains exactly the same ordered pairs as the function except that the coordinates are reversed. So for every point (a, b) on the graph of an invertible function f, there is a corresponding point (b, a) on the graph of f^{-1}. See Fig. 63. This fact causes the graph of f^{-1} to be a reflection of the graph of f with respect to the line $y = x$.

Reflection Property of Inverse Functions

If f is a one-to-one function, then the graph of f^{-1} is a reflection of the graph of f with respect to the line $y = x$.

Only one-to-one functions are invertible. However, sometimes it is possible to restrict the domain of a function that is not one-to-one so that it is one-to-one on the restricted domain. For example, $f(x) = x^2$ for x in $(-\infty, \infty)$ is not one-to-one and not invertible. But $f(x) = x^2$ for $x \geq 0$ is one-to-one and invertible. The inverse of $f(x) = x^2$ for $x \geq 0$ is the square root function $f^{-1}(x) = \sqrt{x}$. Graphing will help you to see when the domain of an inverse function must be restricted.

EXAMPLE 7 Graphing a function and its inverse

Find the inverse of the function $f(x) = \sqrt{x - 1}$ and graph both f and f^{-1} on the same coordinate axes.

Solution

The graph of $f(x) = \sqrt{x - 1}$ is shown in Fig. 64. The domain of f is $[1, \infty)$ and the range is $[0, \infty)$. From the graph, we see that f is one-to-one and invertible. Since f is a composition of subtracting 1 and then taking a square root, f^{-1} must be a composition of squaring and then adding 1. Since the domain of f^{-1} must be the range of f, we have $f^{-1}(x) = x^2 + 1$ for $x \geq 0$. The graph of f^{-1} is half of a parabola, as shown in Fig. 64, and it is a reflection of the graph of f with respect to the line $y = x$. Note that without the restriction on the domain of f^{-1} the reflection property would not hold true.

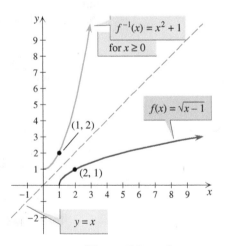

Figure 64

▶**TRY THIS.** Find the inverse of $f(x) = \sqrt{x + 2}$ and graph f and f^{-1}. ∎

The Switch-and-Solve Method

In the inverse function, the roles of x and y are switched. So we can actually switch x and y in the formula, do a bit of rewriting, and we have the inverse function. As you will see, this method is similar to finding an inverse by reversing a composition. Its advantage is that it works on some functions that are not readily viewed as a composition as in Example 8(b).

Functions and Graphs

PROCEDURE

Finding $f^{-1}(x)$ by the Switch-and-Solve Method

To find the inverse of a one-to-one function given in function notation:

1. Replace $f(x)$ by y.

2. Interchange x and y.

3. Solve the equation for y.

4. Replace y by $f^{-1}(x)$.

5. Check that the domain of f is the range of f^{-1} and the range of f is the domain of f^{-1}.

EXAMPLE 8 The switch-and-solve method

Find the inverse of each function.

a. $f(x) = 4x - 1$ **b.** $f(x) = \dfrac{2x + 1}{x - 3}$ **c.** $f(x) = \sqrt{x + 2} - 3$

Solution

a. The graph of $f(x) = 4x - 1$ is a line with slope 4. By the horizontal line test the function is one-to-one and invertible. Replace $f(x)$ with y to get $y = 4x - 1$. Next, interchange x and y to get $x = 4y - 1$. Now solve for y:

$$x = 4y - 1$$

$$x + 1 = 4y$$

$$\frac{x + 1}{4} = y$$

Replace y by $f^{-1}(x)$ to get $f^{-1}(x) = \frac{x + 1}{4}$. The domain of f is $(-\infty, \infty)$ and that is the range of f^{-1}. The range of f is $(-\infty, \infty)$ and that is the domain of f^{-1}.

b. In Example 3(a) we showed that f is a one-to-one function. So we can find f^{-1} by interchanging x and y and solving for y:

$$y = \frac{2x + 1}{x - 3} \quad \text{Replace } f(x) \text{ by } y.$$

$$x = \frac{2y + 1}{y - 3} \quad \text{Interchange } x \text{ and } y.$$

$$x(y - 3) = 2y + 1 \quad \text{Solve for } y.$$

$$xy - 3x = 2y + 1$$

$$xy - 2y = 3x + 1$$

$$y(x - 2) = 3x + 1$$

$$y = \frac{3x + 1}{x - 2}$$

Replace y by $f^{-1}(x)$ to get $f^{-1}(x) = \frac{3x + 1}{x - 2}$. The domain of f is all real numbers except 3. The range of f^{-1} is the set of all real numbers except 3. We exclude 3 because $\frac{3x + 1}{x - 2} = 3$ has no solution. Check that the range of f is equal to the domain of f^{-1}.

223

c. Replace $f(x)$ with y to get $y = \sqrt{x + 2} - 3$. Interchange x and y to get $x = \sqrt{y + 2} - 3$. Now solve for y:

$$x = \sqrt{y + 2} - 3$$

$$x + 3 = \sqrt{y + 2}$$

$$(x + 3)^2 = y + 2 \qquad \text{Square both sides.}$$

$$(x + 3)^2 - 2 = y$$

$$x^2 + 6x + 7 = y$$

The equation obtained by squaring both sides is not equivalent to the one above it. So we must make sure that the domain of the inverse function is the same as the range of the original function. The range of $f(x) = \sqrt{x + 2} - 3$ is the interval $[-3, \infty)$ and so that must be the domain of f^{-1}. So replace y by $f^{-1}(x)$ to get $f^{-1}(x) = x^2 + 6x + 7$ for $x \geq -3$.

▶**TRY THIS.** Use switch-and-solve to find the inverse of $h(x) = x^3 - 5$. ∎

If a function f is defined by a short list of ordered pairs, then we simply write all of the pairs in reverse to find f^{-1}. If two functions are defined by formulas, it may not be obvious whether the ordered pairs of one are the reverse of the ordered pairs of the other. However, we can use the compositions of the functions to make the determination as stated in the following theorem.

Theorem: Verifying Whether f and g Are Inverses

The functions f and g are inverses of each other if and only if

1. $g(f(x)) = x$ for every x in the domain of f and
2. $f(g(x)) = x$ for every x in the domain of g.

EXAMPLE 9 Using composition to verify inverse functions

Determine whether the functions $f(x) = x^3 - 1$ and $g(x) = \sqrt[3]{x + 1}$ are inverse functions.

Solution

Find $f(g(x))$ and $g(f(x))$:

$$f(g(x)) = f\left(\sqrt[3]{x + 1}\right) = \left(\sqrt[3]{x + 1}\right)^3 - 1 = x + 1 - 1 = x$$

$$g(f(x)) = g(x^3 - 1) = \sqrt[3]{x^3 - 1 + 1} = \sqrt[3]{x^3} = x$$

Since $f(g(x)) = x$ is true for any real number (the domain of g) and $g(f(x)) = x$ is true for any real number (the domain of f), the functions f and g are inverses of each other.

▶**TRY THIS.** Determine whether $f(x) = 2x + 1$ and $g(x) = \frac{x - 1}{2}$ are inverse functions.

FUNCTION
gallery... **Some Inverse Functions**

Linear

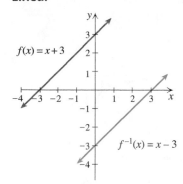

$f(x) = x + 3$

$f^{-1}(x) = x - 3$

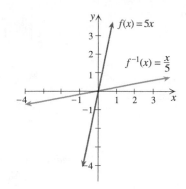

$f(x) = 5x$

$f^{-1}(x) = \frac{x}{5}$

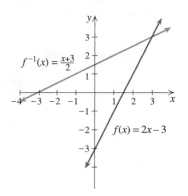

$f^{-1}(x) = \frac{x+3}{2}$

$f(x) = 2x - 3$

Powers and Roots

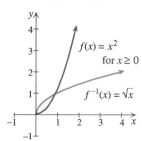

$f(x) = x^2$
for $x \geq 0$

$f^{-1}(x) = \sqrt{x}$

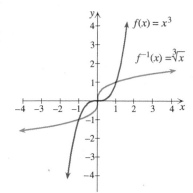

$f(x) = x^3$

$f^{-1}(x) = \sqrt[3]{x}$

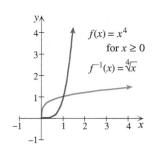

$f(x) = x^4$
for $x \geq 0$

$f^{-1}(x) = \sqrt[4]{x}$

FOR thought... True or False? Explain.

1. The inverse of the function $\{(2, 3), (5, 5)\}$ is $\{(5, 2), (5, 3)\}$.

2. The function $f(x) = -2$ is an invertible function.

3. If $g(x) = x^2$, then $g^{-1}(x) = \sqrt{x}$.

4. The only functions that are invertible are the one-to-one functions.

5. Every function has an inverse function.

6. The function $f(x) = x^4$ is invertible.

7. If $f(x) = 3\sqrt{x - 2}$, then $f^{-1}(x) = \frac{(x + 2)^2}{3}$ for $x \geq 0$.

8. If $f(x) = |x - 3|$, then $f^{-1}(x) = |x| + 3$.

9. According to the horizontal line test, $y = |x|$ is one-to-one.

10. The function $g(x) = -x$ is the inverse of the function $f(x) = -x$.

EXERCISES 5

Fill in the blank.

1. If a function has no two ordered pairs with different first coordinates and the same second coordinate then the function is _____.

2. If a function is one-to-one, then it is _____.

3. If f is one-to-one, then the function obtained by interchanging the coordinates in each ordered pair of f is the _____ of f.

4. The graphs of f and f^{-1} are _____ with respect to the line $y = x$.

Determine whether each function is one-to-one.

5. $\{(3, 3), (5, 5), (6, 6), (9, 9)\}$

6. $\{(3, 4), (5, 6), (7, 8), (9, 10), (11, 15)\}$

7. $\{(-1, 1), (1, 1), (-2, 4), (2, 4)\}$

8. $\{(3, 2), (5, 2), (7, 2)\}$

9. $\{(1, 99), (2, 98), (3, 97), (4, 96), (5, 99)\}$

10. $\{(-1, 9), (-2, 8), (-3, 7), (1, 9), (2, 8), (3, 7)\}$

Use the horizontal line test to determine whether each function is one-to-one.

11. $f(x) = x^2 - 3x$

12. $g(x) = |x - 2| + 1$

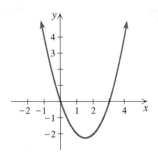

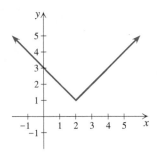

13. $y = \sqrt[3]{x} + 2$

14. $y = (x - 2)^3$

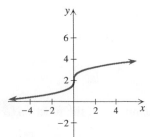

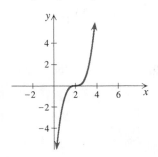

15. $y = x^3 - x$

16. $y = \dfrac{1}{x}$

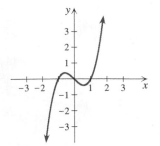

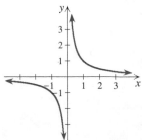

Determine whether each function is one-to-one.

17. $f(x) = 2x - 3$

18. $h(x) = 4x - 9$

19. $q(x) = \dfrac{1 - x}{x - 5}$

20. $g(x) = \dfrac{x + 2}{x - 3}$

21. $p(x) = |x + 1|$

22. $r(x) = 2|x - 1|$

23. $w(x) = x^2 + 3$

24. $v(x) = 2x^2 - 1$

25. $k(x) = \sqrt[3]{x + 9}$

26. $t(x) = \sqrt{x + 3}$

Determine whether each function is invertible. If it is invertible, find the inverse.

27. $\{(9, 3), (2, 2)\}$

28. $\{(4, 5), (5, 6)\}$

29. $\{(-1, 0), (1, 0), (5, 0)\}$

30. $\{(1, 2), (5, 2), (6, 7)\}$

31. $\{(3, 3), (2, 2), (4, 4), (7, 7)\}$

32. $\{(1, 1), (2, 4), (4, 16), (7, 49)\}$

33. $\{(1, 1), (2, 2), (4.5, 2), (5, 5)\}$

34. $\{(0, 2), (2, 0), (1, 0), (4, 6)\}$

Determine whether each function is invertible and explain your answer.

35. The function that pairs the universal product code of an item at Sears with a price.

36. The function that pairs the number of days since your birth with your age in years.

37. The function that pairs the length of a VCR tape in feet with the playing time in minutes.

38. The function that pairs the speed of your car in miles per hour with the speed in kilometers per hour.

39. The function that pairs the number of days of a hotel stay with the total cost for the stay.

40. The function that pairs the number of days that a deposit of $100 earns interest at 6% compounded daily with the amount of interest.

For each function f, find f^{-1}, $f^{-1}(5)$, and $(f^{-1} \circ f)(2)$.

41. $f = \{(2, 1), (3, 5)\}$

42. $f = \{(-1, 5), (0, 0), (2, 6)\}$

43. $f = \{(-3, -3), (0, 5), (2, -7)\}$

44. $f = \{(3.2, 5), (2, 1.99)\}$

Determine whether each function is invertible by inspecting its graph on a graphing calculator.

45. $f(x) = (x + 0.01)(x + 0.02)(x + 0.03)$

46. $f(x) = x^3 - 0.6x^2 + 0.11x - 0.006$

47. $f(x) = |x - 2| - |5 - x|$

48. $f(x) = \sqrt[3]{0.1x + 3} + \sqrt[3]{-0.1x}$

Find the inverse of each function by reversing a composition.

49. a. $f(x) = 5x + 1$ **b.** $f(x) = 3x - 88$

  c. $f(x) = 3x - 7$ **d.** $f(x) = 4 - 3x$

  e. $f(x) = \dfrac{1}{2}x - 9$ **f.** $f(x) = -x$

  g. $f(x) = \sqrt[3]{x} - 9$ **h.** $f(x) = 3x^3 - 7$

  i. $f(x) = \sqrt[3]{x - 1} + 5$ **j.** $f(x) = 2\sqrt[3]{x} - 7$

50. a. $f(x) = \dfrac{x}{2}$ **b.** $f(x) = x + 99$

  c. $f(x) = 5x + 1$ **d.** $f(x) = 5 - 2x$

  e. $f(x) = \dfrac{x}{3} + 6$ **f.** $f(x) = \dfrac{1}{x}$

  g. $f(x) = \sqrt[3]{x - 9}$ **h.** $f(x) = -x^3 + 4$

  i. $f(x) = 3\sqrt[3]{x + 4}$ **j.** $f(x) = \sqrt[3]{x + 3} - 9$

Determine whether each pair of functions f and g are inverses of each other.

51.

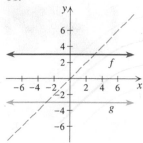

52.

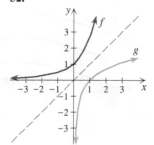

53.

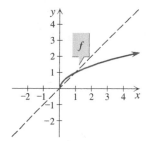

54.

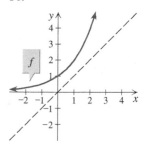

For each function f, sketch the graph of f^{-1}.

55.

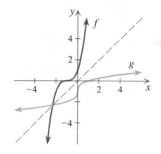

56.

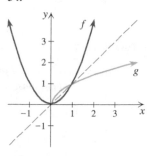

57.

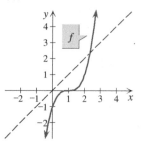

58.

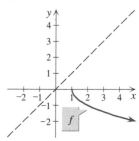

Find the inverse of each function and graph both f and f^{-1} on the same coordinate plane.

59. $f(x) = 3x + 2$ **60.** $f(x) = -x - 8$

61. $f(x) = x^2 - 4$ for $x \geq 0$ **62.** $f(x) = 1 - x^2$ for $x \geq 0$

63. $f(x) = x^3$ **64.** $f(x) = -x^3$

65. $f(x) = \sqrt{x} - 3$ **66.** $f(x) = \sqrt{x - 3}$

Find the inverse of each function using the procedure for the switch-and-solve method in Example 8.

67. $f(x) = 3x - 7$ **68.** $f(x) = -2x + 5$

69. $f(x) = 2 + \sqrt{x - 3}$ **70.** $f(x) = \sqrt{3x - 1}$

71. $f(x) = -x - 9$ **72.** $f(x) = -x + 3$

73. $f(x) = \dfrac{x + 3}{x - 5}$ **74.** $f(x) = \dfrac{2x - 1}{x - 6}$

75. $f(x) = -\dfrac{1}{x}$ **76.** $f(x) = x$

77. $f(x) = \sqrt[3]{x - 9} + 5$ **78.** $f(x) = \sqrt[3]{\dfrac{x}{2}} + 5$

79. $f(x) = (x - 2)^2$ for $x \geq 2$ **80.** $f(x) = x^2$ for $x \leq 0$

In each case find $f(g(x))$ and $g(f(x))$. Then determine whether g and f are inverse functions.

81. $f(x) = 4x + 4, g(x) = 0.25x - 1$

82. $f(x) = 20 - 5x, g(x) = -0.2x + 4$

83. $f(x) = x^2 + 1, g(x) = \sqrt{x - 1}$

84. $f(x) = \sqrt[4]{x}, g(x) = x^4$

85. $f(x) = \dfrac{1}{x} + 3, g(x) = \dfrac{1}{x - 3}$

86. $f(x) = 4 - \dfrac{1}{x}, g(x) = \dfrac{1}{4 - x}$

87. $f(x) = \sqrt[3]{\dfrac{x - 2}{5}}, g(x) = 5x^3 + 2$

88. $f(x) = x^3 - 27, g(x) = \sqrt[3]{x} + 3$

⊞ *For each exercise, graph the three functions on the same screen of a graphing calculator. Enter these functions as shown without simplifying any expressions. Explain what these exercises illustrate.*

89. $y_1 = \sqrt[3]{x} - 1, y_2 = (x + 1)^3, y_3 = (\sqrt[3]{x} - 1 + 1)^3$

90. $y_1 = (2x - 1)^{1/3}, y_2 = (x^3 + 1)/2,$
$y_3 = (2((x^3 + 1)/2) - 1)^{1/3}$

Solve each problem.

91. *Price of a Car* The tax on a new car is 8% of the purchase price P. Express the total cost C as a function of the purchase price P. Express the purchase price P as a function of the total cost C.

92. *Volume of a Cube* Express the volume of a cube $V(x)$ as a function of the length of a side x. Express the length of a side of a cube $S(x)$ as a function of the volume x.

93. *Rowers and Speed* The world record times in the 2000-m race are a function of the number of rowers as shown in the figure (www.cbs.sportsline.com). If r is the number of rowers and t is the time in minutes, then the formula $t = -0.39r + 7.89$ models this relationship. Is this function invertible? Find the inverse. If the time for a 2000-m race was 5.55 min, then how many rowers were probably in the boat?

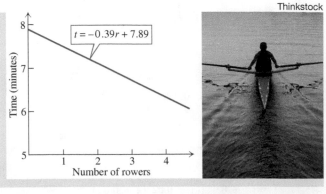

$t = -0.39r + 7.89$

Time (minutes) — Number of rowers

Figure for Exercise 93

94. *Temperature* The function $C = \frac{5}{9}(F - 32)$ expresses the Celsius temperature as a function of the Fahrenheit temperature. Find the inverse function. What is it used for?

95. *Landing Speed* The function $V = \sqrt{1.496w}$ expresses the landing speed V (in feet per second) as a function of the gross weight (in pounds) of the Piper Cheyenne aircraft. Find the inverse function. Use the inverse function to find the gross weight for a Piper Cheyenne for which the proper landing speed is 115 ft/sec.

96. *Poiseuille's Law* Under certain conditions, the velocity V of blood in a vessel at distance r from the center of the vessel is given by $V = 500(5.625 \times 10^{-5} - r^2)$ where $0 \leq r \leq 7.5 \times 10^{-3}$. Write r as a function of V.

97. *Depreciation Rate* The depreciation rate r for a $50,000 new car is given by the function $r = 1 - \left(\dfrac{V}{50,000}\right)^{1/5}$, where V is the value of the car when it is five years old.
   a. What is the depreciation rate for a $50,000 BMW that is worth $28,000 after 5 years?

   b. Write V as a function of r.

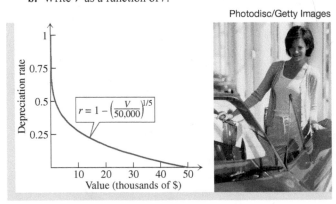

Depreciation rate — $r = 1 - \left(\dfrac{V}{50,000}\right)^{1/5}$ — Value (thousands of $)

Figure for Exercise 97

98. *Annual Growth Rate* One measurement of the quality of a mutual fund is its average annual growth rate over the last 10 years. The function $r = \left(\frac{P}{10,000}\right)^{1/10} - 1$ expresses the average annual growth rate r as a function of the present value P of an investment of $10,000 made 10 years ago. An investment of $10,000 in Fidelity's Contrafund in 1998 was worth $22,402 in 2008 (Fidelity Investments, www.fidelity.com). What was the annual growth rate for that period? Write P as a function of r.

Sebastian Kaulitzki/Shutterstock

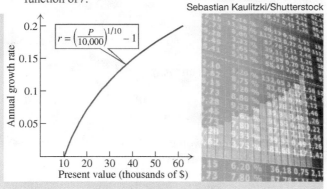

Figure for Exercise 98

FOR WRITING/DISCUSSION

99. If $f(x) = 2x + 1$ and $g(x) = 3x - 5$, verify the equation $(f \circ g)^{-1} = g^{-1} \circ f^{-1}$.

HINT Find formulas for $f \circ g$, $(f \circ g)^{-1}$, f^{-1}, g^{-1}, and $g^{-1} \circ f^{-1}$.

100. Explain why $(f \circ g)^{-1} = g^{-1} \circ f^{-1}$ for any invertible functions f and g. Discuss any restrictions on the domains and ranges of f and g for this equation to be correct.

101. Use a geometric argument to prove that if $a \neq b$, then (a, b) and (b, a) lie on a line perpendicular to the line $y = x$ and are equidistant from $y = x$.

102. Why is it difficult to find the inverse of a function such as $f(x) = (x - 3)/(x + 2)$ mentally?

103. Find an expression equivalent to $(x - 3)/(x + 2)$ in which x appears only once. Explain.

104. Use the result of Exercise 103 to find the inverse of $f(x) = (x - 3)/(x + 2)$ mentally. Explain.

▶ RETHINKING

105. Let $f(x) = \dfrac{2x + 3}{5}$ and $g(x) = 5x - 9$. Find $(f \circ g)(2)$ and $(f \cdot g)(2)$.

106. The graph of $y = \sqrt{x}$ is stretched by a factor of 2, reflected in the x-axis, then translated 5 units to the right. Write the equation of the graph in its final position.

107. Let $f(x) = -\sqrt{9 - x^2}$. Find the domain, range, and the interval on which the function is increasing.

108. Is the set of ordered pairs $\{(1, 3), (3, 5), (9, 0), (1, 4)\}$ a function?

109. Solve $0.125x + 0.75 = 0.225x - 0.8$.

110. Find the equation of the line through $(2, 4)$ that is perpendicular to the line $2x - y = 19$. Write the answer in slope-intercept form.

THINKING OUTSIDE THE BOX XVIII

Costly Computers A school district purchased x computers at y dollars each for a total of $640,000. Both x and y are whole numbers and neither is a multiple of 10. Find the absolute value of the difference between x and y.

▶ POP QUIZ 5

1. Is the function $\{(1, 3), (4, 5), (2, 3)\}$ invertible?

2. If $f = \{(5, 4), (3, 6), (2, 5)\}$, then what is $f^{-1}(5)$?

3. If $f(x) = 2x$, then what is $f^{-1}(8)$?

4. Is $f(x) = x^4$ a one-to-one function?

5. If $f(x) = 2x - 1$, then what is $f^{-1}(x)$?

6. If $g(x) = \sqrt[3]{x + 1} - 4$, then what is $g^{-1}(x)$?

7. Find $(h \circ j)(x)$ if $h(x) = x^3 - 5$ and $j(x) = \sqrt[3]{x + 5}$.

Pay Day Loans

Star Financial Corporation offers short-term loans as shown in the accompanying advertisement. If you borrow P dollars for n days at the annual percentage rate r, then you pay back A dollars where

$$A = P\left(1 + \frac{r}{365}\right)^n.$$

a) Solve the formula for r in terms of A, P, and n.

b) Find the annual percentage rate (APR) for each of the loans described in the advertisement.

c) If you borrowed $200, then how much would you have to pay back in one year using the APR that you determined in part (b)?

d) Find the current annual percentage rates for a car loan, house mortgage, and a credit card.

e) Why do you think Star Financial Corporation charges such high rates?

6 Constructing Functions with Variation

The area of a circle is a function of the radius, $A = \pi r^2$. As the values of r change or vary, the values of A vary also. Certain relationships are traditionally described by indicating how one variable changes according to the values of another variable. In this section we will construct functions for those relationships.

Direct Variation

If we save 3 cubic yards of landfill space for every ton of paper that we recycle, then the volume V of space saved is a linear function of the number of tons recycled n, $V = 3n$. If n is 20 tons, then V is 60 cubic yards. If n is doubled to 40 tons, then V is also doubled to 120 cubic yards. If n is tripled, V is also tripled. This relationship is called **direct variation.**

Definition: Direct Variation

The statement y **varies directly as** x or y **is directly proportional to** x means that

$$y = kx$$

for some fixed nonzero real number k. The constant k is called the **variation constant** or **proportionality constant.**

Compare the landfill savings to a pizza that costs $5 plus $2 per topping. The cost is a linear function of the number of toppings n, $C = 2n + 5$. If $n = 2$,

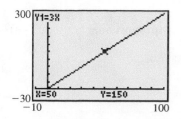

Figure 65

then $C = \$9$ and if $n = 4$, then $C = \$13$. The cost increases as n increases, but doubling n does not double C. The savings in landfill space is directly proportional to the number of tons of paper that is recycled, but the cost of the pizza is not directly proportional to the number of toppings. The graph of $V = 3n$ in Fig. 65 is a straight line through the origin. In general, if y varies directly as x, then y is a linear function of x whose graph is a straight line through the origin. We are merely introducing some new terms to describe an old idea.

EXAMPLE 1 Direct variation

The cost C of a house in Wedgewood Estates is directly proportional to the size of the house s. If a 2850-square-foot house costs \$182,400, then what is the cost of a 3640-square-foot house?

Solution

Because C is directly proportional to s, there is a constant k such that

$$C = ks.$$

We can find the constant by using $C = \$182,400$ when $s = 2850$:

$$182,400 = k(2850)$$

$$64 = k$$

The cost for a house is \$64 per square foot. To find the cost of a 3640-square-foot house, use the formula $C = 64s$:

$$C = 64(3640)$$

$$= 232,960$$

The 3640-square-foot house costs \$232,960.

▶**TRY THIS.** The cost of a smoothie is directly proportional to its size. If a 12-ounce smoothie is \$3.60, then what is the cost of a 16-ounce smoothie? ∎

Since $y = kx$ in a direct variation, we have $\frac{y}{x} = k$. So the ratio of y to x is constant. If (x_1, y_1) and (x_2, y_2) are two ordered pairs in a direct variation, then

$$\frac{y_1}{x_1} = \frac{y_2}{x_2}.$$

We could have used this proportion in Example 1. If a 2850-square-foot house costs \$182,400 and a 3640-square-foot house costs an unknown amount C, we have

$$\frac{182,400}{2850} = \frac{C}{3640}$$

or

$$C = \frac{182,400}{2850} \cdot 3640 = \$232,960.$$

Inverse Variation

The time that it takes to make the 3470-mile trip by air from New York to London is a function of the rate of the airplane, $T = 3470/R$. A Boeing 747 averaging 675 mph can make the trip in about 5 hours. The Concorde, traveling twice as fast at 1350 mph, made it in half the time, about 2.5 hours. If you travel three times as fast as the 747 you could make the trip in one-third the time. This relationship is called **inverse variation.**

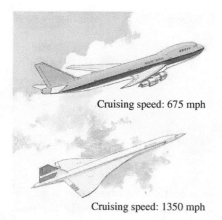

Cruising speed: 675 mph

Cruising speed: 1350 mph

Definition: Inverse Variation

The statement *y* **varies inversely as** *x* or *y* **is inversely proportional to** *x* means that

$$y = \frac{k}{x}$$

for a fixed nonzero real number *k*.

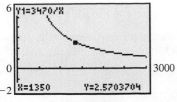

Figure 66

The graph of $T = 3470/R$ is shown in Fig. 66. As the speed increases the time decreases, but it does not reach zero for any speed.

EXAMPLE 2 Inverse variation

The time it takes to remove all of the campaign signs in Bakersfield after an election varies inversely with the number of volunteers working on the job. If 12 volunteers could complete the job in 7 days, then how many days would it take for 15 volunteers?

Solution

Since the time *T* varies inversely as the number of volunteers *n*, we have

$$T = \frac{k}{n}.$$

Since $T = 7$ when $n = 12$, we can find *k*:

$$7 = \frac{k}{12}$$

$$84 = k$$

So the formula is $T = 84/n$. Now if $n = 15$, we get

$$T = \frac{84}{15} = 5.6.$$

It would take 15 volunteers 5.6 days to remove all of the political signs.

▶**TRY THIS.** The time required to rake the grounds at Rockwood Manor varies inversely with the number of rakers. If 4 rakers can complete the job in 12 hours, then how long would it take for 6 rakers to complete the job? ■

Since $y = k/x$ in an inverse variation, we have $xy = k$. So the product of *x* and *y* is constant. If (x_1, y_1) and (x_2, y_2) are two ordered pairs in an inverse variation, then $x_1 y_1 = x_2 y_2$ or

$$\frac{y_1}{y_2} = \frac{x_2}{x_1}.$$

We could have used this inverse proportion in Example 2. If 12 volunteers take 7 days and 15 volunteers take *T* days, then we have

$$\frac{7}{T} = \frac{15}{12}$$

or

$$T = \frac{7 \cdot 12}{15} = 5.6 \text{ days.}$$

Joint Variation

We have been studying functions of one variable, but situations often arise in which one variable depends on the values of two or more variables. For example, the area of a rectangular room depends on the length *and* the width, $A = LW$. If carpeting costs $25 per square yard, then the total cost is a function of the length and width, $C = 25LW$. This example illustrates **joint variation.**

Definition: Joint Variation

> The statement ***y*** **varies jointly as *x* and *z* or *y* is jointly proportional to *x* and *z*** means that
>
> $$y = kxz$$
>
> for a fixed nonzero real number k.

EXAMPLE 3 Joint variation

The cost of constructing a 9-foot by 12-foot patio is $734.40. If the cost varies jointly as the length and width, then what does an 8-foot by 14-foot patio cost?

Solution

Since the cost varies jointly as L and W, we have $C = kLW$ for some constant k. Use $W = 9, L = 12$, and $C = \$734.40$ to find k:

$$734.40 = k(12)(9)$$

$$6.80 = k$$

So the formula is $C = 6.80LW$. Use $W = 8$ and $L = 14$ to find C:

$$C = 6.80(14)(8)$$

$$= 761.60$$

The cost of constructing an 8-foot by 14-foot patio is $761.60.

▶**TRY THIS.** The cost of a fence that is 200 feet long and 5 feet high is $3000. If the cost varies jointly with the length and height, then what is the cost of a fence that is 250 feet long and 6 feet high? ∎

Combined Variation

Some relationships are combinations of direct and inverse variation. For example, the formula $V = kT/P$ expresses the volume of a gas in terms of its temperature T and its pressure P. The volume varies directly as the temperature and inversely as the pressure. The next example gives more illustrations of combining direct, inverse, and joint variation.

EXAMPLE 4 Constructing functions for combined variation

Write each sentence as a function involving a constant of variation k.

a. y varies directly as x and inversely as z.
b. y varies jointly as x and the square root of z.
c. y varies jointly as x and the square of z and inversely as the cube of w.

Solution

a. $y = \dfrac{kx}{z}$ **b.** $y = kx\sqrt{z}$ **c.** $y = \dfrac{kxz^2}{w^3}$

▶**TRY THIS.** Suppose that M varies directly as w and the cube of z. Write a formula that describes this variation with k as the constant. ∎

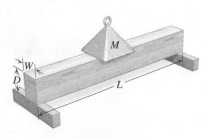

Figure 67

The language of variation evolved as a means of describing functions that involve only multiplication and/or division. The terms "varies directly," "directly proportional," and "jointly proportional" indicate multiplication. The term "inverse" indicates division. The term "variation" is *never* used in this text to refer to a formula involving addition or subtraction. Note that the formula for the cost of a pizza $C = 2n + 5$ is *not* the kind of formula that is described in terms of variation.

EXAMPLE 5 | Solving a combined variation problem

The recommended maximum load for the ceiling joist with rectangular cross section shown in Fig. 67 varies directly as the product of the width and the square of the depth of the cross section, and inversely as the length of the joist. If the recommended maximum load is 800 pounds for a 2-inch by 6-inch joist that is 12 feet long, then what is the recommended maximum load for a 2-inch by 12-inch joist that is 16 feet long?

Solution

The maximum load M varies directly as the product of the width W and the square of the depth D, and inversely as the length L:

$$M = \frac{kWD^2}{L}$$

Because the depth is squared, the maximum load is always obtained by positioning the joist so that the larger dimension is the depth. Use $W = 2, D = 6, L = 12$, and $M = 800$ to find k:

$$800 = \frac{k \cdot 2 \cdot 6^2}{12}$$

$$800 = 6k$$

$$\frac{400}{3} = k$$

Now use $W = 2, D = 12, L = 16$, and $k = 400/3$ in $M = \frac{kWD^2}{L}$ to find M:

$$M = \frac{400 \cdot 2 \cdot 12^2}{3 \cdot 16} = 2400$$

The maximum load on the joist is 2400 pounds. Notice that feet and inches were used in the formula without converting one to the other. If we solve the problem using only feet or only inches, then the value of k is different but we get the same value for M.

▶**TRY THIS.** W varies directly with m and inversely as the square of t. If $W = 480$ when $m = 5$ and $t = 4$, then what is W when $m = 3$ and $t = 6$? ∎

→ FOR thought... True or False? Explain.

1. If the cost of an 800 number is $29.95 per month plus 28 cents per minute, then the monthly cost varies directly as the number of minutes.

2. If bananas are $0.39 per pound, then your cost for a bunch of bananas varies directly with the number of bananas purchased.

3. The area of a circle varies directly as the square of the radius.

4. The area of a triangle varies jointly as the length of the base and the height.

5. The number π is a constant of proportionality.

6. If y is inversely proportional to x, then for $x = 0$, we get $y = 0$.

7. If the cost of potatoes varies directly with the number of pounds purchased, then the proportionality constant is the price per pound.

8. The height of a student in centimeters is directly proportional to the height of the same student in inches.

9. The surface area of a cube varies directly as the square of the length of an edge.

10. The surface area of a rectangular box varies jointly as its length, width, and height.

EXERCISES 6

Fill in the blank.

1. If $y = kx$, then y _____ as x.

2. If $y = kx$, then k is the _____ constant.

3. If $y = k/x$, then y _____ as x.

4. If $y = kxz$, then y _____ as x and z.

Construct a function that expresses the relationship in each statement. Use k as the constant of variation.

5. Your grade on the next test G varies directly with the number of hours n that you study for it.

6. The amount of sales tax on a new car is directly proportional to the purchase price of the car.

7. The volume of a gas in a cylinder V is inversely proportional to the pressure on the gas P.

8. For two lines that are perpendicular and have slopes, the slope of one is inversely proportional to the slope of the other.

9. The cost of constructing a silo varies jointly as the height and the radius.

10. The volume of grain that a silo can hold varies jointly as the height and the square of the radius.

11. Y varies directly as x and inversely as the square root of z.

12. W varies directly with r and t and inversely with v.

For each formula that illustrates a type of variation, write the formula in words using the vocabulary of variation. The letters k and π represent constants, and all other letters represent variables.

13. $A = \pi r^2$

14. $C = \pi D$

15. $y = \dfrac{1}{x}$

16. $m_1 = \dfrac{-1}{m_2}$

17. $T = 3W + 5$

18. $y = k\sqrt{x - 3}$

19. $a = kzw$

20. $V = LWH$

21. $H = \dfrac{k\sqrt{t}}{s}$

22. $B = \dfrac{y^2}{2\sqrt{x}}$

23. $D = \dfrac{2LJ}{W}$

24. $E = mc^2$

Find the constant of variation and construct the function that is expressed in each statement.

25. y varies directly as x, and $y = 5$ when $x = 9$.

26. h is directly proportional to z, and $h = 210$ when $z = 200$.

27. T is inversely proportional to y, and $T = -30$ when $y = 5$.

28. H is inversely proportional to n, and $H = 9$ when $n = -6$.

29. m varies directly as the square of t, and $m = 54$ when $t = 3\sqrt{2}$.

30. p varies directly as the cube root of w, and $p = \sqrt[3]{2}/2$ when $w = 4$.

31. y varies directly as x and inversely as the square root of z, and $y = 2.192$ when $x = 2.4$ and $z = 2.25$.

32. n is jointly proportional to x and the square root of b, and $n = -18.954$ when $x = -1.35$ and $b = 15.21$.

Solve each variation problem.

33. If y varies directly as x, and $y = 9$ when $x = 2$, what is y when $x = -3$?

34. If y is directly proportional to z, and $y = 6$ when $z = \sqrt{12}$, what is y when $z = \sqrt{75}$?

35. If P is inversely proportional to w, and $P = 2/3$ when $w = 1/4$, what is P when $w = 1/6$?

36. If H varies inversely as q, and $H = 0.03$ when $q = 0.01$, what is H when $q = 0.05$?

37. If A varies jointly as L and W, and $A = 30$ when $L = 3$ and $W = 5\sqrt{2}$, what is A when $L = 2\sqrt{3}$ and $W = 1/2$?

38. If J is jointly proportional to G and V, and $J = \sqrt{3}$ when $G = \sqrt{2}$ and $V = \sqrt{8}$, what is J when $G = \sqrt{6}$ and $V = 8$?

39. If y is directly proportional to u and inversely proportional to the square of v, and $y = 7$ when $u = 9$ and $v = 6$, what is y when $u = 4$ and $v = 8$?

40. If q is directly proportional to the square root of h and inversely proportional to the cube of j, and $q = 18$ when $h = 9$ and $j = 2$, what is q when $h = 16$ and $j = 1/2$?

Determine whether the first variable varies directly or inversely with the other variable. Construct a function for the variation using the appropriate variation constant.

41. The length of a car in inches, the length of the same car in feet

42. The time in seconds to pop a bag of microwave popcorn, the time in minutes to pop the same bag of popcorn

43. The price for each person sharing a $20 pizza, the number of hungry people

44. The number of identical steel rods with a total weight of 40,000 lb, the weight of one of those rods

45. The speed of a car in miles per hour, the speed of the same car at the same time in kilometers per hour

46. The weight of a sumo wrestler in pounds, the weight of the same sumo wrestler in kilograms. (Chad Rowan of the United States, at 455 lb, or 206 kg, was the first-ever foreign grand champion in Tokyo's annual tournament.)

Shizuo Kambayashi/AP Images

Figure for Exercise 46

47. The temperature in degrees Celsius, the temperature at the same time and place in degrees Fahrenheit

48. The perimeter of a rectangle with a length of 4 ft, the width of the same rectangle

49. The area of a rectangle with a length of 30 in., the width of the same rectangle

50. The area of a triangle with a height of 10 cm, the base of the same triangle

51. The number of gallons of gasoline that you can buy for $50, the price per gallon of that same gasoline

52. The length of Yolanda's 40 ft^2 closet, the width of that closet

Solve each problem.

53. *First-Class Diver* The pressure exerted by water at a point below the surface varies directly with the depth. The pressure is 4.34 lb/in.^{2} at a depth of 10 ft. What pressure does the sperm whale (the deepest diver among the air-breathing mammals) experience when it dives 6000 ft. below the surface?

54. *Second Place* The elephant seal (second only to the sperm whale) experiences a pressure of 2170 lb/in.^{2} when it makes its deepest dives. At what depth does the elephant seal experience this pressure? See the previous exercise.

55. *Processing Oysters* The time required to process a shipment of oysters varies directly with the number of pounds in the shipment and inversely with the number of workers assigned. If 3000 lb can be processed by 6 workers in 8 hr, then how long would it take 5 workers to process 4000 lb?

56. *View from an Airplane* The view V from the air is directly proportional to the square root of the altitude A. If the view from horizon to horizon at an altitude of 16,000 ft is approximately 154 mi, then what is the view from 36,000 ft?

57. *Simple Interest* The amount of simple interest on a deposit varies jointly with the principal and the time in days. If $20.80 is earned on a deposit of $4000 for 16 days, how much interest would be earned on a deposit of $6500 for 24 days?

58. *Free Fall at Six Flags* Visitors at Six Flags in Atlanta get a brief thrill in the park's "free fall" ride. Passengers seated in a small cab drop from a 10-story tower down a track that eventually curves level with the ground. The distance the cab falls varies directly with the square of the time it is falling. If the cab falls 16 ft in the first second, then how far has it fallen after 2 sec?

59. *Cost of Plastic Sewer Pipe* The cost of a plastic sewer pipe varies jointly as its diameter and its length. If a 20-ft pipe with a diameter of 6 in. costs $18.60, then what is the cost of a 16-ft pipe with a diameter of 8 in.?

60. *Cost of Copper Tubing* A plumber purchasing materials for a renovation observed that the cost of copper tubing varies jointly as the length and the diameter of the tubing. If 20 ft of $\frac{1}{2}$-in.-diameter tubing costs $36.60, then what is the cost of 100 ft of $\frac{3}{4}$-in.-diameter tubing?

61. *Weight of a Can* The weight of a can of baked beans varies jointly with the height and the square of the diameter. If a 4-in.-high can with a 3-in. radius weighs 14.5 oz, then what is the weight of a 5-in.-high can with a diameter of 6 in.?

62. *Nitrogen Gas Shock Absorber* The volume of gas in a nitrogen gas shock absorber varies directly with the temperature of the gas and inversely with the amount of weight on the piston. If the volume is 10 in.^{3} at 80°F with a weight of 600 lb, then what is the volume at 90°F with a weight of 800 lb?

63. *Velocity of Underground Water* Darcy's law states that the velocity V of underground water through sandstone varies directly as the head h and inversely as the length l of the flow. The head is the vertical distance between the point of intake into the rock and the point of discharge such as a spring, and the length is the length of the flow from intake to discharge. In a certain sandstone a velocity of 10 ft per year has been recorded with a head of 50 ft and length of 200 ft. What would we expect the velocity to be if the head is 60 ft and the length is 300 ft?

64. *Cross-Sectional Area of a Well* The rate of discharge of a well, V, varies jointly as the hydraulic gradient, i, and the cross-sectional area of the well wall, A. Suppose that a well with a cross-sectional area of 10 ft^2 discharges 3 gal of water per minute in an area where the hydraulic gradient is 0.3. If we dig another well nearby where the hydraulic gradient is 0.4, and we want a discharge of 5 gal/min, then what should be the cross-sectional area for the well?

65. *Dollars Per Death* The accompanying table shows the annual amount of money that the National Institutes of Health spends on disease research and the annual number of deaths for three diseases (www.nih.gov). Is the annual spending directly proportional to the annual number of deaths? Should it be?

Table for Exercise 65

Disease	Research Spending	Annual Deaths
AIDS	$1.34 billion	42,506
Diabetes	$295 million	59,085
Heart disease	$958 million	738,781

66. *Bicycle Gear Ratio* The gear ratio r for a bicycle varies jointly with the number of teeth on the chainring n, by the pedals, and the diameter of the wheel w (in inches), and inversely with the number of teeth on the cog c, by the wheel (www.harriscyclery.com). Find the missing entries in the accompanying table.

Table for Exercise 66

n	w	c	r
50	27	25	54
40	26	13	
45	27		67.5

Harm Kruyshaar/Shutterstock

67. *Grade on an Algebra Test* Calvin believes that his grade on a college algebra test varies directly with the number of hours spent studying during the week prior to the test and inversely with the number of hours spent at the Beach Club playing volleyball during the week prior to the test. If he scored 76 on a test when he studied 12 hr and played 10 hr during the week prior to the test, then what score should he expect if he studies 9 hr and plays 15 hr?

68. *Carpeting a Room* The cost of carpeting a room varies jointly as the length and width. Julie advertises a price of $263.40 to carpet a 9-ft by 12-ft room with Dupont Stainmaster. Julie gave a customer a price of $482.90 for carpeting a room with a width of 4 yd with that same carpeting, but she has forgotten the length of the room. What is the length of the room?

69. *Pole-Vault Principle* The height a pole-vaulter attains is directly proportional to the square of his velocity on the runway. Given that a speed of 32 ft/sec will loft a vaulter to 16 ft, find the speed necessary for world record holder Sergie Bubka to reach a record height of 20 ft 2.5 in.

70. *Cooperative Learning* Working in groups, drop a ball from various heights and measure the distance that the ball rebounds after hitting the floor. Enter your pairs of data into a graphing calculator and calculate the regression line. What is the value of the correlation coefficient, r? Do you think that the rebound distance is directly proportional to the drop distance? Compare your results with other groups.

71. *Moving Melons* To move more watermelons, a retailer decided to make the price of each watermelon purchased by a single customer inversely proportional to the number of watermelons purchased by the customer. Is this a good idea? Explain.

72. *Common Units* In general we do not perform computations involving inches and feet until they are converted to a common unit of measure. Explain how it is possible to use inches and feet in Example 5 without converting to a common unit of measure.

73. Find the inverse of the function $f(x) = \sqrt[3]{x - 9} + 1$.

74. Write a formula that expresses the diagonal d of a square as a function of the area A.

75. Galdino drove his truck from 8 A.M. to 11 A.M. in the rain. From 11 A.M. to 4 P.M. the skies were clear and he averaged 5 mph more than he did in the rain. If the total distance traveled was 425 miles, then what was his average speed in the rain?

76. Determine the symmetry of the graph of the function $f(x) = x^3 - 8x$.

77. Find the equation of the line through $(-4, 2)$ that is parallel to the line $5x - 10y = 31$. Write the answer in standard form.

78. Solve $|3x - 9| < 6$.

Good Timing Sharon leaves at the same time every day and walks to her 8 o'clock class. On Monday she averaged 4 miles per hour and was one minute late. On Wednesday she averaged 5 miles per hour and was one minute early. Find the exact speed that she should walk on Friday to get to class on time.

POP QUIZ 6

1. Find the constant of variation if y varies directly as x and $y = 4$ when $x = 20$.

2. If a varies inversely as b and the constant is 10, then what is a when $b = 2$?

3. The cost of a round rug varies directly as the square of its radius. If a rug with a 3-foot radius costs $108, then what is the cost of a rug with a 4-foot radius?

4. The cost of a rectangular tapestry varies jointly as its length and width. If a 6×2 foot tapestry costs $180, then what is the cost of a 5×4 foot tapestry?

LINKING
concepts...   For Individual or Group Explorations

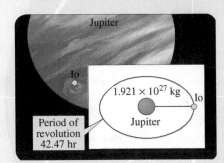

Determining the Mass of a Planet

A result of Kepler's harmonic law is that the mass of a planet with a satellite is directly proportional to the cube of the mean distance from the satellite to the planet, and inversely proportional to the square of the period of revolution. Early astronomers estimated the mass of the earth to be 5.976×10^{24} kg and observed that the moon orbited the earth with a period of 27.322 days at a mean distance of 384.4×10^3 km.

a) Write a formula for the mass of a planet according to Kepler.

b) Find the proportionality constant using the observations and estimates for the earth and the moon.

c) Extend your knowledge across the solar system to find the mass of Mars based on observations that Phobos orbits Mars in 7.65 hr at a mean distance of 9330 km.

d) What is the approximate ratio of the mass of the earth to the mass of Mars?

e) If the mass of Jupiter is 1.921×10^{27} kg and the period of revolution of Io around Jupiter is 42.47 hr, then what is the mean distance between Io and Jupiter?

Highlights

1 Functions

Relation	Any set of ordered pairs	$\{(1, 5), (1, 3), (3, 5)\}$
Function	A relation in which no two ordered pairs have the same first coordinate and different second coordinates	$\{(1, 5), (2, 3), (3, 5)\}$
Vertical Line Test	If no vertical line crosses a graph more than once, then the graph is a function.	Function Not a function

Average Rate of Change	The slope of the line through $(a, f(a))$ and $(b, f(b))$: $\frac{f(b) - f(a)}{b - a}$	Average rate of change of $f(x) = x^2$ on $[2, 9]$ is $\frac{9^2 - 2^2}{9 - 2}$.
Difference Quotient	Average rate of change of f on $[x, x + h]$: $\frac{f(x + h) - f(x)}{h}$	$f(x) = x^2$, difference quotient $= \frac{(x + h)^2 - x^2}{h} = 2x + h$

2 Graphs of Relations and Functions

Graph of a Relation	An illustration of all ordered pairs of a relation	Graph of $y = x + 1$ shows all ordered pairs in this function.
Circle	A circle is not the graph of a function.	Since $(0, \pm 2)$ satisfies $x^2 + y^2 = 4$, it is not a function.
Increasing, Decreasing, or Constant	When going from left to right, a function is increasing if its graph is rising, decreasing if its graph is falling, constant if its graph is staying the same.	$y = |x|$ is increasing on $[0, \infty)$ and decreasing on $(-\infty, 0]$. $y = 5$ is constant on $(-\infty, \infty)$.

3 Families of Functions, Transformations, and Symmetry

Transformations of $y = f(x)$	Horizontal: $y = f(x - h)$ Vertical: $y = f(x) + k$ Stretching: $y = af(x)$ for $a > 1$ Shrinking: $y = af(x)$ for $0 < a < 1$ Reflection: $y = -f(x)$	$y = (x - 4)^2$ $y = x^2 + 9$ $y = 3x^2$ $y = 0.5x^2$ $y = -x^2$
Family of Functions	All functions of the form $f(x) = af(x - h) + k$ $(a \neq 0)$ for a given function $y = f(x)$	The square root family: $y = a\sqrt{x - h} + k$
Even Function	Graph is symmetric with respect to y-axis. $f(-x) = f(x)$	$f(x) = x^2, g(x) = |x|$
Odd Function	Graph is symmetric about the origin. $f(-x) = -f(x)$	$f(x) = x, g(x) = x^3$
Inequalities	$f(x) > 0$ is satisfied on all intervals where the graph of $y = f(x)$ is above the x-axis. $f(x) < 0$ is satisfied on all intervals where the graph of $y = f(x)$ is below the x-axis.	$4 - x^2 > 0$ on $(-2, 2)$ $4 - x^2 < 0$ on $(-\infty, -2) \cup (2, \infty)$

4 Operations with Functions

Sum	$(f + g)(x) = f(x) + g(x)$	$f(x) = x^2 - 4, g(x) = x + 2$ $(f + g)(x) = x^2 + x - 2$
Difference	$(f - g)(x) = f(x) - g(x)$	$(f - g)(x) = x^2 - x - 6$
Product	$(f \cdot g)(x) = f(x) \cdot g(x)$	$(f \cdot g)(x) = x^3 + 2x^2 - 4x - 8$
Quotient	$(f/g)(x) = f(x)/g(x)$	$(f/g)(x) = x - 2$
Composition	$(f \circ g)(x) = f(g(x))$	$(f \circ g)(x) = (x + 2)^2 - 4$ $(g \circ f)(x) = x^2 - 2$

5 Inverse Functions

One-to-One Function	A function that has no two ordered pairs with different first coordinates and the same second coordinate	$\{(1,2),(3,5),(6,9)\}$ $g(x) = x + 3$ is one-to-one. $f(x) = x^2$ is not one-to-one.
Inverse Function	A one-to-one function has an inverse. The inverse function has the same ordered pairs, with the coordinates reversed.	$f = \{(1,2),(3,5),(6,9)\}$ $f^{-1} = \{(2,1),(5,3),(9,6)\}$ $g(x) = x + 3, g^{-1}(x) = x - 3$
Horizontal Line Test	If there is a horizontal line that crosses the graph of f more than once, then f is not invertible.	$y = 4$ crosses $f(x) = x^2$ twice, so f is not invertible.
Graph of f^{-1}	Reflect the graph of f about the line $y = x$ to get the graph of f^{-1}.	

6 Constructing Functions with Variation

Direct Variation	$y = kx$ for a constant $k \neq 0$.	$D = 40T$
Inverse Variation	$y = k/x$ for a constant $k \neq 0$.	$T = 200/R$
Joint Variation	$y = kxz$ for a constant $k \neq 0$.	$C = 25LW$

Chapter Review Exercises

Graph each set of ordered pairs. State the domain and range of each relation. Determine whether each set is a function.

1. $\{(0,0),(1,1),(-2,-2)\}$

2. $\{(0,-3),(1,-1),(2,1),(2,3)\}$

3. $\{(x,y)\,|\,y = 3 - x\}$ 4. $\{(x,y)\,|\,2x + y = 5\}$

5. $\{(x,y)\,|\,x = 2\}$ 6. $\{(x,y)\,|\,y = 3\}$

7. $\{(x,y)\,|\,x^2 + y^2 = 0.01\}$

8. $\{(x,y)\,|\,x^2 + y^2 = 2x - 4y\}$

9. $\{(x,y)\,|\,x = y^2 + 1\}$ 10. $\{(x,y)\,|\,y = |x - 2|\}$

11. $\{(x,y)\,|\,y = \sqrt{x} - 3\}$ 12. $\{(x,y)\,|\,x = \sqrt{y}\}$

Let $f(x) = x^2 + 3$ and $g(x) = 2x - 7$. Find and simplify each expression.

13. $f(-3)$ 14. $g(3)$

15. $g(12)$ 16. $f(-1)$

17. x, if $f(x) = 19$ 18. x, if $g(x) = 9$

19. $(g \circ f)(-3)$ 20. $(f \circ g)(3)$

21. $(f + g)(2)$ 22. $(f - g)(-2)$

23. $(f \cdot g)(-1)$ 24. $(f/g)(4)$

25. $f(g(2))$ 26. $g(f(-2))$

27. $(f \circ g)(x)$ 28. $(g \circ f)(x)$

29. $(f \circ f)(x)$ 30. $(g \circ g)(x)$

31. $f(a + 1)$ 32. $g(a + 2)$

33. $\dfrac{f(3+h) - f(3)}{h}$ 34. $\dfrac{g(5+h) - g(5)}{h}$

35. $\dfrac{f(x+h) - f(x)}{h}$ 36. $\dfrac{g(x+h) - g(x)}{h}$

37. $g\left(\dfrac{x+7}{2}\right)$ 38. $f(\sqrt{x} - 3)$

39. $g^{-1}(x)$ 40. $g^{-1}(-3)$

Use transformations to graph each pair of functions on the same coordinate plane.

41. $f(x) = \sqrt{x}, g(x) = 2\sqrt{x + 3}$

42. $f(x) = \sqrt{x}, g(x) = -2\sqrt{x} + 3$

43. $f(x) = |x|, g(x) = -2|x + 2| + 4$

44. $f(x) = |x|, g(x) = \frac{1}{2}|x - 1| - 3$

45. $f(x) = x^2, g(x) = \frac{1}{2}(x - 2)^2 + 1$

46. $f(x) = x^2, g(x) = -2x^2 + 4$

Let $f(x) = x - 4$, $g(x) = \sqrt{x}$ and $h(x) = x^2$. Find each composition and state its domain.

47. $f \circ g$

48. $g \circ f$

49. $f \circ h$

50. $h \circ f$

51. $g \circ f \circ h$

52. $h \circ f \circ g$

For each exercise, graph the function by transforming the given graph of $y = f(x)$.

53. $y = 2f(x - 2) + 1$ **54.** $y = 2f(x + 3) - 1$

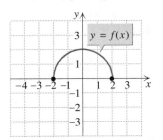   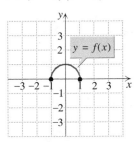

55. $y = -f(x + 1) - 3$ **56.** $y = -f(x - 1) + 2$

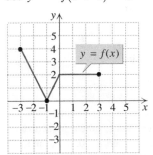   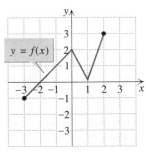

57. $y = -2f(x + 2)$ **58.** $y = -3f(x) + 1$

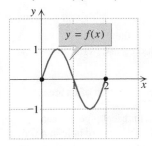   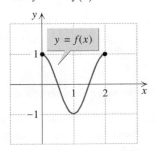

59. $y = -2f(x) + 3$ **60.** $y = 4f(x - 1) + 3$

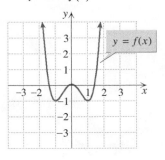   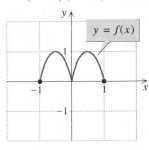

Let $f(x) = \sqrt[3]{x}$, $g(x) = x - 4$, $h(x) = x/3$, and $j(x) = x^2$. Write each function as a composition of the appropriate functions chosen from f, g, h, and j.

61. $F(x) = \sqrt[3]{x - 4}$ **62.** $G(x) = -4 + \sqrt[3]{x}$

63. $H(x) = \sqrt[3]{\dfrac{x^2 - 4}{3}}$ **64.** $M(x) = \left(\dfrac{x - 4}{3}\right)^2$

65. $N(x) = \dfrac{1}{3}x^{2/3}$ **66.** $P(x) = x^2 - 16$

67. $R(x) = \dfrac{x^2}{3} - 4$ **68.** $Q(x) = x^2 - 8x + 16$

Find the difference quotient for each function and simplify it.

69. $f(x) = -5x + 9$ **70.** $f(x) = \sqrt{x - 7}$

71. $f(x) = \dfrac{1}{2x}$ **72.** $f(x) = -5x^2 + x$

Sketch the graph of each function and state its domain and range. Determine the intervals on which the function is increasing, decreasing, or constant.

73. $f(x) = \sqrt{100 - x^2}$ **74.** $f(x) = -\sqrt{7 - x^2}$

75. $f(x) = \begin{cases} -x^2 & \text{for } x \le 0 \\ x^2 & \text{for } x > 0 \end{cases}$

76. $f(x) = \begin{cases} x^2 & \text{for } x \le 0 \\ x & \text{for } 0 < x \le 4 \end{cases}$

77. $f(x) = \begin{cases} -x - 4 & \text{for } x \le -2 \\ -|x| & \text{for } -2 < x < 2 \\ x - 4 & \text{for } x \ge 2 \end{cases}$

78. $f(x) = \begin{cases} -x - 4 & \text{for } x \le -2 \\ -|x| & \text{for } -2 < x < 2 \\ x - 4 & \text{for } x \ge 2 \end{cases}$

Each of the following graphs is from the absolute-value family. Construct a function for each graph and state the domain and range of the function.

79.

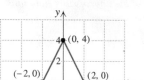

80.

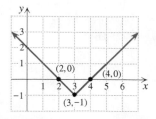

81.

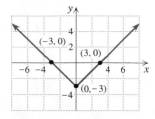

82.

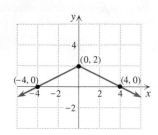

83.

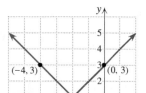

84.

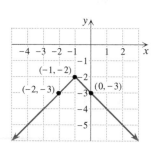

Determine whether the graph of each function is symmetric with respect to the y-axis or the origin.

85. $f(x) = x^4 - 9x^2$

86. $f(x) = |x| - 99$

87. $f(x) = -x^3 - 5x$

88. $f(x) = \dfrac{15}{x}$

89. $f(x) = -x + 1$

90. $f(x) = |x - 1|$

91. $f(x) = \sqrt{x^2}$

92. $f(x) = \sqrt{16 - x^2}$

Use the graph of an appropriate function to find the solution set to each inequality.

93. $|x - 3| \geq 1$

94. $|x + 2| + 1 < 0$

95. $-2x^2 + 4 > 0$

96. $-\dfrac{1}{2}x^2 + 2 \leq 0$

97. $-\sqrt{x + 1} - 2 > 0$

98. $\sqrt{x} - 3 < 0$

Graph each pair of functions on the same coordinate plane. What is the relationship between the functions in each pair?

99. $f(x) = \sqrt{x + 3}, g(x) = x^2 - 3$ for $x \geq 0$

100. $f(x) = (x - 2)^3, g(x) = \sqrt[3]{x} + 2$

101. $f(x) = 2x - 4, g(x) = \dfrac{1}{2}x + 2$

102. $f(x) = -\dfrac{1}{2}x + 4, g(x) = -2x + 8$

Determine whether each function is invertible. If the function is invertible, then find the inverse function, and state the domain and range of the inverse function.

103. $\{(\pi, 0), (\pi/2, 1), (2\pi/3, 0)\}$

104. $\{(-2, 1/3), (-3, 1/4), (-4, 1/5)\}$

105. $f(x) = 3x - 21$

106. $f(x) = 3|x|$

107. $y = \sqrt{9 - x^2}$

108. $y = 7 - x$

109. $f(x) = \sqrt{x - 9}$

110. $f(x) = \sqrt{x} - 9$

111. $f(x) = \dfrac{x - 7}{x + 5}$

112. $f(x) = \dfrac{2x - 3}{5 - x}$

113. $f(x) = x^2 + 1$ for $x \leq 0$ **114.** $f(x) = (x + 3)^4$ for $x \geq 0$

Solve each problem.

115. *Turning a Profit* Mary Beth buys roses for $1.20 each and sells them for $2 each at an outdoor market where she rents space for $40 per day. She buys and sells x roses per day. Construct her daily cost, revenue, and profit functions. How many roses must she sell to make a profit?

116. *Tin Can* The surface area S and volume V for a can with a top and bottom are given by

$$S = 2\pi r^2 + 2\pi rh \quad \text{and} \quad V = \pi r^2 h,$$

where r is the radius and h is the height. Suppose that a can has a volume of 1 ft^3.

a. Write its height as a function of its radius.

b. Write its radius as a function of its height.

c. Write its surface area as a function of its radius.

117. *Dropping the Ball* A ball is dropped from a height of 64 feet. Its height h (in feet) is a function of time t (in seconds), where $h = -16t^2 + 64$ for t in the interval $[0, 2]$. Find the inverse of this function and state the domain of the inverse function.

118. *Sales Tax Function* If S is the subtotal in dollars of your groceries before a 5% sales tax, then the function $T = 1.05S$ gives the total cost in dollars including tax. Write S as a function of T.

119. Write the diameter of a circle d as a function of its area A.

120. *Circle Inscribed in a Square* A cylindrical pipe with an outer radius r must fit snugly through a square hole in a wall. Write the area of the square as a function of the radius of the pipe.

121. *Load on a Spring* When a load of 5 lb is placed on a spring, its length is 6 in., and when a load of 9 lb is placed on the spring, its length is 8 in. What is the average rate of change of the length of the spring as the load varies from 5 lb to 9 lb?

122. *Changing Speed of a Dragster* Suppose that 2 sec after starting, a dragster is traveling 40 mph, and 5 sec after starting, the dragster is traveling 130 mph. What is the average rate of change of the speed of the dragster over the time interval from 2 sec to 5 sec? What are the units for this measurement?

123. Given that D is directly proportional to W and $D = 9$ when $W = 25$, find D when $W = 100$.

124. Given that t varies directly as u and inversely as v, and $t = 6$ when $u = 8$ and $v = 2$, find t when $u = 19$ and $v = 3$.

125. *Dinosaur Speed* R. McNeill Alexander, a British paleontologist, uses observations of living animals to estimate the speed of dinosaurs. Alexander believes that two animals of different sizes but geometrically similar shapes will move in a similar fashion. For animals of similar shapes, their velocity is directly proportional to the square root of their hip height. Alexander has compared a white rhinoceros, with a hip height of 1.5 m, and a member of the genus *Triceratops*, with a hip height of 2.8 m. If a white rhinoceros can move at 45 km/hr, then what is the estimated velocity of the dinosaur?

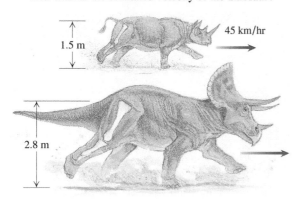

Figure for Exercise 125

126. *Arranging Plants in a Row* Timothy has a shipment of strawberry plants to plant in his field, which is prepared with rows of equal length. He knows that the number of rows that he will need varies inversely with the number of plants per row. If he plants 240 plants per row, then he needs 21 rows. How many rows does he need if he plants 224 plants per row?

127. *Handling Charge for a Globe* The shipping and handling charge for a globe from Mercator's Map Company varies directly as the square of the diameter. If the charge is $4.32 for a 6-in.-diameter globe, then what is the charge for a 16-in.-diameter globe?

128. *Newton's Law of Gravity* Newton's law of gravity states that the force of gravity acting between two objects varies directly as the product of the masses of the two objects and inversely as the square of the distance between their centers. Write an equation for Newton's law of gravity.

FOR WRITING/DISCUSSION

129. Explain what the vertical and horizontal line tests are and how to apply them.

130. Is a vertical line the graph of a linear function? Explain.

THINKING OUTSIDE THE BOX XX & XXI

Area of a Polygon Find the exact area of the polygon bounded by the x-axis, the y-axis, the line $2x + 3y = 7$, and the line $3x - 4y = 18$.

Whole Lotta Shakin' At the start of an economic conference between the eastern delegation and the western delegation, each delegate shook hands with every other member of his own delegation for a total of 466 handshakes. Next, each delegate shook hands with every person in the other delegation for 480 more handshakes. What was the total number of delegates at the conference?

Chapter Test

Determine whether each equation defines y as a function of x.

1. $x^2 + y^2 = 25$

2. $3x - 5y = 20$

3. $x = |y + 2|$

4. $y = x^3 - 3x^2 + 2x - 1$

State the domain and range of each relation.

5. $\{(2, -3), (2, -4), (5, 7)\}$

6. $y = \sqrt{x - 9}$

7. $x = |y - 1|$

Sketch the graph of each function.

8. $3x - 4y = 12$

9. $y = 2x - 3$

10. $y = \sqrt{25 - x^2}$

11. $y = -(x - 2)^2 + 5$

12. $y = 2|x| - 4$

13. $y = \sqrt{x + 3} - 5$

14. $f(x) = \begin{cases} x & \text{for } x < 0 \\ 2 & \text{for } x \geq 0 \end{cases}$

Let $f(x) = \sqrt{x + 2}$ and $g(x) = 3x - 1$. Find and simplify each of the following expressions.

15. $f(7)$

16. $(f \circ g)(2)$

17. $(f \circ g)(x)$

18. $g^{-1}(x)$

19. $(f + g)(14)$

20. $\dfrac{g(x + h) - g(x)}{h}$

Solve each problem.

21. State the intervals on which $f(x) = (x - 3)^2$ is increasing and those on which $f(x)$ is decreasing.

22. Discuss the symmetry of the graph of the function $f(x) = x^4 - 3x^2 + 9$.

23. State the solution set to the inequality $|x - 1| - 3 < 0$ using interval notation.

24. Find the inverse of the function $g(x) = 3 + \sqrt[3]{x - 2}$.

25. Find the inverse of the function $f(x) = \sqrt{x - 5}$.

26. Jang's Postal Service charges $35 for addressing 200 envelopes, and $60 for addressing 400 envelopes. What is the average rate of change of the cost as the number of envelopes goes from 200 to 400?

27. The intensity of illumination I from a light source varies inversely as the square of the distance d from the source. If a flash on a camera has an intensity of 300 candlepower at a distance of 2 m, then what is the intensity of the flash at a distance of 10 m?

28. Construct a function expressing the volume V of a cube as a function of the length of the diagonal d of a side of the cube.

CONCEPTS OF
calculus...

Instantaneous rate of change

Suppose that you start at Amarillo and drive west on I-40 for 500 miles. If this trip takes you 10 hours, then the average rate at which your location is changing is 50 miles per hour. At every instant of your trip your speedometer shows the instantaneous rate at which your location is changing. Your instantaneous rate of change might range from 0 miles per hour to 70 miles per hour or more.

We defined the average rate of change of a function $f(x)$ on the interval $[x, x + h]$ as $\frac{f(x + h) - f(x)}{h}$. We cannot use a speedometer to find the instantaneous rate of change of a function. We use the idea of limits, which was discussed in the Concepts of Calculus at the end of previous chapter. For the instantaneous rate of change we shrink the interval to nothing. So we define the instantaneous rate of change of $f(x)$ as
$$\lim_{h \to 0} \frac{f(x + h) - f(x)}{h}.$$

Exercises

1. Let $f(x) = x^2$.

   a. Find $\dfrac{f(2 + h) - f(2)}{h}$.

   b. Find $\lim_{h \to 0} \dfrac{f(2 + h) - f(2)}{h}$.

2. Let $f(x) = x^2 - 2x$.

   a. Find $\dfrac{f(x + h) - f(x)}{h}$.

   b. Find $\lim_{h \to 0} \dfrac{f(x + h) - f(x)}{h}$.

   c. Find the instantaneous rate of change of $f(x) = x^2 - 2x$ when $x = 5$.

3. Let $f(x) = \sqrt{x}$.

   a. Find $\dfrac{f(x + h) - f(x)}{h}$ and write your answer with a rational numerator.

   b. Find $\lim_{h \to 0} \dfrac{f(x + h) - f(x)}{h}$.

   c. Find the instantaneous rate of change of $f(x) = \sqrt{x}$ when $x = 9$.

4. A ball is tossed into the air from ground level at 128 feet per second. The function $f(t) = -16t^2 + 128t$ gives the height above ground (in feet) as a function of time (in seconds).

   a. Find $f(0)$ and $f(3)$.

   b. How far did the ball travel in the first three seconds of its flight?

   c. Find the average rate of change of the height for the time interval $[0, 3]$.

   d. Find $\dfrac{f(t + h) - f(t)}{h}$.

   e. Find $\lim_{h \to 0} \dfrac{f(t + h) - f(t)}{h}$.

   f. Find the instantaneous rate of change of the height (or the *instantaneous velocity*) of the ball at times $t = 0, 2, 4, 6,$ and 8 seconds.

The average rate of change of the function f on the interval $[c, x]$ is $\frac{f(x) - f(c)}{x - c}$.

5. Let $f(x) = \dfrac{1}{x}$.

   a. Find and simplify $\dfrac{f(x) - f(2)}{x - 2}$.

   b. Find $\lim_{x \to 2} \dfrac{f(x) - f(2)}{x - 2}$.

   c. Find the instantaneous rate of change of $f(x)$ when $x = 2$.

6. Let $f(x) = x^3$.

   a. Find and simplify $\dfrac{f(x) - f(c)}{x - c}$.

   b. Find $\lim_{x \to c} \dfrac{f(x) - f(c)}{x - c}$.

   c. Find the instantaneous rate of change of $f(x)$ when $x = c$.

Answers to Exercises

Section 1

For Thought: 1. F   **2.** F   **3.** T   **4.** F   **5.** F   **6.** F
7. T   **8.** T   **9.** T   **10.** F

Exercises:

1. relation   **3.** independent, dependent   **5.** difference quotient
7. Both   **9.** a is a function of b **11.** b is a function of a
13. Neither   **15.** Both   **17.** No   **19.** Yes   **21.** Yes
23. Yes   **25.** No   **27.** No   **29.** Yes   **31.** Yes
33. Yes   **35.** No   **37.** Yes   **39.** Yes   **41.** No
43. $\{-3, 4, 5\}, \{1, 2, 6\}$ **45.** $(-\infty, \infty), \{4\}$ **47.** $(-\infty, \infty), [5, \infty)$
49. $[-3, \infty), (-\infty, \infty)$ **51.** $[4, \infty), [0, \infty)$ **53.** $(-\infty, 0], (-\infty, \infty)$
55. 6   **57.** 11   **59.** 3   **61.** 7   **63.** 22   **65.** $3a^2 - a$
67. $4a + 6$ **69.** $3x^2 + 5x + 2$ **71.** $4x + 4h - 2$
73. $6x + 2$ **75.** $6xh + 3h^2 - h$ **77.** $-\$2400$ per yr
79. $-32, -48, -62.4, -63.84$, and -63.984 ft/sec
81. -10.1 million hectares per yr   **83.** 4   **85.** 3

87. $2x + h + 1$ **89.** $-2x - h + 1$ **91.** $\dfrac{3}{\sqrt{x + h} + \sqrt{x}}$

93. $\dfrac{1}{\sqrt{x + h + 2} + \sqrt{x + 2}}$ **95.** $\dfrac{-1}{x(x + h)}$

97. $\dfrac{-3}{(x + 2)(x + h + 2)}$

99. a. $A = s^2$ **b.** $s = \sqrt{A}$ **c.** $s = \dfrac{d\sqrt{2}}{2}$ **d.** $d = s\sqrt{2}$

e. $P = 4s$ **f.** $s = P/4$ **g.** $A = \dfrac{P^2}{16}$ **h.** $d = \sqrt{2A}$

101. $C = 50 + 35n$
103. a. Amount spent in 2004, $9.6 billion   **b.** 2010
105. $h = \left(2\sqrt{3} + 2\right)a$
107. At $18/ticket revenue is increasing at $1950 per dollar change in ticket price. At $22/ticket revenue is decreasing at $2050 per dollar change in ticket price.
111. $\{-9/17\}$ **113.** $2\sqrt{10}$ **115.** $\{-6, 7\}$

Section 2

For Thought: 1. T   **2.** F   **3.** T   **4.** T   **5.** F   **6.** T
7. T   **8.** T   **9.** F   **10.** T

Exercises:

1. parabola
3. $(-\infty, \infty), (-\infty, \infty)$, yes   **5.** $(-\infty, \infty), (-\infty, \infty)$, yes

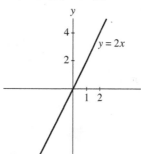

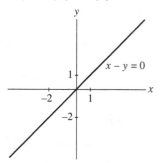

7. $(-\infty, \infty), \{5\}$, yes   **9.** $(-\infty, \infty), [0, \infty)$, yes

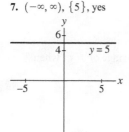

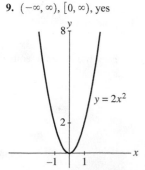

11. $(-\infty, \infty), (-\infty, 1]$, yes   **13.** $[0, \infty), [1, \infty)$, yes

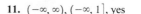
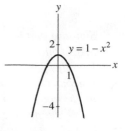

15. $[1, \infty), (-\infty, \infty)$, no   **17.** $[0, \infty), [0, \infty)$, yes

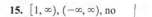
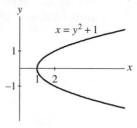
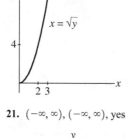
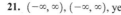

19. $(-\infty, \infty), (-\infty, \infty)$, yes   **21.** $(-\infty, \infty), (-\infty, \infty)$, yes

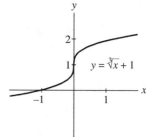
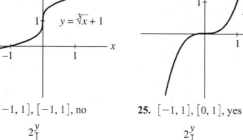

23. $[-1, 1], [-1, 1]$, no   **25.** $[-1, 1], [0, 1]$, yes

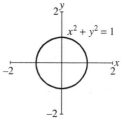
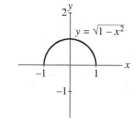

27. $(-\infty, \infty), (-\infty, \infty)$, yes   **29.** $(-\infty, \infty), [0, \infty)$, yes

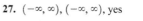
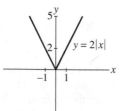
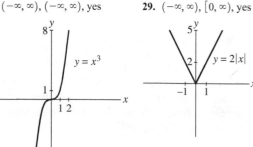

31. $(-\infty, \infty)$, $(-\infty, 0]$, yes

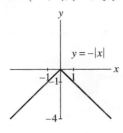
$y = -|x|$

33. $[0, \infty)$, $(-\infty, \infty)$, no

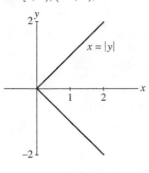
$x = |y|$

49. a. $D(-\infty, \infty)$, $R(-\infty, \infty)$, dec $(-\infty, \infty)$
   b. $D(-\infty, \infty)$, $R(-\infty, 4]$, inc $(-\infty, 0]$, dec $[0, \infty)$
51. a. $D[-2, 6]$, $R[3, 7]$, inc $[-2, 2]$, dec $[2, 6]$
   b. $D(-\infty, 2]$, $R(-\infty, 3]$, inc $(-\infty, -2]$, constant $[-2, 2]$
53. a. $D(-\infty, \infty)$, $R[0, \infty)$, dec $(-\infty, 0]$, inc $[0, \infty)$
   b. $D(-\infty, \infty)$, $R(-\infty, \infty)$, dec$(-\infty, -2]$ and $[-2/3, \infty)$, inc $[-2, -2/3]$
55. a. $D(-\infty, \infty)$, $R(-\infty, \infty)$, inc $(-\infty, \infty)$
   b. $D[-2, 5]$, $R[1, 4]$, dec $[-2, 1]$, inc $[1, 2]$, constant $[2, 5]$

57. $(-\infty, \infty)$, $(-\infty, \infty)$, inc $(-\infty, \infty)$

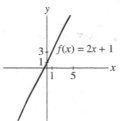
$f(x) = 2x + 1$

59. $(-\infty, \infty)$, $[0, \infty)$, dec $(-\infty, 1]$, inc $[1, \infty)$

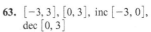
$f(x) = |x - 1|$

35. $(-\infty, \infty)$, $\{-2, 2\}$

$f(x) = \begin{cases} 2 & x < -1 \\ -2 & x \geq -1 \end{cases}$

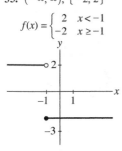

37. $(-\infty, \infty)$, $(-\infty, -2] \cup (2, \infty)$

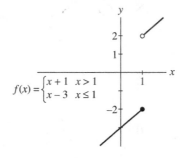
$f(x) = \begin{cases} x + 1 & x > 1 \\ x - 3 & x \leq 1 \end{cases}$

61. $(-\infty, 0) \cup (0, \infty)$, $\{-1, 1\}$, constant $(-\infty, 0)$, $(0, \infty)$

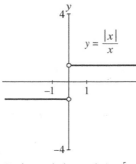
$y = \dfrac{|x|}{x}$

63. $[-3, 3]$, $[0, 3]$, inc $[-3, 0]$, dec $[0, 3]$

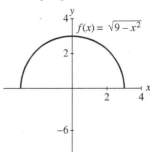
$f(x) = \sqrt{9 - x^2}$

39. $[-2, \infty)$, $(-\infty, 2]$

$f(x) = \begin{cases} \sqrt{x + 2} & -2 \leq x \leq 2 \\ 4 - x & x > 2 \end{cases}$

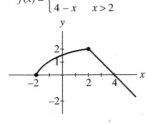

41. $(-\infty, \infty)$, $[0, \infty)$

$f(x) = \begin{cases} \sqrt{-x} & x < 0 \\ \sqrt{x} & x \geq 0 \end{cases}$

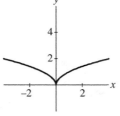

65. $(-\infty, \infty)$, $(-\infty, \infty)$, inc $[-\infty, 3)$, $[3, \infty)$

$f(x) = \begin{cases} x + 1 & x \geq 3 \\ x + 2 & x < 3 \end{cases}$

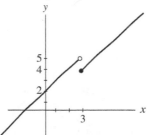

43. $(-\infty, \infty)$, $(-\infty, \infty)$

$f(x) = \begin{cases} x^2 & x < -1 \\ -x & x \geq -1 \end{cases}$

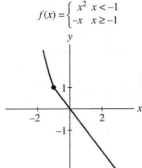

45. $(-\infty, \infty)$, integers

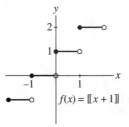
$f(x) = [\![x + 1]\!]$

67. $(-\infty, \infty)$, $(-\infty, 2]$, inc $(-\infty, -2]$, $(-2, 0]$ dec $[0, 2)$, $[2, \infty)$

$f(x) = \begin{cases} x + 3 & x \leq -2 \\ \sqrt{4 - x^2} & -2 < x < 2 \\ -x + 3 & x \geq 2 \end{cases}$

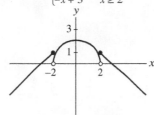

47. $[0, 4)$, $\{2, 3, 4, 5\}$

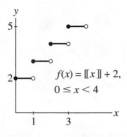
$f(x) = [\![x]\!] + 2$, $0 \leq x < 4$

247

69. $f(x) = \begin{cases} 2 & \text{for } x > -1 \\ -1 & \text{for } x \le -1 \end{cases}$

71. $f(x) = \begin{cases} x - 1 & \text{for } x \ge -1 \\ -x & \text{for } x < -1 \end{cases}$

73. $f(x) = \begin{cases} 2x - 2 & \text{for } x \ge 0 \\ -x - 2 & \text{for } x < 0 \end{cases}$

75. Dec $(-\infty, 0.83]$, inc $[0.83, \infty)$
77. Inc $(-\infty, -1]$, $[1, \infty)$, dec $[-1, 1]$
79. Dec $(-\infty, -1.73]$, $[0, 1.73]$, inc $[-1.73, 0]$, $[1.73, \infty)$
81. Inc $[30, 50]$, $[70, \infty)$, dec $(-\infty, 30]$, $[50, 70]$
83. c   **85.** d
87. Inc $[0, 3]$, $[6, 15]$, dec $[3, 6]$, $[30, 39]$, constant $[15, 30]$

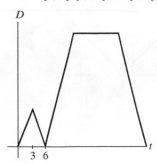

89. Inc $[0, 2]$, dec $[2.5, 4.5]$, constant $[2, 2.5]$

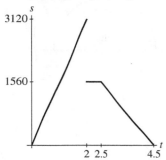

91. 565 million, 800 million, 14.5 million/yr
93. $[0, 10^4]$, $[10^4, \infty)$
95. $[5, \infty)$

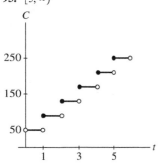

97. $f(x) = \begin{cases} 150 & 0 < x < 3 \\ 50x & 3 \le x \le 10 \end{cases}$

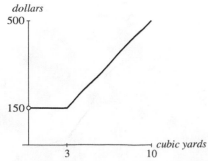

101. $[2, \infty)$, $[3, \infty)$ **103.** $\{55/13\}$ **105.** $\{5/2\}$

Section 3

For Thought: **1.** F   **2.** T   **3.** F   **4.** T   **5.** T   **6.** F
7. T   **8.** F   **9.** T   **10.** T

Exercises:
1. rigid   **3.** parabola   **5.** reflection   **7.** linear   **9.** odd

11.   **13.**

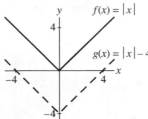

15.   **17.**

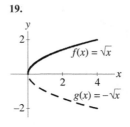

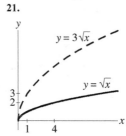

19.   **21.**

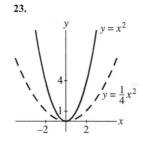

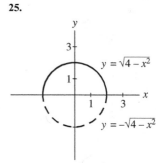

23.   **25.**

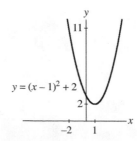

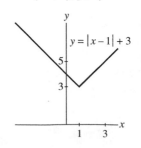

27. g   **29.** b   **31.** c   **33.** f
35. $y = \sqrt{x} + 2$ **37.** $y = (x - 5)^2$ **39.** $y = (x - 10)^2 + 4$
41. $y = -3\sqrt{x} - 5$ **43.** $y = -3|x - 7| + 9$
45. $(-\infty, \infty)$, $[2, \infty)$ **47.** $(-\infty, \infty)$, $[3, \infty)$

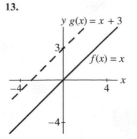

49. $(-\infty, \infty), (-\infty, \infty)$

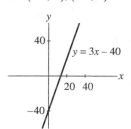

$y = 3x - 40$

51. $(-\infty, \infty), (-\infty, \infty)$

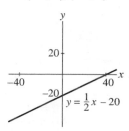

$y = \frac{1}{2}x - 20$

53. $(-\infty, \infty), (-\infty, 40]$

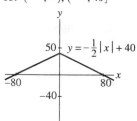

$y = -\frac{1}{2}|x| + 40$

55. $(-\infty, \infty), (-\infty, 0]$

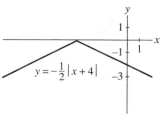

$y = -\frac{1}{2}|x + 4|$

57. $[3, \infty), (-\infty, 1]$

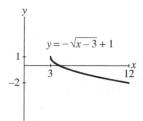

$y = -\sqrt{x - 3} + 1$

59. $[-3, \infty), (-\infty, 2]$

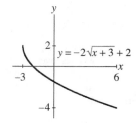

$y = -2\sqrt{x + 3} + 2$

61. y-axis, even   **63.** No symmetry, neither   **65.** $x = -3$, neither
67. $x = 2$, neither   **69.** Origin, odd   **71.** No symmetry, neither
73. No symmetry, neither   **75.** y-axis, even   **77.** No symmetry, neither
79. y-axis, even   **81.** e   **83.** g   **85.** b   **87.** c
89. $(-\infty, -1] \cup [1, \infty)$ **91.** $(-\infty, -1) \cup (5, \infty)$ **93.** $(-2, 4)$
95. $[0, 25]$ **97.** $(-\infty, 2 - \sqrt{3}) \cup (2 + \sqrt{3}, \infty)$ **99.** $(-5, 5)$
101. $(-3.36, 1.55)$
103. a.

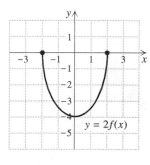

$y = 2f(x)$

b.

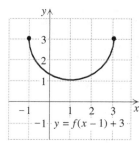

$y = -f(x)$

c.

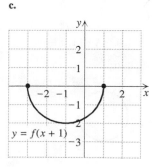

$y = f(x + 1)$

d.

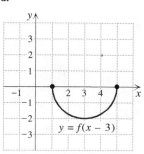

$y = f(x - 3)$

e.

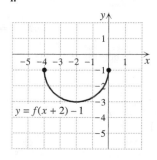

$y = -3f(x)$

f.

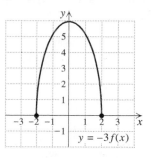

$y = f(x + 2) - 1$

g.

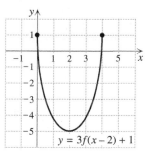

$y = f(x - 1) + 3$

h.

$y = 3f(x - 2) + 1$

105. $N(x) = x + 2000$ **107.** $x > 25\%$ **109. a.** Even function
b. Odd function   **c.** Translation one unit to left
d. Translation two units to right and three units up
111. $4a + 4$ **113.** $(-\infty, -2/3] \cup [2/3, \infty)$

115. $y = \dfrac{-2}{a + b - c}$

Section 4

For Thought: **1.** F   **2.** T   **3.** T   **4.** T   **5.** T   **6.** T
7. F   **8.** T   **9.** F   **10.** T
Exercises:
1. sum   **3.** 1   **5.** -11 **7.** -8 **9.** $1/12$
11. $a^2 - 3$ **13.** $a^3 - 4a^2 + 3a$ **15.** $\{(-3, 3), (2, 6)\}, \{-3, 2\}$
17. $\{(-3, -1), (2, -6)\}, \{-3, 2\}$ **19.** $\{(-3, 2), (2, 0)\}, \{-3, 2\}$
21. $\{(-3, 2)\}, \{-3\}$ **23.** $(f + g)(x) = \sqrt{x} + x - 4, [0, \infty)$

25. $(f - h)(x) = \sqrt{x} - \dfrac{1}{x - 2}, [0, 2) \cup (2, \infty)$

27. $(g \cdot h)(x) = \dfrac{x - 4}{x - 2}, (-\infty, 2) \cup (2, \infty)$

29. $(g/f)(x) = \dfrac{x - 4}{\sqrt{x}}, (0, \infty)$ **31.** $\{(-3, 0), (1, 0), (4, 4)\}$

33. $\{(1, 4)\}$ **35.** $\{(-3, 4), (1, 4)\}$ **37.** 5   **39.** 5
41. 59.8163   **43.** 5   **45.** 5   **47.** a **49.** $3t^2 + 2$
51. $(f \circ g)(x) = \sqrt{x} - 2, [0, \infty)$

53. $(f \circ h)(x) = \dfrac{1}{x} - 2, (-\infty, 0) \cup (0, \infty)$

55. $(h \circ g)(x) = \dfrac{1}{\sqrt{x}}, (0, \infty)$ **57.** $(f \circ f)(x) = x - 4, (-\infty, \infty)$

59. $(h \circ g \circ f)(x) = \dfrac{1}{\sqrt{x - 2}}, (2, \infty)$

61. $(h \circ f \circ g)(x) = \dfrac{1}{\sqrt{x} - 2}, (0, 4) \cup (4, \infty)$

63. $F = g \circ h$ **65.** $H = h \circ g$ **67.** $N = h \circ g \circ f$
69. $P = g \circ f \circ g$ **71.** $S = g \circ g$ **73.** $g(x) = x^3$ and $h(x) = x - 2$
75. $g(x) = x + 5$ and $h(x) = \sqrt{x}$
77. $g(x) = 3x - 1$ and $h(x) = \sqrt{x}$, $g(x) = 3x$ and $h(x) = \sqrt{x - 1}$
79. $g(x) = |x|$ and $h(x) = 4x + 5$, $g(x) = 4|x|$ and $h(x) = x + 5$
81. $y = 6x - 1$ **83.** $y = x^2 + 6x + 7$ **85.** $y = x$
87. $y = (n - 4)^2$ **89.** $y = \sqrt{x + 16}/8$ **91.** $y = -x$, no
93. $[-1, \infty), [-7, \infty)$ **95.** $[1, \infty), [0, \infty)$ **97.** $[0, \infty), [4, \infty)$
99. $P(x) = 28x - 200, x \geq 8$ **101.** $A = d^2/2$

103. $(f \circ f)(x) = 0.899x$, $(f \circ f \circ f)(x) = 0.852x$ **105.** $T(x) = 1.26x$

107. $D = \dfrac{1.16 \times 10^7}{L^3}$ **109.** $W = \dfrac{(8 + \pi)s^2}{8}$ **111.** $s = \dfrac{d\sqrt{2}}{2}$

113. No, composition   **115.** $\dfrac{-3}{x(x + h)}$ **117.** $[3, \infty), (-\infty, 2]$

119. $(-1/5, \infty)$

Section 5

For Thought: **1.** F   **2.** F   **3.** F   **4.** T   **5.** F   **6.** F
7. F   **8.** F   **9.** F   **10.** T

Exercises:
1. one-to-one   **3.** inverse   **5.** Yes   **7.** No   **9.** No
11. Not one-to-one   **13.** One-to-one   **15.** Not one-to-one
17. One-to-one   **19.** One-to-one   **21.** Not one-to-one
23. Not one-to-one   **25.** One-to-one   **27.** Invertible, $\{(3, 9), (2, 2)\}$
29. Not invertible   **31.** Invertible, $\{(3, 3), (2, 2), (4, 4), (7, 7)\}$
33. Not invertible   **35.** Not invertible   **37.** Invertible
39. Invertible   **41.** $\{(1, 2), (5, 3)\}, 3, 2$
43. $\{(-3, -3), (5, 0), (-7, 2)\}, 0, 2$ **45.** Not invertible
47. Not invertible

49. a. $f^{-1}(x) = \dfrac{x - 1}{5}$ **b.** $f^{-1}(x) = (x + 88)/3$

c. $f^{-1}(x) = \dfrac{x + 7}{3}$ **d.** $f^{-1}(x) = \dfrac{x - 4}{-3}$ **e.** $f^{-1}(x) = 2x + 18$

f. $f^{-1}(x) = -x$ **g.** $f^{-1}(x) = (x + 9)^3$ **h.** $f^{-1}(x) = \sqrt[3]{\dfrac{x + 7}{3}}$

i. $f^{-1}(x) = (x - 5)^3 + 1$ **j.** $f^{-1}(x) = \left(\dfrac{x}{2}\right)^3 + 7$

51. No   **53.** Yes
55.

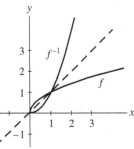

57.

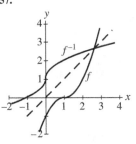

59. $f^{-1}(x) = \dfrac{x - 2}{3}$ **61.** $f^{-1}(x) = \sqrt{x + 4}$

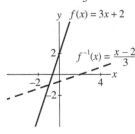

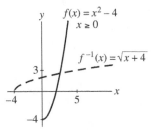

63. $f^{-1}(x) = \sqrt[3]{x}$ **65.** $f^{-1}(x) = (x + 3)^2$ for $x \geq -3$

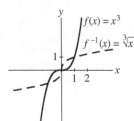

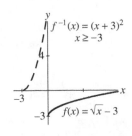

67. $f^{-1}(x) = \dfrac{x + 7}{3}$ **69.** $f^{-1}(x) = (x - 2)^2 + 3$ for $x \geq 2$

71. $f^{-1}(x) = -x - 9$ **73.** $f^{-1}(x) = \dfrac{5x + 3}{x - 1}$

75. $f^{-1}(x) = -\dfrac{1}{x}$ **77.** $f^{-1}(x) = (x - 5)^3 + 9$

79. $f^{-1}(x) = \sqrt{x} + 2$ **81.** $f(g(x)) = x, g(f(x)) = x$, yes
83. $f(g(x)) = x, g(f(x)) = |x|$, no
85. $f(g(x)) = x, g(f(x)) = x$, yes
87. $f(g(x)) = x, g(f(x)) = x$, yes
89. The functions y_1 and y_2 are inverses.

91. $C = 1.08P, P = \dfrac{C}{1.08}$ **93.** Yes, $r = \dfrac{7.89 - t}{0.39}, 6$

95. $w = \dfrac{V^2}{1.496}$, 8840 lb   **97. a.** 10.9%   **b.** $V = 50{,}000(1 - r)^5$

103. $1 + \dfrac{-5}{x + 2}$ **105.** $1, 7/5$ **107.** $[-3, 3], [-3, 0], [0, 3]$

109. $\{15.5\}$

Section 6

For Thought: **1.** F   **2.** F   **3.** T   **4.** T   **5.** T   **6.** F
7. T   **8.** T   **9.** T   **10.** F

Exercises:
1. varies directly   **3.** varies inversely   **5.** $G = kn$

7. $V = \dfrac{k}{P}$ **9.** $C = khr$ **11.** $Y = \dfrac{kx}{\sqrt{z}}$

13. A varies directly as the square of r.
15. The variable y varies inversely as x.
17. No variation   **19.** The variable a varies jointly as z and w.
21. H varies directly as the square root of t and inversely as s.
23. D varies jointly as L and J, and inversely as W.

25. $y = \dfrac{5}{9}x$ **27.** $T = \dfrac{-150}{y}$ **29.** $m = 3t^2$

31. $y = \dfrac{1.37x}{\sqrt{z}}$ **33.** $-27/2$ **35.** 1   **37.** $\sqrt{6}$ **39.** $7/4$

41. Direct, $L_i = 12L_f$ **43.** Inverse, $P = 20/n$
45. Direct, $S_m = 0.6S_k$ **47.** Neither   **49.** Direct, $A = 30W$
51. Inverse, $n = \dfrac{50}{p}$ **53.** 2604 lb/in.^{2} **55.** 12.8 hr
57. \$50.70   **59.** \$19.84   **61.** 18.125 oz   **63.** 8 ft/yr
65. No   **67.** 38   **69.** 35.96 ft/sec
73. $f^{-1}(x) = (x - 1)^3 + 9$ **75.** 50 mph   **77.** $x - 2y = -8$

Chapter Review Exercises

1. $\{-2, 0, 1\}, \{-2, 0, 1\}$, yes   **3.** $(-\infty, \infty), (-\infty, \infty)$, yes

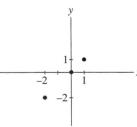

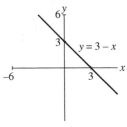

5. $\{2\}, (-\infty, \infty)$, no   **7.** $[-0.1, 0.1], [-0.1, 0.1]$, no

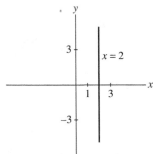

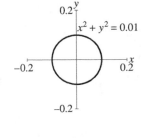

9. $[1, \infty)$, $(-\infty, \infty)$, no

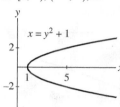

$x = y^2 + 1$

11. $[0, \infty)$, $[-3, \infty)$, yes

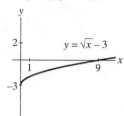

$y = \sqrt{x} - 3$

13. 12   **15.** 17   **17.** ± 4 **19.** 17   **21.** 4   **23.** -36
25. 12   **27.** $4x^2 - 28x + 52$ **29.** $x^4 + 6x^2 + 12$
31. $a^2 + 2a + 4$ **33.** $6 + h$ **35.** $2x + h$ **37.** x
39. $\dfrac{x + 7}{2}$

41.

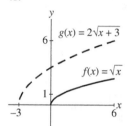

$g(x) = 2\sqrt{x + 3}$

$f(x) = \sqrt{x}$

43.

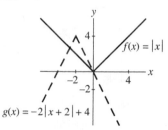

$f(x) = |x|$

$g(x) = -2|x + 2| + 4$

45.

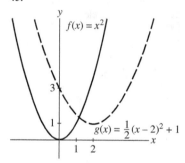

$f(x) = x^2$

$g(x) = \frac{1}{2}(x - 2)^2 + 1$

47. $(f \circ g)(x) = \sqrt{x} - 4$, $[0, \infty)$
49. $(f \circ h)(x) = x^2 - 4$, $(-\infty, \infty)$
51. $(g \circ f \circ h)(x) = \sqrt{x^2 - 4}$, $(-\infty, -2] \cup [2, \infty)$
53.

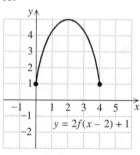

$y = 2f(x - 2) + 1$

55.

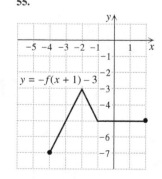

$y = -f(x + 1) - 3$

57.

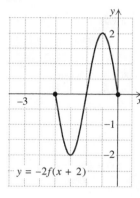

$y = -2f(x + 2)$

59.

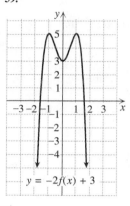

$y = -2f(x) + 3$

61. $F = f \circ g$ **63.** $H = f \circ h \circ g \circ j$
65. $N = h \circ f \circ j$ or $N = h \circ j \circ f$ **67.** $R = g \circ h \circ j$

69. -5 **71.** $\dfrac{-1}{2x(x + h)}$

73. $[-10, 10]$, $[0, 10]$,
    inc $[-10, 0]$, dec $[0, 10]$

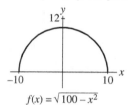

$f(x) = \sqrt{100 - x^2}$

75. $(-\infty, \infty)$, $(-\infty, \infty)$,
    inc $(-\infty, \infty)$

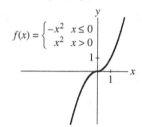

$f(x) = \begin{cases} -x^2 & x \le 0 \\ x^2 & x > 0 \end{cases}$

77. $(-\infty, \infty)$, $[-2, \infty)$,
    inc $[-2, 0]$, $[2, \infty)$,
    dec $(-\infty, -2]$ and $[0, 2]$

$f(x) = \begin{cases} -x - 4 & x \le -2 \\ -|x| & -2 < x < 2 \\ x - 4 & x \ge 2 \end{cases}$

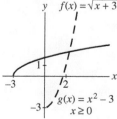

79. $y = |x| - 3$, $(-\infty, \infty)$, $[-3, \infty)$
81. $y = -2|x| + 4$, $(-\infty, \infty)$, $(-\infty, 4]$
83. $y = |x + 2| + 1$, $(-\infty, \infty)$, $[1, \infty)$
85. y-axis   **87.** Origin   **89.** Neither symmetry   **91.** y-axis
93. $(-\infty, 2] \cup [4, \infty)$ **95.** $(-\sqrt{2}, \sqrt{2})$ **97.** $\varnothing$
99. Inverse functions   **101.** Inverse functions

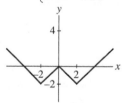

$f(x) = \sqrt{x + 3}$

$g(x) = x^2 - 3$
$x \ge 0$

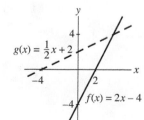

$g(x) = \frac{1}{2}x + 2$

$f(x) = 2x - 4$

103. Not invertible **105.** $f^{-1}(x) = \dfrac{x + 21}{3}, (-\infty, \infty), (-\infty, \infty)$

107. Not invertible **109.** $f^{-1}(x) = x^2 + 9$ for $x \geq 0, [0, \infty), [9, \infty)$

111. $f^{-1}(x) = \dfrac{5x + 7}{1 - x}, (-\infty, 1) \cup (1, \infty), (-\infty, -5) \cup (-5, \infty)$

113. $f^{-1}(x) = -\sqrt{x - 1}, [1, \infty), (-\infty, 0]$

115. $C(x) = 1.20x + 40, R(x) = 2x, P(x) = 0.80x - 40$ where x is the number of roses, 51 or more roses

117. $t = \dfrac{\sqrt{64 - h}}{4}$, domain $[0, 64]$ **119.** $d = 2\sqrt{A/\pi}$

121. 0.5 in./lb **123.** 36 **125.** 61 km/hr **127.** $30.72

Chapter Test

1. No **2.** Yes **3.** No **4.** Yes **5.** $\{2, 5\}, \{-3, -4, 7\}$

6. $[9, \infty), [0, \infty)$ **7.** $[0, \infty), (-\infty, \infty)$

8.

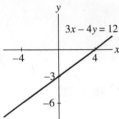

$3x - 4y = 12$

9.

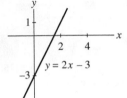

$y = 2x - 3$

10.

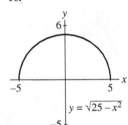

$y = \sqrt{25 - x^2}$

11.

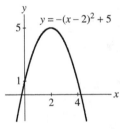

$y = -(x - 2)^2 + 5$

12.

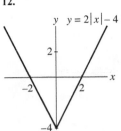

$y = 2|x| - 4$

13.

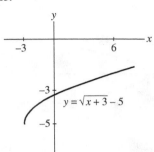

$y = \sqrt{x + 3} - 5$

14.

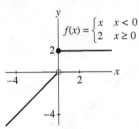

$f(x) = \begin{cases} x & x < 0 \\ 2 & x \geq 0 \end{cases}$

15. 3 **16.** $\sqrt{7}$ **17.** $\sqrt{3x + 1}$ **18.** $\dfrac{x + 1}{3}$ **19.** 45

20. 3 **21.** Inc $[3, \infty)$, dec $(-\infty, 3]$ **22.** y-axis

23. $(-2, 4)$ **24.** $g^{-1}(x) = (x - 3)^3 + 2$

25. $f^{-1}(x) = x^2 + 5$ for $x \geq 0$ **26.** $0.125 per envelope

27. 12 candlepower **28.** $V = \dfrac{\sqrt{2}d^3}{4}$

Solutions to Try This Exercises

1.1 Tax is determined by finding 5% of p and rounding to the nearest cent. So t is a function of p. One cannot determine p from t because 10 cents in tax is paid on an item that costs $2 or $2.01. So p is not a function of t.

1.2 Since no vertical line can be drawn so that it crosses this graph more than once, y is a function of x.

1.3 a. Since $(5, 5)$ and $(5, 7)$ have the same first coordinate and different second coordinates, the relation is not a function.

b. Since no ordered pair in the table has the same first coordinate and different second coordinates, the relation is a function.

1.4 Since $(-1, 1)$ and $(-1, -1)$ both satisfy $x^3 + y^2 = 0$, the equation does not define y as a function of x.

1.5 Since $\sqrt{x + 3}$ is a real number only if $x + 3 \geq 0$ or $x \geq -3$, the domain is $[-3, \infty)$. Since $\sqrt{x + 3} \geq 0$, the range is $[0, \infty)$. Since y is uniquely determined by $y = \sqrt{x + 3}$, this relation is a function.

1.6 a. $f(4) = 4 - 3 = 1$

b. If $f(x) = 9$, then $x - 3 = 9$ and $x = 12$.

1.7 Replace x with $x + 2$ to get
$$
\begin{aligned}
f(x + 2) &= (x + 2)^2 - 4 \\
&= x^2 + 4x + 4 - 4 \\
&= x^2 + 4x
\end{aligned}
$$

1.8 $\dfrac{28{,}645 - 13{,}837}{2003 - 2009} = -2468$

The average rate of change was $-$2468 per year.

1.9
$$
\begin{aligned}
\frac{f(x + h) - f(x)}{h} &= \frac{(x + h)^2 - (x + h) - (x^2 - x)}{h} \\
&= \frac{x^2 + 2xh + h^2 - x - h - x^2 + x}{h} \\
&= \frac{2xh + h^2 - h}{h} = 2x + h - 1
\end{aligned}
$$

1.10 For a square, $P = 4s$. So $s = P/4$ expresses the side as a function of the perimeter.

2.1 Since no vertical line crosses the graph more than once, y is a function of x.

x	-4	-2	0	2	4
$y = \frac{1}{2}x^2$	8	2	0	2	8

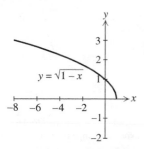

Since any real number can be used for x, the domain is $(-\infty, \infty)$. Since $y \geq 0$, the range is $[0, \infty)$.

2.2 Since no vertical line crosses the graph more than once, y is a function of x.

x	1	0	-3	-8
$y = \sqrt{1 - x}$	0	1	2	3

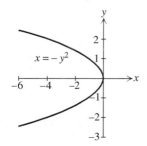

Since $1 - x \geq 0$ or $x \leq 1$ the domain is $(-\infty, 1]$. Since $y \geq 0$, the range is $[0, \infty)$.

2.3 Since $(-1, 1)$ and $(-1, -1)$ both satisfy $x = -y^2$, y is not uniquely determined by x and the equation is not a function. Also, y is not a function of x by the vertical line test.

$x = -y^2$	-4	-1	0	-1	-4
y	-2	-1	0	1	2

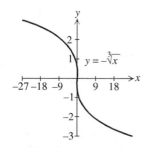

Since any real number can be used for y, the range is $(-\infty, \infty)$. Since $x \leq 0$, the domain is $(-\infty, 0]$.

2.4 Since no vertical line crosses the graph more than once, y is a function of x.

x	0	1	8	27
$y = -\sqrt[3]{x}$	0	-1	-2	-3

Since any real number can be used for x, the domain is $(-\infty, \infty)$. Since any real number can occur for y, the range is $(-\infty, \infty)$.

2.5

x	-3	0	3
$y = -\sqrt{9 - x^2}$	0	-3	0

The graph is a semicircle.

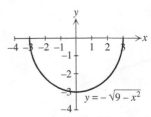

$$y = -\sqrt{9 - x^2}$$

Since x must be between -3 and 3 inclusive, the domain is $[-3, 3]$. Since y is between -3 and 0 inclusive, the range is $[-3, 0]$.

2.6 Since no vertical line crosses the graph more than once, y is a function of x.

x	0	± 1	± 2
$y = |x| + 2$	2	3	4

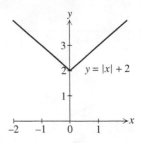

$$y = |x| + 2$$

Since x can be any real number, the domain is $(-\infty, \infty)$. Since $y \geq 2$, the range is $[2, \infty)$.

2.7 For $x \geq 0$ the graph is a line with slope 1 starting at the origin. For $x < 0$ the graph is a line with slope -2.

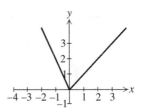

Since x can be any real number, the domain is $(-\infty, \infty)$. Since $y \geq 0$, the range is $[0, \infty)$.

2.8

x	$[0, 1)$	$[1, 2)$	$[2, 3)$
$y = -[x]$	0	-1	-2

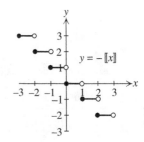

$$y = -[x]$$

Since any real number can be used for x, the domain is $(-\infty, \infty)$. The range is the set of integers.

2.9

x	$[0, 1)$	$[1, 2)$	$[2, 3)$
$y = [x + 2]$	2	3	4

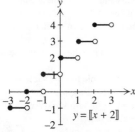

$$y = [x + 2]$$

Since any real number can be used for x, the domain is $(-\infty, \infty)$. The range is the set of integers.

2.10 Graph $f(x) = -3x$ as follows.

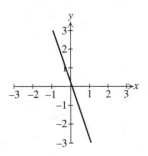

Since the y-coordinates are decreasing as we move from left to right on the graph, the function is decreasing.

2.11 Graph $f(x)$ as follows.

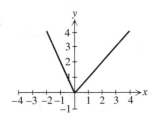

The function is decreasing on $(-\infty, 0]$ and increasing on $[0, \infty)$.

3.1 Note that g lies two units to the right of f and h lies one unit to the left of f.

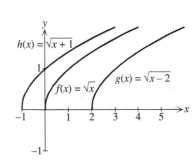

$$h(x) = \sqrt{x + 1}$$
$$f(x) = \sqrt{x}$$
$$g(x) = \sqrt{x - 2}$$

3.2 Note that $f(x) = (x - 2)^2$ goes through $(1, 1)$, $(2, 0)$, and $(3, 1)$ and lies two units to the right of $y = x^2$.

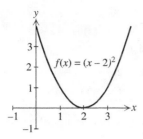

3.3 The graph of $g(x) = -\sqrt{x}$ is a reflection of the graph of $f(x) = \sqrt{x}$. Note that g lies below the x-axis and f lies above the x-axis.

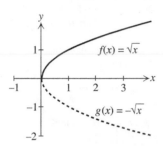

3.4 The graph of $g(x) = 3|x|$ is obtained by stretching the graph of $f(x) = |x|$. The graph of $h(x) = \frac{1}{3}|x|$ is obtained by shrinking the graph of $f(x)$.

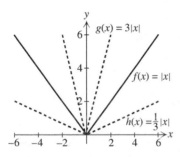

3.5 Note that g lies one unit above f and h lies two units below f.

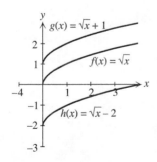

3.6 The graph of $y = |x|$ is translated one unit to the left, stretched by a factor of 2, reflected in the x-axis, and finally translated four units upward to obtain the graph of $y = 4 - 2|x + 1|$. The graph is v-shaped and extends downward from $(-1, 4)$.

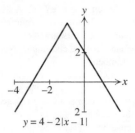

3.7 The graph of $y = x$ is stretched by a factor of 2, reflected in the x-axis, and translated five units upward to obtain the graph of $y = -2x + 5$.

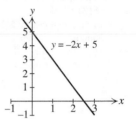

3.8 Since $f(-x) = -2(-x)^2 + 5 = -2x^2 + 5$, we have $f(-x) = f(x)$. So the graph is symmetric about the y-axis.

3.9 The graph of $y = 2 - |x - 1|$ is shown here.

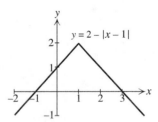

Since the graph is below the x-axis when $x \leq -1$ or when $x \geq 3$, the solution set to the inequality is $(-\infty, -1] \cup [3, \infty)$.

4.1 $(h + j)(5) = h(5) + j(5) = 5^2 + 3 \cdot 5 = 40$,
$(h \cdot j)(2) = h(2) \cdot j(2) = 2^2 \cdot 3(2) = 24$,
$(h/j)(a) = h(a)/j(a) = a^2/(3a) = a/3$

4.2 Note that $(h + j)(2) = h(2) + j(2) = 10 + 5 = 15$,
$(h + j)(6) = h(6) + j(6) = 8 + 0 = 8$, and $(h + j)(4)$ is undefined because 4 is not in the domain of j. So $h + j = \{(2, 15), (6, 8)\}$ and the domain is $\{2, 6\}$. Note that $(h/j)(2) = h(2)/j(2) = 10/5 = 2$, $(h/j)(4)$ is undefined because 4 is not in the domain of j, and $(h/j)(6)$ is undefined because $j(6) = 0$. So $h/j = \{(2, 2)\}$ and the domain is $\{2\}$.

4.3 The domain of $h + j$ is the intersection of the domains of h and j. So $(h + j)(x) = \sqrt{x} + x$ and the domain is $[0, \infty)$. Since $j(0) = 0$, the domain of h/j is $(0, \infty)$ and $(h/j)(x) = \sqrt{x}/x$.

4.4 Note that $(j \circ h)(2) = j(h(2)) = j(0) = 7$, $(j \circ h)(4) = j(h(4)) = j(0) = 7$, and $(j \circ h)(6)$ is undefined. So $j \circ h = \{(2, 7), (4, 7)\}$ and the domain is $\{2, 4\}$.

4.5 Note that $h(5) = \sqrt{5 - 1} = 2$ and $j(5) = 2 \cdot 5 = 10$. So $(h \circ j)(5) = h(j(5)) = h(10) = \sqrt{10 - 1} = 3$ and $(j \circ h)(5) = j(h(5)) = j(2) = 2(2) = 4$.

4.6 Since $(h \circ j)(x) = h(j(x)) = h(3x) = \sqrt{3x + 3}$ we must have $3x + 3 \geq 0$ or $x \geq -1$. So the domain is $[-1, \infty)$.

4.7 The function K is the composition of subtracting 3, taking the square root, and then multiplying by 2, in that order. So $K = h \circ f \circ g$. Check: $h(f(g(x))) = h(f(x - 3)) = h(\sqrt{x - 3}) = 2\sqrt{x - 3}$

4.8 Substitute $r = C/(2\pi)$ into $d = 2r$ to get $d = 2 \cdot \dfrac{C}{2\pi}$ or $d = \dfrac{C}{\pi}$.

4.9 In $C(x) = 0.10x$, x is revenue. Since $R(x) = 80x$, replace x with $80x$ to get $C(x) = 0.10(80x) = 8x$ where x is the number of books.

5.1 This function is one-to-one because no two ordered pairs have different first coordinates and the same second coordinate. Note that π, 3.14, and 22/7 are three different numbers.

5.2 Since no horizontal line can cross the graph in (a) more than once, the function is one-to-one. Since the horizontal line $y = -2$ crosses the graph in (b) more than once, the function is not one-to-one.

5.3 If $h(x_1) = h(x_2)$, then $5x_1^2 = 5x_2^2$ or $x_1^2 = x_2^2$. But $x_1^2 = x_2^2$ does not imply that $x_1 = x_2$, because $2^2 = (-2)^2$. So the function is not one-to-one.

5.4 Since there are no ordered pairs with the same second coordinate and different first coordinates, the function is invertible and $h^{-1} = \{(1, 2), (4, 3), (0, 4)\}$.

5.5 Since $h^{-1} = \{(1, 2), (4, 3), (0, 4)\}$, $h(3) = 4$, $h^{-1}(4) = 3$, and $(h \circ h^{-1})(1) = h(h^{-1}(1)) = h(2) = 1$.

5.6 Since f is a composition of multiplying x by 2/3. and then adding 6, f^{-1} is a composition of subtracting 6 and then dividing by 2/3 (or multiplying by 3/2) so $f^{-1}(x) = \frac{3}{2}(x - 6) = \frac{3}{2}x - 9$.

5.7 The domain of f is $[-2, \infty)$ and the range is $[0, \infty)$. So $f^{-1}(x) = x^2 - 2$ for $x \geq 0$.

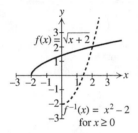

5.8 First switch x and y in $y = x^3 - 5$ then solve for y:
$$x = y^3 - 5$$
$$y^3 = x + 5$$
$$y = \sqrt[3]{x + 5}$$
$$h^{-1}(x) = \sqrt[3]{x + 5}$$

5.9 Find $f(g(x))$ and $g(f(x))$:
$$f(g(x)) = 2\left(\frac{x - 1}{2}\right) + 1 = x - 1 + 1 = x$$
$$g(f(x)) = \frac{(2x + 1) - 1}{2} = \frac{2x}{2} = x$$

Since these equations are correct for any real number x, the functions are inverses of each other.

6.1 Since $c = ks$ and $3.60 = k(12)$, we have $k = 0.30$. So if $s = 16$, then $c = 0.30(16) = 4.80$. The cost of a 16-ounce smoothie is \$4.80.

6.2 Since $t = k/n$ and $12 = k/4$, we have $k = 48$. So if $n = 6$, then $t = 48/6 = 8$. So it takes 6 rakers 8 hours to complete the job.

6.3 Since $c = kLH$ and $3000 = k(200 \cdot 5)$, we have $k = 3$. So if $L = 250$ and $H = 6$, then $c = 3 \cdot 250 \cdot 6 = 4500$. So the cost of a 6-foot fence that is 250 feet long is \$4500.

6.4 Since the variation is direct, we use multiplication: $M = kwz^3$.

6.5 Use $W = 480$, $m = 5$, and $t = 4$ in $W = km/t^2$ to find k:
$$480 = \frac{k(5)}{4^2}$$
$$k = 1536$$

Now use $k = 1536$, $m = 3$, and $t = 6$ to find W:
$$W = \frac{1536(3)}{6^2} = 128$$

Functions and Graphs

For Thought

1. False, since $\{(1,2),(1,3)\}$ is not a function.

2. False, since $f(5)$ is not defined.   **3.**   True

4. False, since a student's exam grade is a function of the student's preparation. If two classmates had the same IQ and only one prepared then the one who prepared will most likely achieve a higher grade.

5. False, since $(x+h)^2 = x^2 + 2xh + h^2$

6. False, since the domain is all real numbers.

7. True   **8.**   True   **9.**   True

10. False, since $\left(\frac{3}{8}, 8\right)$ and $\left(\frac{3}{8}, 5\right)$ are two ordered pairs with the same first coordinate and different second coordinates.

1 Exercises

1. relation

3. independent, dependent

5. difference quotient

7. Note, $b = 2\pi a$ is equivalent to $a = \dfrac{b}{2\pi}$.
Then a is a function of b, and b is a function of a.

9. a is a function of b since a given denomination has a unique length. Since a dollar bill and a five-dollar bill have the same length, then b is not a function of a.

11. Since an item has only one price, b is a function of a. Since two items may have the same price, a is not a function of b.

13. a is not a function of b since it is possible that two different students can obtain the same final exam score but the times spent on studying are different.
b is not a function of a since it is possible that two different students can spend the same time studying but obtain different final exam scores.

15. Since 1 in ≈ 2.54 cm, a is a function of b and b is a function of a.

17. No   **19.**   Yes   **21.**   Yes   **23.**   Yes

25. Not a function since 25 has two different second coordinates.

27. Not a function since 3 has two different second coordinates.

29. Yes

31. Since the ordered pairs in the graph of $y = 3x - 8$ are $(x, 3x - 8)$, there are no two ordered pairs with the same first coordinate and different second coordinates. We have a function.

33. Since $y = (x + 9)/3$, the ordered pairs are $(x, (x + 9)/3)$. Thus, there are no two ordered pairs with the same first coordinate and different second coordinates. We have a function.

35. Since $y = \pm x$, the ordered pairs are $(x, \pm x)$. Thus, there are two ordered pairs with the same first coordinate and different second coordinates. We do not have a function.

37. Since $y = x^2$, the ordered pairs are (x, x^2). Thus, there are no two ordered pairs with the same first coordinate and different second coordinates. We have a function.

39. Since $y = |x| - 2$, the ordered pairs are $(x, |x| - 2)$. Thus, there are no two ordered pairs with the same first coordinate and different second coordinates. We have a function.

41. Since $(2, 1)$ and $(2, -1)$ are two ordered pairs with the same first coordinate and different second coordinates, the equation does not define a function.

43. Domain $\{-3, 4, 5\}$, range $\{1, 2, 6\}$

45. Domain $(-\infty, \infty)$, range $\{4\}$

47. Domain $(-\infty, \infty)$;
since $|x| \geq 0$, the range of $y = |x| + 5$ is $[5, \infty)$

49. Since $x = |y| - 3 \geq -3$, the domain of $x = |y| - 3$ is $[-3, \infty)$; range $(-\infty, \infty)$

51. Since $\sqrt{x-4}$ is a real number whenever $x \geq 4$, the domain of $y = \sqrt{x-4}$ is $[4, \infty)$.

Since $y = \sqrt{x-4} \geq 0$ for $x \geq 4$, the range is $[0, \infty)$.

53. Since $x = -y^2 \leq 0$, the domain of $x = -y^2$ is $(-\infty, 0]$; range is $(-\infty, \infty)$;

55. 6

57. $g(2) = 3(2) + 5 = 11$

59. Since $(3, 8)$ is the ordered pair, one obtains $f(3) = 8$. The answer is $x = 3$.

61. Solving $3x + 5 = 26$, we find $x = 7$.

63. $f(4) + g(4) = 5 + 17 = 22$

65. $3a^2 - a$

67. $4(a+2) - 2 = 4a + 6$

69. $3(x^2 + 2x + 1) - (x + 1) = 3x^2 + 5x + 2$

71. $4(x + h) - 2 = 4x + 4h - 2$

73. $3(x^2 + 2x + 1) - (x + 1) - 3x^2 + x = 6x + 2$

75. $3(x^2 + 2xh + h^2) - (x + h) - 3x^2 + x = $
$6xh + 3h^2 - h$

77. The average rate of change is
$$\frac{8,000 - 20,000}{5} = -\$2,400 \text{ per year.}$$

79. The average rate of change on $[0, 2]$ is
$$\frac{h(2) - h(0)}{2 - 0} = \frac{0 - 64}{2 - 0} = -32 \text{ ft/sec.}$$
The average rate of change on $[1, 2]$ is
$$\frac{h(2) - h(1)}{2 - 1} = \frac{0 - 48}{2 - 1} = -48 \text{ ft/sec.}$$
The average rate of change on $[1.9, 2]$ is
$$\frac{h(2) - h(1.9)}{2 - 1.9} = \frac{0 - 6.24}{0.1} = -62.4 \text{ ft/sec.}$$
The average rate of change on $[1.99, 2]$ is
$$\frac{h(2) - h(1.99)}{2 - 1.99} = \frac{0 - 0.6384}{0.01} = -63.84 \text{ ft/sec.}$$
The average rate of change on $[1.999, 2]$ is
$$\frac{h(2) - h(1.999)}{2 - 1.999} = \frac{0 - 0.063984}{0.001} = -63.984$$
ft/sec.

81. The average rate of change is $\dfrac{1768 - 1970}{20} = $
-10.1 million hectares per year.

83.
$$\frac{f(x+h) - f(x)}{h} = \frac{4(x+h) - 4x}{h}$$
$$= \frac{4h}{h}$$
$$= 4$$

85.
$$\frac{f(x+h) - f(x)}{h} = \frac{3(x+h) + 5 - 3x - 5}{h}$$
$$= \frac{3h}{h}$$
$$= 3$$

87. Let $g(x) = x^2 + x$. Then we obtain
$$\frac{g(x+h) - g(x)}{h} =$$
$$\frac{(x+h)^2 + (x+h) - x^2 - x}{h} =$$
$$\frac{2xh + h^2 + h}{h} =$$
$$2x + h + 1.$$

89. Difference quotient is
$$= \frac{-(x+h)^2 + (x+h) - 2 + x^2 - x + 2}{h}$$
$$= \frac{-2xh - h^2 + h}{h}$$
$$= -2x - h + 1$$

91. Difference quotient is
$$= \frac{3\sqrt{x+h} - 3\sqrt{x}}{h} \cdot \frac{3\sqrt{x+h} + 3\sqrt{x}}{3\sqrt{x+h} + 3\sqrt{x}}$$
$$= \frac{9(x+h) - 9x}{h(3\sqrt{x+h} + 3\sqrt{x})}$$
$$= \frac{9h}{h(3\sqrt{x+h} + 3\sqrt{x})}$$
$$= \frac{3}{\sqrt{x+h} + \sqrt{x}}$$

93. Difference quotient is

$$= \frac{\sqrt{x+h+2}-\sqrt{x+2}}{h} \cdot \frac{\sqrt{x+h+2}+\sqrt{x+2}}{\sqrt{x+h+2}+\sqrt{x+2}}$$

$$= \frac{(x+h+2)-(x+2)}{h(\sqrt{x+h+2}+\sqrt{x+2})}$$

$$= \frac{h}{h(\sqrt{x+h+2}+\sqrt{x+2})}$$

$$= \frac{1}{\sqrt{x+h+2}+\sqrt{x+2}}$$

95. Difference quotient is

$$= \frac{\frac{1}{x+h}-\frac{1}{x}}{h} \cdot \frac{x(x+h)}{x(x+h)}$$

$$= \frac{x-(x+h)}{xh(x+h)}$$

$$= \frac{-h}{xh(x+h)}$$

$$= \frac{-1}{x(x+h)}$$

97. Difference quotient is

$$= \frac{\frac{3}{x+h+2}-\frac{3}{x+2}}{h} \cdot \frac{(x+h+2)(x+2)}{(x+h+2)(x+2)}$$

$$= \frac{3(x+2)-3(x+h+2)}{h(x+h+2)(x+2)}$$

$$= \frac{-3h}{h(x+h+2)(x+2)}$$

$$= \frac{-3}{(x+h+2)(x+2)}$$

99. a) $A = s^2$ **b)** $s = \sqrt{A}$ **c)** $s = \dfrac{d\sqrt{2}}{2}$

d) $d = s\sqrt{2}$ **e)** $P = 4s$ **f)** $s = P/4$

g) $A = P^2/16$ **h)** $d = \sqrt{2A}$

101. $C = 50 + 35n$

103.

   (a) The quantity $C(4) = (0.95)(4) + 5.8 =$ $\$9.6$ billion represents the amount spent on computers in the year 2004.

   (b) By solving $0.95n + 5.8 = 15$, we obtain

$$n = \frac{9.2}{0.95} \approx 10.$$

Thus, spending for computers will be $\$15$ billion in 2010.

105. Let a be the radius of each circle. Note, triangle $\triangle ABC$ is an equilateral triangle with side $2a$ and height $\sqrt{3}a$.

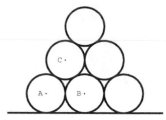

Thus, the height of the circle centered at C from the horizontal line is $\sqrt{3}a + 2a$. Hence, by using a similar reasoning, we obtain that height of the highest circle from the line is

$$2\sqrt{3}a + 2a$$

or equivalently $(2\sqrt{3} + 2)a$.

107. When $x = 18$ and $h = 0.1$, we have

$$\frac{R(18.1) - R(18)}{0.1} = 1,950.$$

The revenue from the concert will increase by approximately $\$1,950$ if the price of a ticket is raised from $\$18$ to $\$19$.

If $x = 22$ and $h = 0.1$, then

$$\frac{R(22.1) - R(22)}{0.1} = -2,050.$$

The revenue from the concert will decrease by approximately $\$2,050$ if the price of a ticket is raised from $\$22$ to $\$23$.

111.

$$\frac{3}{2}x - \frac{5}{9}x = \frac{1}{3} - \frac{5}{6}$$

$$\frac{17}{18}x = -\frac{1}{2}$$

$$x = -\frac{1}{2} \cdot \frac{18}{17}$$

$$x = -\frac{9}{17}$$

113. $\sqrt{(-4+6)^2 + (-3-3)^2} = \sqrt{4+36} =$
$\sqrt{40} = 2\sqrt{10}$

115.

$$
\begin{aligned}
x^2 - x - 6 &= 36 \\
x^2 - x - 42 &= 0 \\
(x-7)(x+6) &= 0
\end{aligned}
$$

The solution set is $\{-6, 7\}$.

For Thought

1. True, since the graph is a parabola opening down with vertex at the origin.

2. False, the graph is decreasing.

3. True

4. True, since $f(-4.5) = [-1.5] = -2$.

5. False, since the range is $\{\pm 1\}$.

6. True **7.** True **8.** True

9. False, since the range is the interval $[0, 4]$.

10. True

2 Exercises

1. parabola

3. Function $y = 2x$ includes the points $(0,0), (1,2)$, domain and range are both $(-\infty, \infty)$

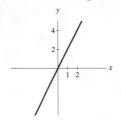

5. Function $x - y = 0$ includes the points $(-1,-1)$, $(0,0), (1,1)$, domain and range are both $(-\infty, \infty)$

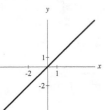

7. Function $y = 5$ includes the points $(0,5)$, $(\pm 2, 5)$, domain is $(-\infty, \infty)$, range is $\{5\}$

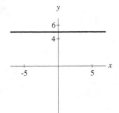

9. Function $y = 2x^2$ includes the points $(0,0)$, $(\pm 1, 2)$, domain is $(-\infty, \infty)$, range is $[0, \infty)$

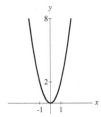

11. Function $y = 1 - x^2$ includes the points $(0,1)$, $(\pm 1, 0)$, domain is $(-\infty, \infty)$, range is $(-\infty, 1]$

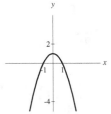

13. Function $y = 1 + \sqrt{x}$ includes the points $(0,1)$, $(1,2), (4,3)$, domain is $[0, \infty)$, range is $[1, \infty)$

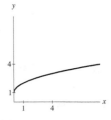

15. $x = y^2 + 1$ is not a function and includes the points $(1,0), (2,\pm 1)$, domain is $[1,\infty)$, range is $(-\infty,\infty)$

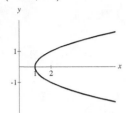

17. Function $x = \sqrt{y}$ goes through $(0,0), (2,4), (3,9)$, domain and range is $[0,\infty)$

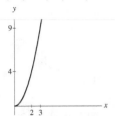

19. Function $y = \sqrt[3]{x} + 1$ goes through $(-1,0), (1,2), (8,3)$, domain $(-\infty,\infty)$, and range $(-\infty,\infty)$

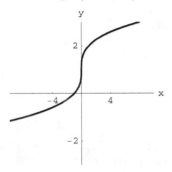

21. Function, $x = \sqrt[3]{y}$ goes through $(0,0), (1,1), (2,8)$, domain $(-\infty,\infty)$, and range $(-\infty,\infty)$

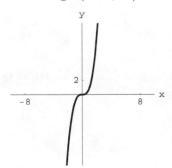

23. Not a function, $y^2 = 1 - x^2$ goes through $(1,0), (0,1), (-1,0)$, domain $[-1,1]$, and range $[-1,1]$

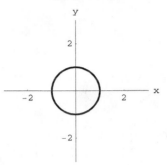

25. Function, $y = \sqrt{1 - x^2}$ goes through $(\pm 1, 0), (0,1)$, domain $[-1,1]$, and range $[0,1]$

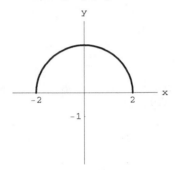

27. Function $y = x^3$ includes the points $(0,0)$, $(1,1), (2,8)$, domain and range are both $(-\infty,\infty)$

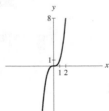

29. Function $y = 2|x|$ includes the points $(0,0)$, $(\pm 1, 2)$, domain is $(-\infty,\infty)$, range is $[0,\infty)$

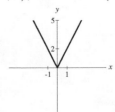

31. Function $y = -|x|$ includes the points $(0,0)$, $(\pm 1, -1)$, domain is $(-\infty, \infty)$, range is $(-\infty, 0]$

33. Not a function, graph of $x = |y|$ includes the points $(0,0), (2,2), (2,-2)$, domain is $[0, \infty)$, range is $(-\infty, \infty)$

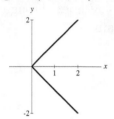

35. Domain is $(-\infty, \infty)$, range is $\{\pm 2\}$, some points are $(-3, -2)$, $(1, -2)$

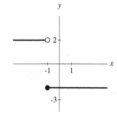

37. Domain is $(-\infty, \infty)$, range is $(-\infty, -2] \cup (2, \infty)$, some points are $(2, 3)$, $(1, -2)$

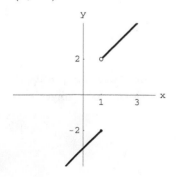

39. Domain is $[-2, \infty)$, range is $(-\infty, 2]$, some points are $(2, 2), (-2, 0), (3, 1)$

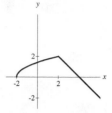

41. Domain is $(-\infty, \infty)$, range is $[0, \infty)$, some points are $(-1, 1), (-4, 2), (4, 2)$

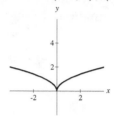

43. Domain is $(-\infty, \infty)$, range is $(-\infty, \infty)$, some points are $(-2, 4), (1, -1)$

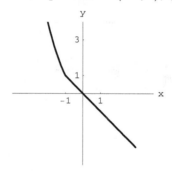

45. Domain is $(-\infty, \infty)$, range is the set of integers, some points are $(0, 1), (1, 2), (1.5, 2)$

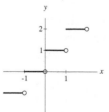

47. Domain $[0, 4)$, range is $\{2, 3, 4, 5\}$, some points are $(0, 2), (1, 3), (1.5, 3)$

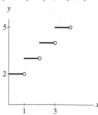

49. a. Domain and range are both $(-\infty, \infty)$, decreasing on $(-\infty, \infty)$

b. Domain is $(-\infty, \infty)$, range is $(-\infty, 4]$ increasing on $(-\infty, 0)$, decreasing on $(0, \infty)$

51. a. Domain is $[-2, 6]$, range is $[3, 7]$ increasing on $(-2, 2)$, decreasing on $(2, 6)$

b. Domain $(-\infty, 2]$, range $(-\infty, 3]$, increasing on $(-\infty, -2)$, constant on $(-2, 2)$

53. a. Domain is $(-\infty, \infty)$, range is $[0, \infty)$ increasing on $(0, \infty)$, decreasing on $(-\infty, 0)$

b. Domain and range are both $(-\infty, \infty)$ increasing on $(-2, -2/3)$, decreasing on $(-\infty, -2)$ and $(-2/3, \infty)$

55. a. Domain and range are both $(-\infty, \infty)$, increasing on $(-\infty, \infty)$

b. Domain is $[-2, 5]$, range is $[1, 4]$ increasing on $(1, 2)$, decreasing on $(-2, 1)$, constant on $(2, 5)$

57. Domain and range are both $(-\infty, \infty)$ increasing on $(-\infty, \infty)$, some points are $(0, 1)$, $(1, 3)$

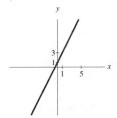

59. Domain is $(-\infty, \infty)$, range is $[0, \infty)$, increasing on $(1, \infty)$, decreasing on $(-\infty, 1)$, some points are $(0, 1)$, $(1, 0)$

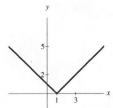

61. Domain is $(-\infty, 0) \cup (0, \infty)$, range is $\{\pm 1\}$, constant on $(-\infty, 0)$ and $(0, \infty)$, some points are $(1, 1)$, $(-1, -1)$

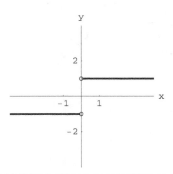

63. Domain is $[-3, 3]$, range is $[0, 3]$, increasing on $(-3, 0)$, decreasing on $(0, 3)$, some points are $(\pm 3, 0)$, $(0, 3)$

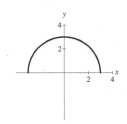

65. Domain and range are both $(-\infty, \infty)$, increasing on $(-\infty, 3)$ and $(3, \infty)$, some points are $(4, 5)$, $(0, 2)$

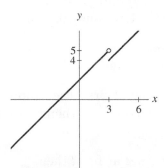

67. Domain is $(-\infty, \infty)$, range is $(-\infty, 2]$, increasing on $(-\infty, -2)$ and $(-2, 0)$, decreasing on $(0, 2)$ and $(2, \infty)$, some points are $(-3, 0)$, $(0, 2)$, $(4, -1)$

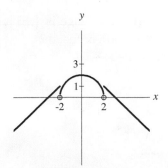

69. $f(x) = \begin{cases} 2 & \text{for} \quad x > -1 \\ -1 & \text{for} \quad x \le -1 \end{cases}$

71. The line joining $(-1, 1)$ and $(-3, 3)$ is $y = -x$, and the line joining $(-1, -2)$ and $(3, 2)$ is $y = x - 1$. The piecewise function is

$$f(x) = \begin{cases} x - 1 & \text{for} \quad x \ge -1 \\ -x & \text{for} \quad x < -1. \end{cases}$$

73. The line joining $(0, -2)$ and $(2, 2)$ is $y = 2x - 2$, and the line joining $(0, -2)$ and $(-3, 1)$ is $y = -x - 2$. The piecewise function is

$$f(x) = \begin{cases} 2x - 2 & \text{for} \quad x \ge 0 \\ -x - 2 & \text{for} \quad x < 0. \end{cases}$$

75. increasing on the interval $[0.83, \infty)$,

decreasing on $(-\infty, 0.83]$

77. increasing on $(-\infty, -1]$ and $[1, \infty)$,

decreasing on $[-1, 1]$

79. increasing on $[-1.73, 0)$ and $[1.73, \infty)$,

decreasing on $(-\infty, -1.73]$ and $(0, 1.73]$

81. increasing on $[30, 50]$, and $[70, \infty)$,

decreasing on $(-\infty, 30]$ and $[50, 70]$

83. c, graph was increasing at first, then suddenly dropped and became constant, then increased slightly

85. d, graph was decreasing at first, then fluctuated between increases and decreases, then the market increased

87. The independent variable is time t where t is the number of minutes after 7:45 and the dependent variable is distance D from the holodeck.

D is increasing on the intervals $[0, 3]$ and $[6, 15]$, decreasing on $[3, 6]$ and $[30, 39]$, and constant on $[15, 30]$.

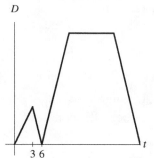

89. Independent variable is time t in years, dependent variable is savings s in dollars

s is increasing on the interval $[0, 2]$; s is constant on $[2, 2.5]$; s is decreasing on $[2.5, 4.5]$.

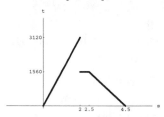

91. In 1988, there were $M(18) = 565$ million cars. In 2010, it is projected that there will be $M(40) = 800$ million cars. The average rate of change from 1984 to 1994 is

$$\frac{M(24) - M(14)}{10} = 14.5$$

in millions of cars per year.

93. Constant on $[0, 10^4]$, increasing on $[10^4, \infty)$

95. The cost is over \$235 for t in $[5, \infty)$.

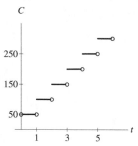

97. $f(x) = \begin{cases} 150 & \text{if} \quad 0 < x < 3 \\ 50x & \text{if} \quad 3 \le x \le 10 \end{cases}$

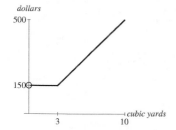

99. A mechanic's fee is \$20 for each half-hour of work with any fraction of a half-hour charged as a half-hour. If y is the fee in dollars and x is the number of hours, then $y = -20[-2x]$.

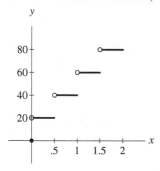

101. Since $x - 2 \ge 0$, the domain is $[2, \infty)$.

Since $\sqrt{x - 2}$ is nonnegative, we find $\sqrt{x - 2} + 3$ is at least three. Thus, the range is $[3, \infty)$.

103. Note, we have $13x - 55 = 0$.

The solution set is $\{55/13\}$.

105. Since we have a perfect square

$$(2x - 5)^2 = 0$$

the solution set is $\{5/2\}$.

For Thought

1. False, it is a reflection in the y-axis.

2. True **3.** False, rather it is a left translation.

4. True **5.** True

6. False, the down shift should come after the reflection. **7.** True

8. False, since their domains are different.

9. True **10.** True

3 Exercises

1. rigid

3. parabola

5. reflection

7. linear

9. odd

11. $f(x) = |x|, g(x) = |x| - 4$

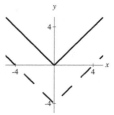

13. $f(x) = x, g(x) = x + 3$

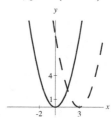

15. $y = x^2, y = (x - 3)^2$

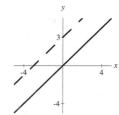

17. $y = \sqrt{x}, y = \sqrt{x + 9}$

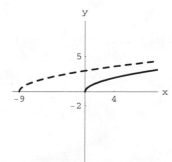

19. $f(x) = \sqrt{x}$, $g(x) = -\sqrt{x}$

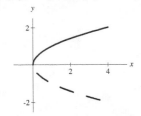

21. $y = \sqrt{x}$, $y = 3\sqrt{x}$

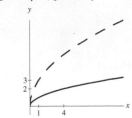

23. $y = x^2$, $y = \dfrac{1}{4}x^2$

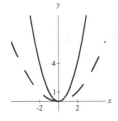

25. $y = \sqrt{4 - x^2}$, $y = -\sqrt{4 - x^2}$

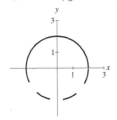

27. g   **29.** b

31. c   **33.** f

35. $y = \sqrt{x} + 2$

37. $y = (x - 5)^2$

39. $y = (x - 10)^2 + 4$

41. $y = -(3\sqrt{x} + 5)$ or $y = -3\sqrt{x} - 5$

43. $y = -3|x - 7| + 9$

45. $y = (x - 1)^2 + 2$; right by 1, up by 2, domain $(-\infty, \infty)$, range $[2, \infty)$

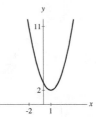

47. $y = |x - 1| + 3$; right by 1, up by 3 domain $(-\infty, \infty)$, range $[3, \infty)$

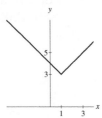

49. $y = 3x - 40$, domain and range are both $(-\infty, \infty)$

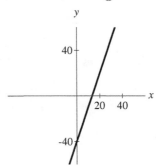

51. $y = \dfrac{1}{2}x - 20$, domain and range are both $(-\infty, \infty)$

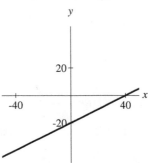

53. $y = -\dfrac{1}{2}|x| + 40$, shrink by 1/2, reflect about x-axis, up by 40, domain $(-\infty, \infty)$, range $(-\infty, 40]$

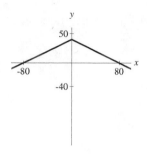

55. $y = -\dfrac{1}{2}|x+4|$, left by 4,

reflect about x-axis, shrink by $1/2$,

domain $(-\infty, \infty)$, range $(-\infty, 0]$

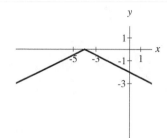

57. $y = -\sqrt{x-3}+1$, right by 3,
reflect about x-axis, up by 1,
domain $[3, \infty)$, range $(-\infty, 1]$

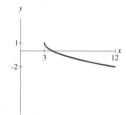

59. $y = -2\sqrt{x+3}+2$, left by 3, stretch by 2,
reflect about x-axis, up by 2,
domain $[-3, \infty)$, range $(-\infty, 2]$

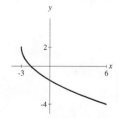

61. Symmetric about y-axis, even function
since $f(-x) = f(x)$

63. No symmetry, neither even nor odd
since $f(-x) \neq f(x)$ and $f(-x) \neq -f(x)$

65. Symmetric about $x = -3$, neither even nor
odd since $f(-x) \neq f(x)$ and $f(-x) \neq -f(x)$

67. Symmetry about $x = 2$, not an even or odd
function since $f(-x) \neq f(x)$ and
$f(-x) \neq -f(x)$

69. Symmetric about the origin, odd function
since $f(-x) = -f(x)$

71. No symmetry, not an even or odd function
since $f(-x) \neq f(x)$ and $f(-x) \neq -f(x)$

73. No symmetry, not an even or odd function
since $f(-x) \neq f(x)$ and $f(-x) \neq -f(x)$

75. Symmetric about the y-axis, even function
since $f(-x) = f(x)$

77. No symmetry, not an even or odd function
since $f(-x) = -f(x)$ and $f(-x) \neq -f(x)$

79. Symmetric about the y-axis, even function
since $f(-x) = f(x)$

81. e   **83.**   g

85. b   **87.**   c

89. $(-\infty, -1] \cup [1, \infty)$

91. $(-\infty, -1) \cup (5, \infty)$

93. Using the graph of $y = (x-1)^2 - 9$, we find
that the solution is $(-2, 4)$.

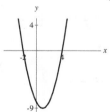

95. From the graph of $y = 5 - \sqrt{x}$, we find that
the solution is $[0, 25]$.

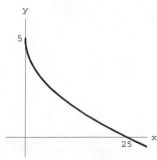

97. Note, the points of intersection of $y = 3$ and $y = (x-2)^2$ are $(2 \pm \sqrt{3}, 3)$. The solution set of $(x-2)^2 > 3$ is $\left(-\infty, 2 - \sqrt{3}\right) \cup \left(2 + \sqrt{3}, \infty\right)$.

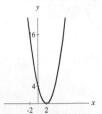

99. From the graph of $y = \sqrt{25 - x^2}$, we conclude that the solution is $(-5, 5)$.

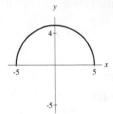

101. From the graph of $y = \sqrt{3}x^2 + \pi x - 9$,

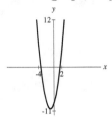

we observe that the solution set of $\sqrt{3}x^2 + \pi x - 9 < 0$ is $(-3.36, 1.55)$.

103. a. Stretch the graph of f by a factor of 2.

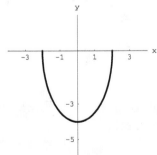

b. Reflect the graph of f about the x-axis.

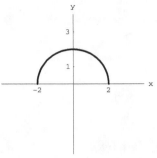

c. Translate the graph of f to the left by 1-unit.

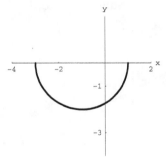

d. Translate the graph of f to the right by 3-units.

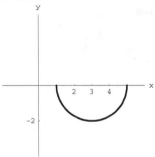

e. Stretch the graph of f by a factor of 3 and reflect about the x-axis.

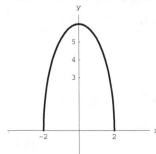

f. Translate the graph of f to the left by 2-units and down by 1-unit.

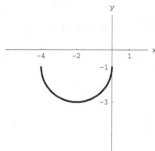

g. Translate the graph of f to the right by 1-unit and up by 3-units.

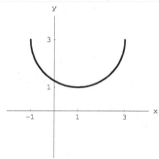

h. Translate the graph of f to the right by 2-units, stretch by a factor of 3, and up by 1-unit.

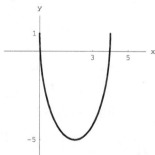

105. $N(x) = x + 2000$

107. If inflation rate is less than 50%, then $1 - \sqrt{x} < \frac{1}{2}$. This simplifies to $\frac{1}{2} < \sqrt{x}$. After squaring we have $\frac{1}{4} < x$ and so $x > 25\%$.

109.

(a) Both functions are even functions and the graphs are identical

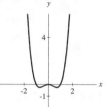

(b) One graph is a reflection of the other about the y-axis. Both functions are odd functions.

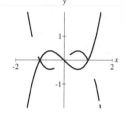

(c) The second graph is obtained by shifting the first one to the left by 1 unit.

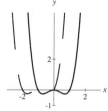

(d) The second graph is obtained by translating the first one to the right by 2 units and 3 units up.

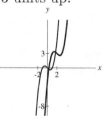

111. If $f(x) = x^2 + 1$, then
$$
\begin{aligned}
f(a+2) - f(a) &= \\
(a+2)^2 + 1 - a^2 - 1 &= \\
a^2 + 4a + 4 - a^2 &= \\
4a + 4
\end{aligned}
$$

113. Note $|x| \geq 2/3$ is equivalent to $x \geq 2/3$ or $x \leq -2/3$. Then the solution set is
$$(-\infty, -2/3] \cup [2/3, \infty).$$

115.

$$ay + by - cy = -2$$
$$y = \frac{-2}{a + b - c}$$

For Thought

1. False, since $f + g$ has an empty domain.

2. True **3.** True **4.** True

5. True, since $A = P^2/16$. **6.** True

7. False, since $(f \circ g)(x) = \sqrt{x - 2}$ **8.** True

9. False, since $(h \circ g)(x) = x^2 - 9$.

10. True, since x belongs to the domain if $\sqrt{x - 2}$ is a real number, i.e., if $x \geq 2$.

4 Exercises

1. sum

3. $-1 + 2 = 1$

5. $-5 - 6 = -11$

7. $(-4) \cdot 2 = -8$

9. $1/12$

11. $(a - 3) + (a^2 - a) = a^2 - 3$

13. $(a - 3)(a^2 - a) = a^3 - 4a^2 + 3a$

15. $f + g = \{(-3, 1 + 2), (2, 0 + 6)\} = \{(-3, 3), (2, 6)\}$, domain $\{-3, 2\}$

17. $f - g = \{(-3, 1 - 2), (2, 0 - 6)\} = \{(-3, -1), (2, -6)\}$, domain $\{-3, 2\}$

19. $f \cdot g = \{(-3, 1 \cdot 2), (2, 0 \cdot 6) = \{(-3, 2), (2, 0)\}$, domain $\{-3, 2\}$

21. $g/f = \{(-3, 2/1)\} = \{(-3, 2)\}$, domain $\{-3\}$

23. $(f + g)(x) = \sqrt{x} + x - 4$, domain is $[0, \infty)$

25. $(f - h)(x) = \sqrt{x} - \frac{1}{x - 2}$, domain is $[0, 2) \cup (2, \infty)$

27. $(g \cdot h)(x) = \frac{x - 4}{x - 2}$, domain is $(-\infty, 2) \cup (2, \infty)$

29. $\left(\frac{g}{f}\right)(x) = \frac{x - 4}{\sqrt{x}}$, domain is $(0, \infty)$

31. $\{(-3, 0), (1, 0), (4, 4)\}$

33. $\{(1, 4)\}$

35. $\{(-3, 4), (1, 4)\}$

37. $f(2) = 5$

39. $f(2) = 5$

41. $f(20.2721) = 59.8163$

43. $(g \circ h \circ f)(2) = (g \circ h)(5) = g(2) = 5$

45. $(f \circ g \circ h)(2) = (f \circ g)(1) = f(2) = 5$

47. $(f \circ h)(a) = f\left(\frac{a + 1}{3}\right) =$
$3\left(\frac{a + 1}{3}\right) - 1 = (a + 1) - 1 = a$

49. $(f \circ g)(t) = f\left(t^2 + 1\right) =$
$3(t^2 + 1) - 1 = 3t^2 + 2$

51. $(f \circ g)(x) = \sqrt{x} - 2$, domain $[0, \infty)$

53. $(f \circ h)(x) = \frac{1}{x} - 2$, domain $(-\infty, 0) \cup (0, \infty)$

55. $(h \circ g)(x) = \frac{1}{\sqrt{x}}$, domain $(0, \infty)$

57. $(f \circ f)(x) = (x - 2) - 2 = x - 4$, domain $(-\infty, \infty)$

59. $(h \circ g \circ f)(x) = h(\sqrt{x - 2}) = \frac{1}{\sqrt{x - 2}}$, domain $(2, \infty)$

61. $(h \circ f \circ g)(x) = h\left(\sqrt{x} - 2\right) = \frac{1}{\sqrt{x} - 2}$, domain $(0, 4) \cup (4, \infty)$

63. $F = g \circ h$

65. $H = h \circ g$

67. $N = h \circ g \circ f$

69. $P = g \circ f \circ g$

71. $S = g \circ g$

73. If $g(x) = x^3$ and $h(x) = x - 2$, then

$$(h \circ g)(x) = g(x) - 2 = x^3 - 2 = f(x).$$

75. If $g(x) = x + 5$ and $h(x) = \sqrt{x}$, then

$$(h \circ g)(x) = \sqrt{g(x)} = \sqrt{x + 5} = f(x).$$

77. If $g(x) = 3x - 1$ and $h(x) = \sqrt{x}$, then

$$(h \circ g)(x) = \sqrt{g(x)} = \sqrt{3x - 1} = f(x).$$

79. If $g(x) = |x|$ and $h(x) = 4x + 5$, then

$$(h \circ g)(x) = 4g(x) + 5 = 4|x| + 5 = f(x).$$

81. $y = 2(3x + 1) - 3 = 6x - 1$

83. $y = (x^2 + 6x + 9) - 2 = x^2 + 6x + 7$

85. $y = 3 \cdot \dfrac{x + 1}{3} - 1 = x + 1 - 1 = x$

87. Since $m = n - 4$ and $y = m^2$, $y = (n - 4)^2$.

89. Since $w = x + 16$, $z = \sqrt{w}$, and $y = \dfrac{z}{8}$,

we obtain $y = \dfrac{\sqrt{x + 16}}{8}$.

91. After multiplying y by $\dfrac{x + 1}{x + 1}$ we have

$$y = \frac{\dfrac{x - 1}{x + 1} + 1}{\dfrac{x - 1}{x + 1} - 1} = \frac{(x - 1) + (x + 1)}{(x - 1) - (x + 1)} = -x$$

The domain of the original function is $(-\infty, -1) \cup (-1, \infty)$ while the domain of the simplified function is $(-\infty, \infty)$. The two functions are not the same.

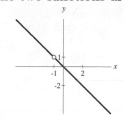

93. Domain $[-1, \infty)$, range $[-7, \infty)$

95. Domain $[1, \infty)$, range $[0, \infty)$

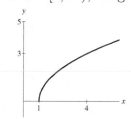

97. Domain $[0, \infty)$, range $[4, \infty)$

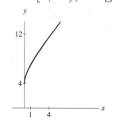

99. $P(x) = 68x - (40x + 200) = 28x - 200$.

Since $200/28 \approx 7.1$, the profit is positive when the number of trimmers satisfies $x \geq 8$.

101. $A = d^2/2$

103. $(f \circ f)(x) = 0.899x$ and $(f \circ f \circ f)(x) = 0.852x$ are the amounts of forest land at the start of 2002 and 2003, respectively.

105. Total cost is

$$(T \circ C)(x) = 1.05(1.20x) = 1.26x.$$

107. Note, $D = \dfrac{d/2240}{x} = \dfrac{d/2240}{L^3/100^3} = \dfrac{100^3 d}{2240 L^3}$

$$= \frac{100^3(26000)}{2240 L^3} = \frac{100^4(26)}{224 L^3} = \frac{100^4(13)}{112 L^3}.$$

Expressing D as a function of L, we write $D = \dfrac{(13)100^4}{112 L^3}$ or $D = \dfrac{1.16 \times 10^7}{L^3}$.

109. The area of a semicircle with radius $s/2$ is $(1/2)\pi(s/2)^2 = \pi s^2/8$. The area of the square is s^2. The area of the window is

$$W = s^2 + \frac{\pi s^2}{8} = \frac{(8+\pi)s^2}{8}.$$

111. Form a right triangle with two sides of length s and a hypotenuse of length d. By the Pythagorean Theorem, we obtain

$$d^2 = s^2 + s^2.$$

Solving for s, we have $s = \dfrac{d\sqrt{2}}{2}$.

113. If a coat is on sale at 25% off and there is an additional 10% off, then the coat will cost $0.90(.75x) = 0.675x$ where x is the regular price. Thus, the discount sale is 32.5% off and not 35% off.

115. The difference quotient is

$$\frac{1 + \frac{3}{x+h} - 1 - \frac{3}{x}}{h} =$$
$$\frac{\frac{3}{x+h} - \frac{3}{x}}{h} =$$
$$\frac{3x - 3x - 3h}{xh(x+h)} =$$
$$\frac{-3}{x(x+h)} =$$

117. Since $x - 3 \geq 0$, the domain is $[3, \infty)$. Since $-5\sqrt{x-3}$ has range $(-\infty, 0]$, the range of $f(x) = -5\sqrt{x-3} + 2$ is $(-\infty, 2]$.

119. Since $5x > -1$, the solution set is $(-1/5, \infty)$.

For Thought

1. False, since the inverse function is $\{(3,2), (5,5)\}$.

2. False, since it is not one-to-one.

3. False, $g^{-1}(x)$ does not exist since g is not one-to-one.

4. True

5. False, a function that fails the horizontal line test has no inverse.

6. False, since it fails the horizontal line test.

7. False, since $f^{-1}(x) = \left(\dfrac{x}{3}\right)^2 + 2$ where $x \geq 0$.

8. False, $f^{-1}(x)$ does not exist since f is not one-to-one.

9. False, since $y = |x|$ is V-shaped and the horizontal line test fails.

10. True

5 Exercises

1. one-to-one

3. inverse

5. Yes, since all second coordinates are distinct.

7. No, since there are repeated second coordinates such as $(-1, 1)$ and $(1, 1)$.

9. No, since there are repeated second coordinates such as $(1, 99)$ and $(5, 99)$.

11. Not one-to-one

13. One-to-one

15. Not one-to-one

17. One-to-one; since the graph of $y = 2x - 3$ shows $y = 2x - 3$ is an increasing function, the Horizontal Line Test implies $y = 2x - 3$ is one-to-one.

19. One-to-one; for if $q(x_1) = q(x_2)$ then

$$\frac{1 - x_1}{x_1 - 5} = \frac{1 - x_2}{x_2 - 5}$$
$$(1 - x_1)(x_2 - 5) = (1 - x_2)(x_1 - 5)$$
$$x_2 - 5 - x_1 x_2 + 5x_1 = x_1 - 5 - x_2 x_1 + 5x_2$$
$$x_2 + 5x_1 = x_1 + 5x_2$$
$$4(x_1 - x_2) = 0$$
$$x_1 - x_2 = 0.$$

Thus, if $q(x_1) = q(x_2)$ then $x_1 = x_2$. Hence, q is one-to-one.

21. Not one-to-one for $p(-2) = p(0) = 1$.

23. Not one-to-one for $w(1) = w(-1) = 4$.

25. One-to-one; for if $k(x_1) = k(x_2)$ then

$$
\begin{aligned}
\sqrt[3]{x_1 + 9} &= \sqrt[3]{x_2 + 9} \\
(\sqrt[3]{x_1 + 9})^3 &= (\sqrt[3]{x_2 + 9})^3 \\
x_1 + 9 &= x_2 + 9 \\
x_1 &= x_2.
\end{aligned}
$$

Thus, if $k(x_1) = k(x_2)$ then $x_1 = x_2$. Hence, k is one-to-one.

27. Invertible, $\{(3,9),(2,2)\}$

29. Not invertible

31. Invertible, $\{(3,3),(2,2),(4,4),(7,7)\}$

33. Not invertible

35. Not invertible, there can be two different items with the same price.

37. Invertible, since the playing time is a function of the length of the VCR tape.

39. Invertible, assuming that cost is simply a multiple of the number of days. If cost includes extra charges, then the function may not be invertible.

41. $f^{-1} = \{(1,2),(5,3)\}$, $f^{-1}(5) = 3$, $(f^{-1} \circ f)(2) = 2$

43. $f^{-1} = \{(-3,-3),(5,0),(-7,2)\}$, $f^{-1}(5) = 0$, $(f^{-1} \circ f)(2) = 2$

45. Not invertible since it fails the Horizontal Line Test.

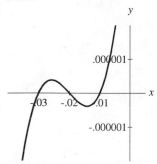

47. Not invertible since it fails the Horizontal Line Test.

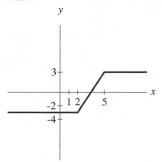

49. a) $f(x)$ is the composition of multiplying x by 5, then subtracting 1.

Reversing the operations, the inverse is
$$f^{-1}(x) = \frac{x-1}{5}$$

b) $f(x)$ is the composition of multiplying x by 3, then subtracting 88.

Reversing the operations, the inverse is
$$f^{-1}(x) = \frac{x+88}{3}$$

c) $f^{-1}(x) = (x+7)/3$

d) $f^{-1}(x) = \dfrac{x-4}{-3}$

e) $f^{-1}(x) = 2(x+9) = 2x + 18$

f) $f^{-1}(x) = -x$

g) $f(x)$ is the composition of taking the cube root of x, then subtracting 9.

Reversing the operations, the inverse is
$$f^{-1}(x) = (x+9)^3$$

h) $f(x)$ is the composition of cubing x, multiplying the result by 3, then subtracting 7.

Reversing the operations, the inverse is
$$f^{-1}(x) = \sqrt[3]{\frac{x+7}{3}}$$

i) $f(x)$ is the composition of subtracting 1 from x, taking the cube root of the result, then adding 5.

Reversing the operations, the inverse is
$$f^{-1}(x) = (x-5)^3 + 1$$

j) $f(x)$ is the composition of subtracting 7 from x, taking the cube root of the result, then multiplying by 2.

Reversing the operations, the inverse is
$$f^{-1}(x) = \left(\frac{x}{2}\right)^3 + 7$$

51. No, since they fail the Horizontal Line Test.

53. Yes, since the graphs are symmetric about the line $y = x$.

55. Graph of f^{-1}

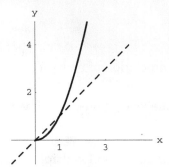

57. Graph of f^{-1}

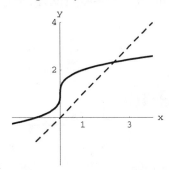

59. $f^{-1}(x) = \dfrac{x-2}{3}$

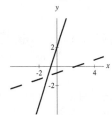

61. $f^{-1}(x) = \sqrt{x+4}$

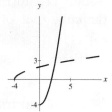

63. $f^{-1}(x) = \sqrt[3]{x}$

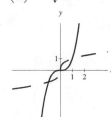

65. $f^{-1}(x) = (x+3)^2$ for $x \geq -3$

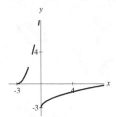

67. Interchange x and y then solve for y.

$$
\begin{aligned}
x &= 3y - 7 \\
\frac{x+7}{3} &= y \\
\frac{x+7}{3} &= f^{-1}(x)
\end{aligned}
$$

69. Interchange x and y then solve for y.

$$
\begin{aligned}
x &= 2 + \sqrt{y-3} \quad \text{for } x \geq 2 \\
(x-2)^2 &= y - 3 \quad \text{for } x \geq 2 \\
f^{-1}(x) &= (x-2)^2 + 3 \quad \text{for } x \geq 2
\end{aligned}
$$

71. Interchange x and y then solve for y.

$$
\begin{aligned}
x &= -y - 9 \\
y &= -x - 9 \\
f^{-1}(x) &= -x - 9
\end{aligned}
$$

73. Interchange x and y then solve for y.

$$
\begin{aligned}
x &= \frac{y+3}{y-5} \\
xy - 5x &= y + 3 \\
xy - y &= 5x + 3 \\
y(x-1) &= 5x + 3 \\
f^{-1}(x) &= \frac{5x+3}{x-1}
\end{aligned}
$$

75. Interchange x and y then solve for y.

$$x = -\frac{1}{y}$$
$$xy = -1$$
$$f^{-1}(x) = -\frac{1}{x}$$

77. Interchange x and y then solve for y.

$$x = \sqrt[3]{y-9} + 5$$
$$x - 5 = \sqrt[3]{y-9}$$
$$(x-5)^3 = y - 9$$
$$f^{-1}(x) = (x-5)^3 + 9$$

79. Interchange x and y then solve for y.

$$x = (y-2)^2 \quad x \geq 0$$
$$\sqrt{x} = y - 2$$
$$f^{-1}(x) = \sqrt{x} + 2$$

81. Note, $(g \circ f)(x) = 0.25(4x+4) - 1 = x$ and $(f \circ g)(x) = 4(0.25x-1) + 4 = x$.

Yes, g and f are inverse functions of each other.

83. Since $(f \circ g)(x) = \left(\sqrt{x-1}\right)^2 + 1 = x$ and and $(g \circ f)(x) = \sqrt{x^2+1-1} = \sqrt{x^2} = |x|$, g and f are not inverse functions of each other.

85. We find

$$(f \circ g)(x) = \frac{1}{1/(x-3)} + 3$$
$$= x - 3 + 3$$
$$(f \circ g)(x) = x$$

and

$$(g \circ f)(x) = \frac{1}{\left(\frac{1}{x}+3\right) - 3}$$
$$= \frac{1}{1/x}$$
$$(g \circ f)(x) = x.$$

Then g and f are inverse functions of each other.

87. We obtain

$$(f \circ g)(x) = \sqrt[3]{\frac{5x^3+2-2}{5}}$$
$$= \sqrt[3]{\frac{5x^3}{5}}$$
$$= \sqrt[3]{x^3}$$
$$(f \circ g)(x) = x$$

and

$$(g \circ f)(x) = 5\left(\sqrt[3]{\frac{x-2}{5}}\right)^3 + 2$$
$$= 5\left(\frac{x-2}{5}\right) + 2$$
$$= (x-2) + 2$$
$$(g \circ f)(x) = x.$$

Thus, g and f are inverse functions of each other.

89. y_1 and y_2 are inverse functions of each other and $y_3 = y_2 \circ y_1$.

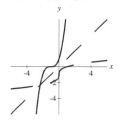

91. $C = 1.08P$ expresses the total cost as a function of the purchase price; and $P = C/1.08$ is the purchase price as a function of the total cost.

93. The graph of t as a function of r satisfies the Horizontal Line Test and is invertible. Solving for r we find,

$$t - 7.89 = -0.39r$$
$$r = \frac{t-7.89}{-0.39}$$

and the inverse function is $r = \frac{7.89-t}{0.39}$.

If $t = 5.55$ min., then $r = \frac{7.89-5.55}{0.39} = 6$ rowers.

95. Solving for w, we obtain

$$1.496w = V^2$$
$$w = \frac{V^2}{1.496}$$

and the inverse function is $w = \frac{V^2}{1.496}$. If

$V = 115$ ft./sec., then $w = \frac{115^2}{1.496} \approx 8,840$ lb.

97. a) Let $V = \$28,000$. The depreciation rate is

$$r = 1 - \left(\frac{28,000}{50,000}\right)^{1/5} \approx 0.109$$

or $r \approx 10.9\%$.

b) Writing V as a function of r we find

$$1 - r = \left(\frac{V}{50,000}\right)^{1/5}$$
$$(1 - r)^5 = \frac{V}{50,000}$$

and $V = 50,000(1 - r)^5$.

99. Since $g^{-1}(x) = \frac{x+5}{3}$ and $f^{-1}(x) = \frac{x-1}{2}$, we have

$$g^{-1} \circ f^{-1}(x) = \frac{\frac{x-1}{2} + 5}{3} = \frac{x+9}{6}.$$

Likewise, since $(f \circ g)(x) = 6x - 9$, we get

$$(f \circ g)^{-1}(x) = \frac{x+9}{6}.$$

Hence, $(f \circ g)^{-1} = g^{-1} \circ f^{-1}$.

101. One can easily see that the slope of the line joining (a, b) to (b, a) is -1, and that their midpoint is $\left(\frac{a+b}{2}, \frac{a+b}{2}\right)$. This midpoint lies on the line $y = x$ whose slope is 1. Then $y = x$ is the perpendicular bisector of the line segment joining the points (a, b) and (b, a)

103. Dividing we get $\frac{x-3}{x+2} = 1 - \frac{5}{x+2}$.

105. $(f \circ g)(2) = f(g(2)) = f(1) = \frac{2+3}{5} = 1$

$$(f \cdot g)(2) = f(2)g(2) = \frac{7}{5} \cdot 1 = \frac{7}{5}$$

107. Observe, the graph of $f(x) = -\sqrt{9 - x^2}$ is a lower semicircle of radius 3 centered at $(0, 0)$.

Then domain is $[-3, 3]$, the range is $[-3, 0]$, and increasing on $[0, 3]$

109.

$$0.75 + 0.80 = 0.225x - 0.125x$$
$$1.55 = 0.1x$$
$$15.5 = x$$

The solution set is $\{15.5\}$.

For Thought

1. False

2. False, since cost varies directly with the number of pounds purchased.

3. True **4.** True

5. True, since the area of a circle varies directly with the square of its radius.

6. False, since $y = k/x$ is undefined when $x = 0$.

7. True **8.** True **9.** True

10. False, the surface area is not equal to

(Surface Area) $= k \cdot$ length $\cdot$ width $\cdot$ height

for some constant k.

6 Exercises

1. varies directly

3. varies inversely

5. $G = kn$ **7.** $V = k/P$ **9.** $C = khr$

11. $Y = \frac{kx}{\sqrt{z}}$

13. A varies directly as the square of r

15. y varies inversely as x

17. Not a variation expression

19. a varies jointly as z and w

21. H varies directly as the square root of t and inversely as s

23. D varies jointly as L and J and inversely as W

25. Since $y = kx$ and $5 = k \cdot 9$, $k = 5/9$. Then $y = 5x/9$.

27. Since $T = k/y$ and $-30 = k/5$, $k = -150$. Thus, $T = -150/y$.

29. Since $m = kt^2$ and $54 = k \cdot 18$, $k = 3$. Thus, $m = 3t^2$.

31. Since $y = kx/\sqrt{z}$ and $2.192 = k(2.4)/\sqrt{2.25}$, we obtain $k = 1.37$. Hence, $y = 1.37x/\sqrt{z}$.

33. Since $y = kx$ and $9 = k(2)$, we obtain
$$y = \frac{9}{2} \cdot (-3) = -27/2.$$

35. Since $P = k/w$ and $2/3 = \dfrac{k}{1/4}$, we find
$$k = \frac{2}{3} \cdot \frac{1}{4} = \frac{1}{6}. \text{ Thus, } P = \frac{1/6}{1/6} = 1.$$

37. Since $A = kLW$ and $30 = k(3)(5\sqrt{2})$, we obtain $A = \sqrt{2}(2\sqrt{3})\dfrac{1}{2} = \sqrt{6}$.

39. Since $y = ku/v^2$ and $7 = k \cdot 9/36$,

we find $y = 28 \cdot 4/64 = 7/4$.

41. Let L_i and L_f be the length in inches and feet, respectively. Then $L_i = 12L_f$ is a direct variation.

43. Let P and n be the cost per person and the number of persons, respectively. Then $P = 20/n$ is an inverse variation.

45. Let S_m and S_k be the speeds of the car in mph and kph, respectively. Then $S_m \approx S_k/1.6 \approx 0.6S_k$ is a direct variation.

47. Not a variation

49. Let A and W be the area and width, respectively. Then $A = 30W$ is a direct variation.

51. Let n and p be the number of gallons and price per gallon, respectively. Since $np = 5$, we obtain that $n = \dfrac{5}{p}$ is an inverse variation.

53. If p is the pressure at depth d, then $p = kd$. Since $4.34 = k(10)$, $k = 0.434$. At $d = 6000$ ft, the pressure is $p = 0.434(6000) = 2604$ lb per square inch.

55. If h is the number of hours, p is the number of pounds, and w is the number of workers then $h = kp/w$. Since $8 = k(3000)/6$, $k = 0.016$. Five workers can process 4000 pounds in $h = (0.016)(4000)/5 = 12.8$ hours.

57. Since $I = kPt$ and $20.80 = k(4000)(16)$, we find $k = 0.000325$. The interest from a deposit of \$6500 for 24 days is
$$I = (0.000325)(6500)(24) \approx \$50.70.$$

59. Since $C = kDL$ and $18.60 = k(6)(20)$, we obtain $k = 0.155$. The cost of a 16 ft pipe with a diameter of 8 inches is
$$C = 0.155(8)(16) = \$19.84.$$

61. Since $w = khd^2$ and $14.5 = k(4)(6^2)$, we find $k = \dfrac{14.5}{144}$. Then a 5-inch high can with a diameter of 6 inches has weight
$$w = \frac{14.5}{144}(5)(6^2) = 18.125 \text{ oz.}$$

63. Since $V = kh/l$ and $10 = k(50)/(200)$, we get $k = 40$. The velocity, if the head is 60 ft and the length is 300 ft, is $V = (40)(60)/(300) = 8$ ft/year.

65. No, it is not directly proportional otherwise the following ratios $\dfrac{42,506}{1.34} \approx 31,720$,

$\dfrac{59,085}{0.295} \approx 200,288$, and

$\dfrac{738,781}{0.958} \approx 771,170$ would be all the same but they are not.

67. Since $g = ks/p$ and $76 = k(12)/(10)$, $k = \dfrac{190}{3}$.

If Calvin studies for 9 hours and plays for 15 hours, then his score is

$$g = \frac{190}{3} \cdot \frac{s}{p} = \frac{190}{3} \cdot \frac{9}{15} = 38.$$

69. Since $h = kv^2$ and $16 = k(32)^2$, we get $k = \dfrac{1}{64}$.

To reach a height of $20'2.5''$, the velocity v must satisfy

$$20 + \frac{2.5}{12} = \frac{1}{64}v^2.$$

Solving for v, we find $v \approx 35.96$ ft/sec.

73. Interchange x and y then solve for y.

$$
\begin{aligned}
x &= \sqrt[3]{y-9} + 1 \\
(x-1)^3 &= y - 9 \\
(x-1)^3 + 9 &= y \\
f^{-1}(x) &= (x-1)^3 + 9
\end{aligned}
$$

75. Let x be the average speed in the rain. Then

$$3x + 5(x+5) = 425$$

Solving for x, we find $x = 50$ mph.

77. The slope of the line is $1/2$. Using $y = mx + b$ and the point $(-4, 2)$, we find

$$
\begin{aligned}
2 &= \frac{1}{2}(-4) + b \\
2 &= -2 + b \\
4 &= b
\end{aligned}
$$

The line is given by $y = \frac{1}{2}x + 4$, or $2y = x + 8$. A standard form is $x - 2y = -8$.

Review Exercises

1. Function, domain and range are both $\{-2, 0, 1\}$

3. $y = 3 - x$ is a function, domain and range are both $(-\infty, \infty)$

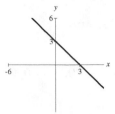

5. Not a function, domain is $\{2\}$, range is $(-\infty, \infty)$

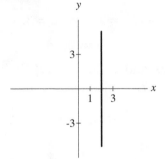

7. $x^2 + y^2 = 0.01$ is not a function, domain and range are both $[-0.1, 0.1]$

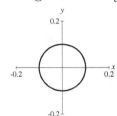

9. $x = y^2 + 1$ is not a function, domain is $[1, \infty)$, range is $(-\infty, \infty)$

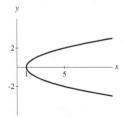

11. $y = \sqrt{x} - 3$ is a function, domain is $[0, \infty)$, range is $[-3, \infty)$

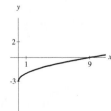

13. $9 + 3 = 12$

15. $24 - 7 = 17$

17. If $x^2 + 3 = 19$, then $x^2 = 16$ or $x = \pm 4$.

19. $g(12) = 17$

21. $7 + (-3) = 4$

23. $(4)(-9) = -36$

25. $f(-3) = 12$

27.

$$
\begin{aligned}
f(g(x)) &= f(2x - 7) \\
&= (2x - 7)^2 + 3 \\
&= 4x^2 - 28x + 52
\end{aligned}
$$

29. $(x^2 + 3)^2 + 3 = x^4 + 6x^2 + 12$

31. $(a + 1)^2 + 3 = a^2 + 2a + 4$

33.

$$
\begin{aligned}
\frac{f(3 + h) - f(3)}{h} &= \frac{(9 + 6h + h^2) + 3 - 12}{h} \\
&= \frac{6h + h^2}{h} \\
&= 6 + h
\end{aligned}
$$

35.

$$
\begin{aligned}
\frac{f(x + h) - f(x)}{h} &= \\
\frac{(x^2 + 2xh + h^2) + 3 - x^2 - 3}{h} &= \\
\frac{2xh + h^2}{h} &= \\
2x + h &=
\end{aligned}
$$

37. $g\left(\dfrac{x + 7}{2}\right) = (x + 7) - 7 = x$

39. $g^{-1}(x) = \dfrac{x + 7}{2}$

41. $f(x) = \sqrt{x}, g(x) = 2\sqrt{x + 3}$; left by 3, stretch by 2

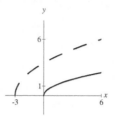

43. $f(x) = |x|, g(x) = -2|x + 2| + 4$; left by 2, stretch by 2, reflect about x-axis, up by 4

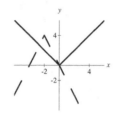

45. $f(x) = x^2, g(x) = \dfrac{1}{2}(x - 2)^2 + 1$; right by 2, stretch by $\dfrac{1}{2}$, up by 1

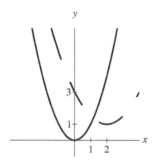

47. $(f \circ g)(x) = \sqrt{x} - 4$, domain $[0, \infty)$

49. $(f \circ h)(x) = x^2 - 4$, domain $(-\infty, \infty)$

51. $(g \circ f \circ h)(x) = g(x^2 - 4) = \sqrt{x^2 - 4}$.

To find the domain, solve $x^2 - 4 \geq 0$. Then the domain is $[2, \infty) \cup (-\infty, -2]$

53. Translate the graph of f to the right by 2-units, stretch by a factor of 2, shift up by 1-unit.

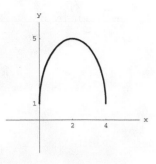

55. Translate the graph of f to the left by 1-unit, reflect about the x-axis, shift down by 3-units.

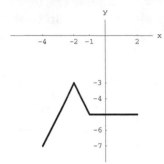

57. Translate the graph of f to the left by 2-units, stretch by a factor of 2, reflect about the x-axis.

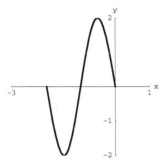

59. Stretch the graph of f by a factor of 2, reflect about the x-axis, shift up by 3-units.

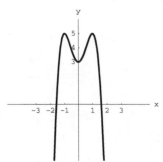

61. $F = f \circ g$

63. $H = f \circ h \circ g \circ j$

65. $N = h \circ f \circ j$ or $N = h \circ j \circ f$

67. $R = g \circ h \circ j$

69.

$$\frac{f(x+h) - f(x)}{h} = \frac{-5(x+h) + 9 + 5x - 9}{h}$$

$$= \frac{-5h}{h}$$

$$= -5$$

71.

$$\frac{f(x+h) - f(x)}{h} =$$

$$= \frac{\dfrac{1}{2x+2h} - \dfrac{1}{2x}}{h} \cdot \frac{(2x+2h)(2x)}{(2x+2h)(2x)}$$

$$= \frac{(2x) - (2x+2h)}{h(2x+2h)(2x)}$$

$$= \frac{-2}{(2x+2h)(2x)}$$

$$= \frac{-1}{(x+h)(2x)}$$

73. Domain is $[-10, 10]$, range is $[0, 10]$, increasing on $[-10, 0]$, decreasing on $[0, 10]$

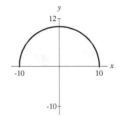

75. Domain and range are both $(-\infty, \infty)$, increasing on $(-\infty, \infty)$

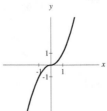

77. Domain is $(-\infty, \infty)$, range is $[-2, \infty)$, increasing on $[-2, 0]$ and $[2, \infty)$, decreasing on $(-\infty, -2]$ and $[0, 2]$

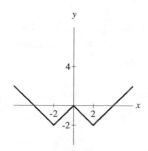

79. $y = |x| - 3$, domain is $(-\infty, \infty)$, range is $[-3, \infty)$

81. $y = -2|x| + 4$, domain is $(-\infty, \infty)$, range is $(-\infty, 4]$

83. $y = |x + 2| + 1$, domain is $(-\infty, \infty)$, range is $[1, \infty)$

85. Symmetry: y-axis

87. Symmetric about the origin

89. Neither symmetry

91. Symmetric about the y-axis

93. From the graph of $y = |x - 3| - 1$, the solution set is $(-\infty, 2] \cup [4, \infty)$

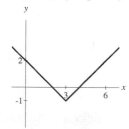

95. From the graph of $y = -2x^2 + 4$, the solution set is $(-\sqrt{2}, \sqrt{2})$

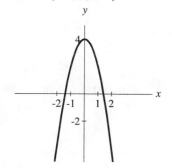

97. No solution since $-\sqrt{x + 1} - 2 \leq -2$

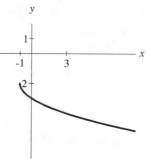

99. Inverse functions, $f(x) = \sqrt{x + 3}, g(x) = x^2 - 3$ for $x \geq 0$

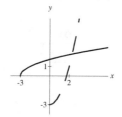

101. Inverse functions, $f(x) = 2x - 4, g(x) = \dfrac{1}{2}x + 2$

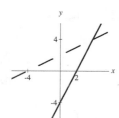

103. Not invertible, since there are two second components that are the same.

105. Inverse is $f^{-1}(x) = \dfrac{x + 21}{3}$ with domain and range both $(-\infty, \infty)$

107. Not invertible

109. Inverse is $f^{-1}(x) = x^2 + 9$ for $x \geq 0$ with domain $[0, \infty)$ and range $[9, \infty)$

111. Inverse is $f^{-1}(x) = \dfrac{5x + 7}{1 - x}$ with domain $(-\infty, 1) \cup (1, \infty)$, and range $(-\infty, -5) \cup (-5, \infty)$

113. Inverse is $f^{-1}(x) = -\sqrt{x - 1}$ with domain $[1, \infty)$ and range $(-\infty, 0]$

115. Let x be the number of roses. The cost function is $C(x) = 1.20x + 40$, the revenue function is $R(x) = 2x$, and the profit function is $P(x) = R(x) - C(x)$ or $P(x) = 0.80x - 40$.

Since $P(50) = 0$, to make a profit she must sell at least 51 roses.

117. Since $h(0) = 64$ and $h(2) = 0$, the range of $h = -16t^2 + 64$ is the interval $[0, 64]$.

Then the domain of the inverse function is $[0, 64]$. Solving for t, we obtain

$$
\begin{aligned}
16t^2 &= 64 - h \\
t^2 &= \frac{64 - h}{16} \\
t &= \frac{\sqrt{64 - h}}{4}.
\end{aligned}
$$

The inverse function is $t = \dfrac{\sqrt{64 - h}}{4}$.

119. Since $A = \pi \left(\dfrac{d}{2}\right)^2$, $d = 2\sqrt{\dfrac{A}{\pi}}$.

121. The average rate of change is

$$\frac{8 - 6}{4} = 0.5 \text{ inch/lb.}$$

123. Since $D = kW$ and $9 = k \cdot 25$, we obtain

$$D = \frac{9}{25}100 = 36.$$

125. Since $V = k\sqrt{h}$ and $45 = k\sqrt{1.5}$, the velocity of a Triceratops is $V = \dfrac{45}{\sqrt{1.5}} \cdot \sqrt{2.8} \approx 61$ kph.

127. Since $C = kd^2$ and $4.32 = k \cdot 36$, a 16-inch diameter globe costs $C = \dfrac{4.32}{36} \cdot 16^2 = \$30.72$.

Chapter Test

1. No, since $(0, 5)$ and $(0, -5)$ are two ordered pairs with the same first coordinate and different second coordinates.

2. Yes, since to each x-coordinate there is exactly one y-coordinate, namely, $y = \dfrac{3x - 20}{5}$.

3. No, since $(1, -1)$ and $(1, -3)$ are two ordered pairs with the same first coordinate and different second coordinates.

4. Yes, since to each x-coordinate there is exactly one y-coordinate, namely, $y = x^3 - 3x^2 + 2x - 1$.

5. Domain is $\{2, 5\}$, range is $\{-3, -4, 7\}$

6. Domain is $[9, \infty)$, range is $[0, \infty)$

7. Domain is $[0, \infty)$, range is $(-\infty, \infty)$

8. Graph of $3x - 4y = 12$ includes the points $(4, 0), (0, -3)$

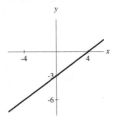

9. Graph of $y = 2x - 3$ includes the points $(3/2, 0), (0, -3)$

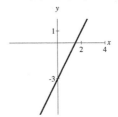

10. $y = \sqrt{25 - x^2}$ is a semicircle with radius 5

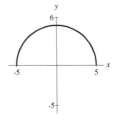

11. $y = -(x - 2)^2 + 5$ is a parabola with vertex $(2, 5)$

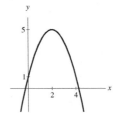

12. $y = 2|x| - 4$ includes the points $(0, -4), (\pm 3, 2)$

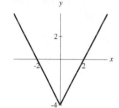

13. $y = \sqrt{x + 3} - 5$ includes the points $(1, -3), (6, -2)$

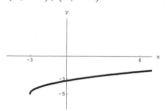

14. Graph includes the points $(-2, -2), (0, 2), (3, 2)$

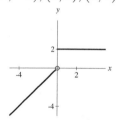

15. $\sqrt{9} = 3$ **16.** $f(5) = \sqrt{7}$

17. $f(3x - 1) = \sqrt{(3x - 1) + 2} = \sqrt{3x + 1}.$

18. $g^{-1}(x) = \dfrac{x + 1}{3}$ **19.** $\sqrt{16} + 41 = 45$

20.

$$
\begin{aligned}
\frac{g(x + h) - g(x)}{h} &= \frac{3(x + h) - 1 - 3x + 1}{h} \\
&= \frac{3h}{h} \\
&= 3
\end{aligned}
$$

21. Increasing on $(3, \infty)$, decreasing on $(-\infty, 3)$

22. Symmetric about the y-axis

23. Add 1 to $-3 < x - 1 < 3$ to obtain $-2 < x < 4$. Thus, the solution set $(-2, 4)$.

24. $f(x)$ is the composition of subtracting 2 from x, taking the cube root of the result, then adding 3. Reversing the operations, the inverse is $f^{-1}(x) = (x - 3)^3 + 2$.

25. The range of $f(x) = \sqrt{x - 5}$ is $[0, \infty)$. Then the domain of $f^{-1}(x)$ is $x \geq 0$ Note, $f(x)$ is the composition of subtracting 5 from x, then taking the square root of the result. Reversing the operations, the inverse is $f^{-1}(x) = x^2 + 5$ for $x \geq 0$.

26. $\dfrac{60 - 35}{200} = \$0.125$ per envelope

27. Since $I = k/d^2$ and $300 = k/4$, we get $k = 1200$. If $d = 10$, then $I = 1200/100 = 12$ candlepower.

28. Let s be the length of one side of the cube. By the Pythagorean Theorem we have

$s^2 + s^2 = d^2$. Then $s = \dfrac{d}{\sqrt{2}}$ and the volume

is $V = \left(\dfrac{d}{\sqrt{2}} \right)^3 = \dfrac{\sqrt{2}d^3}{4}.$

Polynomial and Rational Functions

From Chapter 3 of *Precalculus: Functions and Graphs*. Fourth Edition. Mark Dugopolski. Copyright © 2013 by Pearson Education, Inc.

Polynomial and Rational Functions

Others had died trying, but in May of 1927, Charles Lindbergh claimed the $25,000 prize for flying across the Atlantic Ocean. He was the first aviator to make the 3610-mile nonstop solo flight from New York to Paris.

Lindbergh did not just get in a plane and start flying. He spent years planning, designing, and practicing for his attempt to cross the Atlantic. Lindbergh collected and analyzed a vast amount of data to determine relationships between wind velocity, air speed, fuel consumption, and time elapsed. As he burned fuel, the plane got lighter and he flew slower.

▶WHAT YOU WILL learn... In this chapter we explore polynomial and rational functions and their graphs. We'll learn how to use these basic functions of algebra to model many real-life situations, and we'll see how Lindbergh used them in planning his historic flight.

Library of Congress Prints and Photographs Division [LCUSZ62-13161]

1 Quadratic Functions and Inequalities

A **polynomial function** is defined by a polynomial. A **quadratic function** is defined by a quadratic or second-degree polynomial. So a quadratic function has the form $f(x) = ax^2 + bx + c$ where $a \neq 0$. The form $f(x) = a(x - h)^2 + k$ is an equivalent quadratic function.

Two Forms for Quadratic Functions

It is easy to convert $f(x) = a(x - h)^2 + k$ to the form $f(x) = ax^2 + bx + c$ by squaring the binomial. To convert in the other direction we use completing the square. Recall that the perfect square trinomial whose first two terms are $x^2 + bx$ is $x^2 + bx + \left(\frac{b}{2}\right)^2$. So to get the last term you *take one-half of the coefficient of the middle term and square it.*

Rather than adding the last term of the perfect square trinomial to both sides of the equation, we want to keep $f(x)$ on the left side. To complete the square and change only the right side, we add and subtract on the right side as shown in Example 1(a). Another complication here is that the coefficient of x^2 is not always 1. To overcome this problem, you must factor before completing the square as shown in Example 1(b).

EXAMPLE 1 Completing the square for a quadratic function

Rewrite each function in the form $f(x) = a(x - h)^2 + k$.

a. $f(x) = x^2 + 6x$ **b.** $f(x) = 2x^2 - 20x + 3$

Solution

a. One-half of 6 is 3 and 3^2 is 9. Adding and subtracting 9 on the right side of $f(x) = x^2 + 6x$ does not change the function.

$$f(x) = x^2 + 6x$$
$$= x^2 + 6x + 9 - 9 \quad 9 = \left(\tfrac{1}{2} \cdot 6\right)^2$$
$$= (x + 3)^2 - 9 \quad \text{Factor.}$$

b. First factor 2 out of the first two terms, because the leading coefficient in $(x - h)^2$ is 1.

$$f(x) = 2x^2 - 20x + 3$$
$$= 2(x^2 - 10x) + 3$$
$$= 2(x^2 - 10x + 25 - 25) + 3 \quad 25 = \left(\tfrac{1}{2} \cdot 10\right)^2$$
$$= 2(x^2 - 10x + 25) - 50 + 3 \quad \text{Remove } -25 \text{ from the parentheses.}$$
$$= 2(x - 5)^2 - 47$$

Because of the 2 preceding the parentheses, the second 25 was doubled when it was removed from the parentheses.

▶**TRY THIS.** Rewrite $f(x) = 2x^2 - 8x + 9$ in the form $f(x) = a(x - h)^2 + k$. ∎

In the next example we complete the square and graph a quadratic function.

EXAMPLE 2 Graphing a quadratic function

Rewrite $f(x) = -2x^2 - 4x + 3$ in the form $f(x) = a(x - h)^2 + k$ and sketch its graph.

Solution

Start by completing the square:

$$f(x) = -2(x^2 + 2x) + 3 \qquad \text{Factor out } -2 \text{ from the first two terms.}$$

$$= -2(x^2 + 2x + 1 - 1) + 3 \qquad \text{Complete the square for } x^2 + 2x.$$

$$= -2(x^2 + 2x + 1) + 2 + 3 \qquad \text{Remove } -1 \text{ from the parentheses.}$$

$$= -2(x + 1)^2 + 5$$

The function is now in the form $f(x) = a(x - h)^2 + k$. The number 1 indicates that the graph of $f(x) = x^2$ is translated one unit to the left. Since $a = -2$, the graph is stretched by a factor of 2 and reflected below the x-axis. Finally, the graph is translated five units upward. The graph shown in Fig. 1 includes the points $(0, 3)$, $(-1, 5)$, and $(-2, 3)$.

▶**TRY THIS.** Rewrite $f(x) = -2x^2 - 4x + 1$ in the form $f(x) = a(x - h)^2 + k$ and sketch its graph. ∎

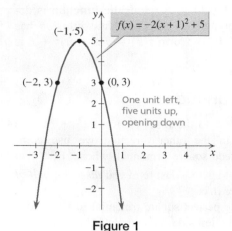

Figure 1

We can use completing the square as in Example 2 to prove the following theorem.

Theorem: Quadratic Functions

The graph of any quadratic function is a transformation of the graph of $f(x) = x^2$.

PROOF Since $f(x) = a(x - h)^2 + k$ is a transformation of $f(x) = x^2$, we will show that $f(x) = ax^2 + bx + c$ can be written in that form:

$$f(x) = ax^2 + bx + c$$

$$= a\left(x^2 + \frac{b}{a}x\right) + c \qquad \text{Factor } a \text{ out of the first two terms.}$$

To complete the square for $x^2 + \frac{b}{a}x$, add and subtract $\frac{b^2}{4a^2}$ inside the parentheses:

$$f(x) = a\left(x^2 + \frac{b}{a}x + \frac{b^2}{4a^2} - \frac{b^2}{4a^2}\right) + c$$

$$= a\left(x^2 + \frac{b}{a}x + \frac{b^2}{4a^2}\right) - \frac{b^2}{4a} + c \qquad \text{Remove } -\frac{b^2}{4a^2} \text{ from the parentheses.}$$

$$= a\left(x + \frac{b}{2a}\right)^2 + \frac{4ac - b^2}{4a} \qquad \text{Factor and get a common denominator.}$$

$$= a(x - h)^2 + k \qquad \text{Let } h = -\frac{b}{2a} \text{ and } k = \frac{4ac - b^2}{4a}.$$

So the graph of any quadratic function is a transformation of $f(x) = x^2$. ∎

We stated that any transformation of $f(x) = x^2$ is called a parabola. Therefore, the graph of any quadratic function is a parabola.

Opening, Vertex, and Axis of Symmetry

If $a > 0$, the graph of $f(x) = a(x - h)^2 + k$ **opens upward**; if $a < 0$, the graph **opens downward** as shown in Fig. 2. Notice that h determines the amount of horizontal translation and k determines the amount of vertical translation of the graph of $f(x) = x^2$. Because of the translations, the point $(0, 0)$ on the graph of $f(x) = x^2$ moves to the point (h, k) on the graph of $f(x) = a(x - h)^2 + k$. Since $(0, 0)$ is the lowest point on the graph of $f(x) = x^2$, the lowest point on any parabola that opens upward is (h, k). Since $(0, 0)$ is the highest point on the graph of $f(x) = -x^2$, the highest point on any parabola that opens downward is (h, k). The point (h, k) is called the **vertex** of the parabola. Since (h, k) is the vertex, $f(x) = a(x - h)^2 + k$ is called the **vertex form** of the equation of a parabola. The form $f(x) = ax^2 + bx + c$ is the **general form** of the equation of a parabola.

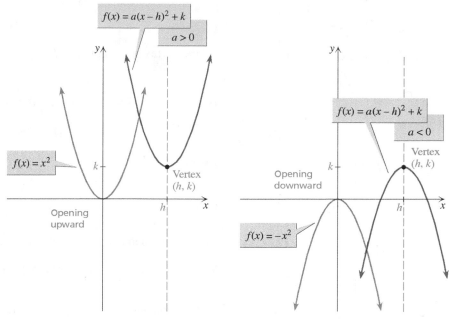

Figure 2

The graph of $f(x) = x^2$ is symmetric about the y-axis, which runs vertically through the vertex of the parabola. Since this symmetry is preserved in transformations, the graph of any quadratic function is symmetric about the vertical line through its vertex, the **axis of symmetry.** See Fig. 2. The equation of the axis of symmetry is $x = h$ or $x = -b/(2a)$, because we used $h = -b/(2a)$ when we converted general form to vertex form.

You can use a graphing calculator to experiment with different values for a, h, and k. Two possibilities are shown in Fig. 3(a) and (b). The graphing calculator allows you to see results quickly and to use values that you would not use otherwise. □

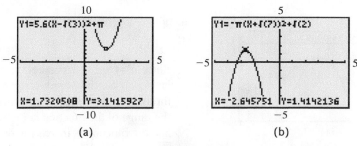

(a)   (b)

Figure 3

It is easy to find the vertex (h, k) if the equation of the parabola is given as $f(x) = a(x - h)^2 + k$. For the parabola $f(x) = ax^2 + bx + c$ we can find the vertex using $x = -b/(2a)$, because the axis of symmetry goes through the vertex.

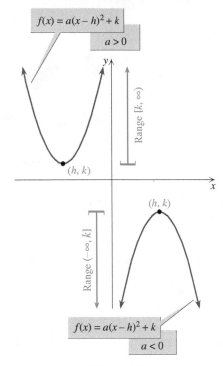

Figure 4

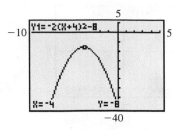

Figure 5

> **SUMMARY**
>
> ### Vertex of a Parabola
>
> 1. For a quadratic function in the form $f(x) = a(x - h)^2 + k$ the vertex of the parabola is (h, k).
>
> 2. For the form $f(x) = ax^2 + bx + c$, the x-coordinate of the vertex is $\frac{-b}{2a}$. The y-coordinate is $f\left(\frac{-b}{2a}\right)$.

> **EXAMPLE 3** Finding the vertex

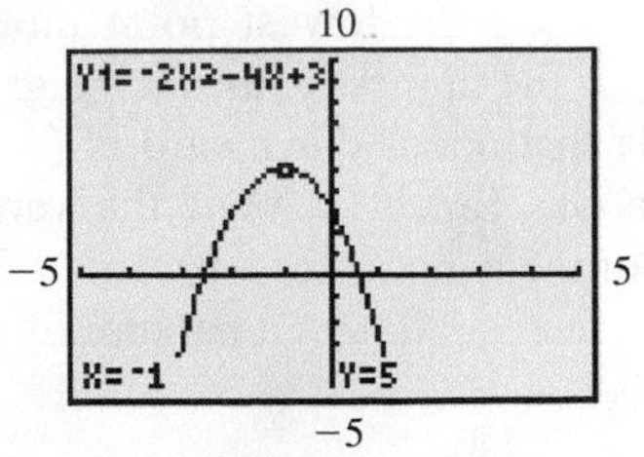

Find the vertex of the graph of $f(x) = -2x^2 - 4x + 3$.

Solution

Use $x = -b/(2a)$ to find the x-coordinate of the vertex:

$$x = \frac{-b}{2a} = \frac{-(-4)}{2(-2)} = -1$$

Now find $f(-1)$:

$$f(-1) = -2(-1)^2 - 4(-1) + 3 = 5$$

The vertex is $(-1, 5)$. In Example 2, $f(x) = -2x^2 - 4x + 3$ was rewritten as $f(x) = -2(x + 1)^2 + 5$. In this form we see immediately that the vertex is $(-1, 5)$. The graph in Fig. 4 supports these conclusions.

▶**TRY THIS.** Find the vertex of the graph of $f(x) = 3x^2 - 12x + 5$. ∎

The domain of every quadratic function $f(x) = a(x - h)^2 + k$ is the set of real numbers, $(-\infty, \infty)$. The range of a quadratic function is determined from the second coordinate of the vertex. If $a > 0$, the range is $[k, \infty)$ and k is called the **minimum value of the function**. The function is decreasing on $(-\infty, h]$ and increasing on $[h, \infty)$. See Fig. 5. If $a < 0$, the range is $(-\infty, k]$ and k is called the **maximum value of the function**. The function is increasing on $(-\infty, h]$ and decreasing on $[h, \infty)$.

> **EXAMPLE 4** Identifying the characteristics of a parabola

For each parabola, determine whether the parabola opens upward or downward, and find the vertex, axis of symmetry, and range of the function. Find the maximum or minimum value of the function and the intervals on which the function is increasing or decreasing.

a. $y = -2(x + 4)^2 - 8$ **b.** $y = 2x^2 - 4x - 9$

Solution

a. Since $a = -2$, the parabola opens downward. In $y = a(x - h)^2 + k$, the vertex is (h, k). So the vertex is $(-4, -8)$. The axis of symmetry is the vertical line through the vertex, $x = -4$. Since the parabola opens downward from $(-4, -8)$, the range of the function is $(-\infty, -8]$. The maximum value of the function is -8, and the function is increasing on $(-\infty, -4]$ and decreasing on $[-4, \infty)$. The graph in Fig. 6 supports these results. □

Figure 6

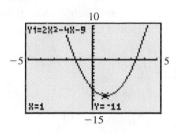

Figure 7

b. Since $a = 2$, the parabola opens upward. In the form $y = ax^2 + bx + c$, the x-coordinate of the vertex is $x = -b/(2a)$. In this case,

$$x = \frac{-b}{2a} = \frac{-(-4)}{2(2)} = 1.$$

Use $x = 1$ to find $y = 2(1)^2 - 4(1) - 9 = -11$. So the vertex is $(1, -11)$, and the axis of symmetry is the vertical line $x = 1$. Since the parabola opens upward, the vertex is the lowest point and the range is $[-11, \infty)$. The function is decreasing on $(-\infty, 1]$ and increasing on $[1, \infty)$. The minimum value of the function is -11. The graph in Fig. 7 supports these results.

▶**TRY THIS.** Identify all of the characteristics of the parabola $y = 3(x - 5)^2 - 4$. ∎

Intercepts

The graph of $y = ax^2 + bx + c$ always has a y-intercept. The y-intercept $(0, c)$ is found by replacing x with 0 in $y = ax^2 + bx + c$. Whether the graph has any x-intercepts depends on whether the quadratic equation $ax^2 + bx + c = 0$ has any solutions. Any quadratic equation can be solved using the quadratic formula:

$$x = \frac{-b \pm \sqrt{b^2 - 4ac}}{2a} \qquad \text{Quadratic formula}$$

Since the quadratic formula could produce 0, 1, or 2 real solutions to the equation, there might be 0, 1, or 2 x-intercepts. Note how the axis of symmetry, $x = -b/(2a)$, appears in this formula. If the graph has two x-intercepts, then they are on opposite sides of the graph and are equidistant from the axis of symmetry as shown in Fig. 8.

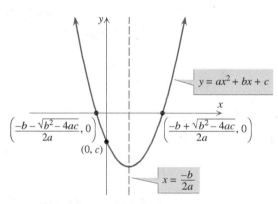

Figure 8

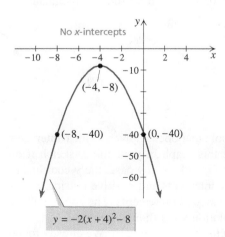

Figure 9

EXAMPLE 5 Finding the intercepts

Find the y-intercept and the x-intercepts for each parabola and sketch the graph of each parabola.

a. $y = -2(x + 4)^2 - 8$ **b.** $y = 2x^2 - 4x - 9$

Solution

a. If $x = 0$, $y = -2(0 + 4)^2 - 8 = -40$. The y-intercept is $(0, -40)$. Because the graph is symmetric about the line $x = -4$, the point $(-8, -40)$ is also on the graph. Since the parabola opens downward from $(-4, -8)$, which is below the x-axis, there are no x-intercepts. If we try to solve $-2(x + 4)^2 - 8 = 0$ to find the x-intercepts, we get $(x + 4)^2 = -4$, which has no real solution. The graph is shown in Fig. 9.

291

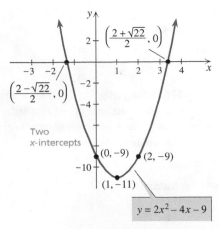

Two
x-intercepts

Figure 10

b. If $x = 0$, $y = 2(0)^2 - 4(0) - 9 = -9$. The y-intercept is $(0, -9)$. From Example 4(b), the vertex is $(1, -11)$. Because the graph is symmetric about the line $x = 1$, the point $(2, -9)$ is also on the graph. The x-intercepts are found by solving $2x^2 - 4x - 9 = 0$:

$$x = \frac{4 \pm \sqrt{(-4)^2 - 4(2)(-9)}}{2(2)} = \frac{4 \pm \sqrt{88}}{4} = \frac{2 \pm \sqrt{22}}{2}$$

The x-intercepts are $\left(\frac{2 + \sqrt{22}}{2}, 0\right)$ and $\left(\frac{2 - \sqrt{22}}{2}, 0\right)$. See Fig. 10.

▶**TRY THIS.** Find all intercepts and sketch the graph of $y = 3(x - 5)^2 - 4$. ∎

Quadratic Inequalities

A **quadratic inequality** is an inequality that involves a quadratic polynomial. To solve a quadratic inequality such as $ax^2 + bx + c > 0$, we can use the graph of the quadratic function $y = ax^2 + bx + c$. The values of x that satisfy the inequality are the same as the values of x for which $y > 0$ on the graph of the function $y = ax^2 + bx + c$. You can use the following strategy for this **graphical method.**

STRATEGY

Solving a Quadratic Inequality by the Graphical Method

1. Get 0 on one side of the inequality and a quadratic polynomial on the other side.

2. Find all roots to the quadratic polynomial.

3. Graph the corresponding quadratic function. The roots from (2) determine the x-intercepts.

4. Read the solution set to the inequality from the graph of the parabola.

EXAMPLE 6 Graphical method for solving quadratic inequalities

Solve each inequality. Write the solution set in interval notation and graph it.

a. $x^2 - x > 6$ **b.** $x^2 - x \leq 6$

Solution

a. Rewrite the inequality as $x^2 - x - 6 > 0$. Then find all roots to the quadratic polynomial:

$$x^2 - x - 6 = 0$$
$$(x - 3)(x + 2) = 0$$
$$x - 3 = 0 \quad \text{or} \quad x + 2 = 0$$
$$x = 3 \quad \text{or} \quad x = -2$$

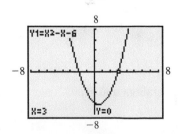

Figure 11

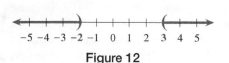

Figure 12

The graph of $y = x^2 - x - 6$ is a parabola that opens upward with x-intercepts at $(-2, 0)$ and $(3, 0)$. You can picture this graph in your mind, sketch it on paper, or use a graphing calculator as in Fig. 11. In any case, the y-coordinates on the parabola are negative between the intercepts and positive outside the intercepts. So this inequality is satisfied outside the intercepts. The solution set is $(-\infty, -2) \cup (3, \infty)$. The graph of the solution set is shown in Fig. 12.

b. The inequality $x^2 - x \leq 6$ is equivalent to $x^2 - x - 6 \leq 0$. We already found the roots to $x^2 - x - 6 = 0$ and the graph of $y = x^2 - x - 6$ in part (a). The

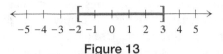

Figure 13

y-coordinates are less than zero between the intercepts and equal to zero at the intercepts. So the endpoints of the interval are included in the solution set. The solution set is $[-2, 3]$ and its graph is shown in Fig. 13.

▶**TRY THIS.** Solve $x^2 + 6x + 8 \geq 0$ by the graphical method. ∎

Note that it is usually not a good idea to make conclusions from a graph. The graph may not show all of the important features of the function. However, we did use the graph in Example 6, because we know that the graph of every quadratic function is a parabola. Once we have found the x-intercepts, we know the precise location of the parabola.

The **test-point method** for solving a quadratic inequality does not involve the graph of the quadratic function. In place of reading the graph, we test points in the intervals determined by the roots to the quadratic polynomial. This method will be used again for polynomial and rational inequalities later in this chapter.

STRATEGY

Solving a Quadratic Inequality Using Test Points

1. Get 0 on one side of the inequality and a quadratic polynomial on the other side.
2. Find all roots to the quadratic polynomial and plot them on a number line.
3. Select a test point in each interval determined by the roots.
4. Evaluate the quadratic function at each test point.
5. Determine the solution set from the signs of the function at the test points.

EXAMPLE 7 | Solving a quadratic inequality using the test-point method

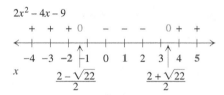

Figure 14

Solve $2x^2 - 4x - 9 < 0$. Write the solution set in interval notation.

Solution

The roots to $2x^2 - 4x - 9 = 0$ were found to be $\frac{2 \pm \sqrt{22}}{2}$ in Example 5(b). Since $\frac{2 - \sqrt{22}}{2} \approx -1.3$ and $\frac{2 + \sqrt{22}}{2} \approx 3.3$, we make the number line as in Fig. 14. Select a convenient test point in each of the three intervals determined by the roots. Our selections -2, 1, and 5 are shown in red on the number line. Now evaluate $2x^2 - 4x - 9$ for each test point:

$$2(-2)^2 - 4(-2) - 9 = 7 \qquad \text{Positive}$$

$$2(1)^2 - 4(1) - 9 = -11 \qquad \text{Negative}$$

$$2(5)^2 - 4(5) - 9 = 21 \qquad \text{Positive}$$

The signs of these results are shown on the number line in Fig. 14. Since $2x^2 - 4x - 9 < 0$ between the roots, the solution set is

$$\left(\frac{2 - \sqrt{22}}{2}, \frac{2 + \sqrt{22}}{2} \right).$$

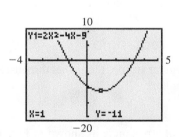

Figure 15

The graph of $y = 2x^2 - 4x - 9$ in Fig. 15 is below the x-axis between the x-intercepts and supports our conclusion. Note that every point that appears on the graph can be viewed as a test point.

▶**TRY THIS.** Solve $x^2 - 2x - 4 < 0$ using the test-point method. ∎

If there are no real solutions to the quadratic equation that corresponds to a quadratic inequality, then the solution set to the inequality is either the empty set or all real numbers. For example, $x^2 + 4 = 0$ has no real solutions. Use any number as a test point to find that the solution set to $x^2 + 4 > 0$ is $(-\infty, \infty)$ and the solution set to $x^2 + 4 < 0$ is the empty set $\varnothing$.

Applications of Maximum and Minimum

If one variable is a quadratic function of another, then the maximum or minimum value of the dependent variable occurs at the vertex of the graph of the quadratic function. A nice application of this idea occurs in modeling projectile motion. The formula $h(t) = -16t^2 + v_0 t + h_0$ is used to find the height in feet at time t in seconds for a projectile that is launched in a vertical direction with initial velocity of v_0 feet per second from an initial height of h_0 feet. Since the height is a quadratic function of time, the maximum height occurs at the vertex of the parabola.

EXAMPLE 8 Finding maximum height of a projectile

A ball is tossed straight upward with an initial velocity of 80 feet per second from a rooftop that is 12 feet above ground level. The height of the ball in feet at time t in seconds is given by $h(t) = -16t^2 + 80t + 12$. Find the maximum height above ground level for the ball.

Solution

Since the height is a quadratic function of t with a negative leading coefficient, the height has a maximum value at the vertex of the parabola. Use $-b/(2a)$ to find the t-coordinate of the vertex. Since $a = -16$ and $b = 80$

$$\frac{-b}{2a} = \frac{-80}{2(-16)} = 2.5.$$

So the ball reaches its maximum height at time $t = 2.5$ seconds. Now

$$h(2.5) = -16(2.5)^2 + 80(2.5) + 12 = 112.$$

So the maximum height of the ball is 112 feet above the ground.

▶TRY THIS. The height (in feet) above the ground for a ball that is tossed straight upward is given by $h(t) = -16t^2 + 96t + 40$, where t is the time in seconds. Find the maximum height above the ground for this ball. ■

In Example 8, the quadratic function was given. In the next example we need to write the quadratic function and then find its maximum value.

EXAMPLE 9 Maximizing area of a rectangle

If 100 m of fencing will be used to fence a rectangular region, then what dimensions for the rectangle will maximize the area of the region?

Solution

Since the 100 m of fencing forms the perimeter of a rectangle as shown in Fig. 16, we have $2L + 2W = 100$, where W is its width and L is its length. Dividing by 2 we get $L + W = 50$ or $W = 50 - L$. Since $A = LW$ for a rectangle, by substituting we get

$$A = LW = L(50 - L) = -L^2 + 50L.$$

L

$50 - L$

Figure 16

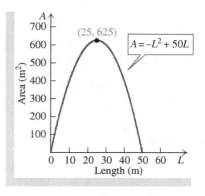

Figure 17

So the area is a quadratic function of the length. The graph of this function is the parabola in Fig. 17. Since the parabola opens downward, the maximum value of A occurs when

$$L = \frac{-b}{2a} = \frac{-50}{2(-1)} = 25.$$

If $L = 25$ then $W = 25$ also, since $W = 50 - L$. So the length should be 25 meters and the width 25 meters to get the maximum area. The rectangle that gives the maximum area is actually a square with an area of 625 m^2.

▶**TRY THIS.** If a rectangle has a perimeter of 50 meters, then what dimensions will maximize its area? ■

FOR thought... True or False? Explain.

1. The domain and range of a quadratic function are $(-\infty, \infty)$.

2. The vertex of the graph of $y = 2(x - 3)^2 - 1$ is $(3, 1)$.

3. The graph of $y = -3(x + 2)^2 - 9$ has no x-intercepts.

4. The maximum value of y in the function $y = -4(x - 1)^2 + 9$ is 9.

5. For $y = 3x^2 - 6x + 7$, the value of y is at its minimum when $x = 1$.

6. The graph of $f(x) = 9x^2 + 12x + 4$ has one x-intercept and one y-intercept.

7. The graph of every quadratic function has exactly one y-intercept.

8. The inequality $\pi(x - \sqrt{3})^2 + \pi/2 \leq 0$ has no solution.

9. The maximum area of a rectangle with fixed perimeter p is $p^2/16$.

10. The function $f(x) = (x - 3)^2$ is increasing on the interval $[-3, \infty)$.

EXERCISES 1

Fill in the blank.

1. If $a > 0$, the graph of $f(x) = a(x - h)^2 + k$ opens _____.

2. If $a < 0$, the graph of $f(x) = a(x - h)^2 + k$ opens _____.

3. The point (h, k) is the _____ of the parabola $y = a(x - h)^2 + k$.

4. For $f(x) = ax^2 + bx + c$ $(a \neq 0)$, the x-coordinate of the _____ is $-b/(2a)$.

5. If $a > 0$ and $f(x) = a(x - h)^2 + k$, then k is the _____ value of the function.

6. If $a < 0$ and $f(x) = a(x - h)^2 + k$, then k is the _____ value of the function.

7. The line $x = -b/(2a)$ is the _____ for the function $f(x) = ax^2 + bx + c$ $(a \neq 0)$.

8. The point $(0, c)$ is the _____ for the function $f(x) = ax^2 + bx + c$ $(a \neq 0)$.

Write each quadratic function in the form $y = a(x - h)^2 + k$ and sketch its graph.

9. $y = x^2 + 4x$

10. $y = x^2 - 6x$

11. $y = x^2 - 3x$

12. $y = x^2 + 5x$

13. $y = 2x^2 - 12x + 22$

14. $y = 3x^2 - 12x + 1$

15. $y = -3x^2 + 6x - 3$

16. $y = -2x^2 - 4x + 8$

17. $y = x^2 + 3x + \dfrac{5}{2}$

18. $y = x^2 - x + 1$

19. $y = -2x^2 + 3x - 1$

20. $y = 3x^2 + 4x + 2$

Find the vertex of the graph of each quadratic function.

21. $f(x) = 3x^2 - 12x + 1$　　**22.** $f(x) = -2x^2 - 8x + 9$

23. $f(x) = -3(x - 4)^2 + 1$　　**24.** $f(x) = \frac{1}{2}(x + 6)^2 - \frac{1}{4}$

25. $y = -\frac{1}{2}x^2 - \frac{1}{3}x$　　**26.** $y = \frac{1}{4}x^2 + \frac{1}{2}x - 1$

From the graph of each parabola, determine whether the parabola opens upward or downward, and find the vertex, axis of symmetry, and range of the function. Find the maximum or minimum value of the function and the intervals on which the function is increasing or decreasing.

27.

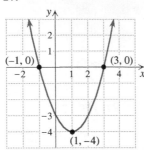

28.

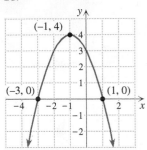

Find the range of each quadratic function and the maximum or minimum value of the function. Identify the intervals on which each function is increasing or decreasing.

29. $f(x) = 3 - x^2$　　**30.** $f(x) = 5 - x^2$

31. $y = (x - 1)^2 - 1$　　**32.** $y = (x + 3)^2 + 4$

33. $y = x^2 + 8x - 2$　　**34.** $y = x^2 - 2x - 3$

35. $y = \frac{1}{2}(x - 3)^2 + 4$　　**36.** $y = -\frac{1}{3}(x + 6)^2 + 37$

37. $f(x) = -2x^2 + 6x + 9$　　**38.** $f(x) = -3x^2 - 9x + 4$

39. $y = -\frac{3}{4}\left(x - \frac{1}{2}\right)^2 + 9$　　**40.** $y = \frac{3}{2}\left(x - \frac{1}{3}\right)^2 - 6$

Identify the vertex, axis of symmetry, y-intercept, x-intercepts, and opening of each parabola, then sketch the graph.

41. $y = x^2 - 3$　　**42.** $y = 8 - x^2$

43. $y = x^2 - x$　　**44.** $y = 2x - x^2$

45. $f(x) = x^2 + 6x + 9$　　**46.** $f(x) = x^2 - 6x$

47. $f(x) = (x - 3)^2 - 4$　　**48.** $f(x) = (x + 1)^2 - 9$

49. $y = -3(x - 2)^2 + 12$　　**50.** $y = -2(x + 3)^2 + 8$

51. $y = -2x^2 + 4x + 1$　　**52.** $y = -x^2 + 2x - 6$

Solve each inequality by using the graphical method. State the solution set in interval notation.

53. $x^2 - 2x - 3 > 0$　　**54.** $x^2 + x - 2 \geq 0$

55. $x^2 - 4x + 1 < 0$　　**56.** $x^2 - 2x - 1 \leq 0$

57. $x + 1 < 6x^2$　　**58.** $x + 6 > 5x^2$

Identify the solution set to each quadratic inequality by inspecting the graphs of $y = x^2 - 2x - 3$ and $y = -x^2 - 2x + 3$ as shown.

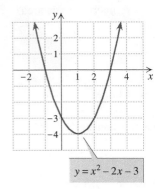

$y = x^2 - 2x - 3$

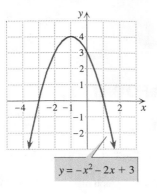

$y = -x^2 - 2x + 3$

59. $x^2 - 2x - 3 \geq 0$　　**60.** $x^2 - 2x - 3 < 0$

61. $-x^2 - 2x + 3 > 0$　　**62.** $-x^2 - 2x + 3 \leq 0$

63. $x^2 + 2x \leq 3$　　**64.** $x^2 \leq 2x + 3$

Solve each inequality by using the test-point method. State the solution set in interval notation and graph it.

65. $x^2 - 4x + 2 < 0$　　**66.** $x^2 - 4x + 1 \leq 0$

67. $x^2 - 9 > 1$　　**68.** $6 < x^2 - 1$

69. $y^2 + 18 > 10y$　　**70.** $y^2 + 3 \geq 6y$

71. $p^2 + 9 > 0$　　**72.** $-5 - s^2 < 0$

73. $a^2 + 20 \leq 8a$　　**74.** $6t \leq t^2 + 25$

75. $-2w^2 + 5w < 6$　　**76.** $-3z^2 - 5 > 2z$

Solve each inequality by using the method of your choice. State the solution set in interval notation and graph it.

77. $2x^2 - x - 3 < 0$　　**78.** $3x^2 - 4x - 4 \leq 0$

79. $2x + 15 < x^2$　　**80.** $5x - x^2 < 4$

81. $w^2 - 4w - 12 \geq 0$　　**82.** $y^2 + 8y + 15 \leq 0$

83. $t^2 \leq 16$　　**84.** $36 \leq h^2$

85. $a^2 + 6a + 9 \leq 0$　　**86.** $c^2 + 4 \leq 4c$

87. $4z^2 - 12z + 9 > 0$　　**88.** $9s^2 + 6s + 1 \geq 0$

The next two exercises incorporate many concepts of quadratics.

89. Let $f(x) = x^2 - 3x - 10$.
  a. Solve $f(x) = 0$.

  b. Solve $f(x) = -10$.

  c. Solve $f(x) > 0$.

  d. Solve $f(x) \leq 0$.

  e. Write f in the form $f(x) = a(x - h)^2 + k$ and describe the graph of f as a transformation of the graph of $y = x^2$.

  f. Graph f and state the domain, range, and the maximum or minimum y-coordinate on the graph.

  g. What is the relationship between the graph of f and the answers to parts (c) and (d)?

  h. Find the intercepts, axis of symmetry, vertex, opening, and intervals on which f is increasing or decreasing.

90. Repeat parts (a) through (h) from the previous exercise for $f(x) = -x^2 + 2x + 1$.

Solve each problem

91. *Maximum Height of a Football* If a football is kicked straight up with an initial velocity of 128 ft/sec from a height of 5 ft, then its height above the earth is a function of time given by $h(t) = -16t^2 + 128t + 5$. What is the maximum height reached by this ball?
  HINT Find the vertex of the graph of the quadratic function.

92. *Maximum Height of a Ball* If a juggler can toss a ball into the air at a velocity of 64 ft/sec from a height of 6 ft, then what is the maximum height reached by the ball?

93. *Shooting an Arrow* If an archer shoots an arrow straight upward with an initial velocity of 160 ft/sec from a height of 8 ft, then its height above the ground in feet at time t in seconds is given by the function

$$h(t) = -16t^2 + 160t + 8.$$

  a. What is the maximum height reached by the arrow?

  b. How long does it take for the arrow to reach the ground?

94. *Rocket-Propelled Grenade* If a soldier in basic training fires a rocket-propelled grenade (RPG) straight up from ground level with an initial velocity of 256 ft/sec, then its height above the ground in feet at time t in seconds is given by the function

$$h(t) = -16t^2 + 256t.$$

  a. What is the maximum height reached by the RPG?

  b. How long does it take for the RPG to reach the ground?

95. *Lindbergh's Air Speed* Flying too fast or slow wastes fuel. For the *Spirit of St. Louis,* miles per pound of fuel M was a function of air speed A in miles per hour, modeled by the formula

$$M = -0.000653A^2 + 0.127A - 5.01.$$

  a. Use the accompanying graph to estimate the most economical air speed.

  b. Use the formula to find the value of A that maximizes M.

  c. How many gallons of fuel did he burn per hour if he flew at 97 mph and got 1.2 mi/lb of fuel, which weighed 6.12 lb/gal?

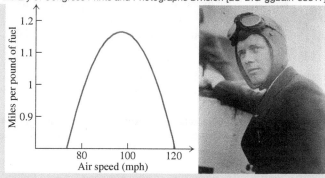

Library of Congress Prints and Photographs Division [LC-DIG-ggbain-35317]

Figure for Exercise 95

96. *Average Farm Size* The average size in acres of a farm in the United States in the year $1994 + x$ can be modeled by the quadratic function

$$A(x) = 0.37x^2 - 3.06x + 440.3.$$

  a. Find the year in which the average size of a farm reached its maximum.

  b. Find the year in which the average size was 470 acres.

  c. For what years shown in the accompanying figure is the average size decreasing? Increasing?

  d. When was the average size less than 435 acres?

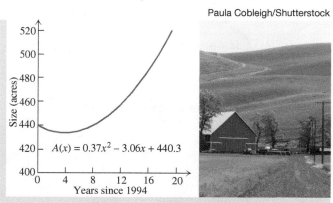

Paula Cobleigh/Shutterstock

Figure for Exercise 96

97. *Maximum Area* Shondra wants to enclose a rectangular garden with 200 yards of fencing. What dimensions for the garden will maximize its area?

> **HINT** Write a quadratic function for the area and find the vertex.

98. *Mirror Mirror* Chantel wants to make a rectangular frame for a mirror using 10 feet of frame molding. What dimensions will maximize the area of the mirror assuming that there is no waste?

99. *Twin Kennels* Martin plans to construct a rectangular kennel for two dogs using 120 feet of chain-link fencing. He plans to fence all four sides and down the middle to keep the dogs separate. What overall dimensions will maximize the total area fenced?

> **HINT** Write a quadratic function for the area and find the vertex.

100. *Cross Fenced* Kim wants to construct rectangular pens for four animals with 400 feet of fencing. To get four separate pens she will fence a large rectangle and then fence through the middle of the rectangle parallel to the length and parallel to the width. What overall dimensions will maximize the total area of the pens?

101. *Big Barn* Mike wants to enclose a rectangular area for his rabbits alongside his large barn using 30 feet of fencing. What dimensions will maximize the area fenced if the barn is used for one side of the rectangle?

102. *Maximum Area* Kevin wants to enclose a rectangular garden using 14 eight-ft railroad ties, which he cannot cut. What are the dimensions of the rectangle that maximize the area enclosed?

103. *Cross Section of a Gutter* Seth has a piece of aluminum that is 10 in. wide and 12 ft long. He plans to form a gutter with a rectangular cross section and an open top by folding up the sides as shown in the figure. What dimensions of the gutter would maximize the amount of water that it can hold.

> **HINT** Write a quadratic function for the cross-sectional area and find the vertex.

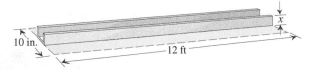

Figure for Exercise 103

104. *Maximum Volume of a Cage* Sharon has a 12-ft board that is 12 in. wide. She wants to cut it into five pieces to make a cage for two pigeons, as shown in the figure. The front and back will be covered with chicken wire. What should be the dimensions of the cage to maximize the volume and use all of the 12-ft board?

Figure for Exercise 104

105. *Maximizing Revenue* Mona Kalini gives a walking tour of Honolulu to one person for $49. To increase her business, she advertised at the National Orthodontist Convention that she would lower the price by $1 per person for each additional person, up to 49 people.

   a. Write the price per person p as a function of the number of people n.

   b. Write her revenue as a function of the number of people on the tour.

> **HINT** Her revenue is the product of n and p.

   c. What is the maximum revenue for her tour?

106. *Concert Tickets* At $10 per ticket, Willie Williams and the Wranglers will fill all 8000 seats in the Assembly Center. The manager knows that for every $1 increase in the price, 500 tickets will go unsold.

   a. Write the number of tickets sold n as a function of ticket price p.

   b. Write the total revenue as a function of the ticket price.

> **HINT** Revenue is the product of n and p.

   c. What ticket price will maximize the revenue?

107. *Variance of the Number of Smokers* If p is the probability that a randomly selected person in Chicago is a smoker, then $1 - p$ is the probability that the person is not a smoker. The variance of the number of smokers in a random sample of 50 Chicagoans is $50p(1 - p)$. What value of p maximizes the variance?

108. *Rate of Flu Infection* In a town of 5000 people the daily rate of infection with a flu virus varies directly with the product of the number of people who have been infected and the number of people not infected. When 1000 people have been infected, the flu is spreading at a rate of 40 new cases per day. For what number of people infected is the daily rate of infection at its maximum?

■ **Foreshadowing Calculus**

In algebra we can maximize or minimize a quadratic function because we can easily find the vertex of a parabola. However, max/min problems involving other functions are usually solved using techniques of calculus.

109. *Altitude and Pressure* At an altitude of h feet the atmospheric pressure a (atm) is given by

$$a = 3.89 \times 10^{-10}h^2 - 3.48 \times 10^{-5}h + 1$$

(Sportscience, www.sportsci.org).
a. Graph this quadratic function.

b. In 1953, Edmund Hillary and Tenzing Norgay were the first persons to climb Mount Everest (see accompanying figure). Was the atmospheric pressure increasing or decreasing as they went to the 29,029-ft summit?

c. Where is the function decreasing? Increasing?

d. Does your answer to part (c) make sense?

e. For what altitudes do you think the function is valid?

Figure for Exercise 109

110. *Increasing Revenue* A company's weekly revenue in dollars is given by $R(x) = 2000x - 2x^2$, where x is the number of items produced during a week.
a. For what x is $R(x) > 0$?

b. On what interval is $R(x)$ increasing? Decreasing?

c. For what number of items is the revenue maximized?

d. What is the maximum revenue?

e. Find the marginal revenue function $MR(x)$, where $MR(x)$ is defined by

$$MR(x) = R(x + 1) - R(x).$$

f. On what interval is $MR(x)$ positive? Negative?

Use a calculator or a computer for the following regression problems.

111. *Quadratic Versus Linear* The average retail price for a used basic 2-door hatchback Corvette depends on the age of the car, as shown in the accompanying table for the summer of 2008 (Edmund's, www.edmunds.com).

Table for Exercise 111

Age (yr)	Price ($)
1	35,243
2	32,102
3	29,616
4	25,215
5	22,648
6	21,051
7	19,942
8	17,585
9	15,924

Drazen Vukelic/Shutterstock

a. Use both linear regression and quadratic regression on a graphing calculator to express the price as a function of the age of the car.

b. Plot the data, the linear function, and the quadratic function on your calculator. Judging from what you see, which function appears to fit the data better?

c. Predict the price of an eleven-year-old car using both the linear function and the quadratic function.

112. *Homicides in the United States* The accompanying table gives the number of homicides per 100,000 population in the United States (Federal Bureau of Investigation, www.fbi.gov).
a. Use quadratic regression on a graphing calculator to express the number of homicides as a function of x, where x is the number of years after 1994.

b. Plot the data and the quadratic function on your calculator. Judging from what you see, does the function appear to be a good model for the data?

c. Use the quadratic function to find the year in which the number of homicides was at a minimum.

d. Use the quadratic function to find the year in which there will be 10 homicides per 100,000 population.

Table for Exercise 112

Year	Homicides per 100,000	Year	Homicides per 100,000
1994	9.0	2001	5.6
1995	8.2	2002	5.6
1996	7.4	2003	5.7
1997	6.8	2004	5.5
1998	6.3	2005	5.6
1999	5.7	2006	5.7
2000	5.5	2007	5.5

▶ RETHINKING

113. If y varies inversely as x and $y = 3$ when $x = 12$, find y when $x = 40$.

114. Is the function $f(x) = x^2 - 4$ one-to-one?

115. If $f(x) = 2x - 9$ and $g(x) = \sqrt{x}$, find $(f + g)(9)$.

116. The graph of $y = x^2$ is reflected in the x-axis, translated 4 units to the left and 5 units upward. What is the equation of the curve in its final position?

117. Find the domain and range for the function $\{(1, 2), (3, 5), (4, 2), (-3, 5)\}$.

118. Find the domain and range for $f(x) = -\sqrt{x - 1} + 2$.

THINKING OUTSIDE THE BOX XXII

Overlapping Region A right triangle with sides of length 3, 4, and 5 is drawn so that the endpoints of the side of length 5 are $(0, 0)$ and $(5, 0)$. A square with sides of length 1 is drawn so that its center is the vertex of the right angle and its sides are parallel to the x- and y-axes. What is the area of the region where the square and the triangle overlap?

POP QUIZ 1

1. Write $y = 2x^2 + 16x - 1$ in the form $y = a(x - h)^2 + k$.

2. Find the vertex of the graph of $y = 3(x + 4)^2 + 8$.

3. Find the range of $f(x) = -x^2 - 4x + 9$.

4. Find the minimum y-value for $y = x^2 - 3x$.

5. Find the x-intercepts and axis of symmetry for $y = x^2 - 2x - 8$.

6. Solve the inequality $x^2 + 4x < 0$.

LINKING concepts... For Individual or Group Explorations

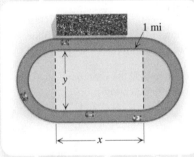

Designing a Race Track

An architect is designing a race track that will be 60 feet wide and have semicircular ends, as shown in the accompanying figure. The length of the track is to be one mile, measured on the inside edge of the track.

a) Find the exact dimensions for x and y in the figure that will maximize the area of the rectangular center section.

b) Round the answers to part (a) to the nearest tenth of a foot and make an accurate drawing of the track.

c) Find the exact dimensions for x and y that will maximize the total area enclosed by the track.

d) Repeat parts (a), (b), and (c) assuming that the one-mile length is measured on the outside edge of the track.

2 Zeros of Polynomial Functions

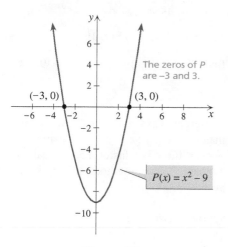

The zeros of P are -3 and 3.

$(-3, 0)$

$(3, 0)$

$P(x) = x^2 - 9$

Figure 18

We have studied linear and quadratic functions extensively. In this section we will study general polynomial functions.

The Remainder Theorem

If $y = P(x)$ is a polynomial function, then a value of x that satisfies $P(x) = 0$ is called a **zero** of the polynomial function or a zero of the polynomial. For example, 3 and -3 are zeros of the function $P(x) = x^2 - 9$, because $P(3) = 0$ and $P(-3) = 0$. Note that the zeros of $P(x) = x^2 - 9$ are the same as the solutions to the equation $x^2 - 9 = 0$. The real zeros of a polynomial function appear on the graph of the function as the x-coordinates of the x-intercepts. The x-intercepts of the graph of $P(x) = x^2 - 9$ shown in Fig. 18 are $(-3, 0)$ and $(3, 0)$.

For polynomial functions of degree 2 or less, the zeros can be found by solving quadratic or linear equations. Our goal in this section is to find all of the zeros of a polynomial function when possible. For polynomials of degree higher than 2, the difficulty of this task ranges from easy to impossible, but we have some theorems to assist us. The remainder theorem relates evaluating a polynomial to division of polynomials.

The Remainder Theorem

> If R is the remainder when a polynomial $P(x)$ is divided by $x - c$, then $R = P(c)$.

PROOF Let $Q(x)$ be the quotient and R be the remainder when $P(x)$ is divided by $x - c$. Since the dividend is equal to the divisor times the quotient plus the remainder, we have

$$P(x) = (x - c)Q(x) + R.$$

This statement is true for any value of x, and so it is also true for $x = c$:

$$P(c) = (c - c)Q(c) + R$$
$$= 0 \cdot Q(c) + R$$
$$= R$$

So $P(c)$ is equal to the remainder when $P(x)$ is divided by $x - c$. ∎

To illustrate the remainder theorem, we will now use long division to evaluate a polynomial.

EXAMPLE 1 Using the remainder theorem to evaluate a polynomial

Use the remainder theorem to find $P(3)$ if $P(x) = 2x^3 - 5x^2 + 4x - 6$.

Solution

By the remainder theorem $P(3)$ is the remainder when $P(x)$ is divided by $x - 3$:

$$
\begin{array}{r}
2x^2 + x + 7 \\
x - 3 \overline{\smash{)}2x^3 - 5x^2 + 4x - 6} \\
\underline{2x^3 - 6x^2} \\
x^2 + 4x \\
\underline{x^2 - 3x} \\
7x - 6 \\
\underline{7x - 21} \\
15
\end{array}
$$

301

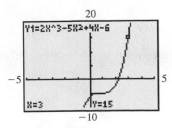

Figure 19

The remainder is 15 and therefore $P(3) = 15$. We can check by finding $P(3)$ in the usual manner:

$$P(3) = 2 \cdot 3^3 - 5 \cdot 3^2 + 4 \cdot 3 - 6 = 54 - 45 + 12 - 6 = 15$$

You can check this with a graphing calculator as shown in Fig. 19.

▶TRY THIS. Use the remainder theorem to find $P(1)$ if $P(x) = x^2 - 7x + 9$. ∎

Synthetic Division

In Example 1 we found $P(3) = 15$ in two different ways. Certainly, evaluating $P(x)$ for $x = 3$ in the usual manner is faster than dividing $P(x)$ by $x - 3$ using the ordinary method of dividing polynomials. However, there is a faster method, called **synthetic division,** for dividing by $x - 3$. Compare the two methods side by side, both showing $2x^3 - 5x^2 + 4x - 6$ divided by $x - 3$:

Ordinary Division of Polynomials

$$\begin{array}{r} 2x^2 + x + 7 \leftarrow \text{Quotient} \\ x - 3 \overline{)2x^3 - 5x^2 + 4x - 6} \\ \underline{2x^3 - 6x^2} \\ x^2 + 4x \\ \underline{x^2 - 3x} \\ 7x - 6 \\ \underline{7x - 21} \\ 15 \leftarrow \text{Remainder} \end{array}$$

Synthetic Division

$$\begin{array}{r|rrrr} 3 & 2 & -5 & 4 & -6 \\ & & 6 & 3 & 21 \\ \hline & 2 & 1 & 7 & 15 \leftarrow \text{Remainder} \end{array}$$
$$\underset{\text{Quotient}}{}$$

Synthetic division certainly looks easier than ordinary division, and in general it is faster than evaluating the polynomial by substitution. Synthetic division is used as a quick means of dividing a polynomial by a binomial of the form $x - c$.

In synthetic division we write just the necessary parts of the ordinary division. Instead of writing $2x^3 - 5x^2 + 4x - 6$, write the coefficients 2, -5, 4, and -6. For $x - 3$, write only the 3. The bottom row in synthetic division gives the coefficients of the quotient and the remainder.

To actually perform the synthetic division, start with the following arrangement of coefficients:

$$\begin{array}{r|rrrr} 3 & 2 & -5 & 4 & -6 \\ & & & & \\ \hline & & & & \end{array}$$

Bring down the first coefficient, 2. Multiply 2 by 3 and write the answer beneath -5. Then add:

$$\begin{array}{r|rrrr} 3 & 2 & -5 & 4 & -6 \\ & \downarrow & 6 & & \\ \hline \text{Multiply} \rightarrow & 2 & 1 & & \\ & & \uparrow & & \\ & & \text{Add} & & \end{array}$$

Using 3 rather than -3 when dividing by $x - 3$ allows us to multiply and add rather than multiply and subtract as in ordinary division. Now multiply 1 by 3 and write the answer beneath 4. Then add. Repeat the multiply-and-add step for the remaining column:

$$\begin{array}{r|rrrr} 3 & 2 & -5 & 4 & -6 \\ & & 6 & 3 & 21 \\ \hline & 2 & 1 & 7 & 15 \end{array}$$

To perform this arithmetic on a graphing calculator, start with the leading coefficient 2 as the answer. Then repeatedly multiply the answer by 3 and add the next coefficient as shown in Fig. 20. □

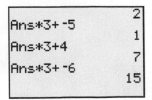

Figure 20

The quotient is $2x^2 + x + 7$, and the remainder is 15. Since the divisor in synthetic division is of the form $x - c$, the degree of the quotient is always one less than the degree of the dividend.

EXAMPLE 2 Synthetic division

Use synthetic division to find the quotient and remainder when $x^4 - 14x^2 + 5x - 9$ is divided by $x + 4$.

Solution

Since $x + 4 = x - (-4)$, we use -4 in the synthetic division. Use 1, 0, -14, 5, and -9 as the coefficients of the polynomial. We use 0 for the coefficient of the missing x^3-term, as we would in ordinary division of polynomials.

$$
\begin{array}{r|rrrrr}
-4 & 1 & 0 & -14 & 5 & -9 \\
   &   & -4 & 16 & -8 & 12 \\
\hline
\text{Multiply} \rightarrow & 1 & -4 & 2 & -3 & 3 \\
   &   &   & \uparrow \\
   &   &   & \text{Add}
\end{array}
$$

The quotient is $x^3 - 4x^2 + 2x - 3$ and the remainder is 3.

▶**TRY THIS.** Use synthetic division to find the quotient and remainder when $x^3 - 7x + 5$ is divided by $x + 2$. ∎

To find the value of a polynomial $P(x)$ for $x = c$, we can divide $P(x)$ by $x - c$ or we can substitute c for x and compute. Using long division to divide by $x - c$ is not an efficient way to evaluate a polynomial. However, if we use synthetic division to divide by $x - c$ we can actually evaluate some polynomials using fewer arithmetic operations than we use in the substitution method. Note that in part (a) of the next example, synthetic division takes more steps than substitution, but in part (b) synthetic division takes fewer steps. To gain a better understanding of why synthetic division gives the value of a polynomial, see Linking Concepts at the end of this section.

EXAMPLE 3 Using synthetic division to evaluate a polynomial

Let $f(x) = x^3$ and $g(x) = x^3 - 3x^2 + 5x - 12$. Use synthetic division to find the following function values.

a. $f(-2)$ **b.** $g(4)$

Solution

a. To find $f(-2)$, divide the polynomial x^3 by $x - (-2)$ or $x + 2$ using synthetic division. Write x^3 as $x^3 + 0x^2 + 0x + 0$, and use 1, 0, 0, and 0 as the coefficients. We use a zero for each power of x below x^3.

$$
\begin{array}{r|rrrr}
-2 & 1 & 0 & 0 & 0 \\
   &   & -2 & 4 & -8 \\
\hline
   & 1 & -2 & 4 & -8
\end{array}
$$

The remainder is -8, so $f(-2) = -8$. To check, find $f(-2) = (-2)^3 = -8$.

b. To find $g(4)$, use synthetic division to divide $x^3 - 3x^2 + 5x - 12$ by $x - 4$:

$$
\begin{array}{r|rrrr}
4 & 1 & -3 & 5 & -12 \\
  &   & 4 & 4 & 36 \\
\hline
  & 1 & 1 & 9 & 24
\end{array}
$$

The remainder is 24, so $g(4) = 24$. Check this answer by finding
$g(4) = 4^3 - 3(4^2) + 5(4) - 12 = 24$.

▶**TRY THIS.** Use synthetic division to find $P(3)$ if $P(x) = x^3 + x^2 - 9$. ■

The Factor Theorem

Consider the polynomial function $P(x) = x^2 - x - 6$. We can find the zeros of the
function by solving $x^2 - x - 6 = 0$ by factoring:

$$(x - 3)(x + 2) = 0$$

$$x - 3 = 0 \quad \text{or} \quad x + 2 = 0$$

$$x = 3 \quad \text{or} \quad x = -2$$

Both 3 and -2 are zeros of the function $P(x) = x^2 - x - 6$. Note how each factor
of the polynomial corresponds to a zero of the function. This example suggests the
following theorem.

The Factor Theorem

> The number c is a zero of the polynomial function $y = P(x)$ if and only if
> $x - c$ is a factor of the polynomial $P(x)$.

PROOF   If c is a zero of the polynomial function $y = P(x)$, then $P(c) = 0$. If
$P(x)$ is divided by $x - c$, we get a quotient $Q(x)$ and a remainder R such that

$$P(x) = (x - c)Q(x) + R.$$

By the remainder theorem, $R = P(c)$. Since $P(c) = 0$, we have $R = 0$ and
$P(x) = (x - c)Q(x)$, which proves that $x - c$ is a factor of $P(x)$.

In Exercise 92 you will be asked to prove that if $x - c$ is a factor of $P(x)$, then
c is a zero of the polynomial function. These two arguments together establish the
truth of the factor theorem. ■

Synthetic division can be used in conjunction with the factor theorem. If the
remainder of dividing $P(x)$ by $x - c$ is 0, then $P(c) = 0$ and c is a zero of the
polynomial function. By the factor theorem, $x - c$ is a factor of $P(x)$.

EXAMPLE 4   Using the factor theorem to factor
a polynomial

Determine whether $x + 4$ is a factor of the polynomial $P(x) = x^3 - 13x + 12$. If
it is a factor, then factor $P(x)$ completely.

Solution

By the factor theorem, $x + 4$ is a factor of $P(x)$ if and only if $P(-4) = 0$. We can
find $P(-4)$ using synthetic division:

$$
\begin{array}{r|rrrr}
-4 & 1 & 0 & -13 & 12 \\
   &   & -4 & 16 & -12 \\
\hline
   & 1 & -4 & 3 & 0
\end{array}
$$

Since $P(-4)$ is equal to the remainder, $P(-4) = 0$ and -4 is a zero of $P(x)$. By
the factor theorem, $x + 4$ is a factor of $P(x)$. Since the other factor is the quotient
from the synthetic division, $P(x) = (x + 4)(x^2 - 4x + 3)$. Factor the quadratic
polynomial to get $P(x) = (x + 4)(x - 1)(x - 3)$.

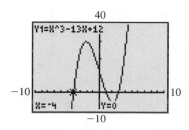

40

Y1=X^3-13X+12

-10   10

X=-4   Y=0

-10

Figure 21

HISTORICAL NOTE

Carl Friedrich Gauss (1777–1855) was a German mathematician and scientist of profound genius who contributed significantly to many fields, including number theory, analysis, differential geometry, geodesy, magnetism, astronomy, and optics. Gauss had a remarkable influence in many fields of mathematics and science and is ranked as one of history's most influential mathematicians.

You can check this result by examining the calculator graph of $y = x^3 - 13x + 12$ shown in Fig. 21. The graph appears to cross the x-axis at -4, 1, and 3, supporting the conclusion that $P(x) = (x + 4)(x - 1)(x - 3)$.

▶**TRY THIS.** Is $x - 1$ a factor of $P(x) = x^3 - 3x + 2$? If it is a factor, then factor $P(x)$ completely. ∎

The Fundamental Theorem of Algebra

Whether a number is a zero of a polynomial function can be determined by synthetic division. But does every polynomial function have a zero? This question was answered in the affirmative by Carl F. Gauss when he proved the fundamental theorem of algebra in his doctoral thesis in 1799 at the age of 22.

The Fundamental Theorem of Algebra

> If $y = P(x)$ is a polynomial function of positive degree, then $y = P(x)$ has at least one zero in the set of complex numbers.

Gauss also proved the n-root theorem of Section 3 that says that the number of zeros of a polynomial (or polynomial function) of degree n is at most n. For example, a fifth-degree polynomial function has at least one zero and at most five.

Note that the zeros guaranteed by Gauss are in the set of complex numbers. So the zero might be real or imaginary. The theorem applies only to polynomial functions of degree 1 or more, because a polynomial function of zero degree such as $P(x) = 7$ has no zeros. A polynomial function of degree 1, $f(x) = ax + b$, has exactly one zero, which is found by solving $ax + b = 0$. A polynomial function of degree 2, $f(x) = ax^2 + bx + c$, has one or two zeros that can be found by the quadratic formula. For higher-degree polynomials the situation is not as simple. The fundamental theorem tells us that a polynomial function has at least one zero but not how to find it. For this purpose we have some other theorems.

The Rational Zero Theorem

Zeros or roots that are rational numbers, the **rational zeros,** are generally the easiest to find. The polynomial function $f(x) = 6x^2 - x - 35$ has two rational zeros that can be found as follows:

$$6x^2 - x - 35 = 0$$

$$(2x - 5)(3x + 7) = 0 \quad \text{Factor.}$$

$$x = \frac{5}{2} \quad \text{or} \quad x = -\frac{7}{3}$$

Note that in 5/2, 5 is a factor of -35 (the constant term) and 2 is a factor of 6 (the leading coefficient). For the zero $-7/3$, -7 is a factor of -35 and 3 is a factor of 6. Of course, these observations are not surprising, because we used these facts to factor the quadratic polynomial in the first place. Note that there are a lot of other factors of -35 and 6 for which the ratio is *not* a zero of this function. This example illustrates the rational zero theorem, which is also called the rational root theorem.

The Rational Zero Theorem

> If $f(x) = a_n x^n + a_{n-1} x^{n-1} + a_{n-2} x^{n-2} + \cdots + a_1 x + a_0$ is a polynomial function with integral coefficients ($a_n \neq 0$ and $a_0 \neq 0$) and p/q (in lowest terms) is a rational zero of $f(x)$, then p is a factor of the constant term a_0 and q is a factor of the leading coefficient a_n.

PROOF If p/q is a zero of $f(x)$, then $f(p/q) = 0$:

$$a_n \left(\frac{p}{q}\right)^n + a_{n-1}\left(\frac{p}{q}\right)^{n-1} + a_{n-2}\left(\frac{p}{q}\right)^{n-2} + \cdots + a_1 \frac{p}{q} + a_0 = 0$$

Subtract a_0 from each side and multiply by q^n to get the following equation:

$$a_n p^n + a_{n-1}p^{n-1}q + a_{n-2}p^{n-2}q^2 + \cdots + a_1 pq^{n-1} = -a_0 q^n$$

Because the coefficients are integers and p and q are integers, both sides of this equation are integers. Since p is a factor of the left side, p must be a factor of the right side, which is the same integer. Since p/q is in lowest terms, p is not a factor of q. So p must be a factor of a_0.

To prove that q is a factor of a_n, rearrange the preceding equation as follows:

$$a_{n-1}p^{n-1}q + a_{n-2}\,p^{n-2}q^2 + \cdots + a_1 pq^{n-1} + a_0 q^n = -a_n p^n$$

Now q is a factor of a_n by the same argument used previously. ∎

The rational zero theorem does not identify exactly which rational numbers are zeros of a function; it only gives *possibilities* for the rational zeros.

EXAMPLE 5 Using the rational zero theorem

Find all possible rational zeros for each polynomial function.

a. $f(x) = 2x^3 - 3x^2 - 11x + 6$ **b.** $g(x) = 3x^3 - 8x^2 - 8x + 8$

Solution

a. If the rational number p/q is a zero of $f(x)$, then p is a factor of 6 and q is a factor of 2. The positive factors of 6 are 1, 2, 3, and 6. The positive factors of 2 are 1 and 2. Take each factor of 6 and divide by 1 to get $1/1$, $2/1$, $3/1$, and $6/1$. Take each factor of 6 and divide by 2 to get $1/2$, $2/2$, $3/2$, and $6/2$. Simplify the ratios, eliminate duplications, and put in the negative factors to get

$$\pm 1, \quad \pm 2, \quad \pm 3, \quad \pm 6, \quad \pm \frac{1}{2}, \quad \text{and} \quad \pm \frac{3}{2}$$

as the possible rational zeros to the function $f(x)$.

b. If the rational number p/q is a zero of $g(x)$, then p is a factor of 8 and q is a factor of 3. The factors of 8 are 1, 2, 4, and 8. The factors of 3 are 1 and 3. If we take all possible ratios of a factor of 8 over a factor of 3, we get

$$\pm 1, \quad \pm 2, \quad \pm 4, \quad \pm 8, \quad \pm \frac{1}{3}, \quad \pm \frac{2}{3}, \quad \pm \frac{4}{3}, \quad \text{and} \quad \pm \frac{8}{3}$$

as the possible rational zeros of the function $g(x)$.

▶**TRY THIS.** Find all possible rational zeros for $h(x) = 2x^3 + x^2 - 4x - 3$. ∎

Our goal is to find all of the zeros to a polynomial function. The zeros to a polynomial function might be rational, irrational, or imaginary. We can determine the rational zeros by simply evaluating the polynomial function for every number in the list of possible rational zeros. If the list is long, looking at a graph of the function can speed up the process. We will use synthetic division to evaluate the polynomial, because synthetic division gives the quotient polynomial as well as the value of the polynomial.

EXAMPLE 6 Finding all zeros of a polynomial function

Find all of the real and imaginary zeros for each polynomial function of Example 5.

a. $f(x) = 2x^3 - 3x^2 - 11x + 6$ **b.** $g(x) = 3x^3 - 8x^2 - 8x + 8$

Solution

a. The possible rational zeros of $f(x)$ are listed in Example 5(a). Use synthetic division to check each possible zero to see whether it is actually a zero. Try 1 first.

$$
\begin{array}{r|rrrr}
1 & 2 & -3 & -11 & 6 \\
  &   & 2 & -1 & -12 \\
\hline
  & 2 & -1 & -12 & -6
\end{array}
$$

Since the remainder is -6, 1 is not a zero of the function. Keep on trying numbers from the list of possible rational zeros. To save space, we will not show any more failures. So try 1/2 next.

$$
\begin{array}{r|rrrr}
\dfrac{1}{2} & 2 & -3 & -11 & 6 \\
  &   & 1 & -1 & -6 \\
\hline
  & 2 & -2 & -12 & 0
\end{array}
$$

Since the remainder in the synthetic division is 0, 1/2 is a zero of $f(x)$. By the factor theorem, $x - 1/2$ is a factor of the polynomial. The quotient is the other factor.

$$2x^3 - 3x^2 - 11x + 6 = 0$$

$$\left(x - \frac{1}{2}\right)(2x^2 - 2x - 12) = 0 \quad \text{Factor.}$$

$$(2x - 1)(x^2 - x - 6) = 0 \quad \begin{array}{l}\text{Factor 2 out of the second "factor"}\\ \text{and distribute it into the first factor.}\end{array}$$

$$(2x - 1)(x - 3)(x + 2) = 0 \quad \text{Factor completely.}$$

$$2x - 1 = 0 \quad \text{or} \quad x - 3 = 0 \quad \text{or} \quad x + 2 = 0$$

$$x = \frac{1}{2} \quad \text{or} \quad x = 3 \quad \text{or} \quad x = -2$$

The zeros of the function f are 1/2, 3, and -2. Note that each zero of f corresponds to an x-intercept on the graph of f shown in Fig. 22. Because this polynomial had three rational zeros, we could have found them all by using synthetic division or by examining the calculator graph. However, it is good to factor the polynomial to see the correspondence between the three zeros, the three factors, and the three x-intercepts.

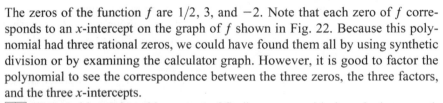 You could speed up this process of finding a zero with the calculator graph shown in Fig. 23. It is not too hard to discover that 1/2 is a zero by looking at the graph and the possible rational zeros that we listed in Example 5. If you use a graph to find that 1/2 is a zero, you still need to do synthetic division to factor the polynomial. □

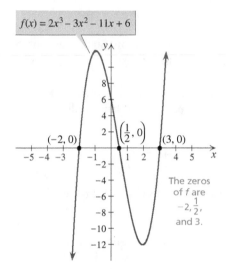

$f(x) = 2x^3 - 3x^2 - 11x + 6$

$(-2, 0)$ $\left(\dfrac{1}{2}, 0\right)$ $(3, 0)$

The zeros of f are $-2, \dfrac{1}{2},$ and 3.

Figure 22

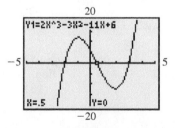

Figure 23

b. The possible rational zeros of $g(x)$ are listed in Example 5(b). First check 2/3 to see whether it produces a remainder of 0.

$$
\begin{array}{r|rrrr}
\dfrac{2}{3} & 3 & -8 & -8 & 8 \\
  &   & 2 & -4 & -8 \\
\hline
  & 3 & -6 & -12 & 0
\end{array}
$$

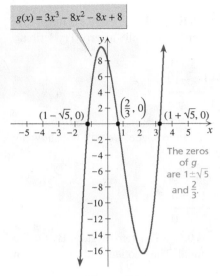

$g(x) = 3x^3 - 8x^2 - 8x + 8$

$(1 - \sqrt{5}, 0)$ $\left(\frac{2}{3}, 0\right)$ $(1 + \sqrt{5}, 0)$

The zeros
of g
are $1 \pm \sqrt{5}$
and $\frac{2}{3}$.

Figure 24

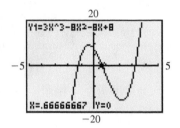

Y1=3X^3-8X2-8X+8

X=.66666667 Y=0

Figure 25

Since the remainder in the synthetic division is 0, 2/3 is a zero of $g(x)$. By the factor theorem, $x - 2/3$ is a factor of the polynomial. The quotient is the other factor.

$$3x^3 - 8x^2 - 8x + 8 = 0$$

$$\left(x - \frac{2}{3}\right)(3x^2 - 6x - 12) = 0$$

$$(3x - 2)(x^2 - 2x - 4) = 0$$

$$3x - 2 = 0 \quad \text{or} \quad x^2 - 2x - 4 = 0$$

$$x = \frac{2}{3} \quad \text{or} \qquad\qquad x = \frac{2 \pm \sqrt{20}}{2}$$

$$x = \frac{2}{3} \quad \text{or} \qquad\qquad x = 1 \pm \sqrt{5}$$

There are one rational and two irrational roots to the equation. So the zeros of the function g are 2/3, $1 + \sqrt{5}$, and $1 - \sqrt{5}$. Each zero corresponds to an x-intercept on the graph of g shown in Fig. 24.

You could graph the function with a calculator as shown in Fig. 25. Keeping in mind the list of possible rational zeros, it is not hard to discover that 2/3 is a zero.

▶**TRY THIS.** Find all zeros for $h(x) = 2x^3 + x^2 - 4x - 3$. ■

Note that in Example 6(a) all of the zeros were rational. All three could have been found by continuing to check the possible rational zeros using synthetic division. In Example 6(b) we would be wasting time if we continued to check the possible rational zeros, because there is only one. When we get a quadratic polynomial, it is best to either factor the quadratic polynomial or use the quadratic formula to find the remaining zeros. Of course, the remaining zeros could be imaginary, as is demonstrated in the next example.

EXAMPLE 7 Finding all zeros of a polynomial function

Find all real and imaginary zeros for each function.

a. $f(x) = 2x^3 - 11x^2 + 22x - 15$ **b.** $g(x) = x^4 + 3x^3 + x^2 + 15x - 20$

Solution

a. The possible rational zeros consist of all possible factors of 15 over factors of 2:

$$\pm 1, \ \pm 3, \ \pm 5, \ \pm 15, \ \pm\frac{1}{2}, \ \pm\frac{3}{2}, \ \pm\frac{5}{2}, \ \pm\frac{15}{2}$$

Now use synthetic division to check if any of these is actually a zero of the function. To save space, we will try 3/2 first:

$$
\begin{array}{r|rrrr}
\frac{3}{2} & 2 & -11 & 22 & -15 \\
  &   & 3 & -12 & 15 \\
\hline
  & 2 & -8 & 10 & 0 \\
\end{array}
$$

Since 0 is the remainder, 3/2 is a zero of $f(x)$. By the factor theorem $x - 3/2$ is a factor of the polynomial. The quotient is the other factor.

$$2x^3 - 11x^2 + 22x - 15 = 0$$

$$\left(x - \frac{3}{2}\right)(2x^2 - 8x + 10) = 0$$

$$(2x - 3)(x^2 - 4x + 5) = 0$$

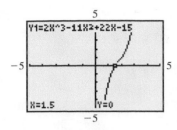

Figure 26

Apply the quadratic formula to $x^2 - 4x + 5 = 0$ to get

$$x = \frac{4 \pm \sqrt{(-4)^2 - 4(1)(5)}}{2(1)} = \frac{4 \pm \sqrt{-4}}{2} = \frac{4 \pm 2i}{2} = 2 \pm i.$$

So the zeros of the function are $3/2$, $2 - i$, and $2 + i$.

Note that the graph of $f(x) = 2x^3 - 11x^2 + 22x - 15$ in Fig. 26 has only one x-intercept because there is only one real zero to the function. □

b. The possible rational zeros consist of all possible factors of 20 over factors of 1:

$$\pm 1, \pm 2, \pm 4, \pm 5, \pm 10, \pm 20$$

Use synthetic division to check if any of these numbers is actually a zero of the function. To save space, we will try 1 and -4 first:

$$
\begin{array}{r|rrrrr}
1 & 1 & 3 & 1 & 15 & -20 \\
  &   & 1 & 4 & 5 & 20 \\
\hline
-4 & 1 & 4 & 5 & 20 & 0 \\
   &   & -4 & 0 & -20 & \\
\hline
   & 1 & 0 & 5 & 0 &
\end{array}
$$

Now we have $g(x) = (x - 1)(x + 4)(x^2 + 5)$. If $x^2 + 5 = 0$, then $x = \pm i\sqrt{5}$. So the zeros of $g(x)$ are 1, -4, and $\pm i\sqrt{5}$.

▶**TRY THIS.** Find all real and imaginary zeros to $f(x) = 3x^3 - 2x^2 + 12x - 8$. ■

►FOR thought... True or False? Explain.

1. The function $f(x) = 1/x$ has at least one zero.

2. If $P(x) = x^4 - 6x^2 - 8$ is divided by $x^2 - 2$, then the remainder is $P(\sqrt{2})$.

3. If $1 - 2i$ and $1 + 2i$ are zeros of $P(x) = x^3 - 5x^2 + 11x - 15$, then $x - 1 - 2i$ and $x - 1 + 2i$ are factors of $P(x)$.

4. If we divide $x^5 - 1$ by $x - 2$, then the remainder is 31.

5. Every polynomial function has at least one zero.

6. If $P(x) = x^3 - x^2 + 4x - 5$ and b is the remainder from division of $P(x)$ by $x - c$, then $b^3 - b^2 + 4b - 5 = c$.

7. If $P(x) = x^3 - 5x^2 + 4x - 15$, then $P(4) = 0$.

8. The equation $\pi^2 x^4 - \frac{1}{\sqrt{2}} x^3 + \frac{1}{\sqrt{7} + \pi} = 0$ has at least one complex solution.

9. The binomial $x - 1$ is a factor of $x^5 + x^4 - x^3 - x^2 - x + 1$.

10. The binomial $x + 3$ is a factor of $3x^4 - 5x^3 + 7x^2 - 9x - 2$.

►EXERCISES 2

Fill in the blank.

1. If $y = P(x)$ is a polynomial function and $P(w) = 0$, then w is a(n) _____ of the function.

2. If R is the _____ when a polynomial $P(x)$ is divided by $x - c$, then $R = P(c)$.

3. The number c is a(n) _____ of the polynomial function $y = P(x)$ if and only if $x - c$ is a(n) _____ of the polynomial $P(x)$.

4. If $y = P(x)$ is a polynomial function of positive degree, then $y = P(x)$ has at least one _____ in the set of _____.

Use ordinary division of polynomials to find the quotient and remainder when the first polynomial is divided by the second.

5. $x^2 - 5x + 7, x - 2$ **6.** $x^2 - 3x + 9, x - 4$

7. $-2x^3 + 4x - 9, x + 3$ **8.** $-4w^3 + 5w^2 - 7, w - 3$

9. $s^4 - 3s^2 + 6, s^2 - 5$ **10.** $h^4 + 3h^3 + h - 5, h^2 - 3$

Use synthetic division to find the quotient and remainder when the first polynomial is divided by the second.

11. $x^2 + 4x + 1, x - 2$ **12.** $2x^2 - 3x + 6, x - 5$

13. $-x^3 + x^2 - 4x + 9, x + 3$

14. $-3x^3 + 5x^2 - 6x + 1, x + 1$

15. $4x^3 - 5x + 2, x - \dfrac{1}{2}$ **16.** $-6x^3 + 25x^2 - 9, x - \dfrac{3}{2}$

17. $2a^3 - 3a^2 + 4a + 3, a + \dfrac{1}{2}$

18. $-3b^3 - b^2 - 3b - 1, b + \dfrac{1}{3}$

19. $x^4 - 3, x - 1$ **20.** $x^4 - 16, x - 2$

21. $x^5 - 6x^3 + 4x - 5, x - 2$

22. $2x^5 - 5x^4 - 5x + 7, x - 3$

Let $f(x) = x^5 - 1, g(x) = x^3 - 4x^2 + 8$, and $h(x) = 2x^4 + x^3 - x^2 + 3x + 3$. Find the following function values by using synthetic division. Check by using substitution.

23. $f(1)$ **24.** $f(-1)$ **25.** $f(-2)$ **26.** $f(3)$

27. $g(1)$ **28.** $g(-1)$ **29.** $g\left(-\dfrac{1}{2}\right)$ **30.** $g\left(\dfrac{1}{2}\right)$

31. $h(-1)$ **32.** $h(2)$ **33.** $h(1)$ **34.** $h(-3)$

Determine whether the given binomial is a factor of the polynomial following it. If it is a factor, then factor the polynomial completely.

35. $x + 3, x^3 + 4x^2 + x - 6$

36. $x + 5, x^3 + 8x^2 + 11x - 20$

37. $x - 4, x^3 + 4x^2 - 17x - 60$

38. $x - 2, x^3 - 12x^2 + 44x - 48$

Determine whether each given number is a zero of the polynomial function following the number.

39. $3, f(x) = 2x^3 - 5x^2 - 4x + 3$

40. $-2, g(x) = 3x^3 - 6x^2 - 3x - 19$

41. $-2, g(d) = d^3 + 2d^2 + 3d + 1$

42. $-1, w(x) = 3x^3 + 2x^2 - 2x - 1$

43. $-1, P(x) = x^4 + 2x^3 + 4x^2 + 6x + 3$

44. $3, G(r) = r^4 + 4r^3 + 5r^2 + 3r + 17$

45. $\dfrac{1}{2}, H(x) = x^3 + 3x^2 - 5x + 7$

46. $-\dfrac{1}{2}, T(x) = 2x^3 + 3x^2 - 3x - 2$

Use the rational zero theorem to find all possible rational zeros for each polynomial function.

47. $f(x) = x^3 - 9x^2 + 26x - 24$

48. $g(x) = x^3 - 2x^2 - 5x + 6$

49. $h(x) = x^3 - x^2 - 7x + 15$

50. $m(x) = x^3 + 4x^2 + 4x + 3$

51. $P(x) = 8x^3 - 36x^2 + 46x - 15$

52. $T(x) = 18x^3 - 9x^2 - 5x + 2$

53. $M(x) = 18x^3 - 21x^2 + 10x - 2$

54. $N(x) = 4x^3 - 10x^2 + 4x + 5$

Find all of the real and imaginary zeros for each polynomial function.

55. $f(x) = x^3 - 9x^2 + 26x - 24$

56. $g(x) = x^3 - 2x^2 - 5x + 6$

57. $h(x) = x^3 - x^2 - 7x + 15$

58. $m(x) = x^3 + 4x^2 + 4x + 3$

59. $P(a) = 8a^3 - 36a^2 + 46a - 15$

60. $T(b) = 18b^3 - 9b^2 - 5b + 2$

61. $M(t) = 18t^3 - 21t^2 + 10t - 2$

62. $N(t) = 4t^3 - 10t^2 + 4t + 5$

63. $y = x^3 - 26x + 60$ **64.** $y = x^3 - x^2 + 2$

65. $S(w) = w^4 + w^3 - w^2 + w - 2$

66. $W(v) = 2v^4 + 5v^3 + 3v^2 + 15v - 9$

67. $V(x) = x^4 + 2x^3 - x^2 - 4x - 2$

68. $U(x) = x^4 - 4x^3 + x^2 + 12x - 12$

69. $f(x) = 24x^3 - 26x^2 + 9x - 1$

70. $f(x) = 30x^3 - 47x^2 - x + 6$

71. $y = 16x^3 - 33x^2 + 82x - 5$

72. $y = 15x^3 - 37x^2 + 44x - 14$

73. $f(x) = 21x^4 - 31x^3 - 21x^2 - 31x - 42$

74. $f(x) = 119x^4 - 5x^3 + 214x^2 - 10x - 48$

75. $f(x) = (x^2 + 9)(x^3 + 6x^2 + 3x - 10)$

76. $f(x) = (x^2 - 5)(x^3 - 5x^2 - 12x + 36)$

77. $f(x) = (x^2 - 4x + 1)(x^3 - 9x^2 + 23x - 15)$

78. $f(x) = (x^2 - 4x + 13)(x^3 - 4x^2 - 17x + 60)$

Use division to write each rational expression in the form quotient + remainder/divisor. Use synthetic division when possible.

79. $\dfrac{2x + 1}{x - 2}$ **80.** $\dfrac{x - 1}{x + 3}$ **81.** $\dfrac{a^2 - 3a + 5}{a - 3}$

82. $\dfrac{2b^2 - 3b + 1}{b + 2}$ **83.** $\dfrac{c^2 - 3c - 4}{c^2 - 4}$ **84.** $\dfrac{2h^2 + h - 2}{h^2 - 1}$

85. $\dfrac{4t - 5}{2t + 1}$ **86.** $\dfrac{6y - 1}{3y - 1}$

Solve each problem.

87. *Drug Testing* The concentration of a drug (in parts per million) in a patient's bloodstream t hours after administration of the drug is given by the function

$$P(t) = -t^4 + 12t^3 - 58t^2 + 132t.$$

a. Use the formula to determine when the drug will be totally eliminated from the bloodstream.

b. Use the graph to estimate the maximum concentration of the drug.

c. Use the graph to estimate the time at which the maximum concentration occurs.

d. Use the graph to estimate the amount of time for which the concentration is above 80 ppm.

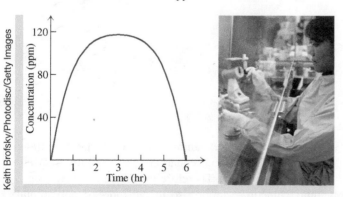

Figure for Exercise 87

88. *Open-Top Box* Joan intends to make an 18-in.³ open-top box out of a 6 in. by 7 in. piece of copper by cutting equal squares (x in. by x in.) from the corners and folding up the sides. Write the difference between the intended volume and the actual volume as a function of x. For what value of x is there no difference between the intended volume and the actual volume?

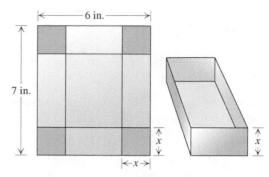

Figure for Exercise 88

89. *Cartridge Box* The height of a box containing an HP Laser Jet III printer cartridge is 4 in. more than the width and the length is 9 in. more than the width. If the volume of the box is 630 in.³, then what are the dimensions of the box?

90. *Computer Case* The width of the case for a 733-megahertz Pentium computer is 4 in. more than twice the height and the depth is 1 in. more than the width. If the volume of the case is 1632 in.³, then what are the dimensions of the case?

FOR WRITING/DISCUSSION

91. *Synthetic Division* Explain how synthetic division can be used to find the quotient and remainder when $3x^3 + 4x^2 + 2x - 4$ is divided by $3x - 2$.

92. Prove that if $x - c$ is a factor of $P(x)$, then c is a zero of the polynomial function.

▶ RETHINKING

93. Write the function $f(x) = 2x^2 - 3x + 1$ in the form $f(x) = a(x - h)^2 + k$.

94. Solve $2x^2 - 3x + 1 = 0$.

95. Solve $|3x + 7| \geq 0$. Write the solution set in interval notation.

96. Solve $2x - 9 = 5 - 4(3x + 2)$.

97. Factor completely.
 a. $24a^3 + 18a^2 - 60a$

 b. $x^5 - 16x$

98. Solve $8 - 6(x - 4) \leq 2(x - 5) - 4(2x - 1)$.

THINKING OUTSIDE THE BOX XXIII

Moving a Refrigerator A box containing a refrigerator is 3 ft wide, 3 ft deep, and 6 ft high. To move it, Wally lays it on its side, then on its top, then on its other side, and finally stands it upright as shown in the figure. Exactly how far has point A traveled in going from its initial location to its final location?

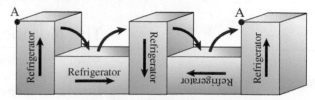

Figure for Thinking Outside the Box XXIII

311

POP QUIZ 2

1. Use ordinary division to find the quotient and remainder when $x^3 - 5x + 7$ is divided by $x + 4$.

2. Use synthetic division to find the quotient and remainder when $x^2 - 3x + 9$ is divided by $x - 5$.

3. Use synthetic division to find $f(3)$ if $f(x) = x^3 - 2x^2 + 4x - 1$.

4. List the possible rational zeros for $f(x) = 2x^3 - 3x + 8$.

5. Find all real and imaginary zeros for $f(x) = 2x^3 - x^2 + 18x - 9$.

LINKING

concepts... For Individual or Group Explorations

Horner's Method

A fourth-degree polynomial in x such as $3x^4 + 5x^3 + 4x^2 + 3x + 1$ contains all of the powers of x from the first through the fourth. However, any polynomial can be written without powers of x. Evaluating a polynomial without powers of x (Horner's method) is somewhat easier than evaluating a polynomial with powers.

a) Show that $\{[(3x + 5)x + 4]x + 3\}x + 1 = 3x^4 + 5x^3 + 4x^2 + 3x + 1$ is an identity.

b) Rewrite the polynomial $P(x) = 6x^5 - 3x^4 + 9x^3 + 6x^2 - 8x + 12$ without powers of x as in part (a).

c) Find $P(2)$ without a calculator using both forms of the polynomial.

d) For which form did you perform fewer arithmetic operations?

e) Explain in detail how to rewrite any polynomial without powers of x.

f) Explain how this new form relates to synthetic division and the remainder theorem.

3 The Theory of Equations

One of the main goals in algebra is to keep expanding our knowledge of solving equations. The solutions (roots) of a polynomial equation $P(x) = 0$ are precisely the zeros of a polynomial function $y = P(x)$. Therefore the theorems of Section 2 concerning zeros of polynomial functions apply also to the roots of polynomial equations. In this section we study several additional theorems that are useful in solving polynomial equations.

The Number of Roots of a Polynomial Equation

When a polynomial equation is solved by factoring, a factor may occur more than once. For example, $x^2 - 10x + 25 = 0$ is equivalent to $(x - 5)^2 = 0$. Since the factor $x - 5$ occurs twice, we say that 5 is a root of the equation with *multiplicity* 2.

Definition: Multiplicity

> If the factor $x - c$ occurs k times in the complete factorization of the polynomial $P(x)$, then c is called a root of $P(x) = 0$ with **multiplicity k**.

If a quadratic equation has a single root, as in $x^2 - 10x + 25 = 0$, then that root has multiplicity 2. If a root with multiplicity 2 is counted as two roots, then every quadratic equation has two roots in the set of complex numbers. This situation is generalized in the following theorem, where the phrase "when multiplicity is considered" means that a root with multiplicity k is counted as k individual roots.

n-Root Theorem

> If $P(x) = 0$ is a polynomial equation with real or complex coefficients and positive degree n, then, when multiplicity is considered, $P(x) = 0$ has n roots.

PROOF By the fundamental theorem of algebra, the polynomial equation $P(x) = 0$ with degree n has at least one complex root c_1. By the factor theorem, $P(x) = 0$ is equivalent to

$$(x - c_1)Q_1(x) = 0,$$

where $Q_1(x)$ is a polynomial with degree $n - 1$ (the quotient when $P(x)$ is divided by $x - c_1$). Again, by the fundamental theorem of algebra, there is at least one complex root c_2 of $Q_1(x) = 0$. By the factor theorem, $P(x) = 0$ can be written as

$$(x - c_1)(x - c_2)Q_2(x) = 0,$$

where $Q_2(x)$ is a polynomial with degree $n - 2$. Reasoning in this manner n times, we get a quotient polynomial that has 0 degree, n factors for $P(x)$, and n complex roots, not necessarily all different. ∎

EXAMPLE 1 Finding all roots of a polynomial equation

State the degree of each polynomial equation. Find all real and imaginary roots of each equation, stating multiplicity when it is greater than one.

a. $6x^5 + 24x^3 = 0$ **b.** $(x - 3)^2(x + 14)^5 = 0$

Solution

a. This fifth-degree equation can be solved by factoring:

$$6x^3(x^2 + 4) = 0$$

$$6x^3 = 0 \quad \text{or} \quad x^2 + 4 = 0$$

$$x^3 = 0 \quad \text{or} \quad x^2 = -4$$

$$x = 0 \quad \text{or} \quad x = \pm 2i$$

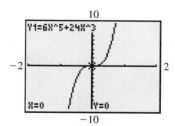

Figure 27

The roots are $\pm 2i$ and 0. Since there are two imaginary roots and 0 is a root with multiplicity 3, there are five roots when multiplicity is considered.

Because 0 is the only real root, the graph of $y = 6x^5 + 24x^3$ has only one x-intercept at $(0, 0)$ as shown in Fig. 27. □

b. The highest power of x in $(x - 3)^2$ is 2, and in $(x + 14)^5$ is 5. By the product rule for exponents, the highest power of x in this equation is 7. The only roots of this seventh-degree equation are 3 and -14. The root 3 has multiplicity 2, and -14 has multiplicity 5. So there are seven roots when multiplicity is considered.

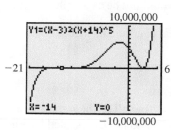

Figure 28

Because the equation has two real solutions, the graph of $y = (x - 3)^2(x + 14)^5$ has two x-intercepts at $(3, 0)$ and $(-14, 0)$ as shown in Fig. 28.

▶**TRY THIS.** Find all roots to $x^3(x + 2)^2(2x - 5) = 0$, including multiplicities. ∎

Note that graphing polynomial functions and solving polynomial equations go hand in hand. The solutions to the equation can help us find an appropriate viewing window for the graph as they did in Example 1, and the graph can help us find solutions to the equation.

The Conjugate Pairs Theorem

For second-degree polynomial equations, the imaginary roots occur in pairs. For example, the roots of $x^2 - 2x + 5 = 0$ are

$$x = \frac{2 \pm \sqrt{(-2)^2 - 4(1)(5)}}{2} = 1 \pm 2i.$$

The roots $1 - 2i$ and $1 + 2i$ are complex conjugates. The $\pm$ symbol in the quadratic formula causes the complex solutions of a quadratic equation with real coefficients to occur in conjugate pairs. The conjugate pairs theorem indicates that this situation occurs also for polynomial equations of higher degree.

Conjugate Pairs Theorem

> If $P(x) = 0$ is a polynomial equation with real coefficients and the complex number $a + bi$ $(b \neq 0)$ is a root, then $a - bi$ is also a root.

The proof for this theorem is left for the exercises.

EXAMPLE 2 | Using the conjugate pairs theorem

Find a polynomial equation with real coefficients that has 2 and $1 - i$ as roots.

Solution

If the polynomial has real coefficients, then its imaginary roots occur in conjugate pairs. So a polynomial with these two roots must actually have at least three roots: $2, 1 - i$, and $1 + i$. Since each root of the equation corresponds to a factor of the polynomial, we can write the following equation.

$$(x - 2)[x - (1 - i)][x - (1 + i)] = 0$$
$$(x - 2)[(x - 1) + i][(x - 1) - i] = 0 \quad \text{Regroup.}$$
$$(x - 2)[(x - 1)^2 - i^2] = 0 \quad (a + b)(a - b) = a^2 - b^2$$
$$(x - 2)[x^2 - 2x + 1 + 1] = 0 \quad i^2 = -1$$
$$(x - 2)(x^2 - 2x + 2) = 0$$
$$x^3 - 4x^2 + 6x - 4 = 0$$

This equation has the required roots and the smallest degree. Any multiple of this equation would also have the required roots but would not be as simple.

▶**TRY THIS.** Find a polynomial equation with real coefficients that has 3 and $-i$ as roots. ■

Descartes's Rule of Signs

None of the theorems in this chapter tells us how to find all of the n roots to a polynomial equation of degree n. However, the theorems and rules presented here add to our knowledge of polynomial equations and help us to predict the type and number of solutions to expect for a particular equation. Descartes's rule of signs is a method for determining the number of positive, negative, and imaginary solutions. For this rule, a solution with multiplicity k is counted as k solutions.

HISTORICAL NOTE

Évariste Galois (1811–1832) was a French mathematician. While still in his teens, he was able to determine a necessary and sufficient condition for a polynomial equation to be solvable by radicals, thereby solving a long-standing problem. His work laid the fundamental foundations for Galois theory, a major branch of abstract algebra.

Galois died in a duel at the age of twenty.

Polynomial and Rational Functions

When a polynomial is written in descending order, a **variation of sign** occurs when the signs of consecutive terms change. For example, if

$$P(x) = 3x^5 - 7x^4 - 8x^3 - x^2 + 3x - 9,$$

there are sign changes in going from the first to the second term, from the fourth to the fifth term, and from the fifth to the sixth term. So there are three variations of sign for $P(x)$. This information determines the number of positive real solutions to $P(x) = 0$. Descartes's rule requires that we look at $P(-x)$ and also count the variations of sign after it is simplified:

$$P(-x) = 3(-x)^5 - 7(-x)^4 - 8(-x)^3 - (-x)^2 + 3(-x) - 9$$
$$= -3x^5 - 7x^4 + 8x^3 - x^2 - 3x - 9$$

In $P(-x)$ the signs of the terms change from the second to the third term and again from the third to the fourth term. So there are two variations of sign for $P(-x)$. This information determines the number of negative real solutions to $P(x) = 0$.

Descartes's Rule of Signs

Suppose $P(x) = 0$ is a polynomial equation with real coefficients and with terms written in descending order.

- The number of positive real roots of the equation is either equal to the number of variations of sign of $P(x)$ or less than that by an even number.
- The number of negative real roots of the equation is either equal to the number of variations of sign of $P(-x)$ or less than that by an even number.

The proof of Descartes's rule of signs is beyond the scope of this text, but we can apply the rule to polynomial equations. Descartes's rule of signs is especially helpful when the number of variations of sign is 0 or 1.

EXAMPLE 3 Using Descartes's rule of signs

Discuss the possibilities for the roots to $2x^3 - 5x^2 - 6x + 4 = 0$.

Solution

The number of variations of sign in

$$P(x) = 2x^3 - 5x^2 - 6x + 4$$

is 2. By Descartes's rule, the number of positive real roots is either 2 or 0. Since

$$P(-x) = 2(-x)^3 - 5(-x)^2 - 6(-x) + 4$$
$$= -2x^3 - 5x^2 + 6x + 4,$$

there is one variation of sign in $P(-x)$. So there is exactly one negative real root.

The equation must have three roots, because it is a third-degree polynomial equation. Since there must be three roots and one is negative, the other two roots must be either both imaginary numbers or both positive real numbers. Table 1 summarizes these two possibilities.

Table 1 Number of roots

Positive	Negative	Imaginary
2	1	0
0	1	2

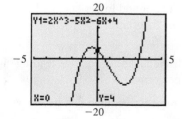

Figure 29

The graph of $y = 2x^3 - 5x^2 - 6x + 4$ shown in Fig. 29 crosses the positive x-axis twice and the negative x-axis once. So the first case in Table 1 is actually correct.

▶**TRY THIS.** Discuss the possibilities for the roots to $x^3 - 5x^2 + 4x + 3 = 0$. ∎

315

EXAMPLE 4 Using Descartes's rule of signs

Discuss the possibilities for the roots to each equation.

a. $3x^4 - 5x^3 - x^2 - 8x + 4 = 0$ **b.** $3x^3 + 4x^2 + 5 = 0$

Solution

a. There are two variations of sign in the polynomial

$$P(x) = 3x^4 - 5x^3 - x^2 - 8x + 4.$$

According to Descartes's rule, there are either two or zero positive real roots to the equation. Since

$$P(-x) = 3(-x)^4 - 5(-x)^3 - (-x)^2 - 8(-x) + 4$$
$$= 3x^4 + 5x^3 - x^2 + 8x + 4,$$

there are two variations of sign in $P(-x)$. So the number of negative real roots is either two or zero. Since the degree of the polynomial is 4, there must be four roots. Each line of Table 2 gives a possible distribution of the type of those four roots. Note that the number of imaginary roots is even in each case, as we would expect from the conjugate pairs theorem.

Table 2 Number of roots

Positive	Negative	Imaginary
2	2	0
2	0	2
0	2	2
0	0	4

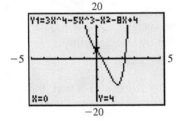

Figure 30

The calculator graph of $y = 3x^4 - 5x^3 - x^2 - 8x + 4$ in Fig. 30 shows two positive intercepts and no negative intercepts. However, we might not have the appropriate viewing window. The negative intercepts might be less than -5. In this case the graph did not allow us to conclude which line in Table 2 is correct. □

b. There are no variations of sign in $P(x) = 3x^3 + 4x^2 + 5$. So there are no positive real roots to the equation. Since

$$P(-x) = -3x^3 + 4x^2 + 5,$$

there is one variation of sign in $P(-x)$. So there is exactly one negative real root. Note that zero is not a root. Since the degree of the polynomial is 3, there must be 3 complex roots. Thus there is one negative real root and two imaginary roots.

▶**TRY THIS.** Discuss the possibilities for the roots to $x^4 - 6x^2 + 10 = 0$. ■

Bounds on the Roots

If a polynomial equation has no roots greater than c, then c is called an **upper bound** for the roots. If there are no roots less than c, then c is called a **lower bound** for the roots. The next theorem is used to determine upper and lower bounds for the roots of a polynomial equation. We will not prove this theorem.

Theorem on Bounds

Suppose that $P(x)$ is a polynomial with real coefficients and a positive leading coefficient, and synthetic division with $x - c$ is performed.

■ If $c > 0$ and all terms in the bottom row are nonnegative, then c is an upper bound for the roots of $P(x) = 0$.

■ If $c < 0$ and the terms in the bottom row alternate in sign, then c is a lower bound for the roots of $P(x) = 0$.

If 0 appears in the bottom row of the synthetic division, then it may be assigned either a positive or negative sign in determining whether the signs alternate. For example, the numbers 3, 0, 5, and -6 would be alternating in sign if we assign a negative sign to 0. The numbers $-7, 5, -8, 0,$ and -2 would be alternating in sign if we assign a positive sign to 0.

EXAMPLE 5 | Finding bounds for the roots

Use the theorem on bounds to establish the best integral bounds for the roots of $2x^3 - 5x^2 - 6x + 4 = 0$.

Solution

Try synthetic division with the integers 1, 2, 3, and so on. The first integer for which all terms on the bottom row are nonnegative is the best upper bound for the roots according to the theorem on bounds. Note that we are not trying fractions because we are looking for integral bounds for the roots and not the actual roots.

$$
\begin{array}{r|rrrr}
1 & 2 & -5 & -6 & 4 \\
  &   & 2 & -3 & -9 \\
\hline
  & 2 & -3 & -9 & -5 \\
\end{array}
\qquad
\begin{array}{r|rrrr}
2 & 2 & -5 & -6 & 4 \\
  &   & 4 & -2 & -16 \\
\hline
  & 2 & -1 & -8 & -12 \\
\end{array}
$$

$$
\begin{array}{r|rrrr}
3 & 2 & -5 & -6 & 4 \\
  &   & 6 & 3 & -9 \\
\hline
  & 2 & 1 & -3 & -5 \\
\end{array}
\qquad
\begin{array}{r|rrrr}
4 & 2 & -5 & -6 & 4 \\
  &   & 8 & 12 & 24 \\
\hline
  & 2 & 3 & 6 & 28 \\
\end{array}
$$

By the theorem on bounds, no number greater than 4 can be a root to the equation. Now try synthetic division with the integers $-1, -2, -3,$ and so on. The first negative integer for which the terms on the bottom row alternate in sign is the best lower bound for the roots.

$$
\begin{array}{r|rrrr}
-1 & 2 & -5 & -6 & 4 \\
   &   & -2 & 7 & -1 \\
\hline
   & 2 & -7 & 1 & 3 \\
\end{array}
\qquad
\begin{array}{r|rrrr}
-2 & 2 & -5 & -6 & 4 \\
   &   & -4 & 18 & -24 \\
\hline
   & 2 & -9 & 12 & -20 \\
\end{array}
$$

By the theorem on bounds, no number less than -2 can be a root to the equation. So all of the real roots to this equation are between -2 and 4.

The graph of $y = 2x^3 - 5x^2 - 6x + 4$ in Fig. 31 shows three x-intercepts between -2 and 4, which supports our conclusion about the bounds for the roots. Note that the bounds for the roots help you determine a good window.

▶**TRY THIS.** Use the theorem on bounds to establish the best integral bounds for the roots to $x^3 + 3x^2 - 5x - 15 = 0$. ■

In the next example we use all of the available information about roots.

EXAMPLE 6 | Using all of the theorems about roots

Find all of the solutions to $2x^3 - 5x^2 - 6x + 4 = 0$.

Solution

In Example 3 we used Descartes's rule of signs on this equation to determine that it has either two positive roots and one negative root or one negative root and two imaginary roots. In Example 5 we used the theorem on bounds to determine that all of the real roots to this equation are between -2 and 4. From the rational zero theorem, the possible rational roots are $\pm 1, \pm 2, \pm 4,$ and $\pm 1/2$. Since there must be one negative root and it must be greater than -2, the only possible numbers from

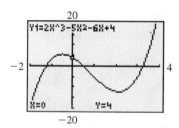

Figure 31

the list are -1 and $-1/2$. So start by checking $-1/2$ and -1 with synthetic division.

$$
\begin{array}{r|rrrr}
-\dfrac{1}{2} & 2 & -5 & -6 & 4 \\
 & & -1 & 3 & \dfrac{3}{2} \\
\hline
 & 2 & -6 & -3 & \dfrac{11}{2}
\end{array}
\qquad
\begin{array}{r|rrrr}
-1 & 2 & -5 & -6 & 4 \\
 & & -2 & 7 & -1 \\
\hline
 & 2 & -7 & 1 & 3
\end{array}
$$

Since neither -1 nor $-1/2$ is a root, the negative root must be irrational. The only rational possibilities for the two positive roots smaller than 4 are $1/2$, 1, and 2.

$$
\begin{array}{r|rrrr}
\dfrac{1}{2} & 2 & -5 & -6 & 4 \\
 & & 1 & -2 & -4 \\
\hline
 & 2 & -4 & -8 & 0
\end{array}
$$

Since $1/2$ is a root of the equation, $x - 1/2$ is a factor of the polynomial. The last line in the synthetic division indicates that the other factor is $2x^2 - 4x - 8$.

$$\left(x - \frac{1}{2}\right)(2x^2 - 4x - 8) = 0$$

$$(2x - 1)(x^2 - 2x - 4) = 0$$

$$2x - 1 = 0 \quad \text{or} \quad x^2 - 2x - 4 = 0$$

$$x = \frac{1}{2} \quad \text{or} \qquad x = \frac{2 \pm \sqrt{4 - 4(1)(-4)}}{2} = 1 \pm \sqrt{5}$$

There are two positive roots, $1/2$ and $1 + \sqrt{5}$. The negative root is $1 - \sqrt{5}$. Note that the roots guaranteed by Descartes's rule of signs are real numbers but not necessarily rational numbers.

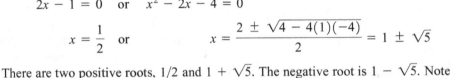 The graph of $y = 2x^3 - 5x^2 - 6x + 4$ in Fig. 32 supports these conclusions, because its x-intercepts appear to be $(1 - \sqrt{5}, 0)$, $(1/2, 0)$, and $(1 + \sqrt{5}, 0)$.

▶**TRY THIS.** Find all solutions to $2x^3 - 5x^2 - 8x + 5 = 0$. ∎

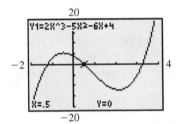

Figure 32

FOR thought... True or False? Explain.

1. The number 1 is a root of $x^3 - 1 = 0$ with multiplicity 3.

2. The equation $x^3 = 125$ has three complex number solutions.

3. For $(x + 1)^3(x^2 - 2x + 1) = 0$, -1 is a root with multiplicity 3.

4. For $(x - 5)^3(x^2 - 3x - 10) = 0$, 5 is a root with multiplicity 3.

5. If $4 - 5i$ is a solution to a polynomial equation with real coefficients, then $5i - 4$ is also a solution to the equation.

6. If $P(x) = 0$ is a polynomial equation with real coefficients and i, $2 - 3i$, and $5 + 7i$ are roots, then the degree of $P(x)$ is at least 6.

7. Both $-3 - i\sqrt{5}$ and $3 - i\sqrt{5}$ are solutions to $5x^3 - 9x^2 + 17x - 23 = 0$.

8. Both $3/2$ and 2 are solutions to $2x^5 - 4x^3 - 6x^2 - 3x - 6 = 0$.

9. The equation $x^3 - 5x^2 + 6x - 1 = 0$ has no negative roots.

10. The equation $5x^3 - 171 = 0$ has two imaginary solutions.

EXERCISES 3

Fill in the blank.

1. If the factor $x - c$ occurs k times in the complete factorization of the polynomial $P(x)$, then c is a root of $P(x) = 0$ with _____ k.

2. If $P(x) = 0$ is a polynomial equation with real or complex coefficients and positive degree n, then, counting multiplicity, $P(x) = 0$ has _____ roots.

3. If $P(x) = 0$ is a polynomial equation with real coefficients and the complex number $a + bi$ $(b \neq 0)$ is a root, then _____ is also a root.

4. If a polynomial equation has no root greater than c, then c is a(n) _____ for the roots.

State the degree of each polynomial equation. Find all of the real and imaginary roots of each equation, stating multiplicity when it is greater than one.

5. $x^2 - 10x + 25 = 0$

6. $x^2 - 18x + 81 = 0$

7. $x^5 - 9x^3 = 0$

8. $x^6 + x^4 = 0$

9. $x^4 - 2x^3 + x^2 = 0$

10. $x^5 - 6x^4 + 9x^3 = 0$

11. $(2x - 3)^2 (3x + 4)^2 = 0$

12. $(2x^2 + x)^2 (3x - 1)^4 = 0$

13. $x^3 - 4x^2 - 6x = 0$

14. $-x^3 + 8x^2 - 14x = 0$

Find each product.

15. $(x - 3i)(x + 3i)$

16. $(x + 6i)(x - 6i)$

17. $[x - (1 + \sqrt{2})][x - (1 - \sqrt{2})]$

18. $[x - (3 - \sqrt{5})][x - (3 + \sqrt{5})]$

19. $[x - (3 + 2i)][x - (3 - 2i)]$

20. $[x - (3 - i)][x - (3 + i)]$

21. $(x - 2)[x - (3 + 4i)][x - (3 - 4i)]$

22. $(x + 1)[x - (1 - i)][x - (1 + i)]$

Find a polynomial equation with real coefficients that has the given roots.

23. $-3, 5$ **24.** $6, -1$ **25.** $-4i, 4i$ **26.** $-9i, 9i$

27. $3 - i$ **28.** $4 + i$ **29.** $-2, i$ **30.** $4, -i$

31. $0, i\sqrt{3}$ **32.** $-2, i\sqrt{2}$ **33.** $3, 1 - i$ **34.** $5, 4 - 3i$

35. $1, 2, 3$ **36.** $-1, 2, -3$ **37.** $1, 2 - 3i$

38. $-1, 4 - 2i$ **39.** $\dfrac{1}{2}, \dfrac{1}{3}, \dfrac{1}{4}$ **40.** $-\dfrac{1}{2}, -\dfrac{1}{3}, 1$

41. $i, 1 + i$ **42.** $3i, 3 - i$

Use Descartes's rule of signs to discuss the possibilities for the roots of each equation. Do not solve the equation.

43. $x^3 + 5x^2 + 7x + 1 = 0$ **44.** $2x^3 - 3x^2 + 5x - 6 = 0$

45. $-x^3 - x^2 + 7x + 6 = 0$ **46.** $-x^4 - 5x^2 - x + 7 = 0$

47. $y^4 + 5y^2 + 7 = 0$ **48.** $-3y^4 - 6y^2 + 7 = 0$

49. $t^4 - 3t^3 + 2t^2 - 5t + 7 = 0$

50. $-5r^4 + 4r^3 + 7r - 16 = 0$

51. $x^5 + x^3 + 5x = 0$ **52.** $x^4 - x^2 + 1 = 0$

Use the theorem on bounds to establish the best integral bounds for the roots of each equation.

53. $2x^3 - 5x^2 + 6 = 0$ **54.** $2x^3 - x^2 - 5x + 3 = 0$

55. $4x^3 + 8x^2 - 11x - 15 = 0$

56. $6x^3 + 5x^2 - 36x - 35 = 0$

57. $w^4 - 5w^3 + 3w^2 + 2w - 1 = 0$

58. $3z^4 - 7z^2 + 5 = 0$

59. $-2x^3 + 5x^2 - 3x + 9 = 0$ **60.** $-x^3 + 8x - 12 = 0$

Use the rational zero theorem, Descartes's rule of signs, and the theorem on bounds as aids in finding all real and imaginary roots to each equation.

61. $x^3 - 4x^2 - 7x + 10 = 0$

62. $x^3 + 9x^2 + 26x + 24 = 0$

63. $x^3 - 10x - 3 = 0$ **64.** $2x^3 - 7x^2 - 16 = 0$

65. $x^4 + 2x^3 - 7x^2 + 2x - 8 = 0$

66. $x^4 - 4x^3 + 7x^2 - 16x + 12 = 0$

67. $6x^3 + 25x^2 - 24x + 5 = 0$

68. $6x^3 - 11x^2 - 46x - 24 = 0$

69. $x^4 + 2x^3 - 3x^2 - 4x + 4 = 0$

70. $x^5 + 3x^3 + 2x = 0$

71. $x^4 - 6x^3 + 12x^2 - 8x = 0$

72. $x^4 + 9x^3 + 27x^2 + 27x = 0$

73. $x^6 - x^5 - x^4 + x^3 - 12x^2 + 12x = 0$

74. $2x^7 - 2x^6 + 7x^5 - 7x^4 - 4x^3 + 4x^2 = 0$

75. $8x^5 + 2x^4 - 33x^3 + 4x^2 + 25x - 6 = 0$

76. $6x^5 + x^4 - 28x^3 - 3x^2 + 16x - 4 = 0$

For each of the following functions use synthetic division and the theorem on bounds to find integers a and b, such that the interval (a, b) contains all real zeros of the function. This method does not necessarily give the shortest interval containing all real zeros. By inspecting the graph of each function, find the shortest interval (c, d) that contains all real zeros of the function with c and d integers. The second interval should be a subinterval of the first.

77. $y = 2x^3 - 3x^2 - 50x + 18$ **78.** $f(x) = x^3 - 33x - 58$

79. $f(x) = x^4 - 26x^2 + 153$

80. $y = x^4 + x^3 - 16x^2 - 10x + 60$

81. $y = 4x^3 - 90x^2 - 2x + 45$

82. $f(x) = x^4 - 12x^3 + 27x^2 - 6x - 8$

Solve each problem.

83. *Growth Rate for Bacteria* The instantaneous growth rate of a population is the rate at which it is growing at every instant in time. The instantaneous growth rate r of a colony of bacteria t hours after the start of an experiment is given by the function

$$r = 0.01t^3 - 0.08t^2 + 0.11t + 0.20$$

for $0 \leq t \leq 7$. Find the times for which the instantaneous growth rate is zero.

84. *Retail Store Profit* The manager of a retail store has figured that her monthly profit P (in thousands of dollars) is determined by her monthly advertising expense x (in tens of thousands of dollars) according to the formula

$$P = x^3 - 20x^2 + 100x \quad \text{for} \quad 0 \leq x \leq 4.$$

For what value of x does she get \$147,000 in profit?

85. *Designing Fireworks* Marshall is designing a rocket for the Red Rocket Fireworks Company. The rocket will consist of a cardboard circular cylinder with a height that is four times as large as the radius. On top of the cylinder will be a cone with a height of 2 in. and a radius equal to the radius of the base as shown in the figure. If he wants to fill the cone and the cylinder with a total of 114π in.^{3} of powder, then what should be the radius of the cylinder?

HINT Use the formulas for the volume of a cone and a cylinder, which can be found inside the back cover of this text.

Figure for Exercise 85

86. *Heating and Air* An observatory is built in the shape of a right circular cylinder with a hemispherical roof as shown in the figure. The heating and air contractor has figured the volume of the structure as 3168π ft^3. If the height of the cylindrical

walls is 2 ft more than the radius of the building, then what is the radius of the building?

HINT Use the formulas for the volume of a sphere and a cylinder.

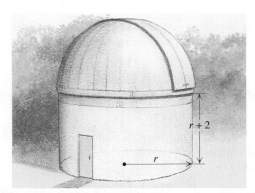

Figure for Exercise 86

FOR WRITING/DISCUSSION

87. *Conjugate of a Sum* Show that the conjugate of the sum of two complex numbers is equal to the sum of their conjugates.

88. *Conjugate of a Product* Show that the conjugate of the product of two complex numbers is equal to the product of their conjugates.

89. *Conjugate of a Real Number* Show that $\bar{a} = a$ for any real number a, where $\bar{a}$ is the conjugate of a.

90. *Conjugate Pairs* Assume that $a + bi$ is a root of $a_nx^n + a_{n-1}x^{n-1} + \cdots + a_1x + a_0 = 0$ and substitute $a + bi$ for x. Take the conjugate of each side of the resulting equation and use the results of Exercises 87–89 to simplify it. Your final equation should show that $a - bi$ is a root of $a_nx^n + a_{n-1}x^{n-1} + \cdots + a_1x + a_0 = 0$. This proves the conjugate pairs theorem.

91. *Finding Polynomials* Find a third-degree polynomial function such that $f(0) = 3$ and whose zeros are 1, 2, and 3. Explain how you found it.

92. *Finding Polynomials* Is there a third-degree polynomial function such that $f(0) = 6$ and $f(-1) = 12$ and whose zeros are 1, 2, and 3? Explain.

▶ RETHINKING

93. Use the rational zeros theorem to list the possible rational zeros to the function $f(x) = 2x^3 - 5x^2 + 7x - 6$.

94. Solve the inequality $x^2 - 4x + 3 \geq 0$. Write the solution set using interval notation.

95. Suppose that b is the number of prime numbers in the interval $(0, a)$ where a is a positive integer. Determine whether a is a function of b, b is a function of a, or neither.

96. A gambler drove from Newark to Atlantic City. On the return trip he was broke and decreased his average speed by one-third to save gas. By what percent did his time increase for the return trip?

97. Let $f(x) = 2x^2 - 9$ and $g(x) = 2x - 4$. Find $(f \circ g)(x)$.

98. Find the equation of the line through $(2, 4)$ that is parallel to the line $x = 6$.

THINKING OUTSIDE THE BOX XXIV

Packing Billiard Balls There are several ways to tightly pack nine billiard balls each with radius 1 into a rectangular box. Find the volume of the box in each of the following cases and determine which box has the least volume.

a. Four balls are placed so that they just fit into the bottom of the box, then another layer of four, then one ball in the middle tangent to all four in the second layer, as shown in this side view.

b. Four balls are placed so that they just fit into the bottom of the box as in (a), then one is placed in the middle on top of the first four. Finally, four more are placed so that they just fit at the top of the box.

c. The box is packed with layers of four, one, and four as in (b), but the box is required to be cubic. In this case, the four balls in

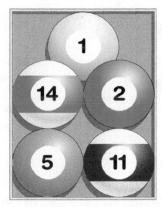

Figure for Thinking Outside the Box XXIV

the bottom layer will not touch each other and the four balls in the top layer will not touch each other. The ball in the middle will be tangent to all of the other eight balls.

► POP QUIZ 3

1. Find all real and imaginary roots to $x^5 - x^3 = 0$, including multiplicities.

2. Find a polynomial equation with real coefficients that has the roots $-4i$ and 5.

3. By Descartes's rule of signs, how many positive roots can $x^4 + x^3 - 3x^2 + 5x + 9 = 0$ have?

4. By Descartes's rule of signs, how many negative roots can $3x^3 + 5x^2 - x + 9 = 0$ have?

5. Find all real and imaginary roots to $x^3 - 3x^2 - 6x + 8 = 0$.

► LINKING

concepts... For Individual or Group Explorations

Designing a Crystal Ball

The wizard Gandalf is creating a massive crystal ball. To achieve maximum power, the orb must be a perfect solid sphere of clear crystal mounted on a square solid silver base, as shown in the figure.

a) Write a formula for the total volume of material used in terms of the radius of the sphere, the thickness of the base, and the length of the side of the base.

b) The wizard has determined that the diameter of the sphere must equal the length of the side of the square base, and the thickness of the base must be π in. Find the exact radius of the sphere if the total amount of material used in the sphere and base must be 1296π in.[3].

c) If it turns out that the sphere in part (b) is not powerful enough, Gandalf plans to make a sphere and base of solid dilithium crystal. For this project the diameter of the sphere must be 2 in. less than the length of the side of the base and the thickness of the base must be 2 in. Find the approximate radius of the sphere if the total volume of material used in the sphere and base must be 5000 in.[3].

4 Miscellaneous Equations

In Section 3 we learned that an nth-degree polynomial equation has n roots. However, it is not always obvious how to find them. In this section we will solve polynomial equations using some new techniques and we will solve several other types of equations. Unfortunately, we cannot generally predict the number of roots to nonpolynomial equations.

Factoring Higher-Degree Equations

We can solve quadratic equations by factoring and setting the factors equal to zero. We use the zero factor property, which we restate here.

Zero Factor Property

> If A and B are algebraic expressions, then the equation $AB = 0$ is equivalent to the compound statement $A = 0$ or $B = 0$.

This property holds true also for any number of factors. So if we can factor a higher-degree polynomial equation, we can set each factor equal to zero and solve the resulting equations. This is often the easiest method for solving a higher-degree polynomial equation.

EXAMPLE 1 Solving an equation by factoring

Solving each equation.

a. $x^3 + 3x^2 + x + 3 = 0$ **b.** $30x^3 + 16x^2 - 24x = 0$

Solution

a. Factor the polynomial on the left-hand side by grouping.

$$x^2(x + 3) + 1(x + 3) = 0 \quad \text{Factor by grouping.}$$
$$(x^2 + 1)(x + 3) = 0 \quad \text{Factor out } x + 3.$$
$$x^2 + 1 = 0 \quad \text{or} \quad x + 3 = 0 \quad \text{Zero factor property}$$
$$x^2 = -1 \quad \text{or} \quad x = -3$$
$$x = \pm i \quad \text{or} \quad x = -3$$

The solution set is $\{-3, -i, i\}$.

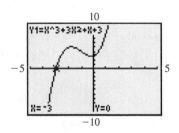

Figure 33

The graph in Fig. 33 supports these solutions. Because there is only one real solution, the graph crosses the x-axis only once. □

b. First factor out the common factor $2x$:

$$30x^3 + 16x^2 - 24x = 0$$
$$2x(15x^2 + 8x - 12) = 0 \quad \text{Factor out the GCF } 2x.$$
$$2x(3x - 2)(5x + 6) = 0 \quad \text{Factor the trinomial.}$$
$$2x = 0 \quad \text{or} \quad 3x - 2 = 0 \quad \text{or} \quad 5x + 6 = 0 \quad \text{Zero factor property}$$
$$x = 0 \quad \text{or} \quad x = \frac{2}{3} \quad \text{or} \quad x = -\frac{6}{5}$$

The solution set is $\left\{-\frac{6}{5}, 0, \frac{2}{3}\right\}$. You should check by graphing the corresponding polynomial function. It should have three x-intercepts.

▶**TRY THIS.** Solve $x^3 - 2x^2 + 5x - 10 = 0$ by factoring. ∎

EXAMPLE 2 Solving an equation by factoring

Solve $2x^5 = 16x^2$.

Solution

Write the equation with 0 on the right-hand side, then factor completely.

$$2x^5 - 16x^2 = 0$$

$$2x^2(x^3 - 8) = 0 \quad \text{Factor out the greatest common factor.}$$

$$2x^2(x - 2)(x^2 + 2x + 4) = 0 \quad \text{Factor the difference of two cubes.}$$

$$2x^2 = 0 \quad \text{or} \quad x - 2 = 0 \quad \text{or} \quad x^2 + 2x + 4 = 0$$

$$x = 0 \quad \text{or} \quad x = 2 \quad \text{or} \quad x = \frac{-2 \pm \sqrt{-12}}{2} = -1 \pm i\sqrt{3}$$

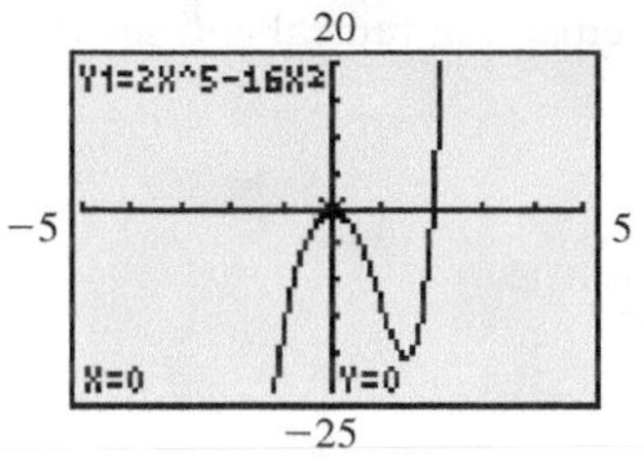

The solution set is $\{0, 2, -1 \pm i\sqrt{3}\}$. Since 0 is a root with multiplicity 2, there are five roots, counting multiplicity, to this fifth-degree equation.
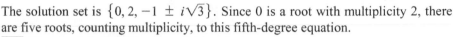 The graph in Fig. 34 supports this solution.

▶**TRY THIS.** Solve $x^5 = 27x^2$. ■

Figure 34

Note that in Example 2, if we had divided each side by x^2 as our first step, we would have lost the solution $x = 0$. *We do not usually divide each side of an equation by a variable expression.* Instead, bring all expressions to the same side and factor out the common factors.

Equations Involving Square Roots

Recall that $\sqrt{x}$ represents the nonnegative square root of x. To solve $\sqrt{x} = 3$ we can use the definition of square root. Since the nonnegative square root of 9 is 3, the solution to $\sqrt{x} = 3$ is 9. To solve $\sqrt{x} = -3$ we again use the definition of square root. Because $\sqrt{x}$ is nonnegative while -3 is negative, this equation has no solution.

More complicated equations involving square roots are usually solved by squaring both sides. However, squaring both sides does not always lead to an equivalent equation. If we square both sides of $\sqrt{x} = 3$, we get $x = 9$, which is equivalent to $\sqrt{x} = 3$. But if we square both sides of $\sqrt{x} = -3$, we also get $x = 9$, which is not equivalent to $\sqrt{x} = -3$. Because 9 appeared in the attempt to solve $\sqrt{x} = -3$, but does not satisfy the equation, it is called an *extraneous root*. This same situation can occur with an equation involving a fourth root or any other even root. So if you raise each side of an equation to an even power, you must check for extraneous roots.

EXAMPLE 3 Squaring each side to solve an equation

Solve $\sqrt{x} + 2 = x$.

Solution

Isolate the radical before squaring each side.

$$\sqrt{x} = x - 2$$

$$(\sqrt{x})^2 = (x - 2)^2 \quad \text{Square each side.}$$

$$x = x^2 - 4x + 4 \quad \text{Use the special product } (a - b)^2 = a^2 - 2ab + b^2.$$

$$0 = x^2 - 5x + 4 \quad \text{Write in the form } ax^2 + bx + c = 0.$$

$$0 = (x - 4)(x - 1) \quad \text{Factor the quadratic polynomial.}$$

$$x - 4 = 0 \quad \text{or} \quad x - 1 = 0 \quad \text{Zero factor property}$$

$$x = 4 \quad \text{or} \quad x = 1$$

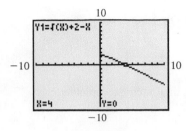

Figure 35

Checking $x = 4$, we get $\sqrt{4} + 2 = 4$, which is correct. Checking $x = 1$, we get $\sqrt{1} + 2 = 1$, which is incorrect. So 1 is an extraneous root and the solution set is $\{4\}$.

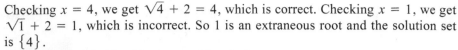 The graph in Fig. 35 supports this solution.

▶**TRY THIS.** Solve $\sqrt{x} + 12 = x$. ∎

The next example involves two radicals. In this example we will isolate the more complicated radical before squaring each side. But not all radicals are eliminated upon squaring each side. So we isolate the remaining radical and square each side again.

EXAMPLE 4 Squaring each side twice

Solve $\sqrt{2x + 1} - \sqrt{x} = 1$.

Solution

First we write the equation so that the more complicated radical is isolated. Then we square each side. On the left side, when we square $\sqrt{2x + 1}$, we get $2x + 1$. On the right side, when we square $1 + \sqrt{x}$, we use the special product rule $(a + b)^2 = a^2 + 2ab + b^2$.

$$\sqrt{2x + 1} = 1 + \sqrt{x}$$
$$(\sqrt{2x + 1})^2 = (1 + \sqrt{x})^2 \qquad \text{Square each side.}$$
$$2x + 1 = 1 + 2\sqrt{x} + x$$
$$x = 2\sqrt{x} \qquad \text{All radicals are not eliminated by the first squaring.}$$
$$x^2 = (2\sqrt{x})^2 \qquad \text{Square each side a second time.}$$
$$x^2 = 4x$$
$$x^2 - 4x = 0$$
$$x(x - 4) = 0$$
$$x = 0 \quad \text{or} \quad x - 4 = 0$$
$$x = 0 \quad \text{or} \quad x = 4$$

Both 0 and 4 satisfy the original equation. So the solution set is $\{0, 4\}$.

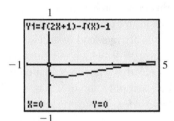 The graph in Fig. 36 supports this solution.

Figure 36

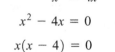

▶**TRY THIS.** Solve $\sqrt{3x - 2} - \sqrt{x} = 2$. ∎

Use the following strategy when solving equations involving square roots.

STRATEGY

Solving Equations Involving Square Roots

1. Isolate the radical if there is only one. Separate the radicals on opposite sides of the equation if there is more than one.
2. Square both sides and simplify.
3. Isolate or separate any remaining radicals and square again.
4. Check all solutions because squaring can produce extraneous solutions.

Equations with Rational Exponents

To solve equations of the form $x^{m/n} = k$ in which m and n are positive integers and m/n is in lowest terms, we adapt the methods of Examples 3 and 4 of raising each side to a power. Cubing each side of $x^{2/3} = 4$, yields $(x^{2/3})^3 = 4^3$ or $x^2 = 64$. By the square root property, $x = \pm 8$. We can shorten this solution by raising each side of the equation to the power $3/2$ (the reciprocal of $2/3$) and inserting the $\pm$ symbol to obtain the two square roots.

$$x^{2/3} = 4$$

$$(x^{2/3})^{3/2} = \pm 4^{3/2} \quad \text{Raise each side to the power } 3/2 \text{ and insert } \pm.$$

$$x = \pm 8$$

The equation $x^{2/3} = 4$ has two solutions because the numerator of the exponent $2/3$ is an even number. An equation such as $x^{-3/2} = 1/8$ has only one solution because the numerator of the exponent $-3/2$ is odd. To solve $x^{-3/2} = 1/8$, raise each side to the power $-2/3$ (the reciprocal of $-3/2$).

$$x^{-3/2} = \frac{1}{8}$$

$$(x^{-3/2})^{-2/3} = \left(\frac{1}{8}\right)^{-2/3} \quad \text{Raise each side to the power } -2/3.$$

$$x = 4$$

To solve equations of the form $x^{m/n} = k$ we can use the following strategy.

STRATEGY

Solving $x^{m/n} = k$ ($k \neq 0$, m/n in lowest terms)

1. Raise each side of the equation to the reciprocal power n/m. Recall that n/m means the nth power of the mth root.

2. Remember that there are two real even roots of any positive real number and there is exactly one real odd root of any real number.

3. If m is even and $k > 0$, then $x = \pm k^{n/m}$. If m is even and $k < 0$ there is no real solution.

4. If m is odd, then there is only one real solution, $x = k^{n/m}$.

EXAMPLE 5 Equations with rational exponents

Solve each equation.

a. $x^{4/3} = 625$ **b.** $(y - 2)^{-5/2} = 32$

Solution

a. Raise each side of the equation to the power $3/4$. Use the $\pm$ symbol because the numerator of $4/3$ is even.

$$x^{4/3} = 625$$

$$(x^{4/3})^{3/4} = \pm 625^{3/4}$$

$$x = \pm 125$$

Check in the original equation. The solution set is $\{-125, 125\}$.
The graph in Fig. 37 supports this solution. □

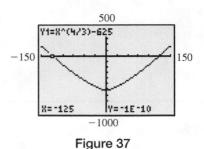

Figure 37

b. Raise each side to the power $-2/5$. Because the numerator in $-5/2$ is an odd number, there is only one solution.

$$(y - 2)^{-5/2} = 32$$

$$((y - 2)^{-5/2})^{-2/5} = 32^{-2/5} \qquad \text{Raise each side to the power } -2/5.$$

$$y - 2 = \frac{1}{4}$$

$$y = 2 + \frac{1}{4} = \frac{9}{4}$$

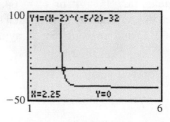

Figure 38

Check $9/4$ in the original equation. The solution set is $\left\{\frac{9}{4}\right\}$.
The graph in Fig. 38 supports this solution.

▶**TRY THIS.** Solve $x^{-4/5} = 16$. ■

Equations of Quadratic Type

In some cases, an equation can be converted to a quadratic equation by substituting a single variable for a more complicated expression. Such equations are called **equations of quadratic type**. An equation of quadratic type has the form $au^2 + bu + c = 0$, where $a \neq 0$ and u is an algebraic expression.

In the next example, the expression x^2 in a fourth-degree equation is replaced by u, yielding a quadratic equation. After the quadratic equation is solved, u is replaced by x^2 so that we find values for x that satisfy the original fourth-degree equation.

$\boxed{\text{EXAMPLE } 6}$ Solving a fourth-degree polynomial equation

Find all real and imaginary solutions to each equation.

a. $x^4 - 14x^2 + 45 = 0$ **b.** $x^4 + 14x^2 - 32 = 0$

Solution

a. We let $u = x^2$ so that $u^2 = (x^2)^2 = x^4$.

$$(x^2)^2 - 14x^2 + 45 = 0$$

$$u^2 - 14u + 45 = 0 \qquad \text{Replace } x^2 \text{ by } u.$$

$$(u - 9)(u - 5) = 0$$

$$u - 9 = 0 \quad \text{or} \quad u - 5 = 0$$

$$u = 9 \quad \text{or} \quad u = 5$$

$$x^2 = 9 \quad \text{or} \quad x^2 = 5 \qquad \text{Replace } u \text{ by}$$

$$x = \pm 3 \quad \text{or} \quad x = \pm\sqrt{5}$$

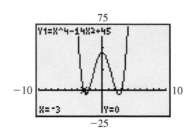

Figure 39

Check in the original equation. The solution set is $\left\{-3, -\sqrt{5}, \sqrt{5}, 3\right\}$.
The graph in Fig. 39 supports this solution. □

b. We could let $u = x^2$ as in part (a) or we can just factor the polynomial as follows.

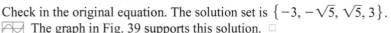

$$x^4 + 14x^2 - 32 = 0$$

$$(x^2 + 16)(x^2 - 2) = 0$$

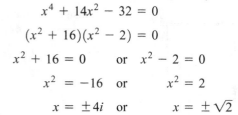

$$x^2 + 16 = 0 \quad \text{or} \quad x^2 - 2 = 0$$

$$x^2 = -16 \quad \text{or} \quad x^2 = 2$$

$$x = \pm 4i \quad \text{or} \quad x = \pm\sqrt{2}$$

The solution set is $\left\{-\sqrt{2}, \sqrt{2}, -4i, 4i\right\}$. Check in the original equation.

▶**TRY THIS.** Solve $x^4 - 9x^2 + 20 = 0$. ■

Note that the equation of Example 6 could be solved by factoring without doing substitution, because $x^4 - 14x^2 + 45 = (x^2 - 9)(x^2 - 5)$. Since the next example involves a more complicated algebraic expression, we use substitution to simplify it, although it too could be solved by factoring, without substitution.

EXAMPLE 7 Another equation of quadratic type

Solve $(x^2 - x)^2 - 18(x^2 - x) + 72 = 0$.

Solution

If we let $u = x^2 - x$, then the equation becomes a quadratic equation.

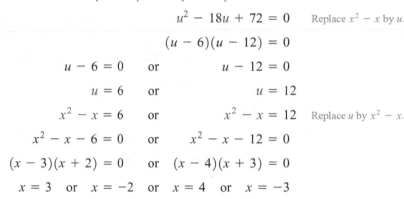

$$(x^2 - x)^2 - 18(x^2 - x) + 72 = 0$$
$$u^2 - 18u + 72 = 0 \qquad \text{Replace } x^2 - x \text{ by } u.$$
$$(u - 6)(u - 12) = 0$$

$u - 6 = 0$	or	$u - 12 = 0$	
$u = 6$	or	$u = 12$	
$x^2 - x = 6$	or	$x^2 - x = 12$	Replace u by $x^2 - x$.
$x^2 - x - 6 = 0$	or	$x^2 - x - 12 = 0$	
$(x - 3)(x + 2) = 0$	or	$(x - 4)(x + 3) = 0$	
$x = 3$ or $x = -2$	or	$x = 4$ or $x = -3$	

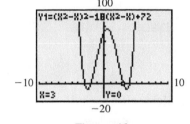

Figure 40

Check in the original equation. The solution set is $\{-3, -2, 3, 4\}$. The graph in Fig. 40 supports this solution.

▶**TRY THIS.** Solve $(x^2 + x)^2 - 8(x^2 + x) + 12 = 0$. ∎

The next equations of quadratic type have rational exponents.

EXAMPLE 8 Quadratic type and rational exponents

Find all real solutions to each equation.

a. $x^{2/3} - 9x^{1/3} + 8 = 0$ **b.** $(11x^2 - 18)^{1/4} = x$

Solution

a. If we let $u = x^{1/3}$, then $u^2 = (x^{1/3})^2 = x^{2/3}$.

$$u^2 - 9u + 8 = 0 \qquad \text{Replace } x^{2/3} \text{ by } u^2 \text{ and } x^{1/3} \text{ by } u.$$
$$(u - 8)(u - 1) = 0$$

$u = 8$	or	$u = 1$	
$x^{1/3} = 8$	or	$x^{1/3} = 1$	Replace u by $x^{1/3}$.
$(x^{1/3})^3 = 8^3$	or	$(x^{1/3})^3 = 1^3$	
$x = 512$	or	$x = 1$	

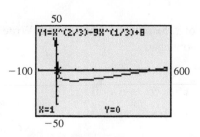

Figure 41

Check in the original equation. The solution set is $\{1, 512\}$. The graph in Fig. 41 supports this solution. □

b. $(11x^2 - 18)^{1/4} = x$

$((11x^2 - 18)^{1/4})^4 = x^4$ Raise each side to the power 4.

$$11x^2 - 18 = x^4$$

$$x^4 - 11x^2 + 18 = 0$$

$$(x^2 - 9)(x^2 - 2) = 0$$

$$x^2 = 9 \quad \text{or} \quad x^2 = 2$$

$$x = \pm 3 \quad \text{or} \quad x = \pm\sqrt{2}$$

Since the exponent 1/4 means principal fourth root, the right-hand side of the equation cannot be negative. So -3 and $-\sqrt{2}$ are extraneous roots. Since 3 and $\sqrt{2}$ satisfy the original equation, the solution set is $\{\sqrt{2}, 3\}$.

The graph in Fig. 42 supports this solution.

▶**TRY THIS.** Solve $x^{2/3} - x^{1/3} - 6 = 0$.   ■

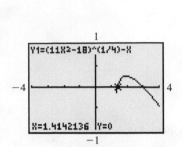

Figure 42

Equations Involving Absolute Value

In the next two examples we solve some more complicated absolute value equations.

(**EXAMPLE 9**) An equation involving absolute value

Solve $|x^2 - 2x - 16| = 8$.

Solution

First write an equivalent statement without using absolute value symbols.

$$x^2 - 2x - 16 = 8 \quad \text{or} \quad x^2 - 2x - 16 = -8$$

$$x^2 - 2x - 24 = 0 \quad \text{or} \quad x^2 - 2x - 8 = 0$$

$$(x - 6)(x + 4) = 0 \quad \text{or} \quad (x - 4)(x + 2) = 0$$

$$x = 6 \quad \text{or} \quad x = -4 \quad \text{or} \quad x = 4 \quad \text{or} \quad x = -2$$

The solution set is $\{-4, -2, 4, 6\}$.

The graph in Fig. 43 supports this solution.

▶**TRY THIS.** Solve $|x^2 - x - 4| = 2$.   ■

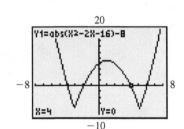

Figure 43

In the next example we have an equation in which an absolute value expression is equal to an expression that could be positive or negative and an equation with two absolute value expressions.

(**EXAMPLE 10**) More equations involving absolute value

Solve each equation.

a. $|x^2 - 6| = 5x$ **b.** $|a - 1| = |2a - 3|$

Solution

a. Since $|x^2 - 6|$ is nonnegative for any value of x, $5x$ must be nonnegative. Write the equivalent statement assuming that $5x$ is nonnegative:

$$x^2 - 6 = 5x \quad \text{or} \quad x^2 - 6 = -5x$$

$$x^2 - 5x - 6 = 0 \quad \text{or} \quad x^2 + 5x - 6 = 0$$

$$(x - 6)(x + 1) = 0 \quad \text{or} \quad (x + 6)(x - 1) = 0$$

$$x = 6 \quad \text{or} \quad x = -1 \quad \text{or} \quad x = -6 \quad \text{or} \quad x = 1$$

The expression $|x^2 - 6|$ is nonnegative for any real number x. But $5x$ is negative if $x = -1$ or if $x = -6$. So -1 and -6 are extraneous roots. They do not satisfy the original equation. The solution set is $\{1, 6\}$.

The graph in Fig. 44 supports this solution. □

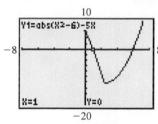

Figure 44

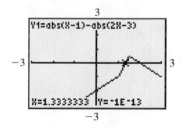

Figure 45

b. The equation $|a - 1| = |2a - 3|$ indicates that $a - 1$ and $2a - 3$ have the same absolute value. If two quantities have the same absolute value, they are either equal or opposites. Use this fact to write an equivalent statement without absolute value signs.

$$a - 1 = 2a - 3 \quad \text{or} \quad a - 1 = -(2a - 3)$$

$$a + 2 = 2a \quad \text{or} \quad a - 1 = -2a + 3$$

$$2 = a \quad \text{or} \quad a = \frac{4}{3}$$

Check that both 2 and $\frac{4}{3}$ satisfy the original absolute value equation. The solution set is $\left\{\frac{4}{3}, 2\right\}$.

The graph in Fig. 45 supports this solution.

▶**TRY THIS.** Solve $|x| = |x - 1|$. ■

Applications

The **break-even point** for a business is the point at which the cost of doing business is equal to the revenue generated by the business. The business is profitable when the revenue is greater than the cost.

EXAMPLE 11 Break-even point for a bus tour

A tour operator uses the equation $C = 3x + \sqrt{50x + 9000}$ to find his cost in dollars for taking x people on a tour of San Francisco.

a. For what value of x is the cost 160?
b. If he charges $10 per person for the tour, then what is his break-even point?

Solution

a. Replace C by 160 and solve the equation.

$$160 = 3x + \sqrt{50x + 9000}$$

$$160 - 3x = \sqrt{50x + 9000} \quad \text{Isolate the radical.}$$

$$25{,}600 - 960x + 9x^2 = 50x + 9000 \quad \text{Square each side.}$$

$$9x^2 - 1010x + 16{,}600 = 0$$

$$x = \frac{-(-1010) \pm \sqrt{1010^2 - 4(9)(16{,}600)}}{2(9)}$$

$$x = 20 \quad \text{or} \quad x \approx 92.2$$

Check that 20 satisfies the original equation but 92.2 does not. The cost is $160 when 20 people take the tour.

b. At $10 per person, the revenue in dollars is given by $R = 10x$. When the revenue is equal to the cost, as shown in Fig. 46, the operator breaks even.

$$10x = 3x + \sqrt{50x + 9000}$$

$$7x = \sqrt{50x + 9000}$$

$$49x^2 = 50x + 9000 \quad \text{Square each side.}$$

$$49x^2 - 50x - 9000 = 0$$

$$x = \frac{50 \pm \sqrt{50^2 - 4(49)(-9000)}}{2(49)}$$

$$x \approx -13.052 \quad \text{or} \quad x \approx 14.072$$

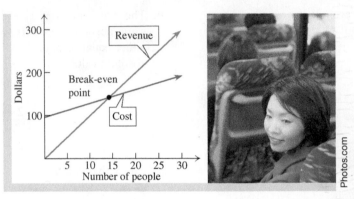

Figure 46

If 14.072 people took the tour, the operator would break even. Since the break-even point is not a whole number, the operator actually needs 15 people to make a profit.

▶**TRY THIS.** The function $D = \sqrt{P} - \sqrt{P - 400}$ gives the monthly demand D for custom-made suits in terms of the price P in dollars. For what price is the demand 10 suits? ■

→ **FOR** thought... True or False? Explain.

1. Squaring each side of $\sqrt{x - 1} + \sqrt{x} = 6$ yields $x - 1 + x = 36$.

2. The equations $(2x - 1)^2 = 9$ and $2x - 1 = 3$ are equivalent.

3. The equations $x^{2/3} = 9$ and $x = 27$ have the same solution set.

4. To solve $2x^{1/4} - x^{1/2} + 3 = 0$, we let $u = x^{1/2}$ and $u^2 = x^{1/4}$.

5. If $(x - 1)^{-2/3} = 4$, then $x = 1 \pm 4^{-3/2}$.

6. No negative number satisfies $x^{-2/5} = 4$.

7. The solution set to $|2x + 10| = 3x$ is $\{-2, 10\}$.

8. No negative number satisfies $|x^2 - 3x + 2| = 7x$.

9. The equation $|2x + 1| = |x|$ is equivalent to $2x + 1 = x$ or $2x + 1 = -x$.

10. The equation $x^9 - 5x^3 + 6 = 0$ is an equation of quadratic type.

EXERCISES 4

Find all real and imaginary solutions to each equation. Check your answers.

1. $x^3 + 3x^2 - 4x - 12 = 0$ **2.** $x^3 - x^2 - 5x + 5 = 0$

3. $2x^3 + 1000x^2 - x - 500 = 0$

4. $3x^3 - 1200x^2 - 2x + 800 = 0$

5. $a^3 + 5a = 15a^2$ **6.** $b^3 + 20b = 9b^2$

7. $3y^4 - 12y^2 = 0$ **8.** $5m^4 - 10m^3 + 5m^2 = 0$

9. $a^4 - 16 = 0$ **10.** $w^4 + 8w = 0$

Find all real solutions to each equation. Check your answers.

11. $\sqrt{x + 1} = x - 5$ **12.** $\sqrt{x - 1} = x - 7$

13. $\sqrt{x - 2} = x - 22$ **14.** $3 + \sqrt{x} = 1 + x$

15. $w = \dfrac{\sqrt{1 - 3w}}{2}$ **16.** $t = \dfrac{\sqrt{2 - 3t}}{3}$

17. $\dfrac{1}{z} = \dfrac{3}{\sqrt{4z + 1}}$ **18.** $\dfrac{1}{p} - \dfrac{2}{\sqrt{9p + 1}} = 0$

19. $\sqrt{x^2 - 2x - 15} = 3$ **20.** $\sqrt{3x^2 + 5x - 3} = x$

21. $\sqrt{x + 40} - \sqrt{x} = 4$

22. $\sqrt{x} + \sqrt{x - 36} = 2$

23. $\sqrt{n + 4} + \sqrt{n - 1} = 5$

24. $\sqrt{y + 10} - \sqrt{y - 2} = 2$

25. $\sqrt{2x + 5} + \sqrt{x + 6} = 9$

26. $\sqrt{3x - 2} - \sqrt{x - 2} = 2$

Find all real solutions to each equation. Check your answers.

27. $x^{2/3} = 2$ **28.** $x^{2/3} = \dfrac{1}{2}$ **29.** $w^{-4/3} = 16$

30. $w^{-3/2} = 27$ **31.** $t^{-1/2} = 7$ **32.** $t^{-1/2} = \dfrac{1}{2}$

33. $(s - 1)^{-1/2} = 2$ **34.** $(s - 2)^{-1/2} = \dfrac{1}{3}$

Find all real and imaginary solutions to each equation. Check your answers.

35. $x^4 - 12x^2 + 27 = 0$ **36.** $x^4 + 10 = 7x^2$

37. $x^4 + 6x^2 - 7 = 0$ **38.** $x^4 - x^2 - 12 = 0$

39. $x^4 - 81 = 0$ **40.** $x^4 - 625 = 0$

41. $\left(\dfrac{2c - 3}{5}\right)^2 + 2\left(\dfrac{2c - 3}{5}\right) = 8$

42. $\left(\dfrac{b - 5}{6}\right)^2 - \left(\dfrac{b - 5}{6}\right) - 6 = 0$

43. $\dfrac{1}{(5x - 1)^2} + \dfrac{1}{5x - 1} - 12 = 0$

44. $\dfrac{1}{(x - 3)^2} + \dfrac{2}{x - 3} - 24 = 0$

45. $(v^2 - 4v)^2 - 17(v^2 - 4v) + 60 = 0$

46. $(u^2 + 2u)^2 - 2(u^2 + 2u) - 3 = 0$

47. $x - 4\sqrt{x} + 3 = 0$ **48.** $2x + 3\sqrt{x} - 20 = 0$

49. $q - 7q^{1/2} + 12 = 0$ **50.** $h + 1 = 2h^{1/2}$

51. $x^{2/3} + 10 = 7x^{1/3}$ **52.** $x^{1/2} - 3x^{1/4} + 2 = 0$

Solve each absolute value equation.

53. $|w^2 - 4| = 3$ **54.** $|a^2 - 1| = 1$

55. $|v^2 - 3v| = 5v$ **56.** $|z^2 - 12| = z$

57. $|x^2 - x - 6| = 6$ **58.** $|2x^2 - x - 2| = 1$

59. $|x + 5| = |2x + 1|$ **60.** $|3x - 4| = |x|$

61. $|x - 2| + 1 = 5x$ **62.** $|x - 4| - 1 = -4x$

63. $|x - 4| = |x - 2|$ **64.** $|2x - 3| = |2x + 7|$

Solve each equation. Find imaginary solutions when possible.

65. $\sqrt{16x + 1} - \sqrt{6x + 13} = -1$

66. $\sqrt{16x + 1} - \sqrt{6x + 13} = 1$

67. $v^6 - 64 = 0$ **68.** $t^4 - 1 = 0$

69. $(7x^2 - 12)^{1/4} = x$ **70.** $(10x^2 - 1)^{1/4} = 2x$

71. $\sqrt[3]{2 + x - 2x^2} = x$

72. $\sqrt{48 + \sqrt{x}} - 4 = \sqrt[4]{x}$

73. $\left(\dfrac{x - 2}{3}\right)^2 - 2\left(\dfrac{x - 2}{3}\right) + 10 = 0$

74. $\dfrac{1}{(x + 1)^2} - \dfrac{2}{x + 1} + 2 = 0$

75. $(3u - 1)^{2/5} = 2$ **76.** $(2u + 1)^{2/3} = 3$

77. $x^2 - 11\sqrt{x^2 + 1} + 31 = 0$

78. $2x^2 - 3\sqrt{2x^2 - 3} - 1 = 0$

79. $|x^2 - 2x| = |3x - 6|$ **80.** $|x^2 + 5x| = |3 - x^2|$

81. $(3m + 1)^{-3/5} = -\dfrac{1}{8}$

82. $(1 - 2m)^{-5/3} = -\dfrac{1}{32}$

83. $|x^2 - 4| = x - 2$

84. $|x^2 + 7x| = x^2 - 4$

Solve each problem.

85. *Maximum Sail Area* According to the International America's Cup Rules, the maximum sail area S for a boat with length L (in meters) and displacement D (in cubic meters) is determined by the equation

$$L + 1.25S^{1/2} - 9.8D^{1/3} = 16.296$$

(America's Cup, www.americascup.org). Find S for a boat with length 21.24 m and displacement 18.34 m³.

Figure for Exercises 85 and 86

86. *Minimum Displacement for a Yacht* The minimum displacement D for a boat with length 21.52 m and a sail area of 310.64 m² is determined by the equation $L + 1.25S^{1/2} - 9.8D^{1/3} = 16.296$. Find this boat's minimum displacement.

87. *Cost of Baking Bread* The daily cost for baking x loaves of bread at Juanita's Bakery is given in dollars by $C = 0.5x + \sqrt{8x + 5000}$. Find the number of loaves for which the cost is $83.50.

88. *Break-Even Analysis* If the bread in Exercise 87 sells for $4.49 per loaf, then what is the minimum number of loaves that Juanita must bake and sell to make a profit?

89. *Square Roots* Find two numbers that differ by 6 and whose square roots differ by 1.

90. *Right Triangle* One leg of a right triangle is 1 cm longer than the other leg. What is the length of the short leg if the total length of the hypotenuse and the short leg is 10 cm?

91. *Perimeter of a Right Triangle* A sign in the shape of a right triangle has one leg that is 7 in. longer than the other leg. What is the length of the shorter leg if the perimeter is 30 in.?

92. *Right Triangle Inscribed in a Semicircle* One leg of a right triangle is 1 ft longer than the other leg. If the triangle is inscribed in a circle and the hypotenuse of the triangle is the diameter of the circle, then what is the length of the radius for which the length of the radius is equal to the length of the shortest side?

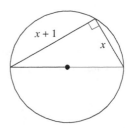

Figure for Exercise 92

93. *Area of a Foundation* The original plans for Jennifer's house called for a square foundation. After increasing one side by 30 ft and decreasing the other by 10 ft, the area of the rectangular foundation was 2100 ft². What was the area of the original square foundation?

94. *Shipping Carton* Heloise designed a cubic box for shipping paper. The height of the box was acceptable, but the paper would not fit into the box. After increasing the length by 0.5 in. and the width by 6 in. the area of the bottom was 119 in.² and the paper would fit. What was the original volume of the cubic box?

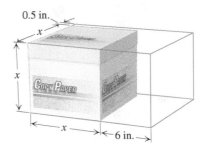

Figure for Exercise 94

95. *Sail Area-Displacement Ratio* The sail area-displacement ratio S is defined as

$$S = A\left(\dfrac{d}{64}\right)^{-2/3},$$

where A is the sail area in square feet and d is the displacement in pounds. The Oceanis 381 is a 39-ft sailboat with a sail area-displacement ratio of 14.26 and a sail area of 598.9 ft². Find the displacement for the Oceanis 381.

96. *Capsize Screening Value* The capsize screening value C is defined as

$$C = b\left(\dfrac{d}{64}\right)^{-1/3},$$

where b is the beam (or width) in feet and d is the displacement in pounds. The Bahia 46 is a 46-ft catamaran with a capsize screening value of 3.91 and a beam of 26.1 ft. Find the displacement for the Bahia 46.

97. *Insulated Carton* Nina is designing a box for shipping frozen shrimp. The box is to have a square base and a height that is 2 in. greater than the width of the base. The box will be surrounded with a 1-in.-thick layer of styrofoam. If the volume of the inside of the box must be equal to the volume of the styrofoam used, then what volume of shrimp can be shipped in the box?

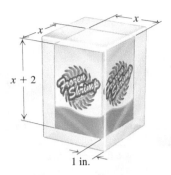

Figure for Exercise 97

98. *Volume of a Cubic Box* If the width of the base of a cubic container is increased by 3 m and the length of the base decreased by 1 m, then the volume of the new container is 6 m^3. What is the height of the cubic container?

99. *Hiking Time* William, Nancy, and Edgar met at the lodge at 8 A.M., and William began hiking west at 4 mph. At 10 A.M., Nancy began hiking north at 5 mph and Edgar went east on a three-wheeler at 12 mph. At what time was the distance between Nancy and Edgar 14 mi greater than the distance between Nancy and William?

100. *Accuracy of Transducers* Setra Systems Inc., of Acton, MA, calculates the accuracy A of its pressure transducers using the formula

$$A = \sqrt{(NL)^2 + (HY)^2 + (NR)^2}$$

where NL represents nonlinearity, HY represents hysteresis, and NR represents nonrepeatability. If the nonlinearity is 0.1%, the hysteresis is 0.05%, and the nonrepeatability is 0.02%, then what is the accuracy? Solve the formula for hysteresis.

101. *Geometric Mean* The geometric mean of the numbers $x_1, x_2, \ldots, x_n$ is defined as

$$GM = \sqrt[n]{x_1 \cdot x_2 \cdot \cdots \cdot x_n}.$$

The accompanying graph shows the quarterly net income for Apple Computer for the first three quarters of 2006.
a. Find the geometric mean of the net income for these three quarters.

b. What would the net income have to be for the next quarter so that the geometric mean for the four quarters would be $500 million?

Photos.com

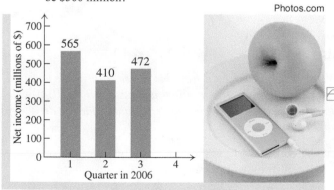

Figure for Exercise 101

■ Foreshadowing calculus
The situation in the next exercise is studied also in calculus. However, in calculus we find the route that minimizes the total time for the trip.

102. *Time Swimming and Running* Lauren is competing in her town's cross-country competition. Early in the event, she must race from point A on the Greenbriar River to point B, which is 5 mi downstream and on the opposite bank. The Greenbriar is 1 mi wide. In planning her strategy, Lauren knows she can use any combination of running and swimming. She can run 10 mph and swim 8 mph. How long would it take if she ran 5 mi downstream and then swam across? Find the time it would take if she swam diagonally from A to B. Find x so that she could run x miles along the bank, swim diagonally to B, and complete the race in 36 min. (Ignore the current in the river.)

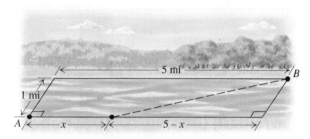

Figure for Exercise 102

103. *Boston Molasses Disaster* In the city of Boston, during the afternoon of January 15, 1919, a cylindrical metal tank containing 25,850,000 kg of molasses ruptured. The sticky liquid poured into the streets in a 9-m-deep stream that knocked down buildings and killed pedestrians and horses (www.discovery.com). If the diameter of the tank was equal to its height and the weight of molasses is 1600 kg/m^3, then what was the height of the tank in meters?

Figure for Exercise 103

104. *Storing Supplies* An army sergeant wants to use a 20-ft by 40-ft piece of canvas to make a two-sided tent for holding supplies as shown in the figure on the next page.
a. Write the volume of the tent as a function of b.

b. For what value of b is the volume 1600 ft^3?

c. Use a graphing calculator to find the values for b and h that will maximize the volume of the tent.

HINT The volume is the area of the triangular end times the length of the tent.

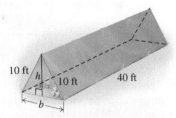

Figure for Exercise 104

105. *Radius of a Pipe* A large pipe is placed next to a wall and a 1-foot-high block is placed 5 feet from the wall to keep the pipe in place as shown in the accompanying figure. What is the radius of the pipe?

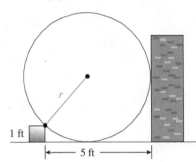

Figure for Exercise 105

106. *Radius of a Pipe* A large pipe is held in place on level ground by using a 1-foot-high block on one side and a 2-foot-high block on the other side. If the distance between the blocks is 6 feet, then what is the radius of the pipe?

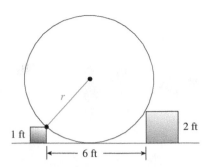

Figure for Exercise 106

▶ RETHINKING

107. Find a polynomial equation with real coefficients, and leading coefficient 1, that has -5 and $2i$ as roots.

108. Find all zeros to the function $f(x) = x^3 + 2x^2 - 13x + 10$.

109. Solve $-x^2 + 2x + 8 > 0$. Write the solution set in interval notation.

110. Let $f(x) = [x - 3]$. Find $f(-5.2)$, $f(6.2)$, and $f(6.9)$.

111. Find the equation (in slope-intercept form) for the line through $(9, 4)$ that is perpendicular to the line $y = \frac{3}{2}x + 7$.

112. Find the additive inverse and multiplicative inverse of $-8i$.

THINKING OUTSIDE THE BOX XXV

Painting Problem A painter has seven 3-ft by 5-ft rectangular drop cloths. If he lays each drop cloth on the carpet as a 3-ft by 5-ft rectangle, without folding, cutting, or tearing them, then what is the maximum area that he can cover with these drop cloths in an 8-ft by 13-ft room?

▶ POP QUIZ 4

Solve each equation. Find imaginary solutions when possible.

1. $x^3 + x^2 + x + 1 = 0$

2. $\sqrt{x + 4} = x - 2$

3. $x^{-2/3} = 4$

4. $x^4 - 3x^2 = 4$

5. $|x + 3| = |2x - 5|$

▶ LINKING

concepts... For Individual or Group Explorations

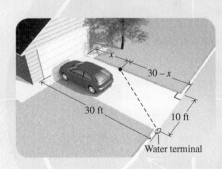

Minimizing Construction Cost

A homeowner needs to run a new water pipe from his house to a water terminal as shown in the accompanying diagram. The terminal is 30 ft down the 10-ft-wide driveway and on the other side. A contractor charges $3/ft alongside the driveway and $4/ft for underneath the driveway.

a) What will it cost if the contractor runs the pipe entirely under the driveway along the diagonal of the 30-ft by 10-ft rectangle?

b) What will it cost if the contractor runs the pipe 30 ft alongside the driveway and then 10 ft straight across?

c) The contractor claims that he can do the job for $120 by going alongside the driveway for some distance and then going under the drive diagonally to the terminal. Find x, the distance alongside the driveway.

d) Write the cost as a function of x and sketch the graph of the function.

e) Use the minimum feature of a graphing calculator to find the approximate value for x that will minimize the cost.

f) What is the minimum cost (to the nearest cent) for which the job can be done?

5 Graphs of Polynomial Functions

The graph of a polynomial function of degree 0 or 1 is a straight line. In Section 1 we learned that the graph of a second-degree polynomial function is a parabola. In this section we will concentrate on graphs of polynomial functions of degree greater than 2.

Drawing Good Graphs

A graph of an equation is a picture of all of the ordered pairs that satisfy the equation. However, it is impossible to draw a perfect picture of any set of ordered pairs. We usually find a few important features of the graph and make sure that our picture brings out those features. For example, you can make a good graph of a linear function by drawing a line through the intercepts using a ruler and a sharp pencil. A good parabola should look smooth and symmetric and pass through the vertex and intercepts.

A graphing calculator is a tremendous aid in graphing because it can quickly plot many points. However, the calculator does not know if it has drawn a graph that shows the important features. For example, the graph of $y = (x + 30)^2 (x - 40)^2$ has x-intercepts at $(-30, 0)$ and $(40, 0)$, but they do not appear on the graph in Fig. 47. □

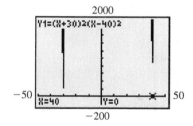

Figure 47

An important theorem for understanding the graphs of polynomial functions is the intermediate value theorem (IVT). The IVT says that *a polynomial function takes on every value between any two of its values*. For example, consider $f(x) = x^3$, for which $f(1) = 1$ and $f(2) = 8$. Select any number between 1 and 8, say 5. By the IVT there is a number c in the interval $(1, 2)$ such that $f(c) = 5$. In this case, c is easy to find: $c = \sqrt[3]{5}$. The IVT allows us to "connect the dots" when drawing a graph. The curve cannot go from $(1, 1)$ to $(2, 8)$ without hitting every y-coordinate between 1 and 8. If one of the values is positive and the other negative, the IVT guarantees that the curve crosses the x-axis on the interval. For example, $f(-2) = -8$ and $f(2) = 8$. By the IVT there is a c in the interval $(-2, 2)$ for which $f(c) = 0$. Of course, in this case $c = 0$ and the x-intercept is $(0, 0)$.

Note that the greatest integer function, which is not a polynomial function, does not obey the IVT. The greatest integer function jumps from one integer to the next without taking on any values between the integers.

We will not prove the IVT here, as it is proved in calculus. The theorem is stated symbolically as follows.

The Intermediate Value Theorem

Suppose that f is a polynomial function and $[a, b]$ is an interval for which $f(a) \neq f(b)$. If k is a number between $f(a)$ and $f(b)$, then there is a number c in the interval (a, b) such that $f(c) = k$.

Symmetry

Symmetry is a very special property of graphs of some functions but not others. Recognizing that the graph of a function has some symmetry usually cuts in half the work required to obtain the graph and also helps cut down on errors in graphing. So far we have discussed the following types of symmetry.

> **SUMMARY**
>
> ## Types of Symmetry
>
> 1. The graph of a function $f(x)$ is *symmetric about the y-axis* and f is an *even function* if $f(-x) = f(x)$ for any value of x in the domain of the function.
>
> 2. The graph of a function $f(x)$ is *symmetric about the origin* and f is an *odd function* if $f(-x) = -f(x)$ for any value of x in the domain of the function.
>
> 3. The graph of a quadratic function $f(x) = ax^2 + bx + c$ is *symmetric about its axis of symmetry*, $x = -b/(2a)$.

The graphs of $f(x) = x^2$ and $f(x) = x^3$ shown in Figs. 48 and 49 are nice examples of symmetry about the y-axis and symmetry about the origin, respectively. The axis of symmetry of $f(x) = x^2$ is the y-axis. The symmetry of the other quadratic functions comes from the fact that the graph of every quadratic function is a transformation of the graph of $f(x) = x^2$.

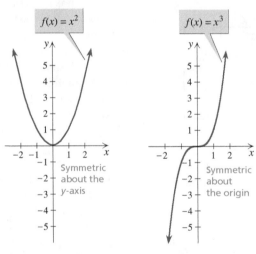

| Figure 48 | Figure 49 |

EXAMPLE 1 Determining the symmetry of a graph

Discuss the symmetry of the graph of each polynomial function.

a. $f(x) = 5x^3 - x$ **b.** $g(x) = 2x^4 - 3x^2$ **c.** $h(x) = x^2 - 3x + 6$
d. $j(x) = x^4 - x^3$

Solution

a. Replace x by $-x$ in $f(x) = 5x^3 - x$ and simplify:

$$f(-x) = 5(-x)^3 - (-x)$$
$$= -5x^3 + x$$

Since $f(-x)$ is the opposite of $f(x)$, the graph is symmetric about the origin. Figure 50 supports this conclusion. □

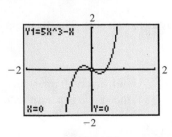

Figure 50

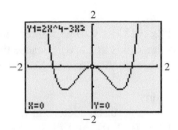

Figure 51

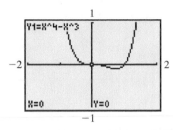

Figure 52

b. Replace x by $-x$ in $g(x) = 2x^4 - 3x^2$ and simplify:

$$g(-x) = 2(-x)^4 - 3(-x)^2$$
$$= 2x^4 - 3x^2$$

Since $g(-x) = g(x)$, the graph is symmetric about the y-axis. Figure 51 supports this conclusion. □

c. Because h is a quadratic function, its graph is symmetric about the line $x = -b/(2a)$, which in this case is the line $x = 3/2$.

d. In this case

$$j(-x) = (-x)^4 - (-x)^3$$
$$= x^4 + x^3.$$

So $j(-x) \neq j(x)$ and $j(-x) \neq -j(x)$. The graph of j is not symmetric about the y-axis and is not symmetric about the origin. Figure 52 supports this conclusion.

▶**TRY THIS.** Discuss the symmetry of $f(x) = -x^3 - 4x$. ∎

Behavior at the x-Intercepts

The x-intercepts are key points for the graph of a polynomial function, as they are for any function. Consider the graph of $y = (x - 2)^2(x + 1)$ in Fig. 53. Near 2 the values of y are positive, as shown in Fig. 54, and the graph does not cross the x-axis. Near -1 the values of y are negative for $x < -1$ and positive for $x > -1$, as shown in Fig. 55, and the graph crosses the x-axis. The reason for this behavior is the exponents in $(x - 2)^2$ and $(x + 1)^1$. Because $(x - 2)^2$ has an even exponent, $(x - 2)^2$ cannot be negative. Because $(x + 1)^1$ has an odd exponent, $(x + 1)^1$ changes sign at -1 but does not change sign at 2. So the product $(x - 2)^2(x + 1)$ does not change sign at 2, but does change sign at -1.

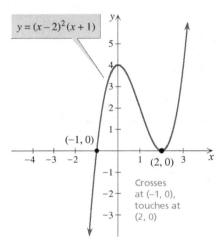

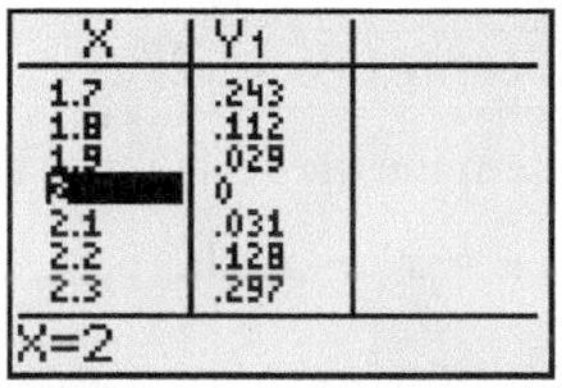

Crosses at $(-1, 0)$, touches at $(2, 0)$

Figure 53

Figure 54 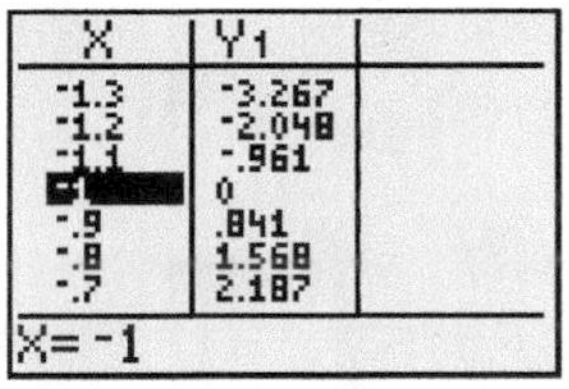   **Figure 55**

Every x-intercept corresponds to a factor of the polynomial and to a root of the polynomial function. Whether the multiplicity of the root is odd or even determines the behavior of the graph at the x-intercept.

Theorem: Behavior at the x-Intercepts

Let a be a root with multiplicity k for a polynomial function.
If k is odd, then the graph crosses the x-axis at $(a, 0)$.
If k is even, then the graph touches but does not cross the x-axis at $(a, 0)$.

As another example, consider the graphs of $f(x) = x^2$ and $f(x) = x^3$ shown in Figs. 48 and 49. Zero is a root with odd multiplicity for $f(x) = x^3$ and even multiplicity for $f(x) = x^2$. The graph of $f(x) = x^3$ crosses the x-axis at $(0, 0)$ but $f(x) = x^2$ does not cross the x-axis at $(0, 0)$.

EXAMPLE 2 Crossing at the x-intercepts

Find the x-intercepts and determine whether the graph of the function crosses the x-axis at each x-intercept.

a. $f(x) = (x - 1)^2(x - 3)$ **b.** $f(x) = x^3 + 2x^2 - 3x$

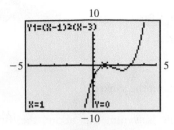

Figure 56

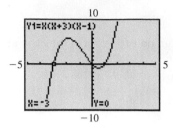

Figure 57

Solution

a. The x-intercepts are found by solving $(x - 1)^2(x - 3) = 0$. The x-intercepts are $(1, 0)$ and $(3, 0)$. The graph does not cross the x-axis at $(1, 0)$ because the factor $x - 1$ occurs to an even power. The graph crosses the x-axis at $(3, 0)$ because $x - 3$ occurs to an odd power.

The graph in Fig. 56 supports these conclusions. □

b. The x-intercepts are found by solving $x^3 + 2x^2 - 3x = 0$. By factoring, we get $x(x + 3)(x - 1) = 0$. The x-intercepts are $(0, 0)$, $(-3, 0)$, and $(1, 0)$. Since each factor occurs an odd number of times (once), the graph crosses the x-axis at each of the x-intercepts.

The graph in Fig. 57 supports these conclusions.

▶**TRY THIS.** Determine whether the graph of $f(x) = (x - 1)^3(x + 5)^2$ crosses the x-axis at each of its x-intercepts. ■

The Leading Coefficient Test

We now consider the behavior of a polynomial function as the x-coordinate goes to or approaches infinity or negative infinity. In symbols, $x \to \infty$ or $x \to -\infty$. Since we seek only an intuitive understanding of the ideas presented here, we will not give precise definitions of these terms. Precise definitions are given in a calculus course.

To say that $x \to \infty$ means that x gets larger and larger without bound. For our purposes we can think of x assuming the values 1, 2, 3, and so on, without end. Similarly, $x \to -\infty$ means that x gets smaller and smaller without bound. Think of x assuming the values -1, -2, -3, and so on, without end.

As x approaches ∞ the y-coordinates of any polynomial function approach ∞ or $-\infty$. Likewise, when $x \to -\infty$ the y-coordinates approach ∞ or $-\infty$. The direction that y goes is determined by the degree of the polynomial and the sign of the leading coefficient. The four possible types of behavior are illustrated in the next example.

EXAMPLE 3 Behavior as $x \to \infty$ or $x \to -\infty$

Determine the behavior of the graph of each function as $x \to \infty$ or $x \to -\infty$.

a. $y = x^3 - x$ **b.** $y = -x^3 + 1$ **c.** $y = x^4 - 4x^2$ **d.** $y = -x^4 + 4x^2 + x$

Solution

a. Consider the following table. If you have a graphing calculator, make a table like this and scroll through it.

x	-30	-20	-10	0	10	20	30
$y = x^3 - x$	$-26{,}970$	-7980	-990	0	990	7980	26{,}970

$\xleftarrow{\qquad y \to -\infty \qquad}$ $\xrightarrow{\qquad y \to \infty \qquad}$

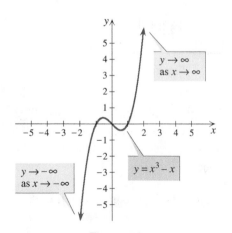

Figure 58

The graph of $y = x^3 - x$ is shown in Fig. 58. As x gets larger and larger $(x \to \infty)$, y increases without bound $(y \to \infty)$. As x gets smaller and smaller $(x \to -\infty)$, y decreases without bound $(y \to -\infty)$. Notice that the degree of the polynomial is odd and the sign of the leading coefficient is positive. The behavior of this function is stated with limit notation as

$$\lim_{x \to \infty} x^3 - x = \infty \quad \text{and} \quad \lim_{x \to -\infty} x^3 - x = -\infty.$$

The notation $\lim_{x \to \infty} x^3 - x = \infty$ is read as "the limit as x approaches ∞ of $x^3 - x$ is ∞." We could also write $\lim_{x \to \infty} y = \infty$ if it is clear that $y = x^3 - x$.

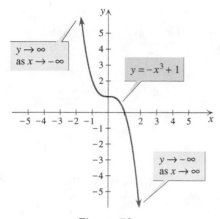

Figure 59

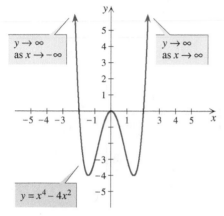

Figure 60

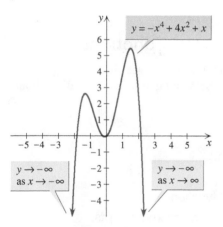

Figure 61

b. Consider the following table. If you have a graphing calculator, make a table like this and scroll through it.

x	-30	-20	-10	0	10	20	30
$y = -x^3 + 1$	27,001	8001	1001	1	-999	-7999	$-26,999$

$\longleftarrow \quad y \to \infty \qquad\qquad y \to -\infty \quad \longrightarrow$

The graph of $y = -x^3 + 1$ is shown in Fig. 59. As x gets larger and larger $(x \to \infty)$, y decreases without bound $(y \to -\infty)$. As x gets smaller and smaller $(x \to -\infty)$, y increases without bound $(y \to \infty)$. Notice that the degree of this polynomial is odd and the sign of the leading coefficient is negative. The behavior of this function is stated with limit notation as

$$\lim_{x \to \infty} -x^3 + 1 = -\infty \qquad \text{and} \qquad \lim_{x \to -\infty} -x^3 + 1 = \infty.$$

c. Consider the following table. If you have a graphing calculator, make a table like this and scroll through it.

x	0	± 10	± 20	± 30	± 40
$y = x^4 - 4x^2$	0	9600	158,400	806,400	2,553,600

$\longrightarrow \quad y \to \infty \quad \longrightarrow$

The graph of $y = x^4 - 4x^2$ is shown in Fig. 60. As $x \to \infty$ or $x \to -\infty$, y increases without bound $(y \to \infty)$. Notice that the degree of this polynomial is even and the sign of the leading coefficient is positive. The behavior of this function is stated with limit notation as

$$\lim_{x \to \infty} x^4 - 4x^2 = \infty \qquad \text{and} \qquad \lim_{x \to -\infty} x^4 - 4x^2 = \infty.$$

d. Consider the following table. If you have a graphing calculator, make a table like this and scroll through it.

x	-20	-10	0	10	20
$y = -x^4 + 4x^2 + x$	$-158,420$	-9610	0	-9590	$-158,380$

$\longleftarrow \quad y \to -\infty \qquad\qquad y \to -\infty \quad \longrightarrow$

The graph of $y = -x^4 + 4x^2 + x$ is shown in Fig. 61. As $x \to \infty$ or $x \to -\infty$, y decreases without bound $(y \to -\infty)$. Notice that the degree of this polynomial is even and the sign of the leading coefficient is negative. The behavior of this function is stated with limit notation as

$$\lim_{x \to \infty} -x^4 + 4x^2 + x = -\infty \qquad \text{and} \qquad \lim_{x \to -\infty} -x^4 + 4x^2 + x = -\infty.$$

▶**TRY THIS.** Discuss the behavior of the graph of $f(x) = -x^3 - 4x$. ∎

As $x \to \infty$ or $x \to -\infty$ all first-degree polynomial functions have "end behavior" like the lines $y = x$ or $y = -x$, all second-degree polynomial functions behave like the parabolas $y = x^2$ or $y = -x^2$, and all third-degree polynomial functions behave like $y = x^3$ or $y = -x^3$, and so on. The end behavior is determined by the degree and the sign of the first term. The smaller-degree terms in the polynomial determine the number of "hills" and "valleys" between the ends of the curve. With degree n there are at most $n - 1$ hills and valleys. The end behavior of polynomial functions is summarized in the **leading coefficient test.**

Leading Coefficient Test

If $f(x) = a_n x^n + a_{n-1} x^{n-1} + \cdots + a_1 x + a_0$, the behavior of the graph of f to the left and right is determined as follows:

For n odd and $a_n > 0$, $\quad \lim\limits_{x \to \infty} f(x) = \infty \quad$ and $\quad \lim\limits_{x \to -\infty} f(x) = -\infty$.

For n odd and $a_n < 0$, $\quad \lim\limits_{x \to \infty} f(x) = -\infty \quad$ and $\quad \lim\limits_{x \to -\infty} f(x) = \infty$.

For n even and $a_n > 0$, $\quad \lim\limits_{x \to \infty} f(x) = \infty \quad$ and $\quad \lim\limits_{x \to -\infty} f(x) = \infty$.

For n even and $a_n < 0$, $\quad \lim\limits_{x \to \infty} f(x) = -\infty \quad$ and $\quad \lim\limits_{x \to -\infty} f(x) = -\infty$.

The leading coefficient test is presented visually in Fig. 62, which shows only the "ends" of the graphs of the polynomial functions.

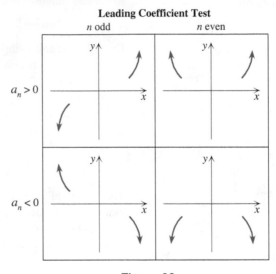

Figure 62

Sketching Graphs of Polynomial Functions

A good graph of a polynomial function should include the features that we have been discussing. The following strategy will help you graph polynomial functions.

STRATEGY

Graphing a Polynomial Function

1. Check for symmetry.
2. Find all real zeros of the polynomial function.
3. Determine the behavior at the corresponding x-intercepts.
4. Determine the behavior as $x \to \infty$ and as $x \to -\infty$.
5. Calculate several ordered pairs including the y-intercept to verify your suspicions about the shape of the graph.
6. Draw a smooth curve through the points to make the graph.

EXAMPLE 4 Graphing polynomial functions

Sketch the graph of each polynomial function.

a. $f(x) = x^3 - 5x^2 + 7x - 3$ **b.** $f(x) = x^4 - 200x^2 + 10{,}000$

Solution

a. First find $f(-x)$ to determine symmetry and the number of negative roots.

$$f(-x) = (-x)^3 - 5(-x)^2 + 7(-x) - 3$$
$$= -x^3 - 5x^2 - 7x - 3$$

From $f(-x)$, we see that the graph has neither type of symmetry. Because $f(-x)$ has no sign changes, $x^3 - 5x^2 + 7x - 3 = 0$ has no negative roots by Descartes's rule of signs. The only possible rational roots are 1 and 3.

$$\begin{array}{r|rrrr} 1 & 1 & -5 & 7 & -3 \\ & & 1 & -4 & 3 \\ \hline & 1 & -4 & 3 & 0 \end{array}$$

From the synthetic division we know that 1 is a root and we can factor $f(x)$:

$$f(x) = (x - 1)(x^2 - 4x + 3)$$
$$= (x - 1)^2(x - 3) \qquad \text{Factor completely.}$$

The x-intercepts are $(1, 0)$ and $(3, 0)$. The graph of f does not cross the x-axis at $(1, 0)$ because $x - 1$ occurs to an even power, while the graph crosses at $(3, 0)$ because $x - 3$ occurs to an odd power. The y-intercept is $(0, -3)$. Since the leading coefficient is positive and the degree is odd, $y \to \infty$ as $x \to \infty$ and $y \to -\infty$ as $x \to -\infty$. Calculate two more ordered pairs for accuracy, say $(2, -1)$ and $(4, 9)$. Draw a smooth curve as in Fig. 63.

The calculator graph shown in Fig. 64 supports these conclusions. □

b. First find $f(-x)$:

$$f(-x) = (-x)^4 - 200(-x)^2 + 10{,}000$$
$$= x^4 - 200x^2 + 10{,}000$$

Since $f(x) = f(-x)$, the graph is symmetric about the y-axis. We can factor the polynomial as follows.

$$f(x) = x^4 - 200x^2 + 10{,}000$$
$$= (x^2 - 100)(x^2 - 100)$$
$$= (x - 10)(x + 10)(x - 10)(x + 10)$$
$$= (x - 10)^2(x + 10)^2$$

The x-intercepts are $(10, 0)$ and $(-10, 0)$. Because each factor for these intercepts has an even power, the graph does not cross the x-axis at the intercepts. The y-intercept is $(0, 10{,}000)$. Since the leading coefficient is positive and the degree is even, $y \to \infty$ as $x \to \infty$ or as $x \to -\infty$. The graph also goes through $(-20, 90{,}000)$ and $(20, 90{,}000)$. Draw a smooth curve through these points and the intercepts as shown in Fig. 65.

The calculator graph shown in Fig. 66 supports these conclusions.

▶**TRY THIS.** Sketch the graph of $f(x) = x^4 - 4x^2$. ■

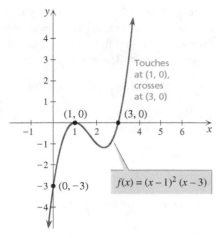

Figure 63

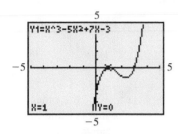

Figure 64

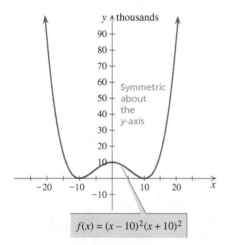

Figure 65

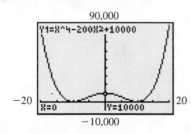

Figure 66

Polynomial Inequalities

We can solve polynomial inequalities using the graphical method or test-point method that we used on quadratic inequalities in Section 1. You should recall that for either of these methods we find all real roots to the corresponding polynomial function. The real roots divide the number line into intervals. With the graphical method we determine the sign of the polynomial in each interval from a graph, whereas with the test-point method we determine the sign of the polynomial by testing an arbitrary point in each interval. We will not use the graphical method here because it is difficult to draw a good graph of some polynomial functions, especially if the x-intercepts are really close together or very far apart. The test-point method is more reliable.

EXAMPLE 5 | Solving a polynomial inequality with test points

Solve $x^4 + x^3 - 15x^2 - 3x + 36 < 0$ using the test-point method.

Solution

Use synthetic division to see that 3 and -4 are zeros of the function $f(x) = x^4 + x^3 - 15x^2 - 3x + 36$:

$$
\begin{array}{r|rrrrr}
3 & 1 & 1 & -15 & -3 & 36 \\
  &   & 3 & 12 & -9 & -36 \\
\hline
-4 & 1 & 4 & -3 & -12 & 0 \\
   &   & -4 & 0 & 12 & \\
\hline
 & 1 & 0 & -3 & 0 &
\end{array}
$$

Since $x^4 + x^3 - 15x^2 - 3x + 36 = (x - 3)(x + 4)(x^2 - 3)$, the other two zeros are $\pm\sqrt{3}$. The four zeros determine five intervals on the number line in Fig. 67. Select an arbitrary test point in each of these intervals. The selected points $-5, -3, 0, 2,$ and 4 are shown in red in the figure:

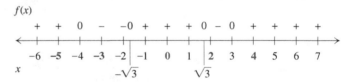

Figure 67

Now evaluate $f(x) = x^4 + x^3 - 15x^2 - 3x + 36$ at each test point:

$$f(-5) = 176, \quad f(-3) = -36, \quad f(0) = 36, \quad f(2) = -6, \quad f(4) = 104$$

These values indicate that the signs of the function are $+, -, +, -,$ and $+$ on the intervals shown in Fig. 67. The values of x that satisfy the original inequality are the values of x for which $f(x)$ is negative. So the solution set is $(-4, -\sqrt{3}) \cup (\sqrt{3}, 3)$. The calculator graph of $y = x^4 + x^3 - 15x^2 - 3x + 36$ in Fig. 68 confirms that y is negative for x in $(-4, -\sqrt{3}) \cup (\sqrt{3}, 3)$. Since the multiplicity of each zero of the function is one, the graph crosses the x-axis at each intercept and the y-coordinates change sign at each intercept.

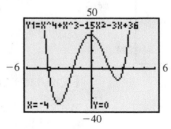

Figure 68

▶**TRY THIS.** Solve $x^4 - 4x^2 < 0$ using test points. ∎

→ FUNCTION
gallery... **Polynomial Functions**

Linear: $f(x) = mx + b$

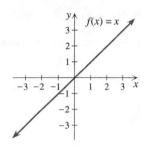

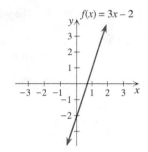

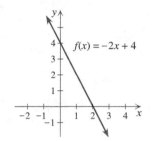

Slope 1, *y*-intercept $(0, 0)$ Slope 3, *y*-intercept $(0, -2)$ Slope -2, *y*-intercept $(0, 4)$

Quadratic: $f(x) = ax^2 + bx + c$ or $f(x) = a(x - h)^2 + k$

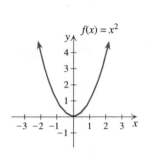

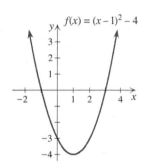

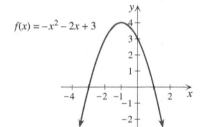

Vertex $(0, 0)$ Vertex $(1, -4)$ Vertex $(-1, 4)$
Range $[0, \infty)$ Range $[-4, \infty)$ Range $(-\infty, 4]$

Cubic: $f(x) = ax^3 + bx^2 + cx + d$

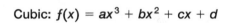

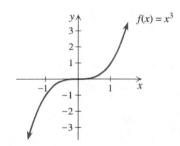

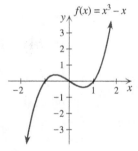

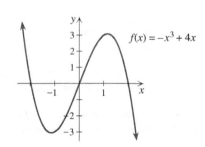

Quartic or Fourth-Degree: $f(x) = ax^4 + bx^3 + cx^2 + dx + e$

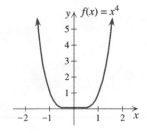

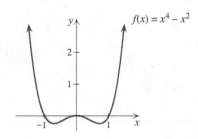

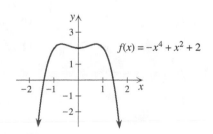

FOR thought... True or False? Explain.

1. If P is a function for which $P(2) = 8$ and $P(-2) = -8$, then the graph of P is symmetric about the origin.

2. If $y = -3x^3 + 4x^2 - 6x + 9$, then $y \to -\infty$ as $x \to \infty$.

3. If the graph of $y = P(x)$ is symmetric about the origin and $P(8) = 4$, then $-P(-8) = 4$.

4. If $f(x) = x^3 - 3x$, then $f(x) = f(-x)$ for any value of x.

5. If $f(x) = x^4 - x^3 + x^2 - 6x + 7$, then $f(-x) = x^4 + x^3 + x^2 + 6x + 7$.

6. The graph of $f(x) = x^2 - 6x + 9$ has only one x-intercept.

7. The x-intercepts for $P(x) = (x - 1)^2(x + 1)$ are $(0, 1)$ and $(0, -1)$.

8. The y-intercept for $P(x) = 4(x - 3)^2 + 2$ is $(0, 2)$.

9. The graph of $f(x) = x^2(x + 8)^2$ has no points in quadrants III and IV.

10. The graph of $f(x) = x^3 - 1$ has three x-intercepts.

EXERCISES 5

Fill in the blank.

1. If $f(-x) = f(x)$ for every value of x in the domain of the function, then the graph of $f(x)$ is symmetric about the _____.

2. If $f(-x) = -f(x)$ for every value of x in the domain of the function, then the graph of $f(x)$ is symmetric about the _____.

3. The graph of a quadratic function $f(x) = ax^2 + bx + c$ is symmetric about the line $x = $ _____.

4. If a is a root with multiplicity 3 for a polynomial function, then the graph of the function _____ the x-axis at $(a, 0)$.

Discuss the symmetry of the graph of each polynomial function. See the summary of the types of symmetry in Section 5.

5. $f(x) = x^6$

6. $f(x) = x^5 - x$

7. $f(x) = x^2 - 3x + 5$

8. $f(x) = 5x^2 + 10x + 1$

9. $f(x) = 3x^6 - 5x^2 + 3x$

10. $f(x) = x^6 - x^4 + x^2 - 8$

11. $f(x) = 4x^3 - x$

12. $f(x) = 7x^3 + x^2$

13. $f(x) = (x - 5)^2$

14. $f(x) = (x^2 - 1)^2$

15. $f(x) = -x$

16. $f(x) = 3x$

Find the x-intercepts and discuss the behavior of the graph of each polynomial function at its x-intercepts.

17. $f(x) = (x - 4)^2$

18. $f(x) = (x - 1)^2(x + 3)^2$

19. $f(x) = (2x - 1)^3$

20. $f(x) = x^6$

21. $f(x) = 4x - 1$

22. $f(x) = x^2 - 5x - 6$

23. $f(x) = x^2 - 3x + 10$

24. $f(x) = x^4 - 16$

25. $f(x) = x^3 - 3x^2$

26. $f(x) = x^3 - x^2 - x + 1$

27. $f(x) = 2x^3 - 5x^2 + 4x - 1$

28. $f(x) = x^3 - 3x^2 + 4$

29. $f(x) = -2x^3 - 8x^2 + 6x + 36$

30. $f(x) = -x^3 + 7x - 6$

For each function use the leading coefficient test to determine whether $y \to \infty$ or $y \to -\infty$ as $x \to \infty$.

31. $y = 2x^3 - x^2 + 9$

32. $y = -3x + 7$

33. $y = -3x^4 + 5$

34. $y = 6x^4 - 5x^2 - 1$

35. $y = x - 3x^3$

36. $y = 5x - 7x^4$

For each function use the leading coefficient test to determine whether $y \to \infty$ or $y \to -\infty$ as $x \to -\infty$.

37. $y = -2x^5 - 3x^2$

38. $y = x^3 + 8x + \sqrt{2}$

39. $y = 3x^6 - 999x^3$

40. $y = -12x^4 - 5x$

For each graph discuss its symmetry, indicate whether the graph crosses the x-axis at each x-intercept, and determine whether $y \to \infty$ or $y \to -\infty$ as $x \to \infty$ and $x \to -\infty$.

41.

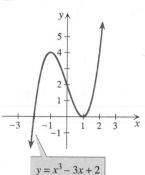

$y = x^3 - 3x + 2$

42.

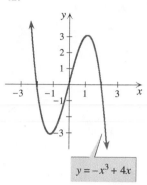

$y = -x^3 + 4x$

43.

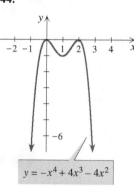

$y = x^4 - 2x^2 + 2$

44.

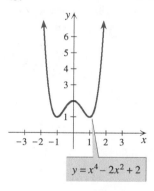

$y = -x^4 + 4x^3 - 4x^2$

Determine whether each limit is equal to ∞ or $-\infty$.

45. $\lim\limits_{x \to \infty} x^2 - 4$

46. $\lim\limits_{x \to \infty} x^3 + x$

47. $\lim\limits_{x \to \infty} -x^5 - x^2$

48. $\lim\limits_{x \to \infty} -3x^4 + 9x^2$

49. $\lim\limits_{x \to -\infty} -3x$

50. $\lim\limits_{x \to -\infty} x^3 - 5$

51. $\lim\limits_{x \to -\infty} -2x^2 + 1$

52. $\lim\limits_{x \to -\infty} 6x^4 - x$

For each given function make a rough sketch of the graph that shows the behavior at the x-intercepts and the behavior as x approaches ∞ and $-\infty$.

53. $f(x) = (x - 1)^2(x + 3)$

54. $f(x) = (x + 2)^2(x - 5)^2$

55. $f(x) = -2(2x - 1)^2(x + 1)^3$

56. $f(x) = -3(3x - 4)^2(2x + 1)^4$

Match each polynomial function with its graph (a)–(h).

57. $f(x) = -2x + 1$

58. $f(x) = -2x^2 + 1$

59. $f(x) = -2x^3 + 1$

60. $f(x) = -2x^2 + 4x - 1$

61. $f(x) = -2x^4 + 6$

62. $f(x) = -2x^4 + 6x^2$

63. $f(x) = x^3 + 4x^2 - x - 4$

64. $f(x) = (x - 2)^4$

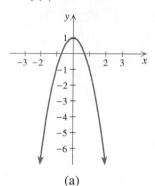

(a)

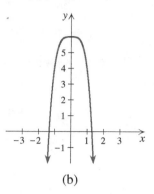

(b)

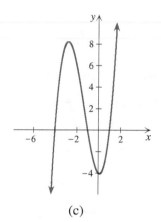

(c)

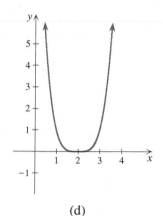

(d)

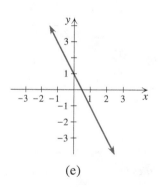

(e)

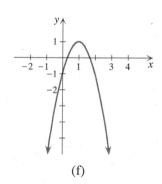

(f)

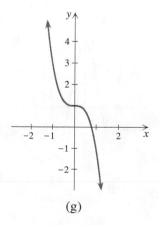

(g)

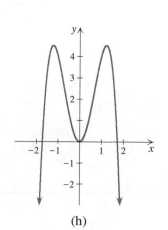

(h)

345

Sketch the graph of each function. See the strategy for graphing polynomial functions.

65. $f(x) = x - 30$ **66.** $f(x) = 40 - x$

67. $f(x) = (x - 30)^2$ **68.** $f(x) = (40 - x)^2$

69. $f(x) = x^3 - 40x^2$ **70.** $f(x) = x^3 - 900x$

71. $f(x) = (x - 20)^2(x + 20)^2$

72. $f(x) = (x - 20)^2(x + 12)$

73. $f(x) = -x^3 - x^2 + 5x - 3$ **74.** $f(x) = -x^4 + 6x^3 - 9x^2$

75. $f(x) = x^3 - 10x^2 - 600x$

76. $f(x) = -x^4 + 24x^3 - 144x^2$

77. $f(x) = x^3 + 18x^2 - 37x + 60$

78. $f(x) = x^3 - 7x^2 - 25x - 50$

79. $f(x) = -x^4 + 196x^2$ **80.** $f(x) = -x^4 + x^2 + 12$

81. $f(x) = x^3 + 3x^2 + 3x + 1$ **82.** $f(x) = -x^3 + 3x + 2$

83. $f(x) = (x - 3)^2(x + 5)^2(x + 7)$

84. $f(x) = x(x + 6)^2(x^2 - x - 12)$

Solve each polynomial inequality using the test-point method.

85. $x^3 - 3x > 0$ **86.** $-x^3 + 3x + 2 < 0$

87. $2x^2 - x^4 \le 0$ **88.** $-x^4 + x^2 + 12 \ge 0$

89. $x^3 + 4x^2 - x - 4 > 0$ **90.** $x^3 + 2x^2 - 2x - 4 < 0$

91. $x^3 - 4x^2 - 20x + 48 \ge 0$ **92.** $x^3 + 7x^2 - 36 \le 0$

93. $x^3 - x^2 + x - 1 < 0$ **94.** $x^3 + x^2 + 2x - 4 > 0$

95. $x^4 - 19x^2 + 90 \le 0$

96. $x^4 - 5x^3 + 3x^2 + 15x - 18 \ge 0$

State the solution sets to the inequalities in Exercises 97–104 by reading the following graphs.

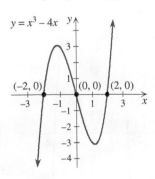

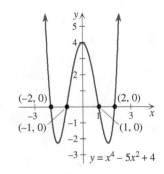

97. $x^3 - 4x > 0$ **98.** $x^3 - 4x \le 0$

99. $x^3 - 4x \ge 0$ **100.** $x^3 - 4x < 0$

101. $x^4 - 5x^2 + 4 < 0$ **102.** $x^4 - 5x^2 + 4 > 0$

103. $x^4 + 4 \ge 5x^2$ **104.** $x^4 + 4 \le 5x^2$

Determine which of the given functions is shown in the accompanying graph.

105. a. $f(x) = (x - 3)(x + 2)$ **b.** $f(x) = (x + 3)(x - 2)$

c. $f(x) = \frac{1}{3}(x - 3)(x + 2)$ **d.** $f(x) = \frac{1}{3}(x + 3)(x - 2)$

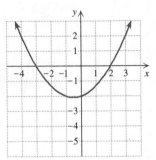

Figure for Exercise 105

106. a. $f(x) = (x + 3)(x + 1)(x - 1)$

b. $f(x) = (x - 3)(x^2 - 1)$

c. $f(x) = \frac{2}{3}(x + 3)(x + 1)(x - 1)$

d. $f(x) = -\frac{2}{3}(x + 3)(x^2 - 1)$

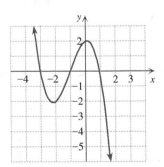

Figure for Exercise 106

Find the equation and sketch the graph for each function.

107. A quadratic function with x-intercepts $(-5, 0)$ and $(4, 0)$ and y-intercept $(0, 3)$

108. A quadratic function with x-intercepts $(3, 0)$ and $(-6, 0)$ and y-intercept $(0, -5)$

109. A quadratic function that passes through $(1, 2)$ and has x-intercepts $(-1, 0)$ and $(3, 0)$

110. A quadratic function that passes through $(-1, -3)$ and has x-intercepts $(2, 0)$ and $(4, 0)$

111. A cubic function (a third-degree polynomial function) with x-intercepts $(2, 0)$, $(-3, 0)$, and $(4, 0)$ and y-intercept $(0, 6)$

112. A cubic function with x-intercepts $(1, 0)$, $(-1/2, 0)$, and $(1/4, 0)$ and y-intercept $(0, 2)$

113. A quartic function (a fourth-degree polynomial function) that passes through the point $(1, 3)$ and has x-intercepts $(\pm 2, 0)$ and $(\pm 4, 0)$

114. A quartic function that passes through the point $(1, 5)$ and has x-intercepts $(1/2, 0)$, $(1/3, 0)$, $(1/4, 0)$, and $(-2/3, 0)$

Solve each problem.

115. *Maximum Profit* A company's weekly profit (in thousands of dollars) is given by the function $P(x) = x^3 - 3x^2 + 2x + 3$, where x is the amount (in thousands of dollars) spent per week on advertising. Use a graphing calculator to estimate the local maximum and the local minimum value for the profit. What amount must be spent on advertising to get the profit higher than the local maximum profit?

116. *Maximum Volume* An open-top box is to be made from a 6 in. by 7 in. piece of copper by cutting equal squares (x in. by x in.) from each corner and folding up the sides. Write the volume of the box as a function of x. Use a graphing calculator to find the maximum possible volume to the nearest hundredth of a cubic inch.

117. *Economic Forecast* The total annual profit (in thousands of dollars) for a department store chain is determined by $P = 90x - 6x^2 + 0.1x^3$, where x is the number of stores in the chain. The company now has 10 stores in operation and plans to pursue an aggressive expansion program. What happens to the total annual profit as the company opens more and more stores? For what values of x is profit increasing?

118. *Contaminated Chicken* The number of bacteria of a certain type found on a chicken t minutes after processing in a contaminated plant is given by the function

$$N = 30t + 25t^2 + 44t^3 - 0.01t^4.$$

Find N for $t = 30$, 300, and 3000. What happens to N as t keeps increasing?

119. *Packing Cheese* Workers at the Green Bay Cheese Factory are trying to cover a block of cheese with an 8 in. by 12 in. piece of foil paper as shown in the figure. The ratio of the length and width of the block must be 4 to 3 to accommodate the label. Find a polynomial function that gives the volume of the block of cheese covered in this manner as a function of the thickness x. Use a graphing calculator to find the dimensions of the block that will maximize the volume.

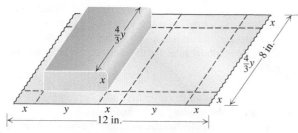

Figure for Exercise 119

120. *Giant Teepee* A casino designer is planning a giant teepee that is 80 ft in diameter and 120 ft high as shown in the figure. Inside the teepee is to be a cylindrical room for slot machines. Write the volume of the cylindrical room as a function of its radius. Use a graphing calculator to find the radius that maximizes the volume of the cylindrical room.

HINT If h is the height of the room and r the radius, then the ratio of h to $40 - r$ is 3 to 1.

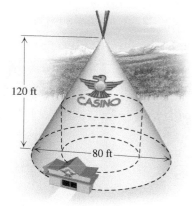

Figure for Exercise 120

121. *Paint Coverage* A one-pint can of spray paint will cover 50 ft^2. Of course a small amount of paint coats the inside of the cylindrical can and it is not used. What would happen if the inside of the can had a surface area of 50 ft^2? Find the dimensions for the two one-pint cans that have a surface area of 50 ft^2.

HINT For a cylinder, $V = \pi r^2 h$ and $S = 2\pi r^2 + 2\pi rh$. Use 1 ft$^3 \approx 7.5$ gallons.

Figure for Exercise 121

122. *Booming Business* When Computer Recyclers opened its doors, business started booming. After a few months, there was a temporary slowdown in sales, after which sales took off again. We can model sales for this business with the function

$$N = 8t^3 - 133t^2 + 653t,$$

where N is the number of computers sold in month t ($t = 0$ corresponds to the opening of the business).

a. Use a graphing calculator to estimate the month in which the temporary slowdown was the worst.

b. What percentage drop in sales occurred at the bottom of the slowdown compared to the previous high point in sales?

▶ **RETHINKING**

123. Solve $\sqrt{x + 12} - \sqrt{x - 9} = 3$.

124. Find a polynomial equation with real coefficients that has the roots $-5, 2 + i$.

125. Use synthetic division to find the quotient and remainder when $x^4 + 3x^3 - 9x^2 + 2x - 5$ is divided by $x + 2$.

126. For the function $y = -4x^2 + 8x + 9$ find the domain, range, and the maximum value for y.

127. Find the domain and range of the relation $x = |y - 5|$.

128. Is the function $\{(0, 3), (-9, 0), (-3, 5), (9, 7)\}$ one-to-one?

THINKING OUTSIDE THE BOX XXVI

Leaning Ladder A 7-ft ladder is leaning against a vertical wall. There is a point near the bottom of the ladder that is 1 ft from the ground and 1 ft from the wall. Find the exact or approximate distance from the top of the ladder to the ground.

1 ft
1 ft

Figure for Thinking Outside the Box XXVI

▶ POP QUIZ 5

1. Discuss the symmetry of the graph of $y = x^4 - 3x^2$.

2. Discuss the symmetry of the graph of $y = x^3 - 3x$.

3. Does $f(x) = (x - 4)^3$ cross the x-axis at $(4, 0)$?

4. If $y = x^4 - 3x^3$, does y go to ∞ or $-\infty$ as $x \to \infty$?

5. If $y = -2x^4 + 5x^2$, does y go to ∞ or $-\infty$ as $x \to -\infty$?

6. Solve $(x - 3)^2(x + 1)^3 > 0$.

▶ LINKING
concepts... For Individual or Group Explorations

x

10 in.

14 in.

Maximizing Volume

A sheet metal worker is planning to make an open-top box by cutting equal squares (x-in. by x-in.) from the corners of a 10-in. by 14-in. piece of copper. A second box is to be made in the same manner from an 8-in. by 10-in. piece of aluminum, but its height is to be one-half that of the first box.

a) Find polynomial functions for the volume of each box.

b) Find the values of x for which the copper box is 72 in.³ larger than the aluminum box.

c) Write the difference between the two volumes d as a function of x and graph it.

d) Find d for $x = 1.5$ in. and $x = 8$ in.

e) For what value of x is the difference between the two volumes the largest?

f) For what value of x is the total volume the largest?

6 Rational Functions and Inequalities

In this section we will use our knowledge of polynomial functions to study functions that are ratios of polynomial functions.

Rational Functions and Their Domains

Functions such as

$$y = \frac{1}{x}, \qquad f(x) = \frac{x - 3}{x - 1}, \qquad \text{and} \qquad g(x) = \frac{2x - 3}{x^2 - 4}$$

are rational functions.

Definition:
Rational Function

> If $P(x)$ and $Q(x)$ are polynomials, then a function of the form
>
> $$f(x) = \frac{P(x)}{Q(x)}$$
>
> is called a **rational function,** provided that $Q(x)$ is not the zero polynomial.

To simplify discussions of rational functions we will assume that $f(x)$ is in lowest terms ($P(x)$ and $Q(x)$ have no common factors) unless it is stated otherwise.

The domain of a polynomial function is the set of all real numbers, while the domain of a rational function is restricted to real numbers that do not cause the denominator to have a value of 0. The domain of $y = 1/x$ is the set of all real numbers except 0.

EXAMPLE 1 The domain of a rational function

Find the domain of each rational function.

a. $f(x) = \dfrac{x - 3}{x - 1}$ **b.** $g(x) = \dfrac{2x - 3}{x^2 - 4}$

Solution

a. Since $x - 1 = 0$ only for $x = 1$, the domain of f is the set of all real numbers except 1. The domain is written in interval notation as $(-\infty, 1) \cup (1, \infty)$.
b. Since $x^2 - 4 = 0$ for $x = \pm 2$, any real number except 2 and -2 can be used for x. So the domain of g is $(-\infty, -2) \cup (-2, 2) \cup (2, \infty)$.

▶**TRY THIS.** Find the domain of $f(x) = \dfrac{x - 1}{x^2 - 9}$. ∎

Horizontal and Vertical Asymptotes

The graph of a rational function such as $f(x) = 1/x$ does not look like the graph of a polynomial function. The domain of $f(x) = 1/x$ is the set of all real numbers except 0. However, 0 is an important number for the graph of this function because of the behavior of the graph when x is close to 0. The following table shows ordered pairs in which x is close to 0.

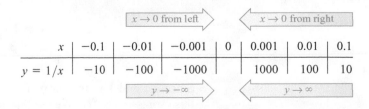

	$x \to 0$ from left				$x \to 0$ from right		
x	-0.1	-0.01	-0.001	0	0.001	0.01	0.1
$y = 1/x$	-10	-100	-1000		1000	100	10
	$y \to -\infty$				$y \to \infty$		

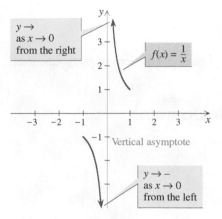

Figure 69

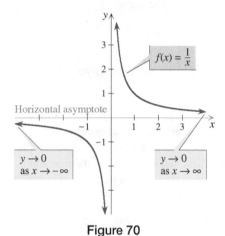

Figure 70

Notice that the closer x is to 0, the farther y is from 0. In symbols, $y \to \infty$ as $x \to 0$ from the right. Using limit notation we write $\lim\limits_{x \to 0^+} \frac{1}{x} = \infty$, where the plus symbol indicates that x is approaching 0 from above or from the right. If $x \to 0$ from the left, $y \to -\infty$. Using limit notation we write $\lim\limits_{x \to 0^-} \frac{1}{x} = -\infty$, where the negative symbol indicates that x is approaching 0 from below or from the left. Plotting the ordered pairs from the table suggests a curve that gets closer and closer to the vertical line $x = 0$ (the y-axis) but never touches it, as shown in Fig. 69. The y-axis is called a *vertical asymptote* for this curve.

The following table shows ordered pairs in which x is far from 0.

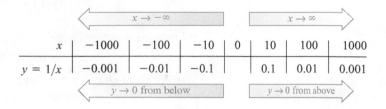

x	-1000	-100	-10	0	10	100	1000
$y = 1/x$	-0.001	-0.01	-0.1		0.1	0.01	0.001

Notice that the farther x is from 0, the closer y is to 0. Using limit notation we write $\lim\limits_{x \to \infty} \frac{1}{x} = 0$ and $\lim\limits_{x \to -\infty} \frac{1}{x} = 0$. Plotting the ordered pairs from the table suggests a curve that lies just above the positive x-axis and just below the negative x-axis. The x-axis is called a *horizontal asymptote* for the graph of f. The complete graph of $f(x) = 1/x$ is shown in Fig. 70. Since $f(-x) = 1/(-x) = -f(x)$, the graph is symmetric about the origin.

For any rational function expressed in lowest terms, a horizontal asymptote is determined by the value approached by the rational expression as $|x| \to \infty$ ($x \to \infty$ or $x \to -\infty$). A vertical asymptote occurs for every number that causes the denominator of the function to have a value of 0, provided the rational function is in lowest terms. As we will learn shortly, not every rational function has a vertical and a horizontal asymptote. We can give a formal definition of asymptotes as described below.

Definition: Vertical and Horizontal Asymptotes

> Let $f(x) = P(x)/Q(x)$ be a rational function written in lowest terms.
>
> If $|f(x)| \to \infty$ as $x \to a$, then the vertical line $x = a$ is a **vertical asymptote.** Using limit notation, $x = a$ is a vertical asymptote if $\lim\limits_{x \to a} |f(x)| = \infty$. The line $y = a$ is a **horizontal asymptote** if $f(x) \to a$ as $x \to \infty$ or $x \to -\infty$. Using limit notation, $y = a$ is a horizontal asymptote if $\lim\limits_{x \to \infty} f(x) = a$ or $\lim\limits_{x \to -\infty} f(x) = a$.

To find a horizontal asymptote we need to approximate the value of a rational expression when x is arbitrarily large. If x is large, then expressions such as

$$\frac{500}{x}, \quad -\frac{14}{x}, \quad \frac{3}{x^2}, \quad \frac{6}{x^3}, \quad \text{and} \quad \frac{4}{x - 5},$$

which consist of a fixed number over a polynomial, are approximately zero. To approximate a ratio of two polynomials that both involve x, such as $\frac{x - 2}{2x + 3}$, we rewrite the expression by dividing by the highest power of x:

$$\frac{x - 2}{2x + 3} = \frac{\dfrac{x}{x} - \dfrac{2}{x}}{\dfrac{2x}{x} + \dfrac{3}{x}} = \frac{1 - \dfrac{2}{x}}{2 + \dfrac{3}{x}}$$

Since $2/x$ and $3/x$ are approximately zero when x is large, the approximate value of this expression is $1/2$. We use this idea in the next example.

EXAMPLE 2 Identifying horizontal and vertical asymptotes

Find the horizontal and vertical asymptotes for each rational function.

a. $f(x) = \dfrac{3}{x^2 - 1}$ **b.** $g(x) = \dfrac{x}{x^2 - 4}$ **c.** $h(x) = \dfrac{2x + 1}{x + 3}$

X Y1
0 -3
10 .0303
20 .00752
30 .00334
40 .00188
50 .0012
60 8.3E-4
$Y_1=3/(X^2-1)$

Figure 71

Solution

a. The denominator $x^2 - 1$ has a value of 0 if $x = \pm 1$. So the lines $x = 1$ and $x = -1$ are vertical asymptotes. As $x \to \infty$ or $x \to -\infty$, $x^2 - 1$ gets larger, making $3/(x^2 - 1)$ the ratio of 3 and a large number. Thus $3/(x^2 - 1) \to 0$ and the x-axis is a horizontal asymptote.

The calculator table shown in Fig. 71 supports the conclusion that the x-axis is a horizontal asymptote. □

b. The denominator $x^2 - 4$ has a value of 0 if $x = \pm 2$. So the lines $x = 2$ and $x = -2$ are vertical asymptotes. As $x \to \infty$, $x/(x^2 - 4)$ is a ratio of two large numbers. The approximate value of this ratio is not clear. However, if we divide the numerator and denominator by x^2, the highest power of x, we can get a clearer picture of the value of this ratio:

$$g(x) = \frac{x}{x^2 - 4} = \frac{\frac{x}{x^2}}{\frac{x^2}{x^2} - \frac{4}{x^2}} = \frac{\frac{1}{x}}{1 - \frac{4}{x^2}}$$

X Y1
0 0
100 .01
200 .005
300 .00333
400 .0025
500 .002
600 .00167
$Y_1=X/(X^2-4)$

Figure 72

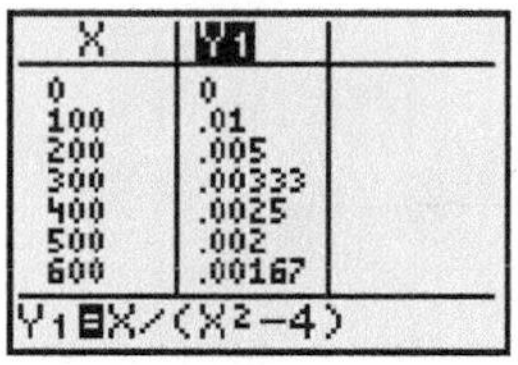

As $|x| \to \infty$, the values of $1/x$ and $4/x^2$ go to 0. So

$$g(x) \to \frac{0}{1 - 0} = 0.$$

Thus the x-axis is a horizontal asymptote.

The calculator table shown in Fig. 72 supports the conclusion that the x-axis is a horizontal asymptote. □

c. The denominator $x + 3$ has a value of 0 if $x = -3$. So the line $x = -3$ is a vertical asymptote. To find any horizontal asymptotes, rewrite the rational expression by dividing the numerator and denominator by the highest power of x:

$$h(x) = \frac{2x + 1}{x + 3} = \frac{\frac{2x}{x} + \frac{1}{x}}{\frac{x}{x} + \frac{3}{x}} = \frac{2 + \frac{1}{x}}{1 + \frac{3}{x}}$$

X Y1
0 .33333
100 1.9515
200 1.9754
300 1.9835
400 1.9876
500 1.9901
600 1.9917
$Y_1=(2X+1)/(X+3)$

Figure 73

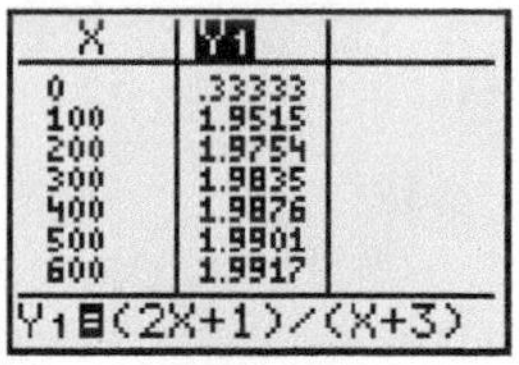

As $x \to \infty$ or $x \to -\infty$ the values of $1/x$ and $3/x$ approach 0. So

$$h(x) \to \frac{2 + 0}{1 + 0} = 2.$$

Thus the line $y = 2$ is a horizontal asymptote.

The calculator table shown in Fig. 73 supports the conclusion that $y = 2$ is a horizontal asymptote.

▶**TRY THIS.** Find all asymptotes for $f(x) = \frac{x - 1}{x^2 - 9}$. ■

If the degree of the numerator of a rational function is less than the degree of the denominator, as in Examples 2(a) and (b), then the x-axis is a horizontal asymptote

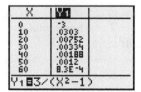

for the graph of the function. If the degree of the numerator is equal to the degree of the denominator, as in Example 2(c), then the x-axis is not a horizontal asymptote. We can see this clearly if we use division to rewrite the expression as quotient + remainder/divisor. For the function of Example 2(c), we get

$$h(x) = \frac{2x + 1}{x + 3} = 2 + \frac{-5}{x + 3}.$$

The graph of h is a translation two units upward of the graph of $y = -5/(x + 3)$, which has the x-axis as a horizontal asymptote. So $y = 2$ is a horizontal asymptote for h. Note that 2 is simply the ratio of the leading coefficients.

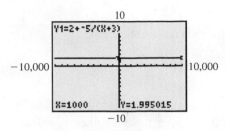 Since the graph of h is very close to $y = 2$, the view of h in Fig. 74 looks like $y = 2$. Note how this choice of viewing window causes some of the important features of the graph to disappear. □

Figure 74

Oblique Asymptotes

Each rational function of Example 2 had one horizontal asymptote and had a vertical asymptote for each zero of the polynomial in the denominator. The horizontal asymptote $y = 0$ occurs because the y-coordinate gets closer and closer to 0 as $x \to \infty$ or $x \to -\infty$. Some rational functions have a nonhorizontal line for an asymptote. An asymptote that is neither horizontal nor vertical is called an **oblique asymptote** or **slant asymptote**. Oblique asymptotes are determined by using long division or synthetic division of polynomials.

(**EXAMPLE** 3) A rational function with an oblique asymptote

Determine all of the asymptotes for $g(x) = \frac{2x^2 + 3x - 5}{x + 2}$.

Solution

If $x + 2 = 0$, then $x = -2$. So the line $x = -2$ is a vertical asymptote. Because the degree of the numerator is larger than the degree of the denominator, we use long division (or in this case, synthetic division) to rewrite the function as quotient + remainder/divisor (dividing the numerator and denominator by x^2 will not work in this case):

$$g(x) = \frac{2x^2 + 3x - 5}{x + 2} = 2x - 1 + \frac{-3}{x + 2}$$

If $|x| \to \infty$, then $-3/(x + 2) \to 0$. So the value of $g(x)$ approaches $2x - 1$ as $|x| \to \infty$. The line $y = 2x - 1$ is an oblique asymptote for the graph of g. You may look ahead to Fig. 83 to see the graph of this function with its oblique asymptote. Note that the wide view of g in Fig. 75 looks like the line $y = 2x - 1$.

▶**TRY THIS.** Find all asymptotes for $f(x) = \frac{3x^2 - 4}{x - 1}$.

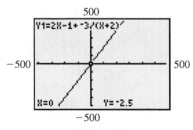

Figure 75

If the degree of $P(x)$ is 1 greater than the degree of $Q(x)$ and the degree of $Q(x)$ is at least 1, then the rational function has an oblique asymptote. In this case use division to rewrite the function as quotient + remainder/divisor. The graph of the equation formed by setting y equal to the quotient is an oblique asymptote. We conclude this discussion of asymptotes with a summary.

SUMMARY

Finding Asymptotes for a Rational Function

Let $f(x) = P(x)/Q(x)$ be a rational function in lowest terms with the degree of $Q(x)$ at least 1.

1. The graph of f has a vertical asymptote corresponding to each root of $Q(x) = 0$.
2. If the degree of $P(x)$ is less than the degree of $Q(x)$, then the x-axis is a horizontal asymptote.
3. If the degree of $P(x)$ equals the degree of $Q(x)$, then the horizontal asymptote is determined by the ratio of the leading coefficients.
4. If the degree of $P(x)$ is greater than the degree of $Q(x)$, then use division to rewrite the function as quotient + remainder/divisor. The graph of the equation formed by setting y equal to the quotient is an asymptote. This asymptote is an oblique or slant asymptote if the degree of $P(x)$ is 1 larger than the degree of $Q(x)$.

Sketching Graphs of Rational Functions

We now use asymptotes and symmetry to help us sketch the graphs of the rational functions discussed in Examples 2 and 3. Use the following steps to graph a rational function.

PROCEDURE

Graphing a Rational Function

To graph a rational function in lowest terms:

1. Determine the asymptotes and draw them as dashed lines.
2. Check for symmetry.
3. Find any intercepts.
4. Plot several selected points to determine how the graph approaches the asymptotes.
5. Draw curves through the selected points, approaching the asymptotes.

EXAMPLE 4 Functions with horizontal and vertical asymptotes

Sketch the graph of each rational function.

a. $f(x) = \dfrac{3}{x^2 - 1}$ **b.** $g(x) = \dfrac{x}{x^2 - 4}$ **c.** $h(x) = \dfrac{2x + 1}{x + 3}$

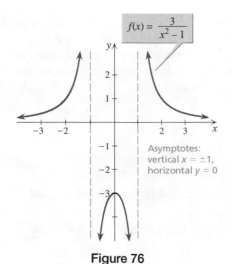

Figure 76

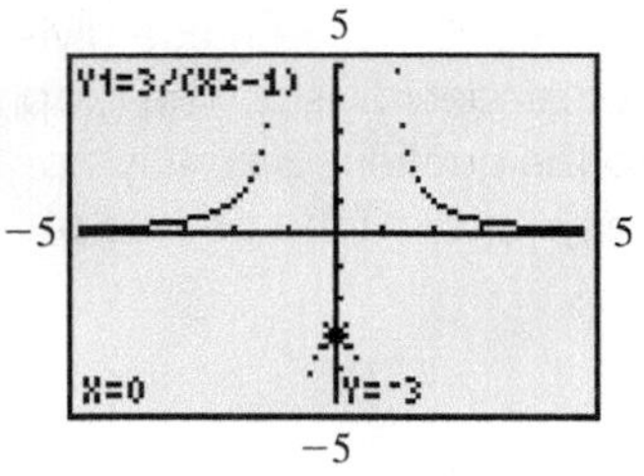

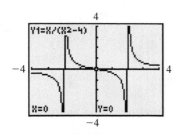

Figure 77

Solution

a. From Example 2(a), $x = 1$ and $x = -1$ are vertical asymptotes, and the x-axis is a horizontal asymptote. Draw the vertical asymptotes using dashed lines. Since all of the powers of x are even, $f(-x) = f(x)$ and the graph is symmetric about the y-axis. The y-intercept is $(0, -3)$. There are no x-intercepts because $f(x) = 0$ has no solution. Evaluate the function at $x = 0.9$ and $x = 1.1$ to see how the curve approaches the asymptote at $x = 1$. Evaluate at $x = 2$ and $x = 3$ to see whether the curve approaches the horizontal asymptote from above or below. We get $(0.9, -15.789)$, $(1.1, 14.286)$, $(2, 1)$, and $(3, 3/8)$. From these points you can see that the curve is going downward toward $x = 1$ from the left and upward toward $x = 1$ from the right. It is approaching its horizontal asymptote from above. Now use the symmetry with respect to the y-axis to draw the curve approaching its asymptotes as shown in Fig. 76.

The calculator graph in dot mode in Fig. 77 supports these conclusions. ☐

b. Draw the vertical asymptotes $x = 2$ and $x = -2$ from Example 2(b) as dashed lines. The x-axis is a horizontal asymptote. Because $f(-x) = -f(x)$, the graph is symmetric about the origin. The x-intercept is $(0, 0)$. Evaluate the function near the vertical asymptote $x = 2$, and for larger values of x to see how the curve approaches the horizontal asymptote. We get $(1.9, -4.872)$, $(2.1, 5.122)$, $(3, 3/5)$, and $(4, 1/3)$. From these points you can see that the curve is going downward toward $x = 2$ from the left and upward toward $x = 2$ from the right. It is approaching its horizontal asymptote from above. Now use the symmetry with respect to the origin to draw the curve approaching its asymptotes as shown in Fig. 78.

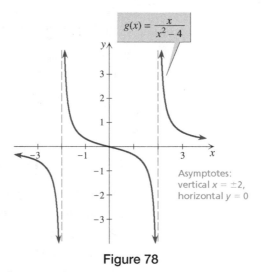

Figure 78

The calculator graph in connected mode in Fig. 79 confirms these conclusions. Note how the calculator appears to draw the vertical asymptotes as it connects the points that are close to but on opposite sides of the asymptotes. ☐

c. Draw the vertical asymptote $x = -3$ and the horizontal asymptote $y = 2$ from Example 2(c) as dashed lines. The x-intercept is $(-1/2, 0)$ and the y-intercept is $(0, 1/3)$. The points $(-2, -3)$, $(7, 1.5)$, $(-4, 7)$, and $(-13, 2.5)$ are also on the graph. From these points we can conclude that the curve goes upward toward $x = -3$ from the left and downward toward $x = -3$ from the right. It approaches

Figure 79

$y = 2$ from above as x goes to $-\infty$ and from below as x goes to ∞. Draw the graph approaching its asymptotes as shown in Fig. 80.

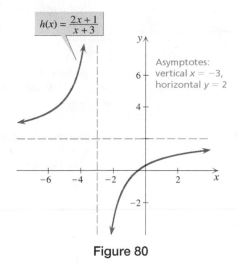

Figure 80

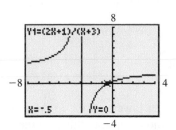

Figure 81

The calculator graph in Fig. 81 supports these conclusions.

▶TRY THIS. Sketch the graph of $f(x) = \dfrac{x-1}{x^2-9}$. ■

The graph of a rational function cannot cross a vertical asymptote, but it can cross a nonvertical asymptote. The graph of a rational function gets closer and closer to a nonvertical asymptote as $|x| \to \infty$, but it can also cross a nonvertical asymptote as illustrated in the next example.

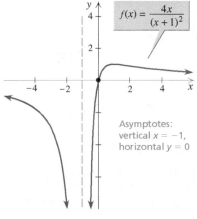

Figure 82

EXAMPLE 5 | A rational function that crosses an asymptote

Sketch the graph of $f(x) = \dfrac{4x}{(x+1)^2}$.

Solution

The graph of f has a vertical asymptote at $x = -1$, and since the degree of the numerator is less than the degree of the denominator, the x-axis is a horizontal asymptote. If $x > 0$ then $f(x) > 0$, and if $x < 0$ then $f(x) < 0$. So the graph approaches the horizontal axis from above for $x > 0$, and from below for $x < 0$. However, the x-intercept is $(0, 0)$. Therefore, the graph crosses its horizontal asymptote at $(0, 0)$. The graph shown in Fig. 82 goes through $(1, 1)$, $(2, 8/9)$, $(-2, -8)$, and $(-3, -3)$.

▶TRY THIS. Sketch the graph of $f(x) = \dfrac{x}{(x-2)^2}$. ■

The graph of any function should illustrate the function's most important features. For a rational function, the most important feature is its asymptotic behavior. The graph of a rational function does not cross its vertical asymptotes, and the graph approaches but does not touch its nonvertical asymptotes as x approaches ∞ or $-\infty$. So be careful with calculator graphs. On some calculators the graph will cross its vertical asymptote in connected mode and, unless the viewing window is selected carefully, the graph will appear to touch its nonvertical asymptotes.

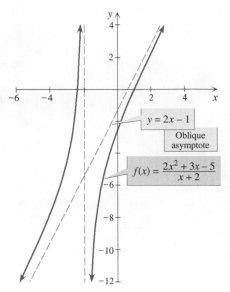

Figure 83

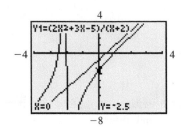

Figure 84

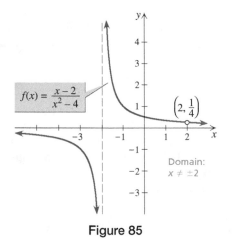

Figure 85

EXAMPLE 6 Graphing a function with an oblique asymptote

Sketch the graph of $f(x) = \dfrac{2x^2 + 3x - 5}{x + 2}$.

Solution

Draw the vertical asymptote $x = -2$ and the oblique asymptote $y = 2x - 1$ determined in Example 3 as dashed lines. The x-intercepts, $(1, 0)$ and $(-2.5, 0)$, are found by solving $2x^2 + 3x - 5 = 0$. The y-intercept is $(0, -2.5)$. The points $(-1, -6)$, $(4, 6.5)$, and $(-3, -4)$ are also on the graph. From these points we can conclude that the curve goes upward toward $x = -2$ from the left and downward toward $x = -2$ from the right. It approaches $y = 2x - 1$ from above as x goes to $-\infty$ and from below as x goes to ∞. Draw the graph approaching its asymptotes as shown in Fig. 83.

The calculator graph in Fig. 84 supports these conclusions.

▶**TRY THIS.** Sketch the graph of $f(x) = \dfrac{3x^2 - 4}{x - 1}$. ∎

All rational functions so far have been given in lowest terms. In the next example the numerator and denominator have a common factor. In this case the graph does not have as many vertical asymptotes as you might expect. The graph is almost identical to the graph of the rational function obtained by reducing the expression to lowest terms.

EXAMPLE 7 A graph with a hole in it

Sketch the graph of $f(x) = \dfrac{x - 2}{x^2 - 4}$.

Solution

Since $x^2 - 4 = (x - 2)(x + 2)$, the domain of f is the set of all real numbers except 2 and -2. Because the rational expression can be reduced, the function f could also be defined as

$$f(x) = \frac{1}{x + 2} \qquad \text{for } x \neq 2 \text{ and } x \neq -2.$$

Note that the domain is determined before the function is simplified. The graph of $y = 1/(x + 2)$ has only one vertical asymptote $x = -2$. In fact, the graph of $y = 1/(x + 2)$ is a translation two units to the left of $y = 1/x$. Since $f(2)$ is undefined, the point $(2, 1/4)$ that would normally be on the graph of $y = 1/(x + 2)$ is omitted. The missing point is indicated on the graph in Fig. 85 as a small open circle. Note that the graph made by a graphing calculator will usually not show the missing point.

▶**TRY THIS.** Sketch the graph of $f(x) = \dfrac{x - 1}{x^2 - 1}$. ∎

Rational Inequalities

An inequality that involves a rational expression, such as $\dfrac{x + 3}{x - 2} \leq 2$, is called a **rational inequality.** Our first thought for solving this inequality might be to clear the denominator by multiplying each side by $x - 2$. But, when we multiply each side of an inequality by a real number, we must know whether the real number is positive or negative. Whether $x - 2$ is positive or negative depends on x. So multiplying by $x - 2$ is not a good idea. *We usually do not multiply a rational inequality* *by an expression that involves a variable.* However, we can solve rational inequalities using the test-point method as we did for quadratic inequalities in Section 1 and polynomial inequalities in Section 5.

We saw in Section 5 that a polynomial function can change sign only at a zero of the function. A rational function can change sign only at a zero of the function or at a vertical asymptote. So to solve a rational inequality we use the following strategy.

STRATEGY

Solving a Rational Inequality with Test Points

1. Rewrite the inequality (if necessary) with zero on one side and a ratio of two polynomials in lowest terms on the other side,

2. Find all zeros for the polynomial functions in the numerator and denominator.

3. The rational function is undefined at the zeros of the denominator. They give the locations of the vertical asymptotes.

4. Locate the zeros from (2) on a number line and test a point in each interval to see whether the rational function is positive or negative on the interval.

EXAMPLE 8 Solving a rational inequality with test points

Solve $\frac{x + 3}{x - 2} \leq 2$. State the solution set using interval notation.

Solution

As with quadratic inequalities, we must have 0 on one side. Note that we do not multiply each side by $x - 2$.

$$\frac{x + 3}{x - 2} \leq 2$$

$$\frac{x + 3}{x - 2} - 2 \leq 0$$

$$\frac{x + 3}{x - 2} - \frac{2(x - 2)}{x - 2} \leq 0 \qquad \text{Get a common denominator.}$$

$$\frac{x + 3 - 2(x - 2)}{x - 2} \leq 0 \qquad \text{Subtract.}$$

$$\frac{7 - x}{x - 2} \leq 0 \qquad \text{Combine like terms.}$$

Now $7 - x = 0$ if $x = 7$ and $x - 2 = 0$ if $x = 2$. Put a 0 above 7 and a "U" (for undefined) above 2 as shown in Fig. 86.

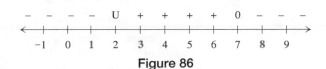

Figure 86

The numbers 2 and 7 divide the number line into three intervals. Select a test point in each interval. We will choose 1, 3, and 8, which are shown in red in Fig. 86. Let $R(x) = \frac{7 - x}{x - 2}$ and evaluate $R(x)$ at each test point:

$$R(1) = \frac{7 - 1}{1 - 2} = -6, \qquad R(3) = \frac{7 - 3}{3 - 2} = 4, \qquad R(8) = \frac{7 - 8}{8 - 2} = -\frac{1}{6}$$

So $-$, $+$, and $-$ are the signs of the rational function in the three intervals in Fig. 86. The inequality $\frac{7 - x}{x - 2} \le 0$ is satisfied whenever $R(x) \le 0$. Note that $R(7) = 0$ but $R(2)$ is undefined. So 7 is included in the solution set, but 2 is not. According to the test points, the solution set is $(-\infty, 2) \cup [7, \infty)$.

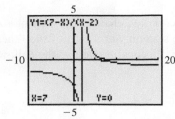

The graph of $y = (7 - x)/(x - 2)$ in Fig. 87 supports our conclusion that the inequality is satisfied if $x < 2$ or if $x \ge 7$.

Figure 87

▶**TRY THIS.** Solve $\frac{1}{x - 1} \ge 1$ using test points. ∎

The test-point method works on any rational inequality for which we can find all zeros of the numerator and denominator. The test-point method depends on the fact that the graph of a rational function can go from one side of the x-axis to the other only at a vertical asymptote (where the function is undefined) or at an x-intercept (where the value of the function is 0).

EXAMPLE **9** | Solving a rational inequality with the test-point method

Solve $\frac{x + 3}{x^2 - 1} \ge 0$. State the solution set using interval notation.

Solution

Since the denominator can be factored, the inequality is equivalent to

$$\frac{x + 3}{(x - 1)(x + 1)} \ge 0.$$

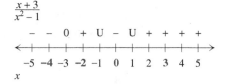

Figure 88

The rational expression is undefined if $x = \pm 1$ and has value 0 if $x = -3$. Above each of these numbers on a number line put a 0 or a "U" (for undefined) as shown in Fig. 88. Now we select -4, -2, 0, and 3 as test points (shown in red in Fig. 88). Let $R(x) = \frac{x + 3}{x^2 - 1}$ and evaluate $R(x)$ at each test point to determine the sign of $R(x)$ in the interval of the test point:

$$R(-4) = -\frac{1}{15}, \qquad R(-2) = \frac{1}{3}, \qquad R(0) = -3, \qquad R(3) = \frac{3}{4}$$

So $-$, $+$, $-$, and $+$ are the signs of the rational expression in the four intervals in Fig. 88. The inequality is satisfied whenever the rational expression has a positive or 0 value. Since $R(-1)$ and $R(1)$ are undefined, -1 and 1 are not in the solution set. The solution set is $[-3, -1) \cup (1, \infty)$.

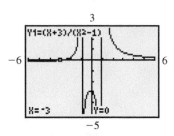

Figure 89

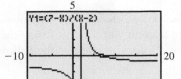

The graph of $y = (x + 3)/(x^2 - 1)$ in Fig. 89 supports the conclusion that the inequality is satisfied if $-3 \le x < -1$ or $x > 1$.

▶**TRY THIS.** Solve $\frac{x + 3}{x - 1} \ge 0$ with test points. ∎

Applications

Rational functions can occur in many applied situations. A horizontal asymptote might indicate that the average cost of producing a product approaches a fixed value in the long run. A vertical asymptote might show that the cost of a project goes up astronomically as a certain barrier is approached.

EXAMPLE 10 | Average cost of a handbook

Eco Publishing spent $5000 to produce an environmental handbook and $8 each for printing. Write a function that gives the average cost to the company per printed handbook. Graph the function for $0 < x \le 500$. What happens to the average cost if the book becomes very, very popular?

Solution

The total cost of producing and printing x handbooks is $8x + 5000$. To find the average cost per book, divide the total cost by the number of books:

$$C = \frac{8x + 5000}{x}$$

This rational function has a vertical asymptote at $x = 0$ and a horizontal asymptote $C = 8$. The graph is shown in Fig. 90. As x gets larger and larger, the $5000 production cost is spread out over more and more books, and the average cost per book approaches $8, as shown by the horizontal asymptote. Using limit notation we write

$$\lim_{x \to \infty} C = 8.$$

▶**TRY THIS.** A truck rents for $100 per day plus $0.80 per mile that it is driven. Write a function that gives the average cost per mile for a one-day rental. What happens to the average cost per mile as the number of miles gets very large? ■

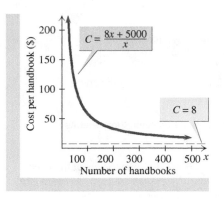

Figure 90

FUNCTION gallery... Some Basic Rational Functions

Horizontal Asymptote *x*-axis and Vertical Asymptote *y*-axis

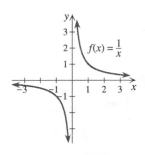

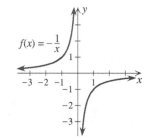

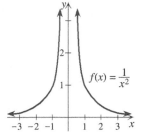

Various Asymptotes

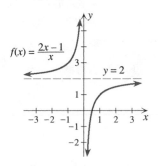

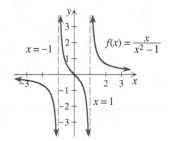

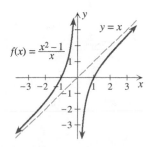

FOR thought... True or False? Explain.

1. The function $f(x) = \dfrac{1}{\sqrt{x-3}}$ is a rational function.

2. The domain of $f(x) = \dfrac{x+2}{x-2}$ is $(-\infty, -2) \cup (-2, 2) \cup (2, \infty)$.

3. The number of vertical asymptotes for a rational function equals the degree of the denominator.

4. The graph of $f(x) = \dfrac{1}{x^4 - 4x^2}$ has four vertical asymptotes.

5. The x-axis is a horizontal asymptote for $f(x) = \dfrac{x^2 - 2x + 7}{x^3 - 4x}$.

6. The x-axis is a horizontal asymptote for the graph of $f(x) = \dfrac{5x-1}{x+2}$.

7. The line $y = x - 3$ is an asymptote for the graph of $f(x) = x - 3 + \dfrac{1}{x-1}$.

8. The graph of a rational function cannot intersect its asymptote.

9. The graph of $f(x) = \dfrac{4}{x^2 - 16}$ is symmetric about the y-axis.

10. The graph of $f(x) = \dfrac{2x+6}{x^2 - 9}$ has only one vertical asymptote.

EXERCISES 6

Fill in the blank.

1. If $P(x)$ and $Q(x)$ are polynomials, then $f(x) = P(x)/Q(x)$ is a(n) _____ function provided $Q(x)$ is not the zero polynomial.

2. If $\lim\limits_{x \to \infty} f(x) = c$, then the line $y = c$ is a(n) _____.

3. If $\lim\limits_{x \to a} |f(x)| = \infty$, then the line $x = a$ is a(n) _____.

4. An asymptote that is neither horizontal nor vertical is a(n) _____ or _____ asymptote.

Find the domain of each rational function.

5. $f(x) = \dfrac{4}{x+2}$

6. $f(x) = \dfrac{-1}{x-2}$

7. $f(x) = \dfrac{-x}{x^2 - 4}$

8. $f(x) = \dfrac{2}{x^2 - x - 2}$

9. $f(x) = \dfrac{2x+3}{x-3}$

10. $f(x) = \dfrac{4-x}{x+2}$

11. $f(x) = \dfrac{x^2 - 2x + 4}{x}$

12. $f(x) = \dfrac{x^3 + 2}{x^2}$

13. $f(x) = \dfrac{3x^2 - 1}{x^3 - x}$

14. $f(x) = \dfrac{x^2 + 1}{8x^3 - 2x}$

15. $f(x) = \dfrac{-x^2 + x}{x^2 + 5x + 6}$

16. $f(x) = \dfrac{-x^2 + 2x - 3}{x^2 + x - 12}$

Determine the domain and the equations of the asymptotes for the graph of each rational function.

17.

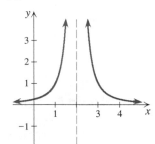

18.

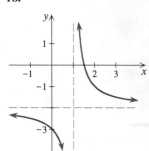

19.

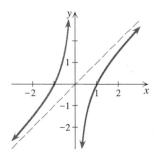

20.

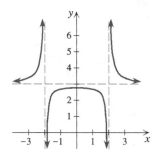

Determine the equations of all asymptotes for the graph of each function. See the summary for finding asymptotes for a rational function.

21. $f(x) = \dfrac{5}{x-2}$

22. $f(x) = \dfrac{-1}{x+12}$

23. $f(x) = \dfrac{-x}{x^2 - 9}$

24. $f(x) = \dfrac{-2}{x^2 - 5x + 6}$

25. $f(x) = \dfrac{2x + 4}{x - 1}$

26. $f(x) = \dfrac{5 - x}{x + 5}$

27. $f(x) = \dfrac{x^2 - 2x + 1}{x}$

28. $f(x) = \dfrac{x^3 - 8}{x^2}$

29. $f(x) = \dfrac{3x^2 + 4}{x + 1}$

30. $f(x) = \dfrac{x^2}{x - 9}$

31. $f(x) = \dfrac{-x^2 + 4x}{x + 2}$

32. $f(x) = \dfrac{-x^2 + 3x - 7}{x - 3}$

Find all asymptotes, x-intercepts, and y-intercepts for the graph of each rational function and sketch the graph of the function. See the procedure for graphing a rational function.

33. $f(x) = \dfrac{-1}{x}$

34. $f(x) = \dfrac{1}{x^2}$

35. $f(x) = \dfrac{1}{x - 2}$

36. $f(x) = \dfrac{-1}{x + 1}$

37. $f(x) = \dfrac{1}{x^2 - 4}$

38. $f(x) = \dfrac{1}{x^2 - 2x + 1}$

39. $f(x) = \dfrac{-1}{(x + 1)^2}$

40. $f(x) = \dfrac{-2}{x^2 - 9}$

41. $f(x) = \dfrac{2x + 1}{x - 1}$

42. $f(x) = \dfrac{3x - 1}{x + 1}$

43. $f(x) = \dfrac{x - 3}{x + 2}$

44. $f(x) = \dfrac{2 - x}{x + 2}$

45. $f(x) = \dfrac{x}{x^2 - 1}$

46. $f(x) = \dfrac{-x}{x^2 - 9}$

47. $f(x) = \dfrac{4x}{x^2 - 2x + 1}$

48. $f(x) = \dfrac{-2x}{x^2 + 6x + 9}$

49. $f(x) = \dfrac{8 - x^2}{x^2 - 9}$

50. $f(x) = \dfrac{2x^2 + x - 8}{x^2 - 4}$

51. $f(x) = \dfrac{2x^2 + 8x + 2}{x^2 + 2x + 1}$

52. $f(x) = \dfrac{-x^2 + 7x - 9}{x^2 - 6x + 9}$

Use a graph or a table to find each limit.

53. $\displaystyle\lim_{x \to \infty} \dfrac{1}{x^2}$

54. $\displaystyle\lim_{x \to -\infty} \dfrac{1}{x^2}$

55. $\displaystyle\lim_{x \to \infty} \dfrac{2x - 3}{x - 1}$

56. $\displaystyle\lim_{x \to \infty} \dfrac{3x^2 - 1}{x^2 - x}$

57. $\displaystyle\lim_{x \to 0^+} \dfrac{1}{x^2}$

58. $\displaystyle\lim_{x \to 0^-} \dfrac{1}{x^2}$

59. $\displaystyle\lim_{x \to 1^+} \dfrac{2}{x - 1}$

60. $\displaystyle\lim_{x \to 1^-} \dfrac{2}{x - 1}$

Find the oblique asymptote and sketch the graph of each rational function.

61. $f(x) = \dfrac{x^2 + 1}{x}$

62. $f(x) = \dfrac{x^2 - 1}{x}$

63. $f(x) = \dfrac{x^3 - 1}{x^2}$

64. $f(x) = \dfrac{x^3 + 1}{x^2}$

65. $f(x) = \dfrac{x^2}{x + 1}$

66. $f(x) = \dfrac{x^2}{x - 1}$

67. $f(x) = \dfrac{2x^2 - x}{x - 1}$

68. $f(x) = \dfrac{-x^2 + x + 1}{x + 1}$

69. $f(x) = \dfrac{x^3 - x^2 - 4x + 5}{x^2 - 4}$

70. $f(x) = \dfrac{x^3 + 2x^2 + x - 2}{x^2 - 1}$

71. $f(x) = \dfrac{-x^3 + x^2 + 5x - 4}{x^2 + x - 2}$

72. $f(x) = \dfrac{x^3 + x^2 - 16x - 24}{x^2 - 2x - 8}$

Match each rational function with its graph (a)–(h), without using a graphing calculator.

73. $f(x) = -\dfrac{3}{x}$

74. $f(x) = \dfrac{1}{3 - x}$

75. $f(x) = \dfrac{x}{x - 3}$

76. $f(x) = \dfrac{x - 3}{x}$

77. $f(x) = \dfrac{1}{x^2 - 3x}$

78. $f(x) = \dfrac{x^2}{x^2 - 9}$

79. $f(x) = \dfrac{x^2 - 3}{x}$

80. $f(x) = \dfrac{-x^3 + 1}{x^2}$

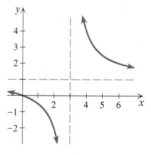

(a)

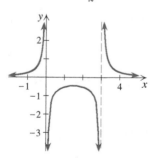

(b)

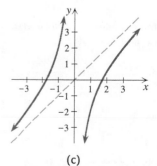

(c)

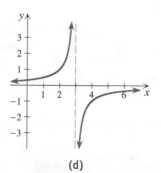

(d)

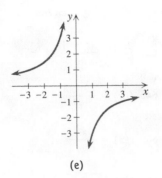

(e)

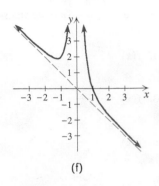

(f)

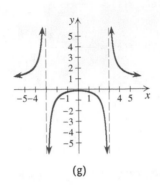

(g)

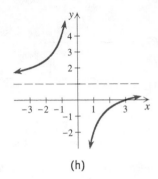

(h)

Sketch the graph of each rational function. Note that the functions are not in lowest terms. Find the domain first.

81. $f(x) = \dfrac{x + 1}{x^2 - 1}$

82. $f(x) = \dfrac{x}{x^2 + 2x}$

83. $f(x) = \dfrac{x^2 - 1}{x - 1}$

84. $f(x) = \dfrac{x^2 - 5x + 6}{x - 2}$

85. $f(x) = \dfrac{x^4 - x^2}{x^2 - 1}$

86. $f(x) = \dfrac{-x^5 + x^3}{x^3 - x}$

87. $f(x) = \dfrac{x^2 - 4}{x^4 - 4x^2}$

88. $f(x) = \dfrac{-x^2 + 1}{x^4 - x^2}$

Sketch the graph of each rational function.

89. $f(x) = \dfrac{2}{x^2 + 1}$

90. $f(x) = \dfrac{x}{x^2 + 1}$

91. $f(x) = \dfrac{x - 1}{x^3 - 9x}$

92. $f(x) = \dfrac{x^2 + 1}{x^3 - 4x}$

93. $f(x) = \dfrac{x + 1}{x^2}$

94. $f(x) = \dfrac{x - 1}{x^2}$

Solve with the test-point method. State the solution set using interval notation. See the strategy for solving a rational inequality.

95. $\dfrac{x - 4}{x + 2} \le 0$

96. $\dfrac{x + 3}{x + 5} \ge 0$

97. $\dfrac{q - 2}{q + 3} < 2$

98. $\dfrac{p + 1}{2p - 1} \ge 1$

99. $\dfrac{w^2 - w - 6}{w - 6} \ge 0$

100. $\dfrac{z - 5}{z^2 + 2z - 8} \le 0$

101. $\dfrac{1}{x + 2} > \dfrac{1}{x - 3}$

102. $\dfrac{1}{x + 1} > \dfrac{2}{x - 1}$

103. $x < \dfrac{3x - 8}{5 - x}$

104. $\dfrac{2}{x + 3} \ge \dfrac{1}{x - 1}$

105. $\dfrac{(x - 3)(x + 1)}{x - 5} \ge 0$

106. $\dfrac{(x + 2)(x - 1)}{(x + 4)^2} \le 0$

107. $\dfrac{x^2 - 7}{2 - x^2} \le 0$

108. $\dfrac{x^2 + 1}{5 - x^2} \ge 0$

109. $\dfrac{x^2 + 2x + 1}{x^2 - 2x - 15} \ge 0$

110. $\dfrac{x^2 - 2x - 8}{x^2 + 10x + 25} \le 0$

111. $\dfrac{1}{w} > \dfrac{1}{w^2}$

112. $\dfrac{1}{w} > w^2$

113. $w > \dfrac{w - 5}{w - 3}$

114. $w < \dfrac{w - 2}{w + 1}$

State the solution sets to the inequalities in Exercises 115–122 by reading the following graphs.

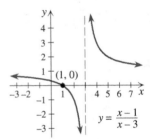

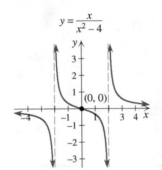

115. $\dfrac{x - 1}{x - 3} > 0$

116. $\dfrac{x - 1}{x - 3} \le 0$

117. $\dfrac{x - 1}{x - 3} \ge 0$

118. $\dfrac{x - 1}{x - 3} < 0$

119. $\dfrac{x}{x^2 - 4} < 0$

120. $\dfrac{x}{x^2 - 4} > 0$

121. $\dfrac{x}{x^2 - 4} \ge 0$

122. $\dfrac{x}{x^2 - 4} \le 0$

Find the equation and sketch the graph of each function.

123. A rational function that passes through $(3, 1)$, has the x-axis as a horizontal asymptote, and has the line $x = 1$ as its only vertical asymptote

124. A rational function that passes through $(0, 4)$, has the x-axis as a horizontal asymptote, and has the line $x = 3$ as its only vertical asymptote

125. A rational function that passes through $(0, 5)$, has the line $y = 1$ as a horizontal asymptote, and has the line $x = 2$ as its only vertical asymptote

126. A rational function that passes through $(-1, 2)$, has the line $y = -2$ as a horizontal asymptote, and has the line $x = -3$ as its only vertical asymptote

127. A rational function that passes through $(0, 0)$ and $(4, 8/7)$, has the x-axis as a horizontal asymptote, and has two vertical asymptotes $x = 3$ and $x = -3$

128. A rational function that passes through $(0, 1)$ and $(2, 1)$, has the x-axis as a horizontal asymptote, and has two vertical asymptotes $x = 3$ and $x = -3$

129. A rational function that passes through $(0, 3)$, has $y = 2x + 1$ as an oblique asymptote, and has $x = 1$ as its only vertical asymptote

130. A rational function that passes through $(3, 3)$, has $y = x - 2$ as an oblique asymptote, and has $x = -5$ as its only vertical asymptote

Solve each problem.

131. *Admission to the Zoo* Winona paid $100 for a lifetime membership to Friends of the Zoo, so that she could gain admittance to the zoo for only $1 per visit. Write Winona's average cost per visit C as a function of the number of visits when she has visited x times. What is her average cost per visit when she has visited the zoo 100 times? Graph the function for $x > 0$. What happens to her average cost per visit if she starts when she is young and visits the zoo every day?

132. *Renting a Car* The cost of renting a car for one day is $39 plus 30 cents per mile. Write the average cost per mile C as a function of the number of miles driven in one day x. Graph the function for $x > 0$. What happens to C as the number of miles gets very large?

133. *Average Speed of an Auto Trip* A 200-mi trip by an electric car must be completed in 4 hr. Let x be the number of hours it takes to travel the first half of the distance and write the average speed for the second half of the trip as a function of x. Graph this function for $0 < x < 4$. What is the significance of the vertical asymptote?
    HINT Average speed is distance divided by time.

134. *Billboard Advertising* An Atlanta marketing agency figures that the monthly cost of a billboard advertising campaign depends on the fraction of the market p that the client wishes to reach. For $0 \le p < 1$ the cost in dollars is determined by the formula $C = (4p - 1200)/(p - 1)$. What is the monthly cost for a campaign intended to reach 95% of the market? Graph this function for $0 \le p < 1$. What happens to the cost for a client who wants to reach 100% of the market?

135. *Carbon Monoxide Poisoning* The accompanying graph shows the relationship between carbon monoxide levels and time for which permanent brain damage will occur (*American Sensors, Carbon Monoxide Detector Owner's Manual*).
    a. At 1800 PPM, how long will it take for permanent brain damage to occur?

    b. What level of carbon monoxide takes 240 minutes to produce permanent brain damage?

c. What are the horizontal and vertical asymptotes for the curve? Explain what these asymptotes mean in simple terms.

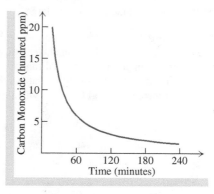

Figure for Exercise 135

136. *Balancing the Costs* A furniture maker buys foam rubber x times per year. The delivery charge is $400 per purchase regardless of the amount purchased. The annual cost of storage is figured as $10,000/x$, because the more frequent the purchase, the less it costs for storage. So the annual cost of delivery and storage is given by

$$C = 400x + \frac{10,000}{x}.$$

a. Graph the function with a graphing calculator.

b. Find the number of purchases per year that minimizes the annual cost of delivery and storage.

137. *Making a Gas Tank* An engineer is designing a cylindrical metal tank that is to hold 500 ft^3 of gasoline.
    a. Write the height h as a function of the radius r.
        HINT The volume is given by $V = \pi r^2 h$.

    b. Use the result of part (a) to write the surface area S as a function of r and graph it.
        HINT The surface area is given by $S = 2\pi r^2 + 2\pi rh$.

    c. Use the minimum feature of a graphing calculator to find the radius to the nearest tenth of a foot that minimizes the surface area. Ignore the thickness of the metal.

    d. If the tank costs $8 per square foot to construct, then what is the minimum cost for making the tank?

138. *Making a Glass Tank* An architect for the Aquarium of the Americas is designing a cylindrical fish tank to hold 1000 ft^3 of water. The bottom and side of the tank will be 3-in.-thick glass and the tank will have no top.
    a. Write the inside surface area of the tank as a function of the inside radius and graph the function.

    b. Use the minimum feature of a graphing calculator to find the inside radius that minimizes that inside surface area.

    c. If Owens Corning will build the tank for $250 per cubic foot of glass used, then what will be the cost for the minimal tank?

FOR WRITING/DISCUSSION

139. *Approximate Value* Given an arbitrary rational function $R(x)$, explain how you can find the approximate value of $R(x)$ when the absolute value of x is very large.

140. *Cooperative Learning* Each student in your small group should write the equations of the horizontal, vertical, and/or oblique asymptotes of an unknown rational function. Then work as a group to find a rational function that has the specified asymptotes. Is there a rational function with any specified asymptotes?

▶ RETHINKING

141. Solve the inequality $(x - 1)^2(x + 5) > 0$.

142. Find all real solutions to $(x - 1)^{2/3} = 8$.

143. Find all real and imaginary solutions to $x^5 + 13x^3 + 36x = 0$.

144. Use Descartes's rule of signs to discuss the possibilities for the roots of the equation $-x^4 - 6x^2 - 3x + 9 = 0$.

145. Find the vertex of the graph of $f(x) = -x^2 + 3x - 10$ and determine the interval on which the function is increasing.

146. Find the inverse of the function $f(x) = -8\sqrt[3]{x - 5} + 4$.

THINKING OUTSIDE THE BOX XXVII

Filling a Triangle Fiber-optic cables just fit inside a triangular pipe as shown in the figure. The cables have circular cross sections and the cross section of the pipe is an equilateral triangle with sides of length 1. Suppose that there are n cables of the same size in the bottom row, $n - 1$ of that size in the next row, and so on.

a. Write the total cross-sectional area of the cables as a function of n.

b. As n approaches infinity, will the triangular pipe get totally filled with cables? Explain.

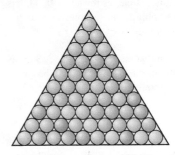

Figure for Thinking Outside the Box XXVII

▶ POP QUIZ 6

1. What is the domain of $f(x) = \frac{x - 1}{x + 4}$?

2. Find the equations of all asymptotes for the graph of $y = \frac{x - 5}{x + 2}$.

3. Find the x-intercept and y-intercept for $f(x) = \frac{x^2 - 9}{x^2 - 1}$.

4. What is the horizontal asymptote for $y = \frac{x - 8}{x + 3}$?

5. What is the oblique asymptote for $f(x) = \frac{x^2 - 2x}{x - 3}$?

6. Solve $\frac{x - 1}{x + 4} \geq 0$.

▶ LINKING

concepts... For Individual or Group Explorations

Modeling Capital and Operating Cost

To decide when to replace company cars, an accountant looks at two cost components: capital cost and operating cost. The capital cost is the difference between the original cost and the salvage value, and the operating cost is the cost of operating the vehicle.

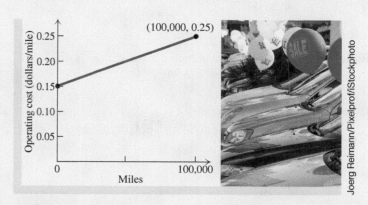

a) For a new Ford Fusion, the capital cost is $3000 plus $0.12 for each mile that the car is driven. Write the capital cost C as a function of the number of miles the car is driven x.

b) If a Ford Fusion is purchased for $19,846 and driven 80,000 miles, then what is its salvage value?

c) The operating cost P for the Fusion starts at $0.15 per mile when the car is new and increases linearly to $0.25 per mile when the car reaches 100,000 miles. Write P as a function of x.

d) What is the operating cost at 70,000 miles?

e) The total cost per mile is given by $T = \frac{C}{x} + P$. Identify all asymptotes and graph T as a function of x.

f) Explain each asymptote in terms of this application.

g) Find T for $x = 20,000$, 30,000, and 90,000 miles.

h) The senior vice president has told the accountant that the goal is to keep the total operating cost less than $0.38 per mile. Is this goal practical?

Highlights

1 Quadratic Functions and Inequalities

Quadratic Function	$y = ax^2 + bx + c$ where $a \neq 0$ Graph is a parabola opening upward for $a > 0$ and downward for $a < 0$.	$y = 2x^2 + 8x - 1$ Opens upward
Vertex	$x = -b/(2a)$ is the x-coordinate of the vertex. Use $y = ax^2 + bx + c$ to find the y-coordinate.	$x = -8/(2 \cdot 2) = -2$ Vertex: $(-2, -9)$
Maximum / Minimum	The y-coordinate of the vertex is the max value of the function if $a < 0$ and the min if $a > 0$.	$y = 2x^2 + 8x - 1$ Min y-value is -9.
Two Forms	General form: $y = ax^2 + bx + c$ Vertex form: $y = a(x - h)^2 + k$, vertex (h, k) By completing the square the general form can be rewritten into vertex form.	$y = 2x^2 + 8x - 1$ $y = 2(x + 2)^2 - 9$
Inequalities	To solve $ax^2 + bx + c > 0$ find all roots to $ax^2 + bx + c = 0$, then test a point in each interval determined by the roots.	$(x - 2)(x + 3) > 0$ Roots are -3 and 2. Solution set: $(-\infty, -3) \cup (2, \infty)$

2 Zeros of Polynomial Functions

Remainder Theorem	The remainder when $P(x)$ is divided by $x - c$ is $P(c)$.	$P(x) = x^2 + 3x - 4$ $P(x)$ divided by $x + 1$ has remainder $P(-1)$ or -6.
Synthetic Division	An abbreviated version of long division, used only for dividing a polynomial by $x - c$.	$\begin{array}{r|rrr} -1 & 1 & 3 & -4 \\ & & -1 & -2 \\ \hline & 1 & 2 & -6 \end{array}$ Dividend $P(x)$, divisor $x + 1$ quotient $x + 2$, remainder -6
Factor Theorem	c is a zero of $y = P(x)$ if and only if $x - c$ is a factor of $P(x)$.	Since $x - 2$ is a factor of $P(x) = x^2 + x - 6$, $P(2) = 0$.
Fundamental Theorem of Algebra	If $y = P(x)$ is a polynomial function of positive degree, then $y = P(x)$ has at least one zero in the set of complex numbers.	$f(x) = x^7 - x^5 + 3x^2 - 9$ has at least one complex zero and in fact has seven of them.
Rational Zero Theorem	If p/q is a rational zero in lowest terms for $y = P(x)$ with integral coefficients, then p is a factor of the constant term and q is a factor of the leading coefficient.	$P(x) = 6x^2 + x - 15$ $P(3/2) = 0$ 3 is a factor of -15; 2 is a factor of 6.

3 The Theory of Equations

n-Root Theorem	If $P(x)$ has positive degree n and complex coefficients, then $P(x) = 0$ has n roots counting multiplicity.	$(x - 2)^3(x^4 - 9) = 0$ has seven complex solutions counting multiplicity.
Conjugate Pairs Theorem	If $P(x)$ has real coefficients, then the imaginary roots of $P(x) = 0$ occur in conjugate pairs.	$x^2 - 4x + 5 = 0$ $x = 2 \pm i$
Descartes's Rule of Signs	The changes in sign of $P(x)$ determine the number of positive roots and the changes in sign of $P(-x)$ determine the number of negative roots to $P(x) = 0$.	$P(x) = x^5 - x^2$ has 1 positive root, no negative roots
Theorem on Bounds	Use synthetic division to obtain an upper bound and lower bound for the roots of $P(x) = 0$.	See Example 5 in Section 3.

4 Miscellaneous Equations

Higher Degree	Solve by factoring.	$x^4 - x^2 - 6 = 0$ $(x^2 - 3)(x^2 + 2) = 0$
Squaring Each Side	Possibly extraneous roots	$\sqrt{x - 3} = -2, x - 3 = 4$ $x = 7$ extraneous root
Rational Exponents	Raise each side to a whole-number power and then apply the even or odd root property.	$x^{2/3} = 4, x^2 = 64, x = \pm 8$
Quadratic Type	Make a substitution to get a quadratic equation.	$x^{1/3} + x^{1/6} - 12 = 0$ $a^2 + a - 12 = 0$ if $a = x^{1/6}$
Absolute Value	Write equivalent equations without absolute value.	$\lvert x^2 - 4 \rvert = 2$ $x^2 - 4 = 2$ or $x^2 - 4 = -2$

5 Graphs of Polynomial Functions

Axis of Symmetry	The parabola $y = ax^2 + bx + c$ is symmetric about the line $x = -b/(2a)$.	Axis of symmetry for $y = x^2 - 4x$ is $x = 2$.
Behavior at the x-Intercepts	A polynomial function crosses the x-axis at $(c, 0)$ if $x - c$ occurs with an odd power or touches the x-axis if $x - c$ occurs with an even power.	$f(x) = (x - 3)^2(x + 1)^3$ crosses at $(-1, 0)$, touches but does not cross at $(3, 0)$.
End Behavior	The leading coefficient and the degree of the polynomial determine the behavior as $x \to -\infty$ or $x \to \infty$.	$y = x^3$ $y \to \infty$ as $x \to \infty$ $y \to -\infty$ as $x \to -\infty$
Polynomial Inequality	Locate all zeros and then test a point in each interval determined by the zeros.	$x^3 - 4x > 0$ when x is in $(-2, 0) \cup (2, \infty)$.

6 Rational Functions and Inequalities

Vertical Asymptote	A rational function in lowest terms has a vertical asymptote wherever the denominator is zero.	$y = x/(x^2 - 4)$ has vertical asymptotes $x = -2$ and $x = 2$.
Horizontal Asymptote	If degree of denominator exceeds degree of numerator, then the x-axis is the horizontal asymptote. If degree of numerator equals degree of denominator, then the ratio of leading coefficients is the horizontal asymptote.	$y = x/(x^2 - 4)$ Horizontal asymptote: $y = 0$ $y = (2x - 1)/(3x - 2)$ Horizontal asymptote: $y = 2/3$
Oblique or Slant Asymptote	If degree of numerator exceeds degree of denominator by 1, then use division to determine the slant asymptote.	$y = \frac{x^2}{x - 1} = x + 1 + \frac{1}{x - 1}$ Slant asymptote: $y = x + 1$
Rational Inequality	Test a point in each interval determined by the zeros and the vertical asymptotes.	$\frac{x - 2}{x + 3} \le 0$ when x is in the interval $(-3, 2]$.

Chapter Review Exercises

Solve each problem.

1. Write the function $f(x) = 3x^2 - 2x + 1$ in the form $f(x) = a(x - h)^2 + k$.

2. Write the function $f(x) = -4\left(x - \frac{1}{3}\right)^2 - \frac{1}{2}$ in the form $f(x) = ax^2 + bx + c$.

3. Find the vertex, axis of symmetry, x-intercepts, and y-intercept for the parabola $y = 2x^2 - 4x - 1$.

4. Find the maximum value of the function $y = -x^2 + 3x - 5$.

5. Write the equation of a parabola that has x-intercepts $(-1, 0)$ and $(3, 0)$ and y-intercept $(0, 6)$.

6. Write the equation of the parabola that has vertex $(1, 2)$ and y-intercept $(0, 5)$.

Find all the real and imaginary zeros for each polynomial function.

7. $f(x) = 3x - 1$

8. $g(x) = 7$

9. $h(x) = x^2 - 8$

10. $m(x) = x^3 - 8$

11. $n(x) = 8x^3 - 1$

12. $C(x) = 3x^2 - 2$

13. $P(t) = t^4 - 100$

14. $S(t) = 25t^4 - 1$

15. $R(s) = 8s^3 - 4s^2 - 2s + 1$

16. $W(s) = s^3 + s^2 + s + 1$

17. $f(x) = x^3 + 2x^2 - 6x$

18. $f(x) = 2x^3 - 4x^2 + 3x$

For each polynomial, find the indicated value in two different ways.

19. $P(x) = 4x^3 - 3x^2 + x - 1, P(3)$

20. $P(x) = 2x^3 + 5x^2 - 3x - 2, P(-2)$

21. $P(x) = -8x^5 + 2x^3 - 6x + 2, P\left(-\dfrac{1}{2}\right)$

22. $P(x) = -4x^4 + 3x^2 + 1, P\left(\dfrac{1}{2}\right)$

Use the rational zero theorem to list all possible rational zeros for each polynomial function.

23. $f(x) = -3x^3 + 6x^2 + 5x - 2$

24. $f(x) = 2x^4 + 9x^2 - 8x - 3$

25. $f(x) = 6x^4 - x^2 - 9x + 3$

26. $f(x) = 4x^3 - 5x^2 - 13x - 8$

Find a polynomial equation with integral coefficients (and lowest degree) that has the given roots.

27. $-\dfrac{1}{2}, 3$

28. $\dfrac{1}{2}, -5$

29. $3 - 2i$

30. $4 + 2i$

31. $2, 1 - 2i$

32. $-3, 3 - 4i$

33. $2 - \sqrt{3}$

34. $1 + \sqrt{2}$

Use Descartes's rule of signs to discuss the possibilities for the roots to each equation. Do not solve the equation.

35. $x^8 + x^6 + 2x^2 = 0$

36. $-x^3 - x - 3 = 0$

37. $4x^3 - 3x^2 + 2x - 9 = 0$

38. $5x^5 + x^3 + 5x = 0$

39. $x^3 + 2x^2 + 2x + 1 = 0$

40. $-x^4 - x^3 + 3x^2 + 5x - 8 = 0$

Establish the best integral bounds for the roots of each equation according to the theorem on bounds.

41. $6x^2 + 5x - 50 = 0$

42. $4x^2 - 12x - 27 = 0$

43. $2x^3 - 15x^2 + 31x - 12 = 0$

44. $x^3 + 6x^2 + 11x + 7 = 0$

45. $12x^3 - 4x^2 - 3x + 1 = 0$

46. $4x^3 - 4x^2 - 9x + 10 = 0$

Find all real and imaginary solutions to each equation, stating multiplicity when it is greater than one.

47. $x^3 - 6x^2 + 11x - 6 = 0$

48. $x^3 + 7x^2 + 16x + 12 = 0$

49. $6x^4 - 5x^3 + 7x^2 - 5x + 1 = 0$

50. $6x^4 + 5x^3 + 25x^2 + 20x + 4 = 0$

51. $x^3 - 9x^2 + 28x - 30 = 0$

52. $x^3 - 4x^2 + 6x - 4 = 0$

53. $x^3 - 4x^2 + 7x - 6 = 0$

54. $2x^3 - 5x^2 + 10x - 4 = 0$

55. $2x^4 - 5x^3 - 2x^2 + 2x = 0$

56. $2x^5 - 15x^4 + 26x^3 - 12x^2 = 0$

Find all real solutions to each equation.

57. $|2v - 1| = 3v$

58. $|2h - 3| = |h|$

59. $x^4 + 7x^2 = 18$

60. $2x^{-2} + 5x^{-1} = 12$

61. $\sqrt{x + 6} - \sqrt{x - 5} = 1$

62. $\sqrt{2x - 1} = \sqrt{x - 1} + 1$

63. $\sqrt{y} + \sqrt[4]{y} = 6$

64. $\sqrt[3]{x^2} + \sqrt[3]{x} = 2$

65. $x^4 - 3x^2 - 4 = 0$

66. $(y - 1)^2 - (y - 1) = 2$

67. $(x - 1)^{2/3} = 4$

68. $(2x - 3)^{-1/2} = \dfrac{1}{2}$

69. $(x + 3)^{-3/4} = -8$

70. $\left(\dfrac{1}{x - 3}\right)^{-1/4} = \dfrac{1}{2}$

71. $\sqrt[3]{3x - 7} = \sqrt[3]{4 - x}$

72. $\sqrt[3]{x + 1} = \sqrt[6]{4x + 9}$

Discuss the symmetry of the graph of each function.

73. $f(x) = 2x^2 - 3x + 9$

74. $f(x) = -3x^2 + 12x - 1$

75. $f(x) = -3x^4 - 2$

76. $f(x) = \dfrac{-x^3}{x^2 - 1}$

77. $f(x) = \dfrac{x}{x^2 + 1}$

78. $f(x) = 2x^4 + 3x^2 + 1$

Find the domain of each rational function.

79. $f(x) = \dfrac{x^2 - 4}{2x + 5}$

80. $f(x) = \dfrac{4x + 1}{x^2 - x - 6}$

81. $f(x) = \dfrac{1}{x^2 + 1}$

82. $f(x) = \dfrac{x - 9}{x^2 - 1}$

Find the x-intercepts, y-intercept, and asymptotes for the graph of each function and sketch the graph.

83. $f(x) = x^2 - x - 2$

84. $f(x) = -2(x - 1)^2 + 6$

85. $f(x) = x^3 - 3x - 2$

86. $f(x) = x^3 - 3x^2 + 4$

87. $f(x) = \dfrac{1}{2}x^3 - \dfrac{1}{2}x^2 - 2x + 2$

88. $f(x) = \frac{1}{2}x^3 - 3x^2 + 4x$ **89.** $f(x) = \frac{1}{4}x^4 - 2x^2 + 4$

90. $f(x) = \frac{1}{2}x^4 + 2x^3 + 2x^2$

91. $f(x) = \frac{2}{x+3}$ **92.** $f(x) = \frac{1}{2-x}$

93. $f(x) = \frac{2x}{x^2-4}$ **94.** $f(x) = \frac{2x^2}{x^2-4}$

95. $f(x) = \frac{x^2-2x+1}{x-2}$ **96.** $f(x) = \frac{-x^2+x+2}{x-1}$

97. $f(x) = \frac{2x-1}{2-x}$ **98.** $f(x) = \frac{1-x}{x+1}$

99. $f(x) = \frac{x^2-4}{x-2}$ **100.** $f(x) = \frac{x^3+x}{x}$

Solve each inequality. State the solution set using interval notation.

101. $8x^2 + 1 < 6x$ **102.** $x^2 + 2x < 63$

103. $(3-x)(x+5) \geq 0$ **104.** $-x^2 - 2x + 15 < 0$

105. $4x^3 - 400x^2 - x + 100 \geq 0$

106. $x^3 - 49x^2 - 52x + 100 < 0$

107. $\frac{x+10}{x+2} < 5$ **108.** $\frac{x-6}{2x+1} \geq 1$

109. $\frac{12-7x}{x^2} > -1$ **110.** $x - \frac{2}{x} \leq -1$

111. $\frac{x^2-3x+2}{x^2-7x+12} \geq 0$ **112.** $\frac{x^2+4x+3}{x^2-2x-15} \leq 0$

Solve each problem.

113. Find the quotient and remainder when $x^3 - 6x^2 + 9x - 15$ is divided by $x - 3$.

114. Find the quotient and remainder when $3x^3 + 4x^2 + 2x - 4$ is divided by $3x - 2$.

115. *Altitude of a Rocket* If the altitude in feet of a model rocket is given by the equation $S = -16t^2 + 156t$, where t is the time in seconds after ignition, then what is the maximum height attained by the rocket?

116. *Antique Saw* Willard is making a reproduction of an antique saw. The handle consists of two pieces of wood joined at a right angle, with the blade being the hypotenuse of the right triangle as shown in the figure. If the total length of the handle is to be 36 in., then what length for each piece would minimize the square of the length of the blade?

Figure for Exercise 116

117. *Bonus Room* A homeowner wants to put a room in the attic of her house. The house is 48 ft wide and the roof has a 7–12 pitch. (The roof rises 7 ft in a horizontal distance of 12 ft.) Find the dimensions of the room that will maximize the area of the cross section shown in the figure.

Figure for Exercise 117

118. *Maximizing Area* An isosceles triangle has one vertex at the origin and a horizontal base below the x-axis with its endpoints on the curve $y = x^2 - 16$. See the figure. Let (a, b) be the vertex in the fourth quadrant and write the area of the triangle as a function of a. Use a graphing calculator to find the point (a, b) for which the triangle has the maximum possible area.

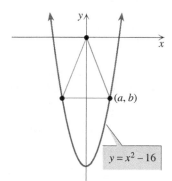

Figure for Exercise 118

119. *Limiting Velocity* As a skydiver falls, his velocity keeps increasing. However, because of air resistance, the rate at which the velocity increases keeps decreasing and there is a limit velocity that the skydiver cannot exceed. To see this behavior, graph

$$V = \frac{1000t}{5t+8}$$

where V is the velocity in feet per second and t is the time in seconds.

a. What is the velocity at time $t = 10$ sec?

b. What is the horizontal asymptote for this graph?

c. What is the limiting velocity that cannot be exceeded?

PhotoLink/Photodisc/Getty Images

Figure for Exercise 119

THINKING OUTSIDE THE BOX XXVIII & XXIX

Polynomial Equation Find a polynomial equation with integral coefficients for which $\sqrt{3} + \sqrt{5}$ is a root.

Bad Arithmetic Each letter in the following addition problem represents a different digit. Find the digits that will make the addition problem correct. There is more than one possibility.

$$\begin{array}{r} S\,E\,V\,E\,N \\ +\,E\,I\,G\,H\,T \\ \hline T\,W\,E\,L\,V\,E \end{array}$$

Chapter Test

Solve each problem.

1. Write $y = 3x^2 - 12x + 1$ in the form $y = a(x - h)^2 + k$.

2. Identify the vertex, axis of symmetry, y-intercept, x-intercepts, and range for $y = 3x^2 - 12x + 1$.

3. What is the minimum value of y in the function $y = 3x^2 - 12x + 1$?

4. Use synthetic division to find the quotient and remainder when $2x^3 - 4x + 5$ is divided by $x + 3$.

5. What is the remainder when

$$x^{98} - 19x^{73} + 17x^{44} - 12x^{23} + 2x^9 - 3$$

is divided by $x - 1$?

6. List the possible rational zeros for the function $f(x) = 3x^3 - 4x^2 + 5x - 6$ according to the rational zero theorem.

7. Find a polynomial equation with real coefficients that has the roots -3 and $4i$.

8. Use Descartes's rule of signs to discuss the possibilities for the roots of $x^3 - 3x^2 + 5x + 7 = 0$.

9. The altitude in feet of a toy rocket t seconds after launch is given by the function $S(t) = -16t^2 + 128t$. Find the maximum altitude reached by the rocket.

Find all real and imaginary zeros for each polynomial function.

10. $f(x) = x^2 - 9$

11. $f(x) = x^4 - 16$

12. $f(x) = x^3 - 4x^2 - x + 10$

Find all real and imaginary roots of each equation. State the multiplicity of a root when it is greater than one.

13. $x^4 + 2x^2 + 1 = 0$

14. $(x^3 - 2x^2)(2x + 3)^3 = 0$

15. $2x^3 - 9x^2 + 14x - 5 = 0$

Sketch the graph of each function.

16. $y = 2(x - 3)^2 + 1$

17. $y = (x - 2)^2(x + 1)$

18. $y = x^3 - 4x$

Find all asymptotes and sketch the graph of each function.

19. $y = \dfrac{1}{x - 2}$

20. $y = \dfrac{2x - 3}{x - 2}$

21. $f(x) = \dfrac{x^2 + 1}{x}$

22. $y = \dfrac{4}{x^2 - 4}$

23. $y = \dfrac{x^2 - 2x + 1}{x - 1}$

Solve each inequality.

24. $x^2 - 2x < 8$

25. $\dfrac{x + 2}{x - 3} > -1$

26. $\dfrac{x + 3}{(4 - x)(x + 1)} \geq 0$

27. $x^3 - 7x > 0$

Find all real solutions to each equation.

28. $(x - 3)^{-2/3} = \dfrac{1}{3}$

29. $\sqrt{x} - \sqrt{x - 7} = 1$

CONCEPTS OF
calculus...

Instantaneous rate of change of the power functions

We define the average rate of change of a function f on the interval $\left[x, x + h\right]$ as

$$\frac{f(x + h) - f(x)}{h}.$$

We then defined the instantaneous rate of change of the function as the limit as h approaches zero of the average rate of change. The notation $f'(x)$, read "f prime of x," is used for the instantaneous rate of change. So

$$f'(x) = \lim_{h \to 0} \frac{f(x + h) - f(x)}{h}.$$

In the following exercises we will find the instantaneous rate of change of the power functions and discover the power rule.

Exercises

1. Let $f(x) = x$.

   a. Find $\dfrac{f(x + h) - f(x)}{h}$ and simplify it.

   b. Find $\lim\limits_{h \to 0} \dfrac{f(x + h) - f(x)}{h}$.

   c. Find $f'(x)$ and $f'(2)$.

2. Let $f(x) = x^2$.

   a. Find $\dfrac{f(x + h) - f(x)}{h}$ and simplify it.

   b. Find $\lim\limits_{h \to 0} \dfrac{f(x + h) - f(x)}{h}$.

   c. Find $f'(x)$ and $f'(2)$.

3. Let $f(x) = x^3$.

   a. Find $\dfrac{f(x + h) - f(x)}{h}$ and simplify it. (*Hint:* To find

   $(x + h)^3$, multiply $x^2 + 2xh + h^2$ by $x + h$.)

   b. Find $\lim\limits_{h \to 0} \dfrac{f(x + h) - f(x)}{h}$.

   c. Find $f'(x)$ and $f'(2)$.

4. Let $f(x) = x^4$.

   a. Find $\dfrac{f(x + h) - f(x)}{h}$ and simplify it.

   b. Find $\lim\limits_{h \to 0} \dfrac{f(x + h) - f(x)}{h}$.

   c. Find $f'(x)$ and $f'(2)$.

5. Look for a pattern in the results for $f'(x)$ in Exercises 1–4. Use the pattern to determine $f'(x)$ for $f(x) = x^5$.

6. Let $f'(x) = x^n$ where n is a positive integer. Use the pattern established in Exercises 1–4 to determine $f'(x)$. This result is known as the *power rule*.

Answers to Exercises

Section 1

For Thought: **1.** F **2.** F **3.** T **4.** T **5.** T **6.** T
7. T **8.** T **9.** T **10.** F

Exercises:
1. upward **3.** vertex **5.** minimum **7.** axis of symmetry

9. $y = (x + 2)^2 - 4$ **11.** $y = \left(x - \dfrac{3}{2}\right)^2 - \dfrac{9}{4}$

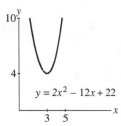

$y = x^2 + 4x$

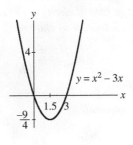

$y = x^2 - 3x$

13. $y = 2(x - 3)^2 + 4$

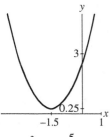

$y = 2x^2 - 12x + 22$

15. $y = -3(x - 1)^2$
$y = -3x^2 + 6x - 3$

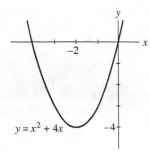

17. $y = \left(x + \dfrac{3}{2}\right)^2 + \dfrac{1}{4}$ **19.** $y = -2\left(x - \dfrac{3}{4}\right)^2 + \dfrac{1}{8}$

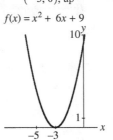

$y = x^2 + 3x + \dfrac{5}{2}$

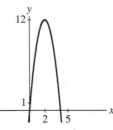

$y = -2x^2 + 3x - 1$

21. $(2, -11)$ **23.** $(4, 1)$ **25.** $(-1/3, 1/18)$
27. Up, $(1, -4)$, $x = 1$, $[-4, \infty)$, min -4, dec $(-\infty, 1]$, inc $[1, \infty)$
29. $(-\infty, 3]$, max 3, inc $(-\infty, 0]$, dec $[0, \infty)$
31. $[-1, \infty)$, min -1, dec $(-\infty, 1]$, inc $[1, \infty)$
33. $[-18, \infty)$, min value -18, dec $(-\infty, -4]$, inc $[-4, \infty)$
35. $[4, \infty)$, min value 4, dec $(-\infty, 3]$, inc $[3, \infty)$
37. $(-\infty, 27/2]$, max $27/2$, inc $(-\infty, 3/2]$, dec $[3/2, \infty)$
39. $(-\infty, 9]$, max 9, inc $(-\infty, 1/2]$, dec $[1/2, \infty)$

41. $(0, -3)$, $x = 0$, $(0, -3)$, $(\pm\sqrt{3}, 0)$, up

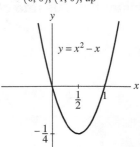

$y = x^2 - 3$

43. $\left(\dfrac{1}{2}, -\dfrac{1}{4}\right)$, $x = \dfrac{1}{2}$, $(0, 0)$, $(1, 0)$, up

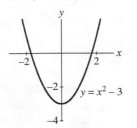

$y = x^2 - x$

45. $(-3, 0)$, $x = -3$, $(0, 9)$, $(-3, 0)$, up

$f(x) = x^2 + 6x + 9$

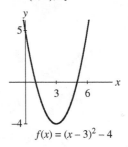

47. $(3, -4)$, $x = 3$, $(0, 5)$, $(1, 0)$, $(5, 0)$, up

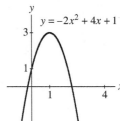

$f(x) = (x - 3)^2 - 4$

49. $(2, 12)$, $x = 2$, $(0, 0)$, $(4, 0)$, down

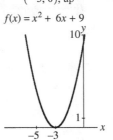

$y = -3(x - 2)^2 + 12$

51. $(1, 3)$, $x = 1$, $(0, 1)$, $\left(1 \pm \dfrac{\sqrt{6}}{2}, 0\right)$, down

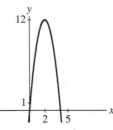

$y = -2x^2 + 4x + 1$

53. $(-\infty, -1) \cup (3, \infty)$ **55.** $(2 - \sqrt{3}, 2 + \sqrt{3})$
57. $(-\infty, -1/3) \cup (1/2, \infty)$ **59.** $(-\infty, -1] \cup [3, \infty)$
61. $(-3, 1)$ **63.** $[-3, 1]$
65. $(2 - \sqrt{2}, 2 + \sqrt{2})$ **67.** $(-\infty, -\sqrt{10}) \cup (\sqrt{10}, \infty)$

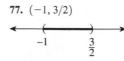

$2 - \sqrt{2} \qquad 2 + \sqrt{2}$

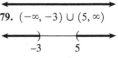

$-\sqrt{10} \qquad \sqrt{10}$

69. $(-\infty, 5 - \sqrt{7}) \cup [5 + \sqrt{7}, \infty]$ **71.** $(-\infty, \infty)$

$5 - \sqrt{7} \qquad 5 + \sqrt{7}$

73. No solution **75.** $(-\infty, \infty)$

77. $(-1, 3/2)$ **79.** $(-\infty, -3) \cup (5, \infty)$

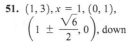

$-1 \qquad \dfrac{3}{2}$

$-3 \qquad 5$

81. $(-\infty, -2] \cup [6, \infty)$

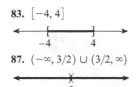

83. $[-4, 4]$

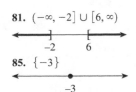

85. $\{-3\}$

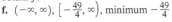

87. $(-\infty, 3/2) \cup (3/2, \infty)$

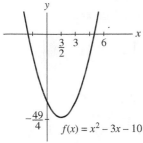

89. a. $\{-2, 5\}$ **b.** $\{0, 3\}$ **c.** $(-\infty, -2) \cup (5, \infty)$ **d.** $[-2, 5]$
e. $f(x) = \left(x - \frac{3}{2}\right)^2 - \frac{49}{4}$; Move $y = x^2$ to the right $\frac{3}{2}$ and down $\frac{49}{4}$ to obtain f.
f. $(-\infty, \infty)$, $\left[-\frac{49}{4}, \infty\right)$, minimum $-\frac{49}{4}$

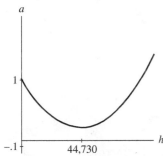

$f(x) = x^2 - 3x - 10$

g. The graph of f is above the x-axis when x is in $(-\infty, -2) \cup (5, \infty)$ and on or below the x-axis when x is in $[-2, 5]$.
h. $(-2, 0)$, $(5, 0)$, $(0, -10)$, $x = \frac{3}{2}$, $\left(\frac{3}{2}, -\frac{49}{4}\right)$, opens upward, dec on $\left(-\infty, \frac{3}{2}\right]$ and inc on $\left[\frac{3}{2}, \infty\right)$
91. 261 ft   **93. a.** 408 ft   **b.** $(10 + \sqrt{102})/2 \approx 10.05$ sec
95. a. Approximately 100 mph   **b.** 97.24 mph   **c.** 13.2 gal/hr
97. 50 yd by 50 yd   **99.** 20 ft by 30 ft   **101.** 7.5 ft by 15 ft
103. 5 in. wide, 2.5 in. high
105. a. $p = 50 - n$ **b.** $R = 50n - n^2$ **c.** $625   **107.** 1/2

109. a.

$a = 3.89 \times 10^{-10} h^2 - 3.48 \times 10^{-5} h + 1$

b. Decreasing   **c.** Dec $[0, 44{,}730]$, inc $[44{,}730, \infty)$ **d.** No
e. Approximately $(0, 30{,}000)$
111. a. $y = -2405.7x + 36{,}397.8$,
$y = 156.4x^2 - 3969.9x + 39{,}265.6$
b. Quadratic

c. $9935, $14,521
113. 9/10   **115.** 12   **117.** $\{-3, 1, 3, 4\}$, $\{2, 5\}$

Section 2

For Thought: **1.** F   **2.** T   **3.** T   **4.** T   **5.** F   **6.** F
7. F   **8.** T   **9.** T   **10.** F

Exercises:
1. zero   **3.** zero, factor   **5.** $x - 3, 1$ **7.** $-2x^2 + 6x - 14, 33$
9. $s^2 + 2, 16$ **11.** $x + 6, 13$ **13.** $-x^2 + 4x - 16, 57$
15. $4x^2 + 2x - 4, 0$ **17.** $2a^2 - 4a + 6, 0$
19. $x^3 + x^2 + x + 1, -2$ **21.** $x^4 + 2x^3 - 2x^2 - 4x - 4, -13$
23. 0   **25.** -33 **27.** 5   **29.** $\frac{55}{8}$ **31.** 0   **33.** 8
35. $(x + 3)(x + 2)(x - 1)$ **37.** $(x - 4)(x + 3)(x + 5)$
39. Yes   **41.** No   **43.** Yes   **45.** No
47. $\pm(1, 2, 3, 4, 6, 8, 12, 24)$ **49.** $\pm(1, 3, 5, 15)$
51. $\pm\left(1, 3, 5, 15, \frac{1}{2}, \frac{1}{4}, \frac{1}{8}, \frac{3}{2}, \frac{3}{4}, \frac{3}{8}, \frac{5}{2}, \frac{5}{4}, \frac{5}{8}, \frac{15}{2}, \frac{15}{4}, \frac{15}{8}\right)$
53. $\pm\left(1, 2, \frac{1}{2}, \frac{1}{3}, \frac{2}{3}, \frac{1}{6}, \frac{1}{9}, \frac{2}{9}, \frac{1}{18}\right)$ **55.** $2, 3, 4$ **57.** $-3, 2 \pm i$
59. $\frac{1}{2}, \frac{3}{2}, \frac{5}{2}$ **61.** $\frac{1}{2}, \frac{1 \pm i}{3}$ **63.** $-6, 3 \pm i$ **65.** $\pm i, 1, -2$
67. $-1, \pm\sqrt{2}$ **69.** $\frac{1}{4}, \frac{1}{3}, \frac{1}{2}$ **71.** $\frac{1}{16}, 1 \pm 2i$ **73.** $-\frac{6}{7}, \frac{7}{3}, \pm i$
75. $-5, -2, 1, \pm 3i$ **77.** $1, 3, 5, 2 \pm \sqrt{3}$ **79.** $2 + \frac{5}{x - 2}$
81. $a + \frac{5}{a - 3}$ **83.** $1 + \frac{-3c}{c^2 - 4}$ **85.** $2 + \frac{-7}{2t + 1}$
87. a. 6 hr   **b.** ≈ 120 ppm   **c.** ≈ 3 hr   **d.** ≈ 4 hr
89. 5 in. by 9 in. by 14 in.   **93.** $f(x) = 2\left(x - \frac{3}{4}\right)^2 - \frac{1}{8}$ **95.** $(-\infty, \infty)$
97. a. $6a(4a - 5)(a + 2)$ **b.** $x(x^2 + 4)(x - 2)(x + 2)$

Section 3

For Thought: **1.** F   **2.** T   **3.** T   **4.** F   **5.** F   **6.** T
7. F   **8.** F   **9.** T   **10.** T

Exercises:
1. multiplicity   **3.** $a - bi$ **5.** Degree 2, 5 with multiplicity 2
7. Degree 5, ± 3, 0 with multiplicity 3
9. Degree 4, 0, 1 each with multiplicity 2
11. Degree 4, $-\frac{4}{3}, \frac{3}{2}$ each with multiplicity 2
13. Degree 3, 0, $2 \pm \sqrt{10}$ **15.** $x^2 + 9$ **17.** $x^2 - 2x - 1$
19. $x^2 - 6x + 13$ **21.** $x^3 - 8x^2 + 37x - 50$
23. $x^2 - 2x - 15 = 0$ **25.** $x^2 + 16 = 0$
27. $x^2 - 6x + 10 = 0$ **29.** $x^3 + 2x^2 + x + 2 = 0$
31. $x^3 + 3x = 0$ **33.** $x^3 - 5x^2 + 8x - 6 = 0$
35. $x^3 - 6x^2 + 11x - 6 = 0$ **37.** $x^3 - 5x^2 + 17x - 13 = 0$
39. $24x^3 - 26x^2 + 9x - 1 = 0$ **41.**
$x^4 - 2x^3 + 3x^2 - 2x + 2 = 0$
43. 3 neg; 1 neg, 2 imag   **45.** 1 pos, 2 neg; 1 pos, 2 imag
47. 4 imag   **49.** 4 pos; 2 pos, 2 imag; 4 imag   **51.** 4 imag and 0
53. $-1 < x < 3$ **55.** $-3 < x < 2$ **57.** $-1 < w < 5$
59. $-1 < x < 3$ **61.** $-2, 1, 5$ **63.** $-3, \frac{3 \pm \sqrt{13}}{2}$
65. $\pm i, 2, -4$ **67.** $-5, \frac{1}{3}, \frac{1}{2}$ **69.** $1, -2$ each with multiplicity 2
71. 0, 2 with multiplicity 3   **73.** 0, 1, ± 2, $\pm i\sqrt{3}$
75. $-2, -1, 1/4, 1, 3/2$ **77.** $-5 < x < 6, -5 < x < 6$
79. $-6 < x < 6, -5 < x < 5$ **81.** $-1 < x < 23, -1 < x < 23$
83. 4 hr and 5 hr   **85.** 3 in.   **91.** $f(x) = -\frac{1}{2}x^3 + 3x^2 - \frac{11}{2}x + 3$
93. $\pm 1, \pm 2, \pm 3, \pm 6, \pm 1/2, \pm 3/2$ **95.** b is a function of a.
97. $(f \circ g)(x) = 8x^2 - 32x + 23$

Section 4

For Thought: 1. F   2. F   3. F   4. F   5. T   6. F
7. F   8. T   9. T   10. F

Exercises:

1. $\{\pm 2, -3\}$ 3. $\left\{-500, \pm \dfrac{\sqrt{2}}{2}\right\}$ 5. $\left\{0, \dfrac{15 \pm \sqrt{205}}{2}\right\}$

7. $\{0, \pm 2\}$ 9. $\{\pm 2, \pm 2i\}$ 11. $\{8\}$ 13. $\{25\}$

15. $\left\{\dfrac{1}{4}\right\}$ 17. $\left\{\dfrac{2 + \sqrt{13}}{9}\right\}$ 19. $\{-4, 6\}$ 21. $\{9\}$

23. $\{5\}$ 25. $\{10\}$ 27. $\{\pm 2\sqrt{2}\}$ 29. $\left\{\pm \dfrac{1}{8}\right\}$

31. $\left\{\dfrac{1}{49}\right\}$ 33. $\left\{\dfrac{5}{4}\right\}$ 35. $\{\pm 3, \pm \sqrt{3}\}$ 37. $\{\pm i\sqrt{7}, \pm 1\}$

39. $\{\pm 3i, \pm 3\}$ 41. $\left\{-\dfrac{17}{2}, \dfrac{13}{2}\right\}$ 43. $\left\{\dfrac{3}{20}, \dfrac{4}{15}\right\}$

45. $\{-2, -1, 5, 6\}$ 47. $\{1, 9\}$ 49. $\{9, 16\}$ 51. $\{8, 125\}$
53. $\{\pm \sqrt{7}, \pm 1\}$ 55. $\{0, 8\}$ 57. $\{-3, 0, 1, 4\}$

59. $\{-2, 4\}$ 61. $\{1/2\}$ 63. $\{3\}$ 65. $\left\{\dfrac{1}{2}\right\}$

67. $\{\pm 2, -1 \pm i\sqrt{3}, 1 \pm i\sqrt{3}\}$ 69. $\{\sqrt{3}, 2\}$

71. $\{-2, \pm 1\}$ 73. $\{5 \pm 9i\}$ 75. $\left\{\dfrac{1 \pm 4\sqrt{2}}{3}\right\}$

77. $\{\pm 2\sqrt{6}, \pm \sqrt{35}\}$ 79. $\{\pm 3, 2\}$ 81. $\{-11\}$ 83. $\{2\}$

85. 279.56 m^2 87. 23   89. $\dfrac{25}{4}$ and $\dfrac{49}{4}$ 91. 5 in.

93. 1600 ft^2 95. 17,419.3 lb   97. 462.89 in.^3 99. 1 P.M.
101. **a.** \$478 million   **b.** \$572 million   103. 27.4 m
105. $6 - \sqrt{10} \text{ ft}$ 107. $x^3 + 5x^2 + 4x + 20 = 0$

109. $(-2, 4)$ 111. $y = -\dfrac{2}{3}x + 10$

Section 5

For Thought: 1. F   2. T   3. T   4. F   5. T   6. T
7. F   8. F   9. T   10. F

Exercises:
1. y-axis   3. $-b/(2a)$ 5. Symmetric about y-axis
7. Symmetric about $x = 3/2$ 9. Neither symmetry
11. Symmetric about origin   13. Symmetric about $x = 5$
15. Symmetric about origin   17. Does not cross at $(4, 0)$

19. Crosses at $(1/2, 0)$ 21. Crosses at $(1/4, 0)$
23. No x-intercepts   25. Does not cross at $(0, 0)$, crosses at $(3, 0)$
27. Crosses at $(1/2, 0)$, does not cross at $(1, 0)$
29. Does not cross at $(-3, 0)$, crosses at $(2, 0)$ 31. $y \to \infty$
33. $y \to -\infty$ 35. $y \to -\infty$ 37. $y \to \infty$ 39. $y \to \infty$
41. Neither symmetry; crosses at $(-2, 0)$; does not cross at $(1, 0)$; $y \to \infty$
as $x \to \infty$; $y \to -\infty$ as $x \to -\infty$
43. Symmetric about y-axis; no x-intercepts; $y \to \infty$ as $x \to \infty$; $y \to \infty$ as
$x \to -\infty$ 45. ∞ 47. $-\infty$ 49. ∞ 51. $-\infty$
53.   55.

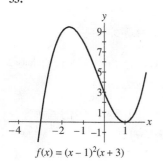

$f(x) = (x - 1)^2(x + 3)$

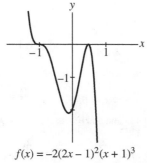

$f(x) = -2(2x - 1)^2(x + 1)^3$

57. (e)   59. (g)   61. (b)   63. (c)
65.   67.

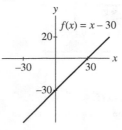

$f(x) = x - 30$

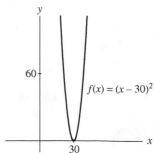

$f(x) = (x - 30)^2$

69.   71.

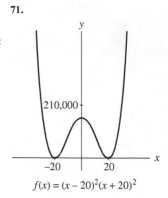

$f(x) = x^3 - 40x^2$

$f(x) = (x - 20)^2(x + 20)^2$

73.   75.

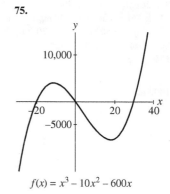

$f(x) = -x^3 - x^2 + 5x - 3$

$f(x) = x^3 - 10x^2 - 600x$

77.   79.

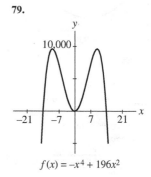

$f(x) = x^3 + 18x^2 - 37x + 60$

$f(x) = -x^4 + 196x^2$

81.

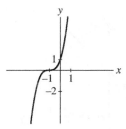

$f(x) = x^3 + 3x^2 + 3x + 1$

83.

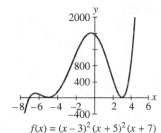

$f(x) = (x-3)^2(x+5)^2(x+7)$

85. $(-\sqrt{3}, 0) \cup (\sqrt{3}, \infty)$ **87.** $(-\infty, -\sqrt{2}] \cup \{0\} \cup [\sqrt{2}, \infty)$
89. $(-4, -1) \cup (1, \infty)$ **91.** $[-4, 2] \cup [6, \infty)$ **93.** $(-\infty, 1)$
95. $[-\sqrt{10}, -3] \cup [3, \sqrt{10}]$ **97.** $(-2, 0) \cup (2, \infty)$
99. $[-2, 0] \cup [2, \infty)$ **101.** $(-2, -1) \cup (1, 2)$
103. $(-\infty, -2] \cup [-1, 1] \cup [2, \infty)$ **105.** d

107.

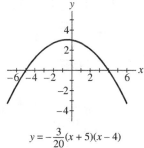

$y = -\frac{3}{20}(x+5)(x-4)$

109.

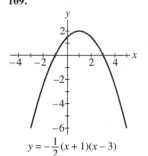

$y = -\frac{1}{2}(x+1)(x-3)$

111.

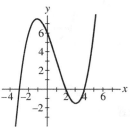

$y = \frac{1}{4}(x-2)(x+3)(x-4)$

113.

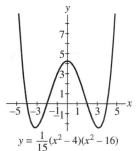

$y = \frac{1}{15}(x^2-4)(x^2-16)$

115. $3,400, $2,600, $x > $2,200
117. Decreases to 0 at 30 stores, then increases
119. $V = 3x^3 - 24x^2 + 48x$, 4/3 in. by 4 in. by 16/3 in.
121. All of the paint coats the inside of can. $r = 6.67 \times 10^{-4}$ ft and $h = 11,924.69$ ft, $r = 2.82$ ft and $h = 6.67 \times 10^{-4}$ ft
123. $\{13\}$ **125.** $x^3 + x^2 - 11x + 24, -53$
127. $[0, \infty), (-\infty, \infty)$

Section 6

For Thought: **1.** F **2.** F **3.** F **4.** F **5.** T **6.** F
7. T **8.** F **9.** T **10.** T
Exercises:
1. rational **3.** vertical asymptote **5.** $(-\infty, -2) \cup (-2, \infty)$
7. $(-\infty, -2) \cup (-2, 2) \cup (2, \infty)$ **9.** $(-\infty, 3) \cup (3, \infty)$
11. $(-\infty, 0) \cup (0, \infty)$ **13.** $(-\infty, -1) \cup (-1, 0) \cup (0, 1) \cup (1, \infty)$
15. $(-\infty, -3) \cup (-3, -2) \cup (-2, \infty)$
17. $(-\infty, 2) \cup (2, \infty), y = 0, x = 2$

19. $(-\infty, 0) \cup (0, \infty), y = x, x = 0$
21. $x = 2, y = 0$ **23.** $x = \pm 3, y = 0$ **25.** $x = 1, y = 2$
27. $x = 0, y = x - 2$ **29.** $x = -1, y = 3x - 3$
31. $x = -2, y = -x + 6$
33. $x = 0, y = 0$ **35.** $x = 2, y = 0, (0, -1/2)$

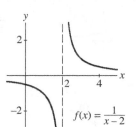

$f(x) = \frac{-1}{x}$

$f(x) = \frac{1}{x-2}$

37. $x = \pm 2, y = 0, (0, -1/4)$

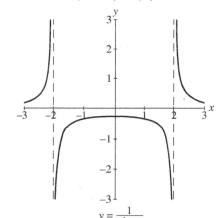

$y = \frac{1}{x^2 - 4}$

39. $x = -1, y = 0, (0, -1)$
$f(x) = \frac{-1}{(x+1)^2}$

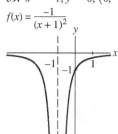

41. $x = 1, y = 2, (0, -1), (-1/2, 0)$

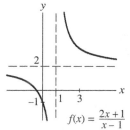

$f(x) = \frac{2x+1}{x-1}$

43. $x = -2, y = 1, (3, 0), (0, -3/2)$

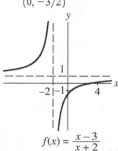

$f(x) = \frac{x-3}{x+2}$

45. $x = \pm 1, y = 0, (0, 0)$

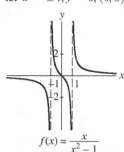

$f(x) = \frac{x}{x^2 - 1}$

47. $x = 1, y = 0, (0, 0)$

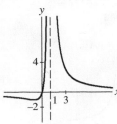

$$f(x) = \frac{4x}{x^2 - 2x + 1}$$

49. $x = \pm 3, y = -1, (0, -8/9),$
$(\pm \sqrt{8}, 0)$

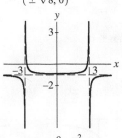

$$f(x) = \frac{8 - x^2}{x^2 - 9}$$

51. $x = -1, y = 2, (0, 2),$
$(-2 \pm \sqrt{3}, 0)$

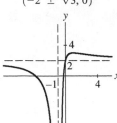

$$f(x) = \frac{2x^2 + 8x + 2}{x^2 + 2x + 1}$$

53. 0 **55.** 2 **57.** ∞ **59.** ∞

61. $y = x$

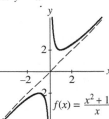

$$f(x) = \frac{x^2 + 1}{x}$$

63. $y = x$

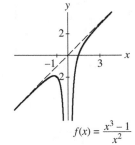

$$f(x) = \frac{x^3 - 1}{x^2}$$

65. $y = x - 1$

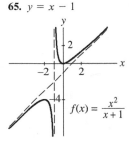

$$f(x) = \frac{x^2}{x + 1}$$

67. $y = 2x + 1$

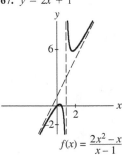

$$f(x) = \frac{2x^2 - x}{x - 1}$$

69. $y = x - 1$

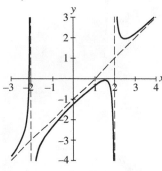

$$f(x) = \frac{x^3 - x^2 - 4x + 5}{x^2 - 4}$$

71. $y = -x + 2$

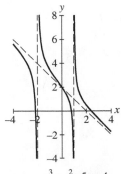

$$f(x) = \frac{-x^3 + x^2 + 5x - 4}{x^2 + x - 2}$$

73. (e) **75.** (a) **77.** (b) **79.** (c)

81. $x \neq \pm 1$

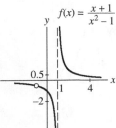

$$f(x) = \frac{x + 1}{x^2 - 1}$$

83. $x \neq 1$

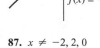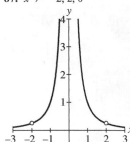

$$f(x) = \frac{x^2 - 1}{x - 1}$$

85. $x \neq -1, 1$

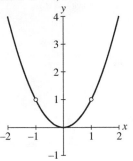

$$f(x) = \frac{x^4 - x^2}{x^2 - 1}$$

87. $x \neq -2, 2, 0$

$$f(x) = \frac{x^2 - 4}{x^4 - 4x^2}$$

89.

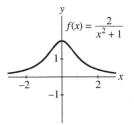

$$f(x) = \frac{2}{x^2 + 1}$$

91.

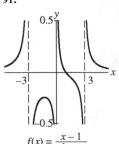

$$f(x) = \frac{x - 1}{x^3 - 9x}$$

93.

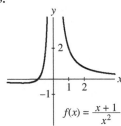

$$f(x) = \frac{x + 1}{x^2}$$

95. $(-2, 4]$ **97.** $(-\infty, -8) \cup (-3, \infty)$ **99.** $[-2, 3] \cup (6, \infty)$
101. $(-2, 3)$ **103.** $(-\infty, -2) \cup (4, 5)$ **105.** $[-1, 3] \cup (5, \infty)$
107. $(-\infty, -\sqrt{7}] \cup (-\sqrt{2}, \sqrt{2}) \cup [\sqrt{7}, \infty)$
109. $(-\infty, -3) \cup \{-1\} \cup (5, \infty)$ **111.** $(1, \infty)$ **113.** $(3, \infty)$
115. $(-\infty, 1) \cup (3, \infty)$ **117.** $(-\infty, 1] \cup (3, \infty)$
119. $(-\infty, -2) \cup (0, 2)$ **121.** $(-2, 0] \cup (2, \infty)$
123.

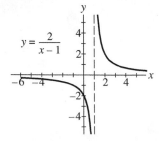

$$y = \frac{2}{x - 1}$$

125.

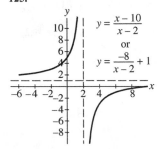

$$y = \frac{x - 10}{x - 2}$$
or
$$y = \frac{-8}{x - 2} + 1$$

127.

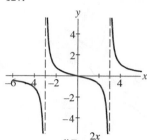

$$y = \frac{2x}{x^2 - 9}$$

129.

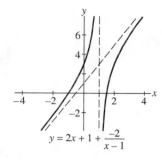

$$y = 2x + 1 + \frac{-2}{x - 1}$$

131. $C = \dfrac{100 + x}{x}, \$2, C \to \$1$ **133.** $S = \dfrac{100}{4 - x}, S \to \infty$ as $x \to 4$

135. a. ≈ 15 min   **b.** ≈ 220 PPM

c. $t = 0$, PPM $= 0$; Low concentration for long time or high concentration for short time will give permanent brain damage.

137. a. $h = 500/(\pi r^2)$

b. $S = 2\pi r^2 + 1000/r$

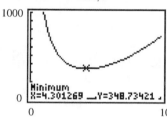

c. 4.3 ft   **d.** \$2789.87

141. $(-5, 1) \cup (1, \infty)$ **143.** $\{0, \pm 2i, \pm 3i\}$

145. $(3/2, -31/4), (-\infty, 3/2]$

Chapter Review Exercises

1. $f(x) = 3\left(x - \dfrac{1}{3}\right)^2 + \dfrac{2}{3}$

3. $(1, -3), x = 1, \left(\dfrac{2 \pm \sqrt{6}}{2}, 0\right), (0, -1)$

5. $y = -2x^2 + 4x + 6$ **7.** $1/3$ **9.** $\pm 2\sqrt{2}$

11. $\dfrac{1}{2}, \dfrac{-1 \pm i\sqrt{3}}{4}$ **13.** $\pm\sqrt{10}, \pm i\sqrt{10}$

15. $-\dfrac{1}{2}, \dfrac{1}{2}$ with multiplicity 2   **17.** $0, -1 \pm \sqrt{7}$ **19.** 83

21. 5   **23.** $\pm\left(1, 2, \dfrac{1}{3}, \dfrac{2}{3}\right)$ **25.** $\pm\left(1, 3, \dfrac{1}{2}, \dfrac{1}{3}, \dfrac{1}{6}, \dfrac{3}{2}\right)$

27. $2x^2 - 5x - 3 = 0$ **29.** $x^2 - 6x + 13 = 0$

31. $x^3 - 4x^2 + 9x - 10 = 0$ **33.** $x^2 - 4x + 1 = 0$

35. 0 with multiplicity 2, 6 imag   **37.** 1 pos, 2 imag; 3 pos

39. 3 neg; 1 neg, 2 imag   **41.** $-4 < x < 3$

43. $-1 < x < 8$ **45.** $-1 < x < 1$ **47.** 1, 2, 3

49. $\dfrac{1}{2}, \dfrac{1}{3}, \pm i$ **51.** $3, 3 \pm i$ **53.** $2, 1 \pm i\sqrt{2}$

55. $0, \dfrac{1}{2}, 1 \pm \sqrt{3}$ **57.** $\{1/5\}$ **59.** $\{\pm\sqrt{2}\}$ **61.** $\{30\}$

63. $\{16\}$ **65.** $\{\pm 2\}$ **67.** $\{-7, 9\}$ **69.** No solution

71. $\{11/4\}$ **73.** $x = 3/4$ **75.** y-axis   **77.** Origin

79. $(-\infty, -2.5) \cup (-2.5, \infty)$ **81.** $(-\infty, \infty)$

83. $(-1, 0), (2, 0), (0, -2)$

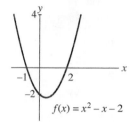

$$f(x) = x^2 - x - 2$$

85. $(-1, 0), (2, 0), (0, -2)$

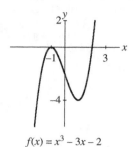

$$f(x) = x^3 - 3x - 2$$

87. $(\pm 2, 0), (1, 0), (0, 2)$

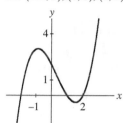

$$f(x) = \dfrac{1}{2}x^3 - \dfrac{1}{2}x^2 - 2x + 2$$

89. $(\pm 2, 0), (0, 4)$

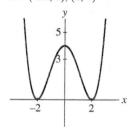

$$f(x) = \dfrac{1}{4}x^4 - 2x^2 + 4$$

91. $(0, 2/3), x = -3, y = 0$

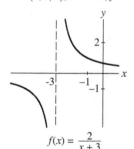

$$f(x) = \dfrac{2}{x + 3}$$

93. $(0, 0), x = \pm 2, y = 0$

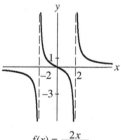

$$f(x) = \dfrac{2x}{x^2 - 4}$$

95. $(1, 0), \left(0, -\dfrac{1}{2}\right), x = 2,$ $y = x$

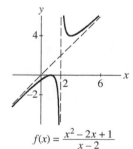

$$f(x) = \dfrac{x^2 - 2x + 1}{x - 2}$$

97. $\left(\dfrac{1}{2}, 0\right), \left(0, -\dfrac{1}{2}\right), x = 2,$ $y = -2$

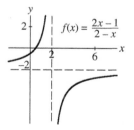

$$f(x) = \dfrac{2x - 1}{2 - x}$$

99. $(-2, 0), (0, 2)$

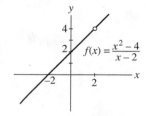

$$f(x) = \dfrac{x^2 - 4}{x - 2}$$

101. $(1/4, 1/2)$ **103.** $[-5, 3]$ **105.** $[-1/2, 1/2] \cup [100, \infty)$
107. $(-\infty, -2) \cup (0, \infty)$ **109.** $(-\infty, 0) \cup (0, 3) \cup (4, \infty)$
111. $(-\infty, 1] \cup [2, 3) \cup (4, \infty)$ **113.** $x^2 - 3x, -15$
115. 380.25 ft   **117.** 24 ft wide, 7 ft high
119. a. 172.4 ft/sec   **b.** $V = 200$ **c.** 200 ft/sec

Chapter Test

1. $y = 3(x - 2)^2 - 11$

2. $(2, -11), x = 2, (0, 1), \left(\dfrac{6 \pm \sqrt{33}}{3}, 0\right), [-11, \infty)$ **3.** -11

4. $2x^2 - 6x + 14, -37$ **5.** -14 **6.** $\pm\left(1, 2, 3, 6, \dfrac{1}{3}, \dfrac{2}{3}\right)$

7. $x^3 + 3x^2 + 16x + 48 = 0$ **8.** 2 pos, 1 neg; 1 neg, 2 imag
9. 256 ft   **10.** ± 3 **11.** $\pm 2, \pm 2i$ **12.** $1 \pm \sqrt{6}, 2$
13. $\pm i$ each with multiplicity 2

14. 2, 0 with multiplicity 2, $-\frac{3}{2}$ with multiplicity 3   **15.** $2 \pm i, \dfrac{1}{2}$

16.

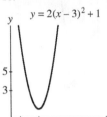

$y = 2(x - 3)^2 + 1$

17.

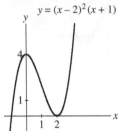

$y = (x - 2)^2(x + 1)$

18.

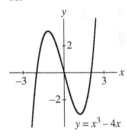

$y = x^3 - 4x$

19. $x = 2, y = 0$

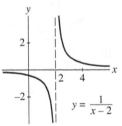

$y = \dfrac{1}{x - 2}$

20. $x = 2, y = 2$

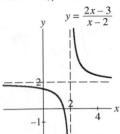

$y = \dfrac{2x - 3}{x - 2}$

21. $x = 0, y = x$

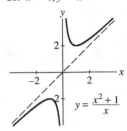

$y = \dfrac{x^2 + 1}{x}$

22. $x = \pm 2, y = 0$

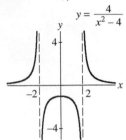

$y = \dfrac{4}{x^2 - 4}$

23.

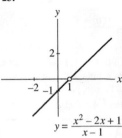

$y = \dfrac{x^2 - 2x + 1}{x - 1}$

24. $(-2, 4)$ **25.** $(-\infty, 1/2) \cup (3, \infty)$ **26.** $(-\infty, -3] \cup (-1, 4)$
27. $(-\sqrt{7}, 0) \cup (\sqrt{7}, \infty)$ **28.** $\{3 \pm 3\sqrt{3}\}$ **29.** $\{16\}$

Solutions to Try This Exercises

1.1 $f(x) = 2x^2 - 8x + 9$
$f(x) = 2(x^2 - 4x) + 9$
$f(x) = 2(x^2 - 4x + 4 - 4) + 9$
$f(x) = 2(x^2 - 4x + 4) - 8 + 9$
$f(x) = 2(x - 2)^2 + 1$

1.2 $f(x) = -2x^2 - 4x + 1$
$f(x) = -2(x^2 + 2x) + 1$
$f(x) = -2(x^2 + 2x + 1 - 1) + 1$
$f(x) = -2(x^2 + 2x + 1) + 2 + 1$
$f(x) = -2(x + 1)^2 + 3$

The graph is a parabola opening downward from $(-1, 3)$. The graph goes through $(0, 1)$ and $(-2, 1)$.

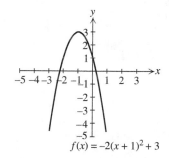

$f(x) = -2(x + 1)^2 + 3$

3.1.3 $x = \dfrac{-b}{2a} = \dfrac{-(-12)}{2(3)} = 2$
$f(2) = 3(2^2) - 12(2) + 5 = -7$
The vertex is $(2, -7)$.

1.4 The vertex is $(5, -4)$ and the axis of symmetry is $x = 5$. Since the parabola opens upward from the vertex, the range is $[-4, \infty)$ and -4 is the minimum value of the function. The function is decreasing on $(-\infty, 5]$ and increasing on $[5, \infty)$.

1.5 If $x = 0$, then $y = 3(0 - 5)^2 - 4 = 71$. If $y = 0$, then
$3(x - 5)^2 - 4 = 0$ or $x = 5 \pm \sqrt{\frac{4}{3}} = 5 \pm \frac{2\sqrt{3}}{3} = \frac{15 \pm 2\sqrt{3}}{3}$.

The intercepts are $(0, 71)$ and $\left(\frac{15 \pm 2\sqrt{3}}{3}, 0\right)$.

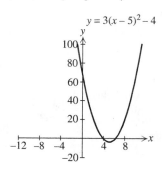

$y = 3(x - 5)^2 - 4$

1.6 Find the x-intercepts for $y = x^2 + 6x + 8$:

$$x^2 + 6x + 8 = 0$$
$$(x + 2)(x + 4) = 0$$
$$x = -2 \quad \text{or} \quad x = -4$$

The x-intercepts are $(-4, 0)$ and $(-2, 0)$. Since the parabola $y = x^2 + 6x + 8$ opens upward, the y-coordinates are positive outside the x-intercepts and zero at the x-intercepts. So the solution set to $x^2 + 6x + 8 \geq 0$ is $(-\infty, -4] \cup [-2, \infty)$.

1.7 Solve $x^2 - 2x - 4 = 0$:

$$x = \frac{2 \pm \sqrt{4 - 4(1)(-4)}}{2(1)} = 1 \pm \sqrt{5}$$

The numbers $1 - \sqrt{5}$ and $1 + \sqrt{5}$ divide the number line into three intervals, $(-\infty, 1 - \sqrt{5})$, $(1 - \sqrt{5}, 1 + \sqrt{5})$, and $(1 + \sqrt{5}, \infty)$. Test one point from each interval in $x^2 - 2x - 4 < 0$ to see that the solution set is $(1 - \sqrt{5}, 1 + \sqrt{5})$.

1.8 For $h(t) = -16t^2 + 96t + 40$ we have $a = -16, b = 96$, and $-b/(2a) = -96/(-32) = 3$. Since $h(3) = -16(3^2) + 96(3) + 40 = 184$, the vertex is $(3, 184)$. Since the parabola opens downward, 184 is the maximum value of the function and the maximum height above the ground is 184 feet.

1.9 Since $L + W = 25$, $W = 25 - L$.
$$A = L(25 - L) = -L^2 + 25L$$
$$L = \frac{-b}{2a} = \frac{-25}{2(-1)} = 12.5$$

If $L = 12.5$, then $W = 12.5$ and the rectangle with the largest area is a 12.5-m by 12.5-m square.

2.1

$$
\begin{array}{r}
x - 6 \\
x - 1 \overline{) x^2 - 7x + 9} \\
\underline{x^2 - x } \\
-6x + 9 \\
\underline{-6x + 6} \\
3
\end{array}
$$

Since the remainder is 3, $P(1) = 3$.

2.2

$$
\begin{array}{r|rrrr}
-2 & 1 & 0 & -7 & 5 \\
   &   & -2 & 4 & 6 \\
\hline
   & 1 & -2 & -3 & 11
\end{array}
$$

The quotient is $x^2 - 2x - 3$ and the remainder is 11.

2.3

$$
\begin{array}{r|rrrr}
3 & 1 & 1 & 0 & -9 \\
  &   & 3 & 12 & 36 \\
\hline
  & 1 & 4 & 12 & 27
\end{array}
$$

$P(3) = 27$

2.4

$$
\begin{array}{r|rrrr}
1 & 1 & 0 & -3 & 2 \\
  &   & 1 & 1 & -2 \\
\hline
  & 1 & 1 & -2 & 0
\end{array}
$$

Since the remainder is 0, $x - 1$ is a factor.
$$P(x) = (x - 1)(x^2 + x - 2)$$
$$= (x - 1)^2(x + 2)$$

2.5 The factors of 2 are 1 and 2. The factors of 3 are 1 and 3. All possible factors of 3 over factors of 2 are $\pm 1, \pm 3, \pm\frac{1}{2}$, and $\pm\frac{3}{2}$.

2.6 Try the possible rational zeros.

$$
\begin{array}{r|rrr}
-1 & 2 & 1 & -4 & -3 \\
   &   & -2 & 1 & 3 \\
\hline
   & 2 & -1 & -3 & 0
\end{array}
$$

$h(x) = (x + 1)(2x^2 - x - 3)$
$= (x + 1)(x + 1)(2x - 3)$
The zeros are -1 and $3/2$.

2.7 The possible rational zeros come from factors of 8 over factors of 3:

$$\pm\left(1, 2, 4, 8, \frac{1}{3}, \frac{2}{3}, \frac{4}{3}, \frac{8}{3}\right)$$

Use synthetic division to find a rational zero:

$$
\begin{array}{r|rrrr}
\frac{2}{3} & 3 & -2 & 12 & -8 \\
   &   & 2 & 0 & 8 \\
\hline
   & 3 & 0 & 12 & 0
\end{array}
$$

Solve $3x^2 + 12 = 0$:

$$3x^2 = -12$$
$$x^2 = -4$$
$$x = \pm\sqrt{-4} = \pm 2i$$

The three zeros are $2/3$ and $\pm 2i$.

3.1 Set each factor equal to zero to get 0 as a root with multiplicity 3, -2 as a root with multiplicity 2, and $5/2$ as a root.

3.2 If the coefficients are to be real, then both $-i$ and its conjugate i must be roots.

$$(x - 3)(x - i)(x + i) = 0$$
$$(x - 3)(x^2 + 1) = 0$$
$$x^3 - 3x^2 + x - 3 = 0$$

3.3 The number of variations in sign for $P(x) = x^3 - 5x^2 + 4x + 3$ is 2. So there are either 0 or 2 positive roots. The number of variations in sign for $P(-x) = -x^3 - 5x^2 - 4x + 3$ is 1. So there is exactly 1 negative root. Since there must be a total of 3 roots, there is one negative root and 2 positive roots or one negative root and 2 imaginary roots.

3.4 The number of variations in sign for $P(x) = x^4 - 6x^2 + 10$ is 2 and for $P(-x) = x^4 - 6x^2 + 10$ it is also 2. So there are either 0 or 2 positive roots and 0 or 2 negative roots. So the possibilities are 0 positive, 0 negative, 4 imaginary; 0 positive, 2 negative, 2 imaginary; 2 positive, 0 negative, 2 imaginary; 2 positive, 2 negative, 0 imaginary.

3.5 The first positive integer for which all terms of the bottom row of synthetic division are nonnegative is 3. So 3 is the best upper bound for the roots. The first negative integer for which the terms of the bottom row alternate in sign is -5. So -5 is the best lower bound for the roots by the theorem on bounds.

3.6 Try possible rational roots with synthetic division:

$$\begin{array}{r|rrrr} \frac{1}{2} & 2 & -5 & -8 & 5 \\ & & 1 & -2 & -5 \\ \hline & 2 & -4 & -10 & 0 \end{array}$$

$$2x^2 - 4x - 10 = 0$$
$$x^2 - 2x - 5 = 0$$
$$x = \frac{2 \pm \sqrt{4 - 4(1)(-5)}}{2(1)} = 1 \pm \sqrt{6}$$

The roots are $1/2$, $1 - \sqrt{6}$, and $1 + \sqrt{6}$.

4.1 $x^3 - 2x^2 + 5x - 10 = 0$
$$x^2(x - 2) + 5(x - 2) = 0$$
$$(x^2 + 5)(x - 2) = 0$$
$$x^2 + 5 = 0 \quad \text{or} \quad x - 2 = 0$$
$$x = \pm i\sqrt{5} \quad \text{or} \quad x = 2$$
The solution set is $\{2, -i\sqrt{5}, i\sqrt{5}\}$.

4.2
$$x^5 = 27x^2$$
$$x^5 - 27x^2 = 0$$
$$x^2(x - 3)(x^2 + 3x + 9) = 0$$
$$x^2 = 0 \quad \text{or} \quad x = 3 \quad \text{or} \quad x = \frac{-3 \pm \sqrt{-27}}{2}$$
$$= -\frac{3}{2} \pm \frac{3}{2}i\sqrt{3}$$
The solution set is $\{0, 3, -\frac{3}{2} \pm \frac{3}{2}i\sqrt{3}\}$.

4.3 $\sqrt{x} + 12 = x$
$$\sqrt{x} = x - 12$$
$$x = x^2 - 24x + 144$$
$$0 = x^2 - 25x + 144$$
$$0 = (x - 9)(x - 16)$$
$$x = 9 \quad \text{or} \quad x = 16$$
Since 9 does not satisfy $\sqrt{x} + 12 = x$ the solution set is $\{16\}$.

4.4 $\sqrt{3x - 2} - \sqrt{x} = 2$
$$\sqrt{3x - 2} = 2 + \sqrt{x}$$
$$3x - 2 = 4 + 4\sqrt{x} + x$$
$$2x - 6 = 4\sqrt{x}$$
$$x - 3 = 2\sqrt{x}$$
$$x^2 - 6x + 9 = 4x$$
$$x^2 - 10x + 9 = 0$$
$$(x - 9)(x - 1) = 0$$
$$x = 9 \quad \text{or} \quad x = 1$$
Since $\sqrt{3x - 2} - \sqrt{x} = 2$ is not satisfied by 1, the solution set is $\{9\}$.

4.5 $\quad x^{-4/5} = 16$
$$(x^{-4/5})^{-5/4} = \pm 16^{-5/4}$$
$$x = \pm\frac{1}{32}$$
The solution set is $\{\pm 1/32\}$.

4.6 $\quad x^4 - 9x^2 + 20 = 0$
$$(x^2 - 5)(x^2 - 4) = 0$$
$$x^2 - 5 = 0 \quad \text{or} \quad x^2 - 4 = 0$$
$$x = \pm\sqrt{5} \quad \text{or} \quad x = \pm 2$$
The solution set is $\{\pm\sqrt{5}, \pm 2\}$.

4.7 $(x^2 + x)^2 - 8(x^2 + x) + 12 = 0$
$$u^2 - 8u + 12 = 0$$
$$(u - 6)(u - 2) = 0$$
$$u - 6 = 0 \quad \text{or} \quad u - 2 = 0$$
$$x^2 + x - 6 = 0 \quad \text{or} \quad x^2 + x - 2 = 0$$
$$(x + 3)(x - 2) = 0 \quad \text{or} \quad (x + 2)(x - 1) = 0$$
$$x = -3 \quad \text{or} \quad x = 2 \quad \text{or} \quad x = -2 \quad \text{or} \quad x = 1$$
The solution set is $\{-3, -2, 1, 2\}$.

4.8 $\quad x^{2/3} - x^{1/3} - 6 = 0$
$$(x^{1/3} - 3)(x^{1/3} + 2) = 0$$
$$x^{1/3} = 3 \quad \text{or} \quad x^{1/3} = -2$$
$$x = 27 \quad \text{or} \quad x = -8$$
The solution set is $\{-8, 27\}$.

4.9 $|x^2 - x - 4| = 2$
$$x^2 - x - 4 = 2 \quad \text{or} \quad x^2 - x - 4 = -2$$
$$x^2 - x - 6 = 0 \quad \text{or} \quad x^2 - x - 2 = 0$$
$$(x - 3)(x + 2) = 0 \quad \text{or} \quad (x - 2)(x + 1) = 0$$
$$x = 3 \quad \text{or} \quad x = -2 \quad \text{or} \quad x = 2 \quad \text{or} \quad x = -1$$
The solution set is $\{-2, -1, 2, 3\}$.

4.10 $|x| = |x - 1|$
$$x = x - 1 \quad \text{or} \quad x = -(x - 1)$$
$$0 = -1 \quad \text{or} \quad 2x = 1$$
$$\text{or} \quad x = \frac{1}{2}$$
The solution set is $\{1/2\}$.

4.11 Let $D = 10$ and solve for P:
$$10 = \sqrt{P} - \sqrt{P - 400}$$
$$\sqrt{P - 400} = \sqrt{P} - 10$$
$$P - 400 = P - 20\sqrt{P} + 100$$
$$-500 = -20\sqrt{P}$$
$$25 = \sqrt{P}$$
$$625 = P$$
At \$625 the demand is 10 suits per month.

5.1 Since $f(-x) = x^3 + 4x$, we have $f(-x) = -f(x)$ and the graph is symmetric about the origin.

5.2 Since $x - 1$ occurs with an odd power, the graph crosses the x-axis at $(1, 0)$. Since $x + 5$ occurs with an even power, the graph does not cross the x-axis at $(-5, 0)$.

5.3 Since the leading coefficient is negative and the degree is odd, as $x \to \infty, y \to -\infty$. As $x \to -\infty, y \to \infty$.

5.4 Since $f(-x) = f(x)$ the graph is symmetric about the y-axis. Since $f(x) = x^2(x-2)(x+2)$ the graph crosses the x-axis at $(2, 0)$ and $(-2, 0)$ and touches but does not cross at $(0, 0)$. As $x \to \pm\infty, y \to \infty$.

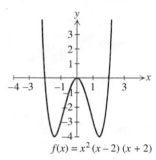

$$f(x) = x^2(x-2)(x+2)$$

5.5 The solutions to $x^4 - 4x^2 = 0$ are $-2, 0$, and 2. They divide the number line into four intervals $(-\infty, -2), (-2, 0), (0, 2)$, and $(2, \infty)$. Testing one number from each interval in $x^4 - 4x^2 < 0$ reveals that the solution set to the inequality is $(-2, 0) \cup (0, 2)$.

6.1 Since $x^2 - 9 = 0$ only if $x = \pm 3$, the domain is $(-\infty, -3) \cup (-3, 3) \cup (3, \infty)$.

6.2 The vertical lines $x = -3$ and $x = 3$ are vertical asymptotes. Since the degree of the denominator is larger than the degree of the numerator, the x-axis is a horizontal asymptote.

6.3

$$
\begin{array}{r}
3x + 3 \\
x - 1 \overline{\smash{)}\, 3x^2 + 0x - 4} \\
\underline{3x^2 - 3x} \\
3x - 4 \\
\underline{3x - 3} \\
-1
\end{array}
$$

$$\frac{3x^2 - 4}{x - 1} = 3x + 3 + \frac{-1}{x - 1}$$

The line $y = 3x + 3$ is an oblique asymptote and the line $x = 1$ is a vertical asymptote.

6.4 The vertical asymptotes are $x = \pm 3$ and the horizontal asymptote is $y = 0$. The x-intercept is $(1, 0)$.

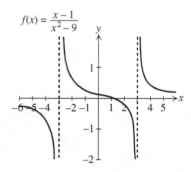

$$f(x) = \frac{x - 1}{x^2 - 9}$$

6.5 The line $x = 2$ is a vertical asymptote and the x-axis is a horizontal asymptote. The x-intercept is $(0, 0)$.

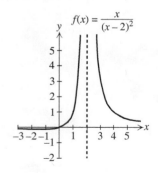

$$f(x) = \frac{x}{(x-2)^2}$$

6.6 From 3.6.3, the oblique asymptote is $y = 3x + 3$ and the vertical asymptote is $x = 1$.

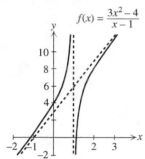

$$f(x) = \frac{3x^2 - 4}{x - 1}$$

6.7 If $x \neq 1$ and $x \neq -1$, then $f(x) = \frac{1}{x + 1}$. So there is a vertical asymptote at $x = -1$ and a hole at $(1, 1/2)$.

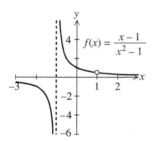

$$f(x) = \frac{x - 1}{x^2 - 1}$$

6.8

$$\frac{1}{x - 1} \geq 1$$

$$\frac{1}{x - 1} - 1 \geq 0$$

$$\frac{1}{x - 1} - \frac{x - 1}{x - 1} \geq 0$$

$$\frac{2 - x}{x - 1} \geq 0$$

The rational expression is undefined if $x = 1$ and has value 0 if $x = 2$. These critical numbers divide the number line into three intervals, $(-\infty, 1)$, $(1, 2)$, and $(2, \infty)$. Test one point in each interval to determine that $\frac{2 - x}{x - 1}$ is positive only on the interval $(1, 2)$. Since the value of $\frac{2 - x}{x - 1}$ is zero if $x = 2$, the solution set is $(1, 2]$.

6.9 The expression is undefined if $x = 1$ and has a value of 0 if $x = -3$. These numbers divide the number line into three intervals, $(-\infty, -3)$, $(-3, 1)$, and $(1, \infty)$. Test one number in each interval to see that $\frac{x + 3}{x - 1} \geq 0$ is satisfied for x in $(-\infty, -3] \cup (1, \infty)$.

6.10 The average cost per mile is given by $C = \frac{0.80x + 100}{x}$ where x is the number of miles. As x increases, C approaches the horizontal asymptote, which is \$0.80 per mile.

Polynomial and Rational Functions

For Thought

1. False, the range of $y = x^2$ is $[0, \infty)$.

2. False, the vertex is the point $(3, -1)$.

3. True **4.** True **5.** True, since $\dfrac{-b}{2a} = \dfrac{6}{2 \cdot 3} = 1$.

6. True, the x-intercept of $y = (3x + 2)^2$ is the vertex $(-2/3, 0)$ and the y-intercept is $(0, 4)$.

7. True

8. True, since $(x - \sqrt{3})^2$ is always nonnegative.

9. True, since if x and $\dfrac{p - 2x}{2}$ are the length and the width, respectively, of a rectangle with perimeter p, then the area is $y = x \cdot \dfrac{p - 2x}{2}$. This is a parabola opening down with vertex $\left(\dfrac{p}{4}, \dfrac{p^2}{16} \right)$. Thus, the maximum area is $\dfrac{p^2}{16}$.

10. False

1 Exercises

1. upward

3. vertex

5. minimum

7. axis of symmetry

9. Completing the square, we get

$$y = \left(x^2 + 4x + \left(\frac{4}{2} \right)^2 \right) - \left(\frac{4}{2} \right)^2$$
$$y = \left(x^2 + 4x + 4 \right) - 4$$
$$y = (x + 2)^2 - 4.$$

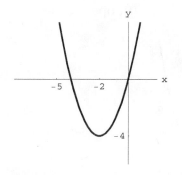

11. $y = \left(x^2 - 3x + \dfrac{9}{4} \right) - \dfrac{9}{4} = \left(x - \dfrac{3}{2} \right)^2 - \dfrac{9}{4}$

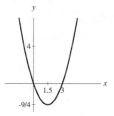

13. Completing the square, we get

$$y = 2 \left(x^2 - 6x + \left(\frac{6}{2} \right)^2 \right) - 2 \left(\frac{6}{2} \right)^2 + 22$$
$$y = 2(x - 3)^2 + 4.$$

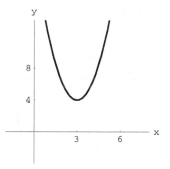

15. Completing the square, we find

$$y = -3 \left(x^2 - 2x + \left(\frac{2}{2} \right)^2 \right) + 3 \left(\frac{2}{2} \right)^2 - 3$$
$$y = -3(x - 1)^2.$$

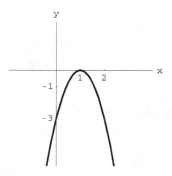

17. $y = \left(x^2 + 3x + \dfrac{9}{4} \right) - \dfrac{9}{4} + \dfrac{5}{2} = \left(x + \dfrac{3}{2} \right)^2 + \dfrac{1}{4}$

From Chapter 3 of *Student's Solutions Manual for Precalculus: Functions and Graphs*, Fourth Edition. Mark Dugopolski.

19. $y = -2\left(x^2 - \dfrac{3}{2}x + \dfrac{9}{16}\right) + \dfrac{9}{8} - 1 =$

$-2\left(x - \dfrac{3}{4}\right)^2 + \dfrac{1}{8}$

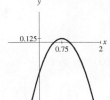

21. Since $\dfrac{-b}{2a} = \dfrac{12}{6} = 2$ and $f(2) = 12 - 24 + 1 =$
-11, the vertex is $(2, -11)$.

23. Vertex: $(4, 1)$

25. Since $\dfrac{-b}{2a} = \dfrac{1/3}{-1} = -\dfrac{1}{3}$ and $f(-1/3) =$
$-\dfrac{1}{18} + \dfrac{1}{9} = \dfrac{1}{18}$, the vertex is $\left(-\dfrac{1}{3}, \dfrac{1}{18}\right)$.

27. Up, vertex $(1, -4)$, axis of symmetry $x = 1$,
range $[-4, \infty)$, minimum value -4, decreasing
on $(-\infty, 1)$, inreasing on $(1, \infty)$.

29. Since it opens down with vertex $(0, 3)$, the
range is $(-\infty, 3]$, maximum value is 3,
decreasing on $(0, \infty)$, and increasing
on $(-\infty, 0)$.

31. Since it opens up with vertex $(1, -1)$, the
range is $[-1, \infty)$, minimum value is -1,
decreasing on $(-\infty, 1)$, and increasing
on $(1, \infty)$.

33. Since it opens up with vertex $(-4, -18)$,
range is $[-18, \infty)$, minimum value is -18,
decreasing on $(-\infty, -4)$, and
increasing on $(-4, \infty)$.

35. Since it opens up with vertex is $(3, 4)$, the
range is $[4, \infty)$, minimum value is 4,
decreasing on $(-\infty, 3)$, and increasing
on $(3, \infty)$.

37. Since it opens down with vertex $(3/2, 27/2)$,
the range is $(-\infty, 27/2]$, maximum value is
$27/2$, decreasing on $(3/2, \infty)$, and
increasing on $(-\infty, 3/2)$.

39. Since it opens down with vertex is $(1/2, 9)$,
the range is $(-\infty, 9]$, maximum value is 9,
decreasing on $(1/2, \infty)$, and
increasing on $(-\infty, 1/2)$.

41. Vertex $(0, -3)$, axis $x = 0$, y-intercept $(0, -3)$,
x-intercepts $(\pm\sqrt{3}, 0)$, opening up

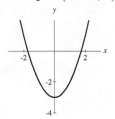

43. Vertex $(1/2, -1/4)$, axis $x = 1/2$, y-intercept
$(0, 0)$, x-intercepts $(0, 0), (1, 0)$, opening up

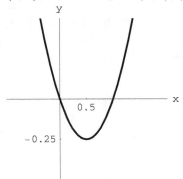

45. Vertex $(-3, 0)$, axis $x = -3$, y-intercept $(0, 9)$,
x-intercept $(-3, 0)$, opening up

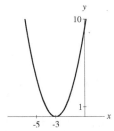

47. Vertex $(3, -4)$, axis $x = 3$, y-intercept $(0, 5)$,
x-intercepts $(1, 0), (5, 0)$, opening up

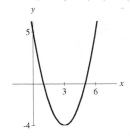

49. Vertex $(2, 12)$, axis $x = 2$, y-intercept $(0, 0)$, x-intercepts $(0, 0), (4, 0)$, opening down

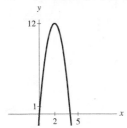

51. Vertex $(1, 3)$, axis $x = 1$, y-intercept $(0, 1)$, x-intercepts $\left(1 \pm \dfrac{\sqrt{6}}{2}, 0\right)$, opening down

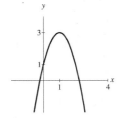

53. The x-intercepts are $x = -1, 3$. Since the parabola opens upward, the solution set for $x^2 - 2x - 3 > 0$ is $(-\infty, -1) \cup (3, \infty)$.

55. Since $x^2 - 4x + 1 = (x - 2)^2 - 3$, the x-intercepts are $x = 2 \pm \sqrt{3}$. Since the parabola opens upward, the solution set for $x^2 - 4x + 1 < 0$ is $(2 - \sqrt{3}, 2 + \sqrt{3})$.

57. Since $6x^2 - x - 1 = (3x + 1)(2x - 1)$, the x-intercepts are $x = -1/3, 1/2$. Then the solution set for $x + 1 < 6x^2$ or $6x^2 - x - 1 > 0$ is $(-\infty, -1/3) \cup (1/2, \infty)$.

59. $(-\infty, -1] \cup [3, \infty)$

61. $(-3, 1)$

63. $[-3, 1]$

65. The roots of $x^2 - 4x + 2 = 0$ are $x_1 = 2 - \sqrt{2}$ and $x_2 = 2 + \sqrt{2}$.

If $x = -5$, then $(-5)^2 - 4(-5) + 2 > 0$.
If $x = 2$, then $(2)^2 - 4(2) + 2 < 0$.
If $x = 5$, then $(5)^2 - 4(5) + 2 > 0$.

$$\begin{array}{ccccccccc} & + & & 0 & & - & & 0 & & + \\ \hline & \text{-5} & & x_1 & & 0 & & x_2 & & 5 \end{array}$$

The solution set of $x^2 - 4x + 2 < 0$ is $(2 - \sqrt{2}, 2 + \sqrt{2})$ and its graph follows.

$$\overset{2-\sqrt{2} \quad 2+\sqrt{2}}{\longleftarrow\!\!(\!\!=\!\!=\!\!=\!\!)\!\!\longrightarrow}$$

67. The roots of $x^2 - 10 = 0$ are $x_1 = -\sqrt{10}$ and $x_2 = \sqrt{10}$.

If $x = -4$, then $(-4)^2 - 10 > 0$.
If $x = 0$, then $(0)^2 - 10 < 0$.
If $x = 4$, then $(4)^2 - 10 > 0$.

$$\begin{array}{ccccccccc} & + & & 0 & & - & & 0 & & + \\ \hline & -4 & & x_1 & & 0 & & x_2 & & 4 \end{array}$$

The solution set of $x^2 - 9 \geq 1$ is $(-\infty, -\sqrt{10}] \cup [\sqrt{10}, \infty)$ and its graph is $\overset{-\sqrt{10} \quad \sqrt{10}}{\longleftarrow\!\!=\!\!]\!\![\!\!=\!\!\longrightarrow}$

69. The roots of $y^2 - 10y + 18 = 0$ are $y_1 = 5 - \sqrt{7}$ and $y_2 = 5 + \sqrt{7}$.

If $y = 2$, then $(2)^2 - 10(2) + 18 > 0$.
If $y = 5$, then $(5)^2 - 10(5) + 18 < 0$.
If $y = 8$, then $(8)^2 - 10(8) + 18 > 0$.

$$\begin{array}{ccccccccc} & + & & 0 & & - & & 0 & & + \\ \hline & 2 & & y_1 & & 5 & & y_2 & & 8 \end{array}$$

The solution set of $y^2 - 10y + 18 > 0$ is $(-\infty, 5 - \sqrt{7}) \cup (5 + \sqrt{7}, \infty)$ and its graph is $\overset{5-\sqrt{7} \; 5+\sqrt{7}}{\longleftarrow\!\!=\!\!)\;(\!\!=\!\!\longrightarrow}$

71. Note, $p^2 + 9 = 0$ has no real roots. If $p = 0$, then $(0)^2 + 9 > 0$. The signs of $p^2 + 9$ are shown below.

$$\begin{array}{c} + \\ \hline 0 \end{array}$$

The solution set of $p^2 + 9 > 0$ is $(-\infty, \infty)$ and its graph follows. $\longleftarrow\!\!=\!\!=\!\!=\!\!\longrightarrow$

73. Note, $a^2 - 8a + 20 = 0$ has no real roots. If $a = 0$, then $(0)^2 - 8(0) + 20 > 0$. The signs of $a^2 - 8a + 20$ are shown below.

$$+$$
$$\longleftrightarrow$$
$$0$$

The solution set of $a^2 - 8a + 20 \le 0$ is $\emptyset$.

75. Note, $2w^2 - 5w + 6 = 0$ has no real roots.
If $w = 0$, then $2(0)^2 - 5(0) + 6 > 0$. The signs of $2w^2 - 5w + 6$ are shown below.

$$+$$
$$\longleftrightarrow$$
$$0$$

The solution set of $2w^2 - 5w + 6 > 0$ is $(-\infty, \infty)$

and its graph follows. $\longleftrightarrow$

77. The zeros of $f(x) = (2x - 3)(x + 1)$ are $x_1 = -1$ and $x_2 = 3/2$.

If $x = -2$, then $f(-2) > 0$.
If $x = 0$, then $f(0) < 0$.
If $x = 2$, then $f(2) > 0$.

$+$	0	$-$	0	$+$
-2	−1	0	3/2	2

The solution set is $(-1, 3/2)$

79. The zeros of $f(x) = x^2 - 2x - 15 = (x+3)(x-5)$ are $x_1 = -3$ and $x_2 = 5$.

If $x = -4$, then $f(-4) > 0$.
If $x = 0$, then $f(0) < 0$.
If $x = 6$, then $f(6) > 0$.

$+$	0	$-$	0	$+$
-4	-3	0	5	6

The solution set is $(-\infty, -3) \cup (5, \infty)$.

81. The zeros of $f(w) = w^2 - 4w - 12 =$ $(w + 2)(w - 6)$ are $w_1 = -2$ and $w_2 = 6$.

If $w = -3$, then $f(-3) > 0$.
If $w = 0$, then $f(0) < 0$.
If $w = 7$, then $f(7) > 0$.

$+$	0	$-$	0	$+$
-3	-2	0	6	7

The solution set is $(-\infty, -2] \cup [6, \infty)$.

83. The zeros of $f(t) = t^2 - 16 =$ $(t + 4)(t - 4)$ are $t_1 = -4$ and $t_2 = 4$.

If $t = -5$, then $f(-5) > 0$.
If $t = 0$, then $f(0) < 0$.
If $t = 5$, then $f(5) > 0$.

$+$	0	$-$	0	$+$
-5	-4	0	4	5

The solution set is $[-4, 4]$.

85. The zero of $f(a) = (a + 3)^2$ is $a_1 = -3$.

If $a = -4$, then $f(-4) > 0$.
If $a = 0$, then $f(0) > 0$.

$+$	0	$+$
-4	-3	0

The solution set is $\{-3\}$.

87. The zero of $f(z) = (2z - 3)^2$ is $z_1 = 3/2$.

If $z = 0$, then $f(0) > 0$.
If $z = 2$, then $f(2) > 0$.

$+$	0	$+$
0	3/2	2

The solution set is $(-\infty, 3/2) \cup (3/2, \infty)$.

89. a) Since $x^2 - 3x - 10 = (x - 5)(x + 2) = 0$, the solution set is $\{-2, 5\}$.

b) Since $x^2 - 3x - 10 = -10$, we get $x^2 - 3x = 0$ or $x(x - 3) = 0$. The solution set is $\{0, 3\}$.

c) If $x = -3$, then $(-3)^2 - 3(-3) - 10 > 0$.
If $x = 0$, then $(0)^2 - 3(0) - 10 < 0$.
If $x = 6$, then $(6)^2 - 3(6) - 10 > 0$.
The signs of $x^2 - 3x - 10$ are shown below.

$+$	0	$-$	0	$+$
−3	−2	0	5	6

The solution set of $x^2 - 3x - 10 > 0$. is $(-\infty, -2) \cup (5, \infty)$

d) Using the sign graph of $x^2 - 3x - 10$ given in part c), the solution set of $x^2 - 3x - 10 \leq 0$ is $[-2, 5]$.

e) By using the method of completing the square, one obtains

$$x^2 - 3x - 10 = \left(x - \frac{3}{2}\right)^2 - 10 - \frac{9}{4}$$

$$x^2 - 3x - 10 = \left(x - \frac{3}{2}\right)^2 - \frac{49}{4}.$$

The graph of f is obtained from the graph of $y = x^2$ by shifting to the right by $\frac{3}{2}$ unit, and down by $\frac{49}{4}$.

f) Domain is $(-\infty, \infty)$, range is $\left[-\frac{49}{4}, \infty\right)$, minimum y-value is $-\frac{49}{4}$

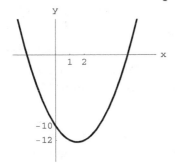

g) The solution to $f(x) > 0$ may be obtained by considering the part of the parabola that is above the x-axis, i.e., when x lies in $(-\infty, -2) \cup (5, \infty)$.

While, the solution to $f(x) \leq 0$ may be obtained by considering the part of the parabola on or below the x-axis. i.e., when x is in $[-2, 5]$.

h) x-intercepts are $(5, 0)$ and $(-2, 0)$, the y-intercept is $(0, -10)$, axis of symmetry $x = \frac{3}{2}$, vertex $\left(\frac{3}{2}, -\frac{49}{4}\right)$, opens up, increasing on $\left(\frac{3}{2}, \infty\right)$, decreasing on $\left(-\infty, \frac{3}{2}\right)$

91. Since $\dfrac{-b}{2a} = \dfrac{-128}{-2(-16)} = 4$, the maximum height is $h(4) = 261$ ft.

93. a) Finding the vertex involves the number

$$\frac{-b}{2a} = \frac{-160}{-32} = 5.$$

Thus, the maximum height is

$$h(5) = -16(5)^2 + 160(5) + 8 = 408 \text{ ft.}$$

b) When the arrow reaches the ground, one has $h(t) = 0$.

$$-16t^2 + 160t + 8 = 0$$

$$t^2 - 10t = \frac{1}{2}$$

$$(t - 5)^2 = 25 + \frac{1}{2}$$

$$t = 5 \pm \sqrt{\frac{51}{2}}$$

Since $t \geq 0$, the arrow reaches the ground in

$$5 + \frac{\sqrt{102}}{2} = \frac{10 + \sqrt{102}}{2} \approx 10.05 \text{ sec.}$$

95. a) About 100 mph

b) The value of A that would maximize M is

$$A = \frac{-b}{2a} = \frac{-0.127}{-0.001306} \approx 97.24 \text{ mph.}$$

c) Lindbergh flying at 97 mph would use $\dfrac{97}{1.2} \approx 80.83$ lbs. of fuel or

$$\frac{80.83 \text{ lbs}}{6.12 \text{ lbs per gal}} \approx 13.2 \text{ gallons per hour.}$$

97. Let x and y be the length and width, respectively. Since $2x + 2y = 200$, we find $y = 100 - x$. The area as a function of x is

$$f(x) = x(100 - x) = 100x - x^2.$$

The graph of f is a parabola and its vertex is $(50, 2500)$. Thus, the maximum area is 2500 yd^2. Using $x = 50$ from the vertex, we get $y = 100 - x = 100 - 50 = 50$. The dimensions are 50 yd by 50 yd.

99. Let the length of the sides be x, x, x, y, y.

Then $3x + 2y = 120$ and $y = \dfrac{120 - 3x}{2}$.

The area of rectangular enclosure is

$$A(x) = xy = x\left(\left(\frac{120 - 3x}{2}\right)\right) = \frac{1}{2}(120x - 3x^2).$$

This is a parabola opening down. Since

$$-\frac{b}{2a} = 20 \text{ and } y = \frac{120 - 3(20)}{2} = 30, \text{ the}$$

optimal dimensions are 20 ft by 30 ft.

101. Let the length of the sides be x, x, and $30 - 2x$. The area of rectangular enclosure is

$$A(x) = x(30 - 2x) = 30x - 2x^2.$$

We have a parabola opening down. Since $-\frac{b}{2a} = 7.5$ and $y = 30 - 2(7.5) = 15$, the optimal dimensions are 15 ft by 7.5 ft.

103. Let x be the length of a folded side. The area of the cross-section is $A = x(10 - 2x)$. This is a parabola opening down with $-b/2a = 2.5$. The dimensions of the cross-section are 2.5 in. high and 5 in. wide.

105. Let n and p be the number of persons and the price of a tour per person, respectively.

a) The function expressing p as a function of n is $p = 50 - n$.

b) The revenue is $R = (50 - n)n$ or

$$R = 50n - n^2.$$

c) Since the graph of R is a parabola opening down with vertex $(25, 625)$, we find that 25 persons will give her the maximum revenue of $625.

107. Since $v = 50p - 50p^2$ is a parabola opening down, to maximize v choose

$$p = \frac{-b}{2a} = \frac{50}{100} = 1/2.$$

109. (a) A graph of atmospheric pressure versus altitude is given below.

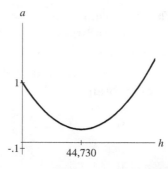

(b) From the graph, one finds the atmospheric pressure is decreasing as they went to $h = 29,029$ feet.

(c) Since $\frac{-b}{2a} = \frac{3.48 \times 10^{-5}}{2(3.89 \times 10^{-10})} \approx 44,730$ feet, the function is decreasing on the interval $[0, 44,730]$ and increasing on $[44,730, \infty)$.

(d) No, it does not make sense to speak of atmospheric pressure at heights that lie in $(44,730, \infty)$ since it is higher than the summit of 29,029 ft.

(e) It is valid for altitudes less than $30,000$ feet which is less than the height of the summit.

111. (a) Using a graphing calculator, we find that the equation of the regression line is

$$y = -2405.7x + 36,397.8.$$

The equation of the quadratic regression curve is $y = 156.4x^2 - 3969.9x + 39,265.6$

(b) Judging from the graph, it is too close to tell which function seems more reasonable. [The green graph is the line, and the pink graph is the parabola.]

The quadratic regression curve seems more reasonable since it is closer to the value of a 9-year-old car.

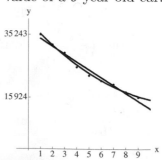

(c) We substitute $x = 11$ into the regression equations in part (a). Using the linear function, the price of an eleven year old car is $9935.

Using the quadratic curve, we obtain $14,521.

113. Let $y = k/x$. If $y = 3$ and $x = 12$, we find $k = 36$. Thus, if $x = 40$ then

$$y = \frac{k}{x} = \frac{36}{40} = \frac{9}{10}.$$

115. Since $f(9) = 2(9) - 9 = 9$ and $g(9) = \sqrt{9} = 3$, we obtain $(f + g)(9) = 9 + 3 = 12$.

117. Domain $\{-3, 1, 3, 4\}$, range $\{2, 5\}$

For Thought

1. False

2. True, by the Remainder Theorem.

3. True, by the Factor Theorem.

4. True, since $2^5 - 1 = 31$.

5. False, since $P(x) = 1$ has no zero.

6. False, rather $c^3 - c^2 + 4c - 5 = b$.

7. False, since $P(4) = -15$.   **8.**   True

9. True, since 1 is a root.

10. False, since -3 is not a root.

2 Exercises

1. zero

3. zero, factor

5. Quotient $x - 3$, remainder 1

$$
\begin{array}{r}
x - 3 \\
x - 2 \overline{\smash{)}x^2 - 5x + 7} \\
\underline{x^2 - 2x} \\
-3x + 7 \\
\underline{-3x + 6} \\
1
\end{array}
$$

7. Quotient $-2x^2 + 6x - 14$, remainder 33

$$
\begin{array}{r}
-2x^2 + 6x - 14 \\
x + 3 \overline{\smash{)}-2x^3 + 0x^2 + 4x - 9} \\
\underline{-2x^3 - 6x^2} \\
6x^2 + 4x \\
\underline{6x^2 + 18x} \\
-14x - 9 \\
\underline{-14x - 42} \\
33
\end{array}
$$

9. Quotient $s^2 + 2$, remainder 16

$$
\begin{array}{r}
s^2 + 2 \\
s^2 - 5 \overline{\smash{)}s^4 - 3s^2 + 6} \\
\underline{s^4 - 5s^2} \\
2s^2 + 6 \\
\underline{2s^2 - 10} \\
16
\end{array}
$$

11. Quotient $x + 6$, remainder 13

$$
\begin{array}{r|rrr}
2 & 1 & 4 & 1 \\
  &   & 2 & 12 \\
\hline
  & 1 & 6 & 13
\end{array}
$$

13. Quotient $-x^2 + 4x - 16$, remainder 57

$$
\begin{array}{r|rrrr}
-3 & -1 & 1 & -4 & 9 \\
   &   & 3 & -12 & 48 \\
\hline
   & -1 & 4 & -16 & 57
\end{array}
$$

15. Quotient $4x^2 + 2x - 4$, remainder 0

$$
\begin{array}{r|rrrr}
1/2 & 4 & 0 & -5 & 2 \\
    &   & 2 & 1 & -2 \\
\hline
    & 4 & 2 & -4 & 0
\end{array}
$$

17. Quotient $2a^2 - 4a + 6$, remainder 0

$$
\begin{array}{r|rrrr}
-1/2 & 2 & -3 & 4 & 3 \\
     &   & -1 & 2 & -3 \\
\hline
     & 2 & -4 & 6 & 0
\end{array}
$$

19. Quotient $x^3 + x^2 + x + 1$, remainder -2

$$
\begin{array}{c|ccccc}
1 & 1 & 0 & 0 & 0 & -3 \\
  &   & 1 & 1 & 1 & 1 \\
\hline
  & 1 & 1 & 1 & 1 & -2
\end{array}
$$

21. Quotient $x^4 + 2x^3 - 2x^2 - 4x - 4$, remainder -13

$$
\begin{array}{c|cccccc}
2 & 1 & 0 & -6 & 0 & 4 & -5 \\
  &   & 2 & 4 & -4 & -8 & -8 \\
\hline
  & 1 & 2 & -2 & -4 & -4 & -13
\end{array}
$$

23. $f(1) = 0$

$$
\begin{array}{c|cccccc}
1 & 1 & 0 & 0 & 0 & 0 & -1 \\
  &   & 1 & 1 & 1 & 1 & 1 \\
\hline
  & 1 & 1 & 1 & 1 & 1 & 0
\end{array}
$$

25. $f(-2) = -33$

$$
\begin{array}{c|cccccc}
-2 & 1 & 0 & 0 & 0 & 0 & -1 \\
   &   & -2 & 4 & -8 & 16 & -32 \\
\hline
   & 1 & -2 & 4 & -8 & 16 & -33
\end{array}
$$

$$
\begin{array}{c|ccccc}
1 & 1 & -4 & 0 & 8 \\
  &   & 1 & -3 & -3 \\
\hline
  & 1 & -3 & -3 & 5
\end{array}
$$

29. $g(-1/2) = 55/8$

$$
\begin{array}{c|cccc}
-1/2 & 1 & -4 & 0 & 8 \\
     &   & -1/2 & 9/4 & -9/8 \\
\hline
     & 1 & -9/2 & 9/4 & 55/8
\end{array}
$$

31. $h(-1) = 0$

$$
\begin{array}{c|ccccc}
-1 & 2 & 1 & -1 & 3 & 3 \\
   &   & -2 & 1 & 0 & -3 \\
\hline
   & 2 & -1 & 0 & 3 & 0
\end{array}
$$

33. $h(1) = 8$

$$
\begin{array}{c|ccccc}
1 & 2 & 1 & -1 & 3 & 3 \\
  &   & 2 & 3 & 2 & 5 \\
\hline
  & 2 & 3 & 2 & 5 & 8
\end{array}
$$

35. Yes, $(x+3)(x^2+x-2) = (x+3)(x+2)(x-1)$

$$
\begin{array}{c|cccc}
-3 & 1 & 4 & 1 & -6 \\
   &   & -3 & -3 & 6 \\
\hline
   & 1 & 1 & -2 & 0
\end{array}
$$

37. Yes, $(x-4)(x^2+8x+15) = (x-4)(x+5)(x+3)$

$$
\begin{array}{c|cccc}
4 & 1 & 4 & -17 & -60 \\
  &   & 4 & 32 & 60 \\
\hline
  & 1 & 8 & 15 & 0
\end{array}
$$

39. Yes, since the remainder below is zero

$$
\begin{array}{c|cccc}
3 & 2 & -5 & -4 & 3 \\
  &   & 6 & 3 & -3 \\
\hline
  & 2 & 1 & -1 & 0
\end{array}
$$

41. No, since the remainder below is not zero

$$
\begin{array}{c|cccc}
-2 & 1 & 2 & 3 & 1 \\
   &   & -2 & 0 & -6 \\
\hline
   & 1 & 0 & 3 & -5
\end{array}
$$

43. Yes, since the remainder below is zero

$$
\begin{array}{c|ccccc}
-1 & 1 & 2 & 4 & 6 & 3 \\
   &   & -1 & -1 & -3 & -3 \\
\hline
   & 1 & 1 & 3 & 3 & 0
\end{array}
$$

45. No, since the remainder below is not zero

$$
\begin{array}{c|cccc}
1/2 & 1 & 3 & -5 & 7 \\
    &   & 1/2 & 7/4 & -13/8 \\
\hline
    & 1 & 7/2 & -13/4 & 43/8
\end{array}
$$

47. $\pm\{1, 2, 3, 4, 6, 8, 12, 24\}$

49. $\pm\{1, 3, 5, 15\}$

51. $\pm\left\{1, 3, 5, 15, \dfrac{1}{2}, \dfrac{1}{4}, \dfrac{1}{8}, \dfrac{3}{2}, \dfrac{3}{4},\right.$

$\left.\dfrac{3}{8}, \dfrac{5}{2}, \dfrac{5}{4}, \dfrac{5}{8}, \dfrac{15}{2}, \dfrac{15}{4}, \dfrac{15}{8}\right\}$

53. $\pm\left\{1, 2, \dfrac{1}{2}, \dfrac{1}{3}, \dfrac{1}{6}, \dfrac{1}{9}, \dfrac{1}{18}, \dfrac{2}{3}, \dfrac{2}{9}\right\}$

55. Zeros are $2, 3, 4$ since

$$
\begin{array}{r|rrrr}
2 & 1 & -9 & 26 & -24 \\
  &   & 2 & -14 & 24 \\
\hline
  & 1 & -7 & 12 & 0
\end{array}
$$

and $x^2 - 7x + 12 = (x - 4)(x - 3)$

57. Zeros are $-3, 2 \pm i$ since

$$
\begin{array}{r|rrrr}
-3 & 1 & -1 & -7 & 15 \\
   &   & -3 & 12 & -15 \\
\hline
   & 1 & -4 & 5 & 0
\end{array}
$$

$x^2 - 4x + 5 = (x - 2)^2 + 1 = 0$ or $x - 2 = \pm i$

59. Zeros are $1/2, 3/2, 5/2$ since

$$
\begin{array}{r|rrrr}
1/2 & 8 & -36 & 46 & -15 \\
    &   & 4 & -16 & 15 \\
\hline
    & 8 & -32 & 30 & 0
\end{array}
$$

and $8a^2 - 32a + 30 = 2(4a^2 - 16a + 15) = 2(2a - 3)(2a - 5)$

61. Zeros are $\dfrac{1}{2}, \dfrac{1 \pm i}{3}$ since

$$
\begin{array}{r|rrrr}
1/2 & 18 & -21 & 10 & -2 \\
    &   & 9 & -6 & 2 \\
\hline
    & 18 & -12 & 4 & 0
\end{array}
$$

and the zeros of $18t^2 - 12t + 4$ are (by the quadratic formula) $\dfrac{1 \pm i}{3}$

63. Zeros are $-6, 3 \pm i$ since

$$
\begin{array}{r|rrrr}
-6 & 1 & 0 & -26 & 60 \\
   &   & -6 & 36 & -60 \\
\hline
   & 1 & -6 & 10 & 0
\end{array}
$$

and the zeros of $x^2 - 6x + 10$ are (by the quadratic formula) $3 \pm i$

65. Zeros are $1, -2, \pm i$ since

$$
\begin{array}{r|rrrrr}
1 & 1 & 1 & -1 & 1 & -2 \\
  &   & 1 & 2 & 1 & 2 \\
\hline
  & 1 & 2 & 1 & 2 & 0
\end{array}
$$

$$
\begin{array}{r|rrrr}
-2 & 1 & 2 & 1 & 2 \\
   &   & -2 & 0 & -2 \\
\hline
   & 1 & 0 & 1 & 0
\end{array}
$$

and the zeros of $w^2 + 1$ are $\pm i$

67. Zeros are $-1, \pm\sqrt{2}$ since

$$
\begin{array}{r|rrrrr}
-1 & 1 & 2 & -1 & -4 & -2 \\
   &   & -1 & -1 & 2 & 2 \\
\hline
   & 1 & 1 & -2 & -2 & 0
\end{array}
$$

$$
\begin{array}{r|rrrr}
-1 & 1 & 1 & -2 & -2 \\
   &   & -1 & 0 & 2 \\
\hline
   & 1 & 0 & -2 & 0
\end{array}
$$

and the zeros of $x^2 - 2$ are $\pm\sqrt{2}$

69. Zeros are $1/2, 1/3, 1/4$ since

$$
\begin{array}{r|rrrr}
1/2 & 24 & -26 & 9 & -1 \\
    &   & 12 & -7 & 1 \\
\hline
    & 24 & -14 & 2 & 0
\end{array}
$$

and $2(12x^2 - 7x + 1) = 2(4x - 1)(3x - 1)$

71. Rational zero is 1/16 since

$$
\begin{array}{r|rrrr}
1/16 & 16 & -33 & 82 & -5 \\
 & & 1 & -2 & 5 \\
\hline
 & 16 & -32 & 80 & 0
\end{array}
$$

and by the quadratic formula $16x^2 - 32x + 80$ has imaginary zeros $1 \pm 2i$.

73. Rational zeros are $7/3, -6/7$ since

$$
\begin{array}{r|rrrrr}
7/3 & 21 & -31 & -21 & -31 & -42 \\
 & & 49 & 42 & 49 & 42 \\
\hline
 & 21 & 18 & 21 & 18 & 0
\end{array}
$$

$$
\begin{array}{r|rrrr}
-6/7 & 21 & 18 & 21 & 18 \\
 & & -18 & 0 & -18 \\
\hline
 & 21 & 0 & 21 & 0
\end{array}
$$

and $21x^2 + 21 = 0$ has imaginary zeros $\pm i$.

75. Dividing $x^3 + 6x^2 + 3x - 10$ by $x - 1$, we find

$$
\begin{array}{r|rrrr}
1 & 1 & 6 & 3 & -10 \\
 & & 1 & 7 & 10 \\
\hline
 & 1 & 7 & 10 & 0
\end{array}
$$

Moreover, $x^2 + 7x + 10 = (x + 5)(x + 2)$.
Note, the zeros of $x^2 + 9$ are $\pm 3i$.
Thus, the zeros of $f(x)$ are $x = -5, -2, 1, \pm 3i$.

77. Dividing $x^3 - 9x^2 + 23x - 15$ by $x - 1$, we find

$$
\begin{array}{r|rrrr}
1 & 1 & -9 & 23 & -15 \\
 & & 1 & -8 & 15 \\
\hline
 & 1 & -8 & 15 & 0
\end{array}
$$

For the quotient, we find

$$x^2 - 8x + 15 = (x - 5)(x - 3).$$

Then the zeros of $x^3 - 9x^2 + 23x - 15$ are $x = 1, 3, 5$.

By using the method of completing the square, we find

$$x^2 - 4x + 1 = (x - 2)^2 - 3.$$

Then the zeros of $(x - 2)^2 - 3$ are $2 \pm \sqrt{3}$.
Thus, all the zeros are $x = 1, 3, 5, 2 \pm \sqrt{3}$.

79.
$$\frac{2x + 1}{x - 2} = 2 + \frac{5}{x - 2} \quad \text{since}$$

$$
\begin{array}{r|rr}
2 & 2 & 1 \\
 & & 4 \\
\hline
 & 2 & 5
\end{array}
$$

81.
$$\frac{a^2 - 3a + 5}{a - 3} = a + \frac{5}{a - 3} \quad \text{since}$$

$$
\begin{array}{r|rrr}
3 & 1 & -3 & 5 \\
 & & 3 & 0 \\
\hline
 & 1 & 0 & 5
\end{array}
$$

83.
$$\frac{c^2 - 3c - 4}{c^2 - 4} = 1 + \frac{-3c}{c^2 - 4} \quad \text{since}$$

$$
\begin{array}{r}
1 \\
c^2 - 4 \overline{) c^2 - 3c - 4} \\
\underline{c^2 + 0c - 4} \\
-3c
\end{array}
$$

85.
$$\frac{4t - 5}{2t + 1} = 2 + \frac{-7}{2t + 1} \quad \text{since}$$

$$
\begin{array}{r}
2 \\
2t + 1 \overline{) 4t - 5} \\
\underline{4t + 2} \\
-7
\end{array}
$$

87. a) Note, $\dfrac{P(t)}{t} = -t^3 + 12t^2 - 58t + 132.$

$$
\begin{array}{r|rrrr}
6 & -1 & 12 & -58 & 132 \\
 & & -6 & 36 & -132 \\
\hline
 & -1 & 6 & -22 & 0
\end{array}
$$

The drug will be eliminated in $t = 6$ hr.

b) About 120 ppm

c) About 3 hours

d) Between 1 and 5 hours approximately, the concentration is above 80 ppm. Thus, the concentration is above 80 ppm for about 4 hours.

89. If w is the width, then $w(w+4)(w+9) = 630$. This can be re-written as

$$w^3 + 13w^2 + 36w - 630 = 0.$$

Using synthetic division, we find

5	1	13	36	-630
		5	90	630
	1	18	126	0

Since $w^2 + 18w + 126 = 0$ has non-real roots, the width of the HP box is $w = 5$ in. The dimensions are 5 in. by 9 in. by 14 in.

91. The quotient and remainder when

$$3x^3 + 4x^2 + 2x - 4 \text{ is divided by } 3x - 2$$

are the same as the quotient and remainder, respectively, when

$$x^3 + \frac{4}{3}x^2 + \frac{2}{3}x - \frac{4}{3} \text{ is divided by } x - \frac{2}{3}.$$

Then one can use sythetic division for the latter case since the divisor is $x - \dfrac{2}{3}$.

93. Using the method of completing the square, we find

$$
\begin{aligned}
f(x) &= 2\left(x^2 - \frac{3}{2}x\right) + 1 \\
&= 2\left(x - \frac{3}{4}\right)^2 - \frac{9}{8} + 1 \\
&= 2\left(x - \frac{3}{4}\right)^2 - \frac{1}{8}.
\end{aligned}
$$

95. Since an absolute value is always nonnegative, the solution set of $|3x + 7| \geq 0$ is $(-\infty, \infty)$.

97. a) $6a(4a^2 + 3a - 10) = 6a(4a - 5)(a + 2)$

b) $x(x^4 - 16) = x(x^2 + 4)(x^2 - 4) =$
$x(x^2 + 4)(x - 2)(x + 2)$

For Thought

1. False, since 1 has multiplicity 1. **2.** True

3. True **4.** False, it factors as $(x - 5)^4(x + 2)$.

5. False, rather $4+5i$ is also a solution. **6.** True

7. False, since they are solutions to a polynomial with real coefficients of degree at least 4.

8. False, 2 is not a solution.

9. True, since $-x^3 - 5x^2 - 6x - 1 = 0$ has no sign changes.

10. True

3 Exercises

1. multiplicity

3. $a - bi$

5. Degree 2; 5 with multiplicity 2 since $(x-5)^2 = 0$

7. Degree 5; 0 with multiplicity 3, and ± 3 since $x^3(x - 3)(x + 3) = 0$

9. Degree 4; 0 and 1 each have multiplicity 2 since $x^2(x^2 - 2x + 1) = x^2(x - 1)^2$

11. Degree 4; 3/2 and $-4/3$ each with multiplicity 2

13. Degree 3; the roots are $0, 2 \pm \sqrt{10}$ since $x(x^2 - 4x - 6) = x((x - 2)^2 - 10) = 0$

15. $x^2 + 9$

17. $\left[(x - 1) - \sqrt{2}\right]\left[(x - 1) + \sqrt{2}\right] = (x-1)^2 - 2 = x^2 - 2x - 1$

19. $[(x - 3) - 2i][(x - 3) + 2i] = (x - 3)^2 + 4 = x^2 - 6x + 13$

21. $(x - 2)[(x - 3) - 4i][(x - 3) + 4i] = (x - 2)[(x - 3)^2 + 16] = x^3 - 8x^2 + 37x - 50$

23. $(x + 3)(x - 5) = 0$ or $x^2 - 2x - 15 = 0$

25. $(x + 4i)(x - 4i) = 0$ or $x^2 + 16 = 0$

27. $(x-(3-i))(x-(3+i)) = 0$ or $x^2 - 6x + 10 = 0$

29. $(x+2)(x-i)(x+i) = 0$ or $x^3 + 2x^2 + x + 2 = 0$

31. $x(x - i\sqrt{3})(x + i\sqrt{3}) = 0$ or $x^3 + 3x = 0$

33. $(x-3)[x-(1-i)][x-(1+i)] = 0$ or
$x^3 - 5x^2 + 8x - 6 = 0$

35. $(x-1)(x-2)(x-3) = 0$ or
$x^3 - 6x^2 + 11x - 6 = 0$

37. $(x-1)[x-(2-3i)][x-(2+3i)] = 0$ or
$x^3 - 5x^2 + 17x - 13 = 0$

39. $(2x-1)(3x-1)(4x-1) = 0$ or
$24x^3 - 26x^2 + 9x - 1 = 0$

41. $(x-i)(x+i)[x-(1+i)][x-(1-i)] = 0$
or $x^4 - 2x^3 + 3x^2 - 2x + 2 = 0$

43. $P(x) = x^3 + 5x^2 + 7x + 1$ has no sign change and $P(-x) = -x^3 + 5x^2 - 7x + 1$ has 3 sign changes. There are (a) 3 negative roots, or (b) 1 negative root & 2 imaginary roots.

45. $P(x) = -x^3 - x^2 + 7x + 6$ has 1 sign change and $P(-x) = x^3 - x^2 - 7x + 6$ has 2 sign changes. There are (a) 1 positive root and 2 negative roots, or (b) 1 positive root and 2 imaginary roots.

47. $P(y) = y^4 + 5y^2 + 7 = P(-y)$ has no sign change. There are 4 imaginary roots.

49. $P(t) = t^4 - 3t^3 + 2t^2 - 5t + 7$ has 4 sign changes and $P(-t) = t^4 + 3t^3 + 2t^2 + 5t + 7$ has no sign change. There are (a) 4 positive roots, or (b) 2 positive roots and 2 imaginary roots, or (c) 4 imaginary roots.

51. $P(x) = x^5 + x^3 + 5x$ and $P(-x) = -x^5 - x^3 - 5x$ have no sign changes; 4 imaginary roots and 0.

53. Best integral bounds are $-1 < x < 3$. One checks that $1, 2$ are not upper bounds and that 3 is a bound.

$$\begin{array}{r|rrrr} 3 & 2 & -5 & 0 & 6 \\ & & 6 & 3 & 9 \\ \hline & 2 & 1 & 3 & 15 \end{array}$$

-1 is a lower bound since

$$\begin{array}{r|rrrr} -1 & 2 & -5 & 0 & 6 \\ & & -2 & 7 & -7 \\ \hline & 2 & -7 & 7 & -1 \end{array}$$

55. Best integral bounds are $-3 < x < 2$. One checks that 1 is not an upper bound and that 2 is a bound.

$$\begin{array}{r|rrrr} 2 & 4 & 8 & -11 & -15 \\ & & 8 & 32 & 42 \\ \hline & 4 & 16 & 21 & 27 \end{array}$$

$-1, -2$ are not lower bounds but -3 is a bound since

$$\begin{array}{r|rrrr} -3 & 4 & 8 & -11 & -15 \\ & & -12 & 12 & -3 \\ \hline & 4 & -4 & 1 & -18 \end{array}$$

57. Best integral bounds are $-1 < x < 5$. One checks that $1, 2, 3, 4$ are not upper bounds and that 5 is a bound

$$\begin{array}{r|rrrrr} 5 & 1 & -5 & 3 & 2 & -1 \\ & & 5 & 0 & 15 & 85 \\ \hline & 1 & 0 & 3 & 17 & 84 \end{array}$$

-1 is a lower bound since

$$\begin{array}{r|rrrrr} -1 & 1 & -5 & 3 & 2 & -1 \\ & & -1 & 6 & -9 & 7 \\ \hline & 1 & -6 & 9 & -7 & 6 \end{array}$$

59. Best integral bounds are $-1 < x < 3$. Multiply equation by -1, this makes the leading coefficient positive. One checks that $1, 2$ are not upper bounds and that 3 is a bound.

$$\begin{array}{r|rrrr} 3 & 2 & -5 & 3 & -9 \\ & & 6 & 3 & 18 \\ \hline & 2 & 1 & 6 & 9 \end{array}$$

-1 is a lower bound since

$$\begin{array}{c|cccc} -1 & 2 & -5 & 3 & -9 \\ & & -2 & 7 & -10 \\ \hline & 2 & -7 & 10 & -19 \end{array}$$

61. Roots are $1, 5, -2$ since

$$\begin{array}{c|cccc} 1 & 1 & -4 & -7 & 10 \\ & & 1 & -3 & -10 \\ \hline & 1 & -3 & -10 & 0 \end{array}$$

and $x^2 - 3x - 10 = (x - 5)(x + 2)$.

63. Roots are $-3, \dfrac{3 \pm \sqrt{13}}{2}$ since

$$\begin{array}{c|cccc} -3 & 1 & 0 & -10 & -3 \\ & & -3 & 9 & 3 \\ \hline & 1 & -3 & -1 & 0 \end{array}$$

and by the quadratic formula the roots

of $x^2 - 3x - 1 = 0$ are $\dfrac{3 \pm \sqrt{13}}{2}$.

65. Roots are $2, -4, \pm i$ since

$$\begin{array}{c|ccccc} 2 & 1 & 2 & -7 & 2 & -8 \\ & & 2 & 8 & 2 & 8 \\ \hline & 1 & 4 & 1 & 4 & 0 \end{array}$$

$$\begin{array}{c|cccc} -4 & 1 & 4 & 1 & 4 \\ & & -4 & 0 & -4 \\ \hline & 1 & 0 & 1 & 0 \end{array}$$

and the root of $x^2 + 1 = 0$ are $\pm i$.

67. Roots are $1/3, 1/2, -5$ since

$$\begin{array}{c|cccc} 1/3 & 6 & 25 & -24 & 5 \\ & & 2 & 9 & -5 \\ \hline & 6 & 27 & -15 & 0 \end{array}$$

and $6x^2 + 27x - 15 = 3(2x - 1)(x + 5)$.

69. $1, -2$ each have multiplicity 2 since

$$\begin{array}{c|ccccc} 1 & 1 & 2 & -3 & -4 & 4 \\ & & 1 & 3 & 0 & -4 \\ \hline & 1 & 3 & 0 & -4 & 0 \end{array}$$

$$\begin{array}{c|cccc} -2 & 1 & 3 & 0 & -4 \\ & & -2 & -2 & 4 \\ \hline & 1 & 1 & -2 & 0 \end{array}$$

and $x^2 + x - 2 = (x + 2)(x - 1)$.

71. Use synthetic division on the cubic factor in $x(x^3 - 6x^2 + 12x - 8) = 0$.

$$\begin{array}{c|cccc} 2 & 1 & -6 & 12 & -8 \\ & & 2 & -8 & 8 \\ \hline & 1 & -4 & 4 & 0 \end{array}$$

Since $x^2 - 4x + 4 = (x - 2)^2$, the roots are 2 (with multiplicity 3) and 0.

73. Use synthetic division on the 5th degree factor in $x(x^5 - x^4 - x^3 + x^2 - 12x + 12) = 0$.

$$\begin{array}{c|cccccc} 1 & 1 & -1 & -1 & 1 & -12 & 12 \\ & & 1 & 0 & -1 & 0 & -12 \\ \hline & 1 & 0 & -1 & 0 & -12 & 0 \end{array}$$

$$\begin{array}{c|ccccc} 2 & 1 & 0 & -1 & 0 & -12 \\ & & 2 & 4 & 6 & 12 \\ \hline & 1 & 2 & 3 & 6 & 0 \end{array}$$

$$\begin{array}{c|cccc} -2 & 1 & 2 & 3 & 6 \\ & & -2 & 0 & -6 \\ \hline & 1 & 0 & 3 & 0 \end{array}$$

Note, the roots of $x^2 + 3 = 0$ are $\pm i\sqrt{3}$.
Thus, the roots are $x = 0, 1, \pm 2, \pm i\sqrt{3}$.

75. The roots are $\pm 1, -2, 1/4, 3/2$ since

$$
\begin{array}{r|rrrrrr}
-1 & 8 & 2 & -33 & 4 & 25 & -6 \\
   &   & -8 & 6 & 27 & -31 & 6 \\
\hline
   & 8 & -6 & -27 & 31 & -6 & 0 \\
\end{array}
$$

$$
\begin{array}{r|rrrrr}
-2 & 8 & -6 & -27 & 31 & -6 \\
   &   & -16 & 44 & -34 & 6 \\
\hline
   & 8 & -22 & 17 & -3 & 0 \\
\end{array}
$$

$$
\begin{array}{r|rrrr}
1 & 8 & -22 & 17 & -3 \\
  &   & 8 & -14 & 3 \\
\hline
  & 8 & -14 & 3 & 0 \\
\end{array}
$$

and the last quotient is

$$8x^2 - 14x + 4 = (4x - 1)(2x - 3).$$

77. By the Theorem of Bounds and the graph below

$$
\begin{array}{r|rrrr}
6 & 2 & -3 & -50 & 18 \\
  &   & 12 & 54 & 24 \\
\hline
  & 2 & 9 & 4 & 42 \\
\end{array}
$$

$$
\begin{array}{r|rrrr}
-5 & 2 & -3 & -50 & 18 \\
   &   & -10 & 65 & -75 \\
\hline
   & 2 & -13 & 15 & -57 \\
\end{array}
$$

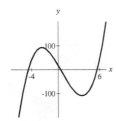

the intervals are $-5 < x < 6, -5 < x < 6$

79. By the Theorem of Bounds and the graph below

$$
\begin{array}{r|rrrrr}
6 & 1 & 0 & -26 & 0 & 153 \\
  &   & 6 & 36 & 60 & 360 \\
\hline
  & 1 & 6 & 10 & 60 & 513 \\
\end{array}
$$

$$
\begin{array}{r|rrrrr}
-6 & 1 & 0 & -26 & 0 & 153 \\
   &   & -6 & 36 & -60 & 360 \\
\hline
   & 1 & -6 & 10 & -60 & 513 \\
\end{array}
$$

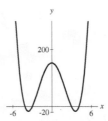

the intervals are $-6 < x < 6, -5 < x < 5$.

81. By the Theorem of Bounds and the graph below

$$
\begin{array}{r|rrrr}
23 & 4 & -90 & -2 & 45 \\
   &   & 92 & 46 & 1012 \\
\hline
   & 4 & 2 & 44 & 1057 \\
\end{array}
$$

$$
\begin{array}{r|rrrr}
-1 & 4 & -90 & -2 & 45 \\
   &   & -4 & 94 & -92 \\
\hline
   & 4 & -94 & 92 & -47 \\
\end{array}
$$

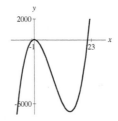

the intervals are $-1 < x < 23, -1 < x < 23$.

83. Multiplying by 100, $t^3 - 8t^2 + 11t + 20 = 0$.

$$
\begin{array}{r|rrrr}
4 & 1 & -8 & 11 & 20 \\
  &   & 4 & -16 & -20 \\
\hline
  & 1 & -4 & -5 & 0 \\
\end{array}
$$

Since $t^2 - 4t - 5 = (t - 5)(t + 1) = 0$, we obtain $t = 4$ hr and $t = 5$ hr.

85. Let x be the radius of the cone.

The volume of the cone is $\dfrac{\pi}{3}x^2 \cdot 2$ and the volume of the cylinder with height $4x$ is

$\pi x^2 \cdot (4x)$. So $114\pi = \dfrac{\pi}{3} 2x^2 + \pi x^2 (4x)$.

Divide by π, multiply by 3, and simplify to obtain $12x^3 + 2x^2 - 342 = 0$.

$$
\begin{array}{r|rrrr}
3 & 12 & 2 & 0 & -342 \\
  &   & 36 & 114 & 342 \\
\hline
  & 12 & 38 & 114 & 0
\end{array}
$$

The radius is $x = 3$ in. since $12x^2 + 38x + 114 = 0$ has no real roots.

87. From the following

$$
\begin{aligned}
\overline{(a+bi)+(c+di)} &= \overline{(a+c)+i(b+d)} \\
&= (a+c) - i(b+d)
\end{aligned}
$$

and

$$
\begin{aligned}
\overline{a+bi} + \overline{c+di} &= (a-bi) + (c-di) \\
&= (a+c) - i(b+d)
\end{aligned}
$$

we obtain that the conjugate of the sum of two complex numbers is equal to the sum of their conjugates.

89. If a is real then $\overline{a} = \overline{a+0i} = a - 0i = a$.

91. Let $f(x) = a(x-1)(x-2)(x-3)$.

Since $f(0) = -6a = 3$, we find $a = -\dfrac{1}{2}$.

Then substitute $a = -\dfrac{1}{2}$ and multiply out $f(x)$ to obtain $f(x) = -\dfrac{1}{2}x^3 + 3x^2 - \dfrac{11}{2}x + 3$.

93. The divisors of the constant term 6 are $p = \pm 1, \pm 2, \pm 3, \pm 6$. The divisors of the leading coefficient 2 are $q = \pm 1, \pm 2$. Then the possible rational zeros are $p/q = \pm 1, \pm 2, \pm 3, \pm 6, \pm 1/2, \pm 3/2$.

95. b is a function of a since there is a unique number of primes less than a.

a is not a function of b since the ordered pairs $(b, a) = (3, 6)$ and $(a, b) = (3, 7)$ have the same first coordinates and different second coordinates.

97. $(f \circ g)(x) = 2(2x-4)^2 - 9 = 8x^2 - 32x + 23$

For Thought

1. False, since

$$
(\sqrt{x-1} + \sqrt{x})^2 = (x-1) + 2\sqrt{x(x-1)} + x.
$$

2. False, since -1 is a solution of the first and not of the second equation.

3. False, since -27 is a solution of the first equation but not of the second.

4. False, rather let $u = x^{1/4}$ and $u^2 = x^{1/2}$.

5. True, since $x - 1 = \pm 4^{-3/2}$.

6. False, $\left(-\dfrac{1}{32}\right)^{-2/5} = (-32)^{2/5} = (-2)^2 = 4$.

7. False, $x = -2$ is not a solution.

8. True

9. True

10. False, since $(x^3)^2 = x^6$.

4 Exercises

1. Factor: $x^2(x+3) - 4(x+3) = 0$
$(x^2 - 4)(x+3) = (x-2)(x+2)(x+3) = 0$
The solution set is $\{\pm 2, -3\}$.

3. Factor: $2x^2(x+500) - (x+500) = 0$
$(2x^2 - 1)(x+500) = 0$
The solution set is $\left\{\pm\dfrac{\sqrt{2}}{2}, -500\right\}$.

5. Set the right-hand side to 0 and factor.

$$
a(a^2 - 15a + 5) = 0
$$

$$
a = \dfrac{15 \pm \sqrt{15^2 - 4(1)(5)}}{2} \quad \text{or} \quad a = 0
$$

$$
a = \dfrac{15 \pm \sqrt{205}}{2} \quad \text{or} \quad a = 0
$$

The solution set is $\left\{\dfrac{15 \pm \sqrt{205}}{2}, 0\right\}$.

7. Factor: $3y^2(y^2 - 4) = 3y^2(y-2)(y+2) = 0$
The solution set is $\{0, \pm 2\}$.

9. Factor: $(a^2 - 4)(a^2 + 4) =$
$(a - 2)(a + 2)(a - 2i)(a + 2i) = 0$.
The solution set is $\{\pm 2, \pm 2i\}$.

11. Squaring each side, we get

$$
\begin{aligned}
x + 1 &= x^2 - 10x + 25 \\
0 &= x^2 - 11x + 24 = (x - 8)(x - 3).
\end{aligned}
$$

Checking $x = 3$, we get $2 \neq -2$. Then $x = 3$ is an extraneous root. The solution set is $\{8\}$.

13. Isolate the radical and then square each side.

$$
\begin{aligned}
x &= x^2 - 40x + 400 \\
0 &= x^2 - 41x + 400 = (x - 25)(x - 16)
\end{aligned}
$$

Checking $x = 16$, we get $2 \neq -6$. Then $x = 16$ is an extraneous root. The solution set is $\{25\}$.

15. Isolate the radical and then square each side.

$$
\begin{aligned}
2w &= \sqrt{1 - 3w} \\
4w^2 &= 1 - 3w \\
4w^2 + 3w - 1 &= (4w - 1)(w + 1) = 0 \\
w &= \frac{1}{4}, -1
\end{aligned}
$$

Checking $w = -1$, we get $-1 \neq 1$.
Then $w = -1$ is an extraneous root.
The solution set is $\left\{\dfrac{1}{4}\right\}$.

17. Multiply both sides by $z\sqrt{4z + 1}$ and square each side.

$$
\begin{aligned}
\sqrt{4z + 1} &= 3z \\
4z + 1 &= 9z^2 \\
0 &= 9z^2 - 4z - 1
\end{aligned}
$$

By the quadratic formula,

$$
\begin{aligned}
z &= \frac{4 \pm \sqrt{16 - 4(9)(-1)}}{18} \\
z &= \frac{4 \pm \sqrt{52}}{18} = \frac{4 \pm 2\sqrt{13}}{18} = \frac{2 \pm \sqrt{13}}{9}
\end{aligned}
$$

Since $z = \dfrac{2 - \sqrt{13}}{9} < 0$ and the right-hand side of the original equation is nonnegative,

$z = \dfrac{2 - \sqrt{13}}{9}$ is an extraneous root.

The solution set is $\left\{\dfrac{2 + \sqrt{13}}{9}\right\}$.

19. Squaring each side, one obtains

$$
\begin{aligned}
x^2 - 2x - 15 &= 9 \\
x^2 - 2x - 24 &= (x - 6)(x + 4) = 0.
\end{aligned}
$$

The solution set is $\{-4, 6\}$.

21. Isolate a radical and square each side.

$$
\begin{aligned}
\sqrt{x + 40} &= \sqrt{x} + 4 \\
x + 40 &= x + 8\sqrt{x} + 16 \\
24 &= 8\sqrt{x} \\
3 &= \sqrt{x} \\
9 &= x
\end{aligned}
$$

The solution set is $\{9\}$.

23. Isolate a radical and square each side.

$$
\begin{aligned}
\sqrt{n + 4} &= 5 - \sqrt{n - 1} \\
n + 4 &= 25 - 10\sqrt{n - 1} + (n - 1) \\
-20 &= -10\sqrt{n - 1} \\
2 &= \sqrt{n - 1} \\
4 &= n - 1
\end{aligned}
$$

The solution set is $\{5\}$.

25. Isolate a radical and square each side.

$$
\begin{aligned}
\sqrt{2x + 5} &= 9 - \sqrt{x + 6} \\
2x + 5 &= 81 - 18\sqrt{x + 6} + (x + 6) \\
x - 82 &= -18\sqrt{x + 6} \\
x^2 - 164x + 6724 &= 324(x + 6) \\
x^2 - 488x + 4780 &= 0 \\
(x - 10)(x - 478) &= 0
\end{aligned}
$$

Checking $x = 478$ we get $53 \neq 9$ and $x = 478$ is an extraneous root. The solution set is $\{10\}$.

27. Raise each side to the power $3/2$.
Then $x = \pm 2^{3/2} = \pm 8^{1/2} = \pm 2\sqrt{2}$.
The solution set is $\left\{\pm 2\sqrt{2}\right\}$.

29. Raise each side to the power $-3/4$.

Thus, $w = \pm (16)^{-3/4} = \pm (2)^{-3} = \pm \dfrac{1}{8}$.

The solution set is $\left\{ \pm \dfrac{1}{8} \right\}$.

31. Raise each side to the power -2.

So, $t = (7)^{-2} = \dfrac{1}{49}$. The solution set is $\left\{ \dfrac{1}{49} \right\}$.

33. Raise each side to the power -2.

Then $s - 1 = (2)^{-2} = \dfrac{1}{4}$ and $s = 1 + \dfrac{1}{4}$.

The solution set is $\left\{ \dfrac{5}{4} \right\}$.

35. Since $(x^2 - 9)(x^2 - 3) = 0$, the solution set is $\left\{ \pm 3, \pm \sqrt{3} \right\}$.

37. Since $(x^2 + 7)(x^2 - 1) = 0$, the solution set is $\left\{ \pm 1, \pm i\sqrt{7} \right\}$.

39. Since $(x^2 + 9)(x^2 - 9) = 0$, the solution set is $\{ \pm 3, \pm 3i \}$.

41. Let $u = \dfrac{2c - 3}{5}$ and $u^2 = \left(\dfrac{2c - 3}{5} \right)^2$. Then

$$u^2 + 2u - 8 = 0$$
$$(u + 4)(u - 2) = 0$$
$$u = -4, 2$$
$$\dfrac{2c - 3}{5} = -4 \quad \text{or} \quad \dfrac{2c - 3}{5} = 2$$
$$2c - 3 = -20 \quad \text{or} \quad 2c - 3 = 10$$
$$c = -\dfrac{17}{2} \quad \text{or} \quad c = \dfrac{13}{2}.$$

The solution set is $\left\{ -\dfrac{17}{2}, \dfrac{13}{2} \right\}$.

43. Let $u = \dfrac{1}{5x - 1}$ and $u^2 = \left(\dfrac{1}{5x - 1} \right)^2$. Then

$$u^2 + u - 12 = (u + 4)(u - 3) = 0$$
$$u = -4, 3$$
$$\dfrac{1}{5x - 1} = -4 \quad \text{or} \quad \dfrac{1}{5x - 1} = 3$$
$$1 = -20x + 4 \quad \text{or} \quad 1 = 15x - 3$$
$$x = \dfrac{3}{20} \quad \text{or} \quad \dfrac{4}{15} = x.$$

The solution set is $\left\{ \dfrac{3}{20}, \dfrac{4}{15} \right\}$.

45. Let $u = v^2 - 4v$ and $u^2 = \left(v^2 - 4v \right)^2$. Then

$$u^2 - 17u + 60 = (u - 5)(u - 12) = 0$$
$$u = 5, 12$$
$$v^2 - 4v = 5 \quad \text{or} \quad v^2 - 4v = 12$$
$$v^2 - 4v - 5 = 0 \quad \text{or} \quad v^2 - 4v - 12 = 0$$
$$(v - 5)(v + 1) = 0 \quad \text{or} \quad (v - 6)(v + 2) = 0.$$

The solution set is $\{ -1, -2, 5, 6 \}$.

47. Factor the left-hand side.

$$\left(\sqrt{x} - 3 \right) \left(\sqrt{x} - 1 \right) = 0$$
$$\sqrt{x} = 3, 1$$
$$x = 9, 1$$

The solution set is $\{ 1, 9 \}$.

49. Factor the left-hand side as $\left(\sqrt{q} - 4 \right) \left(\sqrt{q} - 3 \right) = 0$. Then $\sqrt{q} = 3, 4$ and the solution set is $\{ 9, 16 \}$.

51. Set the right-hand side to 0 and factor.

$$x^{2/3} - 7x^{1/3} + 10 = 0$$
$$\left(x^{1/3} - 5 \right) \left(x^{1/3} - 2 \right) = 0$$
$$x^{1/3} = 5, 2$$

The solution set is $\{ 8, 125 \}$.

53. An equivalent statement is

$$w^2 - 4 = 3 \quad \text{or} \quad w^2 - 4 = -3$$
$$w^2 = 7 \quad \text{or} \quad w^2 = 1.$$

The solution set is $\left\{ \pm \sqrt{7}, \pm 1 \right\}$.

55. An equivalent statement assuming $5v \geq 0$ is

$$v^2 - 3v = 5v \quad \text{or} \quad v^2 - 3v = -5v$$
$$v^2 - 8v = 0 \quad \text{or} \quad v^2 + 2v = 0$$
$$v(v - 8) = 0 \quad \text{or} \quad v(v + 2) = 0$$
$$v = 0, 8, -2.$$

Since $5v \geq 0$, $v = -2$ is an extraneous root and the solution set is $\{ 0, 8 \}$.

57. An equivalent statement is

$$x^2 - x - 6 = 6 \quad \text{or} \quad x^2 - x - 6 = -6$$
$$x^2 - x - 12 = 0 \quad \text{or} \quad x^2 - x = 0$$
$$(x - 4)(x + 3) = 0 \quad \text{or} \quad x(x - 1) = 0.$$

The solution set is $\{-3, 0, 1, 4\}$.

59. An equivalent statement is

$$x + 5 = 2x + 1 \quad \text{or} \quad x + 5 = -(2x + 1)$$
$$4 = x \quad \text{or} \quad x = -2.$$

The solution set is $\{-2, 4\}$.

61. An equivalent statement is

$$x - 2 = 5x - 1 \quad \text{or} \quad x - 2 = -5x + 1$$
$$-1 = 4x \quad \text{or} \quad 6x = 3$$
$$-\frac{1}{4} = x \quad \text{or} \quad x = \frac{1}{2}$$

Note, $x = -\frac{1}{4}$ is an extraneous root. The solution set is $\{1/2\}$.

63. An equivalent statement is

$$x - 4 = x - 2 \quad \text{or} \quad x - 4 = -x + 2$$
$$-4 = -2 \quad \text{or} \quad 2x = 6$$
$$\textit{inconsistent} \quad \text{or} \quad x = 3$$

The solution set is $\{3\}$.

65. Isolate a radical and square both sides.

$$\sqrt{16x + 1} = \sqrt{6x + 13} - 1$$
$$16x + 1 = (6x + 13) - 2\sqrt{6x + 13} + 1$$
$$10x - 13 = -2\sqrt{6x + 13}$$

$$100x^2 - 260x + 169 = 4(6x + 13)$$
$$100x^2 - 284x + 117 = 0$$

$$x = \frac{284 \pm \sqrt{284^2 - 4(100)(117)}}{200}$$
$$x = \frac{284 \pm 184}{200}$$
$$x = \frac{1}{2}, \frac{117}{50}$$

Checking $x = \frac{117}{50}$ we get $\sqrt{\frac{1922}{50}} - \sqrt{\frac{1352}{50}} > 0$ and so $x = \frac{117}{50}$ is an extraneous root.

The solution set is $\left\{\frac{1}{2}\right\}$.

67. Factor as a difference of two squares and then as a sum and difference of two cubes.

$$(v^3 - 8)(v^3 + 8) = 0$$
$$(v - 2)(v^2 + 2v + 4)(v + 2)(v^2 - 2v + 4) = 0$$

Then $v = \pm 2$ or

$$v = \frac{-2 \pm \sqrt{2^2 - 16}}{2} \quad \text{or} \quad v = \frac{2 \pm \sqrt{2^2 - 16}}{2}$$
$$v = \frac{-2 \pm 2i\sqrt{3}}{2} \quad \text{or} \quad v = \frac{2 \pm 2i\sqrt{3}}{2}$$

The solution set is $\left\{\pm 2, -1 \pm i\sqrt{3}, 1 \pm i\sqrt{3}\right\}$.

69. Raise both sides to the power 4. Then

$$7x^2 - 12 = x^4$$
$$0 = x^4 - 7x^2 + 12 = (x^2 - 4)(x^2 - 3)$$
$$x = \pm 2, \pm\sqrt{3}$$

Since the left-hand side of the given equation is nonnegative, $x = -2, -\sqrt{3}$ are extraneous roots. The solution set is $\left\{\sqrt{3}, 2\right\}$.

71. Raise both sides to the power 3.

$$2 + x - 2x^2 = x^3$$
$$x^3 + 2x^2 - x - 2 = 0$$
$$x^2(x + 2) - (x + 2) = (x^2 - 1)(x + 2) = 0$$
$$x = \pm 1, -2$$

The solution set is $\{\pm 1, -2\}$.

73. Let $t = \frac{x - 2}{3}$ and $t^2 = \left(\frac{x - 2}{3}\right)^2$. Then

$$t^2 - 2t + 10 = 0$$
$$t^2 - 2t + 1 = -10 + 1$$
$$(t - 1)^2 = -9$$
$$t = 1 \pm 3i$$
$$\frac{x - 2}{3} = 1 \pm 3i$$
$$x - 2 = 3 \pm 9i$$
$$x = 5 \pm 9i.$$

The solution set is $\{5 \pm 9i\}$.

75. Raise both sides to the power $5/2$. Then

$$3u - 1 = \pm 2^{5/2}$$
$$3u - 1 = \pm 32^{1/2}$$
$$3u = 1 \pm 4\sqrt{2}$$

The solution set is $\left\{ \dfrac{1 \pm 4\sqrt{2}}{3} \right\}$.

77. Factor this quadratic type expression.

$$(x^2 + 1) - 11\sqrt{x^2 + 1} + 30 = 0$$
$$\left(\sqrt{x^2 + 1} - 5\right)\left(\sqrt{x^2 + 1} - 6\right) = 0$$
$$\sqrt{x^2 + 1} = 5 \quad \text{or} \quad \sqrt{x^2 + 1} = 6$$
$$x^2 = 24 \quad \text{or} \quad x^2 = 35$$
$$x = \pm 2\sqrt{6}, \pm\sqrt{35}$$

The solution set is $\left\{\pm\sqrt{35}, \pm 2\sqrt{6}\right\}$.

79. An equivalent statement is

$$x^2 - 2x = 3x - 6 \quad \text{or} \quad x^2 - 2x = -3x + 6$$
$$x^2 - 5x + 6 = 0 \quad \text{or} \quad x^2 + x - 6 = 0$$
$$(x - 3)(x - 2) = 0 \quad \text{or} \quad (x + 3)(x - 2) = 0$$
$$x = 2, \pm 3$$

The solution set is $\{2, \pm 3\}$.

81. Raise both sides to the power $-5/3$. Then

$$3m + 1 = \left(-\dfrac{1}{8}\right)^{-5/3}$$
$$3m + 1 = \left(-\dfrac{1}{2}\right)^{-5}$$
$$3m + 1 = -32.$$

The solution set is $\{-11\}$.

83. An equivalent statement assuming $x - 2 \geq 0$ is

$$x^2 - 4 = x - 2 \quad \text{or} \quad x^2 - 4 = -x + 2$$
$$x^2 - x - 2 = 0 \quad \text{or} \quad x^2 + x - 6 = 0$$
$$(x - 2)(x + 1) = 0 \quad \text{or} \quad (x + 3)(x - 2) = 0$$
$$x = 2, -1, -3.$$

Since $x - 2 \geq 0$, $x = -1, -3$ are extraneous roots and the solution set is $\{2\}$.

85. Solve for S.

$$21.24 + 1.25S^{1/2} - 9.8(18.34)^{1/3} = 16.296$$
$$1.25S^{1/2} - 25.84396 \approx -4.944$$
$$S^{1/2} \approx 16.72$$
$$S \approx 279.56$$

The maximum sailing area is 279.56 m^2.

87. Solve for x with $C = 83.50$.

$$0.5x + \sqrt{8x + 5000} = 83.50$$
$$\sqrt{8x + 5000} = 83.50 - 0.5x$$
$$8x + 5000 = 6972.25 - 83.50x + 0.25x^2$$
$$0 = 0.25x^2 - 91.50x + 1972.25$$

$$x = \dfrac{91.50 \pm \sqrt{(-91.50)^2 - 4(0.25)(1972.25)}}{0.5}$$
$$x = \dfrac{91.50 \pm 80}{0.5}$$
$$x = 23, 343$$

Checking $x = 343$, the value of the left-hand side of the first equation exceeds 83.50 and so $x = 343$ is an extraneous root. Thus, 23 loaves cost $83.50.

89. Let x and $x + 6$ be two numbers. Then

$$\sqrt{x + 6} - \sqrt{x} = 1$$
$$\sqrt{x + 6} = \sqrt{x} + 1$$
$$x + 6 = x + 2\sqrt{x} + 1$$
$$5 = 2\sqrt{x}$$
$$25 = 4x$$
$$x = \dfrac{25}{4}$$

Since $\dfrac{25}{4} + 6 = \dfrac{49}{4}$, the numbers are $\dfrac{25}{4}$ and $\dfrac{49}{4}$.

91. Let x be the length of the short leg. Since $x + 7$ is the other leg, by the Pythagorean Theorem the hypotenuse is $\sqrt{x^2 + (x + 7)^2}$. Then

$$x + (x + 7) + \sqrt{x^2 + (x + 7)^2} = 30$$

$$\begin{aligned}
2x - 23 &= -\sqrt{x^2 + (x+7)^2} \\
4x^2 - 92x + 529 &= 2x^2 + 14x + 49 \\
2x^2 - 106x + 480 &= 0 \\
x^2 - 53x + 240 &= 0 \\
(x-5)(x-48) &= 0 \\
x &= 5, 48
\end{aligned}$$

Since the perimeter is 30 in., $x = 48$ is an extraneous root. The short leg is $x = 5$ in.

93. Let x be the length of one side of the original square foundation. From the 2100 ft^2 we have

$$\begin{aligned}
(x-10)(x+30) &= 2100 \\
x^2 + 20x - 2400 &= 0 \\
(x+60)(x-40) &= 0.
\end{aligned}$$

Since x is nonnegative, $x = 40$ and the area of the square foundation is $x^2 = 1600$ ft^2.

95. Solving for d, we find

$$\begin{aligned}
598.9 \left(\frac{d}{64}\right)^{-2/3} &= 14.26 \\
\left(\frac{d}{64}\right)^{-2/3} &= \frac{14.26}{598.9} \\
\frac{d}{64} &= \left(\frac{14.26}{598.9}\right)^{-3/2} \\
d &= 64 \left(\frac{14.26}{598.9}\right)^{-3/2} \\
d &\approx 17,419.3 \text{ lb.}
\end{aligned}$$

97. Let $x^2(x+2)$ be the volume of shrimp to be shipped. Here, x is the length of one side of the square base and $x+2$ is the height. The volume of the box containing the styrofoam and shrimp is $(x+2)^2(x+4)$. Since the amount of shrimp is one-half of the volume of the box it is to be shipped in, we have

$$\begin{aligned}
2x^2(x+2) &= (x+2)^2(x+4) \\
2x^3 + 4x^2 &= (x^2 + 4x + 4)(x+4) \\
x^3 - 4x^2 - 20x - 16 &= 0.
\end{aligned}$$

By using the Rational Zero Theorem and synthetic division, we obtain

$$x^3 - 4x^2 - 20x - 16 = (x+2)(x^2 - 6x - 8).$$

Note, we have to exclude the zero of $x+2$ which is -2 since a dimension is a positive number. Then by using the method of completing the square, we get

$$\begin{aligned}
x^2 - 6x &= 8 \\
x^2 - 6x + 9 &= 17 \\
(x-3)^2 &= 17 \\
x &= 3 \pm \sqrt{17} \\
x &\approx -1.123, 7.123
\end{aligned}$$

Again, we exclude $x = -1.123$.
So $x = 3 + \sqrt{17}$.
Thus, the volume of shrimp to be shipped is $(3 + \sqrt{17})^2(5 + \sqrt{17}) \approx 462.89$ in.^{3}

99. Let x be the number of hours after 10:00 a.m. so that the distance between Nancy and Edgar is 14 miles greater than the distance between Nancy and William.

By the Pythagorean Theorem,
$\sqrt{(5x)^2 + (12x)^2}$ and $\sqrt{(5x)^2 + [4(x+2)]^2}$ are the distances between Nancy and Edgar and Nancy and William, respectively. Since these distances are equal, we have

$$\begin{aligned}
\sqrt{(5x)^2 + (12x)^2} - 14 &= \sqrt{(5x)^2 + [4(x+2)]^2} \\
\sqrt{169x^2} - 14 &= \sqrt{41x^2 + 64x + 64} \\
13x - 14 &= \sqrt{41x^2 + 64x + 64} \\
169x^2 - 364x + 196 &= 41x^2 + 64x + 64 \\
128x^2 - 428x + 132 &= 0 \\
32x^2 - 107x + 33 &= 0
\end{aligned}$$

$$x = \frac{107 \pm \sqrt{(-107)^2 - 4(32)(33)}}{64} = 3, \frac{11}{32}.$$

Since the left-hand side of the first equation is negative when $x = \frac{11}{32}$, we find that $x = \frac{11}{32}$ is an extraneous root. Thus, $x = 3$ hours and the time is 1:00 p.m.

101. (a) $\sqrt[3]{(565)(410)(472)} \approx \$478$ million

(b) Let p be the net income in the fourth quarter. Then

$$\sqrt[4]{(565)(410)(472)p} = 500$$

$$p = \frac{500^4}{(565)(410)(472)}$$

$$p \approx \$572 \text{ million.}$$

103. The weight of a cylindrical tank is its volume times its density. Then

$$\pi\left(\frac{d}{2}\right)^2 \cdot d \cdot 1600 = 25,850,060$$

$$400\pi d^3 = 25,850,060$$

$$d = \sqrt[3]{\frac{25,850,060}{400\pi}} \approx 27.4.$$

The height of the tank is about 27.4 meters.

105. By choosing an appropriate coordinate system, we can assume the circle is given by

$$(x+r)^2 + (y-r)^2 = r^2$$

where $r > 0$ is the radius of the circle and $(-5, 1)$ is the common point between the block and the circle. Note, the radius is less than 5 feet. Substitute $x = -5$ and $y = 1$. Then we obtain

$$(-5+r)^2 + (1-r)^2 = r^2$$
$$r^2 - 10r + 25 + 1 - 2r + r^2 = r^2$$
$$r^2 - 12r + 26 = 0.$$

The solutions of the last quadratic equation are $r = 6 \pm \sqrt{10}$. Since $r < 5$, the radius of the circle is

$$r = 6 - \sqrt{10} \text{ ft.}$$

107. $(x+5)(x-2i)(x+2i) = (x+5)(x^2+4) = x^3 + 5x^2 + 4x + 20$

109. The x-intercepts are $x = -2, 4$. Since the parabola opens downward, the solution set to $-x^2 + 2x + 8 > 0$ is $(-2, 4)$.

111. The slope of the perpendicular line is $-2/3$. Using $y = mx + b$ and the point $(9, 4)$, we find b as follows:

$$4 = -\frac{2}{3}(9) + b$$
$$4 = -6 + b$$
$$10 = b.$$

The line is $y = -\frac{2}{3}x + 10$

For Thought

1. False, to be symmetric about the origin one must have $P(-x) = -P(x)$ for *all* x in the domain.

2. True   3.   True

4. False, since $f(-x) = -f(x)$.

5. True   6.   True   7.   False

8. False, y-intercept is $(0, 38)$.   9.   True

10. False, only one x-intercept.

5 Exercises

1. y-axis

3. $-\dfrac{b}{2a}$

5. y-axis, since $f(-x) = f(x)$

7. $x = 3/2$, since $\dfrac{3}{2}$ is the x-coordinate of the vertex of a parabola

9. None

11. Origin, since $f(-x) = -f(x)$

13. $x = 5$, since 5 is the x-coordinate of the vertex of a parabola

15. Origin, since $f(-x) = -f(x)$

17. It does not cross $(4, 0)$ since $x - 4$ is raised to an even power.

19. It crosses $(1/2, 0)$.

21. It crosses $(1/4, 0)$

23. No x-intercepts since $x^2 - 3x + 10 = 0$ has no real root.

25. It crosses $(3, 0)$ and not $(0, 0)$ since $x^3 - 3x^2 = x^2(x - 3)$.

27. It crosses $(1/2, 0)$ and not $(1, 0)$ since

1	2	-5	4	-1
		2	-3	1
	2	-3	1	0

and $2x^3 - 5x^2 + 4x - 1 = (x-1)(2x^2 - 3x + 1) = (x-1)^2(2x-1)$.

29. It crosses $(2, 0)$ and not $(-3, 0)$ since

-3	-2	-8	6	36
		6	6	-36
	-2	-2	12	0

and $(x+3)(-2x^2 - 2x + 12) =$
$-2(x+3)(x^2 + x - 6) =$
$-2(x+3)(x+3)(x-2) = -2(x+3)^2(x-2)$.

31. $y \to \infty$ **33.** $y \to -\infty$ **35.** $y \to -\infty$

37. $y \to \infty$ **39.** $y \to \infty$

41. Neither symmetry, crosses $(-2, 0)$,
does not cross $(1, 0)$, $y \to \infty$ as $x \to \infty$,
$y \to -\infty$ as $x \to -\infty$

43. Symmetric about y-axis, no x-intercepts,
$y \to \infty$ as $x \to \infty$, $y \to \infty$ as $x \to -\infty$

45. Applying the leading coefficient test, we find

$$\lim_{x \to \infty} (x^2 - 4) = \infty.$$

47. Applying the leading coefficient test, we obtain

$$\lim_{x \to \infty} (-x^5 - x^2) = -\infty.$$

49. Using the leading coefficient test, we get

$$\lim_{x \to -\infty} (-3x) = \infty.$$

51. Using the leading coefficient test, we get

$$\lim_{x \to -\infty} (-2x^2 + 1) = -\infty.$$

53. The graph of $f(x) = (x-1)^2(x+3)$ is shown below.

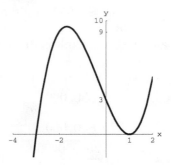

55. The graph of $f(x) = -2(2x-1)^2(x+1)^3$ is given below.

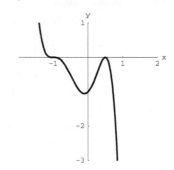

57. e, line

59. g, cubic polynomial and y-intercept $(0, 1)$

61. b, y-intercept $(0, 6)$, 4th degree polynomial

63. c, y-intercept $(0, -4)$, 3rd degree polynomial

65. $f(x) = x - 30$ has x-intercept $(30, 0)$ and y-intercept $(0, -30)$

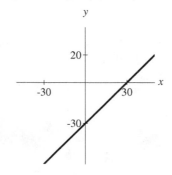

67. $f(x) = (x - 30)^2$ does not cross $(30, 0)$,
y-intercept $(0, 900)$, $y \to \infty$ as $x \to \infty$ and
as $x \to -\infty$

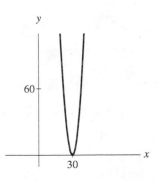

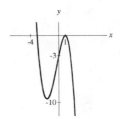

69. $f(x) = x^2(x - 40)$ crosses $(40, 0)$ but does not cross $(0, 0)$, $y \to \infty$ as $x \to \infty$, $y \to -\infty$ as $x \to -\infty$

75. Since $x^3 - 10x^2 - 600x = x(x - 30)(x + 20)$, graph crosses $(0, 0), (30, 0), (-20, 0)$, $y \to \infty$ as $x \to \infty$, $y \to -\infty$ as $x \to -\infty$

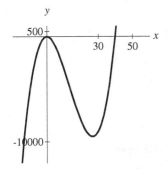

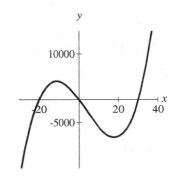

71. $f(x) = (x - 20)^2(x + 20)^2$ does not cross $(20, 0), (-20, 0)$, y-intercept $(0, 160000)$, $y \to \infty$ as $x \to \infty$ and as $x \to -\infty$

77. $f(x) = x^3 + 18x^2 - 37x + 60$ has only one x-intercept since

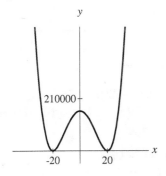

-20	1	18	-37	60
		-20	40	-60
	1	-2	3	0

and $x^2 - 2x + 3$ has no real root.
Graph crosses $(-20, 0)$, y-intercept $(0, 60)$,
$y \to \infty$ as $x \to \infty$, $y \to -\infty$ as $x \to -\infty$

73. Since $f(x) = -x^3 - x^2 + 5x - 3$

1	-1	-1	5	-3
		-1	-2	3
	-1	-2	3	0

$f(x) = (x - 1)(-x^2 - 2x + 3) =$
$-(x-1)(x+3)(x-1)$, the graph crosses $(-3, 0)$
but not $(1, 0)$, y-intercept $(0, -3)$,
$y \to -\infty$ as $x \to \infty$, and $y \to \infty$ as $x \to -\infty$

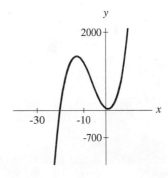

79. Since $-x^2(x^2 - 196) = -x^2(x - 14)(x + 14)$, graph crosses $(\pm 14, 0)$ and does not cross $(0, 0)$, $y \to -\infty$ as $x \to \infty$ and as $x \to -\infty$

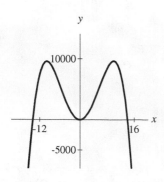

81. Use synthetic division on $f(x) = x^3 + 3x^2 + 3x + 1$ with $c = 1$.

```
-1 | 1    3    3    1
   |     -1   -2   -1
   ------------------------
     1    2    1    0
```

Since $x^2 + 2x + 1 = (x+1)^2$ then $f(x) = (x+1)^3$. Graph crosses $(-1, 0)$, y-intercept $(0, 1)$, $y \to \infty$ as $x \to \infty$, and $y \to -\infty$ as $x \to -\infty$.

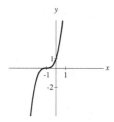

83. The graph crosses $(-7, 0)$, but it does not cross $(3, 0)$ and $(-5, 0)$, y-intercept is $(0, 1575)$, $y \to \infty$ as $x \to \infty$, and $y \to -\infty$ as $x \to -\infty$.

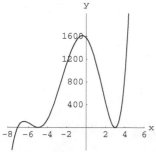

85. The roots of $x(x^2 - 3) = 0$ are $x = 0, \pm\sqrt{3}$.

If $x = 2$, then $(2)^2 - 3(2) > 0$.
If $x = 1$, then $(1)^2 - 3(1) < 0$.
If $x = -1$, then $(-1)^2 - 3(-1) > 0$.
If $x = -2$, then $(-2)^2 - 3(-2) < 0$.

The solution set is $(-\sqrt{3}, 0) \cup (\sqrt{3}, \infty)$.

87. The roots of $x^2(2 - x^2) = 0$ are $x = 0, \pm\sqrt{2}$.

If $x = 3$, then $2(3)^2 - (3)^4 < 0$.
If $x = 1$, then $2(1)^2 - (1)^4 > 0$.
If $x = -1$, then $2(-1)^2 - (-1)^4 > 0$.
If $x = -3$, then $2(-3)^2 - (-3)^4 < 0$.

The solution set is $(-\infty, -\sqrt{2}] \cup \{0\} \cup [\sqrt{2}, \infty)$.

89. Let $f(x) = x^3 + 4x^2 - x - 4$. Since

$$x^2(x+4) - (x+4) = (x+4)(x^2 - 1) = 0,$$

the zeros of $f(x)$ are $x = -4, \pm 1$.

If $x = 2$, then $f(2) > 0$.
If $x = 0$, then $f(0) < 0$.
If $x = -2$, then $f(-2) > 0$.
If $x = -5$, then $f(-5) < 0$.

The solution set is $(-4, -1) \cup (1, \infty)$.

91. Let $f(x) = x^3 - 4x^2 - 20x + 48$.
Since $f(x) = (x+4)(x-2)(x-6)$, the zeros of $f(x)$ are $x = -4, 2, 6$.

If $x = 7$, then $f(7) > 0$.
If $x = 4$, then $f(4) < 0$.
If $x = 0$, then $f(0) > 0$.
If $x = -5$, then $f(-5) < 0$.

The solution set is $[-4, 2] \cup [6, \infty)$.

93. Note, $f(x) = x^3 - x^2 + x - 1 = x^2(x-1) + (x-1) = (x-1)(x^2 + 1) = 0$ has only one solution, namely, $x = 1$.

If $x = 2$, then $f(2) > 0$.
If $x = 0$, then $f(0) < 0$.

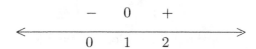

The solution set is $(-\infty, 1)$.

95. Let $f(x) = x^4 - 19x^2 + 90$.
Since $f(x) = (x^2 - 10)(x^2 - 9)$, the zeros
of $f(x)$ are $x = \pm\sqrt{10}, \pm 3$.

If $x = 4$, then $f(4) > 0$.
If $x = 3.1$, then $f(3.1) < 0$.
If $x = 0$, then $f(0) > 0$.
If $x = -3.1$, then $f(-3.1) < 0$.
If $x = -4$, then $f(-4) > 0$.

The solution set is $[-\sqrt{10}, -3] \cup [3, \sqrt{10}]$.

97. $(-2, 0) \cup (2, \infty)$, see the part of the graph above
the x-axis

99. $[-2, 0] \cup [2, \infty)$, see the part of the graph above
the x-axis including the x-intercepts

101. $(-2, -1) \cup (1, 2)$, see the part of the graph
below the x-axis

103. $(-\infty - 2] \cup [-1, 1] \cup [2, \infty)$, see the part of
the graph above the x-axis including the x-intercepts

105. d, since the x-intercepts of

$$f(x) = \frac{1}{3}(x + 3)(x - 2)$$

are -3 and 2 and $f(0) = -2$

107. Since $f(-5) = 0 = f(4)$, the quadratic function f can be expressed as

$$f(x) = a(x + 5)(x - 4).$$

Also, $3 = f(0) = a(5)(-4)$ and so $a = -3/20$.
Thus, we have

$$f(x) = -\frac{3}{20}(x + 5)(x - 4).$$

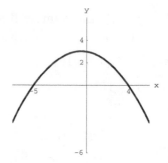

109. Since $f(-1) = 0 = f(3)$, the quadratic function f can be written as

$$f(x) = a(x + 1)(x - 3).$$

Also, $2 = f(1) = a(2)(-2)$ and we find $a = -1/2$. Thus, we obtain

$$f(x) = -\frac{1}{2}(x + 1)(x - 3).$$

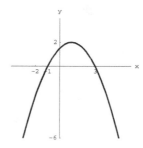

111. Since $f(2) = f(-3) = f(4) = 0$, the cubic
function f can be expressed as

$$f(x) = a(x - 2)(x + 3)(x - 4).$$

Also, $6 = f(0) = a(-2)(3)(-4)$ and we get
$a = 1/4$. Thus, we obtain

$$f(x) = \frac{1}{4}(x - 2)(x + 3)(x - 4).$$

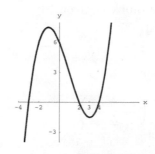

113. Since $f(\pm 2) = 0 = f(\pm 4)$, the quartic function f can be written as

$$f(x) = a(x^2 - 4)(x^2 - 16).$$

Also, $3 = f(1) = a(-3)(-15)$ and we get $a = 1/15$. Thus, we obtain

$$f(x) = \frac{1}{15}(x^2 - 4)(x^2 - 16).$$

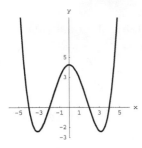

115. From the graph of the profit function, we find a local maximum of \$3400 and a local minimum of \$2600. To get a profit higher than \$3400, the company must spend more than \$2200 on advertising.

117. Note, $P = \dfrac{x}{10}(x^2 - 60x + 900) = \dfrac{x}{10}(x-30)^2$.

The graph of P does not cross the x-intercept $(30, 0)$. Thus, the profit decreases to \$0 at $x = 30$ stores, and the profit increases as more stores (greater than 30) are opened.

A closer look at the graph of P shows that the profit is also increasing for $0 < x < 10$, and is decreasing when $10 < x < 30$.

119. Since $3x + 2y = 12$, we get $y = \dfrac{12 - 3x}{2}$.

The volume V of the block is given by

$$\begin{aligned}
V &= xy\frac{4y}{3} \\[4pt]
&= \frac{4x}{3}y^2 \\[4pt]
&= \frac{4x}{3}\left(\frac{12 - 3x}{2}\right)^2 \\[4pt]
V &= 3x^3 - 24x^2 + 48x.
\end{aligned}$$

One finds from the graph of

$$V = \frac{4x}{3}\left(\frac{12 - 3x}{2}\right)^2$$

that the optimal dimensions of the block are

$$x = \frac{4}{3} \text{ in. by } y = \frac{12 - 4}{2} = 4 \text{ in. by } \frac{16}{3} \text{ in.}.$$

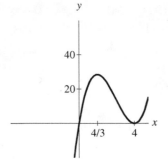

121. If the surface area is 50 square feet, then no paint can be used (since all the paint is used to coat the inside of the can).

Since the amount of paint in a 1-pint can is $\dfrac{1}{8} \cdot \dfrac{1}{7.5}$ or $\dfrac{1}{60}$ feet^3, we get

$$\frac{1}{60} = \pi r^2 h.$$

Solving for h, one obtains $h = \dfrac{1}{60\pi r^2}$. Then

$$\begin{aligned}
2\pi r^2 + 2\pi rh &= 50 \\[4pt]
2\pi r^2 + 2\pi r\left(\frac{1}{60\pi r^2}\right) &= 50 \\[4pt]
2\pi r^2 + \frac{1}{30r} - 50 &= 0.
\end{aligned}$$

With a graphing calculator, one finds

$$r \approx \pm 2.82 \text{ or } r \approx 6.67 \times 10^{-4}.$$

If $r \approx 2.82$, then $h \approx 6.67 \times 10^{-4}$ feet since $h = \dfrac{1}{60\pi r^2}$. Similarly, if $r \approx 6.67 \times 10^{-4}$, then $h \approx 11{,}924.69$ feet. Thus, either the radius and height of the can are

$$r \approx 2.82 \text{ ft and } h \approx 6.67 \times 10^{-4} \text{ ft}$$

or

$$r \approx 6.67 \times 10^{-4} \text{ ft and } h \approx 11{,}924.69 \text{ ft}.$$

123. Isolate one radical and square both sides.

$$
\begin{aligned}
x + 12 &= 9 + 6\sqrt{x-9} + (x-9) \\
12 &= 6\sqrt{x-9} \\
2 &= \sqrt{x-9} \\
4 &= x - 9 \\
13 &= x
\end{aligned}
$$

The solution set is $\{13\}$.

125. Quotient $x^3 + x^2 - 11x + 24$ and

remainder -53 since

-2	1	3	-9	2	-5
		-2	-2	22	-48
	1	1	-11	24	-53

127. Since the absolute value of a number is non-negative and $x = |y - 5|$, the domain or set of all x-values is $[0, \infty)$. The range or set of all permissible y-values in $|y - 5|$ is $(-\infty, \infty)$.

For Thought

1. False, $\sqrt{x} - 3$ is not a polynomial.

2. False, domain is $(-\infty, 2) \cup (2, \infty)$.

3. False

4. False, it has three vertical asymptotes.

5. True

6. False, $y = 5$ is the horizontal asymptote.

7. True   **8.**   False

9. True, it is an even function.

10. True, since $x = -3$ is not a vertical asymptote.

6 Exercises

1. rational

3. vertical asymptote

5. $(-\infty, -2) \cup (-2, \infty)$

7. $(-\infty, -2) \cup (-2, 2) \cup (2, \infty)$

9. $(-\infty, 3) \cup (3, \infty)$

11. $(-\infty, 0) \cup (0, \infty)$

13. $(-\infty, -1) \cup (-1, 0) \cup (0, 1) \cup (1, \infty)$ since

$$
f(x) = \frac{3x^2 - 1}{x(x^2 - 1)}
$$

15. $(-\infty, -3) \cup (-3, -2) \cup (-2, \infty)$ since

$$
f(x) = \frac{-x^2 + x}{(x+3)(x+2)}
$$

17. Domain $(-\infty, 2) \cup (2, \infty)$, asymptotes $y = 0$ and $x = 2$

19. Domain $(-\infty, 0) \cup (0, \infty)$, asymptotes $y = x$ and $x = 0$

21. Asymptotes $x = 2$, $y = 0$

23. Asymptotes $x = \pm 3$, $y = 0$

25. Asymptotes $x = 1$, $y = 2$

27. Asymptotes $x = 0$, $y = x - 2$ since

$$
f(x) = x - 2 + \frac{1}{x}
$$

29. Asymptotes $x = -1$, $y = 3x - 3$ since

$$
\begin{array}{r}
3x - 3 \\
x + 1 \overline{)3x^2 + 0x + 4} \\
\underline{3x^2 + 3x} \\
-3x + 4 \\
\underline{-3x - 3} \\
7
\end{array}
$$

and $f(x) = 3x - 3 + \dfrac{7}{x+1}$

31. Asymptotes $x = -2$, $y = -x + 6$ since

$$
\begin{array}{r}
-x + 6 \\
x + 2 \overline{)-x^2 + 4x + 0} \\
\underline{-x^2 - 2x} \\
6x + 0 \\
\underline{6x + 12} \\
-12
\end{array}
$$

and $f(x) = -x + 6 + \dfrac{-12}{x+2}$

33. Asymptotes $x = 0$, $y = 0$, no x or y-intercept

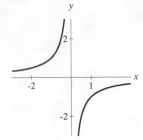

35. Asymptotes $x = 2$, $y = 0$, no x-intercept, y-intercept $(0, -1/2)$

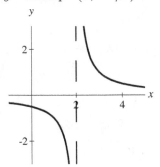

37. Asymptotes $x = \pm 2$, $y = 0$, no x-intercept, y-intercept $(0, -1/4)$

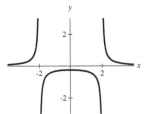

39. Asymptotes $x = -1$, $y = 0$, no x-intercept, y-intercept $(0, -1)$

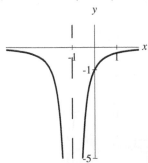

41. Asymptotes $x = 1$, $y = 2$, x-intercept $(-1/2, 0)$, y-intercept $(0, -1)$

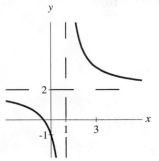

43. Asymptotes $x = -2$, $y = 1$, x-intercept $(3, 0)$, y-intercept $(0, -3/2)$

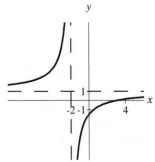

45. Asymptotes $x = \pm 1$, $y = 0$, x- and y-intercept is $(0, 0)$

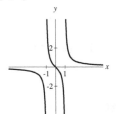

47. Since $f(x) = \dfrac{4x}{(x-1)^2}$, asymptotes are $x = 1$, $y = 0$, x- and y-intercept is $(0, 0)$

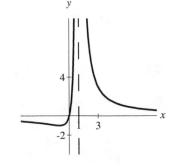

49. Asymptotes are $x = \pm 3$, $y = -1$,
x-intercept $(\pm 2\sqrt{2}, 0)$, y-intercept $(0, -8/9)$

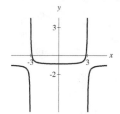

51. Since $f(x) = \dfrac{2x^2 + 8x + 2}{(x + 1)^2}$,

asymptotes are $x = -1$, $y = 2$,
by solving $2x^2 + 8x + 2 = 0$ one gets the
x-intercepts $\left(-2 \pm \sqrt{3}, 0\right)$,
y-intercept $(0, 2)$

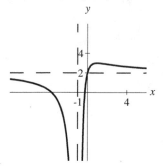

53. We see from the graph that $\displaystyle\lim_{x \to \infty} \dfrac{1}{x^2} = 0$

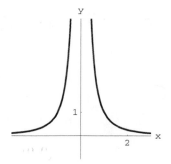

55. From the graph, we find $\displaystyle\lim_{x \to \infty} \dfrac{2x - 3}{x - 1} = 2$

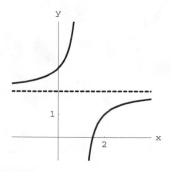

57. From the graph, we find $\displaystyle\lim_{x \to 0^+} \dfrac{1}{x^2} = \infty$

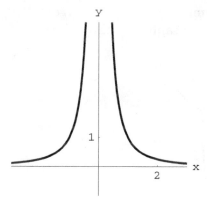

59. We see from the graph that $\displaystyle\lim_{x \to 1^+} \dfrac{2}{x - 1} = \infty$

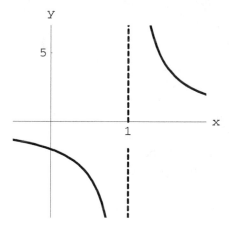

61. Since $f(x) = x + \dfrac{1}{x}$, oblique asymptote is

$y = x$, asymptote $x = 0$, no x-intercept,
no y-intercept, graph goes through
$(1, 2), (-1, -2)$

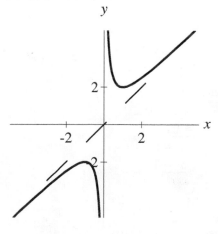

63. Since $f(x) = x - \dfrac{1}{x^2}$, oblique asymptote

is $y = x$, asymptote $x = 0$, x-intercept $(1, 0)$,
no y-intercept, graph goes through $(-1, -2)$

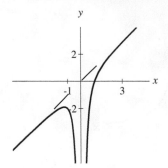

65. $f(x) = x - 1 + \dfrac{1}{x+1}$ since

$$
\begin{array}{r}
x - 1 \\
x + 1 \enclose{longdiv}{x^2 + 0x} \\
\underline{x^2 + x} \\
-x + 0 \\
\underline{-x - 1} \\
1
\end{array}
$$

Oblique asymptote $y = x - 1$,
asymptote $x = -1$, x-intercept $(0, 0)$,
graph goes through $(-2, -4)$

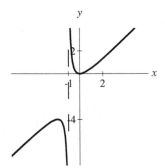

67. $f(x) = 2x + 1 + \dfrac{1}{x-1}$ since

$$
\begin{array}{r}
2x + 1 \\
x - 1 \enclose{longdiv}{2x^2 - x + 0} \\
\underline{2x^2 - 2x} \\
x + 0 \\
\underline{x - 1} \\
1
\end{array}
$$

Oblique asymptote $y = 2x + 1$,
asymptote $x = 1$,
x-intercepts $(0, 0), (1/2, 0)$,
graph goes through $(2, 6)$

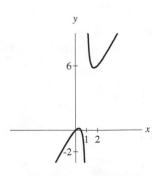

69. Using long division, we find

$$
\frac{x^3 - x^2 - 4x + 5}{x^2 - 4} = (x - 1) + \frac{1}{x^2 - 4}.
$$

The oblique asymptote is $y = x - 1$.

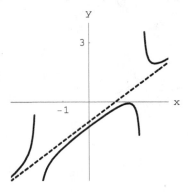

71. Using long division, we find

$$
\frac{-x^3 + x^2 + 5x - 4}{x^2 + x - 2} = (-x + 2) + \frac{x}{x^2 + x - 2}.
$$

The oblique asymptote is $y = -x + 2$.

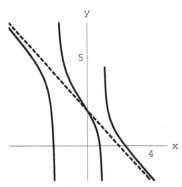

73. e   **75.**   a

77. b   **79.**   c

81. Domain is $\{x : x \neq \pm 1\}$ since

$$f(x) = \frac{x+1}{(x+1)(x-1)} = \frac{1}{x-1} \text{ if } x \neq -1,$$

a 'hole' at $(-1, -1/2)$, asymptotes $x = 1$, $y = 0$, no x-intercept, y-intercept $(0, -1)$

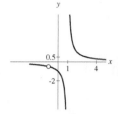

83. The domain is $\{x : x \neq 1\}$ since

$$f(x) = \frac{(x-1)(x+1)}{x-1} = x + 1 \text{ where } x \neq 1,$$

a line with a 'hole' at $(1, 2)$

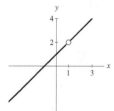

85. Parabola $y = x^2$ with domain $x \neq \pm 1$.

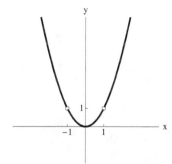

87. The graph of $y = \dfrac{1}{x^2}$ with domain $x \neq \pm 2$

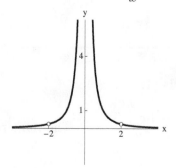

89. Symmetric about y-axis, asymptote $x = 0$, goes through $(0, 2), (1, 1)$

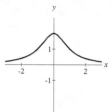

91. Since $f(x) = \dfrac{x-1}{x(x^2-9)}$, asymptotes are

$x = \pm 3, x = 0, y = 0$, crosses $(1, 0)$

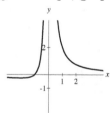

93. Asymptotes $x = 0, y = 0$, x-intercept $(-1, 0)$, no y-intercept, graph goes through $(1, 2)$

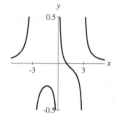

95. Let $f(x) = \dfrac{x-4}{x+2}$.

If $x = -3$, then $f(-3) > 0$.
If $x = 0$, then $f(0) < 0$.
If $x = 5$, then $f(5) > 0$.

$$
\begin{array}{ccccccc}
+ & & \text{UD} & - & 0 & & + \\
\hline
-3 & & -2 & 0 & 4 & & 5
\end{array}
$$

The solution set is $(-2, 4]$.

97. Let $f(q) = \dfrac{q+8}{q+3} > 0$.

If $q = -9$, then $f(-9) > 0$.
If $q = -6$, then $f(-6) < 0$.
If $q = 0$, then $f(0) > 0$.

$$
\begin{array}{ccccccc}
+ & & 0 & - & \text{UD} & & + \\
\hline
-9 & & -8 & -6 & -3 & & 0
\end{array}
$$

The solution set is $(-\infty, -8) \cup (-3, \infty)$.

99. Let $f(w) = \dfrac{(w-3)(w+2)}{w-6} \geq 0$.

If $w = -3$, then $f(-3) < 0$.
If $w = 0$, then $f(0) > 0$.
If $w = 4$, then $f(4) < 0$.
If $w = 7$, then $f(7) > 0$.

$$
\begin{array}{ccccccc}
- & 0 & + & 0 & - & \text{UD} & + \\
\end{array}
$$
$$
\xleftarrow{\qquad} \quad \underset{-3 \;\; -2 \;\; 0 \quad\;\; 3 \quad\;\; 4 \quad\; 6 \;\; 7}{\hspace{4cm}} \xrightarrow{\qquad}
$$

The solution set is $[-2, 3] \cup (6, \infty)$.

101. Let $f(x) = \dfrac{-5}{(x+2)(x-3)} > 0$.

If $x = -3$, then $f(-3) < 0$.
If $x = 0$, then $f(0) > 0$.
If $x = 4$, then $f(4) < 0$.

$$
\begin{array}{ccccc}
- & \text{UD} & + & \text{UD} & - \\
\end{array}
$$
$$
\xleftarrow{\qquad} \quad \underset{-3 \quad\;\; -2 \quad\;\; 0 \quad\;\; 3 \quad\;\; 4}{\hspace{4cm}} \xrightarrow{\qquad}
$$

The solution set is $(-2, 3)$.

103. Let $f(x) = \dfrac{(x-4)(x+2)}{5-x} > 0$.

If $x = -3$, then $f(-3) > 0$.
If $x = 0$, then $f(0) < 0$.
If $x = 4.5$, then $f(4.5) > 0$.
If $x = 6$, then $f(6) < 0$.

$$
\begin{array}{cccccc}
+ & 0 & - & 0 & + & \text{UD} & - \\
\end{array}
$$
$$
\xleftarrow{\qquad} \quad \underset{-3 \;\; -2 \;\; 0 \quad\; 4 \quad\; 4.5 \;\; 5 \quad\; 6}{\hspace{4cm}} \xrightarrow{\qquad}
$$

The solution set is $(-\infty, -2) \cup (4, 5)$.

105. Let $f(x) = \dfrac{(x-3)(x+1)}{x-5} \geq 0$.

If $x = -2$, then $f(-2) < 0$.
If $x = 0$, then $f(0) > 0$.
If $x = 4$, then $f(4) < 0$.
If $x = 7$, then $f(7) > 0$.

$$
\begin{array}{ccccccc}
- & 0 & + & 0 & - & \text{UD} & + \\
\end{array}
$$
$$
\xleftarrow{\qquad} \quad \underset{-2 \;\; -1 \;\; 0 \quad\; 3 \quad\; 4 \quad\; 5 \;\; 7}{\hspace{4cm}} \xrightarrow{\qquad}
$$

The solution set is $[-1, 3] \cup (5, \infty)$.

107. Let $f(x) = \dfrac{(x-\sqrt{7})(x+\sqrt{7})}{(\sqrt{2}-x)(\sqrt{2}+x)}$.

If $x = 3$, then $f(3) < 0$.
If $x = 2$, then $f(2) > 0$.
If $x = 0$, then $f(0) < 0$.
If $x = -2$, then $f(-2) > 0$.
If $x = -3$, then $f(-3) < 0$.

$$
\begin{array}{ccccccc}
- & 0 & + & \text{U} & - & \text{U} & + & 0 & - \\
\end{array}
$$
$$
\xleftarrow{\qquad} \quad \underset{-\sqrt{7} \quad\; -\sqrt{2} \quad\; \sqrt{2} \quad\;\; \sqrt{7}}{\hspace{4cm}} \xrightarrow{\qquad}
$$

The solution set is

$$(-\infty, -\sqrt{7}] \cup (-\sqrt{2}, \sqrt{2}) \cup [\sqrt{7}, \infty).$$

109. Let $R(x) = \dfrac{(x+1)^2}{(x-5)(x+3)} \geq 0$.

Since $R(-4) > 0$, $R(-2) < 0$, $R(0) < 0$,
and $R(6) > 0$, we get

$$
\begin{array}{ccccccc}
+ & \text{U} & - & 0 & - & \text{U} & + \\
\end{array}
$$
$$
\xleftarrow{\qquad} \quad \underset{-4 \;\; -3 \quad\; -2 \quad\; -1 \quad\; 0 \quad\; 5 \quad\; 6}{\hspace{4cm}} \xrightarrow{\qquad}
$$

The solution set is $(-\infty, -3) \cup \{-1\} \cup (5, \infty)$.

111. Let $f(w) = \dfrac{w-1}{w^2} > 0$.

If $w = -1$, then $f(-1) < 0$.
If $w = 0.5$, then $f(0.5) < 0$.
If $w = 2$, then $f(2) > 0$.

$$
\begin{array}{ccccc}
- & \text{U} & - & 0 & + \\
\end{array}
$$
$$
\xleftarrow{\qquad} \quad \underset{-1 \quad\; 0 \quad\;\; 0.5 \quad\; 1 \quad\;\; 2}{\hspace{4cm}} \xrightarrow{\qquad}
$$

The solution set is $(1, \infty)$.

113. Let $f(w) = \dfrac{w^2 - 4w + 5}{w-3} > 0$. The numerator has no real zero.

If $w = 0$, then $f(0) < 0$.
If $w = 4$, then $f(4) > 0$.

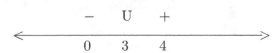

The solution set is $(3, \infty)$.

115. $(-\infty, 1) \cup (3, \infty)$, see the part of the graph above the x-axis

117. $(-\infty, 1] \cup (3, \infty)$, see the part of the graph above the x-axis including the x-intercepts

119. $(-\infty, -2) \cup (0, 2)$, see the part of the graph below the x-axis

121. $(-2, 0] \cup (2, \infty)$, see the part of the graph above the x-axis including the x-intercepts

123. Since $y = 0$ and $x = 1$ are asymptotes, the rational function can be written as

$$y = \frac{a}{x - 1}.$$

Since $(3, 1)$ satifies the equation above, we find $1 = a/2$ or $a = 2$. Thus, the function is

$$y = \frac{2}{x - 1}.$$

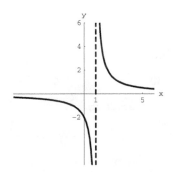

125. Since $y = 1$ and $x = 2$ are asymptotes, the function can be expressed as

$$y = \frac{x - a}{x - 2}.$$

Since $(0, 5)$ satifies the equation above, we obtain $5 = (-a)/(-2)$ or $a = 10$. Thus, the function is

$$y = \frac{x - 10}{x - 2} \text{ or } y = \frac{-8}{x - 2} + 1.$$

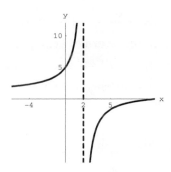

127. Since $y = 0$ and $x = \pm 3$ are asymptotes, the function can be written as

$$y = \frac{ax + b}{x^2 - 9}.$$

Since $(0, 0)$ and $(4, 8/7)$ satifies the equation above, we obtain $0 = (b)/(-9)$ and $8/7 = (4a + b)/7$, respectively. Then $b = 0$ and $8/7 = 4a/7$ or $a = 2$. Thus, the function is

$$y = \frac{2x}{x^2 - 9}.$$

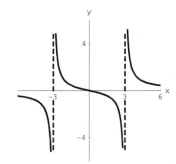

129. Since $y = 2x + 1$ and $x = 1$ are asymptotes, the function can be written as

$$y = (2x + 1) + \frac{a}{x - 1}.$$

Since $(0, 3)$ satifies the equation above, we find $3 = 1 + a/(-1)$ or $a = -2$. Thus, the function is

$$y = 2x + 1 + \frac{-2}{x - 1}.$$

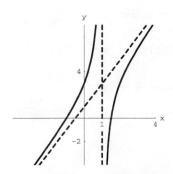

131. Average cost is $C = \dfrac{100 + x}{x}$. If she visits the zoo 100 times, then her average cost per visit is $C = \dfrac{200}{100} = \$2$. Since $C \to \$1$ as $x \to \infty$, over a long period her average cost per visit is $\$1$.

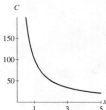

133. Since the second half is 100 miles long and it must be completed in $4 - x$ hours, the average speed for the second half is $S(x) = \dfrac{100}{4 - x}$. The asymptote $x = 4$ implies $S \to \infty$ as the completion time in the first half shortens to four hours.

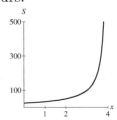

135. a) About 15 minutes

b) About 200 PPM

c) The horizontal asymptote is PPM $= 0$ and the vertical asymptote is $t = 0$. In simple terms, a long exposure to low level carbon monoxide still leads to permanent brain damage, and a very high level carbon monoxide can lead to permanent brain damage in a few minutes.

137.

(a) $h = \dfrac{500}{\pi r^2}$ since $500 = \pi r^2 h$

(b) $S = 2\pi r^2 + 2\pi r h = 2\pi r^2 + 2\pi r \dfrac{500}{\pi r^2}$

or equivalently $S = 2\pi r^2 + \dfrac{1000}{r}$

(c) As can be seen from the graph of $S = 2\pi r^2 + \dfrac{1000}{r}$, S is minimized when $r \approx 4.3$ feet.

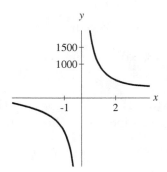

(d) If it costs $\$8$ per ft^2 to construct the tank in part (c), then the cost of the tank is given by

$$8\left(2\pi(4.3)^2 + \frac{1000}{4.3}\right) \approx \$2789.87.$$

141. Let $f(x) = (x - 1)^2(x + 5) > 0$.
If $x = -6$, then $f(-6) < 0$.
If $x = 0$, then $f(0) > 0$.
If $x = 2$, then $f(2) > 0$.

$$
\begin{array}{ccccccccc}
 & - & & 0 & & + & & 0 & & + \\
\hline
 & -6 & & -5 & & 0 & & 1 & & 2
\end{array}
$$

The solution set is $(-5, 1) \cup (1, \infty)$.

143. Factoring, we find

$$x(x^4 + 13x^2 + 36) = x(x^2 + 4)(x^2 + 9)$$

The solution set is $\{0, \pm 2i, \pm 3i\}$.

145. Since $-\dfrac{b}{2a} = \dfrac{3}{2}$ and $f\left(\dfrac{3}{2}\right) = -\dfrac{31}{4}$, the vertex is $\left(\dfrac{3}{2}, -\dfrac{31}{4}\right)$. Since the parabola opens downward, the function is increasing on $\left(-\infty, \dfrac{3}{2}\right]$.

Chapter Review Exercises

1. By using the method of completing the square, we obtain

$$
\begin{aligned}
f(x) &= 3\left(x^2 - \frac{2}{3}x + \frac{1}{9}\right) - \frac{1}{3} + 1 \\
&= 3\left(x - \frac{1}{3}\right)^2 + \frac{2}{3}
\end{aligned}
$$

3. Since $y = 2(x^2 - 2x + 1) - 2 - 1 = 2(x-1)^2 - 3$, the vertex is $(1, -3)$ and axis of symmetry is $x = 1$. Setting $y = 0$, we get $x - 1 = \pm\dfrac{\sqrt{6}}{2}$ and the x-intercepts are $\left(\dfrac{2 \pm \sqrt{6}}{2}, 0\right)$. The y-intercept is $(0, -1)$.

5. From the x-intercepts, $y = a(x+1)(x-3)$. Substitute $(0, 6)$, so $6 = a(-3)$ or $a = -2$. The equation of the parabola is $y = -2(x^2 - 2x - 3)$ or $y = -2x^2 + 4x + 6$.

7. $1/3$ **9.** $\pm 2\sqrt{2}$

11. Factoring, we obtain

$$m(x) = (2x - 1)(4x^2 + 2x + 1).$$

By using the quadratic formula, we obtain the zeros to the second factor. Namely,

$$x = \frac{-2 \pm \sqrt{-12}}{8} = \frac{-2 \pm 2i\sqrt{3}}{8}.$$

The zeros are $\dfrac{1}{2}, \dfrac{-1 \pm i\sqrt{3}}{4}$.

13. Since $P(t) = (t^2 - 10)(t^2 + 10)$, the zeros are $\pm\sqrt{10}, \pm i\sqrt{10}$

15. Factoring, we obtain $R(s) = 4s^2(2s-1) - (2s-1) = (4s^2-1)(2s-1)$.

The zeros are $\dfrac{1}{2}$ (with multiplicity 2) and $-\dfrac{1}{2}$.

17. Find the roots of the second factor of $f(x) = x(x^2 + 2x - 6)$. Since $x^2 + 2x - 6 = (x^2 + 2x + 1) - 6 - 1 = (x+1)^2 - 7$, the zeros are $0, -1 \pm \sqrt{7}$.

19. $P(3) = 108 - 27 + 3 - 1 = 83$. By synthetic division, we get

3	4	-3	1	-1
		12	27	84
	4	9	28	83

Remainder is $P(3) = 83$.

21. $P(-1/2) = \dfrac{1}{4} - \dfrac{1}{4} + 3 + 2 = 5$.

By synthetic division, we obtain

-1/2	-8	0	2	0	-6	2
		4	-2	0	0	3
	-8	4	0	0	-6	5

So the remainder is $P(-1/2) = 5$.

23. $\pm\left\{1, \dfrac{1}{3}, 2, \dfrac{2}{3}\right\}$

25. $\pm\left\{1, \dfrac{1}{2}, \dfrac{1}{3}, \dfrac{1}{6}, 3, \dfrac{3}{2}\right\}$

27.

$$2\left(x + \frac{1}{2}\right)(x - 3) = (2x + 1)(x - 3)$$
$$= 2x^2 - 5x - 3$$

An equation is $2x^2 - 5x - 3 = 0$.

29. $(x - (3 - 2i))(x - (3 + 2i)) =$

$$= ((x - 3) + 2i)((x - 3) - 2i)$$
$$= (x - 3)^2 + 4$$
$$= x^2 - 6x + 13$$

An equation is $x^2 - 6x + 13 = 0$.

31. $(x - 2)(x - (1 - 2i))(x - (1 + 2i)) =$

$$= (x - 2)((x - 1) + 2i)((x - 1) - 2i)$$
$$= (x - 2)\left((x - 1)^2 + 4\right)$$
$$= (x - 2)(x^2 - 2x + 5)$$
$$= x^3 - 4x^2 + 9x - 10$$

Thus, an equation is $x^3 - 4x^2 + 9x - 10 = 0$.

33. $\left(x - (2 - \sqrt{3})\right)\left(x - (2 + \sqrt{3})\right) =$

$$= \left((x - 2) + \sqrt{3}\right)\left((x - 2) - \sqrt{3}\right)$$
$$= \left((x - 2)^2 - 3\right)$$
$$= x^2 - 4x + 1$$

Thus, an equation is $x^2 - 4x + 1 = 0$.

35. $P(x) = P(-x) = x^8 + x^6 + 2x^2$ has no sign variation. There are 6 imaginary roots and 0 has multiplicity 2.

37. $P(x) = 4x^3 - 3x^2 + 2x - 9$ has 3 sign variations and $P(-x) = -4x^3 - 3x^2 - 2x - 9$ has no sign variation. There are
(a) 3 positive roots, or
(b) 1 positive and 2 imaginary roots.

39. $P(x) = x^3 + 2x^2 + 2x + 1$ has no sign variation and $P(-x) = -x^3 + 2x^2 - 2x + 1$ has 3 sign variations. There are
(a) 3 negative roots, or
(b) 1 negative root and 2 imaginary roots.

41. Best integral bounds: $-4 < x < 3$. One checks that $1, 2$ are not upper bounds and that 3 is a bound.

3	6	5	-50
		18	69
	6	23	19

One checks that $-1, -2, -3$ are not lower bounds and that -4 is a bound since

-4	6	5	-50
		-24	76
	6	-19	26

43. Best integral bounds: $-1 < x < 8$. One checks that $1, 2, 3, 4, 5, 6, 7$ are not upper bounds and that 8 is a bound.

8	2	-15	31	-12
		16	8	312
	2	1	39	300

-1 is a lower bound since

-1	2	-15	31	-12
		-2	17	-48
	2	-17	48	-60

45. Best integral bounds: $-1 < x < 1$

1	12	-4	-3	1
		12	8	5
	12	8	5	6

-1	12	-4	-3	1
		-12	16	-13
	12	-16	13	-12

47. Roots are $1, 2, 3$ since

1	1	-6	11	-6
		1	-5	6
	1	-5	6	0

and $x^2 - 5x + 6 = (x - 3)(x - 2)$.

49. Roots are $\pm i, 1/3, 1/2$ since

1/2	6	-5	7	-5	1
		3	-1	3	-1
	6	-2	6	-2	0

1/3	6	-2	6	-2
		2	0	2
	6	0	6	0

and the zeros of $6x^2 + 6 = 6(x^2 + 1) = 0$ are $\pm i$.

51. Roots are $3, 3 \pm i$ since

3	1	-9	28	-30
		3	-18	30
	1	-6	10	0

and the zeros of $x^2 - 6x + 10 = (x - 3)^2 + 1 = 0$ are $3 \pm i$.

53. Roots are $2, 1 \pm i\sqrt{2}$ since

$$\begin{array}{r|rrrr} 2 & 1 & -4 & 7 & -6 \\ & & 2 & -4 & 6 \\ \hline & 1 & -2 & 3 & 0 \end{array}$$

and the zeros of $x^2 - 2x + 3 =$
$(x-1)^2 + 2 = 0$ are $1 \pm i\sqrt{2}$.

55. Apply synthetic division to the second factor in $x(2x^3 - 5x^2 - 2x + 2) = 0$.

$$\begin{array}{r|rrrr} 1/2 & 2 & -5 & -2 & 2 \\ & & 1 & -2 & -2 \\ \hline & 2 & -4 & -4 & 0 \end{array}$$

By completing the square, the zeros of $2x^2 - 4x - 4 = 2(x^2 - 2x) - 4 = 2(x-1)^2 - 6 = 0$ are $1 \pm \sqrt{3}$. All the roots are $x = 0, 1/2, 1 \pm \sqrt{3}$.

57. Solve an equivalent statement assuming $3v \geq 0$.

$$\begin{array}{ccc} 2v - 1 = 3v & \text{or} & 2v - 1 = -3v \\ -1 = v & \text{or} & 5v = 1 \end{array}$$

Since $3v \geq 0$, $v = -1$ is an extraneous root.
The solution set is $\{1/5\}$.

59. Let $w = x^2$ and $w^2 = x^4$.

$$\begin{aligned} w^2 + 7w &= 18 \\ (w+9)(w-2) &= 0 \\ w &= -9, 2 \\ x^2 = -9 \quad \text{or} \quad x^2 &= 2. \end{aligned}$$

Since $x^2 = -9$ has no real solution, the solution set is $\{\pm\sqrt{2}\}$.

61. Isolate a radical and square both sides.

$$\begin{aligned} \sqrt{x+6} &= \sqrt{x-5} + 1 \\ x + 6 &= x - 5 + 2\sqrt{x-5} + 1 \\ 5 &= \sqrt{x-5} \\ 25 &= x - 5 \end{aligned}$$

The solution set is $\{30\}$.

63. Let $w = \sqrt[4]{y}$ and $w^2 = \sqrt{y}$.

$$\begin{aligned} w^2 + w - 6 &= 0 \\ (w+3)(w-2) &= 0 \\ w = -3 \quad \text{or} \quad w &= 2 \\ y^{1/4} = -3 \quad \text{or} \quad y^{1/4} &= 2 \end{aligned}$$

Since $y^{1/4} = -3$ has no real solution, the solution set is $\{16\}$.

65. Let $w = x^2$ and $w^2 = x^4$.

$$\begin{aligned} w^2 - 3w - 4 &= 0 \\ (w+1)(w-4) &= 0 \\ x^2 = -1 \quad \text{or} \quad x^2 &= 4 \end{aligned}$$

Since $x^2 = -1$ has no real solution, the solution set is $\{\pm 2\}$.

67. Raise to the power $3/2$ and get $x - 1 = \pm(4^{1/2})^3$. So, $x = 1 \pm 8$.
The solution set is $\{-7, 9\}$.

69. No solution since $(x+3)^{-3/4}$ is nonnegative.

71. Since $3x - 7 = 4 - x$, we obtain $4x = 11$.
The solution set is $\{11/4\}$.

73. Symmetric about $x = 3/4$ since $\dfrac{-b}{2a} = \dfrac{3}{4}$.

75. Symmetric about y-axis since $f(-x) = f(x)$.

77. Symmetric about the origin for $f(-x) = -f(x)$.

79. $(-\infty, -2.5) \cup (-2.5, \infty)$

81. $(-\infty, \infty)$

83. Since $f(x) = (x-2)(x+1)$, the x-intercepts are $(2, 0), (-1, 0)$, y-intercept is $(0, -2)$.

Since $\dfrac{-b}{2a} = \dfrac{1}{2}$, the vertex is $(1/2, -9/4)$.

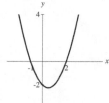

85. Use synthetic division on $f(x) = x^3 - 3x - 2$.

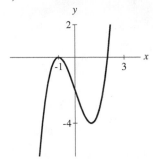

$$\begin{array}{c|cccc} -1 & 1 & 0 & -3 & -2 \\ & & -1 & 1 & 2 \\ \hline & 1 & -1 & -2 & 0 \end{array}$$

Since $x^2 - x - 2 = (x - 2)(x + 1)$,
$f(x) = (x + 1)^2(x - 2)$. Graph crosses $(2, 0)$
but does not cross $(-1, 0)$. y-intercept is $(0, -2)$.

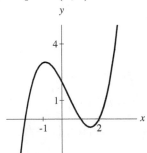

87. Use synthetic division on

$$f(x) = \frac{1}{2}x^3 - \frac{1}{2}x^2 - 2x + 2.$$

$$\begin{array}{c|cccc} 1 & 1/2 & -1/2 & -2 & 2 \\ & & 1/2 & 0 & -2 \\ \hline & 1/2 & 0 & -2 & 0 \end{array}$$

Since the roots of $\frac{1}{2}x^2 - 2 = 0$ are ± 2,
the graph crosses x-intercepts $(\pm 2, 0), (1, 0)$,
y-intercept is $(0, 2)$.

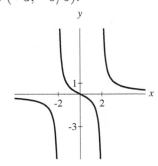

89. Factoring, we get

$$f(x) = \frac{1}{4}(x^4 - 8x^2 + 16) = \frac{1}{4}(x^2 - 4)^2.$$

The graph does not cross through
x-intercepts $(\pm 2, 0)$, y-intercept is $(0, 4)$.

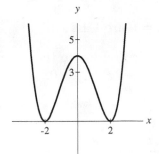

91. $f(x) = \dfrac{2}{x + 3}$ has no x-intercept, y-intercept
is $(0, 2/3)$, asymptotes are $x = -3, y = 0$

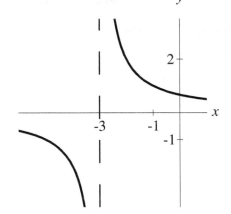

93. $f(x) = \dfrac{2x}{x^2 - 4}$ has x-intercept $(0, 0)$,
asymptotes are $x = \pm 2, y = 0$.
Symmetric about the origin.
Graph goes through $(1, -2/3), (3, 6/5)$,
and $(-3, -6/5)$.

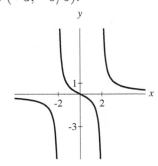

95. $f(x) = \dfrac{(x-1)^2}{x-2}$ has x-intercept $(1,0)$,

y-intercept is $(0,-1/2)$, asymptote $x = 2$, and oblique asymptote $y = x$ since

$$
\begin{array}{r|rrr}
2 & 1 & -2 & 1 \\
  &   & 2 & 0 \\
\hline
  & 1 & 0 & 1
\end{array}
$$

and $f(x) = x + \dfrac{1}{x-2}$.

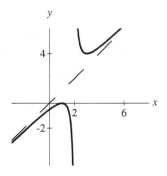

97. $f(x) = \dfrac{2x-1}{2-x}$ has x-intercept $(1/2, 0)$,

y-intercept is $(0, -1/2)$,
asymptotes are $x = 2$ and $y = -2$,
graph goes through $(1, 1), (3, -5)$.

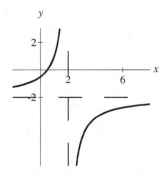

99. Since $f(x) = \dfrac{x^2 - 4}{x - 2} = x + 2$ if $x \neq 2$,

x-intercept is $(-2, 0)$, y-intercept is $(0, 2)$,

no asymptotes

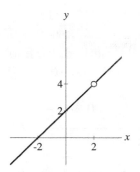

101. Let $f(x) = 8x^2 - 6x + 1 = (4x - 1)(2x - 1) < 0$.

Using the test-point method, we find
$f(0) > 0, f(3/4) < 0,$ and $f(1) > 0.$

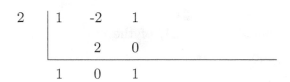

$$
\begin{array}{ccccc}
+ & 0 & - & 0 & + \\
\end{array}
$$

The solution is $(1/4, 1/2)$.

103. Let $f(x) = (3 - x)(x + 5) \geq 0$.

Using the test-point method, we find
$f(-6) < 0, f(0) > 0,$ and $f(4) < 0.$

$$
\begin{array}{ccccc}
- & 0 & + & 0 & - \\
-6 & -5 & 0 & 3 & 4
\end{array}
$$

The solution is $[-5, 3]$.

105. Using the Rational Zero Theorem and synthetic division, we obtain

$$
\begin{array}{r|rrrr}
1/2 & 4 & -400 & -1 & 100 \\
    &   & 2 & -199 & -100 \\
\hline
    & 4 & -398 & -200 & 0
\end{array}
$$

Note, $4x^2 - 398x - 200 = (4x + 2)(x - 100)$.
Let $f(x) = 4x^3 - 400x^2 - x + 100 =$
$(x - \frac{1}{2})(4x + 2)(x - 100) \geq 0$.

Apply the test-point method as follows:

$$
\begin{array}{ccccccc}
- & 0 & + & 0 & - & 0 & + \\
-1 & -\frac{1}{2} & 0 & \frac{1}{2} & 1 & 100 & 101
\end{array}
$$

The solution set is $\left[-\dfrac{1}{2}, \dfrac{1}{2}\right] \cup [100, \infty)$.

107. Let $R(x) = \dfrac{x+10}{x+2} - 5 = \dfrac{-4x}{x+2} < 0.$

Using the test-point method, we find $R(-3) < 0, R(-1) > 0,$ and $R(1) < 0.$

$$
\begin{array}{ccccc}
- & U & + & 0 & - \\
\end{array}
$$

$$
\begin{array}{ccccc}
-3 & -2 & -1 & 0 & 1
\end{array}
$$

The solution is $(-\infty, -2) \cup (0, \infty).$

109. $R(x) = \dfrac{12 - 7x}{x^2} + 1 = \dfrac{(x-3)(x-4)}{x^2} > 0.$

Using the test-point method, we get $R(-1) > 0, R(1) > 0, R(3.5) < 0,$ and $R(5) > 0.$

$$
\begin{array}{cccccc}
+ & U & + & 0 & - & 0 & + \\
\end{array}
$$

$$
\begin{array}{cccccc}
-1 & 0 & 1 & 3 & 3.5 & 4 & 5
\end{array}
$$

the solution is $(-\infty, 0) \cup (0, 3) \cup (4, \infty).$

111. Let $R(x) = \dfrac{(x-1)(x-2)}{(x-3)(x-4)}.$ We will use

the test-point method. Note, $R(0) > 0,$ $R(1.5) < 0, R(2.5) > 0, R(3.5) < 0,$ and $R(5) > 0.$

$$
\begin{array}{ccccccc}
+ & 0 & - & 0 & + & U & - & U & + \\
\end{array}
$$

$$
\begin{array}{ccccccc}
0 & 1 & 1.5 & 2 & 2.5 & 3 & 3.5 & 4 & 5
\end{array}
$$

The solution is $(-\infty, 1] \cup [2, 3) \cup (4, \infty).$

113. Quotient $x^2 - 3x$, remainder -15

$$
\begin{array}{r|rrrr}
3 & 1 & -6 & 9 & -15 \\
 & & 3 & -9 & 0 \\
\hline
 & 1 & -3 & 0 & -15
\end{array}
$$

115. Since $\dfrac{-b}{2a} = \dfrac{-156}{-32} = 4.875$, the maximum

height is $-16(4.875)^2 + 156(4.875) = 380.25$ ft.

117. Let w be the height and let l be the length of the given cross-section of the room. Since the

ratios of corresponding sides of similar triangles are equal, we obtain

$$
\frac{7}{12} = \frac{w}{(48-l)/2}
$$
$$
w = \frac{7}{24}(48-l)
$$

and the area, A, of the cross-section of the room is $A = wl = \dfrac{7}{24}(48-l)l.$ Since $l = 24$ maximizes A, we get $w = \dfrac{7}{24}(48-24) = 7$ ft. The dimensions that will maximize the area are 24 ft by 7 ft.

119.

(a) $V(10) = \dfrac{10,000}{58} \approx 172.4$ feet per second

(b) $V = 200$

(c) 200 feet per second

Chapter Test

1. Use the method of completing the square.

$$
y = 3(x^2 - 4x + 4) + 1 - 12 = 3(x-2)^2 - 11
$$

2. $y = 3(x-2)^2 - 11$ has vertex $(2, -11),$ axis of symmetry $x = 2,$ y-intercept $(0, 1),$ the x-intercepts are

$$
\left(\frac{6 \pm \sqrt{33}}{3}, 0 \right),
$$

and the range is $[-11, \infty)$

3. Minimum value is -11 since vertex is $(2, -11)$

4. Quotient $2x^2 - 6x + 14$, remainder -37

$$
\begin{array}{r|rrrr}
-3 & 2 & 0 & -4 & 5 \\
 & & -6 & 18 & -42 \\
\hline
 & 2 & -6 & 14 & -37
\end{array}
$$

5. By the Remainder Theorem, remainder is $-14.$

6. $\pm \left\{ 1, \dfrac{1}{3}, 2, \dfrac{2}{3}, 3, 6 \right\}$

7.

$$
\begin{aligned}
(x+3)(x-4i)(x+4i) &= (x+3)(x^2+16) \\
&= x^3 + 3x^2 + 16x + 48
\end{aligned}
$$

An equation is $x^3 + 3x^2 + 16x + 48 = 0$.

8. $P(x) = x^3 - 3x^2 + 5x + 7$ has 2 sign variations and $P(-x) = -x^3 - 3x^2 - 5x + 7$ has 1 sign variation. There are
(a) 2 positive roots and 1 negative root, or
(b) 1 negative root and 2 imaginary roots.

9. Since $\dfrac{-b}{2a} = \dfrac{-128}{-32} = 4$,

the maximum height is $S(4) = 256$ feet.

10. ± 3

11. $\pm 2, \pm 2i$

12.

$$
\begin{array}{r|rrrr}
2 & 1 & -4 & -1 & 10 \\
  &   & 2 & -4 & -10 \\
\hline
  & 1 & -2 & -5 & 0
\end{array}
$$

Since $x^2 - 2x - 5 = (x-1)^2 - 6$, the zeros are $2, 1 \pm \sqrt{6}$.

13. Zeros are $x = \pm i$, each with multiplicity 2 since $f(x) = (x^2+1)^2 = (x-i)^2(x+i)^2$

14. The zeros are 2, 0 with multiplicity 2, and $-3/2$ with mulitiplicity 3 since the equation can be written as $x^2(x-2)(2x+3)^3 = 0$.

15.

$$
\begin{array}{r|rrrr}
1/2 & 2 & -9 & 14 & -5 \\
    &   & 1 & -4 & 5 \\
\hline
    & 2 & -8 & 10 & 0
\end{array}
$$

By completing the square, we find that the roots of $2(x^2 - 4x) + 10 = 2(x-2)^2 + 2 = 0$ are $2 \pm i$. The zeros are $x = 2 \pm i, 1/2$.

16. Parabola $y = 2(x-3)^2 + 1$ with vertex $(3,1)$

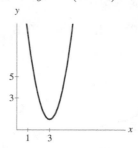

17. $y = (x-2)^2(x+1)$ crosses $(-1,0)$ but does not cross $(2,0)$, y-intercept is $(0,4)$

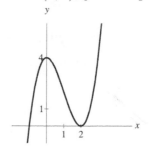

18. $y = x(x-2)(x+2)$ crosses $(0,0), (\pm 2, 0)$, and goes through $(1,-3)$

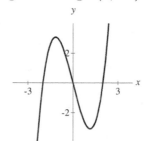

19. $y = \dfrac{1}{x-2}$ has asymptotes $x = 2$, $y = 0$, and goes through $(1,-1), (3,1), (4,1/2)$

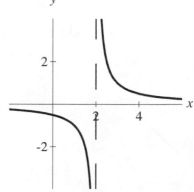

20. $y = \dfrac{2x - 3}{x - 2}$ has asymptotes $x = 2, y = 2$,

x-intercept $(3/2, 0)$, y-intercept $(0, 3/2)$

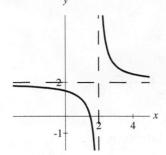

21. $f(x) = x + \dfrac{1}{x}$ has oblique asymptote $y = x$,

asymptote $x = 0$, goes through $(1, 2), (-1, -2)$

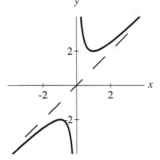

22. $y = \dfrac{4}{x^2 - 4}$ has asymptotes $x = \pm 2, y = 0$,

y-intercept $(0, -1)$

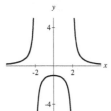

23. Note, $\dfrac{x^2 - 2x + 1}{x - 1} = x - 1$ provided $x \neq 1$;

no x-intercept, y-intercept $(0, -1)$

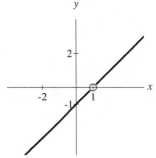

24. Let $f(x) = (x - 4)(x + 2) < 0$.

Using the test-point method, we get $f(-3) > 0, f(0) < 0, f(5) > 0$.

$$
\begin{array}{ccccc}
+ & 0 & - & 0 & + \\
\end{array}
$$

$$
\begin{array}{ccccc}
-3 & -2 & 0 & 4 & 5 \\
\end{array}
$$

The solution set is the interval $(-2, 4)$.

25. Let $f(x) = \dfrac{2x - 1}{x - 3} > 0$.

Using the test-point method we find

$$
\begin{array}{cccc}
+ & 0 & - & U & + \\
\end{array}
$$

$$
\begin{array}{ccccc}
0 & \frac{1}{2} & 1 & 3 & 4 \\
\end{array}
$$

The solution set is $(-\infty, 1/2) \cup (3, \infty)$.

26. Let $f(x) = \dfrac{x + 3}{(4 - x)(x + 1)} \geq 0$.

Using the test-point method we find

$$
\begin{array}{cccccc}
+ & 0 & - & U & + & U & - \\
\end{array}
$$

$$
\begin{array}{ccccccc}
-4 & -3 & -2 & -1 & 2 & 4 & 5 \\
\end{array}
$$

The solution set is $(-\infty, -3] \cup (-1, 4)$.

27. Let $f(x) = x(x^2 - 7) > 0$.

Applying the test-point method, we obtain

$$
\begin{array}{c}
\text{- - - - - - - - - - - - - - } 0 + + + \\
\text{- - - - - - - - - - - } 0 + + + + + + \\
\text{- - - - - } 0 + + + + + + + + + + + \\
\end{array}
$$

$$
\begin{array}{ccc}
-\sqrt{7} & 0 & \sqrt{7} \\
\end{array}
$$

$$
\begin{array}{cccccc}
- & 0 & + & 0 & - & 0 & + \\
\end{array}
$$

$$
\begin{array}{ccccccc}
-4 & -\sqrt{7} & -2 & 0 & 2 & \sqrt{7} & 5 \\
\end{array}
$$

The solution set is $(-\sqrt{7}, 0) \cup (\sqrt{7}, \infty)$.

28. If we raise each side of $(x - 3)^{-2/3} = \dfrac{1}{3}$ to

the power -3, then we obtain $(x - 3)^2 = 27$.

Thus, $x = 3 \pm \sqrt{27}$ and the solution set is $\left\{ 3 \pm 3\sqrt{3} \right\}$.

29. Isolate a radical and square each side.

$$\sqrt{x} - 1 = \sqrt{x - 7}$$
$$x - 2\sqrt{x} + 1 = x - 7$$
$$-2\sqrt{x} = -8$$
$$4x = 64$$

The solution set is $\{16\}$.

Exponential and Logarithmic Functions

In the summer of 2008, scientists discovered a new batch of well-preserved dinosaur bones, petrified trees, and even freshwater clams in southeastern Utah. An excavation revealed at least four sauropods, which are long-necked, long-tailed plant-eating dinosaurs. Although the excavation did not unearth any new species, scientists say that it could provide new clues about life in the region some 150 million years ago.

Paleontologists use data gathered from fossils to determine when and how dinosaurs lived. Sauropods were the largest land animals ever to have lived. Sauropods could be as long as 130 feet and weigh as much as 100 tons. Their remains have been found on every continent except Antarctica.

▶ WHAT YOU WILL learn... In this chapter we learn how scientists use exponential functions to date archaeological finds that are millions of years old. Through applications ranging from population growth to growth of financial investments, we'll see how exponential functions can help us predict the future and discover the past.

Ng Yin Chern/Shutterstock

From Chapter 4 of *Precalculus: Functions and Graphs*. Fourth Edition. Mark Dugopolski. Copyright © 2013 by Pearson Education, Inc.

1 Exponential Functions and Their Applications

The functions that involve some combination of basic arithmetic operations, powers, or roots are called **algebraic functions.** Most of the functions studied so far are algebraic functions. In this chapter we turn to the exponential and logarithmic functions. These functions are used to describe phenomena ranging from growth of investments to the decay of radioactive materials, which cannot be described with algebraic functions. Since the exponential and logarithmic functions transcend what can be described with algebraic functions, they are called **transcendental functions.**

The Definition

In algebraic functions such as

$$j(x) = x^2, \qquad p(x) = x^5, \qquad \text{and} \qquad m(x) = x^{1/3}$$

the base is a variable and the exponent is constant. For the exponential functions the base is constant and the exponent is a variable. The functions

$$f(x) = 2^x, \qquad g(x) = 5^x, \qquad \text{and} \qquad h(x) = \left(\frac{1}{3}\right)^x$$

are exponential functions.

Definition:
Exponential Function

> An **exponential function** with **base β** is a function of the form
>
> $$f(x) = a^x$$
>
> where a and x are real numbers such that $a > 0$ and $a \neq 1$.

We rule out the base $a = 1$ in the definition because $f(x) = 1^x$ is the constant function $f(x) = 1$. Negative numbers and 0 are not used as bases because powers such as $(-4)^{1/2}$ and 0^{-2} are not real numbers or not defined. Other functions with variable exponents, such as $f(x) = 3^{2x+1}$ or $f(x) = 10 \cdot 7^{-x^2}$, may also be called exponential functions.

To evaluate an exponential function we use our knowledge of exponents.

EXAMPLE 1 Evaluating exponential functions

Let $f(x) = 4^x$, $g(x) = 5^{2-x}$, and $h(x) = \left(\frac{1}{3}\right)^x$. Find the following values. Check your answers with a calculator.

a. $f(3/2)$ **b.** $g(3)$ **c.** $h(-2)$

Solution

a. $f(3/2) = 4^{3/2} = (\sqrt{4})^3 = 2^3 = 8$ Take the square root, then cube.

b. $g(3) = 5^{2-3} = 5^{-1} = \frac{1}{5}$ Exponent -1 means reciprocal.

c. $h(-2) = \left(\frac{1}{3}\right)^{-2} = 3^2 = 9$ Find the reciprocal, then square.

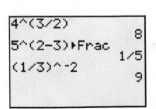

Figure 1

Evaluating these functions with a calculator, as in Fig. 1, yields the same results.

▶**TRY THIS.** Find $f(-2)$ and $f(1/2)$ if $f(x) = 9^x$. ∎

Domain of Exponential Functions

The domain of the exponential function $f(x) = 2^x$ is the set of all real numbers. To understand how this function can be evaluated for any *real* number, first note that the function is evaluated for any *rational* number using powers and roots. For example,

$$f(1.7) = f(17/10) = 2^{17/10} = \sqrt[10]{2^{17}} \approx 3.249009585.$$

Until now, we have not considered *irrational* exponents.

Consider the expression $2^{\sqrt{3}}$ and recall that the irrational number $\sqrt{3}$ is an infinite nonterminating nonrepeating decimal number:

$$\sqrt{3} = 1.7320508075 \ldots$$

If we use rational approximations to $\sqrt{3}$ as exponents, we see a pattern:

$$2^{1.7} = 3.249009585 \ldots$$

$$2^{1.73} = 3.317278183 \ldots$$

$$2^{1.732} = 3.321880096 \ldots$$

$$2^{1.73205} = 3.321995226 \ldots$$

$$2^{1.7320508} = 3.321997068 \ldots$$

As the exponents get closer and closer to $\sqrt{3}$ we get results that are approaching some number. We define $2^{\sqrt{3}}$ to be that number. Of course, it is impossible to write the exact value of $\sqrt{3}$ or $2^{\sqrt{3}}$ as a decimal, but you can use a calculator to get $2^{\sqrt{3}} \approx 3.321997085$. Since any irrational number can be approximated by rational numbers in this same manner, 2^x is defined similarly for any irrational number. This idea extends to any exponential function.

Domain of an Exponential Function

> The domain of $f(x) = a^x$ for $a > 0$ and $a \neq 1$ is the set of all real numbers.

Graphing Exponential Functions

Even though the domain of an exponential function is the set of real numbers, for ease of computation, we generally choose only rational numbers for x to find ordered pairs on the graph of the function.

EXAMPLE 2 Graphing an exponential function ($a > 1$)

Sketch the graph of each exponential function and state the domain and range.

a. $f(x) = 2^x$ **b.** $g(x) = 10^x$

Solution

a. Find some ordered pairs satisfying $f(x) = 2^x$ as follows:

x	-2	-1	0	1	2	3
$y = 2^x$	1/4	1/2	1	2	4	8

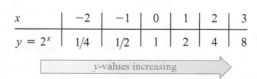

y-values increasing

As $x \to \infty$, so does 2^x. Using limit notation, $\lim\limits_{x \to \infty} 2^x = \infty$. As $x \to -\infty$, 2^x approaches but never reaches 0. Using limit notation, $\lim\limits_{x \to -\infty} 2^x = 0$. So the x-axis is a horizontal asymptote for the curve. It can be shown that the graph of $f(x) = 2^x$ increases in a continuous manner, with no "jumps" or "breaks". So the graph is a smooth curve through the points shown in Fig. 2. The domain of $f(x) = 2^x$ is $(-\infty, \infty)$ and the range is $(0, \infty)$. The function is increasing on $(-\infty, \infty)$.

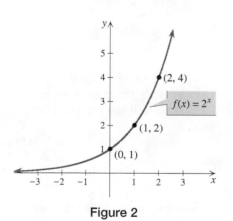

Figure 2

429

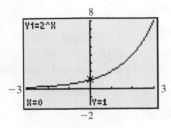

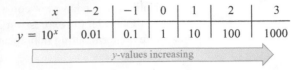

Figure 3

The calculator graph shown in Fig. 3 supports these conclusions. Because of the limited resolution of the calculator screen, the calculator graph appears to touch its horizontal asymptote in this window. You can have a mental picture of a curve that gets closer and closer but never touches its asymptote, but it is impossible to accurately draw such a picture. □

b. Find some ordered pairs satisfying $g(x) = 10^x$ as follows:

x	-2	-1	0	1	2	3
$y = 10^x$	0.01	0.1	1	10	100	1000

y-values increasing

These points indicate that the graph of $g(x) = 10^x$ behaves in the same manner as the graph of $f(x) = 2^x$. We have $\lim_{x \to \infty} 10^x = \infty$ and $\lim_{x \to -\infty} 10^x = 0$. So the *x*-axis is a horizontal asymptote. The domain of $g(x) = 10^x$ is $(-\infty, \infty)$ and the range is $(0, \infty)$. The function is increasing on $(-\infty, \infty)$. Plotting the points in the table yields the curve shown in Fig. 4. In theory the curve never touches the *x*-axis. So we usually try to keep our hand-drawn curve from touching the *x*-axis.

The calculator graph in Fig. 5 supports these conclusions.

▶**TRY THIS.** Graph $f(x) = 9^x$ and state the domain and range. ■

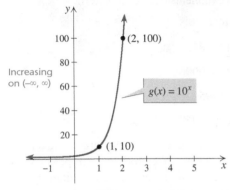

Figure 4

Note the similarities between the graphs shown in Figs. 2 and 4. Both pass through the point $(0, 1)$, both functions are increasing, and both have the *x*-axis as a horizontal asymptote. Since a horizontal line can cross these graphs only once, the functions $f(x) = 2^x$ and $g(x) = 10^x$ are one-to-one by the horizontal line test. All functions of the form $f(x) = a^x$ for $a > 1$ have graphs similar to those in Figs. 2 and 4.

The phrase "growing exponentially" is often used to describe a population or other quantity whose growth can be modeled with an increasing exponential function. For example, the earth's population is said to be growing exponentially because of the shape of the graph shown in Fig. 6

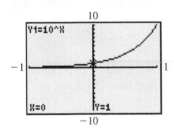

Figure 5

Figure6

If $a > 1$, then the graph of $f(x) = a^x$ is increasing. In the next example we graph exponential functions in which $0 < a < 1$ and we will see that these functions are decreasing.

EXAMPLE 3 Graphing an exponential function $(0 < a < 1)$

Sketch the graph of each function and state the domain and range of the function.

a. $f(x) = (1/2)^x$ **b.** $g(x) = 3^{-x}$

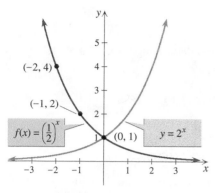

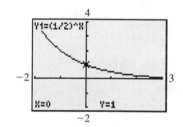

Figure 7

Figure 8

Solution

a. Find some ordered pairs satisfying $f(x) = (1/2)^x$ as follows:

x	-2	-1	0	1	2	3
$y = \left(\dfrac{1}{2}\right)^x$	4	2	1	$1/2$	$1/4$	$1/8$

y-values decreasing →

Plot these points and draw a smooth curve through them as in Fig. 7 Note that $\lim\limits_{x\to\infty}\left(\frac{1}{2}\right)^x = 0$ and $\lim\limits_{x\to-\infty}\left(\frac{1}{2}\right)^x = \infty$. The x-axis is a horizontal asymptote. The domain is $(-\infty, \infty)$ and the range is $(0, \infty)$. The function is decreasing on $(-\infty, \infty)$. Because $(1/2)^x = 2^{-x}$ the graph of $f(x) = (1/2)^x$ is a reflection in the y-axis of the graph of $y = 2^x$.

The calculator graph in Fig. 8 supports these conclusions. □

b. Since $3^{-x} = 1/3^x = (1/3)^x$, this function is of the form $y = a^x$ for $0 < a < 1$. Find some ordered pairs satisfying $g(x) = 3^{-x}$ or $g(x) = (1/3)^x$ as follows:

x	-2	-1	0	1	2	3
$y = 3^{-x}$	9	3	1	$1/3$	$1/9$	$1/27$

y-values decreasing →

Plot these points and draw a smooth curve through them as shown in Fig. 9. Note that $\lim\limits_{x\to\infty} 3^{-x} = 0$ and $\lim\limits_{x\to-\infty} 3^{-x} = \infty$. The domain is $(-\infty, \infty)$ and the range is $(0, \infty)$. The function is decreasing on its entire domain, $(-\infty, \infty)$. The x-axis is again a horizontal asymptote.

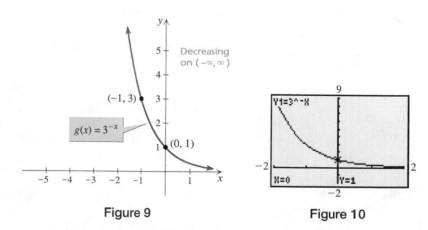

Figure 9   **Figure 10**

The calculator graph in Fig. 10 supports these conclusions.

▶**TRY THIS.** Graph $f(x) = 9^{-x}$ and state the domain and range. ■

Again note the similarities between the graphs in Figs. 7 and 9. Both pass through $(0, 1)$, both functions are decreasing, and both have the x-axis as a horizontal asymptote. By the horizontal line test, these functions are also one-to-one. The base determines whether the exponential function is increasing or decreasing. In general, we have the following properties of exponential functions.

The exponential function $f(x) = a^x$ has the following properties:

1. The function f is increasing for $a > 1$ and decreasing for $0 < a < 1$.
2. The y-intercept of the graph of f is $(0, 1)$.
3. The graph has the x-axis as a horizontal asymptote.
4. The domain of f is $(-\infty, \infty)$, and the range of f is $(0, \infty)$.
5. The function f is one-to-one.

The Exponential Family of Functions

A function of the form $f(x) = a^x$ is an exponential function. Any function of the form $g(x) = b \cdot a^{x-h} + k$ is a member of the **exponential family** of functions. The graph of g is a transformation of the graph of f:

The graph of f moves to the left if $h < 0$ or to the right if $h > 0$.

The graph of f moves upward if $k > 0$ or downward if $k < 0$.

The graph of f is stretched if $b > 1$ and shrunk if $0 < b < 1$.

The graph of f is reflected in the x-axis if b is negative.

EXAMPLE 4 Graphing members of the exponential family

Sketch the graph of each function and state its domain and range.

a. $y = 2^{x-3}$ **b.** $f(x) = -4 + 3^{x+2}$

Solution

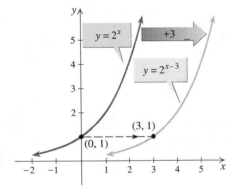

Figure 11

a. The graph of $y = 2^{x-3}$ is a translation three units to the right of the graph of $y = 2^x$. For accuracy, find a few ordered pairs that satisfy $y = 2^{x-3}$:

x	3	4	5
$y = 2^{x-3}$	1	2	4

Draw the graph of $y = 2^{x-3}$ through these points as shown in Fig. 11 The domain of $y = 2^{x-3}$ is $(-\infty, \infty)$, and the range is $(0, \infty)$.

The calculator graph in Fig. 12 supports these conclusions. □

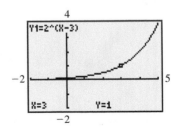

Figure 12

b. The graph of $f(x) = -4 + 3^{x+2}$ is obtained by translating $y = 3^x$ to the left two units and downward four units. For accuracy, find a few points on the graph of $f(x) = -4 + 3^{x+2}$:

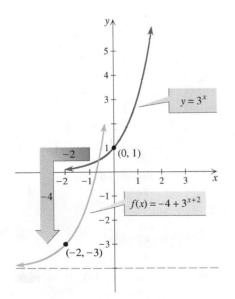

Figure 13

x	-3	-2	-1	0
$y = -4 + 3^{x+2}$	$-11/3$	-3	-1	5

Sketch a smooth curve through these points as shown in Fig. 13 The horizontal asymptote is the line $y = -4$. The domain of f is $(-\infty, \infty)$, and the range is $(-4, \infty)$.

Figure 14

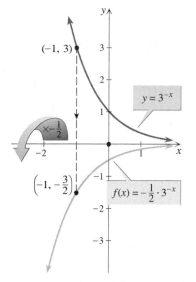

Figure 15

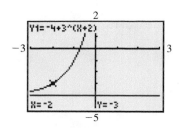The calculator graph of $y = -4 + 3^{x+2}$ and the asymptote $y = -4$ in Fig. 14 support these conclusions.

▶**TRY THIS.** Graph $f(x) = 2^{x-2} + 1$ and state the domain and range. ∎

If you recognize that a function is a transformation of a simpler function, then you know what its graph looks like. This information along with a few ordered pairs will help you to make accurate graphs.

EXAMPLE 5 | Graphing an exponential function with a reflection

Sketch the graph of $f(x) = -\frac{1}{2} \cdot 3^{-x}$ and state the domain and range.

Solution

The graph of $y = 3^{-x}$ is shown in Fig. 9. Multiplying by $-1/2$ shrinks the graph and reflects it below the x-axis. The x-axis is the horizontal asymptote for the graph of f. Find a few ordered pairs as follows:

x	-2	-1	0	1	2
$y = -\frac{1}{2} \cdot 3^{-x}$	$-9/2$	$-3/2$	$-1/2$	$-1/6$	$-1/18$

y-values increasing →

Sketch the curve through these points as in Fig. 15. The domain is $(-\infty, \infty)$ and the range is $(-\infty, 0)$.

▶**TRY THIS.** Graph $f(x) = -4^{-x}$ and state the domain and range. ∎

The form $f(x) = b \cdot a^x$ is often used in applications. In this case b is the initial value of the function, because $f(0) = b \cdot a^0 = b$. For example, if you discover 3 ants in your cookie jar (time 0) and the number of ants doubles after each minute, then the number of ants x minutes after your initial discovery is $3 \cdot 2^x$. If it makes sense to start at $x = 1$, then use $x - 1$ for the exponent. For example, if you get \$2 in tips on your first day at work and your tips increase by 50% on each succeeding day, then the amount on day x is $2 \cdot 1.5^{x-1}$ dollars.

Exponential Equations

From the graphs of exponential functions, we observed that they are one-to-one. For an exponential function, one-to-one means that if two exponential expressions with the same base are equal, then the exponents are equal. For example, if $2^m = 2^n$, then $m = n$.

One-to-One Property of Exponential Functions

> For $a > 0$ and $a \neq 1$,
>
> $$\text{if} \quad a^{x_1} = a^{x_2}, \quad \text{then} \quad x_1 = x_2.$$

The one-to-one property is used in solving simple exponential equations. For example, to solve $2^x = 8$, we recall that $8 = 2^3$. So the equation becomes $2^x = 2^3$. By the one-to-one property, $x = 3$ is the only solution. The one-to-one property applies only to equations in which each side is a power of the same base.

Exponential and Logarithmic Functions

EXAMPLE 6 Solving exponential equations

Solve each exponential equation.

a. $4^x = \dfrac{1}{4}$ **b.** $\left(\dfrac{1}{10}\right)^x = 100$

Solution

a. Since $1/4 = 4^{-1}$, we can write the right-hand side as a power of 4 and use the one-to-one property:

$$4^x = \frac{1}{4} = 4^{-1} \quad \text{Both sides are powers of 4.}$$

$$x = -1 \quad \text{One-to-one property}$$

b. Since $(1/10)^x = 10^{-x}$ and $100 = 10^2$, we can write each side as a power of 10:

$$\left(\frac{1}{10}\right)^x = 100 \quad \text{Original equation}$$

$$10^{-x} = 10^2 \quad \text{Both sides are powers of 10.}$$

$$-x = 2 \quad \text{One-to-one property}$$

$$x = -2$$

▶**TRY THIS.** Solve $2^{-x} = \frac{1}{8}$. ∎

The type of equation that we solved in Example 6 arises naturally when we try to find the first coordinate of an ordered pair of an exponential function when given the second coordinate, as shown in the next example.

EXAMPLE 7 Finding the first coordinate given the second

Let $f(x) = 5^{2-x}$. Find x such that $f(x) = 125$.

Solution

To find x such that $f(x) = 125$, we must solve $5^{2-x} = 125$:

$$5^{2-x} = 5^3 \quad \text{Since } 125 = 5^3$$

$$2 - x = 3 \quad \text{One-to-one property}$$

$$x = -1$$

▶**TRY THIS.** Let $f(x) = 3^{4-x}$. Find x such that $f(x) = \frac{1}{9}$. ∎

The Compound Interest Model

Exponential functions are used to model phenomena such as population growth, radioactive decay, and compound interest. Here we will show how these functions are used to determine the amount of an investment earning compound interest.

If P dollars are deposited in an account with a simple annual interest rate r for t years, then the amount A in the account at the end of t years is found by using the formula $A = P + Prt$ or $A = P(1 + rt)$. If $1000 is deposited at 6% annual rate for one quarter of a year, then at the end of three months the amount is

$$A = 1000\left(1 + 0.06 \cdot \frac{1}{4}\right) = 1000(1.015) = \$1015.$$

434

If the account begins the next quarter with \$1015, then at the end of the second quarter we again multiply by 1.015 to get the amount

$$A = 1000(1.015)^2 \approx \$1030.23.$$

This process is referred to as compound interest because interest is put back into the account and the interest also earns interest. At the end of 20 years, or 80 quarters, the amount is

$$A = 1000(1.015)^{80} \approx \$3290.66.$$

Compound interest can be thought of as simple interest computed over and over. The general **compound interest formula** follows.

Compound Interest Formula

> If a principal P is invested for t years at an annual rate r compounded n times per year, then the amount A, or ending balance, is given by
>
> $$A = P\left(1 + \frac{r}{n}\right)^{nt}.$$

Figure 16

The principal P is also called **present value** and the amount A is called **future value.**

EXAMPLE 8 Using the compound interest formula

Find the amount or future value when a principal of \$20,000 is invested at 6% compounded daily for three years.

Solution

Use $P = \$20{,}000$, $r = 0.06$, $n = 365$, and $t = 3$ in the compound interest formula:

$$A = \$20{,}000\left(1 + \frac{0.06}{365}\right)^{365 \cdot 3} \approx \$23{,}943.99$$

Fig. 16 shows this expression on a graphing calculator.

▶**TRY THIS.** Find the amount when \$9000 is invested at 5.4% compounded monthly for 6 years. ∎

When interest is compounded daily, financial institutions usually use the exact number of days. To keep our discussion of interest simple, we assume that all years have 365 days and ignore leap years. When discussing months we assume that all months have 30 days. There may be other rules involved in computing interest that are specific to the institution doing the computing. One popular method is to compound quarterly and only give interest on money that is on deposit for full quarters. With this rule you could have money on deposit for nearly six months (say January 5 to June 28) and receive no interest.

Continuous Compounding and the Number *e*

The more often that interest is figured during the year, the more interest an investment will earn. The first five lines of Table 1 show the future value of \$10,000 invested at 12% for one year for more and more frequent compounding. The last line shows the limiting amount \$11,274.97, which we cannot exceed no matter how often we compound the interest on this investment for one year.

HISTORICAL NOTE

Leonhard Euler (1707–1783) was a Swiss mathematician and physicist. Euler introduced and popularized several notational conventions through his numerous textbooks. He introduced the concept of a function and was the first to write $f(x)$. He also introduced the modern notation for the trigonometric functions: the letter e (Euler's number) for the base of the natural logarithm, the Greek letter sigma for summations, and the letter i to denote the imaginary unit.

Table 1

Compounding	Future Value in One Year
Annually	$\$10,000\left(1 + \dfrac{0.12}{1}\right)^1 = \$11,200$
Quarterly	$\$10,000\left(1 + \dfrac{0.12}{4}\right)^4 \approx \$11,255.09$
Monthly	$\$10,000\left(1 + \dfrac{0.12}{12}\right)^{12} \approx \$11,268.25$
Daily	$\$10,000\left(1 + \dfrac{0.12}{365}\right)^{365} \approx \$11,274.75$
Hourly	$\$10,000\left(1 + \dfrac{0.12}{8760}\right)^{8760} \approx \$11,274.96$
Continuously	$\$10,000e^{0.12(1)} \approx \$11,274.97$

■ **Foreshadowing Calculus**

There are several ways to define the number e and the function $f(x) = e^x$ in calculus. Calculus can deepen your understanding of many of the concepts that you study in algebra.

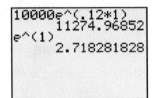

Figure 17

To better understand Table 1, we need to use a fact from calculus. The expression $[1 + r/n]^{nt}$ used in calculating the first five values in the table can be shown to approach e^{rt} as n goes to ∞. Using limit notation,

$$\lim_{n\to\infty}\left[1 + \frac{r}{n}\right]^{nt} = e^{rt}.$$

The number e (like π) is an irrational number that occurs in many areas of mathematics. Using $r = 1$ and $t = 1$ in this limit gives us $\lim_{n\to\infty}[1 + 1/n]^n = e$, which can be used as the definition of the number e. You can find approximate values for powers of e using a calculator with an e^x-key. To find an approximation for e itself, find e^1 on a calculator:

$$e \approx 2.718281828459$$

Figure 17 shows the graphing calculator computation of the future value of $10,000 at 12% compounded continuously for one year and the value of e^1. □

So there is a limit to the results obtained by increasingly frequent compounding. The limit is the product of the principal and e^{rt}. Using $A = P \cdot e^{rt}$ to find the amount is called **continuous compounding.**

Continuous Compounding Formula

If a principal P is invested for t years at an annual rate r compounded continuously, then the amount A, or ending balance, is given by

$$A = P \cdot e^{rt}.$$

EXAMPLE 9 Interest compounded continuously

Find the amount when a principal of $5600 is invested at $6\frac{1}{4}$% annual rate compounded continuously for 5 years and 9 months.

Solution

Convert 5 years and 9 months to 5.75 years. Use $r = 0.0625, t = 5.75,$ and $P = \$5600$ in the continuous compounding formula:

$$A = 5600 \cdot e^{(0.0625)(5.75)} \approx \$8021.63$$

▶**TRY THIS.** Find the amount when $8000 is invested at 6.3% compounded continuously for 7 years and 3 months. ■

The function $f(x) = e^x$ is called the **base-e exponential function.** Variations of this function are used to model many types of growth and decay. The graph of

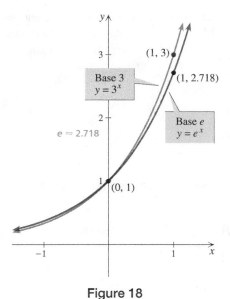

Figure 18

$y = e^x$ looks like the graph of $y = 3^x$, because the value of e is close to 3. Use your calculator to check that the graph of $y = e^x$ shown in Fig. 18 goes approximately through the points $(-1, 0.368)$, $(0, 1)$, $(1, 2.718)$, and $(2, 7.389)$.

The Radioactive Decay Model

The mathematical model of radioactive decay is based on the formula

$$A = A_0 e^{rt},$$

which gives the amount A of a radioactive substance remaining after t years, where A_0 is the initial amount present and r is the annual rate of decay. The only difference between this formula and the continuous compounding formula is that when decay is involved, the rate r is negative.

EXAMPLE 10 Radioactive decay of carbon-14

Finely chipped spear points shaped by nomadic hunters in the Ice Age were found at the scene of a large kill in Lubbock, Texas. From the amount of decay of carbon-14 in the bone fragments of the giant bison, scientists determined that the kill took place about 9833 years ago (*National Geographic*, December 1955). Carbon-14 is a radioactive substance that is absorbed by an organism while it is alive but begins to decay upon the death of the organism. The number of grams of carbon-14 remaining in a fragment of charred bone from the giant bison after t years is given by the formula $A = 3.6e^{rt}$, where $r = -1.21 \times 10^{-4}$. Find the amount present initially and after 9833 years.

Solution

To find the initial amount, let $t = 0$ and $r = -1.21 \times 10^{-4}$ in the formula $A = A_0 e^{rt}$:

$$A = 3.6e^{(-1.21 \times 10^{-4})(0)} = 3.6 \text{ grams}$$

To find the amount present after 9833 years, let $t = 9833$ and $r = -1.21 \times 10^{-4}$:

$$A = 3.6e^{(-1.21 \times 10^{-4})(9833)}$$

$$\approx 1.1 \text{ grams}$$

The initial amount of carbon-14 was 3.6 grams, and after 9833 years, approximately 1.1 grams of carbon-14 remained. See Fig. 19.

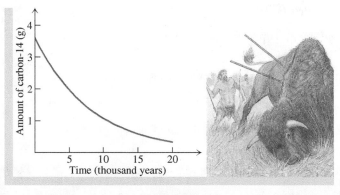

Figure 19

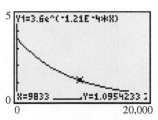

Figure 20

The calculator graph in Fig. 20 can be used to find the amount of radioactive substance present after 9833 years.

▶**TRY THIS.** If the amount (in grams) of carbon-14 present after t years is given by $A = 2.9e^{rt}$, where $r = -1.21 \times 10^{-4}$, then what is the initial amount and what amount is present after 6500 years? ∎

The formula for radioactive decay is used to determine the age of ancient objects such as bones, campfire charcoal, and meteorites. To date objects, we must solve the radioactive decay formula for t, which will be done in Section 4 after we have studied logarithms.

FOR thought... True or False? Explain.

1. The function $f(x) = (-2)^x$ is an exponential function.

2. The function $f(x) = 2^x$ is invertible.

3. If $2^x = \frac{1}{8}$, then $x = -3$.

4. If $f(x) = 3^x$, then $f(0.5) = \sqrt{3}$.

5. If $f(x) = e^x$, then $f(0) = 1$.

6. If $f(x) = e^x$ and $f(t) = e^2$, then $t = 2$.

7. The x-axis is a horizontal asymptote for the graph of $y = e^x$.

8. The function $f(x) = (0.5)^x$ is increasing.

9. The functions $f(x) = 4^{x-1}$ and $g(x) = (0.25)^{1-x}$ have the same graph.

10. $2^{1.73} = \sqrt[100]{2^{173}}$

EXERCISES 1

Fill in the blank.

1. Functions that involve some combination of basic arithmetic operations, powers, or roots are _____ functions.

2. Exponential and logarithmic functions are _____ functions.

3. A function of the form $f(x) = a^x$ where a and x are real numbers with $a > 0$ and $a \neq 1$ is a(n) _____ function.

4. The domain of $f(x) = a^x$ for $a > 0$ is the set of _____.

5. The function $f(x) = a^x$ is _____ if $a > 1$ and _____ if $0 < a < 1$.

6. The graph of $f(x) = a^x$ has the x-axis as a(n) _____.

7. The _____ of $f(x) = a^x$ is $(0, \infty)$.

8. The _____ of functions consists of all functions of the form $f(x) = b \cdot a^{x-h} + k$.

Evaluate each exponential expression without using a calculator.

9. 3^3

10. 2^5

11. -2^0

12. -4^0

13. 2^{-3}

14. 3^{-2}

15. $\left(\frac{1}{2}\right)^{-4}$

16. $\left(\frac{1}{3}\right)^{-2}$

17. $8^{2/3}$

18. $9^{3/2}$

19. $-9^{-3/2}$

20. $-4^{-3/2}$

Let $f(x) = 3^x, g(x) = 2^{1-x}$, and $h(x) = (1/4)^x$. Find the following values.

21. $f(2)$

22. $f(4)$

23. $f(-2)$

24. $f(-3)$

25. $g(2)$

26. $g(1)$

27. $g(-2)$

28. $g(-3)$

29. $h(-1)$

30. $h(-2)$

31. $h(-1/2)$

32. $h(3/2)$

Sketch the graph of each function by finding at least three ordered pairs on the graph. State the domain, the range, and whether the function is increasing or decreasing.

33. $f(x) = 5^x$

34. $f(x) = 4^x$

35. $y = 10^{-x}$

36. $y = e^{-x}$

37. $f(x) = (1/4)^x$

38. $f(x) = (0.2)^x$

Use a graph or a table to find each limit.

39. $\lim\limits_{x \to \infty} 3^x$

40. $\lim\limits_{x \to -\infty} 3^x$

41. $\lim\limits_{x \to \infty} 5^{-x}$

42. $\lim\limits_{x \to -\infty} 5^{-x}$

43. $\lim\limits_{x \to \infty} \left(\frac{1}{3}\right)^x$

44. $\lim\limits_{x \to -\infty} \left(\frac{1}{3}\right)^x$

45. $\lim\limits_{x \to -\infty} e^{-x}$

46. $\lim\limits_{x \to \infty} e^{-x}$

Use transformations to help you graph each function. Identify the domain, range, and horizontal asymptote. Determine whether the function is increasing or decreasing.

47. $f(x) = 2^x - 3$

48. $f(x) = 3^{-x} + 1$

49. $f(x) = 2^{x+3} - 5$

50. $f(x) = 3^{1-x} - 4$

51. $y = -2^{-x}$

52. $y = -10^{-x}$

53. $y = 1 - 2^x$

54. $y = -1 - 2^{-x}$

55. $f(x) = 0.5 \cdot 3^{x-2}$

56. $f(x) = -0.1 \cdot 5^{x+4}$

57. $y = 500(0.5)^x$

58. $y = 100 \cdot 2^x$

Write the equation of each graph in its final position.

59. The graph of $y = 2^x$ is translated five units to the right and then two units downward.

60. The graph of $y = e^x$ is translated three units to the left and then one unit upward.

61. The graph of $y = (1/4)^x$ is translated one unit to the right, reflected in the *x*-axis, and then translated two units downward.

62. The graph of $y = 10^x$ is translated three units upward, two units to the left, and then reflected in the *x*-axis.

Solve each equation.

63. $2^x = 64$

64. $5^x = 1$

65. $10^x = 0.1$

66. $10^{2x} = 1000$

67. $-3^x = -27$

68. $-2^x = -\dfrac{1}{2}$

69. $3^{-x} = 9$

70. $2^x = \dfrac{1}{8}$

71. $8^x = 2$

72. $9^x = 3$

73. $e^x = \dfrac{1}{e^2}$

74. $e^{-x} = \dfrac{1}{e}$

75. $\left(\dfrac{1}{2}\right)^x = 8$

76. $\left(\dfrac{2}{3}\right)^x = \dfrac{9}{4}$

77. $10^{x-1} = 0.01$

78. $10^{|x|} = 1000$

79. $2 \cdot 2^{2x} = 4^x + 64$

80. $\left(\dfrac{4}{9}\right)^x \cdot \left(\dfrac{8}{27}\right)^{1-x} = \dfrac{2}{3}$

Let $f(x) = 2^x$, $g(x) = (1/3)^x$, $h(x) = 10^x$, and $m(x) = e^x$. Find the value of x in each equation.

81. $f(x) = 4$

82. $f(x) = 32$

83. $f(x) = \dfrac{1}{2}$

84. $f(x) = 1$

85. $g(x) = 1$

86. $g(x) = 9$

87. $g(x) = 27$

88. $g(x) = \dfrac{1}{9}$

89. $h(x) = 1000$

90. $h(x) = 10^5$

91. $h(x) = 0.1$

92. $h(x) = 0.0001$

93. $m(x) = e$

94. $m(x) = e^3$

95. $m(x) = \dfrac{1}{e}$

96. $m(x) = 1$

Fill in the missing coordinate in each ordered pair so that the pair is a solution to the given equation.

97. $y = 3^x$ $\quad$ $(2, \;\;), (\;\;, 3), (-1, \;\;), (\;\;, 1/9)$

98. $y = 10^x$ $\quad$ $(3, \;\;), (\;\;, 1), (-1, \;\;), (\;\;, 0.01)$

99. $f(x) = 5^{-x}$ $\quad$ $(0, \;\;), (\;\;, 25), (-1, \;\;), (\;\;, 1/5)$

100. $f(x) = e^{-x}$ $\quad$ $(1, \;\;), (\;\;, e), (0, \;\;), (\;\;, e^2)$

101. $f(x) = -2^x$ $\quad$ $(4, \;\;), (\;\;, -1/4), (-1, \;\;), (\;\;, -32)$

102. $f(x) = -(1/4)^{x-1}$ $\quad$ $(3, \;\;), (\;\;, -4), (-1, \;\;), (\;\;, -1/16)$

Solve each problem. When needed, use 365 days per year and 30 days per month.

103. *Periodic Compounding* A deposit of $5000 earns 8% annual interest. Find the amount in the account at the end of 6 years and the amount of interest earned during the 6 years if the interest is compounded

  a. annually

  b. quarterly

  c. monthly

  d. daily.

104. *Periodic Compounding* Melinda invests her $80,000 winnings from Publishers Clearing House at a 9% annual percentage rate. Find the amount of the investment at the end of 20 years and the amount of interest earned during the 20 years if the interest is compounded

  a. annually

  b. quarterly

  c. monthly

  d. daily.

105. *Compounded Continuously* The Lakewood Savings Bank pays 8% annual interest compounded continuously. How much will a deposit of $5000 amount to for each time period? **HINT** Convert months to days.

  a. 6 years

  b. 8 years 3 months

  c. 5 years 4 months 22 days

  d. 20 years 321 days

106. *Compounding Continuously* The Commercial Federal Credit Union pays $6\frac{3}{4}$% annual interest compounded continuously. How much will a deposit of $9000 amount to for each time period? **HINT** Convert months to days.

  a. 13 years

  b. 12 years 8 months

  c. 10 years 6 months 14 days

  d. 40 years 66 days

107. *Present Value Compounding Daily* A credit union pays 6.5% annual interest compounded daily. What deposit today (present value) would amount to $3000 in 5 years and 4 months?
> **HINT** Solve the compound interest formula for P.

108. *Higher Yields* Federal Savings and Loan offers $6\frac{3}{4}$% annual interest compounded daily on certificates of deposit. What dollar amount deposited now would amount to $40,000 in 3 years and 2 months?

109. *Present Value Compounding Continuously* Peoples Bank offers 5.42% compounded continuously on CDs. What amount invested now would grow to $20,000 in 30 years?
> **HINT** Solve the continuous compounding formula for P.

110. *Saving for Retirement* An investor wants to have a retirement nest egg of $100,000 and estimates that her investment now will grow at 3% compounded continuously for 40 years. What amount should she invest now to achieve this goal?

111. *Working by the Hour* One million dollars is deposited in an account paying 6% compounded continuously.
  a. What amount of interest will it earn in its first hour on deposit?
  > **HINT** One hour is 1/8760 of a year.

  b. What amount of interest will it earn during its 500th hour on deposit?
  > **HINT** Subtract the amount for $t = 499$ from the amount for $t = 500$.

112. *National Debt* The national debt was about $10 trillion in 2008.
  a. If the United States paid 5.5% interest compounded continuously on the debt, then what amount of interest does the government pay in one day?

  b. How much is saved in one day if the interest were 5.5% compounded daily?

113. *Radioactive Decay* The number of grams of a certain radioactive substance present at time t is given by the formula $A = 200e^{-0.001t}$, where t is the number of years. How many grams are present at time $t = 0$? How many grams are present at time $t = 500$?

114. *Population Growth* The function $P = 2.4e^{0.03t}$ models the size of the population of a small country, where P is in millions of people in the year $2000 + t$.
  a. What was the population in 2000?

  b. Use the formula to estimate the population to the nearest tenth of a million in 2020.

115. *Facebook Users* The function $U = 0.1e^{1.45t}$ models the number of Facebook users, where U is in millions of people and t is the number of years since 2005.
  a. How many Facebook users (to the nearest hundred thousand) were there in 2006?

  b. How many Facebook users (to the nearest million) were there in 2011?

116. *Facebook Revenue* The function $R = 52e^{0.91t}$ models the revenue of Facebook, where R is in millions of dollars and t is the number of years since 2006.
  a. What was Facebook's revenue in 2006?

  b. What was Facebook's revenue (to the nearest million) in 2010?

117. *Cell Phone Subscribers* The number of cell phone subscribers (in millions) in the United States is given in the accompanying table (www.infoplease.com).

Table for Exercise 117

Year	Cell Phone Subscribers (millions)
1990	5.3
1995	33.8
2000	109.4
2005	207.9
2006	233.0
2007	255.4
2008	271.6

Jack Hollingsworth/Digital Vision/Getty Images

  a. Use the exponential regression feature of a graphing calculator to find an equation of the form $y = ab^x$ that fits the data, where x is the years since 1990.

  b. Judging from the graph of the data and the curve, does the exponential model look like a good model?

  c. Use the equation to estimate the number of cell phone subscribers in 2010.

118. *Newspaper Circulation* As more and more people turn to Internet and 24-hour cable network news, newspaper circulation has declined. The accompanying table gives the total number of daily papers sold in the United States (www.naa.org).

Table for Exercise 118

Year	Papers Sold (millions)
1990	62.3
1995	58.1
2000	55.8
2005	53.3
2006	52.3
2007	51.2
2008	49.6

Corbis

  a. Use the exponential regression feature of a graphing calculator to find an equation of the form $y = ab^x$ that fits the data, where x is the years since 1990.

  b. Judging from the graph of the data and the curve, does the exponential model look like a good model for these data?

  c. Use the equation to estimate the daily newspaper circulation in 2012.

119. *Position of a Football* The football is on the 10-yard line. Several penalties in a row are given, and each penalty moves the ball half the distance to the closer goal line. Write a formula that gives the ball's position P after the nth such penalty.
HINT First write some ordered pairs starting with $(1, 5)$.

120. *Cost of a Parking Ticket* The cost of a parking ticket on campus is $15 for the first offense. Given that the cost doubles for each additional offense, write a formula for the cost C as a function of the number of tickets n.
HINT First write some ordered pairs starting with $(1, 15)$.

121. *Challenger Disaster* Using data on O-ring damage from 24 previous space shuttle launches, Professor Edward R. Tufte of Yale University concluded that the number of O-rings damaged per launch is an exponential function of the temperature at the time of the launch. If NASA had used a model such as $n = 644e^{-0.15t}$, where t is the Fahrenheit temperature at the time of launch and n is the number of O-rings damaged, then the tragic end to the flight of the space shuttle *Challenger* might have been avoided. Using this model, find the number of O-rings that would be expected to fail at 31°F, the temperature at the time of the *Challenger* launch on January 28, 1986.

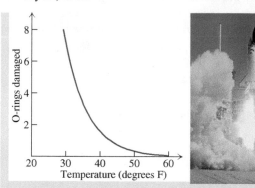

Figure for Exercise 121

122. *Manufacturing Cost* The cost in dollars for manufacturing x units of a certain drug is given by the function $C(x) = xe^{0.001x}$. Find the cost for manufacturing 500 units. Find the function $AC(x)$ that gives the average cost per unit for manufacturing x units. What happens to the average cost per unit as x gets larger and larger?

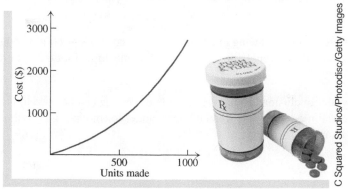

Figure for Exercise 122

FOR WRITING/DISCUSSION

123. *Cooperative Learning* Work in a small group to write a summary (including drawings) of the types of graphs that can be obtained for exponential functions of the form $y = a^x$ for $a > 0$ and $a \neq 1$.

124. *Group Toss* Have all students in your class stand and toss a coin. Those that get heads sit down. Those that are left standing toss again and all who obtain heads must sit down. Repeat until no one is left standing. For each toss record the number of coins that are tossed—for example, $(1, 30)$, $(2, 14)$, and so on. Do not include a pair with zero coins tossed. Enter the data into a graphing calculator and use exponential regression to find an equation of the form $y = a \cdot b^x$ that fits the data. What percent of those standing did you expect would sit down after each toss? Is the value of b close to this number?

▶ RETHINKING

125. Find the equations of the horizontal and vertical asymptotes for the graph of the function $f(x) = \dfrac{2x - 3}{x + 7}$.

126. Solve $|2x - 5| = 7x$.

127. Solve $|2x - 5| > 7$.

128. Solve $2x - 5 = 7x$.

129. Solve $2x - 5 = y$ for x.

130. Find the equation of the line through $(4, 3)$ that is parallel to $y = 2x - 99$

THINKING OUTSIDE THE BOX XXX & XXXI

Swim Meet Two swimmers start out from opposite sides of a pool. Each swims the length of the pool and back at a constant rate. They pass each other for the first time 40 feet from one side of the pool and for the second time 45 feet from the other side of the pool. What is the length of the pool?

One-seventh to One Six matches are arranged to form the fraction one-seventh as shown here:

$$\dfrac{\text{I}}{\text{VII}}$$

Move one match, but not the fraction bar, to make a fraction that is equal to one.

Kennedy Space Center/NASA

C Squared Studios/Photodisc/Getty Images

►POP QUIZ 1

1. What is $f(4)$ if $f(x) = -2^x$?

2. Is $f(x) = 3^{-x}$ increasing or decreasing?

3. Find the domain and range for $y = e^{x-1} + 2$.

4. What is the horizontal asymptote for $y = 2^x - 1$?

5. Solve $(1/4)^x = 64$.

6. What is a, if $f(a) = 8$ and $f(x) = 2^{-x}$?

7. If $1000 earns 4% annual interest compounded quarterly, then what is the amount after 20 years?

8. Find the amount in the last problem if the interest is compounded continuously.

►LINKING concepts... For Individual or Group Explorations

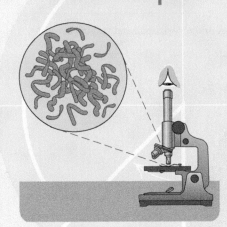

Comparing Exponential and Linear Models

The function $f(t) = 300e^{0.5t}$ gives the number of bacteria present in a culture t hours after the start of an experiment in which the bacteria are growing continuously at a rate of 50% per hour. Let $A[a, b]$ represent the average rate of change of f on the time interval $[a, b]$.

a) Fill in the following table.

Interval $[a, b]$	$f(a)$	$A[a, b]$	$A[a, b]/f(a)$
$[3.00, 3.05]$			
$[7.50, 7.51]$			
$[8.623, 8.624]$			

b) What are the units for the quantity $A[a, b]$?

c) What can you conjecture about the ratio $A[a, b]/f(a)$?

d) Test your conjecture on a few more intervals of various lengths. Explain how the length of the interval affects the ratio.

e) State your conjecture in terms of variation. What is the constant of proportionality?

f) Suppose the bacteria were growing in a linear manner, say $f(t) = 800t + 300$. Make a table like the given table and make a conjecture about the ratio $A[a, b]/f(a)$.

g) Explain how your conclusions about average rate of change can be used to justify an exponential model as better than a linear model for modeling growth of a bacteria (or human) population.

2 Logarithmic Functions and Their Applications

Since exponential functions are one-to-one functions (Section 1), they are invertible. In this section we will study the inverses of the exponential functions.

The Definition

The inverses of the exponential functions are called **logarithmic functions.** Since f^{-1} is a general name for an inverse function, we adopt a more descriptive notation for these inverses. If $f(x) = a^x$, then instead of $f^{-1}(x)$, we write $\log_a(x)$ for the inverse of the base-a exponential function. We read $\log_a(x)$ as "log of x with base a," and we call the expression $\log_a(x)$ a **logarithm.**

The meaning of $\log_a(x)$ will be clearer if we consider the exponential function

$$f(x) = 2^x$$

as an example. Since $f(3) = 2^3 = 8$, the base-2 exponential function pairs the exponent 3 with the value of the exponential expression 8. Since the function $\log_2(x)$ reverses that pairing, we have $\log_2(8) = 3$. So $\log_2(8)$ is the exponent that is used on the base 2 to obtain 8. *In general, $\log_a(x)$ is the exponent that is used on the base a to obtain the value x.*

■ **Foreshadowing Calculus**

In calculus the logarithm functions can be defined geometrically (as area under a certain curve). Then exponential functions are defined as the inverses of the logarithm functions.

Definition:
Logarithmic Function

> For $a > 0$ and $a \neq 1$, the **logarithmic function with base a** is denoted $f(x) = \log_a(x)$, where
>
> $$y = \log_a(x) \qquad \text{if and only if} \qquad a^y = x.$$

EXAMPLE 1 Evaluating logarithmic functions

Find the indicated values of the logarithmic functions.

a. $\log_3(9)$ **b.** $\log_2\left(\dfrac{1}{4}\right)$ **c.** $\log_{1/2}(8)$

Solution

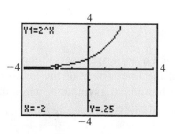

Figure 21

a. By the definition of logarithm, $\log_3(9)$ is the exponent that is used on the base 3 to obtain 9. Since $3^2 = 9$, we have $\log_3(9) = 2$.

b. Since $\log_2(1/4)$ is the exponent that is used on the base 2 to obtain $1/4$, we try various powers of 2 until we find $2^{-2} = 1/4$. So $\log_2(1/4) = -2$.

   You can use the graph of $y = 2^x$ as in Fig. 21 to check that $2^{-2} = 1/4$. □

c. Since $\log_{1/2}(8)$ is the exponent that is used on a base of $1/2$ to obtain 8, we try various powers of $1/2$ until we find $(1/2)^{-3} = 8$. So $\log_{1/2}(8) = -3$.

▶**TRY THIS.** Find $\log_4(1/16)$. ■

Since the exponential function $f(x) = a^x$ has domain $(-\infty, \infty)$ and range $(0, \infty)$, the logarithmic function $f(x) = \log_a(x)$ has domain $(0, \infty)$ and range $(-\infty, \infty)$. So there are no logarithms of negative numbers or zero. Expressions such as $\log_2(-4)$ and $\log_3(0)$ are undefined. Note that $\log_a(1) = 0$ for any base a, because $a^0 = 1$ for any base a.

There are two bases that are used more frequently than the others; they are 10 and e. The notation $\log_{10}(x)$ is abbreviated $\log(x)$, and $\log_e(x)$ is abbreviated $\ln(x)$.

Definition: Common and Natural Logarithms

The **common logarithmic function** is denoted as $f(x) = \log(x)$, where

$$y = \log(x) \quad \text{if and only if} \quad 10^y = x.$$

The **natural logarithmic function** is denoted as $f(x) = \ln(x)$, where

$$y = \ln(x) \quad \text{if and only if} \quad e^y = x.$$

```
log(76)
          1.880813592
10^(1.8808)
          75.99762144
10^(1.880813592)
          75.99999995
```

Figure 22

Most scientific calculators have function keys for the exponential functions 10^x and e^x and their inverses $\log(x)$ and $\ln(x)$. Natural logarithms are also called **Napierian logarithms** after John Napier (1550–1617).

Note that $\log(76)$ is approximately 1.8808 and $10^{1.8808}$ is approximately 76 as shown in Fig. 22. If you use more digits for $\log(76)$ as the power of 10, then the calculator gets closer to 76. □

You can use a calculator to find common or natural logarithms, but you should know how to find the values of logarithms such as those in Examples 1 and 2 without using a calculator.

EXAMPLE 2 Evaluating logarithmic functions

Find the indicated values of the logarithmic functions without a calculator. Use a calculator to check.

a. $\log(1000)$ **b.** $\ln(1)$ **c.** $\ln(-6)$

Solution

```
log(1000)
                    3
ln(1)
                    0
ln(-6)
```

Figure 23

a. To find $\log(1000)$, we must find the exponent that is used on the base 10 to obtain 1000. Since $10^3 = 1000$, we have $\log(1000) = 3$.

b. Since $e^0 = 1$, $\ln(1) = 0$.

c. The expression $\ln(-6)$ is undefined because -6 is not in the domain of the natural logarithm function. There is no power of e that results in -6.

The calculator results for parts (a) and (b) are shown in Fig. 23. If you ask a calculator for $\ln(-6)$, it will give you an error message.

▶**TRY THIS.** Find $\log(100)$. ■

Graphs of Logarithmic Functions

The functions $y = a^x$ and $y = \log_a(x)$ for $a > 0$ and $a \neq 1$ are inverse functions. So the graph of $y = \log_a(x)$ is a reflection about the line $y = x$ of the graph of $y = a^x$. The graph of $y = a^x$ has the x-axis as its horizontal asymptote, while the graph of $y = \log_a(x)$ has the y-axis as its vertical asymptote.

EXAMPLE 3 Graph of a base-a logarithmic function with $a > 1$

Sketch the graphs of $y = 2^x$ and $y = \log_2(x)$ on the same coordinate system. State the domain and range of each function.

Solution

Since these two functions are inverses of each other, the graph $y = \log_2(x)$ is a reflection of the graph of $y = 2^x$ about the line $y = x$. Make a table of ordered pairs for each function:

x	-1	0	1	2
$y = 2^x$	$1/2$	1	2	4

x	$1/2$	1	2	4
$y = \log_2(x)$	-1	0	1	2

Interfoto/Alamy

HISTORICAL NOTE

John Napier (1550–1617) was a Scottish mathematician, physicist, and astronomer/astrologer. He is best remembered as the inventor of logarithms and Napier's bones (a calculating device) and for popularizing the use of the decimal point. Napier described a method of multiplication and division using metal plates, which was the direct antecedent of the slide rule.

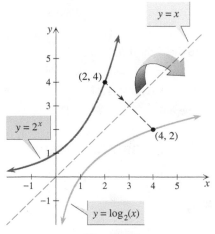

Figure 24

Sketch $y = 2^x$ and $y = \log_2(x)$ through the points given in the table as shown in Fig. 24. Keep in mind that $y = \log_2(x)$ is a reflection of $y = 2^x$ about the line $y = x$. The important features of the two functions are given in the following table:

	Domain	Range	Asymptotes	Limits
$y = 2^x$	$(-\infty, \infty)$	$(0, \infty)$	x-axis	$\lim\limits_{x \to -\infty} 2^x = 0, \ \lim\limits_{x \to \infty} 2^x = \infty$
$y = \log_2(x)$	$(0, \infty)$	$(-\infty, \infty)$	y-axis	$\lim\limits_{x \to 0^+} \log_2(x) = -\infty,$ $\lim\limits_{x \to \infty} \log_2(x) = \infty$

▶**TRY THIS.** Graph $f(x) = \log_6(x)$ and state the domain and range. ■

Note that the function $y = \log_2(x)$ graphed in Fig. 24 is one-to-one by the horizontal line test and it is an increasing function. The graphs of the common logarithm function $y = \log(x)$ and the natural logarithm function $y = \ln(x)$ are shown in Fig. 25 and they are also increasing functions. The function $y = \log_a(x)$ is increasing if $a > 1$. By contrast, if $0 < a < 1$, the function $y = \log_a(x)$ is decreasing, as illustrated in the next example.

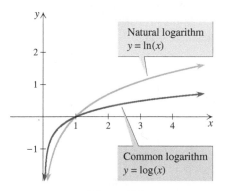

Figure 25

EXAMPLE 4 Graph of a base-a logarithmic function with $0 < a < 1$

Sketch the graph of $f(x) = \log_{1/3}(x)$ and state its domain and range.

Solution

Make a table of ordered pairs for the function:

x	1/9	1/3	1	3	9
$y = \log_{1/3}(x)$	2	1	0	-1	-2

Sketch the curve through these points as shown in Fig. 26 The y-axis is a vertical asymptote for the curve. In terms of limits, $\lim\limits_{x \to 0^+} \log_{1/3}(x) = \infty$ and $\lim\limits_{x \to \infty} \log_{1/3}(x) = -\infty$. The domain is $(0, \infty)$, and its range is $(-\infty, \infty)$.

▶**TRY THIS.** Graph $f(x) = \log_{1/6}(x)$ and state the domain and range. ■

The logarithmic functions have properties corresponding to the properties of the exponential functions stated in Section 1.

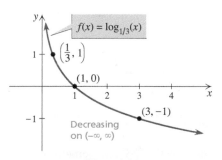

Figure 26

Properties of Logarithmic Functions

The logarithmic function $f(x) = \log_a(x)$ has the following properties:

1. The function f is increasing for $a > 1$ and decreasing for $0 < a < 1$.
2. The x-intercept of the graph of f is $(1, 0)$.
3. The graph has the y-axis as a vertical asymptote.
4. The domain of f is $(0, \infty)$, and the range of f is $(-\infty, \infty)$.
5. The function f is one-to-one.
6. The functions $f(x) = \log_a(x)$ and $f(x) = a^x$ are inverse functions.

The Logarithmic Family of Functions

A function of the form $f(x) = \log_a(x)$ is a logarithmic function. Any function of the form $g(x) = b \cdot \log_a(x - h) + k$ is a member of the **logarithmic family** of functions. The graph of g is a transformation of the graph of f, as discussed in Section 2.3:

The graph of f moves to the left if $h < 0$ or to the right if $h > 0$.

The graph of f moves upward if $k > 0$ or downward if $k < 0$.

The graph of f is stretched if $b > 1$ and shrunk if $0 < b < 1$.

The graph of f is reflected in the x-axis if b is negative.

EXAMPLE 5 | Graphing members of the logarithmic family

Sketch the graph of each function and state its domain and range.

a. $y = \log_2(x - 1)$ **b.** $f(x) = -\dfrac{1}{2}\log_2(x + 3)$

Solution

a. The graph of $y = \log_2(x - 1)$ is obtained by translating the graph of $y = \log_2(x)$ to the right one unit. Since the domain of $y = \log_2(x)$ is $(0, \infty)$, the domain of $y = \log_2(x - 1)$ is $(1, \infty)$. The line $x = 1$ is the vertical asymptote. Calculate a few ordered pairs to get an accurate graph.

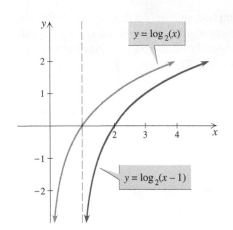

Figure 27

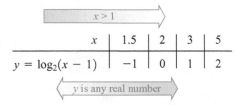

$x > 1$				
x	1.5	2	3	5
$y = \log_2(x - 1)$	-1	0	1	2
y is any real number				

Sketch the curve as shown in Fig. 27 The range is $(-\infty, \infty)$.

b. The graph of f is obtained by translating the graph of $y = \log_2(x)$ to the left three units. The vertical asymptote for f is the line $x = -3$. Multiplication by $-1/2$ shrinks the graph and reflects it in the x-axis. Calculate a few ordered pairs for accuracy.

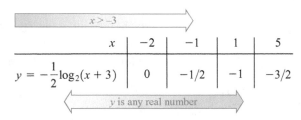

$x > -3$				
x	-2	-1	1	5
$y = -\dfrac{1}{2}\log_2(x + 3)$	0	$-1/2$	-1	$-3/2$
y is any real number				

Sketch the curve through these points as shown in Fig. 28 The domain of f is $(-3, \infty)$, and the range is $(-\infty, \infty)$.

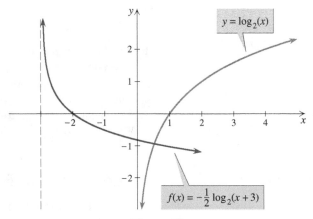

Figure 28

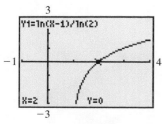

Figure 29

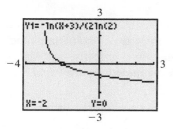

Figure 30

▶**TRY THIS.** Graph $f(x) = -\log_2(x + 1)$ and state the domain and range.   ■

A graphing calculator typically has keys for log and ln only. To graph logarithmic functions with other bases, use the formula $\log_a(x) = \dfrac{\ln(x)}{\ln(a)}$, which will be proven in Section 3. So to check Example 5(a), graph $y = \dfrac{\ln(x - 1)}{\ln(2)}$ as shown in Fig. 29. For Example 5(b) graph $y = -\dfrac{1}{2} \cdot \dfrac{\ln(x + 3)}{\ln(2)}$ or $y = \dfrac{-\ln(x + 3)}{2 \cdot \ln(2)}$ as in Fig. 30.

Logarithmic and Exponential Equations

Some equations involving logarithms can be solved by writing an equivalent exponential equation, and some equations involving exponents can be solved by writing an equivalent logarithmic equation. Rewriting logarithmic and exponential equations is possible because of the definition of logarithms:

$$y = \log_a(x) \qquad \text{if and only if} \qquad a^y = x$$

EXAMPLE 6 Rewriting logarithmic and exponential equations

Write each equation involving logarithms as an equivalent exponential equation, and write each equation involving exponents as an equivalent logarithmic equation.

a. $\log_5(625) = 4$ **b.** $\log_3(n) = 5$ **c.** $3^x = 50$ **d.** $e^{x-1} = 9$

Solution

a. $\log_5(625) = 4$ is equivalent to $5^4 = 625$.
b. $\log_3(n) = 5$ is equivalent to $3^5 = n$.
c. $3^x = 50$ is equivalent to $x = \log_3(50)$.
d. $e^{x-1} = 9$ is equivalent to $x - 1 = \ln(9)$.

▶**TRY THIS.** Write $\log_4(w) = 7$ as an exponential equation.   ■

In the next example we find the inverses of an exponential function and a logarithmic function.

EXAMPLE 7 Finding inverse functions

a. Find f^{-1} for $f(x) = \frac{1}{2} \cdot 6^{x-3}$.
b. Find f^{-1} for $f(x) = \log_2(x - 1) + 4$.

Solution

a. Using the switch-and-solve method, we switch x and y, then solve for y:

$$x = \frac{1}{2} \cdot 6^{y-3} \quad \text{Switch x and y in $y = \frac{1}{2} \cdot 6^{x-3}$.}$$

$$2x = 6^{y-3} \quad \text{Multiply each side by 2.}$$

$$y - 3 = \log_6(2x) \quad \text{Definition of logarithm}$$

$$y = \log_6(2x) + 3 \quad \text{Add 3 to each side.}$$

So $f^{-1}(x) = \log_6(2x) + 3$.

447

b. Switch x and y, then solve for y:

$$x = \log_2(y - 1) + 4 \quad \text{Switch } x \text{ and } y \text{ in } y = \log_2(x - 1) + 4.$$

$$x - 4 = \log_2(y - 1) \quad \text{Subtract 4 from each side.}$$

$$y - 1 = 2^{x-4} \quad \text{Definition of logarithm}$$

$$y = 2^{x-4} + 1 \quad \text{Add 1 to each side.}$$

So $f^{-1}(x) = 2^{x-4} + 1$.

▶**TRY THIS.** Find f^{-1} for $f(x) = 3 \cdot e^{5x-1}$. ∎

The one-to-one property of exponential functions was used to solve exponential equations in Section 1. Likewise, the one-to-one property of logarithmic functions is used in solving logarithmic equations. The one-to-one property says that *if two quantities have the same base-a logarithm, then the quantities are equal.* For example, if $\log_2(m) = \log_2(n)$, then $m = n$.

One-to-One Property of Logarithms

For $a > 0$ and $a \neq 1$,

$$\text{if} \quad \log_a(x_1) = \log_a(x_2), \quad \text{then} \quad x_1 = x_2.$$

The one-to-one properties and the definition of logarithm are at present the only new tools that we have for solving equations. Later in this chapter we will develop more properties of logarithms and solve more complicated equations.

EXAMPLE 8 Solving equations involving logarithms

Solve each equation.

a. $\log_3(x) = -2$ **b.** $\log_x(5) = 2$ **c.** $5^x = 9$ **d.** $\ln(x^2) = \ln(3x)$

Solution

a. Use the definition of logarithm to write the equivalent exponential equation.

$$\log_3(x) = -2 \quad \text{Original equation}$$

$$x = 3^{-2} \quad \text{Definition of logarithm}$$

$$= \frac{1}{9}$$

Since $\log_3(1/9) = -2$ is correct, the solution to the equation is $1/9$.

b. $\log_x(5) = 2 \quad \text{Original equation}$

$$x^2 = 5 \quad \text{Definition of logarithm}$$

$$x = \pm\sqrt{5}$$

Since the base of a logarithm is always nonnegative, the only solution is $\sqrt{5}$.

c. $5^x = 9 \quad \text{Original equation}$

$$x = \log_5(9) \quad \text{Definition of logarithm}$$

The exact solution to $5^x = 9$ is the irrational number $\log_5(9)$. In the next section we will learn how to find a rational approximation for $\log_5(9)$.

d. $\ln(x^2) = \ln(3x) \quad \text{Original equation}$

$$x^2 = 3x \quad \text{One-to-one property of logarithms}$$

$$x^2 - 3x = 0$$

$$x(x - 3) = 0$$

$$x = 0 \quad \text{or} \quad x = 3$$

Checking $x = 0$ in the original equation, we get the undefined expression $\ln(0)$. So the only solution to the equation is 3.

▶**TRY THIS.** Solve $\log_5(2x) = -3$. ∎

EXAMPLE 9 Equations involving common and natural logarithms

Use a calculator to find the value of x rounded to four decimal places.

a. $10^x = 50$ **b.** $2e^{0.5x} = 6$

Solution

a. $10^x = 50$ Original equation

$\quad x = \log(50)$ Definition of logarithm

$\quad x \approx 1.6990$

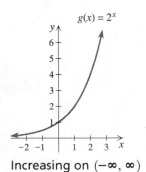

Figure 31

Figure 31 shows how to find the approximate value of $\log(50)$ and how to check the approximate answer and exact answer. □

b. $2e^{0.5x} = 6$ Original equation

$\quad e^{0.5x} = 3$ Divide by 2 to get the form $a^x = y$.

$\quad 0.5x = \ln(3)$ Definition of logarithm

$$x = \frac{\ln(3)}{0.5}$$

$\quad x \approx 2.1972$

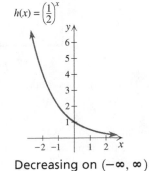

Figure 32

Fig. 32 shows how to find the approximate value of x and how to check it in the original equation.

▶**TRY THIS.** Solve $10^{3x} = 70$. ∎

FUNCTION

gallery... Exponential and Logarithmic Functions

Exponential: $f(x) = a^x$, domain $(-\infty, \infty)$, range $(0, \infty)$

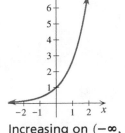

$g(x) = 2^x$

Increasing on $(-\infty, \infty)$
y-intercept $(0, 1)$

$h(x) = \left(\frac{1}{2}\right)^x$

Decreasing on $(-\infty, \infty)$
y-intercept $(0, 1)$

$j(x) = e^x$

Increasing on $(-\infty, \infty)$
y-intercept $(0, 1)$

Logarithmic: $f^{-1}(x) = \log_a(x)$, domain $(0, \infty)$, range $(-\infty, \infty)$

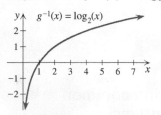

Increasing on $(0, \infty)$
x-intercept $(1, 0)$

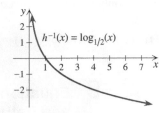

Decreasing on $(0, \infty)$
x-intercept $(1, 0)$

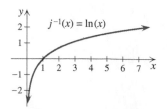

Increasing on $(0, \infty)$
x-intercept $(1, 0)$

Applications

We saw in Section 1 that if a principal of P dollars earns interest at an annual rate r compounded continuously, then the amount after t years is given by

$$A = Pe^{rt}.$$

If either the rate or the time is the only unknown in this formula, then the definition of logarithms can be used to solve for the rate or the time.

EXAMPLE 10 Finding the time in a continuous compounding problem

If $8000 is invested at 9% compounded continuously, then how long will it take for the investment to grow to $20,000?

Solution

Use the formula $A = Pe^{rt}$ with $A = \$20{,}000$, $P = \$8000$, and $r = 0.09$:

$$20{,}000 = 8000e^{0.09t}$$

$$2.5 = e^{0.09t} \qquad \text{Divide by 8000 to get the form } y = a^x.$$

$$0.09t = \ln(2.5) \qquad \text{Definition of logarithm: } y = a^x \text{ if and only if } x = \log_a(y)$$

$$t = \frac{\ln(2.5)}{0.09}$$

$$\approx 10.181 \text{ years}$$

We can multiply 365 by 0.181 to get approximately 66 days. So the investment grows to $20,000 in approximately 10 years and 66 days.

You can use a graphing calculator to check as shown in Fig. 33.

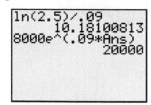

Figure 33

▶**TRY THIS.** How long does it take for $4 to grow to $12 at 5% compounded continuously? ∎

The formula $A = Pe^{rt}$ was introduced to model the continuous growth of money. However, this type of formula is used in a wide variety of applications. In the following exercises you will find problems involving population growth, declining forests, and global warming.

FOR thought... True or False? Explain.

1. The first coordinate of an ordered pair in an exponential function is a logarithm.

2. $\log_{100}(10) = 2$

3. If $f(x) = \log_3(x)$, then $f^{-1}(x) = 3^x$.

4. $10^{\log(1000)} = 1000$

5. The domain of $f(x) = \ln(x)$ is $(-\infty, \infty)$.

6. $\ln(e^{2.451}) = 2.451$

7. For any positive real number x, $e^{\ln(x)} = x$.

8. For any base a, where $a > 0$ and $a \neq 1$, $\log_a(0) = 1$.

9. $\log(10^3) + \log(10^5) = \log(10^8)$

10. $\log_2(32) - \log_2(8) = \log_2(4)$

EXERCISES 2

Fill in the blank.

1. The inverse of an exponential function is a(n) _____ function.

2. A base 10 logarithm is a(n) _____ logarithm.

3. Base e logarithm is a(n) _____ logarithm.

4. The function $f(x) = \log_a(x)$ is _____ if $a > 1$ and _____ if $0 < a < 1$.

5. The y-axis is a(n) _____ for the graph of $f(x) = \log_a(x)$.

6. The _____ of the function $f(x) = \log_a(x)$ is $(0, \infty)$.

7. The _____ of functions consists of all functions of the form $f(x) = b \cdot \log_a(x - h) + k$.

8. The _____ property of logarithms indicates that if $\log_a(m) = \log_a(n)$, then $m = n$.

Determine the number that can be used in place of the question mark to make the equation true.

9. $2^? = 64$

10. $2^? = 16$

11. $3^? = \dfrac{1}{81}$

12. $3^? = 1$

13. $16^? = 2$

14. $16^? = 16$

15. $\left(\dfrac{1}{5}\right)^? = 125$

16. $\left(\dfrac{1}{5}\right)^? = \dfrac{1}{125}$

Find the indicated value of the logarithmic functions.

17. $\log_2(64)$

18. $\log_2(16)$

19. $\log_3(1/81)$

20. $\log_3(1)$

21. $\log_{16}(2)$

22. $\log_{16}(16)$

23. $\log_{1/5}(125)$

24. $\log_{1/5}(1/125)$

25. $\log(0.1)$

26. $\log(10^6)$

27. $\log(1)$

28. $\log(10)$

29. $\ln(e)$

30. $\ln(0)$

31. $\ln(e^{-5})$

32. $\ln(e^9)$

Sketch the graph of each function, and state the domain and range of each function.

33. $y = \log_3(x)$

34. $y = \log_4(x)$

35. $f(x) = \log_5(x)$

36. $g(x) = \log_8(x)$

37. $y = \log_{1/2}(x)$

38. $y = \log_{1/4}(x)$

39. $h(x) = \log_{1/5}(x)$

40. $s(x) = \log_{1/10}(x)$

41. $f(x) = \ln(x - 1)$

42. $f(x) = \log_3(x + 2)$

43. $f(x) = -3 + \log(x + 2)$

44. $f(x) = 4 - \log(x + 6)$

45. $f(x) = -\dfrac{1}{2}\log(x - 1)$

46. $f(x) = -2 \cdot \log_2(x + 2)$

Use a graph or a table to find each limit.

47. $\lim\limits_{x \to \infty} \log_3(x)$

48. $\lim\limits_{x \to 0^+} \log_3(x)$

49. $\lim\limits_{x \to 0^+} \log_{1/2}(x)$

50. $\lim\limits_{x \to \infty} \log_{1/2}(x)$

51. $\lim\limits_{x \to 0^+} \ln(x)$

52. $\lim\limits_{x \to \infty} \ln(x)$

53. $\lim\limits_{x \to \infty} \log(x)$

54. $\lim\limits_{x \to 0^+} \log(x)$

Write the equation of each graph in its final position.

55. The graph of $y = \ln(x)$ is translated three units to the right and then four units downward.

56. The graph of $y = \log(x)$ is translated five units to the left and then seven units upward.

57. The graph of $y = \log_2(x)$ is translated five units to the right, reflected in the x-axis, and then translated one unit downward.

58. The graph of $y = \log_3(x)$ is translated four units upward, six units to the left, and then reflected in the x-axis.

Write each equation as an equivalent exponential equation.

59. $\log_2(32) = 5$ **60.** $\log_3(81) = 4$

61. $\log_5(x) = y$ **62.** $\log_4(a) = b$

63. $\log(1000) = z$ **64.** $\ln(y) = 3$

65. $\ln(5) = x$ **66.** $\log(y) = 2$

67. $\log_a(x) = m$ **68.** $\log_b(q) = t$

Write each equation as an equivalent logarithmic equation.

69. $5^3 = 125$ **70.** $2^7 = 128$

71. $e^3 = y$ **72.** $10^5 = w$

73. $y = 10^m$ **74.** $p = e^x$

75. $y = a^z$ **76.** $w = b^k$

77. $a^{x-1} = n$ **78.** $w^{x+2} = r$

For each function, find f^{-1}.

79. $f(x) = 2^x$ **80.** $f(x) = 5^x$

81. $f(x) = \log_7(x)$ **82.** $f(x) = \log(x)$

83. $f(x) = \ln(x - 1)$ **84.** $f(x) = \log(x + 4)$

85. $f(x) = 3^{x+2}$ **86.** $f(x) = 6^{x-1}$

87. $f(x) = \frac{1}{2} \cdot 10^{x-1} + 5$ **88.** $f(x) = 2^{3x+1} - 6$

Solve each equation. Find the exact solutions.

89. $\log_2(x) = 8$ **90.** $\log_5(x) = 3$

91. $\log_3(x) = \dfrac{1}{2}$ **92.** $\log_4(x) = \dfrac{1}{3}$

93. $\log_x(16) = 2$ **94.** $\log_x(16) = 4$

95. $3^x = 77$ **96.** $\dfrac{1}{2^x} = 5$

97. $\ln(x - 3) = \ln(2x - 9)$ **98.** $\log_2(4x) = \log_2(x + 6)$

99. $\log_x(18) = 2$ **100.** $\log_x(9) = \dfrac{1}{2}$

101. $3^{x+1} = 7$ **102.** $5^{3-x} = 12$

103. $\log(x) = \log(6 - x^2)$ **104.** $\log_3(2x) = \log_3(24 - x^2)$

105. $\log_x\left(\dfrac{1}{9}\right) = -\dfrac{2}{3}$ **106.** $\log_x\left(\dfrac{1}{16}\right) = \dfrac{4}{3}$

107. $4^{2x-1} = \dfrac{1}{2}$ **108.** $e^{3x-4} = 1$

109. $\log_{32}(64) = x$ **110.** $\ln\left(\dfrac{1}{\sqrt{e}}\right) = x$

111. $\log_2(\log_3(\log_4(x))) = 0$ **112.** $\log_2(\log_2(\log_2(2^{(4^x)}))) = 3$

Find the approximate solution to each equation. Round to four decimal places.

113. $10^x = 25$ **114.** $e^x = 2$

115. $e^{2x} = 3$ **116.** $10^{3x} = 5$

117. $5e^x = 4$ **118.** $10^x - 3 = 5$

119. $\dfrac{1}{10^x} = 2$ **120.** $\dfrac{1}{e^{x-1}} = 5$

Solve each problem.

121. *Finding Time* Find the amount of time to the nearest tenth of a year that it would take for $10 to grow to $20 at each of the following annual rates compounded continuously.
  a. 2%   **b.** 4%

  c. 8%   **d.** 16%

122. *Finding Time* Find the amount of time to the nearest tenth of a year that it would take for $10 to grow to $40 at each of the following annual rates compounded continuously.
  a. 1%   **b.** 2%

  c. 8.327%   **d.** $7\dfrac{2}{3}\%$

123. *Finding Rate* Find the annual percentage rate compounded continuously to the nearest tenth of a percent for which $10 would grow to $30 for each of the following time periods.
  a. 5 years   **b.** 10 years

  c. 20 years   **d.** 40 years

124. *Finding Rate* Find the annual percentage rate to the nearest tenth of a percent for which $10 would grow to $50 for each of the following time periods.
  a. 4 years   **b.** 8 years

  c. 16 years   **d.** 32 years

125. *Becoming a Millionaire* Find the amount of time to the nearest day that it would take for a deposit of $1000 to grow to $1 million at 14% compounded continuously.

126. *Doubling Your Money* How long does it take for a deposit of $1000 to double at 8% compounded continuously?

127. *Finding the Rate* Solve the equation $A = Pe^{rt}$ for r, then find the rate at which a deposit of $1000 would double in 3 years compounded continuously.

128. *Finding the Rate* At what interest rate would a deposit of $30,000 grow to $2,540,689 in 40 years with continuous compounding?

129. *Rule of 70*
  a. Find the time that it takes for an investment to double at 10% compounded continuously.

  b. The time that it takes for an investment to double at $r\%$ is approximately 70 divided by r (the rule of 70). So at 10%, an investment will double in about 7 years. Explain why this rule works.

130. *Using the Rule of 70* Find approximate answers to these questions without using a calculator. See Exercise 129.
   a. Connie deposits $1000 in a bank at an annual interest rate of 2%. How long does it take for her money to double?

   b. Celeste invests $1000 in the stock market and her money grows at an annual rate of 10% (the historical average rate of return for the stock market). How long does it take for her money to double?

   c. What is the ratio of the value of Celeste's investment after 35 years to the value of Connie's investment after 35 years?

131. *Miracle in Boston* To illustrate the "miracle" of compound interest, Ben Franklin bequeathed $4000 to the city of Boston in 1790. The fund grew to $4.5 million in 200 years. Find the annual rate compounded continuously that would cause this "miracle" to happen.

132. *Miracle in Philadelphia* Ben Franklin's gift of $4000 to the city of Philadelphia in 1790 was not managed as well as his gift to Boston. The Philadelphia fund grew to only $2 million in 200 years. Find the annual rate compounded continuously that would yield this total value.

133. *Deforestation in Nigeria* In Nigeria, deforestation occurs at the rate of about 5.2% per year. Assume that the amount of forest remaining is determined by the function

$$F = F_0 e^{-0.052t},$$

where F_0 is the present acreage of forest land and t is the time in years from the present. In how many years will there be only 60% of the present acreage remaining?
   HINT Find the amount of time it takes for F_0 to become $0.60F_0$.

134. *Deforestation in El Salvador* It is estimated that at the present rate of deforestation in El Salvador, in 20 years only 53% of the present forest will be remaining. Use the exponential model $F = F_0 e^{rt}$ to determine the annual rate of deforestation in El Salvador.

135. *World Population* The population of the world doubled from 1950 to 1987, going from 2.5 billion to 5 billion people. Using the exponential model,

$$P = P_0 e^{rt},$$

find the annual growth rate r for that period. Although the annual growth rate has declined slightly to 1.63% annually, the population of the world is still growing at a tremendous rate. Using the initial population of 5 billion in 1987 and an annual rate of 1.63%, estimate the world population in the year 2010.

136. *Black Death* Because of the Black Death, or plague, the only substantial period in recorded history when the earth's population was not increasing was from 1348 to 1400. During that period the world population decreased by about 100 million people. Use the exponential model $P = P_0 e^{rt}$ and the data from the accompanying table to find the annual growth rate for the period 1400 to 2000. If the 100 million people had not been lost, then how many people would they have grown to in 600 years using the growth rate that you just found?

Table for Exercise 136

Year	World Population	
1348	0.47×10^9	
1400	0.37×10^9	
1900	1.60×10^9	
2000	6.07×10^9	

Alexander Lukin/Shutterstock

137. *Castle Rock Fire* The 2007 Castle Rock fire in Idaho was said to be growing exponentially after it expanded from 30 acres to 12,058 acres in 5 days (*Idaho Mountain Express*, August 22, 2007). See the accompanying figure. This exponential growth can be modeled by the function

$$a = 30e^{1.2t}$$

where t is the number of days since the start of the fire and a is the size of the fire in acres.
   a. According to the exponential model, what will be the size of the fire after 7 days?

   b. If the fire continues to grow exponentially, then in how many days will the size of the fire be 53,480,960 acres (the size of the state of Idaho)?

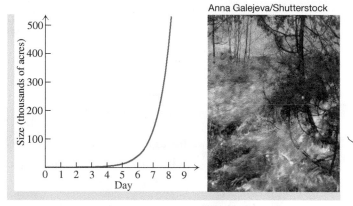

Anna Galejeva/Shutterstock

Figure for Exercise 137

138. *Global Warming* The increasing global temperature can be modeled by the function

$$I = 0.1e^{0.02t},$$

where I is the increase in global temperature in degrees Celsius since 1900, and t is the number of years since 1900 (NASA, www.science.nasa.gov).
   a. How much warmer was it in 2010 than it was in 1950?

   b. In what year will the global temperature be 4° greater than the global temperature in 2000?

139. *Safe Water* The graph on the next page shows the percentage of population without safe water p as a function of per capita income I (World Resources Institute, www.wri.org). Because the horizontal axis has a *log scale* (each mark is 10 times the previous mark), the relationship looks linear but it is not.
   a. Find a formula for this function.
   HINT First find the equation of the line through $(2, 100)$ and $(4, 10)$ in the form $p = mx + b$, then replace x with $\log(I)$.

b. What percent of the population would be expected to be without safe drinking water in a city with a per capita income of $100,000?

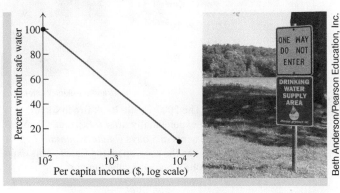

Figure for Exercise 139

140. *Municipal Waste* The accompanying graph shows the amount of municipal waste per capita *w* as a function of per capita income *I* (World Resources Institute, www.wri.org).

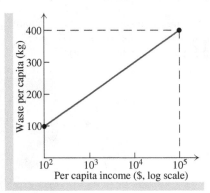

Figure for Exercise 140

a. Use the technique of the previous exercise to find a formula for *w* as a function of *I*.

b. How much municipal waste per capita would you expect in a city where the per capita income is $200,000?

Use the following definition for Exercises 141–144.

In chemistry, the pH of a solution is defined to be

$$pH = -\log[H^+],$$

where H^+ is the hydrogen ion concentration of the solution in moles per liter. Distilled water has a pH of approximately 7. A substance with a pH under 7 is called an acid, and one with a pH over 7 is called a base.

141. *Acidity of Tomato Juice* Tomato juice has a hydrogen ion concentration of $10^{-4.1}$ moles per liter. Find the pH of tomato juice.

142. *Acidity in Your Stomach* The gastric juices in your stomach have a hydrogen ion concentration of 10^{-1} moles per liter. Find the pH of your gastric juices.

143. *Acidity of Orange Juice* The hydrogen ion concentration of orange juice is $10^{-3.7}$ moles per liter. Find the pH of orange juice.

144. *Acidosis* A healthy body maintains the hydrogen ion concentration of human blood at $10^{-7.4}$ moles per liter. What is the pH of normal healthy blood? The condition of low blood pH is called acidosis. Its symptoms are sickly sweet breath, headache, and nausea.

FOR WRITING/DISCUSSION

145. *Different Models* Calculators that perform exponential regression often use $y = a \cdot b^x$ as the exponential growth model instead of $y = a \cdot e^{cx}$. For what value of *c* is $a \cdot b^x = a \cdot e^{cx}$? If a calculator gives $y = 500(1.036)^x$ for a growth model, then what is the continuous growth rate to the nearest hundredth of a percent?

146. *Making Conjectures* Consider the function $y = \log(10^n \cdot x)$ where *n* is an integer. Use a graphing calculator to graph this function for several choices of *n*. Make a conjecture about the relationship between the graph of $y = \log(10^n \cdot x)$ and the graph of $y = \log(x)$. Save your conjecture and attempt to prove it after you have studied the properties of logarithms, which are coming in Section 3. Repeat this exercise with $y = \log(x^n)$ where *n* is an integer.

147. *Increasing or Decreasing* Which exponential and logarithmic functions are increasing? Decreasing? Is the inverse of an increasing function increasing or decreasing? Is the inverse of a decreasing function increasing or decreasing? Explain.

148. *Cooperative Learning* Work in a small group to write a summary (including drawings) of the types of graphs that can be obtained for logarithmic functions of the form $y = \log_a(x)$ for $a > 0$ and $a \neq 1$.

▶ RETHINKING

149. Find the domain and range of the function
$$f(x) = -\frac{1}{2}3^{x-5} + 7.$$

150. Solve $2^{x-3} = 4^{5x-1}$.

151. Evaluate $(2 \times 10^{-9})^3(5 \times 10^3)^2$ without a calculator. Write the answer in scientific notation.

152. A pond contains 2000 fish of which 10% are bass. How many bass must be added so that 20% of the fish in the pond are bass?

153. Find all real and imaginary solutions to $x^3 + 13x = 4x^2$.

154. The cost of installing an oak floor varies jointly with the length and width of the room. If the cost is $875.60 for a room that is 8 feet by 11 feet, what is the cost for a room that is 10 feet by 14 feet?

THINKING OUTSIDE THE BOX XXXII

Seven-Eleven A convenience store sells a gallon of milk for $7 and a loaf of bread for $11. You are allowed to buy any combination of milk and bread, including only milk or only bread. Your total bill is always a whole number of dollars, but there are many whole numbers that cannot be the total. For example, the total cannot be $15. What is the largest whole number of dollars that cannot be the total?

POP QUIZ 2

1. What is x if $2^x = 32$?

2. Find $\log_2(32)$.

3. Is $y = \log_3(x)$ increasing or decreasing?

4. Find all asymptotes for $f(x) = \ln(x - 1)$.

5. Write $3^a = b$ as a logarithmic equation.

6. Find f^{-1} if $f(x) = \log(x + 3)$.

7. Solve $\log_5(x) = 3$.

8. Solve $\log_x(36) = 2$.

9. How long (to the nearest day) does it take for \$2 to grow to \$4 at 5% compounded continuously?

LINKING concepts... For Individual or Group Explorations

Modeling the U.S. Population

To effectively plan for the future one must attempt to predict the future. Government agencies use data about the past to construct a model and predict the future. The following table gives the population of the United States in millions every 10 years since 1900 (Census Bureau, www.census.gov).

Year	Pop.	Year	Pop.
1900	76	1960	180
1910	92	1970	204
1920	106	1980	227
1930	123	1990	249
1940	132	2000	279
1950	152	2010	309

Rafael Ramirez Lee/Shutterstock

a) Draw a bar graph of the data in the accompanying table. Use a computer graphics program if one is available.

b) Enter the data into your calculator and use exponential regression to find an exponential model of the form $y = a \cdot b^x$, where $x = 0$ corresponds to 1900.

c) Make a table (like the given table) that shows the predicted population according to the exponential model rather than the actual population.

d) Plot the points from part (c) on your bar graph and sketch an exponential curve through the points.

e) Use the given population data with linear regression to find a linear model of the form $y = ax + b$ and graph the line on your bar graph.

f) Predict the population in the year 2020 using the exponential model and the linear model.

g) Judging from your exponential curve and the line on your bar graph, in which prediction do you have the most confidence?

h) Use only the fact that the population grew from 76 million at time $t = 0$ (the year 1900) to 309 million at time $t = 110$ (the year 2010) to find a formula of the form $P(t) = P_0 \cdot e^{rt}$ for the population at any time t. Do not use regression.

i) Use the formula from part (h) to predict the population in the year 2020. Compare this prediction to the prediction that you found using exponential regression.

3 Rules of Logarithms

The rules of logarithms are closely related to the rules of exponents, because logarithms are exponents. In this section we use the rules of exponents to develop some rules of logarithms. With these rules of logarithms we will be able to solve more equations involving exponents and logarithms.

The Inverse Rules

The definition of logarithms leads to two rules that are useful in solving equations. If $f(x) = a^x$ and $g(x) = \log_a(x)$, then

$$g(f(x)) = g(a^x) = \log_a(a^x) = x$$

for any real number x. The result of this composition is x because the functions are inverses. If we compose in the opposite order we get

$$f(g(x)) = f(\log_a(x)) = a^{\log_a(x)} = x$$

for any positive real number x. The results are called the **inverse rules.**

Inverse Rules

Figure 34

If $a > 0$ and $a \neq 1$, then

1. $\log_a(a^x) = x$ for any real number x
2. $a^{\log_a(x)} = x$ for $x > 0$.

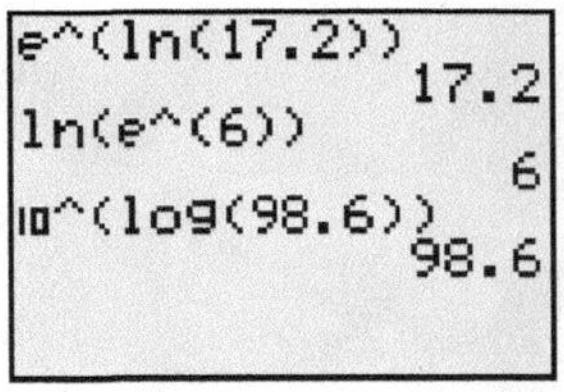

The inverse rules are easy to use if you remember that $\log_a(x)$ is the power of a that produces x. For example, $\log_2(67)$ is the power of 2 that produces 67. So $2^{\log_2(67)} = 67$. Similarly, $\ln(e^{99})$ is the power of e that produces e^{99}. So $\ln(e^{99}) = 99$. You can illustrate the inverse rules with a calculator, as shown in Fig. 34.

EXAMPLE 1 Using the inverse rules

Simplify each expression.

a. $e^{\ln(x^2)}$ **b.** $\log_7(7^{2x-1})$

Solution

By the inverse rules, $e^{\ln(x^2)} = x^2$ and $\log_7(7^{2x-1}) = 2x - 1$.

▶TRY THIS. Simplify $10^{\log(5w)}$ and $\log(10^p)$. ∎

The Logarithm of a Product

By the product rule for exponents, we add exponents when multiplying exponential expressions having the same base. To find a corresponding rule for logarithms, let's examine the equation $2^3 \cdot 2^2 = 2^5$. Notice that the exponents 3, 2, and 5 are the base-2 logarithms of 8, 4, and 32, respectively.

$$\overset{\log_2(8) \quad \log_2(4) \quad \log_2(32)}{2^3 \cdot 2^2 = 2^5}$$

When we add the exponents 3 and 2 to get 5, we are adding logarithms and getting another logarithm as the result. So the base-2 logarithm of 32 (the product of 8 and 4) is the sum of the base-2 logarithms of 8 and 4:

$$\log_2(8 \cdot 4) = \log_2(8) + \log_2(4)$$

Exponential and Logarithmic Functions

This example suggests the **product rule for logarithms.**

Product Rule for Logarithms

For $M > 0$ and $N > 0$,

$$\log_a(MN) = \log_a(M) + \log_a(N).$$

PROOF

$$a^{\log_a M + \log_a N} = a^{\log_a M} \cdot a^{\log_a N} \quad \text{Product rule for exponents}$$

$$= M \cdot N \quad\quad\quad \text{Inverse rule}$$

Now by the definition of logarithm $(a^x = y \Leftrightarrow \log_a y = x)$ we have

$$\log_a(MN) = \log_a(M) + \log_a(N). \quad ■$$

The product rule for logarithms says that *the logarithm of a product of two numbers is equal to the sum of their logarithms*, provided that all of the logarithms are defined and all have the same base. There is no rule about the logarithm of a sum, and the logarithm of a sum is generally *not* equal to the sum of the logarithms. For example, $\log_2(8 + 8) \neq \log_2(8) + \log_2(8)$ because $\log_2(8 + 8) = 4$ while $\log_2(8) + \log_2(8) = 6$.

You can use a calculator to illustrate the product rule, as in Fig. 35 ▢

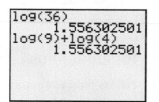

```
log(36)
       1.556302501
log(9)+log(4)
       1.556302501
```

Figure 35

EXAMPLE 2 Using the product rule for logarithms

Write each expression as a single logarithm. All variables represent positive real numbers.

a. $\log_3(x) + \log_3(6)$ **b.** $\ln(3) + \ln(x^2) + \ln(y)$

Solution

a. By the product rule for logarithms, $\log_3(x) + \log_3(6) = \log_3(6x)$.
b. By the product rule for logarithms, $\ln(3) + \ln(x^2) + \ln(y) = \ln(3x^2y)$.

▶**TRY THIS.** Write $\log(x) + \log(y)$ as a single logarithm. ■

The Logarithm of a Quotient

By the quotient rule for exponents, we subtract the exponents when dividing exponential expressions having the same base. To find a corresponding rule for logarithms, examine the equation $2^5/2^2 = 2^3$. Notice that the exponents 5, 2, and 3 are the base-2 logarithms of 32, 4, and 8, respectively:

$$\overset{\log_2(32)}{\underset{\log_2(4)}{\frac{2^5}{2^2}}} = \overset{\log_2(8)}{2^3}$$

When we subtract the exponents 5 and 2 to get 3, we are subtracting logarithms and getting another logarithm as the result. So the base-2 logarithm of 8 (the quotient of 32 and 4) is the difference of the base-2 logarithms of 32 and 4:

$$\log_2\left(\frac{32}{4}\right) = \log_2(32) - \log_2(4)$$

This example suggests the **quotient rule for logarithms.**

Quotient Rule for Logarithms

For $M > 0$ and $N > 0$,

$$\log_a\left(\frac{M}{N}\right) = \log_a(M) - \log_a(N).$$

```
ln(7/9)
       -.2513144283
ln(7)-ln(9)
       -.2513144283
```

Figure 36

The quotient rule for logarithms says that *the logarithm of a quotient of two numbers is equal to the difference of their logarithms*, provided that all logarithms are defined and all have the same base. (The proof of the quotient rule is similar to that of the product rule and so it is left as an exercise.) Note that the quotient rule does not apply to division of logarithms. For example,

$$\frac{\log_2(32)}{\log_2(4)} \neq \log_2(32) - \log_2(4),$$

because $\log_2(32)/\log_2(4) = 5/2$, while $\log_2(32) - \log_2(4) = 3$.

You can use a calculator to illustrate the quotient rule, as shown in Fig. 36. □

EXAMPLE 3 Using the quotient rule for logarithms

Write each expression as a single logarithm. All variables represent positive real numbers.

a. $\log_3(24) - \log_3(4)$ **b.** $\ln(x^6) - \ln(x^2)$

Solution

a. By the quotient rule, $\log_3(24) - \log_3(4) = \log_3(24/4) = \log_3(6)$.

b. $\ln(x^6) - \ln(x^2) = \ln\left(\dfrac{x^6}{x^2}\right)$ By the quotient rule for logarithms

$$= \ln(x^4) \qquad \text{By the quotient rule for exponents}$$

▶**TRY THIS.** Write $\log(5x) - \log(5)$ as a single logarithm. ∎

The Logarithm of a Power

By the power rule for exponents, we multiply the exponents when finding a power of an exponential expression. For example, $(2^3)^2 = 2^6$. Notice that the exponents 3 and 6 are the base-2 logarithms of 8 and 64, respectively.

$$\overset{\displaystyle \log_2(8) \quad \log_2(64)}{\underset{\downarrow \qquad\qquad \downarrow}{(2^3)^2 = 2^6}}$$

So the base-2 logarithm of 64 (the second power of 8) is twice the base-2 logarithm of 8:

$$\log_2(8^2) = 2 \cdot \log_2(8)$$

This example suggests the **power rule for logarithms.**

Power Rule for Logarithms

For $M > 0$ and any real number N,

$$\log_a(M^N) = N \cdot \log_a(M).$$

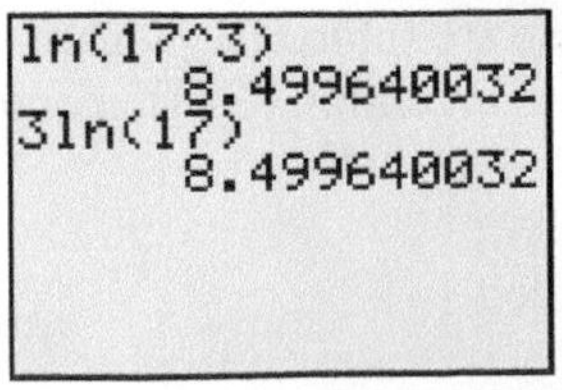

```
ln(17^3)
       8.499640032
3ln(17)
       8.499640032
```

Figure 37

The power rule for logarithms says that *the logarithm of a power of a number is equal to the power times the logarithm of the number*, provided that all logarithms are defined and have the same base. The proof is left as an exercise.

You can illustrate the power rule on a calculator, as shown in Fig. 37. □

EXAMPLE 4 Using the power rule for logarithms

Rewrite each expression in terms of $\log(3)$.

a. $\log(3^8)$ **b.** $\log(\sqrt{3})$ **c.** $\log\left(\dfrac{1}{3}\right)$

Solution

a. $\log(3^8) = 8 \cdot \log(3)$ By the power rule for logarithms

b. $\log(\sqrt{3}) = \log(3^{1/2}) = \dfrac{1}{2}\log(3)$ By the power rule for logarithms

c. $\log\left(\dfrac{1}{3}\right) = \log(3^{-1}) = -\log(3)$ By the power rule for logarithms

▶**TRY THIS.** Write $\ln(27)$ in terms of $\ln(3)$.   ■

Using the Rules

When simplifying or rewriting expressions, we often apply several rules. In the following box we list all of the available rules of logarithms.

Rules of Logarithms with Base a

If M, N, and a are positive real numbers with $a \neq 1$, and x is any real number, then

1. $\log_a(a) = 1$ **2.** $\log_a(1) = 0$
3. $\log_a(a^x) = x$ **4.** $a^{\log_a(N)} = N$
5. $\log_a(MN) = \log_a(M) + \log_a(N)$ **6.** $\log_a(M/N) = \log_a(M) - \log_a(N)$
7. $\log_a(M^x) = x \cdot \log_a(M)$ **8.** $\log_a(1/N) = -\log_a(N)$

Note that rule 1 is a special case of rule 3 with $x = 1$, rule 2 follows from the fact that $a^0 = 1$ for any nonzero base a, and rule 8 is a special case of rule 6 with $M = 1$.

The rules for logarithms with base a in the preceding box apply to all logarithms, including common logarithms (base 10) and natural logarithms (base e). Since natural logarithms are very popular, we list the rules of logarithms again for base e in the following box for easy reference.

Rules of Natural Logarithms

If M and N are positive real numbers and x is any real number, then

1. $\ln(e) = 1$ **2.** $\ln(1) = 0$
3. $\ln(e^x) = x$ **4.** $e^{\ln(N)} = N$
5. $\ln(MN) = \ln(M) + \ln(N)$ **6.** $\ln(M/N) = \ln(M) - \ln(N)$
7. $\ln(M^x) = x \cdot \ln(M)$ **8.** $\ln(1/N) = -\ln(N)$

EXAMPLE 5 Using the rules of logarithms

Rewrite each expression in terms of $\log(2)$ and $\log(3)$.

a. $\log(6)$ **b.** $\log\left(\dfrac{16}{3}\right)$ **c.** $\log\left(\dfrac{1}{3}\right)$

Solution

a. $\log(6) = \log(2 \cdot 3)$ Factor.

$\qquad = \log(2) + \log(3)$ Rule 5

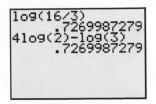

Figure 38

b. $\log\left(\dfrac{16}{3}\right) = \log(16) - \log(3)$ Rule 6

$$= \log(2^4) - \log(3) \quad \text{Write 16 as a power of 2.}$$

$$= 4 \cdot \log(2) - \log(3) \quad \text{Rule 7}$$

   You can check this answer with a calculator, as shown in Fig. 38. ☐

c. $\log\left(\dfrac{1}{3}\right) = -\log(3)$ Rule 8

▶**TRY THIS.** Write $\ln(45)$ in terms of $\ln(3)$ and $\ln(5)$. ■

Be careful to use the rules of logarithms exactly as stated. For example, the logarithm of a product is the sum of the logarithms. The logarithm of a product is generally *not* equal to the product of the logarithms. That is,

$$\log(2 \cdot 3) = \log(2) + \log(3) \quad \text{but} \quad \log(2 \cdot 3) \neq \log(2) \cdot \log(3).$$

EXAMPLE 6 Rewriting a logarithmic expression

Rewrite each expression using a sum or difference of multiples of logarithms.

a. $\ln\left(\dfrac{3x^2}{yz}\right)$ **b.** $\log_3\left(\dfrac{(x-1)^2}{z^{3/2}}\right)$

Solution

a. $\ln\left(\dfrac{3x^2}{yz}\right) = \ln(3x^2) - \ln(yz)$ Quotient rule for logarithms

$$= \ln(3) + \ln(x^2) - \big[\ln(y) + \ln(z)\big] \quad \text{Product rule for logarithms}$$

$$= \ln(3) + 2 \cdot \ln(x) - \ln(y) - \ln(z) \quad \text{Power rule for logarithms}$$

Note that $\ln(y) + \ln(z)$ must be in brackets (or parentheses) because of the subtraction symbol preceding it.

b. $\log_3\left(\dfrac{(x-1)^2}{z^{3/2}}\right) = \log_3((x-1)^2) - \log_3(z^{3/2})$ Quotient rule for logarithms

$$= 2 \cdot \log_3(x-1) - \frac{3}{2}\log_3(z) \quad \text{Power rule for logarithms}$$

▶**TRY THIS.** Write $\log\left(\dfrac{x^2}{5a}\right)$ using sums and/or differences of multiples of logarithms. ■

In Example 7 we use the rules "in reverse" of the way we did in Example 6.

EXAMPLE 7 Rewriting as a single logarithm

Rewrite each expression as a single logarithm.

a. $\ln(x-1) + \ln(3) - 3 \cdot \ln(x)$ **b.** $\dfrac{1}{2}\log(y) - \dfrac{1}{3}\log(z)$

Solution

a. Use the product rule, the power rule, and then the quotient rule for logarithms:

$$\ln(x-1) + \ln(3) - 3 \cdot \ln(x) = \ln[3(x-1)] - \ln(x^3)$$

$$= \ln[3x - 3] - \ln(x^3)$$

$$= \ln\left(\frac{3x-3}{x^3}\right)$$

b. $\dfrac{1}{2}\log(y) - \dfrac{1}{3}\log(z) = \log(y^{1/2}) - \log(z^{1/3})$

$$= \log(\sqrt{y}) - \log(\sqrt[3]{z})$$

$$= \log\!\left(\frac{\sqrt{y}}{\sqrt[3]{z}}\right)$$

▶**TRY THIS.** Write $\ln(x) - \ln(y) - 2 \cdot \ln(z)$ as a single logarithm. ∎

The rules for logarithms correspond to the rules for exponents because *logarithms are exponents*. The following table shows the rules side by side.

	Exponent Rule	**Logarithm Rule**
Product Rule	$a^x a^y = a^{x+y}$	$\log_a(MN) = \log_a(M) + \log_a(N)$
Quotient Rule	$\dfrac{a^x}{a^y} = a^{x-y}$	$\log_a\!\left(\frac{M}{N}\right) = \log_a(M) - \log_a(N)$
Power Rule	$(a^x)^y = a^{xy}$	$\log_a(M^N) = N \cdot \log_a(M)$
Zero Exponent	$a^0 = 1$	$\log_a(1) = 0$

The Base-Change Formula

The exact solution to an exponential equation is often expressed in terms of logarithms. For example, the exact solution to $(1.03)^x = 5$ is $x = \log_{1.03}(5)$. But how do we calculate $\log_{1.03}(5)$? The next example shows how to find a rational approximation for $\log_{1.03}(5)$ using rules of logarithms. In this example we also introduce a new idea in solving equations, *taking the logarithm of each side*. The base-a logarithms of two equal quantities are equal because logarithms are functions.

EXAMPLE 8 A rational approximation for a logarithm

Find an approximate rational solution to $(1.03)^x = 5$. Round to four decimal places.

Solution

Take the logarithm of each side using one of the bases available on a calculator.

$$(1.03)^x = 5$$

$$\log((1.03)^x) = \log(5) \qquad \text{Take the logarithm of each side.}$$

$$x \cdot \log(1.03) = \log(5) \qquad \text{Power rule for logarithms}$$

$$x = \frac{\log(5)}{\log(1.03)} \qquad \text{Divide each side by } \log(1.03).$$

$$\approx 54.4487$$

Divide the logarithms and check with a calculator, as shown in Fig. 39.

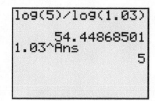

```
log(5)/log(1.03)
          54.44868501
1.03^Ans
                   5
```

Figure 39

▶**TRY THIS.** Solve $5.44^x = 2.3$. Round to four decimal places. ∎

The solution to the equation of Example 8 is a base-1.03 logarithm, but we obtained a rational approximation for it using base-10 logarithms. We can use the procedure of Example 8 to write a base-a logarithm in terms of a base-b logarithm for any bases a and b:

$$a^x = M \qquad \text{Equivalent equation: } x = \log_a(M)$$

$$\log_b(a^x) = \log_b(M) \qquad \text{Take the base-}b\text{ logarithm of each side.}$$

$$x \cdot \log_b(a) = \log_b(M) \qquad \text{Power rule for logarithms}$$

$$x = \frac{\log_b(M)}{\log_b(a)} \qquad \text{Divide each side by } \log_b(a).$$

Since $x = \log_a(M)$, we have the following **base-change formula.**

Base-Change Formula

If $a > 0, b > 0, a \neq 1, b \neq 1$, and $M > 0$, then

$$\log_a(M) = \frac{\log_b(M)}{\log_b(a)}.$$

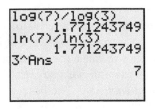

Figure 40

The base-change formula says that the logarithm of a number in one base is equal to the logarithm of the number in the new base divided by the logarithm of the old base. Using this formula, a logarithm such as $\log_3(7)$ can be easily found with a calculator. Let $a = 3$, $b = 10$, and $M = 7$ in the formula to get

$$\log_3(7) = \frac{\log(7)}{\log(3)} \approx 1.7712.$$

Note that you get the same value for $\log_3(7)$ using natural logarithms, as shown in Fig. 40. □

EXAMPLE 9 Using the base-change formula with compound interest

If \$2500 is invested at 6% compounded daily, then how long (to the nearest day) would it take for the investment to double in value?

Solution

We want the number of years for \$2500 to grow to \$5000 at 6% compounded daily. Use $P = \$2500$, $A = \$5000$, $n = 365$, and $r = 0.06$ in the formula for compound interest:

$$A = P\left(1 + \frac{r}{n}\right)^{nt}$$

$$5000 = 2500\left(1 + \frac{0.06}{365}\right)^{365t}$$

$$2 = \left(1 + \frac{0.06}{365}\right)^{365t} \qquad \text{Divide by 2500 to get the form } y = a^x.$$

$$2 \approx (1.000164384)^{365t} \qquad \text{Approximate the base with a decimal number.}$$

$$365t \approx \log_{1.000164384}(2) \qquad \text{Definition of logarithm}$$

$$t \approx \frac{1}{365} \cdot \frac{\ln(2)}{\ln(1.000164384)} \qquad \text{Base-change formula (Use either ln or log.)}$$

$$\approx 11.553 \text{ years}$$

The investment of \$2500 will double in about 11 years, 202 days.

▶**TRY THIS.** How long (to the nearest day) does it take for \$100 to grow to \$400 at 5% compounded daily? ∎

Note that Example 9 can also be solved by taking the log (or ln) of each side and applying the power rule for logarithms.

$$\log(2) = \log((1 + 0.06/365)^{365t})$$

$$\log(2) = 365t \cdot \log(1 + 0.06/365)$$

$$\frac{\log(2)}{365 \cdot \log(1 + 0.06/365)} = t$$

$$11.553 \approx t$$

Finding the Rate

If a variable is a function of time, we are often interested in finding the rate of growth or decay. In the continuous model, $y = ae^{rt}$, the rate r appears as an exponent. If we know the values of the other variables, we find the rate by solving for r using natural logarithms. If $y = ab^t$ is used instead of $y = ae^{rt}$, the rate does not appear in the formula. However, we can write $y = ab^t$ as $y = ae^{\ln(b) \cdot t}$, because $b = e^{\ln(b)}$. Comparing $e^{\ln(b) \cdot t}$ to e^{rt}, we see that the rate is $\ln(b)$.

In the case of interest compounded periodically, the growth is not continuous and we use the formula $A = P(1 + r/n)^{nt}$. Because the rate appears in the base, it can be found without using logarithms, as shown in the next example.

> **EXAMPLE 10** Finding the rate with interest compounded periodically

For what annual percentage rate would \$1000 grow to \$3500 in 20 years compounded monthly?

Solution

Use $A = 3500$, $P = 1000$, $n = 12$, and $t = 20$ in the compound interest formula.

$$A = P\left(1 + \frac{r}{n}\right)^{nt}$$

$$3500 = 1000\left(1 + \frac{r}{12}\right)^{240}$$

$$3.5 = \left(1 + \frac{r}{12}\right)^{240} \qquad \text{Divide each side by 1000.}$$

Since 240 is even, there is a positive and a negative 240th root of 3.5. Ignore the negative root in this application because it gives a negative interest rate.

$$1 + \frac{r}{12} = (3.5)^{1/240} \qquad \text{Logarithms are not needed because the exponent is a constant.}$$

$$\frac{r}{12} = (3.5)^{1/240} - 1$$

$$r = 12((3.5)^{1/240} - 1)$$

$$\approx 0.063$$

If \$1000 earns approximately 6.3% compounded monthly, then it will grow to \$3500 in 20 years.

▶**TRY THIS.** For what annual rate compounded daily would \$100 grow to \$300 in 20 years? ∎

FOR thought... True or False? Explain.

1. $\dfrac{\log(8)}{\log(3)} = \log(8) - \log(3)$

2. $\ln(\sqrt{3}) = \dfrac{\ln(3)}{2}$

3. $\dfrac{\log_{19}(8)}{\log_{19}(2)} = \log_3(27)$

4. $\dfrac{\log_2(7)}{\log_2(5)} = \dfrac{\log_3(7)}{\log_3(5)}$

5. $e^{\ln(x)} = x$ for any real number x.

6. The equations $\log(x - 2) = 4$ and $\log(x) - \log(2) = 4$ are equivalent.

7. The equations $x + 1 = 2x + 3$ and $\log(x + 1) = \log(2x + 3)$ are equivalent.

8. $\ln(e^x) = x$ for any real number x.

9. If $30 = x^{50}$, then x is between 1 and 2.

10. If $20 = a^4$, then $\ln(a) = \frac{1}{4}\ln(20)$.

EXERCISES 3

Fill in the blank.

1. The logarithm of a product of two numbers is equal to the _____ of their logarithms.

2. The logarithm of a(n) _____ of two numbers is equal to the difference of their logarithms.

3. The logarithm of a power of a number is equal to the _____ times the logarithm of the number.

4. According to the _____ formula, the base-a logarithm of a number is equal to the base-b logarithm of the number divided by $\log_b(a)$.

Simplify each expression.

5. $e^{\ln(\sqrt{y})}$

6. $10^{\log(3x+1)}$

7. $\log(10^{y+1})$

8. $\ln(e^{2k})$

9. $7^{\log_7(999)}$

10. $\log_4(2^{300})$

Rewrite each expression as a single logarithm.

11. $\log(5) + \log(3)$

12. $\ln(6) + \ln(2)$

13. $\log_2(x - 1) + \log_2(x)$

14. $\log_3(x + 2) + \log_3(x - 1)$

15. $\log_4(12) - \log_4(2)$

16. $\log_2(25) - \log_2(5)$

17. $\ln(x^8) - \ln(x^3)$

18. $\log(x^2 - 4) - \log(x - 2)$

Rewrite each expression as a sum or difference of logarithms.

19. $\log_2(3x)$

20. $\log_3(xy)$

21. $\log\left(\dfrac{x}{2}\right)$

22. $\log\left(\dfrac{a}{b}\right)$

23. $\log(x^2 - 1)$

24. $\log(a^2 - 9)$

25. $\ln\left(\dfrac{x - 1}{x}\right)$

26. $\ln\left(\dfrac{a + b}{b}\right)$

Rewrite each expression in terms of $\log_a(5)$.

27. $\log_a(5^3)$

28. $\log_a(25)$

29. $\log_a(\sqrt{5})$

30. $\log_a(\sqrt[3]{5})$

31. $\log_a\left(\dfrac{1}{5}\right)$

32. $\log_a\left(\dfrac{1}{125}\right)$

Rewrite each expression in terms of $\log_a(2)$ and $\log_a(5)$.

33. $\log_a(10)$

34. $\log_a(0.4)$

35. $\log_a(2.5)$

36. $\log_a(250)$

37. $\log_a(\sqrt{20})$

38. $\log_a(0.0005)$

39. $\log_a\left(\dfrac{4}{25}\right)$

40. $\log_a(0.1)$

Rewrite each expression as a sum or difference of multiples of logarithms.

41. $\log_3(5x)$

42. $\log_2(xyz)$

43. $\log_2\left(\dfrac{5}{2y}\right)$

44. $\log\left(\dfrac{4a}{3b}\right)$

45. $\log(3\sqrt{x})$

46. $\ln(\sqrt{x/4})$

47. $\log(3 \cdot 2^{x-1})$

48. $\ln\left(\dfrac{5^{-x}}{2}\right)$

49. $\ln\left(\dfrac{\sqrt[3]{xy}}{t^{4/3}}\right)$

50. $\log\left(\dfrac{3x^2}{(ab)^{2/3}}\right)$

51. $\ln\left(\dfrac{6\sqrt{x-1}}{5x^3}\right)$

52. $\log_4\left(\dfrac{3x\sqrt{y}}{\sqrt[3]{x-1}}\right)$

Rewrite each expression as a single logarithm.

53. $\log_2(5) + 3 \cdot \log_2(x)$

54. $\log(x) + 5 \cdot \log(x)$

55. $\log_7(x^5) - 4 \cdot \log_7(x^2)$

56. $\dfrac{1}{3}\ln(6) - \dfrac{1}{3}\ln(2)$

57. $\log(2) + \log(x) + \log(y) - \log(z)$

58. $\ln(2) + \ln(3) + \ln(5) - \ln(7)$

59. $\dfrac{1}{2}\log(x) - \log(y) + \log(z) - \dfrac{1}{3}\log(w)$

60. $\dfrac{5}{6}\log_2(x) + \dfrac{2}{3}\log_2(y) - \dfrac{1}{2}\log_2(x) - \log_2(y)$

61. $3 \cdot \log_4(x^2) - 4 \cdot \log_4(x^{-3}) + 2 \cdot \log_4(x)$

62. $\dfrac{1}{2}\left[\log(x) + \log(y)\right] - \log(z)$

Find an approximate rational solution to each equation. Round answers to four decimal places.

63. $2^x = 9$

64. $3^x = 12$

65. $(0.56)^x = 8$

66. $(0.23)^x = 18.4$

67. $(1.06)^x = 2$

68. $(1.09)^x = 3$

69. $(0.73)^x = 0.5$

70. $(0.62)^x = 0.25$

Use a calculator and the base-change formula to find each logarithm to four decimal places.

71. $\log_4(9)$

72. $\log_3(4.78)$

73. $\log_{9.1}(2.3)$

74. $\log_{1.2}(13.7)$

75. $\log_{1/2}(12)$

76. $\log_{1.05}(3.66)$

Solve each equation. Round answers to four decimal places.

77. $(1.02)^{4t} = 3$

78. $(1.025)^{12t} = 3$

79. $(1.0001)^{365t} = 3.5$

80. $(1.00012)^{365t} = 2.4$

81. $(1 + r)^3 = 2.3$

82. $\left(1 + \dfrac{r}{4}\right)^{20} = 3$

83. $2\left(1 + \dfrac{r}{12}\right)^{360} = 8.4$

84. $5\left(1 + \dfrac{r}{360}\right)^{720} = 12$

Solve each equation. Round answers to four decimal places.

85. $\log_x(33.4) = 5$

86. $\log_x(12.33) = 2.3$

87. $\log_x(0.546) = -1.3$

88. $\log_x(0.915) = -3.2$

For Exercises 89–94 find the time or rate required for each investment given in the table to grow to the specified amount. The letter W represents an unknown principal.

	Principal	Ending Balance	Rate	Compounded	Time
89.	$800	$2000	8%	Daily	?
90.	$10,000	$1,000,000	7.75%	Annually	?
91.	$W	$3W	10%	Quarterly	?
92.	$W	$2W	12%	Monthly	?
93.	$500	$2000	?	Annually	25 yr
94.	$1000	$2500	?	Monthly	8 yr

95. *Ben's Gift to Boston* Ben Franklin's gift of $4000 to Boston grew to $4.5 million in 200 years. At what interest rate compounded annually would this growth occur?

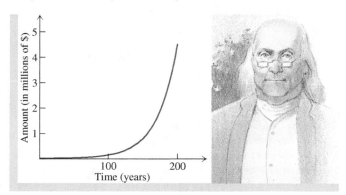

Figure for Exercise 95

96. *Ben's Gift to Philadelphia* Ben Franklin's gift of $4000 to Philadelphia grew to $2 million in 200 years. At what interest rate compounded monthly would this growth occur?

97. *Cheap Cars* One of the cheapest new cars you could buy in 1970 was the Ford Maverick at $1995. In 2009 the cheapest new car was probably the Kia Rio at $10,890. Use the formula for compound interest to find the annual growth rate (to the nearest tenth of a percent) for the price of the cheapest new car.

98. *Price of Milk* In 1960 a gallon of milk was around $0.49. In 2009 a gallon of milk was around $4.59. Use the formula for compound interest to find the annual growth rate (to the nearest tenth of a percent) for the price of a gallon to milk.

99. *Richter Scale* The common logarithm is used to measure the intensity of an earthquake on the Richter scale. The Richter scale rating of an earthquake of intensity I is given by $\log(I) - \log(I_0)$, where I_0 is the intensity of a small "benchmark" earthquake. Write the Richter scale rating as a single logarithm. What is the Richter scale rating of an earthquake for which $I = 1000 \cdot I_0$?

100. *Colombian Earthquake of 1906* At 8.6 on the Richter scale, the Colombian earthquake of January 31, 1906, was one of the strongest earthquakes on record. Use the formula from Exercise 99 to write I as a multiple of I_0 for this earthquake.

101. *Time for Growth* The time in years for a population of size P_0 to grow to size P at the annual growth rate r is given by $t = \ln((P/P_0)^{1/r})$. Use the rules of logarithms to express t in terms of $\ln(P)$ and $\ln(P_0)$.

102. *Formula for pH* The pH of a solution is given by $pH = \log(1/H^+)$, where H^+ is the hydrogen ion concentration of the solution. Use the rules of logarithms to express the pH in terms of $\log(H^+)$.

103. *Rollover Time* The probability that a \$1 ticket does not win the Louisiana Lottery is $\frac{7,059,051}{7,059,052}$. The probability p that n independently sold tickets are all losers and the lottery rolls over is given by

$$p = \left(\frac{7,059,051}{7,059,052}\right)^n.$$

   a. As n increases is p increasing or decreasing?

   b. For what number of tickets sold is the probability of a rollover greater than 50%?

104. *Economic Impact* An economist estimates that 75% of the money spent in Chattanooga is respent in four days on the average in Chattanooga. So if P dollars are spent, then the economic impact I in dollars after n respendings is given by

$$I = P(0.75)^n.$$

When $I < 0.02P$, then P no longer has an impact on the economy. If the Telephone Psychics Convention brings \$1.3 million to the city, then in how many days will that money no longer have an impact on the city?

105. *Marginal Revenue* The revenue in dollars from the sale of x items is given by the function $R(x) = 500 \cdot \log(x + 1)$. The marginal revenue function $MR(x)$ is the difference quotient for $R(x)$ when $h = 1$. Find $MR(x)$ and write it as a single logarithm. What happens to the marginal revenue as x gets larger and larger?

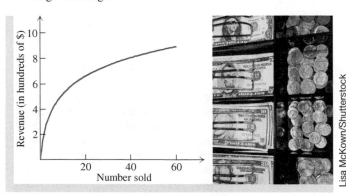

Figure for Exercise 105

106. *Human Memory Model* A class of college algebra students was given a test on college algebra concepts every month for one year after completing a college algebra course. The mean score for the class t months after completing the course can be modeled by the function $m = \ln\left[e^{80}/(t + 1)^7\right]$ for $0 \le t \le 12$. Find the mean score of the class for $t = 0, 5,$ and 12. Use the rules of logarithms to rewrite the function.

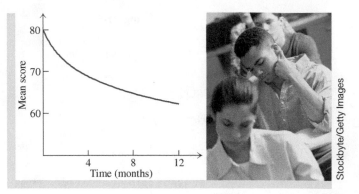

Figure for Exercise 106

107. *Computers per Capita* The number of personal computers per 1000 people in the United States from 1990 through 2010 is given in the accompanying table (*Consumer Industry Almanac,* www.c-i-a.com).

   a. Use exponential regression on a graphing calculator to find the best-fitting curve of the form $y = a \cdot b^x$, where $x = 0$ corresponds to 1990.

   b. Write your equation in the form $y = ae^{cx}$.

   c. Assuming that the number of computers per 1000 people is growing continuously, what is the annual percentage rate?

   d. In what year will the number of computers per 1000 people reach 1500?

   e. Judging from the graph of the data and the curve, does the exponential model look like a good model?

Table for Exercise 107

Year	Computers per 1000
1990	192
1995	321
2000	628
2005	778
2010	932

Digital Vision/Getty Images

108. *Crude Oil Prices* The average cost in dollars of a barrel of domestic crude oil for each year from 2000 to 2008 is shown in the accompanying table (www.inflationdata.com).

Table for Exercise 108

Year	Cost per Barrel
2000	27
2001	23
2002	23
2003	28
2004	38
2005	50
2006	58
2007	64
2008	130

IRC/Shutterstock

a. Use exponential regression on a graphing calculator to find the best-fitting curve of the form $y = a \cdot b^x$, where $x = 0$ corresponds to 2000.

b. Use the exponential model from part (a) to predict the average price of a barrel of domestic crude in 2015.

FOR WRITING/DISCUSSION

109. *Power Rule* Applying the power rule to $y = \log(x^2)$ yields $y = 2 \cdot \log(x)$, but are these functions the same? What is the domain of each function? Graph the functions. Find another example of a function whose domain changes after application of a rule for logarithms.

110. *Quotient Rule* Write a proof for the quotient rule for logarithms that is similar to the proof given in the text for the product rule for logarithms.

111. *Cooperative Learning* Work in a small group to write a proof for the power rule for logarithms.

112. *Finding Relationships* Graph each of the following pairs of functions on the same screen of a graphing calculator. (Use the base-change formula to graph with bases other than 10 or e.) Explain how the functions in each pair are related.
a. $y_1 = \log_3(\sqrt{3}x), y_2 = 0.5 + \log_3(x)$

b. $y_1 = \log_2(1/x), y_2 = -\log_2(x)$

c. $y_1 = 3^{x-1}, y_2 = \log_3(x) + 1$

d. $y_1 = 3 + 2^{x-4}, y_2 = \log_2(x - 3) + 4$

▶ RETHINKING

113. Determine the domain and range of the function $y = \log_2(x - 1)$.

114. Solve $\log_2(x - 3) = 8$.

115. Find the amount when $10,000 is invested for 5 years and 3 months at 4.3% compounded continuously.

116. Find the amount when $10,000 is invested for 5 years and 3 months at 4.3% compounded daily.

117. Solve $\frac{3}{8}(x - 5) = \frac{3}{2}x + \frac{5}{6}$.

118. Evaluate $-4^{3/2}$ and $4^{-3/2}$.

THINKING OUTSIDE THE BOX XXXIII

Unit Fractions The fractions $\frac{1}{2}, \frac{1}{3}, \frac{1}{4}, \frac{1}{5}, \frac{1}{6}, \frac{1}{7}$, etc., are called *unit fractions*. Some rational numbers can be expressed as sums of unit fractions. For example,

$$\frac{4}{7} = \frac{1}{2} + \frac{1}{14} \quad \text{and} \quad \frac{11}{18} = \frac{1}{3} + \frac{1}{6} + \frac{1}{9}.$$

Write each of the following fractions as a sum of unit fractions using the fewest number of unit fractions, and keep the total of all of the denominators in the unit fractions as small as possible.

a. $\frac{6}{23}$ **b.** $\frac{14}{15}$ **c.** $\frac{7}{11}$

➤ POP QUIZ 3

1. Write $\log(9) + \log(3)$ as a single logarithm.

2. Write $\log(9) - \log(3)$ as a single logarithm.

3. Write $3\ln(x) + \ln(y)$ as a single logarithm.

4. Write $\ln(5x)$ as a sum of logarithms.

5. Write $\ln(\sqrt{18})$ in terms of $\ln(2)$ and $\ln(3)$.

Solve each equation. Round answers to four decimal places.

6. $3^x = 11$ **2.** $\log_x(22.5) = 3$

►LINKING
concepts... For Individual or Group Explorations

Niderlander/Shutterstock

A Logarithmic Model for Water Quality

The United States Geological Survey measures the quality of a water sample by using the diversity index d, given by

$$d = -[p_1 \cdot \log_2(p_1) + p_2 \cdot \log_2(p_2) + \cdots + p_n \cdot \log_2(p_n)],$$

where n is the number of different taxons (biological classifications) represented in the sample and p_1 through p_n are the percentages of organisms in each of the n taxons. For example, if 10% of the organisms in a water sample are E. coli and 90% are fecal coliform, then

$$d = -[0.1 \cdot \log_2(0.1) + 0.9 \cdot \log_2(0.9)] \approx 0.5.$$

a) Find the value of d when the only organism found in a sample is *E. coli* bacteria.

b) Let $n = 3$ in the formula and write the diversity index as a single logarithm.

c) If a water sample is found to contain 20% of its organisms of one type, 30% of another type, and 50% of a third type, then what is the diversity index for the water sample?

d) If the organisms in a water sample are equally distributed among 100 different taxons, then what is the diversity index?

e) If 99% of the organisms in a water sample are from one taxon and the other 1% are equally distributed among 99 other taxons, then what is the diversity index?

f) The diversity index can be found for populations other than organisms in a water sample. Find the diversity index for the dogs in the movie *101 Dalmatians* (cartoon version).

g) Identify a population of your choice and different classifications within the population. (For example, the trees on campus can be classified as pine, maple, spruce, or elm.) Gather real data and calculate the diversity index for your population.

4 More Equations and Applications

The rules of Section 3 combined with the techniques that we have already used in Sections 1 and 2 allow us to solve several new types of equations involving exponents and logarithms.

Logarithmic Equations

An equation involving a single logarithm can usually be solved by using the definition of logarithm as we did in Section 2.

EXAMPLE 1 An equation involving a single logarithm

Solve the equation $\log(x - 3) = 4$.

Solution

Write the equivalent equation using the definition of logarithm:

$$\log(x - 3) = 4 \qquad \text{Original equation } \log_a(y) = x \Leftrightarrow y = a^x$$

$$x - 3 = 10^4$$

$$x = 10{,}003$$

Check this number in the original equation. The solution is 10,003.

▶**TRY THIS.** Solve $\log(2x + 1) = 3$. ∎

When more than one logarithm is present, we can use the one-to-one property as in Section 2 or use the other rules of logarithms to combine logarithms.

> **EXAMPLE 2** Equations involving more than one logarithm

Solve each equation.

a. $\log_2(x) + \log_2(x + 2) = \log_2(6x + 1)$ **b.** $\log(x) - \log(x - 1) = 2$
c. $2 \cdot \ln(x) = \ln(x + 3) + \ln(x - 1)$

Solution

a. Since the sum of two logarithms is equal to the logarithm of a product, we can rewrite the left-hand side of the equation.

$$\log_2(x) + \log_2(x + 2) = \log_2(6x + 1)$$

$$\log_2(x(x + 2)) = \log_2(6x + 1) \qquad \text{Product rule for logarithms}$$

$$x^2 + 2x = 6x + 1 \qquad \text{One-to-one property of logarithms}$$

$$x^2 - 4x - 1 = 0 \qquad \text{Solve quadratic equation.}$$

$$x = \frac{4 \pm \sqrt{16 - 4(-1)}}{2} = 2 \pm \sqrt{5}$$

Since $2 - \sqrt{5}$ is a negative number, $\log_2(2 - \sqrt{5})$ is undefined and $2 - \sqrt{5}$ is not a solution. The only solution to the equation is $2 + \sqrt{5}$. Check this solution by using a calculator and the base-change formula.

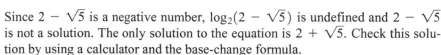 The check is shown with a graphing calculator in Fig. 41. ▢

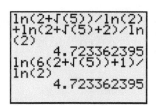

Figure 41

b. Since the difference of two logarithms is equal to the logarithm of a quotient, we can rewrite the left-hand side of the equation:

$$\log(x) - \log(x - 1) = 2$$

$$\log\left(\frac{x}{x - 1}\right) = 2 \qquad \text{Quotient rule for logarithms}$$

$$\frac{x}{x - 1} = 10^2 \qquad \text{Definition of logarithm}$$

$$x = 100x - 100 \qquad \text{Solve for } x.$$

$$-99x = -100$$

$$x = \frac{100}{99}$$

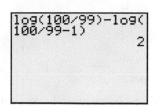

Figure 42

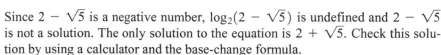 Check 100/99 in the original equation, as shown in Fig. 42. ▢

c. $2 \cdot \ln(x) = \ln(x + 3) + \ln(x - 1)$

$$\ln(x^2) = \ln(x^2 + 2x - 3) \qquad \text{Power rule, product rule}$$

$$x^2 = x^2 + 2x - 3 \qquad \text{One-to-one property}$$

$$0 = 2x - 3$$

$$\frac{3}{2} = x$$

Use a calculator to check 33/22 in the original equation. The only solution to the equation is 3/2.

▶**TRY THIS.** Solve $\log(x - 1) + \log(3) = \log(x) - \log(4)$. ∎

All solutions to logarithmic and exponential equations should be checked in the original equation, because extraneous roots can occur, as in Example 2(a). Use your calculator to check every solution and you will increase your proficiency with your calculator.

Exponential Equations

An exponential equation with a single exponential expression can usually be solved by using the definition of logarithm, as in Section 2.

> **EXAMPLE 3** Equations involving a single exponential expression

Solve the equation $(1.02)^{4t-1} = 5$.

Solution

Write an equivalent equation, using the definition of logarithm.

$$4t - 1 = \log_{1.02}(5)$$

$$t = \frac{1 + \log_{1.02}(5)}{4} \qquad \text{The exact solution}$$

$$= \frac{1 + \dfrac{\ln(5)}{\ln(1.02)}}{4} \qquad \text{Base-change formula}$$

$$\approx 20.5685$$

The approximate solution is 20.5685.

Check with a graphing calculator, as shown in Fig. 43.

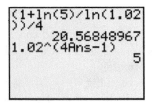

Figure 43

▶**TRY THIS.** Solve $(1.05)^{3t} = 8$. ∎

Note that Example 3 can also be solved by taking the ln (or log) of each side and applying the power rule for logarithms:

$$\ln(1.02^{4t-1}) = \ln(5)$$

$$(4t - 1)\ln(1.02) = \ln(5)$$

$$4t \cdot \ln(1.02) - \ln(1.02) = \ln(5)$$

$$t = \frac{\ln(5) + \ln(1.02)}{4 \cdot \ln(1.02)} \approx 20.5685$$

If an equation has an exponential expression on each side, as in Example 4, then it is best to take the log or ln of each side to solve it.

EXAMPLE 4 Equations involving two exponential expressions

Find the exact and approximate solutions to each equation.

a. $6^x = 7^{x-1}$ **b.** $3^{2x-1} = 5^x$

Solution

a.
$$\log(6^x) = \log(7^{x-1}) \qquad \text{Take the log of each side.}$$
$$x \cdot \log(6) = (x - 1)\log(7) \qquad \text{Power rule for logarithms}$$
$$x \cdot \log(6) = x \cdot \log(7) - \log(7) \qquad \text{Distributive property}$$
$$x \cdot \log(6) - x \cdot \log(7) = -\log(7)$$
$$x(\log(6) - \log(7)) = -\log(7) \qquad \text{Factor.}$$
$$x = \frac{-\log(7)}{\log(6/7)} \qquad \log(6) - \log(7) = \log(6/7)$$
$$x \approx 12.6234$$

b.
$$\ln(3^{2x-1}) = \ln(5^x) \quad \text{Take the natural logarithm of each side.}$$
$$(2x - 1)\ln(3) = x \cdot \ln(5) \quad \text{Power rule for logarithms}$$
$$2x \cdot \ln(3) - \ln(3) = x \cdot \ln(5) \quad \text{Distributive property}$$
$$2x \cdot \ln(3) - x \cdot \ln(5) = \ln(3)$$
$$x[2 \cdot \ln(3) - \ln(5)] = \ln(3)$$
$$x = \frac{\ln(3)}{2 \cdot \ln(3) - \ln(5)} \quad \text{Exact solution}$$
$$\approx 1.8691$$

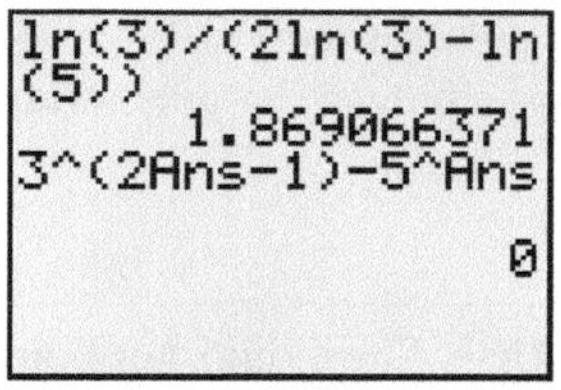

```
ln(3)/(2ln(3)-ln
(5))
         1.869066371
3^(2Ans-1)-5^Ans
                   0
```

Figure 44

⬚ Check the solution in the original equation, as shown in Fig. 44.

▶**TRY THIS.** Solve $3^{x-1} = 2^x$. ∎

The technique of Example 4 can be used on any equation of the form $a^M = b^N$. Take the natural logarithm of each side and apply the power rule, to get an equation of the form $M \cdot \ln(a) = N \cdot \ln(b)$. This last equation usually has no exponents and is relatively easy to solve.

Strategy for Solving Equations

We solved equations involving exponential and logarithmic functions in Sections 1 through 4. There is no formula that will solve every exponential or logarithmic equation, but the following strategy will help you solve exponential and logarithmic equations.

STRATEGY

Solving Exponential and Logarithmic Equations

1. If the equation involves a single logarithm or a single exponential expression, then use the definition of logarithm: $y = \log_a(x)$ if and only if $a^y = x$.
2. Use the one-to-one properties when applicable:
   a) if $a^M = a^N$, then $M = N$.
   b) if $\log_a(M) = \log_a(N)$, then $M = N$.

3. If an equation has several logarithms with the same base, then combine them using the product and quotient rules:

   a) $\log_a(M) + \log_a(N) = \log_a(MN)$

   b) $\log_a(M) - \log_a(N) = \log_a(M/N)$

4. If an equation has only exponential expressions with different bases on each side, then take the natural or common logarithm of each side and use the power rule: $a^M = b^N$ is equivalent to $\ln(a^M) = \ln(b^N)$ or $M \cdot \ln(a) = N \cdot \ln(b)$.

Radioactive Dating

In Section 1, we stated that the amount A of a radioactive substance remaining after t years is given by

$$A = A_0 e^{rt},$$

where A_0 is the initial amount present and r is the annual rate of decay for that particular substance. A standard measurement of the speed at which a radioactive substance decays is its **half-life.** The half-life of a radioactive substance is the amount of time that it takes for one-half of the substance to decay. Of course, when one-half has decayed, one-half remains.

Now that we have studied logarithms, we can use the formula for radioactive decay to determine the age of an ancient object that contains a radioactive substance. One such substance is potassium-40, which is found in rocks. Once the rock is formed, the potassium-40 begins to decay. The amount of time that has passed since the formation of the rock can be determined by measuring the amount of potassium-40 that has decayed into argon-40. Dating rocks using potassium-40 is known as **potassium-argon dating.**

EXAMPLE 5 Sauropods in Utah

Our chapter opener topic was a recent dinosaur find in Utah. Since dinosaur bones are too old to contain organic material for radiocarbon dating, paleontologists estimate the age of bones like those of the sauropods found in Utah by dating volcanic debris in surrounding rock using potassium-argon dating. The half-life of potassium-40 is 1.31 billion years. If 92.4% of the original amount of potassium-40 is still present in the rock, then how old is the rock?

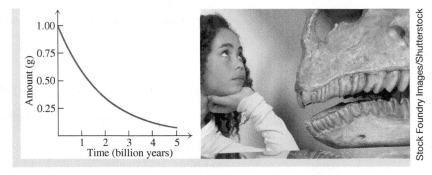

Figure 45

Stock Foundry Images/Shutterstock

Solution

The half-life is the amount of time that it takes for 1 gram to decay to 0.5 gram. Use $A_0 = 1$, $A = 0.5$, and $t = 1.31 \times 10^9$ in the formula $A = A_0 e^{rt}$ to find r.

$$0.5 = 1 \cdot e^{(1.31 \times 10^9)(r)}$$

$$(1.31 \times 10^9)(r) = \ln(0.5) \qquad \text{Definition of logarithm}$$

$$r = \frac{\ln(0.5)}{1.31 \times 10^9}$$

$$\approx -5.29 \times 10^{-10}$$

Now we can find the amount of time that it takes for 1 gram to decay to 0.924 gram. Use $r \approx -5.29 \times 10^{-10}$, $A_0 = 1$, and $A = 0.924$ in the formula.

$$0.924 = 1 \cdot e^{(-5.29 \times 10^{-10})(t)}$$

$$(-5.29 \times 10^{-10})(t) = \ln(0.924) \qquad \text{Definition of logarithm}$$

$$t = \frac{\ln(0.924)}{-5.29 \times 10^{-10}}$$

$$\approx 150 \text{ million years}$$

So the rock and the sauropods are about 150 million years old.

▶**TRY THIS.** If the half-life of a substance is 1 million years and 40% of the original amount is still present in a rock, then how old is the rock? ■

The radioactive decay model is also used to model the manner in which the human body eliminates a drug. If A_0 is the initial dose of a drug, then the amount remaining in the body at time t is given by $A = A_0 e^{rt}$ where r is the elimination rate.

EXAMPLE 6 | Drug elimination

The half-life of the antidepressant Prozac in an average man is 2 days. How long does it take for 95% of the original dose to be eliminated from a man's body?

Solution

First find the elimination rate by using the fact that the initial amount A_0 is reduced to $\frac{1}{2}A_0$ in 2 days:

$$\frac{1}{2}A_0 = A_0 e^{2r} \qquad \text{Use } A = A_0 e^{rt}.$$

$$\frac{1}{2} = e^{2r} \qquad \text{Divide each side by } A_0.$$

$$2r = \ln(1/2) \qquad \text{Definition of logarithm}$$

$$r = \frac{\ln(1/2)}{2} \approx -0.34657$$

Now find the time. When 95% of the drug is eliminated, only 5% remains. So we find the time that it takes for A_0 to be reduced to $0.05A_0$ using the elimination rate -0.34657:

$$0.05A_0 = A_0 e^{-0.34657t} \qquad \text{Use } A = A_0 e^{rt}.$$

$$0.05 = e^{-0.34657t} \qquad \text{Divide each side by } A_0.$$

$$-0.34657t = \ln(0.05) \qquad \text{Definition of logarithm}$$

$$t = \frac{\ln(0.05)}{-0.34657} \approx 8.6$$

Thus, 95% of the original dose is eliminated in about 8.6 days.

▶**TRY THIS.** In a certain woman the half-life of Prozac is 4 days. How long does it take for 99% of the original dose to be eliminated from the woman's body? ■

Newton's Model for Cooling

Newton's law of cooling states that when a warm object is placed in colder surroundings or a cold object is placed in warmer surroundings, then the difference between the two temperatures decreases in an exponential manner. If D_0 is the initial difference in temperature, then the difference D at time t is modeled by the formula

$$D = D_0 e^{kt},$$

where k is a constant that depends on the object and the surroundings. In the next example we use Newton's law of cooling to answer a question that you might have asked yourself as the appetizers were running low.

EXAMPLE 7 Using Newton's law of cooling

A turkey with a temperature of 40°F is moved to a 350° oven. After 4 hours the internal temperature of the turkey is 170°F. If the turkey is done when its temperature reaches 185°, then how much longer must it cook?

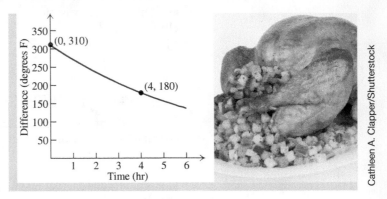

Figure 46

Solution

The initial difference of 310° (350° − 40°) has dropped to a difference of 180° (350° − 170°) after 4 hours. See Fig. 45. With this information we can find k:

$$180 = 310e^{4k}$$

$$e^{4k} = \frac{180}{310} \qquad \text{Isolate } e^{4k} \text{ by dividing by 310.}$$

$$4k = \ln(18/31) \qquad \text{Definition of logarithm: } e^x = y \Leftrightarrow x = \ln(y)$$

$$k = \frac{\ln(18/31)}{4} \approx -0.1359$$

The turkey is done when the difference in temperature between the turkey and the oven is 165° (the oven temperature 350° minus the turkey temperature 185°). Now find the time for which the difference will be 165°:

$$165 = 310e^{-0.1359t}$$

$$e^{-0.1359t} = \frac{165}{310}$$

$$-0.1359t = \ln(165/310) \qquad \text{Definition of logarithm: } e^x = y \Leftrightarrow x = \ln(y)$$

$$t = \frac{\ln(165/310)}{-0.1359} \approx 4.6404$$

The difference in temperature between the turkey and the oven will be 165° when the turkey has cooked approximately 4.6404 hours. So the turkey must cook about 0.6404 hour (38.4 minutes) longer.

▶**TRY THIS.** A cup of boiling water (212°F) is placed outside, where the temperature is 12°F. In 4 minutes the water temperature is 102°F. How much longer will it take for the water temperature to reach 82°F? ■

Paying off a Loan

If n is the number of periods per year, r is the annual percentage rate (APR), t is the number of years, and i is the interest rate per period $(i = r/n)$, then the periodic payment R that will pay off a loan of P dollars is given by

$$R = P \frac{i}{1 - (1 + i)^{-nt}}.$$

The process of paying off a loan using this formula for R is called **amortization.** Homeowners are often interested in how long it will take to pay off an existing loan if they increase the monthly payment. We can answer that question by using logarithms to solve the formula for t.

EXAMPLE 8 Finding the time

A couple still owes $90,000 on a house that is financed at 8% annual percentage rate compounded monthly. If they start paying $1200 per month, when will the loan be paid off?

Solution

Use $R = 1200$, $P = 90,000$, $n = 12$, and $i = 0.08/12$ in the formula for the monthly payment:

$$1200 = 90,000 \frac{0.08/12}{1 - (1 + 0.08/12)^{-12t}}$$

$$1200(1 - (1 + 0.08/12)^{-12t}) = 600$$

$$1 - (1 + 0.08/12)^{-12t} = 0.5$$

$$0.5 = (1 + 0.08/12)^{-12t}$$

$$\ln(0.5) = -12t \cdot \ln(1 + 0.08/12)$$

$$\frac{\ln(0.5)}{-12 \cdot \ln(1 + 0.08/12)} = t$$

$$8.6932 \approx t$$

So in approximately 8.6932 years, or about 8 years and 8 months, the loan will be paid off.

▶**TRY THIS.** How long (to the nearest month) does it take to pay off $120,000 financed at 7.5% APR compounded monthly with payments of $2000 per month? ■

FOR thought... True or False? Explain.

1. The equation $3(1.02)^x = 21$ is equivalent to $x = \log_{1.02}(7)$.

2. If $x - x \cdot \ln(3) = 8$, then $x = \dfrac{8}{1 - \ln(3)}$.

3. The solution to $\ln(x) - \ln(x - 1) = 6$ is $1 - \sqrt{6}$.

4. If $2^{x-3} = 3^{2x+1}$, then $x - 3 = \log_2(3^{2x+1})$.

5. The exact solution to $3^x = 17$ is 2.5789.

6. The equation $\log(x) + \log(x - 3) = 1$ is equivalent to $\log(x^2 - 3x) = 1$.

7. The equation $4^x = 2^{x-1}$ is equivalent to $2x = x - 1$.

8. The equation $(1.09)^x = 2.3$ is equivalent to $x \cdot \ln(1.09) = \ln(2.3)$.

9. $\ln(2) \cdot \log(7) = \log(2) \cdot \ln(7)$

10. $\log(e) \cdot \ln(10) = 1$

EXERCISES 4

Each of these equations involves a single logarithm. Solve each equation. See the strategy for solving exponential and logarithmic equations in Example 4.

1. $\log_2(x) = 3$ **2.** $\log_3(x) = 0$

3. $\log(x + 20) = 2$ **4.** $\log(x - 6) = 1$

5. $\log(x^2 - 15) = 1$ **6.** $\log(x^2 - 5x + 16) = 1$

7. $\log_x(9) = 2$ **8.** $\log_x(16) = 4$

9. $-2 = \log_x(4)$ **10.** $-\dfrac{1}{2} = \log_x(9)$

11. $\log_x(10) = 3$ **12.** $\log_x(5) = 2$

13. $\log_8(x) = -\dfrac{2}{3}$ **14.** $\log_4(x) = -\dfrac{5}{2}$

Each of these equations involves more than one logarithm. Solve each equation. Give exact solutions.

15. $\log_2(x + 2) + \log_2(x - 2) = 5$

16. $\log_6(w - 1) + \log_6(w - 2) = 1$

17. $\log\left(\dfrac{x - 3}{2}\right) + \log\left(\dfrac{x + 2}{7}\right) = 0$

18. $\log_2\left(\dfrac{a - 2}{5}\right) + \log_2\left(\dfrac{a + 3}{10}\right) = 0$

19. $\log(x + 1) - \log(x) = 3$

20. $\log_5(x) - \log_5(x - 2) = 3$

21. $\log_4(x) - \log_4(x + 2) = 2$

22. $\log_3(x - 6) - \log_3(2x) = 4$

23. $\log(5) = 2 - \log(x)$ **24.** $\log(4) = 1 + \log(x - 1)$

25. $\ln(x) + \ln(x + 2) = \ln(8)$

26. $\log_3(x) = \log_3(2) - \log_3(x - 2)$

27. $\log(4) + \log(x) = \log(5) - \log(x)$

28. $\ln(x) - \ln(x + 1) = \ln(x + 3) - \ln(x + 5)$

29. $\log_2(x) - \log_2(3x - 1) = 0$

30. $\log_3(x) + \log_3(1/x) = 0$ **31.** $x \cdot \ln(3) = 2 - x \cdot \ln(2)$

32. $x \cdot \log(5) + x \cdot \log(7) = \log(9)$

Each of these equations involves a single exponential expression. Solve each equation. Round approximate solutions to four decimal places.

33. $2^{x-1} = 7$ **34.** $5^{3x} = 29$ **35.** $(1.09)^{4x} = 3.4$

36. $(1.04)^{2x} = 2.5$ **37.** $3^{-x} = 30$ **38.** $10^{-x+3} = 102$

39. $9 = e^{-3x^2}$ **40.** $25 = 10^{-2x}$

Each of these equations involves more than one exponential expression. Solve each equation. Round approximate solutions to four decimal places.

41. $6^x = 3^{x+1}$ **42.** $2^x = 7^{x-1}$ **43.** $e^{x+1} = 10^x$

44. $e^x = 2^{x+1}$ **45.** $2^{x-1} = 4^{3x}$ **46.** $3^{3x-4} = 9^x$

47. $6^{x+1} = 12^x$ **48.** $2^x \cdot 2^{x+1} = 4^{x^2+x}$

Solve each equation. Round approximate solutions to four decimal places.

49. $e^{-\ln(w)} = 3$ **50.** $10^{2 \cdot \log(y)} = 4$

51. $(\log(z))^2 = \log(z^2)$ **52.** $\ln(e^x) - \ln(e^6) = \ln(e^2)$

53. $4(1.02)^x = 3(1.03)^x$ **54.** $500(1.06)^x = 400(1.02)^{4x}$

55. $e^{3 \cdot \ln(x^2) - 2 \cdot \ln(x)} = \ln(e^{16})$

56. $\sqrt{\log(x) - 3} = \log(x) - 3$

57. $\left(\dfrac{1}{2}\right)^{2x-1} = \left(\dfrac{1}{4}\right)^{3x+2}$ **58.** $\left(\dfrac{2}{3}\right)^{x+1} = \left(\dfrac{9}{4}\right)^{x+2}$

Find the approximate solution to each equation by graphing an appropriate function on a graphing calculator and locating the x-intercept. Note that these equations cannot be solved by the techniques that we have learned in this chapter.

59. $2^x = 3^{x-1} + 5^{-x}$ **60.** $2^x = \log(x + 4)$

61. $\ln(x + 51) = \log(-48 - x)$ **62.** $2^x = 5 - 3^{x+1}$

63. $x^2 = 2^x$ **64.** $x^3 = e^x$

Solve each problem.

65. *Finding the Rate* If the half-life of a radioactive substance is 10,000 years, then at what rate is it decaying?
HINT The amount goes from A_0 to $\frac{1}{2}A_0$ in 10,000 years.

66. *Finding the Rate* If the half-life of a drug is 12 hours, then at what rate is it being eliminated from the body?

67. *Dating a Bone* A piece of bone from an organism is found to contain 10% of the carbon-14 that it contained when the organism was living. If the half-life of carbon-14 is 5730 years, then how long ago was the organism alive?
HINT First find the rate of decay for carbon-14.

68. *Old Clothes* If only 15% of the carbon-14 in a remnant of cloth has decayed, then how old is the cloth?
HINT Use the decay rate for carbon-14 from the previous problem.

69. *Dating a Tree* How long does it take for 12 g of carbon-14 in a tree trunk to be reduced to 10 g of carbon-14 by radioactive decay?

70. *Carbon-14 Dating* How long does it take for 2.4 g of carbon-14 to be reduced to 1.3 g of carbon-14 by radioactive decay?

71. *Radioactive Waste* If 25 g of radioactive waste reduces to 20 g of radioactive waste after 8000 years, then what is the half-life for this radioactive element?
HINT First find the rate of decay, then find the time for half of it to decay.

72. *Finding the Half-Life* If 80% of a radioactive element remains radioactive after 250 million years, then what percent remains radioactive after 600 million years? What is the half-life of this element?

73. *Lorazepam* The drug lorazepam, used to relieve anxiety and nervousness, has a half-life of 14 hours. Its chemical structure is shown in the accompanying figure. If a doctor prescribes one 2.5-milligram tablet every 24 hours, then what percentage of the last dosage remains in the patient's body when the next dosage is taken?

Lorazepam

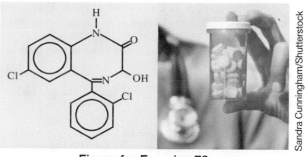

Figure for Exercise 73

74. *Drug Build-Up* The level of a prescription drug in the human body over time can be found using the formula

$$L = \frac{D}{1 - (0.5)^{n/h}}$$

where D is the amount taken every n hours and h is the drug's half-life in hours.

a. If 2.5 milligrams of lorazepam with a half-life of 14 hours is taken every 24 hours, then to what level does the drug build up over time?

b. If a doctor wants the level of lorazepam to build up to a level of 5.58 milligrams in a patient taking 2.5 milligram doses, then how often should the doses be taken?

c. What is the difference between taking 2.5 milligrams of lorazepam every 12 hours and taking 5 milligrams every 24 hours?

75. *Dead Sea Scrolls* Willard Libby, a nuclear chemist from the University of Chicago, developed radiocarbon dating in the 1940s. This dating method, effective on specimens up to about 40,000 years old, works best on objects like shells, charred bones, and plants that contain organic matter (carbon). Libby's first great success came in 1951 when he dated the Dead Sea Scrolls. Carbon-14 has a half-life of 5730 years. If Libby found 79.3% of the original carbon-14 still present, then in about what year were the scrolls made?

76. *Leakeys Date Zinjanthropus* In 1959, archaeologists Louis and Mary Leakey were exploring Olduvai Gorge, Tanzania, when they uncovered the remains of *Zinjanthropus*, an early hominid with traits of both ape and man. Dating of the volcanic rock revealed that 91.2% of the original potassium had not decayed into argon. What age was assigned to the rock and the bones of *Zinjanthropus*? The radioactive decay of potassium-40 to argon-40 occurs with a half-life of 1.31 billion years.

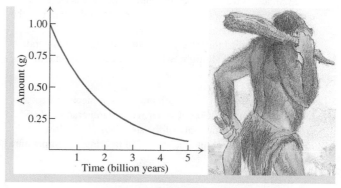

Figure for Exercise 76

77. *Depreciating Camry* Antoinette paid $21,075 for a Toyota Camry. After three years it was worth $11,981. Assume that the price is decreasing according to the continuous exponential decay model $P = P_0 e^{rt}$.

   a. Find the annual depreciation rate to the nearest tenth of a percent.

   b. Find the value of the car after 5 years to the nearest hundred dollars.

78. *Depreciating Porsche* Byron paid $107,500 for a Porsche 911 Turbo. After four years it was worth $49,900. Assume that the price is decreasing according to the continuous exponential decay model $P = P_0 e^{rt}$.

   a. Find the annual depreciation rate to the nearest tenth of a percent.

   b. Find the value of the car after 7 years to the nearest hundred dollars.

79. *Growth of Blogging* In 2009 there were about 0.1 million blog sites on the Internet. In 2011 there were 4.8 million. Assuming that the number of blog sites is experiencing continuous exponential growth, predict the number of blog sites (to the nearest million) in 2014.

80. *Growth of the Internet* Only 1.7% of the world's population used the Internet in 1997, whereas 28.8% of the world's population used it in 2010. Assuming continuous exponential growth, find the year in which the percentage will reach 100%.

81. *Cooking a Roast* James knows that to get well-done beef, it should be brought to a temperature of 170°F. He placed a sirloin tip roast with a temperature of 35°F in an oven with a temperature of 325°, and after 3 hr the temperature of the roast was 140°. How much longer must the roast be in the oven to get it well done? If the oven temperature is set at 170°, how long will it take to get the roast well done?

   HINT The difference between the roast temperature and the oven temperature decreases exponentially.

82. *Room Temperature* Marlene brought a can of polyurethane varnish that was stored at 40°F into her shop, where the temperature was 74°. After 2 hr the temperature of the varnish was 58°. If the varnish must be 68° for best results, then how much longer must Marlene wait until she uses the varnish?

83. *Time of Death* A detective discovered a body in a vacant lot at 7 A.M. and found that the body temperature was 80°F. The county coroner examined the body at 8 A.M. and found that the body temperature was 72°. Assuming that the body temperature was 98° when the person died and that the air temperature was a constant 40° all night, what was the approximate time of death?

84. *Cooling Hot Steel* A blacksmith immersed a piece of steel at 600°F into a large bucket of water with a temperature of 65°. After 1 min the temperature of the steel was 200°. How much longer must the steel remain immersed to bring its temperature down to 100°?

85. *Paying off a Loan* Find the time (to the nearest month) that it takes to pay off a loan of $100,000 at 9% APR compounded monthly with payments of $1250 per month.

86. *Solving for Time* Solve the formula

$$R = P \frac{i}{1 - (1 + i)^{-nt}}$$

for t. Then use the result to find the time (to the nearest month) that it takes to pay off a loan of $48,265 at $8\frac{3}{4}$% APR compounded monthly with payments of $700 per month.

87. *Equality of Investments* Fiona invested $1000 at 6% compounded continuously. At the same time, Maria invested $1100 at 6% compounded daily. How long will it take (to the nearest day) for their investments to be equal in value?

88. *Depreciation and Inflation* Boris won a $35,000 luxury car on *Wheel of Fortune*. He plans to keep it until he can trade it evenly for a new compact car that currently costs $10,000. If the value of the luxury car decreases by 8% each year and the cost of the compact car increases by 5% each year, then in how many years will he be able to make the trade?

89. *Population of Rabbits* The population of rabbits in a national forest is modeled by the formula $P = 12,300 + 1000 \cdot \ln(t + 1)$, where t is the number of years from the present.

   a. How many rabbits are now in the forest?

   b. Use the accompanying graph to estimate the number of years that it will take for the rabbit population to reach 15,000.

   c. Use the formula to determine the number of years that it will take for the rabbit population to reach 15,000.

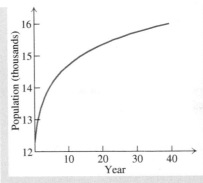

Figure for Exercise 89

90. *Population of Foxes* The population of foxes in the forest of Exercise 89 appears to be growing according to the formula $P = 400 + 50 \cdot \ln(90t + 1)$. When the population of foxes is equal to 5% of the population of rabbits, the system is considered to be out of ecological balance. In how many years will the system be out of balance?

91. *Habitat Destruction* Biologists use the species-area curve $n = k \log(A)$ to estimate the number of species n that live in a region of area A, where k is a constant.
  a. If 2500 species live in a rainforest of 400 square kilometers, then how many species will be left when half of this rainforest is destroyed by logging?

  b. A rainforest of 1200 square kilometers supported 3500 species in 1950. Due to intensive logging, what remains of this forest supported only 1000 species in 2000. What percent of this rainforest has been destroyed?

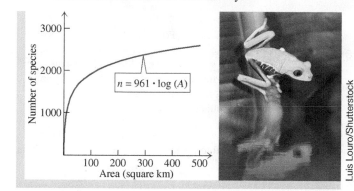

Figure for Exercise 91

92. *Extinction of Species* In 1980 an Amazon rainforest of area A contained n species. In the year 2000, after intensive logging, this rainforest was reduced to an area that contained only half as many species. Use the species-area formula from the previous exercise to find the area in 2000.

93. *Visual Magnitude of a Star* If all stars were at the same distance, it would be a simple matter to compare their brightness. However, the brightness that we see, the apparent visual magnitude m, depends on a star's intrinsic brightness, or absolute visual magnitude M_V, and the distance d from the observer in parsecs (1 parsec = 3.262 light years), according to the formula $m = M_V - 5 + 5 \cdot \log(d)$. The values of M_V range from -8 for the intrinsically brightest stars to $+15$ for the intrinsically faintest stars. The nearest star to the sun, Alpha Centauri, has an apparent visual magnitude of 0 and an absolute visual magnitude of 4.39. Find the distance d in parsecs to Alpha Centauri.

94. *Visual Magnitude of Deneb* The star Deneb is 490 parsecs away and has an apparent visual magnitude of 1.26, which means that it is harder to see than Alpha Centauri. Use the formula from Exercise 93 to find the absolute visual magnitude of Deneb. Is Deneb intrinsically very bright or very faint? If Deneb and Alpha Centauri were both 490 parsecs away, then which would appear brighter?

95. *Price per Gigabyte* According to Moore's law, the performance of electronic parts grows exponentially while the cost of those parts declines exponentially. The accompanying figure shows the decline in price P for a gigabyte of hard drive storage for the years 1982 through 2005. The relationship looks linear because the price axis has a log scale.
  a. Find a formula for P in terms of x, where x is the number of years since 1982. See Exercise 139 of Section 2.

  b. Find P in 1991.

  c. Find the year in which the price will be \$0.25.

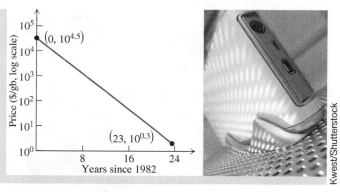

Figure for Exercise 95

96. *Hard Drive Capacity* The accompanying figure shows how hard drive capacity C has increased for the years 1982 through 2005. The relationship looks linear because the capacity axis has a log scale.
  a. Find a formula for C in terms of x, where x is the number of years since 1982. See the previous exercise.

  b. Find C in 1994.

  c. Find the year in which the capacity will be 1000 gigabytes.

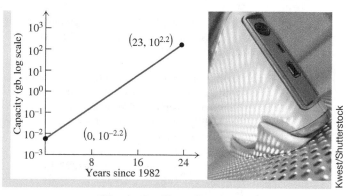

Figure for Exercise 96

97. *Noise Pollution* The level of a sound in decibels (db) is determined by the formula

$$\text{sound level} = 10 \cdot \log(I \times 10^{12})\, \text{db},$$

where I is the intensity of the sound in watts per square meter. To combat noise pollution, a city has an ordinance prohibiting sounds above 90 db on a city street. What value of I gives a sound of 90 db?

98. *Doubling the Sound Level* A small stereo amplifier produces a sound of 50 db at a distance of 20 ft from the speakers. Use the formula from Exercise 97 to find the intensity of the sound at this point in the room. If the intensity just found is doubled, what happens to the sound level? What must the intensity be to double the sound level to 100 db?

99. *Present Value of a CD* What amount (present value) must be deposited today in a certificate of deposit so that the investment will grow to \$20,000 in 18 years at 6% compounded continuously.

100. *Present Value of a Bond* A $50 U.S. Savings Bond paying 6.22% compounded monthly matures in 11 years 2 months. What is the present value of the bond?

101. *Two-Parent Families* The percentage of households with children that consist of two-parent families is shown in the following table (U.S. Census Bureau, www.census.gov).

Table for Exercise 101

Year	Two Parents
1970	85%
1980	77
1990	73
1992	71
1994	69
1996	68
1998	68
2000	68

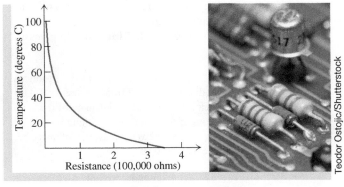

Monkey Business Images/ Shutterstock

a. Use logarithmic regression on a graphing calculator to find the best-fitting curve of the form $y = a + b \cdot \ln(x)$, where $x = 0$ corresponds to 1960.

b. Use your equation to predict the percentage of two-parent families in 2010.

c. In what year will the percentage of two-parent families reach 50%?

d. Graph your equation and the data on your graphing calculator. Does this logarithmic model look like another model that we have used?

102. *Thermistor Resistance* A thermistor is a resistor whose resistance varies with the temperature, as shown in the figure. The relationship between temperature T in °C and resistance R in ohms for a BetaTHERM thermistor model 100K6A1 is given by the Steinhart-Hart equation

$$T = \frac{1}{A + B \cdot \ln(R) + C \cdot \left[\ln(R)\right]^3} - 273.15,$$

where

$$A = 8.27153 \times 10^{-4}$$
$$B = 2.08796 \times 10^{-4}$$
$$C = 8.060985 \times 10^{-8}.$$

Temperature (degrees C) vs. Resistance (100,000 ohms)

Figure for Exercise 102

At what temperature is the resistance 1×10^5 ohms? Use a graphing calculator to find the resistance when $T = 35$°C.

■ **Foreshadowing Calculus**

To evaluate an exponential or logarithmic function we simply press a button on a calculator. But what does the calculator do to find the answer? The next two exercises show formulas from calculus that are used to evaluate e^x and $\ln(1 + x)$.

103. *Infinite Series for e^x* The following formula from calculus is used to compute values of e^x:

$$e^x = 1 + x + \frac{x^2}{2!} + \frac{x^3}{3!} + \frac{x^4}{4!} + \cdots + \frac{x^n}{n!} + \cdots,$$

where $n! = 1 \cdot 2 \cdot 3 \cdot \cdots \cdot n$ for any positive integer n. The notation $n!$ is read "n factorial." For example, $3! = 1 \cdot 2 \cdot 3 = 6$. In calculating e^x, the more terms that we use from the formula, the closer we get to the true value of e^x. Use the first five terms of the formula to estimate the value of $e^{0.1}$ and compare your result to the value of $e^{0.1}$ obtained using the e^x-key on your calculator.

104. *Infinite Series for Logarithms* The following formula from calculus can be used to compute values of natural logarithms:

$$\ln(1 + x) = x - \frac{x^2}{2} + \frac{x^3}{3} - \frac{x^4}{4} + \cdots,$$

where $-1 < x < 1$. The more terms that we use from the formula, the closer we get to the true value of $\ln(1 + x)$. Find $\ln(1.4)$ by using the first five terms of the series and compare your result to the calculator value for $\ln(1.4)$.

▶ **RETHINKING**

105. Simplify $\log_6(4) + \log_6(9)$.

106. Find the approximate rational solution to the equation $1.56^{x-1} = 9.8$. Round the answer to four decimal places.

107. Solve $\log_x(9.8) = 2.4$. Round to four decimal places.

108. The graph of $y = 2^x$ is reflected in the x-axis, translated 5 units to the right, and then 9 units upward. Find the equation of the curve in its final position.

109. Let $f(x) = 3^{x-5}$ and $g(x) = \log_3(x) + 5$. Find $(g \circ f)(x)$.

110. Factor $3x - 9 + wx - 3w$.

THINKING OUTSIDE THE BOX XXXIV

Pile of Pipes Six pipes are placed in a pile as shown in the diagram. The three pipes on the bottom each have a radius of 2 feet. The two pipes on top of those each have a radius of 1 foot. At the top of the pile is a pipe that is tangent to the two smaller pipes and one of the larger pipes. What is its exact radius?

Figure for Thinking Outside the Box XXXIV

POP QUIZ 4

Solve each equation. Round approximate solutions to four decimal places.

1. $\log_5(x) = 4$

2. $\log(x + 1) = 3$

3. $\ln(x) + \ln(x - 1) = \ln(12)$ **4.** $3^{x-5} = 10$

5. $8^x = 3^{x+5}$

LINKING
concepts...   For Individual or Group Explorations

The Logistic Growth Model

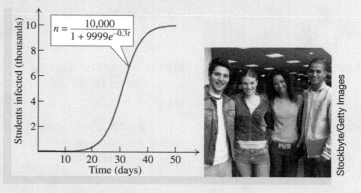

*When a virus infects a finite population of size P in which no one is immune, the virus spreads slowly at first, then more rapidly as more people are infected, and finally slows down when nearly everyone has been infected. This situation is modeled by a **logistic curve** of the form*

$$n = \frac{P}{1 + (P - 1) \cdot e^{-ct}}$$

where n is the number of people who have caught the virus on or before day t, and c is a positive constant.

$$n = \frac{10,000}{1 + 9999e^{-0.3t}}$$

a) According to the model, how many people have caught the virus at time $t = 0$?

b) Now consider what happens when one student carrying a flu virus returns from spring break to a university of 10,000 students. For $c = 0.1, 0.2,$ and so on through $c = 0.9$, graph the logistic curve

$$y_1 = 10000/(1 + 9999e\char94(-cx))$$

and the daily number of new cases

$$y_2 = y_1(x) - y_1(x - 1).$$

For each value of c use the graph of y_2 to find the day on which the flu is spreading most rapidly.

c) The Health Center estimated that the greatest number of new cases of the flu occurred on the 19th day after the students returned from spring break. What value of c should be used to model this situation? How many new cases occurred on the 19th day?

d) Algebraically find the day on which the number of infected students reached 9000.

e) The Health Center has a team of doctors from Atlanta arriving on the 30th day to help with this three-day flu epidemic. What do you think of this plan?

Highlights

1 Exponential Functions and Their Applications

Exponential Function	$f(x) = a^x$ for $a > 0$ and $a \neq 1$ Domain: $(-\infty, \infty)$, Range: $(0, \infty)$ Horizontal asymptote: $y = 0$	$f(x) = 2^x, g(x) = e^x$
Increasing and Decreasing	$f(x) = a^x$ is increasing on $(-\infty, \infty)$ if $a > 1$, decreasing on $(-\infty, \infty)$ if $0 < a < 1$.	$f(x) = 3^x$ is increasing. $g(x) = (0.4)^x$ is decreasing.
One-to-One	If $a^{x_1} = a^{x_2}$, then $x_1 = x_2$.	$2^{x-1} = 2^3 \Rightarrow x - 1 = 3$
Amount Formula	P dollars, annual interest rate r, for t years Compounded periodically: n periods per year, $A = P\left(1 + \frac{r}{n}\right)^{nt}$ Compounded continuously: $A = Pe^{rt}(e \approx 2.718)$	$P = \$1000, r = 5\%, t = 10$ yr Compounded monthly: $A = 1000\left(1 + \frac{0.05}{12}\right)^{120}$ Compounded continuously: $A = 1000e^{0.05(10)}$

2 Logarithmic Functions and Their Applications

Logarithmic Function	$f(x) = \log_a(x)$ for $a > 0$ and $a \neq 1$ $y = \log_a(x) \Leftrightarrow a^y = x$ Domain: $(0, \infty)$, Range: $(-\infty, \infty)$ Vertical asymptote: $x = 0$ Common log: base 10, $f(x) = \log(x)$ Natural log: base e, $f(x) = \ln(x)$	$f(x) = \log_2(x)$ $f(32) = \log_2(32) = 5$ $f(1) = \log_2(1) = 0$ $f(1/4) = \log_2(1/4) = -2$
Increasing and Decreasing	$f(x) = \log_a(x)$ is increasing on $(0, \infty)$ if $a > 1$, decreasing on $(0, \infty)$ if $0 < a < 1$.	$f(x) = \ln(x)$ is increasing. $g(x) = \log_{1/2}(x)$ is decreasing.
One-to-One	If $\log_a(x_1) = \log_a(x_2)$, then $x_1 = x_2$.	$\log_2(3x) = \log_2(4) \Rightarrow 3x = 4$
Inverse Functions	The inverse of a logarithmic function is an exponential function (and vice versa). Find the inverse using switch-and-solve.	$f(x) = \log_2(x) + 3$ $y = \log_2(x) + 3$ $x = \log_2(y) + 3$ $x - 3 = \log_2(y)$ $y = 2^{x-3}$ $f^{-1}(x) = 2^{x-3}$

3 Rules of Logarithms

Inverse Rules	$\log_a(a^x) = x$ and $a^{\log_a(x)} = x$	$\ln(e^5) = 5, 10^{\log(7)} = 7$
Product Rule	$\log_a(MN) = \log_a(M) + \log_a(N)$	$\log_2(8x) = 3 + \log_2(x)$
Quotient Rule	$\log_a(M/N) = \log_a(M) - \log_a(N)$	$\log(1/2) = \log(1) - \log(2)$
Power Rule	$\log_a(M^N) = N \cdot \log_a(M)$	$\ln(e^3) = 3 \cdot \ln(e)$
Base-Change Formula	$\log_a(M) = \frac{\log_b(M)}{\log_b(a)}$	$\log_3(7) = \frac{\ln(7)}{\ln(3)} = \frac{\log(7)}{\log(3)}$

4 More Equations and Applications

Equation-Solving Strategy	1. Use $y = \log_a(x) \Leftrightarrow a^y = x$ on equations with a single logarithm or single exponential. 2. Use the one-to-one properties to eliminate logarithms or exponential expressions. 3. Combine logarithms using the product and quotient rules. 4. Take a logarithm of each side and use the power rule.	$\log_2(x) = 3 \Leftrightarrow x = 2^3$ $\log(x^2) = \log(5) \Leftrightarrow x^2 = 5$ $e^x = e^{2x-1} \Leftrightarrow x = 2x - 1$ $\ln(x) + \ln(2) = 3$ $\quad \ln(2x) = 3$ $3^x = 4^{2x}$ $x \cdot \ln(3) = 2x \cdot \ln(4)$

Chapter Review Exercises

Simplify each expression.

1. 2^6

2. $\ln(e^2)$

3. $\log_2(64)$

4. $3 + 2 \cdot \log(10)$

5. $\log_9(1)$

6. $5^{\log_5(99)}$

7. $\log_2(2^{17})$

8. $\log_2(\log_2(16))$

9. $\sqrt{4^{2/\log_3(4)+2\cdot\log_9(3)}}$

10. $\sqrt[3]{5^{1/\log_2(5)}} + 3^{1/\log_6(3)}$

Let $f(x) = 2^x$, $g(x) = 10^x$, and $h(x) = \log_2(x)$. Simplify each expression.

11. $f(5)$

12. $g(-1)$

13. $\log(g(3))$

14. $g(\log(5))$

15. $(h \circ f)(9)$

16. $(f \circ h)(7)$

17. $g^{-1}(1000)$

18. $g^{-1}(1)$

19. $h(1/8)$

20. $f(1/2)$

22. $f^{-1}(8)$

22. $(f^{-1} \circ f)(13)$

Rewrite each expression as a single logarithm.

23. $\log(x - 3) + \log(x)$

24. $(1/2)\ln(x) - 2 \cdot \ln(y)$

25. $2 \cdot \ln(x) + \ln(y) + \ln(3)$

26. $3 \cdot \log_2(x) - 2 \cdot \log_2(y) + \log_2(z)$

Rewrite each expression as a sum or difference of multiples of logarithms.

27. $\log(3x^4)$

28. $\ln\left(\dfrac{x^5}{y^3}\right)$

29. $\log_3\left(\dfrac{5\sqrt{x}}{y^4}\right)$

30. $\log_2\left(\sqrt{xy^3}\right)$

Rewrite each expression in terms of $\ln(2)$ and $\ln(5)$.

31. $\ln(10)$

32. $\ln(0.4)$

33. $\ln(50)$

34. $\ln(\sqrt{20})$

Find the exact solution to each equation.

35. $\log(x) = 10$

36. $\log_3(x + 1) = -1$

37. $\log_x(81) = 4$

38. $\log_x(1) = 0$

39. $\log_{1/3}(27) = x + 2$

40. $\log_{1/2}(4) = x - 1$

41. $3^{x+2} = \dfrac{1}{9}$

42. $2^{x-1} = \dfrac{1}{4}$

43. $e^{x-2} = 9$

44. $\dfrac{1}{2^{1-x}} = 3$

45. $4^{x+3} = \dfrac{1}{2^x}$

46. $3^{2x-1} \cdot 9^x = 1$

47. $\log(x) + \log(2x) = 5$

48. $\log(x + 90) - \log(x) = 1$

49. $\log_2(x) + \log_2(x - 4) = \log_2(x + 24)$

50. $\log_5(x + 18) + \log_5(x - 6) = 2 \cdot \log_5(x)$

51. $2 \cdot \ln(x + 2) = 3 \cdot \ln(4)$

52. $x \cdot \log_2(12) = x \cdot \log_2(3) + 1$

53. $x \cdot \log(4) = 6 - x \cdot \log(25)$

54. $\log(\log(x)) = 1$

Find the missing coordinate so that each ordered pair satisfies the given equation.

55. $y = \left(\dfrac{1}{3}\right)^x : (-1, \ ), (\ , 27), (-1/2, \ ), (\ , 1)$

56. $y = \log_9(x - 1): (2, \ ), (4, \ ), (\ , 3/2), (\ , -1)$

Match each equation to one of the graphs (a)–(h).

57. $y = 2^x$

58. $y = 2^{-x}$

59. $y = \log_2(x)$

60. $y = \log_{1/2}(x)$

61. $y = 2^{x+2}$

62. $y = \log_2(x + 2)$

63. $y = 2^x + 2$

64. $y = 2 + \log_2(x)$

a.

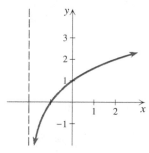

b.

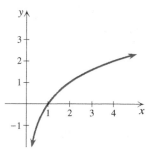

c.

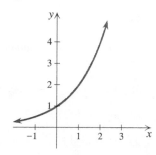

d.

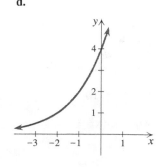

e.

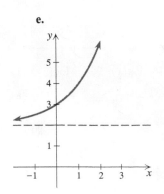

f.

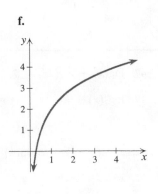

g.

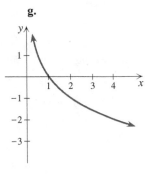

h.

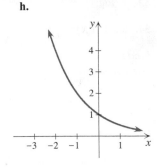

93. $\ln(3^2) = (\ln(3))^2$　　**94.** $\ln\left(\dfrac{5}{8}\right) = \dfrac{\ln(5)}{\ln(8)}$

95. $\log_2(8^4) = 12$

96. $\log(8.2 \times 10^{-9}) = -9 + \log(8.2)$

97. $\log(1006) = 3 + \log(6)$

98. $\dfrac{\log_2(16)}{\log_2(4)} = \log_2(16) - \log_2(4)$

99. $\dfrac{\log_2(8)}{\log_2(16)} = \log_2(8) - \log_2(16)$

100. $\ln(e^{(e^x)}) = e^x$

101. $\log_2(25) = 2 \cdot \log(5)$

102. $\log_3\left(\dfrac{5}{7}\right) = \log(5) - \log(7)$

103. $\log_2(7) = \dfrac{\log(7)}{\log(2)}$　　**104.** $\dfrac{\ln(17)}{\ln(3)} = \dfrac{\log(17)}{\log(3)}$

Sketch the graph of each function. State the domain, the range, and whether the function is increasing or decreasing. Identify any asymptotes.

65. $f(x) = 5^x$　　　　　**66.** $f(x) = e^x$

67. $f(x) = 10^{-x}$　　　　**68.** $f(x) = (1/2)^x$

69. $y = \log_3(x)$　　　　**70.** $y = \log_5(x)$

71. $y = 1 + \ln(x + 3)$　　**72.** $y = 3 - \log_2(x)$

73. $f(x) = 1 + 2^{x-1}$　　**74.** $f(x) = 3 - 2^{x+1}$

75. $y = \log_3(-x + 2)$　　**76.** $y = 1 + \log_3(x + 2)$

For each function f, find f^{-1}.

77. $f(x) = 7^x$　　　　　**78.** $f(x) = 3^x$

79. $f(x) = \log_5(x)$　　　**80.** $f(x) = \log_8(x)$

81. $f(x) = 3 \cdot \log(x - 1)$　**82.** $f(x) = \log_2(x + 3) - 5$

83. $f(x) = e^{x+2} - 3$　　**84.** $f(x) = 2 \cdot 3^x + 1$

Use a calculator to find an approximate solution to each equation. Round answers to four decimal places.

85. $3^x = 10$　　　　　**86.** $4^{2x} = 12$

87. $\log_3(x) = 1.876$　　**88.** $\log_5(x + 2) = 2.7$

89. $5^x = 8^{x+1}$　　　　**90.** $3^x = e^{x+1}$

Use the rules of logarithms to determine whether each equation is true or false. Explain your answer.

91. $\log_3(81) = \log_3(9) \cdot \log_3(9)$　**92.** $\log(81) = \log(9) \cdot \log(9)$

Solve each problem.

105. *Comparing pH* If the hydrogen ion concentration of liquid A is 10 times the hydrogen ion concentration of liquid B, then how does the pH of A compare with the pH of B? See Exercise 141 in Section 2 and Exercise 102 in Section 3.

106. *Solving a Formula* Solve the formula $A = P + Ce^{-kt}$ for t.

107. *Future Value* If $50,000 is deposited in a bank account paying 5% compounded quarterly, then what will be the value of the account at the end of 18 years?

108. *Future Value* If $30,000 is deposited in First American Savings and Loan in an account paying 6.18% compounded continuously, then what will be the value of the account after 12 years and 3 months?

109. *Doubling Time with Quarterly Compounding* How long (to the nearest quarter) will it take for the investment of Exercise 107 to double?

110. *Doubling Time with Continuous Compounding* How long (to the nearest day) will it take for the investment of Exercise 108 to double?

111. *Finding the Half-Life* The number of grams A of a certain radioactive substance present at time t is given by the formula $A = 25e^{-0.00032t}$, where t is the number of years from the present. How many grams are present initially? How many grams are present after 1000 years? What is the half-life of this substance?

112. *Comparing Investments* Shinichi invested $800 at 6% compounded continuously. At the same time, Toshio invested $1000 at 5% compounded monthly. How long (to the nearest month) will it take for their investments to be equal in value?

113. *Learning Curve* According to an educational psychologist, the number of words learned by a student of a foreign language after t hours in the language laboratory is given by $f(t) = 40{,}000(1 - e^{-0.0001t})$. How many hours would it take to learn 10,000 words?

114. *Pediatric Tuberculosis* Health researchers divided the state of Maryland into regions according to per capita income and found a relationship between per capita income i (in thousands) and the percentage of pediatric TB cases P. The equation $P = 31.5(0.935)^i$ can be used to model the data.
  a. What percentage of TB cases would you expect to find in the region with a per capita income of $8000?

  b. What per capita income would you expect in the region where only 2% of the TB cases occurred?

115. *Sea Worthiness* Three measures of a boat's sea worthiness are given in the accompanying table, where A is the sail area in square feet, d is the displacement in pounds, L is the length at the water line in feet, and b is the beam in feet. The Freedom 40 is a $291,560 sailboat with a sail area of 1026 ft^2, a displacement of 25,005 lb, a beam of 13 ft 6 in., and a length at the water line of 35 ft 1 in. Its sail area-displacement ratio is 19.20, its displacement-length ratio is 258.51, and its capsize screening value is 1.85. Find x, y, and z.

Table for Exercise 115

Measure	Expression	
Sail area-displacement ratio	$A\left(\dfrac{d}{64}\right)^x$	
Displacement-length ratio	$\dfrac{d}{2240}\left(\dfrac{L}{100}\right)^y$	
Capsize-screening value	$b\left(\dfrac{d}{64}\right)^z$	

Ventura 2009/Shutterstock

116. *Doubling the Bet* A strategy used by some gamblers when they lose is to play again and double the bet, assuming that the amount won is equal to the amount bet. So if a gambler loses $2, then the gambler plays again and bets $4, then $8, and so on.
  a. Why would the gambler use this strategy?

  b. On the nth bet, the gambler risks 2^n dollars. Estimate the first value of n for which the amount bet is more than $1 million using the accompanying graph of $y = 2^n$.

  c. Use logarithms to find the answer to part (b).

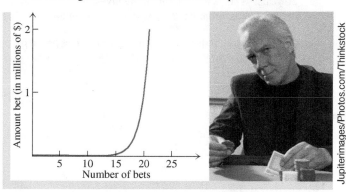

Figure for Exercise 116

THINKING OUTSIDE THE BOX XXXV

Crescent City Three semicircles are drawn so that their diameters are the three sides of a right triangle as shown in the diagram. What is the ratio of the total area of the two crescents A and B to the area of the triangle T?

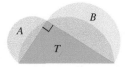

Figure for Thinking Outside the Box XXXV

Chapter Test

Simplify each expression.

1. $\log(1000)$

2. $\log_7(1/49)$

3. $3^{\log_3(6.47)}$

4. $\ln(e^{\sqrt{2}})$

Find the inverse of each function.

5. $f(x) = \ln(x)$

6. $f(x) = 8^{x+1} - 3$

Write each expression as a single logarithm.

7. $\log(x) + 3 \cdot \log(y)$

8. $\dfrac{1}{2} \cdot \ln(x - 1) - \ln(33)$

Write each expression in terms of $\log_a(2)$ and $\log_a(7)$.

9. $\log_a(28)$

10. $\log_a(3.5)$

Find the exact solution to each equation.

11. $\log_2(x) + \log_2(x - 2) = 3$

12. $\log(10x) - \log(x + 2) = 2 \cdot \log(3)$

Find the exact solution and an approximate solution (to four decimal places) for each equation.

13. $3^x = 5^{x-1}$

14. $\log_3(x - 1) = 5.46$

Graph each equation in the xy-plane. State the domain and range of the function and whether the function is increasing or decreasing. Identify any asymptotes.

15. $f(x) = 2^x + 1$

16. $y = \log_{1/2}(x - 1)$

Solve each problem.

17. What is the only ordered pair that satisfies both $y = \log_2(x)$ and $y = \ln(x)$?

18. A student invested $2000 at 8% annual percentage rate for 20 years. What is the amount of the investment if the interest is compounded quarterly? Compounded continuously?

19. A satellite has a radioisotope power supply. The power supply in watts is given by the formula $P = 50e^{-t/250}$, where t is the time in days. How much power is available at the end of 200 days? What is the half-life of the power supply? If the equipment aboard the satellite requires 9 watts of power to operate properly, then what is the operational life of the satellite?

20. If $4000 is invested at 6% compounded quarterly, then how long will it take for the investment to grow to $10,000?

21. An educational psychologist uses the model $t = -50 \cdot \ln(1 - p)$ for $0 \le p < 1$ to predict the number of hours t that it will take for a child to reach level p in the new video game Mario Goes to Mars (MGM). Level $p = 0$ means that the child knows nothing about MGM. What is the predicted level of a child for 100 hr of playing MGM? If $p = 1$ corresponds to mastery of MGM, then is it possible to master MGM?

► TYING IT ALL
together...

Chapters 1–4

Solve each equation.

1. $(x - 3)^2 = 4$

2. $2 \cdot \log(x - 3) = \log(4)$

3. $\log_2(x - 3) = 4$

4. $2^{x-3} = 4$

5. $\sqrt{x - 3} = 4$

6. $|x - 3| = 4$

7. $x^2 - 4x = -2$

8. $2^{x-3} = 4^x$

9. $\sqrt[3]{x - 5} = 5$

10. $2^x = 3$

11. $\log(x - 3) + \log(4) = \log(x)$

12. $x^3 - 4x^2 + x + 6 = 0$

Sketch the graph of each function.

13. $y = x^2$

14. $y = (x - 2)^2$

15. $y = 2^x$

16. $y = x^{-2}$

17. $y = \log_2(x - 2)$

18. $y = x - 2$

19. $y = 2x$

20. $y = \log(2^x)$

21. $y = e^2$

22. $y = 2 - x^2$

23. $y = \dfrac{2}{x}$

24. $y = \dfrac{1}{x - 2}$

Find the inverse of each function.

25. $f(x) = \dfrac{1}{3}x$

26. $f(x) = \dfrac{1}{3^x}$

27. $f(x) = \sqrt{x - 2}$

28. $f(x) = 2 + (x - 5)^3$

29. $f(x) = \log(\sqrt{x} - 3)$

30. $f = \{(3, 1), (5, 4)\}$

31. $f(x) = 3 + \dfrac{1}{x - 5}$

32. $f(x) = 3 - e^{\sqrt{x}}$

Find a formula for each composition function given that $p(x) = e^x$, $m(x) = x + 5$, $q(x) = \sqrt{x}$, and $r(x) = \ln(x)$. State the domain and range of the composition function.

33. $p \circ m$

34. $p \circ q$

35. $q \circ p \circ m$

36. $m \circ r \circ q$

37. $p \circ r \circ m$

38. $r \circ q \circ p$

Express each of the following functions as a composition of the functions f, g, and h, where $f(x) = \log_2(x)$, $g(x) = x - 4$, and $h(x) = x^3$.

39. $F(x) = \log_2(x^3 - 4)$ **40.** $H(x) = (\log_2(x))^3 - 4$ **41.** $G(x) = (\log_2(x) - 4)^3$ **42.** $M(x) = (\log_2(x - 4))^3$

Fill in the blanks.

43. The point at the intersection of the *x*-axis and *y*-axis is called the _____.

44. The set of all points in the plane that lie at a fixed distance from a fixed point is called a(n) _____.

45. The slope of a line is the ratio of its _____ to its _____.

46. The equation $y - y_1 = m(x - x_1)$ is called the _____ of the equation of a line.

47. The equation $y = mx + b$ is called the _____ of the equation of a line.

48. Two lines with slopes m_1 and m_2 are _____ if and only if $m_1 m_2 = -1$.

49. Two lines with slopes m_1 and m_2 are _____ if and only if $m_1 = m_2$.

50. An equation of the form $ax^2 + bx + c = 0$ with $a \neq 0$ is called a(n) _____ equation.

51. The formula $x = \dfrac{-b \pm \sqrt{b^2 - 4ac}}{2a}$ is called the _____ formula.

52. Two equations with the same solution set are called _____ equations.

→ **FUNCTION**

gallery... Some Basic Functions of Algebra with Transformations

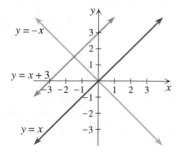

Linear

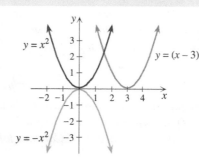

Quadratic

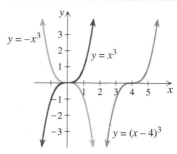

Cubic

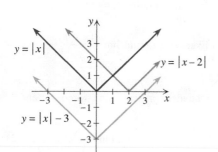

Absolute value

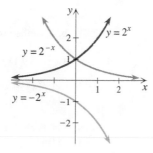

Exponential

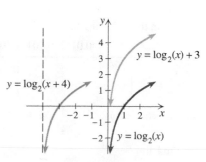

Logarithmic

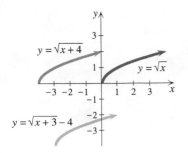

$y = \sqrt{x+4}$

$y = \sqrt{x}$

$y = \sqrt{x+3} - 4$

Square root

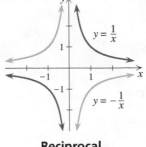

$y = \frac{1}{x}$

$y = -\frac{1}{x}$

Reciprocal

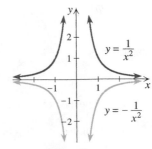

$y = \frac{1}{x^2}$

$y = -\frac{1}{x^2}$

Rational

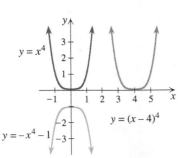

$y = x^4$

$y = (x-4)^4$

$y = -x^4 - 1$

Fourth degree

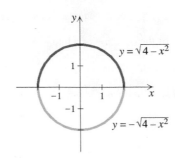

$y = \sqrt{4 - x^2}$

$y = -\sqrt{4 - x^2}$

Semicircle

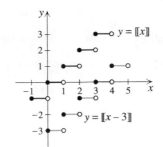

$y = [\![x]\!]$

$y = [\![x-3]\!]$

Greatest integer

CONCEPTS OF
calculus...

The instantaneous rate of change of $f(x) = e^x$

In the Concepts of Calculus for Chapter 2, we defined the average rate of change of a function f on the interval $[x, x + h]$ as

$$\frac{f(x + h) - f(x)}{h}.$$

We then defined the instantaneous rate of change of the function as the limit as h approaches zero of the average rate of change. The notation $f'(x)$, read "f prime of x," is used for the instantaneous rate of change. So

$$f'(x) = \lim_{h \to 0} \frac{f(x + h) - f(x)}{h}.$$

In the following exercises we will find the instantaneous rate of change of the base e exponential function. It will be necessary here to find a limit using a table of values as we did in the Concepts of Calculus for Chapter 1.

Exercises

1. a. Fill in the following table.

h	0.1	0.01	0.001	0.0001
$\dfrac{e^h - 1}{h}$				

b. Can you evaluate $\dfrac{e^h - 1}{h}$ if $h = 0$?

c. Find $\lim\limits_{h \to 0} \dfrac{e^h - 1}{h}$.

2. Let $f(x) = e^x$.

a. Find $\dfrac{f(x + h) - f(x)}{h}$ and simplify it by factoring out e^x.

b. Use the result of Exercise 1 to find $\lim\limits_{h \to 0} \dfrac{f(x + h) - f(x)}{h}$.

c. Find $f'(x)$.

3. Let $f(x) = e^{2x}$. Use the ideas presented in Exercises 1 and 2 to find $f'(x)$.

4. Let $f(x) = e^{3x}$. Use the ideas presented in Exercises 1 and 2 to find $f'(x)$.

5. Let $f(x) = e^{nx}$, where n is a positive integer. What can you conjecture about $f'(x)$?

Answers to Exercises

Section 1

For Thought: **1.** F **2.** T **3.** T **4.** T **5.** T **6.** T
7. T **8.** F **9.** T **10.** T
Exercises:
1. algebraic **3.** exponential **5.** increasing, decreasing **7.** range
9. 27 **11.** -1 **13.** 1/8 **15.** 16 **17.** 4 **19.** $-1/27$
21. 9 **23.** 1/9 **25.** 1/2 **27.** 8 **29.** 4 **31.** 2
33. $(-\infty, \infty)$, $(0, \infty)$, inc **35.** $(-\infty, \infty)$, $(0, \infty)$, dec

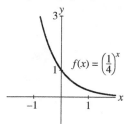

37. $(-\infty, \infty)$, $(0, \infty)$, dec **39.** ∞ **41.** 0 **43.** 0 **45.** ∞

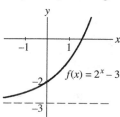

47. $(-\infty, \infty)$, $(-3, \infty)$, $y = -3$, increasing **49.** $(-\infty, \infty)$, $(-5, \infty)$, $y = -5$, increasing

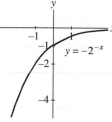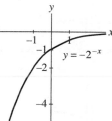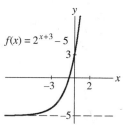

51. $(-\infty, \infty)$, $(-\infty, 0)$, $y = 0$, increasing **53.** $(-\infty, \infty)$, $(-\infty, 1)$, $y = 1$, decreasing

55. $(-\infty, \infty)$, $(0, \infty)$, $y = 0$, increasing **57.** $(-\infty, \infty)$, $(0, \infty)$, $y = 0$, decreasing

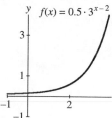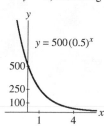

59. $y = 2^{x-5} - 2$ **61.** $y = -(1/4)^{x-1} - 2$ **63.** $\{6\}$
65. $\{-1\}$ **67.** $\{3\}$ **69.** $\{-2\}$ **71.** $\{1/3\}$ **73.** $\{-2\}$
75. $\{-3\}$ **77.** $\{-1\}$ **79.** $\{3\}$ **81.** 2 **83.** -1
85. 0 **87.** -3 **89.** 3 **91.** -1 **93.** 1 **95.** -1
97. 9, 1, 1/3, -2 **99.** 1, -2, 5, 1 **101.** -16, -2, $-1/2$, 5
103. a. \$7934.37, \$2934.37 **b.** \$8042.19, \$3042.19
c. \$8067.51, \$3067.51 **d.** \$8079.95, \$3079.95
105. a. \$8080.37 **b.** \$9671.31 **c.** \$7694.93 **d.** \$26,570.30
107. \$2121.82 **109.** \$3934.30
111. a. \$6.85 **b.** \$6.87 **113.** 200 g, 121.3 g
115. a. 400,000 **b.** 600 million
117. a. $y = 8.44(1.23)^x$ **b.** Yes **c.** 530 million
119. $P = 10\left(\dfrac{1}{2}\right)^n$ **121.** 6 **125.** $y = 2, x = -7$
127. $(-\infty, -1) \cup (6, \infty)$ **129.** $x = \dfrac{y + 5}{2}$

Section 2

For Thought: **1.** T **2.** F **3.** T **4.** T **5.** F **6.** T
7. T **8.** F **9.** T **10.** T
Exercises:
1. logarithmic **3.** natural **5.** vertical asymptote
7. logarithmic family **9.** 6 **11.** -4 **13.** 1/4 **15.** -3
17. 6 **19.** -4 **21.** 1/4 **23.** -3 **25.** -1 **27.** 0
29. 1 **31.** -5

33. $(0, \infty)$, $(-\infty, \infty)$ **35.** $(0, \infty)$, $(-\infty, \infty)$

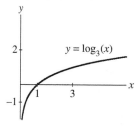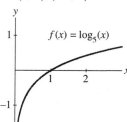

37. $(0, \infty)$, $(-\infty, \infty)$ **39.** $(0, \infty)$, $(-\infty, \infty)$

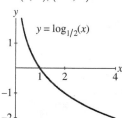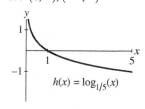

41. $(1, \infty)$, $(-\infty, \infty)$ **43.** $(-2, \infty)$, $(-\infty, \infty)$

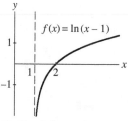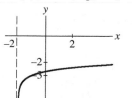

45. $(1, \infty)$, $(-\infty, \infty)$

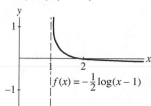

489

47. ∞ **49.** ∞ **51.** $-\infty$ **53.** ∞ **55.** $y = \ln(x-3) - 4$

57. $y = -\log_2(x-5) - 1$ **59.** $2^5 = 32$ **61.** $5^y = x$

63. $10^z = 1000$ **65.** $e^x = 5$ **67.** $x = a^m$ **69.** $\log_5(125) = 3$

71. $\ln(y) = 3$ **73.** $\log(y) = m$ **75.** $z = \log_a(y)$

77. $\log_a(n) = x - 1$ **79.** $f^{-1}(x) = \log_2(x)$ **81.** $f^{-1}(x) = 7^x$

83. $f^{-1}(x) = e^x + 1$ **85.** $f^{-1}(x) = \log_3(x) - 2$

87. $f^{-1}(x) = \log(2x - 10) + 1$ **89.** 256 **91.** $\sqrt{3}$ **93.** 4

95. $\log_3(77)$ **97.** 6 **99.** $3\sqrt{2}$ **101.** $-1 + \log_3(7)$

103. 2 **105.** 27 **107.** 1/4 **109.** 6/5 **111.** 64

113. 1.3979 **115.** 0.5493 **117.** -0.2231 **119.** -0.3010

121. a. 34.7 yr **b.** 17.3 yr **c.** 8.7 yr **d.** 4.3 yr

123. a. 22.0% **b.** 11.0% **c.** 5.5% **d.** 2.7%

125. 49 yr 125 days **127.** $r = \ln(A/P)/t$, 23.1%

129. a. 6.9 yr **131.** 3.5% **133.** 9.8 yr **135.** 1.87%, 7.3 billion

137. a. 133,412 acres **b.** 12 days

139. a. $p = -45 \cdot \log(I) + 190$ **b.** 0%

141. 4.1 **143.** 3.7 **145.** $c = \ln(b)$, 3.54%

149. $(-\infty, \infty), (-\infty, 7)$ **151.** 2×10^{-19} **153.** $\{0, 2 \pm 3i\}$

Section 3

For Thought: **1.** F **2.** T **3.** T **4.** T **5.** F **6.** F

7. F **8.** T **9.** F **10.** F

Exercises:

1. sum **3.** power **5.** $\sqrt{y}$ **7.** $y + 1$ **9.** 999

11. $\log(15)$ **13.** $\log_2(x^2 - x)$ **15.** $\log_4(6)$ **17.** $\ln(x^5)$

19. $\log_2(3) + \log_2(x)$ **21.** $\log(x) - \log(2)$

23. $\log(x-1) + \log(x+1)$ **25.** $\ln(x-1) - \ln(x)$

27. $3 \cdot \log_a(5)$ **29.** $\frac{1}{2} \cdot \log_a(5)$ **31.** $-1 \cdot \log_a(5)$

33. $\log_a(2) + \log_a(5)$ **35.** $\log_a(5) - \log_a(2)$

37. $\log_a(2) + \frac{1}{2} \cdot \log_a(5)$ **39.** $2 \cdot \log_a(2) - 2 \cdot \log_a(5)$

41. $\log_3(5) + \log_3(x)$ **43.** $\log_2(5) - \log_2(2) - \log_2(y)$

45. $\log(3) + \frac{1}{2}\log(x)$ **47.** $\log(3) + (x-1)\log(2)$

49. $\frac{1}{3}\ln(x) + \frac{1}{3}\ln(y) - \frac{4}{3}\ln(t)$

51. $\ln(6) + \frac{1}{2}\ln(x-1) - \ln(5) - 3 \cdot \ln(x)$

53. $\log_2(5x^3)$ **55.** $\log_7(x^{-3})$ **57.** $\log\left(\frac{2xy}{z}\right)$ **59.** $\log\left(\frac{z\sqrt{x}}{y\sqrt[3]{w}}\right)$

61. $\log_4(x^{20})$ **63.** 3.1699 **65.** -3.5864 **67.** 11.8957

69. 2.2025 **71.** 1.5850 **73.** 0.3772 **75.** -3.5850

77. 13.8695 **79.** 34.3240 **81.** 0.3200 **83.** 0.0479, -24.0479

85. 2.0172 **87.** 1.5928 **89.** 11 yr 166 days

91. 44 quarters **93.** 5.7% **95.** 3.58% **97.** 4.4%

99. $\log(I/I_0)$, 3 **101.** $t = \frac{1}{r}\ln(P) - \frac{1}{r}\ln(P_0)$

103. a. Decreasing **b.** $n \le 4{,}892{,}961$

105. $MR(x) = \log\left[\left(\frac{x+2}{x+1}\right)^{500}\right]$, $MR(x) \to 0$

107. a. $y = 217.9(1.084)^x$ **b.** $y = 217.9e^{0.0807x}$ **c.** 8.07%

d. 2014 **e.** No

109. No, $(-\infty, 0) \cup (0, \infty)$, $(0, \infty)$

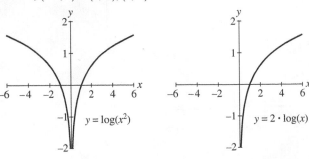
$y = \log(x^2)$ $y = 2 \cdot \log(x)$

113. $(1, \infty), (-\infty, \infty)$ **115.** \$12,532.62 **117.** $\{-65/27\}$

Section 4

For Thought: **1.** T **2.** T **3.** F **4.** T **5.** F **6.** F

7. T **8.** T **9.** T **10.** T

Exercises:

1. 8 **3.** 80 **5.** ± 5 **7.** 3 **9.** 1/2 **11.** $\sqrt[3]{10}$

13. 1/4 **15.** 6 **17.** 5 **19.** 1/999 **21.** $\varnothing$ **23.** 20

25. 2 **27.** $\frac{\sqrt{5}}{2}$ **29.** $\frac{1}{2}$ **31.** $\frac{2}{\ln(6)}$ **33.** 3.8074

35. 3.5502 **37.** -3.0959 **39.** No solution **41.** 1.5850

43. 0.7677 **45.** -0.2 **47.** 2.5850 **49.** 1/3 **51.** 1, 100

53. 29.4872 **55.** 2 **57.** $-5/4$ **59.** 0.194, 2.70

61. -49.73 **63.** $-0.767, 2, 4$ **65.** -6.93×10^{-5}

67. 19,035 yr ago **69.** 1507 yr **71.** 24,850 yr

73. 30.5% **75.** a.d. 34

77. a. -18.8% per year **b.** \$8200 **79.** 1596 million

81. 1 hr 11 min, forever **83.** 5:20 a.m. **85.** 10 yr 3 mo

87. 19,328 yr 307 days

89. a. 12,300 **b.** ≈ 15 yr **c.** 13.9 yr

91. a. 2211 **b.** 99% **93.** 1.32 parsecs

95. a. $P = 10^{-0.1826x+4.5}$ **b.** \$718.79 **c.** 2010

97. 10^{-3} watts/m^2 **99.** \$6791.91

101. a. $y = 114.8 - 12.8 \cdot \ln(x)$ in year $1960 + x$ **b.** 65%

c. 2121 **d.** Quadratic or exponential

103. 1.105170833, 1.105170918 **105.** 2 **107.** $\{2.5883\}$

109. $(g \circ f)(x) = x$

Chapter Review Exercises

1. 64 **3.** 6 **5.** 0 **7.** 17 **9.** 6 **11.** 32 **13.** 3

15. 9 **17.** 3 **19.** -3 **21.** 3 **23.** $\log(x^2 - 3x)$

25. $\ln(3x^2 y)$ **27.** $\log(3) + 4 \cdot \log(x)$

29. $\log_3(5) + \frac{1}{2}\log_3(x) - 4 \cdot \log_3(y)$ **31.** $\ln(2) + \ln(5)$

33. $\ln(2) + 2 \cdot \ln(5)$ **35.** 10^{10} **37.** 3 **39.** -5 **41.** -4

43. $2 + \ln(9)$ **45.** -2 **47.** $100\sqrt{5}$ **49.** 8 **51.** 6 **53.** 3

55. $3, -3, \sqrt{3}, 0$ **57.** (c) **59.** (b) **61.** (d) **63.** (e)

65. $(-\infty, \infty), (0, \infty)$, inc, $y = 0$ **67.** $(-\infty, \infty), (0, \infty)$, dec, $y = 0$

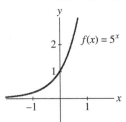
$f(x) = 5^x$

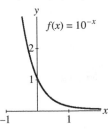
$f(x) = 10^{-x}$

69. $(0, \infty), (-\infty, \infty)$, inc, $x = 0$ **71.** $(-3, \infty), (-\infty, \infty)$, inc, $x = -3$

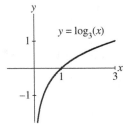
$y = \log_3(x)$

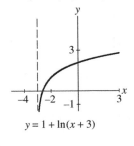
$y = 1 + \ln(x+3)$

73. $(-\infty, \infty)$, $(1, \infty)$, inc, $y = 1$ **75.** $(-\infty, 2)$, $(-\infty, \infty)$, dec, $x = 2$

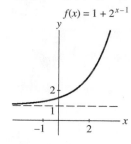

$f(x) = 1 + 2^{x-1}$

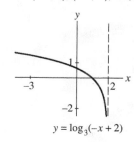

$y = \log_3(-x + 2)$

10. $\log_a(7) - \log_a(2)$ **11.** 4   **12.** 18

13. $\dfrac{\ln(5)}{\ln(5) - \ln(3)} \approx 3.1507$ **14.** $1 + 3^{5.46} \approx 403.7931$

15. $(-\infty, \infty)$, $(1, \infty)$, inc, $y = 1$ **16.** $(1, \infty)$, $(-\infty, \infty)$, dec, $x = 1$

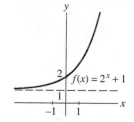

$f(x) = 2^x + 1$

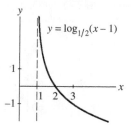

$y = \log_{1/2}(x - 1)$

77. $f^{-1}(x) = \log_7(x)$ **79.** $f^{-1}(x) = 5^x$ **81.** $f^{-1}(x) = 10^{x/3} + 1$
83. $f^{-1}(x) = -2 + \ln(x + 3)$ **85.** 2.0959   **87.** 7.8538
89. -4.4243 **91.** T   **93.** F   **95.** T   **97.** F   **99.** F
101. F   **103.** T   **105.** The pH of A is one less than the pH of B.
107. \$122,296.01   **109.** 56 quarters   **111.** 25 g, 18.15 g, 2166 yr
113. 2877 hr   **115.** $-2/3, -3, -1/3$

17. $(1, 0)$ **18.** \$9750.88, \$9906.06
19. 22.5 watts, 173.3 days, 428.7 days   **20.** 61.5 quarters
21. $p = 0.86$, no

Chapter Test

1. 3   **2.** -2 **3.** 6.47   **4.** $\sqrt{2}$ **5.** $f^{-1}(x) = e^x$
6. $f^{-1}(x) = -1 + \log_8(x + 3)$ **7.** $\log(xy^3)$
8. $\ln\left(\dfrac{\sqrt{x - 1}}{33}\right)$ **9.** $2 \cdot \log_a(2) + \log_a(7)$

Solutions to Try This Exercises

Section 1

1.1 If $f(x) = 9^x$, then $f(-2) = 9^{-2} = 1/81$ and $f(1/2) = 9^{1/2} = 3$.

1.2 The ordered pairs $(-2, 1/81)$, $(0, 1)$, and $(2, 81)$ are on the graph. The domain is $(-\infty, \infty)$ and the range is $(0, \infty)$.

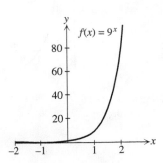

1.3 The ordered pairs $(-2, 81)$, $(0, 1)$, and $(2, 1/81)$ are on the graph. The domain is $(-\infty, \infty)$ and the range is $(0, \infty)$.

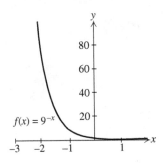

1.4 The ordered pairs $(1, 3/2)$, $(2, 2)$, and $(3, 3)$ are on the graph. The domain is $(-\infty, \infty)$ and the range is $(1, \infty)$.

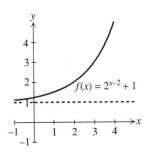

1.5 The ordered pairs $(-1, -4)$, $(0, -1)$, and $(1, -1/4)$ are on the graph. The domain is $(-\infty, \infty)$ and the range is $(-\infty, 0)$.

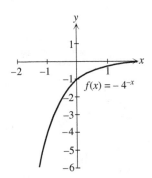

1.6 $2^{-x} = \dfrac{1}{8}$

$2^{-x} = 2^{-3}$

$-x = -3$

$x = 3$

1.7 $3^{4-x} = \dfrac{1}{9}$

$3^{4-x} = 3^{-2}$

$4 - x = -2$

$-x = -6$

$x = 6$

1.8 $A = 9000\left(1 + \dfrac{0.054}{12}\right)^{12 \cdot 6}$

$\approx \$12{,}434.78$

1.9 $A = 8000e^{0.063(7.25)}$

$\approx \$12{,}631.47$

1.10 $A = 2.9e^{-1.21 \times 10^{-4}(0)} = 2.9$

The initial amount is 2.9 grams.

$A = 2.9e^{-1.21 \times 10^{-4}(6500)} \approx 1.3$ grams

Section 2

2.1 Since $4^{-2} = 1/16$, $\log_4(1/16) = -2$.

2.2 Since $10^2 = 100$, $\log(100) = 2$.

2.3 The ordered pairs $(1/6, -1)$, $(1, 0)$, $(6, 1)$, and $(36, 2)$ are on the graph. The domain is $(0, \infty)$ and the range is $(-\infty, \infty)$.

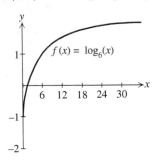

2.4 The ordered pairs $(36, -2)$, $(6, -1)$, $(1, 0)$, $(1/6, 1)$, and $(1/36, 2)$ are on the graph. The domain is $(0, \infty)$ and the range is $(-\infty, \infty)$.

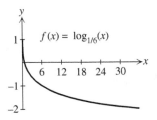

2.5 The ordered pairs $(0, 0)$, $(1, -1)$, $(3, -2)$, $(7, -3)$, and $(-1/2, 1)$ are on the graph. The domain is $(-1, \infty)$ and the range is $(-\infty, \infty)$.

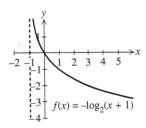

2.6 Since $y = a^x$ is equivalent to $\log_a(y) = x$, $\log_4(w) = 7$ is equivalent to $w = 4^7$.

2.7 $\quad f(x) = 3 \cdot e^{5x-1}$

$\quad y = 3 \cdot e^{5x-1}$

$\quad x = 3 \cdot e^{5y-1}$

$\quad \dfrac{x}{3} = e^{5y-1}$

$\ln\left(\dfrac{x}{3}\right) = 5y - 1$

$\quad 5y = \ln\left(\dfrac{x}{3}\right) + 1$

$\quad y = \dfrac{1}{5}\ln\left(\dfrac{x}{3}\right) + \dfrac{1}{5}$

$f^{-1}(x) = \dfrac{1}{5}\ln\left(\dfrac{x}{3}\right) + \dfrac{1}{5}$

2.8 $\log_5(2x) = -3$

$\quad 2x = 5^{-3}$

$\quad 2x = \dfrac{1}{125}$

$\quad x = \dfrac{1}{250}$

2.9 $10^{3x} = 70$

$\quad 3x = \log(70)$

$\quad x = \dfrac{\log(70)}{3} \approx 0.6150$

2.10 $\quad 12 = 4 \cdot e^{0.05t}$

$\quad 3 = e^{0.05t}$

$\quad 0.05t = \ln(3)$

$\quad t = \dfrac{\ln(3)}{0.05} \approx 21.9722$

The time is 21.9722 years or 21 years and 355 days (to the nearest day).

Section 3

3.1 $10^{\log(5w)} = 5w$, $\log(10^p) = p$

3.2 $\log(x) + \log(y) = \log(xy)$

3.3 $\log(5x) - \log(5) = \log(5x/5)$

$\quad = \log(x)$

3.4 $\ln(27) = \ln(3^3) = 3 \cdot \ln(3)$

3.5 $\ln(45) = \ln(3^2 \cdot 5)$

$\quad = 2 \cdot \ln(3) + \ln(5)$

3.6 $\log\left(\dfrac{x^2}{5a}\right) = \log(x^2) - \log(5a)$

$\quad = 2 \cdot \log(x) - [\log(5) + \log(a)]$

$\quad = 2 \cdot \log(x) - \log(5) - \log(a)$

3.7 $\ln(x) - \ln(y) - 2 \cdot \ln(z)$

$= \ln\left(\dfrac{x}{y}\right) - \ln(z^2)$

$= \ln\left(\dfrac{x}{yz^2}\right)$

3.8 $\quad 5.44^x = 2.3$

$\log(5.44^x) = \log(2.3)$

$x \cdot \log(5.44) = \log(2.3)$

$\quad x = \dfrac{\log(2.3)}{\log(5.44)}$

$\quad x \approx 0.4917$

3.9 $400 = 100\left(1 + \dfrac{0.05}{365}\right)^{365t}$

$\quad 4 = \left(1 + \dfrac{0.05}{365}\right)^{365t}$

$\quad 4 \approx 1.000136986^{365t}$

$365t \approx \log_{1.000136986}(4)$

$\quad t \approx \dfrac{1}{365} \cdot \dfrac{\ln(4)}{\ln(1.000136986)}$

$\quad \approx 27.72778621$ yr

$\quad \approx 27$ years 266 days

3.10 $\quad 300 = 100\left(1 + \dfrac{r}{365}\right)^{365(20)}$

$\quad 3 = \left(1 + \dfrac{r}{365}\right)^{7300}$

$1 + \dfrac{r}{365} = 3^{1/7300}$

$\quad r = 365(3^{1/7300} - 1)$

$\quad r \approx 5.5\%$

Section 4

4.1 $\log(2x + 1) = 3$

$\quad 2x + 1 = 10^3$

$\quad 2x = 999$

$\quad x = 499.5$

4.4.2 $\log(x - 1) + \log(3) = \log(x) - \log(4)$

$\quad \log(3x - 3) = \log(x/4)$

$\quad 3x - 3 = \dfrac{x}{4}$

$\quad 12x - 12 = x$

$\quad 11x = 12$

$\quad x = \dfrac{12}{11}$

4.3 $(1.05)^{3t} = 8$

$\quad 3t = \log_{1.05}(8)$

$\quad t = \dfrac{1}{3} \cdot \dfrac{\ln(8)}{\ln(1.05)}$

$\quad t \approx 14.2067$

4.4 $\quad\quad\quad 3^{x-1} = 2^x$

$\quad\quad \ln(3^{x-1}) = \ln(2^x)$

$\quad (x - 1)\ln(3) = x \cdot \ln(2)$

$\quad x \cdot \ln(3) - \ln(3) = x \cdot \ln(2)$

$x \cdot \ln(3) - x \cdot \ln(2) = \ln(3)$

$\quad x(\ln(3) - \ln(2)) = \ln(3)$

$\quad\quad x \cdot \ln(3/2) = \ln(3)$

$\quad\quad x = \dfrac{\ln(3)}{\ln(3/2)} \approx 2.7095$

4.5 First find r:

$\quad 1 = 2e^{1 \times 10^6 r}$

$\quad 0.5 = e^{1 \times 10^6 r}$

$1 \times 10^6 r = \ln(0.5)$

$\quad r = \dfrac{\ln(0.5)}{1 \times 10^6} \approx -6.93 \times 10^{-7}$

Next find t:

$\quad 0.40 = 1e^{-6.93 \times 10^{-7} t}$

$-6.93 \times 10^{-7} t = \ln(0.40)$

$\quad t = \dfrac{\ln(0.40)}{-6.93 \times 10^{-7}}$

$\quad \approx 1.32 \times 10^6$ years

4.6 $\dfrac{1}{2}A_0 = A_0 e^{4r}$

$\quad \dfrac{1}{2} = e^{4r}$

$\quad 4r = \ln(1/2)$

$\quad r = \dfrac{\ln(1/2)}{4} \approx -0.1732868$

If 99% is eliminated, 1% remains. Now find the time:

$$0.01 A_0 = A_0 e^{-0.1732868t}$$
$$0.01 = e^{-0.1732868t}$$
$$-0.1732868t = \ln(0.01)$$
$$t = \frac{\ln(0.01)}{-0.1732868} \approx 26.6$$

So 99% will be eliminated in 26.6 days.

4.7 The difference in temperature goes from 200° to 90° in 4 minutes.

$$90 = 200 e^{4r}$$
$$e^{4r} = 0.45$$
$$4r = \ln(0.45)$$
$$r = \frac{\ln(0.45)}{4} \approx -0.1996$$

Let t be the time required for the difference to go from 90° to 70°.

$$70 = 90 e^{-0.1996t}$$
$$e^{-0.1996t} = 7/9$$
$$-0.1996t = \ln(7/9)$$
$$t = \frac{\ln(7/9)}{-0.1996}$$
$$\approx 1.2589 \text{ minutes}$$

4.8
$$2000 = 120{,}000 \frac{0.075/12}{1 - (1 + 0.075/12)^{-12t}}$$
$$1 - (1 + 0.075/12)^{-12t} = 0.375$$
$$0.625 = (1 + 0.075/12)^{-12t}$$
$$-12t \cdot \ln(1 + 0.075/12) = \ln(0.625)$$
$$t = \frac{\ln(0.625)}{-12 \cdot \ln(1 + 0.075/12)}$$
$$\approx 6.2863 \text{ yr}$$
$$\approx 6 \text{ years } 3 \text{ mo}$$

Exponential and Logarithmic Functions

For Thought

1. False, the base of an exponential function is positive. **2.** True

3. True, since $2^{-3} = \dfrac{1}{8}$.

4. True **5.** True **6.** True **7.** True

8. False, since it is decreasing.

9. True, since $0.25 = 4^{-1}$.

10. True, since $\sqrt[100]{2^{173}} = \left(2^{173}\right)^{1/100}$.

1 Exercises

1. algebraic

3. exponential

5. increasing, decreasing

7. range

9. 27

11. $-(2^0) = -1$

13. $\dfrac{1}{2^3} = \dfrac{1}{8}$

15. $\left(\dfrac{2}{1}\right)^4 = 2^4 = 16$

17. $\left(8^{1/3}\right)^2 = 2^2 = 4$

19. $-\left(9^{1/2}\right)^{-3} = -(3)^{-3} = -\dfrac{1}{3^3} = -\dfrac{1}{27}$

21. $3^2 = 9$ **23.** $3^{-2} = 1/9$ **25.** $2^{-1} = 1/2$

27. $2^3 = 8$

29. $(1/4)^{-1} = 4$

31. $4^{1/2} = 2$

33. $f(x) = 5^x$ goes through $(-1, 1/5), (0, 1), (1, 5)$, domain is $(-\infty, \infty)$, range is $(0, \infty)$, increasing

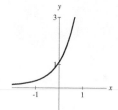

35. $f(x) = 10^{-x}$ goes through $(-1, 10), (0, 1)$, $(1, 1/10)$, domain is $(-\infty, \infty)$, range is $(0, \infty)$, decreasing

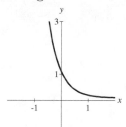

37. $f(x) = (1/4)^x$ goes through $(-1, 4), (0, 1)$, $(1, 1/4)$, domain is $(-\infty, \infty)$, range is $(0, \infty)$, decreasing

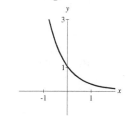

39. From the graph, we find $\lim\limits_{x \to \infty} 3^x = \infty$.

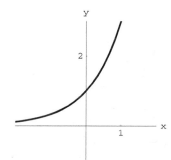

41. Using the graph, we obtain $\lim\limits_{x \to \infty} 5^{-x} = 0$.

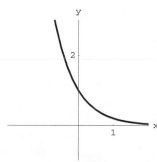

From Chapter 4 of *Student's Solutions Manual for Precalculus: Functions and Graphs*, Fourth Edition. Mark Dugopolski.

43. We see from the graph that $\lim\limits_{x\to\infty}\left(\dfrac{1}{3}\right)^x = 0$.

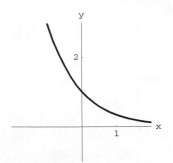

45. Using the graph, we get $\lim\limits_{x\to-\infty} e^{-x} = \infty$.

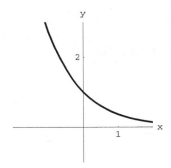

47. Shift $y = 2^x$ down by 3 units; $f(x) = 2^x - 3$
goes through $(-1, -2.5), (0, -2), (2, 1)$,
domain $(-\infty, \infty)$, range $(-3, \infty)$,
asymptote $y = -3$, increasing

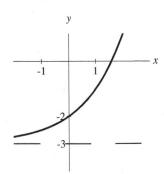

49. Shift $y = 2^x$ to left by 3 units and down by
5 units; $f(x) = 2^{x+3} - 5$ goes through
$(-4, -4.5), (-3, -4), (0, 3)$, domain $(-\infty, \infty)$,
range $(-5, \infty)$, asymptote $y = -5$, increasing

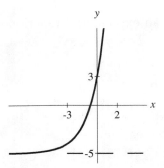

51. Reflect $y = 2^{-x}$ about x-axis, $f(x) = -2^{-x}$
goes through $(-1, -2), (0, -1), (1, -1/2)$,
domain $(-\infty, \infty)$, range $(-\infty, 0)$,
asymptote $y = 0$, increasing

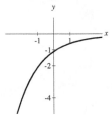

53. Reflect $y = 2^x$ about x-axis and shift
up by 1 unit, $f(x) = 1 - 2^x$ goes through
$(-1, 0.5), (0, 0), (1, -1)$, domain $(-\infty, \infty)$,
range $(-\infty, 1)$, asymptote $y = 1$, decreasing

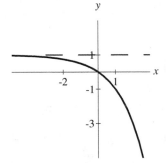

55. Shift $y = 3^x$ to right by 2 and shrink by a
factor of 0.5, $f(x) = 0.5 \cdot 3^{x-2}$ goes through
$(0, 1/18), (2, 0.5), (3, 1.5)$, domain $(-\infty, \infty)$,
range $(0, \infty)$, asymptote $y = 0$, increasing

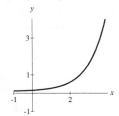

57. Stretch $y = (0.5)^x$ by a factor of 500, $f(x) = 500 \cdot (0.5)^x$ goes through $(0, 500)$, $(1, 250)$, domain $(-\infty, \infty)$, range $(0, \infty)$, asymptote $y = 0$, decreasing

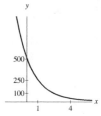

59. $y = 2^{x-5} - 2$

61. $y = -\left(\dfrac{1}{4}\right)^{x-1} - 2$

63. Since $2^x = 2^6$, solution set is $\{6\}$.

65. $\{-1\}$

67. Multiplying the equation by -1, $3^x = 3^3$ and the solution set is $\{3\}$.

69. $\{-2\}$

71. Since $(2^3)^x = 2^{3x} = 2$, $3x = 1$.

The solution set is $\left\{\dfrac{1}{3}\right\}$.

73. $\{-2\}$

75. Since $(2^{-1})^x = 2^{-x} = 2^3$, $-x = 3$. The solution set is $\{-3\}$.

77. Since $10^{x-1} = 10^{-2}$, $x - 1 = -2$. The solution set is $\{-1\}$.

79. Since $2^{2x} = 4^x$, the original equation may be written as $4^x = 64$. Then the solution set is $\{3\}$.

81. Since $2^x = 4$, we find $x = 2$.

83. Since $2^x = \dfrac{1}{2}$, we obtain $x = -1$.

85. Since $\left(\dfrac{1}{3}\right)^x = 1$, we get $x = 0$.

87. Since $\left(\dfrac{1}{3}\right)^x = 3^3$, we find $x = -3$.

89. Since $10^x = 1000$, we obtain $x = 3$.

91. Since $10^x = 0.1 = 10^{-1}$, we find $x = -1$.

93. 1   **95.** -1

97. $(2, 9), (1, 3), (-1, 1/3), (-2, 1/9)$

99. $(0, 1), (-2, 25), (-1, 5), (1, 1/5)$

101. $(4, -16), (-2, -1/4), (-1, -1/2), (5, -32)$

103. When interest is compounded n times a year, the amount at the end of 6 years is

$$A(n) = 5000\left(1 + \frac{0.08}{n}\right)^{6n}$$

and the interest earned after 6 years is

$$I(n) = A(n) - 5000.$$

a) If $n = 1$, then $A(1) = \$7934.37$ and $I(1) = \$2934.37$.

b) If $n = 4$, then $A(4) = \$8042.19$ and $I(4) = \$3042.19$.

c) If $n = 12$, then $A(12) = \$8067.51$ and $I(12) = \$3067.51$.

d) If $n = 365$, then $A(365) = \$8079.95$ and $I(365) = \$3079.95$.

105. After t years, a deposit of \$5000 will amount to

$$A(t) = 5000e^{0.08t}.$$

We use 30 days per month and 365 days per year.

a) After 6 years, the amount is $A(6) = \$8080.37$.

b) After 8 years and 3 months, the amount is $A\left(8 + \dfrac{90}{365}\right) = \$9671.31$.

c) After 5 years, 4 months, and 22 days, the amount is

$$A\left(8 + \frac{4(30) + 22}{365}\right) = \$7694.93.$$

d) After 20 years and 321 days, the amount is

$$A\left(20 + \frac{321}{365}\right) = \$26,570.30.$$

107. Assume there are 365 days in a year and 30 days in a month. The present value is

$$3000 \left(1 + \frac{0.065}{365}\right)^{-(365)(5+120/365)} = \$2121.82.$$

109. $20,000e^{-0.0542(30)} = \$3934.30$

111. a) The interest for first hour is

$$10^6 \cdot e^{0.06\left(\frac{1}{(24)(365)}\right)} - 10^6 = \$6.85.$$

b) The interest for 500th hour is the difference between the amounts in the account at the end of the 500th and 499th hours i.e.

$$10^6 e^{0.06\left(\frac{500}{(24)(365)}\right)} - 10^6 e^{0.06\left(\frac{499}{(24)(365)}\right)} = \$6.87$$

113. If $t = 0$, then $A = 200e^0 = 200$ g.
If $t = 500$, then $A = 200e^{-0.001(500)} \approx 121.3$ g.

115. a) In 2006 when $t = 1$, the number of Facebook users was $0.1e^{1.45}$ million or about 400,000 users.

b) In 2011 when $t = 6$, the number of Facebook users was about $0.1e^{1.45(6)} \approx 600$ million.

117. a) Using a calculator, we find that the exponential regression curve is

$$y = 8.44(1.23)^x$$

b) Yes

c) In 2010 when $t = 20$, the number of subscribers is

$$8.44(1.23)^{20} \approx 530 \text{ million.}$$

119. $P = 10\left(\frac{1}{2}\right)^n$

121. When $t = 31$, the number of damaged O-rings is $n = 644e^{-0.15(31)} \approx 6$.

125. $y = 2$, $x = -7$

127. Rewrite $|2x - 5| > 7$ as follows:

$$2x - 5 > 7 \quad \text{or} \quad 2x - 5 < -7$$
$$2x > 12 \quad \text{or} \quad 2x < -2$$
$$x > 6 \quad \text{or} \quad x < -1$$

The solution set is $(-\infty, -1) \cup (6, \infty)$.

129. Solve for x:

$$2x - 5 = y$$
$$2x = y + 5$$
$$x = \frac{y + 5}{2}$$

For Thought

1. True

2. False, since $\log_{100}(10) = 1/2$.

3. True

4. True

5. False, the domain is $(0, \infty)$.

6. True

7. True

8. False, since $\log_a(0)$ is undefined.

9. True

10. True

2 Exercises

1. logarithmic

3. natural

5. vertical asymptote

7. logarithmic family

9. 6   **11.** -4

13. $\dfrac{1}{4}$ **15.** -3

17. Since $2^6 = 64$, $\log_2(64) = 6$.

19. Since $3^{-4} = \dfrac{1}{81}$, $\log_3\left(\dfrac{1}{81}\right) = -4$.

21. Since $16^{1/4} = 2$, $\log_{16}(2) = \dfrac{1}{4}$.

23. Since $\left(\dfrac{1}{5}\right)^{-3} = 125$, $\log_{1/5}(125) = -3$.

25. Since $10^{-1} = 0.1$, $\log(0.1) = -1$

27. Since $10^0 = 1$, $\log(1) = 0$.

29. Since $e^1 = e$, $\ln(e) = 1$.

31. -5

33. $y = \log_3(x)$ goes through $(1/3, -1)$, $(1, 0)$, $(3, 1)$, domain $(0, \infty)$, range $(-\infty, \infty)$

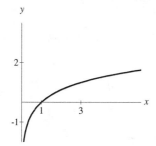

35. $f(x) = \log_5(x)$ goes through $(1/5, -1)$, $(1, 0)$, and $(5, 1)$, domain $(0, \infty)$, range $(-\infty, \infty)$

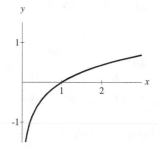

37. $y = \log_{1/2}(x)$ goes through $(2, -1)$, $(1, 0)$, $(1/2, 1)$, domain $(0, \infty)$, range $(-\infty, \infty)$

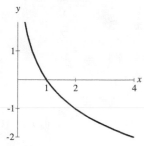

39. $h(x) = \log_{1/5}(x)$ goes through $(5, -1)$, $(1, 0)$, $(1/5, 1)$, domain $(0, \infty)$, range $(-\infty, \infty)$

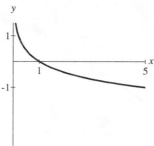

41. $f(x) = \ln(x - 1)$ goes through $\left(1 + \dfrac{1}{e}, -1\right)$, $(2, 0)$, $(1 + e, 1)$, domain $(1, \infty)$, range $(-\infty, \infty)$

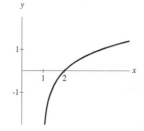

43. $f(x) = -3 + \log(x + 2)$ goes through $(-1.9, -4)$, $(-1, -3)$, $(8, -2)$, domain $(-2, \infty)$, range $(-\infty, \infty)$

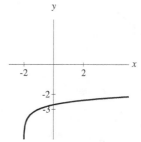

45. $f(x) = -\dfrac{1}{2}\log(x - 1)$ goes through $(1.1, 0.5)$, $(2, 0)$, $(11, -0.5)$, domain $(1, \infty)$, range $(-\infty, \infty)$

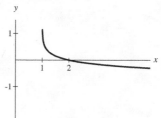

47. From the graph, we find $\lim\limits_{x\to\infty} \log_3 x = \infty$.

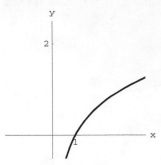

49. Using the graph, we obtain $\lim\limits_{x\to 0^+} \log_{1/2} x = \infty$.

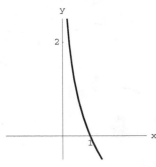

51. From the graph, we get $\lim\limits_{x\to 0^+} \ln x = -\infty$.

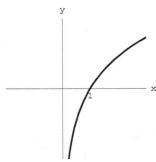

53. From the graph, we find $\lim\limits_{x\to\infty} \log x = \infty$.

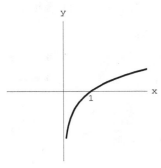

55. $y = \ln(x-3) - 4$

57. $y = -\log_2(x-5) - 1$

59. $2^5 = 32$

61. $5^y = x$

63. $10^z = 1000$

65. $e^x = 5$

67. $a^m = x$

69. $\log_5(125) = 3$

71. $\ln(y) = 3$

73. $\log(y) = m$

75. $\log_a(y) = z$

77. $\log_a(n) = x - 1$

79. $f^{-1}(x) = \log_2(x)$

81. $f^{-1}(x) = 7^x$

83. Replace $f(x)$ by y, interchange x and y, solve for y, and replace y by $f^{-1}(x)$.

$$\begin{aligned} y &= \ln(x-1) \\ x &= \ln(y-1) \\ e^x &= y - 1 \\ y = f^{-1}(x) &= e^x + 1 \end{aligned}$$

85. Replace $f(x)$ by y, interchange x and y, solve for y, and replace y by $f^{-1}(x)$.

$$\begin{aligned} y &= 3^{x+2} \\ x &= 3^{y+2} \\ y + 2 &= \log_3(x) \\ y = f^{-1}(x) &= \log_3(x) - 2 \end{aligned}$$

87. Replace $f(x)$ by y, interchange x and y, solve for y, and replace y by $f^{-1}(x)$.

$$\begin{aligned} x &= \frac{1}{2}10^{y-1} + 5 \\ x - 5 &= \frac{1}{2}10^{y-1} \\ 2x - 10 &= 10^{y-1} \\ \log(2x-10) &= y - 1 \\ \log(2x-10) + 1 &= y \\ f^{-1}(x) &= \log(2x-10) + 1 \end{aligned}$$

89. Since $2^8 = x$, the solution is $x = 256$.

91. Since $3^{1/2} = x$, the solution is $x = \sqrt{3}$.

93. Since $x^2 = 16$ and the base of a logarithm is positive, $x = 4$.

95. By using the definition of the logarithm, we get $x = \log_3(77)$.

97. Since $y = \ln(x)$ is one-to-one, $x - 3 = 2x - 9$. The solution is $x = 6$.

99. Since $x^2 = 18$, we obtain $x = \sqrt{18} = 3\sqrt{2}$. The base of a logarithm is positive.

101. Since $x + 1 = \log_3(7)$, $x = \log_3(7) - 1$.

103. Since $y = \log(x)$ is one-to-one, we get

$$
\begin{aligned}
x &= 6 - x^2 \\
x^2 + x - 6 &= 0 \\
(x + 3)(x - 2) &= 0 \\
x &= -3, 2.
\end{aligned}
$$

But $\log(-3)$ is undefined, so the solution is $x = 2$.

105. Since $x^{-2/3} = \dfrac{1}{9}$, we find

$$
x = \pm \left(\frac{1}{9}\right)^{-3/2} = \pm \left(\frac{1}{3}\right)^{-3} = \pm 27.
$$

The solution is $x = 27$ since a negative number cannot be a base.

107. Since $(2^2)^{2x-1} = 2^{4x-2} = 2^{-1}$, we get

$$
4x - 2 = -1.
$$

The solution is $x = \dfrac{1}{4}$.

109. Since $32^x = 64$, we get

$$
2^{5x} = 2^6.
$$

Thus, the solution is $x = \dfrac{6}{5}$.

111. Since $\log_3(\log_4(x)) = 1$, we obtain

$$
\log_4 x = 3.
$$

Then $x = 4^3 = 64$.

113. $x = \log 25 \approx 1.3979$

115. Solving for x, we obtain

$$
\begin{aligned}
e^{2x} &= 3 \\
2x &= \ln(3) \\
x &= \frac{1}{2}\ln(3) \\
x &\approx 0.5493.
\end{aligned}
$$

117. Solving for x, we get

$$
\begin{aligned}
e^x &= \frac{4}{5} \\
x &= \ln\left(\frac{4}{5}\right) \\
x &\approx -0.2231.
\end{aligned}
$$

119. Solving for x, we find

$$
\begin{aligned}
\frac{1}{10^x} &= 2 \\
\frac{1}{2} &= 10^x \\
x &= \log\left(\frac{1}{2}\right) \\
x &\approx -0.3010.
\end{aligned}
$$

121. Solving for the year t when \$10 grows to \$20, we find

$$
\begin{aligned}
20 &= 10e^{rt} \\
2 &= e^{rt} \\
\ln 2 &= rt \\
\frac{\ln 2}{r} &= t.
\end{aligned}
$$

a) If $r = 2\%$, then $t = \dfrac{\ln 2}{0.02} \approx 34.7$ years.

b) If $r = 4\%$, then $t = \dfrac{\ln 2}{0.04} \approx 17.3$ years.

c) If $r = 8\%$, then $t = \dfrac{\ln 2}{0.08} \approx 8.7$ years.

d) If $r = 16\%$, then $t = \dfrac{\ln 2}{0.16} \approx 4.3$ years.

123. Solving for the annual percentage rate r when $10 becomes $30, we find

$$30 = 10e^{rt}$$
$$3 = e^{rt}$$
$$\ln 3 = rt$$
$$\frac{\ln 3}{t} = r.$$

a) If $t = 5$ years, then $r = \dfrac{\ln 3}{5} \approx 0.2197 \approx 22\%$.

b) If $t = 10$ years, then $r = \dfrac{\ln 3}{10} \approx 0.10986 \approx 11\%$.

c) If $t = 20$ years, then $r = \dfrac{\ln 3}{20} \approx 0.0549 \approx 5.5\%$.

d) If $t = 40$ years, then $r = \dfrac{\ln 3}{40} \approx 0.027465 \approx 2.7\%$.

125. Let t be the number of years.

$$1000 \cdot e^{0.14t} = 10^6$$
$$e^{0.14t} = 1000$$
$$0.14t = \ln(1000)$$
$$t \approx 49.341 \text{ years}$$

Note, $0.341(365) \approx 125$.
It will take 49 years and 125 days.

127. Since $e^{rt} = A/P$, $rt = \ln(A/P)$ and

$$r = \frac{\ln(A/P)}{t}.$$

Thus, $1000 will double in 3 years if the rate is $r = \dfrac{\ln(2000/1000)}{3} \approx 0.231$ or 23.1%.

129.

(a) Let t be the number of years.

$$P \cdot e^{0.1t} = 2P$$
$$e^{0.1t} = 2$$
$$0.1t = \ln(2)$$
$$t = \frac{\ln(2)}{0.1} \approx 6.9$$

An investment at 10% doubles every 6.9 years.

(b) If t is the number of years it takes before an investment doubles, then

$$P \cdot e^{rt} = 2P$$
$$e^{rt} = 2$$
$$rt = \ln(2)$$
$$t = \frac{\ln(2)}{r}$$
$$t \approx \frac{0.70}{r}.$$

In particular, if $r = 0.07$ then

$$t \approx \frac{0.70}{0.07} = 10 \text{ years.}$$

That is, at 10%, an investment will double in about 10 years.

131. Let r be the interest rate.

$$4,000 \cdot e^{200r} = 4,500,000$$
$$e^{200r} = 1,125$$
$$200r = \ln(1,125)$$
$$r = \frac{\ln(1,125)}{200} \approx 0.035$$

The rate is 3.5% .

133. Let t be the number of years.

$$F_o \cdot e^{-0.052t} = 0.6F_o$$
$$e^{-0.052t} = 0.6$$
$$-0.052t = \ln(0.6)$$
$$t = \frac{\ln(0.6)}{-0.052} \approx 9.8$$

Only 60% of the present forest will remain after 9.8 years.

135. Let r be the annual rate from 1950 to 1987.

$$\begin{aligned} 2.5 \cdot e^{37r} &= 5 \\ e^{37r} &= 2 \\ 37r &= \ln(2) \\ r = \frac{\ln(2)}{37} &\approx 0.0187 \end{aligned}$$

The annual rate is 1.87%.

If the annual rate is 1.63% and the initial population is 5 billion in 1987, the world population in year 2010 will be

$$5 \cdot e^{0.0163(23)} \approx 7.3 \text{ billion.}$$

137.

(a) $30e^{1.2(7)} \approx 133,412$ acres

(b) Solve for t:

$$\begin{aligned} 30e^{1.2t} &= 53,480,960 \\ 1.2t &= \ln\left(\frac{53,480,960}{30}\right) \\ t &\approx 11.9 \end{aligned}$$

It will take about 12 days.

139.

a) The function is given by

$$\begin{aligned} p - 100 &= \frac{100 - 10}{2 - 4}(x - 2) \\ p - 100 &= -45(x - 2) \\ p &= -45x + 90 + 100 \\ p &= -45x + 190 \\ p &= -45\log(I) + 190. \end{aligned}$$

b) $p = -45\log(100,000) + 190 = -35\%$ or 0% of the population is expected to be without safe drinking water, i.e., everyone is expected to have safe water.

141. $pH = -\log\left(10^{-4.1}\right) = 4.1$

143. $pH = -\log\left(10^{-3.7}\right) = 3.7$

145. By substituting $x = 1$, we find a formula for c.

$$\begin{aligned} a \cdot b^x &= a \cdot e^{cx} \\ b^x &= e^{cx} \\ b &= e^c \\ c &= \ln b. \end{aligned}$$

By using this formula, we find

$$y = 500(1.036)^x = 500e^{\ln(1.036)x}$$

and the continuous growth rate is

$$\ln(1.036) \cdot 100 \approx 3.54\%.$$

149. Domain $(-\infty, \infty)$, range $(-\infty, 7]$

151. $(8 \times 10^{-27})(25 \times 10^6) = 200 \times 10^{-21} = 2 \times 10^{-19}$

153. Rewrite the equation:

$$\begin{aligned} x(x^2 - 4x + 13) &= 0 \\ x((x - 2)^2 + 9) &= 0 \end{aligned}$$

Then $x = 0$ or $x - 2 = \pm 3i$.

The solution set is $\{0, 2 \pm 3i\}$.

For Thought

1. False, since $\log(8) - \log(3) = \log(8/3) \neq \dfrac{\log(8)}{\log(3)}$.

2. True, since $\ln(3^{1/2}) = \dfrac{1}{2} \cdot \ln(3) = \dfrac{\ln(3)}{2}$.

3. True, since $\dfrac{\log_{19}(8)}{\log_{19}(2)} = \log_2(8) = 3 = \log_3(27)$.

4. True, because of the base-change formula.

5. False

6. False, since $\log(x) - \log(2) = \log(x/2)$.

7. False, since the solution of the first equation is $x = -2$ and the second equation is not defined when $x = -2$.

8. True   **9.**   False, since x can be negative.

10. False, since a can be negative and so $\ln(a)$ will not be a real number.

3 Exercises

1. sum

3. power

5. $\sqrt{y}$ **7.** $y+1$ **9.**   999

11. $\log(15)$

13. $\log_2((x-1)x) = \log_2(x^2 - x)$

15. $\log_4(6)$ **17.** $\ln\left(\dfrac{x^8}{x^3}\right) = \ln(x^5)$

19. $\log_2(3x) = \log_2(3) + \log_2(x)$

21. $\log\left(\dfrac{x}{2}\right) = \log(x) - \log(2)$

23. $\log((x-1)(x+1)) = \log(x-1) + \log(x+1)$

25. $\ln\left(\dfrac{x-1}{x}\right) = \ln(x-1) - \ln(x)$

27. $\log_a(5^3) = 3\log_a(5)$

29. $\log_a(5^{1/2}) = \dfrac{1}{2}\cdot\log_a(5)$

31. $\log_a(5^{-1}) = -\log_a(5)$

33. $\log_a(2) + \log_a(5)$

35. $\log_a(5/2) = \log_a(5) - \log_a(2)$

37. $\log_a\left(\sqrt{2^2\cdot 5}\right) = \dfrac{1}{2}\left(2\log_a(2) + \log_a(5)\right) =$
$\log_a(2) + \dfrac{1}{2}\log_a(5)$

39. $\log_a(4) - \log_a(25) = \log_a(2^2) - \log_a(5^2) =$
$2\log_a(2) - 2\log_a(5)$

41. $\log_3(5) + \log_3(x)$

43. $\log_2(5) - \log_2(2y) = \log_2(5) - \log_2(2) - \log_2(y)$

45. $\log(3) + \dfrac{1}{2}\log(x)$

47. $\log(3) + (x-1)\log(2)$

49. $\dfrac{1}{3}\cdot\ln(xy) - \dfrac{4}{3}\ln(t) = \dfrac{1}{3}\cdot\ln(x) + \dfrac{1}{3}\cdot\ln(y) - \dfrac{4}{3}\ln(t)$

51. $\ln(6\sqrt{x-1}) - \ln(5x^3) =$
$\ln(6) + \dfrac{1}{2}\cdot\ln(x-1) - \ln(5) - 3\cdot\ln(x)$

53. $\log_2(5x^3)$

55. $\log_7(x^5) - \log_7(x^8) = \log(x^5/x^8) = \log_7(x^{-3})$

57. $\log(2xy/z)$

59. $\log\left(\dfrac{\sqrt{x}}{y}\right) + \log\left(\dfrac{z}{\sqrt[3]{w}}\right) = \log\left(\dfrac{z\sqrt{x}}{y\sqrt[3]{w}}\right)$

61. $\log_4(x^6) + \log_4(x^{12}) + \log_4(x^2) = \log_4(x^{20})$

63. Since $2^x = 9$, we get $x = \dfrac{\log 9}{\log 2} \approx 3.1699$.

65. Since $0.56^x = 8$, we get
$x = \dfrac{\log 8}{\log 0.56} \approx -3.5864$.

67. Since $1.06^x = 2$, we get
$x = \dfrac{\log 2}{\log 1.06} \approx 11.8957$.

69. Since $0.73^x = 0.5$, we get
$x = \dfrac{\log 0.5}{\log 0.73} \approx 2.2025$.

71. $\dfrac{\ln(9)}{\ln(4)} \approx \dfrac{2.1972246}{1.3862944} \approx 1.5850$

73. $\dfrac{\ln(2.3)}{\ln(9.1)} \approx \dfrac{0.8329091}{2.2082744} \approx 0.3772$

75. $\dfrac{\ln(12)}{\ln(1/2)} \approx -3.5850$

77. Since $4t = \log_{1.02}(3) = \dfrac{\ln(3)}{\ln(1.02)}$,
we find $t = \dfrac{\ln(3)}{4\cdot\ln(1.02)} \approx 13.8695$.

79. Since $365t = \log_{1.0001}(3.5) = \dfrac{\ln(3.5)}{\ln(1.0001)}$,
we get $t = \dfrac{\ln(3.5)}{365\cdot\ln(1.0001)} \approx 34.3240$.

81. $1 + r = \sqrt[3]{2.3}$, so $r = \sqrt[3]{2.3} - 1 \approx 0.3200$

83.

$$\left(1 + \frac{r}{12}\right)^{360} = 4.2$$

$$1 + \frac{r}{12} = \pm \sqrt[360]{4.2}$$

$$r = 12\left(\pm \sqrt[360]{4.2} - 1\right)$$

$$r \approx 0.0479, -24.0479$$

85. Since $x^5 = 33.4$, we get $x = \sqrt[5]{33.4} \approx 2.0172$.

87. Since $x^{-1.3} = 0.546$, we have $x = 0.546^{1/(-1.3)}$ or $x \approx 1.5928$.

89. Let t be the number of years.

$$800\left(1 + \frac{0.08}{365}\right)^{365t} = 2000$$

$$\left(1 + \frac{0.08}{365}\right)^{365t} = 2.5$$

$$(1.0002192)^{365t} \approx 2.5$$

$$365t \approx \log_{1.0002192}(2.5)$$

$$t \approx \frac{1}{365} \cdot \frac{\ln(2.5)}{\ln(1.0002192)}$$

$$t \approx 11.454889$$

$$t \approx 11 \text{ years, } 166 \text{ days}$$

91. Let t be the number of years.

$$W\left(1 + \frac{0.1}{4}\right)^{4t} = 3W$$

$$(1.025)^{4t} = 3$$

$$4t \approx \log_{1.025}(3)$$

$$t \approx \frac{1}{4} \cdot \frac{\ln(3)}{\ln(1.025)}$$

$$t \approx 11.123 \text{ years}$$

$$t \approx 11.123(4) \approx 44 \text{ quarters}$$

93. Let t be the number of years.

$$500(1 + r)^{25} = 2000$$

$$(1 + r)^{25} = 4$$

$$1 + r \approx \sqrt[25]{4}$$

$$r = \sqrt[25]{4} - 1$$

$$r \approx 0.057 \text{ or } 5.7\%$$

95. Let t be the number of years.

$$4000(1 + r)^{200} = 4.5 \times 10^6$$

$$(1 + r)^{200} = 1125$$

$$r = \sqrt[200]{1125} - 1$$

$$r \approx 0.035752 \text{ or } 3.58\%$$

97. Let r be the annual growth rate.

$$1995(1 + r)^{39} = 10,890$$

$$r = \left(\frac{10,890}{1995}\right)^{1/39} - 1$$

$$r \approx 0.0444$$

$$r \approx 4.4\%$$

99. The Richter scale rating is

$$\log(I) - \log(I_o) = \log\left(\frac{I}{I_o}\right).$$

When $I = 1000 \cdot I_o$, the Richter scale rating is

$$\log\left(\frac{1000 \cdot I_o}{I_o}\right) = \log(1000) = 3.$$

101. $t = \frac{1}{r}\ln(P/P_o) = \frac{1}{r}\ln(P) - \frac{1}{r}\ln(P_o)$

103.

(a) p decreases as n increases

(b) Solving for n, one can take the logarithm of both sides and to note that $y = \log(x)$ is an increasing function.

$$\left(\frac{7,059,051}{7,059,052}\right)^n > \frac{1}{2}$$

$$\log\left(\left(\frac{7,059,051}{7,059,052}\right)^n\right) > \log\left(\frac{1}{2}\right)$$

$$n\log\left(\frac{7,059,051}{7,059,052}\right) > \log\left(\frac{1}{2}\right)$$

$$n < \frac{\log(1/2)}{\log(7,059,051/7,059,052)}$$

$$n < 4,892,962$$

If at most $4,892,961$ tickets are purchsed, then the probability of a rollover is greater than 50%.

105. We note that $MR(x) = R(x+1) - R(x) =$
$500 \cdot \log(x+2) - 500 \cdot \log(x+1) =$

$$500 \cdot \log\left(\frac{x+2}{x+1}\right) = \log\left(\left(\frac{x+2}{x+1}\right)^{500}\right).$$

Hence, as $x \to \infty$, then $\dfrac{x+2}{x+1} \to 1$

and $MR(x) \to 0$.

107.

a) Let x be the number of years since 1990 and let y be the number of computers per 1000 people. With the aid of a calculator, we find that an exponential regression curve is

$$y = 217.9(1.084)^x$$

b) $y = 217.9(e^{\ln 1.084})^x \approx 217.9e^{0.0807x}$

c) From part b), the continuous growth is 8.07%

d) Substitute $y = 1500$ into the equation in part a):

$$1500 = 217.9(1.084)^x$$

$$\frac{1500}{217.9} = 1.084^x$$

$$\ln\left(\frac{1500}{217.9}\right) = x \ln 1.084$$

$$23.9 \approx x$$

In 2014 ($= 1990 + 24$), there will be 1500 computers per 1000 people.

e) No, the data does not look exponential, rather it looks linear.

109. Note, $x^2 \geq 0$ for all real numbers x. Then the domain of $y = \log(x^2)$ is $(-\infty, 0) \cup (0, \infty)$ and the domain of $y = 2\log(x)$ is $(0, \infty)$. Thus, these two functions are not the same. The graph of $y = \log(x^2)$ is shown below

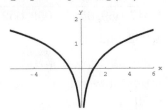

and the graph of $y = 2\log(x)$ is given next.

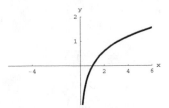

Note, the domain $y = \log(x(x-1))$ and the domain of $y = \log(x) + \log(x-1)$ are not the same.

111. Let $a > 0$, $a \neq 1$. Using the definition of a logarithm and properties of exponents, we have

$$a^{\log_a(M^p)} = M^p = \left(a^{\log_a(M)}\right)^p = a^{p \cdot \log_a(M)}.$$

Then $a^{\log_a(M^p)} = a^{p \cdot \log_a(M)}$. Since $a^s = a^t$ implies $s = t$, we have $\log_a(M^p) = p \cdot \log_a(M)$.

113. Domain $(1, \infty)$, range $(-\infty, \infty)$

115. $10{,}000e^{0.043(5.25)} = \$12{,}532.6$

117. Solve for x:

$$\frac{3}{8}x - \frac{15}{8} = \frac{3}{2}x + \frac{5}{6}$$

$$-\frac{15}{8} - \frac{5}{6} = \frac{3}{2}x - \frac{3}{8}x$$

$$-\frac{65}{24} = \frac{9}{8}x$$

$$-\frac{65}{24} \cdot \frac{8}{9} = x$$

$$-\frac{65}{27} = x$$

The solution set is $\{-\frac{65}{27}\}$.

For Thought

1. True, since $(1.02)^x = 7$ is equivalent to $x = \log_{1.02}(7)$.

2. True, for $x(1 - \ln(3)) = 8$ implies $x = \dfrac{8}{1 - \ln(3)}$.

3. False, $\ln(1 - \sqrt{6})$ is undefined.

4. True, by the definition of a logarithm.

5. False, the exact solution is $x = \log_3(17)$ which is not the same as 2.5789.

6. False, since $x = -2$ is not a solution of the first equation but is a solution of the second one.

7. True, since $4^x = 2^{2x} = 2^{x-1}$ is equivalent to $2x = x - 1$.

8. True, since we may take the ln of both sides of $1.09^x = 2.3$.

9. True, since $\dfrac{\ln(2)}{\ln(7)} = \dfrac{\log(2)}{\log(7)}$.

10. True, since $\log(e) \cdot \ln(10) = \ln\left(10^{\log(e)}\right) = \ln(e) = 1$.

4 Exercises

1. Since $x = 2^3$, we get $x = 8$.

3. Since $10^2 = x + 20$, $x = 80$.

5. Since $10^1 = x^2 - 15$, we get $x^2 = 25$. The solutions are $x = \pm 5$.

7. Note, $x^2 = 9$ and $x = \pm 3$. Since the base of a logarithm is positive, the solution is $x = 3$.

9. Note, $x^{-2} = 4$ or $\dfrac{1}{4} = x^2$. Since the base of a logarithm is positive, the solution is $x = \dfrac{1}{2}$.

11. Since $x^3 = 10$, the solution is $x = \sqrt[3]{10}$.

13. Since $x = \left(8^{-1/3}\right)^2$, the solution is $x = \dfrac{1}{4}$.

15.

$$
\begin{aligned}
\log_2(x^2 - 4) &= 5 \\
x^2 - 4 &= 2^5 \\
x^2 &= 36 \\
x &= \pm 6
\end{aligned}
$$

Checking $x = -6$, one gets $\log_2(-6 + 2)$ which is undefined. The solution is $x = 6$.

17.

$$
\begin{aligned}
\log_6\left(\frac{x^2 - x - 6}{14}\right) &= 0 \\
\frac{x^2 - x - 6}{14} &= 6^0 = 1 \\
x^2 - x - 6 &= 14 \\
x^2 - x - 20 &= 0 \\
(x - 5)(x + 4) &= 0
\end{aligned}
$$

Note, if $x = -4$, then $\log \frac{x-3}{2}$ is undefined. Thus, $x = 5$.

19.

$$
\begin{aligned}
\log\left(\frac{x + 1}{x}\right) &= 3 \\
\frac{x + 1}{x} &= 10^3 \\
x + 1 &= 1000x \\
1 &= 999x \\
x &= \frac{1}{999}
\end{aligned}
$$

21.

$$
\begin{aligned}
\log_4\left(\frac{x}{x + 2}\right) &= 2 \\
\frac{x}{x + 2} &= 16 \\
x &= 16x + 32 \\
-\frac{32}{15} &= x
\end{aligned}
$$

Note, if $x = -32/15$, then $\log_4 x$ is undefined. The solution set is $\emptyset$.

23.

$$
\begin{aligned}
\log(5) + \log(x) &= 2 \\
\log(5x) &= 2 \\
5x &= 10^2 \\
x &= 20
\end{aligned}
$$

25. Since $\ln(x(x + 2)) = \ln(8)$ and $y = \ln(x)$ is one-to-one, we get

$$
\begin{aligned}
x^2 + 2x &= 8 \\
x^2 + 2x - 8 &= 0 \\
(x + 4)(x - 2) &= 0 \\
x &= -4, 2
\end{aligned}
$$

Since $\ln(-4)$ is undefined, the solution is $x = 2$.

27. Since $\log(4x) = \log\left(\dfrac{5}{x}\right)$ and $y = \log(x)$

is one-to-one, we obtain

$$
\begin{aligned}
4x &= \frac{5}{x} \\
4x^2 &= 5 \\
x^2 &= \frac{5}{4} \\
x &= \pm\frac{\sqrt{5}}{2}.
\end{aligned}
$$

But $\log\left(-\dfrac{\sqrt{5}}{2}\right)$ is undefined, so $x = \dfrac{\sqrt{5}}{2}$.

29. Since $\log_2\left(\dfrac{x}{3x-1}\right) = 0$, we get

$$
\begin{aligned}
\frac{x}{3x-1} &= 1 \\
x &= 3x - 1 \\
1 &= 2x \\
x &= \frac{1}{2}.
\end{aligned}
$$

31.

$$
\begin{aligned}
x \cdot \ln(3) + x \cdot \ln(2) &= 2 \\
x(\ln(3) + \ln(2)) &= 2 \\
&= \frac{2}{\ln(3) + \ln(2)} \\
x &= \frac{2}{\ln(6)}
\end{aligned}
$$

33. Since $x - 1 = \log_2(7)$, $x = \dfrac{\ln(7)}{\ln(2)} + 1 \approx 3.8074$.

35. Since $4x = \log_{1.09}(3.4)$, we find

$$
x = \frac{1}{4} \cdot \frac{\ln(3.4)}{\ln(1.09)} \approx 3.5502.
$$

37. Since $-x = \log_3(30)$, we obtain

$$
x = -\frac{\ln(30)}{\ln(3)} \approx -3.0959.
$$

39. Note, $-3x^2 = \ln(9)$. There is no solution since the left-hand side is non-negative and the right-hand side is positive.

41.

$$
\begin{aligned}
\ln(6^x) &= \ln(3^{x+1}) \\
x \cdot \ln(6) &= (x+1) \cdot \ln(3) \\
x \cdot \ln(6) &= x \cdot \ln(3) + \ln(3) \\
x(\ln(6) - \ln(3)) &= \ln(3) \\
x &= \frac{\ln(3)}{\ln(6) - \ln(3)} \\
x &\approx 1.5850
\end{aligned}
$$

43.

$$
\begin{aligned}
\ln(e^{x+1}) &= \ln(10^x) \\
(x+1) \cdot \ln(e) &= x \cdot \ln(10) \\
x + 1 &= x \cdot \ln(10) \\
1 &= x(\ln(10) - 1) \\
x &= \frac{1}{\ln(10) - 1} \\
x &\approx 0.7677
\end{aligned}
$$

45.

$$
\begin{aligned}
2^{x-1} &= (2^2)^{3x} \\
2^{x-1} &= 2^{6x} \\
x - 1 &= 6x \\
-1 &= 5x \\
x &= -0.2
\end{aligned}
$$

47.

$$
\begin{aligned}
\ln(6^{x+1}) &= \ln(12^x) \\
(x+1) \cdot \ln(6) &= x \cdot \ln(12) \\
x \cdot \ln(6) + \ln(6) &= x \cdot \ln(12) \\
\ln(6) &= x(\ln(12) - \ln(6)) \\
x &= \frac{\ln(6)}{\ln(12) - \ln(6)} \\
x &\approx 2.5850
\end{aligned}
$$

49. Since $3 = e^{-\ln(w)} = e^{\ln(1/w)} = 1/w$, we have $\dfrac{1}{w} = 3$ and $w = \dfrac{1}{3}$.

51.

$$(\log(z))^2 = 2 \cdot \log(z)$$
$$(\log(z))^2 - 2 \cdot \log(z) = 0$$
$$\log(z) \cdot (\log(z) - 2) = 0$$
$$\log(z) = 0 \quad \text{or} \quad \log(z) = 2$$
$$z = 10^0 \quad \text{or} \quad z = 10^2$$
$$z = 1 \quad \text{or} \quad z = 100$$

The solutions are $z = 1, 100$.

53. Divide the equation by $4(1.03)^x$.

$$\left(\frac{1.02}{1.03}\right)^x = \frac{3}{4}$$

$$\ln\left(\left(\frac{1.02}{1.03}\right)^x\right) = \ln\left(\frac{3}{4}\right)$$

$$x \cdot \ln\left(\frac{1.02}{1.03}\right) = \ln\left(\frac{3}{4}\right)$$

$$x = \frac{\ln\left(\dfrac{3}{4}\right)}{\ln\left(\dfrac{1.02}{1.03}\right)}$$

$$x \approx 29.4872$$

55. Note that $e^{\ln((x^2)^3) - \ln(x^2)} = e^{\ln(x^6) - \ln(x^2)} = e^{\ln(x^6/x^2)} = e^{\ln(x^4)} = x^4$.
Thus, $x^4 = 16$ and $x = \pm 2$.
But $\ln(-2)$ is undefined, so $x = 2$.

57. Since $\left(\dfrac{1}{2}\right)^2 = \dfrac{1}{4}$, we find

$$\left(\frac{1}{2}\right)^{2x-1} = \left(\frac{1}{2}\right)^{6x+4}$$

$$2x - 1 = 6x + 4$$

$$-5 = 4x$$

$$x = -\frac{5}{4}.$$

59. By approximating the x-intercepts of the graph $y = 2^x - 3^{x-1} - 5^{-x}$, we find that the solutions are $x \approx 0.194, 2.70$.

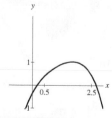

61. By approximating the x-intercept of the graph $y = \ln(x + 51) - \log(-48 - x)$, we obtain that the solution is $x \approx -49.73$.

63. By approximating the x-intercepts of the graph $y = x^2 - 2^x$, we find that the solutions are $x \approx -0.767, 2, 4$.

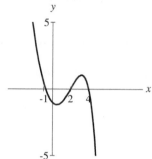

65. Solving for the rate of decay r, we find

$$A_0/2 = A_0 e^{10,000r}$$

$$1/2 = e^{10,000r}$$

$$\ln(1/2) = 10,000r$$

$$\frac{\ln(1/2)}{10,000} = r$$

Approximately, $r \approx -6.93 \times 10^{-5}$.

67. Using $A = A_o e^{rt}$ with $A_o = 1$ and the half-life, we obtain $\dfrac{1}{2} = e^{5730r}$. Thus, $5730r = \ln\left(\dfrac{1}{2}\right)$ and $r \approx -0.000120968$. When $A = 0.1$, we get

$$0.1 = e^{-0.000120968t}$$

$$\ln(0.1) = -0.000120968t$$

$$t = \frac{\ln(0.1)}{-0.000120968} \approx 19,035 \text{ years}$$

69. From Number 67, $r \approx -0.000120968$.
When $A = 10$ and $A_o = 12$, we obtain

$$10 = 12 \cdot e^{-0.000120968t}$$

$$\ln(10/12) = -0.000120968t$$

$$t = \frac{\ln(5/6)}{-0.000120968} \approx 1507 \text{ years}.$$

71. Let $A = A_o e^{rt}$ where $A_o = 25$, $A = 20$, and $t = 8000$. Then

$$
\begin{aligned}
20 &= 25 \cdot e^{8000r} \\
\ln(0.8) &= 8000r \\
r &\approx -0.000027893.
\end{aligned}
$$

To find the half-life, let $A = 12.5$. Thus, we have

$$
\begin{aligned}
12.5 &= 25 \cdot e^{-0.000027893t} \\
\ln(0.5) &= -0.000027893t \\
t &\approx 24,850 \text{ years.}
\end{aligned}
$$

73. $\dfrac{2.5(0.5)^{24/14}}{2.5} \times 100 \approx 30.5\%$, the percentage of the last dosage that remains before the next dosage is taken

75. Since the half-life is $t = 5730$ years and $A_o = 1$ and $A = 0.5$, we get

$$
\begin{aligned}
0.5 &= e^{(5730) \cdot r} \\
\ln(0.5) &= 5730 \cdot r \\
r &\approx -0.000121.
\end{aligned}
$$

If 79.3% of the carbon is still present, then

$$
\begin{aligned}
0.793 &= e^{(-0.000121) \cdot t} \\
\ln(0.793) &= -0.000121 \cdot t \\
t &\approx 1917.
\end{aligned}
$$

The scrolls were made in the year $1951 - 1917 = 34$ AD.

77.

a) Solve for r:

$$
\begin{aligned}
11,981 &= 21,075 e^{3r} \\
\ln\left(\frac{11,981}{21,075}\right) &= 3r \\
-0.188255 &= r \\
-18.8\% &\approx r
\end{aligned}
$$

b) If $t = 5$ years, then

$$
P = 21,075 e^{5(-0.188)} = \$8,200
$$

79. Let $y = 0.1 e^{kt}$, and $y = 4.8$ when $t = 2$. Then

$$
\begin{aligned}
4.8 &= 0.1 e^{2k} \\
e^k &= \sqrt{48}
\end{aligned}
$$

Thus, $y = 0.1(\sqrt{48})^t$. In 2014 or $t = 5$, we find $y = 0.1(48^{2.5}) \approx 1596$ million bloggers.

81. The initial difference in temperature is $325 - 35 = 290$, and after $t = 3$ hours the difference is $325 - 140 = 185$. Then

$$
\begin{aligned}
185 &= 290 \cdot e^{3k} \\
\ln\left(\frac{185}{290}\right) &= 3k \\
k &\approx -0.1498417.
\end{aligned}
$$

The difference in temperature when the roast is well-done is $325 - 170 = 155$. Thus,

$$
\begin{aligned}
155 &= 290 \cdot e^{(-0.1498417) \cdot t} \\
\ln\left(\frac{155}{290}\right) &= (-0.1498417) \cdot t \\
t &\approx 4.18 \text{ hr} \\
t &\approx 4 \text{ hr and } 11 \text{ min.}
\end{aligned}
$$

James must wait 1 hour and 11 minutes longer.

If the oven temperature is set at 170°, then the initial and final differences are 135 and 0, respectively. Since $0 = 135 \cdot e^{(-0.1498417) \cdot t}$ has no solution, James has to wait forever.

83. At 7:00 a.m., the difference in temperature is $80 - 40 = 40$, and $t = 1$ hour later the difference in temperature is $72 - 40 = 32$. Then

$$
\begin{aligned}
32 &= 40 \cdot e^{1 \cdot k} \\
\ln\left(\frac{32}{40}\right) &= k \\
k &\approx -0.2231436.
\end{aligned}
$$

Let n be the number of hours before 7:00 a.m. when death occured. At the time of death, the difference in temperature is $98 - 40 = 58$. Then

$$
\begin{aligned}
40 &= 58 \cdot e^{-0.2231436 \cdot n} \\
\ln\left(\frac{40}{58}\right) &= -0.2231436 \cdot n \\
n &\approx 1.665 \text{ hr} \\
n &\approx 1 \text{ hr and } 40 \text{ min.}
\end{aligned}
$$

The death occured at 5:20 a.m.

85. Since $R = P\dfrac{i}{1 - (1+i)^{-nt}}$, we obtain

$$\begin{aligned}
1 - (1+i)^{-nt} &= Pi/R \\
1 - Pi/R &= (1+i)^{-nt} \\
\ln(1 - Pi/R) &= -nt\ln(1+i) \\
\frac{-\ln(1 - Pi/R)}{n\ln(1+i)} &= t.
\end{aligned}$$

Let $i = 0.09/12 = 0.0075$, $P = 100,000$, and $R = 1250$. Then

$$t = \frac{-\ln(1 - Pi/R)}{n\ln(1+i)} \approx 10.219.$$

It will take 10 yr, 3 mo to pay off the loan.

87. The future values of the $1000 and $1100 investments are equal. Then

$$\begin{aligned}
1,000 \cdot e^{0.06t} &= 1100\left(1 + \frac{0.06}{365}\right)^{365t} \\
e^{0.06t} &= 1.1\left(1 + \frac{0.06}{365}\right)^{365t} \\
.06t &= \ln(1.1) + 365t\ln\left(1 + \frac{0.06}{365}\right)
\end{aligned}$$

$$.06t - 365t\ln\left(1 + \frac{0.06}{365}\right) = \ln(1.1)$$

$$t = \frac{\ln(1.1)}{.06 - 365\ln\left(1 + \frac{0.06}{365}\right)}$$

$$t \approx 19,328.84173 \text{ years}$$

They will be equal after $19,328$ yr, 307 days.

89. a) Let $t = 0$. The present number of rabbits is

$$P = 12,300 + 1000 \cdot \ln(1) = 12,300 + 0 = 12,300.$$

b) In about 15 years.

c) The number of years before there will be 15,000 rabbits is given by

$$\begin{aligned}
12,300 + 1000 \cdot \ln(t+1) &= 15,000 \\
1000 \cdot \ln(t+1) &= 2,700 \\
\ln(t+1) &= 2.7 \\
t+1 &= e^{2.7} \\
t &\approx 13.9 \text{ yr.}
\end{aligned}$$

91. a) Let $n = 2500$ and $A = 400$.
Since $n = k\log(A)$, $2500 = k\log(400)$.
Then $k = \dfrac{2500}{\log(400)}$. When $A = 200$,
the number of species left is

$$n = \frac{2500}{\log(400)}\log(200) \approx 2211 \text{ species.}$$

b) Let $n = 3500$ and $A = 1200$.
Since $n = k\log(A)$, $3500 = k\log(1200)$.
Then $k = \dfrac{3500}{\log(1200)}$. When $n = 1000$,
the remaining forest area is given by

$$1000 = \frac{3500}{\log(1200)}\log(A)$$

$$\frac{1000}{3500}\log(1200) = \log(A)$$

$$\frac{2}{7}\log(1200) = \log(A)$$

$$\log\left(1200^{2/7}\right) = \log(A)$$

$$1200^{2/7} = A$$

Thus, the percentage of forest that has been destroyed is $100 - \dfrac{A}{1200}(100) \approx 99\%$.

93. Since $m = 0$ and $M_v = 4.39$, the distance to α Centauri is given by

$$\begin{aligned}
4.39 - 5 + 5 \cdot \log(d) &= 0 \\
5 \cdot \log(d) &= 0.61 \\
\log(d) &= 0.122 \\
d = 10^{0.122} &\approx 1.32 \text{ parsecs.}
\end{aligned}$$

95.

a) Let $y = \log(P)$. A formula for P is

$$\begin{aligned}
y - 4.5 &= \frac{4.5 - 0.3}{0 - 23}(x - 0) \\
y &= -\frac{21}{115}x + 4.5 \\
\log(P) &= -\frac{21}{115}x + 4.5 \\
P &= 10^{(-21x/115 + 4.5)} \\
P &\approx 10^{-0.1826x + 4.5}
\end{aligned}$$

b) In 1991, $x = 9$ and

$$P \approx 10^{-0.1826(9)+4.5} = \$718.79.$$

c) Solving for x, we derive

$$
\begin{aligned}
0.25 &= 10^{(-21x/115+4.5)} \\
\log(0.25) &= -\frac{21}{115}x + 4.5 \\
\frac{\log(0.25) - 4.5}{-21/115} &= x \\
x &\approx 28
\end{aligned}
$$

In the year $2010 = (1982+28)$, according to this model a 1-gigabit hard drive will cost \$0.25.

97. If the sound level is 90 db, then the intensity of the sound is given by

$$
\begin{aligned}
10 \cdot \log(I \times 10^{12}) &= 90 \\
\log(I) + \log(10^{12}) &= 9 \\
\log(I) + 12 &= 9 \\
\log(I) &= -3 \\
I &= 10^{-3} \text{ watts per/m}^2.
\end{aligned}
$$

99. Since $P \cdot e^{(0.06)18} = 20{,}000$, the investment will grow to $P = \dfrac{20{,}000}{e^{(0.06)18}} \approx \$6791.91.$

101.

a) The logarithmic regression line is

$$y = 114.7865206 - 12.75457939 \ln(x)$$

or approximately is

$$y = 114.8 - 12.8 \ln(x)$$

where the year is $1960 + x$.

b) Let $x = 50$. Since

$$114.7865206 - 12.75457939 \ln(50) \approx 65,$$

the percentage of households in 2010 with two parents is 65%.

c) Let $y = 50$. Then

$$50 = 114.7865206 - 12.75457939 \ln(x)$$

$$
\begin{aligned}
\ln(x) &= \frac{114.7865206 - 50}{12.75457939} \\
x &\approx 161.
\end{aligned}
$$

Since $1960 + 161 = 2121$, the percentage of two-parent families will reach 50% in the year 2121.

d) The data looks like a quadratic or exponential model.

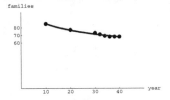

103. By using the first five terms of the formula,

$$
\begin{aligned}
e^{0.1} &\approx 1 + 0.1 + \frac{(0.1)^2}{2} + \frac{(0.1)^3}{6} + \frac{(0.1)^4}{24} \\
&\approx 1.105170833
\end{aligned}
$$

From a calculator, $e^{0.1} \approx 1.105170918$.

105. $\log_6(4 \cdot 9) = \log_6(36) = 2$

107. Convert to exponential form:

$$
\begin{aligned}
x^{2.4} &= 9.8 \\
x &= 9.8^{1/2.4} \\
x &\approx 2.5883
\end{aligned}
$$

The solution set is $\{2.5883\}$.

109. By the identity $\log_3(3^w) = w$, we obtain

$$
\begin{aligned}
(g \circ f)(x) &= \log_3\left(3^{(x-5)}\right) + 5 \\
&= (x-5) + 5 \\
&= x
\end{aligned}
$$

Chapter Review Exercises

1. 64   **3.** 6

5. 0   **7.** 17

9. $4^{1/\log_3 4 + \log_9 3} = 4^{\log_4 3 + 1/2} =$

$4^{\log_4 3} 4^{1/2} = 3 \cdot 2 = 6$

11. $2^5 = 32$

13. $\log(10^3) = 3$

15. $\log_2(2^9) = 9$

17. $\log(1000) = 3$

19. $\log_2(1) - \log_2(8) = 0 - 3 = -3$

21. $\log_2(8) = 3$

23. $\log((x - 3)x) = \log(x^2 - 3x)$

25. $\ln(x^2) + \ln(3y) = \ln(3x^2 y)$

27. $\log(3) + \log(x^4) = \log(3) + 4 \cdot \log(x)$

29. $\log_3(5) + \log_3(x^{1/2}) - \log_3(y^4) =$

$\log_3(5) + \dfrac{1}{2} \cdot \log_3(x) - 4 \cdot \log_3(y)$

31. $\ln(2 \cdot 5) = \ln(2) + \ln(5)$

33. $\ln(5^2 \cdot 2) = \ln(5^2) + \ln(2) = 2 \cdot \ln(5) + \ln(2)$

35. Since $\log_{10}(x) = 10$, we get $x = 10^{10}$.

37. Since $x^4 = 81$ and $x > 0$, $x = 3$.

39. Since $\log_{1/3}(27) = -3 = x + 2$, we get $x = -5$.

41. Since $3^{x+2} = 3^{-2}$, $x + 2 = -2$. So $x = -4$.

43. Since $x - 2 = \ln(9)$, we obtain $x = 2 + \ln(9)$.

45. Since $(2^2)^{x+3} = 2^{2x+6} = 2^{-x}$, we get $2x + 6 = -x$. Then $6 = -3x$ and so $x = -2$.

47.

$$
\begin{aligned}
\log(2x^2) &= 5 \\
2x^2 &= 10^5 \\
x^2 &= 50,000 \\
x &= \pm 100\sqrt{5}
\end{aligned}
$$

Since $\log(-100\sqrt{5})$ is undefined, $x = 100\sqrt{5}$.

49.

$$
\begin{aligned}
\log_2\left(x^2 - 4x\right) &= \log_2(x + 24) \\
x^2 - 4x &= x + 24 \\
x^2 - 5x - 24 &= 0 \\
(x - 8)(x + 3) &= 0 \\
x &= 8, -3
\end{aligned}
$$

Since $\log(-3)$ is undefined, $x = 8$.

51. Since $\ln((x + 2)^2) = \ln(4^3)$ and $y = \ln(x)$ is a one-to-one function, we obtain

$$
\begin{aligned}
(x + 2)^2 &= 64 \\
x + 2 &= \pm 8 \\
x &= -2 \pm 8 \\
x &= 6, -10.
\end{aligned}
$$

Checking $x = -10$ one gets $2\ln(-8)$ which is undefined. So $x = 6$.

53.

$$
\begin{aligned}
x \cdot \log(4) + x \cdot \log(25) &= 6 \\
x(\log(4) + \log(25)) &= 6 \\
x \cdot \log(100) &= 6 \\
x \cdot 2 &= 6 \\
x &= 3
\end{aligned}
$$

55. The missing coordinates are

(i) 3 since $\left(\dfrac{1}{3}\right)^{-1} = 3$,

(ii) -3 since $\left(\dfrac{1}{3}\right)^{-3} = 27$,

(iii) $\sqrt{3}$ since $\left(\dfrac{1}{3}\right)^{-1/2} = \sqrt{3}$, and

(iv) 0 since $\left(\dfrac{1}{3}\right)^{0} = 1$.

57. c

59. b

61. d

63. e

65. Domain $(-\infty, \infty)$, range $(0, \infty)$, increasing, asymptote $y = 0$

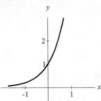

67. Domain $(-\infty, \infty)$, range $(0, \infty)$, decreasing, asymptote $y = 0$

69. Domain $(0, \infty)$, range $(-\infty, \infty)$, increasing, asymptote $x = 0$

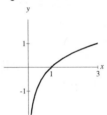

71. Domain $(-3, \infty)$, range $(-\infty, \infty)$, increasing, asymptote $x = -3$

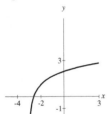

73. Domain $(-\infty, \infty)$, range $(1, \infty)$, increasing, asymptote $y = 1$

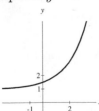

75. Domain $(-\infty, 2)$, range $(-\infty, \infty)$, decreasing, asymptote $x = 2$

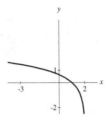

77. $f^{-1}(x) = \log_7(x)$

79. $f^{-1}(x) = 5^x$

81. Replace $f(x)$ by y, interchange x and y, solve for y, and replace y by $f^{-1}(x)$.

$$
\begin{aligned}
y &= 3\log(x - 1) \\
x &= 3\log(y - 1) \\
\frac{x}{3} &= \log(y - 1) \\
10^{x/3} &= y - 1 \\
10^{x/3} + 1 &= y \\
f^{-1}(x) &= 10^{x/3} + 1
\end{aligned}
$$

83. Replace $f(x)$ by y, interchange x and y, solve for y, and replace y by $f^{-1}(x)$.

$$
\begin{aligned}
y &= e^{x+2} - 3 \\
x &= e^{y+2} - 3 \\
x + 3 &= e^{y+2} \\
\ln(x + 3) &= y + 2 \\
\ln(x + 3) - 2 &= y \\
f^{-1}(x) &= \ln(x + 3) - 2
\end{aligned}
$$

85. Since $3^x = 10$, $x = \log_3(10) = \dfrac{\ln(10)}{\ln(3)} \approx 2.0959$

.

87. Since $\log_3(x) = 1.876$, $x = 3^{1.876} \approx 7.8538$.

89. After taking the natural logarithm of both sides,
we have

$$
\begin{aligned}
\ln(5^x) &= \ln(8^{x+1}) \\
x \cdot \ln(5) &= (x + 1) \cdot \ln(8) \\
x \cdot \ln(5) &= x \cdot \ln(8) + \ln(8) \\
x \cdot (\ln(5) - \ln(8)) &= \ln(8) \\
x &= \frac{\ln(8)}{\ln(5) - \ln(8)} \\
x &\approx -4.4243.
\end{aligned}
$$

91. True, since $\log_3(81) = 4$ and $2 = \log_3(9)$.

93. False, since $\ln(3^2) = 2 \cdot \ln(3) \neq (\ln(3))^2$.

95. True, since $4 \cdot \log_2(8) = 4 \cdot 3 = 12$.

97. False, since $3 + \log(6) = \log(10^3) + \log(6) = \log(6000)$.

99. False, since $\log_2(16) = 4$, $\log_2(8) = 3$, and $\dfrac{3}{4} \neq 3 - 4$.

101. False, since $\log_2(25) = 2\log_2(5) = 2 \cdot \dfrac{\log(5)}{\log(2)} \neq 2 \cdot \log(5)$.

103. True, because of the base-changing formula.

105. If H_B^+ is the hydrogen ion concentration of liquid B then $10 \cdot H_B^+$ is the hydrogen ion concentration of liquid A. The pH of A is

$$-\log(10 \cdot H_B^+) = -1 - \log(H_B^+)$$

i.e. the pH of A is one less than the pH of B.

107. The value at the end of 18 years is

$$50,000 \left(1 + \frac{0.05}{4}\right)^{18 \cdot 4} \approx \$122,296.01.$$

109. Let t be the number of years.

$$50,000 \left(1 + \frac{0.05}{4}\right)^{4t} = 100,000$$
$$(1.0125)^{4t} = 2$$
$$4t = \log_{1.0125}(2)$$
$$t = \frac{1}{4} \cdot \frac{\ln(2)}{\ln(1.0125)}$$
$$t \approx 13.9 \text{ years}$$

It doubles in $4 \cdot 13.9 \approx 56$ quarters.

111. The present amount is $A = 25 \cdot e^0 = 25$ g. After $t = 1000$ years, the amount left is $A = 25 \cdot e^{-0.32} \approx 18.15$ g.

To find the half-life, let $A = 12.5$.

$$25 \cdot e^{-0.00032t} = 12.5$$
$$e^{-0.00032t} = 0.5$$
$$-0.00032t = \ln(0.5)$$
$$t \approx 2166$$

The half-life is 2166 years.

113. Let $f(t) = 10,000$.

$$40,000 \cdot (1 - e^{-0.0001t}) = 10,000$$
$$1 - e^{-0.0001t} = 0.25$$
$$0.75 = e^{-0.0001t}$$
$$\ln(0.75) = -0.0001t$$
$$t \approx 2877 \text{ hr}$$

It takes 2877 hours to learn $10,000$ words.

115. In the following equations, we solve for x.

$$1026 \left(\frac{25,005}{64}\right)^x = 19.2$$
$$\left(\frac{25,005}{64}\right)^x = \frac{19.2}{1026}$$
$$x \ln \left(\frac{25,005}{64}\right) = \ln \left(\frac{19.2}{1026}\right)$$
$$x = \frac{\ln \left(\frac{19.2}{1026}\right)}{\ln \left(\frac{25,005}{64}\right)}$$
$$x \approx -0.667 \quad \text{or} \quad x \approx -\frac{2}{3}$$

In the following equations, we obtain y.

$$\frac{25005}{2240} \left(\frac{35 + \frac{1}{12}}{100}\right)^y = 258.51$$
$$\left(\frac{35 + \frac{1}{12}}{100}\right)^y = \frac{258.51(2240)}{25005}$$
$$y = \frac{\ln \left(\frac{258.51(2240)}{25005}\right)}{\ln \left(\frac{35 + \frac{1}{12}}{100}\right)}$$
$$y \approx -3$$

Next, we solve for z.

$$13.5 \left(\frac{25005}{64}\right)^z = 1.85$$
$$\left(\frac{25005}{64}\right)^z = \frac{1.85}{13.5}$$
$$z \ln \left(\frac{25005}{64}\right) = \ln \left(\frac{1.85}{13.5}\right)$$
$$z = \frac{\ln (1.85/13.5)}{\ln (25005/64)}$$
$$z \approx -0.333 \quad \text{or} \quad z \approx -\frac{1}{3}$$

Chapter Test

1. 3   **2.** -2 **3.** 6.47   **4.** $\sqrt{2}$

5. $f^{-1}(x) = e^x$

6. Replace $f(x)$ by y, interchange x and y, solve for y, and replace y by $f^{-1}(x)$.

$$
\begin{aligned}
y &= 8^{x+1} - 3 \\
x &= 8^{y+1} - 3 \\
x + 3 &= 8^{y+1} \\
\log_8(x+3) &= y + 1 \\
\log_8(x+3) - 1 &= y \\
f^{-1}(x) &= \log_8(x+3) - 1
\end{aligned}
$$

7. $\log(x) + \log(y^3) = \log(xy^3)$

8. $\ln(\sqrt{x-1}) - \ln(33) = \ln\left(\dfrac{\sqrt{x-1}}{33}\right)$

9. $\log_a(2^2 \cdot 7) = \log_a(2^2) + \log_a(7) = 2 \cdot \log_a(2) + \log_a(7)$

10. $\log_a\left(\dfrac{7}{2}\right) = \log_a(7) - \log_a(2)$

11.

$$
\begin{aligned}
\log_2(x^2 - 2x) &= 3 \\
x^2 - 2x &= 2^3 \\
x^2 - 2x - 8 &= 0 \\
(x-4)(x+2) &= 0 \\
x &= 4, -2
\end{aligned}
$$

But $\log_2(-2)$ is undefined, so $x = 4$.

12.

$$
\begin{aligned}
\log\left(\dfrac{10x}{x+2}\right) &= \log(3^2) \\
\dfrac{10x}{x+2} &= 9 \\
10x &= 9x + 18 \\
x &= 18
\end{aligned}
$$

13.

$$
\begin{aligned}
\ln(3^x) &= \ln(5^{x-1}) \\
x \cdot \ln(3) &= (x-1) \cdot \ln(5) \\
x \cdot \ln(3) &= x \cdot \ln(5) - \ln(5) \\
x(\ln(3) - \ln(5)) &= -\ln(5) \\
x(\ln(5) - \ln(3)) &= \ln(5) \\
x &= \dfrac{\ln(5)}{\ln(5) - \ln(3)} \\
x &\approx 3.1507
\end{aligned}
$$

14. By the definition of a logarithm, we obtain $x - 1 = 3^{5.46}$. Then $x = 1 + 3^{5.46} \approx 403.7931$.

15. Domain $(-\infty, \infty)$, range $(1, \infty)$, increasing, asymptote $y = 1$

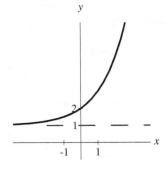

16. Domain $(1, \infty)$, range $(-\infty, \infty)$, decreasing, asymptote $x = 1$

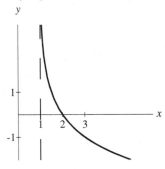

17. $(1, 0)$

18. Compounded quarterly, the investment is worth

$$
2000\left(1 + \dfrac{0.08}{4}\right)^{80} \approx \$9750.88.
$$

Compounded continuously, the investment is worth

$$
2000 \cdot e^{0.08(20)} \approx \$9906.06.
$$

19. The amount of power at the end of $t = 200$ days is $P = 50 \cdot e^{-200/250} \approx 22.5$ watts.

To find the half-life, let $P = 25$.

$$
\begin{aligned}
50 \cdot e^{-t/250} &= 25 \\
e^{-t/250} &= 0.5 \\
-\frac{t}{250} &= \ln(0.5) \\
t &\approx 173.3
\end{aligned}
$$

The half-life is 173.3 days.

The operational life for a power of $P = 9$ watts is given by

$$
\begin{aligned}
50 \cdot e^{-t/250} &= 9 \\
e^{-t/250} &= \frac{9}{50} \\
-\frac{t}{250} &= \ln\left(\frac{9}{50}\right) \\
t &\approx 428.7 \text{ days.}
\end{aligned}
$$

20.

$$
\begin{aligned}
4{,}000 \cdot \left(1 + \frac{0.06}{4}\right)^{4t} &= 10{,}000 \\
(1.015)^{4t} &= 2.5 \\
4t &= \log_{1.015}(2.5) \\
t &\approx 15.38576 \text{ years} \\
t &\approx 61.5 \text{ quarters}
\end{aligned}
$$

21. Substituting $t = 100$, we obtain

$$
\begin{aligned}
-50 \cdot \ln(1-p) &= 100 \\
\ln(1-p) &= -2 \\
1-p &= e^{-2} \\
p &= 1 - e^{-2} \\
p &\approx 0.86.
\end{aligned}
$$

The level reached after 100 hr is $p = 0.86$. When $p = 1$, then $t = -50\ln(0)$ which is undefined, so it is impossible to master MGM.

Systems of Equations and Inequalities

Throughout history humans have been directly or indirectly influenced by the world's oceans. Ocean waters serve as a source of food and valuable minerals, as a vast highway for commerce, and as a place for both recreation and waste disposal.

The world ocean has an area of 139 million square miles and occupies 70% of the surface of the earth. Yet, it has been said that we know more about outer space than we do about the oceans. The oceans hold the answers to many important questions about the development of the earth and the history of life on earth.

▶WHAT YOU WILL learn... In this chapter we will use systems of equations to solve problems involving two or more variables. In particular, we will learn how geophysicists use systems of equations in their effort to map the ocean floor and expand their knowledge of this important resource.

1 Systems of Linear Equations in Two Variables

2 Systems of Linear Equations in Three Variables

3 Nonlinear Systems of Equations

4 Partial Fractions

5 Inequalities and Systems of Inequalities in Two Variables

6 The Linear Programming Model

Georgette Douwma/
Digital Vision/Getty Images

From Chapter 8 of *Precalculus: Functions and Graphs*. Fourth Edition. Mark Dugopolski. Copyright © 2013 by Pearson Education, Inc. All rights reserved.

1 Systems of Linear Equations in Two Variables

A linear equation in two variables has the form

$$Ax + By = C,$$

where A and B are not both zero, and we discussed numerous applications of linear equations. There are infinitely many ordered pairs that satisfy a single linear equation. In applications, however, we are often interested in finding a single ordered pair that satisfies a *pair* of linear equations. In this section we discuss several methods for solving this problem.

Solving a System by Graphing

Any collection of two or more equations is called a **system of equations.** For example, the system of equations consisting of $x + 2y = 6$ and $2x - y = -8$ is written as follows:

$$x + 2y = 6$$
$$2x - y = -8$$

The **solution set** of a system of two linear equations in two variables is the set of all ordered pairs that satisfy *both* equations of the system. The graph of an equation shows all ordered pairs that satisfy it, so we can solve some systems by graphing the equations and observing which points (if any) satisfy all of the equations.

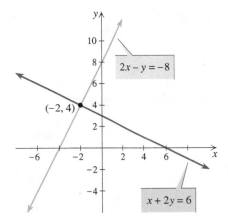

Figure 1

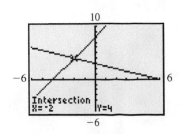

Figure 2

EXAMPLE 1 | Solving a system by graphing

Solve each system by graphing.

a. $x + 2y = 6$ **b.** $3x - y = 2$ **c.** $y = \dfrac{1}{2}x + 2$

    $2x - y = -8$ $2y - 6x = -4$ $x - 2y = 4$

Solution

a. Graph the straight line

$$x + 2y = 6$$

by using its intercepts, $(0, 3)$ and $(6, 0)$. Graph the straight line

$$2x - y = -8$$

by using its intercepts, $(0, 8)$ and $(-4, 0)$. The graphs are shown in Fig. 1. The lines appear to intersect at $(-2, 4)$. Check $(-2, 4)$ in both equations. Since

$$-2 + 2(4) = 6 \quad \text{and} \quad 2(-2) - 4 = -8$$

are both correct, we can be certain that $(-2, 4)$ satisfies both equations. The solution set of the system is $\{(-2, 4)\}$.

You can check by graphing the equations on a calculator and finding the intersection, as shown in Fig. 2. $\square$

b. Solve each equation for y.

$$3x - y = 2 \qquad\qquad 2y - 6x = -4$$
$$-y = -3x + 2 \qquad\qquad 2y = 6x - 4$$
$$y = 3x - 2 \qquad\qquad y = 3x - 2$$

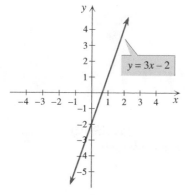

Figure 3

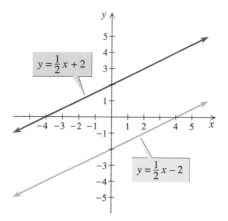

Figure 4

The system consists of two equations for the same line. So the graph of the system is the line $y = 3x - 2$ shown in Fig. 3. There are infinitely many solutions to this system. All points on the line satisfy both equations of the system. Thus the solution set is $\{(x, y) \mid y = 3x - 2\}$. We could also write the solution set as $\{(x, y) \mid 3x - y = 2\}$.

c. Use the y-intercept $(0, 2)$ and the slope $1/2$ to graph

$$y = \frac{1}{2}x + 2,$$

as shown in Fig. 4. Since $x - 2y = 4$ is equivalent to

$$y = \frac{1}{2}x - 2,$$

its graph has y-intercept $(0, -2)$ and is parallel to the first line. Since the lines are parallel, there is no point that satisfies both equations of the system. In fact, if you substitute any value of x in the two equations, the corresponding y-values will differ by 4.

▶**TRY THIS.** Solve the system $y = x - 3$ and $x + y = 7$ by graphing. ■

Types of Systems

A system of equations that has at least one solution is **consistent** (Example 1a and 1b). A system with no solutions is **inconsistent** (Example 1c). There are two types of consistent systems. A consistent system with exactly one solution is **independent** (Example 1a) and a consistent system with infinitely many solutions is **dependent** (Example 1b). These ideas are summarized in Fig. 5.

Consistent system
Independent
Exactly one solution

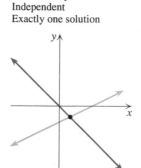

Lines have different slopes.

Consistent system
Dependent
Infinitely many solutions

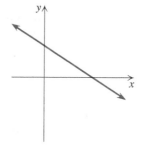

Lines have same slope, same y-intercept.

Inconsistent system

No solution

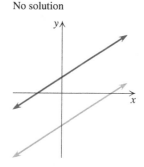

Lines have same slope, different y-intercepts.

Figure 5

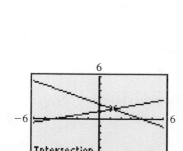

Figure 6

The Substitution Method

Graphing the equations of a system helps us to visualize the system and determine how many solutions it has. However, solving systems of linear equations by graphing is not very accurate unless the solution is fairly simple. The accuracy of graphing can be improved with a graphing calculator, but even with a graphing calculator, we generally get only approximate solutions. For example, the solution to $y_1 = (28 - 7x)/13$ and $y_2 = (29 + 7x)/26$ is $(9/7, 19/13)$, but the graphing calculator solution in Fig. 6 does not give this exact answer. However, by using an algebraic technique such as the substitution method, we can get exact solutions quickly. In this method, shown in Example 2, we eliminate a variable from one equation by substituting an expression for that variable from the other equation.

EXAMPLE 2 Solving a system by substitution

Solve each system by substitution.

a. $3x - y = 6$ **b.** $y = 2x + 1000$
$6x + 5y = -23$ $0.05x + 0.06y = 400$

Solution

a. Since y occurs with coefficient -1 in $3x - y = 6$, it is simpler to isolate y in this equation than to isolate any other variable in the system.

$$-y = -3x + 6$$

$$y = 3x - 6$$

Use $3x - 6$ in place of y in the equation $6x + 5y = -23$:

$$6x + 5(3x - 6) = -23 \quad \text{Substitution}$$

$$6x + 15x - 30 = -23$$

$$21x = 7$$

$$x = \frac{1}{3}$$

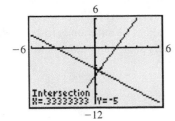

Figure 7

The x-coordinate of the solution is $\frac{1}{3}$. To find y, use $x = \frac{1}{3}$ in $y = 3x - 6$:

$$y = 3\left(\frac{1}{3}\right) - 6$$

$$y = -5$$

Check that $\left(\frac{1}{3}, -5\right)$ satisfies both of the original equations. The solution set is $\left\{\left(\frac{1}{3}, -5\right)\right\}$.

The graphs of $y_1 = 3x - 6$ and $y_2 = (-23 - 6x)/5$ in Fig. 7 support this solution. □

b. The first equation, $y = 2x + 1000$, already has one variable isolated. So we can replace y by $2x + 1000$ in $0.05x + 0.06y = 400$:

$$0.05x + 0.06(2x + 1000) = 400 \quad \text{Substitution}$$

$$0.05x + 0.12x + 60 = 400$$

$$0.17x = 340$$

$$x = 2000$$

Use $x = 2000$ in $y = 2x + 1000$ to find y:

$$y = 2(2000) + 1000$$

$$y = 5000$$

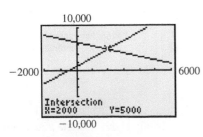

Figure 8

Check $(2000, 5000)$ in the original equations. The solution set is $\{(2000, 5000)\}$.
The graphs of $y_1 = 2x + 1000$ and $y_2 = (400 - 0.05x)/0.06$ in Fig. 8 support this solution.

▶**TRY THIS.** Solve $y = 2x - 3$ and $x + 2y = -1$ by substitution. ∎

If substitution results in a false statement, then the system is inconsistent. If substitution results in an identity, then the system is dependent. In the next example we solve an inconsistent system and a dependent system by substitution.

EXAMPLE 3 | Inconsistent and dependent systems

Solve each system by substitution.

a. $3x - y = 9$ **b.** $\frac{1}{2}x - \frac{2}{3}y = -2$

   $\quad 2y - 6x = 7$ $\qquad\qquad 4y = 3x + 12$

Solution

a. Solve $3x - y = 9$ for y to get $y = 3x - 9$. Replace y by $3x - 9$ in the equation $2y - 6x = 7$:

$$2(3x - 9) - 6x = 7$$

$$6x - 18 - 6x = 7$$

$$-18 = 7$$

Since the last statement is false, the system is inconsistent and has *no solution*. The graphs of $y_1 = 3x - 9$ and $y_2 = (6x + 7)/2$ in Fig. 9 appear to be parallel lines and support the conclusion that the system is inconsistent. ☐

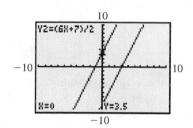

Figure 9

b. Solve $4y = 3x + 12$ for y to get $y = \frac{3}{4}x + 3$. Replace y by $\frac{3}{4}x + 3$ in the first equation:

$$\frac{1}{2}x - \frac{2}{3}\left(\frac{3}{4}x + 3\right) = -2$$

$$\frac{1}{2}x - \frac{1}{2}x - 2 = -2$$

$$-2 = -2$$

Since the last statement is an identity, the system is dependent. The solution set is $\{(x, y) \mid 4y = 3x + 12\}$.

▶**TRY THIS.** Solve $y = 3x - 5$ and $6x - 2y = 1$ by substitution. ■

Note that there are many ways of writing the solution set in Example 3(b). Since $4y = 3x + 12$ is equivalent to $y = \frac{3}{4}x + 3$ or to $x = \frac{4}{3}y - 4$, we could write the solution set as $\left\{\left(x, \frac{3}{4}x + 3\right) \mid x \text{ is any real number}\right\}$ or $\left\{\left(\frac{4}{3}y - 4, y\right) \mid y \text{ is any real number}\right\}$. The variable used in describing the solution set does not matter. We could even use another variable and write $\left\{\left(t, \frac{3}{4}t + 3\right) \mid t \text{ is any real number}\right\}$. All of these sets contain exactly the same ordered pairs.

The Addition Method

In the substitution method we eliminate a variable in one equation by substituting from the other equation. In the addition method we eliminate a variable by adding the two equations. It might be necessary to multiply each equation by an appropriate number so that a variable will be eliminated by the addition.

EXAMPLE 4 | Solving systems by addition

Solve each system by addition.

a. $3x - y = 9$ **b.** $2x - 3y = -2$

   $\quad 2x + y = 1$ $\qquad 3x - 2y = 12$

Solution

a. Add the equations to eliminate the y-variable:

$$3x - y = 9$$
$$\underline{2x + y = 1}$$
$$5x \quad\;\; = 10$$
$$x \quad\;\;\;\; = 2$$

Use $x = 2$ in $2x + y = 1$ to find y:

$$2(2) + y = 1$$
$$y = -3$$

Substituting the values $x = 2$ and $y = -3$ in the original equation yields $3(2) - (-3) = 9$ and $2(2) + (-3) = 1$, which are both correct. So $(2, -3)$ satisfies both equations, and the solution set to the system is $\{(2, -3)\}$.

b. To eliminate x upon addition, we multiply the first equation by 3 and the second equation by -2:

$$3(2x - 3y) = 3(-2)$$
$$-2(3x - 2y) = -2(12)$$

This multiplication produces $6x$ in one equation and $-6x$ in the other. So the x-variable is eliminated upon addition of the equations.

$$6x - 9y = -6$$
$$\underline{-6x + 4y = -24}$$
$$-5y = -30$$
$$y = 6$$

Use $y = 6$ in $2x - 3y = -2$ to find x:

$$2x - 3(6) = -2$$
$$2x - 18 = -2$$
$$2x = 16$$
$$x = 8$$

If $y = 6$ is used in the other equation, $3x - 2y = 12$, we would also get $x = 8$. Substituting $x = 8$ and $y = 6$ in both of the original equations yields $2(8) - 3(6) = -2$ and $3(8) - 2(6) = 12$, which are both correct. So the solution set to the system is $\{(8, 6)\}$.

▶**TRY THIS.** Solve $x + y = 3$ and $3x - 2y = 4$ by addition. ∎

In Example 4(b), we started with the given system and multiplied the first equation by 3 and the second equation by -2 to get

$$6x - 9y = -6$$
$$-6x + 4y = -24.$$

Since each equation of the new system is equivalent to an equation of the old system, the solution sets to these systems are identical. Two systems with the same solution set are **equivalent systems.** If we had multiplied the first equation by 2 and the second by -3, we would have obtained the equivalent system

$$4x - 6y = -4$$
$$-9x + 6y = -36$$

and we would have eliminated y by adding the equations.

When we have a choice of which method to use for solving a system, we generally avoid graphing because it is often inaccurate. Substitution and addition both yield exact solutions, but sometimes one method is easier to apply than the other. Substitution is usually used when one equation gives one variable in terms of the other, as in Example 2. Addition is usually used when both equations are in the form $Ax + By = C$, as in Example 4. By doing the exercises, you will soon discover which method works best on a given system.

When a system is solved by the addition method, an inconsistent system results in a false statement and a dependent system results in an identity, just as they did for the substitution method.

EXAMPLE 5 | Inconsistent and dependent systems

Solve each system by addition.

a. $0.2x - 0.4y = 0.5$ **b.** $\dfrac{1}{2}x - \dfrac{2}{3}y = -2$

$x - 2y = 1.3$ $-3x + 4y = 12$

Solution

a. It is usually a good idea to eliminate the decimals in the coefficients, so we multiply the first equation by 10:

$$2x - 4y = 5 \qquad \text{First equation multiplied by 10}$$

$$x - 2y = 1.3$$

Now multiply the second equation by -2 and add to eliminate x:

$$2x - 4y = 5$$
$$\underline{-2x + 4y = -2.6}$$
$$0 = 2.4$$

Since $0 = 2.4$ is false, there is no solution to the system.

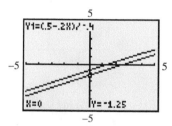 The graphs of $y_1 = (0.5 - 0.2x)/(-0.4)$ and $y_2 = (1.3 - x)/(-2)$ in Fig. 10 appear to be parallel lines and support the conclusion that there is no solution to the system. □

b. To eliminate fractions in the coefficients, multiply the first equation by the LCD 6:

$$3x - 4y = -12$$
$$\underline{-3x + 4y = 12}$$
$$0 = 0$$

Since $0 = 0$ is an identity, the solution set is $\{(x, y)\,|\,-3x + 4y = 12\}$.

▶**TRY THIS.** Solve $\frac{1}{2}x - \frac{1}{4}y = 1$ and $2x - y = 3$ by addition. ∎

Note that there are many ways to solve a system by addition. In Example 5(a), we could have multiplied the first equation by -5 or the second equation by -0.2. In either case, x would be eliminated upon addition. Try this for yourself.

Modeling with a System of Equations

We solved many problems involving linear equations in the past, but we always wrote all unknown quantities in terms of a single variable. Now that we can solve systems of equations, we can model situations involving two unknown quantities by using two variables and a system of equations.

Figure 10

EXAMPLE 6 Modeling with a system of equations

At Starbucks, an Orange Mango Banana Blend smoothie contains 16 grams of protein and 5 grams of fiber. A Banana Chocolate Blend smoothie contains 21 grams of protein and 6 grams of fiber. How many smoothies of each type would you have to consume to get exactly 243 grams of protein and 72 grams of fiber?

Solution

Let x be the number of Orange Mango Banana Blend smoothies and y be the number of Banana Chocolate Blend smoothies. We can write an equation for the total amount of protein and another for the total amount of fiber.

$$16x + 21y = 243$$
$$5x + 6y = 72$$

To eliminate x, multiply the first equation by -5 and the second by 16:

$$-5(16x + 21y) = -5(243)$$
$$16(5x + 6y) = 16(72)$$

Add the two resulting equations:

$$-80x - 105y = -1215$$
$$\underline{80x + 96y = 1152}$$
$$-9y = -63$$
$$y = 7$$

Use $y = 7$ in $5x + 6y = 72$ to find x:

$$5x + 6(7) = 72$$
$$5x + 42 = 72$$
$$5x = 30$$
$$x = 6$$

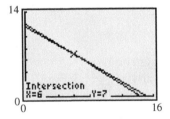

Figure 11

Check that 6 Orange Mango Banana Blend smoothies and 7 Banana Chocolate Blend smoothies satisfy the statements in the original problem.

The graphs of $y_1 = (243 - 16x)/21$ and $y_2 = (72 - 5x)/6$ in Fig. 11 support this conclusion.

▶**TRY THIS.** Two DVDs and three CDs cost $78. One DVD and four CDs cost $74. What is the cost of a DVD? ∎

EXAMPLE 7 Investing in mutual funds

Ruby invested a total of $100,000 in two mutual funds at the beginning of 2008. At the end of 2008 she lost 32% of the amount invested in the Fidelity Balanced Fund and lost 50% of the amount she invested in the Fidelity Value Fund. If her losses totaled $42,800, then how much did she invest in each fund?

Solution

Let x represent the amount invested in the Fidelity Balanced Fund and y represent the amount invested in the Fidelity Value Fund. We can write two equations:

$$x + y = 100,000 \quad \text{Total investment}$$
$$0.32x + 0.50y = 42,800 \quad \text{Total loss}$$

Rewrite the first equation as $y = 100,000 - x$ and substitute:

$$0.32x + 0.50(100,000 - x) = 42,800$$
$$0.32x + 50,000 - 0.50x = 42,800$$
$$-0.18x = -7200$$
$$x = 40,000$$

Substitute $x = 40,000$ into the first equation to get $y = 60,000$. So she invested $40,000 in the Fidelity Balanced Fund and $60,000 in the Fidelity Value Fund.

▶**TRY THIS.** Willard invested a total of $200,000 in stocks and bonds. After one year he lost 24% on his stocks and gained 8% on his bonds, and he still had exactly $200,000. How much did he invest in each category? ∎

FOR thought... True or False? Explain.

The following systems are referenced in these statements.

(a) $x + y = 5$ **(b)** $x - 2y = 4$ **(c)** $x = 5 + 3y$

    $x - y = 1$ $3x - 6y = 8$ $9y - 3x = -15$

1. The ordered pair $(2, 3)$ is in the solution set to $x + y = 5$.

2. The ordered pair $(2, 3)$ is in the solution set to system (a).

3. System (a) is inconsistent.

4. There is no solution to system (b).

5. Adding the equations in system (a) would eliminate y.

6. To solve system (c), we could substitute $5 + 3y$ for x in $9y - 3x = -15$.

7. System (c) is inconsistent.

8. The solution set to system (c) is the set of all real numbers.

9. The graphs of the equations of system (c) intersect at a single point.

10. The graphs of the equations of system (b) are parallel.

EXERCISES 1

Fill in the blank.

1. A collection of two or more equations is a(n) _____ of equations.

2. A system of equations that has at least one solution is _____.

3. A system of equations with no solution is _____.

4. A system of equations with exactly one solution is _____.

5. A system of equations with infinitely many solutions is _____.

6. Two systems with the same solution set are _____ systems.

Determine whether the given point is in the solution set to the given system.

7. $(1, 3)$
    $x + y = 4$
    $x - y = -2$

8. $(-1, 2)$
    $x + y = 1$
    $2x - 3y = -8$

9. $(-1, 5)$
    $2x + y = 3$
    $x - 2y = -9$

10. $(3, 2)$
    $3x - y = 7$
    $2x + 4y = 16$

Solve each system by inspecting the graphs of the equations.

11. $2x - 3y = -4$
$y = -2x + 4$

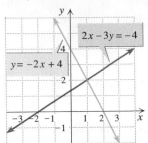

12. $x + 2y = -1$
$2x + 3y = -3$

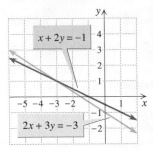

13. $3x - 4y = 0$
$y = \frac{3}{4}x + 2$

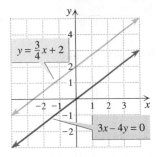

14. $x - 2y = -3$
$y = \frac{1}{2}x + \frac{3}{2}$

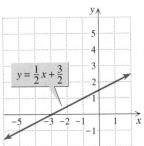

Solve each system by graphing.

15. $x + y = 5$
$x - y = 1$

16. $2x + y = -1$
$y - x = 5$

17. $y = x - 2$
$y = -x + 4$

18. $y = -3x$
$x - 2y = 7$

19. $3y + 2x = 6$
$y = -\frac{2}{3}x - 1$

20. $2x + 4y = 12$
$2y = 6 - x$

21. $y = \frac{1}{2}x - 3$
$2x - 4y = 12$

22. $y = -2x + 6$
$4x + 2y = 8$

Solve each system by substitution. Determine whether each system is independent, inconsistent, or dependent.

23. $y = 2x + 1$
$3x - 4y = 1$

24. $5x - 6y = 23$
$x = 6 - 3y$

25. $x + y = 1$
$2x - 3y = 8$

26. $x + 2y = 3$
$2x + y = 5$

27. $y - 3x = 5$
$3(x + 1) = y - 2$

28. $2y = 1 - 4x$
$2x + y = 0$

29. $2y = 6 - 3x$
$\frac{1}{2}x + \frac{1}{3}y = 3$

30. $2x = 10 - 5y$
$\frac{1}{5}x + \frac{1}{2}y = 1$

31. $x + y = 200$
$0.05x + 0.06y = 10.50$

32. $2x + y = 300$
$\frac{1}{2}x + \frac{1}{3}y = 80$

33. $y = 3x + 1$
$y = 3x - 7$

34. $2x + y = 9$
$4x + 2y = 10$

35. $\frac{1}{2}x - \frac{1}{3}y = 12$
$\frac{1}{4}x - \frac{1}{2}y = 1$

36. $0.05x + 0.1y = 10$
$0.06x + 0.2y = 16$

Solve each system by addition. Determine whether each system is independent, dependent, or inconsistent.

37. $x + y = 20$
$x - y = 6$

38. $3x - 2y = 7$
$-3x + y = 5$

39. $x - y = 5$
$3x + 2y = 10$

40. $x - 4y = -3$
$-3x + 5y = 2$

41. $x - y = 7$
$y - x = 5$

42. $2x - y = 6$
$-4x + 2y = 9$

43. $2x + 3y = 1$
$3x - 5y = -8$

44. $-2x + 5y = 14$
$7x + 6y = -2$

45. $0.05x + 0.1y = 0.6$
$x + 2y = 12$

46. $0.02x - 0.04y = 0.08$
$x - 2y = 4$

47. $\frac{x}{2} + \frac{y}{2} = 5$
$\frac{3x}{2} - \frac{2y}{3} = 2$

48. $\frac{x}{4} + \frac{y}{3} = 0$
$\frac{x}{8} - \frac{y}{6} = 2$

49. $3x - 2.5y = -4.2$
$0.12x + 0.09y = 0.4932$

50. $1.5x - 2y = 8.5$
$3x + 1.5y = 6$

Classify each system as independent, dependent, or inconsistent without doing any written work.

51. $y = 5x - 6$
$y = -5x - 6$

52. $y = 5x - 6$
$y = 5x + 4$

53. $5x - y = 6$
$y = 5x - 6$

54. $5x - y = 6$
$y = -5x + 6$

 Solve each system by graphing the equations on a graphing calculator and estimating the point of intersection.

55. $y = 0.5x + 3$
$y = 0.499x + 2$

56. $y = 2x - 3$
$y = 1.9999x - 2$

57. $0.23x + 0.32y = 1.25$
$0.47x - 1.26y = 3.58$

58. $342x - 78y = 474$
$123x + 145y = 397$

Solve each problem using two variables and a system of two equations. Solve the system by the method of your choice. Note that some of these problems lead to dependent or inconsistent systems.

59. *Two-Income Family* Althea has a higher income than Vaughn and their total income is $82,000. If their salaries differ by $16,000, then what is the income of each?

60. *Males and Females* A total of 76 young Republicans attended a strategy meeting. The number of females exceeded the number of males by 2. How many of each gender were at the meeting?

61. *Income on Investments* Carmen made $25,000 profit on the sale of her condominium. She lent part of the profit to Jim's Orange Grove at 10% interest and the remainder to Ricky's Used Cars at 8% interest. If she received $2200 in interest after one year, then how much did she lend to each business?

62. *Stock Market Losses* In 2008 Gerhart lost twice as much in the futures market as he did in the stock market. If his losses totaled $18,630, then how much did he lose in each market?

63. *Zoo Admission Prices* The Springfield Zoo has different admission prices for adults and children. When Mr. and Mrs. Weaver went with their five children, the bill was $33. If Mrs. Wong and her three children got in for $18.50, then what is the price of an adult's ticket and what is the price of a child's ticket?

64. *Book Prices* At the Book Exchange, all paperbacks sell for one price and all hardbacks sell for another price. Tanya got six paperbacks and three hardbacks for $8.25, while Gretta got four paperbacks and five hardbacks for $9.25. What was Todd's bill for seven paperbacks and nine hardbacks?

65. *Getting Fit* The Valley Health Club sold a dozen memberships in one week for a total of $6000. If male memberships cost $500 and female memberships cost $500, then how many male memberships and how many female memberships were sold?

66. *Quality Time* Mr. Thomas and his three children paid a total of $65.75 for admission to Water World. Mr. and Mrs. Li and their six children paid a total of $131.50. What is the price of an adult's ticket and what is the price of a child's ticket?

67. *Cows and Ostriches* A farmer has some cows and ostriches. One day he observed that his animals, which are normal, have 84 eyes and 122 legs. How many animals of each type does he have?

68. *Snakes and Iguanas* The farmer's wife collects snakes and iguanas. One day she observed that her reptiles, which are normal, have a total of 60 eyes and 68 feet. How many reptiles of each type does she have?

69. *Cows and Horses* A rancher has some normal cows and horses. One day he observed that his animals have a total of 96 legs and 24 tails. How many animals of each type does he have?

70. *Snakes and Mice* The rancher's wife raises snakes and white mice. One day she observed that her animals have a total of 78 eyes and 38 tails. How many animals of each type does she have?

71. *Coffee and Muffins* On Monday the office staff paid a total of $7.77 including tax for 3 coffees and 7 muffins. On Tuesday the bill was $14.80 including tax for 6 coffees and 14 muffins. If the sales tax rate is 7%, then what is the price of a coffee and what is the price of a muffin?

72. *Graduating Seniors* In Sociology 410 there are 55 more males than there are females. Two-thirds of the males and two-thirds of the females are graduating seniors. If there are 30 more graduating senior males than graduating senior females, then how many males and how many females are in the class?

73. *Political Party Preference* The results of a survey of students at Central High School concerning political party preference are given in the accompanying table. If 230 students preferred the Democratic party and 260 students preferred the Republican party, then how many students are there at CHS?

Table for Exercise 73

	M	F	
Democrat	50%	30%	
Republican	20%	60%	
Other	30%	10%	

S. Meltzer/PhotoLink/Photodisc/Getty Images

74. *Protein and Carbohydrates* Nutritional information for Rice Krispies and Grape-nuts is given in the accompanying table. How many servings of each would it take to get exactly 23 g of protein and 215 g of carbohydrates?

HINT Write an equation for protein and another for carbohydrates.

Table for Exercise 74

	Rice Krispies	Grape-nuts	
Protein (g/serving)	2	3	
Carbohydrates (g/serving)	25	23	

Lise Gagne/iStockphoto

75. *Distribution of Coin Types* Isabelle paid for her $1.75 lunch with 87 coins. If all of the coins were nickels and pennies, then how many were there of each type?

76. *Coin Collecting* Theodore has a collection of 166 old coins consisting of quarters and dimes. If he figures that each coin is worth two and a half times its face value, then his collection is worth $61.75. How many of each type of coin does he have?

77. *Bird Mobile* A wood carver is making a bird mobile, as shown in the accompanying figure. The weights of the horizontal bars and strings are negligible. The mobile will balance if the product of the weight and distance on one side of the balance point is equal to the product of the weight and distance on the other side. For what values of x and y will the mobile be balanced? HINT Write an equation for each balancing point.

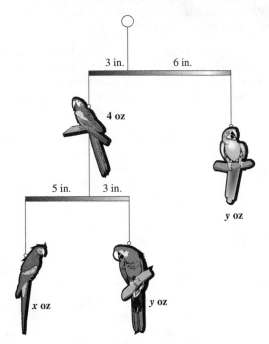

Figure for Exercise 77

78. *Doubles and Singles* The Executive Inn rents a double room for $20 more per night than a single. One night the motel took in $3949 by renting 15 doubles and 26 singles. What is the rental price for each type of room?

79. *Furniture Rental* A civil engineer has a choice of two plans for renting furniture for her new office. Under Plan A she pays $800 plus $150 per month, while under Plan B she pays $200 plus $200 per month. For each plan, write the cost as a function of the number of months. Which plan is cheaper in the long run? For what number of months do the two plans cost the same?

80. *Flat Tax* The 2008 tax rate schedule for a single taxpayer is given in the accompanying table (Internal Revenue Service, www.irs.ustreas.gov). Suppose the federal tax were simplified to be $100 plus 25% of taxable income. Use a system of equations to find the taxable income at which a single taxpayer would pay the same amount of tax under the simplified plan as under the 2008 schedule.

Table for Exercise 80 2008 Tax rate schedule–single taxpayers (in dollars)

If taxable income is over	but not over	your tax is	of the amount over
$0	$8025	0 + 10%	$0
8025	32,550	802.50 + 15%	8025
32,550	78,850	4481.25 + 25%	32,550
78,850	164,550	16,056.25 + 28%	78,850
164,550	357,700	40,052.25 + 33%	164,550
357,700	No limit	103,791.75 + 35%	357,700

81. *Prescribing Drugs* Doctors often prescribe the same drugs for children as they do for adults. If a is the age of a child and D is the adult dosage, then to find the child's dosage d, doctors can use the formula $d = 0.08aD$ (Fried's rule) or $d = D(a + 1)/24$ (Cowling's rule). For what age do the two formulas give the same child's dosage?

82. *Tax Reform* One plan for federal income tax reform is to tax an individual's income in excess of $15,000 at a 17% rate. Another plan is to institute a national retail sales tax of 15%. If an individual spends 75% of his or her income in retail stores where it is taxed at 15%, then for what income would the amount of tax be the same under either plan?

83. *Approaching Trucks* A 60-ft truck doing 40 mph is approaching a 40-ft truck doing 50 mph on a two-lane road. How long (in seconds) does it take them to pass each other?

84. *Passing Trucks* A 40-ft truck doing 50 mph and a 60-ft truck doing 40 mph are traveling in the same direction in adjacent lanes on an interstate highway. How long (in seconds) does it take the faster truck to pass the slower truck?

A system of equations can be used to find the equation of a line that goes through two points. For example, if $y = ax + b$ goes through $(3, 5)$, then a and b must satisfy $3a + b = 5$. For each given pair of points, find the equation of the line $y = ax + b$ that goes through the points by solving a system of equations.

85. $(-3, 9), (2, -1)$ **86.** $(1, -1), (3, 7)$

87. $(-2, 3), (4, -7)$ **88.** $(-3, -1), (4, 9)$

FOR WRITING/DISCUSSION

89. *Number of Solutions* Explain how you can tell (without graphing) whether a system of linear equations has one solution, no solutions, or infinitely many solutions. Be sure to account for linear equations that are not functions.

90. *Cooperative Learning* Write a step-by-step procedure (or algorithm) based on the addition method that will solve any system of two equations of the form $Ax + By = C$. Ask a classmate to solve a system using your procedure.

91. *Cooperative Learning* Write an independent system of two linear equations for which $(2, -3)$ is the solution. Ask a classmate to solve your system.

92. *Cooperative Learning* Write a dependent system of two linear equations for which $\{(t, t + 5) \mid t \text{ is any real number}\}$ is the solution set. Ask a classmate to solve your system.

▶ **RETHINKING**

93. Let $f(x) = 8^x$ and $g(x) = 4^{2-x}$. Find the following.
  a. $f(2/3)$

  b. $g(3)$

  c. $(f \circ g)(2)$

94. What is the equation of the horizontal asymptote to the graph of $f(x) = 3e^{x-4} + 5$?

95. Solve $8^{x-3} = 4^{x+5}$.

96. Find the equation of the axis of symmetry for the graph of $g(x) = -3x^2 - 5x + 9$.

97. Solve $15x^2 - 28x + 12 \leq 0$.

98. Find the remainder when $x^8 - 2x + 1$ is divided by $x - 2$.

THINKING OUTSIDE THE BOX LX & LXI

Many Means The mean score for those who passed the last test was 65, whereas the mean score for those who failed that test was 35. The mean for the entire class was 53. What percentage of the students in the class passed the test?

Cubic Power Find all real solutions to the equation
$$(x^2 + 2x - 24)^{x^3 - 9x^2 + 20x} = 1.$$

▶ **POP QUIZ** 1

Solve each system and classify each system as independent, inconsistent, or dependent.

1. $7x - 3y = 4$
  $y = 2x$

2. $3x - 5y = 11$
  $7x + 5y = 19$

3. $5x - 2y = -1$
  $4x + 3y = 13$

4. $3x = 1 - 9y$
  $3y + x = 8$

5. $y = x + 1$
  $5x - 5y + 5 = 0$

▶ **LINKING**

concepts... For Individual or Group Explorations

Modeling Life Expectancy

The accompanying table gives the life expectancy at birth for U.S. men and women (Centers for Disease Control, www.cdc.gov).

Gladskikh Tatiana/Shutterstock

Year of Birth	Life Expectancy (Male)	Life Expectancy (Female)
1930	58.1	61.6
1940	60.8	65.2
1950	65.6	71.1
1960	66.6	73.1
1970	67.1	74.7
1980	70.0	77.4
1990	71.1	78.6
2000	74.4	79.7

a) Use linear regression on your graphing calculator to find the life expectancy for men as a function of the year of birth.

b) Use linear regression on your graphing calculator to find the life expectancy for women as a function of the year of birth.

(continued on next page)

c) Graph the functions that you found in parts (a) and (b) on the same coordinate system.

d) According to this model, will men ever catch up to women in life expectancy?

e) For what year of birth did men and women have the same life expectancy?

f) Interpret the slope of these two lines.

g) Why do you think that life expectancy for women is increasing at a greater rate than life expectancy for men?

2 Systems of Linear Equations in Three Variables

Systems of many linear equations in many variables are used to model a variety of situations ranging from airline scheduling to allocating resources in manufacturing. The same techniques that we are studying with small systems can be extended to much larger systems. In this section we use the techniques of substitution and addition from Section 1 to solve systems of linear equations in three variables.

Definitions

A **linear equation in three variables** x, y, and z is an equation of the form

$$Ax + By + Cz = D,$$

where A, B, C, and D are real numbers with A, B, and C not all equal to zero. For example,

$$x + y + 2z = 9$$

is a linear equation in three variables. The equation is called *linear* because its form is similar to that of a linear equation in two variables. A solution to a linear equation in three variables is an **ordered triple** of real numbers in the form (x, y, z) that satisfies the equation. For instance, the ordered triple $(1, 2, 3)$ is a solution to

$$x + y + 2z = 9$$

because $1 + 2 + 2(3) = 9$. Other ordered triples, such as $(4, 5, 0)$ or $(3, 4, 1)$, are also in the solution set to $x + y + 2z = 9$. In fact, there are infinitely many ordered triples in the solution set to a linear equation in three variables.

The graph of the solution set of a linear equation in three variables requires a three-dimensional coordinate system. A three-dimensional coordinate system has a z-axis through the origin of the xy-plane, as shown in Fig. 12. The third coordinate of a point indicates its distance above or below the xy-plane. The point $(1, 2, 3)$ is shown in Fig. 12.

The graph of a linear equation in three variables is a plane and not a line as the name might suggest. We think of a plane as an infinite sheet of paper (with no edges), but that is difficult to draw. One way to draw a representation of a plane in a three-dimensional coordinate system is to draw a triangle whose vertices are the points of intersection of the plane and the axes.

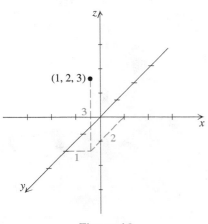

Figure 12

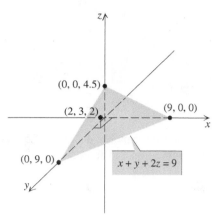

Figure 13

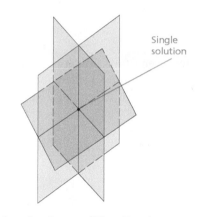

Independent System of Three Equations

Figure 14

EXAMPLE 1 | Graphing a plane

Sketch the graph of $x + y + 2z = 9$ in a three-dimensional coordinate system by locating the three intercepts. Find one additional point that satisfies the equation and plot it.

Solution

Let x and y both be zero in the equation:

$$0 + 0 + 2z = 9$$

$$z = 4.5$$

So $(0, 0, 4.5)$ is the z-intercept of the plane. If x and z are both zero, then we get $y = 9$. Thus $(0, 9, 0)$ is the y-intercept. If y and z are both zero, then we get $x = 9$. So $(9, 0, 0)$ is the x-intercept. Plot the three intercepts and draw a triangle, as shown in Fig. 13. If $x = 2$ and $y = 3$, then $z = 2$. Therefore $(2, 3, 2)$ satisfies the equation and appears to be on the plane when it is plotted as in Fig. 13. Of course there is more to a plane than the triangle in Fig. 13, but the triangle gives us an idea of the location of the plane.

▶**TRY THIS.** Graph $x + 2y + z = 6$ in a three-dimensional coordinate system. ■

It is fairly easy to draw a triangle through the intercepts to represent a plane, as we did in Example 1. However, if we were to draw two or three planes in this manner, it could be very difficult to see how they intersect. So we will often refer to the graphs of the equations to aid in understanding a system, but we will not attempt to solve a system in three variables by graphing. We will solve systems by using the algebraic methods of substitution, addition, or a combination of both.

Independent Systems

As with linear systems in two variables, a linear system in three variables can have one, infinitely many, or zero solutions. If the three equations correspond to three planes that intersect at a single point, as in Fig. 14, then the solution to the system is a single ordered triple. In this case, the system is called **independent.** Note that for simplicity, Fig. 14 is drawn without showing the coordinate axes.

Use the following strategy for solving an independent system of three equations involving three variables.

STRATEGY

Solving Independent Systems in Three Variables

1. Reduce the problem to a system of two equations in two variables.
2. Look for the easiest variable to eliminate.
3. Use addition or substitution to eliminate the chosen variable from two pairs of the original equations.
4. You can eliminate the chosen variable from the first and second, the second and third, or the first and third equations.
5. Solve the system of two equations in two variables. Then find the value of the third variable using one of the original equations.
6. Check in the original system.

$\boxed{\textbf{EXAMPLE 2}}$ An independent system of equations

Solve the system.

(1) $\quad x + y - z = 0$

(2) $\quad 3x - y + 3z = -2$

(3) $\quad x + 2y - 3z = -1$

Solution

Look for a variable that is easy to eliminate by addition. Since y occurs in Eq. (1) and $-y$ occurs in Eq. (2), we can eliminate y by adding Eqs. (1) and (2):

$$x + y - z = 0$$
$$\underline{3x - y + 3z = -2}$$
$$(4)\quad 4x \qquad + 2z = -2$$

Now repeat the process to eliminate y from Eqs. (1) and (3). Multiply Eq. (1) by -2 and add the result to Eq. (3):

$$-2x - 2y + 2z = 0 \qquad \text{Eq. (1) multiplied by } -2$$
$$\underline{x + 2y - 3z = -1} \qquad \text{Eq. (3)}$$
$$(5)\quad -x \qquad - z = -1$$

Equations (4) and (5) are a system of two linear equations in two variables. We could solve this system by substitution or addition. To solve by addition, multiply Eq. (5) by 2 and add to Eq. (4) to eliminate z:

$$4x + 2z = -2 \qquad \text{Eq. (4)}$$
$$\underline{-2x - 2z = -2} \qquad \text{Eq. (5) multiplied by 2}$$
$$2x \qquad = -4$$
$$x = -2$$

Use $x = -2$ in $4x + 2z = -2$ to find z:

$$4(-2) + 2z = -2$$
$$2z = 6$$
$$z = 3$$

To find y, use $x = -2$ and $z = 3$ in $x + y - z = 0$ (Eq. 1):

$$-2 + y - 3 = 0$$
$$y = 5$$

Check that the ordered triple $(-2, 5, 3)$ satisfies all three of the original equations:

(1) $\qquad -2 + 5 - 3 = 0 \qquad$ Correct

(2) $\quad 3(-2) - 5 + 3(3) = -2 \qquad$ Correct

(3) $\quad -2 + 2(5) - 3(3) = -1 \qquad$ Correct

The solution set is $\{(-2, 5, 3)\}$.

▶**TRY THIS.** Solve $x + y + z = 9$, $x - y + 2z = 1$, and $x + y - z = 5$. ■

Systems with Infinite Solution Sets

Two planes in three-dimensional space either are parallel or intersect along a line, as shown in Fig. 15. If the planes are parallel, there is no common point and no solution to the system. If the two planes intersect along a line, then there are infinitely many

Infinite solution: line of intersection

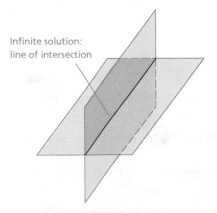

Dependent System of Two Equations

Figure 15

points on that line that satisfy both equations of the system. In our next example we solve a system of two equations whose graphs are planes that intersect along a line.

EXAMPLE 3 Two linear equations in three variables

Solve the system.

$$(1) \quad -2x + 3y - z = -1$$
$$(2) \quad x - 2y + z = 3$$

Solution

Add the equations to eliminate z:

$$-2x + 3y - z = -1$$
$$\underline{x - 2y + z = 3}$$
$$-x + y \qquad = 2$$
$$(3) \qquad y = x + 2$$

Equation (3) indicates that (x, y, z) satisfies both equations if and only if $y = x + 2$. Write Eq. (2) as $z = 3 - x + 2y$ and substitute $y = x + 2$ into this equation:

$$z = 3 - x + 2(x + 2)$$
$$z = x + 7$$

Now (x, y, z) satisfies (1) and (2) if and only if $y = x + 2$ and $z = x + 7$. So the solution set to the system could be written as

$$\{(x, y, z) \mid y = x + 2 \quad \text{and} \quad z = x + 7\}$$

or more simply

$$\{(x, x + 2, x + 7) \mid x \text{ is any real number}\}.$$

We write the solution set in this manner, because the system has infinitely many solutions. Every real number corresponds to a solution. For example, if $x = 1, 2$, or 3 in $(x, x + 2, x + 7)$ we get the solutions $(1, 3, 8)$, $(2, 4, 9)$, and $(3, 5, 10)$. Note that we can write the solution set in terms of x, y, or z. Since $z = x + 7$ and $y = x + 2$, we have $x = z - 7$ and $y = z - 7 + 2 = z - 5$. So the solution set can also be written as

$$\{(z - 7, z - 5, z) \mid z \text{ is any real number}\}.$$

Now if $z = 8, 9$, or 10 we get the solutions $(1, 3, 8)$, $(2, 4, 9)$, and $(3, 5, 10)$.

▶**TRY THIS.** Solve $x + y + z = 2$ and $x - 2y - z = 4$. ∎

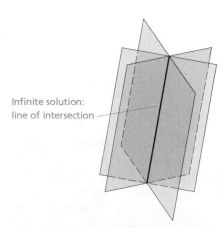

Infinite solution: line of intersection

Dependent System of Three Equations

Figure 16

A line in three-dimensional space does not have a simple equation like a line in a two-dimensional coordinate system. In Example 3, the triple $(x, x + 2, x + 7)$ is a point on the line of intersection of the two planes, for any real number x. For example, the points $(0, 2, 7)$, $(1, 3, 8)$, and $(-2, 0, 5)$ all satisfy both equations of the system and lie on the line of intersection of the planes.

In the next example we solve a system consisting of three planes that intersect along a single line, as shown in Fig. 16. This example is similar to Example 3.

EXAMPLE 4 A dependent system of three equations

Solve the system.

$$(1) \qquad 2x + y - z = 1$$
$$(2) \quad -3x - 3y + 2z = 1$$
$$(3) \quad -10x - 14y + 8z = 10$$

Solution

Examine the system and decide which variable to eliminate. If Eq. (1) is multiplied by 2, then $-2z$ will appear in Eq. (1) and $2z$ in Eq. (2). So, multiply Eq. (1) by 2 and add the result to Eq. (2) to eliminate z:

$$4x + 2y - 2z = 2 \quad \text{Eq. (1) multiplied by 2}$$

$$\underline{-3x - 3y + 2z = 1} \quad \text{Eq. (2)}$$

$$(4) \qquad x - y \qquad = 3$$

Now eliminate z from Eqs. (2) and (3) by multiplying Eq. (2) by -4 and adding the result to Eq. (3):

$$12x + 12y - 8z = -4 \quad \text{Eq. (2) multiplied by } -4$$

$$\underline{-10x - 14y + 8z = 10} \quad \text{Eq. (3)}$$

$$(5) \qquad 2x - 2y \qquad = 6$$

Note that Eq. (5) is a multiple of Eq. (4). Since Eqs. (4) and (5) are dependent, the original system has infinitely many solutions. We can describe all solutions in terms of the single variable x. To do this, get $y = x - 3$ from Eq. (4). Then substitute $x - 3$ for y in Eq. (1) to find z in terms of x:

$$z = 2x + y - 1 \qquad \text{Eq. (1) solved for } z.$$

$$z = 2x + (x - 3) - 1 \quad \text{Replace } y \text{ with } x - 3.$$

$$z = 3x - 4$$

An ordered triple (x, y, z) satisfies the system provided $y = x - 3$ and $z = 3x - 4$. So the solution set to the system is $\{(x, x - 3, 3x - 4) \mid x \text{ is any real number}\}$.

▶**TRY THIS.** Solve $x + y + z = 1$, $x - y - z = 3$, and $3x + y + z = 5$. ∎

If all of the original equations are equivalent, then the solution set to the system is the set of all points that satisfy one of the equations. For example, the system

$$x + y + z = 1$$

$$2x + 2y + 2z = 2$$

$$3x + 3y + 3z = 3$$

has solution set $\{(x, y, z) \mid x + y + z = 1\}$.

Inconsistent Systems

There are several ways that three planes can be positioned so that there is no point that is on all three planes. For example, Fig. 17 corresponds to a system where there are ordered triples that satisfy two equations, but no ordered triple that satisfies all three equations. Whatever the configuration of the planes, if there are no points in common to all three, the corresponding system is called **inconsistent** and has no solution. It is easy to identify a system that has no solution because a false statement will occur when we try to solve the system.

EXAMPLE 5 | A system with no solution

Solve the system.

$$(1) \quad x + y - z = 5$$

$$(2) \quad x + 2y - 3z = 9$$

$$(3) \quad x - y + 3z = 3$$

■ **Foreshadowing Calculus**

Throughout mathematics we encounter the situation of trying to simultaneously determine more than one unknown quantity or function. In general, the more objects that are unknown, the more facts we must have to find them.

No solution: no point on all three planes

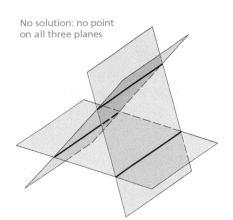

Inconsistent System of Three Equations

Figure 17

Solution

Multiply Eq. (1) by -2 and add the result to Eq. (2):

$$-2x - 2y + 2z = -10 \quad \text{Eq. (1) multiplied by } -2$$
$$\underline{x + 2y - 3z = 9} \quad \text{Eq. (2)}$$
$$(4) \quad -x \qquad - z = -1$$

Add Eq. (1) and Eq. (3) to eliminate y:

$$x + y - z = 5 \quad \text{Eq. (1)}$$
$$\underline{x - y + 3z = 3} \quad \text{Eq. (3)}$$
$$2x \qquad + 2z = 8$$
$$(5) \qquad x + z = 4$$

Now add Eq. (4) and Eq. (5):

$$-x - z = -1 \quad \text{Eq. (4)}$$
$$\underline{x + z = 4} \quad \text{Eq. (5)}$$
$$0 = 3$$

Since $0 = 3$ is false, the system is inconsistent. There is no solution.

▶**TRY THIS.** Solve $x + y + z = 1$, $x - y - z = 3$, and $3x + y + z = 7$. ■

Just as we find the equation of a line from two given points, we can find the equation of a parabola of the form $y = ax^2 + bx + c$ from three given points. Each of the three points determines a linear equation in the three variables a, b, and c. As long as the three points are not colinear, this system of three equations in three unknowns will have a unique solution as demonstrated in the next example.

EXAMPLE 6 | Finding the equation of a parabola given three points

Find the equation of the parabola opening upward or downward through $(-1, 10)$, $(1, 4)$, and $(2, 7)$.

Solution

Letting $x = -1$ and $y = 10$ in $y = ax^2 + bx + c$, we get $10 = a(-1)^2 + b(-1) + c$ or $10 = a - b + c$. For $x = 1$ and $y = 4$ we get $4 = a + b + c$, and for $x = 2$ and $y = 7$ we get $7 = 4a + 2b + c$. The three points determine the following system.

$$(1) \qquad a - b + c = 10$$
$$(2) \qquad a + b + c = 4$$
$$(3) \quad 4a + 2b + c = 7$$

Multiply (1) by -1 and add the result to (2) and to (3) to eliminate c:

$$(4) \qquad 2b = -6$$
$$(5) \quad 3a + 3b = -3$$

Equation (4) yields $b = -3$. Substitute $b = -3$ into (5) to get $a = 2$. Substitute $a = 2$ and $b = -3$ into (2) to get $2 - 3 + c = 4$ or $c = 5$. So the equation of the parabola through these three points is $y = 2x^2 - 3x + 5$.

▶**TRY THIS.** Find the equation of the parabola that goes through $(-1, 1)$, $(1, 3)$, and $(2, 7)$. ■

Modeling with a System of Three Equations

Problems that involve three unknown quantities can often be modeled with a system of three linear equations in three variables.

EXAMPLE 7 A problem involving three unknowns

Lionel delivers milk, bread, and eggs to Marcie's Camp Store. On Monday the bill for eight half-gallons of milk, four loaves of bread, and six dozen eggs was $42.86. On Tuesday the bill for five half-gallons of milk, ten loaves of bread, and three dozen eggs was $47.57. On Wednesday the bill for two half-gallons of milk, five loaves of bread, and seven dozen eggs was $34.72. How much is Thursday's bill for one half-gallon of milk, two loaves of bread, and one dozen eggs?

Solution

Let x represent the price of a half-gallon of milk, y represent the price of a loaf of bread, and z represent the price of a dozen eggs. We can write an equation for the bill on each of the three days:

$$(1) \quad 8x + 4y + 6z = 42.86$$

$$(2) \quad 5x + 10y + 3z = 47.57$$

$$(3) \quad 2x + 5y + 7z = 34.72$$

Multiply Eq. (2) by -2 and add the result to Eq. (1):

$$8x + 4y + 6z = 42.86 \qquad \text{Eq. (1)}$$
$$\underline{-10x - 20y - 6z = -95.14} \qquad \text{Eq. (2) multiplied by } -2$$
$$-2x - 16y \qquad\quad = -52.28$$
$$(4) \qquad x + 8y \qquad\quad = 26.14$$

Multiply Eq. (2) by -7, multiply Eq. (3) by 3, and add the results:

$$-35x - 70y - 21z = -332.99 \qquad \text{Eq. (2) multiplied by } -7$$
$$\underline{6x + 15y + 21z = 104.16} \qquad \text{Eq. (3) multiplied by } 3$$
$$(5) \quad -29x - 55y \qquad\quad = -228.83$$

Multiply Eq. (4) by 29 and add the result to Eq. (5) to eliminate x:

$$29x + 232y = 758.06 \qquad \text{Eq. (4) multiplied by } 29$$
$$\underline{-29x - 55y = -228.83} \qquad \text{Eq. (5)}$$
$$177y = 529.23$$
$$y = 2.99$$

Use $y = 2.99$ in $x + 8y = 26.14$ (Eq. 4):

$$x + 8(2.99) = 26.14$$
$$x + 23.92 = 26.14$$
$$x = 2.22$$

Use $x = 2.22$ and $y = 2.99$ in $8x + 4y + 6z = 42.86$ (Eq. 1) to find z:

$$8(2.22) + 4(2.99) + 6z = 42.86$$
$$6z = 13.14$$
$$z = 2.19$$

Milk is $2.22 per half-gallon, bread is $2.99 per loaf, and eggs are $2.19 per dozen. Thursday's bill should be $10.39.

▶**TRY THIS.** Two adults with one student and one child paid a total of $14 for admission to the zoo. One adult with two students and one child paid a total of $12. Two adults with two students and three children paid a total of $19. Find the admission prices for adults, students, and children. ■

► FOR thought... True or False? Explain.

The following systems are referenced in statements 1–7:

(a) $x + y - z = 2$
$-x - y + z = 4$
$x - 2y + 3z = 9$

(b) $x + y - z = 6$
$x + y + z = 4$
$x - y - z = 8$

(c) $x - y + z = 1$
$-x + y - z = -1$
$2x - 2y + 2z = 2$

1. The point $(1, 1, 0)$ is in the solution set to $x + y - z = 2$.

2. The point $(1, 1, 0)$ is in the solution set to system (a).

3. System (a) is inconsistent.

4. The point $(2, 3, -1)$ satisfies all equations of system (b).

5. The point $(6, -1, -1)$ satisfies all equations of system (b).

6. The solution set to system (c) is $\{(x, y, z) \mid x - y + z = 1\}$.

7. System (c) is dependent.

8. The solution set to $y = 2x + 3$ is $\{(x, 2x + 3) \mid x \text{ is any real number}\}$.

9. $(3, 1, 0) \in \{(x + 2, x, x - 1) \mid x \text{ is any real number}\}$.

10. x nickels, y dimes, and z quarters are worth $5x + 10y + 25z$ dollars.

► EXERCISES 2

Fill in the blank.

1. An equation of the form $Ax + By + Cz = D$ is a(n) _____ equation in three variables.

2. A system of three linear equations in three variables that has a single ordered triple in its solution set is a(n) _____ system.

Sketch the graph of each equation in a three-dimensional coordinate system.

3. $x + y + z = 5$

4. $x + 2y + z = 6$

5. $x + y - z = 3$

6. $2x + y - z = 6$

Determine whether the given point is in the solution set to the given system.

7. $(1, 3, 2)$
$x + y + z = 6$
$x - y - z = -4$
$2x + y - z = 3$

8. $(-1, 2, 4)$
$x + y - z = -3$
$2x - 3y + z = -4$
$x - y + 3z = 9$

9. $(-1, 5, 2)$
$2x + y - z = 1$
$x - 2y + z = -9$
$x - y - 2z = -8$

10. $(3, 2, 1)$
$3x - y + z = 8$
$2x + y - z = 9$
$x - 3y + z = -2$

Solve each system of equations.

11. $x + y + z = 6$
$2x - 2y - z = -5$
$3x + y - z = 2$

12. $3x - y + 2z = 14$
$x + y - z = 0$
$2x - y + 3z = 18$

13. $3x + 2y + z = 1$
$x + y - 2z = -4$
$2x - 3y + 3z = 1$

14. $4x - 2y + z = 13$
$3x - y + 2z = 13$
$x + 3y - 3z = -10$

15. $2x + y - 2z = -15$
$4x - 2y + z = 15$
$x + 3y + 2z = -5$

16. $x - 2y - 3z = 4$
$2x - 4y + 5z = -3$
$5x - 6y + 4z = -7$

Find three ordered triples that belong to each of the following sets. Answers may vary.

17. $\{(x, x + 3, x - 5) \mid x \text{ is any real number}\}$

18. $\{(x, 2x - 4, x - 9) \mid x \text{ is any real number}\}$

19. $\{(2y, y, y - 7) \mid y \text{ is any real number}\}$

20. $\{(3 - z, 2 - z, z) \mid z \text{ is any real number}\}$

Fill in the blanks so that the two sets are equal.

21. $\{(x, x + 3, x - 5) \mid x \text{ is any real number}\}$
$= \{(\quad, y, \quad) \mid y \text{ is any real number}\}$

22. $\{(x, 2x, 3x) \mid x \text{ is any real number}\}$
$= \left\{\left(\quad, y, \quad\right) \mid y \text{ is any real number}\right\}$

23. $\{(x, x + 1, x - 1) \mid x \text{ is any real number}\}$
$= \{(\quad, \quad, z) \mid z \text{ is any real number}\}$

24. $\{(x, x - 1, x + 5) \mid x \text{ is any real number}\}$
$= \{(\quad, \quad, z) \mid z \text{ is any real number}\}$

25. $\{(x, 2x + 1, 3x - 1) \mid x \text{ is any real number}\}$
$= \left\{\left(\quad, y, \quad\right) \mid y \text{ is any real number}\right\}$

26. $\{(x, 3x, 2x - 4) \mid x \text{ is any real number}\}$
$= \left\{\left(\quad, \quad, z\right) \mid z \text{ is any real number}\right\}$

Solve each system.

27. $\begin{aligned} x + 2y - 3z &= -17 \\ 3x - 2y - z &= -3 \end{aligned}$

28. $\begin{aligned} x + 2y + z &= 4 \\ 2x - y - z &= 3 \end{aligned}$

29. $\begin{aligned} x + y - z &= 2 \\ x - 2y + z &= 5 \end{aligned}$

30. $\begin{aligned} 2x - 3y - z &= -9 \\ x - y - z &= 3 \end{aligned}$

31. $\begin{aligned} 2x - y + z &= 7 \\ y + z &= 5 \end{aligned}$

32. $\begin{aligned} 3x - 2y - z &= -20 \\ x - z &= -10 \end{aligned}$

33. $\begin{aligned} x + 2y - 3z &= 5 \\ -x - 2y + 3z &= -5 \\ 2x + 4y - 6z &= 10 \end{aligned}$

$\begin{aligned} 3x - 9y + 6z &= 12 \\ 5x - 15y + 10z &= 20 \end{aligned}$

34. $\quad 2x - 6y + 4z = 8$

35. $\begin{aligned} x - 2y + 3z &= 5 \\ 2x - 4y + 6z &= 3 \\ 2x - 3y + z &= 9 \end{aligned}$

36. $\begin{aligned} -2x + y - 3z &= 6 \\ 4x - y + z &= 2 \\ 2x - y + 3z &= 1 \end{aligned}$

37. $\begin{aligned} x + y - z &= 2 \\ 2x - y + z &= 4 \end{aligned}$

38. $\begin{aligned} -2x + 2y - z &= 4 \\ 2x - y + z &= 1 \end{aligned}$

39. $\begin{aligned} x + y &= 5 \\ y - z &= 2 \\ x + z &= 3 \end{aligned}$

40. $\begin{aligned} 2x - y &= -1 \\ -2x + z &= 1 \\ y - z &= 0 \end{aligned}$

41. $\begin{aligned} x - y + z &= 7 \\ 2y - 3z &= -13 \\ 3x - 2z &= -3 \end{aligned}$

42. $\begin{aligned} 2x + y - z &= 5 \\ 2y + 3z &= -14 \\ -3y - 2z &= 11 \end{aligned}$

43. $\begin{aligned} x + y + 2z &= 7.5 \\ 3x + 4y + z &= 12 \\ 5x + 2y + 5z &= 21 \end{aligned}$

44. $\begin{aligned} 100x + 200y + 500z &= 47 \\ 350x + 5y + 250z &= 33.9 \\ 200x + 80y + 100z &= 23.4 \end{aligned}$

45. $\begin{aligned} x + y + z &= 9000 \\ 0.05x + 0.06y + 0.09z &= 710 \\ z &= 3y \end{aligned}$

46. $\begin{aligned} x + y + z &= 200{,}000 \\ 0.09x + 0.08y + 0.12z &= 20{,}200 \\ z &= x + y \end{aligned}$

47. $\begin{aligned} x &= 2y - 1 \\ y &= 3z + 2 \\ z &= 2x - 3 \end{aligned}$

48. $\begin{aligned} x + 2y - 3z &= 0 \\ 2x - y + z &= 0 \\ 3x + y - 4z &= 0 \end{aligned}$

Use a system of equations to find the parabola of the form $y = ax^2 + bx + c$ that goes through the three given points.

49. $(-1, -2), (2, 1), (-2, 1)$ **50.** $(1, 2), (2, 3), (3, 6)$

51. $(0, 0), (1, 3), (2, 2)$

52. $(0, -6), (1, -3), (2, 6)$

53. $(0, 4), (-2, 0), (-3, 1)$

54. $(0, 6), (3, 0), (-1, 12)$

Write a linear equation in three variables that is satisfied by all three of the given ordered triples.

55. $(0, 0, 1), (0, 1, 0), (1, 0, 0)$

56. $(0, 0, 2), (0, 1, 0), (1, 0, 0)$

57. $(1, 1, 1), (0, 2, 0), (1, 0, 0)$

58. $(1, 0, 1), (2, 1, 0), (0, 2, 1)$

Solve each problem by using a system of three linear equations in three variables.

59. *Just Numbers* The sum of three numbers is 40. The difference between the largest and the smallest is 12, and the largest is equal to the sum of the two smaller numbers. Find the numbers.

60. *Perimeter* The perimeter of a triangle is 40 meters. The sum of the two shorter sides is 2 meters more than the longest side, and the longest side is 11 meters longer than the shortest side. Find the sides.

61. *Quizzes* The Rabbit had an average (mean) score of 7 on the first three College Algebra 101 quizzes. His second quiz score was one point higher than the first quiz score and the third was 4 points higher than the second. What were the three scores?
HINT Mean is the total of the scores divided by the number of scores.

62. *More Quizzes* Dr. M had an average (mean) score of 8 on the first two Chemistry 302 quizzes. After she took the third quiz her average was 12. If her score on the third quiz was 13 points higher than her score on the first quiz, then what were the three quiz scores?

63. *Stocks, Bonds, and a Mutual Fund* Marita invested a total of $25,000 in stocks, bonds, and a mutual fund. In one year she earned 8% on her stock investment, 10% on her bond investment, and 6% on her mutual fund, with a total return of $1860. Unfortunately, the amount invested in the mutual fund was twice as large as the amount she invested in the bonds. How much did she invest in each?

64. *Age Groups* In 1980 the population of Springfield was 1911. In 1990 the number of people under 20 years old increased by 10%, while the number of people in the 20 to 60 category decreased by 8%, and the number of people over 60 increased by one-third. If the 1990 population was 2136 and in 1990 the number of people over 60 was equal to the number of people 60 and under, then how many were in each age group in 1980?

65. *Fast Food Inflation* One year ago you could get a hamburger, fries, and a Coke at Francisco's Drive-In for $3.80. Since then, the price of a hamburger has increased 10%, the price of fries has increased 20%, and the price of a Coke has increased 25%. The same meal now costs $4.49. If the price of a Coke is now 7 cents less than the price of a hamburger, then what was the price of each item one year ago?

66. *Misplaced House Numbers* Angelo on Elm Street removed his three-digit house number for painting and noticed that the sum of the digits was 9 and that the units digit was three times as large as the hundreds digit. When the painters put the house number back up, they reversed the digits. The new house number was now 396 larger than the correct house number. What is Angelo's correct address?

67. *Weight Distribution* A driver of a 1200-pound race car wants to have 51% of the car's weight on the left front and left rear tires and 48% of the car's weight on the left rear and right rear tires. If there must be at least 280 pounds on every tire, then find three possible weight distributions. Answers may vary.

68. *Burgers, Fries, and Cokes* Jennifer bought 5 burgers, 7 orders of fries, and 6 Cokes for $11.25. Marylin bought 6 burgers, 8 orders of fries, and 7 Cokes for $13.20. John wants to buy an order of fries from Marylin for $0.80, but Marylin says that she paid more than that for the fries. What do you think? Find three possibilities for the prices of the burgers, fries, and Cokes. Answers may vary.

69. *Distribution of Coins* Emma paid the $10.36 bill for her lunch with 232 coins consisting of pennies, nickels, and dimes. If the number of nickels plus the number of dimes was equal to the number of pennies, then how many coins of each type did she use?

70. *Students, Teachers, and Pickup Trucks* Among the 564 students and teachers at Jefferson High School, 128 drive to school each day. One-fourth of the male students, one-sixth of the female students, and three-fourths of the teachers drive. Among those who drive to school, there are 41 who drive pickup trucks. If one-half of the driving male students, one-tenth of the driving female students, and one-third of the driving teachers drive pickups, then how many male students, female students, and teachers are there?

71. *Milk, Coffee, and Doughnuts* The employees from maintenance go for coffee together every day at 9 A.M. On Monday, Hector paid $5.45 for three cartons of milk, four cups of coffee, and seven doughnuts. On Tuesday, Guillermo paid $5.30 for four milks, two coffees, and eight doughnuts. On Wednesday, Anna paid $5.15 for two milks, five coffees, and six doughnuts. On Thursday, Alphonse had to pay for five milks, two coffees, and nine doughnuts. How much change did he get back from his $10 bill?

72. *Average Age of Vehicles* The average age of the Johnsons' cars is eight years. Three years ago the Toyota was twice as old as the Ford. Two years ago the sum of the Buick's and the Ford's ages was equal to the age of the Toyota. How old is each car now?

73. *Fish Mobile* A sculptor is designing a fish mobile, as shown in the accompanying figure. The weights of the horizontal bars and strings are negligible compared to the cast-iron fish. The mobile will balance if the product of the weight and distance on one side of the balance point is equal to the product of the weight and distance on the other side. How much must the bottom three fish weigh for the mobile to be balanced?
HINT Write an equation for each balancing point.

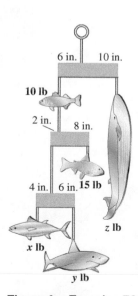

6 in. 10 in.

10 lb

2 in. 8 in.

4 in. 6 in. **15 lb**

z lb

x lb

y lb

Figure for Exercise 73

74. *Efficiency for Descending Flight* In studying the flight of birds, Vance Tucker measured the efficiency (the relationship between power input and power output) for parakeets flying at various speeds in a descending flight pattern. He recorded an efficiency of 0.18 at 12 mph, 0.23 at 22 mph, and 0.14 at 30 mph. Tucker's measurements suggest that efficiency E is a quadratic function of the speed s. Find the quadratic function whose graph goes through the three given ordered pairs, and find the speed that gives the maximum efficiency for descending flight.

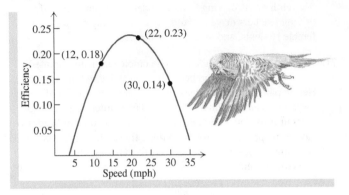

Figure for Exercise 74

75. *Path of an Arrow* An arrow shot into the air follows the parabolic path shown in the figure. When the arrow is 10 meters from the origin, its altitude is 40 meters. When the arrow is 20 meters from the origin, its altitude is 70 meters.

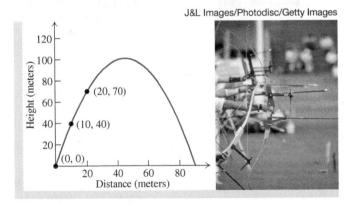

J&L Images/Photodisc/Getty Images

Figure for Exercise 75

a. Find the equation of the parabola.

b. What is the highest altitude reached by the arrow?

c. How many meters from the origin will the arrow land?

76. *Quadratic Regression* Use the data from Exercise 74 and quadratic regression on a graphing calculator to find the equation of the parabola that passes through the given points. Then use your calculator to find the x-coordinate corresponding to the maximum y-coordinate on the graph of the parabola. Compare your results to those in Exercise 74.

FOR WRITING/DISCUSSION

77. *Cooperative Learning* Write a system of three linear equations in three unknowns for which $(1/2, 1/3, 1/4)$ is the only solution. Ask a classmate to solve the system.

78. *Cooperative Learning* Write a word problem for which a system of three linear equations in three unknowns can be used to find the solution. Ask a classmate to solve the problem.

▶ RETHINKING

79. Solve the system of equations $2x - 3y = 20$ and $x + 4y = -1$.

80. Is the system of equations $y = 3x - 5$ and $y = 3x - 9$ independent, dependent, or inconsistent?

81. Find the amount when a principal of $10,000 is invested for 6 years at 3.5% annual percentage rate compounded quarterly.

82. Let $f(x) = \log_2(x)$.
  a. Find $f(1/8)$.

  b. Find a if $f(a) = 4$.

83. Determine whether the equation $x^2 + y^2 = 25$ defines y as a function of x.

84. Find the difference quotient for the function $f(x) = x^2 + x$.

THINKING OUTSIDE THE BOX LXII

Hungry Workers Two bricklayers and a contractor went to a fast food restaurant for lunch. The first bricklayer paid $14.25 for 8 hamburgers, 5 orders of fries, and 2 Cokes. The second bricklayer paid $8.51 for 5 hamburgers, 3 orders of fries, and 1 Coke. What did the contractor pay for 1 hamburger, 1 order of fries, and 1 Coke?

▶ POP QUIZ 2

Solve each system.

1. $x + y + z = 22$

$x + 2y - z = 11$

$x - y + z = 8$

2. $2x - y + 2z = 4$

$x + y - z = 2$

concepts... For Individual or Group Explorations

Sean Locke/iStockphoto

Accounting Problems

For Class C corporations in Louisiana the amount of state income tax is deductible on the federal income tax return and the amount of federal income tax is deductible on the state return. Assume that the state tax rate is 5%, the federal tax rate is 30%, and the corporation has an income of $200,000 before taxes.

a) Write the amount of state tax as a function of the amount of federal tax.

b) Write the amount of federal tax as a function of the amount of state tax.

c) Solve your system to find the amount of state tax and the amount of federal tax.

d) If the corporation wants to give a 20% bonus to employees, the accountant deducts the amount of the bonus, the state tax, and the federal tax from the $200,000 income to get the amount on which a 20% bonus is computed. The bonus and state tax are deductible before the federal tax is computed, and the federal tax and bonus are deductible before the state tax is computed. Find the amount of the bonus, the federal tax, and the state tax for this corporation.

3 Nonlinear Systems of Equations

In Sections 1 and 2 we solved linear systems of equations, but we have seen many equations in two variables that are not linear. Equations such as

$$y = 3x^2, \qquad y = \sqrt{x}, \qquad y = |x|, \qquad y = 10^x, \qquad \text{and} \qquad y = \log(x)$$

are called *nonlinear equations* because their graphs are not straight lines. If a system has at least one nonlinear equation, it is called a **nonlinear system.** Systems of nonlinear equations arise in applications just as systems of linear equations do. In this section we will use the techniques that we learned for linear systems to solve nonlinear systems. We are seeking only the real solutions to the systems in this section.

Solving by Elimination of Variables

To solve nonlinear systems, we combine equations to eliminate variables just as we did for linear systems. However, since the graphs of nonlinear equations are not straight lines, the graphs might intersect at more than one point, and the solution set might contain more than one point. The next examples show systems whose solution sets contain two points, four points, and one point.

EXAMPLE 1 A parabola and a line

Solve the system of equations and sketch the graph of each equation on the same coordinate plane.

$$y = x^2 + 1$$
$$y - x = 2$$

Solution

The graph of $y = x^2 + 1$ is a parabola opening upward. The graph of $y = x + 2$ is a line with y-intercept $(0, 2)$ and slope 1. The graphs are shown in Fig. 18. To find

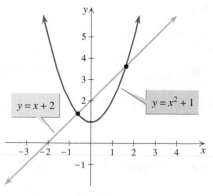

$y = x + 2$

$y = x^2 + 1$

Figure 18

543

the exact coordinates of the points of intersection of the graphs, we solve the system by substitution. Substitute $y = x^2 + 1$ into $y - x = 2$:

$$x^2 + 1 - x = 2$$
$$x^2 - x - 1 = 0$$

Solve this quadratic equation using the quadratic formula:

$$x = \frac{1 \pm \sqrt{1 - 4(1)(-1)}}{2(1)} = \frac{1 \pm \sqrt{5}}{2}$$

Use $x = (1 \pm \sqrt{5})/2$ in $y = x + 2$ to find y:

$$y = \frac{1 \pm \sqrt{5}}{2} + 2 = \frac{5 \pm \sqrt{5}}{2}$$

The solution set to the system is

$$\left\{ \left(\frac{1 + \sqrt{5}}{2}, \frac{5 + \sqrt{5}}{2} \right), \left(\frac{1 - \sqrt{5}}{2}, \frac{5 - \sqrt{5}}{2} \right) \right\}.$$

To check the solution, use a calculator to find the approximations $(1.62, 3.62)$ and $(-0.62, 1.38)$. These points of intersection are consistent with Fig. 18. You should also check the decimal approximations in the original equations. Note that we could have solved this system by solving the second equation for x (or for y) and then substituting into the first.

▶**TRY THIS.** Solve $y = x^2 - 1$ and $x + y = 5$. ∎

In the next example we find the points of intersection for the graph of an absolute value function and a parabola.

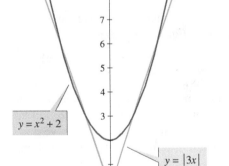

Figure 19

EXAMPLE 2 | An absolute value function and a parabola

Solve the system of equations and sketch the graph of each equation on the same coordinate plane.

$$y = |3x|$$
$$y = x^2 + 2$$

Solution

The graph of $y = x^2 + 2$ is a parabola opening upward with vertex at $(0, 2)$. The graph of $y = |3x|$ is V-shaped and passes through $(0, 0)$ and $(\pm 1, 3)$. Both graphs are shown in Fig. 19. To eliminate y, we can substitute $|3x|$ for y in the second equation:

$$|3x| = x^2 + 2$$

Write an equivalent compound equation without absolute value and solve:

$$3x = x^2 + 2 \quad \text{or} \quad 3x = -(x^2 + 2)$$
$$x^2 - 3x + 2 = 0 \quad \text{or} \quad x^2 + 3x + 2 = 0$$
$$(x - 2)(x - 1) = 0 \quad \text{or} \quad (x + 2)(x + 1) = 0$$
$$x = 2 \quad \text{or} \quad x = 1 \quad \text{or} \quad x = -2 \quad \text{or} \quad x = -1$$

Using each of these values for x in the equation $y = |3x|$ yields the solution set $\{(-2, 6), (-1, 3), (1, 3), (2, 6)\}$. This solution set is consistent with what we see on the graphs in Fig. 19.

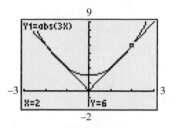

Figure 20

Check with a calculator as shown in Fig. 20. It is hard to see from this calculator graph that there are four solutions.

▶**TRY THIS.** Solve $y = |2x|$ and $y = -x^2 + 2x + 5$.   ∎

It is not necessary to draw the graphs of the equations of a nonlinear system to solve it. However, the graphs give us an idea of how many solutions to expect for the system. So graphs can be used to support our solutions.

$\boxed{\text{EXAMPLE } 3}$ Solving a nonlinear system

Solve the system of equations.

$$(1) \qquad x^2 + y^2 = 25$$

$$(2) \qquad \frac{x^2}{18} + \frac{y^2}{32} = 1$$

Solution

Write Eq. (1) as $y^2 = 25 - x^2$ and substitute into Eq. (2):

$$\frac{x^2}{18} + \frac{25 - x^2}{32} = 1$$

$$288\left(\frac{x^2}{18} + \frac{25 - x^2}{32}\right) = 288 \cdot 1 \qquad \text{The LCD for 18 and 32 is 288.}$$

$$16x^2 + 9(25 - x^2) = 288$$

$$7x^2 + 225 = 288$$

$$7x^2 = 63$$

$$x^2 = 9$$

$$x = \pm 3$$

Use $x = 3$ in $y^2 = 25 - x^2$: $\quad y^2 = 25 - 3^2$

$$y^2 = 16$$

$$y = \pm 4$$

Use $x = -3$ in $y^2 = 25 - x^2$: $\quad y^2 = 25 - (-3)^2$

$$y^2 = 16$$

$$y = \pm 4$$

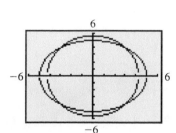

Figure 21

The solution set is $\{(-3, 4), (-3, -4), (3, 4), (3, -4)\}$. Check that all four ordered pairs satisfy both equations of the original system.

The graphs of $y = \pm\sqrt{25 - x^2}$ and $y = \pm\sqrt{32 - 32x^2/18}$ in Fig. 21 intersect at four points and support the conclusion that there are four solutions to the system.

▶**TRY THIS.** Solve $x^2 + y^2 = 5$ and $4x^2 + 9y^2 = 35$.   ∎

$\boxed{\text{EXAMPLE } 4}$ Solving a nonlinear system

Solve the system of equations.

$$(1) \qquad \frac{2}{x} + \frac{3}{y} = \frac{1}{2}$$

$$(2) \qquad \frac{4}{x} + \frac{1}{y} = \frac{2}{3}$$

Solution

Since these equations have the same form, we can use addition to eliminate a variable. Multiply Eq. (2) by -3 and add the result to Eq. (1):

$$\frac{2}{x} + \frac{3}{y} = \frac{1}{2}$$

$$\frac{-12}{x} + \frac{-3}{y} = -2$$

$$\overline{\qquad\qquad\qquad\qquad}$$

$$\frac{-10}{x} \qquad\quad = -\frac{3}{2}$$

$$3x = 20$$

$$x = \frac{20}{3}$$

Use $x = 20/3$ in Eq. (1) to find y:

$$\frac{2}{20/3} + \frac{3}{y} = \frac{1}{2}$$

$$\frac{3}{10} + \frac{3}{y} = \frac{1}{2}$$

$$3y + 30 = 5y \qquad \text{Multiply each side by } 10y.$$

$$30 = 2y$$

$$15 = y$$

The solution set is $\{(20/3, 15)\}$. Check this solution in the original system.

▶**TRY THIS.** Solve $\dfrac{1}{x} + \dfrac{1}{y} = 2$ and $\dfrac{1}{x} - \dfrac{1}{y} = 4$. ∎

In the next example we use the properties of logarithms to solve a system involving logarithms.

EXAMPLE 5 | Solving a nonlinear system

Find the exact solution to the system.

$$y = \log_2(x + 2)$$

$$y = 1 - \log_2(x - 2)$$

Solution

Replace y in the second equation with $\log_2(x + 2)$:

$$\log_2(x + 2) = 1 - \log_2(x - 2)$$

$$\log_2(x + 2) + \log_2(x - 2) = 1$$

$$\log_2((x + 2)(x - 2)) = 1 \qquad\qquad \text{Product rule}$$

$$\log_2(x^2 - 4) = 1$$

$$x^2 - 4 = 2 \qquad\qquad \text{If } \log_2(a) = b, \text{then } a = 2^b.$$

$$x^2 = 6$$

$$x = \pm\sqrt{6}$$

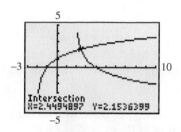

Figure 22

If $x = -\sqrt{6}$, we have a logarithm of a negative number. So $x = \sqrt{6}$ and $y = \log_2(\sqrt{6} + 2)$. The solution set is $\{(\sqrt{6}, \log_2(\sqrt{6} + 2))\}$.

You can find an approximate solution with a calculator as shown in Fig. 22. Using the base-change formula we graph the equations $y = \ln(x + 2)/\ln(2)$ and $y = 1 - \ln(x - 2)/\ln(2)$.

▶**TRY THIS.** Find the exact solution to the system $y = \log(x + 1)$ and $y = 1 + \log(x - 1)$. ∎

Modeling with a Nonlinear System

In the next example we solve a problem using a nonlinear system.

Figure 23

EXAMPLE 6 | Application of a nonlinear system

The screen on a 50-inch LG plasma HD TV has an aspect ratio of 16 to 9. Find the length and width of the screen to the nearest tenth of an inch.

Solution

Let x be the width and let y be the length of the screen as shown in Fig. 23. The diagonal measure of the screen is 50 inches. An aspect ratio of 16 to 9 means that the ratio of the length to the width is 16 to 9. So we can use the Pythagorean theorem to write one equation and the aspect ratio to write a second equation:

$$x^2 + y^2 = 50^2$$

$$\frac{y}{x} = \frac{16}{9}$$

Write the second equation as $y = \frac{16}{9}x$ and substitute into the first equation:

$$x^2 + \left(\frac{16}{9}x\right)^2 = 50^2$$

$$x^2 + \frac{256}{81}x^2 = 2500$$

$$\frac{337}{81}x^2 = 2500$$

$$x^2 = \frac{81}{337} \cdot 2500$$

$$x = \sqrt{\frac{202{,}500}{337}} \approx 24.5$$

$$y = \frac{16}{9}x = \frac{16}{9}\sqrt{\frac{202{,}500}{337}} \approx 43.6$$

Thus the width is approximately 24.5 inches and the length is approximately 43.6 inches.

▶**TRY THIS.** The screen on a 42-inch LCD TV has an aspect ratio of 16 to 10. Find the length and width of the screen to the nearest tenth of an inch. ∎

FOR thought... True or False? Explain.

1. The line $y = x$ intersects the circle $x^2 + y^2 = 1$ at two points.

2. A line and a circle intersect at two points or not at all.

3. A parabola and a circle can intersect at three points.

4. The parabolas $y = x^2 - 1$ and $y = 1 - x^2$ do not intersect.

5. The line $y = x$ intersects $x^2 + y^2 = 2$ at $(1, 1)$, $(1, -1)$, $(-1, 1)$, and $(-1, -1)$.

6. Two distinct circles can intersect at more than two points.

7. The area of a right triangle is half the product of the lengths of its legs.

8. The surface area of a rectangular solid with length L, width W, and height H is $2LW + 2LH + 2WH$.

9. Two numbers with a sum of 6 and a product of 7 are $3 - \sqrt{2}$ and $3 + \sqrt{2}$.

10. It is impossible to find two numbers with a sum of 7 and a product of 1.

EXERCISES 3

Determine whether the given point is in the solution set to the given system.

1. $(-1, 4)$
   $y - 2x = 6$
   $y = x^2 + 3$

2. $(2, -3)$
   $y = x - 5$
   $y = |x - 3| - 4$

3. $(4, -5)$
   $y = \sqrt{x} - 7$
   $x - y = 1$

4. $(-3, -4)$
   $x^2 + y^2 = 25$
   $2x - 3y = 18$

Solve each system algebraically. Then graph both equations on the same coordinate system to support your solution.

5. $y = x^2$
   $y = x$

6. $y = -x^2$
   $y = -2x$

7. $5x - y = 6$
   $y = x^2$

8. $2x^2 - y = 8$
   $7x + y = -4$

9. $y - x = 3$
   $y = |x|$

10. $y = |x| - 1$
    $2y - x = 1$

11. $y = |x|$
    $y = x^2$

12. $y = 2|x| - 1$
    $y = x^2$

13. $y = \sqrt{x}$
    $y = 2x$

14. $y = \sqrt{x + 3}$
    $x - 4y = -7$

15. $y = x^3$
    $y = 4x$

16. $y = x^2$
    $x = y^2$

17. $y = x^3 - x$
    $y = x$

18. $y = x^4 - x^2$
    $y = x^2$

19. $x^2 + y^2 = 1$
    $y = x$

20. $x^2 + y^2 = 25$
    $2x - 3y = -6$

Solve each system.

21. $x + y = -4$
    $xy = 1$

22. $x + y = 10$
    $xy = 21$

23. $2x^2 - y^2 = 1$
    $x^2 - 2y^2 = -1$

24. $x^2 + y^2 = 5$
    $x^2 + 4y^2 = 14$

25. $xy - 2x = 2$
    $2x - y = 1$

26. $y - xy = -10$
    $x - 2y = -7$

27. $\dfrac{3}{x} - \dfrac{1}{y} = \dfrac{13}{10}$
    $\dfrac{1}{x} + \dfrac{2}{y} = \dfrac{9}{10}$

28. $\dfrac{2}{x} + \dfrac{3}{2y} = \dfrac{11}{4}$
    $\dfrac{5}{2x} - \dfrac{2}{y} = \dfrac{3}{2}$

29. $x^2 + xy - y^2 = -5$
    $x + y = 1$

30. $x^2 + xy + y^2 = 12$
    $x + y = 2$

31. $x^2 + 2xy - 2y^2 = -11$
    $-x^2 - xy + 2y^2 = 9$

32. $-3x^2 + 2xy - y^2 = -9$
    $3x^2 - xy + y^2 = 15$

33. $\dfrac{4}{x} + \dfrac{5}{y^2} = 12$

$\dfrac{3}{x} + \dfrac{7}{y^2} = 22$

34. $\dfrac{3}{x^2} - \dfrac{5}{y} = 33$

$\dfrac{5}{x^2} + \dfrac{1}{y} = 83$

35. $xy^2 = 10^{11}$

$\dfrac{x^3}{y} = 10^{12}$

36. $x^2 y^3 = 10^{23}$

$\dfrac{x^4}{y^2} = 10^{6}$

Solve each system of exponential or logarithmic equations.

37. $y = 2^{x+1}$

$y = 4^{-x}$

38. $y = 3^{2x+1}$

$y = 9^{-x}$

39. $y = \log_2(x)$

$y = \log_4(x + 2)$

40. $y = \log_2(-x)$

$y = \log_2(x + 4)$

41. $y = \log_2(x + 2)$

$y = 3 - \log_2(x)$

42. $y = \log(2x + 4)$

$y = 1 + \log(x - 2)$

43. $y = 3^x$

$y = 2^x$

44. $y = 6^{x-1}$

$y = 2^{x+1}$

45. $y = 2^x$

$x = \log_4(y)$

46. $y = 8^x$

$x = \log_2(2y)$

47. $x + \log_{16}(y + 1) = \dfrac{1}{2}$

$x + \log_{16}(y) = \dfrac{1}{4}$

48. $y + \log_2(x) = 4$

$y + \log_8(x) = 2$

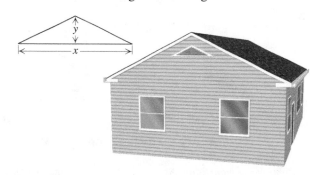 *Using a graphing calculator, we can solve systems that are too difficult to solve algebraically. Solve each system by graphing its equations on a graphing calculator and finding points of intersection to the nearest tenth.*

49. $y = \log_2(x)$

$y = 2^x - 3$

50. $x^2 - y^2 = 1$

$y = 2^{x-3}$

51. $x^2 + y^2 = 4$

$y = \log_3(x)$

52. $y = \dfrac{x^3}{6} + \dfrac{x^2}{2} + x + 1$

$y = e^x$

53. $y = x^2$

$y = 2^x$

54. $y = e^x$

$y = x^3 + 1$

Solve each system.

55. $x + 2y - z = 5$

$3x + 2y + z = 11$

$(x + 2y)^2 - z^2 = 15$

56. $x + y - z = 10$

$2x - y + 3z = 13$

$(x + y)^2 + z^2 = 122$

57. $xy = z^2$

$x + y + z = 7$

$x^2 + y^2 + z^2 = 133$

58. $2xy = z^2$

$x - y + z = -1$

$x^2 + y^2 - 2z^2 = 13$

Solve each problem using a system of two equations in two unknowns.

59. *Big Screen* The screen on a 42-inch LCD TV has an aspect ratio of 15 to 9. Find the length and width of the screen to the nearest tenth of an inch.

60. *Little Screen* The screen on a 4G iPod has an aspect ratio of 5 to 4. The diagonal measure of the screen is 51.83 millimeters. Find the length and width of the screen to the nearest tenth of a millimeter.

61. *Unknown Numbers* Find two numbers whose sum is 6 and whose product is -16.

62. *More Unknown Numbers* Find two numbers whose sum is -8 and whose product is -20.

63. *Legs of a Right Triangle* Find the lengths of the legs of a right triangle whose hypotenuse is 15 m and whose area is 54 m².

64. *Sides of a Rectangle* What are the length and width of a rectangle that has a perimeter of 98 cm and a diagonal of 35 cm?

65. *Sides of a Triangle* Find the lengths of the sides of a triangle whose perimeter is 12 ft and whose angles are 30°, 60°, and 90°.

HINT Use a, $a/2$, and b to represent the lengths of the sides.

66. *Size of a Vent* Kwan is constructing a triangular vent in the gable end of a house, as shown in the accompanying diagram. If the pitch of the roof is 6–12 (run 12 ft and rise 6 ft) and the vent must have an area of 4.5 ft², then what size should he make the base and height of the triangle?

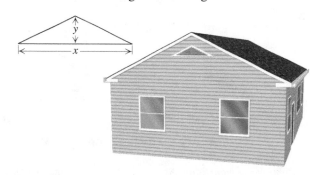

Figure for Exercise 66

67. *Air Mobile* A hobbyist is building a mobile out of model airplanes, as shown in the accompanying figure. Find x and y so that the mobile will balance. Ignore the weights of the horizontal bars and the strings. The mobile will be in balance if the product of the weight and distance on one side of the balance point is equal to the product of the weight and distance on the other side.

HINT Write an equation for each balancing point.

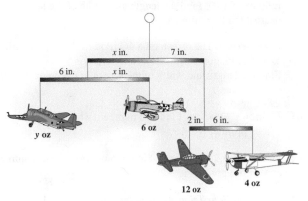

Figure for Exercise 67

68. *Making an Arch* A bricklayer is constructing a circular arch with a radius of 9 ft, as shown in the figure. If the height h must be 1.5 times as large as the width w, then what are h and w?

HINT The center of the circle is the midpoint of w.

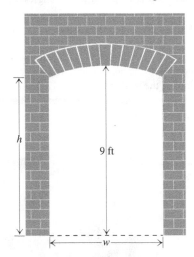

Figure for Exercise 68

69. *Pumping Tomato Soup* At the Acme Soup Company a large vat of tomato soup can be filled in 8 min by pump A and pump B working together. Pump B can be reversed so that it empties the vat at the same rate at which it fills the vat. One day a worker filled the vat in 12 min using pumps A and B, but accidentally ran pump B in reverse. How long does it take each pump to fill the vat working alone?

70. *Planting Strawberries* Blanche and Morris can plant an acre of strawberries in 8 hr working together. Morris takes 2 hr longer to plant an acre of strawberries working alone than it takes Blanche working alone. How long does it take Morris to plant an acre by himself?

71. *Lost Numbers* Find two complex numbers whose sum is 6 and whose product is 10.

72. *More Lost Numbers* Find two complex numbers whose sum is 1 and whose product is 5.

73. *Voyage of the Whales* In one of Captain James Kirk's most challenging missions, he returned to late-twentieth-century San Francisco to bring back a pair of humpback whales. Chief Engineer Scotty built a tank of transparent aluminum to hold the time-traveling cetaceans. If Scotty's 20-ft-high tank had a volume of 36,000 ft^3, and it took 7200 ft^2 of transparent aluminum to cover all six sides, then what were the length and width of the tank?

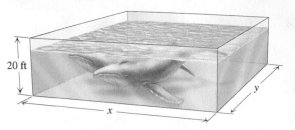

Figure for Exercise 73

74. *Dimensions of a Laundry Room* The plans call for a rectangular laundry room in the Wilsons' new house. Connie wants to increase the width by 1 ft and the length by 2 ft, which will increase the area by 30 ft^2. Christopher wants to increase the width by 2 ft and decrease the length by 3 ft, which will decrease the area by 6 ft^2. What are the original dimensions for the laundry room?

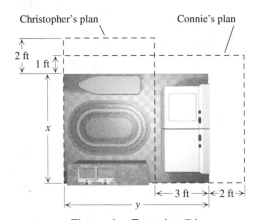

Figure for Exercise 74

75. *Two Models* One demographer believes that the population growth of a certain country is best modeled by the function $P(t) = 20e^{0.07t}$, while a second demographer believes that the population growth of that same country is best modeled by the function $P(t) = 20 + 2t$. In each case t is the number of years from the present and $P(t)$ is given in millions of people. For what values of t do these two models give the same population? In how many years is the population predicted by the exponential model twice as large as the population predicted by the linear model?

76. *Simple or Compound* Harvey borrowed $2000 from Chet (his brother-in-law) and made no payments. After t years

Harvey won the lottery and decided to pay up. However, Chet figured the value of the debt at twice what Harvey figured it. They both used 5% annual interest, but Harvey used simple interest and Chet used interest compounded continuously. Find *t* to the nearest day.

77. *Mixed Signals* Sally and Bob live quite far from each other on Interstate 75 and decide to get together on Saturday. However, they get their signals crossed and they each start out at sunrise for the other's house. At noon they pass each other on the freeway. At 4 P.M. Sally arrives at Bob's house and at 9 P.M. Bob arrives at Sally's house. At what time did the sun rise? See the figure.

Sally's house

Noon

Bob's house

Figure for Exercise 77

78. *Westward Ho* A wagon train that is one mile long advances one mile at a constant rate. During the same time period, the wagon master rides his horse at a constant rate from the front of the wagon train to the rear, and then back to the front. How far did the wagon master ride?

79. *Traveling Mouse* A rectangular train car that is 40 feet long and 10 feet wide is traveling north at a constant rate. A mouse starts from the left rear corner (southwest corner) of the car and runs around the perimeter of the car in a clockwise direction (first going north) at a constant rate. The mouse is back where he started when the train has advanced 40 feet. On the

train car the mouse has traveled 100 feet, but how far did he travel relative to the ground?

80. *Online Dating* A young woman met an older man in a chat room. The difference of their ages is 20 and the difference of the squares of their ages is 1160. What are their ages?

FOR WRITING/DISCUSSION

81. *How Many?* Explain why the system

$$y = 3 + \log_2(x - 1)$$
$$8x - 8 = 2^y$$

has infinitely many solutions.

82. *Line and Circle* For what values of *b* does the solution set to $y = x + b$ and $x^2 + y^2 = 1$ consist of one point, two points, and no points? Explain.

▶ RETHINKING

83. Solve the system of equations $x + y - z = 7$, $3x + y - 2z = 12$, and $x + 2y + z = 44$.

84. Solve the system of equations $3x - 5y = 1$ and $6x - 2 = 10y$.

85. Solve $\log_3(x + 1) + \log_3(x - 5) = 3$.

86. Solve $e^{x^2 - x} = 1$.

87. Solve $2x^3 + x^2 - 41x + 20 = 0$.

88. Find the domain and range for the function $y = \sqrt{3x - 1} + 4$.

THINKING OUTSIDE THE BOX LXIII & LXIV

Perfect Squares Solve the system:

$$x + \sqrt{y} = 32$$
$$y + \sqrt{x} = 54$$

From Left to Right Find the smallest positive integer whose first digit on the left is 1, such that multiplying the number by 3 simply moves the 1 to the first position on the right.

HINT If 147 times 3 were 471, we would have the required number.

➤ POP QUIZ 3

Solve each system.

1. $y = x^2$

   $y = x$

2. $y = |x| + 1$

   $y = \dfrac{1}{2}x + 4$

3. $x^2 - y^2 = 5$

   $x^2 + y^2 = 13$

concepts... For Individual or Group Explorations

Measuring Ocean Depth

Geophysicists who map the ocean floor use sound reflection to measure the depth of the ocean. The problem is complicated by the fact that the speed of sound in water is not constant, but depends on the temperature and other conditions of the water. Let v be the velocity of sound through the water and d_1 be the depth of the ocean below the ship, as shown in the figure.

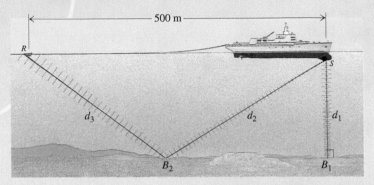

a)   The time that it takes for sound to travel to the ocean floor at point B_1 and back to the ship at point S is measured as 0.280 sec. Write d_1 as a function of v.

b)   It takes 0.446 sec for sound to travel from point S to point B_2 and then to a receiver at R, which is towed 500 meters behind the ship. Assuming that $d_2 = d_3$, write d_2 as a function of v.

c)   Write d_1 as a function of d_2.

d)   Solve your system to find the ocean depth d_1.

4 Partial Fractions

In algebra we usually learn a process and then learn to reverse it. For example, we multiply two binomials, and then we factor trinomials into a product of two binomials. We solve polynomial equations, and we write polynomial equations with given solutions. After we studied functions, we learned about their inverses. We have learned how to add rational expressions. Now we will reverse the process of addition. We start with a rational expression and write it as a sum of two or more simpler rational expressions. This technique shows a nice application of systems of equations.

The Basic Idea

Before trying to reverse addition of rational expressions, recall how to add them.

EXAMPLE 1 | Adding rational expressions

Perform the indicated operation.

$$\frac{3}{x-3} + \frac{-2}{x+1}$$

Solution

The least common denominator (LCD) for $x - 3$ and $x + 1$ is $(x - 3)(x + 1)$. We convert each rational expression or fraction into an equivalent fraction with this denominator:

$$\frac{3}{x - 3} + \frac{-2}{x + 1} = \frac{3(x + 1)}{(x - 3)(x + 1)} + \frac{-2(x - 3)}{(x + 1)(x - 3)}$$

$$= \frac{3x + 3}{(x - 3)(x + 1)} + \frac{-2x + 6}{(x - 3)(x + 1)}$$

$$= \frac{x + 9}{(x - 3)(x + 1)}$$

■ **Foreshadowing Calculus**

In mathematics, it is often useful to express a complicated object in simpler terms. Using the technique of partial fractions, a rational function can be expressed as a sum of simpler rational functions. This technique is used in calculus to find areas of regions.

▶**TRY THIS.** Find the sum $\dfrac{4}{x - 2} + \dfrac{3}{x + 5}$. ■

The following rational expression is similar to the result in Example 1.

$$\frac{8x - 7}{(x + 1)(x - 2)}$$

Thus, it is possible that this fraction is the sum of two fractions with denominators $x + 1$ and $x - 2$. In the next example, we will find those two fractions.

EXAMPLE 2 Reversing the addition of rational expressions

Write the following rational expression as a sum of two rational expressions.

$$\frac{8x - 7}{(x + 1)(x - 2)}$$

Solution

To write the given expression as a sum, we need numbers A and B such that

$$\frac{8x - 7}{(x + 1)(x - 2)} = \frac{A}{x + 1} + \frac{B}{x - 2}.$$

Simplify this equation by multiplying each side by the LCD, $(x + 1)(x - 2)$:

$$(x + 1)(x - 2)\,\frac{8x - 7}{(x + 1)(x - 2)} = (x + 1)(x - 2)\left(\frac{A}{x + 1} + \frac{B}{x - 2}\right)$$

$$8x - 7 = A(x - 2) + B(x + 1)$$

$$8x - 7 = Ax - 2A + Bx + B$$

$$8x - 7 = (A + B)x - 2A + B \quad \text{Combine like terms.}$$

Since the last equation is an identity, the coefficient of x on one side equals the coefficient of x on the other, and the constant on one side equals the constant on the other. So A and B satisfy the following two equations.

$$A + B = 8$$

$$-2A + B = -7$$

553

We can solve this system of two linear equations in two unknowns by addition:

$$A + B = 8$$

$$\underline{2A - B = 7} \quad \text{Second equation multiplied by } -1$$

$$3A = 15$$

$$A = 5$$

If $A = 5$, then $B = 3$, and we have

$$\frac{8x - 7}{(x + 1)(x - 2)} = \frac{5}{x + 1} + \frac{3}{x - 2}.$$

Check by adding the fractions on the right-hand side of the equation.

▶**TRY THIS.** Write $\dfrac{2x - 3}{(x - 1)(x + 3)}$ as a sum of two rational expressions. ■

Each of the two fractions on the right-hand side of the equation

$$\frac{8x - 7}{(x + 1)(x - 2)} = \frac{5}{x + 1} + \frac{3}{x - 2}$$

is called a **partial fraction**. This equation shows the **partial fraction decomposition** of the rational expression on the left-hand side.

General Decomposition

In general, let $N(x)$ be the polynomial in the numerator and $D(x)$ be the polynomial in the denominator of the fraction that is to be decomposed. *We will decompose only fractions for which the degree of the numerator is smaller than the degree of the denominator.* If the degree of $N(x)$ is not smaller than the degree of $D(x)$, we can use long division to write the rational expression as quotient + remainder/divisor. For example,

$$\frac{x^3 + x^2 - x + 5}{x^2 + x - 6} = x + \frac{5x + 5}{x^2 + x - 6} = x + \frac{A}{x + 3} + \frac{B}{x - 2}.$$

You should find the values of A and B in the above equation as we did in Example 2, and check.

If a factor of $D(x)$ is repeated n times, then all powers of the factor from 1 through n might occur as denominators in the partial fractions. To understand the reason for this statement, look at

$$\frac{7}{8} = \frac{1}{2} + \frac{1}{4} + \frac{1}{8} = \frac{1}{2} + \frac{1}{2^2} + \frac{1}{2^3}.$$

Here the factor 2 is repeated three times in $D(x) = 8$. Notice that each of the powers of 2 $(2^1, 2^2, 2^3)$ occurs in the denominators of the partial fractions.

Now consider a fraction $N(x)/D(x)$, where $D(x) = (x - 1)(x + 3)^2$. Since the factor $x + 3$ occurs to the second power, both $x + 3$ and $(x + 3)^2$ occur in the partial fraction decomposition of $N(x)/D(x)$. For example, we write the partial fraction decomposition for $(3x^2 + 17x + 12)/D(x)$ as follows:

$$\frac{3x^2 + 17x + 12}{(x - 1)(x + 3)^2} = \frac{A}{x - 1} + \frac{B}{x + 3} + \frac{C}{(x + 3)^2}.$$

It is possible that we do not need the fraction $B/(x + 3)$, but we do not know this until we find the value of B. If $B = 0$, then the decomposition does not include a fraction with denominator $x + 3$. This decomposition is completed in Example 3.

To find the partial fraction decomposition of a rational expression, the denominator must be factored into a product of prime polynomials. *If a quadratic prime polynomial occurs in the denominator, then the numerator of the partial fraction for that polynomial is of the form $Ax + B$.* For example, if $D(x) = x^3 + x^2 + 4x + 4$, then $D(x) = (x^2 + 4)(x + 1)$. The partial fraction decomposition for $(5x^2 + 3x + 13)/D(x)$ is written as follows:

$$\frac{5x^2 + 3x + 13}{x^3 + x^2 + 4x + 4} = \frac{Ax + B}{x^2 + 4} + \frac{C}{x + 1}$$

This decomposition is completed in Example 4.

The main points to remember for partial fraction decomposition are summarized as follows.

STRATEGY

Decomposition into Partial Fractions

To decompose a rational expression $N(x)/D(x)$ into partial fractions, use the following strategies:

1. If the degree of the numerator $N(x)$ is greater than or equal to the degree of the denominator $D(x)$ use division to express $N(x)/D(x)$ as quotient + remainder/divisor and decompose the resulting fraction.

2. If the degree of $N(x)$ is less than the degree of $D(x)$ factor the denominator completely into prime factors that are either linear $(ax + b)$ or quadratic $(ax^2 + bx + c)$.

3. For each linear factor of the form $(ax + b)^n$, the partial fraction decomposition must include the following fractions:

$$\frac{A_1}{ax + b} + \frac{A_2}{(ax + b)^2} + \cdots + \frac{A_n}{(ax + b)^n}$$

4. For each quadratic factor of the form $(ax^2 + bx + c)^m$, the partial fraction decomposition must include the following fractions:

$$\frac{B_1x + C_1}{ax^2 + bx + c} + \frac{B_2x + C_2}{(ax^2 + bx + c)^2} + \cdots + \frac{B_mx + C_m}{(ax^2 + bx + c)^m}$$

5. Set up and solve a system of equations involving the As, Bs, and/or Cs.

The strategy for decomposition applies to very complicated rational expressions. To actually carry out the decomposition, we must be able to solve the system of equations that arises. Theoretically, we can solve systems of many equations in many unknowns. Practically, we are limited to fairly simple systems of equations. Large systems of equations are generally solved by computers or calculators using techniques that we will develop in the next chapter.

EXAMPLE 3 | Repeated linear factor

Find the partial fraction decomposition for the rational expression

$$\frac{3x^2 + 17x + 12}{(x - 1)(x + 3)^2}.$$

Solution

Since the factor $x + 3$ occurs twice in the original denominator, it might occur in the partial fractions with powers 1 and 2:

$$\frac{3x^2 + 17x + 12}{(x - 1)(x + 3)^2} = \frac{A}{x - 1} + \frac{B}{x + 3} + \frac{C}{(x + 3)^2}$$

Multiply each side of the equation by the LCD, $(x - 1)(x + 3)^2$.

$$3x^2 + 17x + 12 = A(x + 3)^2 + B(x - 1)(x + 3) + C(x - 1)$$
$$= Ax^2 + 6Ax + 9A + Bx^2 + 2Bx - 3B + Cx - C$$
$$= (A + B)x^2 + (6A + 2B + C)x + 9A - 3B - C$$

Next, write a system of equations by equating the coefficients of like terms from opposite sides of the equation. The corresponding coefficients are highlighted above.

$$A + B \qquad = 3$$
$$6A + 2B + C = 17$$
$$9A - 3B - C = 12$$

We can solve this system of three equations in the variables A, B, and C by first eliminating C. Add the last two equations to get $15A - B = 29$. Add this equation to $A + B = 3$:

$$15A - B = 29$$
$$\underline{A + B = 3}$$
$$16A \qquad = 32$$
$$A = 2$$

If $A = 2$ and $A + B = 3$, then $B = 1$. Use $A = 2$ and $B = 1$ in the equation $6A + 2B + C = 17$:

$$6(2) + 2(1) + C = 17$$
$$C = 3$$

The partial fraction decomposition is written as follows:

$$\frac{3x^2 + 17x + 12}{(x - 1)(x + 3)^2} = \frac{2}{x - 1} + \frac{1}{x + 3} + \frac{3}{(x + 3)^2}$$

▶**TRY THIS.** Find the partial fraction decomposition for $\dfrac{4x^2 + 4x - 4}{(x + 1)^2(x - 1)}$. ∎

EXAMPLE 4 │ Single prime quadratic factor

Find the partial fraction decomposition for the rational expression

$$\frac{5x^2 + 3x + 13}{x^3 + x^2 + 4x + 4}.$$

Solution

Factor the denominator by grouping:

$$x^3 + x^2 + 4x + 4 = x^2(x + 1) + 4(x + 1) = (x^2 + 4)(x + 1)$$

Write the partial fraction decomposition:

$$\frac{5x^2 + 3x + 13}{x^3 + x^2 + 4x + 4} = \frac{Ax + B}{x^2 + 4} + \frac{C}{x + 1}$$

Note that $Ax + B$ is used over the prime quadratic polynomial $x^2 + 4$. Multiply each side of this equation by the LCD, $(x^2 + 4)(x + 1)$:

$$5x^2 + 3x + 13 = (Ax + B)(x + 1) + C(x^2 + 4)$$
$$= Ax^2 + Bx + Ax + B + Cx^2 + 4C$$
$$= (A + C)x^2 + (A + B)x + B + 4C$$

Write a system of equations by equating the coefficients of like terms from opposite sides of the last equation:

$$A + C = 5$$
$$A + B = 3$$
$$B + 4C = 13$$

One way to solve the system is to substitute $C = 5 - A$ and $B = 3 - A$ into $B + 4C = 13$:

$$3 - A + 4(5 - A) = 13$$
$$3 - A + 20 - 4A = 13$$
$$23 - 5A = 13$$
$$-5A = -10$$
$$A = 2$$

Since $A = 2$, we get $C = 5 - 2 = 3$ and $B = 3 - 2 = 1$. So the partial fraction decomposition is written as follows:

$$\frac{5x^2 + 3x + 13}{x^3 + x^2 + 4x + 4} = \frac{2x + 1}{x^2 + 4} + \frac{3}{x + 1}$$

▶TRY THIS. Find the partial fraction decomposition for $\dfrac{5x^2 - 4x + 11}{(x^2 + 2)(x - 1)}$. ■

$\boxed{\text{EXAMPLE } 5}$ Repeated prime quadratic factor

Find the partial fraction decomposition for the rational expression

$$\frac{4x^3 - 2x^2 + 7x - 6}{4x^4 + 12x^2 + 9}.$$

Solution

The denominator factors as $(2x^2 + 3)^2$, and $2x^2 + 3$ is prime. Write the partial fractions using denominators $2x^2 + 3$ and $(2x^2 + 3)^2$.

$$\frac{4x^3 - 2x^2 + 7x - 6}{(2x^2 + 3)^2} = \frac{Ax + B}{2x^2 + 3} + \frac{Cx + D}{(2x^2 + 3)^2}$$

Multiply each side of the equation by the LCD, $(2x^2 + 3)^2$, to get the following equation:

$$4x^3 - 2x^2 + 7x - 6 = (Ax + B)(2x^2 + 3) + Cx + D$$
$$= 2Ax^3 + 2Bx^2 + 3Ax + 3B + Cx + D$$
$$= 2Ax^3 + 2Bx^2 + (3A + C)x + 3B + D$$

Equating the coefficients produces the following system of equations:

$$2A = 4$$
$$2B = -2$$
$$3A + C = 7$$
$$3B + D = -6$$

From the first two equations $2A = 4$ and $2B = -2$, we get $A = 2$ and $B = -1$. Using $A = 2$ in $3A + C = 7$ gives $C = 1$. Using $B = -1$ in $3B + D = -6$ gives $D = -3$. So the partial fraction decomposition is written as follows:

$$\frac{4x^3 - 2x^2 + 7x - 6}{(2x^2 + 3)^2} = \frac{2x - 1}{2x^2 + 3} + \frac{x - 3}{(2x^2 + 3)^2}$$

▶**TRY THIS.** Find the partial fraction decomposition for $\dfrac{3x^3 + 3x^2 + x - 2}{(3x^2 - 1)^2}$. ∎

FOR thought... True or False? Explain.

1. $\frac{1}{x} + \frac{3}{x + 1} = \frac{4x + 1}{x^2 + x}$ for any real number x except 0 and -1.

2. $x + \frac{3x}{x^2 - 1} = \frac{x^3 + 2x}{x^2 - 1}$ for any real number x except -1 and 1.

3. The partial fraction decomposition of $\frac{x^2}{x^2 - 9}$ is $\frac{x^2}{x^2 - 9} = \frac{A}{x - 3} + \frac{B}{x + 3}$.

4. In the decomposition $\frac{5}{8} = \frac{A}{2} + \frac{B}{2^2} + \frac{C}{2^3}$, $A = 1, B = 0$, and $C = 1$.

5. The partial fraction decomposition of $\frac{3x - 1}{x^3 + x}$ is $\frac{3x - 1}{x^3 + x} = \frac{A}{x} + \frac{B}{x^2 + 1}$.

6. $\frac{1}{x^2 - 1} = \frac{1}{x - 1} + \frac{1}{x + 1}$ for any real number except 1 and -1.

7. $\frac{x^3 + 1}{x^2 + x - 2} = x - 1 + \frac{3x - 1}{x^2 + x - 2}$ for any real number except 1 and -2.

8. $x^3 - 8 = (x - 2)(x^2 + 4x + 4)$ for any real number x.

9. $\frac{x^2 + 2x}{x^3 - 1} = \frac{1}{x - 1} + \frac{1}{x^2 + x + 1}$ for any real number except 1.

10. There is no partial fraction decomposition for $\frac{2x}{x^2 + 9}$.

EXERCISES 4

Perform the indicated operations.

1. $\dfrac{3}{x - 2} + \dfrac{4}{x + 1}$

2. $\dfrac{-1}{x + 5} + \dfrac{-3}{x - 4}$

3. $\dfrac{1}{x - 1} + \dfrac{-3}{x^2 + 2}$

4. $\dfrac{x + 3}{x^2 + x + 1} + \dfrac{1}{x - 1}$

5. $\dfrac{2x + 1}{x^2 + 3} + \dfrac{x^3 + 2x + 2}{(x^2 + 3)^2}$

6. $\dfrac{3x - 1}{x^2 + x - 3} + \dfrac{x^3 + x - 1}{(x^2 + x - 3)^2}$

7. $\dfrac{1}{x - 1} + \dfrac{2x + 3}{(x - 1)^2} + \dfrac{x^2 + 1}{(x - 1)^3}$

8. $\dfrac{3}{x + 2} + \dfrac{x - 1}{(x + 2)^2} + \dfrac{1}{x^2 + 2}$

Find A and B for each partial fraction decomposition.

9. $\dfrac{12}{x^2 - 9} = \dfrac{A}{x - 3} + \dfrac{B}{x + 3}$

10. $\dfrac{5x + 2}{x^2 - 4} = \dfrac{A}{x - 2} + \dfrac{B}{x + 2}$

Find the partial fraction decomposition for each rational expression.

11. $\dfrac{5x - 1}{(x + 1)(x - 2)}$

12. $\dfrac{-3x - 5}{(x + 3)(x - 1)}$

13. $\dfrac{2x + 5}{x^2 + 6x + 8}$

14. $\dfrac{x + 2}{x^2 + 12x + 32}$

15. $\dfrac{2}{x^2 - 9}$

16. $\dfrac{1}{9x^2 - 1}$

17. $\dfrac{1}{x^2 - x}$

18. $\dfrac{2}{x^2 - 2x}$

Find A, B, and C for each partial fraction decomposition.

19. $\dfrac{x^2 + x - 31}{(x + 3)^2(x - 2)} = \dfrac{A}{x + 3} + \dfrac{B}{(x + 3)^2} + \dfrac{C}{x - 2}$

20. $\dfrac{-x^2 - 9x - 12}{(x + 1)^2(x - 3)} = \dfrac{A}{x + 1} + \dfrac{B}{(x + 1)^2} + \dfrac{C}{x - 3}$

Find each partial fraction decomposition.

21. $\dfrac{4x - 1}{(x - 1)^2(x + 2)}$

22. $\dfrac{5x^2 - 15x + 7}{(x - 2)^2(x + 1)}$

23. $\dfrac{20 - 4x}{(x + 4)(x - 2)^2}$

24. $\dfrac{x^2 - 3x + 14}{(x + 3)(x - 1)^2}$

25. $\dfrac{3x^2 + 3x - 2}{x^3 + x^2 - x - 1}$

26. $\dfrac{-2x^2 + 8x + 6}{x^3 - 3x^2 - 9x + 27}$

Find A, B, and C for each partial fraction decomposition.

27. $\dfrac{x^2 - x - 7}{(x + 1)(x^2 + 4)} = \dfrac{A}{x + 1} + \dfrac{Bx + C}{x^2 + 4}$

28. $\dfrac{4x^2 - 3x + 7}{(x - 1)(x^2 + 3)} = \dfrac{A}{x - 1} + \dfrac{Bx + C}{x^2 + 3}$

Find each partial fraction decomposition.

29. $\dfrac{5x^2 + 5x}{(x + 2)(x^2 + 1)}$

30. $\dfrac{3x^2 - 2x + 11}{(x^2 + 5)(x - 1)}$

31. $\dfrac{x^2 - 2}{(x + 1)(x^2 + x + 1)}$

32. $\dfrac{3x^2 + 7x - 4}{(x^2 + 3x + 1)(x - 2)}$

Find each partial fraction decomposition.

33. $\dfrac{-2x - 7}{x^2 + 4x + 4}$

34. $\dfrac{-3x + 2}{x^2 - 2x + 1}$

35. $\dfrac{6x^2 - x + 1}{x^3 + x^2 + x + 1}$

36. $\dfrac{3x^2 - 2x + 8}{x^3 + 2x^2 + 4x + 8}$

37. $\dfrac{3x^3 - x^2 + 19x - 9}{x^4 + 18x^2 + 81}$

38. $\dfrac{-x^3 - 10x - 3}{x^4 + 10x^2 + 25}$

39. $\dfrac{3x^2 + 17x + 14}{x^3 - 8}$

40. $\dfrac{2x^2 + 17x - 21}{x^3 + 27}$

41. $\dfrac{2x^3 + x^2 + 3x - 2}{x^2 - 1}$

42. $\dfrac{2x^3 - 19x - 9}{x^2 - 9}$

43. $\dfrac{3x^3 - 2x^2 + x - 2}{(x^2 + x + 1)^2}$

44. $\dfrac{x^3 - 8x^2 - 5x - 33}{(x^2 + x + 4)^2}$

45. $\dfrac{3x^3 + 4x^2 - 12x + 16}{x^4 - 16}$

46. $\dfrac{9x^2 + 3}{81x^4 - 1}$

47. $\dfrac{5x^3 + x^2 + x - 3}{x^4 - x^3}$

48. $\dfrac{2x^3 + 3x^2 - 8x + 4}{x^4 - 4x^2}$

49. $\dfrac{6x^2 - 28x + 33}{(x - 2)^2(x - 3)}$

50. $\dfrac{7x^2 + 45x + 58}{(x + 3)^2(x + 1)}$

51. $\dfrac{9x^2 + 21x - 24}{x^3 + 4x^2 - 11x - 30}$

52. $\dfrac{3x^2 + 24x + 6}{2x^3 - x^2 - 13x - 6}$

53. $\dfrac{x^2 - 2}{x^3 - 3x^2 + 3x - 1}$

54. $\dfrac{2x^2}{x^3 + 3x^2 + 3x + 1}$

Find the partial fraction decomposition for each rational expression. Assume that a, b, and c are nonzero constants.

55. $\dfrac{x}{(ax + b)^2}$

56. $\dfrac{x^2}{(ax + b)^3}$

57. $\dfrac{x + c}{ax^2 + bx}$

58. $\dfrac{1}{x^3(ax + b)}$

59. $\dfrac{1}{x^2(ax + b)}$

60. $\dfrac{1}{x^2(ax + b)^2}$

▶ RETHINKING

61. Solve the system $x^2 + y^2 = 34$ and $y = x + 2$.

62. Solve the system $x - y - z = 5$, $2x - y + 2z = 10$, and $3x - 2y + z = 15$.

63. Solve the system $5x - y = 8$ and $2y = 10x - 16$.

64. The graph of $y = x^2$ is reflected about the x-axis, translated 5 units upward, and then translated 6 units to the left. Write the equation of the curve in its final position.

559

65. Write the equation $y = \dfrac{1}{2}x^2 + 4x - 9$ in the form

$y = a(x - h)^2 + k$.

66. Find the domain and range of the function $y = \dfrac{1}{2}x^2 + 4x - 9$.

THINKING OUTSIDE THE BOX LXV

The Lizard and the Fly A cylindrical garbage can has a height of 4 ft and a circumference of 6 ft. On the inside of the can, 1 ft from the top, is a fly. On the opposite side of the can, 1 ft from the bottom and on the outside, is a lizard. What is the shortest distance that the lizard must walk to reach the fly?

Figure for Thinking Outside the Box LXV

POP QUIZ 4

Find the partial fraction decomposition.

1. $\dfrac{6x - 10}{x^2 - 25}$

2. $\dfrac{4x^2 + 2x + 6}{(x + 1)(x^2 + 3)}$

LINKING
concepts...   For Individual or Group Explorations

Modeling Work

Lisa F. Young/Shutterstock

Suppose that Andrew can paint a garage by himself in a hours and Betty can paint the same garage by herself in b hours. Working together they can paint the garage in 2 hr 24 min.

a) What is the sum of $1/a$ and $1/b$?

b) Write a as a function of b and graph it.

c) What are the horizontal and vertical asymptotes? Interpret the asymptotes in the context of this situation.

d) Use a graphing calculator to make a table for a and b. If a and b are positive integers, find all possible values for a and b from the table.

e) Now suppose that the time it takes for Andrew, Betty, or Carl to paint a garage working alone is a, b, or c hours, respectively, where a, b, and c are positive integers. If they paint the garage together in 1 hr 15 min, then what are the possible values of a, b, and c? Explain your solution.

5 Inequalities and Systems of Inequalities in Two Variables

Earlier in this chapter we solved systems of equations in two variables. In this section we turn to linear and nonlinear inequalities in two variables and systems of inequalities in two variables. In the next section systems of linear inequalities will be used to solve linear programming problems.

Linear Inequalities

Three hamburgers and two Cokes cost at least \$5.50. If a hamburger costs x dollars and a Coke costs y dollars, then this sentence can be written as the linear inequality

$$3x + 2y \geq 5.50.$$

A linear inequality in two variables is simply a linear equation in two variables with the equal sign replaced by an inequality symbol.

Definition: Linear Inequality

> If A, B, and C are real numbers with A and B not both zero, then
>
> $$Ax + By < C$$
>
> is called a **linear inequality in two variables.** In place of $<$ we can also use the symbols $\leq$, $>$, or $\geq$.

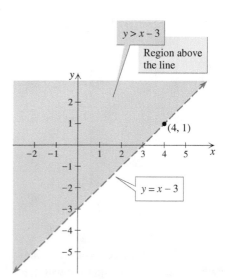

Figure 24

Some examples of linear inequalities are

$$y > x - 3, \qquad 2x - y \geq 1, \qquad x + y < 0, \qquad \text{and} \qquad y \leq 3.$$

The inequality $y \leq 3$ is considered an inequality in two variables because it can be written in the form $0 \cdot x + y \leq 3$.

An ordered pair (a, b) is a **solution to an inequality** if the inequality is true when x is replaced by a and y is replaced by b. Ordered pairs such as $(9, 1)$ and $(7, 3)$ satisfy $y \leq 3$. Ordered pairs such as $(4, 2)$ and $(-1, -2)$ satisfy $y > x - 3$.

The ordered pairs satisfying $y = x - 3$ form a line in the rectangular coordinate system, but what does the solution set to $y > x - 3$ look like? An ordered pair satisfies $y > x - 3$ whenever the y-coordinate is *greater than* the x-coordinate minus 3. For example, $(4, 1)$ satisfies the equation $y = x - 3$ and is on the line, while $(4, 1.001)$ satisfies $y > x - 3$ and is above the line. In fact, any point in the coordinate plane directly above $(4, 1)$ satisfies $y > x - 3$ (and any point directly below $(4, 1)$ satisfies $y < x - 3$). Since this fact holds true for every point on the line $y = x - 3$, the solution set to the inequality is the set of all points *above* the line. The graph of $y > x - 3$ is indicated by shading the region above the line, as shown in Fig. 24. We draw a dashed line for $y = x - 3$ because it is not part of the solution set to $y > x - 3$. However, the graph of $y \geq x - 3$ in Fig. 25 has a solid boundary line because the line is included in its solution set. Notice also that the region below the line is the solution set to $y < x - 3$.

EXAMPLE 1 Graphing linear inequalities

Graph the solution set to each inequality.

a. $y < -\dfrac{1}{2}x + 2$ **b.** $2x - y \geq 1$ **c.** $y > 2$ **d.** $x \leq 3$

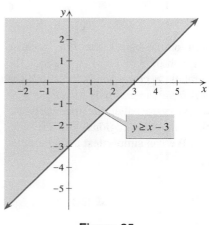

Figure 25

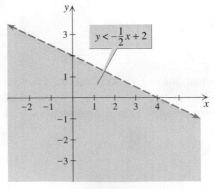

Figure 26

Solution

a. Graph the corresponding equation

$$y = -\frac{1}{2}x + 2$$

as a dashed line by using its intercept $(0, 2)$ and slope $-\frac{1}{2}$. Since the inequality symbol is $<$, the solution set to the inequality is the region below this line, as shown in Fig. 26.

b. Solve the inequality for y:

$$2x - y \geq 1$$

$$-y \geq -2x + 1$$

$$y \leq 2x - 1 \qquad \text{Multiply by } -1 \text{ and reverse the inequality.}$$

Graph the line $y = 2x - 1$ by using its intercept $(0, -1)$ and its slope 2. Because of the symbol $\leq$, we use a solid line and shade the region below it, as shown in Fig. 27.

c. Every point in the region above the horizontal line $y = 2$ satisfies $y > 2$. See Fig. 28.

d. Every point on or to the left of the vertical line $x = 3$ satisfies $x \leq 3$. See Fig. 29.

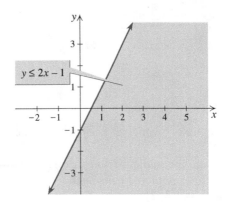

Figure 27

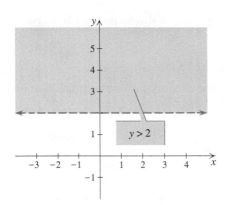

Figure 28

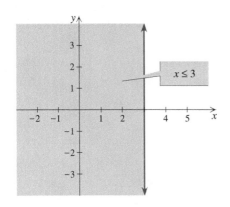

Figure 29

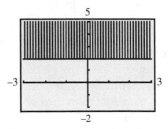

Figure 30

A graphing calculator can graph a linear inequality. However, you must indicate whether to shade above or below the line when you enter the equation using the Y = key. Figure 30 shows $y = 2$ and shading above the line.

▶**TRY THIS.** Graph the solution set to $y \leq -2x + 4$. ∎

The graph in Example 1(b) is the region on or below the line because $2x - y \geq 1$ is equivalent to $y \leq 2x - 1$. The graph of $y > mx + b$ is above the line and $y < mx + b$ is below the line. The symbol $>$ corresponds to "above the line" and $<$ corresponds to "below the line" *only if the inequality is solved for y.*

With the **test point method** it is not necessary to solve the inequality for y. The graph of $Ax + By = C$ divides the plane into two regions. On one side, $Ax + By > C$; and on the other, $Ax + By < C$. We can simply test a single point in one of the regions to see which is which.

EXAMPLE 2 Graphing an inequality using test points

Use the test point method to graph $3x - 6y > 9$.

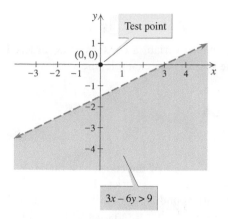

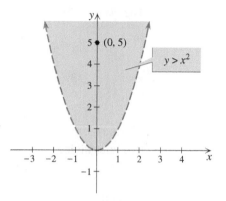

Figure 31

Figure 32

Solution

First graph $3x - 6y = 9$, using a dashed line going through its intercepts $\left(0, -\frac{3}{2}\right)$ and $(3, 0)$. Select a test point that is not on the line, say, $(0, 0)$. Test $(0, 0)$ in $3x - 6y > 9$:

$$3 \cdot 0 - 6 \cdot 0 > 9$$

$$0 > 9 \quad \text{Incorrect}$$

Since $(0, 0)$ does not satisfy $3x - 6y > 9$, any point on the *other* side of the line satisfies $3x - 6y > 9$. So we shade the region that does not contain $(0, 0)$, as shown in Fig. 31.

▶**TRY THIS.** Graph the solution set to $2x - 5y < 20$. ∎

Nonlinear Inequalities

Any nonlinear equation in two variables becomes a nonlinear inequality in two variables when the equal sign is replaced by an inequality symbol. The test point method is generally the easiest to use for graphing nonlinear inequalities in two variables.

EXAMPLE 3 Graphing nonlinear inequalities in two variables

Graph the solution set to each nonlinear inequality.

a. $y > x^2$ **b.** $x^2 + y^2 \le 4$ **c.** $y < \log_2(x)$

Solution

a. The graph of $y = x^2$ is a parabola opening upward with vertex at $(0, 0)$. Draw the parabola dashed, as shown in Fig. 32, and select a point that is not on the parabola, say, $(0, 5)$. Since $5 > 0^2$ is correct, the region of the plane containing $(0, 5)$ is shaded.

b. The graph of $x^2 + y^2 = 4$ is a circle of radius 2 centered at $(0, 0)$. Select $(0, 0)$ as a test point. Since $0^2 + 0^2 \le 4$ is correct, we shade the region inside the circle, as shown in Fig. 33.

c. The graph of $y = \log_2(x)$ is a curve through the points $(1, 0), (2, 1)$, and $(4, 2)$, as shown in Fig. 34. Select $(4, 0)$ as a test point. Since $0 < \log_2(4)$ is correct, shade the region shown in Fig. 34.

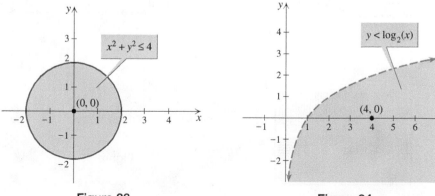

Figure 33   **Figure 34**

▶**TRY THIS.** Graph the solution set to $y < |x|$. ∎

Systems of Inequalities

The solution set to a system of inequalities in two variables consists of all ordered pairs that satisfy *all* of the inequalities in the system. For example, the system

$$x + y > 5$$
$$x - y < 9$$

has $(4, 2)$ as a solution because $4 + 2 > 5$ and $4 - 2 < 9$. There are infinitely many solutions to this system.

The solution set to a system is generally a region of the coordinate plane. It is the intersection of the solution sets to the individual inequalities. To find the solution set to a system, we graph the equation corresponding to each inequality in the system and then test a point in each region to see whether it satisfies all inequalities of the system.

EXAMPLE 4 | Solving a system of linear inequalities

Graph the solution set to the system.

$$x + 2y \le 4$$
$$y \ge x - 3$$

Solution

The graph of $x + 2y = 4$ is a line through $(0, 2)$ and $(4, 0)$. The graph of $y = x - 3$ is a line through $(0, -3)$ with slope 1. These two lines divide the plane into four regions, as shown in Fig. 35. Select a test point in each of the four regions. We use $(0, 0), (0, 5), (0, -5)$, and $(5, 0)$ as test points. Only $(0, 0)$ satisfies both of the inequalities of the system. So we shade the region containing $(0, 0)$ including its boundaries, as shown in Fig. 36.

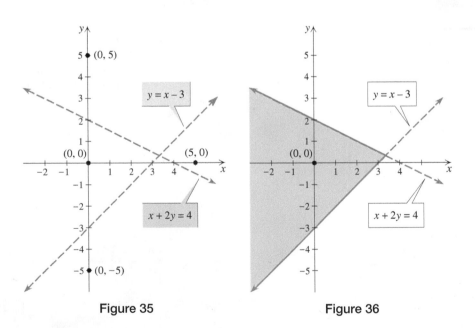

Figure 35   **Figure 36**

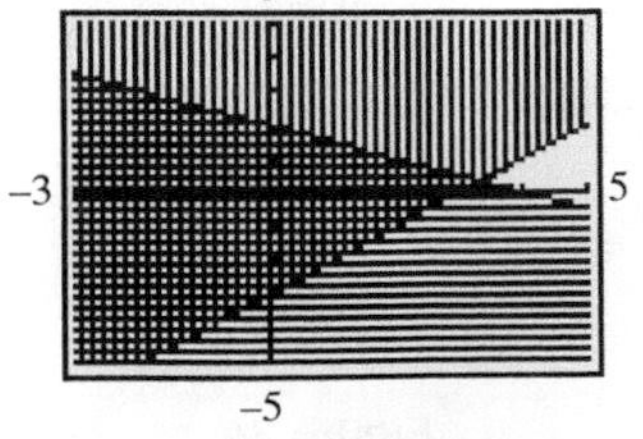

Figure 37

To get the calculator graph in Fig. 37, shade above the line $y = x - 3$ and below the line $y = (4 - x)/2$.

▶**TRY THIS.** Graph the solution set to $y < x$ and $y > 3 - x$. ∎

Note that the set of points indicated in Fig. 36 is the intersection of the set of points on or below the line $x + 2y = 4$ with the set of points on or above the line $y = x - 3$. If you can visualize how these regions intersect, then you can find the solution set without test points.

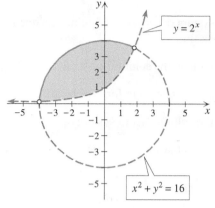

Figure 38

EXAMPLE 5 | Solving a system of nonlinear inequalities

Graph the solution set to the system.

$$x^2 + y^2 \leq 16$$
$$y > 2^x$$

Solution

Points that satisfy $x^2 + y^2 \leq 16$ are on or inside the circle of radius 4 centered at $(0, 0)$. Points that satisfy $y > 2^x$ are above the curve $y = 2^x$. Points that satisfy both inequalities are on or inside the circle and above the curve $y = 2^x$, as shown in Fig. 38. Note that the circular boundary of the solution set is drawn as a solid curve because of the $\leq$ symbol. We could also find the solution set by using test points.

▶**TRY THIS.** Graph the solution set to $y < 1 - |x|$ and $y > x^2 - 1$. ∎

EXAMPLE 6 | Solving a system of three inequalities

Graph the solution set to the system.

$$y > x^2$$
$$y < x + 6$$
$$y < -x + 6$$

Solution

Points that satisfy $y > x^2$ are above the parabola $y = x^2$. Points that satisfy $y < x + 6$ are below the line $y = x + 6$. Points that satisfy $y < -x + 6$ are below the line $y = -x + 6$. Points that satisfy all three inequalities lie in the region shown in Fig. 39.

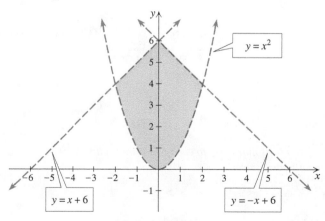

Figure 39

▶**TRY THIS.** Graph the solution set to $y < 3$, $x < 2$, and $y > -x$. ∎

FOR thought... True or False? Explain.

1. The point $(1, 3)$ satisfies the inequality $y > x + 2$.

2. The graph of $x - y < 2$ is the region below the line $x - y = 2$.

3. The graph of $x + y > 2$ is the region above the line $x + y = 2$.

4. The graph of $x^2 + y^2 > 5$ is the region outside the circle of radius 5.

The following systems are referenced in statements 5–10:
(a) $x - 2y < 3$ (b) $x^2 + y^2 > 9$ (c) $y \geq x^2 - 4$
    $y - 3x > 5$ $y < x + 2$ $y < x + 2$

5. The point $(-2, 1)$ is in the solution set to system (a).

6. The solution to system (b) consists of points outside a circle and below a line.

7. The point $(-2, 0)$ is in the solution set to system (c).

8. The point $(-1, 2)$ is a test point for system (a).

9. The origin is in the solution set to system (c).

10. The point $(2, 3)$ is in the solution set to system (b).

EXERCISES 5

Match each inequality with one of the graphs (a)–(d).

1. $y > x - 2$
2. $x < 2 - y$
3. $x - y > 2$
4. $x + y > 2$

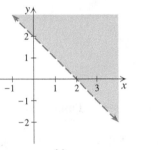

(a)

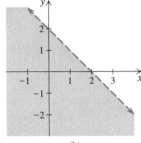

(b)

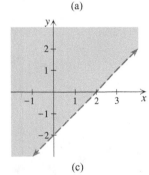

(c)

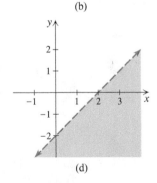

(d)

Sketch the graph of the solution set to each linear inequality in the rectangular coordinate system.

5. $y < 2x$
6. $x > y$
7. $x + y > 3$
8. $2x + y < 1$

9. $2x - y \leq 4$
10. $x - 2y \geq 6$

11. $y < -3x - 4$
12. $y > \frac{2}{3}x - 3$

13. $x - 3 \geq 0$
14. $y + 1 \leq 0$

15. $20x - 30y \leq 6000$
16. $30y + 40x > 1200$

17. $y < 3$
18. $x > 0$

Sketch the graph of each nonlinear inequality.

19. $y > -x^2$
20. $y < 4 - x^2$
21. $x^2 + y^2 \geq 1$

22. $x^2 + y^2 < 36$
23. $x > |y|$
24. $y < x^{1/3}$

25. $x \geq y^2$
26. $y^2 > x - 1$
27. $y \geq x^3$

28. $y < |x - 1|$
29. $y > 2^x$
30. $y < \log_2(x)$

Sketch the graph of the solution set to each system of inequalities.

31. $y > x - 4$
    $y < -x - 2$

32. $y < \frac{1}{2}x + 1$
    $y < -\frac{1}{3}x + 1$

33. $3x - 4y \leq 12$
    $x + y \geq -3$

34. $2x + y \geq -1$
    $y - 2x \leq -3$

35. $3x - y < 4$
    $y < 3x + 5$

36. $x - y > 0$
    $y + 4 > x$

37. $y + x < 0$

$\quad\ y > 3 - x$

38. $3x - 2y \le 6$

$\quad\ 2y - 3x \le -8$

39. $x + y < 5$

$\quad\ y \ge 2$

40. $x \le 2$

$\quad\ y > -2$

41. $y < x - 3$

$\quad\ x \le 4$

42. $y > 0$

$\quad\ y \le x$

Sketch the graph of the solution set to each nonlinear system of inequalities.

43. $y > x^2 - 3$

$\quad\ y < x + 1$

44. $y < 5 - x^2$

$\quad\ y > (x - 1)^2$

45. $x^2 + y^2 \ge 4$

$\quad\ x^2 + y^2 \le 16$

46. $x^2 + y^2 \le 9$

$\quad\ y \ge x - 1$

47. $(x - 3)^2 + y^2 \le 25$

$\quad\ (x + 3)^2 + y^2 \le 25$

48. $x^2 + y^2 \ge 64$

$\quad\ x^2 + y^2 \le 16$

49. $x^2 + y^2 > 4$

$\quad\ |x| \le 4$

50. $x^2 + y^2 < 36$

$\quad\ |y| < 3$

51. $y > |2x| - 4$

$\quad\ y \le \sqrt{4 - x^2}$

52. $y < 4 - |x|$

$\quad\ y \ge |x| - 4$

53. $|x - 1| < 2$

$\quad\ |y - 1| < 4$

54. $x \ge y^2 - 1$

$\quad\ (x + 1)^2 + y^2 \ge 4$

Solve each system of inequalities.

55. $\quad\ x \ge 0$

$\quad\quad\ y \ge 0$

$\quad\ x + y \le 4$

56. $x \ge 0$

$\quad\ y \ge 0$

$\quad\ y \ge -\dfrac{1}{2}x + 2$

57. $x \ge 0, y \ge 0$

$\quad\ x + y \ge 4$

$\quad\ y \ge -2x + 6$

58. $x \ge 0, y \ge 0$

$\quad\ 4x + 3y \le 12$

$\quad\ 3x + 4y \le 12$

59. $x^2 + y^2 \ge 9$

$\quad\ x^2 + y^2 \le 25$

$\quad\ y \ge |x|$

60. $x - 2 < y < x + 2$

$\quad\ x^2 + y^2 < 16$

$\quad\ x > 0, y > 0$

61. $y > (x - 1)^3$

$\quad\ y > 1$

$\quad\ x + y > -2$

62. $x \ge |y|$

$\quad\ y \ge -3$

$\quad\ 2y - x \le 4$

63. $y > 2^x$

$\quad\ y < 6 - x^2$

$\quad\ x + y > 0$

64. $x^2 + y \le 5$

$\quad\ y \ge x^3 - x$

$\quad\ y \le 4$

Write a system of inequalities whose solution set is the region shown.

65.

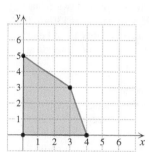

66.

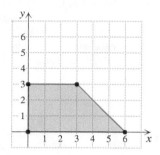

67.

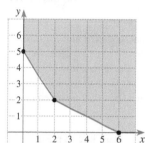

68.

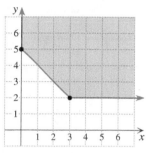

Find a system of inequalities to describe the given region.

69. Points inside the square that has vertices $(2, 2)$, $(-2, 2)$, $(-2, -2)$, and $(2, -2)$.

70. Points inside the triangle that has vertices $(0, 0)$, $(0, 6)$, and $(3, 0)$.

71. Points in the first quadrant less than nine units from the origin.

72. Points that are closer to the x-axis than they are to the y-axis.

Use a graphing calculator to graph the equation corresponding to each inequality. From the display of the graphing calculator, locate one ordered pair in the solution set to the system and check that it satisfies all inequalities of the system. Answers may vary.

73. $y > 2^{x+2}$

$\quad\ y < x^3 - 3x$

74. $y > e^{x-0.8}$

$\quad\ y < \log(x + 2.5)$

75. $y < -0.5x^2 + 150x - 11{,}226.6$

$\quad\ y > -0.11x + 38$

76. $y < x^2$

$\quad\ y > 2^x$

$\quad\ y < 5x - 6$

Write a system of inequalities that describes the possible solutions to each problem and graph the solution set to the system.

77. *Size Restrictions* United Parcel Service defines the girth of a box as the sum of the length, twice the width, and twice the height. The maximum girth that UPS will accept is 130 in. If the length of a box is 50 in., then what inequality must be satisfied by the width and height? Draw a graph showing the acceptable widths and heights for a length of 50 in.

78. *More Restrictions* United Parcel Service defines the girth of a box as the sum of the length, twice the width, and twice the height. The maximum girth that UPS will accept is 130 in. A shipping clerk wants to ship parts in a box that has a height of 24 in. For easy handling, he wants the box to have a width that is less than or equal to two-thirds of the length. Write a system of inequalities that the box must satisfy and draw a graph showing the possible lengths and widths.

79. *Inventory Control* A car dealer stocks mid-size and full-size cars on her lot, which cannot hold more than 110 cars. On the average, she borrows $10,000 to purchase a mid-size car and $15,000 to purchase a full-size car. How many cars of each type could she stock if her total debt cannot exceed $1.5 million?

80. *Delicate Balance* A fast food restaurant must have a minimum of 30 employees and a maximum of 50. To avoid charges of sexual bias, the company has a policy that the number of employees of one sex must never exceed the number of employees of the other sex by more than six. How many persons of each sex could be employed at this restaurant?

81. *Political Correctness* A political party is selling $50 tickets and $100 tickets for a fund-raising banquet in a hall that cannot hold more than 500 people. To show that the party represents the people, the number of $100 tickets must not be greater than 20% of the total number of tickets sold. How many tickets of each type can be sold?

82. *Mixing Alloys* A metallurgist has two alloys available. Alloy A is 20% zinc and 80% copper, while alloy B is 60% zinc and 40% copper. He wants to melt down and mix x ounces of alloy

A with y ounces of alloy B to get a metal that is at most 50% zinc and at most 60% copper. How many ounces of each alloy should he use if the new piece of metal must not weigh more than 20 ounces?

▶ **RETHINKING**

83. Find the partial fraction decomposition for $\dfrac{x^2 + 5x + 3}{x^3 + x^2}$.

84. Solve the system $x - y - 3z = 9$, $2x + y - 4z = 12$, and $2x - 2y - 6z = 8$.

85. Solve the system $5x - 9y = 12$ and $18y - 10x = 20$.

86. Solve the system $y = x^2 + 1$ and $y = x + 1$.

87. Find the amount after 3 years and 6 months for an investment of $20,000 that returns 5% compounded continuously.

88. How long does it take (to the nearest day) for a population of rabbits to grow from 5000 to 8000 if they are growing at an annual rate of 5% compounded continuously?

THINKING OUTSIDE THE BOX LXVI

Changing Places Five men and five women are rowing a long boat with 11 seats in a row. The five men are in front, the five women are in the back, and there is an empty seat in the middle. The five men in the front of the boat want to exchange seats with the five women in back. A rower can move from his/her seat to the next empty seat or he/she can step over one person without capsizing the boat. What is the minimum number of moves needed for the five men in front to change places with the five women in back?

POP QUIZ 5

1. Does the graph of $x - 2y > 0$ consist of the region above or below the line $x - 2y = 0$?

2. Does the graph of $x^2 + y^2 < 9$ consist of the region inside or outside of the circle $x^2 + y^2 = 9$?

3. Does $(0, 1)$ satisfy the system $x + 6y \geq 2$ and $x + 2y \leq -5$?

4. Write a system of inequalities whose solution set consists of points in the second quadrant that are less than 5 units from the origin.

5. What is the area of the graph of the solution set to $|x - 2| \leq 5$ and $|y - 3| \leq 2$?

concepts...

For Individual or Group Explorations

Describing Regular Polygons

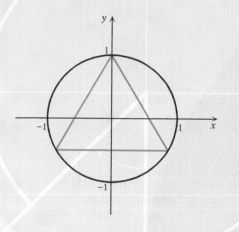

The equilateral triangle in the figure is inscribed in the circle $x^2 + y^2 = 1$.

a) Write a system of inequalities whose graph consists of all points on and inside the equilateral triangle.

b) Write a system of inequalities whose graph consists of all points on and inside a square inscribed in $x^2 + y^2 = 1$. Position the square in any manner that you choose.

c) Write a system of inequalities whose graph consists of all points on and inside a regular pentagon inscribed in $x^2 + y^2 = 1$. You will need trigonometry for this one.

d) Write a system of inequalities whose graph consists of all points on and inside a regular hexagon inscribed in $x^2 + y^2 = 1$.

6 The Linear Programming Model

In this section we apply our knowledge of systems of linear inequalities to solving linear programming problems. Linear programming is a method that can be used to solve many practical business problems. Linear programming can tell us how to allocate resources to achieve a maximum profit, a minimum labor cost, or a most nutritious meal.

Graphing the Constraints

In the simplest linear programming applications we have two variables that must satisfy several linear inequalities. These inequalities are called the **constraints** because they restrict the variables to only certain values. The graph of the solution set to the system is used to indicate the points that satisfy all of the constraints. Any point that satisfies all of the constraints is called a **feasible solution** to the problem.

EXAMPLE 1 Graphing the constraints

Graph the solution set to the system of inequalities and identify each vertex of the region.

$$x \geq 0, \quad y \geq 0$$
$$2x + y \leq 6$$
$$x + y \leq 4$$

Solution

The points on or to the right of the y-axis satisfy $x \geq 0$. The points on or above the x-axis satisfy $y \geq 0$. The points on or below the line $2x + y = 6$ satisfy $2x + y \leq 6$. The points on or below the line $x + y = 4$ satisfy $x + y \leq 4$. Graph

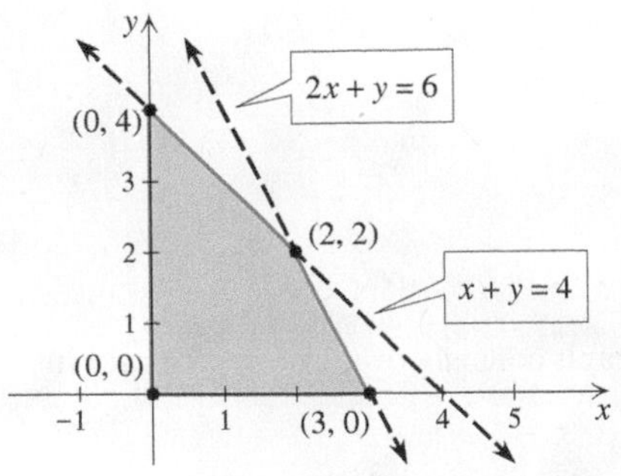

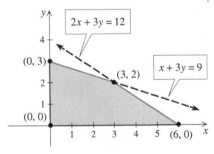

Figure 40

each straight line and shade the region that satisfies all four inequalities, as shown in Fig. 40. Three of the vertices are easily identified as $(0, 0)$, $(0, 4)$, and $(3, 0)$. The fourth vertex is at the intersection of $x + y = 4$ and $2x + y = 6$. Multiply $x + y = 4$ by -1 and add the result to $2x + y = 6$:

$$-x - y = -4$$
$$\underline{2x + y = 6}$$
$$x = 2$$

If $x = 2$ and $x + y = 4$, then $y = 2$. So the fourth vertex is $(2, 2)$.

▶**TRY THIS.** Graph the solution set to $x \geq 0$, $y \geq 0$, $x + y \leq 6$, and $x + 2y \leq 8$ and identify each vertex of the region. ■

In linear programming, the constraints usually come from physical limitations of resources described within the specific problem. Constraints that are always satisfied are called **natural constraints.** For example, the requirement that the number of employees be greater than or equal to zero is a natural constraint. In the next example we write the constraints and then graph the points in the coordinate plane that satisfy all of the constraints.

EXAMPLE 2 Finding and graphing the constraints

Bruce builds portable storage buildings. He uses 10 sheets of plywood and 15 studs in a small building, and he uses 15 sheets of plywood and 45 studs in a large building. Bruce has available only 60 sheets of plywood and 135 studs. Write the constraints on the number of small and large portable buildings that he can build with the available supplies, and graph the solution set to the system of constraints.

Solution

Let x represent the number of small buildings and y represent the number of large buildings. The natural constraints are

$$x \geq 0 \quad \text{and} \quad y \geq 0$$

because he cannot build a negative number of buildings. Since he has only 60 sheets of plywood available, we must have

$$10x + 15y \leq 60$$
$$2x + 3y \leq 12 \quad \text{Divide each side by 5.}$$

Since he has only 135 studs available, we must have

$$15x + 45y \leq 135$$
$$x + 3y \leq 9 \quad \text{Divide each side by 15.}$$

The conditions stated lead to the following system of constraints:

$$x \geq 0, \quad y \geq 0 \quad \text{Natural constraints}$$
$$2x + 3y \leq 12 \quad \text{Constraint on amount of plywood}$$
$$x + 3y \leq 9 \quad \text{Constraint on number of studs}$$

The graph of the solution set to this system is shown in Fig. 41.

Figure 41

▶**TRY THIS.** A small shop assembles electronic components. Component X uses 4 transistors and 6 diodes. Component Y uses 8 transistors and 2 diodes. The shop has on hand only 40 transistors and 30 diodes. Write the constraints on the number of components that can be assembled and graph the system. ■

Maximizing or Minimizing a Linear Function

In Example 2, any ordered pair within the shaded region of Fig. 41 is a feasible solution to the problem of deciding how many buildings of each type could be built. For each feasible solution within the shaded region, Bruce makes some amount of profit. Of course, Bruce wants to find a feasible solution that will yield the maximum possible profit. In general, the function that we wish to maximize or minimize, subject to the constraints, is called the **objective function.**

If Bruce makes a profit of \$400 on a small building and \$500 on a large building, then the total profit from x small and y large buildings is

$$P = 400x + 500y.$$

Since the profit is a function of x and y, we write the objective function as

$$P(x, y) = 400x + 500y.$$

The function P is a linear function of x and y. The domain of P is the region graphed in Fig. 41.

Definition: Linear Function in Two Variables

> A **linear function in two variables** is a function of the form
>
> $$f(x, y) = Ax + By + C,$$
>
> where A, B, and C are real numbers such that A and B are not both zero.

Bruce is interested in the maximum profit, subject to the constraints on x and y. Suppose $x = 1$ and $y = 1$; then the profit is

$$P(1, 1) = 400(1) + 500(1) = \$900.$$

In fact, the profit is \$900 for any x and y that satisfy

$$400x + 500y = 900.$$

If he wants \$1300 profit, then x and y must satisfy

$$400x + 500y = 1300,$$

and the profit is \$1800 if x and y satisfy

$$400x + 500y = 1800.$$

The graphs of these lines are shown in Fig. 42. Notice that the larger profit is found on the higher profit line and all of the profit lines are parallel. Think of the profit lines (or the objective function) as sliding across the graph. As the line slides upward the profit increases. So we want to slide it as far upward as possible while

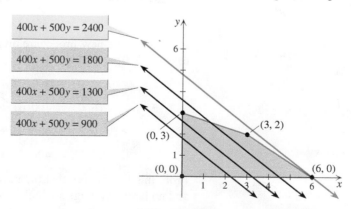

Figure 42

keeping it in contact with the region of feasible solutions. You can see in Fig. 42 that the highest line that intersects the region and is parallel to the other profit lines will intersect the region at the vertex $(6, 0)$. If you slide the profit line any higher it will not intersect the region. So Bruce should build six small buildings and no large buildings to maximize his profit. The maximum profit is $2400, because $P(6, 0) = 400(6) + 500(0) = 2400$. If we slide the profit line downward as far as possible we can find the minimum profit. The lowest profit line that intersects the region will pass through $(0, 0)$. Thus the minimum profit is zero dollars, which occurs when he builds no buildings.

The situation in any linear programming problem is similar to the example of Bruce's buildings. The region of feasible solutions is a region bounded by straight line segments, because the constraints are linear inequalities. Since the objective function is also linear, possible values for the objective function will produce a series of parallel straight lines like the ones in Fig. 42. As we slide the line for the objective function across the region, the final contact with the region must include a vertex of the region. (If one of the sides of the region is parallel to the objective function, then the final intersection of the objective function and the region might be a line segment, which includes two vertices of the region.) In any case, we can find the maximum or minimum value of the objective function by simply evaluating it at each vertex of the region.

Theorem: The Principle of Linear Programming

> The maximum or minimum value of a linear objective function subject to linear constraints occurs at a vertex of the region determined by the constraints.

It is a bit cumbersome and possibly inaccurate to graph parallel lines and then find the highest (or lowest) one that intersects the region determined by the constraints. Instead, we can use the following procedure for linear programming, which does not depend as much on graphing.

PROCEDURE

Linear Programming

Use the following steps to find the maximum or minimum value of a linear function subject to linear constraints.

1. Graph the region that satisfies all of the constraints.
2. Determine the coordinates of each vertex of the region.
3. Evaluate the function at each vertex of the region.
4. Identify which vertex gives the maximum or minimum value of the function.

To use the new procedure on Bruce's buildings, note that in Fig. 42 the vertices are $(0, 0)$, $(6, 0)$, $(0, 3)$, and $(3, 2)$. Compute the profit at each vertex:

$$P(0, 0) = 400(0) + 500(0) = \$0 \quad \text{Minimum profit}$$

$$P(6, 0) = 400(6) + 500(0) = \$2400 \quad \text{Maximum profit}$$

$$P(0, 3) = 400(0) + 500(3) = \$1500$$

$$P(3, 2) = 400(3) + 500(2) = \$2200$$

From this list, we see that the maximum profit is $2400, when six small buildings and no large buildings are built, and the minimum profit is $0, when no buildings of either type are built.

■ Foreshadowing Calculus

In multivariate calculus we study functions of more than one variable and determine how the function is changing with respect to each variable. We can solve problems that are similar to the problems presented here, but involve nonlinear functions.

In the next example we use the linear programming technique to find the minimum value of a linear function subject to a system of constraints.

EXAMPLE 3 | Finding the minimum value of a linear function

One serving of Muesli breakfast cereal contains 4 grams of protein and 30 grams of carbohydrates. One serving of Multi Bran Chex contains 2 grams of protein and 25 grams of carbohydrates. A dietitian wants to mix these two cereals to make a batch that contains at least 44 grams of protein and at least 450 grams of carbohydrates. If the cost of Muesli is 21 cents per serving and the cost of Multi Bran Chex is 14 cents per serving, then how many servings of each cereal would minimize the cost and satisfy the constraints?

Solution

Let x = the number of servings of Muesli and y = the number of servings of Multi Bran Chex. If the batch is to contain at least 44 grams of protein, then

$$4x + 2y \geq 44.$$

If the batch is to contain at least 450 grams of carbohydrates, then

$$30x + 25y \geq 450.$$

Simplify each inequality and use the two natural constraints to get the following system:

$$x \geq 0, \quad y \geq 0$$
$$2x + y \geq 22$$
$$6x + 5y \geq 90$$

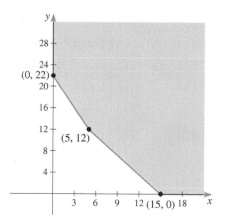

Figure 43

The graph of the constraints is shown in Fig. 43. The vertices are $(0, 22)$, $(5, 12)$, and $(15, 0)$. The cost in dollars for x servings of Muesli and y servings of Multi Bran Chex is $C(x, y) = 0.21x + 0.14y$. Evaluate the cost at each vertex.

$$C(0, 22) = 0.21(0) + 0.14(22) = \$3.08$$
$$C(5, 12) = 0.21(5) + 0.14(12) = \$2.73 \quad \text{Minimum cost}$$
$$C(15, 0) = 0.21(15) + 0.14(0) = \$3.15$$

The minimum cost of \$2.73 is attained by using 5 servings of Muesli and 12 servings of Multi Bran Chex. Note that $C(x, y)$ does not have a maximum value on this region. The cost increases without bound as x and y increase.

▶TRY THIS. The shop described in the Try This for Example 2 gets \$2 for each X-component assembled and \$3 for each Y-component assembled. How many components of each type would maximize the revenue and satisfy the constraints? ■

The examples of linear programming given in this text are simple examples. Problems in linear programming in business can involve a hundred or more variables subject to as many inequalities. These problems are solved by computers using matrix methods, but the basic idea is the same as we have seen in this section.

1. The graph of $x \geq 0$ in the coordinate plane consists only of points on the x-axis that are at or to the right of the origin.

2. The graph of $y \geq 2$ in the coordinate plane consists of the points on or to the right of the line $y = 2$.

3. The graph of $x + y \leq 5$ does not include the origin.

4. The graph of $2x + 3y = 12$ has x-intercept $(0, 4)$ and y-intercept $(6, 0)$.

5. The graph of a system of inequalities is the intersection of their individual solution sets.

6. In linear programming, constraints are inequalities that restrict the values of the variables.

7. The function $f(x, y) = 4x^2 + 9y^2 + 36$ is a linear function of x and y.

8. The value of $R(x, y) = 30x + 15y$ at the point $(1, 3)$ is 75.

9. If $C(x, y) = 7x + 9y + 3$, then $C(0, 5) = 45$.

10. To solve a linear programming problem, we evaluate the objective function at the vertices of the region determined by the constraints.

→ EXERCISES 6

Fill in the blank.

1. The inequalities involved in linear programming are _____.

2. Any point that satisfies all of the constraints is a(n) _____ solution to the problem.

3. Constraints that are always satisfied are _____ constraints.

4. In linear programming we seek to maximize or minimize the _____ function.

Graph the solution set to each system of inequalities and identify each vertex of the region.

5. $x \geq 0, y \geq 0$
   $x + y \leq 4$

6. $x \geq 0, y \geq 0$
   $2x + y \leq 4$

7. $x \geq 0, y \geq 0$
   $x \leq 1, y \leq 3$

8. $x \geq 0, y \geq 0$
   $y \leq x, x \leq 3$

9. $x \geq 0, y \geq 0$
   $x + y \leq 4$
   $2x + y \leq 6$

10. $x \geq 0, y \geq 0$
    $50x + 40y \leq 200$
    $10x + 20y \leq 60$

11. $x \geq 0, y \geq 0$
    $2x + y \geq 4$
    $x + y \geq 3$

12. $x \geq 0, y \geq 0$
    $20x + 10y \geq 40$
    $5x + 5y \geq 15$

13. $x \geq 0, y \geq 0$
    $3x + y \geq 6$
    $x + y \geq 4$

14. $x \geq 0, y \geq 0$
    $2x + y \geq 6$
    $x + 2y \geq 6$

15. $x \geq 0, y \geq 0$
    $3x + y \geq 8$
    $x + y \geq 6$

16. $x \geq 0, y \geq 0$
    $x + 4y \leq 20$
    $4x + y \leq 64$

Find the maximum value of the objective function $T(x, y) = 2x + 3y$ on each given region.

17.

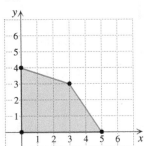

18.

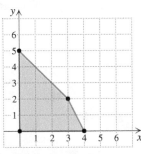

Find the minimum value of the objective function $H(x, y) = 2x + 2y$ on each given region.

19.

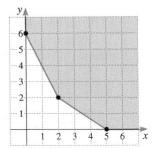

20.

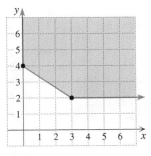

Find the maximum or minimum value of each objective function subject to the given constraints.

21. Maximize $P(x, y) = 5x + 9y$ subject to $x \geq 0, y \geq 0$, and $x + 2y \leq 6$.

22. Maximize $P(x, y) = 25x + 31y$ subject to $x \geq 0, y \geq 0$, and $5x + 6y \leq 30$.

23. Minimize $C(x, y) = 3x + 2y$ subject to $x \geq 0, y \geq 0$, $x + y \geq 4$.

24. Minimize $C(x, y) = 2x + 5y$ subject to $x \geq 0, y \geq 0$, and $2x + y \geq 8$.

25. Minimize $C(x, y) = 10x + 20y$ subject to $x \geq 0, y \geq 0, x + y \geq 8$, and $3x + 5y \geq 30$.

26. Maximize $R(x, y) = 50x + 20y$ subject to $x \geq 0, y \geq 0, 3x + y \leq 18$, and $2x + y \leq 14$.

Solve each problem. See the procedure for linear programming following Example 2.

27. *Maximizing Revenue* Bob and Betty make bird houses and mailboxes in their craft shop near Gatlinburg. Each bird house requires 3 hr of work from Bob and 1 hr from Betty. Each mailbox requires 4 hr of work from Bob and 2 hr of work from Betty. Bob cannot work more than 48 hr per week and Betty cannot work more than 20 hr per week. If each bird house sells for $12 and each mailbox sells for $20, then how many of each should they make to maximize their revenue?

HINT Write an inequality about the amount of time Bob can work and another for Betty.

28. *Maximizing Revenue* At Taco Town a taco contains 2 oz of ground beef and 1 oz of chopped tomatoes. A burrito contains 1 oz of ground beef and 3 oz of chopped tomatoes. Near closing time the cook discovers that they have only 22 oz of ground beef and 36 oz of tomatoes left. The manager directs the cook to use the available resources to maximize their revenue for the remainder of the shift. If a taco sells for 40 cents and a burrito sells for 65 cents, then how many of each should they make to maximize their revenue?

HINT Write an inequality about the amount of available beef and another for the tomatoes.

29. *Bird Houses and Mailboxes* If a bird house sells for $18 and a mailbox for $20, then how many of each should Bob and Betty build to maximize their revenue, subject to the constraints of Exercise 27?

30. *Tacos and Burritos* If a taco sells for 20 cents and a burrito for 65 cents, then how many of each should be made to maximize the revenue, subject to the constraints of Exercise 28?

31. *Minimizing Operating Costs* Kimo's Material Company hauls gravel to a construction site using a small truck and a large truck. The carrying capacity and operating cost per load are given in the accompanying table. Kimo must deliver a minimum of 120 yd^3 per day to satisfy his contract with the

builder. The union contract with his drivers requires that the total number of loads per day be a minimum of 8. How many loads should be made in each truck per day to minimize the total cost?

Table for Exercise 31

	Small Truck	Large Truck	
Capacity (yd^3)	12	20	
Cost per load	$70	$60	

Prism68/Shutterstock

32. *Minimizing Labor Costs* Tina's Telemarketing employs part-time and full-time workers. The number of hours worked per week and the pay per hour for each is given in the accompanying table. Tina needs at least 1200 hr of work done per week. To qualify for certain tax breaks, she must have at least 45 employees. How many part-time and full-time employees should be hired to minimize Tina's weekly labor cost?

Table for Exercise 32

	Part-time	Full-time	
Hours per week	20	40	
Pay per hour	$6	$8	

Neustockimages/iStockphoto

33. *Small Trucks and Large Trucks* If it costs $70 per load to operate the small truck and $75 per load to operate the large truck, then how many loads should be made in each truck per day to minimize the total cost, subject to the constraints of Exercise 31?

34. *Part-Time and Full-Time Workers* If the labor cost for a part-timer is $9/hr and the labor cost for a full-timer is $8/hr, then how many of each should be employed to minimize the weekly labor cost, subject to the constraints of Exercise 32?

▶ **RETHINKING**

35. Solve the system $y > x^2 - 2x$ and $y < -1 - x$.

36. Find the partial fraction decomposition for $\dfrac{11x - 3}{x^2 - x - 6}$.

37. Solve $\dfrac{1}{x} + \dfrac{1}{x - 1} = \dfrac{3}{2}$.

38. Solve $5 - 4(x - 2) > 9$.

39. Solve $\dfrac{3x - 2}{x - 2} > 1$.

40. Find the annual percentage rate at which $4 will grow to $6 in 500 days if the interest is compounded daily. Round to the nearest tenth of a percent.

THINKING OUTSIDE THE BOX LXVII

Ten Tangents In the accompanying figure, $AB = 7$, $AC = 12$, and $BC = 10$. There is a point D on BC such that the circles inscribed in triangles ABD and ACD are both tangent to line AD at a common point E. Find the length of BD.

HINT Two tangent segments from a point to a circle are equal in length.

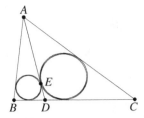

Figure for Thinking Outside the Box LXVII

POP QUIZ 6

1. Find all vertices of the region $x \geq 0, y \geq 0$, and $x + 2y \leq 6$.

2. On the region in the previous problem, find the maximum value of $P(x, y) = 20x + 50y - 100$.

3. Find all vertices of the region $x \geq 0, y \geq 0, x + 2y \geq 6$, and $2x + y \geq 9$.

4. Find the minimum value of $C(x, y) = 5x + 4y$ on the region of the previous problem.

LINKING
concepts... For Individual or Group Explorations

Modeling Numerous Constraints

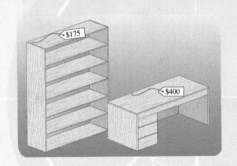

Lucy's Woodworks makes desks and bookcases for furniture stores. Lucy sells the desks for \$400 and the bookcases for \$175. Each desk takes 30 ft² of oak plywood, 12 ft of molding, 1 quart of stain, 3 pints of lacquer, 9 drawer pulls, 7 drawer glides, and 20 hours of labor. Each bookcase requires 20 ft² of oak plywood, 15 ft of molding, 1 pint of stain, 1 quart of lacquer, 20 shelf pins, and 12 hours of labor. Lucy has available only 960 ft² of oak plywood, 480 ft of molding, 8 gallons of stain, 15 gallons of lacquer, 270 drawer pulls, 350 drawer glides, 580 shelf pins, and 720 hours of labor.

a) How many desks and how many bookcases should Lucy make to maximize her revenue?

b) Suppose Lucy could increase her supply of one item. Which item would have the most significant impact on her revenue? Explain your answer.

Highlights

1 Systems of Linear Equations in Two Variables

System	Two equations of the form $Ax + By = C$ where A and B are not both zero	$3x - y = 5$ $3x + y = 13$
Solution Set	The set of ordered pairs that satisfy all equations of the system	$\{(3, 4)\}$
Addition Method	Add the equations (or appropriate multiples of the equations) to eliminate a variable.	$3x - y = 5$ $\underline{3x + y = 13}$ $6x \quad\quad = 18$

Substitution Method	Substitute one equation into the other to eliminate a variable.	$y = 3x - 5$ $3x + (3x - 5) = 13$
Independent	A system with one solution	$y = 2x - 3, y = -2x - 3$
Inconsistent	A system with no solutions	$y = 2x - 3, y = 2x - 4$
Dependent	A system with infinitely many solutions	$y = 2x - 3, 2y = 4x - 6$

2 Systems of Linear Equations in Three Variables

System	Two or three equations of the form $Ax + By + Cz = D$, where A, B, and C are not all zero	$x + y - z = 0$ $x - y + z = 2$ $x - 2y + z = 1$
Solution Set	Single-ordered triple, no solution, or infinitely many solutions	$\{(1, 1, 2)\}$
Methods	Use a combination of addition and/or substitution to eliminate variables.	

3 Nonlinear Systems of Equations

Nonlinear System	Two equations in two variables, where at least one is not linear	$x + y = 12$ $y = x^2$
Solving	Use a combination of addition and/or substitution to eliminate variables.	$x + x^2 = 12$

4 Partial Fractions

Partial Fraction Decomposition	Reverses the addition of rational expressions	$\dfrac{3x - 2}{x(x - 1)} = \dfrac{2}{x} + \dfrac{1}{x - 1}$

5 Inequalities and Systems of Inequalities in Two Variables

Linear Inequalities	$y > mx + b$ is the region above $y = mx + b$.	$y > x$ is above $y = x$.
	$y < mx + b$ is the region below $y = mx + b$.	$y < x$ is below $y = x$.
	$x > k$ is the region to the right of $x = k$.	$x > 2$ is to the right of $x = 2$.
	$x < k$ is the region to the left of $x = k$.	$x < 2$ is to the left of $x = 2$.
Including Boundaries	For $\leq$ or $\geq$ the boundary lines are included and drawn with solid lines.	$x \geq 2$ includes the line $x = 2$.
System of Inequalities	Test a point in each region determined by the boundary lines or curves.	$y > 2$ and $y < 3$ is the region between $y = 2$ and $y = 3$.

6 The Linear Programming Model

Constraints	Inequalities concerning the variables in a linear programming problem	
Principle of Linear Programming	The maximum or minimum of a linear function subject to linear constraints occurs at a vertex of the region determined by the constraints.	

Chapter Review Exercises

Solve each system by graphing.

1. $2x - 3y = -9$
$3x + y = 14$

2. $3x - 2y = 0$
$y = -2x - 7$

3. $x + y = 2$
$2y - 3x = 9$

4. $x - y = 30$
$2x + 3y = 10$

Solve each system by the method of your choice. Indicate whether each system is independent, dependent, or inconsistent.

5. $3x - 5y = 19$
$y = x$

6. $x + y = 9$
$y = x - 3$

7. $4x - 3y = 6$
$3x + 2y = 9$

8. $3x - 2y = 4$
$5x + 7y = 1$

9. $6x + 2y = 2$
$y = -3x + 1$

10. $x - y = 9$
$2y - 2x = -18$

11. $3x - 4y = 12$
$8y - 6x = 9$

12. $y = -5x + 3$
$5x + y = 6$

Solve each system.

13. $x + y - z = 8$
$2x + y + z = 1$
$x + 2y + 3z = -5$

14. $2x + 3y - 2z = 8$
$3x - y + 4z = -20$
$x + y - z = 3$

15. $x + y + z = 1$
$2x - y + 2z = 2$
$2x + 2y + 2z = 2$

16. $x - y - z = 9$
$x + y + 2z = -9$
$-2x + 2y + 2z = -18$

17. $x + y + z = 1$
$2x - y + 3z = 5$
$x + y + z = 4$

18. $2x - y + z = 4$
$x - y + z = -1$
$-x + y - z = 0$

Solve each nonlinear system of equations. Find real solutions only.

19. $x^2 + y^2 = 4$
$x = y^2$

20. $x^2 - y^2 = 9$
$x^2 + y^2 = 7$

21. $y = |x|$
$y = x^2$

22. $y = 2x^2 + x - 3$
$6x + y = 12$

Find the partial fraction decomposition for each rational expression.

23. $\dfrac{7x - 7}{(x - 3)(x + 4)}$

24. $\dfrac{x - 13}{x^2 - 6x + 5}$

25. $\dfrac{7x^2 - 7x + 23}{x^3 - 3x^2 + 4x - 12}$

26. $\dfrac{10x^2 - 6x + 2}{(x - 1)^2(x + 2)}$

Graph the solution set to each inequality.

27. $x^2 + (y - 3)^2 < 9$

28. $2x - 9y \le 18$

29. $x \le (y - 1)^2$

30. $y < 6 - 2x^2$

Graph the solution set to each system of inequalities.

31. $2x - 3y \ge 6$
$x \le 2$

32. $x \le 3, y \ge 1$
$x - y \ge -5$

33. $y \ge 2x^2 - 6$
$x^2 + y^2 \le 9$

34. $x^2 + y^2 \ge 16$
$2y \ge x^2 - 16$

35. $x \ge 0, y \ge 1$
$x + 2y \le 10$
$3x + 4y \le 24$

36. $x \ge 0, y \ge 0$
$30x + 60y \le 1200$
$x + y \le 30$

37. $x \ge 0, y \ge 0$
$x + 6y \ge 60$
$x + y \ge 35$

38. $x \ge 0$
$y \ge x + 1$
$x + y \le 5$

Solve each problem, using a system of equations.

39. Find the equation of the line through $(-2, 3)$ and $(4, -1)$.

40. Find the equation of the line through $(4, 7)$ and $(-2, -3)$.

41. Find the equation of the parabola through $(1, 4)$, $(3, 20)$, and $(-2, 25)$.

42. Find the equation of the parabola through $(-1, 10)$, $(2, -5)$, and $(3, -18)$.

43. *Tacos and Burritos* At Taco Town a taco contains 1 oz of meat and 2 oz of cheese, while a burrito contains 2 oz of meat and 3 oz of cheese. In 1 hr the cook used 181 oz of meat and 300 oz of cheese making tacos and burritos. How many of each were made?

44. *Imported and Domestic Cars* Nicholas had 10% imports on his used car lot, and Seymour had 30% imports on his used car lot. After Nicholas bought Seymour's entire stock, Nicholas had 300 cars, of which 22% were imports. How many cars were on each lot originally?

45. *Daisies, Carnations, and Roses* Esther's Flower Shop sells a bouquet containing five daisies, three carnations, and two roses for $3.05. Esther also sells a bouquet containing three daisies, one carnation, and four roses for $2.75. Her Valentine's Day Special contains four daisies, two carnations, and one rose for $2.10. How much should she charge for her Economy Special, which contains one daisy, one carnation, and one rose?

Lynn Watson/Shutterstock

46. *Peppers, Tomatoes, and Eggplants* Ngan planted 81 plants in his garden at a total cost of $23.85. The 81 plants consisted of peppers at 20 cents each, tomatoes at 35 cents each, and eggplants at 30 cents each. If the total number of peppers and tomatoes was only half the number of eggplants, then how many of each did he plant?

Solve each linear programming problem.

47. *Minimum* Find the minimum value of the function $C(x, y) = 0.42x + 0.84y$ subject to the constraints $x \geq 0, y \geq 0, x + 6y \geq 60$, and $x + y \geq 35$.

48. *Maximum* Find the maximum value of the function $P(x, y) = 1.23x + 1.64y$ subject to the constraints $x \geq 0, y \geq 0, x + 2y \leq 40$, and $x + y \leq 30$.

49. *Pipeline or Barge* A refinery gets its oil from a pipeline or from barges. The refinery needs at least 12 million barrels per day. The maximum capacity of the pipeline is 12 million barrels per day, and the maximum that can be delivered by barge is 8 million barrels per day. The refinery has a contract to buy at least 6 million barrels per day through the pipeline. If the cost of oil by barge is $90 per barrel and the cost of oil from the pipeline is $100 per barrel, then how much oil should be purchased from each source to minimize the cost and satisfy the constraints?

50. *Fluctuating Costs* If the cost of oil by barge goes up to $105 per barrel while the cost of oil by pipeline stays at $100 per barrel, then how much oil should be purchased from each source to minimize the cost and satisfy the constraints of Exercise 49?

THINKING OUTSIDE THE BOX LXVIII & LXIX

Maximizing Mileage Dan knows that tires on the front of his SUV will wear out in 20,000 miles, whereas tires on the rear of his SUV will wear out in 30,000 miles. If Dan buys five new tires for his SUV, then what is the maximum mileage that he can get out of the set of tires by rotating them? Describe how and when they should be rotated.

Tree Farming A tree farmer is planting pine seedlings in a rectangular field that is 1000 ft by 3000 ft. The trees can be planted on the very edge of the field, but the trees must be at least 10 ft apart. What is the maximum number of trees that can be planted in this field?

Chapter Test

Solve the system by the indicated method.

1. Graphing:

$2x + 3y = 6$

$y = \dfrac{1}{3}x + 5$

2. Substitution:

$2x + y = 4$

$3x - 4y = 9$

3. Addition:

$10x - 3y = 22$

$7x + 2y = 40$

Determine whether each of the following systems is independent, inconsistent, or dependent.

4. $x = 6 - y$

$3x + 3y = 4$

5. $y = \dfrac{1}{2}x + 3$

$x - 2y = -6$

6. $y = 2x - 1$

$y = 3x + 20$

7. $y = -x + 2$

$y = -x + 5$

Find the solution set to each system of equations in three variables.

8. $2x - y + z = 4$

$-x + 2y - z = 6$

9. $x - 2y - z = 2$

$2x + 3y + z = -1$

$3x - y - 3z = -4$

10. $x + y + z = 1$

$x + y - z = 4$

$-x - y + z = 2$

Solve each system.

11. $x^2 + y^2 = 16$
$x^2 - 4y^2 = 16$

12. $x + y = -2$
$y = x^2 - 5x$

Find the partial fraction decomposition for each rational expression.

13. $\dfrac{2x + 10}{x^2 - 2x - 8}$

14. $\dfrac{4x^2 + x - 2}{x^3 - x^2}$

Graph the solution set to each inequality or system of inequalities.

15. $2x - y < 8$

16. $x + y \le 5$
$x - y < 0$

17. $x^2 + y^2 \le 9$
$y \le 1 - x^2$

Solve each problem.

18. In a survey of 52 students in the cafeteria, it was found that 15 were commuters. If one-quarter of the female students and one-third of the male students in the survey were commuters, then how many of each sex were surveyed?

19. General Hospital is planning an aggressive advertising campaign to bolster the hospital's image in the community. Each television commercial reaches 14,000 people and costs $9000, while each newspaper ad reaches 6000 people and costs $3000. The advertising budget for the campaign is limited to $99,000, and the advertising agency has the capability of producing a maximum of 23 ads and/or commercials during the time allotted for the campaign. What mix of television commercials and newspaper ads will maximize the audience exposure, subject to the given constraints?

CONCEPTS OF
calculus...

**Instantaneous rate
of change and
partial fractions**

The average rate of change of a function f on the interval $[x, x + h]$ is

$$\frac{f(x + h) - f(x)}{h}.$$

*The instantaneous rate of change $f'(x)$ as the limit as h approaches zero of the
average rate of change is*

$$f'(x) = \lim_{h \to 0} \frac{f(x + h) - f(x)}{h}.$$

*In the following exercises you will first find the instantaneous rate of a rational
function without using partial fractions and then with using partial fractions.*

Exercises

1. Let $f(x) = \dfrac{2x + 1}{x^2 + x}$.

   a. Find $\dfrac{f(x + h) - f(x)}{h}$ and simplify it.

   b. Use the result of part (a) to find $f'(x)$.

2. Use the idea of partial fractions to write $f(x)$ as the sum of
two simpler rational expressions.

3. a. Use the result of Exercise 2 to show that

$$\frac{f(x + h) - f(x)}{h} = \frac{-1}{x(x + h)} + \frac{-1}{(x + 1)(x + h + 1)}.$$

   b. Use the result of part (a) to find $f'(x)$.

4. Show that $f'(x)$ found in Exercise 3(b) is the same as $f'(x)$
found in Exercise 1(b).

Answers to Exercises

Section 1

For Thought: **1.** T **2.** F **3.** F **4.** T **5.** T **6.** T
7. F **8.** F **9.** F **10.** T
Exercises:
1. system **3.** inconsistent **5.** dependent **7.** Yes **9.** No
11. $\{(1, 2)\}$ **13.** $\varnothing$ **15.** $\{(3, 2)\}$ **17.** $\{(3, 1)\}$
19. $\varnothing$ **21.** $\{(x, y)|x - 2y = 6\}$ **23.** $\{(-1, -1)\}$, independent
25. $\{(11/5, -6/5)\}$, independent
27. $\{(x, y)|y = 3x + 5\}$, dependent **29.** $\varnothing$, inconsistent
31. $\{(150, 50)\}$, independent **33.** $\varnothing$, inconsistent
35. $\{(34, 15)\}$, independent **37.** $\{(13, 7)\}$, independent
39. $\{(4, -1)\}$, independent **41.** $\varnothing$, inconsistent
43. $\{(-1, 1)\}$, independent **45.** $\{(x, y)|x + 2y = 12\}$, dependent
47. $\{(4, 6)\}$, independent **49.** $\{(1.5, 3.48)\}$, independent
51. Independent **53.** Dependent **55.** $(-1000, -497)$
57. $(6.18, -0.54)$ **59.** Althea $49,000, Vaughn $33,000
61. $10,000 at 10%, $15,000 at 8% **63.** $6.50 adult, $4 child
65. Dependent, m = number of male and $12 - m$ = number of female
memberships, $0 \le m \le 12$
67. 23 ostriches, 19 cows **69.** Dependent, lots of solutions
71. Inconsistent, no solution **73.** 600 students
75. 65 pennies, 22 nickels **77.** $x = 6$ oz, $y = 10$ oz
79. Plan A, 12 mo **81.** 1.1 yr **83.** 25/33 sec ≈ 0.76 sec
85. $y = -2x + 3$ **87.** $y = -\dfrac{5}{3}x - \dfrac{1}{3}$
93. a. 4 **b.** 1/4 **c.** 8 **95.** $\{19\}$ **97.** $[2/3, 6/5]$

Section 2

For Thought: **1.** T **2.** F **3.** T **4.** F **5.** T **6.** T
7. T **8.** T **9.** T **10.** F
Exercises:
1. linear
3. **5.**

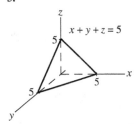

$x + y + z = 5$ $x + y - z = 3$

7. Yes **9.** No **11.** $\{(1, 2, 3)\}$ **13.** $\{(-1, 1, 2)\}$
15. $\{(0, -5, 5)\}$ **17.** $(1, 4, -4), (2, 5, -3), (3, 6, -2)$
19. $(2, 1, -6), (4, 2, -5), (6, 3, -4)$ **21.** $y - 3, y - 8$
23. $z + 1, z + 2$ **25.** $\dfrac{y - 1}{2}, \dfrac{3y - 5}{2}$
27. $\{(x, x - 1, x + 5)|x \text{ is any real number}\}$
29. $\{(x, 2x - 7, 3x - 9)|x \text{ is any real number}\}$
31. $\{(6 - z, 5 - z, z)|z \text{ is any real number}\}$
33. $\{(x, y, z)|x + 2y - 3z = 5\}$ **35.** $\varnothing$
37. $\{(2, y, y)|y \text{ is any real number}\}$
39. $\{(x, 5 - x, 3 - x)|x \text{ is any real number}\}$
41. $\{(5, 7, 9)\}$ **43.** $\{(1.2, 1.5, 2.4)\}$
45. $\{(1000, 2000, 6000)\}$ **47.** $\{(15/11, 13/11, -3/11)\}$
49. $y = x^2 - 3$ **51.** $y = -2x^2 + 5x$ **53.** $y = x^2 + 4x + 4$
55. $x + y + z = 1$ **57.** $2x + y - z = 2$
59. 8, 12, 20 **61.** 5, 6, 10
63. $4000 in stocks, $7000 in bonds, $14,000 in mutual fund
65. Hamburger $1.20, fries $1.60, Coke $1.00

67. Weight in pounds

LR	LF	RR	RF
280	332	296	292
285	327	291	297
290	322	286	302

69. 116 pennies, 48 nickels, 68 dimes
71. $3.95 **73.** $x = 36$ lb, $y = 24$ lb, $z = 51$ lb
75. a. $y = -\dfrac{1}{20}x^2 + \dfrac{9}{2}x$ **b.** 101.25 m **c.** 90 m
79. $\{(7, -2)\}$ **81.** $12,325.52 **83.** Not a function

Section 3

For Thought: **1.** T **2.** F **3.** T **4.** F **5.** F **6.** F
7. T **8.** T **9.** T **10.** F
Exercises:
1. Yes **3.** No **5.** $\{(0, 0), (1, 1)\}$ **7.** $\{(2, 4), (3, 9)\}$
9. $\left\{\left(-\dfrac{3}{2}, \dfrac{3}{2}\right)\right\}$ **11.** $\{(-1, 1), (0, 0), (1, 1)\}$
13. $\left\{(0, 0), \left(\dfrac{1}{4}, \dfrac{1}{2}\right)\right\}$ **15.** $\{(0, 0), (2, 8), (-2, -8)\}$
17. $\{(0, 0), (\sqrt{2}, \sqrt{2}), (-\sqrt{2}, -\sqrt{2})\}$
19. $\left\{\left(\dfrac{\sqrt{2}}{2}, \dfrac{\sqrt{2}}{2}\right)\left(-\dfrac{\sqrt{2}}{2}, -\dfrac{\sqrt{2}}{2}\right)\right\}$
21. $\{(-2 + \sqrt{3}, -2 - \sqrt{3}), (-2 - \sqrt{3}, -2 + \sqrt{3})\}$
23. $\{(1, \pm 1), (-1, \pm 1)\}$ **25.** $\left\{\left(-\dfrac{1}{2}, -2\right), (2, 3)\right\}$
27. $\{(2, 5)\}$ **29.** $\{(4, -3), (-1, 2)\}$
31. $\{(1, -2), (-1, 2)\}$ **33.** $\left\{\left(-\dfrac{1}{2}, \dfrac{1}{2}\right), \left(-\dfrac{1}{2}, -\dfrac{1}{2}\right)\right\}$
35. $\{(10^5, 10^3)\}$ **37.** $\left\{\left(-\dfrac{1}{3}, 2^{2/3}\right)\right\}$ **39.** $\{(2, 1)\}$
41. $\{(2, 2)\}$ **43.** $\{(0, 1)\}$ **45.** $\{(0, 1)\}$ **47.** $\{(1/4, 1)\}$
49. $\{(2, 1), (0.3, -1.8)\}$ **51.** $\{(1.9, 0.6), (0.1, -2.0)\}$
53. $\{(-0.8, 0.6), (2, 4), (4, 16)\}$ **55.** $\{(4, 0, -1)\}$
57. $\{(9, 4, -6), (4, 9, -6)\}$ **59.** 36.0 in., 21.6 in.
61. $-2, 8$ **63.** 9 m and 12 m
65. $6 - 2\sqrt{3}$ ft, $6\sqrt{3} - 6$ ft, $12 - 4\sqrt{3}$ ft
67. $x = 8$ in. and $y = 8$ oz **69.** A 9.6 min, B 48 min
71. $3 + i$ and $3 - i$ **73.** 60 ft and 30 ft
75. 0 and 9.65 yr, 29.5 yr **77.** 6 A.M.
79. $80 + 4\sqrt{29} \approx 101.54$ ft **83.** $\{(9, 11, 13)\}$
85. $\{8\}$ **87.** $\{-5, 1/2, 4\}$

Section 4

For Thought: **1.** T **2.** T **3.** F **4.** T **5.** F **6.** F
7. T **8.** F **9.** T **10.** T
Exercises:
1. $\dfrac{7x - 5}{(x - 2)(x + 1)}$ **3.** $\dfrac{x^2 - 3x + 5}{(x - 1)(x^2 + 2)}$
5. $\dfrac{3x^3 + x^2 + 8x + 5}{(x^2 + 3)^2}$ **7.** $\dfrac{4x^2 - x - 1}{(x - 1)^3}$
9. $A = 2, B = -2$ **11.** $\dfrac{2}{x + 1} + \dfrac{3}{x - 2}$
13. $\dfrac{1/2}{x + 2} + \dfrac{3/2}{x + 4}$ **15.** $\dfrac{1/3}{x - 3} + \dfrac{-1/3}{x + 3}$
17. $\dfrac{-1}{x} + \dfrac{1}{x - 1}$ **19.** $A = 2, B = 5, C = -1$
21. $\dfrac{1}{x - 1} + \dfrac{1}{(x - 1)^2} + \dfrac{-1}{x + 2}$ **23.** $\dfrac{1}{x + 4} + \dfrac{-1}{x - 2} + \dfrac{2}{(x - 2)^2}$
25. $\dfrac{1}{x - 1} + \dfrac{2}{x + 1} + \dfrac{1}{(x + 1)^2}$ **27.** $A = -1, B = 2, C = -3$

29. $\dfrac{2}{x + 2} + \dfrac{3x - 1}{x^2 + 1}$ **31.** $\dfrac{-1}{x + 1} + \dfrac{2x - 1}{x^2 + x + 1}$

33. $\dfrac{-3}{(x + 2)^2} + \dfrac{-2}{x + 2}$ **35.** $\dfrac{4}{x + 1} + \dfrac{2x - 3}{x^2 + 1}$

37. $\dfrac{-8x}{(x^2 + 9)^2} + \dfrac{3x - 1}{x^2 + 9}$ **39.** $\dfrac{5}{x - 2} + \dfrac{-2x + 3}{x^2 + 2x + 4}$

41. $2x + 1 + \dfrac{2}{x - 1} + \dfrac{3}{x + 1}$ **43.** $\dfrac{3x + 3}{(x^2 + x + 1)^2} + \dfrac{3x - 5}{x^2 + x + 1}$

45. $\dfrac{3x}{x^2 + 4} + \dfrac{1}{x - 2} + \dfrac{-1}{x + 2}$ **47.** $\dfrac{1}{x} + \dfrac{2}{x^2} + \dfrac{3}{x^3} + \dfrac{4}{x - 1}$

49. $\dfrac{3}{x - 2} + \dfrac{-1}{(x - 2)^2} + \dfrac{3}{x - 3}$ **51.** $\dfrac{4}{x + 5} + \dfrac{2}{x + 2} + \dfrac{3}{x - 3}$

53. $\dfrac{-1}{(x - 1)^3} + \dfrac{2}{(x - 1)^2} + \dfrac{1}{x - 1}$ **55.** $\dfrac{-b/a}{(ax + b)^2} + \dfrac{1/a}{ax + b}$

57. $\dfrac{c/b}{x} + \dfrac{1 - ac/b}{ax + b}$ **59.** $\dfrac{1/b}{x^2} + \dfrac{-a/b^2}{x} + \dfrac{a^2/b^2}{ax + b}$

61. $\{(-5, -3), (3, 5)\}$ **63.** $\{(x, 5x - 8)\,|\,x \text{ is any real number}\}$

65. $y = \dfrac{1}{2}(x + 4)^2 - 17$

Section 5

For Thought: **1.** F   **2.** F   **3.** T   **4.** F   **5.** T   **6.** T
7. F   **8.** F   **9.** T   **10.** T
Exercises:
1. (c)   **3.** (d)

5.
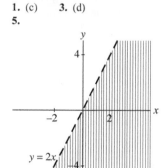

7.
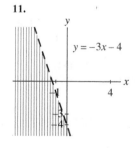

9.
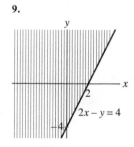

11.
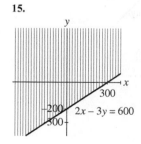

13.
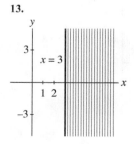

15.
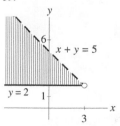

17.
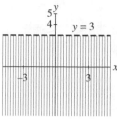

19.
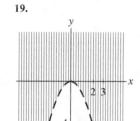

21.
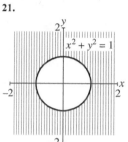

23.
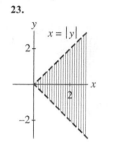

25.

27.
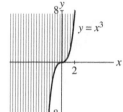

29.
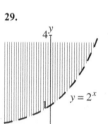

31.
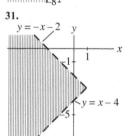

33.
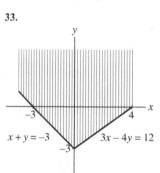

35.
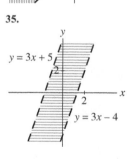

37. No solution
39.
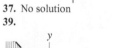

41.
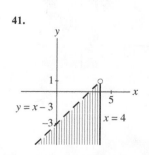

43.

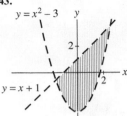

$y = x^2 - 3$

$y = x + 1$

45.

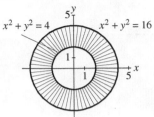

$x^2 + y^2 = 4$ $x^2 + y^2 = 16$

63.

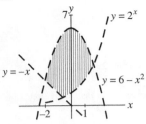

$y = 2^x$

$y = -x$ $y = 6 - x^2$

47.

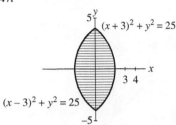

$(x + 3)^2 + y^2 = 25$

$(x - 3)^2 + y^2 = 25$

65. $x \geq 0, y \geq 0, y \leq -\dfrac{2}{3}x + 5, y \leq -3x + 12$

67. $y \geq 0, x \geq 0, y \geq -\dfrac{1}{2}x + 3, y \geq -\dfrac{3}{2}x + 5$

69. $|x| < 2, |y| < 2$ **71.** $x > 0, y > 0, x^2 + y^2 < 81$

73. $(-1.17, 1.84)$ **75.** $(150, 22.4)$

77. $w + h \leq 40$ **79.**

49.

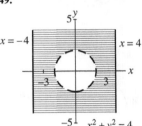

$x = -4$ $x = 4$

$x^2 + y^2 = 4$

51.

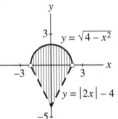

$y = \sqrt{4 - x^2}$

$y = |2x| - 4$

79.

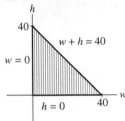

$x + 1.5y = 150$

$x + y = 110$

Number full-size / Number mid-size

77.

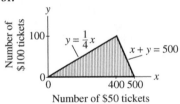

$w + h = 40$

$w = 0$

$h = 0$

81.

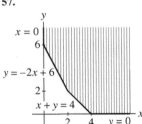

Number of $100 tickets

$y = \dfrac{1}{4}x$

$x + y = 500$

Number of $50 tickets

53.

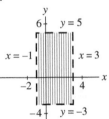

$y = 5$

$x = -1$ $x = 3$

$y = -3$

55.

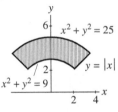

$x + y = 4$

$x = 0$

$y = 0$

83. $\dfrac{2}{x} + \dfrac{3}{x^2} + \dfrac{-1}{x + 1}$ **85.** $\varnothing$ **87.** \$23,824.92

Section 6

For Thought: **1.** F   **2.** F   **3.** F   **4.** F   **5.** T   **6.** T
7. F   **8.** T   **9.** F   **10.** T

Exercises:

1. constraints   **3.** natural

5. $(0, 0), (0, 4), (4, 0)$ **7.** $(0, 0), (0, 3), (1, 3), (1, 0)$

57.

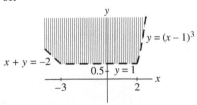

$x = 0$

$y = -2x + 6$

$x + y = 4$ $y = 0$

59.

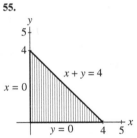

$x^2 + y^2 = 25$

$y = |x|$

$x^2 + y^2 = 9$

7.

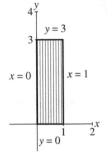

$x + y = 4$

$x = 0$ $x = 1$ $y = 3$ $y = 0$

61.

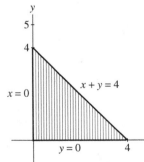

$y = (x - 1)^3$

$x + y = -2$ $y = 1$

9. $(0, 0), (0, 4), (2, 2), (3, 0)$

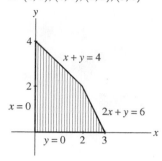

11. $(0, 4), (1, 2), (3, 0)$

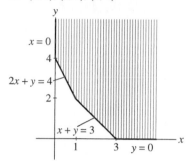

13. $(0, 6), (1, 3), (4, 0)$

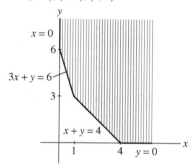

15. $(0, 8), (1, 5), (6, 0)$

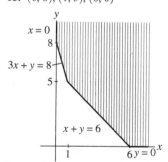

17. 15   **19.** 8   **21.** 30   **23.** 8   **25.** 100
27. 8 bird houses, 6 mailboxes   **29.** 16 bird houses, 0 mailboxes
31. 0 small, 8 large   **33.** 5 small, 3 large   **35.** $\varnothing$
37. $\{1/3, 2\}$ **39.** $(-\infty, 0) \cup (2, \infty)$

Chapter Review Exercises

1. $\{(3, 5)\}$ **3.** $\{(-1, 3)\}$ **5.** $\{(-19/2, -19/2)\}$, independent
7. $\{(39/17, 18/17)\}$, independent
9. $\{(x, y) | y = -3x + 1\}$, dependent   **11.** $\varnothing$, inconsistent
13. $\{(1, 3, -4)\}$ **15.** $\{(x, 0, 1 - x) | x$ is any real number$\}$

17. $\varnothing$ **19.** $\left\{ \left(\dfrac{-1 + \sqrt{17}}{2}, \pm\sqrt{\dfrac{-1 + \sqrt{17}}{2}} \right) \right\}$

21. $\{(0, 0), (1, 1), (-1, 1)\}$ **23.** $\dfrac{2}{x - 3} + \dfrac{5}{x + 4}$

25. $\dfrac{2x - 1}{x^2 + 4} + \dfrac{5}{x - 3}$

27.

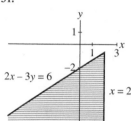

29.

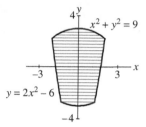

31.

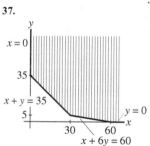

33.

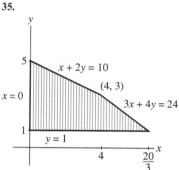

35.

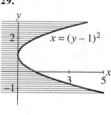

37.

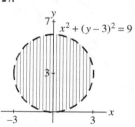

39. $y = -\dfrac{2}{3}x + \dfrac{5}{3}$ **41.** $y = 3x^2 - 4x + 5$
43. 57 tacos, 62 burritos   **45.** \$0.95   **47.** 16.8
49. 6 million barrels per day from each source

Chapter Test

1. $\{(-3, 4)\}$ **2.** $\{(25/11, -6/11)\}$ **3.** $\{(4, 6)\}$
4. Inconsistent   **5.** Dependent   **6.** Independent
7. Inconsistent   **8.** $\{(x, 10 - x, 14 - 3x) | x$ is any real number$\}$
9. $\{(1, -2, 3)\}$ **10.** $\varnothing$ **11.** $\{(4, 0), (-4, 0)\}$
12. $\{(2 + \sqrt{2}, -4 - \sqrt{2}), (2 - \sqrt{2}, -4 + \sqrt{2})\}$
13. $\dfrac{3}{x - 4} + \dfrac{-1}{x + 2}$ **14.** $\dfrac{2}{x^2} + \dfrac{1}{x} + \dfrac{3}{x - 1}$

15.

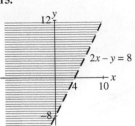

16.

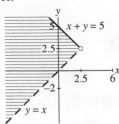

17.

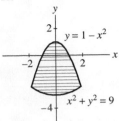

18. 24 males, 28 females
19. 5 television, 18 newspaper

Solutions to Try This Exercises

1.1 Graph $y = x - 3$ through $(0, -3)$ and $(1, -2)$. Graph $x + y = 7$ through $(0, 7)$ and $(7, 0)$.

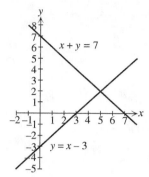

Check $(5, 2)$ in both equations to be sure that the solution set is $\{(5, 2)\}$.

1.2 Substitute $y = 2x - 3$ into $x + 2y = -1$:

$$x + 2(2x - 3) = -1$$
$$5x - 6 = -1$$
$$5x = 5$$
$$x = 1$$
$$y = 2(1) - 3 = -1$$

The solution set is $\{(1, -1)\}$.

1.3 Substitute $y = 3x - 5$ into $6x - 2y = 1$:
$$6x - 2(3x - 5) = 1$$
$$10 = 1$$
The system is inconsistent and has no solution.

1.4 Multiply $x + y = 3$ by 2 to get $2x + 2y = 6$, then add:

$$\begin{array}{r} 2x + 2y = 6 \\ 3x - 2y = 4 \\ \hline 5x \quad\quad = 10 \\ x = 2 \end{array}$$

If $x = 2$ and $x + y = 3$, then $2 + y = 3$ and $y = 1$. The solution set is $\{(2, 1)\}$.

1.5 Multiply $\frac{1}{2}x - \frac{1}{4}y = 1$ by 4 to get $2x - y = 4$. Multiply $2x - y = 3$ by -1, then add:

$$\begin{array}{r} 2x - y = 4 \\ -2x + y = -3 \\ \hline 0 = 1 \end{array}$$

The system is inconsistent and has no solution.

1.6 If d is the cost of a DVD and c is the cost of a CD, then $2d + 3c = 78$ and $d + 4c = 74$. Substitute $d = 74 - 4c$ into the first equation:

$$2(74 - 4c) + 3c = 78$$
$$148 - 8c + 3c = 78$$
$$-5c = -70$$
$$c = 14$$
$$d = 74 - 4(14) = 18$$

The cost of a DVD is \$18.

1.7 Let x be the amount invested in stocks and y be the amount invested in bonds. We have $x + y = 200,000$. Since his gains were equal to his losses, $0.24x = 0.08y$ or $3x = y$. Solve by substitution:

$$x + 3x = 200,000$$
$$4x = 200,000$$
$$x = 50,000$$
$$y = 150,000$$

He invested \$50,000 in stocks and \$150,000 in bonds.

2.1 The intercepts are $(0, 0, 6)$, $(0, 3, 0)$, and $(6, 0, 0)$.

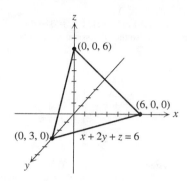

2.2 Eliminate y from the first and second and then the second and third equations:

$$\begin{array}{r} x + y + z = 9 \\ x - y + 2z = 1 \\ \hline 2x \quad\quad + 3z = 10 \end{array} \qquad \begin{array}{r} x - y + 2z = 1 \\ x + y - z = 5 \\ \hline 2x \quad\quad + z = 6 \end{array}$$

$$\begin{array}{r} 2x + 3z = 10 \\ -2x - z = -6 \\ \hline 2z = 4 \\ z = 2 \end{array}$$

If $z = 2$, then $2x + 2 = 6$ and $x = 2$. If $z = 2$ and $x = 2$, then $2 + y + 2 = 9$ and $y = 5$. The solution set is $\{(2, 5, 2)\}$.

2.3
$$x + y + z = 2$$
$$x - 2y - z = 4$$
$$2x - y \quad\quad = 6$$
$$y = 2x - 6$$
$$z = 2 - x - y$$
$$= 2 - x - (2x - 6)$$
$$= -3x + 8$$

The solution set is $\{(x, 2x - 6, -3x + 8) | x \text{ is any real number}\}$.

2.4
$$x + y + z = 1$$
$$x - y - z = 3$$
$$\overline{2x \quad\quad = 4}$$
$$x = 2$$

Replacing x with 2 in any of the three equations yields $y + z = -1$ or $z = -y - 1$. So the solution set is $\{(2, y, -y - 1) | y \text{ is any real number}\}$.

2.5
$$x + y + z = 1$$
$$x - y - z = 3$$
$$\overline{2x \quad\quad = 4}$$
$$x = 2$$

Replacing x with 2 in the first equation yields $y + z = -1$ and in the third equation $y + z = 1$. Substitution yields $-1 = 1$. So there is no solution to the system.

2.6 Using the form $y = ax^2 + bx + c$ and the three points yields the following system.

$$a - b + c = 1 \quad (1)$$
$$a + b + c = 3 \quad (2)$$
$$4a + 2b + c = 7 \quad (3)$$

Subtracting (1) from (2) yields $2b = 2$ or $b = 1$. Use $b = 1$ in (1) and (3) to get $a + c = 2$ and $4a + c = 5$. Subtracting yields $3a = 3$ or $a = 1$. If $a = 1$, then $c = 1$ and $y = x^2 + x + 1$.

2.7
$$2a + s + c = 14 \quad (1)$$
$$a + 2s + c = 12 \quad (2)$$
$$2a + 2s + 3c = 19 \quad (3)$$

Subtract twice (2) from (1) and (3) from (1):

$$\begin{array}{r} 2a + s + c = 14 \\ 2a + 4s + 2c = 24 \\ \hline -3s - c = -10 \end{array} \qquad \begin{array}{r} 2a + s + c = 14 \\ 2a + 2s + 3c = 19 \\ \hline -s - 2c = -5 \end{array}$$

Multiply $-3s - c = -10$ by -2 and add:

$$
\begin{aligned}
6s + 2c &= 20 \\
-s - 2c &= -5 \\
\hline
5s &= 15 \\
s &= 3
\end{aligned}
$$

If $s = 3$, then $6(3) + 2c = 20$ or $c = 1$. If $s = 3$ and $c = 1$, then $2a + 3 + 1 = 14$ or $a = 5$. So the admissions are adults \$5, students \$3, and children \$1.

3.1 Substitute $y = x^2 - 1$ into $x + y = 5$:

$$
\begin{aligned}
x + x^2 - 1 &= 5 \\
x^2 + x - 6 &= 0 \\
(x + 3)(x - 2) &= 0 \\
x = -3 \quad &\text{or} \quad x = 2 \\
y = 8 \quad\;\; &\text{or} \quad y = 3
\end{aligned}
$$

The solution set to the system is $\{(-3, 8), (2, 3)\}$.

3.2 Substitution yields $|2x| = -x^2 + 2x + 5$, which is equivalent to $2x = -x^2 + 2x + 5$ or $2x = -(-x^2 + 2x + 5)$. Solve each of these equations:

$$
\begin{aligned}
2x &= -x^2 + 2x + 5 \\
x^2 &= 5 \\
x &= \pm\sqrt{5}
\end{aligned}
$$

$$
\begin{aligned}
2x &= -(-x^2 + 2x + 5) \\
x^2 - 4x - 5 &= 0 \\
(x - 5)(x + 1) &= 0 \\
x = 5 \text{ or } x &= -1
\end{aligned}
$$

Only $\sqrt{5}$ and -1 yield points that satisfy both systems. So the solution set is $\{(-1, 2), (\sqrt{5}, 2\sqrt{5})\}$.

3.3 Multiplying the first equation by -4 and adding yields $5y^2 = 15$ or $y = \pm\sqrt{3}$. If $y = \pm\sqrt{3}$, then $x^2 + 3 = 5$ or $x = \pm\sqrt{2}$. There are four ordered pairs in the solution set: $(\sqrt{2}, \sqrt{3})$, $(\sqrt{2}, -\sqrt{3})$, $(-\sqrt{2}, \sqrt{3})$, and $(-\sqrt{2}, -\sqrt{3})$.

3.4 Adding the equations yields $\frac{2}{x} = 6$ or $x = 1/3$. If $x = 1/3$, then $3 + \frac{1}{y} = 2$ or $y = -1$. So the solutions set is $\{(1/3, -1)\}$.

3.5 Use substitution to eliminate y:

$$
\begin{aligned}
\log(x + 1) &= 1 + \log(x - 1) \\
\log(x + 1) - \log(x - 1) &= 1 \\
\log\left(\frac{x + 1}{x - 1}\right) &= 1 \\
\frac{x + 1}{x - 1} &= 10 \\
x + 1 &= 10x - 10 \\
-9x &= -11 \\
x &= 11/9 \\
y = \log(11/9 + 1) &= \log(20/9)
\end{aligned}
$$

The solution set is $\{(11/9, \log(20/9)\}$.

3.6 Let x be the length and y be the width. We have $x^2 + y^2 = 42^2$ and $\frac{x}{y} = \frac{16}{10}$ or $y = \frac{5}{8}x$. Solve by substitution:

$$
\begin{aligned}
x^2 + \left(\frac{5}{8}x\right)^2 &= 1764 \\
\frac{89}{64}x^2 &= 1764 \\
x &\approx 35.6 \\
y &\approx 22.3
\end{aligned}
$$

So the screen is 35.6 in by 22.3 in.

4.1 $\dfrac{4}{x - 2} + \dfrac{3}{x + 5}$

$$
\begin{aligned}
&= \frac{4(x + 5)}{(x - 2)(x + 5)} + \frac{3(x - 2)}{(x + 5)(x - 2)} \\
&= \frac{7x + 14}{(x + 5)(x - 2)}
\end{aligned}
$$

4.2 $\dfrac{2x - 3}{(x - 1)(x + 3)} = \dfrac{A}{x - 1} + \dfrac{B}{x + 3}$

Multiply each side by $(x - 1)(x + 3)$:

$$
\begin{aligned}
2x - 3 &= A(x + 3) + B(x - 1) \\
2x - 3 &= (A + B)x + 3A - B
\end{aligned}
$$

So $A + B = 2$ and $3A - B = -3$.

$$
\begin{aligned}
A + B &= 2 \\
3A - B &= -3 \\
\hline
4A &= -1 \\
A &= -1/4
\end{aligned}
$$

If $A = -1/4$, then $-1/4 + B = 2$ and $B = 9/4$.

$$
\frac{2x - 3}{(x - 1)(x + 3)} = \frac{-1/4}{x - 1} + \frac{9/4}{x + 3}
$$

4.3 $\dfrac{4x^2 + 4x - 4}{(x + 1)^2(x - 1)}$

$$
= \frac{A}{x + 1} + \frac{B}{(x + 1)^2} + \frac{C}{x - 1}
$$

Multiply each side by $(x + 1)^2(x - 1)$:

$$
\begin{aligned}
4x^2 &+ 4x - 4 \\
&= A(x^2 - 1) + B(x - 1) + C(x + 1)^2 \\
&= (A + C)x^2 + (B + 2C)x + (-A - B + C)
\end{aligned}
$$

$$
\begin{aligned}
A + C &= 4 \\
B + 2C &= 4 \\
-A - B + C &= -4
\end{aligned}
$$

Substitute $A = 4 - C$ and $B = 4 - 2C$ into the last equation:

$$
\begin{aligned}
-(4 - C) - (4 - 2C) + C &= -4 \\
4C &= 4 \\
C &= 1
\end{aligned}
$$

If $C = 1$, then $B = 2$ and $A = 3$ and

$$
\begin{aligned}
&\frac{4x^2 + 4x - 4}{(x + 1)^2(x - 1)} \\
&= \frac{3}{x + 1} + \frac{2}{(x + 1)^2} + \frac{1}{x - 1}.
\end{aligned}
$$

4.4 $\dfrac{5x^2 - 4x + 11}{(x^2 + 2)(x - 1)}$

$$
= \frac{Ax + B}{x^2 + 2} + \frac{C}{x - 1}
$$

Multiply each side by $(x^2 + 2)(x - 1)$:

$$
\begin{aligned}
5x^2 &- 4x + 11 \\
&= (Ax + B)(x - 1) + C(x^2 + 2) \\
&= (A + C)x^2 + (-A + B)x + (-B + 2C) \\
A + C &= 5 \quad (1) \\
-A + B &= -4 \quad (2) \\
-B + 2C &= 11 \quad (3)
\end{aligned}
$$

Adding (1) and (2) yields $B + C = 1$. Add this result and (3) to get $3C = 12$ or $C = 4$. If $C = 4$, then $A = 1$ and $B = -3$. So

$$
\frac{5x^2 - 4x + 11}{(x^2 + 2)(x - 1)} = \frac{x - 3}{x^2 + 2} + \frac{4}{x - 1}.
$$

4.5 $\dfrac{3x^3 + 3x^2 + x - 2}{(3x^2 - 1)^2}$

$$
= \frac{Ax + B}{3x^2 - 1} + \frac{Cx + D}{(3x^2 - 1)^2}
$$

Multiply each side by $(3x^2 - 1)^2$:

$$
\begin{aligned}
3x^3 &+ 3x^2 + x - 2 \\
&= (Ax + B)(3x^2 - 1) + Cx + D \\
&= 3Ax^3 + 3Bx^2 + (-A + C)x + (-B + D) \\
3A &= 3 \quad (1) \\
3B &= 3 \quad (2) \\
-A + C &= 1 \quad (3) \\
-B + D &= -2 \quad (4)
\end{aligned}
$$

Since $3A = 3$, we have $A = 1$ and $C = 2$. Since $3B = 3$, we have $B = 1$ and $D = -1$. So

$$\frac{3x^3 + 3x^2 + x - 2}{(3x^2 - 1)^2} = \frac{x + 1}{3x^2 - 1} + \frac{2x - 1}{(3x^2 - 1)^2}.$$

5.1 Graph the solid line $y = -2x + 4$ through $(0, 4)$ and $(2, 0)$. Shade below the line for $y \le -2x + 4$.

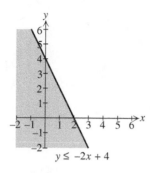

$$y \le -2x + 4$$

5.2 Graph the dashed line $2x - 5y = 20$ through $(0, -4)$ and $(10, 0)$. Since $(0, 0)$ satisfies $2x - 5y < 20$, shade the region containing $(0, 0)$.

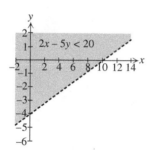

5.3 Draw the v-shaped graph of $y = |x|$. Then shade below for $y < |x|$.

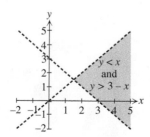

5.4 Graph dashed lines for $y = x$ and $y = 3 - x$. Test a point in each of the four regions. The only region that satisfies both inequalities is the region containing $(5, 0)$.

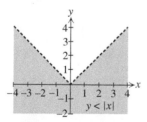

5.5 Draw a v-shaped graph through $(\pm 1, 0)$ and $(0, 1)$ for $y = 1 - |x|$. Draw a parabola through $(\pm 1, 0)$ and $(0, -1)$ for $y = x^2 - 1$. The inequality is satisfied only in the region containing $(0, 0)$.

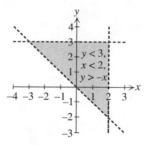

5.6 Graph the horizontal dashed line $y = 3$, the vertical dashed line $x = 2$, and the dashed line $y = -x$ through $(0, 0)$. The only region that satisfies all three inequalities is the region containing $(0, 2)$.

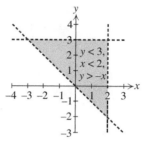

6.1 Graph $x + y = 6$ through $(0, 6)$ and $(6, 0)$. Graph $x + 2y = 8$ through $(0, 4)$ and $(8, 0)$. The region that satisfies all inequalities is below both of these lines and in the first quadrant. The vertices are $(0, 0)$, $(0, 4)$, $(4, 2)$, and $(6, 0)$.

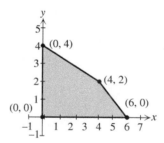

6.2 Let x be the number of X-components and y be the number of Y-components. The inequalities are
$x \ge 0, y \ge 0, 4x + 8y \le 40$, and $6x + 2y \le 30$, or
$x \ge 0, y \ge 0, x + 2y \le 10$, and $3x + y \le 15$.

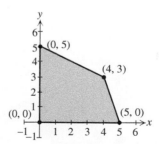

6.3 The revenue in dollars is given by $R(x, y) = 2x + 3y$. Find R at each vertex of the region graphed in the solution to 6.2. Since $R(0, 0) = 0$, $R(0, 5) = 15$, $R(4, 3) = 17$, and $R(5, 0) = 10$, the maximum revenue occurs when four X-components and three Y-components are assembled.

Systems of Equations and Inequalities

For Thought

1. True, since if $x = 2$ and $y = 3$ we get $2 + 3 = 5$.

2. False, since $(2, 3)$ does not satisfy $x - y = 1$.

3. False, it is independent since the two lines are perpendicular and intersect at only one point.

4. True. Multiply $x - 2y = 4$ by -3 and add to the second equation.

$$\begin{array}{rcr} -3x + 6y &=& -12 \\ 3x - 6y &=& 8 \\ \hline 0 &=& -4 \end{array}$$

Since $0 = -4$ is false, there is no solution.

5. True, adding gives $2x = 6$. **6.** True

7. False, it is dependent because substituting $x = 5 + 3y$ results in an identity.

$$\begin{array}{rcl} 9y - 3(5 + 3y) &=& -15 \\ 9y - 15 - 9y &=& -15 \\ -15 &=& -15 \end{array}$$

8. False, it is dependent and the solution set is $\{(5 + 3y, y) | y \text{ is any real number}\}$.

9. False, it is dependent, there are an infinite number of solutions.

10. True, since both lines have slope $1/2$.

1 Exercises

1. system

3. inconsistent

5. dependent

7. Note, $x = 1$ and $y = 3$ satisfies both $x + y = 4$ and $x - y = -2$. Yes, $(1, 2)$ is a solution.

9. Note, $x = -1$ and $y = 5$ does not satisfy $x - 2y = -9$. Thus, $(-1, 5)$ is not a solution.

11. $\{(1, 2)\}$

13. No solution since the lines are parallel. The solution set is $\emptyset$.

15. $\{(3, 2)\}$

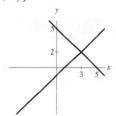

17. $\{(3, 1)\}$

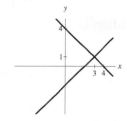

19. No solution since the lines are parallel. The solution set is $\emptyset$.

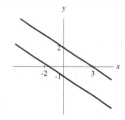

21. Since the lines are identical, the solution set is $\{(x, y) \,|\, x - 2y = 6\}$.

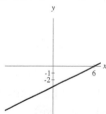

23. Substitute $y = 2x + 1$ into $3x - 4y = 1$.

$$\begin{array}{rcl} 3x - 4(2x + 1) &=& 1 \\ 3x - 8x - 4 &=& 1 \\ -5x &=& 5 \\ x &=& -1 \end{array}$$

From $y = 2x + 1$, $y = 2(-1) + 1 = -1$. Independent and solution set is $\{(-1, -1)\}$.

From Chapter 8 of *Student's Solutions Manual for Precalculus: Functions and Graphs*, Fourth Edition. Mark Dugopolski.

25. Substitute $y = 1 - x$ into $2x - 3y = 8$.

$$\begin{aligned} 2x - 3(1 - x) &= 8 \\ 2x - 3 + 3x &= 8 \\ 5x &= 11 \\ x &= 11/5 \end{aligned}$$

From $y = 1 - x$, $y = 1 - 11/5 = -6/5$.
Independent and solution set is
$\{(11/5, -6/5)\}$.

27. Substitute $y = 3x + 5$ into $3(x + 1) = y - 2$.

$$\begin{aligned} 3x + 3 &= (3x + 5) - 2 \\ 3x + 3 &= 3x + 3 \\ 3 &= 3 \end{aligned}$$

Dependent and solution set is
$\{(x, y) \mid y = 3x + 5\}$.

29. Multiplying $\frac{1}{2}x + \frac{1}{3}y = 3$ by 6, we get $3x + 2y = 18$. Then substitute $2y = 6 - 3x$ into $3x + 2y = 18$. So

$$\begin{aligned} 3x + (6 - 3x) &= 18 \\ 6 &= 18 \end{aligned}$$

Inconsistent and the solution set is $\emptyset$.

31. Multiplying $0.05x + 0.06y = 10.50$ by 100, we obtain $5x + 6y = 1050$. Then substitute $y = 200 - x$ into $5x + 6y = 1050$.

$$\begin{aligned} 5x + 6(200 - x) &= 1050 \\ 5x + 1200 - 6x &= 1050 \\ -x &= -150 \\ x &= 150 \end{aligned}$$

From $y = 200 - x$, $y = 200 - 150 = 50$.
Independent and solution set is $\{(150, 50)\}$.

33. Since $3x + 1 = 3x - 7$ leads to $1 = -7$, the system is inconsistent and the solution set is $\emptyset$.

35. Multiplying the first and second equations by 6 and 4, respectively, we have

—

$3x - 2y = 72$ and $x - 2y = 4$.
Substitute $2y = x - 4$ into $3x - 2y = 72$.

$$\begin{aligned} 3x - (x - 4) &= 72 \\ 2x + 4 &= 72 \\ 2x &= 68 \\ x &= 34 \end{aligned}$$

From $2y = x - 4$, $y = \dfrac{34 - 4}{2} = 15$.
Independent and solution set is $\{(34, 15)\}$.

37. Adding the two equations, we get $2x = 26$.
So $x = 13$ and from $x + y = 20$,
we obtain $13 + y = 20$ or $y = 7$.
Independent and solution set is $\{(13, 7)\}$.

39. Multiplying $x - y = 5$ by 2 and by adding to the second equation, we obtain

$$\begin{aligned} 2x - 2y &= 10 \\ 3x + 2y &= 10 \\ \hline 5x &= 20 \\ x &= 4 \end{aligned}$$

From $x - y = 5$, $4 - y = 5$ or $y = -1$.
Independent and solution set is $\{(4, -1)\}$.

41. Adding the two equations leads to $0 = 12$.
Inconsistent and the solution set is $\emptyset$.

43. Multiply $2x + 3y = 1$ by -3 and $3x - 5y = -8$ by 2. Then add the equations.

$$\begin{aligned} -6x - 9y &= -3 \\ 6x - 10y &= -16 \\ \hline -19y &= -19 \\ y &= 1 \end{aligned}$$

Since $2x + 3y = 1$, $2x + 3 = 1$ or $x = -1$.
Independent and solution set is $\{(-1, 1)\}$.

45. Multiply $0.05x + 0.1y = 0.6$ by -100 and $x + 2y = 12$ by 5. Then add the equations.

$$\begin{aligned} -5x - 10y &= -60 \\ 5x + 10y &= 60 \\ \hline 0 &= 0 \end{aligned}$$

Dependent and the solution set is
$\{(x, y) \mid x + 2y = 12\}$.

47. Multiplying $\dfrac{x}{2} + \dfrac{y}{2} = 5$ by 2 and

$\dfrac{3x}{2} - \dfrac{2y}{3} = 2$ by 6, we have $x + y = 10$

and $9x - 4y = 12$, respectively. Then multiply $x + y = 10$ by 4 and add to the second equation.

$$
\begin{array}{rcl}
4x + 4y &=& 40 \\
9x - 4y &=& 12 \\
\hline
13x &=& 52 \\
x &=& 4
\end{array}
$$

Since $x + y = 10$, $4 + y = 10$ and $y = 6$. Independent and the solution set is $\{(4, 6)\}$.

49. Multiply $3x - 2.5y = -4.2$ by -4 and $0.12x + 0.09y = 0.4932$ by 100. Then add the equations.

$$
\begin{array}{rcl}
-12x + 10y &=& 16.8 \\
12x + 9y &=& 49.32 \\
\hline
19y &=& 66.12 \\
y &=& 3.48
\end{array}
$$

From $3x - 2.5y = -4.2$, we find

$$
\begin{array}{rcl}
3x - 2.5(3.48) &=& -4.2 \\
3x - 8.7 &=& -4.2 \\
3x &=& 4.5 \\
x &=& 1.5.
\end{array}
$$

Independent and the solution set is $\{(1.5, 3.48)\}$.

51. Independent

53. Dependent

55. The point of intersection is $(-1000, -497)$.

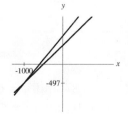

57. The point of intersection is approximately $(6.18, -0.54)$

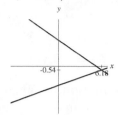

59. Let x and y be Althea's and Vaughn's incomes, respectively. Then $x + y = 82{,}000$ and $x - y = 16{,}000$. By adding these two equations, we get $2x = 98{,}000$ or $x = 49{,}000$. Thus, Althea's income is \$49,000 and Vaughn's income is \$33,000.

61. Let x and y be the amounts invested at 10% and 8%, respectively.

$$
\begin{array}{rcl}
x + y &=& 25{,}000 \\
0.1x + 0.08y &=& 2200
\end{array}
$$

Multiply the second equation by -10 and add to the first.

$$
\begin{array}{rcl}
x + y &=& 25{,}000 \\
-x - 0.8y &=& -22{,}000 \\
\hline
0.2y &=& 3000 \\
y &=& 15{,}000
\end{array}
$$

Carmen invested \$15,000 at 8% and \$10,000 at 10%.

63. Let x and y be the prices of an adult ticket and child ticket, respectively.

$$
\begin{array}{rcl}
2x + 5y &=& 33 \\
x + 3y &=& 18.50
\end{array}
$$

Multiply the second equation by -2 and add to the first equation.

$$
\begin{array}{rcl}
2x + 5y &=& 33 \\
-2x - 6y &=& -37 \\
\hline
-y &=& -4 \\
y &=& 4
\end{array}
$$

A child's ticket costs \$4. Since $x + 3y = 18.50$, $x + 12 = 18.50$ and so an adult's ticket costs $x = \$6.50$.

65. If m and f are the number of male and female memberships, respectively, then a system of equations is

$$m + f = 12$$
$$500m + 500f = 6,000.$$

Dividing the second equation by 500,one finds $m + f = 12$; the system of equations is dependent. Therefore, one cannot conclude the number of female memberships and male memberships.

All we know is that m and $12-m$ are the number of male and female memberships where $0 \leq m \leq 12$.

67. Let x and y be the number of cows and ostriches, respectively.

$$2x + 2y = 84$$
$$4x + 2y = 122$$

Subtract the first equation from the second equation.

$$2x = 38$$
$$x = 19$$

Consequently, we have

$$2x + 2y = 84$$
$$38 + 2y = 84$$
$$2y = 46$$
$$y = 23$$

Hence, there are $x = 19$ cows and $y = 23$ ostriches.

69. Let x and y be the number of cows and horses, respectively.

$$4x + 4y = 96$$
$$x + y = 24$$

Divide the first equation by 4.

$$x + y = 24$$
$$x + y = 24$$

Since the two equations are identical, the system of equations is dependent and there are infinitely many possible solutions.

71. If c and m are the prices of a coffee and a muffin, respectively, then a system of equations is

$$3c + 7m = 7.77$$
$$6c + 14m = 14.80.$$

But if one multiplies the second equation by two, then one obtains $6c + 14m = 15.54$; this last equation contradicts the second equation in the system. Therefore, the system of equations is inconsistent and has no solution.

73. Let x and y be the number of male and female students, respectively.

$$0.5x + 0.3y = 230$$
$$0.2x + 0.6y = 260$$

Multiply the first equation by -2 and the second by 5. Then add the resulting equations.

$$-x - 0.6y = -460$$
$$x + 3y = 1300$$
$$2.4y = 840$$
$$y = 350$$

From $0.2x + 0.6y = 260$, $0.2x + 210 = 260$ and so $x = 250$. There are $250 + 350 = 600$ students at CHS.

75. Let x and y be the number of nickels and pennies, respectively. We obtain

$$x + y = 87$$
$$0.05x + 0.01y = 1.75.$$

Multiply the second equation by -100 and then add it to the first equation.

$$x + y = 87$$
$$-5x - y = -175$$
$$-4x = -88$$
$$x = 22$$

From $x + y = 87$, $22 + y = 87$ and $y = 65$. Isabelle has 22 nickels and 65 pennies.

77. The weights x and y must satisfy

$$5x = 3y$$
$$3(4 + x + y) = 6y.$$

The second equation can be written as $12 + 3x = 3y$. Substituting into the first equation one finds

$$
\begin{aligned}
12 + 3x &= 5x \\
12 &= 2x \\
6 &= x.
\end{aligned}
$$

Then $x = 6$ oz and $y = 10$ oz since

$$y = \frac{5x}{3} = \frac{5(6)}{3}.$$

79. Let x be the number of months. Plan A costs $150x + 800$ and Plan B costs $200x + 200$. Thus, Plan A is cheaper in the long run. The number of months for which the costs are the same is given by

$$
\begin{aligned}
150x + 800 &= 200x + 200 \\
600 &= 50x \\
x &= 12 \text{ months.}
\end{aligned}
$$

81. If we set the formulas equal to each other, then we find

$$
\begin{aligned}
0.08aD &= \frac{D(a+1)}{24} \\
0.08a &= \frac{(a+1)}{24} \\
1.92a &= a + 1 \\
a &= \frac{1}{0.92} \\
a &\approx 1.09.
\end{aligned}
$$

The dosage is the same if the age is 1.1 yr.

83. Suppose the fronts of the trucks are at the same points. Let t be the number of hours before the trucks pass each other. They will be passing each other when the ends of the trucks are at the same position, i.e., when the total distance driven by the trucks is 100 feet.

$$
\begin{aligned}
40(5280)t + 50(5280)t &= 100 \\
40t + 50t &= \frac{100}{5280} \\
90t &= \frac{100}{5280}
\end{aligned}
$$

$$
\begin{aligned}
t &= \frac{100}{(90)5280} \text{ hour} \\
t &= \frac{100}{(90)5280(3600)} \text{ sec} \\
t &= \frac{25}{33} \text{ sec} \\
t &\approx 0.76 \text{ sec}
\end{aligned}
$$

Hence, the trucks pass each other in 0.76 sec, approximately.

85. Solve for a and b.

$$
\begin{aligned}
-3a + b &= 9 \\
2a + b &= -1.
\end{aligned}
$$

Multiply the second equation by -1 and add to the first equation.

$$
\begin{aligned}
-3a + b &= 9 \\
-2a - b &= 1 \\
\hline
-5a &= 10 \\
a &= -2
\end{aligned}
$$

Substituting $a = -2$ into $2a + b = -1$, one finds $b = 3$. An equation of the line is $y = -2x + 3$.

87. Solve for a and b.

$$
\begin{aligned}
-2a + b &= 3 \\
4a + b &= -7
\end{aligned}
$$

Multiply the first equation by -1 and add to the second equation.

$$
\begin{aligned}
2a - b &= -3 \\
4a + b &= -7 \\
\hline
6a &= -10 \\
a &= -\frac{5}{3}
\end{aligned}
$$

Substituting $a = -\frac{5}{3}$ into $-2a + b = 3$, one gets $b = -\frac{1}{3}$. An equation of the line is

$$y = -\frac{5}{3}x - \frac{1}{3}.$$

91. Independent system with solution $(2, -3)$:

$$\begin{aligned} x + y &= -1 \\ x - y &= 5 \end{aligned}$$

93. a) $f\left(\frac{2}{3}\right) = \left(8^{1/3}\right)^2 = 2^2 = 4$

b) $g(3) = 4^{2-3} = 4^{-1} = \dfrac{1}{4}$

c) $(f \circ g)(2) = f(g(2)) = f(1) = 8$

95. Since $2^3 = 8$ and $2^2 = 4$, we find

$$\begin{aligned} \left(2^3\right)^{x-3} &= \left(2^2\right)^{x+5} \\ 2^{3x-9} &= 2^{2x+10} \\ 3x - 9 &= 2x + 10 \\ x &= 19 \end{aligned}$$

The solution set is $\{19\}$.

97. The zeros of

$$f(x) = (3x - 2)(5x - 6).$$

are $x = 2/3, 6/5$.

If $x = 0$, then $f(0) > 0$.
If $x = 1$, then $f(1) < 0$.
If $x = 2$, then $f(2) > 0$.

$$\begin{array}{ccccccccc} & + & & 0 & & - & & 0 & & + \\ \hline & & & & & & & & & \\ & 0 & & \frac{2}{3} & & 1 & & \frac{6}{5} & & 2 \end{array}$$

The solution set of $f(x) \le 0$ is $\left[\frac{2}{3}, \frac{6}{5}\right]$.

For Thought

1. True

2. False, since $(1, 1, 0)$ does not satisfy
$-x - y + z = 4$.

3. True, adding the first two equations gives
$0 = 6$ which is false.

4. False, since $(2, 3, -1)$ does not satisfy
$x - y - z = 8$.

5. True

6. True, adding the first two equations gives
an identity. Also, multiplying the first
by -2 and then adding to the third
equation gives an identity.

$$\begin{aligned} x - y + z &= 1 \\ -x + y - z &= -1 \\ \hline 0 &= 0 \end{aligned}$$

$$\begin{aligned} -2x + 2y - 2z &= -2 \\ 2x - 2y + 2z &= 2 \\ \hline 0 &= 0 \end{aligned}$$

7. True. The calculations in Exercise 6 above
show system (c) is dependent.

8. True

9. True, if $x = 1$ then $(x + 2, x, x - 1) = (3, 1, 0)$.

10. False, the value is $0.05x + 0.10y + 0.25z$ dollars.

2 Exercises

1. linear

3. Points on the plane are $(5, 0, 0)$, $(0, 5, 0)$, and
$(0, 0, 5)$.

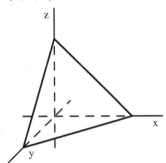

5. Points on the plane are $(3, 0, 0)$, $(0, 3, 0)$,
and $(0, 0, -3)$.

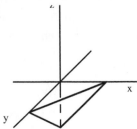

7. Note, $x = 1$, $y = 3$, and $z = 2$ satisfy all the three equations in the system . Yes, $(1, 3, 2)$ is a solution.

9. Note, $x = -1$, $y = 5$, and $z = 2$ does not satisfy $x - y - 2z = -8$. No, $(-1, 5, 2)$ is not a solution.

11. Add the first and second equations and add the first and third equations.

$$
\begin{array}{rcr}
x + y + z &=& 6 \\
2x - 2y - z &=& -5 \\
\hline
3x - y &=& 1
\end{array}
$$

$$
\begin{array}{rcr}
x + y + z &=& 6 \\
3x + y - z &=& 2 \\
\hline
4x + 2y &=& 8
\end{array}
$$

Divide $4x + 2y = 8$ by 2 and add to $3x - y = 1$.

$$
\begin{array}{rcr}
2x + y &=& 4 \\
3x - y &=& 1 \\
\hline
5x &=& 5
\end{array}
$$

So $x = 1$. From $3x - y = 1$, $3 - y = 1$ and $y = 2$. From $x + y + z = 6$, $1 + 2 + z = 6$ and $z = 3$. The solution set is $\{(1, 2, 3)\}$.

13. Multiply the first equation by 2 and add to the second. Then multiply the first equation by -3 and add to the third equation.

$$
\begin{array}{rcr}
6x + 4y + 2z &=& 2 \\
x + y - 2z &=& -4 \\
\hline
7x + 5y &=& -2
\end{array}
$$

$$
\begin{array}{rcr}
-9x - 6y - 3z &=& -3 \\
2x - 3y + 3z &=& 1 \\
\hline
-7x - 9y &=& -2
\end{array}
$$

Add $7x + 5y = -2$ to $-7x - 9y = -2$.

$$
\begin{array}{rcr}
7x + 5y &=& -2 \\
-7x - 9y &=& -2 \\
\hline
-4y &=& -4
\end{array}
$$

So $y = 1$. From $7x + 5y = -2$, $7x + 5 = -2$ and $x = -1$. From $3x + 2y + z = 1$, $-3 + 2 + z = 1$ and $z = 2$. The solution set is $\{(-1, 1, 2)\}$.

15. Add first equation to third equation. Multiply second equation by 2 and add to the first.

$$
\begin{array}{rcr}
2x + y - 2z &=& -15 \\
x + 3y + 2z &=& -5 \\
\hline
3x + 4y &=& -20
\end{array}
$$

$$
\begin{array}{rcr}
8x - 4y + 2z &=& 30 \\
2x + y - 2z &=& -15 \\
\hline
10x - 3y &=& 15
\end{array}
$$

Multiply $3x + 4y = -20$ by 3 and $10x - 3y = 15$ by 4 and then add the equations.

$$
\begin{array}{rcr}
9x + 12y &=& -60 \\
40x - 12y &=& 60 \\
\hline
49x &=& 0
\end{array}
$$

So $x = 0$. From $3x + 4y = -20$, $4y = -20$ and $y = -5$. From $2x + y - 2z = -15$, we get $-5 - 2z = -15$ and $z = 5$. The solution set is $\{(0, -5, 5)\}$.

17. If we substitute $x = 1, 2, 3$ in $(x, x + 3, x - 5)$, we obtain

$$(1, 4, -4), \ (2, 5, -3), \ \text{and} \ (3, 6, -2),$$

respectively.

19. If we substitute $y = 1, 2, 3$ in $(2y, y, y - 7)$, we obtain

$$(2, 1, -6), \ (4, 2, -5), \ \text{and} \ (6, 3, -4),$$

respectively.

21. Let $y = x + 3$. Then $x = y - 3$, $x - 5 = y - 8$, and

$$(x, x + 3, x - 5) = (y - 3, y, y - 8).$$

23. Let $z = x - 1$. Then $x = z + 1$, $x + 1 = z + 2$, and

$$(x, x + 1, x - 1) = (z + 1, z + 2, z).$$

25. Let $y = 2x + 1$. Then $x = (y - 1)/2$, $3x - 1 = (3y - 5)/2$, and

$$(x, 2x + 1, 3x - 1) = \left(\frac{y - 1}{2}, y, \frac{3y - 5}{2}\right).$$

27. Adding the two equations, we have
$4x - 4z = -20$ or $z = x + 5$.
From $x + 2y - 3z = -17$, we obtain

$$
\begin{aligned}
x + 2y - 3(x + 5) &= -17 \\
2y - 2x - 15 &= -17 \\
2y &= 2x - 2 \\
y &= x - 1.
\end{aligned}
$$

The solution set is
$\{(x, x - 1, x + 5) | x \text{ is any real number}\}$.

29. Adding the two equations, we obtain
$2x - y = 7$ or $y = 2x - 7$.
From $x + y - z = 2$, we obtain

$$
\begin{aligned}
z &= x + y - 2 \\
z &= x + (2x - 7) - 2 \\
z &= 3x - 9.
\end{aligned}
$$

The solution set is
$\{(x, 2x - 7, 3x - 9) | x \text{ is any real number}\}$.

31. Adding the two equations, we find
$2x + 2z = 12$ or $x = 6 - z$.
From $y + z = 5$, we obtain

$$
y = 5 - z.
$$

The solution set is
$\{(6 - z, 5 - z, z) | z \text{ is any real number}\}$.

33. Adding the first two equations, we have
$0 = 0$, which is an identity. Multiply the
second equation by 2 and add to the
third equation.

$$
\begin{array}{rcr}
-2x - 4y + 6z &=& -10 \\
2x + 4y - 6z &=& 10 \\
\hline
0 &=& 0
\end{array}
$$

The system is dependent and the solution
set is $\{(x, y, z) | x + 2y - 3z = 5\}$.

35. Multiply first equation by -2 and add
to the second equation.

$$
\begin{array}{rcr}
-2x + 4y - 6z &=& -10 \\
2x - 4y + 6z &=& 3 \\
\hline
0 &=& -7
\end{array}
$$

This is false, so the solution set is $\emptyset$.

37. Adding the two equations, we get $3x = 6$ or
$x = 2$. Substitute into the two equations.
Then

$$
\begin{aligned}
2 + y - z &= 2 \\
y - z &= 0
\end{aligned}
$$

and

$$
\begin{aligned}
4 - y + z &= 4 \\
-y + z &= 0.
\end{aligned}
$$

In any case $y = z$. The solution set is
$\{(2, y, y) | y \text{ is any real number}\}$.

39. If the second equation is multiplied by -1 and
added to the first equation, the result is the
third equation.

$$
\begin{array}{rcr}
x + y &=& 5 \\
-y + z &=& -2 \\
\hline
x + z &=& 3
\end{array}
$$

There ae infinitely number many solutions.
Since $y = 5 - x$ and $z = 3 - x$, the solution set
$\{(x, 5 - x, 3 - x) | x \text{ is any real number}\}$.

41. Multiply the first equation by 2 and add
to the second equation.

$$
\begin{array}{rcr}
2x - 2y + 2z &=& 14 \\
2y - 3z &=& -13 \\
\hline
2x - z &=& 1
\end{array}
$$

Multiply $2x - z = 1$ by -2 and add
to the third equation.

$$
\begin{array}{rcr}
-4x + 2z &=& -2 \\
3x - 2z &=& -3 \\
\hline
-x &=& -5
\end{array}
$$

So $x = 5$. From $2x - z = 1$, we get $10 - z = 1$
and $z = 9$. Since $2y - 3z = -13$, $2y - 27 = -13$
and $y = 7$. The solution set is $\{(5, 7, 9)\}$.

43. Multiply first equation by -2 and add to third
equation. Then multiply first equation by -4
and add to the second.

$$
\begin{array}{rcr}
-2x - 2y - 4z &=& -15 \\
5x + 2y + 5z &=& 21 \\
\hline
3x + z &=& 6
\end{array}
$$

$$-4x - 4y - 8z = -30$$
$$3x + 4y + z = 12$$
$$-x - 7z = -18$$

Multiply $-x - 7z = -18$ by 3 and add to $3x + z = 6$.

$$-3x - 21z = -54$$
$$3x + z = 6$$
$$-20z = -48$$

So $z = 48/20 = 2.4$. From $3x + z = 6$, we get $3x + 2.4 = 6$ and $x = 1.2$. From $x + y + 2z = 7.5$, $1.2 + y + 4.8 = 7.5$ and $y = 1.5$. The solution set is $\{(1.2, 1.5, 2.4)\}$.

45. Multiply the first equation by -5 and add to 100 times the second one.

$$-5x - 5y - 5z = -45,000$$
$$5x + 6y + 9z = 71,000$$
$$y + 4z = 26,000$$

Substitute $z = 3y$ into $y + 4z = 26,000$.

$$y + 12y = 26,000$$
$$13y = 26,000$$
$$y = 2,000$$

From $z = 3y$, we obtain $z = 6000$. From $x + y + z = 9,000$, we have $x + 2000 + 6000 = 9000$ and $x = 1000$. The solution set is $\{(1000, 2000, 6000)\}$.

47. Substitute $x = 2y - 1$ into $z = 2x - 3$ to get $z = 4y - 5$. Then substitute $z = 4y - 5$ into $y = 3z + 2$.

$$y = 3(4y - 5) + 2$$
$$y = 12y - 13$$
$$-11y = -13$$
$$y = 13/11$$

From $z = 4y - 5$, we obtain $z = 52/11 - 5 = -3/11$. Since $x = 2y - 1$, $x = 26/11 - 1 = 15/11$. The solution set is $\{(15/11, 13/11, -3/11)\}$.

49. Substitute $(-1, -2)$, $(2, 1)$, $(-2, 1)$ into $y = ax^2 + bx + c$. So

$$a - b + c = -2$$
$$4a + 2b + c = 1$$
$$4a - 2b + c = 1.$$

Multiply first equation by -1 and add to the second and third equations.

$$-a + b - c = 2$$
$$4a + 2b + c = 1$$
$$3a + 3b = 3$$

$$-a + b - c = 2$$
$$4a - 2b + c = 1$$
$$3a - b = 3$$

Multiply $3a + 3b = 3$ by -1 and add to $3a - b = 3$.

$$-3a - 3b = -3$$
$$3a - b = 3$$
$$-4b = 0$$

So $b = 0$. From $3a - b = 3$, we get $3a = 3$ and $a = 1$. From $a - b + c = -2$, $1 + c = -2$ and $c = -3$. Since the solution is $(a, b, c) = (1, 0, -3)$, the parabola is $y = x^2 - 3$.

51. Substitute $(0, 0)$, $(1, 3)$, $(2, 2)$ into $y = ax^2 + bx + c$. Then

$$c = 0$$
$$a + b + c = 3$$
$$4a + 2b + c = 2.$$

Multiply second one by -2 and add to third equation.

$$-2a - 2b - 2c = -6$$
$$4a + 2b + c = 2$$
$$2a - c = -4$$

Substituting $c = 0$ into $2a - c = -4$, we get $2a = -4$ and $a = -2$. From $a + b + c = 3$, $-2 + b = 3$ and $b = 5$. Since $(a, b, c) = (-2, 5, 0)$, the parabola is $y = -2x^2 + 5x$.

53. Substitute $(0,4)$, $(-2,0)$, $(-3,1)$ into $y = ax^2 + bx + c$. Then

$$
\begin{aligned}
c &= 4 \\
4a - 2b + c &= 0 \\
9a - 3b + c &= 1.
\end{aligned}
$$

Multiply second and third equations by 3 and -2, respectively, then add the equations.

$$
\begin{aligned}
12a - 6b + 3c &= 0 \\
-18a + 6b - 2c &= -2 \\
\hline
-6a + c &= -2
\end{aligned}
$$

Substituting $c = 4$ into $-6a + c = -2$, $-6a + 4 = -2$ and $a = 1$. From $4a - 2b + c = 0$, $4 - 2b + 4 = 0$ and $b = 4$. Since $(a, b, c) = (1, 4, 4)$, the parabola is $y = x^2 + 4x + 4$.

55. By substituting the coordinates of the points $(1,0,0)$, $(0,1,0)$, and $(0,0,1)$ into $ax + by + cz = 1$, we get $a = 1$, $b = 1$, and $c = 1$. A linear equation satisfied by the ordered triples is $x + y + z = 1$.

57. By substituting the coordinates of the points $(1,1,1)$, $(0,2,0)$, and $(1,0,0)$ into $ax + by + cz = 1$, we get $a + b + c = 1$, $2b = 1$, and $a = 1$. Then $b = \frac{1}{2}$ and $c = -\frac{1}{2}$. A linear equation satisfied by the ordered triples is $x + \frac{1}{2}y - \frac{1}{2}z = 1$ or $2x + y - z = 2$

59. Let x, y, z be the three numbers listed in increasing order.

$$
\begin{aligned}
x + y + z &= 40 \\
-x \quad + z &= 12 \\
x + y - z &= 0.
\end{aligned}
$$

If we add the first two equations and add the last two equations, we obtain (by subtracting the 2nd sum from the 1st sum)

$$
\begin{aligned}
y + 2z &= 52 \\
y &= 12 \\
\hline
2z &= 40
\end{aligned}
$$

Then $z = 20$. Since $-x + z = 12$, we find $-x + 20 = 12$ or $x = 8$. Thus, the numbers are $8, 12$, and 20.

61. Let x, y, z be the scores in the 1st, 2nd, and 3rd quizzes, respectively.

$$
\begin{aligned}
x + y + z &= 21 \\
x - y &= -1 \\
y - z &= -4.
\end{aligned}
$$

If we add the first two equations and add the last two equations, we obtain

$$
\begin{aligned}
2x + z &= 20 \\
x - z &= -5 \\
\hline
3x &= 15
\end{aligned}
$$

Since $x = 5$, the scores on the quizzes are 5, 6, and 10.

63. Let x, y, and z be the amounts invested in stocks, bonds, and a mutual fund. Then

$$
\begin{aligned}
x + y + z &= 25,000 \\
0.08x + 0.10y + 0.06z &= 1,860 \\
2y &= z.
\end{aligned}
$$

Multiply the first equation by -8 and add to 100 times the second.

$$
\begin{aligned}
-8x - 8y - 8z &= -200,000 \\
8x + 10y + 6z &= 186,000 \\
\hline
2y - 2z &= -14,000
\end{aligned}
$$

Substitute $z = 2y$ into $2y - 2z = -14,000$.

$$
\begin{aligned}
2y - 4y &= -14,000 \\
-2y &= -14,000 \\
y &= 7,000
\end{aligned}
$$

Since $z = 2y$, we obtain $z = 14,000$. Since $x + y + z = 25,000$, $x = 4000$. Marita invested $\$4,000$ in stocks, $\$7000$ in bonds, and $\$14,000$ in a mutual fund.

65. Let x, y, and z be the prices last year of a hamburger, fries, and a Coke, respectively. So

$$
\begin{aligned}
x + y + z &= 3.80 \\
1.1x + 1.2y + 1.25z &= 4.49 \\
1.25z &= 1.1x - 0.07.
\end{aligned}
$$

Multiply first equation by -12 and add to 10 times the second equation.

$$\begin{array}{rcl} -12x - 12y - 12z & = & -45.6 \\ 11x + 12y + 12.5z & = & 44.9 \\ \hline -x + 0.5z & = & -0.7 \end{array}$$

Substitute $x = 0.5z + 0.7$ into $1.25z = 1.1x - 0.07$.

$$\begin{array}{rcl} 1.25z & = & 1.1(0.5z + 0.7) - 0.07 \\ 0.7z & = & 0.7 \\ z & = & 1 \end{array}$$

Since $x = 0.5z + 0.7$, we find $x = 0.5(1) + 0.7 = 1.20$. From $x + y + z = 3.80$, we have $y = 1.60$. The prices last year of a hamburger, fries and Coke are \$1.20, \$1.60, and \$1, respectively.

67. Let L_f and L_r be the weights on the left front tire and left rear tire, respectively. Let R_f and R_r be the weights on the right front tire and right rear tire, respectively. Since $1200(0.51) = 612$ and $1200(0.48) = 576$, we obtain

$$\begin{array}{rcl} L_f + L_r & = & 612 \\ R_r + L_r & = & 576 \\ L_f, L_r, R_f, R_r & \geq & 280. \end{array}$$

Three possible weight distributions are $(L_r, L_f, R_r, R_f) = (280, 332, 296, 292)$, $(L_r, L_f, R_r, R_f) = (285, 327, 291, 297)$, and $(L_r, L_f, R_r, R_f) = (290, 322, 286, 302)$.

69. Let x, y, and z be the number of pennies, nickels, and dimes, respectively. Then

$$\begin{array}{rcl} x + y + z & = & 232 \\ y + z & = & x \\ 0.01x + 0.05y + 0.10z & = & 10.36. \end{array}$$

Multiply first equation by -1 and add to 10 times the third equation. Also combine first two equations.

$$\begin{array}{rcl} -x - y - z & = & -232 \\ 0.1x + 0.5y + z & = & 103.6 \\ \hline -0.9x - 0.5y & = & -128.4 \end{array}$$

$$\begin{array}{rcl} -x - y - z & = & -232 \\ -x + y + z & = & 0 \\ \hline -2x & = & -232 \end{array}$$

Then $x = 116$. Substituting into $-0.9x - 0.5y = -128.4$, we obtain

$$\begin{array}{rcl} -0.9(116) - 0.5y & = & -128.4 \\ -104.4 - 0.5y & = & -128.4 \\ 24 & = & 0.5y \\ 48 & = & y. \end{array}$$

Since $x + y + z = 232$, $116 + 48 + z = 232$ and $z = 68$. Emma used 116 pennies, 48 nickels, and 68 dimes.

71. Let x, y, and z be the prices of a carton of milk, a cup of coffee, and a doughnut, respectively. So

$$\begin{array}{rcl} 3x + 4y + 7z & = & 5.45 \\ 4x + 2y + 8z & = & 5.30 \\ 2x + 5y + 6z & = & 5.15. \end{array}$$

Multiply third equation by -2 and add to second equation. Also, multiply first equation by -4 and add to 3 times the second equation.

$$\begin{array}{rcl} -4x - 10y - 12z & = & -10.30 \\ 4x + 2y + 8z & = & 5.30 \\ \hline -8y - 4z & = & -5 \end{array}$$

$$\begin{array}{rcl} -12x - 16y - 28z & = & -21.80 \\ 12x + 6y + 24z & = & 15.90 \\ \hline -10y - 4z & = & -5.90 \end{array}$$

Multiply $-8y - 4z = -5$ by -1 and add to $-10y - 4z = -5.90$.

$$\begin{array}{rcl} 8y + 4z & = & 5 \\ -10y - 4z & = & -5.90 \\ \hline -2y & = & -0.90 \end{array}$$

Then $y = 0.45$. Substitute into $-8y - 4z = -5$ to get $-3.60 - 4z = -5$ and $z = 0.35$. Since $3x + 4y + 7z = 5.45$, we have $3x + 1.80 + 2.45 = 5.45$ and $x = 0.40$.

Alphonse's bill was $5(0.40) + 2(0.45) + 9(0.35) = \$6.05$. His change is \$3.95.

73. A system of equations is

$$4x = 6y$$
$$2(x+y) = 15(8)$$
$$6(x+y+15+10) = 10z.$$

Rewriting the first two equations, one obtains

$$2x - 3y = 0$$
$$x + y = 60.$$

Solving this smaller system, one finds $x = 36$ lb, $y = 24$ lb. Substituting into the third equation, one finds

$$z = \frac{6(x+y+25)}{10} = \frac{6(60+25)}{10} = 51 \text{ lb.}$$

75.

a) Substitute $(0,0)$, $(10,40)$, $(20,70)$ into $y = ax^2+bx+c$. Consequently, we obtain the
following system of equations:

$$c = 0$$
$$100a + 10b + c = 40$$
$$400a + 20b + c = 70.$$

Multiply the second equation by -2 and add to third equation.

$$\begin{array}{rcl} -200a - 20b - 2c &=& -80 \\ 400a + 20b + c &=& 70 \\ \hline 200a - c &=& -10 \end{array}$$

Substitute $c = 0$ into $200a - c = -10$. Then $a = -\dfrac{1}{20}$. From $100a+10b+c = 40$,

we obtain $-5 + 10b = 40$ and $b = \dfrac{9}{2}$.

The parabola is $y = -\dfrac{1}{20}x^2 + \dfrac{9}{2}x$.

b) Since $-b/(2a) = 45$, the maximum height is

$$-\frac{1}{20}(45)^2 + \frac{9}{2}(45) = 101.25 \text{ m.}$$

c) Since the zeros of $y = -\dfrac{x}{20}(x - 90)$ are $x = 0, 90$, the missile will strike 90 m from the origin.

79. Multiply the second equation by -2 and add the result to the first equation.

$$\begin{array}{rcl} 2x - 3y &=& 20 \\ -2x - 8y &=& 2 \\ \hline -11y &=& 22 \end{array}$$

Then $y = -2$ and $x = -4y-1 = -4(-2)-1 = 7$. The solution set is $\{(7,-2)\}$.

81. $10,000 \left(1 + \dfrac{0.035}{4}\right)^{24} = \$12,325.52$

83. No, the Vertical Line Test fails for a circle.

For Thought

1. True, since the line $y = x$ passes through the center of the circle.

2. False, when a line is tangent to a circle it intersects the circle at only one point.

3. True, the parabola $y = 2x^2 - 4$ intersects the circle $x^2 + y^2 = 16$ at three points.

4. False, they intersect at $(\pm 1, 0)$.

5. False, they intersect at $(1, 1)$ and $(-1, -1)$.

6. False, since three noncollinear points determine a unique circle through the points.

7. True, since either leg can serve as base and the other leg as altitude.

8. True   **9.**   True

10. False, two such numbers are $\dfrac{1}{2}\left(7 \pm \sqrt{45}\right)$.

3 Exercises

1. Since $x = -1$ and $y = 4$ satisfy both equations in the system , $(-1, 4)$ is a solution.

3. Since $x = 4$ and $y = -5$ does not satisfy $x - y = 1$, $(4, -5)$ is not a solution.

5. Since $y = x$ and $y = x^2$, we obtain

$$x = x^2$$
$$x - x^2 = 0$$
$$x(x - 1) = 0.$$

Then $x = 0, 1$ and the solution set is

$$\{(0,0),\ (1,1)\}.$$

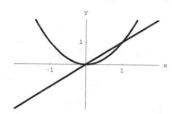

7. Substitute $y = x^2$ into $5x - y = 6$.

$$5x - x^2 = 6$$
$$x^2 - 5x = -6$$
$$x^2 - 5x + 6 = 0$$
$$(x - 3)(x - 2) = 0$$

If $x = 3, 2$ in $y = x^2$, then $y = 9, 4$.
The solution set is $\{(2,4),\ (3,9)\}$.

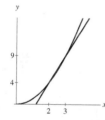

9. Substitute $y = |x|$ into $y = x + 3$.

$$|x| = x + 3$$
$$x = x + 3 \quad \text{or} \quad -x = x + 3$$
$$0 = 3 \quad \text{or} \quad -2x = 3$$

Then $x = -3/2$. Since $y = |x|$, $y = 3/2$.
The solution set is $\{(-3/2, 3/2)\}$.

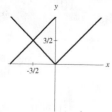

11. Substitute $y = x^2$ into $y = |x|$.

$$x^2 = |x|$$
$$x^2 = x \quad \text{or} \quad x^2 = -x$$
$$x^2 - x = 0 \quad \text{or} \quad x^2 + x = 0$$
$$x(x - 1) = 0 \quad \text{or} \quad x(x + 1) = 0$$
$$x = 0, -1 \quad \text{or} \quad x = 0, -1$$

Using $x = 0, \pm 1$ in $y = x^2$, one finds
$y = 0, 1$. The solution set is
$\{(-1,1), (0,0), (1,1)\}$.

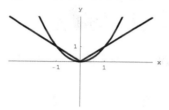

13. Substitute $y = \sqrt{x}$ into $y = 2x$ to obtain

$$\sqrt{x} = 2x$$
$$x = 4x^2$$
$$x - 4x^2 = 0$$
$$x(1 - 4x) = 0.$$

Using $x = 0, 1/4$ in $y = 2x$, $y = 0, 1/2$.
The solution set is

$$\{(0,0), (1/4, 1/2)\}.$$

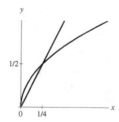

15. Substitute $y = x^3$ into $y = 4x$ to get

$$x^3 = 4x$$
$$x^3 - 4x = 0$$
$$x(x^2 - 4) = 0$$
$$x = 0, \pm 2.$$

Substituting $x = 0, 2, -2$ into $y = 4x$,
we get $y = 0, 8, -8$.
The solution set is

$$\{(0,0), (2,8), (-2,-8).$$

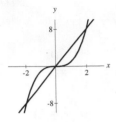

17. Substitute $y = x$ into $y = x^3 - x$.

$$
\begin{aligned}
x &= x^3 - x \\
2x - x^3 &= 0 \\
x(2 - x^2) &= 0 \\
x &= 0, \sqrt{2}, -\sqrt{2}
\end{aligned}
$$

Since $y = x$, the solution set is

$$\{(0,0), (\sqrt{2}, \sqrt{2}), (-\sqrt{2}, -\sqrt{2})\}.$$

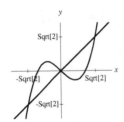

19. Substitute $y = x$ into $x^2 + y^2 = 1$.

$$
\begin{aligned}
x^2 + x^2 &= 1 \\
2x^2 &= 1 \\
x^2 &= \frac{1}{2} \\
x &= \pm\frac{\sqrt{2}}{2}
\end{aligned}
$$

Since $y = x$, the solution set is

$$\left\{\left(\frac{\sqrt{2}}{2}, \frac{\sqrt{2}}{2}\right), \left(-\frac{\sqrt{2}}{2}, -\frac{\sqrt{2}}{2}\right)\right\}.$$

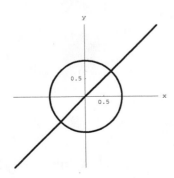

21. Substitute $y = -x - 4$ into $xy = 1$.

$$
\begin{aligned}
x(-x - 4) &= 1 \\
-x^2 - 4x &= 1 \\
x^2 + 4x &= -1 \\
x^2 + 4x + 4 &= 3 \\
(x + 2)^2 &= 3 \\
x &= -2 \pm \sqrt{3}
\end{aligned}
$$

Using $x = -2 + \sqrt{3}, -2 - \sqrt{3}$ in $y = -x - 4$, we find $y = -2 - \sqrt{3}, -2 + \sqrt{3}$.
The solution set is
$$\left\{(-2 + \sqrt{3}, -2 - \sqrt{3}), (-2 - \sqrt{3}, -2 + \sqrt{3})\right\}.$$

23. Substitute $x^2 = 2y^2 - 1$ into $2x^2 - y^2 = 1$.

$$
\begin{aligned}
2(2y^2 - 1) - y^2 &= 1 \\
3y^2 - 2 &= 1 \\
3y^2 &= 3 \\
y^2 &= 1 \\
y &= \pm 1
\end{aligned}
$$

Using $y = 1$ in $x^2 = 2y^2 - 1$, we get $x^2 = 1$ or $x = \pm 1$. Also, if $y = -1$ then $x = \pm 1$.
The solution set is $\{(1, \pm 1), (-1, \pm 1)\}$.

25. Since $2x - y = 1$, we obtain $y = 2x - 1$.
Then substitute into $xy - 2x = 2$.

$$
\begin{aligned}
x(2x - 1) - 2x &= 2 \\
2x^2 - 3x - 2 &= 0 \\
(2x + 1)(x - 2) &= 0 \\
x &= -\frac{1}{2}, 2
\end{aligned}
$$

Since $y = 2x - 1$, we get $y = 2 \cdot \left(-\frac{1}{2}\right) - 1 = -2$

and $x = 2(2) - 1 = 3$. The solution set

is $\left\{\left(-\frac{1}{2}, -2\right), (2, 3)\right\}$.

27. Multiply the first equation by 2 and add to the second.

$$
\begin{aligned}
\frac{6}{x} - \frac{2}{y} &= \frac{26}{10} \\
\frac{1}{x} + \frac{2}{y} &= \frac{9}{10} \\
\hline
\frac{7}{x} &= \frac{35}{10}
\end{aligned}
$$

So $70 = 35x$ and $x = 2$.

Substituting into $\dfrac{3}{x} - \dfrac{1}{y} = \dfrac{13}{10}$, we obtain

$$
\begin{aligned}
\frac{3}{2} - \frac{1}{y} &= \frac{13}{10} \\
-\frac{1}{y} &= \frac{13}{10} - \frac{15}{10} \\
-\frac{1}{y} &= -\frac{2}{10} \\
y &= 5.
\end{aligned}
$$

The solution set is $\{(2, 5)\}$.

29. Substitute $y = 1 - x$ into $x^2 + xy - y^2 = -5$.

$$
\begin{aligned}
x^2 + x(1 - x) - (1 - x)^2 &= -5 \\
x^2 + x - x^2 - (1 - 2x + x^2) &= -5 \\
-x^2 + 3x - 1 &= -5 \\
x^2 - 3x + 1 &= 5 \\
x^2 - 3x - 4 &= 0 \\
(x - 4)(x + 1) &= 0 \\
x &= 4, -1
\end{aligned}
$$

Using $x = 4, -1$ in $y = 1 - x$, we get $y = -3, 2$. The solution set is $\{(4, -3), (-1, 2)\}$.

31. Add the two given equations to obtain $xy = -2$. Substitute $y = -2/x$ into $x^2 + 2xy - 2y^2 = -11$.

$$
\begin{aligned}
x^2 + 2x\left(-\frac{2}{x}\right) - 2 \cdot \frac{4}{x^2} &= -11 \\
x^2 - 4 - \frac{8}{x^2} &= -11 \\
x^4 + 7x^2 - 8 &= 0 \\
(x^2 + 8)(x^2 - 1) &= 0 \\
x &= \pm 1
\end{aligned}
$$

Using $x = 1, -1$ in $y = -2/x$, $y = -2, 2$. The solution set is $\{(1, -2), (-1, 2)\}$.

33. Multiply the first equation by 7 and multiply

the second equation by -5.

$$
\begin{aligned}
\frac{28}{x} + \frac{35}{y^2} &= 84 \\
-\frac{15}{x} - \frac{35}{y^2} &= -110 \\
\hline
\frac{13}{x} &= -26 \\
x &= -\frac{1}{2}
\end{aligned}
$$

Then substitute into $\dfrac{4}{x} + \dfrac{5}{y^2} = 12$.

$$
\begin{aligned}
-8 + \frac{5}{y^2} &= 12 \\
\frac{5}{y^2} &= 20 \\
y^2 &= \frac{1}{4} \\
y &= \pm\frac{1}{2}.
\end{aligned}
$$

The solution set is $\left\{\left(-\dfrac{1}{2}, \dfrac{1}{2}\right), \left(-\dfrac{1}{2}, -\dfrac{1}{2}\right)\right\}$.

35. Since $x = \dfrac{10^{11}}{y^2}$ and $\dfrac{x^3}{y} = 10^{12}$, we find

$$
\begin{aligned}
\frac{10^{33}}{y^7} &= 10^{12} \\
10^{21} &= y^7 \\
y &= 10^3.
\end{aligned}
$$

Substitute into $x = \dfrac{10^{11}}{y^2}$. Then

$$
x = \frac{10^{11}}{10^6} = 10^5.
$$

The solution set is $\{(10^5, 10^3)\}$.

37. Substitute $y = 2^{x+1}$ into $y = 4^{-x}$.

$$
\begin{aligned}
2^{x+1} &= (2^2)^{-x} \\
2^{x+1} &= 2^{-2x} \\
x + 1 &= -2x \\
3x &= -1
\end{aligned}
$$

Using $x = -1/3$ in $y = 2^{x+1}$, we get

$y = 2^{2/3}$. The solution set is $\left\{\left(-\dfrac{1}{3}, 2^{2/3}\right)\right\}$.

39. Substitute $y = \log_2(x)$ into $y = \log_4(x+2)$ and use the base-changing formula.

$$
\begin{aligned}
\log_2(x) &= \log_4(x+2) \\
\log_2(x) &= \frac{\log_2(x+2)}{\log_2(4)} \\
\log_2(x) &= \frac{\log_2(x+2)}{2} \\
2 \cdot \log_2(x) &= \log_2(x+2) \\
2 \cdot \log_2(x) - \log_2(x+2) &= 0 \\
\log_2\left(\frac{x^2}{x+2}\right) &= 0 \\
\frac{x^2}{x+2} &= 1 \\
x^2 &= x+2 \\
x^2 - x - 2 &= 0 \\
(x-2)(x+1) &= 0 \\
x &= 2, -1
\end{aligned}
$$

But $x = -1$ is an extraneous root since $\log_2(-1)$ is undefined. Using $x = 2$ in $y = \log_2(x)$, we have $y = 1$. The solution set is $\{(2,1)\}$.

41. Substitute $y = \log_2(x+2)$ into $y = 3 - \log_2(x)$.

$$
\begin{aligned}
\log_2(x+2) &= 3 - \log_2(x) \\
\log_2(x+2) + \log_2(x) &= 3 \\
\log_2(x^2 + 2x) &= 3 \\
x^2 + 2x &= 2^3 \\
x^2 + 2x - 8 &= 0 \\
(x+4)(x-2) &= 0 \\
x &= -4, 2
\end{aligned}
$$

But $x = -4$ is an extraneous root since $\log_2(-4)$ is undefined. Using $x = 2$ in $y = \log_2(x+2)$, we get $y = \log_2(4) = 2$. The solution set is $\{(2,2)\}$.

43. Substitute $y = 3^x$ into $y = 2^x$.

$$3^x = 2^x$$

$$
\begin{aligned}
\log(3^x) &= \log(2^x) \\
x \cdot \log(3) &= x \cdot \log(2) \\
x\,[\log(3) - \log(2)] &= 0 \\
x &= 0
\end{aligned}
$$

Using $x = 0$ in $y = 3^x$, we obtain $y = 3^0 = 1$. The solution set is $\{(0,1)\}$.

45. Substitute $y = 2^x$ into $x = \log_4(y)$.

$$x = \log_4\left(2^x\right) = x\log_4(2) = x \cdot \frac{1}{2}$$

SInce $x = \frac{x}{2}$, we find $x = 0$. Then

$$y = 2^x = 2^0 = 1.$$

The solution set is $\{(0,1)\}$.

47. If we subtract the second equation from the first, we find

$$
\begin{aligned}
x + \log_{16}(y+1) &= \frac{1}{2} \\
x + \log_{16}(y) &= \frac{1}{4} \\
\hline
\log_{16}\left(\frac{y+1}{y}\right) &= \frac{1}{4} \\
\frac{y+1}{y} &= 2 \\
y &= 1
\end{aligned}
$$

Substitute into $x + \log_{16} y = \dfrac{1}{4}$. Then

$$x + 0 = \frac{1}{4}.$$

The solution set is $\left\{\left(\dfrac{1}{4}, 1\right)\right\}$.

49. From the graphs, the solution set is $\{(2,1), (0.3, -1.8)\}$.

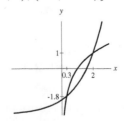

51. From the graphs, the solution set is $\{(1.9, 0.6), (0.1, -2.0)\}$.

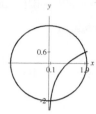

53. From the graphs, the solution set is $\{(-0.8, 0.6), (2, 4), (4, 16)\}$.

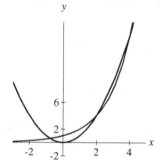

55. From the first equation, we find

$$x + 2y = z + 5.$$

Substitute into the third equation:

$$(x + 2y)^2 - z^2 = 15$$
$$(z + 5)^2 - z^2 = 15$$

Solving for z, we find $z = -1$. Then substitute $z = -1$ into the first two equations, and subtract as follows:

$$
\begin{aligned}
x + 2y &= 4 \\
3x + 2y &= 12 \\
\hline
-2x &= -8 \\
x &= 4
\end{aligned}
$$

Since $x + 2y = 4$ and $x = 4$, we find $y = 0$. The solution set is $\{(4, 0)\}$.

57. If we square the second equation and use the third equation

$$x^2 + y^2 + z^2 = 133$$

we obtain

$$
\begin{aligned}
(x + y + z)^2 &= 49 \\
133 + 2(xy + yz + xz) &= 49 \\
2(xy + yz + xz) &= -84
\end{aligned}
$$

Using the first equation $xy = z^2$, we find

$$
\begin{aligned}
2(z^2 + yz + xz) &= -84 \\
(z + y + x)z &= -42 \\
7z &= -42 \\
z &= -6
\end{aligned}
$$

for $x + y + z = 7$.

Since $z = -6$, we may rewrite the first two given equations as follows:

$$
\begin{aligned}
xy &= 36 \\
x + y &= 13
\end{aligned}
$$

Since $y = \dfrac{36}{x}$, we substitute and find:

$$
\begin{aligned}
x + \frac{36}{x} &= 13 \\
x^2 - 13x + 36z &= 0 \\
(x - 4)(x - 9) &= 0 \\
x &= 4, 9
\end{aligned}
$$

If $x = 4$, then $y = \dfrac{36}{x} = \dfrac{36}{4} = 9$.

If $x = 9$, then $y = \dfrac{36}{x} = \dfrac{36}{9} = 4$.

The solution set is $\{(4, 9, -6), (9, 4, -6)\}$.

59. Let x and y be the base and height of a 42-inch LCD TV, respectively.

$$
\begin{aligned}
\frac{y}{x} &= \frac{9}{15} \\
x^2 + y^2 &= 42^2
\end{aligned}
$$

Then we find $x \approx 36.0$ in. and $y \approx 21.6$ in.

61. Let x and $6 - x$ be the two numbers.

$$
\begin{aligned}
x(6 - x) &= -16 \\
x^2 - 6x &= 16
\end{aligned}
$$

$$x^2 - 6x + 9 = 25$$
$$(x - 3)^2 = 25$$
$$x - 3 = \pm 5$$
$$x = 3 \pm 5$$
$$x = -2, 8$$

The numbers are -2 and 8.

63. Let x and y be the lengths of the legs of the triangle.

$$x^2 + y^2 = 15^2$$
$$\frac{1}{2}xy = 54$$

Substitute $y = \dfrac{108}{x}$ into $x^2 + y^2 = 225$ and use the quadratic formula.

$$x^2 + \frac{11664}{x^2} = 225$$
$$x^4 - 225x^2 + 11,664 = 0$$

$$x^2 = \frac{225 \pm \sqrt{225^2 - 4(11,664)}}{2}$$

$$x^2 = \frac{225 \pm 63}{2}$$
$$x^2 = 144, 81$$
$$x = 12, 9$$

Using $x = 12, 9$ in $y = \dfrac{108}{x}$, we get $y = 9, 12$.

The sides are 9 m and 12 m.

65. If x is the length of the hypotenuse, then $\dfrac{x}{2}$ and $\dfrac{x\sqrt{3}}{2}$ are the lengths of the sides opposite the $30°$ and $60°$ angles.

$$x + \frac{x}{2} + \frac{x\sqrt{3}}{2} = 12$$
$$2x + x + \sqrt{3}x = 24$$
$$(3 + \sqrt{3})x = 24$$
$$x = \frac{24}{3 + \sqrt{3}} \cdot \frac{3 - \sqrt{3}}{3 - \sqrt{3}}$$
$$x = 12 - 4\sqrt{3}$$

Substituting $x = 12 - 4\sqrt{3}$ in $\dfrac{x}{2}$ and $\dfrac{x\sqrt{3}}{2}$, we find $6 - 2\sqrt{3}$ ft and $6\sqrt{3} - 6$ ft are the lengths of the two sides and the hypotenuse is $12 - 4\sqrt{3}$ ft.

67. The values of x and y must satisfy

$$6y = 6x$$
$$x(6 + y) = 7(4 + 12).$$

Since $x = y$ as seen from the first equation, upon substitution into the second equation one obtains

$$6x + x^2 = 112$$
$$x^2 + 6x - 112 = 0$$
$$(x + 14)(x - 8) = 0.$$

Then $x = 8$ in. and $y = 8$ oz. One must exclude the negative value $x = -14$.

69. Let x and y be the number of minutes it takes for pump A and pump B, respectively, to fill the vat.

$$\frac{1}{x} + \frac{1}{y} = \frac{1}{8}$$
$$\frac{1}{x} - \frac{1}{y} = \frac{1}{12}$$

Adding the two equations, we get

$$\frac{2}{x} = \frac{3}{24} + \frac{2}{24}$$
$$\frac{2}{x} = \frac{5}{24}$$
$$5x = 48$$
$$x = 9.6.$$

Substituting $x = \dfrac{48}{5}$ into $\dfrac{1}{x} + \dfrac{1}{y} = \dfrac{1}{8}$, we find

$$\frac{5}{48} + \frac{1}{y} = \frac{1}{8}$$
$$\frac{1}{y} = \frac{6}{48} - \frac{5}{48}$$
$$\frac{1}{y} = \frac{1}{48}$$
$$y = 48.$$

Pump A can fill the vat by itself in $x = 9.6$ min while Pump B will take $y = 48$ min.

71. Let x and y be two numbers satisfying

$$\begin{aligned} x + y &= 6 \\ xy &= 10. \end{aligned}$$

Substituting $y = 6 - x$ into $xy = 10$,

$$\begin{aligned} x(6 - x) &= 10 \\ 6x - x^2 &= 10 \\ x^2 - 6x &= -10 \\ x^2 - 6x + 9 &= -1 \\ (x - 3)^2 &= -1 \\ x &= 3 \pm i. \end{aligned}$$

If $x = 3 + i$, then $y = 6 - (3 + i) = 3 - i$.
If $x = 3 - i$, then $y = 6 - (3 - i) = 3 + i$.
The two numbers are $3 + i$ and $3 - i$.

73. Let x and y be the length and width.

$$\begin{aligned} 20xy &= 36,000 \\ 40x + 40y + 2xy &= 7200 \end{aligned}$$

Substitute $x = \dfrac{1800}{y}$ into $40x + 40y + 2xy = 7200$.

$$\begin{aligned} 40 \cdot \frac{1800}{y} + 40y + 2 \cdot \frac{1800}{y} \cdot y &= 7200 \\ \frac{72,000}{y} + 40y + 3600 &= 7200 \\ \frac{72,000}{y} + 40y &= 3600 \\ 40y^2 - 3600y + 72,000 &= 0 \\ y^2 - 90y + 1800 &= 0 \\ (y - 60)(y - 30) &= 0 \end{aligned}$$

Using $y = 30$ and $y = 60$ in $x = \dfrac{1800}{w}$, we get $x = 60$ and $x = 30$. Thus, the length is 60 ft and the width is 30 ft.

75. From the graphs, the two models give the same population for $t = 0$ and $t = 9.65$ years. The exponential population model is twice the linear model when $t \approx 29.5$ years.

77. Let x be the time of the sunrise or the number of hours since midnight. Let S and B be Sally's and Bob's speeds. The number of miles Sally and Bob drove are $(16 - x)S$ and $(21 - x)B$, respectively. Since they met at noon, the distance between Sally's house and Bob's house is $(12 - x)S + (12 - x)B$; or equivalently $(12 - x)(S + B)$. Then

$$\begin{aligned} (16 - x)S &= (12 - x)(S + B) \\ (16 - x)S &= (16 - x)(S + B) - 4(S + B) \\ 0 &= (16 - x)B - 4(S + B) \\ (16 - x)B &= 4(S + B). \end{aligned}$$

Likewise,

$$\begin{aligned} (21 - x)B &= (21 - x)(S + B) - 9(S + B) \\ (21 - x)S &= 9(S + B). \end{aligned}$$

Combining, one obtains

$$\frac{(16 - x)B}{(21 - x)S} = \frac{4(S + B)}{9(S + B)}. \text{ So, } \frac{(16 - x)9B}{(21 - x)4S} = 1.$$

Furthermore, since $(16 - x)S = (21 - x)B$ one finds $\dfrac{B}{S} = \dfrac{16 - x}{21 - x}$. Then

$$\begin{aligned} \frac{9(16 - x)}{4(21 - x)} \cdot \frac{B}{S} &= 1 \\ \frac{9}{4}\left(\frac{16 - x}{21 - x}\right)^2 &= 1 \\ \frac{16 - x}{21 - x} &= \frac{2}{3} \quad \text{since } 16 - x > 0 \\ 48 - 3x &= 42 - 2x \\ x &= 6. \end{aligned}$$

The sunrise was at 6:00 A.M.

79. By the time the mouse reaches the northeast corner (50 feet from the southwest corner) of the train, the train would have traveled 20 feet which is one-half the distance the train travels before the mouse returns to the southeast corner. So, when the mouse reaches the northwest corner (40 feet from the southwest corner) the train (in proportion to 20 feet) would have traveled 16 feet.

As the distance traveled by the train ranges from 16 feet to 20 feet, the path the mouse takes will be the hypotenuse of a right triangle whose sides are 10 feet and 4 feet. So, in this range, the mouse travels a distance of $\sqrt{10^2 + 4^2}$ feet on the ground, or equivalently $2\sqrt{29}$ feet on the ground.

Thus, the total diagonal ground distance (including the diagonal ground distance as the mouse moves from the southeast corner to the southwest corner) traveled by the mouse is twice of $2\sqrt{29}$ feet, or $4\sqrt{29}$ feet. Since the north-south distance traveled by the mouse is 80 feet on the ground, the total distance on the ground traveled by the mouse is $80 + 4\sqrt{29}$ feet, or about 101.54 ft.

83. If we add the first and third equations, we obtain

$$2x + 3y = 51$$

If we add the second equation to three times the third equation, we find

$$5x + 5y = 100.$$

If we multiply the above equation by $-2/5$, we obtain

$$-2x - 2y = -40.$$

If we add the last equation to $2x + 3y = 51$, we obtain $y = 11$. Working backwards, we find $x = 9$ and $z = 13$. The solution set is $\{(9, 11, 13)\}$.

85. Combine the logarithms as follows:

$$
\begin{aligned}
\log_3((x+1)(x-5)) &= 3 \\
\log_3(x^2 - 4x - 5) &= 3 \\
x^2 - 4x - 5 &= 27 \\
x^2 - 4x - 32 &= \\
(x-8)(x+4) &= 0 \\
x &= 8, -4
\end{aligned}
$$

Note, -4 is an extraneous root. The solution set is $\{8\}$.

87. Let $p(x) = 2x^3 + x^2 - 41x + 20$.

4	2	1	-41	20
		8	36	-20
	2	9	-5	0

Since the quotient factors as

$$2x^2 + 9x - 5 = (2x - 1)(x + 5)$$

the solution set is $\left\{ \left(4, \dfrac{1}{2}, -5 \right) \right\}$

For Thought

1. True, $\dfrac{1}{x} + \dfrac{3}{x+1} = \dfrac{(x+1) + 3x}{x(x+1)} = \dfrac{4x+1}{x(x+1)}$.

2. True, $x + \dfrac{3x}{x^2 - 1} = \dfrac{x(x^2 - 1) + 3x}{x^2 - 1} = \dfrac{x^3 + 2x}{x^2 - 1}$.

3. False, by using long division we obtain
$$\dfrac{x^2}{x^2 - 9} = 1 + \dfrac{9}{x^2 - 9} = 1 + \dfrac{A}{x - 3} + \dfrac{B}{x + 3}$$

4. True, since $\dfrac{1}{2} + \dfrac{1}{2^3} = \dfrac{2^2 + 1}{2^3} = \dfrac{5}{8}$.

5. False, since $\dfrac{3x - 1}{x^3 + x} = \dfrac{A}{x} + \dfrac{Bx + C}{x^2 + 1}$.

6. False, since $\dfrac{1}{x^2 - 1} = \dfrac{1/2}{x - 1} - \dfrac{1/2}{x + 1}$.

7. True, by using long division we get

$$
\begin{array}{r}
x - 1 \\
x^2 + x - 2 \overline{\smash{)}\, x^3 + 0x^2 + 0x + 1} \\
\underline{x^3 + x^2 - 2x} \\
-x^2 + 2x + 1 \\
\underline{-x^2 - x + 2} \\
3x - 1
\end{array}
$$

So $\dfrac{x^3 + 1}{x^2 + x - 2} = x - 1 + \dfrac{3x - 1}{x^2 + x - 2}$.

8. False, since $x^3 - 8 = (x - 2)(x^2 + 2x + 4)$.

9. True, since $\dfrac{1}{x - 1} + \dfrac{1}{x^2 + x + 1} =$
$$\dfrac{(x^2 + x + 1) + (x - 1)}{x^3 - 1} = \dfrac{x^2 + 2x}{x^3 - 1}.$$

10. True, it is already in the form $\dfrac{Ax + B}{x^2 + 9}$.

4 Exercises

1. $\dfrac{3(x+1)+4(x-2)}{(x-2)(x+1)} = \dfrac{7x-5}{(x-2)(x+1)}$

3. $\dfrac{(x^2+2)-3(x-1)}{(x-1)(x^2+2)} = \dfrac{x^2-3x+5}{(x-1)(x^2+2)}$

5.

$$\dfrac{(2x+1)(x^2+3)+(x^3+2x+2)}{(x^2+3)^2} =$$

$$\dfrac{(2x^3+x^2+6x+3)+(x^3+2x+2)}{(x^2+3)^2} =$$

$$\dfrac{3x^3+x^2+8x+5}{(x^2+3)^2}$$

7.

$$\dfrac{(x-1)^2+(2x+3)(x-1)+(x^2+1)}{(x-1)^3} =$$

$$\dfrac{(x^2-2x+1)+(2x^2+x-3)+(x^2+1)}{(x-1)^3} =$$

$$\dfrac{4x^2-x-1}{(x-1)^3}$$

9. Multiply the equation by $(x-3)(x+3)$.

$$\begin{aligned}
12 &= A(x+3)+B(x-3) \\
12 &= (A+B)x+(3A-3B)
\end{aligned}$$

$A+B=0$ and $3A-3B=12$

Divide $3A-3B=12$ by 3 and add to $A+B=0$.

$$\begin{aligned}
A-B &= 4 \\
A+B &= 0 \\
\hline
2A &= 4
\end{aligned}$$

Using $A=2$ in $A+B=0$, $B=-2$. Then $A=2$ and $B=-2$.

11. $\dfrac{5x-1}{(x+1)(x-2)} = \dfrac{A}{x+1} + \dfrac{B}{x-2}$

$$\begin{aligned}
5x-1 &= A(x-2)+B(x+1) \\
5x-1 &= (A+B)x+(-2A+B)
\end{aligned}$$

$A+B=5$ and $-2A+B=-1$

Multiply $-2A+B=-1$ by -1 and add to $A+B=5$.

$$\begin{aligned}
2A-B &= 1 \\
A+B &= 5 \\
\hline
3A &= 6
\end{aligned}$$

Using $A=2$ in $A+B=5$, $B=3$.

The answer is $\dfrac{2}{x+1} + \dfrac{3}{x-2}$.

13. $\dfrac{2x+5}{(x+4)(x+2)} = \dfrac{A}{x+4} + \dfrac{B}{x+2}$

$$\begin{aligned}
2x+5 &= A(x+2)+B(x+4) \\
2x+5 &= (A+B)x+(2A+4B)
\end{aligned}$$

$A+B=2$ and $2A+4B=5$

Multiply $A+B=2$ by -2 and add to $2A+4B=5$.

$$\begin{aligned}
-2A-2B &= -4 \\
2A+4B &= 5 \\
\hline
2B &= 1
\end{aligned}$$

Using $B=1/2$ in $A+B=2$, we find $A=3/2$.

The answer is $\dfrac{3/2}{x+4} + \dfrac{1/2}{x+2}$.

15. $\dfrac{2}{(x-3)(x+3)} = \dfrac{A}{x-3} + \dfrac{B}{x+3}$

$$\begin{aligned}
2 &= A(x+3)+B(x-3) \\
2 &= (A+B)x+(3A-3B)
\end{aligned}$$

$A+B=0$ and $3A-3B=2$

Multiply $A+B=0$ by 3 and add to $3A-3B=2$.

$$\begin{aligned}
3A+3B &= 0 \\
3A-3B &= 2 \\
\hline
6A &= 2
\end{aligned}$$

Using $A=1/3$ in $A+B=0$, we get $B=-1/3$.

The answer is $\dfrac{1/3}{x-3} + \dfrac{-1/3}{x+3}$.

17.

$$\begin{aligned}
\dfrac{1}{x(x-1)} &= \dfrac{A}{x} + \dfrac{B}{x-1} \\
1 &= A(x-1)+Bx \\
1 &= (A+B)x-A
\end{aligned}$$

$A+B=0$ and $-A=1$

Using $A=-1$ in $A+B=0$, we find $B=1$.

The answer is $\dfrac{-1}{x} + \dfrac{1}{x-1}$.

19. Multiplying the equation by $(x+3)^2(x-2)$, we obtain $x^2+x-31 =$

$$= A(x+3)(x-2) + B(x-2) + C(x+3)^2$$
$$= A(x^2+x-6) + B(x-2) + C(x^2+6x+9)$$
$$= (A+C)x^2 + (A+B+6C)x + (-6A-2B+9C).$$

Equate the coefficients and solve the system.

$$A + C = 1$$
$$A + B + 6C = 1$$
$$-6A - 2B + 9C = -31$$

Multiply $A+B+6C=1$ by 2 and add to $-6A-2B+9C=-31$.

$$\begin{array}{rcr} 2A+2B+12C &=& 2 \\ -6A-2B+9C &=& -31 \\ \hline -4A+21C &=& -29 \end{array}$$

Multiply $A+C=1$ by 4 and add to $-4A+21C=-29$.

$$\begin{array}{rcr} 4A+4C &=& 4 \\ -4A+21C &=& -29 \\ \hline 25C &=& -25 \end{array}$$

Using $C=-1$ in $A+C=1$, we obtain $A=2$. From $A+B+6C=1$, $2+B-6=1$ and $B=5$. So $A=2, B=5$, and $C=-1$.

21. $\dfrac{4x-1}{(x-1)^2(x+2)} = \dfrac{A}{x-1} + \dfrac{B}{(x-1)^2} + \dfrac{C}{x+2}$

$$4x-1 = A(x-1)(x+2) + B(x+2) + C(x-1)^2$$
$$4x-1 = A(x^2+x-2) + B(x+2) + C(x^2-2x+1)$$
$$4x-1 = (A+C)x^2 + (A+B-2C)x + (-2A+2B+C)$$

If we equate the coefficients of x, we obtain

$$A + C = 0$$
$$A + B - 2C = 4$$
$$-2A + 2B + C = -1.$$

Solving the system, we get $A=1, B=1$, and $C=-1$. The answer is

$$\frac{1}{x-1} + \frac{1}{(x-1)^2} + \frac{-1}{x+2}.$$

23. $\dfrac{20-4x}{(x-2)^2(x+4)} = \dfrac{A}{x-2} + \dfrac{B}{(x-2)^2} + \dfrac{C}{x+4}$

$$\begin{aligned} 20-4x &= A(x-2)(x+4) + B(x+4) + \\ &\quad C(x-2)^2 \end{aligned}$$
$$\begin{aligned} 20-4x &= A(x^2+2x-8) + B(x+4) + \\ &\quad C(x^2-4x+4) \end{aligned}$$
$$\begin{aligned} 20-4x &= (A+C)x^2 + (2A+B-4C)x + \\ &\quad (-8A+4B+4C) \end{aligned}$$

If we equate the coefficients of x, we obtain

$$A + C = 0$$
$$2A + B - 4C = -4$$
$$-8A + 4B + 4C = 20$$

Solving the system, we get $A=-1, B=2$, and $C=1$. The answer is

$$\frac{-1}{x-2} + \frac{2}{(x-2)^2} + \frac{1}{x+4}.$$

25. Note, $\dfrac{3x^2+3x-2}{(x+1)^2(x-1)} = \dfrac{A}{x+1} + \dfrac{B}{(x+1)^2} + \dfrac{C}{x-1}$

$$\begin{aligned} 3x^2+3x-2 &= A(x+1)(x-1) + B(x-1) + \\ &\quad C(x+1)^2 \end{aligned}$$
$$\begin{aligned} 3x^2+3x-2 &= A(x^2-1) + B(x-1) + \\ &\quad C(x^2+2x+1) \end{aligned}$$
$$\begin{aligned} 3x^2+3x-2 &= (A+C)x^2 + (B+2C)x + \\ &\quad (-A-B+C) \end{aligned}$$

If we equate the coefficients of x, we obtain

$$A + C = 3$$
$$B + 2C = 3$$
$$-A - B + C = -2.$$

Solving the system, we get $A=2, B=1$, and $C=1$. The answer is $\dfrac{2}{x+1} + \dfrac{1}{(x+1)^2} + \dfrac{1}{x-1}$.

27. Multiplying the equation by $(x+1)(x^2+4)$, we get

$$x^2-x-7 = A(x^2+4) + (Bx+C)(x+1)$$
$$x^2-x-7 = (A+B)x^2 + (B+C)x + (4A+C).$$

Equating the coefficients, we have

$$\begin{aligned} A + B &= 1 \\ B + C &= -1 \\ 4A + C &= -7. \end{aligned}$$

Multiply $A + B = 1$ by -1 and add to $B + C = -1$.

$$\begin{aligned} -A - B &= -1 \\ \underline{B + C} &= \underline{-1} \\ -A + C &= -2 \end{aligned}$$

Multiply $4A + C = -7$ by -1 and add to $-A + C = -2$.

$$\begin{aligned} -A + C &= -2 \\ \underline{-4A - C} &= \underline{7} \\ -5A &= 5 \end{aligned}$$

Using $A = -1$ in $A + B = 1$, $B = 2$.
Using $B = 2$ in $B + C = -1$, $C = -3$.
So $A = -1, B = 2$, and $C = -3$.

29. Note, $\dfrac{5x^2 + 5x}{(x+2)(x^2+1)} = \dfrac{A}{x+2} + \dfrac{Bx+C}{x^2+1}$.

$$\begin{aligned} 5x^2 + 5x &= A(x^2+1) + (Bx+C)(x+2) \\ 5x^2 + 5x &= (A+B)x^2 + (2B+C)x + \\ &\quad (A+2C) \end{aligned}$$

If we equate the coefficients of x, we obtain

$$\begin{aligned} A + B &= 5 \\ 2B + C &= 5 \\ A + 2C &= 0 \end{aligned}$$

Solving the system, we obtain $A = 2$, $B = 3$, and $C = -1$. The answer is $\dfrac{2}{x+2} + \dfrac{3x-1}{x^2+1}$.

31. Note,

$$\dfrac{x^2-2}{(x+1)(x^2+x+1)} = \dfrac{A}{x+1} + \dfrac{Bx+C}{x^2+x+1}.$$

$$\begin{aligned} x^2 - 2 &= A(x^2+x+1) + (Bx+C)(x+1) \\ x^2 - 2 &= (A+B)x^2 + (A+B+C)x + \\ &\quad (A+C) \end{aligned}$$

If we equate the coefficients of x, we obtain

$$\begin{aligned} A + B &= 1 \\ A + B + C &= 0 \\ A + C &= -2. \end{aligned}$$

Solving the system, we obtain $A = -1$, $B = 2$, and $C = -1$. The answer is

$$\dfrac{-1}{x+1} + \dfrac{2x-1}{x^2+x+1}.$$

33. $\dfrac{-2x-7}{(x+2)^2} = \dfrac{A}{x+2} + \dfrac{B}{(x+2)^2}$

$$\begin{aligned} -2x - 7 &= A(x+2) + B \\ -2x - 7 &= Ax + (2A+B) \\ A = -2 \quad &\text{and} \quad 2A + B = -7 \end{aligned}$$

Using $A = -2$ in $2A + B = -7$, we get $B = -3$. The answer is

$$\dfrac{-3}{(x+2)^2} + \dfrac{-2}{x+2}.$$

35. Note that $x^3 + x^2 + x + 1 = x^2(x+1) + (x+1) = (x^2+1)(x+1)$. Then we obtain

$$\dfrac{6x^2 - x + 1}{(x^2+1)(x+1)} = \dfrac{A}{x+1} + \dfrac{Bx+C}{x^2+1}$$

$$\begin{aligned} 6x^2 - x + 1 &= A(x^2+1) + (Bx+C)(x+1) \\ 6x^2 - x + 1 &= (A+B)x^2 + (B+C)x + (A+C). \end{aligned}$$

Equating the coefficients, we get

$$\begin{aligned} A + B &= 6 \\ B + C &= -1 \\ A + C &= 1. \end{aligned}$$

Multiply $A + B = 6$ by -1 and add to $B + C = -1$.

$$\begin{aligned} -A - B &= -6 \\ \underline{B + C} &= \underline{-1} \\ -A + C &= -7 \end{aligned}$$

Adding $-A + C = -7$ and $A + C = 1$, $2C = -6$. Using $C = -3$ in $B + C = -1$ and $A + C = 1$, we obtain $B = 2$ and $A = 4$.

The answer is $\dfrac{4}{x+1} + \dfrac{2x-3}{x^2+1}$.

37. Note,

$$\frac{3x^3 - x^2 + 19x - 9}{(x^2 + 9)^2} = \frac{Ax + B}{x^2 + 9} + \frac{Cx + D}{(x^2 + 9)^2}.$$

So $3x^3 - x^2 + 19x - 9 =$
$(Ax + B)(x^2 + 9) + (Cx + D) =$
$Ax^3 + Bx^2 + (9A + C)x + (9B + D).$

Then $A = 3$ and $B = -1$. Since $9A + C = 19$ and $9B + D = -9$, we get $C = -8$ and $D = 0$.

The answer is $\dfrac{-8x}{(x^2 + 9)^2} + \dfrac{3x - 1}{x^2 + 9}.$

39. Observe that

$$\frac{3x^2 + 17x + 14}{(x - 2)(x^2 + 2x + 4)} = \frac{A}{x - 2} + \frac{Bx + C}{x^2 + 2x + 4}.$$

Then $3x^2 + 17x + 14 =$
$A(x^2 + 2x + 4) + (Bx + C)(x - 2) =$
$(A + B)x^2 + (2A - 2B + C)x + (4A - 2C)$

Equating the coefficients, we obtain

$$\begin{aligned} A + B &= 3 \\ 2A - 2B + C &= 17 \\ 4A - 2C &= 14. \end{aligned}$$

Multiply $A + B = 3$ by 2 and add to $2A - 2B + C = 17$.

$$\begin{aligned} 2A + 2B &= 6 \\ 2A - 2B + C &= 17 \\ \hline 4A + C &= 23 \end{aligned}$$

Multiplying $4A - 2C = 14$ by -1 and adding to $4A + C = 23$, $3C = 9$. So $C = 3$ and from $4A - 2C = 14$, $A = 5$. Using these values in $2A - 2B + C = 17$, we get

$B = -2$. The answer is $\dfrac{5}{x - 2} + \dfrac{-2x + 3}{x^2 + 2x + 4}.$

41. Divide $2x^3 + x^2 + 3x - 2$ by $x^2 - 1$ by long division.

$$\begin{array}{r} 2x + 1 \\ x^2 - 1 \overline{)2x^3 + x^2 + 3x - 2} \\ \underline{2x^3 + 0x^2 - 2x} \\ x^2 + 5x - 2 \\ \underline{x^2 + 0x - 1} \\ 5x - 1 \end{array}$$

Then $\dfrac{2x^3 + x^2 + 3x - 2}{x^2 - 1} = 2x + 1 + \dfrac{5x - 1}{x^2 - 1}.$

Decompose $\dfrac{5x - 1}{x^2 - 1} = \dfrac{A}{x - 1} + \dfrac{B}{x + 1}.$

$$\begin{aligned} 5x - 1 &= A(x + 1) + B(x - 1) \\ 5x - 1 &= (A + B)x + (A - B) \end{aligned}$$

So $A + B = 5$ and $A - B = -1$.

Adding $A + B = 5$ and $A - B = -1$, $2A = 4$. Using $A = 2$ in $A + B = 5$, we find $B = 3$.

The answer is $2x + 1 + \dfrac{2}{x - 1} + \dfrac{3}{x + 1}.$

43.

Since $\dfrac{3x^3 - 2x^2 + x - 2}{(x^2 + x + 1)^2} =$

$\dfrac{Ax + B}{x^2 + x + 1} + \dfrac{Cx + D}{(x^2 + x + 1)^2}$, we get

$3x^3 - 2x^2 + x - 2 = (Ax + B)(x^2 + x + 1) +$
$(Cx + D)$
$\quad = Ax^3 + (A + B)x^2 + (A + B + C)x + (B + D).$

Equating the coefficients, we find $A = 3$. Since $A + B = -2$, we get $B = -5$. From $A + B + C = 1$ and $B + D = -2$, we have $C = 3$ and $D = 3$.

The answer is $\dfrac{3x - 5}{x^2 + x + 1} + \dfrac{3x + 3}{(x^2 + x + 1)^2}.$

45.

Since $\dfrac{3x^3 + 4x^2 - 12x + 16}{(x - 2)(x + 2)(x^2 + 4)} =$

$\dfrac{A}{x - 2} + \dfrac{B}{x + 2} + \dfrac{Cx + D}{x^2 + 4}$, we obtain

$3x^3 + 4x^2 - 12x + 16 =$
$\quad = A(x + 2)(x^2 + 4) + B(x - 2)(x^2 + 4) +$
$\quad (Cx + D)(x^2 - 4)$
$\quad = (A + B + C)x^3 + (2A - 2B + D)x^2 +$
$\quad (4A + 4B - 4C)x + (8A - 8B - 4D).$

Equating the coefficients, we get

$$\begin{aligned} A + B + C &= 3 \\ 2A - 2B + D &= 4 \\ 4A + 4B - 4C &= -12 \\ 8A - 8B - 4D &= 16. \end{aligned}$$

Multiply first equation by -4 and add to the third. Multiply second equation by -4 and add to the fourth. Also multiply first equation by 2 and add to the second.

$$\begin{array}{rcl} -4A - 4B - 4C &=& -12 \\ 4A + 4B - 4C &=& -12 \\ \hline -8C &=& -24 \end{array}$$

$$\begin{array}{rcl} -8A + 8B - 4D &=& -16 \\ 8A - 8B - 4D &=& 16 \\ \hline -8D &=& 0 \end{array}$$

$$\begin{array}{rcl} 2A + 2B + 2C &=& 6 \\ 2A - 2B + D &=& 4 \\ \hline 4A + 2C + D &=& 10 \end{array}$$

So $C = 3$ and $D = 0$. From $4A + 2C + D = 10$, we find $A = 1$ and from $2A - 2B + D = 4$, we get $B = -1$.

The answer is $\dfrac{1}{x-2} + \dfrac{-1}{x+2} + \dfrac{3x}{x^2+4}$.

47.

$$\frac{5x^3 + x^2 + x - 3}{x^3(x-1)} = \frac{A}{x} + \frac{B}{x^2} + \frac{C}{x^3} + \frac{D}{x-1},$$

$$\begin{aligned} 5x^3 + x^2 + x - 3 &= \\ &= Ax^2(x-1) + Bx(x-1) + C(x-1) + Dx^3 \\ &= (A+D)x^3 + (-A+B)x^2 + (-B+C)x - C \end{aligned}$$

Equating the coefficients, we get $C = 3$.
From $-B + C = 1$, we find $B = 2$.
From $-A + B = 1$, we obtain $A = 1$.
From $A + D = 5$, we have $D = 4$.

The answer is $\dfrac{1}{x} + \dfrac{2}{x^2} + \dfrac{3}{x^3} + \dfrac{4}{x-1}$.

49. Note,

$$\frac{6x^2 - 28x + 33}{(x-2)^2(x-3)} = \frac{A}{x-2} + \frac{B}{(x-2)^2} + \frac{C}{x-3}.$$

Then $6x^2 - 28x + 33 =$
$$\begin{aligned} &= A(x-2)(x-3) + B(x-3) + C(x-2)^2 \\ &= (A+C)x^2 + (-5A + B - 4C)x + \\ &\quad (6A - 3B + 4C). \end{aligned}$$

Equating the coefficients, we obtain

$$\begin{array}{rcl} A + C &=& 6 \\ -5A + B - 4C &=& -28 \\ 6A - 3B + 4C &=& 33. \end{array}$$

Multiply second equation by 3 and add to the third.

$$\begin{array}{rcl} -15A + 3B - 12C &=& -84 \\ 6A - 3B + 4C &=& 33 \\ \hline -9A - 8C &=& -51 \end{array}$$

Multiply $A + C = 6$ by 8 and add to $-9A - 8C = -51$

$$\begin{array}{rcl} -9A - 8C &=& -51 \\ 8A + 8C &=& 48 \\ \hline -A &=& -3 \end{array}$$

Using $A = 3$ in $A + C = 6$, we find $C = 3$.
From $6A - 3B + 4C = 33$, we obtain $B = -1$.

The answer is $\dfrac{3}{x-2} + \dfrac{-1}{(x-2)^2} + \dfrac{3}{x-3}$.

51. Use synthetic division to factor the denominator.

$$\begin{array}{r|rrrr} -5 & 1 & 4 & -11 & -30 \\ & & -5 & 5 & 30 \\ \hline & 1 & -1 & -6 & 0 \end{array}$$

$$\begin{aligned} x^3 + 4x^2 - 11x - 30 &= (x+5)(x^2 - x - 6) \\ &= (x+5)(x+2)(x-3) \end{aligned}$$

Decomposing, $\dfrac{9x^2 + 21x - 24}{(x+5)(x+2)(x-3)} =$

$$= \frac{A}{x+5} + \frac{B}{x+2} + \frac{C}{x-3}.$$

Then $9x^2 + 21x - 24 =$
$$\begin{aligned} &= A(x+2)(x-3) + B(x+5)(x-3) + \\ &\quad C(x+5)(x+2) \end{aligned}$$

and substituting $x = -2, 3, -5$, we obtain

$$\begin{array}{rcl} -30 &=& -15B \\ 2 &=& B \end{array}$$

$$\begin{array}{rcl} 120 &=& 40C \\ 3 &=& C \end{array}$$

$$\begin{array}{rcl} 96 &=& -24A \\ 4 &=& A. \end{array}$$

The answer is $\dfrac{4}{x+5} + \dfrac{2}{x+2} + \dfrac{3}{x-3}$.

53. Note that $x^3 - 3x^2 + 3x - 1 = (x-1)^3$.

Then $\dfrac{x^2 - 2}{(x-1)^3} = \dfrac{A}{x-1} + \dfrac{B}{(x-1)^2} + \dfrac{C}{(x-1)^3}$.

$$\begin{aligned} x^2 - 2 &= A(x-1)^2 + B(x-1) + C \\ &= Ax^2 + (-2A + B)x + (A - B + C) \end{aligned}$$

Then $A = 1$. Since $-2A + B = 0$, $B = 2$. Since $A - B + C = -2$, we find $1 - 2 + C = -2$ and $C = -1$.

The answer is $\dfrac{1}{x-1} + \dfrac{2}{(x-1)^2} + \dfrac{-1}{(x-1)^3}$.

55.

$$\begin{aligned} \dfrac{x}{(ax+b)^2} &= \dfrac{A}{ax+b} + \dfrac{B}{(ax+b)^2} \\ x &= A(ax+b) + B \\ &= aAx + (bA + B) \end{aligned}$$

So $aA = 1$ and $A = 1/a$. Since $bA + B = 0$, we obtain $\dfrac{b}{a} + B = 0$ and $B = -b/a$.

The answer is $\dfrac{-b/a}{(ax+b)^2} + \dfrac{1/a}{ax+b}$.

57. Since $\dfrac{x+c}{x(ax+b)} = \dfrac{A}{x} + \dfrac{B}{ax+b}$, we have

$$\begin{aligned} x + c &= A(ax+b) + Bx \\ &= (aA + B)x + bA. \end{aligned}$$

So $bA = c$ and $A = \dfrac{c}{b}$. Since $aA + B = 1$, we have $\dfrac{ac}{b} + B = 1$ and $B = 1 - \dfrac{ac}{b}$.

Answer is $\dfrac{c/b}{x} + \dfrac{1 - ac/b}{ax+b}$.

59. Since $\dfrac{1}{x^2(ax+b)} = \dfrac{A}{x} + \dfrac{B}{x^2} + \dfrac{C}{ax+b}$, we get

$$1 = Ax(ax+b) + B(ax+b) + Cx^2$$
$$1 = (aA + C)x^2 + (bA + aB)x + bB.$$

So $bB = 1$ and $B = \dfrac{1}{b}$. Since $bA + aB = 0$, we obtain $bA + \dfrac{a}{b} = 0$ and $A = -\dfrac{a}{b^2}$.

Since $aA + C = 0$, $-\dfrac{a^2}{b^2} + C = 0$ and $C = \dfrac{a^2}{b^2}$.

The answer is

$$\dfrac{-a/b^2}{x} + \dfrac{1/b}{x^2} + \dfrac{a^2/b^2}{ax+b}.$$

61. If we substitute $y = x + 2$ into the other equation, we find

$$\begin{aligned} x^2 + (x+2)^2 &= 34 \\ 2x^2 + 4x - 30 &= 0 \\ x^2 + 2x - 15 &= 0 \\ (x+5)(x-3) &= 0 \\ x &= -5, 3 \end{aligned}$$

If $x = -5$, then $y = x + 2 = -5 + 2 = -3$. Similarly, if $x = 3$ then $y = 5$.

The solution set is $\{(-5, -3), (3, 5)\}$.

63. We may rewrite $2y = 10x - 6$ as $16 = 10x - 2y$ or $8 = 5x - y$. Then the system of two equations are dependent. Since $y = 5x - 8$, the solution set is

$$\{(x, 5x - 8) \mid x \text{ is a real number}\}.$$

65. Apply the method of completing the square.

$$\begin{aligned} y &= \dfrac{1}{2}\left(x^2 + 8x\right) - 9 \\ y &= \dfrac{1}{2}\left(x^2 + 8x + 16\right) - 9 - 8 \\ y &= \dfrac{1}{2}(x+4)^2 - 17 \end{aligned}$$

For Thought

1. False, since $3 > 1 + 2$ is false.

2. False **3.** True

4. False, because $x^2 + y^2 > 5$ is the region outside of a circle of radius $\sqrt{5}$.

5. True, since $(-2, 1)$ satisfies both equations in system (a).

6. True

7. False, $(-2, 0)$ does not satisfy $y < x + 2$.

8. False, $(-1, 2)$ lies on the line $y - 3x = 5$.

9. True

10. True

5 Exercises

1. c   **3.**   d

5. $y < 2x$

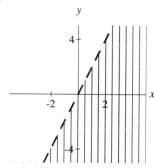

7. $x + y > 3$

9. $2x - y \leq 4$

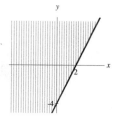

11. $y < -3x - 4$

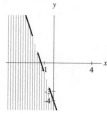

13. $x - 3 \geq 0$

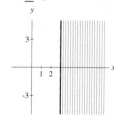

15. $20x - 30y \leq 6000$

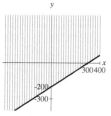

17. $y < 3$

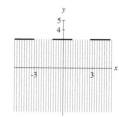

19. $y > -x^2$

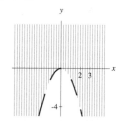

21. $x^2 + y^2 \geq 1$

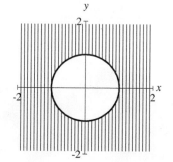

23. $x > |y|$

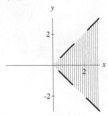

25. $x \geq y^2$

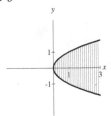

27. $y \geq x^3$

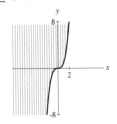

29. $y > 2^x$

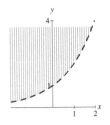

31. $y > x - 4$, $y < -x - 2$

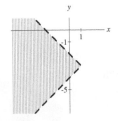

33. $3x - 4y \leq 12$, $x + y \geq -3$

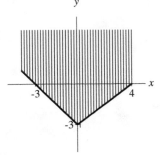

35. $3x - y < 4$, $y < 3x + 5$

37. No solution since the graphs of $y + x < 0$ and $y > 3 - x$ do not overlap.

39. $x + y < 5$, $y \geq 2$

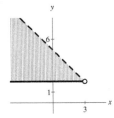

41. $y < x - 3$, $x \leq 4$

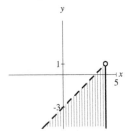

43. $y > x^2 - 3$, $y < x + 1$

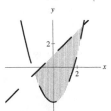

45. $x^2 + y^2 \geq 4$, $x^2 + y^2 \leq 16$

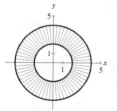

47. $(x-3)^2 + y^2 \leq 25$, $(x+3)^2 + y^2 \leq 25$

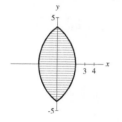

49. $x^2 + y^2 > 4$, $|x| \leq 4$

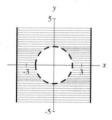

51. $y > |2x| - 4$, $y \leq \sqrt{4 - x^2}$

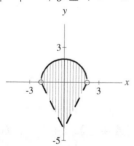

53. $|x - 1| < 2$, $|y - 1| < 4$

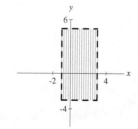

55. $x \geq 0$, $y \geq 0$, $x + y \leq 4$

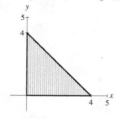

57. $x \geq 0$, $y \geq 0$, $x + y \geq 4$, $y \geq -2x + 6$

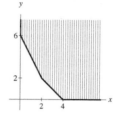

59. $x^2 + y^2 \geq 9$, $x^2 + y^2 \leq 25$, $y \geq |x|$

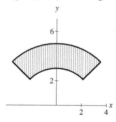

61. $y > (x-1)^3$, $y > 1$, $x + y > -2$

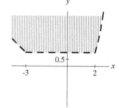

63. $y > 2^x$, $y < 6 - x^2$, $x + y > 0$

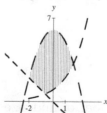

65. $x \geq 0$, $y \geq 0$, $y \leq -\dfrac{2}{3}x + 5$, $y \leq -3x + 12$

67. $x \geq 0$, $y \geq 0$, $y \geq -\dfrac{1}{2}x + 3$, $y \geq -\dfrac{3}{2}x + 5$

69. The system is

$$|x| \; < 2$$
$$|y| \; < 2.$$

71. Since a circle of radius 9 with center at the origin is given by $x^2 + y^2 = 81$, the system is

$$x^2 + y^2 < 81$$
$$x > 0$$
$$y > 0.$$

73. $(-1.17,\ 1.84)$ is a solution.

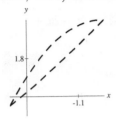

75. $(150,\ 22.4)$ is a solution.

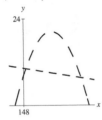

77. Let w and h be the width and height, respectively. Then $50 + 2w + 2h \leq 130$. The system is

$$w + h \leq 40$$
$$w, h \geq 0.$$

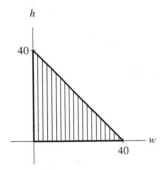

79. Let x and y be the number of mid-size and full-size cars, respectively. Divide $10,000x + 15,000y \leq 1,500,000$ by 1000. The system is

$$x + y \leq 110$$
$$x + 1.5y \leq 150$$
$$x \geq 0$$
$$y \geq 0.$$

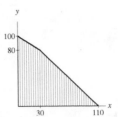

81. Let x and y be the number of \$50 tickets and \$100 tickets, respectively. Simplifying $y \leq 0.2(x + y)$, we get $0.8y \leq 0.2x$. Then $y \leq \frac{1}{4}x$. The system is

$$y \leq \frac{1}{4}x$$
$$x + y \leq 500$$
$$x \geq 0, y \geq 0.$$

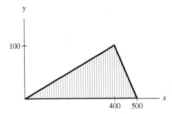

83. From the equation

$$\frac{x^2 + 5x + 3}{x^2(x + 1)} = \frac{A}{x} + \frac{B}{x^2} + \frac{C}{x + 1}$$

we find

$$x^2 + 5x + 3 = Ax(x + 1) + B(x + 1) + Cx^2$$
$$x^2 + 5x + 3 = (A + C)x^2 + (A + B)x + B.$$

Equating the coefficients, we obtain a system of equations.

$$B = 3$$
$$A + B = 5$$
$$A + C = 1$$

The solutions of the above system of equations are $B = 3$, $A = 2$, and $C = -1$.

The partial fraction decomposition is

$$\frac{2}{x} + \frac{3}{x^2} + \frac{-1}{x + 1}.$$

85. The second equation $18y - 10x = 20$ is equivalent to $9y - 5x = 10$ or $5x - 9y = -10$. This contradicts the first equation $5x - 9y = 12$. The solution set is $\emptyset$.

87. $\$20,000e^{0.05(3.5)} = \$23,824.92$

For Thought

1. False, $x \geq 0$ include points on the x-axis and the first and fourth quadrants.

2. False, $y \geq 2$ include points on or above the line $y = 2$. **3.** False

4. False, since x-intercept is $(6,0)$ and y-intercept is $(0,4)$. **5.** True **6.** True **7.** False

8. True, since $R(1,3) = 30(1) + 15(3) = 75$.

9. False, since $C(0,5) = 7(0) + 9(5) + 3 = 48$.

10. True

6 Exercises

1. constraints

3. natural

5. Vertices are $(0,0), (0,4), (4,0)$

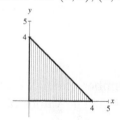

7. Vertices are $(0,0), (1,3), (1,0), (0,3)$

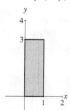

9. Vertices are $(0,0), (2,2), (0,4), (3,0)$

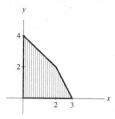

11. Vertices are $(3,0), (1,2), (0,4)$

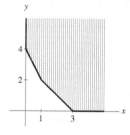

13. Vertices are $(1,3), (4,0), (0,6)$

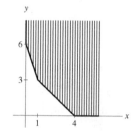

15. Vertices are $(1,5), (6,0), (0,8)$

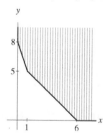

17. The values of $T(x,y) = 2x + 3y$ at the vertices are $T(0,0) = 0$, $T(0,4) = 12$, $T(3,3) = 15$, and $T(5,0) = 10$. The maximum value is 15.

19. The values of $H(x,y) = 2x + 2y$ at the vertices are $T(0,6) = 12$, $T(2,2) = 8$, and $T(5,0) = 10$. The minimum value is 8.

21. The values of $P(x,y) = 5x + 9y$ at the vertices are $P(0,0) = 0$, $P(6,0) = 30$, $P(0,3) = 27$. Maximum value is 30.

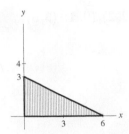

23. The values of $C(x, y) = 3x + 2y$ at the vertices are $C(0, 4) = 8$ and $C(4, 0) = 12$. The minimum value is 8.

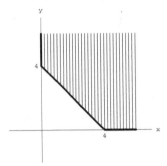

25. The values of $C(x, y) = 10x + 20y$ at the vertices are $C(0, 8) = 160$, $C(5, 3) = 110$, and $C(10, 0) = 100$. Minimum value is 100.

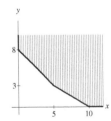

27. Let x and y be the number of bird houses and mailboxes, respectively.

$$\text{Maximize } 12x + 20y$$
$$\text{subject to } 3x + 4y \leq 48$$
$$x + 2y \leq 20$$
$$x, y \geq 0$$

The values of $R(x, y) = 12x + 20y$ at the vertices are $R(0, 0) = 0$, $R(0, 10) = 200$, $R(8, 6) = 216$, and $R(16, 0) = 192$. To maximize revenue, they must sell 8 bird houses and 6 mailboxes.

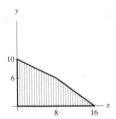

29. Let x and y be the number of bird houses and mailboxes, respectively. The values of $R(x, y) = 18x + 20y$ at the vertices are $R(0, 0) = 0$, $R(0, 10) = 200$, $R(8, 6) = 264$, and $R(16, 0) = 288$. To maximize revenue, they must sell 16 bird houses and 0 mailboxes.

31. Let x and y be the number of small and large truck loads, respectively.

$$\text{Minimize } 70x + 60y$$
$$\text{subject to } 12x + 20y \geq 120$$
$$x + y \geq 8$$
$$x, y \geq 0$$

The values of $C(x, y) = 70x + 60y$ at the vertices are $C(0, 8) = 480$, $C(10, 0) = 700$, and $C(5, 3) = 530$, To minimize costs, they must make 8 large truck loads and 0 small truck loads.

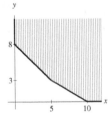

33. Let x and y be the number of small and large truck loads, respectively. The values of $C(x, y) = 70x + 75y$ at the vertices are $C(0, 8) = 600$, $C(10, 0) = 700$, and $C(5, 3) = 575$.

To minimize costs, they must make 5 small truck loads and 3 large truck loads.

35. The points (x, y) satisfying $y > x^2 - 2x$ lie in the region enclosed by the parabola $y = x^2 - 2x$. While the points (x, y) satisfying $y < -1 - x$ lie in the region below the line $y = -1 - x$. Since the line lies to the left of the parabola, the system $y > x^2 - 2x$ and $y < -1 - x$ has no solution. The solution set is $\emptyset$.

37. Multiply by the LCD as follows:

$$\frac{1}{x} + \frac{1}{x-1} = \frac{3}{2}$$

$$2(x-1) + 2x = 3x(x-1)$$
$$4x - 2 = 3x^2 - 3x$$
$$0 = 3x^2 - 7x + 2$$
$$0 = (3x-1)(x-2)$$

Then the solution set is $\{1/3, 2\}$.

39. Rewrite the inequality.

$$\frac{3x-2}{x-2} - 1 > 0$$

$$\frac{2x}{x-2} > 0$$

Let $f(x) = \frac{2x}{x-2} > 0$, and use test points.

If $x = -1$, then $f(-1) > 0$.
If $x = 1$, then $f(1) < 0$.
If $x = 3$, then $f(3) > 0$.

```
    +    0    -    UD   +
<———————————————————————————>
   -1    0    1    2    3
```

The solution set is $(-\infty, 0) \cup (2, \infty)$.

Review Exercises

1. The solution set is $\{(3,5)\}$.

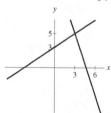

3. The solution set is $\{(-1,3)\}$

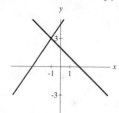

5. Substitute $y = x$ into $3x - 5y = 19$.

$$3x - 5x = 19$$
$$-2x = 19$$
$$x = -19/2$$

Independent and the solution set is $\{(-19/2, -19/2)\}$.

7. Multiply $4x - 3y = 6$ by 2 and $3x + 2y = 9$ by 3, then add the equations.

$$8x - 6y = 12$$
$$9x + 6y = 27$$
$$\overline{17x = 39}$$

Substitute $x = 39/17$ into $4x - 3y = 6$.

$$\frac{156}{17} - 3y = 6$$
$$\frac{54}{17} = 3y$$
$$\frac{18}{17} = y$$

Independent and the solution set is $\{(39/17, 18/17)\}$.

9. Substitute $y = -3x + 1$ into $6x + 2y = 2$.

$$6x + 2(-3x+1) = 2$$
$$6x - 6x + 2 = 2$$
$$2 = 2$$

Dependent and the solution set is $\{(x,y) \mid y = -3x + 1\}$.

11. Multiply $3x - 4y = 12$ by 2 and add to the second equation.

$$6x - 8y = 24$$
$$-6x + 8y = 9$$
$$\overline{0 = 33}$$

Inconsistent and the solution set is $\emptyset$.

13. Add the first and second equations. Multiply $2x + y + z = 1$ by -3 and add to the third equation.

$$x + y - z = 8$$
$$2x + y + z = 1$$
$$\overline{3x + 2y = 9}$$

$$\begin{aligned} -6x - 3y - 3z &= -3 \\ x + 2y + 3z &= -5 \\ \hline -5x - y &= -8 \end{aligned}$$

Multiply $-5x - y = -8$ by 2 and add to $3x + 2y = 9$.

$$\begin{aligned} -10x - 2y &= -16 \\ 3x + 2y &= 9 \\ \hline -7x &= -7 \end{aligned}$$

Using $x = 1$ in $3x + 2y = 9$, $3 + 2y = 9$ or $y = 3$. From $x + y - z = 8$, $1 + 3 - z = 8$ or $z = -4$. The Solution set is $\{(1, 3, -4)\}$.

15. Multiply first equation by -2 and add to the second equation. Multiply first equation by -2 and add to the third one.

$$\begin{aligned} -2x - 2y - 2z &= -2 \\ 2x - y + 2z &= 2 \\ \hline -3y &= 0 \\ y &= 0 \end{aligned}$$

$$\begin{aligned} -2x - 2y - 2z &= -2 \\ 2x + 2y + 2z &= 2 \\ \hline 0 &= 0 \end{aligned}$$

Using $y = 0$ in $x + y + z = 1$, $x + z = 1$ and $z = 1 - x$. The solution set is $\{(x, 0, 1 - x) \mid x \text{ is any real number}\}$.

17. Multiply first equation by -1 and add to the third equation.

$$\begin{aligned} -x - y - z &= -1 \\ x + y + z &= 4 \\ \hline 0 &= 3 \end{aligned}$$

Inconsistent and the solution set is $\emptyset$.

19. Substitute $x = y^2$ into $x^2 + y^2 = 4$ and use the quadratic formula.

$$\begin{aligned} y^4 + y^2 &= 4 \\ y^4 + y^2 - 4 &= 0 \\ y^2 &= \frac{-1 + \sqrt{17}}{2} \\ y &= \pm\sqrt{\frac{-1 + \sqrt{17}}{2}} \end{aligned}$$

Thus, $x = y^2 = \dfrac{-1 + \sqrt{17}}{2}$.

The solution set is

$$\left\{ \left(\frac{-1 + \sqrt{17}}{2}, \pm\sqrt{\frac{-1 + \sqrt{17}}{2}} \right) \right\}.$$

21. Substitute $y = x^2$ into $y = |x|$.

$$\begin{aligned} x^2 &= \sqrt{x^2} \\ x^4 &= x^2 \\ x^2(x^2 - 1) &= 0 \\ x &= 0, \pm 1 \end{aligned}$$

Using $x = 0, 1, -1$ in $y = x^2$, we get $y = 0, 1, 1$, respectively. The solution set is $\{(0, 0), (1, 1), (-1, 1)\}$.

23. Note, $\dfrac{7x - 7}{(x - 3)(x + 4)} = \dfrac{A}{x - 3} + \dfrac{B}{x + 4}$. Then

$$\begin{aligned} 7x - 7 &= A(x + 4) + B(x - 3) \\ 7x - 7 &= (A + B)x + (4A - 3B). \end{aligned}$$

Equating the coefficients, we obtain

$$\begin{aligned} A + B &= 7 \\ 4A - 3B &= -7. \end{aligned}$$

The solution of this system is $A = 2$, $B = 5$. The answer is $\dfrac{2}{x - 3} + \dfrac{5}{x + 4}$.

25. Factoring the denominator, we obtain

$$\begin{aligned} x^3 - 3x^2 + 4x - 12 &= x^2(x - 3) + 4(x - 3) \\ &= (x^2 + 4)(x - 3), \end{aligned}$$

and so $\dfrac{7x^2 - 7x + 23}{(x - 3)(x^2 + 4)} = \dfrac{A}{x - 3} + \dfrac{Bx + C}{x^2 + 4}$.

Then $7x^2 - 7x + 23 =$
$A(x^2 + 4) + (Bx + C)(x - 3) =$
$= (A + B)x^2 + (-3B + C)x + (4A - 3C)$.
Equating the coefficients, we have

$$\begin{aligned} A + B &= 7 \\ -3B + C &= -7 \\ 4A - 3C &= 23. \end{aligned}$$

The solution of this system is $A = 5$, $B = 2$, and $C = -1$. The answer is $\dfrac{5}{x - 3} + \dfrac{2x - 1}{x^2 + 4}$.

27. $x^2 + (y - 3)^2 < 9$

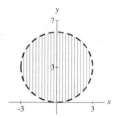

29. $x \leq (y - 1)^2$

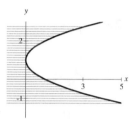

31. $2x - 3y \geq 6$, $x \leq 2$

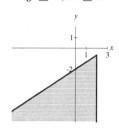

33. $y \geq 2x^2 - 6$, $x^2 + y^2 \leq 9$

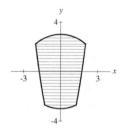

35. $x \geq 0$, $y \geq 1$, $x + 2y \leq 10$, $3x + 4y \leq 24$

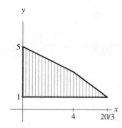

37. $x \geq 0$, $y \geq 0$, $x + 6y \geq 60$, $x + y \geq 35$

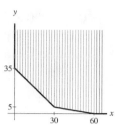

39. Substitute $(-2, 3)$ and $(4, -1)$ into $y = mx + b$.

$$-2m + b = 3$$
$$4m + b = -1$$

Multiply first equation by -1 and add to the second equation.

$$2m - b = -3$$
$$\underline{4m + b = -1}$$
$$6m = -4$$

Using $m = -2/3$ in $-2m + b = 3$, $4/3 + b = 3$ and $b = 5/3$. Equation of line is $y = -\dfrac{2}{3}x + \dfrac{5}{3}$.

41. Substitute $(1, 4)$, $(3, 20)$, and $(-2, 25)$ into $y = ax^2 + bx + c$.

$$a + b + c = 4$$
$$9a + 3b + c = 20$$
$$4a - 2b + c = 25$$

The solution of the above system is $a = 3$, $b = -4$, $c = 5$. The parabola is given by $y = 3x^2 - 4x + 5$.

43. Let x and y be the number of tacos and burritos, respectively.

$$x + 2y = 181$$
$$2x + 3y = 300$$

Solving the above system, we find $x = 57$ tacos and $y = 62$ burritos.

45. Let x, y and z be the selling price of a daisy, carnation, and a rose, respectively. Then

$$5x + 3y + 2z = 3.05$$
$$3x + y + 4z = 2.75$$
$$4x + 2y + z = 2.10.$$

Solving the above system, we find $x = 0.30$, $y = 0.25$, and $z = 0.40$. Esther's economy special sells for $x + y + z = \$0.95$.

47. The values of $C(x,y) = 0.42x + 0.84y$ at the vertices are $C(0,35) = 29.4$, $C(30,5) = 16.8$, and $C(60,0) = 25.2$. The minimum value is 16.8.

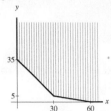

49. Let x and y be the number of barrels of oil obtained through the pipeline and barges, respectively.

Minimize $100x + 90y$

$$\text{subject to } x + y \geq 12{,}000{,}000$$
$$x \leq 12{,}000{,}000$$
$$x \geq 6{,}000{,}000$$
$$y \leq 8{,}000{,}000$$
$$x, y \geq 0$$

The values of $C(x,y) = 20x + 18y$ at the vertices are
$C(12 \text{ million}, 0) = 1200$ million,
$C(12 \text{ million}, 8 \text{ million}) = 1920$ million,
$C(6 \text{ million}, 8 \text{ million}) = 1320$ million, and
$C(6 \text{ million}, 6 \text{ million}) = 1140$ million.
To minimize cost, purchase 6 million barrels from each source.

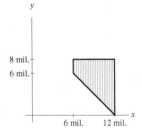

Chapter Test

1. Solution set is $\{(-3, 4)\}$.

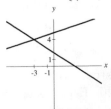

2. Substitute $y = 4 - 2x$ into $3x - 4y = 9$.

$$3x - 4(4 - 2x) = 9$$
$$3x - 16 + 8x = 9$$
$$11x = 25$$
$$x = 25/11$$

Using $x = 25/11$ in $y = 4 - 2x$, we have $y = 4 - 50/11 = -6/11$. Solution set is $\{(25/11, -6/11)\}$.

3. Multiply $10x - 3y = 22$ by 2 and $7x + 2y = 40$ by 3. Then add the equations.

$$\begin{aligned} 20x - 6y &= 44 \\ 21x + 6y &= 120 \\ \hline 41x &= 164 \\ x &= 4 \end{aligned}$$

Using $x = 4$ in $10x - 3y = 22$, we get $40 - 3y = 22$ and $y = 6$. The solution set is $\{(4, 6)\}$.

4. Substitute $x = 6 - y$ into $3x + 3y = 4$.

$$3(6 - y) + 3y = 4$$
$$18 - 3y + 3y = 4$$
$$18 = 4$$

The system is inconsistent.

5. Substitute $y = \dfrac{1}{2}x + 3$ into $x - 2y = -6$.

$$x - 2\left(\frac{1}{2}x + 3\right) = -6$$
$$x - x - 6 = -6$$
$$-6 = -6$$

The system is dependent.

6. Substitute $y = 2x - 1$ into $y = 3x + 20$.

$$2x - 1 = 3x + 20$$
$$-21 = x$$

Using $x = -21$ in $y = 2x - 1$, we get $y = -43$. The system is independent.

7. Substitute $y = -x + 2$ into $y = -x + 5$.

$$\begin{aligned} -x + 2 &= -x + 5 \\ 2 &= 5 \end{aligned}$$

The system is inconsistent.

8. Add the two equations.

$$\begin{aligned} 2x - y + z &= 4 \\ -x + 2y - z &= 6 \\ \hline x + y &= 10 \end{aligned}$$

Using $y = 10 - x$ in $2x - y + z = 4$, we find $2x - (10 - x) + z = 4$ and $z = 14 - 3x$. The solution set is
$\{(x, 10 - x, 14 - 3x) \mid x \text{ is any real number}\}$.

9. Add the first two equations. Also, multiply second equation by 3 and add to the third.

$$\begin{aligned} x - 2y - z &= 2 \\ 2x + 3y + z &= -1 \\ \hline 3x + y &= 1 \end{aligned}$$

$$\begin{aligned} 6x + 9y + 3z &= -3 \\ 3x - y - 3z &= -4 \\ \hline 9x + 8y &= -7 \end{aligned}$$

Multiply $3x + y = 1$ by -3 and add to $9x + 8y = -7$.

$$\begin{aligned} -9x - 3y &= -3 \\ 9x + 8y &= -7 \\ \hline 5y &= -10 \end{aligned}$$

Using $y = -2$ in $3x + y = 1$, we get $3x - 2 = 1$ or $x = 1$. From $x - 2y - z = 2$, we have $1 + 4 - z = 2$ or $z = 3$. The solution set is $\{(1, -2, 3)\}$.

10. Add the second and third equations.

$$\begin{aligned} x + y - z &= 4 \\ -x - y + z &= 2 \\ \hline 0 &= 6 \end{aligned}$$

Inconsistent and the solution set is $\emptyset$.

11. Multiply $x^2 + y^2 = 16$ by -1 and add to $x^2 - 4y^2 = 16$.

$$\begin{aligned} -x^2 - y^2 &= -16 \\ x^2 - 4y^2 &= 16 \\ \hline -5y^2 &= 0 \\ y &= 0 \end{aligned}$$

Using $y = 0$ in $x^2 + y^2 = 16$, we find $x^2 = 16$ and $x = \pm 4$. Solution set is $\{(4, 0), (-4, 0)\}$.

12. Substitute $y = x^2 - 5x$ into $x + y = -2$.

$$\begin{aligned} x + (x^2 - 5x) &= -2 \\ x^2 - 4x &= -2 \\ x^2 - 4x + 4 &= -2 + 4 \\ (x - 2)^2 &= 2 \\ x &= 2 \pm \sqrt{2} \end{aligned}$$

Using $x = 2 + \sqrt{2}$ and $x = 2 - \sqrt{2}$ in $y = -2 - x$, we have $y = -4 - \sqrt{2}$ and $y = -4 + \sqrt{2}$, respectively. The solution set is

$$\{(2 + \sqrt{2}, -4 - \sqrt{2}), (2 - \sqrt{2}, -4 + \sqrt{2})\}.$$

13.

$$\begin{aligned} \frac{2x + 10}{(x - 4)(x + 2)} &= \frac{A}{x - 4} + \frac{B}{x + 2} \\ 2x + 10 &= A(x + 2) + B(x - 4) \\ 2x + 10 &= (A + B)x + (2A - 4B) \end{aligned}$$

Equating the coefficients, we obtain

$$\begin{aligned} A + B &= 2 \\ 2A - 4B &= 10. \end{aligned}$$

The solution of this system is $A = 3, B = -1$.
The answer is $\dfrac{3}{x - 4} + \dfrac{-1}{x + 2}$.

14. Note, $\dfrac{4x^2 + x - 2}{x^2(x - 1)} = \dfrac{A}{x} + \dfrac{B}{x^2} + \dfrac{C}{x - 1}$. Then

$$\begin{aligned} 4x^2 + x - 2 &= Ax(x - 1) + B(x - 1) + Cx^2 \\ &= (A + C)x^2 + (-A + B)x - B. \end{aligned}$$

Equating the coefficients, we have

$$\begin{aligned} A + C &= 4 \\ -A + B &= 1 \\ -B &= -2. \end{aligned}$$

The solution of this system is $B = 2$, $A = 1$, and $C = 3$. The answer is $\dfrac{1}{x} + \dfrac{2}{x^2} + \dfrac{3}{x-1}$.

15. $2x - y < 8$

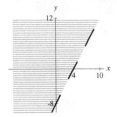

16. $x + y \leq 5$, $x - y < 0$

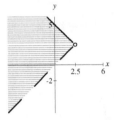

17. $x^2 + y^2 \leq 9$, $y \leq 1 - x^2$

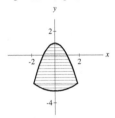

18. Let x and y be the number of male and female students, respectively. Then

$$\begin{aligned} \frac{1}{3}x + \frac{1}{4}y &= 15 \\ x + y &= 52. \end{aligned}$$

Multiply the first equation by 12 and multiply the second equation by -3. Then add the resulting equations.

$$\begin{aligned} 4x + 3y &= 180 \\ \underline{-3x - 3y} &= \underline{-156} \\ x &= 24 \end{aligned}$$

The solution of this system is $x = 24$ males and $y = 28$ females.

19. Let x and y be the number of TV commercials and newspaper ads, respectively. The linear program is given below.

$$\begin{aligned} \text{Maximize } & 14{,}000x + 6000y \\ \text{subject to } 9000x + 3000y &\leq 99{,}000 \\ x + y &\leq 23 \\ x, y &\geq 0 \end{aligned}$$

The values of $N(x, y) = 14{,}000x + 6000y$ at the vertices are $N(0, 0) = 0$, $N(0, 23) = 138{,}000$, $N(5, 18) = 178{,}000$, and $N(11, 0) = 154{,}000$. To obtain maximum audience exposure, the hospital must have 5 TV commercials and 18 newspaper ads.

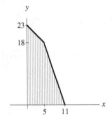

Matrices and Determinants

From Chapter 9 of *Precalculus: Functions and Graphs*. Fourth Edition. Mark Dugopolski. Copyright © 2013 by Pearson Education, Inc. All rights reserved.

Matrices and Determinants

In the year 2020, traffic gridlocks in our major cities will be a thing of the past. At least that is the vision of urban planners, who see mathematics and computers playing an ever increasing role in traffic management.

In the future, powerful computers will pinpoint drivers' locations, select routes and speeds, display maps, prevent collisions, and even issue weather reports. Drivers will simply relax and let the computer do the work.

▶ WHAT YOU WILL learn... To perform such feats, computer systems must instantly solve huge linear programming problems involving hundreds of thousands of variables. In this chapter we will study matrices and several methods for solving linear systems that are used on computers.

1 Solving Linear Systems Using Matrices

2 Operations with Matrices

3 Multiplication of Matrices

4 Inverses of Matrices

5 Solution of Linear Systems in Two Variables Using Determinants

6 Solution of Linear Systems in Three Variables Using Determinants

Stacy Gold/National Geographic/Getty Images

1 Solving Linear Systems Using Matrices

In this section we learn a method for solving systems of linear equations that is an improved version of the addition method. The new method requires some new terminology.

Matrices

Twenty-six female students and twenty-four male students responded to a survey on income in a college algebra class. Among the female students, 5 classified themselves as low-income, 10 as middle-income, and 11 as high-income. Among the male students, 9 were low-income, 2 were middle-income, and 13 were high-income. Each student is classified in two ways, according to gender and income. This information can be written in a *matrix*:

$$
\begin{array}{c}
 \\
\text{Female} \\
\text{Male}
\end{array}
\begin{array}{ccc}
\text{L} & \text{M} & \text{H} \\
\left[\begin{array}{ccc}
5 & 10 & 11 \\
9 & 2 & 13
\end{array}\right]
\end{array}
$$

In this matrix we can see the class makeup according to gender and income. A matrix provides a convenient way to organize a two-way classification of data.

A **matrix** is a rectangular array of real numbers. The **rows** of a matrix run horizontally, and the **columns** run vertically. A matrix with only one row is a **row matrix** or **row vector,** and a matrix with only one column is a **column matrix** or **column vector.** A matrix with m rows and n columns has **size $m \times n$** (read "m by n"). The number of rows is always given first. For example, the matrix used to classify the students is a 2×3 matrix.

EXAMPLE 1 Finding the size of a matrix

Determine the size of each matrix.

a. $\begin{bmatrix} -4 & 3 & -2 \end{bmatrix}$ **b.** $\begin{bmatrix} 3 & -1 \\ 4 & 2 \end{bmatrix}$ **c.** $\begin{bmatrix} -5 & 19 \\ 14 & 2 \\ 0 & -1 \end{bmatrix}$ **d.** $\begin{bmatrix} -4 & 46 & 8 \\ 1 & 0 & 13 \\ -12 & -5 & 2 \end{bmatrix}$

Solution

Matrix (a) is a row matrix with size 1×3. Matrix (b) has size 2×2, matrix (c) has size 3×2, and matrix (d) has size 3×3.

▶**TRY THIS.** Determine the size of the matrix $\begin{bmatrix} 1 & 3 & 5 & 7 \\ 2 & 4 & 6 & 8 \end{bmatrix}$. ∎

A **square matrix** has an equal number of rows and columns. Matrices (b) and (d) of Example 1 are square matrices. Each number in a matrix is called an **entry** or an **element.** The matrix $\begin{bmatrix} 5 \end{bmatrix}$ is a 1×1 matrix with only one entry, 5.

The Augmented Matrix

We now see how matrices are used to represent systems of linear equations. The solution to a system of linear equations such as

$$x - 3y = 11$$

$$2x + y = 1$$

depends on the coefficients of x and y and the constants on the right-hand side of the equation. The **coefficient matrix** for this system is the matrix

$$\begin{bmatrix} 1 & -3 \\ 2 & 1 \end{bmatrix},$$

whose entries are the coefficients of the variables. (The coefficient of y in $x - 3y = 11$ is -3.) The constants from the right-hand side of the system are attached to the matrix of coefficients, to form the **augmented matrix** of the system:

$$\left[\begin{array}{cc|c} 1 & -3 & 11 \\ 2 & 1 & 1 \end{array}\right]$$

Each row of the augmented matrix represents an equation of the system, while the columns represent the coefficients of x, the coefficients of y, and the constants, respectively. The vertical line represents the equal signs.

EXAMPLE 2 Determining the augmented matrix

Write the augmented matrix for each system of equations.

a. $x = y + 3$
$\quad y = 4 - x$

b. $x + 2y - z = 1$
$\quad 2x \quad\quad + 3z = 5$
$\quad 3x - 2y + z = 0$

c. $x - y = 2$
$\quad y - z = 3$

Solution

a. To write the augmented matrix, the equations must be in standard form with the variables on the left-hand side and constants on the right-hand side:

$$x - y = 3$$
$$x + y = 4$$

We write the augmented matrix using the coefficients of the variables and the constants:

$$\left[\begin{array}{cc|c} 1 & -1 & 3 \\ 1 & 1 & 4 \end{array}\right]$$

b. Use the coefficient 0 for each variable that is missing:

$$\left[\begin{array}{ccc|c} 1 & 2 & -1 & 1 \\ 2 & 0 & 3 & 5 \\ 3 & -2 & 1 & 0 \end{array}\right]$$

c. The augmented matrix for this system is a 2×4 matrix:

$$\left[\begin{array}{ccc|c} 1 & -1 & 0 & 2 \\ 0 & 1 & -1 & 3 \end{array}\right]$$

▶**TRY THIS.** Write the augmented matrix for the system $\begin{array}{l} x - y = -2 \\ 2x + y = 3 \end{array}$. ■

EXAMPLE 3 Writing a system for an augmented matrix

Write the system of equations represented by each augmented matrix.

a. $\left[\begin{array}{cc|c} 1 & 3 & -5 \\ 2 & -3 & 1 \end{array}\right]$ **b.** $\left[\begin{array}{cc|c} 1 & 0 & 7 \\ 0 & 1 & 3 \end{array}\right]$ **c.** $\left[\begin{array}{ccc|c} 2 & 5 & 1 & 2 \\ -3 & 0 & 4 & -1 \\ 4 & -5 & 2 & 3 \end{array}\right]$

Solution

a. Use the first two numbers in each row as the coefficients of x and y and the last number as the constant to get the following system:

$$x + 3y = -5$$
$$2x - 3y = 1$$

b. The augmented matrix represents the following system:

$$x = 7$$
$$y = 3$$

c. Use the first three numbers in each row as the coefficients of x, y, and z and the last number as the constant to get the following system:

$$2x + 5y + z = 2$$
$$-3x \quad\quad + 4z = -1$$
$$4x - 5y + 2z = 3$$

▶**TRY THIS.** Write the system for the matrix $\begin{bmatrix} 2 & 1 & | & 5 \\ -1 & 4 & | & 6 \end{bmatrix}$. ■

Two systems of linear equations are **equivalent** if they have the same solution set, whereas two augmented matrices are **equivalent** if the systems they represent are equivalent. The augmented matrices

$$\begin{bmatrix} 1 & 1 & | & 5 \\ 2 & 3 & | & 13 \end{bmatrix} \quad \text{and} \quad \begin{bmatrix} 1 & 1 & | & 5 \\ 0 & 1 & | & 3 \end{bmatrix}$$

are equivalent because their corresponding systems

$$\begin{array}{lcl} x + y = 5 & \text{and} & x + y = 5 \\ 2x + 3y = 13 & & y = 3 \end{array}$$

are equivalent. Each system has solution set $\{(2, 3)\}$.

To solve a single equation, we write simpler and simpler equivalent equations to get an equation whose solution is obvious. Similarly, to solve a system of equations, we write simpler and simpler equivalent systems to get a system whose solution is obvious. We now look at operations that can be performed on augmented matrices to obtain simpler equivalent augmented matrices.

The Gaussian Elimination Method

The rows of an augmented matrix represent the equations of a system. Since the equations of a system can be written in any order, two rows of an augmented matrix can be interchanged if necessary. Since multiplication of both sides of an equation by the same nonzero number produces an equivalent equation, multiplying each entry in a row of the augmented matrix by a nonzero number produces an equivalent augmented matrix. In the augmented matrix, elimination of variables is accomplished by adding the entries in one row to the corresponding entries in another row. These two row operations can be combined to add a multiple of one row to another, just as was done in solving systems by addition. The three **row operations** for an augmented matrix are summarized as follows.

Row Operations

Any of the following row operations on an augmented matrix gives an equivalent augmented matrix:

1. Interchanging two rows of the matrix.

   Abbreviated $R_i \leftrightarrow R_j$ (interchange rows i and j).

2. Multiplying every entry in a row by the same nonzero real number.

   Abbreviated $aR_i \rightarrow R_i$ (a times row i replaces row i).

3. Adding to a row a nonzero multiple of another row.

   Abbreviated $aR_i + R_j \rightarrow R_j$ ($aR_i + R_j$ replaces R_j).

To solve a system of two linear equations in two variables using the **Gaussian elimination method,** we use row operations to obtain simpler and simpler augmented matrices. We want to get an augmented matrix that corresponds to a system whose solution is obvious. An augmented matrix of the following form is the simplest:

$$\left[\begin{array}{cc|c} 1 & 0 & a \\ 0 & 1 & b \end{array}\right]$$

Notice that this augmented matrix corresponds to the system $x = a$ and $y = b$, for which the solution set is $\{(a, b)\}$.

The **diagonal** of a matrix consists of the entries in the first row first column, second row second column, third row third column, and so on. A square matrix with ones on the diagonal and zeros elsewhere is an **identity matrix:**

$$\begin{bmatrix} a_{11} & a_{12} \\ a_{21} & a_{22} \end{bmatrix} \qquad \begin{bmatrix} 1 & 0 \\ 0 & 1 \end{bmatrix} \qquad \begin{bmatrix} 1 & 0 & 0 \\ 0 & 1 & 0 \\ 0 & 0 & 1 \end{bmatrix}$$

| The diagonal of a 2×2 matrix | The 2×2 identity matrix | The 3×3 identity matrix |

The goal of the Gaussian elimination method is to convert the coefficient matrix (in the augmented matrix) into an identity matrix using row operations. If the system has a unique solution, then it will appear in the rightmost column of the final augmented matrix. Keep in mind that Gaussian elimination is just a variation of the addition method, performed on the augmented matrix rather than the original equations.

EXAMPLE 4 | Using the Gaussian elimination method

Use row operations to solve the system.

$$2x - 4y = 16$$
$$3x + y = 3$$

Solution

Start with the augmented matrix:

$$\left[\begin{array}{cc|c} 2 & -4 & 16 \\ 3 & 1 & 3 \end{array}\right]$$

The first step is to multiply the first row R_1 by $\frac{1}{2}$ to get a 1 in the first position on the diagonal. Think of this step as replacing R_1 by $\frac{1}{2}R_1$. We show this in symbols as $\frac{1}{2}R_1 \rightarrow R_1$. Read the arrow as "replaces."

$$\left[\begin{array}{cc|c} 1 & -2 & 8 \\ 3 & 1 & 3 \end{array}\right] \quad \tfrac{1}{2}R_1 \rightarrow R_1$$

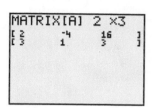

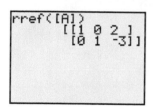

(a)

(b)

Figure 1

To get a 0 in the first position of R_2, multiply R_1 by -3 and add the result to R_2. Since $-3R_1 = [-3, 6, -24]$ and $R_2 = [3, 1, 3]$, $-3R_1 + R_2 = [0, 7, -21]$. We are replacing R_2 with $-3R_1 + R_2$:

$$\begin{bmatrix} 1 & -2 & | & 8 \\ 0 & 7 & | & -21 \end{bmatrix} \quad {\scriptstyle -3R_1 + R_2 \to R_2}$$

To get a 1 in the second position on the diagonal, multiply R_2 by $\frac{1}{7}$:

$$\begin{bmatrix} 1 & -2 & | & 8 \\ 0 & 1 & | & -3 \end{bmatrix} \quad {\scriptstyle \frac{1}{7}R_2 \to R_2}$$

Now row 2 is in the form needed to solve the system. We next get a 0 as the second entry in R_1. Multiply row 2 by 2 and add the result to row 1. Since $2R_2 = [0, 2, -6]$ and $R_1 = [1, -2, 8]$, $2R_2 + R_1 = [1, 0, 2]$. We get the following matrix.

$$\begin{bmatrix} 1 & 0 & | & 2 \\ 0 & 1 & | & -3 \end{bmatrix} \quad {\scriptstyle 2R_2 + R_1 \to R_1}$$

Note that the coefficient of y in the first equation is now 0. The system associated with the last augmented matrix is $x = 2$ and $y = -3$. So the solution set to the system is $\{(2, -3)\}$. Check in the original system.

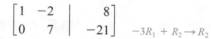 To check with a calculator, define matrix A on your calculator using the matrix edit feature as in Fig. 1(a). Then under the matrix math menu, select rref (row-reduced echelon form) and choose A from the matrix names menu as in Fig. 1(b). The calculator performs all of the computations in Example 4. All you have to do is read off the answer.

▶**TRY THIS.** Use row operations to solve the system $\begin{aligned} 2x - y &= 7 \\ x + 3y &= 14 \end{aligned}$. ■

The procedure used in Example 4 to solve a system that has a unique solution is summarized below. For consistent and dependent systems, see Examples 5 and 6.

PROCEDURE

The Gaussian Elimination Method for an Independent System of Two Equations

To solve a system of two linear equations in two variables using Gaussian elimination, perform the following row operations on the augmented matrix.

1. If necessary, interchange R_1 and R_2 so that R_1 begins with a nonzero entry.

2. Get a 1 in the first position on the diagonal by multiplying R_1 by the reciprocal of the first entry in R_1.

3. Add an appropriate multiple of R_1 to R_2 to get 0 below the first 1.

4. Get a 1 in the second position on the diagonal by multiplying R_2 by the reciprocal of the second entry in R_2.

5. Add an appropriate multiple of R_2 to R_1 to get 0 above the second 1.

6. Read the unique solution from the last column of the final augmented matrix.

Inconsistent and Dependent Equations in Two Variables

A system is independent if it has a single solution. The coefficient matrix of an independent system is equivalent to an identity matrix. A system is inconsistent if it has no solution and dependent if it has infinitely many solutions. The coefficient matrix for an inconsistent or dependent system is not equivalent to an identity matrix. However, we can still use Gaussian elimination to simplify the coefficient matrix and determine the solution.

EXAMPLE 5 An inconsistent system in two variables

Solve the system.

$$x = y + 3$$
$$2y = 2x + 5$$

Solution

Write both equations in the form $Ax + By = C$:

$$x - y = 3$$
$$-2x + 2y = 5$$

Start with the augmented matrix:

$$\begin{bmatrix} 1 & -1 & | & 3 \\ -2 & 2 & | & 5 \end{bmatrix}$$

To get a 0 in the first position of R_2, multiply R_1 by 2 and add the result to R_2:

$$\begin{bmatrix} 1 & -1 & | & 3 \\ 0 & 0 & | & 11 \end{bmatrix} \quad 2R_1 + R_2 \rightarrow R_2$$

It is impossible to convert this augmented matrix to the desired form of the Gaussian elimination method. However, we can obtain the solution by observing that the second row corresponds to the equation $0 = 11$. So the system is inconsistent, and there is no solution.

▶**TRY THIS.** Use row operations to solve the system $\begin{aligned} 3x - y &= 1 \\ -6x + 2y &= 4 \end{aligned}$. ∎

Applying Gaussian elimination to an inconsistent system (as in Example 5) causes a row to appear with 0 as the entry for each coefficient but a nonzero entry for the constant. For a dependent system of two equations in two variables (as in the next example), a 0 will appear in every entry of some row.

EXAMPLE 6 A dependent system in two variables

Solve the system.

$$2x + y = 4$$
$$4x + 2y = 8$$

Solution

Start with the augmented matrix:

$$\begin{bmatrix} 2 & 1 & | & 4 \\ 4 & 2 & | & 8 \end{bmatrix}$$

Notice that the second row is twice the first row. So instead of getting a 1 in the first position on the diagonal, we multiply R_1 by -2 and add the result to R_2:

$$\begin{bmatrix} 2 & 1 & | & 4 \\ 0 & 0 & | & 0 \end{bmatrix} \quad -2R_1 + R_2 \rightarrow R_2$$

The second row of this augmented matrix gives us the equation $0 = 0$. So the system is dependent. Every ordered pair that satisfies the first equation satisfies both equations. The solution set is $\{(x, y)|2x + y = 4\}$. Since $y = 4 - 2x$, every ordered pair of the form $(x, 4 - 2x)$ is a solution. So the solution set can be written also as $\{(x, 4 - 2x)\}$.

▶**TRY THIS.** Use row operations to solve the system $\begin{aligned} 4x + y &= 5 \\ 8x + 2y &= 10 \end{aligned}$. ∎

Gaussian Elimination with Three Variables

In the next example, Gaussian elimination is used on a system involving three variables. For three linear equations in three variables, x, y, and z, we try to get the augmented matrix into the form

$$\begin{bmatrix} 1 & 0 & 0 & | & a \\ 0 & 1 & 0 & | & b \\ 0 & 0 & 1 & | & c \end{bmatrix},$$

from which we conclude that $x = a$, $y = b$, and $z = c$.

EXAMPLE 7 Gaussian elimination with three variables

Use the Gaussian elimination method to solve the following system:

$$2x - y + z = 1$$
$$x + y - 2z = 5$$
$$3x - y - z = 8$$

Solution

Write the augmented matrix:

$$\begin{bmatrix} 2 & -1 & 1 & | & 1 \\ 1 & 1 & -2 & | & 5 \\ 3 & -1 & -1 & | & 8 \end{bmatrix}$$

To get the first 1 on the diagonal, we could multiply R_1 by $\frac{1}{2}$ or interchange R_1 and R_2. Interchanging R_1 and R_2 is simpler because it avoids getting fractions in the entries:

$$\begin{bmatrix} 1 & 1 & -2 & | & 5 \\ 2 & -1 & 1 & | & 1 \\ 3 & -1 & -1 & | & 8 \end{bmatrix} \quad R_1 \leftrightarrow R_2$$

Now use the first row to get 0's below the first 1 on the diagonal. First, to get a 0 in the first position of the second row, multiply the first row by -2 and add the result to the second row. Then, to get a 0 in the first position of the third row, multiply the first row by -3 and add the result to the third row. These two steps eliminate the variable x from the second and third rows.

$$\begin{bmatrix} 1 & 1 & -2 & | & 5 \\ 0 & -3 & 5 & | & -9 \\ 0 & -4 & 5 & | & -7 \end{bmatrix} \quad \begin{array}{l} -2R_1 + R_2 \to R_2 \\ -3R_1 + R_3 \to R_3 \end{array}$$

To get a 1 in the second position on the diagonal, multiply the second row by $-\frac{1}{3}$:

$$\begin{bmatrix} 1 & 1 & -2 & | & 5 \\ 0 & 1 & -\frac{5}{3} & | & 3 \\ 0 & -4 & 5 & | & -7 \end{bmatrix} \quad -\frac{1}{3}R_2 \to R_2$$

To get a 0 above the second 1 on the diagonal, multiply R_2 by -1 and add the result to R_1. To get a 0 below the second 1 on the diagonal, multiply R_2 by 4 and add the result to the third row:

$$\left[\begin{array}{ccc|c} 1 & 0 & -\frac{1}{3} & 2 \\ 0 & 1 & -\frac{5}{3} & 3 \\ 0 & 0 & -\frac{5}{3} & 5 \end{array}\right] \begin{array}{l} -1R_2 + R_1 \rightarrow R_1 \\ \\ 4R_2 + R_3 \rightarrow R_3 \end{array}$$

To get a 1 in the third position on the diagonal, multiply R_3 by $-\frac{3}{5}$:

$$\left[\begin{array}{ccc|c} 1 & 0 & -\frac{1}{3} & 2 \\ 0 & 1 & -\frac{5}{3} & 3 \\ 0 & 0 & 1 & -3 \end{array}\right] \begin{array}{l} \\ \\ -\frac{3}{5}R_3 \rightarrow R_3 \end{array}$$

Use the third row to get 0's above the third 1 on the diagonal:

$$\left[\begin{array}{ccc|c} 1 & 0 & 0 & 1 \\ 0 & 1 & 0 & -2 \\ 0 & 0 & 1 & -3 \end{array}\right] \begin{array}{l} \frac{1}{3}R_3 + R_1 \rightarrow R_1 \\ \frac{5}{3}R_3 + R_2 \rightarrow R_2 \\ \end{array}$$

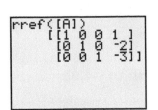

Figure 2

This last matrix corresponds to $x = 1$, $y = -2$, and $z = -3$. So the solution set to the system is $\{(1, -2, -3)\}$. Check in the original system.

To check with a calculator, define matrix A on your calculator using the matrix edit feature. Then under the matrix math menu, select rref (row-reduced echelon form) and choose A from the matrix names menu as in Fig. 2. The calculator performs all of the computations in Example 7.

▶**TRY THIS.** Use Gaussian elimination to solve $\begin{array}{rcl} x + y - z &=& 0 \\ -x + y &=& 4 \\ -x + y + z &=& 10 \end{array}$. ■

In Example 7, there were two different row operations that would produce the first 1 on the diagonal. When doing Gaussian elimination by hand, you should choose the row operations that make the computations the simplest. When this method is performed by a computer, the same sequence of steps is used on every system. Any system of three equations that has a unique solution can be solved with the following sequence of steps.

PROCEDURE

The Gaussian Elimination Method for an Independent System of Three Equations

To solve a system of three linear equations in three variables using Gaussian elimination, perform the following row operations on the augmented matrix.

1. Get a 1 in the first position on the diagonal by multiplying R_1 by the reciprocal of the first entry in R_1. (First interchange rows if necessary.)

2. Add appropriate multiples of R_1 to R_2 and R_3 to get 0's below the first 1.

3. Get a 1 in the second position on the diagonal by multiplying R_2 by the reciprocal of the second entry in R_2. (First interchange rows R_2 and R_3 if necessary.)

4. Add appropriate multiples of R_2 to R_1 and R_3 to get 0's above and below the second 1.

5. Get a 1 in the third position on the diagonal by multiplying R_3 by the reciprocal of the third entry in R_3.

6. Add appropriate multiples of R_3 to R_1 and R_2 to get 0's above the third 1.

7. Read the unique solution from the last column of the final augmented matrix.

Inconsistent and Dependent Systems in Three Variables

Applying Gaussian elimination to inconsistent or dependent systems in two or three variables is similar. If a system is inconsistent, then a row will appear with 0 as the entry for each coefficient but a nonzero entry for the constant. If a system of three equations in three variables is dependent then a row will appear in which all entries are 0. The next example shows a system with fewer equations than variables. In this case we do not necessarily get a row in which all entries are 0.

EXAMPLE 8 A dependent system in three variables

Solve the system.

$$x - y + z = 2$$
$$-2x + y + 2z = 5$$

Solution

Start with the augmented matrix:

$$\begin{bmatrix} 1 & -1 & 1 & \bigm| & 2 \\ -2 & 1 & 2 & \bigm| & 5 \end{bmatrix}$$

Perform the following row operations to get ones and zeros in the first two columns, as you would for a 2×2 matrix:

$$\begin{bmatrix} 1 & -1 & 1 & \bigm| & 2 \\ 0 & -1 & 4 & \bigm| & 9 \end{bmatrix} \qquad 2R_1 + R_2 \rightarrow R_2$$

$$\begin{bmatrix} 1 & -1 & 1 & \bigm| & 2 \\ 0 & 1 & -4 & \bigm| & -9 \end{bmatrix} \qquad -1R_2 \rightarrow R_2$$

$$\begin{bmatrix} 1 & 0 & -3 & \bigm| & -7 \\ 0 & 1 & -4 & \bigm| & -9 \end{bmatrix} \qquad R_2 + R_1 \rightarrow R_1$$

The last matrix corresponds to the system.

$$x - 3z = -7$$
$$y - 4z = -9$$

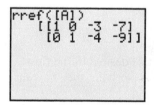

Figure 3

or $x = 3z - 7$ and $y = 4z - 9$. The system is dependent, and the solution set is

$$\left\{ (3z - 7, 4z - 9, z) \mid z \text{ is any real number} \right\}.$$

Replace x by $3z - 7$ and y by $4z - 9$ in the original equations to check.

To check enter the augmented matrix into your calculator and find rref (A) as shown in Fig. 3.

▶**TRY THIS.** Use Gaussian elimination to solve $\begin{aligned} x - y + 2z &= 3 \\ -x + 2y + z &= 2 \end{aligned}$. ■

The Gaussian elimination method can be applied to a system of n linear equations in m unknowns. However, it is a rather tedious method to perform when n and m are greater than 2, especially when fractions are involved. Computers can be programmed to work with matrices, and Gaussian elimination is frequently used for computer solutions.

You can enter matrices into a graphing calculator and perform row operations with the calculator. However, performing row operations with a calculator is still rather tedious. In Section 4 we will see a much simpler method for solving systems with a calculator. □

639

Applications

There is much discussion among city planners and transportation experts about automated highways (*Scientific American*, www.sciamarchive.com). An automated highway system would use a central computer and computers within vehicles to manage traffic flow by controlling traffic lights, rerouting traffic away from congested areas, and perhaps even driving the vehicle for you. It is easy to say that computers will control the complex traffic system of the future, but a computer does only what it is programmed to do. The next example shows one type of problem that a computer would be continually solving in order to control traffic flow.

EXAMPLE 9 | Traffic control in the future

Figure 4 shows the intersections of four one-way streets. The numbers on the arrows represent the number of cars per hour that desire to enter each intersection and leave each intersection. For example, 400 cars per hour want to enter intersection P from the north on First Avenue while 300 cars per hour want to head east from intersection Q on Elm Street. The letters w, x, y, and z represent the number of cars per hour passing the four points between these four intersections, as shown in Fig. 4.

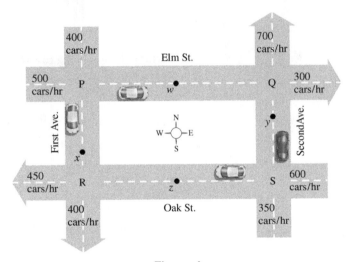

Figure 4

a. Find values for w, x, y, and z that would realize this desired traffic flow.
b. If construction on Oak Street limits z to 300 cars per hour, then how many cars per hour would have to pass w, x, and y?

Solution

a. The solution to the problem is based on the fact that the number of cars entering an intersection per hour must equal the number leaving that intersection per hour, if the traffic is to keep flowing. Since 900 cars $(400 + 500)$ enter intersection P, 900 must leave, $x + w = 900$. Writing a similar equation for each intersection yields the system shown next.

$$w + x = 900$$

$$w + y = 1000$$

$$x + z = 850$$

$$y + z = 950$$

For this system, the augmented matrix is

$$\begin{bmatrix} 1 & 1 & 0 & 0 & | & 900 \\ 1 & 0 & 1 & 0 & | & 1000 \\ 0 & 1 & 0 & 1 & | & 850 \\ 0 & 0 & 1 & 1 & | & 950 \end{bmatrix}.$$

Use row operations to get the equivalent matrix:

$$\begin{bmatrix} 1 & 0 & 0 & -1 & | & 50 \\ 0 & 1 & 0 & 1 & | & 850 \\ 0 & 0 & 1 & 1 & | & 950 \\ 0 & 0 & 0 & 0 & | & 0 \end{bmatrix}$$

The system is a dependent system and does not have a unique solution. From this matrix we get $w = 50 + z$, $x = 850 - z$, and $y = 950 - z$. The problem is solved by any ordered 4-tuple of the form $(50 + z, 850 - z, 950 - z, z)$ where z is a nonnegative integer. (In general, n numbers or expressions separated by commas within parentheses is called an n-tuple.)

b. If z is limited to 300 because of construction, then the solution is (350, 550, 650, 300). To keep traffic flowing when $z = 300$, the system must route 350 cars past w, 550 past x, and 650 past y.

▶**TRY THIS.** A small gift basket contains 3 apples and 5 pears. A large gift basket contains 8 apples and 7 pears. If 30 apples and 31 pears were used, then how many baskets of each type were made? Use Gaussian elimination. ■

One-way streets were used in Example 9 to keep the problem simple, but you can imagine two-way streets where at each intersection there are three ways to route traffic. You can also imagine many streets and many intersections all subject to systems of equations, with computers continually controlling flow to keep all traffic moving. Computerized traffic control may be a few years away, but similar problems are being solved today at AT&T to route long-distance calls and at American Airlines to schedule flight crews and equipment.

▶ FOR thought... True or False? Explain.

1. The augmented matrix for a system of two linear equations in two unknowns is a 2×2 matrix.

2. The augmented matrix
   for $\begin{array}{l} x - y = 4 \\ 3x + y = 5 \end{array}$ is $\begin{bmatrix} x & -y & | & 4 \\ 3x & y & | & 5 \end{bmatrix}$.

3. The augmented matrix
   for $\begin{array}{l} 3x - 2y = 4 \\ x + y = 6 \end{array}$ is $\begin{bmatrix} 3 & -2 & | & 4 \\ 1 & 1 & | & 6 \end{bmatrix}$.

4. The matrix $\begin{bmatrix} 1 & 0 & | & 2 \\ 1 & -1 & | & -3 \end{bmatrix}$ corresponds to the
   system $\begin{array}{l} x = 2 \\ x - y = -3. \end{array}$

5. The matrix $\begin{bmatrix} 1 & 3 & | & -2 \\ -1 & -5 & | & 4 \end{bmatrix}$ is equivalent
   to $\begin{bmatrix} 1 & 3 & | & -2 \\ 0 & -2 & | & 2 \end{bmatrix}$.

6. The matrix $\begin{bmatrix} 1 & 2 & | & 3 \\ 1 & -3 & | & 2 \end{bmatrix}$ is equivalent

to $\begin{bmatrix} 1 & 2 & | & 3 \\ 0 & -5 & | & -1 \end{bmatrix}$.

7. The matrix $\begin{bmatrix} 1 & 0 & | & 2 \\ 0 & 1 & | & 7 \end{bmatrix}$ corresponds to the

system $\begin{array}{l} x + y = 2 \\ x + y = 7. \end{array}$

8. The system corresponding to $\begin{bmatrix} 1 & 3 & | & 5 \\ 0 & 0 & | & 7 \end{bmatrix}$ is inconsistent.

9. The system corresponding to $\begin{bmatrix} -1 & 2 & | & -3 \\ 0 & 0 & | & 0 \end{bmatrix}$ is inconsistent.

10. The notation $2R_1 + R_3 \rightarrow R_3$ means to replace R_3 by $2R_1 + R_3$.

► EXERCISES 1

Fill in the blank.

1. A rectangular array of real numbers is a(n) _____.

2. In a matrix, the _____ run horizontally and the _____ run vertically.

3. The _____ of a matrix is the number of rows and columns in the matrix.

4. A matrix with an equal number of rows and columns is a(n) _____ matrix.

5. Each number in a matrix is a(n) _____ or _____ of the matrix.

6. A matrix consisting of the coefficients and the constants from a system of equations is a(n) _____ matrix.

7. The _____ of a 2 × 2 matrix consists of the entries in the first row first column and the second row second column.

8. A square matrix with ones on the diagonal and zeros elsewhere is the _____ matrix.

Determine the size of each matrix.

9. $\begin{bmatrix} 1 & 5 & 8 \end{bmatrix}$

10. $\begin{bmatrix} -3 \\ y \\ 5 \end{bmatrix}$

11. $\begin{bmatrix} 7 \end{bmatrix}$

12. $\begin{bmatrix} x & y \\ z & w \end{bmatrix}$

13. $\begin{bmatrix} -5 & 12 \\ 99 & 6 \\ 0 & 0 \end{bmatrix}$

14. $\begin{bmatrix} 1 & 5 & 7 \\ 3 & 0 & 5 \\ 2 & -6 & -3 \end{bmatrix}$

Write the augmented matrix for each system of equations.

15. $\begin{array}{l} x - 2y = 4 \\ 3x + 2y = -5 \end{array}$

16. $\begin{array}{l} 4x - y = 1 \\ x + 3y = 5 \end{array}$

17. $\begin{array}{l} x - y - z = 4 \\ x + 3y - z = 1 \\ 2y - 5z = -6 \end{array}$

18. $\begin{array}{l} x + 3y = 5 \\ y - 4z = 8 \\ -2x + 5z = 7 \end{array}$

19. $\begin{array}{l} x + 3y - z = 5 \\ x + z = 0 \end{array}$

20. $\begin{array}{l} x - y = 6 \\ x + z = 7 \end{array}$

Write the system of equations represented by each augmented matrix.

21. $\begin{bmatrix} 3 & 4 & | & -2 \\ 3 & -5 & | & 0 \end{bmatrix}$

22. $\begin{bmatrix} 1 & 0 & | & -7 \\ 0 & 1 & | & 5 \end{bmatrix}$

23. $\begin{bmatrix} 5 & 0 & 0 & | & 6 \\ -4 & 0 & 2 & | & -1 \\ 4 & 4 & 0 & | & 7 \end{bmatrix}$

24. $\begin{bmatrix} 1 & 0 & 1 & | & 2 \\ 0 & 1 & -1 & | & -6 \\ 1 & -1 & 1 & | & 5 \end{bmatrix}$

25. $\begin{bmatrix} 1 & -1 & 2 & | & 1 \\ 0 & 1 & 4 & | & 3 \\ 0 & 0 & 0 & | & 0 \end{bmatrix}$

26. $\begin{bmatrix} 1 & 1 & 1 & | & 3 \\ 0 & 1 & 2 & | & 7 \\ 0 & 0 & 0 & | & 0 \end{bmatrix}$

Perform the indicated row operation on the given augmented matrix. See the summary of row operations in Example 4.

27. $R_1 \leftrightarrow R_2$: $\begin{bmatrix} -2 & 4 & | & 1 \\ 1 & 2 & | & 0 \end{bmatrix}$

28. $R_1 \leftrightarrow R_2$: $\begin{bmatrix} 4 & 9 & | & 3 \\ 1 & 0 & | & 5 \end{bmatrix}$

29. $\frac{1}{2}R_1 \rightarrow R_1$: $\begin{bmatrix} 2 & 8 & | & 2 \\ 0 & 3 & | & 6 \end{bmatrix}$

30. $-\frac{1}{3}R_1 \rightarrow R_1$: $\begin{bmatrix} -3 & 6 & | & 12 \\ 0 & 9 & | & 3 \end{bmatrix}$

31. $3R_1 + R_2 \rightarrow R_2$: $\begin{bmatrix} 1 & -2 & | & 1 \\ -3 & 5 & | & 0 \end{bmatrix}$

32. $-2R_2 + R_1 \rightarrow R_1$: $\begin{bmatrix} 1 & 2 & | & 7 \\ 0 & 1 & | & 4 \end{bmatrix}$

For each given sequence of augmented matrices determine the system that has been solved, the solution, and the row operation that was used on each matrix to obtain the next matrix in the sequence. For the row operations use the notation that was introduced in the examples.

33. $\begin{bmatrix} 2 & 4 & | & 14 \\ 5 & 4 & | & 5 \end{bmatrix}$

$\begin{bmatrix} 1 & 2 & | & 7 \\ 5 & 4 & | & 5 \end{bmatrix}$

$\begin{bmatrix} 1 & 2 & | & 7 \\ 0 & -6 & | & -30 \end{bmatrix}$

$\begin{bmatrix} 1 & 2 & | & 7 \\ 0 & 1 & | & 5 \end{bmatrix}$

$\begin{bmatrix} 1 & 0 & | & -3 \\ 0 & 1 & | & 5 \end{bmatrix}$

34. $\begin{bmatrix} 3 & 5 & | & -2 \\ 1 & 2 & | & -1 \end{bmatrix}$

$\begin{bmatrix} 1 & 2 & | & -1 \\ 3 & 5 & | & -2 \end{bmatrix}$

$\begin{bmatrix} 1 & 2 & | & -1 \\ 0 & -1 & | & 1 \end{bmatrix}$

$\begin{bmatrix} 1 & 2 & | & -1 \\ 0 & 1 & | & -1 \end{bmatrix}$

$\begin{bmatrix} 1 & 0 & | & 1 \\ 0 & 1 & | & -1 \end{bmatrix}$

Solve each system using Gaussian elimination. State whether each system is independent, dependent, or inconsistent. See the procedure for the Gaussian elimination method for two equations in Example 4.

35. $\begin{aligned} x + y &= 5 \\ -2x + y &= -1 \end{aligned}$

36. $\begin{aligned} x - y &= 2 \\ 3x - y &= 12 \end{aligned}$

37. $\begin{aligned} 2x + 2y &= 8 \\ -3x - y &= -6 \end{aligned}$

38. $\begin{aligned} 3x - 6y &= 9 \\ 2x + y &= -4 \end{aligned}$

39. $\begin{aligned} 2x - y &= 3 \\ 3x + 2y &= 15 \end{aligned}$

40. $\begin{aligned} 2x - 3y &= -1 \\ 3x - 2y &= 1 \end{aligned}$

41. $\begin{aligned} 0.4x - 0.2y &= 0 \\ x + 1.5y &= 2 \end{aligned}$

42. $\begin{aligned} 0.2x + 0.6y &= 0.7 \\ 0.5x - y &= 0.5 \end{aligned}$

43. $\begin{aligned} 3a - 5b &= 7 \\ -3a + 5b &= 4 \end{aligned}$

44. $\begin{aligned} 2s - 3t &= 9 \\ 4s - 6t &= 1 \end{aligned}$

45. $\begin{aligned} 0.5u + 1.5v &= 2 \\ 3u + 9v &= 12 \end{aligned}$

46. $\begin{aligned} m - 2.5n &= 0.5 \\ -4m + 10n &= -2 \end{aligned}$

47. $\begin{aligned} y &= 4 - 2x \\ x &= 8 + y \end{aligned}$

48. $\begin{aligned} 3x &= 1 + 2y \\ y &= 2 - x \end{aligned}$

Solve each system using Gaussian elimination. State whether each system is independent, dependent, or inconsistent. See the procedure for the Gaussian elimination method for three equations in Example 7.

49. $\begin{aligned} x + y + z &= 6 \\ x - y - z &= 0 \\ 2y - z &= 3 \end{aligned}$

50. $\begin{aligned} x - y + z &= 2 \\ -x + y + z &= 4 \\ -x + z &= 2 \end{aligned}$

51. $\begin{aligned} 2x + y &= 2 + z \\ x + 2y &= 2 + z \\ x + 2z &= 2 + y \end{aligned}$

52. $\begin{aligned} 3x &= 4 + y \\ x + y &= z - 1 \\ 2z &= 3 - x \end{aligned}$

53. $\begin{aligned} 2a - 2b + c &= -2 \\ a + b - 3c &= 3 \\ a - 3b + c &= -5 \end{aligned}$

54. $\begin{aligned} r - 3s - t &= -3 \\ -r - s + 2t &= 1 \\ -r + 2s - t &= -2 \end{aligned}$

55. $\begin{aligned} 3y &= x + z \\ x - y - 3z &= 4 \\ x + y + 2z &= -1 \end{aligned}$

56. $\begin{aligned} z &= 2 + x \\ 2x - y &= 1 \\ y + 3z &= 15 \end{aligned}$

57. $\begin{aligned} x - 2y + 3z &= 1 \\ 2x - 4y + 6z &= 2 \\ -3x + 6y - 9z &= -3 \end{aligned}$

58. $\begin{aligned} 4x - 2y + 6z &= 4 \\ 2x - y + 3z &= 2 \\ -2x + y - 3z &= -2 \end{aligned}$

59. $\begin{aligned} x - y + z &= 2 \\ 2x + y - z &= 1 \\ 2x - 2y + 2z &= 5 \end{aligned}$

60. $\begin{aligned} x - y + z &= 4 \\ x + y - z &= 1 \\ x + y - z &= 3 \end{aligned}$

61. $\begin{aligned} x + y - z &= 3 \\ 3x + y + z &= 7 \\ x - y + 3z &= 1 \end{aligned}$

62. $\begin{aligned} x + 2y + 2z &= 4 \\ 2x + y + z &= 1 \\ -x + y + z &= 3 \end{aligned}$

63. $\begin{aligned} 2x - y + 3z &= 1 \\ x + y - z &= 4 \end{aligned}$

64. $\begin{aligned} x + 3y + z &= 6 \\ -x + y - z &= 2 \end{aligned}$

65. $\begin{aligned} x - y + z - w &= 2 \\ -x + 2y - z - w &= -1 \\ 2x - y - z + w &= 4 \\ x + 3y - 2z - 3w &= 6 \end{aligned}$

66. $\begin{aligned} 3a - 2b + c + d &= 0 \\ a - b + c - d &= -4 \\ -2a + b + 3c - 2d &= 5 \\ 2a + 3b - c - d &= -3 \end{aligned}$

Write a system of linear equations for each problem and solve the system using Gaussian elimination.

67. *Wages from Two Jobs* Mike works a total of 60 hr per week at his two jobs. He makes $8 per hour at Burgers-R-Us and $9 per hour at the Soap Opera Laundromat. If his total pay for one week is $502 before taxes, then how many hours does he work at each job?

68. *Postal Rates* Noriko spent $23.20 on postage inviting a total of 60 guests to her promotion party. Each woman was sent a picture postcard showing the company headquarters in Tokyo while each man was invited with a letter. If she put a 28-cent stamp on each postcard and a 44-cent stamp on each letter, then how many guests of each gender were invited?

69. *Investment Portfolio* Petula invested a total of $40,000 in a no-load mutual fund, treasury bills, and municipal bonds. Her total return of $3660 came from an 8% return on her investment in the no-load mutual fund, a 9% return on the treasury bills, and 12% return on the municipal bonds. If her total investment in treasury bills and municipal bonds was equal to her investment in the no-load mutual fund, then how much did she invest in each?

70. *Nutrition* The accompanying table shows the percentage of U.S. Recommended Daily Allowances (RDA) for phosphorus (P), magnesium (Mg), and calcium (Ca) in one ounce of three breakfast cereals (without milk). If Hulk Hogan got 98% of the RDA of phosphorus, 84% of the RDA of magnesium, and 38% of the RDA of calcium by eating a large bowl of each (without milk), then how many ounces of each cereal did he eat?

HINT Write an equation for P, one for Mg, and one for Ca.

Table for Exercise 70

	P	Mg	Ca	
Kix	4%	2%	4%	
Quick Oats	10%	10%	0%	
Muesli	8%	8%	2%	

Floortje/iStockphoto

71. *Cubic Curve Fitting* Find a, b, and c such that the graph of $y = ax^3 + bx + c$ goes through the points $(-1, 4)$, $(1, 2)$, and $(2, 7)$.

72. *Quadratic Curve Fitting* Find a, b, and c such that the graph of $y = ax^2 + bx + c$ goes through the points $(-1, 0)$, $(1, 0)$, and $(3, 2)$.

73. *Traffic Control I* The diagram shows the number of cars that desire to enter and leave each of three intersections on three one-way streets in a 60-minute period. The letters x, y, and z represent the number of cars passing the three points between these three intersections, as shown in the diagram. Find values for x, y, and z that would realize this desired traffic flow. If construction on JFK Boulevard limits the value of z to 50, then what values for x and y would keep the traffic flowing?

74. *Traffic Control II* Southbound M. L. King Drive in the figure leads to another intersection that cannot always handle 700 cars in a 60-minute period. Change 700 to 600 in the figure and write a system of three equations in x, y, and z. What is the solution to this system? If you had control over the 400 cars coming from the north into the first intersection on M. L. King Drive, what number would you use in place of 400 to get the system flowing again?

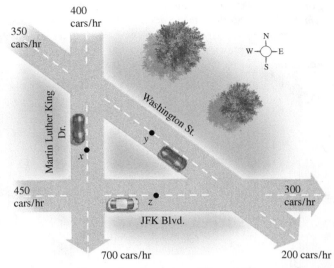

Figure for Exercises 73 and 74

▶ **RETHINKING**

75. Determine whether $(-2, 1)$ satisfies the system of inequalities $x^2 + y^2 < 9$, $y > x + 1$, and $x + y > 2$.

76. Solve the system $3x - 5y = -5$ and $4x + 3y = -26$.

77. Solve the system $x + y = 4$, $y + z = -3$, and $x + z = -17$.

78. Evaluate each expression.
   a. $\log_5(1/25)$ **b.** $\log(\sqrt{10})$ **c.** $\ln(e^3)$

79. Solve $|x - 3| = |2x + 5|$.

80. Solve $15(2x - 1)^2 - 2(2x - 1) - 8 = 0$.

THINKING OUTSIDE THE BOX LXX

The Gigantic The ocean liner *Gigantic* began taking on water after hitting an iceberg. Water was coming in at a uniform rate and some amount had already accumulated. The captain looked in some tables and found that 12 identical pumps could pump out all of the water in 3 hours, while 5 of those same pumps could do it in 10 hours. To calm the passengers, the captain wanted all of the water out in 2 hours. How many pumps are needed?

→ **POP QUIZ 1**

1. Determine the size of $\begin{bmatrix} 1 & 2 & 3 \\ 4 & 5 & 6 \end{bmatrix}$.

2. Write the augmented matrix for $\begin{array}{l} 2x - 3y = -9 \\ x + 4y = 23 \end{array}$.

Solve by Gaussian elimination.

3. $\begin{array}{l} 2x - 3y = -9 \\ x + 4y = 23 \end{array}$

4. $\begin{array}{rcl} x - y + z &=& 4 \\ -x + 2y + z &=& -1 \\ -x + y + 4z &=& 6 \end{array}$

►LINKING
concepts... For Individual or Group Explorations

Modeling Traffic Flow

The accompanying figure shows two one-way streets and two two-way streets. The numbers and arrows represent the number of cars per hour that desire to enter or leave each intersection. The variables a, b, c, d, e, and f represent the number of cars per hour that pass the six points between the four intersections. To keep traffic flowing, the number of cars per hour that enter an intersection must equal the number per hour that leave an intersection.

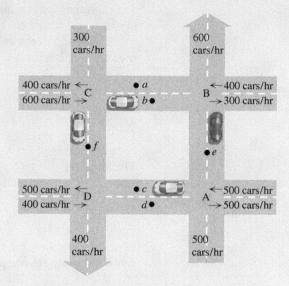

a) Write four equations (one for each intersection) with the six variables.

b) Does the system have a unique solution?

c) If $a = 300$, $c = 400$, and $f = 200$ cars/hr, find b, d, and e.

d) If the number of cars entering intersection A from the south is changed from 500 to 800 cars/hr, then what happens to the system and why?

2 Operations with Matrices

In Section 1, matrices were used to keep track of the coefficients and constants in systems of equations. Matrices are also useful for simplifying and organizing information ranging from inventories to win-loss records of sports teams. In this section we study matrices in more detail and learn how operations with matrices are used in applications.

Notation

In Section 1 a matrix was defined as a rectangular array of numbers. Capital letters are used to name matrices and lowercase letters to name their entries. A general $m \times n$ matrix with m rows and n columns is given as follows:

$$A = \begin{bmatrix} a_{11} & a_{12} & a_{13} & \cdots & a_{1n} \\ a_{21} & a_{22} & a_{23} & \cdots & a_{2n} \\ a_{31} & a_{32} & a_{33} & \cdots & a_{3n} \\ \vdots & \vdots & \vdots & & \vdots \\ a_{m1} & a_{m2} & a_{m3} & \cdots & a_{mn} \end{bmatrix}$$

The subscripts indicate the position of each entry. For example, a_{32} is the entry in the third row and second column. The entry in the ith row and jth column is denoted by a_{ij}.

Two matrices are **equal** if they have the same size and the corresponding entries are equal. We write

$$\begin{bmatrix} 0.5 \\ 0.25 \end{bmatrix} = \begin{bmatrix} \frac{1}{2} \\ \frac{1}{4} \end{bmatrix}$$

because these matrices have the same size and their corresponding entries are equal. The matrices

$$\begin{bmatrix} 4 & 3 \\ 2 & 1 \end{bmatrix} \quad \text{and} \quad \begin{bmatrix} 1 & 3 \\ 2 & 1 \end{bmatrix}$$

have the same size, but they are not equal because the entries in the first row and first column are not equal. The matrices

$$\begin{bmatrix} 3 & 5 \end{bmatrix} \quad \text{and} \quad \begin{bmatrix} 3 \\ 5 \end{bmatrix}$$

are not equal because the first has size 1×2 (a row matrix) and the second has size 2×1 (a column matrix).

EXAMPLE 1 Equal matrices

Determine the values of x, y, and z that make the following matrix equation true:

$$\begin{bmatrix} x & y - 1 \\ z & 7 \end{bmatrix} = \begin{bmatrix} 1 & 3 \\ 2 & 7 \end{bmatrix}$$

Solution

If these matrices are equal, then the corresponding entries are equal. So $x = 1$, $y = 4$, and $z = 2$.

▶TRY THIS. If $\begin{bmatrix} x & 2 \\ 3 & z + 1 \end{bmatrix} = \begin{bmatrix} 1 & y + 1 \\ 3 & 2z - 1 \end{bmatrix}$, then what are x, y, and z? ■

Addition and Subtraction of Matrices

Matrices are rectangular arrays of real numbers, and in many ways they behave like real numbers. We can define matrix operations that have many properties similar to the properties of the real numbers.

Definition: Matrix Addition

> The sum of two $m \times n$ matrices A and B is the $m \times n$ matrix denoted $A + B$ whose entries are the sums of the corresponding entries of A and B.

Note that only matrices that have the same size can be added. There is no definition for the sum of matrices of different sizes.

EXAMPLE 2 Sum of matrices

Find $A + B$ given that $A = \begin{bmatrix} -4 & 3 \\ 5 & -2 \end{bmatrix}$ and $B = \begin{bmatrix} 7 & -3 \\ 2 & -5 \end{bmatrix}$.

Solution

To find $A + B$, add the corresponding entries of A and B:

$$A + B = \begin{bmatrix} -4 & 3 \\ 5 & -2 \end{bmatrix} + \begin{bmatrix} 7 & -3 \\ 2 & -5 \end{bmatrix} = \begin{bmatrix} -4 + 7 & 3 + (-3) \\ 5 + 2 & -2 + (-5) \end{bmatrix} = \begin{bmatrix} 3 & 0 \\ 7 & -7 \end{bmatrix}$$

To check, define matrices A and B on your graphing calculator using the matrix edit feature. Then use the matrix names feature to display $A + B$ and find the sum as in Fig. 5(a), (b), and (c).

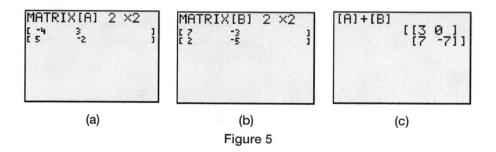

(a)   (b)   (c)

Figure 5

▶**TRY THIS.** Find $A + B$ if $A = \begin{bmatrix} 3 & 4 \\ -1 & 5 \end{bmatrix}$ and $B = \begin{bmatrix} 5 & -4 \\ 1 & 4 \end{bmatrix}$. ■

If all of the entries of a matrix are zero, the matrix is called a **zero matrix.** There is a zero matrix for every size. In matrix addition, the zero matrix behaves just like the additive identity 0 in the set of real numbers. For example,

$$\begin{bmatrix} 5 & -2 \\ 3 & -4 \end{bmatrix} + \begin{bmatrix} 0 & 0 \\ 0 & 0 \end{bmatrix} = \begin{bmatrix} 5 & -2 \\ 3 & -4 \end{bmatrix}.$$

In general, an $n \times n$ zero matrix is called the **additive identity** for $n \times n$ matrices.

For any matrix A, the **additive inverse** of A, denoted $-A$, is the matrix of the same size as A such that each entry of $-A$ is the opposite of the corresponding entry of A. Since corresponding entries are added in matrix addition, $A + (-A)$ is a zero matrix.

EXAMPLE 3 Additive inverses of matrices

Find $-A$ and $A + (-A)$ for $A = \begin{bmatrix} -1 & 2 & 0 \\ 4 & -3 & 5 \\ 2 & 0 & -9 \end{bmatrix}$.

Solution

To find $-A$, find the opposite of every entry of A:

$$-A = \begin{bmatrix} 1 & -2 & 0 \\ -4 & 3 & -5 \\ -2 & 0 & 9 \end{bmatrix}$$

$$A + (-A) = \begin{bmatrix} -1 & 2 & 0 \\ 4 & -3 & 5 \\ 2 & 0 & -9 \end{bmatrix} + \begin{bmatrix} 1 & -2 & 0 \\ -4 & 3 & -5 \\ -2 & 0 & 9 \end{bmatrix} = \begin{bmatrix} 0 & 0 & 0 \\ 0 & 0 & 0 \\ 0 & 0 & 0 \end{bmatrix}$$

Therefore, the sum of A and $-A$ is the additive identity for 3×3 matrices.

▶**TRY THIS.** Find $-A$ and $-A + A$ if $A = \begin{bmatrix} 2 & 3 \\ -4 & 1 \end{bmatrix}$. ∎

The difference of two real numbers a and b is defined by $a - b = a + (-b)$. The difference of two matrices of the same size is defined similarly.

Definition:	
Matrix Subtraction	The difference of two $m \times n$ matrices A and B is the $m \times n$ matrix denoted $A - B$, where $A - B = A + (-B)$.

Even though subtraction is defined as addition of the additive inverse, we can certainly find the difference for two matrices by subtracting their corresponding entries. Note that we can subtract corresponding entries only if the matrices have the same size.

EXAMPLE 4 | Subtraction of matrices

Let $A = \begin{bmatrix} 3 & 5 & 8 \end{bmatrix}$, $B = \begin{bmatrix} 3 & -1 & 6 \end{bmatrix}$, $C = \begin{bmatrix} -3 \\ 5 \\ 6 \end{bmatrix}$, and $D = \begin{bmatrix} 4 \\ 7 \\ 2 \end{bmatrix}$. Find the following matrices.

a. $A - B$ **b.** $C - D$ **c.** $A - C$

Solution

a. To find $A - B$, subtract the corresponding entries of the matrices:

$$A - B = \begin{bmatrix} 3 & 5 & 8 \end{bmatrix} - \begin{bmatrix} 3 & -1 & 6 \end{bmatrix} = \begin{bmatrix} 0 & 6 & 2 \end{bmatrix}$$

b. To find $C - D$, subtract the corresponding entries:

$$C - D = \begin{bmatrix} -3 \\ 5 \\ 6 \end{bmatrix} - \begin{bmatrix} 4 \\ 7 \\ 2 \end{bmatrix} = \begin{bmatrix} -7 \\ -2 \\ 4 \end{bmatrix}$$

c. Since A and C do not have the same size, $A - C$ is not defined.

▶**TRY THIS.** Find $A - B$ if $A = \begin{bmatrix} 1 & -2 & 4 \end{bmatrix}$ and $B = \begin{bmatrix} 1 & 2 & 3 \end{bmatrix}$. ∎

Scalar Multiplication

A matrix of size 1×1 is a matrix with only one entry. To distinguish a 1×1 matrix from a real number, a real number is called a **scalar** when we are dealing with matrices. We define multiplication of a matrix by a scalar as follows.

Definition:
Scalar Multiplication

> If A is an $m \times n$ matrix and b is a scalar, then the matrix bA is the $m \times n$ matrix obtained by multiplying each entry of A by the real number b.

EXAMPLE 5 Scalar multiplication

Given that $A = \begin{bmatrix} -2 & 3 & 5 \end{bmatrix}$ and $B = \begin{bmatrix} -3 & 4 \\ 2 & -6 \end{bmatrix}$, find the following matrices.

a. $3A$ **b.** $-2B$ **c.** $-1A$

Solution

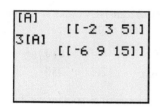

Figure 6

a. The matrix $3A$ is the 1×3 matrix formed by multiplying each entry of A by 3:

$$3A = \begin{bmatrix} -6 & 9 & 15 \end{bmatrix}$$

To check, define A on your calculator and perform scalar multiplication as in Fig. 6. □

b. Multiply each entry of B by -2:

$$-2B = \begin{bmatrix} 6 & -8 \\ -4 & 12 \end{bmatrix}$$

c. Multiply each entry of A by -1:

$$-1A = \begin{bmatrix} 2 & -3 & -5 \end{bmatrix}$$

The scalar product of A and -1 is the additive inverse of A, $-1A = -A$.

▶**TRY THIS.** Find $4C$ if $C = \begin{bmatrix} 1 & -2 & 9 \end{bmatrix}$. ∎

In Section 3 multiplication of matrices will be defined in a manner that is very different from scalar multiplication.

Modeling with matrices

In Section 1 we saw how a matrix is used to represent a system of equations. Just the essential parts of the system, the coefficients, are listed in the matrix. Matrices are also very useful in two-way classifications of data. The matrix just contains the essentials, and we must remember what the entries represent.

EXAMPLE 6 Applications of matrices

The following table shows the number of transistors and resistors purchased by a manufacturer from suppliers A and B for the first week of January.

	A	B
Transistors	400	800
Resistors	600	500

a. Write the data in the table as a 2×2 matrix S_1.
b. Use scalar multiplication to find a matrix S_2 whose entries are all 10% larger than the corresponding entries of S_1.
c. Suppose that S_2 is the supply matrix for the second week of January. Find $S_1 + S_2$ and explain what its entries represent.

Solution

a. The supply table can be written as the following 2×2 matrix:

$$S_1 = \begin{bmatrix} 400 & 800 \\ 600 & 500 \end{bmatrix}$$

b. If the entries of S_2 are 10% larger than the entries of S_1, then $S_2 = S_1 + 0.10S_1 = 1.1S_1$:

$$S_2 = 1.1S_1 = 1.1\begin{bmatrix} 400 & 800 \\ 600 & 500 \end{bmatrix} = \begin{bmatrix} 440 & 880 \\ 660 & 550 \end{bmatrix}$$

c. The entries of $S_1 + S_2$ give the total number of transistors and resistors purchased from suppliers A and B for the first two weeks of January.

$$S_1 + S_2 = \begin{bmatrix} 400 & 800 \\ 600 & 500 \end{bmatrix} + \begin{bmatrix} 440 & 880 \\ 660 & 550 \end{bmatrix} = \begin{bmatrix} 840 & 1680 \\ 1260 & 1050 \end{bmatrix}$$

▶**TRY THIS.** A small post office delivered 11,000 pieces of first class mail, 20,000 pieces of second class mail, and 16,000 pieces of third class mail in 2005. Write this data as a 3×1 matrix. For 2015 the post office expects a 50% increase in each class. Use scalar multiplication to find the matrix whose entries give the expected number in each class. ■

Example 6 is a simple example of how matrices are used with real data. You can imagine the same example with a matrix showing many different items from many different suppliers. Of course, computers, and even graphing calculators, are used to perform the operations when the matrices are large.

➤ FOR thought... True or False? Explain.

The following statements refer to the matrices

$$A = \begin{bmatrix} 1 \\ 3 \end{bmatrix}, \quad B = \begin{bmatrix} 1 \\ 3 \end{bmatrix}, \quad C = \begin{bmatrix} 1 & 1 \\ 3 & 3 \end{bmatrix},$$

$$D = \begin{bmatrix} -3 & 5 \\ 1 & -2 \end{bmatrix} \quad \text{and} \quad E = \begin{bmatrix} -2 & 6 \\ 4 & 1 \end{bmatrix}.$$

1. $A = B$ **2.** $A = C$ **3.** $A + B = C$

4. $C + D = E$

5. $A - B = \begin{bmatrix} 0 \\ 0 \end{bmatrix}$

6. $3B = \begin{bmatrix} 3 \\ 3 \end{bmatrix}$

7. $-A = \begin{bmatrix} 3 \\ 1 \end{bmatrix}$

8. $A + C = \begin{bmatrix} 2 & 1 \\ 6 & 3 \end{bmatrix}$

9. $C - A = \begin{bmatrix} 1 & 0 \\ 3 & 0 \end{bmatrix}$

10. $C + 2D = \begin{bmatrix} -5 & 11 \\ 4 & 1 \end{bmatrix}$

➤ EXERCISES 2

Determine the values of x, y, and z that make each matrix equation true.

1. $\begin{bmatrix} x \\ 5 \end{bmatrix} = \begin{bmatrix} 2 \\ y \end{bmatrix}$

2. $\begin{bmatrix} 2z \\ 5x \end{bmatrix} = \begin{bmatrix} -1 \\ 2 \end{bmatrix}$

3. $\begin{bmatrix} 2x & 4y \\ 3z & 8 \end{bmatrix} = \begin{bmatrix} 6 & 16 \\ z + y & 8 \end{bmatrix}$

4. $\begin{bmatrix} -x & 2y \\ 3 & x + y \end{bmatrix} = \begin{bmatrix} 3 & -6 \\ 3 & 4z \end{bmatrix}$

Find the following sums.

5. $\begin{bmatrix} 3 \\ 5 \end{bmatrix} + \begin{bmatrix} 2 \\ 1 \end{bmatrix}$

6. $\begin{bmatrix} -1 \\ 2 \end{bmatrix} + \begin{bmatrix} 0 \\ 3 \end{bmatrix}$

7. $\begin{bmatrix} -0.5 & -0.03 \\ 2 & -0.33 \end{bmatrix} + \begin{bmatrix} 2 & 1 \\ -0.05 & 1 \end{bmatrix}$

8. $\begin{bmatrix} -0.05 & -0.1 \\ 0.2 & -1 \end{bmatrix} + \begin{bmatrix} 1 & -2 \\ -3 & 0.01 \end{bmatrix}$

9. $\begin{bmatrix} 2 & -3 & 4 \\ 4 & -6 & 8 \\ 6 & -3 & 1 \end{bmatrix} + \begin{bmatrix} 1 & -1 & 1 \\ 0 & 1 & -1 \\ 0 & 0 & 1 \end{bmatrix}$

10. $\begin{bmatrix} -3 & 5 & 1 \\ -8 & 2 & 4 \\ 4 & 5 & -3 \end{bmatrix} + \begin{bmatrix} -4 & -8 & -3 \\ 5 & 0 & -6 \\ -3 & 4 & -1 \end{bmatrix}$

For each matrix A find −A and A + (−A).

11. $A = \begin{bmatrix} 1 & -4 \\ -5 & 6 \end{bmatrix}$

12. $A = \begin{bmatrix} -3 & 5 \\ 0 & 2 \end{bmatrix}$

13. $A = \begin{bmatrix} 3 & 0 & -1 \\ 8 & -2 & 1 \\ -3 & 6 & 3 \end{bmatrix}$

14. $A = \begin{bmatrix} 4 & 8 & 3 \\ -5 & 0 & 6 \\ -1 & 1 & -9 \end{bmatrix}$

Let $A = \begin{bmatrix} -4 & 1 \\ 3 & 0 \end{bmatrix}$, $B = \begin{bmatrix} -1 & -2 \\ 7 & 4 \end{bmatrix}$, $C = \begin{bmatrix} -3 & -4 \\ 2 & -5 \end{bmatrix}$,

$D = \begin{bmatrix} -4 \\ 5 \end{bmatrix}$, *and* $E = \begin{bmatrix} -1 \\ 2 \end{bmatrix}$. *Find each of the following matrices, if possible.*

15. $B - A$

16. $A - B$

17. $B - C$

18. $C - B$

19. $B - E$

20. $A - D$

21. $3A$

22. $5B$

23. $-1D$

24. $-3E$

25. $3A + 3C$

26. $3(A + C)$

27. $2A - B$

28. $-C - 3B$

29. $2D - 3E$

30. $4D + 0E$

31. $D + A$

32. $E + C$

33. $(A + B) + C$

34. $A + (B + C)$

Perform the following operations. If it is not possible to perform an operation, explain.

35. $\begin{bmatrix} 0.2 & 0.1 \\ 0.4 & 0.3 \end{bmatrix} + \begin{bmatrix} 0.2 & 0.05 \\ 0.3 & 0.8 \end{bmatrix}$

36. $\begin{bmatrix} \frac{1}{2} & \frac{1}{3} \\ \frac{1}{4} & 1 \end{bmatrix} - \begin{bmatrix} -\frac{1}{2} & \frac{1}{6} \\ 1 & \frac{1}{3} \end{bmatrix}$

37. $3\begin{bmatrix} \frac{1}{6} & \frac{1}{2} \\ 1 & -4 \end{bmatrix}$

38. $-2\begin{bmatrix} -1 & 4 \\ 3 & 1 \end{bmatrix}$

39. $\begin{bmatrix} -2 & 4 \\ 6 & 8 \end{bmatrix} - 4\begin{bmatrix} -3 & 1 \\ 2 & -2 \end{bmatrix}$

40. $2\begin{bmatrix} \frac{1}{4} \\ \frac{1}{3} \end{bmatrix} + 3\begin{bmatrix} \frac{1}{4} \\ \frac{1}{6} \end{bmatrix}$

41. $\begin{bmatrix} 1 & 3 & 7 \end{bmatrix} + \begin{bmatrix} -1 \\ 2 \\ 3 \end{bmatrix}$

42. $\begin{bmatrix} -1 & 3 \\ 2 & 5 \end{bmatrix} + 5\begin{bmatrix} -2 \\ 4 \end{bmatrix}$

43. $\begin{bmatrix} -5 & 4 \\ -2 & 3 \\ 0 & 1 \end{bmatrix} - \begin{bmatrix} -4 & -9 \\ 7 & 0 \\ -6 & 3 \end{bmatrix}$

44. $\begin{bmatrix} 2 & 3 & 4 \\ 4 & 6 & 8 \\ 6 & 3 & 1 \end{bmatrix} + \begin{bmatrix} 1 & 0 & 0 \\ 0 & 1 & 0 \\ 0 & 0 & 1 \end{bmatrix}$

45. $\begin{bmatrix} \sqrt{2} & 4 & \sqrt{12} \end{bmatrix} + \begin{bmatrix} \sqrt{8} & -2 & \sqrt{3} \end{bmatrix}$

46. $2\begin{bmatrix} -\sqrt{2} \\ \sqrt{5} \\ \sqrt{27} \end{bmatrix} - \begin{bmatrix} -\sqrt{8} \\ \sqrt{20} \\ -\sqrt{3} \end{bmatrix}$

47. $2\begin{bmatrix} a \\ b \end{bmatrix} + 3\begin{bmatrix} 2a \\ 4b \end{bmatrix} - 5\begin{bmatrix} -a \\ 3b \end{bmatrix}$

48. $2\begin{bmatrix} -a \\ b \\ c \end{bmatrix} - \begin{bmatrix} -3a \\ 4b \\ -c \end{bmatrix} - 6\begin{bmatrix} a \\ -b \\ 2c \end{bmatrix}$

49. $0.4\begin{bmatrix} -x & y \\ 2x & 8y \end{bmatrix} - 0.3\begin{bmatrix} 2x & 3y \\ 5x & -y \end{bmatrix}$

50. $a\begin{bmatrix} a & b \\ c & 2b \end{bmatrix} - b\begin{bmatrix} b & a \\ 0 & 3a \end{bmatrix}$

51. $2\begin{bmatrix} x & y & z \\ -x & 2y & 3z \\ x & -y & -3z \end{bmatrix} - \begin{bmatrix} -x & 0 & 3z \\ 4x & y & -z \\ 2x & 5y & z \end{bmatrix}$

52. $\frac{1}{2}\begin{bmatrix} 2 & -8 & -4 \\ 14 & 16 & 10 \\ 4 & -6 & 2 \end{bmatrix} + \frac{1}{3}\begin{bmatrix} 6 & -9 & 0 \\ 0 & 12 & -6 \\ 21 & -18 & -3 \end{bmatrix}$

Each of the following matrix equations corresponds to a system of linear equations. Write the system of equations and solve it by the method of your choice.

53. $\begin{bmatrix} x + y \\ x - y \end{bmatrix} = \begin{bmatrix} 5 \\ 1 \end{bmatrix}$

54. $\begin{bmatrix} x - y \\ 2x + y \end{bmatrix} = \begin{bmatrix} -1 \\ 4 \end{bmatrix}$

55. $\begin{bmatrix} 2x + 3y \\ x - 4y \end{bmatrix} = \begin{bmatrix} 7 \\ -13 \end{bmatrix}$

56. $\begin{bmatrix} x - 3y \\ 2x + y \end{bmatrix} = \begin{bmatrix} 1 \\ -5 \end{bmatrix}$

57. $\begin{bmatrix} x + y + z \\ x - y - z \\ x - y + z \end{bmatrix} = \begin{bmatrix} 8 \\ -7 \\ 2 \end{bmatrix}$

58. $\begin{bmatrix} 2x + y + z \\ x - 2y - z \\ x - y + z \end{bmatrix} = \begin{bmatrix} 7 \\ -6 \\ 2 \end{bmatrix}$

651

Solve each problem.

59. *Budgeting* In January, Terry spent $120 on food, $30 on clothing, and $40 on utilities. In February she spent $130 on food, $70 on clothing, and $50 on utilities. In March she spent $140 on food, $60 on clothing, and $45 on utilities. Write a 3×1 matrix for each month's expenditures and find the sum of the three matrices. What do the entries in the sum represent?

60. *Nutritional Content* According to manufacturers' labels, one serving of Kix contains 110 calories, 2 g of protein, and 40 mg of potassium. One serving of Quick Oats contains 100 calories, 4 g of protein, and 100 mg of potassium. One serving of Muesli contains 120 calories, 3 g of protein, and 115 mg of potassium. Write 1×3 matrices K, Q, and M, which express the nutritional content of each cereal. Find $2K + 2Q + 3M$ and indicate what the entries represent.

61. *Arming the Villagers* In preparation for an attack by rampaging warlords, Xena accumulated 40 swords, 30 longbows, and 80 arrows to arm the villagers. Her companion Gabrielle obtained 80 swords, 90 longbows, and 200 arrows from a passing arms dealer. Write this information as a 3×2 matrix. One week later both Xena and Gabrielle managed to increase their supplies in each category by 50%. Write a 3×2 matrix for the supply of armaments in the second week.

62. *Recommended Daily Allowances* The percentages of the U.S. Recommended Daily Allowances for phosphorus, magnesium, and calcium for a 1-oz serving of Kix are 4, 2, and 4, respectively. The percentages of the U.S. Recommended Daily Allowances for phosphorus, magnesium, and calcium in 1/2 cup of milk are 11, 4, and 16, respectively. Write a 1×3 matrix K giving the percentages for 1 oz of Kix and a 1×3 matrix M giving the percentages for 1/2 cup of milk. Find the matrix $K + 2M$; indicate what its entries represent.

FOR WRITING/DISCUSSION

Let $A = \begin{bmatrix} a_{11} & a_{12} \\ a_{21} & a_{22} \end{bmatrix}$, $B = \begin{bmatrix} b_{11} & b_{12} \\ b_{21} & b_{22} \end{bmatrix}$, *and* $C = \begin{bmatrix} c_{11} & c_{12} \\ c_{21} & c_{22} \end{bmatrix}$ *for the following problems.*

63. Is $A + B = B + A$? Is addition of 2×2 matrices commutative? Explain.

64. Is addition of 3×3 matrices commutative? Explain.

65. Is $(A + B) + C = A + (B + C)$? Is addition of 2×2 matrices associative? Explain.

66. Is addition of 3×3 matrices associative? Explain.

67. Is $k(A + B) = kA + kB$ for any constant k? Is scalar multiplication distributive over addition of 2×2 matrices?

68. Is scalar multiplication distributive over addition of $n \times n$ matrices for each natural number n?

69. In the set of 2×2 matrices, which matrix is the additive identity?

70. Does every 2×2 matrix have an additive inverse with respect to the appropriate additive identity?

▶ RETHINKING

71. Use Gaussian elimination to solve the system of equations $2x + 3y = 4$ and $x - 4y = -31$. Classify the system as independent, dependent, or inconsistent.

72. Find the partial fraction decomposition for $\dfrac{8x^2 + 17x + 12}{x^3 + 3x^2 + 2x}$.

73. Factor each polynomial completely.
   a. $abx^2 + bxy + axz + yz$

   b. $6x^3 - 23x^2y + 20xy^2$

74. Rewrite $\dfrac{1}{2}\ln(x) - 3\ln(y) + \ln(z)$ as a single logarithm.

75. Write $\log_7(x)$ in terms of natural logarithms.

76. Solve $x^4 - 10x^2 + 9 < 0$.

THINKING OUTSIDE THE BOX LXXI AND LXXII

Shade-Tree Mechanic Bubba has filled his 8-quart radiator with antifreeze, but he should have put in only 4 quarts of antifreeze and 4 quarts of water. He has an empty 5-quart container and an empty 3-quart container, but no other way of measuring the antifreeze. How can he get only 4 quarts of antifreeze in his radiator?

Four Pipes Four pipes with circular cross sections are placed in a V-shaped trench so that they all just fit as shown in the accompanying figure. If the radius of the smallest pipe is 16 inches and the radius of the largest is 54 inches, then what are the radii of the two pipes in between?

Figure for Thinking Outside the Box LXXII

► POP QUIZ 2

$A = \begin{bmatrix} 1 \\ 3 \end{bmatrix}, B = \begin{bmatrix} -1 \\ 5 \end{bmatrix}, C = \begin{bmatrix} 1 & 2 \\ 3 & 4 \end{bmatrix}, D = \begin{bmatrix} 1 & 0 \\ 0 & 1 \end{bmatrix}.$ *Perform the*
matrix operations if possible.

1. $A + B$

2. $3A - B$

3. $-A + A$

4. $A + C$

5. $C + 2D$

3 Multiplication of Matrices

In Sections 1 and 2 we saw how matrices are used for solving equations and for representing two-way classifications of data. We saw how addition and scalar multiplication of matrices could be useful in applications. In this section you will learn to find the product of two matrices. Matrix multiplication is more complicated than addition or subtraction, but it is also very useful in applications.

An Application

Before presenting the general definition of multiplication, let us look at an example where multiplication of matrices is useful. Table 1 shows the number of economy, mid-size, and large cars rented by individuals and corporations at a rental agency in a single day. Table 2 shows the number of bonus points and free miles given in a promotional program for each of the three car types.

Table 1

	Econo	Mid	Large
Individuals	3	2	6
Corporations	5	2	4

Table 2

	Bonus Points	Free Miles
Econo	20	50
Mid	30	100
Large	40	150

The 1×3 row matrix $\begin{bmatrix} 3 & 2 & 6 \end{bmatrix}$ from Table 1 represents the number of economy, mid-size, and large cars rented by individuals. The 3×1 column matrix $\begin{bmatrix} 20 \\ 30 \\ 40 \end{bmatrix}$ from Table 2 represents the bonus points given for each economy, mid-size, and large car that is rented. The product of these two matrices is a 1×1 matrix whose entry is the sum of the products of the corresponding entries:

$$\begin{bmatrix} 3 & 2 & 6 \end{bmatrix} \begin{bmatrix} 20 \\ 30 \\ 40 \end{bmatrix} = \begin{bmatrix} 3(20) + 2(30) + 6(40) \end{bmatrix} = \begin{bmatrix} 360 \end{bmatrix}$$

The product of this row matrix and this column matrix gives the total number of bonus points given to individuals on the rental of the 11 cars.

Now write Table 1 as a 2×3 matrix giving the number of cars of each type rented by individuals and corporations and write Table 2 as a 3×2 matrix giving the number of bonus points and free miles for each type of car rented.

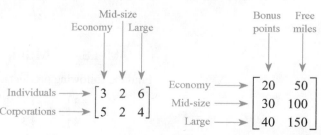

653

The product of these two matrices is a 2×2 matrix that gives the total bonus points and free miles both for individuals and corporations.

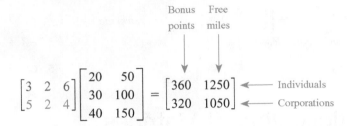

The product of the 2×3 matrix and the 3×2 matrix is a 2×2 matrix. Take a careful look at where the entries in the 2×2 matrix come from:

$$3(20) + 2(30) + 6(40) = 360 \quad \text{Total bonus points for individuals}$$

$$3(50) + 2(100) + 6(150) = 1250 \quad \text{Total free miles for individuals}$$

$$5(20) + 2(30) + 4(40) = 320 \quad \text{Total bonus points for corporations}$$

$$5(50) + 2(100) + 4(150) = 1050 \quad \text{Total free miles for corporations}$$

Each entry in the 2×2 matrix is found by multiplying the entries of a *row* of the first matrix by the corresponding entries of a *column* of the second matrix and adding the results. To multiply any matrices, the number of entries in a row of the first matrix must equal the number of entries in a column of the second matrix.

Matrix Multiplication

The product of two matrices is illustrated by the previous example of the rental cars. The general definition of matrix multiplication follows.

Definition:
Matrix Multiplication

> The product of an $m \times n$ matrix A and an $n \times p$ matrix B is an $m \times p$ matrix AB whose entries are found as follows. The entry in the ith row and jth column of AB is found by multiplying each entry in the ith row of A by the corresponding entry in the jth column of B and adding the results.

Note that by the definition we can multiply an $m \times n$ matrix and an $n \times p$ matrix to get an $m \times p$ matrix. To find a product AB, *each row of A must have the same number of entries as each column of B*. The entry c_{ij} in AB comes from the ith row of A and the jth column of B as shown below.

$$\begin{array}{ccc} i\text{th row of } A & j\text{th column of } B & ij\text{th entry of } AB \end{array}$$

$$\begin{bmatrix} * & * & * \end{bmatrix} \begin{bmatrix} * \\ * \\ * \end{bmatrix} = \begin{bmatrix} c_{ij} \end{bmatrix}$$

EXAMPLE 1 Multiplying matrices

Find the following products.

a. $\begin{bmatrix} 2 & 3 \end{bmatrix} \begin{bmatrix} -3 \\ 4 \end{bmatrix}$ **b.** $\begin{bmatrix} 1 & 2 \\ 3 & 4 \end{bmatrix} \begin{bmatrix} -2 \\ 5 \end{bmatrix}$ **c.** $\begin{bmatrix} 1 & 3 \\ 5 & 7 \end{bmatrix} \begin{bmatrix} 2 & 4 \\ 6 & 8 \end{bmatrix}$

Solution

a. The product of a **1 × 2** matrix and a **2 × 1** matrix is a **1 × 1** matrix. The only entry in the product is found by multiplying the first row of the first matrix by the first column of the second matrix:

$$[2 \quad 3]\begin{bmatrix} -3 \\ 4 \end{bmatrix} = [2(-3) + 3(4)] = [6]$$

b. The product of a **2 × 2** matrix and **2 × 1** matrix is a **2 × 1** matrix. Multiply the corresponding entries in each row of the first matrix and the only column of the second matrix:

$$\begin{bmatrix} 1 & 2 \\ 3 & 4 \end{bmatrix}\begin{bmatrix} -2 \\ 5 \end{bmatrix} = \begin{bmatrix} 8 \\ 14 \end{bmatrix} \qquad \begin{matrix} 1(-2) + 2(5) = 8 \\ 3(-2) + 4(5) = 14 \end{matrix}$$

c. The product of a **2 × 2** matrix and a **2 × 2** matrix is a **2 × 2** matrix. Multiply the corresponding entries in each row of the first matrix and each column of the second matrix.

$$\begin{bmatrix} 1 & 3 \\ 5 & 7 \end{bmatrix}\begin{bmatrix} 2 & 4 \\ 6 & 8 \end{bmatrix} = \begin{bmatrix} 20 & 28 \\ 52 & 76 \end{bmatrix} \qquad \begin{matrix} 1 \cdot 2 + 3 \cdot 6 = 20 \\ 1 \cdot 4 + 3 \cdot 8 = 28 \\ 5 \cdot 2 + 7 \cdot 6 = 52 \\ 5 \cdot 4 + 7 \cdot 8 = 76 \end{matrix}$$

▶**TRY THIS.** Find AB if $A = \begin{bmatrix} 1 & 2 \\ 3 & 4 \end{bmatrix}$ and $B = \begin{bmatrix} 5 & 6 \\ 7 & 8 \end{bmatrix}$. ■

EXAMPLE 2 | Multiplying matrices

Find AB and BA in each case.

a. $A = \begin{bmatrix} 1 & 3 \\ 5 & 7 \\ 8 & 2 \end{bmatrix}$, $B = \begin{bmatrix} 2 & 4 & -1 \\ 6 & -3 & 2 \end{bmatrix}$

b. $A = \begin{bmatrix} 1 & 3 & 4 \\ 2 & 5 & 6 \\ 7 & 8 & 9 \end{bmatrix}$, $B = \begin{bmatrix} 1 & 0 & 1 \\ 0 & 1 & 0 \\ 0 & 1 & 1 \end{bmatrix}$

Solution

a. The product of 3×2 matrix A and 2×3 matrix B is the 3×3 matrix AB. The first row of AB is found by multiplying the corresponding entries in the first row of A and each column of B:

$$1 \cdot 2 + 3 \cdot 6 = 20, \qquad 1 \cdot 4 + 3(-3) = -5, \qquad \text{and} \qquad 1(-1) + 3 \cdot 2 = 5$$

So 20, −5, and 5 form the first row of AB. The second row of AB is formed from multiplying the second row of A and each column from B:

$$5 \cdot 2 + 7 \cdot 6 = 52, \qquad 5 \cdot 4 + 7(-3) = -1, \qquad \text{and} \qquad 5(-1) + 7 \cdot 2 = 9$$

So 52, −1, and 9 form the second row of AB. The third row of AB is formed by multiplying corresponding entries in the third row of A and each column of B.

$$AB = \begin{bmatrix} 1 & 3 \\ 5 & 7 \\ 8 & 2 \end{bmatrix}\begin{bmatrix} 2 & 4 & -1 \\ 6 & -3 & 2 \end{bmatrix} = \begin{bmatrix} 20 & -5 & 5 \\ 52 & -1 & 9 \\ 28 & 26 & -4 \end{bmatrix}$$

The product of 2×3 matrix B and 3×2 matrix A is the 2×2 matrix BA:

$$BA = \begin{bmatrix} 2 & 4 & -1 \\ 6 & -3 & 2 \end{bmatrix} \begin{bmatrix} 1 & 3 \\ 5 & 7 \\ 8 & 2 \end{bmatrix}$$

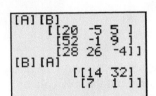

Figure 7

$$= \begin{bmatrix} 14 & 32 \\ 7 & 1 \end{bmatrix} \quad \begin{aligned} 2(1) + 4(5) + (-1)(8) &= 14 \\ 2(3) + 4(7) + (-1)(2) &= 32 \\ 6(1) + (-3)(5) + 2(8) &= 7 \\ 6(3) + (-3)(7) + 2(2) &= 1 \end{aligned}$$

To check, enter A and B into a graphing calculator and find the products, as shown in Fig. 7. □

b. The product of 3×3 matrix A and 3×3 matrix B is the 3×3 matrix AB:

$$AB = \begin{bmatrix} 1 & 3 & 4 \\ 2 & 5 & 6 \\ 7 & 8 & 9 \end{bmatrix} \begin{bmatrix} 1 & 0 & 1 \\ 0 & 1 & 0 \\ 0 & 1 & 1 \end{bmatrix} = \begin{bmatrix} 1 & 7 & 5 \\ 2 & 11 & 8 \\ 7 & 17 & 16 \end{bmatrix}$$

The product of 3×3 matrix B and 3×3 matrix A is the 3×3 matrix BA:

$$BA = \begin{bmatrix} 1 & 0 & 1 \\ 0 & 1 & 0 \\ 0 & 1 & 1 \end{bmatrix} \begin{bmatrix} 1 & 3 & 4 \\ 2 & 5 & 6 \\ 7 & 8 & 9 \end{bmatrix} = \begin{bmatrix} 8 & 11 & 13 \\ 2 & 5 & 6 \\ 9 & 13 & 15 \end{bmatrix}$$

▶**TRY THIS.** Find AB and BA if $A = \begin{bmatrix} 2 \\ 3 \end{bmatrix}$ and $B = \begin{bmatrix} 7 & 4 \end{bmatrix}$. ∎

Example 2(a) shows matrices A and B where $AB \neq BA$. In Example 2(a), AB and BA are not even the same size. It can also happen that AB is defined but BA is undefined because of the sizes of A and B. So multiplication of matrices is generally not commutative. Operations with matrices have some properties that are similar to the properties of operations with real numbers. We will not study the properties of matrices extensively in this text, but some properties for 2×2 matrices are discussed in the exercises.

Matrix Equations

Recall that two matrices are equal provided they are the same size and their corresponding entries are equal. This definition is used to solve matrix equations.

EXAMPLE 3 Solving a matrix equation

Find the values of x and y that satisfy the matrix equation

$$\begin{bmatrix} 3 & 2 \\ 4 & -1 \end{bmatrix} \begin{bmatrix} x \\ y \end{bmatrix} = \begin{bmatrix} 1 \\ -6 \end{bmatrix}.$$

Solution

Multiply the matrices on the left-hand side to get the matrix equation

$$\begin{bmatrix} 3x + 2y \\ 4x - y \end{bmatrix} = \begin{bmatrix} 1 \\ -6 \end{bmatrix}.$$

Since matrices of the same size are equal only when all of their corresponding entries are equal, we have the following system of equations:

$$(1) \quad 3x + 2y = 1$$

$$(2) \quad 4x - y = -6$$

Solve by eliminating y:

$$3x + 2y = 1$$

$$\underline{8x - 2y = -12} \quad \text{Eq. (2) multiplied by 2}$$

$$11x \qquad = -11$$

$$x = -1$$

Now use $x = -1$ in Eq. (1):

$$3(-1) + 2y = 1$$

$$2y = 4$$

$$y = 2$$

You should check that the matrix equation is satisfied if $x = -1$ and $y = 2$.

▶**TRY THIS.** Solve $\begin{bmatrix} 1 & 1 \\ 1 & -1 \end{bmatrix} \begin{bmatrix} x \\ y \end{bmatrix} = \begin{bmatrix} 15 \\ -3 \end{bmatrix}$. ∎

In Example 3, we rewrote a matrix equation as a system of equations. We will now write a system of equations as a matrix equation. In fact, any system of linear equations can be written as a matrix equation in the form $AX = B$, where A is a matrix of coefficients, X is a column matrix of variables, and B is a column matrix of constants. In the next example we write a system of two equations as a matrix equation. In Section 4 we will solve systems of equations by using matrix operations on the corresponding matrix equations.

EXAMPLE 4 Writing a matrix equation

Write the following system as an equivalent matrix equation in the form of $AX = B$.

$$2x + y = 5$$

$$x - y = 4$$

Solution

Let $A = \begin{bmatrix} 2 & 1 \\ 1 & -1 \end{bmatrix}$, $X = \begin{bmatrix} x \\ y \end{bmatrix}$, and $B = \begin{bmatrix} 5 \\ 4 \end{bmatrix}$. The system of equations is equivalent to the matrix equation

$$\begin{bmatrix} 2 & 1 \\ 1 & -1 \end{bmatrix} \begin{bmatrix} x \\ y \end{bmatrix} = \begin{bmatrix} 5 \\ 4 \end{bmatrix},$$

which is of the form $AX = B$. Check by multiplying the two matrices on the left-hand side to get

$$\begin{bmatrix} 2x + y \\ x - y \end{bmatrix} = \begin{bmatrix} 5 \\ 4 \end{bmatrix}.$$

By the definition of equal matrices, this matrix equation is correct provided that $2x + y = 5$ and $x - y = 4$, which is the original system.

▶**TRY THIS.** Write $\begin{array}{r} x - y = 3 \\ x + 2y = 5 \end{array}$ as the matrix equation $AX = B$. ∎

► FOR thought... True or False? Explain.

The following statements refer to the matrices

$$A = \begin{bmatrix} 1 \\ 6 \end{bmatrix}, B = \begin{bmatrix} 7 & 9 \end{bmatrix}, C = \begin{bmatrix} 2 & 3 \\ 4 & 5 \end{bmatrix},$$

$$D = \begin{bmatrix} 1 & 0 \\ 0 & 1 \end{bmatrix}, \text{ and } E = \begin{bmatrix} 2 & -1 \\ 0 & 3 \end{bmatrix}.$$

1. The size of AB is 2×2.

2. The size of BA is 1×1.

3. The size of AC is 1×2.

4. The size of CA is 2×2.

5. $DC = C$ and $CD = C$.

6. $BC = \begin{bmatrix} 50 & 66 \end{bmatrix}$

7. $AB = \begin{bmatrix} 7 & 9 \\ 42 & 54 \end{bmatrix}$
   8. $CE = \begin{bmatrix} 4 & 7 \\ 8 & 11 \end{bmatrix}$

9. $BA = \begin{bmatrix} 61 \end{bmatrix}$
   10. $CE = EC$

► EXERCISES 3

Find the size of AB in each case if the matrices can be multiplied.

1. A has size 3×2, B has size 2×5

2. A has size 3×1, B has size 1×3

3. A has size 1×4, B has size 4×1

4. A has size 4×2, B has size 2×5

5. A has size 5×1, B has size 1×5

6. A has size 2×1, B has size 1×6

7. A has size 3×3, B has size 3×3

8. A has size 4×4, B has size 4×1

9. A has size 3×4, B has size 3×4

10. A has size 4×2, B has size 3×4

Find the following products.

11. $\begin{bmatrix} -3 & 2 \end{bmatrix} \begin{bmatrix} 4 \\ 1 \end{bmatrix}$
   12. $\begin{bmatrix} -1 & 2 \end{bmatrix} \begin{bmatrix} 4 \\ 2 \end{bmatrix}$

13. $\begin{bmatrix} 1 & 3 \\ 2 & -4 \end{bmatrix} \begin{bmatrix} 1 \\ 3 \end{bmatrix}$
   14. $\begin{bmatrix} 0 & 2 \\ -3 & 1 \end{bmatrix} \begin{bmatrix} 2 \\ 5 \end{bmatrix}$

15. $\begin{bmatrix} 5 & 1 \\ 2 & 1 \end{bmatrix} \begin{bmatrix} 1 & 2 \\ 3 & 1 \end{bmatrix}$
   16. $\begin{bmatrix} 3 & 1 \\ 4 & 0 \end{bmatrix} \begin{bmatrix} 0 & 3 \\ 1 & 6 \end{bmatrix}$

17. $\begin{bmatrix} 3 \\ 1 \end{bmatrix} \begin{bmatrix} 5 & 6 \end{bmatrix}$
   18. $\begin{bmatrix} -2 \\ 2 \end{bmatrix} \begin{bmatrix} 4 & 3 \end{bmatrix}$

Find AB and BA in each case.

19. $A = \begin{bmatrix} 1 & 3 \\ 2 & 4 \\ 5 & 6 \end{bmatrix}, B = \begin{bmatrix} 1 & 0 & 1 \\ -1 & 1 & 0 \end{bmatrix}$

20. $A = \begin{bmatrix} 1 & 1 \\ -1 & 0 \\ 1 & -1 \end{bmatrix}, B = \begin{bmatrix} 2 & 1 & 0 \\ 3 & 2 & 0 \end{bmatrix}$

21. $A = \begin{bmatrix} 1 & 2 & 3 \\ 2 & 1 & 3 \\ 3 & 2 & 1 \end{bmatrix}, B = \begin{bmatrix} 1 & 1 & 1 \\ 0 & 1 & 1 \\ 0 & 0 & 1 \end{bmatrix}$

22. $A = \begin{bmatrix} 2 & 0 & 0 \\ 2 & 2 & 0 \\ 2 & 2 & 2 \end{bmatrix}, B = \begin{bmatrix} 0 & 0 & 1 \\ 2 & 0 & 0 \\ 0 & 3 & 0 \end{bmatrix}$

Let $A = \begin{bmatrix} 2 \\ -3 \\ 1 \end{bmatrix}, B = \begin{bmatrix} 2 & 3 & 4 \end{bmatrix}, C = \begin{bmatrix} 2 & 3 \\ 4 & 5 \\ 1 & 0 \end{bmatrix},$

$D = \begin{bmatrix} 2 & -1 & 1 \\ 0 & 3 & 2 \end{bmatrix}, \text{ and } E = \begin{bmatrix} 1 & 1 & 1 \\ 0 & 1 & 1 \\ 0 & 0 & 1 \end{bmatrix}.$ *Find the following if*

possible.

23. AB 24. BC 25. BE 26. BA

27. CE 28. DE 29. EC 30. BD

31. DC 32. CD 33. ED 34. EE

35. EA 36. DA 37. AE 38. EB

39. $AB + 2E$ 40. $EA - 2A$

If A is a square matrix then $A^2 = AA$, $A^3 = AAA$, and so on.
Let $A = \begin{bmatrix} 1 & 0 \\ 1 & 1 \end{bmatrix}$. *Find the following.*

41. A^2 **42.** A^3 **43.** A^4 **44.** A^5

Find each product if possible.

45. $\begin{bmatrix} 2 & 0 \\ 3 & 1 \end{bmatrix}\begin{bmatrix} 1 & 1 \\ 0 & 1 \end{bmatrix}$

46. $\begin{bmatrix} -1 & 2 \\ 3 & 4 \end{bmatrix}\begin{bmatrix} 2 & -1 \\ 5 & 2 \end{bmatrix}$

47. $\begin{bmatrix} 7 & 4 \\ 5 & 3 \end{bmatrix}\begin{bmatrix} 3 & -4 \\ -5 & 7 \end{bmatrix}$

48. $\begin{bmatrix} -2 & -3 \\ 5 & 8 \end{bmatrix}\begin{bmatrix} -8 & -3 \\ 5 & 2 \end{bmatrix}$

49. $\begin{bmatrix} -0.5 & 4 \\ 9 & 0.7 \end{bmatrix}\begin{bmatrix} 1 & 0 \\ 0 & 1 \end{bmatrix}$

50. $\begin{bmatrix} 1 & 0 \\ 0 & 1 \end{bmatrix}\begin{bmatrix} -0.7 & 1.2 \\ 3 & 1.1 \end{bmatrix}$

51. $\begin{bmatrix} -2 & 3 \end{bmatrix}\begin{bmatrix} a & 3b \\ 2a & b \end{bmatrix}$

52. $\begin{bmatrix} -2 & 5 \\ 6 & 4 \end{bmatrix}\begin{bmatrix} x \\ y \end{bmatrix}$

53. $\begin{bmatrix} a & 0 \\ 0 & b \end{bmatrix}\begin{bmatrix} -2 & 5 & 3 \\ 1 & 4 & 6 \end{bmatrix}$

54. $\begin{bmatrix} 1 & 1 \\ 1 & -1 \end{bmatrix}\begin{bmatrix} x \\ y \end{bmatrix}$

55. $\begin{bmatrix} 1 & 2 & 3 \end{bmatrix}\begin{bmatrix} 1 & 0 & 1 \\ 0 & 1 & 1 \\ 1 & 0 & 1 \end{bmatrix}$

56. $\begin{bmatrix} 1 & 1 & 0 \\ 1 & 0 & 1 \\ 0 & 1 & 1 \end{bmatrix}\begin{bmatrix} -2 \\ 3 \\ 5 \end{bmatrix}$

57. $\begin{bmatrix} -1 & 0 & 3 \end{bmatrix}\begin{bmatrix} -5 \\ 1 \\ 4 \end{bmatrix}$

58. $\begin{bmatrix} -5 \\ 1 \\ 4 \end{bmatrix}\begin{bmatrix} -1 & 0 & 3 \end{bmatrix}$

59. $\begin{bmatrix} x \\ y \end{bmatrix}\begin{bmatrix} x & y \end{bmatrix}$

60. $\begin{bmatrix} x & y \end{bmatrix}\begin{bmatrix} x \\ y \end{bmatrix}$

61. $\begin{bmatrix} -1 & 2 & 3 \\ 3 & 4 & 4 \end{bmatrix}\begin{bmatrix} \sqrt{2} \\ 0 \\ \sqrt{2} \end{bmatrix}$

62. $\begin{bmatrix} 2 & 3 \end{bmatrix}\begin{bmatrix} 0 & \sqrt{2} & 5 \\ -1 & \sqrt{8} & 0 \end{bmatrix}$

63. $\begin{bmatrix} \frac{1}{2} & \frac{1}{3} \\ \frac{1}{4} & \frac{1}{5} \end{bmatrix}\begin{bmatrix} -8 & 12 \\ -5 & 15 \end{bmatrix}$

64. $\begin{bmatrix} \frac{1}{4} & \frac{1}{2} \\ \frac{1}{8} & -\frac{1}{2} \end{bmatrix}\begin{bmatrix} -\frac{1}{2} & \frac{1}{4} \\ \frac{1}{2} & \frac{1}{4} \end{bmatrix}$

65. $\begin{bmatrix} 3 & 0 & 3 \end{bmatrix}\begin{bmatrix} 2 & 4 & 6 \end{bmatrix}$

66. $\begin{bmatrix} 2 \\ 5 \end{bmatrix}\begin{bmatrix} 7 & 2 \\ 3 & 1 \end{bmatrix}$

67. $\begin{bmatrix} 1 & 0 & -1 \\ 0 & 1 & 0 \\ 1 & 1 & 1 \end{bmatrix}\begin{bmatrix} 9 & 8 & 10 \\ 3 & 5 & 2 \\ 7 & 8 & 4 \end{bmatrix}$

68. $\begin{bmatrix} 1 & 1 & 1 \\ 0 & 1 & 1 \\ 0 & 0 & 1 \end{bmatrix}\begin{bmatrix} -2 & 3 & -4 \\ 2 & 5 & 7 \\ -3 & 0 & -6 \end{bmatrix}$

69. $\begin{bmatrix} 5 & -3 & -2 \\ 4 & 2 & 6 \\ 2 & 3 & -8 \end{bmatrix}\begin{bmatrix} 0.2 & 0.3 \\ 0.2 & -0.4 \\ 0.3 & 0.5 \end{bmatrix}$

70. $\begin{bmatrix} 0.2 & 0.1 & 0.7 \\ 0.3 & 0.3 & 0.4 \end{bmatrix}\begin{bmatrix} 20 & 30 & 40 \\ 10 & 20 & 50 \\ 60 & 50 & 40 \end{bmatrix}$

Write each matrix equation as a system of equations and solve the system by the method of your choice.

71. $\begin{bmatrix} 2 & -3 \\ 1 & 2 \end{bmatrix}\begin{bmatrix} x \\ y \end{bmatrix} = \begin{bmatrix} 0 \\ 7 \end{bmatrix}$

72. $\begin{bmatrix} 1 & 5 \\ -2 & 4 \end{bmatrix}\begin{bmatrix} x \\ y \end{bmatrix} = \begin{bmatrix} 2 \\ 10 \end{bmatrix}$

73. $\begin{bmatrix} 2 & 3 \\ 4 & 6 \end{bmatrix}\begin{bmatrix} x \\ y \end{bmatrix} = \begin{bmatrix} 5 \\ 9 \end{bmatrix}$

74. $\begin{bmatrix} 1 & -3 \\ -2 & 6 \end{bmatrix}\begin{bmatrix} x \\ y \end{bmatrix} = \begin{bmatrix} 1 \\ -2 \end{bmatrix}$

75. $\begin{bmatrix} 1 & 1 & 1 \\ 0 & 1 & 1 \\ 0 & 0 & 1 \end{bmatrix}\begin{bmatrix} x \\ y \\ z \end{bmatrix} = \begin{bmatrix} 4 \\ 5 \\ 6 \end{bmatrix}$

76. $\begin{bmatrix} 2 & 3 & 1 \\ 0 & 1 & 4 \\ 0 & 0 & 2 \end{bmatrix}\begin{bmatrix} x \\ y \\ z \end{bmatrix} = \begin{bmatrix} 0 \\ 3 \\ 6 \end{bmatrix}$

Write a matrix equation of the form $AX = B$ that corresponds to each system of equations.

77. $2x + 3y = 9$
$4x - y = 6$

78. $x - y = -7$
$x + 2y = 8$

79. $x + 2y - z = 3$
$3x - y + 3z = 1$
$2x + y - 4z = 0$

80. $x + y + z = 1$
$2x + y - z = 4$
$x - y - 3z = 2$

Solve each problem.

81. *Building Costs* A contractor builds two types of houses. The costs for labor and materials for the economy model and the deluxe model in thousands of dollars are shown in the table. Write the information in the table as a matrix A. Suppose that the contractor built four economy models and seven deluxe models. Write a matrix Q of the appropriate size containing the quantity of each type. Find the product matrix AQ. What do the entries of AQ represent?

Table for Exercise 81

	Economy	Deluxe	
Labor Cost	$24	$40	
Material Cost	$38	$70	

AbleStock/Hemera Technologies/Getty Images

82. *Nutritional Information* According to the manufacturers, the breakfast cereals Almond Delight and Basic 4 contain the grams of protein, carbohydrates, and fat per serving listed in the table. Write the information in the table as a matrix A. In one week Julia ate four servings of Almond Delight and three servings of Basic 4. Write a matrix Q of the appropriate size expressing the quantity of each type that Julia ate. Find the product AQ. What do the entries of AQ represent?

Table for Exercise 82

	Almond Delight	Basic 4
Protein	2	3
Carbohydrates	23	28
Fat	2	2

FOR WRITING/DISCUSSION

Let $A = \begin{bmatrix} a_{11} & a_{12} \\ a_{21} & a_{22} \end{bmatrix}$, $B = \begin{bmatrix} b_{11} & b_{12} \\ b_{21} & b_{22} \end{bmatrix}$, and $C = \begin{bmatrix} c_{11} & c_{12} \\ c_{21} & c_{22} \end{bmatrix}$. *Determine whether each of the following statements is true, and explain your answer.*

83. $AB = BA$ (commutative)

84. $(AB)C = A(BC)$ (associative)

85. For any real number k, $k(A + B) = kA + kB$.

86. $A(B + C) = AB + AC$ (distributive)

87. For any real numbers s and t, $sA + tA = (s + t)A$.

88. Multiplication of 1×1 matrices is commutative.

▶ RETHINKING

89. Let $A = \begin{bmatrix} 1 & 2 \\ -3 & 5 \end{bmatrix}$ and $B = \begin{bmatrix} -1 & 3 \\ 2 & 4 \end{bmatrix}$. Find $A + 3B$.

90. Use Gaussian elimination to solve the system $x + y - z = 5$, $y + z = 7$, and $y - z = 6$.

91. Determine whether the system $y = -9x + 2$ and $y = 500x - 98$ is independent, dependent, or inconsistent.

92. Let $y = -x^4 - 3x^3 + x^2 - 9x + 8$. Does y approach ∞ or $-\infty$ as x approaches ∞?

93. Solve $\dfrac{x - 9}{x + 99} \le 0$.

94. Simplify $\left(\dfrac{2x^3 y^3}{8x^{11} y^{21}} \right)^{-1/2}$.

THINKING OUTSIDE THE BOX LXXIII

Statewide Play-Offs Twenty-four teams competed in the statewide soccer play-offs. To reduce the amount of travel, the teams were divided into a north section and a south section, with the winner from each section to meet in a final match. Within each section, each team played every other team once, getting 1 point for a win, 1/2 point for a tie, and no points for a loss. There were 69 more games played in the north than in the south. In the south, Springville scored 5.5 points in the play-offs and was not defeated. How many games did Springville win?

▶ POP QUIZ 3

$A = \begin{bmatrix} 2 \\ 4 \end{bmatrix}$, $B = \begin{bmatrix} 1 \\ 3 \end{bmatrix}$, $C = \begin{bmatrix} 1 & 3 \\ 5 & 7 \end{bmatrix}$, $D = \begin{bmatrix} 2 & 4 \\ 0 & 8 \end{bmatrix}$.

Perform the matrix operations if possible.

1. AB

2. AC

3. CA

4. CD

5. DC

▶ LINKING

concepts... For Individual or Group Explorations

Sandro Donda/Shutterstock

Using Matrices to Rank Teams

The table shown here gives the records of all four teams in a soccer league. An entry of 1 indicates that the row team has defeated the column team. (There are no ties.) The teams are ranked, not by their percentage of victories, but by the number of points received under a ranking scheme that gives a team credit for the quality of the team it defeats. Since team A defeated B and C, A gets two points. Since B defeated C and D, and C defeated D, A gets 3 more secondary points for a total of 5 points.

Since D's only victory is over A, D gets 1 point for that victory plus 2 secondary points for A's defeats of B and C, giving D a total of 3 points.

a) Write the table as a 4×4 matrix M and find M^2.

b) Explain what the entries of M^2 represent.

c) Now let T be a 4×1 matrix with a 1 in every entry. Find $(M + M^2)T$.

d) Explain what the entries of $(M + M^2)T$ represent.

e) Is it possible for one team to have a better win-loss record than another, but end up ranked lower than the other because of this point scheme? Give an example to support your answer.

f) Make up a win-loss table (with no ties) for a six-team soccer league like the given table. Use a graphing calculator to find $(M + M^2)T$. Compare the percentage of games won by each team with its ranking by this scheme. Is it possible for a team to have a higher percentage of wins but still be ranked lower than another team?

g) Find $(2M + M^2)T$ for the matrix M from part (f) and explain its entries. What is the significance of the number 2?

h) Compare the ranking of the six teams using $(2M + M^2)T$ and $(M + M^2)T$. Is it possible that $(2M + M^2)T$ could change the order of the teams?

	A	B	C	D
A	0	1	1	0
B	0	0	1	1
C	0	0	0	1
D	1	0	0	0

4 Inverses of Matrices

In previous sections we learned to add, subtract, and multiply matrices. There is no definition for division of matrices. In Section 1 we defined the identity matrix to be a square matrix with ones on the diagonal and zeros elsewhere. In this section we will see that the identity matrix behaves like the multiplicative identity 1 in the real number system ($1 \cdot a = a$ and $a \cdot 1 = a$ for any real number a). That is why it is called the identity matrix. We will also see that for certain matrices there are inverse matrices such that the product of a matrix and its inverse matrix is the identity matrix.

The Identity Matrix

If $A = \begin{bmatrix} a_{11} & a_{12} \\ a_{21} & a_{22} \end{bmatrix}$ and $I = \begin{bmatrix} 1 & 0 \\ 0 & 1 \end{bmatrix}$, then

$$\begin{bmatrix} a_{11} & a_{12} \\ a_{21} & a_{22} \end{bmatrix}\begin{bmatrix} 1 & 0 \\ 0 & 1 \end{bmatrix} = \begin{bmatrix} a_{11} & a_{12} \\ a_{21} & a_{22} \end{bmatrix} \quad \text{and} \quad \begin{bmatrix} 1 & 0 \\ 0 & 1 \end{bmatrix}\begin{bmatrix} a_{11} & a_{12} \\ a_{21} & a_{22} \end{bmatrix} = \begin{bmatrix} a_{11} & a_{12} \\ a_{21} & a_{22} \end{bmatrix}.$$

So $AI = A$ and $IA = A$ for any 2×2 matrix A. Note that the 2×2 identity matrix is not an identity matrix for 3×3 matrices, but a 3×3 matrix with ones on the diagonal and zeros elsewhere is the identity matrix for 3×3 matrices.

Definition:
Identity Matrix

For each positive integer n, the $n \times n$ **identity matrix** I is an $n \times n$ matrix with ones on the diagonal and zeros elsewhere. In symbols,

$$I = \begin{bmatrix} 1 & 0 & 0 & \cdots & 0 \\ 0 & 1 & 0 & \cdots & 0 \\ 0 & 0 & 1 & \cdots & 0 \\ \vdots & \vdots & \vdots & & \vdots \\ 0 & 0 & 0 & \cdots & 1 \end{bmatrix}.$$

We use the letter I for the identity matrix for any size, but the size of I should be clear from the context.

EXAMPLE 1 Using an identity matrix

Show that $BI = B$ and $IB = B$ where I is the 3×3 identity matrix and

$$B = \begin{bmatrix} 2 & 3 & 5 \\ 1 & 0 & 4 \\ 5 & 7 & 2 \end{bmatrix}.$$

Solution

Check that $BI = B$:

$$\begin{bmatrix} 2 & 3 & 5 \\ 1 & 0 & 4 \\ 5 & 7 & 2 \end{bmatrix} \begin{bmatrix} 1 & 0 & 0 \\ 0 & 1 & 0 \\ 0 & 0 & 1 \end{bmatrix} = \begin{bmatrix} 2 & 3 & 5 \\ 1 & 0 & 4 \\ 5 & 7 & 2 \end{bmatrix} \qquad \begin{matrix} 2 \cdot 1 + 3 \cdot 0 + 5 \cdot 0 = 2 \\ 2 \cdot 0 + 3 \cdot 1 + 5 \cdot 0 = 3 \\ 2 \cdot 0 + 3 \cdot 0 + 5 \cdot 1 = 5 \end{matrix}$$

The computations at the right show that 2, 3, and 5 form the first row of BI. The second and third rows are found similarly. Now check that $IB = B$:

$$\begin{bmatrix} 1 & 0 & 0 \\ 0 & 1 & 0 \\ 0 & 0 & 1 \end{bmatrix} \begin{bmatrix} 2 & 3 & 5 \\ 1 & 0 & 4 \\ 5 & 7 & 2 \end{bmatrix} = \begin{bmatrix} 2 & 3 & 5 \\ 1 & 0 & 4 \\ 5 & 7 & 2 \end{bmatrix}$$

▶**TRY THIS.** Find AB and BA if $A = \begin{bmatrix} 1 & 3 \\ 8 & 9 \end{bmatrix}$ and $B = \begin{bmatrix} 1 & 0 \\ 0 & 1 \end{bmatrix}$. ∎

The Inverse of a Matrix

If the product of two $n \times n$ matrices is the $n \times n$ identity matrix, then the two matrices are *multiplicative inverses* of each other. Matrices also have additive inverses. Since we are discussing only multiplicative inverses in this section, we will simply call them inverses.

Definition:
Inverse of a Matrix

The **inverse** of an $n \times n$ matrix A is an $n \times n$ matrix A^{-1} (if it exists) such that $AA^{-1} = I$ and $A^{-1}A = I$. (Read A^{-1} as "A inverse.")

If A has an inverse, then A is **invertible.** Before we learn how to find the inverse of a matrix, we use the definition to determine whether two given matrices are inverses.

EXAMPLE 2 Using the definition of inverse matrices

Determine whether $A = \begin{bmatrix} 3 & 4 \\ 5 & 7 \end{bmatrix}$ and $B = \begin{bmatrix} 7 & -4 \\ -5 & 3 \end{bmatrix}$ are inverses of each other.

Solution

Find the products AB and BA:

$$AB = \begin{bmatrix} 3 & 4 \\ 5 & 7 \end{bmatrix}\begin{bmatrix} 7 & -4 \\ -5 & 3 \end{bmatrix} = \begin{bmatrix} 1 & 0 \\ 0 & 1 \end{bmatrix}$$

$$BA = \begin{bmatrix} 7 & -4 \\ -5 & 3 \end{bmatrix}\begin{bmatrix} 3 & 4 \\ 5 & 7 \end{bmatrix} = \begin{bmatrix} 1 & 0 \\ 0 & 1 \end{bmatrix}$$

A and B are inverses because $AB = BA = I$, where I is the 2×2 identity matrix.

▶**TRY THIS.** Find AB and BA if $A = \begin{bmatrix} 3 & 5 \\ 1 & 2 \end{bmatrix}$ and $B = \begin{bmatrix} 2 & -5 \\ -1 & 3 \end{bmatrix}$. ∎

If we are given the matrix

$$A = \begin{bmatrix} 3 & 4 \\ 5 & 7 \end{bmatrix}$$

from Example 2, how do we find its inverse if it is not already known? According to the definition, A^{-1} is a 2×2 matrix such that $AA^{-1} = I$ and $A^{-1}A = I$. So if

$$A^{-1} = \begin{bmatrix} x & y \\ z & w \end{bmatrix},$$

then

$$\begin{bmatrix} 3 & 4 \\ 5 & 7 \end{bmatrix}\begin{bmatrix} x & y \\ z & w \end{bmatrix} = \begin{bmatrix} 1 & 0 \\ 0 & 1 \end{bmatrix} \quad \text{and} \quad \begin{bmatrix} x & y \\ z & w \end{bmatrix}\begin{bmatrix} 3 & 4 \\ 5 & 7 \end{bmatrix} = \begin{bmatrix} 1 & 0 \\ 0 & 1 \end{bmatrix}.$$

To find A^{-1} we solve these matrix equations. If A is invertible, both equations will have the same solution. We will work with the first one. Multiply the two matrices on the left-hand side of the first equation to get the following equation:

$$\begin{bmatrix} 3x + 4z & 3y + 4w \\ 5x + 7z & 5y + 7w \end{bmatrix} = \begin{bmatrix} 1 & 0 \\ 0 & 1 \end{bmatrix}$$

Equate the corresponding terms from these equal matrices to get the following two systems:

$$3x + 4z = 1 \qquad\qquad 3y + 4w = 0$$
$$5x + 7z = 0 \qquad\qquad 5y + 7w = 1$$

We can solve these two systems by using the Gaussian elimination method from Section 1. The augmented matrices for these systems are

$$\begin{bmatrix} 3 & 4 & | & 1 \\ 5 & 7 & | & 0 \end{bmatrix} \quad \text{and} \quad \begin{bmatrix} 3 & 4 & | & 0 \\ 5 & 7 & | & 1 \end{bmatrix}.$$

Note that the two augmented matrices have the same coefficient matrix. Since we would use the same row operations on each of them, we can solve the systems simultaneously by combining the two systems into one augmented matrix denoted $[A\,|\,I]$:

$$[A\,|\,I] = \begin{bmatrix} 3 & 4 & | & 1 & 0 \\ 5 & 7 & | & 0 & 1 \end{bmatrix}$$

So the problem of finding A^{-1} is equivalent to the problem of solving two systems by Gaussian elimination. A is invertible if and only if these systems have a solution. Multiply the first row of $[A\,|\,I]$ by $\frac{1}{3}$ to get a 1 in the first row, first column:

$$\begin{bmatrix} 1 & \frac{4}{3} & | & \frac{1}{3} & 0 \\ 5 & 7 & | & 0 & 1 \end{bmatrix} \quad \frac{1}{3}R_1 \to R_1$$

663

Now multiply row 1 by -5 and add the result to row 2:

$$\left[\begin{array}{cc|cc} 1 & \frac{4}{3} & \frac{1}{3} & 0 \\ 0 & \frac{1}{3} & -\frac{5}{3} & 1 \end{array}\right] \quad -5R_1 + R_2 \rightarrow R_2$$

Multiply row 2 by 3:

$$\left[\begin{array}{cc|cc} 1 & \frac{4}{3} & \frac{1}{3} & 0 \\ 0 & 1 & -5 & 3 \end{array}\right] \quad 3R_2 \rightarrow R_2$$

Multiply row 2 by $-\frac{4}{3}$ and add the result to row 1:

$$\left[\begin{array}{cc|cc} 1 & 0 & 7 & -4 \\ 0 & 1 & -5 & 3 \end{array}\right] \quad -\frac{4}{3}R_2 + R_1 \rightarrow R_1$$

The numbers in the first column to the right of the bar give the values of x and z, while the numbers in the second column give the values of y and w. So $x = 7$, $y = -4$, $z = -5$, and $w = 3$ give the solutions to the two systems, and

$$A^{-1} = \begin{bmatrix} 7 & -4 \\ -5 & 3 \end{bmatrix}.$$

Since A^{-1} is the same matrix that was called B in Example 2, we can be sure that $AA^{-1} = I$ and $A^{-1}A = I$. Note that the matrix A^{-1} actually appeared on the right-hand side of the final augmented matrix, while the 2×2 identity matrix I appeared on the left-hand side. So A^{-1} is found by simply using row operations to convert the matrix $[A|I]$ into the matrix $[I|A^{-1}]$.

The essential steps for finding the inverse of a matrix are listed as follows.

PROCEDURE

Finding A^{-1}

Use the following steps to find the inverse of a square matrix A.

1. Write the augmented matrix $[A|I]$, where I is the identity matrix of the same size as A.

2. Use row operations (the Gaussian elimination method) to convert the left-hand side of the augmented matrix into I.

3. If the left-hand side can be converted to I, then $[A|I]$ becomes $[I|A^{-1}]$, and A^{-1} appears on the right-hand side of the augmented matrix.

4. If the left-hand side cannot be converted to I, then A is not invertible.

EXAMPLE 3 | Finding the inverse of a matrix

Find the inverse of the matrix

$$A = \begin{bmatrix} 2 & -3 \\ 1 & 1 \end{bmatrix}.$$

Solution

Write the augmented matrix $[A|I]$:

$$\left[\begin{array}{cc|cc} 2 & -3 & 1 & 0 \\ 1 & 1 & 0 & 1 \end{array}\right]$$

Use row operations to convert $[A\,|\,I\,]$ into $[I\,|\,A^{-1}]$:

$$\begin{bmatrix} 1 & 1 & | & 0 & 1 \\ 2 & -3 & | & 1 & 0 \end{bmatrix} \quad R_1 \leftrightarrow R_2$$

$$\begin{bmatrix} 1 & 1 & | & 0 & 1 \\ 0 & -5 & | & 1 & -2 \end{bmatrix} \quad -2R_1 + R_2 \to R_2$$

$$\begin{bmatrix} 1 & 1 & | & 0 & 1 \\ 0 & 1 & | & -\frac{1}{5} & \frac{2}{5} \end{bmatrix} \quad -\frac{1}{5}R_2 \to R_2$$

$$\begin{bmatrix} 1 & 0 & | & \frac{1}{5} & \frac{3}{5} \\ 0 & 1 & | & -\frac{1}{5} & \frac{2}{5} \end{bmatrix} \quad -R_2 + R_1 \to R_1$$

Since the last matrix is in the form $[I\,|\,A^{-1}]$, we get

$$A^{-1} = \begin{bmatrix} \frac{1}{5} & \frac{3}{5} \\ -\frac{1}{5} & \frac{2}{5} \end{bmatrix}.$$

Check that $AA^{-1} = A^{-1}A = I$.

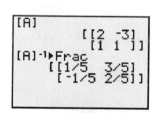 The inverse of a matrix can be found with a graphing calculator. Enter the matrix A from Example 3 into a calculator. Then use the x^{-1} key to find A^{-1}, as shown in Fig. 8.

Figure 8

▶**TRY THIS.** Find the inverse of $\begin{bmatrix} 3 & 2 \\ 7 & 5 \end{bmatrix}$. ∎

(**EXAMPLE 4**) A noninvertible matrix

Find the inverse of the matrix

$$A = \begin{bmatrix} 1 & -3 \\ -1 & 3 \end{bmatrix}.$$

Solution

Use row operations on the augmented matrix $[A\,|\,I\,]$:

$$\begin{bmatrix} 1 & -3 & | & 1 & 0 \\ -1 & 3 & | & 0 & 1 \end{bmatrix}$$

$$\begin{bmatrix} 1 & -3 & | & 1 & 0 \\ 0 & 0 & | & 1 & 1 \end{bmatrix} \quad R_1 + R_2 \to R_2$$

The row containing all zeros on the left-hand side of the augmented matrix indicates that the left-hand side (the matrix A) cannot be converted to I using row operations. So A is not invertible. Note that the row of zeros in the augmented matrix means that there is no solution to the systems that must be solved to find A^{-1}.

▶**TRY THIS.** Find the inverse of $\begin{bmatrix} 3 & -1 \\ -3 & 1 \end{bmatrix}$. ∎

(**EXAMPLE 5**) The inverse of a 3 × 3 matrix

Find the inverse of the matrix

$$A = \begin{bmatrix} 0 & 1 & 2 \\ 1 & 0 & 3 \\ 0 & 1 & 4 \end{bmatrix}.$$

Solution

Perform row operations to convert $[A|I]$ into $[I|A^{-1}]$, where I is the 3×3 identity matrix.

$$\left[\begin{array}{ccc|ccc} 0 & 1 & 2 & 1 & 0 & 0 \\ 1 & 0 & 3 & 0 & 1 & 0 \\ 0 & 1 & 4 & 0 & 0 & 1 \end{array}\right] \quad \text{The augmented matrix}$$

Interchange the first and second rows to get the first 1 on the diagonal:

$$\left[\begin{array}{ccc|ccc} 1 & 0 & 3 & 0 & 1 & 0 \\ 0 & 1 & 2 & 1 & 0 & 0 \\ 0 & 1 & 4 & 0 & 0 & 1 \end{array}\right] \quad R_1 \leftrightarrow R_2$$

Since the first column is now in the desired form, we work on the second column:

$$\left[\begin{array}{ccc|ccc} 1 & 0 & 3 & 0 & 1 & 0 \\ 0 & 1 & 2 & 1 & 0 & 0 \\ 0 & 0 & 2 & -1 & 0 & 1 \end{array}\right] \quad -R_2 + R_3 \rightarrow R_3$$

We now get a 1 in the last position on the diagonal and zeros above it:

$$\left[\begin{array}{ccc|ccc} 1 & 0 & 3 & 0 & 1 & 0 \\ 0 & 1 & 2 & 1 & 0 & 0 \\ 0 & 0 & 1 & -0.5 & 0 & 0.5 \end{array}\right] \quad \tfrac{1}{2}R_3 \rightarrow R_3$$

$$\left[\begin{array}{ccc|ccc} 1 & 0 & 0 & 1.5 & 1 & -1.5 \\ 0 & 1 & 0 & 2 & 0 & -1 \\ 0 & 0 & 1 & -0.5 & 0 & 0.5 \end{array}\right] \quad \begin{array}{l} -3R_3 + R_1 \rightarrow R_1 \\ -2R_3 + R_2 \rightarrow R_2 \end{array}$$

So

$$A^{-1} = \left[\begin{array}{ccc} 1.5 & 1 & -1.5 \\ 2 & 0 & -1 \\ -0.5 & 0 & 0.5 \end{array}\right].$$

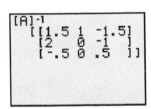

Figure 9

Check that $AA^{-1} = I$ and $A^{-1}A = I$.

Of course it is a lot simpler to find A^{-1} with a calculator, as shown in Fig. 9.

►TRY THIS. Find the inverse of $\left[\begin{array}{ccc} 1 & 1 & 3 \\ -1 & 0 & 0 \\ -1 & -1 & -2 \end{array}\right]$. ∎

Finding the inverse of matrices larger than 2×2 is rather tedious, but technology can be used to great advantage here. We will now see why inverse matrices are so important.

Solving Systems of Equations Using Matrix Inverses

In Section 3 we saw that a system of n linear equations in n unknowns could be written as a matrix equation of the form $AX = B$, where A is a matrix of coefficients, X is a matrix of variables, and B is a matrix of constants. If A^{-1} exists, then we can multiply each side of this equation by A^{-1}. Since matrix multiplication is not commutative in general, A^{-1} is placed to the left of the matrices on each side:

$$AX = B$$

$$A^{-1}(AX) = A^{-1}B \quad \text{Multiply each side by } A^{-1}.$$

$$(A^{-1}A)X = A^{-1}B \quad \text{Matrix multiplication is associative.}$$

$$IX = A^{-1}B \quad \text{Since } A^{-1}A = I$$

$$X = A^{-1}B \quad \text{Since } I \text{ is the identity matrix}$$

The last equation indicates that the values of the variables in the matrix X are equal to the entries in the matrix $A^{-1}B$. So solving the system is equivalent to finding $A^{-1}B$. This result is summarized in the following theorem.

Theorem: Solving a System Using A^{-1}

If a system of n linear equations in n variables has a unique solution, then the solution is given by

$$X = A^{-1}B,$$

where A is the matrix of coefficients, B is the matrix of constants, and X is the matrix of variables.

If there is no solution or there are infinitely many solutions, the matrix of coefficients is not invertible.

EXAMPLE 6 Using the inverse of a matrix to solve a system

Solve the system by using A^{-1}.

$$2x - 3y = 1$$

$$x + y = 8$$

Solution

For this system,

$$A = \begin{bmatrix} 2 & -3 \\ 1 & 1 \end{bmatrix}, \qquad X = \begin{bmatrix} x \\ y \end{bmatrix}, \qquad \text{and} \qquad B = \begin{bmatrix} 1 \\ 8 \end{bmatrix}.$$

Since the matrix A is the same as in Example 3, use A^{-1} from Example 3. Multiply A^{-1} and B to obtain

$$\begin{bmatrix} \frac{1}{5} & \frac{3}{5} \\ -\frac{1}{5} & \frac{2}{5} \end{bmatrix} \begin{bmatrix} 1 \\ 8 \end{bmatrix} = \begin{bmatrix} 5 \\ 3 \end{bmatrix}.$$

Since $X = A^{-1}B$, we have

$$X = \begin{bmatrix} x \\ y \end{bmatrix} = \begin{bmatrix} 5 \\ 3 \end{bmatrix}.$$

Therefore $x = 5$ and $y = 3$. Check this solution in the original system. With a calculator you can enter A and B, then find $A^{-1}B$, as shown in Fig. 10.

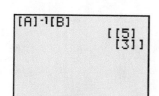

[A]⁻¹[B]
[[5]
[3]]

Figure 10

▶**TRY THIS.** Solve $\begin{aligned} 3x + 2y &= 4 \\ 7x + 5y &= 1 \end{aligned}$ by using A^{-1}. ∎

Since computers and even pocket calculators can find inverses of matrices, the method of solving an equation by first finding A^{-1} is a popular one for use with machines. By hand, this method may seem somewhat tedious. However, it is useful when there are many systems to solve with the same coefficients. The following system has the same coefficients as the system of Example 6:

$$2x - 3y = -1$$
$$x + y = -3$$

So

$$X = A^{-1}B = \begin{bmatrix} \frac{1}{5} & \frac{3}{5} \\ -\frac{1}{5} & \frac{2}{5} \end{bmatrix} \begin{bmatrix} -1 \\ -3 \end{bmatrix} = \begin{bmatrix} -2 \\ -1 \end{bmatrix}$$

or $x = -2$ and $y = -1$. As long as the coefficients of x and y are unchanged, the same A^{-1} is used to solve the system.

Application of Matrices to Secret Codes

There are many ways of encoding a message so that no one other than the intended recipient can understand the message. One way is to use a matrix to encode the message and the inverse matrix to decode the message. Assume that a space is 0, A is 1, B is 2, C is 3, and so on. The numerical equivalent of the word HELP is **8, 5, 12, 16.** List these numbers in two 2×1 matrices. Then multiply the matrices by a coding matrix. We will use the 2×2 matrix A from Example 6:

$$\begin{bmatrix} 2 & -3 \\ 1 & 1 \end{bmatrix} \begin{bmatrix} 8 \\ 5 \end{bmatrix} = \begin{bmatrix} 1 \\ 13 \end{bmatrix} \quad \text{and} \quad \begin{bmatrix} 2 & -3 \\ 1 & 1 \end{bmatrix} \begin{bmatrix} 12 \\ 16 \end{bmatrix} = \begin{bmatrix} -24 \\ 28 \end{bmatrix}$$

So the encoded message sent is 1, 13, −24, 28. The person receiving the message must know that

$$A^{-1} = \begin{bmatrix} \frac{1}{5} & \frac{3}{5} \\ -\frac{1}{5} & \frac{2}{5} \end{bmatrix}.$$

To decode this message, we find

$$\begin{bmatrix} \frac{1}{5} & \frac{3}{5} \\ -\frac{1}{5} & \frac{2}{5} \end{bmatrix} \begin{bmatrix} 1 \\ 13 \end{bmatrix} = \begin{bmatrix} 8 \\ 5 \end{bmatrix} \quad \text{and} \quad \begin{bmatrix} \frac{1}{5} & \frac{3}{5} \\ -\frac{1}{5} & \frac{2}{5} \end{bmatrix} \begin{bmatrix} -24 \\ 28 \end{bmatrix} = \begin{bmatrix} 12 \\ 16 \end{bmatrix}.$$

So the message is 8, 5, 12, 16, or HELP. Of course, any invertible matrix of any size and its inverse could be used for this coding scheme, and all of the encoding and decoding could be done by a computer. If a person or computer didn't know A or A^{-1} or even their size, then how hard do you think it would be to break this code?

➤ FOR thought... True or False? Explain.

The following statements refer to the matrices

$$A = \begin{bmatrix} 2 & 3 \\ 3 & 5 \end{bmatrix}, \quad B = \begin{bmatrix} 5 & -3 \\ -3 & 2 \end{bmatrix}, \quad C = \begin{bmatrix} 4 & 6 \\ 3 & 5 \\ 2 & 1 \end{bmatrix},$$

$$D = \begin{bmatrix} 11 \\ 19 \end{bmatrix}, \quad \text{and} \quad I = \begin{bmatrix} 1 & 0 \\ 0 & 1 \end{bmatrix}.$$

1. $AB = BA = I$

2. $B = A^{-1}$

3. B is an invertible matrix.

4. $AC = CA$

5. $CI = C$

6. C is an invertible matrix.

7. The system $\begin{array}{l} 2x + 3y = 11 \\ 3x + y = 19 \end{array}$ is equivalent to

$$A\begin{bmatrix} x \\ y \end{bmatrix} = D.$$

8. $A^{-1}D = \begin{bmatrix} -2 \\ 5 \end{bmatrix}$

9. The solution set to the system $\begin{array}{l} 2x + 3y = 11 \\ 3x + y = 19 \end{array}$ is $\{(-2, 5)\}$.

10. The solution set to the system $\begin{array}{l} 2x + 3y = 3 \\ 3x + y = -7 \end{array}$ is obtained from $A^{-1}\begin{bmatrix} 3 \\ -7 \end{bmatrix}$.

EXERCISES 4

For each given matrix A, show that AI = A and IA = A where I is the identity matrix of the appropriate size.

1. $A = \begin{bmatrix} 1 & 3 \\ 4 & 6 \end{bmatrix}$

2. $A = \begin{bmatrix} 3 & 2 \\ 5 & 9 \end{bmatrix}$

3. $A = \begin{bmatrix} 3 & 2 & 1 \\ 5 & 6 & 2 \\ 7 & 8 & 3 \end{bmatrix}$

4. $A = \begin{bmatrix} 3 & 4 & 1 \\ 2 & 2 & 5 \\ 0 & 3 & 6 \end{bmatrix}$

Find the following products.

5. $\begin{bmatrix} 1 & 0 \\ 0 & 1 \end{bmatrix}\begin{bmatrix} -3 & 5 \\ 12 & 6 \end{bmatrix}$

6. $\begin{bmatrix} 4 & 8 \\ 9 & -2 \end{bmatrix}\begin{bmatrix} 1 & 0 \\ 0 & 1 \end{bmatrix}$

7. $\begin{bmatrix} -2 & -3 \\ 3 & 4 \end{bmatrix}\begin{bmatrix} 4 & 3 \\ -3 & -2 \end{bmatrix}$

8. $\begin{bmatrix} 3 & 2 \\ 3 & 3 \end{bmatrix}\begin{bmatrix} 1 & -\frac{2}{3} \\ -1 & 1 \end{bmatrix}$

9. $\begin{bmatrix} 3 & 4 \\ 3 & 5 \end{bmatrix}\begin{bmatrix} \frac{5}{3} & -\frac{4}{3} \\ -1 & 1 \end{bmatrix}$

10. $\begin{bmatrix} 1 & 2 \\ 4 & 5 \end{bmatrix}\begin{bmatrix} -\frac{5}{3} & \frac{2}{3} \\ \frac{4}{3} & -\frac{1}{3} \end{bmatrix}$

11. $\begin{bmatrix} 3 & 5 & 1 \\ 4 & 5 & 7 \\ 4 & 9 & 2 \end{bmatrix}\begin{bmatrix} 1 & 0 & 0 \\ 0 & 1 & 0 \\ 0 & 0 & 1 \end{bmatrix}$

12. $\begin{bmatrix} 1 & 0 & 0 \\ 0 & 1 & 0 \\ 0 & 0 & 1 \end{bmatrix}\begin{bmatrix} 4 & 0 & 5 \\ 0 & 7 & 9 \\ 3 & 1 & 2 \end{bmatrix}$

13. $\begin{bmatrix} 1 & 0 & 2 \\ 1 & 3 & 0 \\ 0 & 1 & 0 \end{bmatrix}\begin{bmatrix} 0 & 1 & -3 \\ 0 & 0 & 1 \\ 0.5 & -0.5 & 1.5 \end{bmatrix}$

14. $\begin{bmatrix} 2 & 1 & 0 \\ 1 & 0 & 2 \\ 0 & 1 & 1 \end{bmatrix}\begin{bmatrix} 0.4 & 0.2 & -0.4 \\ 0.2 & -0.4 & 0.8 \\ -0.2 & 0.4 & 0.2 \end{bmatrix}$

15. $\begin{bmatrix} 1 & 1 & 0 \\ 0 & 1 & 1 \\ 1 & 0 & 1 \end{bmatrix}\begin{bmatrix} 0.5 & -0.5 & 0.5 \\ 0.5 & 0.5 & -0.5 \\ -0.5 & 0.5 & 0.5 \end{bmatrix}$

16. $\begin{bmatrix} 0.4 & 0.2 & -0.4 \\ 0.2 & -0.4 & 0.8 \\ -0.2 & 0.4 & 0.2 \end{bmatrix}\begin{bmatrix} 2 & 1 & 0 \\ 1 & 0 & 2 \\ 0 & 1 & 1 \end{bmatrix}$

Determine whether the matrices in each pair are inverses of each other.

17. $\begin{bmatrix} 3 & 1 \\ 11 & 4 \end{bmatrix}, \begin{bmatrix} 4 & -1 \\ -11 & 3 \end{bmatrix}$

18. $\begin{bmatrix} \frac{1}{2} & 0 \\ 0 & \frac{1}{2} \end{bmatrix}, \begin{bmatrix} 2 & 0 \\ 0 & 2 \end{bmatrix}$

19. $\begin{bmatrix} \frac{1}{2} & -1 \\ 3 & -12 \end{bmatrix}, \begin{bmatrix} 4 & 2 \\ 1 & 1 \end{bmatrix}$

20. $\begin{bmatrix} 1 & 2 & 3 \\ 0 & 1 & 2 \\ 0 & 0 & 1 \end{bmatrix}, \begin{bmatrix} 1 & -2 & 1 \\ 0 & 1 & -2 \\ 0 & 0 & 1 \end{bmatrix}$

21. $\begin{bmatrix} 1 & 0 & 0 \\ 0 & \frac{1}{2} & 0 \end{bmatrix}, \begin{bmatrix} 1 & 0 \\ 0 & 2 \\ 3 & 4 \end{bmatrix}$

22. $\begin{bmatrix} 1 & 2 \\ 3 & 4 \\ 5 & 6 \end{bmatrix}, \begin{bmatrix} 1 & \frac{1}{2} \\ \frac{1}{3} & \frac{1}{4} \\ \frac{1}{5} & \frac{1}{6} \end{bmatrix}$

Find the inverse of each matrix A if possible. Check that $AA^{-1} = I$ and $A^{-1}A = I$. See the procedure for finding A^{-1} in Example 2..

23. $\begin{bmatrix} 1 & 4 \\ 0 & 2 \end{bmatrix}$

24. $\begin{bmatrix} 1 & 3 \\ 0 & -1 \end{bmatrix}$

25. $\begin{bmatrix} 1 & 6 \\ 1 & 9 \end{bmatrix}$

26. $\begin{bmatrix} 1 & 4 \\ 3 & 8 \end{bmatrix}$

27. $\begin{bmatrix} -2 & -3 \\ 3 & 4 \end{bmatrix}$

28. $\begin{bmatrix} 3 & 4 \\ 4 & 5 \end{bmatrix}$

29. $\begin{bmatrix} 1 & -5 \\ -1 & 3 \end{bmatrix}$

30. $\begin{bmatrix} 4 & 3 \\ -3 & -2 \end{bmatrix}$

31. $\begin{bmatrix} -1 & 5 \\ 2 & -10 \end{bmatrix}$

32. $\begin{bmatrix} 2 & 6 \\ 1 & 3 \end{bmatrix}$

33. $\begin{bmatrix} 1 & 1 & 0 \\ 0 & -1 & -1 \\ 1 & 0 & -1 \end{bmatrix}$

34. $\begin{bmatrix} 1 & -1 & 2 \\ 1 & 2 & 3 \\ 2 & 1 & 5 \end{bmatrix}$

35. $\begin{bmatrix} 1 & 1 & 1 \\ 1 & -1 & -1 \\ 1 & -1 & 1 \end{bmatrix}$

36. $\begin{bmatrix} 1 & 0 & 2 \\ 0 & 2 & 0 \\ 1 & 3 & 0 \end{bmatrix}$

37. $\begin{bmatrix} 0 & 2 & 0 \\ 3 & 3 & 2 \\ 2 & 5 & 1 \end{bmatrix}$

38. $\begin{bmatrix} 4 & 1 & -3 \\ 0 & 1 & 0 \\ -3 & 1 & 2 \end{bmatrix}$

39. $\begin{bmatrix} 1 & 0 & 1 \\ 0 & 2 & 2 \\ 2 & 1 & 0 \end{bmatrix}$

40. $\begin{bmatrix} 1 & 3 & 0 \\ 0 & 3 & -2 \\ 0 & -5 & 3 \end{bmatrix}$

41. $\begin{bmatrix} 0 & 4 & 2 \\ 0 & 3 & 2 \\ 1 & -1 & 1 \end{bmatrix}$ **42.** $\begin{bmatrix} 1 & 2 & 0 \\ 2 & 3 & -1 \\ 0 & 1 & 2 \end{bmatrix}$

43. $\begin{bmatrix} 1 & 2 & 3 & 4 \\ 0 & 1 & 2 & 3 \\ 0 & 0 & 1 & 2 \\ 0 & 0 & 0 & 1 \end{bmatrix}$ **44.** $\begin{bmatrix} 1 & 0 & 0 & 0 \\ -2 & 1 & 0 & 0 \\ 3 & -2 & 1 & 0 \\ 5 & 3 & -2 & 1 \end{bmatrix}$

Solve each system of equations by using A^{-1}. Note that the matrix of coefficients in each system is a matrix from Exercises 23–44.

45. $x + 6y = -3$
$x + 9y = -6$

46. $x + 4y = 5$
$3x + 8y = 7$

47. $x + 6y = 4$
$x + 9y = 5$

48. $x + 4y = 1$
$3x + 8y = 5$

49. $-2x - 3y = 1$
$3x + 4y = -1$

50. $3x + 4y = 1$
$4x + 5y = 2$

51. $x - 5y = -5$
$-x + 3y = 1$

52. $4x + 3y = 2$
$-3x - 2y = -1$

53. $x + y + z = 3$
$x - y - z = -1$
$x - y + z = 5$

54. $x + 2z = -4$
$2y = 6$
$x + 3y = 7$

55. $2y = 6$
$3x + 3y + 2z = 16$
$2x + 5y + z = 19$

56. $4x + y - 3z = 3$
$y = -2$
$-3x + y + 2z = -5$

Solve each system of equations by using A^{-1} if possible.

57. $0.3x = 3 - 0.1y$
$4y = 7 - 2x$

58. $2x = 3y - 7$
$y = x + 4$

59. $x - y + z = 5$
$2x - y + 3z = 1$
$y + z = -9$

60. $x + y - z = 4$
$2x - 3y + z = 2$
$4x - y - z = 6$

61. $x + y + z = 1$
$2x + 4y + z = 2$
$x + 3y + 6z = 3$

62. $0.5x - 0.25y + 0.1z = 3$
$0.2x - 0.5y + 0.2z = -2$
$0.1x + 0.3y - 0.5z = -8$

⊞ *Most graphing calculators can perform operations with matrices, including matrix inversion and multiplication. Solve the following systems, using a graphing calculator to find A^{-1} and the product $A^{-1}B$.*

63. $0.1x + 0.2y + 0.1z = 27$
$0.5x + 0.2y + 0.3z = 9$
$0.4x + 0.8y + 0.1z = 36$

64. $3x + 6y + 4z = 9$
$x + 2y - 2z = -18$
$-x + 4y + 3z = 54$

65. $1.5x - 5y + 3z = 16$
$2.25x - 4y + z = 24$
$2x + 3.5y - 3z = -8$

66. $2.1x - 3.4y + 5z = 100$
$1.3x + 2y - 8z = 250$
$2.5x + 3y - 9.1z = 300$

Solve each problem.

67. Find all matrices A such that $A = \begin{bmatrix} a & 7 \\ 3 & b \end{bmatrix}$, $A^{-1} = \begin{bmatrix} -b & 7 \\ 3 & -a \end{bmatrix}$, and a and b are positive integers.

68. Find all matrices of the form $A = \begin{bmatrix} a & a \\ 0 & c \end{bmatrix}$ such that $A^2 = I$.

Write a system of equations for each problem. Solve the system using an inverse matrix.

69. *Eggs and Magazines* Stephanie bought a dozen eggs and a magazine at the Handy Mart. Her bill including tax was $8.79. If groceries are taxed at 5% and magazines at 8% and she paid 59 cents in tax on the purchase, then what was the price of each item?

70. *Dogs and Suds* The French Club sold 48 hot dogs and 120 soft drinks at the game on Saturday for a total of $206.40. If the price of a hot dog was 80 cents more than the price of a soft drink, then what was the price of each item?

71. *Plywood and Insulation* A contractor purchased four loads of plywood and six loads of insulation on Monday for $2500, and three loads of plywood and five loads of insulation on Tuesday for $1950. Find the cost of one load of plywood and the cost of one load of insulation.

72. *iPhone and iPod* On Monday, ElectriCity received a shipment of 12 iPhones and 6 iPods for a total cost of $3300. Tuesday's shipment contained 4 iPhones and 8 iPods for a total cost of $2000. Wednesday's shipment of 25 iPhones and 33 iPods did not include an invoice. What was the cost of Wednesday's shipment?

The following messages were encoded by using the matrix $A = \begin{bmatrix} 3 & 1 \\ 5 & 2 \end{bmatrix}$ and the coding scheme described in this section. Find A^{-1} and use it to decode the messages.

73. 36, 65, 49, 83, 12, 24, 66, 111, 33, 55

74. 15, 29, 26, 45, 24, 46, 3, 5, 46, 83, 6, 12, 77, 133

⊞ *Write a system of equations for each of the following problems and solve the system using matrix inversion and matrix multiplication on a graphing calculator.*

75. *Mixing Investments* The Asset Manager Fund keeps 76% of its money in stocks while the Magellan Fund keeps 90% of its money in stocks. How should an investor divide $60,000 between these two mutual funds so that 86% of the money is in stocks?

76. *Mixing Investments* The Asset Manager Mutual Fund investment mix is 76% stocks, 20% bonds, and 4% cash. The Magellan Fund mix is 90% stocks, 9% bonds, and 1% cash. The Puritan Fund mix is 60% stocks, 33% bonds, and 7% cash. How should an investor divide $50,000 between these three funds so that 74% of the money is in stocks, 21.7% is in bonds, and 4.3% is in cash?

77. *Stocking Supplies* Fernando purchases supplies for an import store. His first shipment on Monday was for 24 animal totems, 33 trade-bead necklaces, and 12 tribal masks for a total price of $202.23. His second shipment was for 19 animal totems, 40 trade-bead necklaces, and 22 tribal masks for a total price of $209.38. His third shipment was for 30 animal totems,

9 trade-bead necklaces, and 19 tribal masks for a total price of $167.66. For the fourth shipment the computer was down, and Fernando did not know the price of each item. What is the price of each item?

78. *On the Bayou* A-Bear's Catering Service charges its customers according to the number of servings of each item that is supplied at the party. The table shows the number of servings of jambalaya, crawfish pie, filé gumbo, iced tea, and dessert for the last five customers, along with the total cost of each party. What amount does A-Bear's charge per serving of each item?

HINT Write a system of five equations in five unknowns and use a graphing calculator to solve it.

Table for Exercise 78

	Jambalaya	Crawfish Pie	Filé Gumbo	Iced Tea	Dessert	Cost
Boudreaux	36	28	35	90	68	$344.35
Thibodeaux	37	19	56	84	75	$369.10
Fontenot	49	55	70	150	125	$588.90
Arceneaux	58	34	52	122	132	$529.50
Gautreaux	44	65	39	133	120	$521.65

▶ **RETHINKING**

79. Solve the system $x + y + 2z = 9$ and $x + 2y + 3z = 12$ by Gaussian elimination.

80. Let $A = \begin{bmatrix} 1 & 2 \\ -3 & 5 \end{bmatrix}$ and $B = \begin{bmatrix} -1 & 3 \\ 2 & 4 \end{bmatrix}$. Find AB.

81. Let $A = \begin{bmatrix} 1 & 2 \\ 3 & 4 \\ 5 & 6 \end{bmatrix}$ and $B = \begin{bmatrix} 0 & 1 & 0 \\ 1 & 0 & 1 \end{bmatrix}$. Find BA.

82. Find the exact solution to $e^x = 2^{x-1}$.

83. Solve $x^2 - 4x + 1 = 0$.

84. Find the imaginary solutions to $x^2 - 8x + 20 = 0$.

THINKING OUTSIDE THE BOX LXXIV

Maximizing Products

a) What is the maximum product for two whole numbers whose sum is 10? What are the numbers?

b) What is the maximum product for any number of whole numbers whose sum is 10? What are the numbers?

c) What is the maximum product for any number of whole numbers whose sum is 18? What are the numbers?

POP QUIZ 4

1. Find the product $\begin{bmatrix} 1 & 0 \\ 0 & 1 \end{bmatrix}\begin{bmatrix} 2 & 4 \\ 6 & 8 \end{bmatrix}$.

2. Find the inverse of $\begin{bmatrix} 2 & 5 \\ 3 & 8 \end{bmatrix}$.

3. Solve $\begin{aligned} 2x + 5y &= 4 \\ 3x + 8y &= 3 \end{aligned}$ using an inverse matrix.

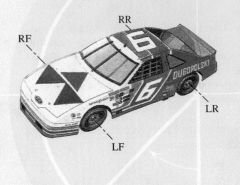

RR

RF

LR

LF

→ LINKING
concepts... For Individual or Group Explorations

Weight Distribution of a Race Car

Race car drivers adjust the weight distribution of their cars according to track conditions. However, according to a NASCAR rule, no more than 52% of a car's weight can be on any pair of tires.

a) A driver of a 1250-pound car wants to have 50% of its weight on the left rear and left front tires and 48% of its weight on the left rear and right front tires. If the right front weight is fixed at 288 pounds, then what amount of weight should be on the other three tires?

b) Is the NASCAR rule satisfied with the weight distribution found in part (a)?

c) A driver of a 1300-pound car wants to have 50% of the car's weight on the left front and left rear tires, 48% on the left rear and right front tires, and 51% on the left rear and right rear tires. How much weight should be on each of the four tires?

d) The driver of the 1300-pound car wants to satisfy the NASCAR 52% rule and have as much weight as possible on the left front tire. What is the maximum amount of weight that can be on that tire?

5 Solution of Linear Systems in Two Variables Using Determinants

We have solved linear systems of equations by graphing, substitution, addition, Gaussian elimination, and inverse matrices. Graphing, substitution, and addition are feasible only with relatively simple systems. By contrast, the Gaussian elimination and inverse matrix methods are readily performed by computers or even hand-held calculators. With a machine doing the work, they can be applied to complicated systems such as those in Exercises 77 and 78 of Section 4. Determinants, which we now discuss, can also be used by computers and calculators and give us another method that is not limited to simple systems.

The Determinant of a 2 × 2 Matrix

Before we can solve a system of equations by using determinants, we need to learn what a determinant is and how to find it. The **determinant** of a square matrix is a real number associated with the matrix. Every square matrix has a determinant. The determinant of a 1×1 matrix is the single entry of the matrix. For a 2×2 matrix the determinant is defined as follows.

Definition: Determinant of a 2 × 2 Matrix

> The **determinant** of the matrix $\begin{bmatrix} a_{11} & a_{12} \\ a_{21} & a_{22} \end{bmatrix}$ is the real number $a_{11}a_{22} - a_{21}a_{12}$.
>
> In symbols,
>
> $$\begin{vmatrix} a_{11} & a_{12} \\ a_{21} & a_{22} \end{vmatrix} = a_{11}a_{22} - a_{21}a_{12}.$$

If a matrix is named A, then the determinant of that matrix is denoted as $|A|$ or $\det(A)$. Even though the symbol for determinant looks like the absolute value symbol, the value of a determinant may be any real number. For a 2×2 matrix, that number is found by subtracting the products of the diagonal entries:

$$\begin{vmatrix} a_{11} & a_{12} \\ a_{21} & a_{22} \end{vmatrix} = a_{11}a_{22} - a_{21}a_{12}$$

EXAMPLE 1 The determinant of a 2×2 matrix

Find the determinant of each matrix.

a. $\begin{bmatrix} 3 & -1 \\ 4 & -5 \end{bmatrix}$ **b.** $\begin{bmatrix} 4 & -6 \\ 2 & -3 \end{bmatrix}$

Solution

a. $\begin{vmatrix} 3 & -1 \\ 4 & -5 \end{vmatrix} = 3(-5) - (4)(-1) = -15 + 4 = -11$

b. $\begin{vmatrix} 4 & -6 \\ 2 & -3 \end{vmatrix} = 4(-3) - (2)(-6) = -12 + 12 = 0$

To find these determinants with a calculator, enter the matrices A and B, then use the determinant function, as in Fig. 11.

▶**TRY THIS.** Find the determinant of $\begin{bmatrix} 2 & 4 \\ -3 & 1 \end{bmatrix}$. ∎

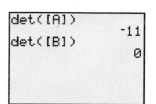

Figure 11

Cramer's Rule for Systems in Two Variables

We will now see how determinants arise in the solution of a system of two linear equations in two unknowns. Consider a general system of two linear equations in two unknowns, x and y,

$$(1) \quad a_1 x + b_1 y = c_1$$
$$(2) \quad a_2 x + b_2 y = c_2$$

where a_1, a_2, b_1, b_2, c_1 and c_2 are real numbers.

To eliminate y, multiply Eq. (1) by b_2 and Eq. (2) by $-b_1$:

$$b_2 a_1 x + b_2 b_1 y = b_2 c_1 \qquad \text{Eq. (1) is multiplied by } b_2.$$
$$\underline{-b_1 a_2 x - b_1 b_2 y = -b_1 c_2} \qquad \text{Eq. (2) is multiplied by } -b_1.$$
$$a_1 b_2 x - a_2 b_1 x = c_1 b_2 - c_2 b_1 \qquad \text{Add.}$$
$$(a_1 b_2 - a_2 b_1) x = c_1 b_2 - c_2 b_1 \qquad \text{Factor out } x.$$
$$x = \frac{c_1 b_2 - c_2 b_1}{a_1 b_2 - a_2 b_1} \qquad \text{Provided that } a_1 b_2 - a_2 b_1 \neq 0$$

This formula for x can be written using determinants as

$$x = \frac{\begin{vmatrix} c_1 & b_1 \\ c_2 & b_2 \end{vmatrix}}{\begin{vmatrix} a_1 & b_1 \\ a_2 & b_2 \end{vmatrix}}, \qquad \text{provided } a_1 b_2 - a_2 b_1 \neq 0.$$

The same procedure is used to eliminate x and get the following formula for y in terms of determinants:

$$y = \frac{\begin{vmatrix} a_1 & c_1 \\ a_2 & c_2 \end{vmatrix}}{\begin{vmatrix} a_1 & b_1 \\ a_2 & b_2 \end{vmatrix}}, \qquad \text{provided } a_1b_2 - a_2b_1 \neq 0$$

Notice that there are three determinants involved in solving for x and y. Let

$$D = \begin{vmatrix} a_1 & b_1 \\ a_2 & b_2 \end{vmatrix}, \qquad D_x = \begin{vmatrix} c_1 & b_1 \\ c_2 & b_2 \end{vmatrix}, \qquad \text{and} \qquad D_y = \begin{vmatrix} a_1 & c_1 \\ a_2 & c_2 \end{vmatrix}.$$

Note that D is the determinant of the original matrix of coefficients of x and y. D appears in the denominator for both x and y. D_x is the determinant D with the constants c_1 and c_2 replacing the first column of D. D_y is the determinant D with the constants c_1 and c_2 replacing the second column of D. These formulas for solving a system of two linear equations in two variables are known as **Cramer's rule.**

Cramer's Rule for Systems in Two Variables

For the system of equations

$$a_1x + b_1y = c_1$$
$$a_2x + b_2y = c_2$$

let

$$D = \begin{vmatrix} a_1 & b_1 \\ a_2 & b_2 \end{vmatrix}, \qquad D_x = \begin{vmatrix} c_1 & b_1 \\ c_2 & b_2 \end{vmatrix}, \qquad \text{and} \qquad D_y = \begin{vmatrix} a_1 & c_1 \\ a_2 & c_2 \end{vmatrix}.$$

If $D \neq 0$, then the solution to the system is given by

$$x = \frac{D_x}{D} \qquad \text{and} \qquad y = \frac{D_y}{D}.$$

Note that D_x is obtained from D by replacing the x-column with the constants c_1 and c_2, whereas D_y is obtained from D by replacing the y-column with the constants c_1 and c_2.

EXAMPLE 2 Applying Cramer's rule

Use Cramer's rule to solve the system.

$$3x = 2y + 9$$
$$3y = x + 3$$

Solution

To apply Cramer's rule, rewrite both equations in the form $Ax + By = C$:

$$3x - 2y = 9$$
$$-x + 3y = 3$$

First find the determinant of the coefficient matrix using the coefficients of x and y:

$$D = \begin{vmatrix} 3 & -2 \\ -1 & 3 \end{vmatrix} = 3(3) - (-1)(-2) = 7$$

Next we find the determinants D_x and D_y. For D_x, use 9 and 3 in the x-column, and for D_y, use 9 and 3 in the y-column:

$$D_x = \begin{vmatrix} 9 & -2 \\ 3 & 3 \end{vmatrix} = 33 \qquad \text{and} \qquad D_y = \begin{vmatrix} 3 & 9 \\ -1 & 3 \end{vmatrix} = 18$$

By Cramer's rule,

$$x = \frac{D_x}{D} = \frac{33}{7} \qquad \text{and} \qquad y = \frac{D_y}{D} = \frac{18}{7}.$$

Check that $x = 33/7$ and $y = 18/7$ satisfy the original system.

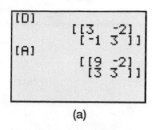

(a)

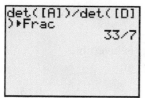

(b)

Figure 12

To check this result with a calculator, define matrices D and A, as in Fig. 12(a). Find x with Cramer's rule, as in Fig. 12(b). You can find y in a similar manner.

▶**TRY THIS.** Solve $\begin{array}{r} 2x + 5y = 17 \\ -3x + y = 0 \end{array}$ by using Cramer's rule. ■

A system of two linear equations in two unknowns may have a unique solution, no solution, or infinitely many solutions. Cramer's rule works only on systems that have a unique solution. For inconsistent or dependent systems, $D = 0$ and Cramer's rule will not give the solution. If $D = 0$, then another method must be used to determine the solution set.

EXAMPLE 3 Inconsistent and dependent systems

Use Cramer's rule to solve each system if possible.

a. $\begin{array}{r} 2x - 4y = 8 \\ -x + 2y = -4 \end{array}$ **b.** $\begin{array}{r} 2x - 4y = 8 \\ -x + 2y = 6 \end{array}$

Solution

The coefficient matrix is the same for both systems:

$$D = \begin{vmatrix} 2 & -4 \\ -1 & 2 \end{vmatrix} = 0$$

So Cramer's rule does not apply to either system. Multiply the second equation in each system by 2 and add the equations:

a. $\begin{array}{r} 2x - 4y = 8 \\ -2x + 4y = -8 \\ \hline 0 = 0 \end{array}$ **b.** $\begin{array}{r} 2x - 4y = 8 \\ -2x + 4y = 12 \\ \hline 0 = 20 \end{array}$

System (a) is dependent, and the solution set is $\{(x, y) \mid -x + 2y = -4\}$. System (b) is inconsistent and has no solution.

▶**TRY THIS.** Solve $\begin{array}{r} x + y = 6 \\ -2x - 2y = 5 \end{array}$ by Cramer's rule if possible. ■

A system of two linear equations in two variables has a unique solution if and only if the determinant of the matrix of coefficients is nonzero. We have not yet seen how to find a determinant of a larger matrix, but the same result is true for a system of n linear equations in n variables. In Section 4 we learned that a system of n linear equations in n variables has a unique solution if and only if the matrix of coefficients is invertible. These two results are combined in the following theorem to give a means of identifying whether a matrix is invertible.

Theorem: Invertible Matrices

A matrix is invertible if and only if it has a nonzero determinant.

EXAMPLE 4 Determinants and inverse matrices

Are the matrices $A = \begin{bmatrix} 2 & -3 \\ 4 & 5 \end{bmatrix}$ and $B = \begin{bmatrix} 3 & 5 \\ 6 & 10 \end{bmatrix}$ invertible?

Solution

Since $|A| = 10 - (-12) = 22$, A is an invertible matrix. However, because $|B| = 30 - 30 = 0$, B is not an invertible matrix.

▶**TRY THIS.** Determine whether $\begin{bmatrix} 1 & 6 \\ -2 & 9 \end{bmatrix}$ has an inverse. ■

→ FOR thought... True of False? Explain.

The following statements refer to the matrices

$A = \begin{bmatrix} 3 & -5 \\ 1 & 4 \end{bmatrix}, \quad B = \begin{bmatrix} 4 & -2 \\ -10 & 5 \end{bmatrix},$

$C = \begin{bmatrix} 2 & -5 \\ 6 & 4 \end{bmatrix}, \quad$ and $\quad E = \begin{bmatrix} 3 & 2 \\ 1 & 6 \end{bmatrix}.$

1. $|A| = 7$

2. A is invertible.

3. $|B| = 0$

4. B is invertible.

5. The system $\begin{array}{l} 3x - 5y = 2 \\ x + 4y = 6 \end{array}$ is independent.

6. $|CE| = |C| \cdot |E|$

7. The solution to the system $\begin{array}{l} 3x^2 - 5y^2 = 2 \\ x^2 + 4y = 6 \end{array}$ is $x = \dfrac{|C|}{|A|}$ and $y = \dfrac{|E|}{|A|}$.

8. The determinant of the 2×2 identity matrix I is 1.

9. The matrix $\begin{bmatrix} 2 & 0.1 \\ 100 & 5 \end{bmatrix}$ is invertible.

10. $\begin{bmatrix} 5 & 3 \\ 1 & 6 \end{bmatrix} = 27$

→ EXERCISES 5

Find the determinant of each matrix.

1. $\begin{bmatrix} 1 & 3 \\ 0 & 2 \end{bmatrix}$

2. $\begin{bmatrix} 0 & 4 \\ 2 & -1 \end{bmatrix}$

3. $\begin{bmatrix} 3 & 4 \\ 2 & 9 \end{bmatrix}$

4. $\begin{bmatrix} 7 & 2 \\ 3 & -2 \end{bmatrix}$

5. $\begin{bmatrix} -0.3 & -0.5 \\ -0.7 & 0.2 \end{bmatrix}$

6. $\begin{bmatrix} -\frac{1}{3} & \frac{4}{3} \\ -3 & \frac{2}{3} \end{bmatrix}$

7. $\begin{bmatrix} \frac{1}{8} & -\frac{3}{8} \\ 2 & -\frac{1}{4} \end{bmatrix}$

8. $\begin{bmatrix} -1 & -3 \\ -5 & -8 \end{bmatrix}$

9. $\begin{bmatrix} 0.02 & 0.4 \\ 1 & 20 \end{bmatrix}$

10. $\begin{bmatrix} -0.3 & 0.4 \\ 3 & -4 \end{bmatrix}$

11. $\begin{bmatrix} 3 & -5 \\ -9 & 15 \end{bmatrix}$

12. $\begin{bmatrix} -6 & 2 \\ 3 & -1 \end{bmatrix}$

Find all values for a that make each equation correct.

13. $\begin{vmatrix} a & 2 \\ 3 & 4 \end{vmatrix} = 10$

14. $\begin{vmatrix} 1 & 7 \\ 3 & a \end{vmatrix} = 5$

15. $\begin{vmatrix} a & 8 \\ 2 & a \end{vmatrix} = 0$

16. $\begin{vmatrix} a & 1 \\ a & a \end{vmatrix} = 0$

Solve each system, using Cramer's rule when possible.

17. $\begin{array}{l} 2x + y = 5 \\ x + 2y = 7 \end{array}$

18. $\begin{array}{l} 3x + y = 10 \\ x + y = 6 \end{array}$

19. $\begin{array}{l} x - 2y = 7 \\ x + 2y = -5 \end{array}$

20. $\begin{array}{l} x - y = 1 \\ 3x + y = 7 \end{array}$

21. $\begin{array}{l} 2x - y = -11 \\ x + 3y = 12 \end{array}$

22. $\begin{array}{l} 3x - 2y = -4 \\ -5x + 4y = -1 \end{array}$

23. $\begin{array}{l} x = y + 6 \\ x + y = 5 \end{array}$

24. $\begin{array}{l} 3x + y = 7 \\ 4x = y - 4 \end{array}$

25. $\begin{array}{l} \frac{1}{2}x - \frac{1}{3}y = 4 \\ \frac{1}{4}x + \frac{1}{2}y = 6 \end{array}$

26. $\begin{array}{l} \frac{1}{4}x + \frac{2}{3}y = 25 \\ \frac{3}{5}x - \frac{1}{10}y = 12 \end{array}$

27. $\begin{array}{l} 0.2x + 0.12y = 148 \\ x + y = 900 \end{array}$

28. $\begin{array}{l} 0.08x + 0.05y = 72 \\ 2x - y = 0 \end{array}$

29. $\begin{array}{l} 3x + y = 6 \\ -6x - 2y = -12 \end{array}$

30. $\begin{array}{l} 8x - 4y = 2 \\ 4x - 2y = 1 \end{array}$

31. $\begin{array}{l} 8x - y = 9 \\ -8x + y = 10 \end{array}$

32. $\begin{array}{l} 12x + 3y = 9 \\ 4x + y = 6 \end{array}$

33. $\begin{array}{l} y = x - 3 \\ y = 3x + 9 \end{array}$

34. $\begin{array}{l} y = \frac{x - 3}{2} \\ x + 2y = 15 \end{array}$

35. $\begin{array}{l} \sqrt{2}x + \sqrt{3}y = 4 \\ \sqrt{18}x - \sqrt{12}y = -3 \end{array}$

36. $\begin{array}{l} \frac{\sqrt{3}x}{3} + y = 1 \\ x - \sqrt{3}y = 0 \end{array}$

37. $\begin{array}{l} x^2 + y^2 = 25 \\ x^2 - y = 5 \end{array}$

38. $\begin{array}{l} x^2 + y = 8 \\ x^2 - y = 4 \end{array}$

39. $\begin{array}{l} x - 2y = y^2 \\ \frac{1}{2}x - y = 2 \end{array}$

40. $\begin{array}{l} y = x^2 \\ x + y = 30 \end{array}$

Determine whether each matrix is invertible by finding the determinant of the matrix.

41. $\begin{bmatrix} 4 & 0.5 \\ 2 & 3 \end{bmatrix}$

42. $\begin{bmatrix} -5 & 2 \\ 4 & -1 \end{bmatrix}$

43. $\begin{bmatrix} 3 & -4 \\ 9 & -12 \end{bmatrix}$

44. $\begin{bmatrix} \frac{1}{2} & 12 \\ \frac{1}{3} & 8 \end{bmatrix}$

Solve the following systems using Cramer's rule and a graphing calculator.

45. $\begin{aligned} 3.47x + 23.09y &= 5978.95 \\ 12.48x + 3.98y &= 2765.34 \end{aligned}$

46. $\begin{aligned} 0.0875x + 0.1625y &= 564.40 \\ x + y &= 4232 \end{aligned}$

Solve each problem, using two linear equations in two variables and Cramer's rule.

47. *The Survey Says* A survey of 615 teenagers found that 44% of the boys and 35% of the girls would like to be taller. If altogether 231 teenagers in the survey wished they were taller, how many boys and how many girls were in the survey?

48. *Consumer Confidence* A survey of 900 Americans found that 680 of them had confidence in the economy. If 80% of the women and 70% of the men surveyed expressed confidence in the economy, then how many men and how many women were surveyed.

49. *Acute Angles* One acute angle of a right triangle is 1° larger than twice the other acute angle. What are the measures of the acute angles?

50. *Isosceles Triangle* If the smallest angle of an isosceles triangle is 2° smaller than any other angle, then what is the measure of each angle?

51. *Average Salary* The average salary for the president and vice-president of Intermax Office Supply is $200,000. If the president's salary is $100,000 more than the vice president's, then what is the salary of each?

52. *A Losing Situation.* Morton Motor Express lost a full truckload (2350 ft^3) of LCD TVs and Blu-ray players valued at $147,500. Each TV was worth $400 and was in a box with a volume of 8 ft^3. Each Blu-ray player was worth $225 and was in a box with a volume of 2.5 ft^3. How many TVs and Blu-ray players were in the shipment?

FOR WRITING/DISCUSSION

The following exercises investigate some of the properties of determinants. For these exercises let $M = \begin{bmatrix} 3 & 2 \\ 5 & 4 \end{bmatrix}$ *and* $N = \begin{bmatrix} 2 & 7 \\ 1 & 5 \end{bmatrix}$.

53. Find $|M|$, $|N|$, and $|MN|$. Is $|MN| = |M| \cdot |N|$?

54. Find M^{-1} and $|M^{-1}|$. Is $|M^{-1}| = 1/|M|$?

55. Prove that the determinant of a product of two 2×2 matrices is equal to the product of their determinants.

56. Prove that if A is any 2×2 invertible matrix, then the determinant of A^{-1} is the reciprocal of the determinant of A.

57. Find $|-2M|$. Is $|-2M| = -2 \cdot |M|$?

58. Prove that if k is any scalar and A is any 2×2 matrix, then $|kA| = k^2 \cdot |A|$.

▶ **RETHINKING**

59. Let $A = \begin{bmatrix} 1 & 1 \\ 1 & 3 \end{bmatrix}$. Find A^{-1}.

60. Let $A = \begin{bmatrix} 1 & 2 \\ 1 & 3 \end{bmatrix}$ and $B = \begin{bmatrix} 3 & -2 \\ -1 & 1 \end{bmatrix}$. Find AB.

61. Solve the system $x + y + z = 6$, $x + 2y - z = 9$, and $2x + 3y = 10$.

62. Solve the system $y = -3x - 99$ and $y = 12x - 99$.

63. Solve the equation $x - 0.09x = 72,800$.

64. Find a polynomial function whose zeros are -1, -3, and 3.

THINKING OUTSIDE THE BOX LXXV

Ponder These Pills A blind man must take two pills every morning; one is type A and the other is type B. Since the pills are identical to the blind man, he keeps them in bottles of different sizes to tell them apart. One day he places one pill of type A on the counter and accidentally drops two pills of type B next to it. Now he has three pills on the counter that he cannot tell apart. They are identical in size, shape, texture, and weight. He is poor and cannot waste these pills, he cannot put them back in the bottles, and he must take his medications. What can he do?

▶ **POP QUIZ 5**

1. Find the determinant of $\begin{bmatrix} 4 & 2 \\ 3 & -1 \end{bmatrix}$.

2. Solve $\begin{aligned} 4x + 2y &= 3 \\ 3x - y &= 1 \end{aligned}$ using Cramer's rule.

3. Is $\begin{bmatrix} 9 & 2 \\ 6 & 8 \end{bmatrix}$ invertible?

6 Solution of Linear Systems in Three Variables Using Determinants

The determinant can be defined for any square matrix. In this section we define the determinant of a 3×3 matrix by extending the definition of the determinant for 2×2 matrices. We can then solve linear systems of three equations in three unknowns, using an extended version of Cramer's rule. The first step is to define a determinant of a certain part of a matrix, a *minor*.

Minors

To each entry of a 3×3 matrix there corresponds a 2×2 matrix, which is obtained by deleting the row and column in which that entry appears. The determinant of this 2×2 matrix is called the **minor** of that entry.

EXAMPLE 1 Finding the minor of an entry

Find the minors for the entries $-2, 5$, and 6 in the 3×3 matrix $\begin{bmatrix} -2 & -3 & -1 \\ -7 & 4 & 5 \\ 0 & 6 & 1 \end{bmatrix}$.

Solution

To find the minor for the entry -2, delete the first row and first column.

$$\begin{bmatrix} -2 & -3 & -1 \\ -7 & 4 & 5 \\ 0 & 6 & 1 \end{bmatrix}$$

The minor for -2 is $\begin{vmatrix} 4 & 5 \\ 6 & 1 \end{vmatrix} = 4 - (30) = -26$. To find the minor for the entry 5, delete the second row and third column.

$$\begin{bmatrix} -2 & -3 & -1 \\ -7 & 4 & 5 \\ 0 & 6 & 1 \end{bmatrix}$$

The minor for 5 is $\begin{vmatrix} -2 & -3 \\ 0 & 6 \end{vmatrix} = -12 - (0) = -12$. To find the minor for the entry 6, delete the third row and second column.

$$\begin{bmatrix} -2 & -3 & -1 \\ -7 & 4 & 5 \\ 0 & 6 & 1 \end{bmatrix}$$

The minor for 6 is $\begin{vmatrix} -2 & -1 \\ -7 & 5 \end{vmatrix} = -10 - (7) = -17$.

▶**TRY THIS.** Find the minor for 7 in the matrix $\begin{bmatrix} 1 & 2 & 3 \\ 4 & 5 & 6 \\ 7 & 8 & 9 \end{bmatrix}$. ∎

The Determinant of a 3 × 3 Matrix

The determinant of a 3×3 matrix is defined in terms of minors. Let M_{ij} be the 2×2 matrix obtained from M by deleting the ith row and jth column. The determinant of M_{ij}, $|M_{ij}|$, is the minor for a_{ij}.

Definition: Determinant of a 3 × 3 Matrix

If $A = \begin{bmatrix} a_{11} & a_{12} & a_{13} \\ a_{21} & a_{22} & a_{23} \\ a_{31} & a_{32} & a_{33} \end{bmatrix}$, then the determinant of A, $|A|$, is defined as

$$|A| = a_{11}|M_{11}| - a_{21}|M_{21}| + a_{31}|M_{31}|.$$

To find the determinant of A, each entry in the first column of A is multiplied by its minor. This process is referred to as **expansion by minors** about the first column. Note the sign change on the middle term in the expansion.

EXAMPLE 2 | The determinant of a 3 × 3 matrix

Find $|A|$, given that $A = \begin{bmatrix} -2 & -3 & -1 \\ -7 & 4 & 5 \\ 0 & 6 & 1 \end{bmatrix}$.

Solution

Use the definition to expand by minors about the first column.

$$|A| = -2 \cdot \begin{vmatrix} 4 & 5 \\ 6 & 1 \end{vmatrix} - (-7) \cdot \begin{vmatrix} -3 & -1 \\ 6 & 1 \end{vmatrix} + 0 \cdot \begin{vmatrix} -3 & -1 \\ 4 & 5 \end{vmatrix}$$

$$= -2(-26) + 7(3) + 0(-11)$$

$$= 73$$

▶**TRY THIS.** Find $|A|$ if $A = \begin{bmatrix} 1 & 2 & 3 \\ 4 & 5 & 6 \\ 7 & 8 & 9 \end{bmatrix}$. ∎

The value of the determinant of a 3 × 3 matrix can be found by expansion by minors about any row or column. However, you must use alternating plus and minus signs to precede the coefficients of the minors according to the following **sign array:**

$$\begin{bmatrix} + & - & + \\ - & + & - \\ + & - & + \end{bmatrix}$$

The signs in the sign array are used for the determinant of *any* 3 × 3 matrix and they are independent of the signs of the entries in the matrix. Notice that in Example 2, when we expanded by minors about the first column, we used the signs "+ − +" from the first column of the sign array. These signs were used in addition to the signs that appear on the entries themselves (-2, -7, and 0).

EXAMPLE 3 | Expansion by minors about the second column

Expand by minors using the second column to find $|A|$, given that

$$A = \begin{bmatrix} -2 & -3 & -1 \\ -7 & 4 & 5 \\ 0 & 6 & 1 \end{bmatrix}.$$

Solution

Use the signs "− + −" from the second column of the sign array:

$$\begin{bmatrix} + & - & + \\ - & + & - \\ + & - & + \end{bmatrix}$$

The coefficients $-3, 4,$ and 6 from the second column of A are preceded by the signs from the second column of the sign array:

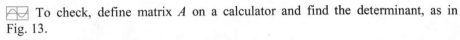

$$|A| = -(-3) \cdot \begin{vmatrix} -7 & 5 \\ 0 & 1 \end{vmatrix} + (4) \cdot \begin{vmatrix} -2 & -1 \\ 0 & 1 \end{vmatrix} - (6) \cdot \begin{vmatrix} -2 & -1 \\ -7 & 5 \end{vmatrix}$$

From second column of A

$$= 3(-7) + 4(-2) - 6(-17)$$

$$= 73$$

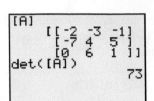

Figure 13

To check, define matrix A on a calculator and find the determinant, as in Fig. 13.

▶**TRY THIS.** Expand by minors using the second column to find $|A|$ if

$$A = \begin{bmatrix} 1 & 2 & 3 \\ 5 & -7 & 4 \\ -6 & 0 & 8 \end{bmatrix}.$$ ∎

In Examples 2 and 3 we got the same value for $|A|$ by using two different expansions. Expanding about any row or column gives the same result, but the computations can be easier if we examine the matrix and choose the row or column that contains the most zeros. Using zeros for the coefficients of one or more minors simplifies the work, because we do not have to evaluate the minors that are multiplied by zero. If a row or column of a matrix contains all zeros, then the determinant of the matrix is 0.

EXAMPLE 4 | Expansion by minors using the simplest row or column

Find $|B|$, given that $B = \begin{bmatrix} 4 & 2 & 1 \\ -6 & 3 & 5 \\ 0 & 0 & -7 \end{bmatrix}$.

Solution

Since the third row has two zeros, we expand by minors about the third row. Use the signs "+ − +" from the third row of the sign array and the coefficients $0, 0,$ and -7 from the third row of B:

$$|B| = 0 \cdot \begin{vmatrix} 2 & 1 \\ 3 & 5 \end{vmatrix} - 0 \cdot \begin{vmatrix} 4 & 1 \\ -6 & 5 \end{vmatrix} + (-7) \cdot \begin{vmatrix} 4 & 2 \\ -6 & 3 \end{vmatrix}$$

$$= -7(24)$$

$$= -168$$

▶**TRY THIS.** Find $|A|$ if $A = \begin{bmatrix} 3 & 5 & 2 \\ -1 & 7 & 0 \\ 4 & 9 & 0 \end{bmatrix}.$ ∎

Determinant of a 4 × 4 Matrix

The determinant of a 4×4 matrix is also found by expanding by minors about a row or column. The following 4×4 sign array of alternating + and

$-$ signs (starting with $+$ in the upper-left position) is used for the signs in the expansion:

$$\begin{bmatrix} + & - & + & - \\ - & + & - & + \\ + & - & + & - \\ - & + & - & + \end{bmatrix}$$

The minor for an entry of a 4×4 matrix is the determinant of the 3×3 matrix found by deleting the row and column of that entry. In general, the determinant of an $n \times n$ matrix is defined in terms of determinants of $(n - 1) \times (n - 1)$ matrices in the same manner.

EXAMPLE 5 Determinant of a 4×4 matrix

Find $|A|$, given that $A = \begin{bmatrix} -2 & -3 & 0 & 4 \\ 1 & -6 & 1 & -1 \\ 2 & 0 & 1 & 5 \\ 4 & 0 & 3 & 1 \end{bmatrix}$.

Solution

Since the second column has two zeros, we expand by minors about the second column, using the signs "$- + - +$" from the second column of the sign array:

$$|A| = -(-3)\begin{vmatrix} 1 & 1 & -1 \\ 2 & 1 & 5 \\ 4 & 3 & 1 \end{vmatrix} + (-6)\begin{vmatrix} -2 & 0 & 4 \\ 2 & 1 & 5 \\ 4 & 3 & 1 \end{vmatrix}$$

$$- 0\begin{vmatrix} -2 & 0 & 4 \\ 1 & 1 & -1 \\ 4 & 3 & 1 \end{vmatrix} + 0\begin{vmatrix} -2 & 0 & 4 \\ 1 & 1 & -1 \\ 2 & 1 & 5 \end{vmatrix}$$

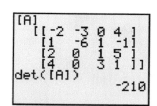

Evaluate the determinant of the first two 3×3 matrices to get

$$|A| = 3(2) - 6(36) = -210.$$

Figure 14

To check, enter A into your calculator and find its determinant, as in Fig. 14.

▶**TRY THIS.** Find $|A|$ if $A = \begin{bmatrix} 1 & 6 & 0 & 0 \\ 0 & 1 & 7 & 9 \\ 0 & 0 & 1 & 0 \\ 0 & 0 & 0 & 1 \end{bmatrix}$. ■

Cramer's Rule for Systems in Three Variables

Cramer's rule for solving a system of three linear equations in three variables consists of formulas for finding x, y, and z in terms of determinants.

Cramer's Rule for Systems in Three Variables

For the system of equations

$$a_1x + b_1y + c_1z = d_1$$
$$a_2x + b_2y + c_2z = d_2$$
$$a_3x + b_3y + c_3z = d_3$$

(continued on next page)

let

$$D = \begin{vmatrix} a_1 & b_1 & c_1 \\ a_2 & b_2 & c_2 \\ a_3 & b_3 & c_3 \end{vmatrix}, \quad D_x = \begin{vmatrix} d_1 & b_1 & c_1 \\ d_2 & b_2 & c_2 \\ d_3 & b_3 & c_3 \end{vmatrix}$$

$$D_y = \begin{vmatrix} a_1 & d_1 & c_1 \\ a_2 & d_2 & c_2 \\ a_3 & d_3 & c_3 \end{vmatrix}, \quad \text{and} \quad D_z = \begin{vmatrix} a_1 & b_1 & d_1 \\ a_2 & b_2 & d_2 \\ a_3 & b_3 & d_3 \end{vmatrix}.$$

If $D \neq 0$, then the solution to the system is given by

$$x = \frac{D_x}{D}, \quad y = \frac{D_y}{D}, \quad \text{and} \quad z = \frac{D_z}{D}.$$

The development of this rule is similar to the development for Cramer's rule in two variables in Section 5, and so we will omit it.

Note that D_x, D_y, and D_z are obtained by replacing, respectively, the first, second, and third columns of D by the constants d_1, d_2, and d_3.

EXAMPLE 6 | Solving a system using Cramer's rule

Use Cramer's rule to solve the system

$$x + y + z = 0$$
$$2x - y + z = -1$$
$$-x + 3y - z = -8.$$

Solution

To use Cramer's rule, we first evaluate D, D_x, D_y, and D_z:

$$D = \begin{vmatrix} 1 & 1 & 1 \\ 2 & -1 & 1 \\ -1 & 3 & -1 \end{vmatrix} = 1 \cdot \begin{vmatrix} -1 & 1 \\ 3 & -1 \end{vmatrix} - 2 \cdot \begin{vmatrix} 1 & 1 \\ 3 & -1 \end{vmatrix} + (-1) \cdot \begin{vmatrix} 1 & 1 \\ -1 & 1 \end{vmatrix}$$

$$= 1(-2) - 2(-4) - 1(2)$$

$$= 4$$

To find D_x, D_y, or D_z, expand by minors about the first row because the first row contains a zero in each case:

$$D_x = \begin{vmatrix} 0 & 1 & 1 \\ -1 & -1 & 1 \\ -8 & 3 & -1 \end{vmatrix} = 0 \cdot \begin{vmatrix} -1 & 1 \\ 3 & -1 \end{vmatrix} - (1) \cdot \begin{vmatrix} -1 & 1 \\ -8 & -1 \end{vmatrix} + (1) \cdot \begin{vmatrix} -1 & -1 \\ -8 & 3 \end{vmatrix}$$

$$= -1(9) + 1(-11)$$

$$= -20$$

$$D_y = \begin{vmatrix} 1 & 0 & 1 \\ 2 & -1 & 1 \\ -1 & -8 & -1 \end{vmatrix} = 1 \cdot \begin{vmatrix} -1 & 1 \\ -8 & -1 \end{vmatrix} - (0) \cdot \begin{vmatrix} 2 & 1 \\ -1 & -1 \end{vmatrix} + (1) \cdot \begin{vmatrix} 2 & -1 \\ -1 & -8 \end{vmatrix}$$

$$= 1(9) + 1(-17)$$

$$= -8$$

$$D_z = \begin{vmatrix} 1 & 1 & 0 \\ 2 & -1 & -1 \\ -1 & 3 & -8 \end{vmatrix} = 1 \cdot \begin{vmatrix} -1 & -1 \\ 3 & -8 \end{vmatrix} - (1) \cdot \begin{vmatrix} 2 & -1 \\ -1 & -8 \end{vmatrix} + (0) \cdot \begin{vmatrix} 2 & -1 \\ -1 & 3 \end{vmatrix}$$

$$= 1(11) - 1(-17)$$

$$= 28$$

Now, by Cramer's rule,

$$x = \frac{D_x}{D} = \frac{-20}{4} = -5, \quad y = \frac{D_y}{D} = \frac{-8}{4} = -2, \quad \text{and} \quad z = \frac{D_z}{D} = \frac{28}{4} = 7.$$

Check that the ordered triple $(-5, -2, 7)$ satisfies all three equations. The solution set to the system is $\{(-5, -2, 7)\}$.

▶**TRY THIS.** Use Cramer's rule to solve
$$\begin{aligned} x + y - z &= 0 \\ -x + y &= 4 \\ -x + y + z &= 10 \end{aligned}.$$ ∎

Cramer's rule can provide the solution to any system of three linear equations in three variables that has a unique solution. Its advantage is that it can give the value of any one of the variables without having to solve for the others. If $D = 0$, then Cramer's rule does not give the solution to the system, but it does indicate that the system is either dependent or inconsistent. If $D = 0$, then we must use another method to complete the solution to the system.

EXAMPLE 7 | Solving a system with $D = 0$

Use Cramer's rule to solve the system.

$$\begin{aligned} (1) \quad 2x + y - z &= 3 \\ (2) \quad 4x + 2y - 2z &= 6 \\ (3) \quad 6x + 3y - 3z &= 9 \end{aligned}$$

Solution

To use Cramer's rule, we first evaluate D:

$$D = \begin{vmatrix} 2 & 1 & -1 \\ 4 & 2 & -2 \\ 6 & 3 & -3 \end{vmatrix} = 2 \cdot \begin{vmatrix} 2 & -2 \\ 3 & -3 \end{vmatrix} - 4 \cdot \begin{vmatrix} 1 & -1 \\ 3 & -3 \end{vmatrix} + 6 \cdot \begin{vmatrix} 1 & -1 \\ 2 & -2 \end{vmatrix}$$

$$= 2(0) - 4(0) + 6(0)$$

$$= 0$$

Because $D = 0$, Cramer's rule cannot be used to solve the system. We could use the Gaussian elimination method, but note that Eqs. (2) and (3) are obtained by multiplying Eq. (1) by 2 and 3, respectively. Since all three equations are equivalent, the solution set to the system is $\{(x, y, z) \mid 2x + y - z = 3\}$.

▶**TRY THIS.** Use Cramer's rule to solve
$$\begin{aligned} x - y + z &= 2 \\ 2x - 2y + 2z &= 4 \\ 3x - 3y + 3z &= 6 \end{aligned}$$ if possible. ∎

In the last two chapters we have discussed several different methods for solving systems of linear equations. Studying different methods increases our understanding of systems of equations. A small system can usually be solved by any of these methods, but for large systems that are solved with computers, the most efficient and popular method is probably the Gaussian elimination method or a variation of it. Since you can find determinants, invert matrices, and perform operations with them on a graphing calculator, you can use either Cramer's rule or inverse matrices with a graphing calculator.

FOR thought... True or False? Explain.

Statements 1–5 reference the matrix $A = \begin{bmatrix} 2 & -3 & 1 \\ 3 & 4 & 2 \\ 0 & 0 & 1 \end{bmatrix}$.

1. The sign array is used to determine whether $|A|$ is positive or negative.

2. $|A| = 2 \cdot \begin{vmatrix} 4 & 2 \\ 0 & 1 \end{vmatrix} - (-3) \cdot \begin{vmatrix} 3 & 2 \\ 0 & 1 \end{vmatrix} + 1 \cdot \begin{vmatrix} 2 & -3 \\ 3 & 4 \end{vmatrix}$

3. We can find $|A|$ by expanding about any row or column.

4. $|A| = \begin{vmatrix} 2 & -3 \\ 3 & 4 \end{vmatrix}$

5. We can find $|A|$ by expanding by minors about the diagonal.

6. A minor is a 2×2 matrix.

7. By Cramer's rule, the value of x is D/D_x.

8. If a matrix has a row in which all entries are zero, then the determinant of the matrix is 0.

9. By Cramer's rule, there is no solution to a system for which $D = 0$.

10. Cramer's rule works on any system of nonlinear equations.

EXERCISES 6

Find the indicated minors, using the matrix $\begin{bmatrix} 2 & -3 & 1 \\ 4 & 5 & -6 \\ 7 & 9 & -8 \end{bmatrix}$.

1. Minor for 2   2. Minor for -3 3. Minor for 1

4. Minor for 4   5. Minor for 5   6. Minor for -6

7. Minor for 9   8. Minor for -8

Find the determinant of each 3×3 matrix, using expansion by minors about the first column.

9. $\begin{bmatrix} 1 & -4 & 0 \\ -3 & 1 & -2 \\ 3 & -1 & 5 \end{bmatrix}$

10. $\begin{bmatrix} 1 & -3 & 2 \\ 3 & 1 & -4 \\ 2 & 3 & 6 \end{bmatrix}$

11. $\begin{bmatrix} 3 & -1 & 2 \\ 0 & 4 & -1 \\ 5 & 1 & -2 \end{bmatrix}$

12. $\begin{bmatrix} -1 & 3 & -1 \\ 0 & 2 & -3 \\ 2 & 6 & -9 \end{bmatrix}$

13. $\begin{bmatrix} -2 & 5 & 1 \\ -3 & 0 & -1 \\ 0 & 2 & -7 \end{bmatrix}$

14. $\begin{bmatrix} 0 & -6 & 2 \\ -1 & 4 & -2 \\ 5 & 3 & -1 \end{bmatrix}$

15. $\begin{bmatrix} 0.1 & 30 & 1 \\ 0.4 & 20 & 6 \\ 0.7 & 90 & 8 \end{bmatrix}$

16. $\begin{bmatrix} 3 & 0.3 & 10 \\ 5 & 0.5 & 30 \\ 8 & 0.1 & 80 \end{bmatrix}$

Evaluate the following determinants, using expansion by minors about the row or column of your choice.

17. $\begin{vmatrix} -1 & 3 & 5 \\ -2 & 0 & 0 \\ 4 & 3 & -4 \end{vmatrix}$

18. $\begin{vmatrix} 8 & -9 & 1 \\ 3 & 4 & 0 \\ -2 & 1 & 0 \end{vmatrix}$

19. $\begin{vmatrix} 1 & 1 & 1 \\ 2 & 2 & 2 \\ 4 & 4 & 4 \end{vmatrix}$

20. $\begin{vmatrix} 4 & -1 & 3 \\ 4 & -1 & 3 \\ 4 & -1 & 3 \end{vmatrix}$

21. $\begin{vmatrix} 0 & -1 & 0 \\ 3 & 4 & 6 \\ -2 & 3 & -5 \end{vmatrix}$

22. $\begin{vmatrix} 2 & 0 & 0 \\ 56 & 3 & -4 \\ 88 & 5 & -2 \end{vmatrix}$

23. $\begin{vmatrix} 2 & 0 & 1 \\ 4 & 0 & 6 \\ -7 & 9 & -8 \end{vmatrix}$

24. $\begin{vmatrix} 2 & -3 & 1 \\ -2 & 5 & -6 \\ 0 & 0 & 0 \end{vmatrix}$

25. $\begin{vmatrix} 3 & 0 & 1 & 5 \\ 2 & -3 & 2 & 0 \\ -2 & 3 & 1 & 2 \\ 2 & -4 & 1 & 3 \end{vmatrix}$

26. $\begin{vmatrix} 1 & -4 & 2 & 0 \\ -2 & -1 & 0 & -3 \\ 2 & 2 & 4 & 1 \\ 3 & 0 & -3 & 1 \end{vmatrix}$

27. $\begin{vmatrix} 2 & -3 & 4 & 6 \\ 1 & -5 & 0 & 0 \\ 1 & 3 & 1 & -3 \\ -2 & 0 & 2 & 1 \end{vmatrix}$

28. $\begin{vmatrix} -2 & 4 & 0 & 5 \\ 2 & -1 & 0 & 7 \\ 3 & 2 & 0 & -1 \\ 2 & 2 & -3 & 4 \end{vmatrix}$

Solve each system, using Cramer's rule where possible.

29. $\begin{aligned} x + y + z &= 6 \\ x - y + z &= 2 \\ 2x + y + z &= 7 \end{aligned}$

30. $\begin{aligned} 2x - 2y + 3z &= 7 \\ x + y - z &= -2 \\ 3x + y - 2z &= 5 \end{aligned}$

31. $\begin{aligned} x + 2y &= 8 \\ x - 3y + z &= -2 \\ 2x - y &= 1 \end{aligned}$

32. $\begin{aligned} 2x + y &= -4 \\ 3y - z &= -1 \\ x + 3z &= -16 \end{aligned}$

33. $2x - 3y + z = 1$
$x + 4y - z = 0$
$3x - y + 2z = 0$

34. $-2x + y - z = 0$
$x - y + 3z = 1$
$3x + 3y + 2z = 0$

35. $x + y + z = 2$
$2x - y + 3z = 0$
$3x + y - z = 0$

36. $x - 2y - z = 0$
$-x + y + 3z = 0$
$x + 3y + z = 3$

37. $x + y - 2z = 1$
$x - 2y + z = 2$
$2x - y - z = 3$

38. $x + y + z = 4$
$-2x - y + 3z = 1$
$y + 5z = 9$

39. $x - y + z = 5$
$x + 2y + 3z = 8$
$2x - 2y + 2z = 16$

40. $3x + 6y + 9z = 12$
$x + 2y + 3z = 0$
$x - y - 3z = 0$

Solve each problem, using a system of three equations in three unknowns and Cramer's rule.

41. *Age Disclosure* Jackie, Rochelle, and Alisha will not disclose their ages. However, the average of the ages of Jackie and Rochelle is 33, the average for Rochelle and Alisha is 25, and the average for Jackie and Alisha is 19. How old is each?

42. *Bennie's Coins* Bennie emptied his pocket of 49 coins to pay for his $5.50 lunch. He used only nickels, dimes, and quarters, and the total number of dimes and quarters was one more than the number of nickels. How many of each type of coin did he use?

43. *What a Difference a Weight Makes* A sociology professor gave two one-hour exams and a final exam. Ian was distressed with his average score of 60 for the three tests and went to see the professor. Because of Ian's improvement during the semester, the professor offered to count the final exam as 60% of the grade and the two tests equally, giving Ian a weighted average of 76. Ian countered that since he improved steadily during the semester, the first test should count 10%, the second 20%, and the final 70% of the grade, giving a weighted average of 83. What were Ian's actual scores on the two tests and the final exam?

44. *Cookie Time* Cheryl, of Cheryl's Famous Cookies, set out 18 cups of flour, 14 cups of sugar, and 13 cups of shortening for her employees to use to make some batches of chocolate chip, oatmeal, and peanut butter cookies. She left for the day without telling them how many batches of each type to bake. The table gives the number of cups of each ingredient required for one batch of each type of cookie. How many batches of each were they supposed to bake?

Table for Exercise 44

	Flour	Sugar	Shortening
Chocolate Chip	2	2	1
Oatmeal	1	1	2
Peanut Butter	4	2	1

Stephen Coburn/Shutterstock

Use the determinant feature of a graphing calculator to solve each system by Cramer's rule.

45. $0.2x - 0.3y + 1.2z = 13.11$
$0.25x + 0.35y - 0.9z = -1.575$
$2.4x - y + 1.25z = 42.02$

46. $3.6x + 4.5y + 6.8z = 45,300$
$0.09x + 0.05y + 0.04z = 474$
$x + y - z = 0$

Solve each problem, using Cramer's rule and a graphing calculator.

47. *Gasoline Sales* The Runway Deli sells regular unleaded, plus unleaded, and supreme unleaded Shell gasoline. The number of gallons of each grade and the total receipts for gasoline are shown in the table for the first three weeks of February. What was the price per gallon for each grade?

Table for Exercise 47

	Regular	Plus	Supreme	Receipts
Week 1	1270	980	890	$12,204.86
Week 2	1450	1280	1050	$14,698.22
Week 3	1340	1190	1060	$13,969.41

48. *Gasoline Sales* John's Curb Market sells regular, plus, and supreme unleaded Citgo gasoline. John sold the same amount of each grade of gasoline each week for the first three weeks of February. The prices that he charged and the receipts for each week are shown in the accompanying table. How many gallons of each grade did he sell each week?

Table for Exercise 48

	Regular	Plus	Supreme	Receipts
Week 1	$3.799	$3.899	$3.999	$17,996.37
Week 2	$3.749	$3.849	$3.949	$17,764.87
Week 3	$3.759	$3.899	$3.949	$17,856.07

Extend Cramer's rule to four linear equations in four unknowns. Solve each system, using the extended Cramer's rule.

49. $w + x + y + z = 4$
$2w - x + y + 3z = 13$
$w + 2x - y + 2z = -2$
$w - x - y + 4z = 8$

50. $2w + 2x - 2y + z = 11$
$w + x + y + z = 10$
$4w - 3x + 2y - 5z = 6$
$w + 3x - y + 9z = 20$

The equation of a line through two points can be expressed as an equation involving a determinant.

51. Show that the following equation is equivalent to the equation of the line through $(3, -5)$ and $(-2, 6)$.

$$\begin{vmatrix} x & y & 1 \\ 3 & -5 & 1 \\ -2 & 6 & 1 \end{vmatrix} = 0$$

52. Show that the following equation is equivalent to the equation of the line through (x_1, y_1) and (x_2, y_2).

$$\begin{vmatrix} x & y & 1 \\ x_1 & y_1 & 1 \\ x_2 & y_2 & 1 \end{vmatrix} = 0$$

FOR WRITING/DISCUSSION

Prove each of the following statements for any 3×3 matrix A.

53. If all entries in any row or column of A are zero, then $|A| = 0$.

54. If A has two identical rows (or columns), then $|A| = 0$.

55. If all entries in a row (or column) of A are multiplied by a constant k, then the determinant of the new matrix is $k \cdot |A|$.

56. If two rows (or columns) of A are interchanged, then the determinant of the new matrix is $-|A|$.

▶ RETHINKING

57. Find the determinant of the matrix $\begin{bmatrix} 3 & -2 \\ -1 & 4 \end{bmatrix}$.

58. Find the determinant of the matrix $\begin{bmatrix} 1 & 2 & 3 \\ 2 & 0 & 4 \\ 0 & 5 & 7 \end{bmatrix}$.

59. Determine whether the system $5x - 9y + 11z = 44$ and $13x - 12y + 31z = -9$ is independent, dependent, or inconsistent.

60. Let $A = \begin{bmatrix} 1 & 2 \\ 3 & 4 \\ 5 & 6 \end{bmatrix}$ and $B = \begin{bmatrix} 0 & 1 & 0 \\ 1 & 0 & 1 \end{bmatrix}$. Find AB.

61. Solve the system $y = (x - 4)^2$ and $y = x^2$.

62. A population of bacteria in a controlled experiment doubles every 15 minutes. How many minutes will it take for 1000 bacteria to grow to 2500? Round to the nearest tenth of a minute.

THINKING OUTSIDE THE BOX LXXVI

The Missing Dollar Three students each pay \$10 for a \$30 room at the Magnolia Inn. After the students are in their room, the night clerk realizes that the student rate is actually only \$25. She gives the bellboy five singles to give back to the students. The bellboy can't decide how to split five singles among three students, so he gives each student one dollar and keeps the other two for himself. Now the students have paid \$9 apiece and the bellboy has \$2. Three times 9 is 27 plus 2 is 29. So where is the other dollar? Explain.

POP QUIZ 6

1. Find the determinant of $\begin{bmatrix} 1 & 2 & 3 \\ 2 & 1 & 1 \\ 3 & 3 & 4 \end{bmatrix}$.

2. Solve the system using Cramer's rule.

$$\begin{aligned} x + y - z &= 1 \\ x - y + 2z &= 9 \\ 2x + y + z &= 12 \end{aligned}$$

3. Is $\begin{bmatrix} 1 & 2 & 3 \\ 0 & 2 & 6 \\ 0 & 5 & 15 \end{bmatrix}$ invertible?

Highlights

1 Solving Linear Systems Using Matrices

Matrix	An $m \times n$ matrix is a rectangular array of numbers with m rows and n columns.	$\begin{bmatrix} 1 & 2 \\ 3 & 4 \end{bmatrix}$
Augmented Matrix	The coefficients of the variables together with the constants from a linear system	$x + 2y = 4$ $3x - y = 5$ $\begin{bmatrix} 1 & 2 & \mid & 4 \\ 3 & -1 & \mid & 5 \end{bmatrix}$

| Gaussian Elimination | Row operations are used to simplify the augmented matrix. | $\begin{bmatrix} 1 & 0 & \vert & 2 \\ 0 & 1 & \vert & 1 \end{bmatrix}$
$x = 2, y = 1$ |

2 Operations with Matrices

Equal Matrices	The same size and all corresponding entries are equal.	$\begin{bmatrix} 1 & 2 \\ 3 & 4 \end{bmatrix} = \begin{bmatrix} 1 & 2 \\ 3 & 4 \end{bmatrix}$
Addition or Subtraction	Add or subtract the corresponding entries for matrices of the same size.	$\begin{bmatrix} 1 & 2 \\ 3 & 4 \end{bmatrix} + \begin{bmatrix} 2 & 3 \\ 4 & 5 \end{bmatrix} = \begin{bmatrix} 3 & 5 \\ 7 & 9 \end{bmatrix}$
Scalar Multiple	To find the product of a scalar and a matrix multiply each entry by the scalar.	$3\begin{bmatrix} 1 & 2 \\ 3 & 4 \end{bmatrix} = \begin{bmatrix} 3 & 6 \\ 9 & 12 \end{bmatrix}$

3 Multiplication of Matrices

| Multiplication | The ijth entry of AB is the sum of the products of the corresponding entries in the ith row of A and the jth column of B. | $\begin{bmatrix} 1 & 0 \\ 2 & 1 \end{bmatrix}\begin{bmatrix} 0 & 1 \\ 3 & 4 \end{bmatrix} = \begin{bmatrix} 0 & 1 \\ 3 & 6 \end{bmatrix}$ |

4 Inverses of Matrices

Identity Matrix	An $n \times n$ matrix with ones on the diagonal and zeros elsewhere	$I = \begin{bmatrix} 1 & 0 \\ 0 & 1 \end{bmatrix}$
Inverse Matrix	The inverse of A is a matrix A^{-1} such that $AA^{-1} = I$.	$\begin{bmatrix} 1 & 1 \\ 5 & 4 \end{bmatrix}\begin{bmatrix} -4 & 1 \\ 5 & -1 \end{bmatrix} = \begin{bmatrix} 1 & 0 \\ 0 & 1 \end{bmatrix}$
Solution to Systems	The solution to $AX = B$ is $X = A^{-1}B$.	$\begin{bmatrix} -4 & 1 \\ 5 & -1 \end{bmatrix}\begin{bmatrix} x \\ y \end{bmatrix} = \begin{bmatrix} 5 \\ 6 \end{bmatrix}$ $\begin{bmatrix} x \\ y \end{bmatrix} = \begin{bmatrix} 1 & 1 \\ 5 & 4 \end{bmatrix}\begin{bmatrix} 5 \\ 6 \end{bmatrix} = \begin{bmatrix} 11 \\ 49 \end{bmatrix}$

5 Solution of Linear Systems in Two Variables Using Determinants

Determinant	$\begin{vmatrix} a & b \\ c & d \end{vmatrix} = ad - cb$	$\begin{vmatrix} 1 & 2 \\ 3 & -1 \end{vmatrix} = -1 - 6 = -7$ $\begin{vmatrix} 4 & 2 \\ 5 & -1 \end{vmatrix} = -14, \begin{vmatrix} 1 & 4 \\ 3 & 5 \end{vmatrix} = -7$
Cramer's Rule	If $\begin{array}{l} a_1x_1 + b_1y_1 = c_1 \\ a_2x_2 + b_2y_2 = c_2 \end{array}$ is an independent system, then $x = \dfrac{\begin{vmatrix} c_1 & b_1 \\ c_2 & b_2 \end{vmatrix}}{\begin{vmatrix} a_1 & b_1 \\ a_2 & b_2 \end{vmatrix}}$ and $y = \dfrac{\begin{vmatrix} a_1 & c_1 \\ a_2 & c_2 \end{vmatrix}}{\begin{vmatrix} a_1 & b_1 \\ a_2 & b_2 \end{vmatrix}}$.	$\begin{array}{l} x + 2y = 4 \\ 3x - y = 5 \end{array}$ $x = \dfrac{-14}{-7} = 2, \quad y = \dfrac{-7}{-7} = 1$

6 Solution of Linear Systems in Three Variables Using Determinants

| Cramer's Rule | $\begin{array}{l} a_1x_1 + b_1y_1 + c_1z_1 = d_1 \\ \text{If } a_2x_2 + b_2y_2 + c_2z_2 = d_2 \text{ is an independent system and} \\ a_3x_3 + b_3y_3 + c_3z_3 = d_3 \end{array}$

$D = \begin{vmatrix} a_1 & b_1 & c_1 \\ a_2 & b_2 & c_2 \\ a_3 & b_3 & c_3 \end{vmatrix}, \quad D_x = \begin{vmatrix} d_1 & b_1 & c_1 \\ d_2 & b_2 & c_2 \\ d_3 & b_3 & c_3 \end{vmatrix}, \quad D_y = \begin{vmatrix} a_1 & d_1 & c_1 \\ a_2 & d_2 & c_2 \\ a_3 & d_3 & c_3 \end{vmatrix}, \quad \text{and} \quad D_z = \begin{vmatrix} a_1 & b_1 & d_1 \\ a_2 & b_2 & d_2 \\ a_3 & b_3 & d_3 \end{vmatrix},$

then $x = D_x/D$, $y = D_y/D$, and $z = D_z/D$. |

Chapter Review Exercises

Let $A = \begin{bmatrix} 2 & -3 \\ -2 & 4 \end{bmatrix}$, $B = \begin{bmatrix} 3 & 7 \\ 1 & 2 \end{bmatrix}$, $C = \begin{bmatrix} -1 \\ 3 \end{bmatrix}$,

$D = \begin{bmatrix} 5 \\ -3 \end{bmatrix}$, $E = \begin{bmatrix} 1 \\ -4 \\ 3 \end{bmatrix}$, $F = \begin{bmatrix} 3 & 2 & -1 \end{bmatrix}$, and

$G = \begin{bmatrix} -1 & 0 & 0 \\ 1 & 1 & 0 \\ -2 & 3 & 1 \end{bmatrix}$. Find each of the following matrices or

determinants if possible.

1. $A + B$ 　　2. $A - B$ 　　3. $2A - B$ 　　4. $2A + 3B$

5. AB 　　6. BA 　　7. $D + E$ 　　8. $F + G$

9. AC 　　10. BD 　　11. EF 　　12. FE

13. FG 　　14. GE 　　15. GF 　　16. EG

17. A^{-1} 　　18. B^{-1} 　　19. G^{-1} 　　20. $A^{-1}C$

21. $(AB)^{-1}$ 　　22. $A^{-1}B^{-1}$ 　　23. AA^{-1} 　　24. GG^{-1}

25. $|A|$ 　　26. $|B|$ 　　27. $|G|$ 　　28. $|C|$

Solve each of the following systems by all three methods: Gaussian elimination, matrix inversion, and Cramer's rule.

29. $x + y = 9$
    $2x - y = 1$

30. $x - 2y = 3$
    $x + 2y = 2$

31. $2x + y = -1$
    $3x + 2y = 0$

32. $3x - y = 1$
    $-2x + y = 1$

33. $x - 5y = 9$
    $-2x + 10y = -18$

34. $3x - y = 4$
    $6x - 2y = 6$

35. $0.05x + 0.1y = 1$
    $10x + 20y = 20$

36. $0.04x - 0.2y = 3$
    $2x - 10y = 150$

37. $x + y - 2z = -3$
    $-x + 2y - z = 0$
    $-x - y + 3z = 6$

38. $x - y + z = 5$
    $x + y + 3z = 11$
    $-x + 2y - z = -5$

39. $y - 3z = 1$
    $x + 2y = 5$
    $x + 4z = 1$

40. $3x + y - 2z = 0$
    $-2y + z = 0$
    $y + 3z = 14$

41. $x - y + z = 2$
    $x - 2y - z = 1$
    $2x - 3y = 3$

42. $x + 2y + z = 1$
    $2x + 4y + 2z = 0$
    $-x - 2y - z = 2$

43. $x - 3y - z = 2$
    $x - 3y - z = 1$
    $x - 3y - z = 0$

44. $2x - y - z = 0$
    $x + y + z = 3$
    $3x = 3$

Find the values of x, y, and z that make each of the equations true.

45. $\begin{bmatrix} x \\ x + y \end{bmatrix} = \begin{bmatrix} 9 \\ -3 \end{bmatrix}$

46. $\begin{bmatrix} x^2 \\ x - y \end{bmatrix} = \begin{bmatrix} 4 \\ 1 \end{bmatrix}$

47. $\begin{bmatrix} 1 & 1 \\ 2 & 1 \end{bmatrix} \begin{bmatrix} x \\ y \end{bmatrix} = \begin{bmatrix} 6 \\ 8 \end{bmatrix}$

48. $\begin{bmatrix} 0 & 0.5 \\ 1 & 1 \end{bmatrix} \begin{bmatrix} x \\ y \end{bmatrix} = \begin{bmatrix} 7 \\ 9 \end{bmatrix}$

49. $\begin{bmatrix} x \\ y \end{bmatrix} + \begin{bmatrix} y \\ -x \end{bmatrix} = \begin{bmatrix} -3 \\ y \end{bmatrix}$

50. $\begin{bmatrix} y \\ x \end{bmatrix} - \begin{bmatrix} x \\ y \end{bmatrix} = \begin{bmatrix} 4 \\ 5 \end{bmatrix}$

51. $\begin{bmatrix} x + y & 0 & 0 \\ 0 & y + z & 0 \\ 0 & 0 & x + z \end{bmatrix} = \begin{bmatrix} 1 & 0 & 0 \\ 0 & 1 & 0 \\ 0 & 0 & 1 \end{bmatrix}$

52. $\begin{bmatrix} 0 & x - y & 2z \\ 0 & 0 & y - z \\ 0 & 0 & 0 \end{bmatrix} = \begin{bmatrix} 0 & 2 & 5 \\ 0 & 0 & 3 \\ 0 & 0 & 0 \end{bmatrix}$

53. $\begin{bmatrix} 1 & 1 & 0 \\ 0 & 1 & 2 \\ 1 & 0 & 3 \end{bmatrix} \begin{bmatrix} x \\ y \\ z \end{bmatrix} = \begin{bmatrix} -1 \\ 7 \\ 17 \end{bmatrix}$

54. $\begin{bmatrix} 1 & 1 & 1 \\ -1 & 1 & -1 \\ 1 & 0 & 2 \end{bmatrix} \begin{bmatrix} x \\ y \\ z \end{bmatrix} = \begin{bmatrix} 0 \\ 0 \\ 0 \end{bmatrix}$

Solve each problem, using a system of linear equations in two or three variables. Use the method of your choice from this chapter.

55. *Fine for Polluting* A small manufacturing plant must pay a fine of $10 for each gallon of pollutant A and $6 for each gallon of pollutant B per day that it discharges into a nearby stream. If the manufacturing process produces three gallons of pollutant A for every four gallons of pollutant B and the daily fine is $4060, then how many gallons of each are discharged each day?

56. *Friends* Ross, Joey, and Chandler spent a total of $216 on coffee and pastry last month at the Central Perk coffee shop. Joey and Ross's expenses totaled only half as much as Chandler's. If Joey spent $12 more than Ross, then how much did each spend?

57. *Utility Bills* Bette's total expense for water, gas, and electricity for one month including tax was $189.83. There is a 6% state tax on electricity, a 5% city tax on gas, and a 4% county tax on water. If her total expenses included $9.83 in taxes and her electric bill including tax was twice the gas bill including tax, then how much was each bill including tax?

58. *Predicting Car Sales* In the first three months of the year, West Coast Cadillac sold 38, 42, and 49 new cars, respectively. Find the equation of the parabola of the form $y = ax^2 + bx + c$

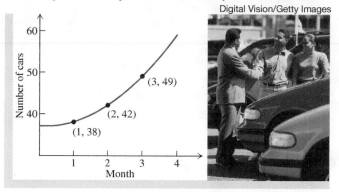

Digital Vision/Getty Images

Figure for Exercise 58

that passes through $(1, 38)$, $(2, 42)$, and $(3, 49)$, as shown in the accompanying figure. (The fact that each point satisfies $y = ax^2 + bx + c$ gives three linear equations in a, b, and c.) Assuming that the fourth month's sales will fall on that same parabola, what would be the predicted sales for the fourth month?

THINKING OUTSIDE THE BOX LXXVII

Disappearing Dogs Someone opened up the cages at Pet Depot and more than 100 puppies got away! There were exactly 300 puppies to begin with. The Daily Mixup reported: "Of the pups that remained, a third were Dobermans, a quarter were schnauzers, a fifth were beagles, a seventh were poodles, and a ninth were dachshunds. The original number of beagles was three times the number of dachshunds that stayed." The Daily Mixup got just one of the fractions wrong. How many beagles escaped?

Chapter Test

Solve each system, using Gaussian elimination.

1. $2x - 3y = 1$
$x + 9y = 4$

2. $2x - y + z = 5$
$x - 2y - z = -2$
$3x - y - z = 6$

3. $x - y - z = 1$
$2x + y - z = 0$
$5x - 2y - 4z = 3$

Let $A = \begin{bmatrix} 1 & -1 \\ -2 & 4 \end{bmatrix}$, $B = \begin{bmatrix} 2 & -3 \\ -4 & 6 \end{bmatrix}$, $C = \begin{bmatrix} -2 \\ 1 \end{bmatrix}$,

$D = \begin{bmatrix} 3 \\ -2 \end{bmatrix}$, $E = \begin{bmatrix} 2 \\ 3 \\ -1 \end{bmatrix}$, $F = \begin{bmatrix} 1 & 0 & -1 \end{bmatrix}$, *and*

$G = \begin{bmatrix} -2 & 3 & 1 \\ -3 & 1 & 3 \\ 0 & 2 & -1 \end{bmatrix}$. *Find each of the following matrices or*

determinants if possible.

4. $A + B$ **5.** $2A - B$ **6.** AB **7.** AC

8. CB **9.** FG **10.** EF **11.** A^{-1}

12. G^{-1} **13.** $|A|$ **14.** $|B|$ **15.** $|G|$

Solve each system, using Cramer's rule.

16. $x - y = 2$
$-2x + 4y = 2$

17. $2x - 3y = 6$
$-4x + 6y = 1$

18. $-2x + 3y + z = -2$
$-3x + y + 3z = -4$
$2y - z = 0$

Solve each system by using inverse matrices.

19. $x - y = 1$
$-2x + 4y = -8$

20. $-2x + 3y + z = 1$
$-3x + y + 3z = 0$
$2y - z = -1$

Solve by using a method from this chapter.

21. The manager of a computer store bought x copies of the program Math Skillbuilder for \$10 each at the beginning of the year and sold y copies of the program for \$35 each. At the end of the year, the program was obsolete and she destroyed 12 unsold copies. If her net profit for the year was \$730, then how many were bought and how many were sold?

22. Find a, b, and c such that the graph of $y = ax^2 + b\sqrt{x} + c$ goes through the points $(0, 3)$, $(1, -1/2)$, and $(4, 3)$.

Answers to Exercises

Section 1

For Thought: **1.** F **2.** F **3.** T **4.** T **5.** T **6.** T
7. F **8.** T **9.** F **10.** T

Exercises:

1. matrix **3.** size **5.** entry, element **7.** diagonal **9.** 1×3

11. 1×1 **13.** 3×2 **15.** $\begin{bmatrix} 1 & -2 & | & 4 \\ 3 & 2 & | & -5 \end{bmatrix}$

17. $\begin{bmatrix} 1 & -1 & -1 & | & 4 \\ 1 & 3 & -1 & | & 1 \\ 0 & 2 & -5 & | & -6 \end{bmatrix}$ **19.** $\begin{bmatrix} 1 & 3 & -1 & | & 5 \\ 1 & 0 & 1 & | & 0 \end{bmatrix}$

21. $3x + 4y = -2$ **23.** $5x = 6$ **25.** $x - y + 2z = 1$
$\quad\ 3x - 5y = 0$ $\qquad -4x + 2z = -1$ $\qquad y + 4z = 3$
$\qquad\qquad\qquad\qquad\quad 4x + 4y = 7$

27. $\begin{bmatrix} 1 & 2 & | & 0 \\ -2 & 4 & | & 1 \end{bmatrix}$ **29.** $\begin{bmatrix} 1 & 4 & | & 1 \\ 0 & 3 & | & 6 \end{bmatrix}$ **31.** $\begin{bmatrix} 1 & -2 & | & 1 \\ 0 & -1 & | & 3 \end{bmatrix}$

33. $2x + 4y = 14, 5x + 4y = 5, \{(-3, 5)\}, \frac{1}{2}R_1 \to R_1,$
$-5R_1 + R_2 \to R_2, -\frac{1}{6}R_2 \to R_2, -2R_2 + R_1 \to R_1$

35. $\{(2, 3)\}$, independent **37.** $\{(1, 3)\}$, independent
39. $\{(3, 3)\}$, independent **41.** $\{(0.5, 1)\}$, independent
43. $\varnothing$, inconsistent **45.** $\{(u, v) \mid u + 3v = 4\}$, dependent
47. $\{(4, -4)\}$, independent **49.** $\{(3, 2, 1)\}$, independent
51. $\{(1, 1, 1)\}$, independent **53.** $\{(1, 2, 0)\}$, independent
55. $\{(1, 0, -1)\}$, independent
57. $\{(x, y, z) \mid x - 2y + 3z = 1\}$, dependent **59.** $\varnothing$, inconsistent
61. $\{(x, 5 - 2x, 2 - x) \mid x \text{ is any real number}\}$, dependent
63. $\left\{\left(x, \dfrac{13 - 5x}{2}, \dfrac{5 - 3x}{2}\right) \mid x \text{ is any real number}\right\}$, dependent
65. $\{(4, 3, 2, 1)\}$, independent
67. 38 hr at Burgers-R-Us, 22 hr at Soap Opera
69. \$20,000 mutual fund, \$11,333.33 treasury bills, \$8,666.67 bonds
71. $a = 1, b = -2, c = 3$
73. $y = 750 - x, z = x - 250$, and $250 \le x \le 750$. If $z = 50$,
then $x = 300$ and $y = 450$.
75. No **77.** $\{(-5, 9, -12)\}$ **79.** $\{-2/3, -8\}$

Section 2

For Thought: **1.** T **2.** F **3.** F **4.** T **5.** T **6.** F
7. F **8.** F **9.** F **10.** F

Exercises:

1. $x = 2, y = 5$
3. $x = 3, y = 4, z = 2$

5. $\begin{bmatrix} 5 \\ 6 \end{bmatrix}$ **7.** $\begin{bmatrix} 1.5 & 0.97 \\ 1.95 & 0.67 \end{bmatrix}$ **9.** $\begin{bmatrix} 3 & -4 & 5 \\ 4 & -5 & 7 \\ 6 & -3 & 2 \end{bmatrix}$

11. $\begin{bmatrix} -1 & 4 \\ 5 & -6 \end{bmatrix}, \begin{bmatrix} 0 & 0 \\ 0 & 0 \end{bmatrix}$ **13.** $\begin{bmatrix} -3 & 0 & 1 \\ -8 & 2 & -1 \\ 3 & -6 & -3 \end{bmatrix}, \begin{bmatrix} 0 & 0 & 0 \\ 0 & 0 & 0 \\ 0 & 0 & 0 \end{bmatrix}$

15. $\begin{bmatrix} 3 & -3 \\ 4 & 4 \end{bmatrix}$ **17.** $\begin{bmatrix} 2 & 2 \\ 5 & 9 \end{bmatrix}$ **19.** Undefined **21.** $\begin{bmatrix} -12 & 3 \\ 9 & 0 \end{bmatrix}$

23. $\begin{bmatrix} 4 \\ -5 \end{bmatrix}$ **25.** $\begin{bmatrix} -21 & -9 \\ 15 & -15 \end{bmatrix}$ **27.** $\begin{bmatrix} -7 & 4 \\ -1 & -4 \end{bmatrix}$

29. $\begin{bmatrix} -5 \\ 4 \end{bmatrix}$ **31.** Undefined **33.** $\begin{bmatrix} -8 & -5 \\ 12 & -1 \end{bmatrix}$

35. $\begin{bmatrix} 0.4 & 0.15 \\ 0.7 & 1.1 \end{bmatrix}$ **37.** $\begin{bmatrix} 1/2 & 3/2 \\ 3 & -12 \end{bmatrix}$ **39.** $\begin{bmatrix} 10 & 0 \\ -2 & 16 \end{bmatrix}$

41. Undefined **43.** $\begin{bmatrix} -1 & 13 \\ -9 & 3 \\ 6 & -2 \end{bmatrix}$ **45.** $\begin{bmatrix} 3\sqrt{2} & 2 & 3\sqrt{3} \end{bmatrix}$

47. $\begin{bmatrix} 13a \\ -b \end{bmatrix}$ **49.** $\begin{bmatrix} -x & -0.5y \\ -0.7x & 3.5y \end{bmatrix}$ **51.** $\begin{bmatrix} 3x & 2y & -z \\ -6x & 3y & 7z \\ 0 & -7y & -7z \end{bmatrix}$

53. $\{(3, 2)\}$ **55.** $\{(-1, 3)\}$ **57.** $\{(0.5, 3, 4.5)\}$

59. $\begin{bmatrix} \$390 \\ \$160 \\ \$135 \end{bmatrix}$ **61.** $\begin{bmatrix} 40 & 80 \\ 30 & 90 \\ 80 & 200 \end{bmatrix}, \begin{bmatrix} 60 & 120 \\ 45 & 135 \\ 120 & 300 \end{bmatrix}$ **63.** Yes, yes

65. Yes, yes **67.** Yes, yes **69.** $\begin{bmatrix} 0 & 0 \\ 0 & 0 \end{bmatrix}$

71. $\{(-7, 6)\}$, independent
73. a. $(ax + y)(bx + z)$ **b.** $x(3x - 4y)(2x - 5y)$
75. $\dfrac{\ln(x)}{\ln(7)}$

Section 3

For Thought: **1.** T **2.** T **3.** F **4.** F **5.** T **6.** T
7. T **8.** T **9.** T **10.** F

Exercises:

1. 3×5 **3.** 1×1 **5.** 5×5 **7.** 3×3

9. AB is undefined. **11.** $\begin{bmatrix} -10 \end{bmatrix}$ **13.** $\begin{bmatrix} 10 \\ -10 \end{bmatrix}$ **15.** $\begin{bmatrix} 8 & 11 \\ 5 & 5 \end{bmatrix}$

17. $\begin{bmatrix} 15 & 18 \\ 5 & 6 \end{bmatrix}$ **19.** $\begin{bmatrix} -2 & 3 & 1 \\ -2 & 4 & 2 \\ -1 & 6 & 5 \end{bmatrix}, \begin{bmatrix} 6 & 9 \\ 1 & 1 \end{bmatrix}$

21. $\begin{bmatrix} 1 & 3 & 6 \\ 2 & 3 & 6 \\ 3 & 5 & 6 \end{bmatrix}, \begin{bmatrix} 6 & 5 & 7 \\ 5 & 3 & 4 \\ 3 & 2 & 1 \end{bmatrix}$ **23.** $\begin{bmatrix} 4 & 6 & 8 \\ -6 & -9 & -12 \\ 2 & 3 & 4 \end{bmatrix}$

25. $\begin{bmatrix} 2 & 5 & 9 \end{bmatrix}$ **27.** Undefined **29.** $\begin{bmatrix} 7 & 8 \\ 5 & 5 \\ 1 & 0 \end{bmatrix}$ **31.** $\begin{bmatrix} 1 & 1 \\ 14 & 15 \end{bmatrix}$

33. Undefined **35.** $\begin{bmatrix} 0 \\ -2 \\ 1 \end{bmatrix}$ **37.** Undefined

39. $\begin{bmatrix} 6 & 8 & 10 \\ -6 & -7 & -10 \\ 2 & 3 & 6 \end{bmatrix}$ **41.** $\begin{bmatrix} 1 & 0 \\ 2 & 1 \end{bmatrix}$ **43.** $\begin{bmatrix} 1 & 0 \\ 4 & 1 \end{bmatrix}$

45. $\begin{bmatrix} 2 & 2 \\ 3 & 4 \end{bmatrix}$ **47.** $\begin{bmatrix} 1 & 0 \\ 0 & 1 \end{bmatrix}$ **49.** $\begin{bmatrix} -0.5 & 4 \\ 9 & 0.7 \end{bmatrix}$ **51.** $\begin{bmatrix} 4a & -3b \end{bmatrix}$

53. $\begin{bmatrix} -2a & 5a & 3a \\ b & 4b & 6b \end{bmatrix}$ **55.** $\begin{bmatrix} 4 & 2 & 6 \end{bmatrix}$ **57.** $\begin{bmatrix} 17 \end{bmatrix}$ **59.** $\begin{bmatrix} x^2 & xy \\ xy & y^2 \end{bmatrix}$

61. $\begin{bmatrix} 2\sqrt{2} \\ 7\sqrt{2} \end{bmatrix}$ **63.** $\begin{bmatrix} -17/3 & 11 \\ -3 & 6 \end{bmatrix}$ **65.** Undefined

67. $\begin{bmatrix} 2 & 0 & 6 \\ 3 & 5 & 2 \\ 19 & 21 & 16 \end{bmatrix}$ **69.** $\begin{bmatrix} -0.2 & 1.7 \\ 3 & 3.4 \\ -1.4 & -4.6 \end{bmatrix}$ **71.** $\{(3, 2)\}$

73. $\varnothing$ **75.** $\{(-1, -1, 6)\}$ **77.** $\begin{bmatrix} 2 & 3 \\ 4 & -1 \end{bmatrix}\begin{bmatrix} x \\ y \end{bmatrix} = \begin{bmatrix} 9 \\ 6 \end{bmatrix}$

79. $\begin{bmatrix} 1 & 2 & -1 \\ 3 & -1 & 3 \\ 2 & 1 & -4 \end{bmatrix}\begin{bmatrix} x \\ y \\ z \end{bmatrix} = \begin{bmatrix} 3 \\ 1 \\ 0 \end{bmatrix}$

81. $AQ = \begin{bmatrix} \$376,000 \\ \$642,000 \end{bmatrix}$. The entries of AQ are the total cost of labor and total cost of material for four economy and seven deluxe models.

83. F **85.** T **87.** T **89.** $\begin{bmatrix} -2 & 11 \\ 3 & 17 \end{bmatrix}$ **91.** Independent
93. $(-99, 9]$

Section 4

For Thought: **1.** T **2.** T **3.** T **4.** F **5.** T **6.** F
7. F **8.** T **9.** F **10.** F

Exercises:

1. $\begin{bmatrix} 1 & 3 \\ 4 & 6 \end{bmatrix}\begin{bmatrix} 1 & 0 \\ 0 & 1 \end{bmatrix} = \begin{bmatrix} 1 & 3 \\ 4 & 6 \end{bmatrix}, \begin{bmatrix} 1 & 0 \\ 0 & 1 \end{bmatrix}\begin{bmatrix} 1 & 3 \\ 4 & 6 \end{bmatrix} = \begin{bmatrix} 1 & 3 \\ 4 & 6 \end{bmatrix}$

3. $\begin{bmatrix} 3 & 2 & 1 \\ 5 & 6 & 2 \\ 7 & 8 & 3 \end{bmatrix}\begin{bmatrix} 1 & 0 & 0 \\ 0 & 1 & 0 \\ 0 & 0 & 1 \end{bmatrix} = \begin{bmatrix} 3 & 2 & 1 \\ 5 & 6 & 2 \\ 7 & 8 & 3 \end{bmatrix}$,

$\begin{bmatrix} 1 & 0 & 0 \\ 0 & 1 & 0 \\ 0 & 0 & 1 \end{bmatrix}\begin{bmatrix} 3 & 2 & 1 \\ 5 & 6 & 2 \\ 7 & 8 & 3 \end{bmatrix} = \begin{bmatrix} 3 & 2 & 1 \\ 5 & 6 & 2 \\ 7 & 8 & 3 \end{bmatrix}$

5. $\begin{bmatrix} -3 & 5 \\ 12 & 6 \end{bmatrix}$ **7.** $\begin{bmatrix} 1 & 0 \\ 0 & 1 \end{bmatrix}$ **9.** $\begin{bmatrix} 1 & 0 \\ 0 & 1 \end{bmatrix}$ **11.** $\begin{bmatrix} 3 & 5 & 1 \\ 4 & 5 & 7 \\ 4 & 9 & 2 \end{bmatrix}$

13. $\begin{bmatrix} 1 & 0 & 0 \\ 0 & 1 & 0 \\ 0 & 0 & 1 \end{bmatrix}$ **15.** $\begin{bmatrix} 1 & 0 & 0 \\ 0 & 1 & 0 \\ 0 & 0 & 1 \end{bmatrix}$ **17.** Yes   **19.** No

21. No   **23.** $\begin{bmatrix} 1 & -2 \\ 0 & 0.5 \end{bmatrix}$ **25.** $\begin{bmatrix} 3 & -2 \\ -1/3 & 1/3 \end{bmatrix}$ **27.** $\begin{bmatrix} 4 & 3 \\ -3 & -2 \end{bmatrix}$

29. $\begin{bmatrix} -1.5 & -2.5 \\ -0.5 & -0.5 \end{bmatrix}$ **31.** No inverse   **33.** No inverse

35. $\begin{bmatrix} 0.5 & 0.5 & 0 \\ 0.5 & 0 & -0.5 \\ 0 & -0.5 & 0.5 \end{bmatrix}$ **37.** $\begin{bmatrix} -3.5 & -1 & 2 \\ 0.5 & 0 & 0 \\ 4.5 & 2 & -3 \end{bmatrix}$

39. $\begin{bmatrix} 1/3 & -1/6 & 1/3 \\ -2/3 & 1/3 & 1/3 \\ 2/3 & 1/6 & -1/3 \end{bmatrix}$ **41.** $\begin{bmatrix} 2.5 & -3 & 1 \\ 1 & -1 & 0 \\ -1.5 & 2 & 0 \end{bmatrix}$

43. $\begin{bmatrix} 1 & -2 & 1 & 0 \\ 0 & 1 & -2 & 1 \\ 0 & 0 & 1 & -2 \\ 0 & 0 & 0 & 1 \end{bmatrix}$ **45.** $\{(3,-1)\}$ **47.** $\{(2,1/3)\}$

49. $\{(1,-1)\}$ **51.** $\{(5,2)\}$ **53.** $\{(1,-1,3)\}$
55. $\{(1,3,2)\}$ **57.** $\{(11.3,-3.9)\}$
59. $\{(-2z-4,-z-9,z)\,|\,z$ is any real number$\}$
61. $\{(1/2,1/6,1/3)\}$ **63.** $\{(-165,97.5,240)\}$
65. $\{(-1.6842,-9.2632,-9.2632)\}$
67. $\begin{bmatrix} 1 & 7 \\ 3 & 20 \end{bmatrix},\begin{bmatrix} 2 & 7 \\ 3 & 10 \end{bmatrix},\begin{bmatrix} 4 & 7 \\ 3 & 5 \end{bmatrix},\begin{bmatrix} 20 & 7 \\ 3 & 1 \end{bmatrix},\begin{bmatrix} 10 & 7 \\ 3 & 2 \end{bmatrix},\begin{bmatrix} 5 & 7 \\ 3 & 4 \end{bmatrix}$
69. \$2.20 eggs, \$6.00 magazine   **71.** \$400 plywood, \$150 insulation
73. Good luck   **75.** \$17,142.86 Asset Manager; \$42,857.14 Magellan
77. \$4.20 animal totems, \$2.75 necklaces, \$0.89 tribal masks
79. $\{(6-z,3-z,z)\,|\,z$ is any real number$\}$ **81.** $\begin{bmatrix} 3 & 4 \\ 6 & 8 \end{bmatrix}$
83. $\{2 \pm \sqrt{3}\}$

Section 5

For Thought: **1.** F   **2.** T   **3.** T   **4.** F   **5.** T   **6.** T
7. F   **8.** T   **9.** F   **10.** F
Exercises:
1. 2   **3.** 19   **5.** −0.41   **7.** 23/32   **9.** 0   **11.** 0
13. 4   **15.** ±4   **17.** $\{(1,3)\}$ **19.** $\{(1,-3)\}$
21. $\{(-3,5)\}$ **23.** $\{(11/2,-1/2)\}$ **25.** $\{(12,6)\}$
27. $\{(500,400)\}$ **29.** $\{(x,y)\,|\,3x+y=6\}$ **31.** ∅
33. $\{(-6,-9)\}$ **35.** $\{(\sqrt{2}/2,\sqrt{3})\}$ **37.** $\{(0,-5),(\pm3,4)\}$
39. $\{(8,2),(0,-2)\}$ **41.** Invertible   **43.** Not invertible
45. $\{(146,237)\}$ **47.** 175 boys, 440 girls
49. 89/3 degrees and 181/3 degrees
51. Vice-president \$150,000, president \$250,000   **53.** 2, 3, 6, yes
57. 8, no   **59.** $\begin{bmatrix} 3/2 & -1/2 \\ -1/2 & 1/2 \end{bmatrix}$ **61.** ∅   **63.** $\{80,000\}$

Section 6

For Thought: **1.** F   **2.** F   **3.** T   **4.** T   **5.** F   **6.** F
7. F   **8.** T   **9.** F   **10.** F
Exercises:
1. 14   **3.** 1   **5.** −23   **7.** −16   **9.** −33   **11.** −56
13. −115   **15.** 14   **17.** −54   **19.** 0   **21.** −3
23. −72   **25.** −137   **27.** −293   **29.** $\{(1,2,3)\}$
31. $\{(2,3,5)\}$ **33.** $\{(7/16,-5/16,-13/16)\}$
35. $\{(-2/7,11/7,5/7)\}$
37. $\{(x,x-5/3,x-4/3)\,|\,x$ is any real number$\}$ **39.** ∅
41. Jackie 27, Alisha 11, Rochelle 39
43. 30, 50, 100   **45.** $\{(16.8,12.3,11.2)\}$
47. \$3.799 regular, \$3.899 plus, \$3.999 supreme   **49.** $\{(1,-2,3,2)\}$
57. 10   **59.** Dependent   **61.** $\{(2,4)\}$

Chapter Review Exercises

1. $\begin{bmatrix} 5 & 4 \\ -1 & 6 \end{bmatrix}$ **3.** $\begin{bmatrix} 1 & -13 \\ -5 & 6 \end{bmatrix}$ **5.** $\begin{bmatrix} 3 & 8 \\ -2 & -6 \end{bmatrix}$ **7.** Undefined

9. $\begin{bmatrix} -11 \\ 14 \end{bmatrix}$ **11.** $\begin{bmatrix} 3 & 2 & -1 \\ -12 & -8 & 4 \\ 9 & 6 & -3 \end{bmatrix}$ **13.** $\begin{bmatrix} 1 & -1 & -1 \end{bmatrix}$

15. Undefined   **17.** $\begin{bmatrix} 2 & 1.5 \\ 1 & 1 \end{bmatrix}$ **19.** $\begin{bmatrix} -1 & 0 & 0 \\ 1 & 1 & 0 \\ -5 & -3 & 1 \end{bmatrix}$

21. $\begin{bmatrix} 3 & 4 \\ -1 & -1.5 \end{bmatrix}$ **23.** $\begin{bmatrix} 1 & 0 \\ 0 & 1 \end{bmatrix}$ **25.** 2   **27.** −1

29. $\{(10/3,17/3)\}$ **31.** $\{(-2,3)\}$ **33.** $\{(x,y)\,|\,x-5y=9\}$
35. ∅   **37.** $\{(1,2,3)\}$ **39.** $\{(-3,4,1)\}$
41. $\left\{\left(\dfrac{3y+3}{2},y,\dfrac{1-y}{2}\right)\,\middle|\,y$ is any real number$\right\}$ **43.** ∅
45. $\{(9,-12)\}$ **47.** $\{(2,4)\}$ **49.** $\{(0,-3)\}$
51. $\{(0.5,0.5,0.5)\}$ **53.** $\{(2,-3,5)\}$
55. 225.56 gal A, 300.74 gal B
57. \$22.88 water, \$55.65 gas, \$111.30 electric

Chapter Test

1. $\{(1,1/3)\}$ **2.** $\{(3,2,1)\}$
3. $\left\{\left(x,\dfrac{-x-1}{2},\dfrac{3x-1}{2}\right)\,\middle|\,x$ is any real number$\right\}$
4. $\begin{bmatrix} 3 & -4 \\ -6 & 10 \end{bmatrix}$ **5.** $\begin{bmatrix} 0 & 1 \\ 0 & 2 \end{bmatrix}$ **6.** $\begin{bmatrix} 6 & -9 \\ -20 & 30 \end{bmatrix}$ **7.** $\begin{bmatrix} -3 \\ 8 \end{bmatrix}$

8. Undefined   **9.** $\begin{bmatrix} -2 & 1 & 2 \end{bmatrix}$ **10.** $\begin{bmatrix} 2 & 0 & -2 \\ 3 & 0 & -3 \\ -1 & 0 & 1 \end{bmatrix}$

11. $\begin{bmatrix} 2 & 0.5 \\ 1 & 0.5 \end{bmatrix}$ **12.** $\begin{bmatrix} 7 & -5 & -8 \\ 3 & -2 & -3 \\ 6 & -4 & -7 \end{bmatrix}$ **13.** 2   **14.** 0   **15.** −1

16. $\{(5,3)\}$ **17.** ∅   **18.** $\{(6,2,4)\}$ **19.** $\{(-2,-3)\}$
20. $\{(15,6,13)\}$ **21.** Bought 46, sold 34
22. $y = 0.5x^2 - 4\sqrt{x} + 3$

1.1 Since the matrix has 2 rows and 4 columns, its size is 2×4.

1.2 Write the coefficients and the constants in a matrix as $\begin{bmatrix} 1 & -1 & -2 \\ 2 & 1 & 3 \end{bmatrix}$.

1.3 Using the first two columns for the coefficients and the last column for the constants, the system is $\begin{array}{c} 2x + y = 5 \\ -x + 4y = 6 \end{array}$.

1.4 $\begin{bmatrix} 2 & -1 & 7 \\ 1 & 3 & 14 \end{bmatrix}$

$\begin{bmatrix} 1 & 3 & 14 \\ 2 & -1 & 7 \end{bmatrix}$ $R_1 \leftrightarrow R_2$

$\begin{bmatrix} 1 & 3 & 14 \\ 0 & -7 & -21 \end{bmatrix}$ $-2R_1 + R_2 \to R_2$

$\begin{bmatrix} 1 & 3 & 14 \\ 0 & 1 & 3 \end{bmatrix}$ $-\dfrac{1}{7}R_2 \to R_2$

$\begin{bmatrix} 1 & 0 & 5 \\ 0 & 1 & 3 \end{bmatrix}$ $-3R_2 + R_1 \to R_1$

The solution set to the system is $\{(5, 3)\}$.

1.5 Multiply the first row by 2 and add to the second.

$\begin{bmatrix} 3 & -1 & 1 \\ -6 & 2 & 4 \end{bmatrix}$ $\begin{bmatrix} 3 & -1 & 1 \\ 0 & 0 & 6 \end{bmatrix}$

The second row corresponds to the equation $0 = 6$. So the system is inconsistent and there is no solution.

1.6 Multiply the first row by -2 and add to the second.

$\begin{bmatrix} 4 & 1 & 5 \\ 8 & 2 & 10 \end{bmatrix}$ $\begin{bmatrix} 4 & 1 & 5 \\ 0 & 0 & 0 \end{bmatrix}$

The second row corresponds to the equation $0 = 0$. So the system is dependent. The solution set is $\{(x, y) \mid 4x + y = 5\}$ or $\{(x, 5 - 4x) \mid x$ is any real number$\}$.

1.7 $\begin{bmatrix} 1 & 1 & -1 & 0 \\ -1 & 1 & 0 & 4 \\ -1 & 1 & 1 & 10 \end{bmatrix}$

$\begin{bmatrix} 1 & 1 & -1 & 0 \\ 0 & 2 & -1 & 4 \\ 0 & 2 & 0 & 10 \end{bmatrix}$ $\begin{array}{c} R_1 + R_2 \to R_2 \\ R_1 + R_3 \to R_3 \end{array}$

$\begin{bmatrix} 1 & 1 & -1 & 0 \\ 0 & 2 & 0 & 10 \\ 0 & 2 & -1 & 4 \end{bmatrix}$ $R_2 \leftrightarrow R_3$

$\begin{bmatrix} 1 & 1 & -1 & 0 \\ 0 & 1 & 0 & 5 \\ 0 & 2 & -1 & 4 \end{bmatrix}$ $\frac{1}{2}R_2 \to R_2$

$\begin{bmatrix} 1 & 0 & -1 & -5 \\ 0 & 1 & 0 & 5 \\ 0 & 0 & -1 & -6 \end{bmatrix}$ $\begin{array}{c} -R_2 + R_1 \to R_1 \\ -2R_2 + R_3 \to R_3 \end{array}$

$\begin{bmatrix} 1 & 0 & 0 & 1 \\ 0 & 1 & 0 & 5 \\ 0 & 0 & 1 & 6 \end{bmatrix}$ $\begin{array}{c} -R_3 + R_1 \to R_1 \\ -R_3 \to R_3 \end{array}$

The solution set is $\{(1, 5, 6)\}$.

1.8 $\begin{bmatrix} 1 & -1 & 2 & 3 \\ -1 & 2 & 1 & 2 \end{bmatrix}$

$\begin{bmatrix} 1 & -1 & 2 & 3 \\ 0 & 1 & 3 & 5 \end{bmatrix}$ $R_1 + R_2 \to R_2$

$\begin{bmatrix} 1 & 0 & 5 & 8 \\ 0 & 1 & 3 & 5 \end{bmatrix}$ $R_2 + R_1 \to R_1$

So $x + 5z = 8$ and $y + 3z = 5$. So the solution set is $\{(8 - 5z, 5 - 3z, z) \mid z$ is any real number$\}$. In terms of x the solution set is $\{(x, \frac{3x + 1}{5}, \frac{8 - x}{5}) \mid x$ is any real number$\}$.

1.9 $\begin{array}{c} 3S + 8L = 30 \\ 5S + 7L = 31 \end{array}$

$\begin{bmatrix} 3 & 8 & 30 \\ 5 & 7 & 31 \end{bmatrix}$

Use Gaussian elimination to get the following equivalent augmented matrix.

$\begin{bmatrix} 1 & 0 & 2 \\ 0 & 1 & 3 \end{bmatrix}$

So there were 2 small and 3 large baskets made.

2.1 If the matrices are equal, then the corresponding entries are equal. So $x = 1$, $y + 1 = 2$ or $y = 1$, and $z + 1 = 2z - 1$ or $z = 2$.

2.2 Add the corresponding entries to get

$$A + B = \begin{bmatrix} 8 & 0 \\ 0 & 9 \end{bmatrix}.$$

2.3 If $A = \begin{bmatrix} 2 & 3 \\ -4 & 1 \end{bmatrix}$, then

$$-A = \begin{bmatrix} -2 & -3 \\ 4 & -1 \end{bmatrix} \text{ and } -A + A = \begin{bmatrix} 0 & 0 \\ 0 & 0 \end{bmatrix}.$$

2.4 Subtract the corresponding entries to get $A - B = \begin{bmatrix} 0 & -4 & 1 \end{bmatrix}$.

2.5 Multiply each entry by 4 to get $4C = \begin{bmatrix} 4 & -8 & 36 \end{bmatrix}$.

2.6 The matrix $\begin{bmatrix} 11{,}000 \\ 20{,}000 \\ 16{,}000 \end{bmatrix}$ represents the amount of mail in each class.

Multiply by 1.5 to get a 50% increase:

$$1.5 \begin{bmatrix} 11{,}000 \\ 20{,}000 \\ 16{,}000 \end{bmatrix} = \begin{bmatrix} 16{,}500 \\ 30{,}000 \\ 24{,}000 \end{bmatrix}$$

3.1 Multiply each row of A by each column of B. For example, $1 \cdot 5 + 2 \cdot 7 = 19$ and $1 \cdot 6 + 2 \cdot 8 = 22$.

$$AB = \begin{bmatrix} 19 & 22 \\ 43 & 50 \end{bmatrix}$$

3.2 $AB = \begin{bmatrix} 2 \\ 3 \end{bmatrix} \begin{bmatrix} 7 & 4 \end{bmatrix} = \begin{bmatrix} 14 & 8 \\ 21 & 12 \end{bmatrix}$

$BA = \begin{bmatrix} 7 & 4 \end{bmatrix} \begin{bmatrix} 2 \\ 3 \end{bmatrix} = \begin{bmatrix} 26 \end{bmatrix}$

3.3 Multiply and set the corresponding entries equal to get $x + y = 15$ and $x - y = -3$. Solving this system by addition yields $x = 6$ and $y = 9$.

3.4 The system $\begin{array}{c} x - y = 3 \\ x + 2y = 5 \end{array}$ can be written as $\begin{bmatrix} 1 & -1 \\ 1 & 2 \end{bmatrix} \begin{bmatrix} x \\ y \end{bmatrix} = \begin{bmatrix} 3 \\ 5 \end{bmatrix}$.

4.1 Since B is the 2×2 identity matrix, $AB = A$ and $BA = A$.

4.2 $AB = \begin{bmatrix} 3 & 5 \\ 1 & 2 \end{bmatrix} \begin{bmatrix} 2 & -5 \\ -1 & 3 \end{bmatrix} = \begin{bmatrix} 1 & 0 \\ 0 & 1 \end{bmatrix}$

$BA = \begin{bmatrix} 2 & -5 \\ -1 & 3 \end{bmatrix} \begin{bmatrix} 3 & 5 \\ 1 & 2 \end{bmatrix} = \begin{bmatrix} 1 & 0 \\ 0 & 1 \end{bmatrix}$

4.3 $\begin{bmatrix} 3 & 2 & 1 & 0 \\ 7 & 5 & 0 & 1 \end{bmatrix}$

$\begin{bmatrix} 3 & 2 & 1 & 0 \\ 1 & 1 & -2 & 1 \end{bmatrix}$ $-2R_1 + R_2 \to R_2$

$\begin{bmatrix} 1 & 1 & -2 & 1 \\ 3 & 2 & 1 & 0 \end{bmatrix}$ $R_1 \leftrightarrow R_2$

$\begin{bmatrix} 1 & 1 & -2 & 1 \\ 0 & -1 & 7 & -3 \end{bmatrix}$ $-3R_1 + R_2 \to R_2$

$$\begin{bmatrix} 1 & 0 & 5 & -2 \\ 0 & 1 & -7 & 3 \end{bmatrix} \quad \begin{matrix} R_1 + R_2 \rightarrow R_1 \\ -R_2 \rightarrow R_2 \end{matrix}$$

The inverse matrix is $\begin{bmatrix} 5 & -2 \\ -7 & 3 \end{bmatrix}$.

4.4 $\begin{bmatrix} 3 & -1 & 1 & 0 \\ -3 & 1 & 0 & 1 \end{bmatrix}$

$$\begin{bmatrix} 3 & -1 & 1 & 0 \\ 0 & 0 & 1 & 1 \end{bmatrix} \quad R_1 + R_2 \rightarrow R_2$$

Since the left-hand side of the augmented matrix has a row of zeros, it cannot be converted to the identity and there is no inverse to the matrix.

4.5 $\begin{bmatrix} 1 & 1 & 3 & 1 & 0 & 0 \\ -1 & 0 & 0 & 0 & 1 & 0 \\ -1 & -1 & -2 & 0 & 0 & 1 \end{bmatrix}$

$$\begin{bmatrix} 1 & 1 & 3 & 1 & 0 & 0 \\ 0 & 1 & 3 & 1 & 1 & 0 \\ 0 & 0 & 1 & 1 & 0 & 1 \end{bmatrix} \quad \begin{matrix} R_1 + R_2 \rightarrow R_2 \\ R_1 + R_3 \rightarrow R_3 \end{matrix}$$

$$\begin{bmatrix} 1 & 0 & 0 & 0 & -1 & 0 \\ 0 & 1 & 3 & 1 & 1 & 0 \\ 0 & 0 & 1 & 1 & 0 & 1 \end{bmatrix} \quad -R_2 + R_1 \rightarrow R_1$$

$$\begin{bmatrix} 1 & 0 & 0 & 0 & -1 & 0 \\ 0 & 1 & 0 & -2 & 1 & -3 \\ 0 & 0 & 1 & 1 & 0 & 1 \end{bmatrix} \quad -3R_3 + R_2 \rightarrow R_2$$

The inverse matrix is $\begin{bmatrix} 0 & -1 & 0 \\ -2 & 1 & -3 \\ 1 & 0 & 1 \end{bmatrix}$.

4.6 The inverse of the matrix of coefficients was found in 4.3. So

$$\begin{bmatrix} x \\ y \end{bmatrix} = A^{-1}B = \begin{bmatrix} 5 & -2 \\ -7 & 3 \end{bmatrix}\begin{bmatrix} 4 \\ 1 \end{bmatrix}$$
$$= \begin{bmatrix} 18 \\ -25 \end{bmatrix}$$

5.1 $\begin{vmatrix} 2 & 4 \\ -3 & 1 \end{vmatrix} = 2 \cdot 1 - (-3)(4) = 14$

5.2 $D = \begin{vmatrix} 2 & 5 \\ -3 & 1 \end{vmatrix} = 2 \cdot 1 - (-3)(5) = 17$

$D_x = \begin{vmatrix} 17 & 5 \\ 0 & 1 \end{vmatrix} = 17 \cdot 1 - (0)(5) = 17$

$D_y = \begin{vmatrix} 2 & 17 \\ -3 & 0 \end{vmatrix} = 2 \cdot 0 - (-3)(17) = 51$

$x = D_x/D = 1, y = D_y/D = 3$

So the solution set to the system is $\{(1, 3)\}$.

5.3 Since $D = \begin{vmatrix} 1 & 1 \\ -2 & -2 \end{vmatrix} = 1(-2) - (-2)(1) = 0$, the system cannot be solved by Cramer's rule. Multiplying the first equation by 2 and adding to the second yields $0 = 17$. So there is no solution to the system.

5.4 A matrix has an inverse if and only if its determinant is nonzero. Since $\begin{vmatrix} 1 & 6 \\ -2 & 9 \end{vmatrix} = 1(9) - (-2)(6) = 21$, the matrix has an inverse.

6.1 The minor for 7 is $\begin{vmatrix} 2 & 3 \\ 5 & 6 \end{vmatrix}$ or -3.

6.2 Expand by minors about the first column:

$$|A| = 1\begin{vmatrix} 5 & 6 \\ 8 & 9 \end{vmatrix} - 4\begin{vmatrix} 2 & 3 \\ 8 & 9 \end{vmatrix} + 7\begin{vmatrix} 2 & 3 \\ 5 & 6 \end{vmatrix}$$
$$= 1(-3) - 4(-6) + 7(-3) = 0$$

6.3 Expand by minors about the second column:

$$|A| = -(2)\begin{vmatrix} 5 & 4 \\ -6 & 8 \end{vmatrix} + (-7)\begin{vmatrix} 1 & 3 \\ -6 & 8 \end{vmatrix} - 0\begin{vmatrix} 1 & 3 \\ 5 & 4 \end{vmatrix}$$
$$= -2(64) - 7(26) - 0(-11) = -310$$

6.4 Expand by minors about the third column:

$$|A| = 2\begin{vmatrix} -1 & 7 \\ 4 & 9 \end{vmatrix} - 0\begin{vmatrix} 3 & 5 \\ 4 & 9 \end{vmatrix} + 0\begin{vmatrix} 3 & 5 \\ -1 & 7 \end{vmatrix}$$
$$= 2(-37) = -74$$

6.5 Expand by minors about the first column:

$$|A| = 1\begin{vmatrix} 1 & 7 & 9 \\ 0 & 1 & 0 \\ 0 & 0 & 1 \end{vmatrix} = 1 \cdot 1\begin{vmatrix} 1 & 0 \\ 0 & 1 \end{vmatrix} = 1$$

6.6 First find the determinants $D = 2, D_x = 2, D_y = 10, D_z = 12$. Then find $x = D_x/D = 1, y = D_y/D = 5$, and $z = D_z/D = 6$.

6.7 Since $D = 0$, the system cannot be solved by Cramer's rule. Since the second and third equations are multiples of the first, the equations are dependent. The solution set is $\{(x, y, z) \mid x - y + z = 2\}$.

Matrices and Determinants

For Thought

1. False, the augmented matrix is a 2×3 matrix.

2. False, the required matrix is $\begin{bmatrix} 1 & -1 & 4 \\ 3 & 1 & 5 \end{bmatrix}$.

3. True   **4.**   True

5. True, since the row operation done is $R_1 + R_2 \rightarrow R_2$.

6. True, since the row operation done is $-R_1 + R_2 \rightarrow R_2$.

7. False, since it corresponds to
$$x = 2$$
$$y = 7.$$

8. True, since $0 \cdot x + 0 \cdot y = 7$ has no solution.

9. False, the system is dependent.   **10.**   True

1 Exercises

1. matrix

3. size

5. entry, element

7. diagonal

9. 1×3 **11.** 1×1 **13.** 3×2

15.
$$\begin{bmatrix} 1 & -2 & 4 \\ 3 & 2 & -5 \end{bmatrix}$$

17.
$$\begin{bmatrix} 1 & -1 & -1 & 4 \\ 1 & 3 & -1 & 1 \\ 0 & 2 & -5 & -6 \end{bmatrix}$$

19.
$$\begin{bmatrix} 1 & 3 & -1 & 5 \\ 1 & 0 & 1 & 0 \end{bmatrix}$$

21.
$$3x + 4y = -2$$
$$3x - 5y = 0$$

23.
$$5x = 6$$
$$-4x + 2z = -1$$
$$4x + 4y = 7$$

25.
$$x - y + 2z = 1$$
$$y + 4z = 3$$

27. Interchange R_1 and R_2
$$\begin{bmatrix} 1 & 2 & 0 \\ -2 & 4 & 1 \end{bmatrix}$$

29. Multiply $\dfrac{1}{2}$ to R_1
$$\begin{bmatrix} 1 & 4 & 1 \\ 0 & 3 & 6 \end{bmatrix}$$

31. Multiply 3 to R_1 then add the product to R_2. This is the new R_2.

$$\begin{bmatrix} 1 & -2 & 1 \\ -3 & 5 & 0 \end{bmatrix} =$$
$$\begin{bmatrix} 1 & -2 & 1 \\ 3 \cdot 1 + (-3) & 3 \cdot (-2) + 5 & 3 \cdot 1 + 0 \end{bmatrix} =$$
$$\begin{bmatrix} 1 & -2 & 1 \\ 0 & -1 & 3 \end{bmatrix}$$

33. From the augmented matrix
$$\begin{bmatrix} 2 & 4 & 14 \\ 5 & 4 & 5 \end{bmatrix}$$

the system is
$$2x + 4y = 14$$
$$5x + 4y = 5.$$

From the final augmented matrix
$$\begin{bmatrix} 1 & 0 & -3 \\ 0 & 1 & 5 \end{bmatrix}$$

we obtain that the solution set is $\{(-3, 5)\}$.

The row operations are $\frac{1}{2}R_1 \rightarrow R_1$,

$-5R_1 + R_2 \rightarrow R_2$, $-\frac{1}{6}R_2 \rightarrow R_2$,

and $-2R_2 + R_1 \rightarrow R_1$.

35. On $\begin{bmatrix} 1 & 1 & | & 5 \\ -2 & 1 & | & -1 \end{bmatrix}$ use $2R_1 + R_2 \rightarrow R_2$ to get

$\begin{bmatrix} 1 & 1 & | & 5 \\ 0 & 3 & | & 9 \end{bmatrix}$, use $\frac{1}{3}R_2 \rightarrow R_2$ to get

$\begin{bmatrix} 1 & 1 & | & 5 \\ 0 & 1 & | & 3 \end{bmatrix}$, use $-R_2 + R_1 \rightarrow R_1$ to get

$\begin{bmatrix} 1 & 0 & | & 2 \\ 0 & 1 & | & 3 \end{bmatrix}$, solution set is $\{(2,3)\}$,

and the system is independent.

37. On $\begin{bmatrix} 2 & 2 & | & 8 \\ -3 & -1 & | & -6 \end{bmatrix}$ use $\frac{1}{2}R_1 \rightarrow R_1$ to get

$\begin{bmatrix} 1 & 1 & | & 4 \\ -3 & -1 & | & -6 \end{bmatrix}$, use $3R_1 + R_2 \rightarrow R_2$ to get

$\begin{bmatrix} 1 & 1 & | & 4 \\ 0 & 2 & | & 6 \end{bmatrix}$, use $\frac{1}{2}R_2 \rightarrow R_2$ to get

$\begin{bmatrix} 1 & 1 & | & 4 \\ 0 & 1 & | & 3 \end{bmatrix}$, use $-1R_2 + R_1 \rightarrow R_1$ to get

$\begin{bmatrix} 1 & 0 & | & 1 \\ 0 & 1 & | & 3 \end{bmatrix}$, solution set is $\{(1,3)\}$,

and the system is independent.

39. On $\begin{bmatrix} 2 & -1 & | & 3 \\ 3 & 2 & | & 15 \end{bmatrix}$ use $-R_1 + R_2 \rightarrow R_1$ to get

$\begin{bmatrix} 1 & 3 & | & 12 \\ 3 & 2 & | & 15 \end{bmatrix}$, use $-3R_1 + R_2 \rightarrow R_2$ to get

$\begin{bmatrix} 1 & 3 & | & 12 \\ 0 & -7 & | & -21 \end{bmatrix}$, use $-\frac{1}{7}R_2 \rightarrow R_2$ to get

$\begin{bmatrix} 1 & 3 & | & 12 \\ 0 & 1 & | & 3 \end{bmatrix}$, use $-3R_2 + R_1 \rightarrow R_1$ to get

$\begin{bmatrix} 1 & 0 & | & 3 \\ 0 & 1 & | & 3 \end{bmatrix}$, solution set is $\{(3,3)\}$,

and the system is independent.

41. On $\begin{bmatrix} 0.4 & -0.2 & | & 0 \\ 1 & 1.5 & | & 2 \end{bmatrix}$ use $5R_1 \rightarrow R_1$ and

$2R_2 \rightarrow R_2$ to get

$\begin{bmatrix} 2 & -1 & | & 0 \\ 2 & 3 & | & 4 \end{bmatrix}$, use $R_1 + (-R_2) \rightarrow R_2$ to get

$\begin{bmatrix} 2 & -1 & | & 0 \\ 0 & -4 & | & -4 \end{bmatrix}$, use $-\frac{1}{4}R_2 \rightarrow R_2$ to get

$\begin{bmatrix} 2 & -1 & | & 0 \\ 0 & 1 & | & 1 \end{bmatrix}$, use $R_1 + R_2 \rightarrow R_1$ to get

$\begin{bmatrix} 2 & 0 & | & 1 \\ 0 & 1 & | & 1 \end{bmatrix}$, use $\frac{1}{2}R_1 \rightarrow R_1$ to get

$\begin{bmatrix} 1 & 0 & | & 0.5 \\ 0 & 1 & | & 1 \end{bmatrix}$, solution set is $\{(0.5, 1)\}$,

and the system is independent.

43. On $\begin{bmatrix} 3 & -5 & | & 7 \\ -3 & 5 & | & 4 \end{bmatrix}$ use $R_1 + R_2 \rightarrow R_2$ to get

$\begin{bmatrix} 3 & -5 & | & 7 \\ 0 & 0 & | & 11 \end{bmatrix}$, inconsistent system, and

the solution set is $\emptyset$.

45. On $\begin{bmatrix} 0.5 & 1.5 & | & 2 \\ 3 & 9 & | & 12 \end{bmatrix}$ use $2R_1 \rightarrow R_1$ to get

$\begin{bmatrix} 1 & 3 & | & 4 \\ 3 & 9 & | & 12 \end{bmatrix}$, use $-3R_1 + R_2 \rightarrow R_2$ to get

$\begin{bmatrix} 1 & 3 & | & 4 \\ 0 & 0 & | & 0 \end{bmatrix}$, dependent system, and

solution set is $\{(u, v) \mid u + 3v = 4\}$.

47. Rewrite system as

$$2x + y = 4$$
$$x - y = 8.$$

On $\begin{bmatrix} 2 & 1 & | & 4 \\ 1 & -1 & | & 8 \end{bmatrix}$ use $R_1 + (-2R_2) \rightarrow R_2$ to get

$\begin{bmatrix} 2 & 1 & | & 4 \\ 0 & 3 & | & -12 \end{bmatrix}$, use $\frac{1}{3}R_2 \rightarrow R_2$ to get

$\begin{bmatrix} 2 & 1 & | & 4 \\ 0 & 1 & | & -4 \end{bmatrix}$, use $-1R_2 + R_1 \rightarrow R_1$ to get

$\begin{bmatrix} 2 & 0 & | & 8 \\ 0 & 1 & | & -4 \end{bmatrix}$, use $\dfrac{1}{2}R_1 \to R_1$ to get

$\begin{bmatrix} 1 & 0 & | & 4 \\ 0 & 1 & | & -4 \end{bmatrix}$, solution set is $\{(4, -4)\}$,

and the system is independent.

49.

On $\begin{bmatrix} 1 & 1 & 1 & | & 6 \\ 1 & -1 & -1 & | & 0 \\ 0 & 2 & -1 & | & 3 \end{bmatrix}$ use $-1R_2 + R_1 \to R_2$ to get

$\begin{bmatrix} 1 & 1 & 1 & | & 6 \\ 0 & 2 & 2 & | & 6 \\ 0 & 2 & -1 & | & 3 \end{bmatrix}$, use $\dfrac{1}{2}R_2 \to R_2$ to get

$\begin{bmatrix} 1 & 1 & 1 & | & 6 \\ 0 & 1 & 1 & | & 3 \\ 0 & 2 & -1 & | & 3 \end{bmatrix}$, use $-1R_2 + R_1 \to R_1$ to get

$\begin{bmatrix} 1 & 0 & 0 & | & 3 \\ 0 & 1 & 1 & | & 3 \\ 0 & 2 & -1 & | & 3 \end{bmatrix}$, use $-2R_2 + R_3 \to R_3$ to get

$\begin{bmatrix} 1 & 0 & 0 & | & 3 \\ 0 & 1 & 1 & | & 3 \\ 0 & 0 & -3 & | & -3 \end{bmatrix}$, use $-\dfrac{1}{3}R_3 \to R_3$ to get

$\begin{bmatrix} 1 & 0 & 0 & | & 3 \\ 0 & 1 & 1 & | & 3 \\ 0 & 0 & 1 & | & 1 \end{bmatrix}$, use $-1R_3 + R_2 \to R_2$ to get

$\begin{bmatrix} 1 & 0 & 0 & | & 3 \\ 0 & 1 & 0 & | & 2 \\ 0 & 0 & 1 & | & 1 \end{bmatrix}$, solution set is $\{(3, 2, 1)\}$,

and the system is independent.

51.

Rewrite system as

$$\begin{aligned} 2x + y - z &= 2 \\ x + 2y - z &= 2 \\ x - y + 2z &= 2. \end{aligned}$$

On $\begin{bmatrix} 2 & 1 & -1 & | & 2 \\ 1 & 2 & -1 & | & 2 \\ 1 & -1 & 2 & | & 2 \end{bmatrix}$, use $-1R_2 + R_1 \to R_1$

and $-1R_3 + R_2 \to R_3$ to get

$\begin{bmatrix} 1 & -1 & 0 & | & 0 \\ 1 & 2 & -1 & | & 2 \\ 0 & 3 & -3 & | & 0 \end{bmatrix}$, use $-1R_2 + R_1 \to R_2$

and $\dfrac{1}{3}R_3 \to R_3$ to get

$\begin{bmatrix} 1 & -1 & 0 & | & 0 \\ 0 & -3 & 1 & | & -2 \\ 0 & 1 & -1 & | & 0 \end{bmatrix}$, use $R_1 + R_3 \to R_1$

and $R_3 + R_2 \to R_2$ to get

$\begin{bmatrix} 1 & 0 & -1 & | & 0 \\ 0 & -2 & 0 & | & -2 \\ 0 & 1 & -1 & | & 0 \end{bmatrix}$, use $-\dfrac{1}{2}R_2 \to R_2$ to get

$\begin{bmatrix} 1 & 0 & -1 & | & 0 \\ 0 & 1 & 0 & | & 1 \\ 0 & 1 & -1 & | & 0 \end{bmatrix}$, use $-1R_3 + R_2 \to R_3$ to get

$\begin{bmatrix} 1 & 0 & -1 & | & 0 \\ 0 & 1 & 0 & | & 1 \\ 0 & 0 & 1 & | & 1 \end{bmatrix}$, use $R_1 + R_3 \to R_1$ to get

$\begin{bmatrix} 1 & 0 & 0 & | & 1 \\ 0 & 1 & 0 & | & 1 \\ 0 & 0 & 1 & | & 1 \end{bmatrix}$, solution set is $\{(1, 1, 1)\}$,

and the system is independent.

53.

Interchange rows of $\begin{bmatrix} 2 & -2 & 1 & | & -2 \\ 1 & 1 & -3 & | & 3 \\ 1 & -3 & 1 & | & -5 \end{bmatrix}$ to get

$\begin{bmatrix} 1 & 1 & -3 & | & 3 \\ 1 & -3 & 1 & | & -5 \\ 2 & -2 & 1 & | & -2 \end{bmatrix}$, use $-1R_2 + R_1 \to R_2$

and $-1R_3 + R_1 + R_2 \to R_3$ to get

$\begin{bmatrix} 1 & 1 & -3 & | & 3 \\ 0 & 4 & -4 & | & 8 \\ 0 & 0 & -3 & | & 0 \end{bmatrix}$, use $\dfrac{1}{4}R_2 \to R_2$

and $-\dfrac{1}{3}R_3 \to R_3$ to get

$\begin{bmatrix} 1 & 1 & -3 & | & 3 \\ 0 & 1 & -1 & | & 2 \\ 0 & 0 & 1 & | & 0 \end{bmatrix}$, use $R_2 + R_3 \to R_2$ to get

$$\begin{bmatrix} 1 & 1 & -3 & | & 3 \\ 0 & 1 & 0 & | & 2 \\ 0 & 0 & 1 & | & 0 \end{bmatrix}, \text{ use } -1R_2 + R_1 \to R_1 \text{ to}$$

get

$$\begin{bmatrix} 1 & 0 & -3 & | & 1 \\ 0 & 1 & 0 & | & 2 \\ 0 & 0 & 1 & | & 0 \end{bmatrix}, \text{ use } 3R_3 + R_1 \to R_1 \text{ to get}$$

$$\begin{bmatrix} 1 & 0 & 0 & | & 1 \\ 0 & 1 & 0 & | & 2 \\ 0 & 0 & 1 & | & 0 \end{bmatrix}, \text{ solution set is } \{(1,2,0)\},$$

and the system is independent.

55.

Rewrite system as

$$\begin{aligned} x - 3y + z &= 0 \\ x - y - 3z &= 4 \\ x + y + 2z &= -1. \end{aligned}$$

$$\text{On } \begin{bmatrix} 1 & -3 & 1 & | & 0 \\ 1 & -1 & -3 & | & 4 \\ 1 & 1 & 2 & | & -1 \end{bmatrix}, \text{ use}$$

$-1R_2 + R_1 \to R_2$ and $-1R_3 + R_1 \to R_3$ to get

$$\begin{bmatrix} 1 & -3 & 1 & | & 0 \\ 0 & -2 & 4 & | & -4 \\ 0 & -4 & -1 & | & 1 \end{bmatrix}, \text{ use } -\frac{1}{2}R_2 \to R_2$$

and $-1R_3 \to R_3$ to get

$$\begin{bmatrix} 1 & -3 & 1 & | & 0 \\ 0 & 1 & -2 & | & 2 \\ 0 & 4 & 1 & | & -1 \end{bmatrix}, \text{ use } -1R_3 + R_1 \to R_1$$

to get

$$\begin{bmatrix} 1 & -7 & 0 & | & 1 \\ 0 & 1 & -2 & | & 2 \\ 0 & 4 & 1 & | & -1 \end{bmatrix}, \text{ use } -4R_2 + R_3 \to R_3$$

to get

$$\begin{bmatrix} 1 & -7 & 0 & | & 1 \\ 0 & 1 & -2 & | & 2 \\ 0 & 0 & 9 & | & -9 \end{bmatrix}, \text{ use } \frac{1}{9}R_3 \to R_3 \text{ to get}$$

$$\begin{bmatrix} 1 & -7 & 0 & | & 1 \\ 0 & 1 & -2 & | & 2 \\ 0 & 0 & 1 & | & -1 \end{bmatrix}, \text{ use } 2R_3 + R_2 \to R_2$$

to get

$$\begin{bmatrix} 1 & -7 & 0 & | & 1 \\ 0 & 1 & 0 & | & 0 \\ 0 & 0 & 1 & | & -1 \end{bmatrix}, \text{ use } R_1 + 7R_2 \to R_1 \text{ to}$$

get

$$\begin{bmatrix} 1 & 0 & 0 & | & 1 \\ 0 & 1 & 0 & | & 0 \\ 0 & 0 & 1 & | & -1 \end{bmatrix}, \text{ solution set is } \{(1,0,-1)\},$$

and the system is independent.

57.

$$\text{On } \begin{bmatrix} 1 & -2 & 3 & | & 1 \\ 2 & -4 & 6 & | & 2 \\ -3 & 6 & -9 & | & -3 \end{bmatrix}, \text{ use } \frac{1}{2}R_2 \to R_2$$

and $-\frac{1}{3}R_3 \to R_3$ to get

$$\begin{bmatrix} 1 & -2 & 3 & | & 1 \\ 1 & -2 & 3 & | & 1 \\ 1 & -2 & 3 & | & 1 \end{bmatrix}, \text{ use } -1R_1 + R_2 \to R_2$$

and $-1R_1 + R_3 \to R_3$ to get

$$\begin{bmatrix} 1 & -2 & 3 & | & 1 \\ 0 & 0 & 0 & | & 0 \\ 0 & 0 & 0 & | & 0 \end{bmatrix}, \text{ dependent system,}$$

and solution set is $\{(x,y,z) \mid x - 2y + 3z = 1\}$.

59.

$$\text{On } \begin{bmatrix} 1 & -1 & 1 & | & 2 \\ 2 & 1 & -1 & | & 1 \\ 2 & -2 & 2 & | & 5 \end{bmatrix}, \text{ use } -\frac{1}{2}R_3 + R_1 \to R_3$$

to get $\begin{bmatrix} 1 & -1 & 1 & | & 2 \\ 2 & 1 & -1 & | & 1 \\ 0 & 0 & 0 & | & -1/2 \end{bmatrix}$, inconsistent,

and the solution set is $\emptyset$.

61.

$$\text{On } \begin{bmatrix} 1 & 1 & -1 & | & 3 \\ 3 & 1 & 1 & | & 7 \\ 1 & -1 & 3 & | & 1 \end{bmatrix}, \text{ use } -1R_3 + R_1 \to R_3$$

and $3R_1 + (-1R_2) \to R_2$ to get

$$\begin{bmatrix} 1 & 1 & -1 & | & 3 \\ 0 & 2 & -4 & | & 2 \\ 0 & 2 & -4 & | & 2 \end{bmatrix}, \text{ use } -1R_3 + R_2 \to R_3 \text{ to}$$

get

$$\begin{bmatrix} 1 & 1 & -1 & | & 3 \\ 0 & 2 & -4 & | & 2 \\ 0 & 0 & 0 & | & 0 \end{bmatrix}, \text{ use } \frac{1}{2}R_2 \to R_2 \text{ to get}$$

$$\begin{bmatrix} 1 & 1 & -1 & | & 3 \\ 0 & 1 & -2 & | & 1 \\ 0 & 0 & 0 & | & 0 \end{bmatrix}, \text{ use } -1R_2 + R_1 \to R_1 \text{ to}$$

get

$$\begin{bmatrix} 1 & 0 & 1 & | & 2 \\ 0 & 1 & -2 & | & 1 \\ 0 & 0 & 0 & | & 0 \end{bmatrix}. \text{ Substitute } z = 2 - x$$

into $y = 1 + 2z$. Then $y = 1 + 2(2 - x) = 5 - 2x$. The solution set is

$$\{(x, 5 - 2x, 2 - x) \mid x \text{ is any real number}\}$$

and the system is dependent.

63.

On $\begin{bmatrix} 2 & -1 & 3 & | & 1 \\ 1 & 1 & -1 & | & 4 \end{bmatrix}$, use $-2R_2 + R_1 \to R_2$

to get

$\begin{bmatrix} 2 & -1 & 3 & | & 1 \\ 0 & -3 & 5 & | & -7 \end{bmatrix}$, use $-3R_1 + R_2 \to R_1$

to get

$\begin{bmatrix} -6 & 0 & -4 & | & -10 \\ 0 & -3 & 5 & | & -7 \end{bmatrix}$, use $-\dfrac{1}{6}R_1 \to R_1$

and $-\dfrac{1}{3}R_2 \to R_2$ to get

$\begin{bmatrix} 1 & 0 & 2/3 & | & 5/3 \\ 0 & 1 & -5/3 & | & 7/3 \end{bmatrix}$. Note $x = \dfrac{5 - 2z}{3}$ and

$y = \dfrac{7 + 5z}{3}$. Solving for z, we get $z = \dfrac{5 - 3x}{2}$.

Then $y = \dfrac{7 + 5 \cdot \frac{5-3x}{2}}{3} = \dfrac{7 + 5 \cdot \frac{5-3x}{2}}{3} \cdot \dfrac{2}{2} =$

$\dfrac{39 - 15x}{6} = \dfrac{13 - 5x}{2}$. The solution set is

$$\left\{ \left(x, \dfrac{13 - 5x}{2}, \dfrac{5 - 3x}{2} \right) \mid x \text{ is any real number} \right\}$$

and the system is dependent.

65.

On $\begin{bmatrix} 1 & -1 & 1 & -1 & | & 2 \\ -1 & 2 & -1 & -1 & | & -1 \\ 2 & -1 & -1 & 1 & | & 4 \\ 1 & 3 & -2 & -3 & | & 6 \end{bmatrix}$,

use $2R_2 + R_3 \to R_3$ and $R_2 + R_4 \to R_4$ to get

$\begin{bmatrix} 1 & -1 & 1 & -1 & | & 2 \\ 0 & 1 & 0 & -2 & | & 1 \\ 0 & 3 & -3 & -1 & | & 2 \\ 0 & 5 & -3 & -4 & | & 5 \end{bmatrix}$, use

$-3R_2 + R_3 \to R_3$ and $-5R_2 + R_4 \to R_4$ to get

$\begin{bmatrix} 1 & -1 & 1 & -1 & | & 2 \\ 0 & 1 & 0 & -2 & | & 1 \\ 0 & 0 & -3 & 5 & | & -1 \\ 0 & 0 & -3 & 6 & | & 0 \end{bmatrix}$, use

$R_1 + R_2 \to R_1$ and $-\dfrac{1}{3}R_4 \to R_4$ to get

$\begin{bmatrix} 1 & 0 & 1 & -3 & | & 3 \\ 0 & 1 & 0 & -2 & | & 1 \\ 0 & 0 & -3 & 5 & | & -1 \\ 0 & 0 & 1 & -2 & | & 0 \end{bmatrix}$, use $R_3 \to R_4$

and $R_4 \to R_3$ to get

$\begin{bmatrix} 1 & 0 & 1 & -3 & | & 3 \\ 0 & 1 & 0 & -2 & | & 1 \\ 0 & 0 & 1 & -2 & | & 0 \\ 0 & 0 & -3 & 5 & | & -1 \end{bmatrix}$, use

$-3R_3 + (-1R_4) \to R_4$ to get

$\begin{bmatrix} 1 & 0 & 1 & -3 & | & 3 \\ 0 & 1 & 0 & -2 & | & 1 \\ 0 & 0 & 1 & -2 & | & 0 \\ 0 & 0 & 0 & 1 & | & 1 \end{bmatrix}$, use $-1R_3 + R_1 \to R_1$

to get

$\begin{bmatrix} 1 & 0 & 0 & -1 & | & 3 \\ 0 & 1 & 0 & -2 & | & 1 \\ 0 & 0 & 1 & -2 & | & 0 \\ 0 & 0 & 0 & 1 & | & 1 \end{bmatrix}$, use $2R_4 + R_3 \to R_3$ to

get

$\begin{bmatrix} 1 & 0 & 0 & -1 & | & 3 \\ 0 & 1 & 0 & -2 & | & 1 \\ 0 & 0 & 1 & 0 & | & 2 \\ 0 & 0 & 0 & 1 & | & 1 \end{bmatrix}$, use $2R_4 + R_2 \to R_2$ to

get

$\begin{bmatrix} 1 & 0 & 0 & -1 & | & 3 \\ 0 & 1 & 0 & 0 & | & 3 \\ 0 & 0 & 1 & 0 & | & 2 \\ 0 & 0 & 0 & 1 & | & 1 \end{bmatrix}$, use $R_4 + R_1 \to R_1$ to

get

$\begin{bmatrix} 1 & 0 & 0 & 0 & | & 4 \\ 0 & 1 & 0 & 0 & | & 3 \\ 0 & 0 & 1 & 0 & | & 2 \\ 0 & 0 & 0 & 1 & | & 1 \end{bmatrix}$, the solution set is

{(4, 3, 2, 1)}, and the system is independent.

67. Let x and y be the number of hours Mike worked at Burgers and the Soap Opera, respectively. The augmented matrix is

$A = \begin{bmatrix} 1 & 1 & 60 \\ 8 & 9 & 502 \end{bmatrix}$. On A use

$-8R_1 + R_2 \to R_2$ to get

$\begin{bmatrix} 1 & 1 & 60 \\ 0 & 1 & 22 \end{bmatrix}$, use $-R_2 + R_1 \to R_1$ to get

$\begin{bmatrix} 1 & 0 & 38 \\ 0 & 1 & 22 \end{bmatrix}$. Mike worked $x = 38$ hours

at Burgers and $y = 22$ hours at Soap Opera.

69. Let x, y, and z be the amounts invested in a mutual fund, in treasury bills, and in bonds, respectively. Augmented matrix is

$A = \begin{bmatrix} 1 & 1 & 1 & 40,000 \\ 0.08 & 0.09 & 0.12 & 3,660 \\ 1 & -1 & -1 & 0 \end{bmatrix}$.

On A use $100R_2 \to R_2$ to get

$\begin{bmatrix} 1 & 1 & 1 & 40,000 \\ 8 & 9 & 12 & 366,000 \\ 1 & -1 & -1 & 0 \end{bmatrix}$, use

$-8R_1 + R_2 \to R_2$ to get

$\begin{bmatrix} 1 & 1 & 1 & 40,000 \\ 0 & 1 & 4 & 46,000 \\ 1 & -1 & -1 & 0 \end{bmatrix}$, use

$-1R_3 + R_1 \to R_3$ and $-1R_2 + R_1 \to R_1$ to get

$\begin{bmatrix} 1 & 0 & -3 & -6,000 \\ 0 & 1 & 4 & 46,000 \\ 0 & 2 & 2 & 40,000 \end{bmatrix}$, use $\frac{1}{2}R_3 \to R_3$ to

get

$\begin{bmatrix} 1 & 0 & -3 & -6,000 \\ 0 & 1 & 4 & 46,000 \\ 0 & 1 & 1 & 20,000 \end{bmatrix}$, use

$-1R_3 + R_2 \to R_3$ to get

$\begin{bmatrix} 1 & 0 & -3 & -6,000 \\ 0 & 1 & 4 & 46,000 \\ 0 & 0 & 3 & 26,000 \end{bmatrix}$, use

$-1R_3 + R_2 \to R_2$ and $\frac{1}{3}R_3 \to R_3$ to get

$\begin{bmatrix} 1 & 0 & -3 & -6,000 \\ 0 & 1 & 1 & 20,000 \\ 0 & 0 & 1 & 8,666.67 \end{bmatrix}$, use $3R_3 + R_1 \to R_1$

and $-1R_3 + R_2 \to R_2$ to get

$\begin{bmatrix} 1 & 0 & 0 & 20,000 \\ 0 & 1 & 0 & 11,333.33 \\ 0 & 0 & 1 & 8,666.67 \end{bmatrix}$. Investments were

$x = \$20,000$ in a mutual fund, $y = \$11,333.33$ in treasury bills, and $z = \$8,666.67$ in bonds.

71. The augmented matrix is

$$A = \begin{bmatrix} -1 & -1 & 1 & 4 \\ 1 & 1 & 1 & 2 \\ 8 & 2 & 1 & 7 \end{bmatrix}.$$

On A use $R_1 \to R_2$ and $R_2 \to R_1$ to get

$\begin{bmatrix} 1 & 1 & 1 & 2 \\ -1 & -1 & 1 & 4 \\ 8 & 2 & 1 & 7 \end{bmatrix}$, use $8R_1 + (-1R_3) \to R_3$

and $-\frac{8}{3}R_2 + \left(-\frac{1}{3}R_3\right) \to R_2$ to get

$\begin{bmatrix} 1 & 1 & 1 & 2 \\ 0 & 2 & -3 & -13 \\ 0 & 6 & 7 & 9 \end{bmatrix}$, use $-3R_2 + R_3 \to R_3$

to get

$\begin{bmatrix} 1 & 1 & 1 & 2 \\ 0 & 2 & -3 & -13 \\ 0 & 0 & 16 & 48 \end{bmatrix}$, use $\frac{1}{2}R_2 \to R_2$

and $\frac{1}{16}R_3 \to R_3$ to get

$\begin{bmatrix} 1 & 1 & 1 & 2 \\ 0 & 1 & -3/2 & -13/2 \\ 0 & 0 & 1 & 3 \end{bmatrix}$, use

$\frac{3}{2}R_3 + R_2 \to R_2$ to get

$\begin{bmatrix} 1 & 1 & 1 & 2 \\ 0 & 1 & 0 & -2 \\ 0 & 0 & 1 & 3 \end{bmatrix}$, use $-1R_3 + R_1 \to R_1$

to get

$\begin{bmatrix} 1 & 1 & 0 & -1 \\ 0 & 1 & 0 & -2 \\ 0 & 0 & 1 & 3 \end{bmatrix}$, use $-1R_2 + R_1 \to R_1$

to get

$$\begin{bmatrix} 1 & 0 & 0 & | & 1 \\ 0 & 1 & 0 & | & -2 \\ 0 & 0 & 1 & | & 3 \end{bmatrix}.$$

Then $a = 1, b = -2$, and $c = 3$.

73. Since the number of cars entering M.L. King Dr. and Washington St. is 750 and $x + y$ is the number of cars leaving the intersection of M.L. King Dr. and Washington St. then $x + y = 750$.

On the intersection of M.L. King Dr. and JFK Blvd., the number of cars entering this intersection is $450 + x$ and the number of cars leaving is $700 + z$. So $450 + x = 700 + z$.

Simplifying, one gets $y = 750 - x$ and $z = x - 250$; and since y and z are nonnegative, $250 \le x \le 750$. The values of x, y, and z that realizes this traffic flow must satisfy

$$\begin{aligned} y &= 750 - x \\ z &= x - 250 \\ 250 \le x &\le 750 \end{aligned}$$

If $z = 50$, then $50 = x - 250$ or $x = 300$, and $y = 750 - 300 = 450$.

75. No, since $(-2, 1)$ does not satisfy $y > x + 1$.

77.

On $\begin{bmatrix} 1 & 1 & 0 & | & 4 \\ 0 & 1 & 1 & | & -3 \\ 1 & 0 & 1 & | & -17 \end{bmatrix}$, use $-R_1 + R_3 \rightarrow R_3$

to get $\begin{bmatrix} 1 & 1 & 0 & | & 4 \\ 0 & 1 & 1 & | & -3 \\ 0 & -1 & 1 & | & -21 \end{bmatrix}.$

Use $R_2 + R_3 \rightarrow R_3$ to get

$$\begin{bmatrix} 1 & 1 & 0 & | & 4 \\ 0 & 1 & 1 & | & -3 \\ 0 & 0 & 2 & | & -24 \end{bmatrix}$$

Use $\dfrac{1}{2}R_3 \rightarrow R_3$ to get

$$\begin{bmatrix} 1 & 1 & 0 & | & 4 \\ 0 & 1 & 1 & | & -3 \\ 0 & 0 & 1 & | & -12 \end{bmatrix}$$

Use $-R_3 + R_2 \rightarrow R_2$ to get

$$\begin{bmatrix} 1 & 1 & 0 & | & 4 \\ 0 & 1 & 0 & | & 9 \\ 0 & 0 & 1 & | & -12 \end{bmatrix}.$$

Use $-R_2 + R_1 \rightarrow R_1$ to get

$$\begin{bmatrix} 1 & 0 & 0 & | & -5 \\ 0 & 1 & 0 & | & 9 \\ 0 & 0 & 1 & | & -12 \end{bmatrix}$$

The solution set is $\{(-5, 9, -12)\}$.

79. Rewrite without absolute values:

$$\begin{array}{ccccccc} x - 3 &=& 2x + 5 & \text{or} & x - 3 &=& -2x - 5 \\ -8 &=& x & \text{or} & 3x &=& -2 \end{array}$$

The solution set is $\{-2/3, -8\}$.

For Thought

1. True

2. False, since the orders of matrices A and C are different.

3. False, $A + B = \begin{bmatrix} 2 \\ 6 \end{bmatrix}.$

4. True, $C + D = \begin{bmatrix} 1-3 & 1+5 \\ 3+1 & 3-2 \end{bmatrix} =$

$= \begin{bmatrix} -2 & 6 \\ 4 & 1 \end{bmatrix}.$

5. True, $A - B = \begin{bmatrix} 1-1 \\ 3-3 \end{bmatrix} = \begin{bmatrix} 0 \\ 0 \end{bmatrix}.$

6. False, $3B = 3\begin{bmatrix} 1 \\ 3 \end{bmatrix} = \begin{bmatrix} 3 \\ 9 \end{bmatrix}.$

7. False, $-A = -\begin{bmatrix} 1 \\ 3 \end{bmatrix} = \begin{bmatrix} -1 \\ -3 \end{bmatrix}.$

8. False, matrices of different orders cannot be added. **9.** False, matrices of different orders cannot be subtracted.

10. False, $C + 2D = \begin{bmatrix} 1 & 1 \\ 3 & 3 \end{bmatrix} + \begin{bmatrix} -6 & 10 \\ 2 & -4 \end{bmatrix} =$

$= \begin{bmatrix} -5 & 11 \\ 5 & -1 \end{bmatrix}.$

2 Exercises

1. $x = 2,\ y = 5$

3. Since $2x = 6$ and $4y = 16$, $x = 3$ and $y = 4$.
Also $3z = z + y$ and so $z = y/2 = 4/2 = 2$.
Then $x = 3$, $y = 4$, and $z = 2$.

5. $\begin{bmatrix} 3+2 \\ 5+1 \end{bmatrix} = \begin{bmatrix} 5 \\ 6 \end{bmatrix}$

7. $\begin{bmatrix} -0.5+2 & -0.03+1 \\ 2-0.05 & -0.33+1 \end{bmatrix} = \begin{bmatrix} 1.5 & 0.97 \\ 1.95 & 0.67 \end{bmatrix}$

9. $\begin{bmatrix} 2+1 & -3-1 & 4+1 \\ 4+0 & -6+1 & 8-1 \\ 6+0 & -3+0 & 1+1 \end{bmatrix} = \begin{bmatrix} 3 & -4 & 5 \\ 4 & -5 & 7 \\ 6 & -3 & 2 \end{bmatrix}$

11. $-A = -\begin{bmatrix} 1 & -4 \\ -5 & 6 \end{bmatrix} = \begin{bmatrix} -1 & 4 \\ 5 & -6 \end{bmatrix}$

and $A + (-A) = \begin{bmatrix} 0 & 0 \\ 0 & 0 \end{bmatrix}$

13. $-A = -\begin{bmatrix} 3 & 0 & -1 \\ 8 & -2 & 1 \\ -3 & 6 & 3 \end{bmatrix} =$

$\begin{bmatrix} -3 & 0 & 1 \\ -8 & 2 & -1 \\ 3 & -6 & -3 \end{bmatrix}$ and

$A + (-A) = \begin{bmatrix} 0 & 0 & 0 \\ 0 & 0 & 0 \\ 0 & 0 & 0 \end{bmatrix}$

15. $B - A = \begin{bmatrix} -1+4 & -2-1 \\ 7-3 & 4-0 \end{bmatrix} = \begin{bmatrix} 3 & -3 \\ 4 & 4 \end{bmatrix}$

17. $B - C = \begin{bmatrix} -1+3 & -2+4 \\ 7-2 & 4+5 \end{bmatrix} = \begin{bmatrix} 2 & 2 \\ 5 & 9 \end{bmatrix}$

19. $B-E$ is undefined since B and E have different sizes

21. $3A = 3\begin{bmatrix} -4 & 1 \\ 3 & 0 \end{bmatrix} = \begin{bmatrix} -12 & 3 \\ 9 & 0 \end{bmatrix}$

23. $-1D = -1\begin{bmatrix} -4 \\ 5 \end{bmatrix} = \begin{bmatrix} 4 \\ -5 \end{bmatrix}$

25.

$3A + 3C = \begin{bmatrix} -12 & 3 \\ 9 & 0 \end{bmatrix} + \begin{bmatrix} -9 & -12 \\ 6 & -15 \end{bmatrix} =$

$\begin{bmatrix} -21 & -9 \\ 15 & -15 \end{bmatrix}$

27.

$2A - B = \begin{bmatrix} -8 & 2 \\ 6 & 0 \end{bmatrix} - \begin{bmatrix} -1 & -2 \\ 7 & 4 \end{bmatrix} =$

$\begin{bmatrix} -7 & 4 \\ -1 & -4 \end{bmatrix}$

29.

$2D - 3E = \begin{bmatrix} -8 \\ 10 \end{bmatrix} - \begin{bmatrix} -3 \\ 6 \end{bmatrix} = \begin{bmatrix} -5 \\ 4 \end{bmatrix}$

31. $D+A$ is undefined since D and A have different sizes

33.

$(A + B) + C = \begin{bmatrix} -5 & -1 \\ 10 & 4 \end{bmatrix} + \begin{bmatrix} -3 & -4 \\ 2 & -5 \end{bmatrix} =$

$\begin{bmatrix} -8 & -5 \\ 12 & -1 \end{bmatrix}$

35. $\begin{bmatrix} 0.2+0.2 & 0.1+0.05 \\ 0.4+0.3 & 0.3+0.8 \end{bmatrix} = \begin{bmatrix} 0.4 & 0.15 \\ 0.7 & 1.1 \end{bmatrix}$

37. $\begin{bmatrix} 1/2 & 3/2 \\ 3 & -12 \end{bmatrix}$

39. $\begin{bmatrix} -2 & 4 \\ 6 & 8 \end{bmatrix} - \begin{bmatrix} -12 & 4 \\ 8 & -8 \end{bmatrix} = \begin{bmatrix} 10 & 0 \\ -2 & 16 \end{bmatrix}$

41. Undefined since we cannot add matrices with different sizes

43. $\begin{bmatrix} -1 & 13 \\ -9 & 3 \\ 6 & -2 \end{bmatrix}$

45. $\begin{bmatrix} 3\sqrt{2} & 2 & 3\sqrt{3} \end{bmatrix}$

47.

$$\begin{bmatrix} 2a \\ 2b \end{bmatrix} + \begin{bmatrix} 6a \\ 12b \end{bmatrix} + \begin{bmatrix} 5a \\ -15b \end{bmatrix} = \begin{bmatrix} 13a \\ -b \end{bmatrix}$$

49.

$$\begin{bmatrix} -0.4x - 0.6x & 0.4y - 0.9y \\ 0.8x - 1.5x & 3.2y + 0.3y \end{bmatrix} =$$

$$\begin{bmatrix} -x & -0.5y \\ -0.7x & 3.5y \end{bmatrix}$$

51.

$$\begin{bmatrix} 2x & 2y & 2z \\ -2x & 4y & 6z \\ 2x & -2y & -6z \end{bmatrix} - \begin{bmatrix} -x & 0 & 3z \\ 4x & y & -z \\ 2x & 5y & z \end{bmatrix} =$$

$$\begin{bmatrix} 3x & 2y & -z \\ -6x & 3y & 7z \\ 0 & -7y & -7z \end{bmatrix}$$

53. Equate the corresponding entries.

$$x + y = 5$$
$$x - y = 1$$

Adding the two equations, we get $2x = 6$. Substitute $x = 3$ into $x + y = 5$. Then $3 + y = 5$ and $y = 2$. Solution set is $\{(3, 2)\}$.

55. Equate the corresponding entries.

$$2x + 3y = 7$$
$$x - 4y = -13$$

Multiply second equation by -2 and add to the first one.

$$\begin{aligned} 2x + 3y &= 7 \\ -2x + 8y &= 26 \\ \hline 11y &= 33 \\ y &= 3 \end{aligned}$$

Substitute $y = 3$ into $x - 4y = -13$. Then $x - 12 = -13$ and $x = -1$. The solution set is $\{(-1, 3)\}$.

57. Equate the corresponding entries.

$$x + y + z = 8$$
$$x - y - z = -7$$
$$x - y + z = 2$$

Adding the first and second equations, $2x = 1$ and $x = 0.5$. Multiply second equation by -1 and add to the third.

$$\begin{aligned} -x + y + z &= 7 \\ x - y + z &= 2 \\ \hline 2z &= 9 \\ z &= 4.5 \end{aligned}$$

Substitute $x = 0.5$ and $z = 4.5$ into $x + y + z = 8$. Then $y + 5 = 8$ and $y = 3$. The solution set is $\{(0.5, 3, 4.5)\}$.

59. The matrices for January, February and March are, respectively,

$$J = \begin{bmatrix} 120 \\ 30 \\ 40 \end{bmatrix}, F = \begin{bmatrix} 130 \\ 70 \\ 50 \end{bmatrix}, \text{ and}$$

$$M = \begin{bmatrix} 140 \\ 60 \\ 45 \end{bmatrix}. \text{ The sum}$$

$$J + F + M = \begin{bmatrix} \$390 \\ \$160 \\ \$135 \end{bmatrix} \text{ represents the}$$

total expenses on food, clothing and utilities for the three months.

61. The supply matrix for the first week is

$$S = \begin{bmatrix} 40 & 80 \\ 30 & 90 \\ 80 & 200 \end{bmatrix}. \text{ Next week's supply matrix}$$

is $S + 0.5S = \begin{bmatrix} 40 & 80 \\ 30 & 90 \\ 80 & 200 \end{bmatrix} + \begin{bmatrix} 20 & 40 \\ 15 & 45 \\ 40 & 100 \end{bmatrix}$

$$= \begin{bmatrix} 60 & 120 \\ 45 & 135 \\ 120 & 300 \end{bmatrix}.$$

63. yes, yes

65. yes, yes

67. yes, yes

69. $\begin{bmatrix} 0 & 0 \\ 0 & 0 \end{bmatrix}$

71. On $\begin{bmatrix} 2 & 3 & | & 4 \\ 1 & -4 & | & -31 \end{bmatrix}$, apply

$-2R_2 + R_1 \to R_2$ to get $\begin{bmatrix} 2 & 3 & | & 4 \\ 0 & 11 & | & 66 \end{bmatrix}$.

Use $\dfrac{1}{11}R_2 \to R_2$ to get $\begin{bmatrix} 2 & 3 & | & 4 \\ 0 & 1 & | & 6 \end{bmatrix}$.

Use $-3R_2 + R_1 \to R_2$ to get

$$\begin{bmatrix} 2 & 0 & | & -14 \\ 0 & 1 & | & 6 \end{bmatrix}.$$

Use $\dfrac{1}{2}R_1 \to R_1$ to get $\begin{bmatrix} 1 & 0 & | & -7 \\ 0 & 1 & | & 6 \end{bmatrix}$.

The solution set is $\{(-7, 6)\}$.

73. a) $bx(ax + y) + z(ax + y) = (ax + y)(bx + z)$

b) $x(6x^2 - 23xy + 20y^2) = x(3x - 4y)(2x - 5y)$

75. $\dfrac{\ln x}{\ln 7}$

For Thought

1. True **2.** True **3.** False, they cannot be multiplied since the number of columns of A is not the same as the number of rows of C.

4. False, the order of CA is 2×1. **5.** True

6. True, $BC = [7 \cdot 2 + 9 \cdot 4 \quad 7 \cdot 3 + 9 \cdot 5] =$
$= [14 + 36 \quad 21 + 45] = [50 \quad 66]$.

7. True, $AB = \begin{bmatrix} 1 \\ 6 \end{bmatrix}[7 \quad 9] = \begin{bmatrix} 1 \cdot 7 & 1 \cdot 9 \\ 6 \cdot 7 & 6 \cdot 9 \end{bmatrix} =$

$= \begin{bmatrix} 7 & 9 \\ 42 & 54 \end{bmatrix}$.

8. True, $\begin{bmatrix} 2 & 3 \\ 4 & 5 \end{bmatrix}\begin{bmatrix} 2 & -1 \\ 0 & 3 \end{bmatrix} =$

$\begin{bmatrix} 4+0 & -2+9 \\ 8+0 & -4+15 \end{bmatrix} = \begin{bmatrix} 4 & 7 \\ 8 & 11 \end{bmatrix}$.

9. True, $BA = [7 \quad 9]\begin{bmatrix} 1 \\ 6 \end{bmatrix} = [7 + 54] = [61]$.

10. False, since $EC = \begin{bmatrix} 2 & -1 \\ 0 & 3 \end{bmatrix}\begin{bmatrix} 2 & 3 \\ 4 & 5 \end{bmatrix} =$

$= \begin{bmatrix} 4-4 & 6-5 \\ 0+12 & 0+15 \end{bmatrix} = \begin{bmatrix} 0 & 1 \\ 12 & 15 \end{bmatrix}$ and from

Exercise 8 one sees $EC \neq CE$.

3 Exercises

1. 3×5 **3.** 1×1 **5.** 5×5

7. 3×3

9. undefined

11. $[-3(4) + 2(1)] = [-10]$

13. $\begin{bmatrix} 1(1) + 3(3) \\ 2(1) + (-4)(3) \end{bmatrix} = \begin{bmatrix} 10 \\ -10 \end{bmatrix}$

15. $\begin{bmatrix} 5(1) + 1(3) & 5(2) + 1(1) \\ 2(1) + 1(3) & 2(2) + 1(1) \end{bmatrix} = \begin{bmatrix} 8 & 11 \\ 5 & 5 \end{bmatrix}$

17. $\begin{bmatrix} 3(5) & 3(6) \\ 1(5) & 1(6) \end{bmatrix} = \begin{bmatrix} 15 & 18 \\ 5 & 6 \end{bmatrix}$

19. $AB = \begin{bmatrix} 1(1) + 3(-1) & 1(0) + 3(1) & 1(1) + 3(0) \\ 2(1) + 4(-1) & 2(0) + 4(1) & 2(1) + 4(0) \\ 5(1) + 6(-1) & 5(0) + 6(1) & 5(1) + 6(0) \end{bmatrix}$

$= \begin{bmatrix} -2 & 3 & 1 \\ -2 & 4 & 2 \\ -1 & 6 & 5 \end{bmatrix}$ and

$BA = \begin{bmatrix} 1(1) + 0(2) + 1(5) & 1(3) + 0(4) + 1(6) \\ -1(1) + 1(2) + 0(5) & -1(3) + 1(4) + 0(6) \end{bmatrix}$

$= \begin{bmatrix} 6 & 9 \\ 1 & 1 \end{bmatrix}$

21. $AB =$

$\begin{bmatrix} 1(1) + 2(0) + 3(0) & 1(1) + 2(1) + 3(0) & 1(1) + 2(1) + 3(1) \\ 2(1) + 1(0) + 3(0) & 2(1) + 1(1) + 3(0) & 2(1) + 1(1) + 3(1) \\ 3(1) + 2(0) + 1(0) & 3(1) + 2(1) + 1(0) & 3(1) + 2(1) + 1(1) \end{bmatrix}$

$= \begin{bmatrix} 1 & 3 & 6 \\ 2 & 3 & 6 \\ 3 & 5 & 6 \end{bmatrix}$ and

$BA =$

$\begin{bmatrix} 1(1) + 1(2) + 1(3) & 1(2) + 1(1) + 1(2) & 1(3) + 1(3) + 1(1) \\ 0(1) + 1(2) + 1(3) & 0(2) + 1(1) + 1(2) & 0(3) + 1(3) + 1(1) \\ 0(1) + 0(2) + 1(3) & 0(2) + 0(1) + 1(2) & 0(3) + 0(3) + 1(1) \end{bmatrix}$

$$= \begin{bmatrix} 6 & 5 & 7 \\ 5 & 3 & 4 \\ 3 & 2 & 1 \end{bmatrix}$$

23.

$$AB = \begin{bmatrix} 2\cdot2 & 2\cdot3 & 2\cdot4 \\ -3\cdot2 & -3\cdot3 & -3\cdot4 \\ 1\cdot2 & 1\cdot3 & 1\cdot4 \end{bmatrix} =$$

$$\begin{bmatrix} 4 & 6 & 8 \\ -6 & -9 & -12 \\ 2 & 3 & 4 \end{bmatrix}$$

25. $\begin{bmatrix} 2+0+0 & 2+3+0 & 2+3+4 \end{bmatrix} =$

$$\begin{bmatrix} 2 & 5 & 9 \end{bmatrix}$$

27. Undefined

29.

$$EC = \begin{bmatrix} 2+4+1 & 3+5+0 \\ 0+4+1 & 0+5+0 \\ 0+0+1 & 0+0+0 \end{bmatrix} = \begin{bmatrix} 7 & 8 \\ 5 & 5 \\ 1 & 0 \end{bmatrix}$$

31.

$$DC = \begin{bmatrix} 4-4+1 & 6-5+0 \\ 0+12+2 & 0+15+0 \end{bmatrix} =$$

$$\begin{bmatrix} 1 & 1 \\ 14 & 15 \end{bmatrix}$$

33. Undefined

35.

$$EA = \begin{bmatrix} 2-3+1 \\ 0-3+1 \\ 0+0+1 \end{bmatrix} = \begin{bmatrix} 0 \\ -2 \\ 1 \end{bmatrix}$$

37. undefined

39. We will use the answer in Exercise 23.

$$AB + 2E =$$

$$\begin{bmatrix} 4 & 6 & 8 \\ -6 & -9 & -12 \\ 2 & 3 & 4 \end{bmatrix} + \begin{bmatrix} 2 & 2 & 2 \\ 0 & 2 & 2 \\ 0 & 0 & 2 \end{bmatrix}$$

$$= \begin{bmatrix} 6 & 8 & 10 \\ -6 & -7 & -10 \\ 2 & 3 & 6 \end{bmatrix}$$

41. $A^2 = \begin{bmatrix} 1 & 0 \\ 1 & 1 \end{bmatrix}\begin{bmatrix} 1 & 0 \\ 1 & 1 \end{bmatrix} =$

$$\begin{bmatrix} 1(1)+0(1) & 1(0)+0(1) \\ 1(1)+1(1) & 1(0)+1(1) \end{bmatrix} = \begin{bmatrix} 1 & 0 \\ 2 & 1 \end{bmatrix}$$

43. We will use the answer in Exercise 42.

$$A^4 = A^3 A = \begin{bmatrix} 1 & 0 \\ 3 & 1 \end{bmatrix}\begin{bmatrix} 1 & 0 \\ 1 & 1 \end{bmatrix} =$$

$$\begin{bmatrix} 1(1)+0(1) & 1(0)+0(1) \\ 3(1)+1(1) & 3(0)+1(1) \end{bmatrix} = \begin{bmatrix} 1 & 0 \\ 4 & 1 \end{bmatrix}$$

45.

$$\begin{bmatrix} 2\cdot1+0\cdot0 & 2\cdot1+0\cdot1 \\ 3\cdot1+1\cdot0 & 3\cdot1+1\cdot1 \end{bmatrix} = \begin{bmatrix} 2 & 2 \\ 3 & 4 \end{bmatrix}$$

47.

$$\begin{bmatrix} 7\cdot3+4\cdot(-5) & 7\cdot(-4)+4\cdot7 \\ 5\cdot3+3\cdot(-5) & 5\cdot(-4)+3\cdot7 \end{bmatrix} =$$

$$\begin{bmatrix} 1 & 0 \\ 0 & 1 \end{bmatrix}$$

49.

$$\begin{bmatrix} -0.5\cdot1+4\cdot0 & -0.5\cdot0+4\cdot1 \\ 9\cdot1+0.7\cdot0 & 9\cdot0+0.7\cdot1 \end{bmatrix} =$$

$$\begin{bmatrix} -0.5 & 4 \\ 9 & 0.7 \end{bmatrix}$$

51. $\begin{bmatrix} -2a+6a & -6b+3b \end{bmatrix} = \begin{bmatrix} 4a & -3b \end{bmatrix}$

53.

$$\begin{bmatrix} -2a+0\cdot1 & 5a+0\cdot4 & 3a+0\cdot6 \\ 0\cdot(-2)+b & 0\cdot5+4b & 0\cdot3+6b \end{bmatrix} =$$

$$\begin{bmatrix} -2a & 5a & 3a \\ b & 4b & 6b \end{bmatrix}$$

55. $\begin{bmatrix} 1\cdot1+2\cdot0+3\cdot1 & 1\cdot0+2\cdot1+3\cdot0 & 1\cdot1+2\cdot1+3\cdot1 \end{bmatrix}$
$= \begin{bmatrix} 4 & 2 & 6 \end{bmatrix}$

57. $[-1\cdot(-5)+0\cdot1+3\cdot4] = [17]$

59.

$$\begin{bmatrix} x^2 & xy \\ xy & y^2 \end{bmatrix}$$

61.

$$\begin{bmatrix} -1\cdot\sqrt{2}+2\cdot0+3\sqrt{2} \\ 3\cdot\sqrt{2}+4\cdot0+4\sqrt{2} \end{bmatrix} = \begin{bmatrix} 2\sqrt{2} \\ 7\sqrt{2} \end{bmatrix}$$

63.
$$\begin{bmatrix} (1/2)\cdot(-8)+(1/3)\cdot(-5) & 6+(1/3)\cdot 15 \\ (1/4)\cdot(-8)+(1/5)\cdot(-5) & 3+(1/5)\cdot 15 \end{bmatrix}$$
$$=\begin{bmatrix} -4-(5/3) & 6+5 \\ -2-1 & 3+3 \end{bmatrix}=\begin{bmatrix} -17/3 & 11 \\ -3 & 6 \end{bmatrix}$$

65. undefined

67.
$$\begin{bmatrix} 9+0-7 & 8+0-8 & 10+0-4 \\ 0+3+0 & 0+5+0 & 0+2+0 \\ 9+3+7 & 8+5+8 & 10+2+4 \end{bmatrix}=$$
$$\begin{bmatrix} 2 & 0 & 6 \\ 3 & 5 & 2 \\ 19 & 21 & 16 \end{bmatrix}$$

69.
$$\begin{bmatrix} 1-0.6-0.6 & 1.5+1.2-1 \\ 0.8+0.4+1.8 & 1.2-0.8+3 \\ 0.4+0.6-2.4 & 0.6-1.2-4 \end{bmatrix}=$$
$$\begin{bmatrix} -0.2 & 1.7 \\ 3 & 3.4 \\ -1.4 & -4.6 \end{bmatrix}$$

71. System of equations is
$$\begin{aligned} 2x-3y &= 0 \\ x+2y &= 7. \end{aligned}$$

Multiply second equation by -2 and add to the first one.
$$\begin{aligned} 2x-3y &= 0 \\ -2x-4y &= -14 \\ \hline -7y &= -14 \end{aligned}$$

Substitute $y=2$ into $x+2y=7$. Then $x+4=7$ and $x=3$. Solution set is $\{(3,2)\}$.

73. System of equations is
$$\begin{aligned} 2x+3y &= 5 \\ 4x+6y &= 9 \end{aligned}$$

Multiply first equation by -2 and add to the second one.
$$\begin{aligned} -4x-6y &= -10 \\ 4x+6y &= 9 \\ \hline 0 &= -1 \end{aligned}$$

Inconsistent and the solution set is $\emptyset$.

75. System of equations is
$$\begin{aligned} x+y+z &= 4 \\ y+z &= 5 \\ z &= 6. \end{aligned}$$

Substitute $z=6$ into $y+z=5$ to get $y+6=5$ and $y=-1$. From $x+y+z=4$, we have $x-1+6=4$ and $x=-1$. Solution set is $\{(-1,-1,6)\}$.

77.
$$\begin{bmatrix} 2 & 3 \\ 4 & -1 \end{bmatrix}\begin{bmatrix} x \\ y \end{bmatrix}=\begin{bmatrix} 9 \\ 6 \end{bmatrix}$$

79.
$$\begin{bmatrix} 1 & 2 & -1 \\ 3 & -1 & 3 \\ 2 & 1 & -4 \end{bmatrix}\begin{bmatrix} x \\ y \\ z \end{bmatrix}=\begin{bmatrix} 3 \\ 1 \\ 0 \end{bmatrix}$$

81.
$$A=\begin{bmatrix} \$24,000 & \$40,000 \\ \$38,000 & \$70,000 \end{bmatrix}, Q=\begin{bmatrix} 4 \\ 7 \end{bmatrix}, \text{ and}$$

matrix product $AQ=\begin{bmatrix} \$376,000 \\ \$642,000 \end{bmatrix}$

represents the costs for labor and material for building 4 economy houses and 7 deluxe models.

83. False

85. True

87. True

89. $A+3B=\begin{bmatrix} 1 & 2 \\ -3 & 5 \end{bmatrix}+\begin{bmatrix} -3 & 9 \\ 6 & 12 \end{bmatrix}=$
$$\begin{bmatrix} -2 & 11 \\ 3 & 17 \end{bmatrix}$$

91. Independent since the lines have different slopes, namely, -9 and 500.

93. Let $f(x)=\dfrac{x-9}{x+99}\le 0$.

If $x=10$, then $f(10)>0$.
If $x=0$, then $f(0)<0$.
If $x=-100$, then $f(100)>0$.

$$+ \quad U \quad - \quad 0 \quad +$$

$$0 \quad -99 \ 10 \quad 9 \quad 100$$

The solution set is $(-99, 9]$.

For Thought

1. True, $AB = \begin{bmatrix} 10-9 & -6+6 \\ 15-15 & -9+10 \end{bmatrix} =$

$$= \begin{bmatrix} 1 & 0 \\ 0 & 1 \end{bmatrix} = \begin{bmatrix} 10-9 & 15-15 \\ -6+6 & -9+10 \end{bmatrix} = BA.$$

2. True, $AB = BA = I$ by Exercise 1.

3. True, A is the inverse of B by Exercise 1.

4. False, AC is undefined, although CA is defined. **5.** True

6. False, a non-square matrix has no inverse.

7. False, the coefficient matrix is $\begin{bmatrix} 2 & 3 \\ 3 & 1 \end{bmatrix}$.

8. True, since $A^{-1} = B$ then $A^{-1}D =$

$$= \begin{bmatrix} 5 & -3 \\ -3 & 2 \end{bmatrix} \begin{bmatrix} 11 \\ 19 \end{bmatrix} = \begin{bmatrix} -2 \\ 5 \end{bmatrix}.$$

9. False, $(-2, 5)$ does not satisfy $3x + y = 19$.

10. False, the solution is $\begin{bmatrix} 2 & 3 \\ 3 & 1 \end{bmatrix}^{-1} \begin{bmatrix} 3 \\ -7 \end{bmatrix}$.

4 Exercises

1.

$$AI = \begin{bmatrix} 1 & 3 \\ 4 & 6 \end{bmatrix} \begin{bmatrix} 1 & 0 \\ 0 & 1 \end{bmatrix}$$

$$= \begin{bmatrix} 1(1) + 3(0) & 1(0) + 3(1) \\ 4(1) + 6(0) & 4(0) + 6(1) \end{bmatrix}$$

$$= \begin{bmatrix} 1 & 3 \\ 4 & 6 \end{bmatrix}$$

$$= A$$

and

$$IA = \begin{bmatrix} 1 & 0 \\ 0 & 1 \end{bmatrix} \begin{bmatrix} 1 & 3 \\ 4 & 6 \end{bmatrix}$$

$$= \begin{bmatrix} 1(1) + 0(4) & 1(3) + 0(6) \\ 0(1) + 1(4) & 0(3) + 1(6) \end{bmatrix}$$

$$= \begin{bmatrix} 1 & 3 \\ 4 & 6 \end{bmatrix}$$

$$= A$$

3. $AI = \begin{bmatrix} 3 & 2 & 1 \\ 5 & 6 & 2 \\ 7 & 8 & 3 \end{bmatrix} \begin{bmatrix} 1 & 0 & 0 \\ 0 & 1 & 0 \\ 0 & 0 & 1 \end{bmatrix} =$

$$\begin{bmatrix} 3(1) + 2(0) + 1(0) & 3(0) + 2(1) + 1(0) & 3(0) + 2(0) + 1(1) \\ 5(1) + 6(0) + 2(0) & 5(0) + 6(1) + 2(0) & 5(0) + 6(0) + 2(1) \\ 7(1) + 8(0) + 3(0) & 7(0) + 8(1) + 3(0) & 7(0) + 8(0) + 3(1) \end{bmatrix}$$

$$= \begin{bmatrix} 3 & 2 & 1 \\ 5 & 6 & 2 \\ 7 & 8 & 3 \end{bmatrix} = A$$

and

$$IA = \begin{bmatrix} 1 & 0 & 0 \\ 0 & 1 & 0 \\ 0 & 0 & 1 \end{bmatrix} \begin{bmatrix} 3 & 2 & 1 \\ 5 & 6 & 2 \\ 7 & 8 & 3 \end{bmatrix} =$$

$$\begin{bmatrix} 1(3) + 0(5) + 0(7) & 1(2) + 0(6) + 0(8) & 1(1) + 0(2) + 0(3) \\ 0(3) + 1(5) + 0(7) & 0(2) + 1(6) + 0(8) & 0(1) + 1(2) + 0(3) \\ 0(3) + 0(5) + 1(7) & 0(2) + 0(6) + 1(8) & 0(1) + 0(2) + 1(3) \end{bmatrix}$$

$$= \begin{bmatrix} 3 & 2 & 1 \\ 5 & 6 & 2 \\ 7 & 8 & 3 \end{bmatrix} = A$$

5.

$$I \begin{bmatrix} -3 & 5 \\ 12 & 6 \end{bmatrix} = \begin{bmatrix} -3 & 5 \\ 12 & 6 \end{bmatrix}$$

7.

$$\begin{bmatrix} -8+9 & -6+6 \\ 12-12 & 9-8 \end{bmatrix} = \begin{bmatrix} 1 & 0 \\ 0 & 1 \end{bmatrix}$$

9.

$$\begin{bmatrix} 5-4 & -4+4 \\ 5-5 & -4+5 \end{bmatrix} = \begin{bmatrix} 1 & 0 \\ 0 & 1 \end{bmatrix}$$

11.

$$\begin{bmatrix} 3 & 5 & 1 \\ 4 & 5 & 7 \\ 4 & 9 & 2 \end{bmatrix} I = \begin{bmatrix} 3 & 5 & 1 \\ 4 & 5 & 7 \\ 4 & 9 & 2 \end{bmatrix}$$

13.

$$\begin{bmatrix} 0+0+1 & 1+0-1 & -3+0+3 \\ 0+0+0 & 1+0+0 & -3+3+0 \\ 0+0+0 & 0+0+0 & 0+1+0 \end{bmatrix} =$$

$$\begin{bmatrix} 1 & 0 & 0 \\ 0 & 1 & 0 \\ 0 & 0 & 1 \end{bmatrix}$$

15.

$$\begin{bmatrix} 0.5+0.5+0 & -0.5+0.5+0 & 0.5-0.5+0 \\ 0+0.5-0.5 & 0+0.5+0.5 & 0-0.5+0.5 \\ 0.5+0-0.5 & -0.5+0+0.5 & 0.5+0+0.5 \end{bmatrix} =$$

$$\begin{bmatrix} 1 & 0 & 0 \\ 0 & 1 & 0 \\ 0 & 0 & 1 \end{bmatrix}$$

17.

Yes, since $\begin{bmatrix} 3 & 1 \\ 11 & 4 \end{bmatrix} \begin{bmatrix} 4 & -1 \\ -11 & 3 \end{bmatrix} =$

$\begin{bmatrix} 12-11 & -3+3 \\ 44-44 & -11+12 \end{bmatrix} = \begin{bmatrix} 1 & 0 \\ 0 & 1 \end{bmatrix}$ and

similarly $\begin{bmatrix} 4 & -1 \\ -11 & 3 \end{bmatrix} \begin{bmatrix} 3 & 1 \\ 11 & 4 \end{bmatrix} = I.$

19.

No, since $\begin{bmatrix} 1/2 & -1 \\ 3 & -12 \end{bmatrix} \begin{bmatrix} 4 & 2 \\ 1 & 1 \end{bmatrix} =$

$\begin{bmatrix} 2-1 & 1-1 \\ 12-12 & 6-12 \end{bmatrix} = \begin{bmatrix} 1 & 0 \\ 0 & -6 \end{bmatrix} \neq I.$

21. No, since only square matrices may have inverses.

23.

On $\begin{bmatrix} 1 & 4 & | & 1 & 0 \\ 0 & 2 & | & 0 & 1 \end{bmatrix}$, use $-2R_2 + R_1 \to R_1$ to get

$\begin{bmatrix} 1 & 0 & | & 1 & -2 \\ 0 & 2 & | & 0 & 1 \end{bmatrix}$, use $\frac{1}{2}R_2 \to R_2$ to get

$\begin{bmatrix} 1 & 0 & | & 1 & -2 \\ 0 & 1 & | & 0 & 1/2 \end{bmatrix}$. Then $A^{-1} = \begin{bmatrix} 1 & -2 \\ 0 & 1/2 \end{bmatrix}.$

25.

On $\begin{bmatrix} 1 & 6 & | & 1 & 0 \\ 1 & 9 & | & 0 & 1 \end{bmatrix}$, use $-1R_1 + R_2 \to R_2$ to get

$\begin{bmatrix} 1 & 6 & | & 1 & 0 \\ 0 & 3 & | & -1 & 1 \end{bmatrix}$, use $-2R_2 + R_1 \to R_1$ to get

$\begin{bmatrix} 1 & 0 & | & 3 & -2 \\ 0 & 3 & | & -1 & 1 \end{bmatrix}$, use $\frac{1}{3}R_2 \to R_2$ to get

$\begin{bmatrix} 1 & 0 & | & 3 & -2 \\ 0 & 1 & | & -1/3 & 1/3 \end{bmatrix}.$

Thus, $A^{-1} = \begin{bmatrix} 3 & -2 \\ -1/3 & 1/3 \end{bmatrix}.$

27.

On $\begin{bmatrix} -2 & -3 & | & 1 & 0 \\ 3 & 4 & | & 0 & 1 \end{bmatrix}$, use $R_2 + R_1 \to R_1$ to get

$\begin{bmatrix} 1 & 1 & | & 1 & 1 \\ 3 & 4 & | & 0 & 1 \end{bmatrix}$, use $-3R_1 + R_2 \to R_2$ to get

$\begin{bmatrix} 1 & 1 & | & 1 & 1 \\ 0 & 1 & | & -3 & -2 \end{bmatrix}$, use $-1R_2 + R_1 \to R_1$ to get

$\begin{bmatrix} 1 & 0 & | & 4 & 3 \\ 0 & 1 & | & -3 & -2 \end{bmatrix}.$ So $A^{-1} = \begin{bmatrix} 4 & 3 \\ -3 & -2 \end{bmatrix}.$

29.

On $\begin{bmatrix} 1 & -5 & | & 1 & 0 \\ -1 & 3 & | & 0 & 1 \end{bmatrix}$, use $R_1 + R_2 \to R_2$ to get

$\begin{bmatrix} 1 & -5 & | & 1 & 0 \\ 0 & -2 & | & 1 & 1 \end{bmatrix}$, use $-\frac{1}{2}R_2 \to R_2$ to get

$\begin{bmatrix} 1 & -5 & | & 1 & 0 \\ 0 & 1 & | & -1/2 & -1/2 \end{bmatrix}$, use

$5R_2 + R_1 \to R_1$ to get

$\begin{bmatrix} 1 & 0 & | & -3/2 & -5/2 \\ 0 & 1 & | & -1/2 & -1/2 \end{bmatrix}.$

Then $A^{-1} = \begin{bmatrix} -3/2 & -5/2 \\ -1/2 & -1/2 \end{bmatrix}.$

31.

On $\begin{bmatrix} -1 & 5 & | & 1 & 0 \\ 2 & -10 & | & 0 & 1 \end{bmatrix}$, use $R_1 + R_2 \to R_1$

and $\frac{1}{2}R_2 \rightarrow R_2$ to get

$$\begin{bmatrix} 1 & -5 & | & 1 & 1 \\ 1 & -5 & | & 0 & 1/2 \end{bmatrix}, \text{ use } -1R_2 + R_1 \rightarrow R_1 \text{ to}$$

get

$$\begin{bmatrix} 0 & 0 & | & 1 & 1/2 \\ 1 & -5 & | & 0 & 1/2 \end{bmatrix}. \text{ So } A \text{ has no inverse.}$$

33.

On $\begin{bmatrix} 1 & 1 & 0 & | & 1 & 0 & 0 \\ 0 & -1 & -1 & | & 0 & 1 & 0 \\ 1 & 0 & -1 & | & 0 & 0 & 1 \end{bmatrix}$, use

$R_2 + R_1 \rightarrow R_1$ and $-1R_3 + R_1 \rightarrow R_3$ to get

$\begin{bmatrix} 1 & 0 & -1 & | & 1 & 1 & 0 \\ 0 & -1 & -1 & | & 0 & 1 & 0 \\ 0 & 1 & 1 & | & 1 & 0 & -1 \end{bmatrix}$, use

$R_2 + R_3 \rightarrow R_2$ to get

$\begin{bmatrix} 1 & 0 & -1 & | & 1 & 1 & 0 \\ 0 & 0 & 0 & | & 1 & 1 & -1 \\ 0 & 1 & 1 & | & 1 & 0 & 1 \end{bmatrix}$. So A^{-1} does not

exist.

35.

On $\begin{bmatrix} 1 & 1 & 1 & | & 1 & 0 & 0 \\ 1 & -1 & -1 & | & 0 & 1 & 0 \\ 1 & -1 & 1 & | & 0 & 0 & 1 \end{bmatrix}$, use

$R_1 + R_2 \rightarrow R_2$ and $R_2 + (-1R_3) \rightarrow R_3$ to get

$\begin{bmatrix} 1 & 1 & 1 & | & 1 & 0 & 0 \\ 2 & 0 & 0 & | & 1 & 1 & 0 \\ 0 & 0 & -2 & | & 0 & 1 & -1 \end{bmatrix}$, use

$-2R_1 + R_2 \rightarrow R_2$ and $-\frac{1}{2}R_3 \rightarrow R_3$ to get

$\begin{bmatrix} 1 & 1 & 1 & | & 1 & 0 & 0 \\ 0 & -2 & -2 & | & -1 & 1 & 0 \\ 0 & 0 & 1 & | & 0 & -1/2 & 1/2 \end{bmatrix}$, use

$-\frac{1}{2}R_2 \rightarrow R_2$ to get

$\begin{bmatrix} 1 & 1 & 1 & | & 1 & 0 & 0 \\ 0 & 1 & 1 & | & 1/2 & -1/2 & 0 \\ 0 & 0 & 1 & | & 0 & -1/2 & 1/2 \end{bmatrix}$, use

$-1R_2 + R_1 \rightarrow R_1$ to get

$\begin{bmatrix} 1 & 0 & 0 & | & 1/2 & 1/2 & 0 \\ 0 & 1 & 1 & | & 1/2 & -1/2 & 0 \\ 0 & 0 & 1 & | & 0 & -1/2 & 1/2 \end{bmatrix}$, use

$-1R_3 + R_2 \rightarrow R_2$ to get

$$\begin{bmatrix} 1 & 0 & 0 & | & 1/2 & 1/2 & 0 \\ 0 & 1 & 0 & | & 1/2 & 0 & -1/2 \\ 0 & 0 & 1 & | & 0 & -1/2 & 1/2 \end{bmatrix}.$$

So $A^{-1} = \begin{bmatrix} 1/2 & 1/2 & 0 \\ 1/2 & 0 & -1/2 \\ 0 & -1/2 & 1/2 \end{bmatrix}.$

37.

On $\begin{bmatrix} 0 & 2 & 0 & | & 1 & 0 & 0 \\ 3 & 3 & 2 & | & 0 & 1 & 0 \\ 2 & 5 & 1 & | & 0 & 0 & 1 \end{bmatrix}$, use

$-1R_3 + R_2 \rightarrow R_3$ to get

$\begin{bmatrix} 0 & 2 & 0 & | & 1 & 0 & 0 \\ 3 & 3 & 2 & | & 0 & 1 & 0 \\ 1 & -2 & 1 & | & 0 & 1 & -1 \end{bmatrix}$, use

$R_3 \rightarrow R_1$ and $R_1 \rightarrow R_3$ to get

$\begin{bmatrix} 1 & -2 & 1 & | & 0 & 1 & -1 \\ 3 & 3 & 2 & | & 0 & 1 & 0 \\ 0 & 2 & 0 & | & 1 & 0 & 0 \end{bmatrix}$, use

$R_3 + R_1 \rightarrow R_1$ and $-1R_3 + R_2 \rightarrow R_2$ to get

$\begin{bmatrix} 1 & 0 & 1 & | & 1 & 1 & -1 \\ 3 & 1 & 2 & | & -1 & 1 & 0 \\ 0 & 2 & 0 & | & 1 & 0 & 0 \end{bmatrix}$, use

$-3R_1 + R_2 \rightarrow R_2$ to get

$\begin{bmatrix} 1 & 0 & 1 & | & 1 & 1 & -1 \\ 0 & 1 & -1 & | & -4 & -2 & 3 \\ 0 & 2 & 0 & | & 1 & 0 & 0 \end{bmatrix}$, use

$-2R_2 + R_3 \rightarrow R_3$ to get

$\begin{bmatrix} 1 & 0 & 1 & | & 1 & 1 & -1 \\ 0 & 1 & -1 & | & -4 & -2 & 3 \\ 0 & 0 & 2 & | & 9 & 4 & -6 \end{bmatrix}$, use

$\frac{1}{2}R_3 \rightarrow R_3$ to get

$\begin{bmatrix} 1 & 0 & 1 & | & 1 & 1 & -1 \\ 0 & 1 & -1 & | & -4 & -2 & 3 \\ 0 & 0 & 1 & | & 9/2 & 2 & -3 \end{bmatrix}$, use

$R_2 + R_3 \rightarrow R_2$ to get

$\begin{bmatrix} 1 & 0 & 1 & | & 1 & 1 & -1 \\ 0 & 1 & 0 & | & 1/2 & 0 & 0 \\ 0 & 0 & 1 & | & 9/2 & 2 & -3 \end{bmatrix}$, use

$-1R_3 + R_1 \rightarrow R_1$ to get

$$\begin{bmatrix} 1 & 0 & 0 & \bigm| & -7/2 & -1 & 2 \\ 0 & 1 & 0 & \bigm| & 1/2 & 0 & 0 \\ 0 & 0 & 1 & \bigm| & 9/2 & 2 & -3 \end{bmatrix}.$$

So $A^{-1} = \begin{bmatrix} -7/2 & -1 & 2 \\ 1/2 & 0 & 0 \\ 9/2 & 2 & -3 \end{bmatrix}.$

39.

On $\begin{bmatrix} 1 & 0 & 1 & \bigm| & 1 & 0 & 0 \\ 0 & 2 & 2 & \bigm| & 0 & 1 & 0 \\ 2 & 1 & 0 & \bigm| & 0 & 0 & 1 \end{bmatrix}$, use

$2R_1 + (-1R_3) \to R_3$ and $\dfrac{1}{2}R_2 \to R_2$ to get

$\begin{bmatrix} 1 & 0 & 1 & \bigm| & 1 & 0 & 0 \\ 0 & 1 & 1 & \bigm| & 0 & 1/2 & 0 \\ 0 & -1 & 2 & \bigm| & 2 & 0 & -1 \end{bmatrix}$, use

$R_2 + R_3 \to R_3$ to get

$\begin{bmatrix} 1 & 0 & 1 & \bigm| & 1 & 0 & 0 \\ 0 & 1 & 1 & \bigm| & 0 & 1/2 & 0 \\ 0 & 0 & 3 & \bigm| & 2 & 1/2 & -1 \end{bmatrix}$, use

$\dfrac{1}{3}R_3 \to R_3$ to get

$\begin{bmatrix} 1 & 0 & 1 & \bigm| & 1 & 0 & 0 \\ 0 & 1 & 1 & \bigm| & 0 & 1/2 & 0 \\ 0 & 0 & 1 & \bigm| & 2/3 & 1/6 & -1/3 \end{bmatrix}$, use

$-1R_3 + R_2 \to R_2$ and $-1R_3 + R_1 \to R_1$ to get

$\begin{bmatrix} 1 & 0 & 0 & \bigm| & 1/3 & -1/6 & 1/3 \\ 0 & 1 & 0 & \bigm| & -2/3 & 1/3 & 1/3 \\ 0 & 0 & 1 & \bigm| & 2/3 & 1/6 & -1/3 \end{bmatrix}.$

Then $A^{-1} = \begin{bmatrix} 1/3 & -1/6 & 1/3 \\ -2/3 & 1/3 & 1/3 \\ 2/3 & 1/6 & -1/3 \end{bmatrix}.$

41.

On $\begin{bmatrix} 0 & 4 & 2 & \bigm| & 1 & 0 & 0 \\ 0 & 3 & 2 & \bigm| & 0 & 1 & 0 \\ 1 & -1 & 1 & \bigm| & 0 & 0 & 1 \end{bmatrix}$, use

$R_1 \to R_3$ and $R_3 \to R_1$ to get

$\begin{bmatrix} 1 & -1 & 1 & \bigm| & 0 & 0 & 1 \\ 0 & 3 & 2 & \bigm| & 0 & 1 & 0 \\ 0 & 4 & 2 & \bigm| & 1 & 0 & 0 \end{bmatrix}$, use

$-1R_2 + R_3 \to R_2$ to get

$\begin{bmatrix} 1 & -1 & 1 & \bigm| & 0 & 0 & 1 \\ 0 & 1 & 0 & \bigm| & 1 & -1 & 0 \\ 0 & 4 & 2 & \bigm| & 1 & 0 & 0 \end{bmatrix}$, use

$R_1 + R_2 \to R_1$ to get

$\begin{bmatrix} 1 & 0 & 1 & \bigm| & 1 & -1 & 1 \\ 0 & 1 & 0 & \bigm| & 1 & -1 & 0 \\ 0 & 4 & 2 & \bigm| & 1 & 0 & 0 \end{bmatrix}$, use

$-4R_2 + R_3 \to R_3$ to get

$\begin{bmatrix} 1 & 0 & 1 & \bigm| & 1 & -1 & 1 \\ 0 & 1 & 0 & \bigm| & 1 & -1 & 0 \\ 0 & 0 & 2 & \bigm| & -3 & 4 & 0 \end{bmatrix}$, use

$\dfrac{1}{2}R_3 \to R_3$ to get

$\begin{bmatrix} 1 & 0 & 1 & \bigm| & 1 & -1 & 1 \\ 0 & 1 & 0 & \bigm| & 1 & -1 & 0 \\ 0 & 0 & 1 & \bigm| & -3/2 & 2 & 0 \end{bmatrix}$, use

$-1R_3 + R_1 \to R_1$ to get

$\begin{bmatrix} 1 & 0 & 0 & \bigm| & 5/2 & -3 & 1 \\ 0 & 1 & 0 & \bigm| & 1 & -1 & 0 \\ 0 & 0 & 1 & \bigm| & -3/2 & 2 & 0 \end{bmatrix}.$

Then $A^{-1} = \begin{bmatrix} 5/2 & -3 & 1 \\ 1 & -1 & 0 \\ -3/2 & 2 & 0 \end{bmatrix}.$

43.

On $\begin{bmatrix} 1 & 2 & 3 & 4 & \bigm| & 1 & 0 & 0 & 0 \\ 0 & 1 & 2 & 3 & \bigm| & 0 & 1 & 0 & 0 \\ 0 & 0 & 1 & 2 & \bigm| & 0 & 0 & 1 & 0 \\ 0 & 0 & 0 & 1 & \bigm| & 0 & 0 & 0 & 1 \end{bmatrix}$, use

$-2R_2 + R_1 \to R_1$ to get

$\begin{bmatrix} 1 & 0 & -1 & -2 & \bigm| & 1 & -2 & 0 & 0 \\ 0 & 1 & 2 & 3 & \bigm| & 0 & 1 & 0 & 0 \\ 0 & 0 & 1 & 2 & \bigm| & 0 & 0 & 1 & 0 \\ 0 & 0 & 0 & 1 & \bigm| & 0 & 0 & 0 & 1 \end{bmatrix}$, use

$-2R_4 + R_3 \to R_3$ to get

$\begin{bmatrix} 1 & 0 & -1 & -2 & \bigm| & 1 & -2 & 0 & 0 \\ 0 & 1 & 2 & 3 & \bigm| & 0 & 1 & 0 & 0 \\ 0 & 0 & 1 & 0 & \bigm| & 0 & 0 & 1 & -2 \\ 0 & 0 & 0 & 1 & \bigm| & 0 & 0 & 0 & 1 \end{bmatrix}$, use

$-2R_3 + R_2 \to R_2$ and $-2R_4 + R_3 \to R_3$ to get

$\begin{bmatrix} 1 & 0 & -1 & -2 & \bigm| & 1 & -2 & 0 & 0 \\ 0 & 1 & 0 & 3 & \bigm| & 0 & 1 & -2 & 4 \\ 0 & 0 & 1 & -2 & \bigm| & 0 & 0 & 1 & -4 \\ 0 & 0 & 0 & 1 & \bigm| & 0 & 0 & 0 & 1 \end{bmatrix}$, use

$R_1 + R_3 \to R_1$ to get

$$\begin{bmatrix} 1 & 0 & 0 & -4 & | & 1 & -2 & 1 & -4 \\ 0 & 1 & 0 & 3 & | & 0 & 1 & -2 & 4 \\ 0 & 0 & 1 & -2 & | & 0 & 0 & 1 & -4 \\ 0 & 0 & 0 & 1 & | & 0 & 0 & 0 & 1 \end{bmatrix}, \text{ use}$$

$2R_4 + R_3 \to R_3$, $-3R_4 + R_2 \to R_2$ and
$4R_4 + R_1 \to R_1$ to get

$$\begin{bmatrix} 1 & 0 & 0 & 0 & | & 1 & -2 & 1 & 0 \\ 0 & 1 & 0 & 0 & | & 0 & 1 & -2 & 1 \\ 0 & 0 & 1 & 0 & | & 0 & 0 & 1 & -2 \\ 0 & 0 & 0 & 1 & | & 0 & 0 & 0 & 1 \end{bmatrix}.$$

Then $A^{-1} = \begin{bmatrix} 1 & -2 & 1 & 0 \\ 0 & 1 & -2 & 1 \\ 0 & 0 & 1 & -2 \\ 0 & 0 & 0 & 1 \end{bmatrix}.$

45.

Since the coefficient matrix is $A = \begin{bmatrix} 1 & 6 \\ 1 & 9 \end{bmatrix}$,

$$A^{-1}\begin{bmatrix} -3 \\ -6 \end{bmatrix} = \begin{bmatrix} 3 & -2 \\ -1/3 & 1/3 \end{bmatrix}\begin{bmatrix} -3 \\ -6 \end{bmatrix} =$$

$$= \begin{bmatrix} 3 \\ -1 \end{bmatrix}. \text{ The solution set is } \{(3, -1)\}.$$

47.

Since the coefficient matrix is $A = \begin{bmatrix} 1 & 6 \\ 1 & 9 \end{bmatrix}$,

$$A^{-1}\begin{bmatrix} 4 \\ 5 \end{bmatrix} = \begin{bmatrix} 3 & -2 \\ -1/3 & 1/3 \end{bmatrix}\begin{bmatrix} 4 \\ 5 \end{bmatrix} =$$

$$= \begin{bmatrix} 2 \\ 1/3 \end{bmatrix}. \text{ The solution set is } \{(2, 1/3)\}.$$

49.

Since the coefficient matrix is

$A = \begin{bmatrix} -2 & -3 \\ 3 & 4 \end{bmatrix}$, we get

$$A^{-1}\begin{bmatrix} 1 \\ -1 \end{bmatrix} = \begin{bmatrix} 4 & 3 \\ -3 & -2 \end{bmatrix}\begin{bmatrix} 1 \\ -1 \end{bmatrix} =$$

$$= \begin{bmatrix} 1 \\ -1 \end{bmatrix}. \text{ The solution set is } \{(1, -1)\}.$$

51.

Since the coefficient matrix is

$A = \begin{bmatrix} 1 & -5 \\ -1 & 3 \end{bmatrix}$, we obtain

$$A^{-1}\begin{bmatrix} -5 \\ 1 \end{bmatrix} = \begin{bmatrix} -3/2 & -5/2 \\ -1/2 & -1/2 \end{bmatrix}\begin{bmatrix} -5 \\ 1 \end{bmatrix} =$$

$$= \begin{bmatrix} 5 \\ 2 \end{bmatrix}. \text{ The solution set is } \{(5, 2)\}.$$

53.

Since coefficient matrix is

$A = \begin{bmatrix} 1 & 1 & 1 \\ 1 & -1 & -1 \\ 1 & -1 & 1 \end{bmatrix}$, we find $A^{-1}\begin{bmatrix} 3 \\ -1 \\ 5 \end{bmatrix} =$

$$= \begin{bmatrix} 1/2 & 1/2 & 0 \\ 1/2 & 0 & -1/2 \\ 0 & -1/2 & 1/2 \end{bmatrix}\begin{bmatrix} 3 \\ -1 \\ 5 \end{bmatrix} = \begin{bmatrix} 1 \\ -1 \\ 3 \end{bmatrix}.$$

The solution set is $\{(1, -1, 3)\}$.

55.

Since the coefficient matrix is

$A = \begin{bmatrix} 0 & 2 & 0 \\ 3 & 3 & 2 \\ 2 & 5 & 1 \end{bmatrix}$, we get $A^{-1}\begin{bmatrix} 6 \\ 16 \\ 19 \end{bmatrix} =$

$$= \begin{bmatrix} -7/2 & -1 & 2 \\ 1/2 & 0 & 0 \\ 9/2 & 2 & -3 \end{bmatrix}\begin{bmatrix} 6 \\ 16 \\ 19 \end{bmatrix} = \begin{bmatrix} 1 \\ 3 \\ 2 \end{bmatrix}.$$

The solution set is $\{(1, 3, 2)\}$.

57. The coefficient matrix of

$$0.3x + 0.1y = 3$$
$$2x + 4y = 7$$

is $A = \begin{bmatrix} 0.3 & 0.1 \\ 2 & 4 \end{bmatrix}$. Note $A^{-1}\begin{bmatrix} 3 \\ 7 \end{bmatrix} =$

$$\begin{bmatrix} 4 & -0.1 \\ -2 & 0.3 \end{bmatrix}\begin{bmatrix} 3 \\ 7 \end{bmatrix} = \begin{bmatrix} 11.3 \\ -3.9 \end{bmatrix}.$$

The solution set is $\{(11.3, -3.9)\}$.

59. Use the Gauss-Jordan method. On the

augmented matrix $\begin{bmatrix} 1 & -1 & 1 & | & 5 \\ 2 & -1 & 3 & | & 1 \\ 0 & 1 & 1 & | & -9 \end{bmatrix}$, use $-1R_1 + R_2 \rightarrow R_1$ to get

$$\left[\begin{array}{ccc|c} 1 & 0 & 2 & -4 \\ 2 & -1 & 3 & 1 \\ 0 & 1 & 1 & -9 \end{array}\right], \text{ use}$$

$-2R_1 + R_2 \rightarrow R_2$ to get

$$\left[\begin{array}{ccc|c} 1 & 0 & 2 & -4 \\ 0 & -1 & -1 & 9 \\ 0 & 1 & 1 & -9 \end{array}\right], \text{ use}$$

$R_2 + R_3 \rightarrow R_3$ and $-1R_2 \rightarrow R_2$ to get

$$\left[\begin{array}{ccc|c} 1 & 0 & 2 & -4 \\ 0 & 1 & 1 & -9 \\ 0 & 0 & 0 & 0 \end{array}\right]. \text{ Since } y + z = -9$$

and $x + 2z = -4$, the solution set is

$$\{(-2z - 4, -z - 9, z) \mid z \text{ is any real number }\}.$$

61.

Note coefficient matrix is $A = \begin{bmatrix} 1 & 1 & 1 \\ 2 & 4 & 1 \\ 1 & 3 & 6 \end{bmatrix}$

and $A^{-1} \begin{bmatrix} 1 \\ 2 \\ 3 \end{bmatrix} =$

$$\begin{bmatrix} 7/4 & -1/4 & -1/4 \\ -11/12 & 5/12 & 1/12 \\ 1/6 & -1/6 & 1/6 \end{bmatrix} \begin{bmatrix} 1 \\ 2 \\ 3 \end{bmatrix} = \begin{bmatrix} 1/2 \\ 1/6 \\ 1/3 \end{bmatrix}.$$

The solution set is $\{(1/2, 1/6, 1/3)\}$.

63.

Note $A^{-1} = \begin{bmatrix} -55/6 & 5/2 & 5/3 \\ 35/12 & -5/4 & 5/6 \\ 40/3 & 0 & -10/3 \end{bmatrix}$

and $A^{-1} \begin{bmatrix} 27 \\ 9 \\ 16 \end{bmatrix} = \begin{bmatrix} -165 \\ 97.5 \\ 240 \end{bmatrix}.$

The solution set is

$$\{(-165, 97.5, 240)\}.$$

65.

We get $A^{-1} = \begin{bmatrix} 68/133 & -36/133 & 8/19 \\ 10/19 & -12/19 & 6/19 \\ 127/133 & -122/133 & 6/19 \end{bmatrix}$

and $A^{-1} \begin{bmatrix} 16 \\ 24 \\ -8 \end{bmatrix} \approx \begin{bmatrix} -1.6842 \\ -9.2632 \\ -9.2632 \end{bmatrix}.$

The solution set is approximately

$$\{(-1.6842, -9.2632, -9.2632)\}.$$

67.

Since $AA^{-1} = \begin{bmatrix} a & 7 \\ 3 & b \end{bmatrix} \begin{bmatrix} -b & 7 \\ 3 & -a \end{bmatrix} =$

$$= \begin{bmatrix} 21 - ab & 0 \\ 0 & 21 - ab \end{bmatrix}, 21 - ab = 1 \text{ and}$$

$ab = 20$. List of permissible pairs (a, b):

a	1	2	4	5	10	20
b	20	10	5	4	2	1

The matrices are $\begin{bmatrix} 1 & 7 \\ 3 & 20 \end{bmatrix}$, $\begin{bmatrix} 2 & 7 \\ 3 & 10 \end{bmatrix}$,

$$\begin{bmatrix} 4 & 7 \\ 3 & 5 \end{bmatrix}, \begin{bmatrix} 5 & 7 \\ 3 & 4 \end{bmatrix},$$

$$\begin{bmatrix} 10 & 7 \\ 3 & 2 \end{bmatrix}, \text{ and } \begin{bmatrix} 20 & 7 \\ 3 & 1 \end{bmatrix}.$$

69. Let x and y be the costs of a dozen eggs and a magazine before taxes. Then

$$\begin{aligned} 0.08x + 0.05y &= 0.59 \\ x + y &= 8.79 - 0.59. \end{aligned}$$

If $A = \begin{bmatrix} .08 & .05 \\ 1 & 1 \end{bmatrix}$, then $A^{-1} \begin{bmatrix} .59 \\ 8.20 \end{bmatrix} =$

$$= \begin{bmatrix} 100/3 & -5/3 \\ -100/3 & 8/3 \end{bmatrix} \begin{bmatrix} .59 \\ 8.20 \end{bmatrix} = \begin{bmatrix} 6 \\ 2.20 \end{bmatrix}.$$

The eggs cost $2.20 a dozen and the magazine costs $6.

71. Let x and y be the costs of one load of plywood and a load insulation, respectively. So

$$\begin{aligned} 4x + 6y &= 2500 \\ 3x + 5y &= 1950. \end{aligned}$$

If $A = \begin{bmatrix} 4 & 6 \\ 3 & 5 \end{bmatrix}$ then $A^{-1} \begin{bmatrix} 2500 \\ 1950 \end{bmatrix} =$

$$= \begin{bmatrix} 5/2 & -3 \\ -3/2 & 2 \end{bmatrix} \begin{bmatrix} 2500 \\ 1950 \end{bmatrix} = \begin{bmatrix} 400 \\ 150 \end{bmatrix}.$$

One load of plywood costs $400 and a load of insulation costs $150 .

73.

One computes $A^{-1} = \begin{bmatrix} 2 & -1 \\ -5 & 3 \end{bmatrix}$. To decode the message, we find

$$\begin{bmatrix} 2 & -1 \\ -5 & 3 \end{bmatrix}\begin{bmatrix} 36 \\ 65 \end{bmatrix} = \begin{bmatrix} 7 \\ 15 \end{bmatrix} = \begin{bmatrix} g \\ o \end{bmatrix},$$

$$\begin{bmatrix} 2 & -1 \\ -5 & 3 \end{bmatrix}\begin{bmatrix} 49 \\ 83 \end{bmatrix} = \begin{bmatrix} 15 \\ 4 \end{bmatrix} = \begin{bmatrix} o \\ d \end{bmatrix},$$

$$\begin{bmatrix} 2 & -1 \\ -5 & 3 \end{bmatrix}\begin{bmatrix} 12 \\ 24 \end{bmatrix} = \begin{bmatrix} 0 \\ 12 \end{bmatrix} = \begin{bmatrix} space \\ l \end{bmatrix},$$

$$\begin{bmatrix} 2 & -1 \\ -5 & 3 \end{bmatrix}\begin{bmatrix} 66 \\ 111 \end{bmatrix} = \begin{bmatrix} 21 \\ 3 \end{bmatrix} = \begin{bmatrix} u \\ c \end{bmatrix},$$

$$\begin{bmatrix} 2 & -1 \\ -5 & 3 \end{bmatrix}\begin{bmatrix} 33 \\ 55 \end{bmatrix} = \begin{bmatrix} 11 \\ 0 \end{bmatrix} = \begin{bmatrix} k \\ space \end{bmatrix}.$$

The message is 'Good luck'.

75. Let x and y be the amounts invested in the Asset Manager Fund and Magellan Fund, respectively. Since $0.86(60,000) = 51,600$, we get

$$\begin{aligned} x + y &= 60,000 \\ 0.76x + 0.90y &= 51,600. \end{aligned}$$

If $A = \begin{bmatrix} 1 & 1 \\ 0.76 & 0.90 \end{bmatrix}$, then

$$A^{-1} = \begin{bmatrix} 45/7 & -50/7 \\ -38/7 & 50/7 \end{bmatrix} \text{ and}$$

$$A^{-1}\begin{bmatrix} 60,000 \\ 51,600 \end{bmatrix} = \begin{bmatrix} 17,142.86 \\ 42,857.14 \end{bmatrix}. \text{ In the}$$

Asset Manager Fund the amount invested was $17,142.86; in the Magellan Fund the amount invested was $42,857.14.

77. Let $x, y,$ and z be the prices of an animal totem, a trade-bead necklace, and a tribal mask, respectively. Then we obtain the system

$$\begin{aligned} 24x + 33y + 12z &= 202.23 \\ 19x + 40y + 22z &= 209.38 \\ 30x + 9y + 19z &= 167.66. \end{aligned}$$

The inverse of the coefficient matrix A is

$$A^{-1} = \frac{1}{11,007}\begin{bmatrix} 562 & -519 & 246 \\ 299 & 96 & -300 \\ 1029 & 774 & 333 \end{bmatrix}.$$

Since $A^{-1}\begin{bmatrix} 202.23 \\ 209.38 \\ 167.66 \end{bmatrix} \approx \begin{bmatrix} \$4.20 \\ \$2.75 \\ \$0.89 \end{bmatrix}$, we find animal totem costs $4.20, a necklace costs $2.75, and a tribal mask costs $0.89.

79.

On $\begin{bmatrix} 1 & 1 & 2 & | & 9 \\ 1 & 2 & 3 & | & 12 \end{bmatrix}$, apply

$-R_1 + R_2 \to R_2$ to get

$$\begin{bmatrix} 1 & 1 & 2 & | & 9 \\ 0 & 1 & 1 & | & 3 \end{bmatrix}$$

Use $-R_2 + R_1 \to R_1$ to get

$$\begin{bmatrix} 1 & 0 & 1 & | & 6 \\ 0 & 1 & 1 & | & 3 \end{bmatrix}$$

Then the solution set is

$$\{(6 - z, 3 - z, z) : z \text{ is real}\}.$$

81.

$$\begin{bmatrix} 0 & 1 & 0 \\ 1 & 0 & 1 \end{bmatrix}\begin{bmatrix} 1 & 2 \\ 3 & 4 \\ 5 & 6 \end{bmatrix} =$$

$$\begin{bmatrix} 1(3) & 1(4) \\ 1(1) + 1(5) & 1(2) + 1(6) \end{bmatrix} =$$

$$\begin{bmatrix} 3 & 4 \\ 6 & 8 \end{bmatrix}$$

83. Use the method of completing the square.

$$\begin{aligned} x^2 - 4x &= -1 \\ x^2 - 4x + 4 &= 3 \\ (x - 2)^2 &= 3 \\ x - 2 &= \pm\sqrt{3} \end{aligned}$$

The solution set is $\left\{2 \pm \sqrt{3}\right\}$.

For Thought

1. False, $|A| = 12 - (-5) = 17$.

2. True, for $|A| \neq 0$.

3. True, $|B| = 4 \cdot 5 - (-2)(-10) = 0$.

4. False, since $|B| = 0$.

5. True, since the determinant of the coefficient matrix A is nonzero.

6. True, in general $|LM| = |L||M|$ for any square matrices L and M of the same size.

7. False, the system is not linear.   **8.**   True

9. False, $\begin{vmatrix} 2 & 0.1 \\ 100 & 5 \end{vmatrix} = 2 \cdot 5 - 100(0.1) = 0$.

10. False, because a 2×2 matrix is not equal to the number 27.

5 Exercises

1.
$$\begin{vmatrix} 1 & 3 \\ 0 & 2 \end{vmatrix} = 1 \cdot 2 - 0 \cdot 3 = 2$$

3.
$$\begin{vmatrix} 3 & 4 \\ 2 & 9 \end{vmatrix} = 3(9) - 2(4) = 19$$

5.
$$\begin{vmatrix} -0.3 & -0.5 \\ -0.7 & 0.2 \end{vmatrix} = (-0.3)(0.2) - (-0.7)(-0.5)$$
$$= -0.41$$

7.
$$\begin{vmatrix} 1/8 & -3/8 \\ 2 & -1/4 \end{vmatrix} = (1/8)(-1/4) - (2)(-3/8)$$
$$= -1/32 + 3/4 = 23/32$$

9.
$$\begin{vmatrix} 0.02 & 0.4 \\ 1 & 20 \end{vmatrix} = (.02)(20) - (.4)(1) = 0$$

11.
$$\begin{vmatrix} 3 & -5 \\ -9 & 15 \end{vmatrix} = (3)(15) - (-9)(-5) = 0$$

13.

Since $\begin{vmatrix} a & 2 \\ 3 & 4 \end{vmatrix} = 4a - 6 = 10$, we find

$4a = 16$ or $a = 4$.

15.

Since $\begin{vmatrix} a & 8 \\ 2 & a \end{vmatrix} = a^2 - 16 = 0$, we find

$a^2 = 16$ or $a = \pm 4$.

17.

Note $D = \begin{vmatrix} 2 & 1 \\ 1 & 2 \end{vmatrix} = 3$, $D_x = \begin{vmatrix} 5 & 1 \\ 7 & 2 \end{vmatrix} = 3$,

and $D_y = \begin{vmatrix} 2 & 5 \\ 1 & 7 \end{vmatrix} = 9$.

Then $x = \dfrac{D_x}{D} = \dfrac{3}{3} = 1$ and $y = \dfrac{D_y}{D} = \dfrac{9}{3} = 3$.

Solution set is $\{(1, 3)\}$.

19.

Note $D = \begin{vmatrix} 1 & -2 \\ 1 & 2 \end{vmatrix} = 4$, $D_x = \begin{vmatrix} 7 & -2 \\ -5 & 2 \end{vmatrix} =$

4, and $D_y = \begin{vmatrix} 1 & 7 \\ 1 & -5 \end{vmatrix} = -12$.

So $x = \dfrac{D_x}{D} = \dfrac{4}{4} = 1$ and $y = \dfrac{D_y}{D} = \dfrac{-12}{4} =$

-3. The solution set is $\{(1, -3)\}$.

21.

Note $D = \begin{vmatrix} 2 & -1 \\ 1 & 3 \end{vmatrix} = 7$, $D_x = \begin{vmatrix} -11 & -1 \\ 12 & 3 \end{vmatrix}$

$= -21$, and $D_y = \begin{vmatrix} 2 & -11 \\ 1 & 12 \end{vmatrix} = 35$. Then

$x = \dfrac{D_x}{D} = -\dfrac{21}{7} = -3$ and $y = \dfrac{D_y}{D} = \dfrac{35}{7} = 5$.

Solution set is $\{(-3, 5)\}$.

23. Rewrite system as

$$\begin{aligned} x - y &= 6 \\ x + y &= 5. \end{aligned}$$

Note $D = \begin{vmatrix} 1 & -1 \\ 1 & 1 \end{vmatrix} = 2$, $D_x = \begin{vmatrix} 6 & -1 \\ 5 & 1 \end{vmatrix}$

$= 11$, and $D_y = \begin{vmatrix} 1 & 6 \\ 1 & 5 \end{vmatrix} = -1$.

So $x = \dfrac{D_x}{D} = \dfrac{11}{2}$ and $y = \dfrac{D_y}{D} = -\dfrac{1}{2}$.

Solution set is $\{(11/2, -1/2)\}$.

25.

Note $D = \begin{vmatrix} 1/2 & -1/3 \\ 1/4 & 1/2 \end{vmatrix} = 1/3$,

$D_x = \begin{vmatrix} 4 & -1/3 \\ 6 & 1/2 \end{vmatrix} = 4$, and

$D_y = \begin{vmatrix} 1/2 & 4 \\ 1/4 & 6 \end{vmatrix} = 2$. So $x = \dfrac{D_x}{D}$

$= \dfrac{4}{1/3} = 12$ and $y = \dfrac{D_y}{D} = \dfrac{2}{1/3} = 6$.

Solution set is $\{(12, 6)\}$.

27.

Note $D = \begin{vmatrix} 0.2 & 0.12 \\ 1 & 1 \end{vmatrix} = 0.08$,

$D_x = \begin{vmatrix} 148 & 0.12 \\ 900 & 1 \end{vmatrix} = 40$, and

$D_y = \begin{vmatrix} 0.2 & 148 \\ 1 & 900 \end{vmatrix} = 32$. Then

$x = \dfrac{D_x}{D} = \dfrac{40}{0.08} = 500$ and

$y = \dfrac{D_y}{D} = \dfrac{32}{0.08} = 400$.

Solution set is $\{(500, 400)\}$.

29. Cramer's rule does not apply since

$D = \begin{vmatrix} 3 & 1 \\ -6 & -2 \end{vmatrix} = 0$. Dividing the second

equation by -2, one gets the first equation.

Solution set is $\{(x, y) \mid 3x + y = 6 \}$.

31. Cramer's Rule does not apply since the determinant D is zero.

Adding the two equations, one gets $0 = 19$. Inconsistent and the solution set is $\emptyset$.

33. We use Cramer's Rule on the system

$$\begin{aligned} x - y &= 3 \\ 3x - y &= -9. \end{aligned}$$

Note, $D = \begin{vmatrix} 1 & -1 \\ 3 & -1 \end{vmatrix} = 2$,

$D_x = \begin{vmatrix} 3 & -1 \\ -9 & -1 \end{vmatrix} = -12$, and

$D_y = \begin{vmatrix} 1 & 3 \\ 3 & -9 \end{vmatrix} = -18$.

So $x = \dfrac{D_x}{D} = \dfrac{-12}{2} = -6$ and

$y = \dfrac{D_y}{D} = \dfrac{-18}{2} = -9$.

Solution set is $\{(-6, -9)\}$.

35. Note, $D = \begin{vmatrix} \sqrt{2} & \sqrt{3} \\ 3\sqrt{2} & -2\sqrt{3} \end{vmatrix} = -5\sqrt{6}$,

$D_x = \begin{vmatrix} 4 & \sqrt{3} \\ -3 & -2\sqrt{3} \end{vmatrix} = -5\sqrt{3}$, and

$D_y = \begin{vmatrix} \sqrt{2} & 4 \\ 3\sqrt{2} & -3 \end{vmatrix} = -15\sqrt{2}$.

So $x = \dfrac{D_x}{D} = \dfrac{-5\sqrt{3}}{-5\sqrt{6}} = \dfrac{1}{\sqrt{2}} = \dfrac{\sqrt{2}}{2}$

and $y = \dfrac{D_y}{D} = \dfrac{-15\sqrt{2}}{-5\sqrt{6}} = \dfrac{3}{\sqrt{3}} = \sqrt{3}$.

The solution set is $\{(\sqrt{2}/2, \sqrt{3})\}$.

37. Multiply second equation by -1 and add to the first one.

$$\begin{aligned} x^2 + y^2 &= 25 \\ -x^2 + y &= -5 \\ \hline y^2 + y &= 20 \\ y^2 + y - 20 &= 0 \\ (y + 5)(y - 4) &= 0 \end{aligned}$$

If $y = -5$, then $x^2 = 0$ and $x = 0$.
If $y = 4$, then $x^2 = 9$ and $x = \pm 3$.
The solution set is $\{(0, -5), (\pm 3, 4)\}$.

39. Solving for x in the second equation, we find $x = 4 + 2y$. Substituting into the first equation, we obtain

$$\begin{aligned} 4 + 2y - 2y &= y^2 \\ 4 &= y^2 \\ \pm 2 &= y. \end{aligned}$$

Using $y = 2$ in $x = 4 + 2y$, we get $x = 8$.
Similarly, if $y = -2$ then $x = 0$.
Solution set is $\{(8, 2), (0, -2)\}$.

41.

Invertible, since $\begin{vmatrix} 4 & 0.5 \\ 2 & 3 \end{vmatrix} = 12 - 1 = 11 \neq 0$

43.

Not invertible, for $\begin{vmatrix} 3 & -4 \\ 9 & -12 \end{vmatrix} = -36 + 36 = 0$

45. Note, $D = \begin{vmatrix} 3.47 & 23.09 \\ 12.48 & 3.98 \end{vmatrix} = -274.3526$,

$D_x = \begin{vmatrix} 5978.95 & 23.09 \\ 2765.34 & 3.98 \end{vmatrix} = -40,055.4796$,

and

$D_y = \begin{vmatrix} 3.47 & 5978.95 \\ 12.48 & 2765.34 \end{vmatrix} = -65,021.5662$.

Then $x = \dfrac{D_x}{D} = 146$ and $y = \dfrac{D_y}{D} = 237$.

The solution set is $\{(146, 237)\}$.

47. Let x and y be the number of boys and girls, respectively. Then

$$\begin{aligned} 0.44x + 0.35y &= 231 \\ x + y &= 615. \end{aligned}$$

Note, $D = \begin{vmatrix} 0.44 & 0.35 \\ 1 & 1 \end{vmatrix} = 0.09$,

$D_x = \begin{vmatrix} 231 & 0.35 \\ 615 & 1 \end{vmatrix} = 15.75$, and

$D_y = \begin{vmatrix} 0.44 & 231 \\ 1 & 615 \end{vmatrix} = 39.6$.

There were $x = \dfrac{D_x}{D} = \dfrac{15.75}{0.09} = 175$ boys

and $y = \dfrac{D_y}{D} = \dfrac{39.6}{0.09} = 440$ girls.

49. Let x and y be the measurements of the two acute angles. Then we obtain

$$\begin{aligned} x + y &= 90 \\ x - 2y &= 1. \end{aligned}$$

Note, $D = \begin{vmatrix} 1 & 1 \\ 1 & -2 \end{vmatrix} = -3$,

$D_x = \begin{vmatrix} 90 & 1 \\ 1 & -2 \end{vmatrix} = -181$, and

$D_y = \begin{vmatrix} 1 & 90 \\ 1 & 1 \end{vmatrix} = -89$.

The acute angles are $x = \dfrac{D_x}{D} = \dfrac{181}{3}$ degrees

and $y = \dfrac{D_y}{D} = \dfrac{89}{3}$ degrees.

51. Let x and y be the salaries of the president and vice-president, respectively. Then we have

$$\begin{aligned} x + y &= 400,000 \\ x - y &= 100,000. \end{aligned}$$

Note, $D = \begin{vmatrix} 1 & 1 \\ 1 & -1 \end{vmatrix} = -2$,

$D_x = \begin{vmatrix} 400,000 & 1 \\ 100,000 & -1 \end{vmatrix} = -500,000$, and

$D_y = \begin{vmatrix} 1 & 400,000 \\ 1 & 100,000 \end{vmatrix} = -300,000$.

Thus, $x = \dfrac{D_x}{D} = \dfrac{-500,000}{-2} = 250,000$ and

$y = \dfrac{D_y}{D} = \dfrac{-300,000}{-2} = 150,000$.

The president's salary is $250,000 and the vice-president's salary is $150,000.

53. Yes, $|MN| = |M||N|$ since $|M| = 2$, $|N| = 3$,

and $|MN| = \begin{vmatrix} 8 & 31 \\ 14 & 55 \end{vmatrix} = 6$.

55.

$\left| \begin{bmatrix} a & b \\ c & d \end{bmatrix} \begin{bmatrix} e & f \\ g & h \end{bmatrix} \right| =$

$\begin{vmatrix} ae + bg & af + bh \\ ce + dg & cf + dh \end{vmatrix} =$

$(ae + bg)(cf + dh) - (ce + dg)(af + bh) =$
$aecf + bgcf + aedh + bgdh - ceaf - dgaf -$
$cebh - dgbh = bgcf + aedh - dgaf - cebh =$
$ad(eh - gf) - bc(eh - gf) = (ad - bc)(eh - gf) =$

$= \begin{vmatrix} a & b \\ c & d \end{vmatrix} \begin{vmatrix} e & f \\ g & h \end{vmatrix}$

57.

No, since $|-2M| = \begin{vmatrix} -6 & -4 \\ -10 & -8 \end{vmatrix} = 8$

and $-2|M| = -4$.

59.

On $\left[\begin{array}{cc|cc} 1 & 1 & 1 & 0 \\ 1 & 3 & 0 & 1 \end{array}\right]$, use $-R_1 + R_2 \to R_2$

to get

$\left[\begin{array}{cc|cc} 1 & 1 & 1 & 0 \\ 0 & 2 & -1 & 1 \end{array}\right]$, use $\frac{1}{2}R_2 \to R_2$

to get

$\left[\begin{array}{cc|cc} 1 & 1 & 1 & 0 \\ 0 & 1 & -\frac{1}{2} & \frac{1}{2} \end{array}\right]$, use $-R_2 + R_1 \to R_1$

to get

$\left[\begin{array}{cc|cc} 1 & 0 & \frac{3}{2} & -\frac{1}{2} \\ 0 & 1 & -\frac{1}{2} & \frac{1}{2} \end{array}\right].$

Then $A^{-1} = \begin{bmatrix} 3/2 & -1/2 \\ -1/2 & 1/2 \end{bmatrix}.$

61. If we add the first two equations, the sum is $2x + 3y = 15$. Note, the third equation is similar to the sum but the right side is different, i.e., is $2x + 36 = 10$. Thus, there are no solutions. The solution set is the empty set

63. Since $0.91x = 72,800$, we find

$$x = \frac{72,800}{0.91} = 80,000.$$

The solution set is $\{80,000\}$.

For Thought

1. False, the sign array of A is used in evaluating $|A|$.

2. False, the last term should be $1 \cdot \begin{vmatrix} 3 & 4 \\ 0 & 0 \end{vmatrix}.$

3. True

4. True, $|A|$ was expanded about the third row.

5. False, $|A|$ can be expanded only about a row or column. **6.** False, a minor is a 2×2 matrix only if it comes from a 3×3 matrix.

7. False, $x = \dfrac{D_x}{D}$. **8.** True

9. False, it can happen that $D = 0$ and there are infinitely many solutions.

10. False, Cramer's Rule applies only to a system of linear equations.

6 Exercises

1.

$\begin{vmatrix} 5 & -6 \\ 9 & -8 \end{vmatrix} = -40 + 54 = 14$

3.

$\begin{vmatrix} 4 & 5 \\ 7 & 9 \end{vmatrix} = 36 - 35 = 1$

5.

$\begin{vmatrix} 2 & 1 \\ 7 & -8 \end{vmatrix} = -16 - 7 = -23$

7.

$\begin{vmatrix} 2 & 1 \\ 4 & -6 \end{vmatrix} = -12 - 4 = -16$

9.

$1\begin{vmatrix} 1 & -2 \\ -1 & 5 \end{vmatrix} - (-3)\begin{vmatrix} -4 & 0 \\ -1 & 5 \end{vmatrix} + 3\begin{vmatrix} -4 & 0 \\ 1 & -2 \end{vmatrix}$

$= 1(3) - (-3)(-20) + 3(8) = -33$

11.

$3\begin{vmatrix} 4 & -1 \\ 1 & -2 \end{vmatrix} - 0\begin{vmatrix} -1 & 2 \\ 1 & -2 \end{vmatrix} + 5\begin{vmatrix} -1 & 2 \\ 4 & -1 \end{vmatrix}$

$= 3(-7) - 0 + 5(-7) = -56$

13.

$-2\begin{vmatrix} 0 & -1 \\ 2 & -7 \end{vmatrix} - (-3)\begin{vmatrix} 5 & 1 \\ 2 & -7 \end{vmatrix} + 0\begin{vmatrix} 5 & 1 \\ 0 & -1 \end{vmatrix}$

$= -2(2) - (-3)(-37) + 0 = -115$

15.

$0.1\begin{vmatrix} 20 & 6 \\ 90 & 8 \end{vmatrix} - 0.4\begin{vmatrix} 30 & 1 \\ 90 & 8 \end{vmatrix} + 0.7\begin{vmatrix} 30 & 1 \\ 20 & 6 \end{vmatrix}$

$= 0.1(-380) - 0.4(150) + 0.7(160) = 14$

17. Expanding about the second row,

$D = -(-2)\begin{vmatrix} 3 & 5 \\ 3 & -4 \end{vmatrix} = -(-2)(-27) = -54.$

19. Expanding about the first row,

$$D = 1 \begin{vmatrix} 2 & 2 \\ 4 & 4 \end{vmatrix} - 1 \begin{vmatrix} 2 & 2 \\ 4 & 4 \end{vmatrix} + 1 \begin{vmatrix} 2 & 2 \\ 4 & 4 \end{vmatrix}$$

$$= 1(0) - 1(0) + 1(0) = 0.$$

21. Expanding about the first row,

$$D = -(-1) \begin{vmatrix} 3 & 6 \\ -2 & -5 \end{vmatrix} = -(-1)(-3) = -3.$$

23. Expanding about the second column,

$$D = -9 \begin{vmatrix} 2 & 1 \\ 4 & 6 \end{vmatrix} = -9(8) = -72.$$

25. Expanding about the first row,

$$3 \begin{vmatrix} -3 & 2 & 0 \\ 3 & 1 & 2 \\ -4 & 1 & 3 \end{vmatrix} + 0 + 1 \begin{vmatrix} 2 & -3 & 0 \\ -2 & 3 & 2 \\ 2 & -4 & 3 \end{vmatrix} -$$

$$5 \begin{vmatrix} 2 & -3 & 2 \\ -2 & 3 & 1 \\ 2 & -4 & 1 \end{vmatrix} =$$

$$= 3(-37) + 1(4) - 5(6) = -137.$$

27. Expand the determinant about the second row.

$$-(1) \begin{vmatrix} -3 & 4 & 6 \\ 3 & 1 & -3 \\ 0 & 2 & 1 \end{vmatrix} + (-5) \begin{vmatrix} 2 & 4 & 6 \\ 1 & 1 & -3 \\ -2 & 2 & 1 \end{vmatrix} =$$

$$= -(1)(3) + (-5)(58) = -293.$$

29.

One finds $D = \begin{vmatrix} 1 & 1 & 1 \\ 1 & -1 & 1 \\ 2 & 1 & 1 \end{vmatrix} = 2,$

$$D_x = \begin{vmatrix} 6 & 1 & 1 \\ 2 & -1 & 1 \\ 7 & 1 & 1 \end{vmatrix} = 2, \quad D_y = \begin{vmatrix} 1 & 6 & 1 \\ 1 & 2 & 1 \\ 2 & 7 & 1 \end{vmatrix} =$$

4, and $D_z = \begin{vmatrix} 1 & 1 & 6 \\ 1 & -1 & 2 \\ 2 & 1 & 7 \end{vmatrix} = 6.$

Since $x = \dfrac{D_x}{D} = 2/2 = 1$, $y = \dfrac{D_y}{D} = 4/2 = 2,$

and $z = \dfrac{D_z}{D} = 6/2 = 3,$

the solution set is $\{(1, 2, 3)\}.$

31.

One finds $D = \begin{vmatrix} 1 & 2 & 0 \\ 1 & -3 & 1 \\ 2 & -1 & 0 \end{vmatrix} = 5,$

$$D_x = \begin{vmatrix} 8 & 2 & 0 \\ -2 & -3 & 1 \\ 1 & -1 & 0 \end{vmatrix} = 10,$$

$$D_y = \begin{vmatrix} 1 & 8 & 0 \\ 1 & -2 & 1 \\ 2 & 1 & 0 \end{vmatrix} = 15,$$

and $D_z = \begin{vmatrix} 1 & 2 & 8 \\ 1 & -3 & -2 \\ 2 & -1 & 1 \end{vmatrix} = 25.$

Since $x = \dfrac{D_x}{D} = 10/5 = 2,$

$$y = \dfrac{D_y}{D} = 15/5 = 3,$$

and $z = \dfrac{D_z}{D} = 25/5 = 5,$

the solution set is $\{(2, 3, 5)\}.$

33.

One finds $D = \begin{vmatrix} 2 & -3 & 1 \\ 1 & 4 & -1 \\ 3 & -1 & 2 \end{vmatrix} = 16,$

$$D_x = \begin{vmatrix} 1 & -3 & 1 \\ 0 & 4 & -1 \\ 0 & -1 & 2 \end{vmatrix} = 7,$$

$$D_y = \begin{vmatrix} 2 & 1 & 1 \\ 1 & 0 & -1 \\ 3 & 0 & 2 \end{vmatrix} = -5,$$

and $D_z = \begin{vmatrix} 2 & -3 & 1 \\ 1 & 4 & 0 \\ 3 & -1 & 0 \end{vmatrix} = -13.$

Then $x = \dfrac{D_x}{D} = 7/16,$

$y = \dfrac{D_y}{D} = -5/16$, and $z = \dfrac{D_z}{D} = -13/16.$

The solution set is $\{(7/16, -5/16, -13/16)\}.$

35.

One finds $D = \begin{vmatrix} 1 & 1 & 1 \\ 2 & -1 & 3 \\ 3 & 1 & -1 \end{vmatrix} = 14,$

$$D_x = \begin{vmatrix} 2 & 1 & 1 \\ 0 & -1 & 3 \\ 0 & 1 & -1 \end{vmatrix} = -4,$$

$$D_y = \begin{vmatrix} 1 & 2 & 1 \\ 2 & 0 & 3 \\ 3 & 0 & -1 \end{vmatrix} = 22,$$

and $D_z = \begin{vmatrix} 1 & 1 & 2 \\ 2 & -1 & 0 \\ 3 & 1 & 0 \end{vmatrix} = 10.$

Then $x = \dfrac{D_x}{D} = -4/14 = -2/7,$

$y = \dfrac{D_y}{D} = 22/14 = 11/7,$ and

$z = \dfrac{D_z}{D} = 10/14 = 5/7.$

The solution set is $\{(-2/7, 11/7, 5/7)\}.$

37. This system is dependent since the sum of the first two equations is the third equation. Adding the first and third equations, we get $3x - 3z = 4$ or $z = x - 4/3$. Substituting into the first equation, we find

$$x + y - 2\left(x - \frac{4}{3}\right) = 1$$

$$y = 1 - \frac{8}{3} + x$$

$$y = x - \frac{5}{3}.$$

Solution set is

$$\left\{ \left(x, x - \frac{5}{3}, x - \frac{4}{3} \right) \mid x \text{ is any real number} \right\}.$$

39. Multiply the first equation by -2 and add to the third equation.

$$\begin{aligned} -2x + 2y - 2z &= -10 \\ \underline{2x - 2y + 2z} &= \underline{16} \\ 0 &= 6 \end{aligned}$$

Inconsistent and the solution set is $\emptyset.$

41. Let $x, y,$ and z be the ages of Jackie, Rochelle, and Alisha, respectively. Since $\dfrac{x + y}{2} = 33,$

$\dfrac{y + z}{2} = 25,$ and $\dfrac{x + z}{2} = 19,$ we obtain

$$\begin{aligned} x + y &= 66 \\ y + z &= 50 \\ x + z &= 38. \end{aligned}$$

One finds $D = \begin{vmatrix} 1 & 1 & 0 \\ 0 & 1 & 1 \\ 1 & 0 & 1 \end{vmatrix} = 2,$

$$D_x = \begin{vmatrix} 66 & 1 & 0 \\ 50 & 1 & 1 \\ 38 & 0 & 1 \end{vmatrix} = 54, \ D_y = \begin{vmatrix} 1 & 66 & 0 \\ 0 & 50 & 1 \\ 1 & 38 & 1 \end{vmatrix} =$$

78, and $D_z = \begin{vmatrix} 1 & 1 & 66 \\ 0 & 1 & 50 \\ 1 & 0 & 38 \end{vmatrix} = 22.$

So Jackie is $x = \dfrac{D_x}{D} = 54/2 = 27$ years old,

Rochelle is $y = \dfrac{D_y}{D} = 78/2 = 39$ years old,

and Alisha is $z = \dfrac{D_z}{D} = 22/2 = 11$ years old.

43. Let $x, y,$ and z be the scores in the first test, second test, and final exam, respectively. Then

$$\begin{aligned} x + y + z &= 180 \\ 0.2x + 0.2y + 0.6z &= 76 \\ 0.1x + 0.2y + 0.7z &= 83. \end{aligned}$$

One finds $D = \begin{vmatrix} 1 & 1 & 1 \\ 0.2 & 0.2 & 0.6 \\ 0.1 & 0.2 & 0.7 \end{vmatrix} = -0.04,$

$$D_x = \begin{vmatrix} 180 & 1 & 1 \\ 76 & 0.2 & 0.6 \\ 83 & 0.2 & 0.7 \end{vmatrix} = -1.2,$$

$$D_y = \begin{vmatrix} 1 & 180 & 1 \\ 0.2 & 76 & 0.6 \\ 0.1 & 83 & 0.7 \end{vmatrix} = -2,$$

and $D_z = \begin{vmatrix} 1 & 1 & 180 \\ 0.2 & 0.2 & 76 \\ 0.1 & 0.2 & 83 \end{vmatrix} = -4.$

Test scores are $x = \dfrac{D_x}{D} = 1.2/(0.04) = 30,$

$y = \dfrac{D_y}{D} = 2/(0.04) = 50,$ and

the final exam is $z = \dfrac{D_z}{D} = 4/(0.04) = 100$.

45. One finds $D = \begin{vmatrix} 0.2 & -0.3 & 1.2 \\ 0.25 & 0.35 & -0.9 \\ 2.4 & -1 & 1.25 \end{vmatrix} = -\dfrac{527}{800}$,

$D_x = \begin{vmatrix} 13.11 & -0.3 & 1.2 \\ -1.575 & 0.35 & -0.9 \\ 42.02 & -1 & 1.25 \end{vmatrix} = -\dfrac{11,067}{1000}$,

$D_y = \begin{vmatrix} 0.2 & 13.11 & 1.2 \\ 0.25 & -1.575 & -0.9 \\ 2.4 & 42.02 & 1.25 \end{vmatrix} = -\dfrac{64,821}{8000}$,

and $D_z = \begin{vmatrix} 0.2 & -0.3 & 13.11 \\ 0.25 & 0.35 & -1.575 \\ 2.4 & -1 & 42.02 \end{vmatrix} = -\dfrac{3689}{500}$.

Note, $\dfrac{D_x}{D} = 16.8$, $\dfrac{D_y}{D} = 12.3$, and $\dfrac{D_z}{D} = 11.2$.
The solution set is $\{(16.8, 12.3, 11.2)\}$.

47. Let x, y, and z be the prices per gallon of regular, plus, and supreme gasoline, respectively. We find

$D = \begin{vmatrix} 1270 & 980 & 890 \\ 1450 & 1280 & 1050 \\ 1340 & 1190 & 1060 \end{vmatrix} = 18,038,000$,

$D_x = \begin{vmatrix} 12,204.86 & 980 & 890 \\ 14,698.22 & 1280 & 1050 \\ 13,969.41 & 1190 & 1060 \end{vmatrix} =$

$68,526,400$,

$D_y = \begin{vmatrix} 1270 & 12,204.86 & 890 \\ 1450 & 14,698.22 & 1050 \\ 1340 & 13,969.41 & 1060 \end{vmatrix} =$

$70,330,200$,

$D_z = \begin{vmatrix} 1270 & 980 & 12,204.86 \\ 1450 & 1280 & 14,698.22 \\ 1340 & 1190 & 13,969.41 \end{vmatrix} =$

$72,134,000$.

Regular gas costs $\dfrac{D_x}{D} \approx \$3.799$,

plus costs $\dfrac{D_y}{D} \approx \$3.899$, and

supreme costs $\dfrac{D_z}{D} \approx \$3.999$ per gallon.

49.

One finds $D = \begin{vmatrix} 1 & 1 & 1 & 1 \\ 2 & -1 & 1 & 3 \\ 1 & 2 & -1 & 2 \\ 1 & -1 & -1 & 4 \end{vmatrix} = 11$,

$D_w = \begin{vmatrix} 4 & 1 & 1 & 1 \\ 13 & -1 & 1 & 3 \\ -2 & 2 & -1 & 2 \\ 8 & -1 & -1 & 4 \end{vmatrix} = 11$,

$D_x = \begin{vmatrix} 1 & 4 & 1 & 1 \\ 2 & 13 & 1 & 3 \\ 1 & -2 & -1 & 2 \\ 1 & 8 & -1 & 4 \end{vmatrix} = -22$,

$D_y = \begin{vmatrix} 1 & 1 & 4 & 1 \\ 2 & -1 & 13 & 3 \\ 1 & 2 & -2 & 2 \\ 1 & -1 & 8 & 4 \end{vmatrix} = 33$,

and $D_z = \begin{vmatrix} 1 & 1 & 1 & 4 \\ 2 & -1 & 1 & 13 \\ 1 & 2 & -1 & -2 \\ 1 & -1 & -1 & 8 \end{vmatrix} = 22$.

Note, $\dfrac{D_w}{D} = 1$, $\dfrac{D_x}{D} = -2$, $\dfrac{D_y}{D} = 3$, and

$\dfrac{D_z}{D} = 2$. The solution set is $\{(1, -2, 3, 2)\}$.

51.

Note, $\begin{vmatrix} x & y & 1 \\ 3 & -5 & 1 \\ -2 & 6 & 1 \end{vmatrix} = 8 - 11x - 5y = 0$.

Since both points $(3, -5)$ and $(-2, 6)$ satisfies $8 - 11x - 5y = 0$, this is an equation of the line through the two points.

53. We will show it for one particular case and the other cases can proved similarly.

Let us suppose $A = \begin{bmatrix} a & b & c \\ 0 & 0 & 0 \\ g & h & i \end{bmatrix}$.

Then $|A| = a \cdot 0 \cdot i + b \cdot 0 \cdot g + c \cdot 0 \cdot h - g \cdot 0 \cdot c - h \cdot 0 \cdot a - i \cdot 0 \cdot b = 0$

55. We will prove it for one particular case and the other cases can be shown similarly.

Let us suppose $A = \begin{bmatrix} a & b & c \\ d & e & f \\ g & h & i \end{bmatrix}$ and

$B = \begin{bmatrix} a & b & c \\ d & e & f \\ kg & kh & ki \end{bmatrix}$. Then $|B| =$

$aeki + bfkg + cdkh - kgec - khfa - kidb =$
$k(aei + bfg + cdh - gec - hfa - idb) = k|A|.$

57.
$\begin{vmatrix} 3 & -2 \\ -1 & 4 \end{vmatrix} = 3(4) - (-1)(-2) = 10$

59. For each value of z, the system below

$$5x - 9y = 44 - 11z$$
$$13x - 12y = -9 - 31z$$

has unique solution since the coefficient matrix $\begin{bmatrix} 5 & -9 \\ 13 & -12 \end{bmatrix}$ has a nonzero determinant. Then the given system of three equations is not independent since the solution is not unique. Hence, in addition since the system is not inconsistent, it follows by elimination that the system is dependent.

61. If $(x - 4)^2 = x^2$, then $x - 4 = \pm x$. Since $x - 4 = x$ is inconsistent, we have $x - 4 = -x$ or $2x = 4$. Then $x = 2$. Thus, $y = x^2 = 2^2 = 4$. The solution set is $\{2, 4\}$.

Review Exercises

1.
$\begin{bmatrix} 2+3 & -3+7 \\ -2+1 & 4+2 \end{bmatrix} = \begin{bmatrix} 5 & 4 \\ -1 & 6 \end{bmatrix}$

3.
$\begin{bmatrix} 4 & -6 \\ -4 & 8 \end{bmatrix} - \begin{bmatrix} 3 & 7 \\ 1 & 2 \end{bmatrix} =$
$\begin{bmatrix} 1 & -13 \\ -5 & 6 \end{bmatrix}$

5.
$AB = \begin{bmatrix} 6-3 & 14-6 \\ -6+4 & -14+8 \end{bmatrix} =$
$\begin{bmatrix} 3 & 8 \\ -2 & -6 \end{bmatrix}$

7. $D + E$ is undefined

9.
$AC = \begin{bmatrix} -2-9 \\ 2+12 \end{bmatrix} = \begin{bmatrix} -11 \\ 14 \end{bmatrix}$

11.
$EF = \begin{bmatrix} 3 & 2 & -1 \\ -12 & -8 & 4 \\ 9 & 6 & -3 \end{bmatrix}$

13. $FG = [-3+2+2 \quad 2-3 \quad -1] =$
$[1 \quad -1 \quad -1]$

15. GF is undefined

17.
On $\begin{bmatrix} 2 & -3 & | & 1 & 0 \\ -2 & 4 & | & 0 & 1 \end{bmatrix}$, use $R_1 + R_2 \to R_2$
to get
$\begin{bmatrix} 2 & -3 & | & 1 & 0 \\ 0 & 1 & | & 1 & 1 \end{bmatrix}$, use $3R_2 + R_1 \to R_1$ to get
$\begin{bmatrix} 2 & 0 & | & 4 & 3 \\ 0 & 1 & | & 1 & 1 \end{bmatrix}$, use $\frac{1}{2}R_1 \to R_1$ to get
$\begin{bmatrix} 1 & 0 & | & 2 & 1.5 \\ 0 & 1 & | & 1 & 1 \end{bmatrix}$. So $A^{-1} = \begin{bmatrix} 2 & 1.5 \\ 1 & 1 \end{bmatrix}$.

19.
On $\begin{bmatrix} -1 & 0 & 0 & | & 1 & 0 & 0 \\ 1 & 1 & 0 & | & 0 & 1 & 0 \\ -2 & 3 & 1 & | & 0 & 0 & 1 \end{bmatrix}$,
use $R_1 + R_2 \to R_2$, $2R_2 + R_3 \to R_3$, and $-1R_1 \to R_1$ to get
$\begin{bmatrix} 1 & 0 & 0 & | & -1 & 0 & 0 \\ 0 & 1 & 0 & | & 1 & 1 & 0 \\ 0 & 5 & 1 & | & 0 & 2 & 1 \end{bmatrix}$,
use $-5R_2 + R_3 \to R_3$ to get
$\begin{bmatrix} 1 & 0 & 0 & | & -1 & 0 & 0 \\ 0 & 1 & 0 & | & 1 & 1 & 0 \\ 0 & 0 & 1 & | & -5 & -3 & 1 \end{bmatrix}$.
So $G^{-1} = \begin{bmatrix} -1 & 0 & 0 \\ 1 & 1 & 0 \\ -5 & -3 & 1 \end{bmatrix}$.

21.
From Exercise 5, $(AB)^{-1} = \begin{bmatrix} 3 & 8 \\ -2 & -6 \end{bmatrix}^{-1}$.

On $\begin{bmatrix} 3 & 8 & | & 1 & 0 \\ -2 & -6 & | & 0 & 1 \end{bmatrix}$, use $-\dfrac{1}{2}R_2 \to R_2$

to get

$\begin{bmatrix} 3 & 8 & | & 1 & 0 \\ 1 & 3 & | & 0 & -0.5 \end{bmatrix}$, use $-3R_2 + R_1 \to R_1$

to get

$\begin{bmatrix} 0 & -1 & | & 1 & 1.5 \\ 1 & 3 & | & 0 & -0.5 \end{bmatrix}$, use $3R_1 + R_2 \to R_2$

to get

$\begin{bmatrix} 0 & -1 & | & 1 & 1.5 \\ 1 & 0 & | & 3 & 4 \end{bmatrix}$, use $R_1 \leftrightarrow R_2$ to get

$\begin{bmatrix} 1 & 0 & | & 3 & 4 \\ 0 & -1 & | & 1 & 1.5 \end{bmatrix}$, use $-1R_2 \to R_2$ to get

$\begin{bmatrix} 1 & 0 & | & 3 & 4 \\ 0 & 1 & | & -1 & -1.5 \end{bmatrix}$.

So $(AB)^{-1} = \begin{bmatrix} 3 & 4 \\ -1 & -1.5 \end{bmatrix}$.

23.

$$AA^{-1} = I = \begin{bmatrix} 1 & 0 \\ 0 & 1 \end{bmatrix}$$

25. $|A| = 8 - 6 = 2$

27. Expanding about the third column,

$$|G| = 1 \cdot \begin{vmatrix} -1 & 0 \\ 1 & 1 \end{vmatrix} = 1(-1) = -1.$$

29. The solution set is $\{(10/3, 17/3)\}$.

First solution is by Gaussian elimination.

On $\begin{bmatrix} 1 & 1 & | & 9 \\ 2 & -1 & | & 1 \end{bmatrix}$, use $-2R_1 + R_2 \to R_2$ to

get

$\begin{bmatrix} 1 & 1 & | & 9 \\ 0 & -3 & | & -17 \end{bmatrix}$, use $-\dfrac{1}{3}R_2 \to R_2$ to get

$\begin{bmatrix} 1 & 1 & | & 9 \\ 0 & 1 & | & 17/3 \end{bmatrix}$, use $-1R_2 + R_1 \to R_1$ to get

$\begin{bmatrix} 1 & 0 & | & 10/3 \\ 0 & 1 & | & 17/3 \end{bmatrix}$.

Secondly, by matrix inversion note $A^{-1} =$

$\begin{bmatrix} 1/3 & 1/3 \\ 2/3 & -1/3 \end{bmatrix}$ and $A^{-1}\begin{bmatrix} 9 \\ 1 \end{bmatrix} = \begin{bmatrix} 10/3 \\ 17/3 \end{bmatrix}$.

Thirdly, by Cramer's Rule note

$$D = \begin{vmatrix} 1 & 1 \\ 2 & -1 \end{vmatrix} = -3, \quad D_x = \begin{vmatrix} 9 & 1 \\ 1 & -1 \end{vmatrix} = -10,$$

and $D_y = \begin{vmatrix} 1 & 9 \\ 2 & 1 \end{vmatrix} = -17.$

So $\dfrac{D_x}{D} = 10/3, \dfrac{D_y}{D} = 17/3.$

31. The solution set is $\{(-2, 3)\}$.

First solution is by Gaussian elimination. On

$\begin{bmatrix} 2 & 1 & | & -1 \\ 3 & 2 & | & 0 \end{bmatrix}$, use $-\dfrac{3}{2}R_1 + R_2 \to R_2$ to get

$\begin{bmatrix} 2 & 1 & | & -1 \\ 0 & 1/2 & | & 3/2 \end{bmatrix}$, use $-2R_2 + R_1 \to R_1$

and $2R_2 \to R_2$ to get

$\begin{bmatrix} 2 & 0 & | & -4 \\ 0 & 1 & | & 3 \end{bmatrix}$, use $\dfrac{1}{2}R_2 \to R_2$ to get

$\begin{bmatrix} 1 & 0 & | & -2 \\ 0 & 1 & | & 3 \end{bmatrix}$.

Secondly, by matrix inversion note $A^{-1} =$

$\begin{bmatrix} 2 & -1 \\ -3 & 2 \end{bmatrix}$ and $A^{-1}\begin{bmatrix} -1 \\ 0 \end{bmatrix} = \begin{bmatrix} -2 \\ 3 \end{bmatrix}$.

Thirdly, by Cramer's Rule note

$$D = \begin{vmatrix} 2 & 1 \\ 3 & 2 \end{vmatrix} = 1, \quad D_x = \begin{vmatrix} -1 & 1 \\ 0 & 2 \end{vmatrix} = -2,$$

and $D_y = \begin{vmatrix} 2 & -1 \\ 3 & 0 \end{vmatrix} = 3.$

So $\dfrac{D_x}{D} = -2, \dfrac{D_y}{D} = 3.$

33. Solution set is $\{(x, y) | x - 5y = 9\}$.

Solution is by Gaussian elimination.

On $\begin{bmatrix} 1 & -5 & | & 9 \\ -2 & 10 & | & -18 \end{bmatrix}$, use $2R_1 + R_2 \to R_2$

to get $\begin{bmatrix} 1 & -5 & | & 9 \\ 0 & 0 & | & 0 \end{bmatrix}$. Dependent system.

This cannot be solved by matrix inversion

since $A^{-1} = \begin{bmatrix} 1 & -5 \\ -2 & 10 \end{bmatrix}^{-1}$ does not exist.

Nor can it be solved by Cramer's rule

since $|D| = \begin{vmatrix} 1 & -5 \\ -2 & 10 \end{vmatrix} = 0.$

35. The solution set is $\emptyset$.

First, apply the Gaussian elimination method.

On $\begin{bmatrix} 0.05 & 0.1 & | & 1 \\ 10 & 20 & | & 20 \end{bmatrix}$, use

$-200R_1 + R_2 \to R_2$ to get

$\begin{bmatrix} 0.05 & 0.1 & | & 1 \\ 0 & 0 & | & -180 \end{bmatrix}$, which is inconsistent.

This cannot be solved by matrix inversion since

$A^{-1} = \begin{bmatrix} 0.05 & 0.1 \\ 10 & 20 \end{bmatrix}^{-1}$ does not exist.

Nor can it be solved by Cramer's rule

since $|D| = \begin{vmatrix} 0.05 & 0.1 \\ 10 & 20 \end{vmatrix} = 0.$

37. Solution set is $\{(1, 2, 3)\}$.

First solution is by Gaussian elimination.

On $\begin{bmatrix} 1 & 1 & -2 & | & -3 \\ -1 & 2 & -1 & | & 0 \\ -1 & -1 & 3 & | & 6 \end{bmatrix}$, use

$R_1 + R_2 \to R_2$ to get

$\begin{bmatrix} 1 & 1 & -2 & | & -3 \\ 0 & 3 & -3 & | & -3 \\ 0 & 0 & 1 & | & 3 \end{bmatrix}$, use

$\frac{1}{3}R_2 \to R_2$ to get

$\begin{bmatrix} 1 & 1 & -2 & | & -3 \\ 0 & 1 & -1 & | & -1 \\ 0 & 0 & 1 & | & 3 \end{bmatrix}$, use

$R_3 + R_2 \to R_2$ and $2R_3 + R_1 \to R_1$ to get

$\begin{bmatrix} 1 & 1 & 0 & | & 3 \\ 0 & 1 & 0 & | & 2 \\ 0 & 0 & 1 & | & 3 \end{bmatrix}$, use $-1R_2 + R_1 \to R_1$

to get $\begin{bmatrix} 1 & 0 & 0 & | & 1 \\ 0 & 1 & 0 & | & 2 \\ 0 & 0 & 1 & | & 3 \end{bmatrix}$.

Secondly, by matrix inversion note $A^{-1} =$

$\begin{bmatrix} 5/3 & -1/3 & 1 \\ 4/3 & 1/3 & 1 \\ 1 & 0 & 1 \end{bmatrix}$ and $A^{-1} \begin{bmatrix} -3 \\ 0 \\ 6 \end{bmatrix} = \begin{bmatrix} 1 \\ 2 \\ 3 \end{bmatrix}.$

Thirdly, by Cramer's Rule note

$D = \begin{vmatrix} 1 & 1 & -2 \\ -1 & 2 & -1 \\ -1 & -1 & 3 \end{vmatrix} = 3,$

$D_x = \begin{vmatrix} -3 & 1 & -2 \\ 0 & 2 & -1 \\ 6 & -1 & 3 \end{vmatrix} = 3,$

$D_y = \begin{vmatrix} 1 & -3 & -2 \\ -1 & 0 & -1 \\ -1 & 6 & 3 \end{vmatrix} = 6,$

and $D_z = \begin{vmatrix} 1 & 1 & -3 \\ -1 & 2 & 0 \\ -1 & -1 & 6 \end{vmatrix} = 9.$

Then $\dfrac{D_x}{D} = 1$, $\dfrac{D_y}{D} = 2$, and $\dfrac{D_z}{D} = 3.$

39. The solution set is $\{(-3, 4, 1)\}$.

First solution is by Gaussian elimination.

On $\begin{bmatrix} 0 & 1 & -3 & | & 1 \\ 1 & 2 & 0 & | & 5 \\ 1 & 0 & 4 & | & 1 \end{bmatrix}$, use

$-1R_3 + R_2 \to R_2$ and $R_1 \leftrightarrow R_3$ to get

$\begin{bmatrix} 1 & 0 & 4 & | & 1 \\ 0 & 2 & -4 & | & 4 \\ 0 & 1 & -3 & | & 1 \end{bmatrix}$, use $\frac{1}{2}R_2 \to R_2$ to get

$\begin{bmatrix} 1 & 0 & 4 & | & 1 \\ 0 & 1 & -2 & | & 2 \\ 0 & 1 & -3 & | & 1 \end{bmatrix}$, use $-1R_2 + R_3 \to R_3$

to get

$\begin{bmatrix} 1 & 0 & 4 & | & 1 \\ 0 & 1 & -2 & | & 2 \\ 0 & 0 & -1 & | & -1 \end{bmatrix}$, use

$-2R_3 + R_2 \to R_2$, $4R_3 + R_1 \to R_1$, and

$-1R_3 \to R_3$ to get

$\begin{bmatrix} 1 & 0 & 0 & | & -3 \\ 0 & 1 & 0 & | & 4 \\ 0 & 0 & 1 & | & 1 \end{bmatrix}$.

Secondly, by matrix inversion

$$A^{-1} = \begin{bmatrix} 4 & -2 & 3 \\ -2 & 3/2 & -3/2 \\ -1 & 1/2 & -1/2 \end{bmatrix}$$

and $A^{-1} \begin{bmatrix} 1 \\ 5 \\ 1 \end{bmatrix} = \begin{bmatrix} -3 \\ 4 \\ 1 \end{bmatrix}$.

Thirdly, by Cramer's Rule note

$$D = \begin{vmatrix} 0 & 1 & -3 \\ 1 & 2 & 0 \\ 1 & 0 & 4 \end{vmatrix} = 2,$$

$$D_x = \begin{vmatrix} 1 & 1 & -3 \\ 5 & 2 & 0 \\ 1 & 0 & 4 \end{vmatrix} = -6,$$

$$D_y = \begin{vmatrix} 0 & 1 & -3 \\ 1 & 5 & 0 \\ 1 & 1 & 4 \end{vmatrix} = 8,$$

and $D_z = \begin{vmatrix} 0 & 1 & 1 \\ 1 & 2 & 5 \\ 1 & 0 & 1 \end{vmatrix} = 2$.

Then $\dfrac{D_x}{D} = -3$, $\dfrac{D_y}{D} = 4$, and $\dfrac{D_z}{D} = 1$.

41. The solution set is

$$\left\{ \left(\frac{3y+3}{2}, y, \frac{1-y}{2} \right) \mid y \text{ is any real number} \right\}.$$

First, apply the Gaussian elimination method.

On $\begin{bmatrix} 1 & -1 & 1 & | & 2 \\ 1 & -2 & -1 & | & 1 \\ 2 & -3 & 0 & | & 3 \end{bmatrix}$, use

$-1R_1 + R_2 \to R_2$ and $-2R_1 + R_3 \to R_3$ to get

$\begin{bmatrix} 1 & -1 & 1 & | & 2 \\ 0 & -1 & -2 & | & -1 \\ 0 & -1 & -2 & | & -1 \end{bmatrix}$, use

$-1R_2 + R_3 \to R_3$, $-1R_2 + R_1 \to R_1$,

and $-1R_2 \to R_2$ to get

$\begin{bmatrix} 1 & 0 & 3 & | & 3 \\ 0 & 1 & 2 & | & 1 \\ 0 & 0 & 0 & | & 0 \end{bmatrix}$. Since $z = \dfrac{1-y}{2}$, we get

$x = 3 - 3z = 3 - 3\left(\dfrac{1-y}{2} \right) = \dfrac{3y+3}{2}$.

This cannot be solved by matrix inversion

since $A^{-1} = \begin{bmatrix} 1 & -1 & 1 \\ 1 & -2 & -1 \\ 2 & -3 & 0 \end{bmatrix}^{-1}$ does not exist.

Nor can it be solved by Cramer's rule

since $|D| = \begin{vmatrix} 1 & -1 & 1 \\ 1 & -2 & -1 \\ 2 & -3 & 0 \end{vmatrix} = 0$.

43. Solution set is $\emptyset$ as seen by an application of the Gaussian elimination method.

On $\begin{bmatrix} 1 & -3 & -1 & | & 2 \\ 1 & -3 & -1 & | & 1 \\ 1 & -3 & -1 & | & 0 \end{bmatrix}$, use

$-1R_1 + R_2 \to R_2$ and $-1R_1 + R_3 \to R_3$ to get

$\begin{bmatrix} 1 & -3 & -1 & | & 2 \\ 0 & 0 & 0 & | & -1 \\ 0 & 0 & 0 & | & -2 \end{bmatrix}$. Inconsistent.

This cannot be solved by matrix inversion

since $A^{-1} = \begin{bmatrix} 1 & -3 & -1 \\ 1 & -3 & -1 \\ 1 & -3 & -1 \end{bmatrix}^{-1}$ does not exist.

Nor can it be solved by Cramer's rule

since $|D| = \begin{vmatrix} 1 & -3 & -1 \\ 1 & -3 & -1 \\ 1 & -3 & -1 \end{vmatrix} = 0$.

45. Using $x = 9$ in $x + y = -3$, we find $9 + y = -3$ and $y = -12$. The solution set is $\{(9, -12)\}$.

47.

Note $\begin{bmatrix} x \\ y \end{bmatrix} = \begin{bmatrix} 1 & 1 \\ 2 & 1 \end{bmatrix}^{-1} \begin{bmatrix} 6 \\ 8 \end{bmatrix} =$

$\begin{bmatrix} -1 & 1 \\ 2 & -1 \end{bmatrix} \begin{bmatrix} 6 \\ 8 \end{bmatrix} = \begin{bmatrix} 2 \\ 4 \end{bmatrix}$.

The solution set is $\{(2, 4)\}$.

49. System of equations can be written as

$$\begin{aligned} x + y &= -3 \\ -x &= 0. \end{aligned}$$

Using $x = 0$ in $x + y = -3$, we get $y = -3$. Solution set is $\{(0, -3)\}$.

51. System of equations can be written as

$$\begin{bmatrix} 1 & 1 & 0 \\ 0 & 1 & 1 \\ 1 & 0 & 1 \end{bmatrix} \begin{bmatrix} x \\ y \\ z \end{bmatrix} = \begin{bmatrix} 1 \\ 1 \\ 1 \end{bmatrix}.$$

By using matrix inversion, we obtain

$$\begin{bmatrix} x \\ y \\ z \end{bmatrix} = \begin{bmatrix} 1/2 & -1/2 & 1/2 \\ 1/2 & 1/2 & -1/2 \\ -1/2 & 1/2 & 1/2 \end{bmatrix} \begin{bmatrix} 1 \\ 1 \\ 1 \end{bmatrix} =$$

$$\begin{bmatrix} 1/2 \\ 1/2 \\ 1/2 \end{bmatrix}.$$ The solution set is $\{(1/2, 1/2, 1/2)\}$.

53. By using the inverse of the coefficient matrix, we get

$$\begin{bmatrix} x \\ y \\ z \end{bmatrix} = \begin{bmatrix} 3/5 & -3/5 & 2/5 \\ 2/5 & 3/5 & -2/5 \\ -1/5 & 1/5 & 1/5 \end{bmatrix} \begin{bmatrix} -1 \\ 7 \\ 17 \end{bmatrix} =$$

$$\begin{bmatrix} 2 \\ -3 \\ 5 \end{bmatrix}.$$ The solution set is $\{(2, -3, 5)\}$.

55. Let x and y be the number of gallons of pollutant A and pollutant B, respectively. Then

$$\begin{aligned} 10x + 6y &= 4060 \\ \frac{3}{4} &= \frac{x}{y}. \end{aligned}$$

Substitute $x = \dfrac{3}{4}y$ in $10x + 6y = 4060$. Solving for x, one finds the quantities discharged are $x \approx 225.56$ gallons of pollutant A and $y \approx 300.74$ gallons of pollutant B.

57. Let $x, y,$ and z be the expenses including tax for water, gas, and electricity, respectively.

$$\begin{aligned} x + y + z &= 189.83 \\ \frac{x}{1.04} + \frac{y}{1.05} + \frac{z}{1.06} &= 180 \\ z &= 2y \end{aligned}$$

Solving the system, one finds the expenses including taxes are $x = \$22.88$ for water, $y = \$55.65$ for gas, and $z = \$111.30$ for electricity.

Chapter Test

1.

On $\begin{bmatrix} 2 & -3 & | & 1 \\ 1 & 9 & | & 4 \end{bmatrix}$, use $-2R_2 + R_1 \to R_2$

to get

$\begin{bmatrix} 2 & -3 & | & 1 \\ 0 & -21 & | & -7 \end{bmatrix}$, use $\dfrac{1}{2}R_1 \to R_1$ and

$-\dfrac{1}{21}R_2 \to R_2$ to get

$\begin{bmatrix} 1 & -3/2 & | & 1/2 \\ 0 & 1 & | & 1/3 \end{bmatrix}$, use $\dfrac{3}{2}R_2 + R_1 \to R_1$

to get

$\begin{bmatrix} 1 & 0 & | & 1 \\ 0 & 1 & | & 1/3 \end{bmatrix}$. Solution set is $\{(1, 1/3)\}$.

2.

On $\begin{bmatrix} 2 & -1 & 1 & | & 5 \\ 1 & -2 & -1 & | & -2 \\ 3 & -1 & -1 & | & 6 \end{bmatrix}$, use

$-\dfrac{1}{2}R_1 + R_2 \to R_2$ and

$-\dfrac{3}{2}R_1 + R_3 \to R_3$ to get

$\begin{bmatrix} 2 & -1 & 1 & | & 5 \\ 0 & -3/2 & -3/2 & | & -9/2 \\ 0 & 1/2 & -5/2 & | & -3/2 \end{bmatrix}$, use

$-\dfrac{2}{3}R_2 \to R_2$ and $3R_3 + R_2 \to R_3$ to get

$\begin{bmatrix} 2 & -1 & 1 & | & 5 \\ 0 & 1 & 1 & | & 3 \\ 0 & 0 & -9 & | & -9 \end{bmatrix}$,

use $-\dfrac{1}{9}R_3 \to R_3$ and $R_2 + R_1 \to R_1$ to get

$\begin{bmatrix} 2 & 0 & 2 & | & 8 \\ 0 & 1 & 1 & | & 3 \\ 0 & 0 & 1 & | & 1 \end{bmatrix}$, use

$-1R_3 + R_2 \to R_2$ and $\dfrac{1}{2}R_1 \to R_1$ to get

$\begin{bmatrix} 1 & 0 & 1 & | & 4 \\ 0 & 1 & 0 & | & 2 \\ 0 & 0 & 1 & | & 1 \end{bmatrix}$, use $-1R_3 + R_1 \to R_1$

to get $\begin{bmatrix} 1 & 0 & 0 & | & 3 \\ 0 & 1 & 0 & | & 2 \\ 0 & 0 & 1 & | & 1 \end{bmatrix}$.

The solution set is $\{(3, 2, 1)\}$.

3.

On $\begin{bmatrix} 1 & -1 & -1 & | & 1 \\ 2 & 1 & -1 & | & 0 \\ 5 & -2 & -4 & | & 3 \end{bmatrix}$, use

$-2R_1 + R_2 \to R_2$ and

$-5R_1 + R_3 \to R_3$ to get

$\begin{bmatrix} 1 & -1 & -1 & | & 1 \\ 0 & 3 & 1 & | & -2 \\ 0 & 3 & 1 & | & -2 \end{bmatrix}$, use

$-1R_3 + R_2 \to R_3$ and $\frac{1}{3}R_2 \to R_2$ to get

$\begin{bmatrix} 1 & -1 & -1 & | & 1 \\ 0 & 1 & 1/3 & | & -2/3 \\ 0 & 0 & 0 & | & 0 \end{bmatrix}$, use

$R_2 + R_1 \to R_1$ to get

$\begin{bmatrix} 1 & 0 & -2/3 & | & 1/3 \\ 0 & 1 & 1/3 & | & -2/3 \\ 0 & 0 & 0 & | & 0 \end{bmatrix}$.

Since $x = \frac{2}{3}z + \frac{1}{3}$, we find $3x = 2z + 1$ and

$z = \frac{3x - 1}{2}$. Since $y = -\frac{1}{3}z - \frac{2}{3}$, we get

$$\begin{aligned} y &= -\frac{1}{3}\left(\frac{3x - 1}{2}\right) - \frac{2}{3} \\ y &= \frac{-3x - 3}{6} \\ y &= \frac{-x - 1}{2} \end{aligned}$$

The solution set is

$$\left\{ \left(x, \frac{-x - 1}{2}, \frac{3x - 1}{2} \right) \mid x \text{ is any real number} \right\}.$$

4.

$A + B = \begin{bmatrix} 3 & -4 \\ -6 & 10 \end{bmatrix}$

5.

$2A - B = \begin{bmatrix} 2 & -2 \\ -4 & 8 \end{bmatrix} - \begin{bmatrix} 2 & -3 \\ -4 & 6 \end{bmatrix} =$

$\begin{bmatrix} 0 & 1 \\ 0 & 2 \end{bmatrix}$

6.

$AB = \begin{bmatrix} 2+4 & -3-6 \\ -4-16 & 6+24 \end{bmatrix} = \begin{bmatrix} 6 & -9 \\ -20 & 30 \end{bmatrix}$

7.

$AC = \begin{bmatrix} -2-1 \\ 4+4 \end{bmatrix} = \begin{bmatrix} -3 \\ 8 \end{bmatrix}$

8. CB is undefined

9. $FG = [-2 \quad 3-2 \quad 1+1] = [-2 \quad 1 \quad 2]$

10.

$EF = \begin{bmatrix} 2(1) & 2(0) & 2(-1) \\ 3(1) & 3(0) & 3(-1) \\ -1(1) & -1(0) & -1(-1) \end{bmatrix}$

$= \begin{bmatrix} 2 & 0 & -2 \\ 3 & 0 & -3 \\ -1 & 0 & 1 \end{bmatrix}$

11.

On $\begin{bmatrix} 1 & -1 & | & 1 & 0 \\ -2 & 4 & | & 0 & 1 \end{bmatrix}$, use

$2R_1 + R_2 \to R_2$ to get

$\begin{bmatrix} 1 & -1 & | & 1 & 0 \\ 0 & 2 & | & 2 & 1 \end{bmatrix}$, use

$\frac{1}{2}R_2 + R_1 \to R_1$ and $\frac{1}{2}R_2 \to R_2$

to get $\begin{bmatrix} 1 & 0 & | & 2 & 1/2 \\ 0 & 1 & | & 1 & 1/2 \end{bmatrix}$.

Then $A^{-1} = \begin{bmatrix} 2 & 1/2 \\ 1 & 1/2 \end{bmatrix}$.

12.

On $\begin{bmatrix} -2 & 3 & 1 & | & 1 & 0 & 0 \\ -3 & 1 & 3 & | & 0 & 1 & 0 \\ 0 & 2 & -1 & | & 0 & 0 & 1 \end{bmatrix}$,

use $-\frac{1}{2}R_1 \to R_1$ and $-\frac{3}{2}R_1 + R_2 \to R_2$ to get

$\begin{bmatrix} 1 & -3/2 & -1/2 & | & -1/2 & 0 & 0 \\ 0 & -7/2 & 3/2 & | & -3/2 & 1 & 0 \\ 0 & 2 & -1 & | & 0 & 0 & 1 \end{bmatrix}$, use

$\frac{4}{7}R_2 + R_3 \to R_3,\ -\frac{3}{7}R_2 + R_1 \to R_1,$

and $-\dfrac{2}{7}R_2 \to R_2$ to get

$$\left[\begin{array}{ccc|ccc} 1 & 0 & -8/7 & 1/7 & -3/7 & 0 \\ 0 & 1 & -3/7 & 3/7 & -2/7 & 0 \\ 0 & 0 & -1/7 & -6/7 & 4/7 & 1 \end{array}\right], \text{ use}$$

$-3R_3 + R_2 \to R_2, -8R_3 + R_1 \to R_1,$

and $-7R_3 \to R_3$ to get

$$\left[\begin{array}{ccc|ccc} 1 & 0 & 0 & 7 & -5 & -8 \\ 0 & 1 & 0 & 3 & -2 & -3 \\ 0 & 0 & 1 & 6 & -4 & -7 \end{array}\right].$$

Then $G^{-1} = \begin{bmatrix} 7 & -5 & -8 \\ 3 & -2 & -3 \\ 6 & -4 & -7 \end{bmatrix}.$

13. $|A| = 4 - 2 = 2$

14. $|B| = 12 - 12 = 0$

15. Expanding about the third row, we find

$$|G| = -2 \begin{vmatrix} -2 & 1 \\ -3 & 3 \end{vmatrix} + (-1) \begin{vmatrix} -2 & 3 \\ -3 & 1 \end{vmatrix} =$$

$-2(-3) + (-1)(7) = -1$

16.

One finds $D = \begin{vmatrix} 1 & -1 \\ -2 & 4 \end{vmatrix} = 2,$

$D_x = \begin{vmatrix} 2 & -1 \\ 2 & 4 \end{vmatrix} = 10, \ D_y = \begin{vmatrix} 1 & 2 \\ -2 & 2 \end{vmatrix} = 6.$

Then $\dfrac{D_x}{D} = 5$ and $\dfrac{D_y}{D} = 3.$

The solution set is $\{(5, 3)\}.$

17. Cramer's Rule is not applicable since

$D = \begin{vmatrix} 2 & -3 \\ -4 & 6 \end{vmatrix} = 0.$ Rather, multiply first

equation by 2 and add to the second one.

$$\begin{array}{rcl} 4x - 6y & = & 12 \\ -4x + 6y & = & 1 \\ \hline 0 & = & 13 \end{array}$$

Inconsistent and the solution set is $\emptyset.$

18.

One finds $D = \begin{vmatrix} -2 & 3 & 1 \\ -3 & 1 & 3 \\ 0 & 2 & -1 \end{vmatrix} = -1,$

$D_x = \begin{vmatrix} -2 & 3 & 1 \\ -4 & 1 & 3 \\ 0 & 2 & -1 \end{vmatrix} = -6,$

$D_y = \begin{vmatrix} -2 & -2 & 1 \\ -3 & -4 & 3 \\ 0 & 0 & -1 \end{vmatrix} = -2, \text{ and}$

$D_z = \begin{vmatrix} -2 & 3 & -2 \\ -3 & 1 & -4 \\ 0 & 2 & 0 \end{vmatrix} = -4.$

Then $\dfrac{D_x}{D} = 6, \dfrac{D_y}{D} = 2,$ and $\dfrac{D_z}{D} = 4.$

The solution set is $\{(6, 2, 4)\}.$

19. The inverse of coefficient matrix is given

by $A^{-1} = \begin{bmatrix} 2 & 1/2 \\ 1 & 1/2 \end{bmatrix}.$ Since

$A^{-1} \begin{bmatrix} 1 \\ -8 \end{bmatrix} = \begin{bmatrix} -2 \\ -3 \end{bmatrix},$ the solution

set is $\{(-2, -3)\}.$

20. The inverse of coefficient matrix was found

in Exercise 12: $A^{-1} = \begin{bmatrix} 7 & -5 & -8 \\ 3 & -2 & -3 \\ 6 & -4 & -7 \end{bmatrix}.$

Since $A^{-1} \begin{bmatrix} 1 \\ 0 \\ -1 \end{bmatrix} = \begin{bmatrix} 15 \\ 6 \\ 13 \end{bmatrix},$ the

solution set is $\{(15, 6, 13)\}.$

21. Corresponding system of equations is

$$\begin{array}{rcl} x - y & = & 12 \\ 35y - 10x & = & 730. \end{array}$$

Solving this system, one finds $x = 46$ copies were bought and $y = 34$ copies were sold.

22. Substitute $(0, 3), (1, -1/2),$ and $(4, 3)$ into $y = ax^2 + b\sqrt{x} + c.$ Then we obtain

$$\begin{array}{rcl} c & = & 3 \\ a + b + c & = & -\dfrac{1}{2} \\ 16a + 2b + c & = & 3. \end{array}$$

Solving this system, one finds $a = 0.5$, $b = -4$, $c = 3$, and the graph is given by

$$y = 0.5x^2 - 4\sqrt{x} + 3.$$

Appendix

Basic Algebra Review

1 Real Numbers and Their Properties

The real numbers and their properties form the foundation for the study of algebra.

The Real Numbers

The set of **real numbers** is the set of numbers that correspond to points on the number line. There are several important subsets of the real numbers.

Subsets of the Real Numbers

Counting or natural numbers	$\{1, 2, 3, \dots\}$
Whole numbers	$\{0, 1, 2, 3, \dots\}$
Integers	$\{\dots, -3, -2, -1, 0, 1, 2, 3, \dots\}$
Rational numbers	Numbers of the form $\frac{a}{b}$, where a and b are integers with $b \neq 0$
Irrational numbers	Real numbers that are not rational

Using decimal notation, the rational numbers are the numbers that are repeating or terminating decimals, and the irrational numbers are the nonrepeating nonterminating decimals. For example, the number $0.595959\dots$ is a rational number because the three dots after the 9 mean that the pair 59 repeats indefinitely. In the number $5.010010001\dots$, the three dots mean that the pattern continues indefinitely. So each group of zeros contains one more zero than the previous group. Because no group of digits repeats, $5.010010001\dots$ is an irrational number.

The square root of any positive integer that is not a perfect square is irrational. So $\sqrt{2}$, $\sqrt{3}$, and $\sqrt{5}$ are irrational. The number π is irrational also. However, it is difficult to see that numbers like $\sqrt{2}$ and π are irrational because their decimal representations are not apparent. Since a calculator operates with a fixed number of decimal places, it gives us only a *rational approximation* for an irrational number such as $\sqrt{2}$ or π.

EXAMPLE 1 Classifying numbers

Determine whether each statement is true or false and explain.

a. The number 0 is a real number.
b. The number π is a rational number.
c. Every real number is rational.
d. No rational number is irrational.

Solution

a. True, because 0 is a whole number and the whole numbers are real.
b. False, because π is irrational.
c. False, because the irrational numbers are real numbers.
d. True, because the irrational numbers and the rational numbers have no numbers in common. ∎

From Appendix B of *Precalculus: Functions and Graphs*. Fourth Edition. Mark Dugopolski. Copyright © 2013 by Pearson Education, Inc. All rights reserved.

Properties of the Real Numbers

The operations of addition and multiplication on the real numbers have the following properties.

Properties of the Real Numbers

For any real numbers a, b, and c:

$a + b$ and ab are real numbers	**Closure Property**
$a + b = b + a$ and $ab = ba$	**Commutative Properties**
$a + (b + c) = (a + b) + c$ and $a(bc) = (ab)c$	**Associative Properties**
$a(b + c) = ab + ac$	**Distributive Property**
$0 + a = a$ and $1 \cdot a = a$	**Identity Properties**
$0 \cdot a = 0$	**Multiplication Property of Zero**
For each real number a, there is a unique real number $-a$ such that $a + (-a) = 0$.	**Additive Inverse Property**
For each nonzero number a, there is a unique real number $1/a$ such that $a \cdot 1/a = 1$.	**Multiplicative Inverse Property**

Zero is the **additive identity** and 1 is the **multiplicative identity.** The number $-a$ is the **additive inverse** or **opposite** of a, and $1/a$ is the **multiplicative inverse** or **reciprocal** of a.

Note that the properties stated here involve only addition and multiplication. We define subtraction as $a - b = a + (-b)$ and division as $a \div b = a \cdot 1/b$ for $b \neq 0$. Note that $a - b$ is called the **difference** of a and b and $a \div b$ is called the **quotient** of a and b.

EXAMPLE 2 Using the properties

Complete each statement using the property named.

a. $a7 = $ _____, commutative   **b.** $2x + 4 = $ _____, distributive

c. $8($_____$) = 1$, multiplicative inverse   **d.** $\frac{1}{3}(3x) = $ _____, associative

Solution

a. $a7 = 7a$ **b.** $2x + 4 = 2(x + 2)$

c. $8\left(\dfrac{1}{8}\right) = 1$ **d.** $\dfrac{1}{3}(3x) = \left(\dfrac{1}{3} \cdot 3\right)x$ ∎

Additive Inverses

We read -7 as negative 7, but we do not read $-a$ as negative a. The symbol $-a$ is read as the additive inverse or opposite of a. If a is positive, then $-a$ is negative. If a is negative, then $-a$ is positive. Some useful properties of additive inverses or opposites follow.

Properties of Opposites

For any real numbers a and b:

1. $-1 \cdot a = -a$	The product of -1 and a is the opposite of a.
2. $-(-a) = a$	The opposite of the opposite of a is a.
3. $-(a - b) = b - a$	The opposite of $a - b$ is $b - a$.

EXAMPLE 3 Using properties of opposites

Use the properties of opposites to complete each equation.

a. $-(-\pi) = $ _____ **b.** $-1(-2) = $ _____
c. $-1(x - h) = $ _____

Solution

a. $-(-\pi) = \pi$
b. $-1(-2) = -(-2) = 2$
c. $-1(x - h) = -(x - h) = h - x$ ∎

Absolute Value

The **absolute value** of a (in symbols $|a|$) is the distance from a to 0 on a number line. Since both 3 and -3 are three units from 0 on the number line, $|3| = 3$ and $|-3| = 3$. A symbolic definition of absolute value follows.

Definition: Absolute Value

For any real number a, $|a| = \begin{cases} a & \text{if } a \geq 0 \\ -a & \text{if } a < 0. \end{cases}$

Note that if $a < 0$, then $-a$ is positive. So $|a| \geq 0$ for any real number a.

EXAMPLE 4 Finding the absolute value of a number

Use the symbolic definition of absolute value to simplify each expression.

a. $|5.6|$ **b.** $|0|$ **c.** $|-3|$

Solution

a. Since $5.6 \geq 0$, we use the equation $|a| = a$ to get $|5.6| = 5.6$.
b. Since $0 \geq 0$, we use the equation $|a| = a$ to get $|0| = 0$.
c. Since $-3 < 0$, we use $|a| = -a$ to get $|-3| = -(-3) = 3$. ∎

Absolute value has the following properties.

Properties of Absolute Value

For any real numbers a and b:

1. $|a| \geq 0$ — The absolute value of any number is nonnegative.
2. $|-a| = |a|$ — Additive inverses have the same absolute value.
3. $|a \cdot b| = |a| \cdot |b|$ — The absolute value of a product is the product of the absolute values.
4. $\left|\dfrac{a}{b}\right| = \dfrac{|a|}{|b|}, b \neq 0$ — The absolute value of a quotient is the quotient of the absolute values.
5. The distance between a and b on a number line is $|a - b|$.

Exponential Expressions

We use positive integral exponents to indicate the number of times a number occurs in a product. For example, $2 \cdot 2 \cdot 2 \cdot 2$ is written as 2^4. We read 2^4 as "the fourth power of 2" or "2 to the fourth power."

Definition: Positive Integral Exponents

For any positive integer n:

$$a^n = \underbrace{a \cdot a \cdot a \cdot \cdots \cdot a}_{n \text{ factors of } a}$$

We call a the **base,** n the **exponent** or **power,** and a^n an **exponential expression.**

We read a^n as "a to the nth power." For a^1 we usually omit the exponent and just write a. We refer to the exponents 2 and 3 as squares and cubes. For example, 3^2 is read "3 squared," 2^3 is read "2 cubed," x^4 is read "x to the fourth," b^5 is read "b to the fifth," and so on. To evaluate an expression such as -3^2, we square 3 first, then take the opposite. So $-3^2 = -9$ and $(-3)^2 = (-3)(-3) = 9$.

EXAMPLE 5 Evaluating exponential expressions

Evaluate.

a. 4^3 **b.** $(-2)^4$ **c.** -2^4

Solution

a. $4^3 = 4 \cdot 4 \cdot 4 = 16 \cdot 4 = 64$
b. $(-2)^4 = (-2)(-2)(-2)(-2) = 16$
c. $-2^4 = -(2 \cdot 2 \cdot 2 \cdot 2) = -16$ ∎

Arithmetic Expressions

The result of writing numbers in a meaningful combination with the ordinary operations of arithmetic is called an **arithmetic expression** or simply an **expression.** The **value** of an arithmetic expression is the real number obtained when all operations are performed. Symbols such as parentheses, brackets, braces, absolute value bars, and fraction bars are called **grouping symbols.** Operations within grouping symbols are performed first.

EXAMPLE 6 Evaluating an arithmetic expression with grouping symbols

Evaluate each expression.

a. $(-7 \cdot 3) + (5 \cdot 8)$ **b.** $\dfrac{3 - 9}{-2 - (-5)}$ **c.** $3 - |5 - (2 \cdot 9)|$

Solution

a. Perform the operations within the parentheses first and remove the parentheses:

$$(-7 \cdot 3) + (5 \cdot 8) = -21 + 40 = 19$$

b. Since the fraction bar acts as a grouping symbol, we evaluate the numerator and denominator before dividing.

$$\frac{3 - 9}{-2 - (-5)} = \frac{-6}{3} = -2$$

c. First evaluate within the innermost grouping symbols:

$$3 - |5 - (2 \cdot 9)| = 3 - |5 - 18| \qquad \text{Innermost grouping symbols}$$
$$= 3 - |-13| \qquad \text{Innermost grouping symbols}$$
$$= 3 - 13 \qquad \text{Evaluate the absolute value.}$$
$$= -10 \qquad \text{Subtract.} \qquad \blacksquare$$

The Order of Operations

When some or all grouping symbols are omitted in an expression, we evaluate the expression using the following order of operations.

Order of Operations

> 1. Evaluate exponential expressions.
> 2. Perform multiplication and division in order from left to right.
> 3. Perform addition and subtraction in order from left to right.

EXAMPLE 7 Using the order of operations to evaluate an expression

Evaluate each expression.

a. $3 - 4 \cdot 2^3$ **b.** $5 \cdot 8 \div 4 \cdot 2$ **c.** $3 - 4 + 9 - 2$

Solution

a. By the order of operations evaluate 2^3, then multiply, and then subtract:

$$3 - 4 \cdot 2^3 = 3 - 4 \cdot 8 = 3 - 32 = -29$$

b. In an expression with only multiplication and division, the operations are performed from left to right:

$$5 \cdot 8 \div 4 \cdot 2 = 40 \div 4 \cdot 2 = 10 \cdot 2 = 20$$

c. In an expression with only addition and subtraction, the operations are performed from left to right:

$$3 - 4 + 9 - 2 = -1 + 9 - 2 = 8 - 2 = 6 \qquad \blacksquare$$

Algebraic Expressions

When we write numbers and one or more variables in a meaningful combination with the ordinary operations of arithmetic, the result is called an **algebraic expression,** or simply an expression. The **value of an algebraic expression** is the value of the arithmetic expression that is obtained when the variables are replaced by real numbers.

EXAMPLE 8 Evaluating an algebraic expression

Find the value of $b^2 - 4ac$ when $a = -1$, $b = -2$, and $c = 3$.

Solution

Replace the variables by the appropriate numbers:

$$b^2 - 4ac = (-2)^2 - 4(-1)(3) = 16 \qquad \blacksquare$$

The **domain** of an algebraic expression in one variable is the set of all real numbers that can be used for the variable. For example, the domain of $1/x$ is the set of nonzero real numbers, because division by 0 is undefined. Two algebraic expressions in one variable are **equivalent** if they have the same domain and if they have the same value for each member of the domain. The expressions $1/x$ and x/x^2 are equivalent.

An expression that is the product of a number and one or more variables raised to powers is called a **term**. Expressions such as $3x$, $2kab^3$, and πr^2 are terms. In the term $3x$, 3 and x are called **factors**. The **coefficient** of any variable part of a term is the product of the remaining factors in the term. For example, the coefficient of x in $3x$ is 3. The coefficient of ab^3 in $2kab^3$ is $2k$ and the coefficient of b^3 is $2ka$. If two terms contain the same variables with the same exponents, then they are called **like terms**. The distributive property allows us to **combine like terms:** $3x + 2x = (3 + 2)x = 5x$.

To **simplify** an expression means to find a simpler-looking equivalent expression. The properties of the real numbers are used to simplify expressions.

EXAMPLE 9 | Using properties to simplify an expression

Simplify each expression.

a. $-4x - (6 - 7x)$ **b.** $\dfrac{1}{2}x - \dfrac{3}{4}x$ **c.** $-6(x - 3) - 3(5 - 7x)$

Solution

a.
$$-4x - (6 - 7x) = -4x + \left[-(6 + (-7x))\right] \quad \text{Definition of subtraction}$$
$$= -4x + \left[-1(6 + (-7x))\right] \quad \text{First property of opposites}$$
$$= -4x + \left[(-6) + 7x\right] \quad \text{Distributive property}$$
$$= \left[-4x + 7x\right] + (-6) \quad \text{Commutative and associative properties}$$
$$= 3x - 6 \quad \text{Combine like terms.}$$

b.
$$\dfrac{1}{2}x - \dfrac{3}{4}x = \dfrac{2}{4}x - \dfrac{3}{4}x \quad \text{Write } \dfrac{1}{2} \text{ as } \dfrac{2}{4} \text{ to obtain a common denominator.}$$
$$= -\dfrac{1}{4}x \quad \text{Combine like terms.}$$

c.
$$-6(x - 3) - 3(5 - 7x) = -6x + 18 - 15 + 21x \quad \text{Distributive property}$$
$$= 15x + 3 \quad \text{Combine like terms.} \quad \blacksquare$$

EXERCISES 1

Determine which numbers in the set $\{-3.5, -\sqrt{2}, -1, 0, 1, \sqrt{3},$ $3.14, \pi, 4.3535\ldots, 5.090090009\ldots\}$ are members of the following sets.

1. Real numbers

2. Rational numbers

3. Irrational numbers

4. Integers   5. Whole numbers

6. Natural numbers

Complete each statement using the property named.

7. $7 + x =$ _____, commutative

8. $5(4y) =$ _____, associative

9. $5(x + 3) =$ _____, distributive

10. $-3(x - 4) =$ _____, distributive

11. $\dfrac{1}{2}x + \dfrac{1}{2} =$ _____, distributive

12. $-5x + 10 =$ _____, distributive

13. $-13 + (4 + x) = $ _____, associative

14. $yx = $ _____, commutative

15. $0.125($ _____ $) = 1$, multiplicative inverse

16. $-3 + ($ _____ $) = 0$, additive inverse

Use the properties of opposites to complete each equation.

17. $-(-\sqrt{3}) = $

18. $-1(-6.4) = $

19. $-1(x^2 - y^2) = $

20. $-(1 - a^2) = $

Use the symbolic definition of absolute value to simplify each expression.

21. $|7.2|$ **22.** $|0/3|$ **23.** $|-\sqrt{5}|$ **24.** $|-3/4|$

Evaluate each expression.

25. 4^3 **26.** 3^4 **27.** -7^2

28. -9^2 **29.** $(-4)^2$ **30.** $(-10)^4$

Evaluate each expression.

31. $(2 \cdot 5) - (3 \cdot 6)$ **32.** $(5 - 3)(2 - 6)$

33. $|3 - (4 \cdot 5)| - 5$ **34.** $5 - |4 - (2 \cdot 3)|$

35. $|-4 \cdot 3| - |-3 \cdot 5|$ **36.** $(-8 \cdot 3) - |-3 \cdot 7|$

37. $\dfrac{-2 - (-6)}{-5 - (-9)}$ **38.** $\dfrac{4 - (-3)}{-3 - (-1)}$

Use the order of operations to evaluate each expression.

39. $4 - 5 \cdot 3^2$ **40.** $4 + 2(-6)^2$

41. $3 - 4 + 5 - 7 - 4$ **42.** $4 - 3 + 2 - 5 + 6$

43. $3 \cdot 6 + 2 \cdot 4$ **44.** $-2 \cdot 9 + 3 \cdot 5$

45. $26 \cdot \dfrac{1}{5} \div \dfrac{1}{2} \cdot 5$ **46.** $\dfrac{4}{3} \cdot 50(0.75) \div 2$

47. $(3 \cdot 4 - 1)(1 + 2 \cdot 4)$ **48.** $-2 - 3(5 - 2 \cdot 8)$

49. $2 - 3|3 - 4 \cdot 6|$ **50.** $1 - (3 - |1 - 2 \cdot 3|)$

51. $7^2 - 2(-3)(-6)$ **52.** $(-3)^2 - 4(-2)(-5)$

53. $(-2 - 3)^2 - (4 - (-1))^2$

54. $-(5 - (-2))^2 + (6 - 7)^2$

Evaluate each expression if $a = -2$, $b = 3$, and $c = 4$.

55. $b^2 - 4ac$ **56.** $(b - 4ac)^2$

57. $\dfrac{a - c}{b - c}$ **58.** $\dfrac{a^2 - c}{b^3 + c^4}$

Use the properties of the real numbers to simplify each expression.

59. $-5x + 3x$ **60.** $-5x - (-8x)$

61. $x - 0.15x$ **62.** $x + 3 - 0.9x$

63. $-3(2xy)$ **64.** $\dfrac{1}{2}(8wz)$

65. $\dfrac{1}{2}(6 - 4x)$ **66.** $\dfrac{1}{4}(8x - 4)$

67. $\dfrac{6x - 2y}{2}$ **68.** $\dfrac{-9 - 6x}{-3}$

69. $(3 - 4x) + (x - 9)$ **70.** $(9x - 3) + (4 - 6x)$

71. $x - 0.03(x + 200)$ **72.** $y - 0.9(y - 3000)$

73. $-2(4 - x) - 3(3 - 3x)$ **74.** $5(4 - 2x) - 2(x - 5)$

2 Exponents and Radicals

We reviewed positive integral exponents in the last section. In this section we review negative integral exponents, rational exponents, and radicals.

Negative Integral Exponents

We use a negative sign in an exponent to represent multiplicative inverses or reciprocals. For negative exponents we do not allow the base to be zero because zero does not have a reciprocal.

Definition: Negative Integral Exponents

If a is a nonzero real number and n is a positive integer, then $a^{-n} = \dfrac{1}{a^n}$.

Appendix: Basic Algebra Review

EXAMPLE 1 Evaluating expressions that have negative exponents

Simplify each expression without using a calculator, then check with a calculator.

a. $4 \cdot 2^{-3}$ **b.** $\left(\dfrac{2}{3}\right)^{-3}$ **c.** $\dfrac{6^{-2}}{2^{-3}}$

Solution

a. $4 \cdot 2^{-3} = 4 \cdot \dfrac{1}{2^3} = 4 \cdot \dfrac{1}{8} = \dfrac{1}{2}$

b. $\left(\dfrac{2}{3}\right)^{-3} = \dfrac{1}{\left(\dfrac{2}{3}\right)^3} = \dfrac{1}{\dfrac{2}{3} \cdot \dfrac{2}{3} \cdot \dfrac{2}{3}} = \dfrac{1}{\dfrac{8}{27}} = \dfrac{27}{8}$ Note that $\left(\dfrac{2}{3}\right)^{-3} = \left(\dfrac{3}{2}\right)^{3}$.

c. $\dfrac{6^{-2}}{2^{-3}} = \dfrac{\dfrac{1}{6^2}}{\dfrac{1}{2^3}} = \dfrac{1}{6^2} \cdot \dfrac{2^3}{1} = \dfrac{8}{36} = \dfrac{2}{9}$ Note that $\dfrac{6^{-2}}{2^{-3}} = \dfrac{2^3}{6^2}$. ∎

Example 1(b) illustrates the fact that a fractional base can be inverted, if the sign of the exponent is changed. Example 1(c) illustrates the fact that a factor of the numerator or denominator can be moved from the numerator to the denominator or vice versa as long as we change the sign of the exponent.

Rules for Negative Exponents and Fractions

If a and b are nonzero real numbers and m and n are integers, then

$$\left(\dfrac{a}{b}\right)^{-m} = \left(\dfrac{b}{a}\right)^{m} \qquad \text{and} \qquad \dfrac{a^{-m}}{b^{-n}} = \dfrac{b^n}{a^m}.$$

Be careful with the rules of exponents when sums or differences are involved. For example, $\dfrac{2^{-1}-1}{3^{-1}} \neq \dfrac{3^1-1}{2^1}$ because

$$\dfrac{2^{-1}-1}{3^{-1}} = \dfrac{\dfrac{1}{2}-1}{\dfrac{1}{3}} = -\dfrac{3}{2} \qquad \text{and} \qquad \dfrac{3^1-1}{2^1} = 1.$$

Rules of Exponents

So far we have defined positive and negative integral exponents. Zero as an exponent is defined as follows.

Definition: Zero Exponent

If a is a nonzero real number, then $a^0 = 1$.

Using the definitions of positive, negative, and zero exponents, we can show that the following rules hold for any integral exponents.

Rules for Integral Exponents

If a and b are nonzero real numbers and m and n are integers, then

1. $a^m a^n = a^{m+n}$ **Product Rule**
2. $\dfrac{a^m}{a^n} = a^{m-n}$ **Quotient Rule**
3. $(a^m)^n = a^{mn}$ **Power of a Power Rule**
4. $(ab)^n = a^n b^n$ **Power of a Product Rule**
5. $\left(\dfrac{a}{b}\right)^n = \dfrac{a^n}{b^n}$ **Power of a Quotient Rule**

736

The rules for integral exponents are used to simplify expressions in the next example.

EXAMPLE 2 Simplifying expressions with integral exponents

Simplify each expression. Write your answer without negative exponents. Assume that all variables represent nonzero real numbers.

a. $(3x^2)^3(-2x^{-2})$ **b.** $\left(\dfrac{a^5b^{-1}}{a^7}\right)^4$

Solution

a. $(3x^2)^3(-2x^{-2}) = 3^3(x^2)^3(-2x^{-2})$ Power of a product rule

$= 27x^6(-2x^{-2})$ Power of a power rule

$= -54x^4$ Product rule

b. $\left(\dfrac{a^5b^{-1}}{a^7}\right)^4 = \dfrac{(a^5b^{-1})^4}{(a^7)^4}$ Power of a quotient rule

$= \dfrac{(a^5)^4(b^{-1})^4}{(a^7)^4}$ Power of a product rule

$= \dfrac{a^{20}b^{-4}}{a^{28}}$ Power of a power rule

$= a^{-8}b^{-4}$ Quotient rule

$= \dfrac{1}{a^8b^4}$ Definition of negative exponent ∎

Roots

Since $2^4 = 16$ and $(-2)^4 = 16$, both 2 and -2 are fourth roots of 16. The nth root of a number is defined in terms of the nth power.

Definition: *n*th Roots

> If n is a positive integer and $a^n = b$, then a is called an **nth root** of b.
>
> If $a^2 = b$, then a is a **square root** of b. If $a^3 = b$, then a is the **cube root** of b.

If n is even and a is an nth root of b, then a is called an **even root** of b. If n is odd and a is an nth root of b, then a is called an **odd root** of b. Every positive real number has *two* real even roots, a positive root and a negative root. For example, both 5 and -5 are square roots of 25 because $5^2 = 25$ and $(-5)^2 = 25$. Moreover, every real number has exactly *one* real odd root. For example, because $2^3 = 8$ and 3 is odd, 2 is the only real cube root of 8. Because $(-2)^3 = -8$ and 3 is odd, -2 is the only real cube root of -8.

Finding an nth root is the reverse of finding an nth power, so we use the notation $a^{1/n}$ for the nth root of a. For example, since the positive square root of 25 is 5, we write $25^{1/2} = 5$.

Definition: Exponent 1/*n*

> If n is a positive even integer and a is positive, then $a^{1/n}$ denotes the **positive real nth root of a** and is called the **principal nth root of a**.
>
> If n is a positive odd integer and a is any real number, then $a^{1/n}$ denotes the real nth root of a.
>
> If n is a positive integer, then $0^{1/n} = 0$.

EXAMPLE 3 Evaluating expressions involving exponent $1/n$

Evaluate each expression.

a. $4^{1/2}$ **b.** $(-8)^{1/3}$ **c.** $(-4)^{1/2}$

Solution

a. Because the positive real square root of 4 is 2, $4^{1/2} = 2$.
b. Because the real cube root of -8 is -2, $(-8)^{1/3} = -2$.
c. Since the definition of nth root does not include an even root of a negative number, $(-4)^{1/2}$ has not yet been defined. Even roots of negative numbers do exist in the complex number system, but an even root of a negative number is not a real number. ∎

Rational Exponents

A rational exponent indicates both a root and a power. The expression $a^{m/n}$ is defined as the mth power of the nth root of a.

Definition: Rational Exponents

If m and n are positive integers, then

$$a^{m/n} = (a^{1/n})^m,$$

provided that $a^{1/n}$ is a real number.

Note that $a^{1/n}$ is not real when a is negative and n is even. According to the definition of rational exponents, expressions such as $(-25)^{-3/2}$, $(-43)^{1/4}$, and $(-1)^{2/2}$ are not defined because each of them involves an even root of a negative number. Note that some authors define $a^{m/n}$ only for m/n in lowest terms. In that case the fourth power of the square root of three could *not* be written as $3^{4/2}$. This author prefers the more general definition given above.

A negative rational exponent indicates a reciprocal just as a negative integral exponent does. So $7^{-2/3} = 1/7^{2/3}$. The root or the power indicated by a rational exponent can be evaluated in either order. That is, $(a^{1/n})^m = (a^m)^{1/n}$, provided $a^{1/n}$ is real. However, for mental evaluation the following order is best.

Procedure: Evaluating $a^{-m/n}$

To evaluate $a^{-m/n}$ mentally,

1. find the nth root of a,   **2.** raise it to the m power,   **3.** find the reciprocal.

EXAMPLE 4 Evaluating expressions with rational exponents

Evaluate each expression.

a. $(-8)^{2/3}$ **b.** $27^{-2/3}$ **c.** $100^{6/4}$

Solution

a. Mentally, the cube root of -8 is -2 and the square of -2 is 4. In symbols:

$$(-8)^{2/3} = ((-8)^{1/3})^2 = (-2)^2 = 4$$

b. Mentally, the cube root of 27 is 3, the square of 3 is 9, and the reciprocal of 9 is $\frac{1}{9}$. In symbols:

$$27^{-2/3} = \frac{1}{(27^{1/3})^2} = \frac{1}{3^2} = \frac{1}{9}$$

c. $100^{6/4} = 100^{3/2} = 10^3 = 1000$ ∎

Note how we reduced the exponent in Example 4(c). However, exponents can be reduced only on expressions that are defined. For example, $(-1)^{2/2} \neq (-1)^1$ because $(-1)^{2/2}$ is an undefined expression.

The rules for integral exponents stated previously in this section also hold for rational exponents. Note that the power of a power rule can fail if the base is negative. For example, $(x^2)^{1/2} = x$ according to the rule. However, if x is a negative number the left side of this equation is positive and the right side is negative. So $(x^2)^{1/2} = x$ is only correct if x is nonnegative. The equation $(x^2)^{1/2} = |x|$ is correct for any x.

EXAMPLE 5 Simplifying expressions with rational exponents

Use the rules of exponents to simplify each expression. Assume that the variables represent positive real numbers. Write answers without negative exponents.

a. $x^{2/3}x^{4/3}$ **b.** $(x^4 y^{1/2})^{1/4}$ **c.** $\left(\dfrac{a^{3/2}b^{2/3}}{a^2}\right)^3$

Solution

a. $x^{2/3}x^{4/3} = x^{6/3}$ Product rule

$\qquad\qquad = x^2$ Simplify the exponent.

b. $(x^4 y^{1/2})^{1/4} = (x^4)^{1/4}(y^{1/2})^{1/4}$ Power of a product rule

$\qquad\qquad\quad = xy^{1/8}$ Power of a power rule

c. $\left(\dfrac{a^{3/2}b^{2/3}}{a^2}\right)^3 = \dfrac{(a^{3/2})^3(b^{2/3})^3}{(a^2)^3}$ Power of a quotient rule

$\qquad\qquad\quad = \dfrac{a^{9/2}b^2}{a^6}$ Power of power rule

$\qquad\qquad\quad = a^{-3/2}b^2$ Quotient rule $\left(\dfrac{9}{2} - 6 = -\dfrac{3}{2}\right)$

$\qquad\qquad\quad = \dfrac{b^2}{a^{3/2}}$ Definition of negative exponents ∎

Radical Notation

The exponent $1/n$ and the **radical sign** $\sqrt[n]{\ }$ are both used to indicate the nth root.

Definition:
Radical Notation

> If n is a positive integer and a is a number for which $a^{1/n}$ is defined, then the expression $\sqrt[n]{a}$ is called a **radical,** and
>
> $$\sqrt[n]{a} = a^{1/n}.$$
>
> If $n = 2$, we write $\sqrt{a}$ rather than $\sqrt[2]{a}$.

The number a is called the **radicand** and n is the **index** of the radical. Expressions such as $\sqrt{-3}$, $\sqrt[4]{-81}$, and $\sqrt[6]{-1}$ do not represent real numbers because each is an even root of a negative number.

EXAMPLE 6 Evaluating radicals

Evaluate each expression.

a. $\sqrt{49}$ **b.** $\sqrt[3]{-1000}$ **c.** $\sqrt[4]{\dfrac{16}{81}}$ **d.** $\sqrt[3]{125^2}$

Solution

a. The symbol $\sqrt{49}$ indicates the positive square root of 49. So $\sqrt{49} = 49^{1/2} = 7$. Writing $\sqrt{49} = \pm 7$ is incorrect.

b. $\sqrt[3]{-1000} = (-1000)^{1/3} = -10$ Check that $(-10)^3 = -1000$.

c. $\sqrt[4]{\dfrac{16}{81}} = \left(\dfrac{16}{81}\right)^{1/4} = \dfrac{2}{3}$ Check that $\left(\dfrac{2}{3}\right)^4 = \dfrac{16}{81}$.

d. $\sqrt[3]{125^2} = (125^2)^{1/3} = 125^{2/3} = 5^2 = 25$ ■

Since $a^{1/n} = \sqrt[n]{a}$, expressions involving rational exponents can be written with radicals.

Rule: Converting $a^{m/n}$ to Radical Notation

If a is a real number and m and n are integers for which $\sqrt[n]{a}$ is real, then

$$a^{m/n} = (\sqrt[n]{a})^m = \sqrt[n]{a^m}.$$

EXAMPLE 7 Converting rational exponents to radicals

Write each expression in radical notation. Assume that all variables represent positive real numbers. Simplify the radicand if possible.

a. $2^{2/3}$ **b.** $(3x)^{3/4}$ **c.** $2(x^2 + 3)^{-1/2}$

Solution

a. $2^{2/3} = \sqrt[3]{2^2} = \sqrt[3]{4}$

b. $(3x)^{3/4} = \sqrt[4]{(3x)^3} = \sqrt[4]{27x^3}$

c. $2(x^2 + 3)^{-1/2} = 2 \cdot \dfrac{1}{(x^2 + 3)^{1/2}} = \dfrac{2}{\sqrt{x^2 + 3}}$ ■

The Product and Quotient Rules for Radicals

Using the power of a product and the power of a quotient rules for rational exponents, we can write

$$(ab)^{1/n} = a^{1/n}b^{1/n} \quad \text{and} \quad \left(\dfrac{a}{b}\right)^{1/n} = \dfrac{a^{1/n}}{b^{1/n}}.$$

These rules are expressed in radical notation as follows.

Rules: Product and Quotient Rules for Radicals

For any positive integer n and real numbers a and b ($b \neq 0$),

1. $\sqrt[n]{ab} = \sqrt[n]{a} \cdot \sqrt[n]{b}$ **Product Rule for Radicals**

2. $\sqrt[n]{\dfrac{a}{b}} = \dfrac{\sqrt[n]{a}}{\sqrt[n]{b}}$ **Quotient Rule for Radicals**

provided that all of the roots are real.

In words, the nth root of a product (or quotient) is the product (or quotient) of the nth roots.

An expression that is the square of a term that is free of radicals is called a **perfect square.** For example, $9x^6$ is a perfect square because $9x^6 = (3x^3)^2$. Likewise, $27y^{12}$ is a **perfect cube.** In general, an expression that is the nth power of an expression free of radicals is a **perfect nth power.** In the next example, the product and quotient rules for radicals are used to simplify radicals containing perfect squares, cubes, and so on.

EXAMPLE 8 | Using the product and quotient rules for radicals

Simplify each radical expression. Assume that all variables represent positive real numbers.

a. $\sqrt[3]{125a^6}$ **b.** $\sqrt{\dfrac{3}{16x^2}}$

Solution

a. Both 125 and a^6 are perfect cubes. So use the product rule to simplify:

$$\sqrt[3]{125a^6} = \sqrt[3]{125} \cdot \sqrt[3]{a^6} = 5a^2 \quad \text{Since } \sqrt[3]{a^6} = a^{6/3} = a^2$$

b. Since 16 is a perfect square, use the quotient rule to simplify the radical:

$$\sqrt{\dfrac{3}{16x^2}} = \dfrac{\sqrt{3}}{\sqrt{16x^2}} = \dfrac{\sqrt{3}}{4x}$$

$\blacksquare$

Simplified Form and Rationalizing the Denominator

We have been simplifying radical expressions by just making them look simpler. However, a radical expression is in *simplified form* only if it satisfies the following three specific conditions.

Definition: Simplified Form for Radicals of Index n

A radical of index n in **simplified form** has

1. *no* perfect nth powers as factors of the radicand,
2. *no* fractions inside the radical, and
3. *no* radicals in a denominator.

The process of removing radicals from a denominator is called **rationalizing the denominator.**

EXAMPLE 9 | Simplified form of a radical expression

Write each radical expression in simplified form. Assume that all variables represent positive real numbers.

a. $\sqrt{20x^8y^9}$ **b.** $\dfrac{9}{\sqrt{3}}$ **c.** $\sqrt[3]{\dfrac{3}{5a^4}}$

Solution

a. Use the product rule to factor the radical, putting all perfect squares in the first factor:

$$\sqrt{20x^8y^9} = \sqrt{4x^8y^8}\,\sqrt{5y} \quad \text{Product rule}$$

$$= 2x^4y^4\,\sqrt{5y} \quad \text{Simplify the first radical.}$$

b. Since $\sqrt{3}$ appears in the denominator, we multiply the numerator and denominator by $\sqrt{3}$ to rationalize the denominator:

$$\frac{9}{\sqrt{3}} = \frac{9\sqrt{3}}{\sqrt{3}\sqrt{3}} = \frac{9\sqrt{3}}{3} = 3\sqrt{3}$$

c. To rationalize this denominator, we must get a perfect cube in the denominator. The radicand $5a^4$ can be made into the perfect cube $125a^6$ by multiplying by $25a^2$.

$$\sqrt[3]{\frac{3}{5a^4}} = \frac{\sqrt[3]{3}}{\sqrt[3]{5a^4}} \qquad \text{Quotient rule for radicals}$$

$$= \frac{\sqrt[3]{3}\sqrt[3]{25a^2}}{\sqrt[3]{5a^4}\sqrt[3]{25a^2}} \qquad \text{Multiply numerator and denominator by } \sqrt[3]{25a^2}.$$

$$= \frac{\sqrt[3]{75a^2}}{\sqrt[3]{125a^6}} \qquad \text{Product rule for radicals}$$

$$= \frac{\sqrt[3]{75a^2}}{5a^2} \qquad \text{Since } (5a^2)^3 = 125a^6$$

Operations with Radical Expressions

We can use the properties of radicals to add, subtract, multiply, and divide radical expressions with the same index.

EXAMPLE 10 Operations with radicals of the same index

Perform each operation and write the answer in simplified form for radicals. Assume that each variable represents a positive real number.

a. $\sqrt{20} + \sqrt{5}$ **b.** $\sqrt[4]{4y^3}\sqrt[4]{12y^2}$ **c.** $\sqrt{40} \div \sqrt{5}$

Solution

a. $\sqrt{20} + \sqrt{5} = \sqrt{4}\sqrt{5} + \sqrt{5}$ Product rule for radicals

$\qquad\qquad = 2\sqrt{5} + \sqrt{5}$ Simplify.

$\qquad\qquad = (2 + 1)\sqrt{5}$ Distributive property

$\qquad\qquad = 3\sqrt{5}$ Simplify.

b. $\sqrt[4]{4y^3}\sqrt[4]{12y^2} = \sqrt[4]{48y^5}$ Product rule for radicals

$\qquad\qquad = \sqrt[4]{16y^4}\sqrt[4]{3y}$ Factor out the perfect fourth powers.

$\qquad\qquad = 2y\sqrt[4]{3y}$ Simplify.

c. $\sqrt{40} \div \sqrt{5} = \sqrt{\dfrac{40}{5}}$ Quotient rule for radicals

$\qquad\qquad = \sqrt{8}$ Divide.

$\qquad\qquad = \sqrt{4}\sqrt{2}$ Product rule for radicals

$\qquad\qquad = 2\sqrt{2}$ Simplify.

Radical expressions that can be added or subtracted using the distributive property as in Example 10(a) are called **like radicals**. Note that it is not necessary to write out the distributive step. We can simply write $2\sqrt{5} + \sqrt{5} = 3\sqrt{5}$ just like we write $2x + x = 3x$.

EXERCISES 2

Evaluate each expression.

1. 3^{-4}

2. $\dfrac{1}{2^{-3}}$

3. $6^{-1} + 5^{-1}$

4. $2^0 + 2^{-1}$

5. $\dfrac{3^{-2}}{6^{-3}}$

6. $\dfrac{3^{-1}}{2^3}$

7. $\left(\dfrac{1}{2}\right)^{-3}$

8. $\left(-\dfrac{1}{10}\right)^{-4}$

Simplify each expression. Write answers without negative exponents. Assume that all variables represent nonzero real numbers.

9. $(-3x^2y^3)(2x^9y^8)$

10. $(-6a^7b^4)(3a^3b^5)$

11. $y^3y^2 + 2y^4y$

12. $x^2x^5 + x^3x^4$

13. $-1(2x^3)^2$

14. $(-3y^{-1})^{-1}$

15. $\left(\dfrac{-2x^2}{3}\right)^3$

16. $\left(\dfrac{-1}{2a}\right)^{-2}$

17. $\dfrac{6x^7}{2x^3}$

18. $\dfrac{-9x^2y}{3xy^2}$

19. $\left(\dfrac{y^2}{5}\right)^{-2}$

20. $\left(-\dfrac{y^2}{2a}\right)^4$

21. $\left(\dfrac{1}{2}x^{-4}y^3\right)\left(\dfrac{1}{3}x^4y^{-6}\right)$

22. $\left(\dfrac{1}{3}a^{-5}b\right)(a^4b^{-1})$

23. $\left(\dfrac{-3m^{-1}n}{-6m^{-1}n^{-1}}\right)^2$

24. $\left(\dfrac{-p^{-1}q^{-1}}{-3pq^{-3}}\right)^{-2}$

Evaluate each expression.

25. $-9^{1/2}$

26. $27^{1/3}$

27. $64^{1/2}$

28. $-144^{1/2}$

29. $(-64)^{1/3}$

30. $81^{1/4}$

31. $(-27)^{4/3}$

32. $125^{-2/3}$

33. $8^{-4/3}$

34. $4^{-3/2}$

Simplify each expression. Assume that all variables represent positive real numbers. Write your answers without negative exponents.

35. $(x^4y)^{1/2}$

36. $(a^{1/2}b^{1/3})^2$

37. $(2a^{1/2})(3a)$

38. $(-3y^{1/3})(-2y^{1/2})$

39. $\dfrac{6a^{1/2}}{2a^{1/3}}$

40. $\dfrac{-4y}{2y^{2/3}}$

41. $(a^2b^{1/2})(a^{1/3}b^{1/2})$

42. $(4^{3/4}a^2b^3)(4^{3/4}a^{-2}b^{-5})$

43. $\left(\dfrac{x^6y^3}{z^9}\right)^{1/3}$

44. $\left(\dfrac{x^{1/2}y}{y^{1/2}}\right)^3$

Evaluate each radical expression.

45. $\sqrt{900}$

46. $\sqrt{400}$

47. $\sqrt[3]{-8}$

48. $\sqrt[3]{64}$

49. $\sqrt[3]{-\dfrac{8}{1000}}$

50. $\sqrt[4]{\dfrac{1}{625}}$

51. $\sqrt[4]{16^3}$

52. $\sqrt[3]{8^5}$

Write each expression involving rational exponents in radical notation, and each expression involving radicals in exponential notation.

53. $10^{2/3}$

54. $-2^{3/4}$

55. $3y^{-3/5}$

56. $a(b^4 + 1)^{-1/2}$

57. $\dfrac{1}{\sqrt{x}}$

58. $-4\sqrt{x^3}$

59. $\sqrt[5]{x^3}$

60. $\sqrt[3]{x^3 + y^3}$

Simplify each radical expression. Assume that all variables represent positive real numbers.

61. $\sqrt{16x^2}$

62. $\sqrt{121y^4}$

63. $\sqrt[3]{8y^9}$

64. $\sqrt[3]{125x^{18}}$

65. $\sqrt{\dfrac{xy}{100}}$

66. $\sqrt{\dfrac{t}{81}}$

67. $\sqrt[3]{\dfrac{-8a^3}{b^{15}}}$

68. $\sqrt[4]{\dfrac{16t^4}{y^8}}$

Write each radical expression in simplified form. Assume that all variables represent positive real numbers.

69. $\sqrt{28}$

70. $\sqrt{50}$

71. $\dfrac{1}{\sqrt{5}}$

72. $\dfrac{7}{\sqrt{7}}$

73. $\sqrt{\dfrac{x}{8}}$

74. $\sqrt{\dfrac{3y}{20}}$

75. $\sqrt[3]{40}$

76. $\sqrt[3]{54}$

77. $\sqrt[3]{-250x^4}$

78. $\sqrt[3]{-24a^5}$

79. $\sqrt[3]{\dfrac{1}{2}}$

80. $\sqrt[3]{\dfrac{3x}{25}}$

Perform the indicated operations and simplify your answer. Assume that all variables represent positive real numbers.

81. $3\sqrt{6} + 9 - 5\sqrt{6}$

82. $3\sqrt{2} + 8 - 5\sqrt{2}$

83. $\sqrt{8} + \sqrt{20} - \sqrt{12}$

84. $\sqrt{18} - \sqrt{50} + \sqrt{12} - \sqrt{75}$

85. $(-2\sqrt{3})(5\sqrt{6})$

86. $(-3\sqrt{2})(-2\sqrt{3})$

87. $(3\sqrt{5a})(4\sqrt{5a})$

88. $(-2\sqrt{6})(3\sqrt{6})$

89. $\sqrt{18a} \div \sqrt{2a^4}$

90. $\sqrt{21x^7} \div \sqrt{3x^2}$

91. $\sqrt{20x^3} + \sqrt{45x^3}$

92. $\sqrt[3]{16a^4} + \sqrt[3]{54a^4}$

3 Polynomials

In this section we will review some basic facts about polynomials.

Definitions

A term was defined in Section 1 as the product of a number and one or more variables raised to powers. A **polynomial** is simply a single term or a finite sum of terms in which the powers of the variables are whole numbers. A polynomial in one variable is defined as follows.

Definition: Polynomial in One Variable x

> If n is a nonnegative integer and $a_0, a_1, a_2, \ldots, a_n$ are real numbers, then
>
> $$a_n x^n + a_{n-1} x^{n-1} + a_{n-2} x^{n-2} + \cdots + a_1 x + a_0$$
>
> is a **polynomial** in one variable x.

In algebra a single number is often referred to as a **constant.** The last term a_0 is called the **constant term.**

Polynomials with one, two, and three terms are called **monomials, binomials, and trinomials,** respectively. We usually write the terms of a polynomial in a single variable so that the exponents are in descending order from left to right. When a polynomial is written in this manner, the coefficient of the first term is the **leading coefficient.** The **degree** of a polynomial in one variable is the highest power of the variable in the polynomial. A constant such as 5 is a monomial with zero degree because $5 = 5x^0$. First-, second-, and third-degree polynomials are called **linear, quadratic,** and **cubic polynomials,** respectively.

> **EXAMPLE 1** Using the definitions

Find the degree and leading coefficient of each polynomial and determine whether the polynomial is a monomial, binomial, or trinomial.

a. $\dfrac{x^3}{2} - \dfrac{1}{8}$ **b.** $5y^2 + y - 9$ **c.** $3w$

Solution

Polynomial (a) is a third-degree binomial, (b) is a second-degree trinomial, and (c) is a first-degree monomial. The leading coefficients are 1/2, 5, and 3, respectively. We can also describe (a) as a cubic polynomial, (b) as a quadratic polynomial, and (c) as a linear polynomial. ■

Naming and Evaluating Polynomials

Polynomials are often used to model quantities such as profit, revenue, and cost. A profit polynomial might be named P. For example, if the expression $3x - 10$ is a profit polynomial, we write $P = 3x - 10$ or $P(x) = 3x - 10$. P and $P(x)$ (read "P of x") both represent the profit when x units are sold. If $x = 6$, then the value of the polynomial is $3 \cdot 6 - 10$ or 8. If $x = 7$ the value is 11. Using the $P(x)$ notation we write $P(6) = 8$ and $P(7) = 11$. With the $P(x)$ notation it is clear that the profit for six units is 8 and the profit for seven units is 11. The $P(x)$ notation is called **function notation.**

EXAMPLE 2 Evaluating a polynomial

Let $P(x) = x^2 - 5$ and $C(x) = -x^3 + 5x - 3$. Find the following.

a. $P(3)$ **b.** $C(10)$

Solution

a. $P(3) = 3^2 - 5 = 4$
b. $C(10) = -10^3 + 5(10) - 3 = -1000 + 50 - 3 = -953$ ∎

Addition and Subtraction of Polynomials

We add or subtract polynomials by adding or subtracting the like terms. You can arrange the work horizontally, as in Example 3, or vertically, as in Example 4.

EXAMPLE 3 Adding and subtracting polynomials horizontally

Find each sum or difference.

a. $(3x^3 - x + 5) + (-8x^3 + 3x - 9)$ **b.** $(x^2 - 5x) - (3x^2 - 4x - 1)$

Solution

a. We use the commutative and associative properties of addition to rearrange the terms.

$$(3x^3 - x + 5) + (-8x^3 + 3x - 9) = (3x^3 - 8x^3) + (-x + 3x) + (5 - 9)$$
$$= -5x^3 + 2x - 4 \quad \text{Combine like terms.}$$

b. The first step is to distribute the multiplication by -1 over the three terms of the second polynomial, changing the sign of every term.

$$(x^2 - 5x) - (3x^2 - 4x - 1) = x^2 - 5x - 3x^2 + 4x + 1 \quad \text{Distributive property}$$
$$= -2x^2 - x + 1 \quad \text{Combine like terms.}$$

∎

EXAMPLE 4 Adding and subtracting polynomials vertically

Find each sum or difference.

a. $(3x^3 - x + 5) + (-8x^3 + 3x - 9)$ **b.** $(x^2 - 5x) - (3x^2 - 4x - 1)$

Solution

a. Add:
$$\begin{array}{r} 3x^3 - x + 5 \\ -8x^3 + 3x - 9 \\ \hline -5x^3 + 2x - 4 \end{array}$$

b. Subtract:
$$\begin{array}{r} x^2 - 5x \\ 3x^2 - 4x - 1 \\ \hline -2x^2 - x + 1 \end{array}$$

∎

Multiplication of Polynomials

To multiply two polynomials, we use the distributive property.

EXAMPLE 5 Multiplying polynomials

Use the distributive property to find each product.

a. $-3x(2x - 3)$ **b.** $(x^2 - 3x + 4)(2x - 3)$ **c.** $(x + 5)(2x - 3)$

Solution

a. $-3x(2x - 3) = -6x^2 + 9x$ Distributive property

b. $(x^2 - 3x + 4)(2x - 3) = x^2(2x - 3) - 3x(2x - 3) + 4(2x - 3)$ Distributive property

$$= 2x^3 - 3x^2 - 6x^2 + 9x + 8x - 12$$ Distributive property

$$= 2x^3 - 9x^2 + 17x - 12$$ Combine like terms.

c. $(x + 5)(2x - 3) = x(2x - 3) + 5(2x - 3)$ Distributive property

$$= 2x^2 - 3x + 10x - 15$$ Distributive property

$$= 2x^2 + 7x - 15$$ Combine like terms. ∎

Using FOIL

The product of two binomials (as in Example 5c) results in four terms:

the product of the <u>First</u> term of each,

the product of the <u>Outer</u> terms,

the product of the <u>Inner</u> terms, and

the product of the <u>Last</u> term of each.

We use FOIL as a memory aid for these four products. The FOIL method allows us to quickly obtain the product of two binomials.

EXAMPLE 6 Multiplying binomials using FOIL

Find each product using FOIL.

a. $(x + 4)(2x - 3)$

b. $(a^2 - 3)(2a - 3)$

Solution

$$\overset{F}{} \quad \overset{O}{} \quad \overset{I}{} \quad \overset{L}{}$$

a. $(x + 4)(2x - 3) = 2x^2 - 3x + 8x - 12 = 2x^2 + 5x - 12$

b. $(a^2 - 3)(2a - 3) = 2a^3 - 3a^2 - 6a + 9$ ∎

Special Products

The products $(a + b)^2$, $(a - b)^2$, and $(a + b)(a - b)$ are called the **special products**. We could use FOIL to find these products, but it is better to memorize the following rules for finding these products quickly.

The Special Products

$(a + b)^2 = a^2 + 2ab + b^2$	**The Square of a Sum**
$(a - b)^2 = a^2 - 2ab + b^2$	**The Square of a Difference**
$(a + b)(a - b) = a^2 - b^2$	**The Product of a Sum and a Difference**

EXAMPLE 7 Finding special products

Find each product by using the special product rules.

a. $(2x + 3)^2$ b. $(x^3 - 9)^2$ c. $(3x + 5)(3x - 5)$

Appendix: Basic Algebra Review

Solution

a. To find $(2x + 3)^2$ substitute $2x$ for a and 3 for b in $(a + b)^2 = a^2 + 2ab + b^2$:

$$(2x + 3)^2 = (2x)^2 + 2(2x)(3) + 3^2$$
$$= 4x^2 + 12x + 9$$

b. To find $(x^3 - 9)^2$ substitute x^3 for a and 9 for b in $(a - b)^2 = a^2 - 2ab + b^2$:

$$(x^3 - 9)^2 = (x^3)^2 - 2(x^3)(9) + 9^2$$
$$= x^6 - 18x^3 + 81$$

c. $(3x + 5)(3x - 5) = (3x)^2 - 5^2 = 9x^2 - 25$ ∎

The expressions $3 - \sqrt{6}$ and $3 + \sqrt{6}$ are called **conjugates.** Their product is a rational number because of the rule $(a + b)(a - b) = a^2 - b^2$. This fact is used to rationalize a denominator in the next example.

EXAMPLE 8 Using conjugates to rationalize a denominator

Simplify the expression $\dfrac{\sqrt{3}}{3 - \sqrt{6}}$.

Solution

Multiply the numerator and denominator by $3 + \sqrt{6}$, the conjugate of $3 - \sqrt{6}$:

$$\frac{\sqrt{3}}{3 - \sqrt{6}} = \frac{\sqrt{3}(3 + \sqrt{6})}{(3 - \sqrt{6})(3 + \sqrt{6})} = \frac{3\sqrt{3} + \sqrt{18}}{9 - 6}$$
$$= \frac{3\sqrt{3} + 3\sqrt{2}}{3} = \sqrt{3} + \sqrt{2}$$ ∎

Division of Polynomials

If 20 is divided by 3, the quotient is 6 and the remainder is 2. So we can write $20 = 6 \cdot 3 + 2$. If the **dividend** $P(x)$ and the **divisor** $D(x)$ are polynomials such that $D(x) \neq 0$ and the degree of $P(x)$ is greater than or equal to the degree of $D(x)$, then there exist unique polynomials, the **quotient** $Q(x)$ and the **remainder** $R(x)$, such that

$$P(x) = Q(x)D(x) + R(x),$$

where $R(x) = 0$ or the degree of $R(x)$ is less than the degree of $D(x)$. To find the quotient and remainder polynomials, we use an algorithm that is similar to the well-known algorithm for dividing whole numbers.

EXAMPLE 9 Using the division algorithm to divide polynomials

Find the quotient and remainder when $x^3 - 8$ is divided by $x - 2$.

Solution

To keep the division organized, insert $0x^2$ and $0x$ for the missing x^2 and x terms.

$$
\begin{array}{r}
x^2 + 2x + 4 \\
x - 2 \overline{)x^3 + 0x^2 + 0x - 8} \\
\underline{x^3 - 2x^2} \\
2x^2 + 0x \\
\underline{2x^2 - 4x} \\
4x - 8 \\
\underline{4x - 8} \\
0
\end{array}
$$

$x^3 \div x = x^2$
$x^2(x - 2) = x^3 - 2x^2$
$0x^2 - (-2x^2) = 2x^2$
$2x(x - 2) = 2x^2 - 4x$
$4(x - 2) = 4x - 8$

747

The quotient is $x^2 + 2x + 4$ and the remainder is 0. To check, find the product $(x^2 + 2x + 4)(x - 2)$.

The dividend is equal to the quotient times the divisor plus the remainder:

$$\text{dividend} = (\text{quotient})(\text{divisor}) + \text{remainder}$$

We can also express this relationship as follows:

$$\frac{\text{dividend}}{\text{divisor}} = \text{quotient} + \frac{\text{remainder}}{\text{divisor}}$$

EXERCISES 3

Find the degree and leading coefficient of each polynomial. Determine whether the polynomial is a monomial, binomial, or trinomial.

1. $x^3 - 4x^2 + \sqrt{5}$ **2.** $-x^7 - 6x^4$

3. $x - 3x^2$ **4.** $x + 5 + x^2$

5. 79   **6.** $-\dfrac{x}{\sqrt{2}}$

Let $P(x) = x^2 - 3x + 2$ and $M(x) = -x^3 + 5x^2 - x + 2$. Find the following.

7. $P(-2)$ **8.** $P(-1)$ **9.** $M(-3)$ **10.** $M(50)$

Find each sum or difference.

11. $(3x^2 - 4x) + (5x^2 + 7x - 1)$

12. $(-3x^2 - 4x + 2) + (5x^2 - 8x - 7)$

13. $(4x^2 - 3x) - (9x^2 - 4x + 3)$

14. $(x^2 + 2x + 4) - (x^2 + 4x + 4)$

15. $(4ax^3 - a^2x) - (5a^2x^3 - 3a^2x + 3)$

16. $(x^2y^2 - 3xy + 2x) - (6x^2y^2 + 4y - 6x)$

Perform the indicated operation.

17. Add: $3x - 4$
$\underline{-x + 3}$

18. Add: $-2x^2 - 5$
$\underline{3x^2 - 6}$

19. Subtract:
$x^2 \qquad - 8$
$\underline{-2x^2 + 3x - 2}$

20. Subtract:
$-2x^2 - 5x + 9$
$\underline{4x^2 - 7x}$

Use the distributive property to find each product.

21. $-3a^3(6a^2 - 5a + 2)$ **22.** $-2m(m^2 - 3m + 9)$

23. $(3b^2 - 5b + 2)(b - 3)$

24. $(-w^2 - 5w + 6)(w + 5)$

25. $(2x - 1)(4x^2 + 2x + 1)$ **26.** $(3x - 2)(9x^2 + 6x + 4)$

27. $(x + 5)(x^2 - 5x + 25)$ **28.** $(a + 3)(a^2 - 3a + 9)$

29. $(x - 4)(z + 3)$ **30.** $(a - 3)(b + c)$

31. $(a - b)(a^2 + ab + b^2)$ **32.** $(a + b)(a^2 - ab + b^2)$

Find each product using FOIL.

33. $(a + 9)(a - 2)$ **34.** $(z - 3)(z - 4)$

35. $(2y - 3)(y + 9)$ **36.** $(2y - 1)(3y + 4)$

37. $(2x - 9)(2x + 9)$ **38.** $(4x - 6y)(4x + 6y)$

39. $(2x^2 + 4)(3x^2 + 5)$

40. $(3x^3 - 2)(5x^3 + 6)$

41. $(2x + 5)^2$

42. $(5x - 3)^2$

Find each product using the special product rules.

43. $(3x + 5)^2$

44. $(x^3 - 2)^2$

45. $(x^2 - 3)(x^2 + 3)$ **46.** $(2z^3 + 1)(2z^3 - 1)$

47. $(\sqrt{2} - 5)(\sqrt{2} + 5)$ **48.** $(6 - \sqrt{3})(6 + \sqrt{3})$

49. $(3x^3 - 4)^2$ **50.** $(2x^2y^3 + 1)^2$

51. $(2xy - 5)^2$ **52.** $(-3x^4 - 2)^2$

Simplify each expression by rationalizing the denominator.

53. $\dfrac{\sqrt{10}}{\sqrt{5} - 2}$ **54.** $\dfrac{\sqrt{3}}{\sqrt{2} - \sqrt{3}}$

55. $\dfrac{\sqrt{6}}{6 + \sqrt{3}}$ **56.** $\dfrac{\sqrt{2}}{\sqrt{8} + \sqrt{3}}$

Find the quotient and remainder when the first polynomial is divided by the second.

57. $x^2 + 6x + 9$, $x + 3$

58. $x^2 - 3x - 54$, $x - 9$

59. $a^3 - 1$, $a - 1$

60. $b^6 + 8$, $b^2 + 2$

61. $x^2 + 3x + 3$, $x - 2$

62. $3x^2 - x + 4$, $x + 2$

63. $2x^2 - 5$, $x + 3$

64. $-4x^2 + 1$, $x - 1$

65. $x^3 - 2x^2 - 2x - 3$, $x - 3$

66. $x^3 + 3x^2 - 3x + 4$, $x + 4$

67. $6x^2 - 7x + 2$, $2x + 1$

68. $-3x^2 + 4x + 9$, $2 - x$

69. $2x^3 + 3x^2 - 7x - 12$, $x^2 - 4$

70. $x^3 + 2x^2 + x - 3$, $x^2 - 1$

71. $x^3 + 2x^2 - 7x - 6$, $x^2 - x - 2$

72. $2x^3 - 3x^2 - 19x - 8$, $x^2 - 2x - 8$

Perform the indicated operations mentally. Write down only the answer.

73. $(x - 4)(x + 6)$

74. $(z^4 + 5)(z^4 - 4)$

75. $(2a^5 - 9)(a^5 + 3)$

76. $(3b^2 + 1)(2b^2 + 5)$

77. $(y - 3) - (2y + 6)$

78. $(a^2 + 3) - (a^2 - 6)$

79. $(w + 4)^2$

80. $(t - 2)^2$

81. $3y^2(y^3 - 3x)$

82. $a^4b(a^2b^2 + 1)$

83. $(6b^3 - 3b^2) \div (3b^2)$

84. $(3w - 8) \div (8 - 3w)$

85. $(3w^2 - 2n)^2$

86. $(7y^2 - 3x)^2$

4 Factoring Polynomials

In this section we will factor polynomials. **Factoring** "reverses" multiplication.

Factoring Out the Greatest Common Factor

To factor $6x^2 - 3x$, notice that $3x$ is a monomial that can be divided evenly into each term. We can use the distributive property to write

$$6x^2 - 3x = 3x(2x - 1).$$

We call this process **factoring out** $3x$. Both $3x$ and $2x - 1$ are **factors** of $6x^2 - 3x$. Since 3 is a factor of $6x^2$ and $3x$, 3 is a **common factor** of the terms of the polynomial. The **greatest common factor** (GCF) is a monomial that includes every number or variable that is a factor of all terms of the polynomial. The monomial $3x$ is the greatest common factor of $6x^2 - 3x$. Usually the common factor has a positive coefficient, but at times it is useful to factor out a common factor with a negative coefficient.

> **EXAMPLE 1** Factoring out the greatest common factor

Factor out the greatest common factor from each polynomial, first using the GCF with a positive coefficient and then using a negative coefficient.

a. $9x^4 - 6x^3 + 12x^2$ **b.** $x^2y + 10xy + 25y$

Solution

a. $9x^4 - 6x^3 + 12x^2 = 3x^2(3x^2 - 2x + 4)$

$$= -3x^2(-3x^2 + 2x - 4)$$

b. $x^2y + 10xy + 25y = y(x^2 + 10x + 25)$

$$= -y(-x^2 - 10x - 25)$$

■

749

Factoring by Grouping

Some four-term polynomials can be factored by **grouping** the terms in pairs and factoring out a common factor from each pair of terms.

> **EXAMPLE 2** Factoring four-term polynomials by grouping

Factor each polynomial by grouping.

a. $x^3 + x^2 + 3x + 3$ **b.** $aw + bc - bw - ac$

Solution

a. Factor the common factor x^2 out of the first two terms and the common factor 3 out of the last two terms:

$$x^3 + x^2 + 3x + 3 = x^2(x + 1) + 3(x + 1) \quad \text{Factor out common factors.}$$
$$= (x + 1)(x^2 + 3) \qquad \text{Factor out the common factor } (x + 1).$$

b. We must first arrange the polynomial so that the first group of two terms has a common factor and the last group of two terms also has a common factor.

$$aw + bc - bw - ac = aw - bw - ac + bc \qquad \text{Rearrange.}$$
$$= w(a - b) - c(a - b) \quad \text{Factor out common factors.}$$
$$= (w - c)(a - b) \qquad \text{Factor out } a - b. \qquad \blacksquare$$

Factoring $ax^2 + bx + c$

Factoring by grouping can be used also to factor a trinomial that is the product of two binomials.

> **EXAMPLE 3** Factoring $ax^2 + bx + c$ with $a = 1$

Factor each trinomial.

a. $x^2 - 5x - 14$ **b.** $x^2 + 4x - 21$

Solution

a. First find two numbers that have a product of -14 and a sum of -5. The numbers are -7 and 2. To get four terms that we can factor by grouping, we replace $-5x$ with $-7x + 2x$.

$$x^2 - 5x - 14 = x^2 - 7x + 2x - 14 \qquad \text{Replace } -5x \text{ with } -7x + 2x.$$
$$= (x - 7)x + (x - 7)2 \quad \text{Factor out common factors.}$$
$$= (x - 7)(x + 2) \qquad \text{Factor out } (x - 7).$$

Check by using FOIL. Note that once we have found -7 and 2, we can skip the grouping step and simply write the answer $(x - 7)(x + 2)$.

b. Two numbers that have a product of -21 and a sum of 4 are 7 and -3.

$$x^2 + 4x - 21 = (x + 7)(x - 3)$$

Check by using FOIL. $\qquad \blacksquare$

To factor $ax^2 + bx + c$ with $a \neq 1$, we can use the **ac-method**.

Procedure: The *ac*-Method
for Factoring $ax^2 + bx + c$
with $a \neq 1$

To factor $ax^2 + bx + c$ with $a \neq 1$:

1. Find two numbers whose sum is b and whose product is ac.
2. Replace b with the sum of these two numbers.
3. Factor the resulting four-term polynomial by grouping.

$\boxed{\textbf{EXAMPLE } 4}$ Factoring $ax^2 + bx + c$ with $a \neq 1$

Factor each trinomial using the *ac*-method.

a. $2x^2 + 5x + 2$ **b.** $6x^2 - x - 12$

Solution

a. Since $ac = 2 \cdot 2 = 4$ and $b = 5$, we need two numbers that have a product of 4 and a sum of 5. The numbers are 4 and 1.

$$2x^2 + 5x + 2 = 2x^2 + 4x + x + 2 \qquad \text{Replace } 5x \text{ by } 4x + x.$$
$$= (x + 2)2x + (x + 2)1 \qquad \text{Factor by grouping.}$$
$$= (x + 2)(2x + 1) \qquad \text{Check using FOIL.}$$

b. Since $ac = 6(-12) = -72$ and $b = -1$, we need two numbers that have a product of -72 and a sum of -1. The numbers are 8 and -9.

$$6x^2 - x - 12 = 6x^2 - 9x + 8x - 12 \qquad \text{Replace } -x \text{ by } -9x + 8x.$$
$$= (2x - 3)3x + (2x - 3)4 \qquad \text{Factor by grouping.}$$
$$= (2x - 3)(3x + 4) \qquad \text{Check using FOIL.} \qquad \blacksquare$$

Factoring the Special Products

Trinomials of the form $a^2 + 2ab + b^2$ and $a^2 - 2ab + b^2$ are called **perfect square trinomials.** We can factor the perfect square trinomials and the difference of two squares by using the same rules that we used to obtain these special products.

$a^2 - b^2 = (a + b)(a - b)$	**Difference of Two Squares**
$a^2 + 2ab + b^2 = (a + b)^2$	**Perfect Square Trinomial**
$a^2 - 2ab + b^2 = (a - b)^2$	**Perfect Square Trinomial**

$\boxed{\textbf{EXAMPLE } 5}$ Factoring the special products

Factor each polynomial.

a. $4x^2 - 1$ **b.** $x^2 - 6x + 9$ **c.** $9y^2 + 30y + 25$

Solution

a. $4x^2 - 1 = (2x)^2 - 1^2 \qquad$ Recognize the difference of two squares.
$$= (2x + 1)(2x - 1)$$

b. $x^2 - 6x + 9 = x^2 - 2 \cdot 3 \cdot x + 3^2 \qquad$ Recognize the perfect square trinomial.
$$= (x - 3)^2$$

c. $9y^2 + 30y + 25 = (3y)^2 + 2(3y)(5) + 5^2 \qquad$ Recognize the perfect square trinomial.
$$= (3y + 5)^2 \qquad \blacksquare$$

Factoring the Difference and Sum of Two Cubes

The following formulas are used to factor the difference of two cubes and the sum of two cubes. You should verify these formulas using multiplication.

Factoring the Difference and Sum of Two Cubes

$$a^3 - b^3 = (a - b)(a^2 + ab + b^2) \quad \textbf{Difference of Two Cubes}$$
$$a^3 + b^3 = (a + b)(a^2 - ab + b^2) \quad \textbf{Sum of Two Cubes}$$

EXAMPLE 6 Factoring differences and sums of two cubes

Factor each polynomial.

a. $x^3 - 27$ **b.** $8w^6 + 125z^3$

Solution

a. Since $x^3 - 27 = x^3 - 3^3$, we use $a = x$ and $b = 3$ in the formula for factoring the difference of two cubes.

$$x^3 - 27 = (x - 3)(x^2 + 3x + 9)$$

b. Since $8w^6 + 125z^3 = (2w^2)^3 + (5z)^3$, we use $a = 2w^2$ and $b = 5z$ in the formula for factoring the sum of two cubes.

$$8w^6 + 125z^3 = (2w^2 + 5z)(4w^4 - 10w^2z + 25z^2) \quad \blacksquare$$

Factoring Completely

Polynomials that cannot be factored using integral coefficients are called **prime** or **irreducible over the integers.** For example, $a^2 + 1, b^2 + b + 1$, and $x + 5$ are prime polynomials because they cannot be expressed as a product (in a nontrivial manner). A polynomial is **factored completely** when it is written as a product of prime polynomials. When factoring polynomials, we usually do not factor integers that are common factors. For example, $4x^2(2x - 3)$ is factored completely even though the coefficient 4 could be factored.

EXAMPLE 7 Factoring completely

Factor each polynomial completely.

a. $2w^4 - 32$ **b.** $-6x^7 + 6x$

Solution

a. $2w^4 - 32 = 2(w^4 - 16)$ Factor out the greatest common factor.

$$= 2(w^2 - 4)(w^2 + 4) \quad \text{Difference of two squares}$$

$$= 2(w - 2)(w + 2)(w^2 + 4) \quad \text{Difference of two squares}$$

The polynomial is now factored completely because $w^2 + 4$ is prime.

b. $-6x^7 + 6x = -6x(x^6 - 1)$ Greatest common factor

$$= -6x(x^3 - 1)(x^3 + 1) \quad \text{Difference of two squares}$$

$$= -6x(x - 1)(x^2 + x + 1)(x + 1)(x^2 - x + 1) \quad \text{Difference of two cubes; sum of two cubes}$$

The polynomial is factored completely because all of the factors are prime. $\blacksquare$

EXERCISES 4

Factor out the greatest common factor from each polynomial, first using a positive coefficient on the GCF and then using a negative coefficient.

1. $6x^3 - 12x^2$

2. $12x^2 + 18x^3$

3. $-ax^3 + 5ax^2 - 6ax$

4. $-sa^3 + sb^3 - sb$

5. $m - n$ 6. $y - x$

Factor each polynomial by grouping.

7. $x^3 + 2x^2 + 5x + 10$ 8. $2w^3 - 2w^2 + 3w - 3$

9. $y^3 - y^2 - 3y + 3$ 10. $x^3 + x^2 - 7x - 7$

11. $ady - w + d - awy$ 12. $xy + ab + by + ax$

13. $x^2y^2 + ab - ay^2 - bx^2$ 14. $6yz - 3y - 10z + 5$

Factor each trinomial.

15. $x^2 + 10x + 16$ 16. $x^2 + 7x + 12$

17. $x^2 - 4x - 12$ 18. $y^2 + 3y - 18$

19. $m^2 - 12m + 20$ 20. $n^2 - 8n + 7$

21. $t^2 + 5t - 84$ 22. $s^2 - 6s - 27$

23. $2x^2 - 7x - 4$ 24. $3x^2 + 5x - 2$

25. $8x^2 - 10x - 3$ 26. $18x^2 - 15x + 2$

27. $6y^2 + 7y - 5$ 28. $15x^2 - 14x - 8$

29. $12b^2 + 17b + 6$ 30. $8h^2 + 22h + 9$

Factor each special product.

31. $t^2 - u^2$ 32. $9t^2 - v^2$

33. $t^2 + 2t + 1$ 34. $m^2 + 10m + 25$

35. $4w^2 - 4w + 1$ 36. $9x^2 - 12xy + 4y^2$

37. $9z^2x^2 + 24zx + 16$ 38. $25t^2 - 20tw^3 + 4w^6$

Factor each sum or difference of two cubes.

39. $t^3 - u^3$ 40. $m^3 + n^3$

41. $a^3 - 8$ 42. $b^3 + 1$

43. $27y^3 + 8$ 44. $1 - 8a^6$

45. $27x^3y^6 - 8z^9$

46. $8t^3h^3 + n^9$

Factor each polynomial completely.

47. $-3x^3 + 27x$ 48. $a^4b^2 - 16b^2$

49. $16t^4 + 54w^3t$ 50. $8a^6 - a^3b^3$

51. $a^3 + a^2 - 4a - 4$

52. $2b^3 + 3b^2 - 18b - 27$

53. $x^4 - 2x^3 - 8x + 16$ 54. $a^4 - a^3 + a - 1$

55. $-36x^3 + 18x^2 + 4x$ 56. $-6a^4 - a^3 + 15a^2$

57. $a^7 - a^6 - 64a + 64$

58. $a^5 - 4a^4 - 4a + 16$

59. $-6x^2 - x + 15$ 60. $-6x^2 - 9x + 42$

5 Rational Expressions

In this section we will review the basic operations with rational expressions.

Reducing

A **rational expression** is a ratio of two polynomials in which the denominator is not the zero polynomial. The **domain** of a rational expression is the set of all real numbers that can be used in place of the variable.

EXAMPLE 1 Domain of a rational expression

Find the domain of each rational expression.

a. $\dfrac{2x - 1}{x + 3}$ **b.** $\dfrac{2x + 4}{(x + 2)(x + 3)}$ **c.** $\dfrac{1}{x^2 + 8}$

Solution

a. The domain is the set of all real numbers except those that cause $x + 3$ to have a value of 0. So -3 is excluded from the domain, because $x + 3$ has a value of 0 for $x = -3$. We write the domain in set notation as $\{x \mid x \neq -3\}$.

b. The domain is the set of all real numbers except -2 and -3, because replacing x by either of these numbers would cause the denominator to be 0. The domain is written in set notation as $\{x \mid x \neq -2 \text{ and } x \neq -3\}$.

c. The value of $x^2 + 8$ is positive for any real number x. So the domain is the set of all real numbers, R. ∎

In arithmetic we learned that each rational number has infinitely many equivalent forms. This fact is due to the **basic principle of rational numbers.**

Basic Principle of Rational Numbers

> If a, b, and c are integers with $b \neq 0$ and $c \neq 0$, then
> $$\frac{ac}{bc} = \frac{a}{b}.$$

The basic principle holds true when a, b, and c are real numbers as well as when they are integers, but we use it most often with integers, when we reduce fractions. For example, we reduce 3/6 as follows:

$$\frac{3}{6} = \frac{1 \cdot 3}{2 \cdot 3} = \frac{1}{2}$$

Note that since 3 and 6 have a common factor of 3, we divide both the numerator and denominator by 3 to reduce the fraction. We reduce rational expressions in the same manner. Factor the numerator and denominator completely, then *divide out* the common factors. A rational expression is in *lowest terms* when all common factors have been divided out.

EXAMPLE 2 Reducing to lowest terms

Reduce each rational expression to lowest terms.

a. $\dfrac{2x + 4}{x^2 + 5x + 6}$

b. $\dfrac{b - a}{a^3 - b^3}$

c. $\dfrac{x^2 z^3}{x^5 z}$

Solution

a. $\dfrac{2x + 4}{x^2 + 5x + 6} = \dfrac{2(x + 2)}{(x + 2)(x + 3)}$ Factor the numerator and denominator.

$\qquad\qquad\qquad\; = \dfrac{2}{x + 3}$ Divide out the common factor $x + 2$.

b. $\dfrac{b - a}{a^3 - b^3} = \dfrac{-1(a - b)}{(a - b)(a^2 + ab + b^2)}$ Factor -1 out of $b - a$.

$\qquad\qquad = \dfrac{-1}{a^2 + ab + b^2}$

c. $\dfrac{x^2 z^3}{x^5 z} = \dfrac{(x^2 z)(z^2)}{(x^2 z)(x^3)} = \dfrac{z^2}{x^3}$ (The quotient rule yields the same result.)   ∎

Be careful when reducing. The <u>only</u> way to reduce rational expressions is to factor and divide out the common *factors*. Identical terms that are not factors cannot be eliminated from a rational expression. For example,

$$\frac{x + 3}{3} \neq x$$

for all real numbers, because 3 is not a factor of the numerator.

Multiplication and Division

We multiply two rational numbers by multiplying their numerators and their denominators. For example, $\frac{2}{3} \cdot \frac{5}{7} = \frac{10}{21}$.

Definition: Multiplication of Rational Numbers

> If a/b and c/d are rational numbers, then
>
> $$\frac{a}{b} \cdot \frac{c}{d} = \frac{ac}{bd}.$$

We multiply rational expressions in the same manner as rational numbers. Of course, any common factor can be divided out as we do when reducing rational expressions.

EXAMPLE 3 Multiplying rational expressions

Find each product.

a. $\dfrac{2a - 2b}{6} \cdot \dfrac{9a}{a^2 - b^2}$ **b.** $\dfrac{x - 1}{x^2 + 4x + 4} \cdot \dfrac{x + 2}{x^2 + 2x - 3}$

Solution

a. $\dfrac{2a - 2b}{6} \cdot \dfrac{9a}{a^2 - b^2} = \dfrac{2(a - b)}{2 \cdot 3} \cdot \dfrac{3 \cdot 3a}{(a - b)(a + b)}$ Factor completely.

$\qquad\qquad\qquad\qquad = \dfrac{3a}{a + b}$ Divide out common factors.

b. $\dfrac{x - 1}{x^2 + 4x + 4} \cdot \dfrac{x + 2}{x^2 + 2x - 3} = \dfrac{x - 1}{(x + 2)^2} \cdot \dfrac{x + 2}{(x + 3)(x - 1)}$ Factor completely.

$\qquad\qquad\qquad\qquad\qquad = \dfrac{1}{x^2 + 5x + 6}$ Divide out common factors.   ∎

We divide rational numbers by multiplying by the reciprocal of the divisor, or *invert and multiply*. For example, $6 \div \frac{1}{2} = 6 \cdot 2 = 12$.

Definition: Division of Rational Numbers

> If a/b and c/d are rational numbers with $c \neq 0$, then
>
> $$\frac{a}{b} \div \frac{c}{d} = \frac{a}{b} \cdot \frac{d}{c}.$$

Rational expressions are divided in the same manner as rational numbers.

EXAMPLE 4 Dividing rational expressions

Perform the indicated operations.

a. $\dfrac{9}{2x} \div \dfrac{3}{x}$ **b.** $\dfrac{4 - x^2}{6} \div \dfrac{x - 2}{2}$

Solution

a. $\dfrac{9}{2x} \div \dfrac{3}{x} = \dfrac{9}{2x} \cdot \dfrac{x}{3}$ Invert and multiply.

$= \dfrac{3 \cdot 3}{2x} \cdot \dfrac{x}{3}$ Factor completely.

$= \dfrac{3}{2}$ Divide out common factors.

b. $\dfrac{4 - x^2}{6} \div \dfrac{x - 2}{2} = \dfrac{-1(x - 2)(x + 2)}{2 \cdot 3} \cdot \dfrac{2}{x - 2}$ Invert and multiply.

$= \dfrac{-x - 2}{3}$ Divide out common factors. ∎

Note that the division in Example 4(a) is valid only if $x \neq 0$. The division in Example 4(b) is valid only if $x \neq 2$ because $x - 2$ appears in the denominator after the rational expression is inverted.

Building Up the Denominator

The addition of fractions can be carried out only when their denominators are identical. To get a required denominator, we may **build up** the denominator of a fraction. To build up the denominator, we use the basic principle of rational numbers in the reverse of the way we use it for reducing. We multiply the numerator and denominator of a fraction by the same nonzero number to get an equivalent fraction.

EXAMPLE 5 Writing equivalent rational expressions

Convert the first rational expression into an equivalent one that has the indicated denominator.

a. $\dfrac{3}{2a}, \dfrac{?}{6ab}$ **b.** $\dfrac{x - 1}{x + 2}, \dfrac{?}{x^2 + 6x + 8}$ **c.** $\dfrac{a}{3b - a}, \dfrac{?}{a^2 - 9b^2}$

Solution

a. Compare the two denominators. Since $6ab = 2a(3b)$, we multiply the numerator and denominator of the first expression by $3b$:

$$\dfrac{3}{2a} = \dfrac{3 \cdot 3b}{2a \cdot 3b} = \dfrac{9b}{6ab}$$

b. Factor the second denominator and compare it to the first. Since $x^2 + 6x + 8 = (x + 2)(x + 4)$, we multiply the numerator and denominator by $x + 4$:

$$\dfrac{x - 1}{x + 2} = \dfrac{(x - 1)(x + 4)}{(x + 2)(x + 4)} = \dfrac{x^2 + 3x - 4}{x^2 + 6x + 8}$$

c. Factor the second denominator as

$$a^2 - 9b^2 = (a - 3b)(a + 3b) = -1(3b - a)(a + 3b).$$

Since $3b - a$ is a factor of $a^2 - 9b^2$, we multiply the numerator and denominator by $-1(a + 3b)$:

$$\frac{a}{3b - a} = \frac{a(-1)(a + 3b)}{(3b - a)(-1)(a + 3b)} = \frac{-a^2 - 3ab}{a^2 - 9b^2} \qquad \blacksquare$$

Addition and Subtraction

Fractions can be added or subtracted only if their denominators are identical. For example, $\frac{1}{3} + \frac{1}{3} = \frac{2}{3}$ and $\frac{7}{12} - \frac{2}{12} = \frac{5}{12}$.

Definition: Addition and Subtraction of Rational Numbers

> If a/b and c/d are rational numbers, then
>
> $$\frac{a}{b} + \frac{c}{b} = \frac{a + c}{b} \qquad \text{and} \qquad \frac{a}{b} - \frac{c}{b} = \frac{a - c}{b}.$$

For fractions with different denominators, we build up one or both denominators to get denominators that are equal to the least common multiple (LCM) of the denominators. The **least common denominator (LCD)** is the smallest number that is a multiple of all of the denominators. Use the following steps to find the LCD.

Procedure: Finding the LCD

> 1. Factor each denominator completely.
> 2. Write a product using each factor that appears in a denominator.
> 3. For each factor, use the highest power of that factor that occurs in the denominators.

For example, to find the LCD for 10 and 12, we write $10 = 2 \cdot 5$ and $12 = 2^2 \cdot 3$. The LCD contains the factors 2, 3, and 5. Using the highest power of each we get $2^2 \cdot 3 \cdot 5 = 60$ for the LCD. So, to add fractions with denominators of 10 and 12, we build up each fraction to a denominator of 60:

$$\frac{1}{10} + \frac{1}{12} = \frac{1 \cdot 6}{10 \cdot 6} + \frac{1 \cdot 5}{12 \cdot 5} = \frac{6}{60} + \frac{5}{60} = \frac{11}{60}$$

We use the same method to add or subtract rational expressions.

EXAMPLE 6 Adding and subtracting rational expressions

Perform the indicated operations.

a. $\dfrac{x}{x - 1} + \dfrac{2x + 3}{x^2 - 1}$ **b.** $\dfrac{x}{x^2 + 6x + 9} - \dfrac{x - 3}{x^2 + 5x + 6}$

Solution

a.
$$\frac{x}{x - 1} + \frac{2x + 3}{x^2 - 1} = \frac{x}{x - 1} + \frac{2x + 3}{(x - 1)(x + 1)} \qquad \text{Factor denominators completely}$$

$$= \frac{x(x + 1)}{(x - 1)(x + 1)} + \frac{2x + 3}{(x - 1)(x + 1)} \qquad \text{Build up using the LCD } (x - 1)(x + 1).$$

$$= \frac{x^2 + x + 2x + 3}{(x - 1)(x + 1)} \qquad \text{Add the fractions.}$$

$$= \frac{x^2 + 3x + 3}{(x - 1)(x + 1)} \qquad \text{Simplify the numerator.}$$

b. $\dfrac{x}{x^2 + 6x + 9} - \dfrac{x-3}{x^2 + 5x + 6} = \dfrac{x}{(x+3)^2} - \dfrac{x-3}{(x+2)(x+3)}$

$$= \dfrac{x(x+2)}{(x+3)^2(x+2)} - \dfrac{(x-3)(x+3)}{(x+2)(x+3)(x+3)}$$

$$= \dfrac{x^2 + 2x}{(x+3)^2(x+2)} - \dfrac{x^2 - 9}{(x+3)^2(x+2)}$$

$$= \dfrac{2x + 9}{(x+3)^2(x+2)} \qquad \blacksquare$$

EXERCISES 5

Find the domain of each rational expression.

1. $\dfrac{x-3}{x+2}$

2. $\dfrac{x^2 - 1}{x - 5}$

3. $\dfrac{x^2 - 9}{(x-4)(x+2)}$

4. $\dfrac{2x - 3}{(x+1)(x-3)}$

5. $\dfrac{x+1}{(x-3)(x+3)}$

6. $\dfrac{x+2}{(x+2)(x+1)}$

7. $\dfrac{3x^2 - 2x + 1}{x^2 + 3}$

8. $\dfrac{-2x^2 - 7}{3x^2 + 8}$

Reduce each rational expression to lowest terms.

9. $\dfrac{3x - 9}{x^2 - x - 6}$

10. $\dfrac{-2x - 4}{x^2 - 3x - 10}$

11. $\dfrac{10a - 8b}{12b - 15a}$

12. $\dfrac{a^2 - b^2}{b - a}$

13. $\dfrac{a^3b^6}{a^2b^3 - a^4b^2}$

14. $\dfrac{18u^6v^5 + 24u^3v^3}{42u^2v^5}$

15. $\dfrac{x^4y^5z^2}{x^7y^3z}$

16. $\dfrac{t^3u^7}{-t^8u^5}$

17. $\dfrac{a^3 - b^3}{a^2 - b^2}$

18. $\dfrac{a^3 + b^3}{a^2 + b^2}$

19. $\dfrac{ab + 3a - by - 3y}{a^2 - 2ay + y^2}$

20. $\dfrac{x^4 - 16}{x^4 + 8x^2 + 16}$

Find the products or quotients.

21. $\dfrac{2a}{3b^2} \cdot \dfrac{9b}{14a^2}$

22. $\dfrac{14w}{51y} \cdot \dfrac{3w}{7y}$

23. $\dfrac{12a}{7} \div \dfrac{2a^3}{49}$

24. $\dfrac{20x}{y^3} \div \dfrac{30}{y^5}$

25. $\dfrac{a^2 - 9}{3a - 6} \cdot \dfrac{a^2 - 4}{a^2 - a - 6}$

26. $\dfrac{6x^2 + x - 1}{6x + 3} \cdot \dfrac{15}{9x^2 - 1}$

27. $\dfrac{x^2 - y^2}{9} \div \dfrac{x^2 + 2xy + y^2}{18}$

28. $\dfrac{a^3 - b^3}{a^2 - 2ab + b^2} \div \dfrac{2a^2 + 2ab + 2b^2}{9a^2 - 9b^2}$

29. $\dfrac{x^2 - y^2}{-3xy} \cdot \dfrac{6x^2y^3}{2y - 2x}$

30. $\dfrac{a^2 - a - 2}{2} \cdot \dfrac{1}{4 - a^2}$

31. $\dfrac{wx - x}{x^2} \div \dfrac{1 - w^2}{2}$

32. $\dfrac{2 + x}{2} \div \dfrac{x^2 - 4}{4}$

Convert the first rational expression into an equivalent one that has the indicated denominator.

33. $\dfrac{4}{3a}, \dfrac{?}{12a^2}$

34. $\dfrac{a + 2}{4a^2}, \dfrac{?}{20a^3b}$

35. $\dfrac{x - 5}{x + 3}, \dfrac{?}{x^2 - 9}$

36. $\dfrac{x + 2}{x - 8}, \dfrac{?}{16 - 2x}$

37. $\dfrac{x}{x + 5}, \dfrac{?}{x^2 + 6x + 5}$

38. $\dfrac{3a - b}{a + b}, \dfrac{?}{9b^2 - 9a^2}$

39. $\dfrac{t}{2t + 2}, \dfrac{?}{2t^2 + 4t + 2}$

40. $\dfrac{x - 1}{2x + 4}, \dfrac{?}{4x^2 - 16x - 48}$

Find the least common denominator (LCD) for each given pair of rational expressions.

41. $\dfrac{1}{4ab^2}, \dfrac{7}{6a^2b^3}$

42. $\dfrac{3}{2x^2y}, \dfrac{a}{5xy}$

43. $\dfrac{-7a}{3a + 3b}, \dfrac{5b}{2a + 2b}$

44. $\dfrac{1}{3a - 3b}, \dfrac{2}{a^2 - b^2}$

45. $\dfrac{2x}{x^2 + 5x + 6}, \dfrac{3x}{x^2 - x - 6}$

46. $\dfrac{x + 7}{2x^2 + 7x - 15}, \dfrac{x - 5}{2x^2 - 5x + 3}$

Perform the indicated operations.

47. $\dfrac{3}{2x} + \dfrac{1}{6}$

48. $\dfrac{-7}{3a^2b} + \dfrac{4}{6ab^2}$

49. $\dfrac{x+3}{x-1} - \dfrac{x+4}{x+1}$

50. $\dfrac{x+2}{x-3} - \dfrac{x^2+3x-2}{x^2-9}$

51. $3 + \dfrac{1}{a}$

52. $-1 - \dfrac{3}{c}$

53. $t - 1 - \dfrac{1}{t+1}$

54. $w + \dfrac{1}{w-1}$

55. $\dfrac{x}{x^2+3x+2} + \dfrac{x-1}{x^2+5x+6}$

56. $\dfrac{x-1}{x^2+x-6} - \dfrac{x-2}{x^2+4x+3}$

57. $\dfrac{1}{x-3} - \dfrac{5}{6-2x}$

58. $\dfrac{5}{4-x^2} - \dfrac{2x}{x-2}$

59. $\dfrac{y^2}{x^3-y^3} + \dfrac{x+y}{x^2+xy+y^2}$

60. $\dfrac{ab}{a^3+b^3} + \dfrac{a}{2a^2-2ab+2b^2}$

61. $\dfrac{x-2}{2x^2+7x-15} - \dfrac{x+1}{2x^2-5x+3}$

62. $\dfrac{x-1}{2x^2-5x-3} - \dfrac{x}{4x^2-1}$

Answers to Exercises

Section 1

Exercises:

1. All   **3.** $\{-\sqrt{2}, \sqrt{3}, \pi, 5.090090009\ldots\}$

5. $\{0, 1\}$ **7.** $x + 7$ **9.** $5x + 15$ **11.** $\frac{1}{2}(x + 1)$

13. $(-13 + 4) + x$ **15.** 8   **17.** $\sqrt{3}$ **19.** $y^2 - x^2$

21. 7.2   **23.** $\sqrt{5}$ **25.** 64   **27.** -49 **29.** 16   **31.** -8

33. 12   **35.** -3 **37.** 1   **39.** -41 **41.** -7 **43.** 26

45. 52   **47.** 99   **49.** -61 **51.** 13   **53.** 0   **55.** 41

57. 6   **59.** $-2x$ **61.** $0.85x$ **63.** $-6xy$ **65.** $3 - 2x$

67. $3x - y$ **69.** $-3x - 6$ **71.** $0.97x - 6$ **73.** $11x - 17$

Section 2

Exercises:

1. $1/81$ **3.** $11/30$ **5.** 24   **7.** 8   **9.** $-6x^{11}y^{11}$ **11.** $3y^5$

13. $-4x^6$ **15.** $-\frac{8}{27}x^6$ **17.** $3x^4$ **19.** $\frac{25}{y^4}$ **21.** $\frac{1}{6y^3}$

23. $\frac{n^4}{4}$ **25.** -3 **27.** 8   **29.** -4 **31.** 81   **33.** $1/16$

35. $x^2y^{1/2}$ **37.** $6a^{3/2}$ **39.** $3a^{1/6}$ **41.** $a^{7/3}b$ **43.** $\frac{x^2y}{z^3}$

45. 30   **47.** -2 **49.** $-\frac{1}{5}$ **51.** 8   **53.** $\sqrt[3]{10^2}$

55. $\frac{3}{\sqrt[5]{y^3}}$ **57.** $x^{-1/2}$ **59.** $x^{3/5}$ **61.** $4x$ **63.** $2y^3$

65. $\frac{\sqrt{xy}}{10}$ **67.** $\frac{-2a}{b^5}$ **69.** $2\sqrt{7}$ **71.** $\frac{\sqrt{5}}{5}$ **73.** $\frac{\sqrt{2x}}{4}$

75. $2\sqrt[3]{5}$ **77.** $-5x\sqrt[3]{2x}$ **79.** $\frac{\sqrt[3]{4}}{2}$ **81.** $9 - 2\sqrt{6}$

83. $2\sqrt{2} + 2\sqrt{5} - 2\sqrt{3}$ **85.** $-30\sqrt{2}$ **87.** $60a$

89. $\frac{3\sqrt{a}}{a^2}$ **91.** $5x\sqrt{5x}$

Section 3

Exercises:

1. 3, 1, trinomial   **3.** 2, -3, binomial   **5.** 0, 79, monomial

7. 12   **9.** 77   **11.** $8x^2 + 3x - 1$ **13.** $-5x^2 + x - 3$

15. $(-5a^2 + 4a)x^3 + 2a^2x - 3$ **17.** $2x - 1$

19. $3x^2 - 3x - 6$ **21.** $-18a^5 + 15a^4 - 6a^3$

23. $3b^3 - 14b^2 + 17b - 6$ **25.** $8x^3 - 1$ **27.** $x^3 + 125$

29. $xz - 4z + 3x - 12$ **31.** $a^3 - b^3$ **33.** $a^2 + 7a - 18$

35. $2y^2 + 15y - 27$ **37.** $4x^2 - 81$ **39.** $6x^4 + 22x^2 + 20$

41. $4x^2 + 20x + 25$ **43.** $9x^2 + 30x + 25$ **45.** $x^4 - 9$

47. -23 **49.** $9x^6 - 24x^3 + 16$ **51.** $4x^2y^2 - 20xy + 25$

53. $5\sqrt{2} + 2\sqrt{10}$ **55.** $\frac{2\sqrt{6} - \sqrt{2}}{11}$ **57.** $x + 3, 0$

59. $a^2 + a + 1, 0$ **61.** $x + 5, 13$ **63.** $2x - 6, 13$

65. $x^2 + x + 1, 0$ **67.** $3x - 5, 7$ **69.** $2x + 3, x$

71. $x + 3, -2x$ **73.** $x^2 + 2x - 24$ **75.** $2a^{10} - 3a^5 - 27$

77. $-y - 9$ **79.** $w^2 + 8w + 16$ **81.** $3y^5 - 9xy^2$

83. $2b - 1$ **85.** $9w^4 - 12w^2n + 4n^2$

Section 4

Exercises:

1. $6x^2(x - 2), -6x^2(-x + 2)$

3. $ax(-x^2 + 5x - 6), -ax(x^2 - 5x + 6)$

5. $1(m - n), -1(-m + n)$ **7.** $(x^2 + 5)(x + 2)$

9. $(y^2 - 3)(y - 1)$ **11.** $(d - w)(ay + 1)$

13. $(y^2 - b)(x^2 - a)$ **15.** $(x + 2)(x + 8)$

17. $(x - 6)(x + 2)$ **19.** $(m - 2)(m - 10)$

21. $(t - 7)(t + 12)$ **23.** $(2x + 1)(x - 4)$

25. $(4x + 1)(2x - 3)$ **27.** $(3y + 5)(2y - 1)$

29. $(3b + 2)(4b + 3)$ **31.** $(t - u)(t + u)$ **33.** $(t + 1)^2$

35. $(2w - 1)^2$ **37.** $(3zx + 4)^2$

39. $(t - u)(t^2 + tu + u^2)$ **41.** $(a - 2)(a^2 + 2a + 4)$

43. $(3y + 2)(9y^2 - 6y + 4)$

45. $(3xy^2 - 2z^3)(9x^2y^4 + 6xy^2z^3 + 4z^6)$ **47.** $-3x(x - 3)(x + 3)$

49. $2t(2t + 3w)(4t^2 - 6tw + 9w^2)$ **51.** $(a - 2)(a + 2)(a + 1)$

53. $(x - 2)^2(x^2 + 2x + 4)$ **55.** $-2x(6x + 1)(3x - 2)$

57. $(a - 2)(a^2 + 2a + 4)(a + 2)(a^2 - 2a + 4)(a - 1)$

59. $-(3x + 5)(2x - 3)$

Section 5

Exercises:

1. $\{x | x \neq -2\}$ **3.** $\{x | x \neq 4 \text{ and } x \neq -2\}$

5. $\{x | x \neq 3 \text{ and } x \neq -3\}$ **7.** All real numbers   **9.** $\frac{3}{x + 2}$

11. $-\frac{2}{3}$ **13.** $\frac{ab^4}{b - a^2}$ **15.** $\frac{y^2z}{x^3}$ **17.** $\frac{a^2 + ab + b^2}{a + b}$

19. $\frac{b + 3}{a - y}$ **21.** $\frac{3}{7ab}$ **23.** $\frac{42}{a^2}$ **25.** $\frac{a + 3}{3}$ **27.** $\frac{2x - 2y}{x + y}$

29. $x^2y^2 + xy^3$ **31.** $\frac{-2}{x + wx}$ **33.** $\frac{16a}{12a^2}$

35. $\frac{x^2 - 8x + 15}{x^2 - 9}$ **37.** $\frac{x^2 + x}{x^2 + 6x + 5}$ **39.** $\frac{t^2 + t}{2t^2 + 4t + 2}$

41. $12a^2b^3$ **43.** $6(a + b)$ **45.** $(x + 2)(x + 3)(x - 3)$

47. $\frac{9 + x}{6x}$ **49.** $\frac{x + 7}{(x - 1)(x + 1)}$ **51.** $\frac{3a + 1}{a}$

53. $\frac{t^2 - 2}{t + 1}$ **55.** $\frac{2x^2 + 3x - 1}{(x + 1)(x + 2)(x + 3)}$ **57.** $\frac{7}{2x - 6}$

59. $\frac{x^2}{x^3 - y^3}$ **61.** $\frac{-9x - 3}{(2x - 3)(x + 5)(x - 1)}$

Formulas

Geometry

Rectangle

Area = LW

Perimeter = $2L + 2W$

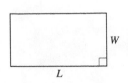

Square

Area = s^2

Perimeter = $4s$

Triangle

Area = $\frac{1}{2}bh$

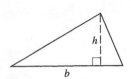

Right Triangle

Area = $\frac{1}{2}ab$

Pythagorean theorem:
$c^2 = a^2 + b^2$

Parallelogram

Area = bh

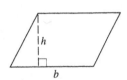

Trapezoid

Area = $\frac{1}{2}h(b_1 + b_2)$

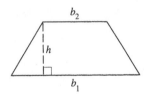

Circle

Area = πr^2

Circumference = $2\pi r$

Right Circular Cone

Volume = $\frac{1}{3}\pi r^2 h$

Lateral surface area = $\pi r\sqrt{r^2 + h^2}$

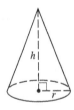

Right Circular Cylinder

Volume = $\pi r^2 h$

Lateral surface area = $2\pi rh$

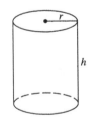

Sphere

Volume = $\frac{4}{3}\pi r^3$

Surface area = $4\pi r^2$

Metric Abbreviations

Length		Volume		Weight	
mm	millimeter	mL	milliliter	mg	milligram
cm	centimeter	cL	centiliter	cg	centigram
dm	decimeter	dL	deciliter	dg	decigram
m	meter	L	liter	g	gram
dam	dekameter	daL	dekaliter	dag	dekagram
hm	hectometer	hL	hectoliter	hg	hectogram
km	kilometer	kL	kiloliter	kg	kilogram

English-Metric Conversion

Length	Volume (U.S.)	Weight
1 in. = 2.540 cm	1 pt = 0.4732 L	1 oz = 28.35 g
1 ft = 30.48 cm	1 qt = 0.9464 L	1 lb = 453.6 g
1 yd = 0.9144 m	1 gal = 3.785 L	1 lb = 0.4536 kg
1 mi = 1.609 km		

Length	Volume (U.S.)	Weight
1 cm = 0.3937 in.	1 L = 2.2233 pt	1 g = 0.0353 oz
1 cm = 0.03281 ft	1 L = 1.0567 qt	1 g = 0.002205 lb
1 m = 1.0936 yd	1 L = 0.2642 gal	1 kg = 2.205 lb
1 km = 0.6215 mi		

Algebra

Subsets of the Real Numbers

Natural numbers $= \{1, 2, 3, \ldots\}$
Whole numbers $= \{0, 1, 2, 3, \ldots\}$
Integers $= \{\ldots -3, -2, -1, 0, 1, 2, 3, \ldots\}$
Rational $= \left\{ \dfrac{a}{b} \middle| a \text{ and } b \text{ are integers with } b \neq 0 \right\}$
Irrational $= \{x | x \text{ is not rational}\}$

Properties of the Real Numbers

For all real numbers a, b, and c

$a + b$ and ab are real numbers.	Closure
$a + b = b + a$; $a \cdot b = b \cdot a$	Commutative
$(a + b) + c = a + (b + c)$; $(ab)c = a(bc)$	Associative
$a(b + c) = ab + ac$; $a(b - c) = ab - ac$	Distributive
$a + 0 = a$; $1 \cdot a = a$	Identity
$a + (-a) = 0$; $a \cdot \dfrac{1}{a} = 1$ $\quad (a \neq 0)$	Inverse
$a \cdot 0 = 0$	Multiplication property of 0

Absolute Value

$$|a| = \begin{cases} a & \text{for } a \geq 0 \\ -a & \text{for } a < 0 \end{cases}$$

$\sqrt{x^2} = |x|$ for any real x

$|x| = k \Leftrightarrow x = k \text{ or } x = -k \qquad (k > 0)$

$|x| < k \Leftrightarrow -k < x < k \qquad (k > 0)$

$|x| > k \Leftrightarrow x < -k \text{ or } x > k \qquad (k > 0)$

(The symbol $\Leftrightarrow$ means "if and only if.")

Interval Notation

$(a, b) = \{x | a < x < b\}$
$(a, b] = \{x | a < x \leq b\}$
$(-\infty, a) = \{x | x < a\}$
$(-\infty, a] = \{x | x \leq a\}$

$[a, b] = \{x | a \leq x \leq b\}$
$[a, b) = \{x | a \leq x < b\}$
$(a, \infty) = \{x | x > a\}$
$[a, \infty) = \{x | x \geq a\}$

Exponents

$a^n = a \cdot a \cdot \cdots \cdot a$ (n factors of a)

$a^0 = 1$ $\qquad a^{-n} = \dfrac{1}{a^n}$

$a^r a^s = a^{r+s}$ $\qquad \dfrac{a^r}{a^s} = a^{r-s}$

$(a^r)^s = a^{rs}$ $\qquad (ab)^r = a^r b^r$

$\left(\dfrac{a}{b}\right)^r = \dfrac{a^r}{b^r}$ $\qquad \left(\dfrac{a}{b}\right)^{-r} = \left(\dfrac{b}{a}\right)^r$

Radicals

$a^{1/n} = \sqrt[n]{a}$ $\qquad a^{m/n} = \left(\sqrt[n]{a}\right)^m = \sqrt[n]{a^m}$

$\sqrt[n]{ab} = \sqrt[n]{a} \cdot \sqrt[n]{b}$ $\qquad \sqrt[n]{\dfrac{a}{b}} = \dfrac{\sqrt[n]{a}}{\sqrt[n]{b}}$

Factoring

$a^2 + 2ab + b^2 = (a + b)^2$
$a^2 - 2ab + b^2 = (a - b)^2$
$a^2 - b^2 = (a + b)(a - b)$
$a^3 - b^3 = (a - b)(a^2 + ab + b^2)$
$a^3 + b^3 = (a + b)(a^2 - ab + b^2)$

Rational Expressions

$\dfrac{ac}{bc} = \dfrac{a}{b}$ $\qquad \dfrac{a}{b} + \dfrac{c}{d} = \dfrac{ad + bc}{bd}$

$\dfrac{a}{b} \cdot \dfrac{c}{d} = \dfrac{ac}{bd}$ $\qquad \dfrac{a}{b} \div \dfrac{c}{d} = \dfrac{a}{b} \cdot \dfrac{d}{c}$

Quadratic Formula

The solutions to $ax^2 + bx + c = 0$ with $a \neq 0$ are
$$x = \frac{-b \pm \sqrt{b^2 - 4ac}}{2a}.$$

Distance Formula

The distance from (x_1, y_1) to (x_2, y_2), is
$$\sqrt{(x_2 - x_1)^2 + (y_2 - y_1)^2}.$$

◇ Algebra

Midpoint Formula

The midpoint of the line segment with endpoints (x_1, y_1) and (x_2, y_2) is

$$\left(\frac{x_1 + x_2}{2}, \frac{y_1 + y_2}{2} \right).$$

Slope Formula

The slope of the line through (x_1, y_1) and (x_2, y_2) is

$$\frac{y_2 - y_1}{x_2 - x_1} \quad \text{(for } x_1 \neq x_2\text{)}.$$

Linear Function

$f(x) = mx + b$ with $m \neq 0$

Graph is a line with slope m.

Quadratic Function

$f(x) = ax^2 + bx + c$ with $a \neq 0$

Graph is a parabola.

Polynomial Function

$f(x) = a_n x^n + a_{n-1} x^{n-1} + \cdots + a_1 x + a_0$ for n a nonnegative integer

Rational Function

$f(x) = \dfrac{p(x)}{q(x)}$, where p and q are polynomial functions with $q(x) \neq 0$

Exponential and Logarithmic Functions

$f(x) = a^x$ for $a > 0$ and $a \neq 1$

$f(x) = \log_a(x)$ for $a > 0$ and $a \neq 1$

Properties of Logarithms

Base-a logarithm:	$y = \log_a(x) \Leftrightarrow a^y = x$
Natural logarithm:	$y = \ln(x) \Leftrightarrow e^y = x$
Common logarithm:	$y = \log(x) \Leftrightarrow 10^y = x$
One-to-one:	$a^{x_1} = a^{x_2} \Leftrightarrow x_1 = x_2$
	$\log_a(x_1) = \log_a(x_2) \Leftrightarrow x_1 = x_2$

$\log_a(a) = 1 \qquad \log_a(1) = 0$

$\log_a(a^x) = x \qquad a^{\log_a(N)} = N$

$\log_a(MN) = \log_a(M) + \log_a(N)$

$\log_a(M/N) = \log_a(M) - \log_a(N)$

$\log_a(M^x) = x \cdot \log_a(M)$

$\log_a(1/N) = -\log_a(N)$

$$\log_a(M) = \frac{\log_b(M)}{\log_b(a)} = \frac{\ln(M)}{\ln(a)} = \frac{\log(M)}{\log(a)}$$

Compound Interest

P = principal, t = time in years, r = annual interest rate, and A = amount:

$$A = P\left(1 + \frac{r}{n}\right)^{nt} \text{ (compounded } n \text{ times/year)}$$

$A = Pe^{rt}$ (compounded continuously)

Variation

Direct: $y = kx \qquad (k \neq 0)$

Inverse: $y = k/x \qquad (k \neq 0)$

Joint: $y = kxz \qquad (k \neq 0)$

Straight Line

Slope-intercept form: $y = mx + b$

Slope: m \qquad y-intercept: $(0, b)$

Point-slope form: $y - y_1 = m(x - x_1)$

Standard form: $Ax + By = C$

Horizontal: $y = k$ \qquad Vertical: $x = k$

◈Algebra

Parabola

$y = a(x - h)^2 + k \qquad (a \neq 0)$

Vertex: (h, k)

Axis of symmetry: $x = h$

Focus: $(h, k + p)$, where $a = \dfrac{1}{4p}$

Directrix: $y = k - p$

Circle

$(x - h)^2 + (y - k)^2 = r^2 \qquad (r > 0)$

Center: (h, k) Radius: r

$x^2 + y^2 = r^2$

Center $(0, 0)$ Radius: r

Ellipse

$\dfrac{x^2}{a^2} + \dfrac{y^2}{b^2} = 1 \qquad (a > b > 0)$

Center: $(0, 0)$ Major axis: horizontal

Foci: $(\pm c, 0)$, where $c^2 = a^2 - b^2$

$\dfrac{x^2}{b^2} + \dfrac{y^2}{a^2} = 1 \qquad (a > b > 0)$

Center: $(0, 0)$ Major axis: vertical

Foci: $(0, \pm c)$, where $c^2 = a^2 - b^2$

Hyperbola

$\dfrac{x^2}{a^2} - \dfrac{y^2}{b^2} = 1$

Center: $(0, 0)$ Vertices: $(\pm a, 0)$

Foci: $(\pm c, 0)$, where $c^2 = a^2 + b^2$

Asymptotes: $y = \pm \dfrac{b}{a} x$

$\dfrac{y^2}{a^2} - \dfrac{x^2}{b^2} = 1$

Center: $(0, 0)$ Vertices: $(0, \pm a)$

Foci: $(0, \pm c)$, where $c^2 = a^2 + b^2$

Asymptotes: $y = \pm \dfrac{a}{b} x$

Arithmetic Sequence

$a_1, a_1 + d, a_1 + 2d, a_1 + 3d, \ldots$

Formula for nth term: $a_n = a_1 + (n - 1)d$

Sum of n terms:

$$S_n = \sum_{i=1}^{n} [a_1 + (i - 1)d] = \frac{n}{2}(a_1 + a_n)$$

Geometric Sequence

$a_1, a_1 r, a_1 r^2, a_1 r^3, \ldots$

Formula for nth term: $a_n = a_1 r^{n-1}$

Sum of n terms when $r \neq 1$:

$$S_n = \sum_{i=1}^{n} a_1 r^{i-1} = \frac{a_1 - a_1 r^n}{1 - r}$$

Sum of all terms when $|r| < 1$:

$$S = \sum_{i=1}^{\infty} a_1 r^{i-1} = \frac{a_1}{1 - r}$$

Counting Formulas

Factorial notation: $n! = 1 \cdot 2 \cdot 3 \cdots (n - 1) \cdot n$

Permutation: $P(n, r) = \dfrac{n!}{(n - r)!}$ for $0 \leq r \leq n$

Combination: $C(n, r) = \dbinom{n}{r} = \dfrac{n!}{(n - r)!r!}$ for $0 \leq r \leq n$

Binomial Expansion

$(a + b)^2 = a^2 + 2ab + b^2$

$(a + b)^3 = a^3 + 3a^2 b + 3ab^2 + b^3$

$(a + b)^4 = a^4 + 4a^3 b + 6a^2 b^2 + 4ab^3 + b^4$

$(a + b)^n = \displaystyle\sum_{r=0}^{n} \binom{n}{r} a^{n-r} b^r$, where $\dbinom{n}{r} = \dfrac{n!}{(n - r)!r!}$

Trigonometry

Trigonometric Functions

If the angle α (in standard position) intersects the unit circle at (x, y), then

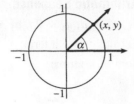

$$\sin \alpha = y \qquad \cos \alpha = x \qquad \tan \alpha = \frac{y}{x}$$

$$\csc \alpha = \frac{1}{y} \qquad \sec \alpha = \frac{1}{x} \qquad \cot \alpha = \frac{x}{y}$$

Trigonometric Ratios

If (x, y) is any point other than the origin on the terminal side of α and $r = \sqrt{x^2 + y^2}$, then

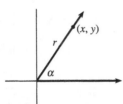

$$\sin \alpha = \frac{y}{r} \qquad \cos \alpha = \frac{x}{r} \qquad \tan \alpha = \frac{y}{x}$$

$$\csc \alpha = \frac{r}{y} \qquad \sec \alpha = \frac{r}{x} \qquad \cot \alpha = \frac{x}{y}$$

Right Triangle Trigonometry

If α is an acute angle of a right triangle, then

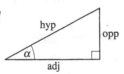

$$\sin \alpha = \frac{\text{opp}}{\text{hyp}} \qquad \cos \alpha = \frac{\text{adj}}{\text{hyp}} \qquad \tan \alpha = \frac{\text{opp}}{\text{adj}}$$

$$\csc \alpha = \frac{\text{hyp}}{\text{opp}} \qquad \sec \alpha = \frac{\text{hyp}}{\text{adj}} \qquad \cot \alpha = \frac{\text{adj}}{\text{opp}}$$

Special Right Triangles

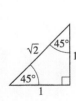 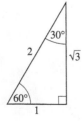

Exact Values of Trigonometric Functions

x degrees	x radians	$\sin x$	$\cos x$	$\tan x$
$0°$	0	0	1	0
$30°$	$\frac{\pi}{6}$	$\frac{1}{2}$	$\frac{\sqrt{3}}{2}$	$\frac{\sqrt{3}}{3}$
$45°$	$\frac{\pi}{4}$	$\frac{\sqrt{2}}{2}$	$\frac{\sqrt{2}}{2}$	1
$60°$	$\frac{\pi}{3}$	$\frac{\sqrt{3}}{2}$	$\frac{1}{2}$	$\sqrt{3}$
$90°$	$\frac{\pi}{2}$	1	0	—

Basic Identities

$$\tan x = \frac{\sin x}{\cos x} = \frac{1}{\cot x} \qquad \cot x = \frac{\cos x}{\sin x} = \frac{1}{\tan x}$$

$$\sin x = \frac{1}{\csc x} \qquad \csc x = \frac{1}{\sin x}$$

$$\cos x = \frac{1}{\sec x} \qquad \sec x = \frac{1}{\cos x}$$

Pythagorean Identities

$$\sin^2 x + \cos^2 x = 1 \qquad 1 + \cot^2 x = \csc^2 x$$

$$\tan^2 x + 1 = \sec^2 x$$

Odd Identities

$$\sin(-x) = -\sin(x) \qquad \csc(-x) = -\csc(x)$$

$$\tan(-x) = -\tan(x) \qquad \cot(-x) = -\cot(x)$$

Even Identities

$$\cos(-x) = \cos(x) \qquad \sec(-x) = \sec(x)$$

◈ Trigonometry

Cofunction Identities

$$\sin\left(\frac{\pi}{2} - u\right) = \cos u \qquad \cos\left(\frac{\pi}{2} - u\right) = \sin u$$

$$\tan\left(\frac{\pi}{2} - u\right) = \cot u \qquad \cot\left(\frac{\pi}{2} - u\right) = \tan u$$

$$\sec\left(\frac{\pi}{2} - u\right) = \csc u \qquad \csc\left(\frac{\pi}{2} - u\right) = \sec u$$

Cosine of a Sum or Difference

$$\cos(\alpha + \beta) = \cos \alpha \cos \beta - \sin \alpha \sin \beta$$
$$\cos(\alpha - \beta) = \cos \alpha \cos \beta + \sin \alpha \sin \beta$$

Sine of a Sum or Difference

$$\sin(\alpha + \beta) = \sin \alpha \cos \beta + \cos \alpha \sin \beta$$
$$\sin(\alpha - \beta) = \sin \alpha \cos \beta - \cos \alpha \sin \beta$$

Tangent of a Sum or Difference

$$\tan(\alpha + \beta) = \frac{\tan \alpha + \tan \beta}{1 - \tan \alpha \tan \beta}$$

$$\tan(\alpha - \beta) = \frac{\tan \alpha - \tan \beta}{1 + \tan \alpha \tan \beta}$$

Double-Angle Identities

$$\sin 2x = 2 \sin x \cos x$$
$$\cos 2x = \cos^2 x - \sin^2 x = 2 \cos^2 x - 1 = 1 - 2 \sin^2 x$$
$$\tan 2x = \frac{2 \tan x}{1 - \tan^2 x}$$

Half-Angle Identities

$$\sin \frac{x}{2} = \pm\sqrt{\frac{1 - \cos x}{2}} \qquad \cos \frac{x}{2} = \pm\sqrt{\frac{1 + \cos x}{2}}$$

$$\tan \frac{x}{2} = \pm\sqrt{\frac{1 - \cos x}{1 + \cos x}} = \frac{\sin x}{1 + \cos x} = \frac{1 - \cos x}{\sin x}$$

Product-to-Sum Identities

$$\sin A \cos B = \frac{1}{2}[\sin(A + B) + \sin(A - B)]$$

$$\sin A \sin B = \frac{1}{2}[\cos(A - B) - \cos(A + B)]$$

$$\cos A \sin B = \frac{1}{2}[\sin(A + B) - \sin(A - B)]$$

$$\cos A \cos B = \frac{1}{2}[\cos(A - B) + \cos(A + B)]$$

Sum-to-Product Identities

$$\sin x + \sin y = 2 \sin\left(\frac{x + y}{2}\right)\cos\left(\frac{x - y}{2}\right)$$

$$\sin x - \sin y = 2 \cos\left(\frac{x + y}{2}\right)\sin\left(\frac{x - y}{2}\right)$$

$$\cos x + \cos y = 2 \cos\left(\frac{x + y}{2}\right)\cos\left(\frac{x - y}{2}\right)$$

$$\cos x - \cos y = -2 \sin\left(\frac{x + y}{2}\right)\sin\left(\frac{x - y}{2}\right)$$

Reduction Formula

If α is an angle in standard position whose terminal side contains (a, b), then for any real number x

$$a \sin x + b \cos x = \sqrt{a^2 + b^2} \sin(x + \alpha).$$

Oblique Triangle

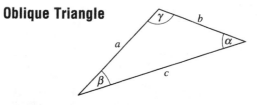

Law of Sines

In any triangle, $\dfrac{\sin \alpha}{a} = \dfrac{\sin \beta}{b} = \dfrac{\sin \gamma}{c}$.

Law of Cosines

$$a^2 = b^2 + c^2 - 2bc \cos \alpha$$
$$b^2 = a^2 + c^2 - 2ac \cos \beta$$
$$c^2 = a^2 + b^2 - 2ab \cos \gamma$$

Index

Page references followed by "f" indicate illustrated figures or photographs; followed by "t" indicates a table.